World Literature
and Its Times

VOLUME **5**

Spanish and Portuguese

Literatures and

Their Times

(The Iberian Peninsula)

World Literature and Its Times

Profiles of Notable Literary Works and the
Historical Events That Influenced Them

Joyce Moss

GALE GROUP

THOMSON LEARNING

Detroit • New York • San Diego • San Francisco
Boston • New Haven, Conn. • Waterville, Maine
London • Munich

World Literature and Its Times

Profiles of Notable Literary Works and the Historical Events That Influenced Them

VOLUME 5

Volume 5: Spanish and Portuguese Literatures and Their Times (The Iberian Peninsula)

JOYCE MOSS

STAFF

Michael L. LaBlanc, *Production Editor*

Joyce Nakamura, *Literature Content Capture Managing Editor*
Sara Constantakis, *Image Editor*
Mary Ruby, *Image Editor*
Arlene Johnson, *Associate Image Editor*
Michelle Kazensky, *Associate Image Editor*
Madeline S. Harris, *Associate Image Editor*
Maikue Vang, *Assistant Image Editor*

Maria Franklin, *Permissions Manager*
Kim Davis, *Permissions Associate*

Barbara J. Yarrow, *Graphic Services Supervisor*
Pamela A. Reed, *Imaging Coordinator*
Dan Newell, *Imaging Specialist*
Luke Rademacher, *Imaging Specialist*
Robyn V. Young, *Senior Image Editor*
Kelly A. Quin, *Image Editor*
Leitha Etheridge-Sims, *Image Cataloger*
Mary K. Grimes, *Image Cataloger*
David G. Oblender, *Image Cataloger*
Christine O'Bryan, *Image Cataloger*

Michael Logusz, *Graphic Artist*

Mary Beth Trimper, *Manager, Composition and Electronic Prepress*
Evi Seoud, *Assistant Manager, Composition Purchasing and Electronic Prepress*

∞™The paper used in this publication meets the minimum requirements of American National Standard for Information Sciences Permanence Paper for Printed Library Materials, ANSI Z39.48-1984.

ISBN 0-7876-3730-0

Printed in the United States of America
10 9 8 7 6 5 4 3 2 1

Library of Congress Control Number: 2001054742

Contents

General Preface

The world at the dawn of the twenty-first century is a shrinking sphere. Innovative modes of transmission make communication from one continent to another virtually instantaneous, quickening the development of an increasingly global society, heightening the urgency of the need for mutual understanding. At the foundation of *World Literature and Its Times* is the belief that within a people's literature are keys to their perspectives, their emotions, and the formative events that have brought them to the present point.

As manifested in their literary works, societies experience phenomena that are in some respects universal and in other respects tied to time and place. T. S. Eliot's poem *The Waste Land,* for example, is set in post-World War I London, when Europe was rife with disenchantment. Coincidentally, Juan Rulfo's novel *Pedro Páramo,* set in Latin America over a spread of decades that includes the post-World War I era, features a protagonist whose last name means "bleak plain" or "waste land." The two literary works, though written oceans apart, conjure a remarkably similar atmosphere. Likewise Aphra Behn's novel *Oroonoko,* set largely in the British colony of Surinam in the early 1660s, and Miguel Barnet's *Biography of a Runaway Slave,* beginning in 1860 in the Spanish colony of Cuba, both feature defiant slaves. The plots in this case take place two centuries apart, suggesting that time, as well as place, is of little consequence. A close look at the two slaves, however—and the two waste lands referred to above—exposes illuminating differences, indeed related to the times and places in which the respective works are set.

World Literature and Its Times regards both fiction and nonfiction as rich mediums for understanding the differences, as well as the similarities, among people and societies. In its view, full understanding of a literary work demands attention to events and attitudes of the period in which the work takes place and of the one in which it is written. The series therefore examines novels, short stories, biographies, essays, speeches, poems, and plays by contextualizing a given work within these two periods. Each volume covers some 50 literary works that span a mix of centuries and genres. The literary work itself takes center stage, with its contents determining which issues—social, political, psychological, economic, or cultural—are covered in a given entry. Every entry discusses the relevant issues apart from the literary work, making connections to it when merited, and allowing for comparisons between the literary and the historical realities. Close attention is given to the literary work as well, in the interest of extracting historical understandings from it.

Of course, the function of literature is not necessarily to represent history accurately. Nevertheless, the images and ideas promoted by a powerful literary work—be it José Hernandez's poem *The Gaucho Martín Fierro* (set in Argentina), Isak Dinesen's memoir *Out of Africa* (Kenya), or William Shakespeare's play *Macbeth* (Scotland)—

leave impressions commonly taken to be historical. In taking literature as fact, one risks acquiring a mistaken notion of history. The gaucho of Argentina is a case in point, having inspired poetry by non-gauchos whose verse conveys a highly romanticized image of these cowboy-like nomads, albeit one that includes some realistic details. To adjust for such discrepancies, this series distinguishes between historical fact and its literary reworkings.

On the other hand, literary works can broaden our understanding of history. They are able to convey more than the cut-and-dried record by portraying events in a way that captures the fears and challenges of a period or that draws attention to groups of people who are generally left out of standard histories. Many of the literary works covered in this series—from Miguel de Cervantes's *Don Quixote* (Spain) to Nelson Mandela's "The Rivonia Trial Speech" (South Africa)—draw attention to elements of society that have been neglected in standard histories. This may be best illustrated by writings that concern the position of women in different societies, from Flora Nwapa's novel *Efuru* (Nigeria), to Charlotte Brontë's *Jane Eyre* (Britain), to Lídia Jorge's *The Murmuring Coast* (Portugal). As illustrated by these works, literature in various societies engages in a vigorous dialog with mainstream texts, offering alternative perspectives. Often it defies stereotypes by featuring characters or notions that are contrary to preconceptions; it may even attack deeply engrained stereotypes directly. Spanish essayist Benito Jerónimo Feijóo takes the direct approach in his early-eighteenth-century "An Essay on Woman," as does British essayist Mary Wollstonecraft a half century later in her *A Vindication of the Rights of Woman*.

Even nonfiction must be anchored in its place and time to derive its full value. José Ortega y Gasset's set of essays *Meditations on Quixote* concerns itself with the search for Spanish identity in light of recent imperial losses and in relation to a European philosophy of the day. A second entry, on Albert Memmi's *Pillar of Salt*, uses the less direct genre of biography to describe the life of a Tunisian Jew during the Nazi occupation of North Africa. A third entry relates Charles Darwin's *On the Origin of Species* to scientific and religious developments in Britain at the time, and to challenges to its empire abroad.

The task of reconstructing the historical context of a literary work can be problematic. An author may present events out of chronological order, as Carlos Fuentes does in *The Death of Artemio Cruz* (Mexico). Other works feature legendary heroes who defy attempts to fit them into a strict time slot (such as the warrior Beowulf of Denmark, glorified in England's epic poetry; or Sunjata, founder of the empire of Mali in the Western Sudan; or the Christian navigator Vasco da Gama, who in Portugal's *The Lusiads* appeals to pagan gods). In the first case, *World Literature and Its Times* unscrambles the plot, providing a linear rendering of events and associated historical information. In the second, the series profiles customs particular to the culture at the times the epic is set and written, arming the reader with details that inform the hero's adventures. The approach sheds light on the relationship between fact and fiction, both of which are shown to provide insight into a people and their epics. As always, this approach is taken with a warm appreciation for the beauty of a literary work independent of historical facts, but also in the belief that ultimate regard is shown for that work by placing it in the context of pertinent events.

Beyond this underlying belief, the series is founded on the notion that a command of world literature bolsters knowledge of the writings produced by one's own society. Long before the present century, writers from different locations influenced one another through trends and strategies in their literatures. In our postcolonial age, such cross-fertilization has quickened. Latin American literature, having been influenced by French and Spanish trends among others, itself influences Chinese writers of today. Likewise, Africa's literary tradition has affected and been affected by France's, and the same relationship holds true for the writings of Spain and Germany and of India and Great Britain. The degree of such literary intermixture promises only to multiply given our increasingly global society. In the process, world literatures and their landmark texts gain even greater significance, attaining the potential to promote understanding not only of others, but also of ourselves.

The Selection of Literary Works

The works chosen for *World Literature and Its Times 5: Spanish and Portuguese Literatures and Their Times* have been carefully selected by professors in the field at the universities listed in the Acknowledgements. Keeping the literature-history connection in mind, the team made its selections based on a combination of factors: how frequently a literary work is studied, how closely it is tied to pivotal events in the past or present, and how strong and enduring its appeal has been to readers in and out of the society that produced it. Attention has been paid to contemporary as well as to classic works that have met with critical and/or popular acclaim. There has also been a careful effort to represent female as well as male authors, to cover a mix of genres, and to include an initial core of works from Portugal and from various reaches of Spain. Selections were limited to those literary works currently available in English. In the interest of presenting a well-developed core of Spanish works, the selection for this volume was limited to those originally written in Castilian. Space limitations precluded the inclusion of well-developed cores from other literatures of Spain. There are, of course, many more integral works by pivotal writers from Spain and Portugal than could be included in the volume. The inclusion of selected works at the expense of others has been made with the above-detailed concerns in mind.

Format and Arrangement of Entries

The volumes in *World Literature and Its Times* are arranged geographically. Within each volume, the collection is arranged alphabetically by title of the literary work. The setting of a literary work is specified at the beginning of the entry. Each entry is organized as follows:

1. **Introduction**—provides identifying information in three parts:

   The literary work—specifies genre of a work, place and time period in which it is set, when it was written and/or first published, and when it was first translated into English; also provided is the title of the work in its original language.

   Synopsis—summarizes the storyline or contents of the work.

   Introductory paragraph—introduces the literary work in relation to the author's life.

2. **Events in History at the Time the Literary Work Takes Place**—describes social and political events that relate to the plot or contents of the literary work. The section may discuss background information as well as relevant events during the period in which the work is set. The subsections in this section vary, depending on the particular literary work. In general, the section takes a deductive approach, starting with events in history and telescoping inward to events in the literary work.

3. **The Literary Work in Focus**—summarizes in detail the plot or contents of the literary work, describes how it illuminates history, and identifies sources used to generate the work, as well as the literary context surrounding it. After a detailed summary of the work comes a subsection that focuses on an aspect that illuminates our understanding of events or attitudes of the period. This subsection takes an inductive approach, starting with the literary work and broadening outward to events in history. It is followed by a third subsection, which specifies sources that inspired elements of the work and which discusses its literary context, or relation to other works.

4. **Events in History at the Time the Literary Work Was Written**—describes social, political, and/or literary events in the author's lifetime that relate to the plot or contents of a work. Also discussed in this section are the reviews or reception accorded the literary work.

5. **For More Information**—provides a list of all sources that have been cited in the entry as well as sources for further reading about the different issues or personalities featured in the entry.

If the literary work is set and written in the same time period, sections 2 and 4 of the entry on that work ("Events in History at the Time the Literary Work Takes Place" and "Events in History at the Time the Literary Work Was Written") are combined into the single section "Events in History at the Time of the Literary Work."

Additional Features

Whenever possible, primary-source material is provided through quotations in the text and material in sidebars. There are also sidebars with historical details that amplify issues raised in the text, and with anecdotes that promote understanding of the temporal context. At the front of the volume is a set of timelines that provides a historical overview of the societies highlighted and that includes a correlation to the literary works covered in the volume. Timelines also appear within entries when needed to summarize intricate periods. Finally, historically relevant illustrations enrich and further clarify information in the entries.

Comments and Suggestions

Your comments on this series and suggestions for future editions are welcome. Please write: Editors, *World Literature and Its Times,* The Gale Group, Inc., 27500 Drake Road, Farmington Hills, Michigan 48331-3535.

Acknowledgments

World Literature and Its Times 5: Spanish and Portuguese Literatures and Their Times is the result of an intensively collaborative effort that evolved through several stages, each of which was monitored by a team of experts in Spanish and Portuguese literatures. A special thank you goes to Professors Ana Paula Ferreira, in Portuguese literature at the University of California at Irvine, and Jesús Torrecilla, in Spanish literature at the University of California at Los Angeles, for their careful and enthusiastic guidance at every stage, from inception to the end of the development process.

Gratitude is extended as well to those who contributed to the process at multiple stages, including refinement of the volume's front matter: for Spanish literature, Professors Michael McGaha of Pomona College, and Nelson Orringer and David K. Herzberger of the University of Connecticut; for Portuguese literature, António Ladeira, lecturer at Yale University, and Professor Frederick Williams of Brigham Young University; and for Spanish and Portuguese history, Teofilo Ruiz of the University of California at Los Angeles.

For their incisive participation in selecting the literary works to cover in the volume, the editors extend deep appreciation to the following professors:

Mary Lee Bretz, Rutgers University, Department of Spanish and Portuguese

Ana Paula Ferreira, University of California at Irvine, Chair, Department of Spanish and Portuguese

David K. Herzberger, University of Connecticut, Department Head, Department of Modern and Classical Languages

Michael McGaha, Pomona College, Romance Languages and Literatures-Spanish Section

José Monleón, University of California at Los Angeles, Department of Spanish and Portuguese

Janet Pérez, Texas Tech University, Department of Classical and Modern Languages and Literatures

Joseph Ricapito, Louisiana State University, Department of Foreign Languages and Literatures

Jesús Torrecilla, University of California at Los Angeles, Department of Spanish and Portuguese

Warm gratitude is extended to the following professors for their careful review of the entries to insure accuracy and completeness of information:

Mary Lee Bretz, Rutgers University, Department of Spanish and Portuguese

Malcolm Compitello, University of Arizona, Department Head, Department of Spanish and Portuguese

Frank C. Fagundes, University of Massachusetts, Amherst, Department of Spanish and Portuguese

Ana Paula Ferreira, University of California at Irvine, Chair, Department of Spanish and Portuguese

Acknowledgments

David William Foster, Arizona State University, Department of Languages and Literatures

Julia B. Grinstein, Texas Tech University, Department of Classical and Modern Languages and Literatures

David K. Herzberger, Department Head, University of Connecticut, Department of Modern and Classical Languages

Edmund King, Professor Emeritus, Princeton University, Department of Classical and Modern Languages and Cultures

Ricardo Landeira, University of Colorado at Boulder, Department of Spanish and Portuguese

Michael McGaha, Pomona College, Romance Languages and Literatures—Spanish Section

José Monleón, University of California at Los Angeles, Department of Spanish and Portuguese

C. Brian Morris, University of California at Los Angeles, Department of Spanish and Portuguese

Nelson Orringer, University of Connecticut, Department of Modern and Classical Languages

Janet Pérez, Texas Tech University, Department of Classical and Modern Languages and Literatures

Joseph Ricapito, Louisiana State University, Department of Foreign Languages and Literatures

Teofilo Ruiz, University of California at Los Angeles, Department of History

Robert Sumpter, Mira Costa High School, History Department

Jesús Torrecilla, University of California at Los Angeles, Department of Spanish and Portuguese

Lisa Vollendorf, Wayne State University, Department of Romance Languages and Literatures

Barbara Zecchi, St. Mary's College, Department of Modern Languages and Women's Studies Program

For their painstaking research and composition, the editors thank the writers whose names appear at the close of the entries they contributed. A complete listing follows:

Jorge Aladro, Associate Professor, University of California at Santa Cruz

Onésimo T. Almeida, Professor, Department Chair, Brown University

Claudia Pazos-Alonso, Lecturer, University of Oxford

Damian Bacich, Ph.D. candidate, University of California at Los Angeles

Matthew Brosamer, Lecturer, Mount St. Mary's College

Alice R. Clemente, Adjunct Professor, Brown University

David Frier, Lecturer, University of Leeds

René P. Garay, Associate Professor, City College, City University of New York

Benito Gómez-Madrid, Ph.D. candidate, University of California at Los Angeles

Julia B. Grinstein, Assistant Professor, Texas Tech University

Michael Hammer, Ph.D. candidate, University of California at Los Angeles

David K. Herzberger, Professor, Department Head, University of Connecticut

António Ladeira, Lecturer, Yale University

Ricardo Landeira, Professor, University of Colorado at Boulder

Margarita M. Lezcano, Associate Professor, Eckerd College

Pamela S. Loy, Ph.D., University of California at Santa Barbara; professional writer

Christopher C. Lund, Professor, Brigham Young University

Mary McGlynn, Assistant Professor, Baruch College, City University of New York

Stephen Miller, Professor, Texas A & M University

José Ornelas, Professor, Department Chair, University of Massachusetts, Amherst

Nelson Orringer, Professor, University of Connecticut

Hilary Owen, Lecturer, University of Manchester

Mehl Penrose, Assistant Professor, Miami University

Diane Renée, B.A., University of California at Los Angeles; Professional writer

Enrique Rodríguez-Cepeda, Professor, University of California at Los Angeles

Kathryn Bishop Sanchez, Assistant Professor, University of Wisconsin, Madison

Ellen W. Sapega, Associate Professor, University of Wisconsin, Madison

María P. Tajes, Lecturer, Rutgers University

Michelle Tannenbaum, Ph.D. candidate, University of California at Los Angeles

Eric Thau, Ph.D. candidate, University of California at Los Angeles

Allison Weisz, M.Phil, Cambridge University; M.A. candidate, Stanford University

Colin Wells, M.A., Oxford University; professional writer

Frederick Williams, Professor, Brigham Young University

James Wojtaszek, Assistant Professor, University of Minnesota, Morris

David Wood, Ph.D. candidate, University of California at Los Angeles

Deep appreciation is extended to Michael L. LaBlanc and to Joyce Nakamura of The Gale Group for his careful editing and for her painstaking compilation of illustrations. Anne Leach indexed the volume with great sensitivity to readers and subject matter. Lastly the editors thank Monica Riordan for her deft copy editing, and Lisa Blai for her proficient proofreading, word processing, and organizational management.

Acknowledgments

Introduction

Across central Iberia runs a majestic cordillera, a mountain range full of roughly hewn slopes, whose peaks tower ever higher from east to west until they reach Mount Almanzor. Soft patches of green, yellow, and pink lichen nestle in the range's rugged surfaces, eagles and wild goats frequent its heights, and age-old villages dot the brown-gray earth below. At its westernmost ridge, the range seems to rest at the edge of the known world. "This is my Spain," declares Miguel de Unamuno in a poem that celebrates the magnificent Gredos, as the sierra is called. "A naked heart of living rock / Of most rough granite / That with its crests touching the sky / In mutual solitude seeks the sun; / This is my Spain, / A hermit country, / That as to its nest turns always to the truth" (Miguel de Unamuno, "On Gredos." *Ten Centuries of Spanish Poetry* [Baltimore: Johns Hopkins Press, 1955], 401, 403).

It is an elusive truth, this essence to which Spain perpetually turns, largely through its literatures. Today its homeland, the Iberian Peninsula, is politically divided into two nations, Spain and Portugal, but the history leading to this configuration involves many more political entities. Historians speak of Spain's consisting of several *patrias chicas*, or small nations within the larger body, each with its own language, history, and literature. Chief among these are Catalonia in the northeast (where the language is Catalan), the Basque provinces in the north and over the Pyrenees Mountains into France (the language is

Basque), and Galicia in northwest Spain (the language is Galician). These and other Iberian languages and cultures were aggressively suppressed under Franco's twentieth-century dictatorship, but the small nations have since become politically autonomous, and they are now enjoying a linguistic and literary revival.

Over the centuries poets, novelists, essayists, dramatists, and historians have struggled to define Spain, peering far back into the waning years of the second century B.C.E., when the Romans first appeared. The Romans would go on to rule for some 600 years, ensconcing among the scattered peoples of the peninsula a few stubbornly enduring building blocks—the Latin language, Christianity, Roman law, a system of highways and aqueducts, and municipal government. Overrun a few centuries later by a Germanic people, the Visigoths, the peninsula saw another building block fall into place when their king, Recared, adopted from the conquered Hispano-Romans their variety of Christianity, thereby linking his Visigothic minority to the conquered majority. *Roman* Spain had begun to evolve into a *Visigothic* Spain heavily influenced by its predecessor. But the land was not yet Spain alone, without any preceding adjective; nor would it be for the next several hundred years, during which another momentous building block fell into place, that of *Muslim* Spain. Invading from North Africa in 711, the Muslim conquerors gave rise to a society that would not be totally extinguished until eight centuries later, at the end of a sporadic anti-Muslim response—the Christian Reconquest.

For more than a hundred years after the advent of the Muslims, the peninsula stood at a crossroads. Not a single city of consequence remained free of Muslim control. With the invaders came the Arabic language and the Islamic faith to a land not yet fully unified or even fully Christian. (A sizeable Jewish community resided in Spain by the end of the first century C.E.; within the next millennium, Spain would become home to 90 percent of the world's Jewish population.) The Muslims introduced a perplexing quandary. Especially at the southern Mediterranean shore, their presence led to a fairly thorough immersion into Arab culture that could have easily determined the region's future. But to the north, in none-too-accessible mountains, there survived pockets of Hispano-Roman-Visigoth life. These small enclaves chose to hold fast to their Christian faith and associated traditions (the Latin language, European customs), stubbornly resisting Islamization (the Arabic language, North African customs). Not yet formed into kingdoms, they would emerge as such during the Reconquest. By the end of the twelfth century, five of them—Aragon, Castile, León, Navarre, and Portugal—formed what came to be perceived as a political entity, the so-called Five Kingdoms, otherwise known as *Spain,* without any preceding adjective. The kingdoms underwent permutations over time. Aragon, established as a kingdom in the eleventh century, allied with the powerful principality of Catalonia in 1137. Castile, which also became a kingdom in the eleventh century, united with León, then separated from it, then reunited with it in 1230, with Castile as dominant partner.

Of the five kingdoms, Castile emerged as pre-eminent. It is important, however, to remember that Castile was forever a kingdom in development, affected as much by its interaction with the other kingdoms as they were by Castile's language and its reconquering zeal. Against the Muslims, Castile distinguished itself by waging battle with a special vengeance, its territory growing ever larger as the decades passed, its language becoming dominant in most of the other kingdoms. Portugal would prove a conspicuous exception, carving out for itself an insistently separate destiny, maintaining an aloofness and maturing into an imperial power whose explorations (evoked in Luis de Camões's epic *The Lusiads* and Fernando Pessoa's *Message*) changed world history. First, however, Portugal too fought the Muslims, concluding its own Reconquest by the end of the thirteenth century.

Meanwhile, Castile led the way in the rest of the peninsula, memorializing the feat of one of its legendary medieval reconquerers in an epic of its own—*Poem of the Cid.* The fourteenth and fifteenth centuries would see Castile grow even more pre-eminent. It triggered a momentous advance in the unification process when Isabella of Castile married Ferdinand of Aragon and the two began a joint rule of their allied-but-still-separate realms that was to endure for three decades (1474-1504). By this time, León had united with Castile, and Navarre would do so shortly after Isabella's death. Events had brought to the forefront three major Christian kingdoms—Aragon, Castile, and Portugal, each with an empire of its own, each with its own set of problems and possibilities. In Castile, unrest would mount after the death of Queen Isabella. Local magnates showed a fractiousness that was ultimately quelled by royal force, the Crown functioning to unify the realm, as it does in Lope de Vega's play *Fuente Ovejuna* (also spelled *Fuenteovejuna*). The function was one Isabella herself had done much to establish, not only through her marriage but also through Castile's reconquering zeal, which led to a final anti-Muslim victory in Granada in 1492.

The effort had been a patently Christian one. Spain owed its very existence to the anti-Muslim wars, a reality built into the fiber of its being and reaffirmed thereafter. The Catholic Monarchs, as Ferdinand and Isabella were called, proceeded to consolidate their land's staunchly Christian identity, demanding the conversion or expulsion of all Jews in 1492. Exactly one decade later they would offer all remaining Muslims the same choice—conversion or expulsion. Were there backsliders among the converts? Isabella set up an Inquisition, a tribunal to ferret them out, and the idea took hold that now that Spain was finally one, a land full of Christian realms, to be a Spaniard, one had to be Christian; anything less amounted to disloyalty. Mindful of having forced the issue of conversion, the authorities looked askance at any convert. First official policy, then the larger population, made purity of Christian blood a priority in the sixteenth and seventeenth centuries. Was one's ancestor a convert? Such a taint could blight one's career or marriage or other life goal, a reality greatly aggravated by the sixteenth-century Reformation in Europe. Spain responded to this Reformation with its old missionary zeal, directed now at a new Protestant threat. The land's Catholic standard bearers set out to advance their old faith in the peninsula's twin-tracked (Spanish and Portuguese) global empire, newly stretched from Asia and Africa to Europe and the Americas. Meanwhile, back in Spain, the response to the Reformation was a Counter-Reformation, a drive to reform the Church from within, which produced stunning mystical literature by clerics like Saint Teresa of Avila (*Interior Castle*) and Saint John of the Cross ("The Dark Night" and Other Poems).

Less saintly literature helped reveal abuses in the sixteenth-century Church, not openly, but clandestinely, since the Inquisition curbed freedom of expression in Spain. Officials curbed this freedom in earnest after the discovery of some Protestants in Castile in 1558. The monarchy called for strict censorship, demanding that manuscripts be checked before and after publication, but clever writers managed anyway to expose the abuses, to get at the elusive truth, cloaking it in fiction that was just as stunning as the age's mystical literature. Not only did *Lazarillo de Tormes*, for instance, satirize the corrupt behavior of priests as well as other foibles of society; it also forged a new literary genre, the picaresque novel. Like other European nations, Spain had produced medieval fiction that prescribed behaviors by example (see *The Book of Count Lucanor and Patronio* and *Libro de Buen Amor [Book of Good Love]*). Now, sticking to its deliberately chosen European path, Spain showed the same self-critical, humanist bent that characterized the rest of the continent in the Renaissance era. Aside from religious corruption, authors found fault with other aspects of society, again cloaking their criticism in fiction, as Miguel de Cervantes does in his *Don Quixote,* which, like *Lazarillo,* forged a new genre, becoming the first modern novel.

Actually the critical bent was nothing new to the peninsula. It had been exercised a half century earlier, at the close of the medieval era, by Portugal's Gil Vicente, whose *The India Play* faulted Portuguese society for the domestic consequences of society's mania for exploration. A farcical play with a serious message, it focuses on empire, as do other Portuguese titles (for example, *The Lusiads, The Murmuring Coast,* and *South of Nowhere*). Portuguese works likewise show a recurring concern for social justice (*Stormy Isles, Baltasar and Blimunda*) and for varieties of repression (*Doomed Love, Ballad of Dog's Beach, New Portuguese Letters*). Other—sometimes similar, sometimes different—issues resurface in Spanish literary works from the 1500s forward:

- **Honor**—*Lazarillo de Tormes, The Swindler, Life Is a Dream, House of Bernarda Alba*
- **Relations between the sexes**—*La Celestina, The Trickster of Seville and the Stone Guest, Disenchantments of Love*
- **Ideal vs. the real**—*Don Quixote, The Infinite Passion, Meditations on Quixote*
- **Social inequity/social barriers**—*The Swindler, The Quest, Time of Silence*
- **Women's status/women's rights**—"An Essay on Woman," *Fortunata and Jacinta, The Maiden's Consent*
- **Social and personal violence**—*Bohemian Lights, The Family of Pascual Duarte*
- **Civil War**—*Nada, Requiem for a Spanish Peasant*
- **Exile**—*Poet in New York, Marks of Identity*
- **Art vs. life**—*Don Quixote, Mist, Back Room*
- **Modernization/national identity**—*The House of Ulloa, The Fields of Castile, The Spaniards*

The way in which a particular issue resurfaces reveals concerns of the era that produced it—the legendary Don Juan is perhaps the clearest case in point. First appearing in print as *The Trickster of Seville* around 1630, during Spain's literary Golden Age, the story of this unredeemed, seductive rake underwent transformation in the 1840s. *Don Juan Tenorio,* a wildly popular play, transformed him into a soul who could be saved, and the poem *The Student of Salamanca* into a representative of the Romantic era's burning desire to know, as well as its skeptical approach to religion and other aspects of life. Repression took on different casts too, depending on time and place, from the Inquisition in 1700s Portugal (*Baltasar and Blimunda*), to personal repression in early 1900s Spain (*The House of Bernarda Alba,* written just before Federico García Lorca and other intellectuals were murdered at the start of the Civil War), to the question of what authors such as Carmen Laforet left out of post-Civil-War novels like *Nada* because of a new 1938 Press Law. (The law censored literary works not supportive of the Franco dictatorship, the Church, or "proper" morals and language.)

Twentieth-century Spain grew isolated, setting up barriers against "dangerous" influences from other societies, committing itself to an insular life. In doing so, Spain picked up on and magnified a thread woven into its fabric much earlier, during the sixteenth-century Reformation, when Castile banned books and prevented students from attending certain foreign universities, mostly contenting itself with the Spanish empire, an entity that seemed to grow ever larger. The empire even subsumed Portugal and its territories, which became part of Spain for 60 years (1580-1640), then wrested itself free. Afterwards the two countries diverged. Portugal turned outward toward the sea, its own colonies, and the effort needed to sustain itself in the face of scant resources and the constant threat of Spanish domination. Spain seemed meanwhile to enter a lengthy era of decline and separation from the rest of Europe. On one hand, the country's domestic consolidation progressed; Spain finally achieved internal unity (only since 1785 has there been a Spanish flag). On the other hand, the general population turned inward, so to speak, sticking doggedly to traditional ways and beliefs, although Spain's new, French-related Bourbon monarchy imported fresh ideas and fashions. Shaken out of their quietude in the early 1800s by Napoleon's invasion, the Spanish suffered French rule for a few years before his forces were ousted, then settled down to decades of soul-searching and the rise of a middle class, suffering the same growing pains experienced elsewhere in Europe at the time. Spaniards too divided into liberal and conservative camps, experimenting with government from the nineteenth into the twentieth century, shifting from absolute monarchy, to First Republic, constitutional monarchy favoring landed interests, military dictatorship, Second Republic, military dictatorship, and democratic constitutional monarchy.

If nineteenth-century government was tumultuous, there was energetic creativity in literature to match. The Inquisition ended early in the century, censorship was relaxed, and literature responded with a creative vigor that approached that of the Golden Age. Again like the rest of Europe, Spain produced literary works that became the driving force of a succession of genres—from Romanticism and *costumbrismo* (the portrayal of local customs, as in "The Old-Fashioned Castilian"), to realism (*La Regenta*), naturalism (*The House of Ulloa*), post-Romantic poetry (*Beside the River Sar*), and finally the Generation of 1898. A pivotal group this generation was, one that would have a cataclysmic effect on Spanish letters and intellectual life. Was the truth of what it meant to be a Spaniard elusive? This generation would address the question more directly than ever before. It would struggle in this freshly post-imperial era (Spain had just lost its final American and Asian colonies) to work out the answer and make up for any time lost during the earlier withdrawal of Spain from European life. Pursued in litera-

ture, the struggle gave rise to writings such as José Ortega y Gasset's *Meditations on Quixote* and Miguel de Unamuno's *Mist*, which—again at the same time as the rest of Europe—helped establish in Spain the genre of modernism. Then came devastating civil war and stifling dictatorship, which muffled but did not silence the literary voices, though many went into exile and the search for truth through writing was forced to retreat into indirect discourse again.

A few years before Spain, Portugal began living under a dictatorship that would become entrenched for four decades, until 1974. Spain's ended in 1975, so that both lands spent much of the twentieth century under autocratic rule. Portugal too produced distinguished literature in the various genres (e.g., Romanticism—*Travels in My Homeland*; realism—*The Maias*; modernism—*Message*). As in Spain, other writers produced works that refused to fit neatly into the prevailing genre yet brought to life a particular era or environment in Portugal (see *Stormy Isles—An Azorean Tale*). Remarkable in Portugal since the 1970s is a host of literary works that, with astounding honesty, subject society to self-scrutiny for past misdeeds. Novel after novel brings to light injustice—in Portugal's treatment of women (*New Portuguese Letters*), in its imperial rule in Africa (*Murmuring Coast*), and even within what was a sometimes unholy revolutionary effort to topple the Salazar dictatorship (*Ballad of Dogs' Beach*).

Meanwhile, post-dictatorship writers in Spain have produced fiction that struggles with the disorienting experience of exile (*Marks of Identity*) and with the search for the still elusive truth, this time after decades of fascistic propaganda (*The Back Room*). In fiction, poetry, and prose, writers continue to perform a crucial service, sorting out the past, bringing present-day vision into ever clearer focus. Until now, there has been a primary reliance on Castilian literature to achieve this end. Yet in the present, as in the past, when the medieval Jewish and Arabic cultures flourished, people in Spain speak various languages that have rich literary traditions of their own. Catalonia boasts a prodigious collection of Catalan poetry and prose; Galician and Basque writers have penned memorable works in their languages too. Consideration of these traditions alongside the already rich Castilian canon promises only to deepen insights into Spain's past and present. The original Castile, says philosopher Julián Marías, was never a well-defined kingdom but a "*project which constantly traveled*," a notion one must bear in mind to understand Spain (Julián Marías, *Understanding Spain* [Ann Arbor: The University of Michigan Press, 1990], 128). In keeping with this notion, presented in *World Literature and Its Times 5* is a literary core by writers from Portugal and from various reaches of Spain who employed the Castilian language. Future years might see this core expand to include works from other languages, works also generated in and expressive of this land over the centuries.

Chronology of Relevant Events

Spanish and Portuguese Literatures and Their Times

BEGINNINGS TO MUSLIM INVASION

Life on the Iberian Peninsula is ancient. The emergence of an enduring culture in the area, a specifically Iberian culture, that is, can be traced back to shards of pottery dated *c.* 1,200 B.C.E. According to most historians today, these ancient Iberians were native to the peninsula. They appear to have been the most advanced of a number of early peninsular groups including the Celts, Basques, and Celtiberians as well as the Iberians. The lives of these groups were impacted by ancient and medieval invaders; most notably the Romans and their Visigoth (Germanic) successors. Becoming the first to establish "Hispania" as a single administrative and political unit, the Romans introduced a common Latin language, system of laws (including popular municipal government), network of roads, bridges, and aqueducts, and also a single religion, Christianity. Tradition holds that Saints Peter and Paul consecrated seven bishops to evangelize the peoples of Spain and that Saint James, patron of Spain, fought alongside the defenders of Christianity against their enemies in the land, though neither of these claims is verifiable. Altogether the Roman presence in Spain lasted for six centuries, after which the Visigoths, a Germanic people who subscribed to Arianism, a different form of Christianity, invaded and conquered the land. In time the Visigoths adopted the Roman (Catholic) religion, language, and law, leaving as their legacy the ideal, if the not the reality, of a single kingdom that would encompass the entire land. After their conversion to Catholicism, the faith of the Visigothic kings became linked to the ideal of peninsular unity. But in 711 Muslims from North Africa overcame the not-yet-unified Visigoths, conquering most parts of the peninsula. Ultimately the ideal of unity would reassert itself, but not before peninsular life had been changed forever.

Historical Events		Related Literary Works in *WLAIT 5* (correlated to times in which works are set and/or written)
c. 798,000 B.C.E.	Remains of Homo antecessor unearthed near Burgos, Spain	
c. 60,000 B.C.E.	Discoveries of early Neanderthal Man in Gibraltar and Girona	
c. 16,000 B.C.E.	Evidence of prehistoric cave paintings, most notably at Altamira, portraying bison, mammoths, reindeer, and bears	
c. 1200 B.C.E.	Pottery shards testify to emergence of Iberian culture	
c. 800 B.C.E.	Phoenician traders establish Gadir (Cadiz) on the southwest coast and begin trade	
c. 700-500 B.C.E.	Tartessian culture in southern Spain	
c. 575 B.C.E.	Greek colonization begins	
237-206 B.C.E.	Carthaginian Empire in Spain	
218	Roman conquest begins; start of Second Punic War between Rome and Carthage, whose defeat will end in its surrendering to Rome all remaining overseas territories	
197 B.C.E.	Roman rule is established with creation of two provinces in the Iberian Peninsula	*The Spaniards: An Introduction to Their History* by Américo Castro
c. 100-300 C.E.	Introduction of Christianity and Judaism to the Iberian Peninsula	
409 C.E. dominance	First Germanic invasion signifies end of general Roman	
414 C.E.	Appearance of Visigoths in Roman Spain, first as allies, ultimately as conquerors of the Romans	
476-711 C.E.	Visigothic kingdom	
587 C.E.	Roman form of Christianity becomes official state religion following the conversion of King Recared	

CONQUEST AND RECONQUEST

The Muslim conquest of Spain in 711 touched off sporadic territorial conflict as the defeated Christians set out to reconquer lost territory, achieving isolated victories as time passed, first adopting the full-blown rationale of "crusader" in the eleventh century. Until then, the Muslims, or Moors, as they were called in Spain, remained dominant in al-Andalus, the name given to the Muslim domain in Spain. It was a domain that would diminish over the nearly eight centuries of Muslim presence, mostly because of the onslaughts of three Christian kingdoms—Aragon, Castile, and Portugal. These Christian kingdoms, along with León and Navarre, came into existence during the centuries of Reconquest. Gaining a collective identity because of their common opposition to the Muslims, they became known as the "Five Kingdoms." Castile emerged as the dominant kingdom linguistically, gaining even more prominence once it allied with the powerful kingdom of Aragon through the marriage of Ferdinand and Isabella. This emergence occurred over centuries, during which three cultures lived in close proximity in Castile as well as elsewhere in Christian Spain and in Muslim Spain. The three groups—Muslims, Christians, and Jews—co-existed in uneasy peace, influencing cultural, social, and economic development to greater and lesser degrees. Established early in Muslim rule, tolerance eroded over the years, dissolving into a peninsula-wide deadly rash of pogroms, or anti-Jewish massacres, in 1391, then deteriorating even further over the following century. The Christian drive for orthodoxy that prompted the pogroms afterward led to the founding of the Spanish Inquisition, a tribunal of priests established to test conformity to the teachings of the Roman Catholic Church. Overseen by the Crown, the Inquisition targeted peoples as well as ideas, its aim being to cleanse Spanish lands of all "subversive" elements. Though the tribunal would endure off and on for more than three centuries, it conducted most of its executions in the first 50 years, claiming perhaps 2,000 victims from 1481-1530. Meanwhile, in 1492, the Christians achieved their final political victory in Spain, conquering the last remnant of Muslim rule, the kingdom of Granada. Christian dominance was complete.

711-18	Muslim conquest of Spain begins with Muslim victory at battle of Guadalete	
711-1031	Rise and height of Muslim rule in Spain	
716	Muslim capital established in Córdoba	
718	Pelayo, the Visigothic Christian leader, establishes kingdom of Asturias; he succeeds in defending it against Moors	
722	Led by Pelayo, Christians win victory at battle of Covadonga	
750s	First Christian counteroffensive under Alfonso I of Asturias	
756	Under Abd-al-Rahman, the Muslims' Ummayad dynasty forms rule based on religious and ethnic toleration; establishes unified government in Muslim Spain; dynasty lasts until 1031	
c. 796-98	Independent state of Navarre is established as territory of the Basques	
850-950	Kingdom of Asturias expands; capital is moved to León and kingdom becomes known as Asturias and León, or just León	
899	After the discovery of St. James's remains in Galicia, the site becomes an important Christian shrine	
900-1200	Flowering of Muslim learning and philosophy in Spain	
900s-1400s	Interactions between Jews, Muslims, and Christians shape medieval Spanish culture	*The Book of Good Love* by Juan Ruiz; *The Book of Count Lucanor and Patronio* by Don Juan Manuel; *The Spaniards: An Introduction to Their History* by Américo Castro
912-61	Abd al-Rahman III reigns as first caliph of Córdoba; under his rule Umayyad dynasty begins to peak, winning renown for poetry, music, botany, medicine, astronomy, mathematics, and ivory-carving	
1031	Collapse of caliphate; Muslim Spain becomes series of *taifas*, or petty kingdoms	
1043-99	Life of the Castilian knight Rodrigo Díaz de Vivar, known as El Cid; highlight of his career is the conquest of Valencia in 1094 *Poem of the Cid*	
1085	Alfonso VI of Castile, aided by Christian crusaders, captures Toledo, a key Muslim stronghold	
1086-1143	Almoravids—fundamentalist Muslims—invade from Morocco, reestablish dominance of Muslims in al-Andalus	
1128-85	Afonso Henriques establishes kingdom of Portugal	

1137	The kingdom of Aragon and principality of Catalonia unite through marriage of their rulers	
early 1140s	Break-up of Almoravid empire; reemergence of *taifa* kingdoms	
1148-73	Almohads from Morocco subjugate *taifa* kingdoms	
1158-70	The monastic knightly Orders of Calatrava (1158), Alcántara (1166), and Santiago (1170) are created to defend Spain's Christian states against the Muslims	
1188	Establishment of the Cortes (Spanish parliament) in León, first meeting of a medieval parliament	
1195	The Almohads defeat Alfonso VIII at Alarcos	
1212	Alfonso VIII leads Christian kingdoms to a great victory at Las Navas de Tolosa; century of Christian reconquest of the southern peninsula begins	
1217-52	Reign of Ferdinand III in Castile; progress in the Reconquest; victories at Córdoba, Murcia, Jaén, and Seville make Granada the only remaining Muslim stronghold in Spain; Muslim kingdom of Granada comes into existence, with capital at palace of Alhambra	
c. 1220	Alfonso IX establishes University of Salamanca	
1221-84	Life span of Alfonso X the "Wise" of Castile: Alfonso brings together Christian clerics with Jewish and Arab sages to write *eatables of Astronomy*, which influenced Europe for centuries; sponsors histories and the *aced Paribas* (Seven Parts), first great code of law in Spain; in Galician dialect, writes *Songs in Praise of the Saint Mary*, a collection of laudatory poetry to the Virgin	
1229-76	Jaime I of Aragon conquers Valencia and the Balearic Islands	
1230	Castile and León unite under Ferdinand III of Castile	
1230-31	End of Almohad power in Spain	
1340	Alfonso XI of Castile defeats Muslims at the battle of Salado	
1348-51	The Black Death spreads through Europe	
1391	Anti-Jewish feeling leads to rash of pogroms in Castile, Aragon, and other parts of Iberian Peninsula	
1442	Alfonso V of Aragon gains control of Naples	
1449	Movement against *conversos* (converted Jews) surfaces in Toledo	
1469	Marriage of Ferdinand of Aragon to Isabella of Castile	
1473	Massacre of Conversos in Andalusian towns in southern Spain	
1474	Enrique IV dies; his sister Isabella is crowned queen of Castile, empowers Ferdinand to serve as her co-ruler in Castile	
1478-81	The Spanish Inquisition is formed to examine religious faith of Conversos; first auto de fe, or sentencing, in Seville; six people are burned at the stake	*The Swindler* by Francisco de Quevedo
1479	Ferdinand accedes to throne of Aragon; Aragon, as well as Castile, falls under the joint rule of Ferdinand and Isabella	
1492	Conquest of Granada—the last Moorish outpost in Spain falls to the Christians; Jews are expelled; the Pope dubs Ferdinand and Isabella "the Catholic Monarchs"	*Lazarillo de Tormes*; *La Celestina* by Fernando de Rojas

IMPERIAL SPAIN: FROM THE DISCOVERY OF THE NEW WORLD TO THE LAST HABSBURG MONARCHS

Christopher Columbus's discovery of the New World in 1492 initiated a period of exploration and conquest for Spain. Conquistadors such as Francisco Pizarro and Hernán Cortés subdued indigenous peoples like the Incas and Aztecs and planted Spanish outposts in Latin America. Collected from this so-called "New World," silver and other riches poured into Spanish coffers, enriching the colonizers. The fifteenth and sixteenth centuries witnessed Spain's growth into a supreme empire, in contention with other European nations, including Great Britain and France, for wealth, territory, and international prestige. During the reigns of Charles I and Philip II, Spain emerged as one of the richest, most powerful nations on the Continent. In the same spirit with which they had embarked on the Reconquest, Spaniards zealously attempted to convert their new imperial subjects to Christianity, meanwhile continuing to "cleanse" their own homeland of religious deviation. In 1609 they expelled the last Muslim descendants, the Moriscos, who were converts to Christianity, for the most part, just on the surface. Spain's project, world empire and as much religious unity as possible, was a grand one, too grand, it turned out, to handle. So large did the empire grow, and so contrary were parts of it, that it became impossible to manage. By the 1650s, ineffective government, poorly conducted and costly wars, and extravagant spending had begun to undermine Spain's dominance on the world stage.

1492	Christopher Columbus discovers the New World, claiming it for Spain	
1492-c. 1823	Spain builds worldwide empire, including territories in the Americas, Asia, Africa, and Europe	
1500s-1600s	Mines in Spanish colonies triple the amount of gold and silver possessed by Europe; religious fervor stimulates mystical	*Interior Castle* by Saint Teresa of Avila; "The Dark Night" and Other Poems by Saint John of the Crosswritings by Spanish clerics
1502	Muslims forced to choose between conversion or expulsion from Spain	
1512	King Ferdinand annexes Navarre—independent since 840	
1516-24	Accession of Charles V to throne of Castile sparks armed resistance in Castile and Aragon; resistance is ultimately suppressed	
1516-56	Reign of Charles I, the first Habsburg ruler of Spain; in 1519	*Lazarillo de Tormes*made the Holy Roman Emperor (as Charles V); conquistadors discover and exploit New World wealth
1517	Martin Luther begins Reformation, the Christian division into Protestant and Catholic factions, by posting list of grievances on church door in Germany	
1519-22	Hernán Cortés conquers Aztecs of Mexico	
1521	Charles V cements the power of the Crown in Castile in his victory at battle of Villalar	
1531-34	Pizarro conquers Incas of Peru	
1534	Ignatius Loyola founds Order of the Jesuits, avid defenders of the pope, religious teachers, and proselytizers	

Historical Events		Related Literary Works in *WLAIT 5*
1545	Discovery of silver mountain at Potosi, Bolivia	
1545-63	Councils in Trent introduce reforms of Catholic Church, initiate Counter Reformation movement to modify Church from within and restore prominence of Catholicism in northern Europe	*The Trickster of Seville* by Tirso de Molina; *Life is a Dream* by Pedro Calderón de la Barca
1546	Silver mine developed at Zacatecas, Mexico	
1556-98	Philip II accedes to throne of Spain after his father Charles V abdicates; Spain enjoys era of military supremacy; Madrid is established as capital of Spain	
1563-84	Construction of the monastery-palace of San Lorenzo del Escorial (the Escorial), on which Philip spends six million ducats	
1564-65	Spain begins to colonize the Philippines, named in honor of Philip II	
1568-1649	The Netherlands begins 80-year war, culminating in independence from Spain	
1571	Under Philip II's half-brother John of Austria, combined fleets of Spain, Venice, and the Pope defeat the Turkish navy at Lepanto in the Mediterranean; victory ends threat of Turkish invasion of Western Europe	
1580	Philip II joins Portugal and the Portuguese empire to that of Spain	
1588	Spanish Armada fails in its attempt to invade England; is nearly destroyed	
1598-1621	Reign of Philip III; less adept than Philip II, he delegates duties to the Duke of Lerma; Golden Age begins to draw to a close	*The Swindler* by Francisco de Quevedo
1599-1600	An epidemic of plague claims half a million victims in Castile	
1609	Spain expels the Moriscos, last remaining Muslims in Spain	
1618-48	Spain and other European nations fight Thirty Years' War following a political crisis in Bohemia	
1621-65	Reign of Philip IV, who also delegates duties to a favorite, the Count-Duke of Olivares; Spain enters period of decline as a world power	
1621-1700	Philip IV and Charles II wage unsuccessful wars, weakening Spanish rule	
1639	Spanish fleet suffers decisive defeat at hands of the Dutch in Battle of the Downs	
1640	Portugal regains independence from Spain; Catalonians in northwest Spain revolt, drive out royal troops; French occupy Catalonia in 1642; it becomes French protectorate	
1651-52	Spanish army retakes Catalan city of Barcelona	
1650s	American slave trade lends new vigor to institution of slavery in Spain	*The Disenchantments of Love* by María de Zayas y Sotomayor
1659	Treaty confirms restoration to Spain of Catalonia, except for region north of the Pyrenees Mountains, which is lost forever	
1665	Death of Philip IV; accession of sickly Charles II creates the problem of future succession to Spanish throne	
1665-1700	Reign of Charles II	

BOURBON SPAIN TO IMPERIAL DECLINE

With the accession of Philip V (1700-46) came the end of the Habsburg monarchy and the beginning of the Bourbon dynasty on the Spanish throne. This new dynasty was related to the one in France, whose Louis XIV was grandfather to Spain's Philip V. It is thus hardly surprising that the eighteenth and nineteenth centuries saw an infusion of many things French into Spain, from fashion to attitudes toward science and education. The Spanish army, for instance, adopted French-style uniforms and equipment. In other ways the monarchy and its regime remained distinctly Spanish. Nevertheless, many in the general population bristled at all the foreign-inspired innovation, forming a backlash. They balked at the cultural "invasion" favored by the king and his court, staunchly resisting new customs. Meanwhile, Spain's political decline continued, mushrooming into a long era of decadence, during which the country lost European and American territories and began viewing itself as second rate. Yet until the 1820s, Spain maintained control of most of its valuable possessions, remaining globally important, even if it was no longer a foremost power in Europe. The Spanish, despite this still encouraging reality, harbored a sense of fading prominence. No longer did they feel the same sense of self-confidence exhibited in the Imperial Age; the sense was replaced by an ambivalence in how they felt about Spain. This mostly new ambivalence encouraged a minority to open their minds to fresh ideas and cultural reforms. Slowly the minority grew, particularly in the political arena. By the early nineteenth century, government had become an arena for experimentation, paralleling and influenced by similar developments elsewhere in Europe, especially in post-Revolutionary France.

Historical Events	Related Literary Works in *WLAIT 5*
1700 Death of Charles II, after naming the grandson of Louis XIV of France as his heir	
1700-46 Reign of Philip V, first Bourbon ruler, introduces innovations into Spanish society; Philip founds Royal Library and Spanish Academy; clashes with the Catholic Church	"An Essay on Woman" by Benito Jerónimo Feijóo
1702-14 War of the Spanish Succession—Austrians and British attempt to replace Philip V with Archduke Charles of Austria; Philip retains his throne but Austrians take over most of Spain's European possessions and British obtain Gibraltar and Menorca; Aragon, Valencia, and Catalonia lose autonomy	
1713 Philip V passes edict barring women from the throne	
1716 The Decree of Nueva Planta replaces government of Catalonia with authorities tied to Madrid	
1740-48 War of the Austrian Succession—Spain allied to France against Austria; Philip V conquers Milan in 1744 but is driven out in 1745; Spain's future Carlos III (Charles III) becomes king of the Two Sicilies; involvement in Italian conflicts ends	
1759-88 Reign of Charles III, considered Spain's most enlightened despot	
1762-69 Seven Years' War with Great Britain; Spain loses Florida to Britain but gains Louisiana from France	
1766 Famine in central Spain due to three years of bad harvest; riots break out in Madrid over government attempt to ban traditional capes and hats and over the cost of bread	

	Historical Events	Related Literary Works in *WLAIT 5*
1767	Charles III orders the expulsion of the Jesuits from Spain, blaming them for inciting the Madrid riots	
1779-83	Spain sides with America in its war of independence against Great Britain; Spain secures control of Florida and Menorca from Britain	
1785	Adoption of a Spanish flag, replacing separate flags and banners of military orders, old kingdoms, and the like	
1788-1808	Reign of Charles IV	
1793-95	Charles IV declares war on France after French revolutionaries execute his kinsman, Louis XVI; Spain loses Caribbean possession of Santo Domingo to France	*The Maiden's Consent* by Leandro Fernández de Moratín
1793-1805	French troops invade Spain, forcing it into an alliance against Britain; in 1796-1802 Spain joins France in war against Great Britain; British blockade devastates trade between Spain and its empire and Europe	
1797	British defeat Spanish fleet at Cape St. Vincent on western coast of Madagascar	
1804-1808	Allied again with France, now under control of Napoleon Bonaparte, Spain renews hostilities with Great Britain	
1805	French-Spanish forces defeated by British at sea in Battle of Trafalgar; some 2,000 Spaniards and French die, followed by innumerable drownings in week-long gale	
1808-14	French emperor, Napoleon, forces Charles IV and Ferdinand VII to abdicate, places brother Joseph on Spanish throne, provoking Spanish guerrilla warfare against French and Peninsular War between Britain (Spain's ally) and France; Spain conducts War of Independence	
1813	Battle of Vitoria becomes decisive battle of Peninsular War; Joseph loses 7,000 men; battle ends Napoleon's rule in Spain and French retreat across Pyrenees	
1810-26	Most colonies of Spanish America are lost to independence movements; Spain retains Cuba, Puerto Rico, the Philippines, Guam, the Caroline Islands, and outposts in North Africa	
1812	First Spanish constitution is promulgated at Cadiz; abolishes aristocratic legal privileges; establishes one-house legislature, giving crown only veto; constitutes one of most advanced documents of its time in Europe	
1814	Restored to the throne, Ferdinand VII abolishes constitution of 1812	
1814-33	Absolutist reign of Ferdinand VII drives many Spanish liberals into exile	
1820-1823	Liberals revolt, leading to restoration of 1812 constitution; French invade Spain, re-establish Ferdinand VII as monarch	
1833	Death of Ferdinand VII leaves his three-year-old daughter, Isabel, heir to the throne	
1833-40	Regency of Queen Mother María Cristina; Spanish Inquisition is formally dissolved by royal decree in 1834	
1834-39	Onset of civil wars—first Carlist War in favor of Ferdinand's brother, Don Carlos, pits reactionaries against liberals	*The Sea Gull* by Fernán Caballero
1843-68	Reign of Isabella II, marked by unstable government, political turmoil, and popular rebellions; *pronunciamientos* (changes of government effected by military)	
1848-49	Second Carlist War erupts after Isabella II marries her cousin, heir to the Duke of Cadiz; war ends a year later	

Historical Events		Related Literary Works in *WLAIT 5*
1868	Isabel II is deposed; so-called "Glorious Revolution" drives her and royal family into exile	*The House of Ulloa* by Emilia Pardo Bazán; *The Infinite Passion* by Gustavo Adolfo Bécquer
1868-78	First Cuban War of Independence	
1869	Constitution of 1869 establishes constitutional monarchy that includes religious tolerance and universal suffrage; becomes one of many short-lived constitutions promulgated in nineteenth-century Spain	
1870	Amadeo, son of Victor Emmanuel of Italy, chosen as king of Spain	
1872-76	Third Carlist War grows out of uprisings in Basque provinces, Navarre, and parts of Catalonia; after Alfonso XII accedes to the throne, he mounts large-scale offensive that drives many Carlist rebels to flee to France	
1873	King Amadeo abdicates	
1873-74	Formation and dissolution of First Spanish Republic	
1875	Restoration of Bourbon monarchy	*Fortunata and Jacinta* by Benito Pérez Galdós; *La Regenta* (The Judge's Wife) by Leopoldo Alas ("Clarín")
1875-85	Reign of Alfonso XII, son of Isabella II	
1878	Clandestine Socialist Party is formed	
1885-1909	Era of *turno pacífico* system—Liberal and Conservative parties alternate in power via elections managed by minister of interior and local bosses	
1886	Alfonso XIII becomes king, under regency of his mother	
1888	Socialists form General Union of Workers	
1890	Universal suffrage is granted to Spanish males	

POST-IMPERIALISM TO EUROPEAN UNION

The outcome of the Spanish-American War in 1898 dealt a death blow to the erstwhile Spanish empire—in the aftermath, Cuba became independent, while Guam, Puerto Rico, and the Philippines were ceded to the victorious United States. With the loss of its last overseas territories, Spain was forced to acknowledge and come to terms with its inferior status as a world power. The twentieth century saw numerous attempts by committed voices to define Spain as a nation in the post-imperial era. Attempts at forging a national identity ran the gamut from distinct intellectual and cultural movements—the Generations of 1898 and 1927—to social and political redefinition of the government. By turns, Spain operated as a constitutional monarchy, a republic, and a dictatorship under General Francisco Franco. After Franco's death in 1975, Spain re-established itself as both a hereditary monarchy (with the accession of Juan Carlos I) and a democracy (with the passage of the Law of Political Reform). In 1977 the Kingdom of Spain, a constitutional monarchy modeled after the United Kingdom, held its first free elections in 40 years; the center-right political faction was victorious. Since then, experimentation has continued, with conservative and socialist administrations providing alternate styles of leadership in government throughout the 1980s and 1990s. Meanwhile, in 1986, Spain joined the European Community (as did Portugal). Spain made Europeanization a priority of national policy, a goal that has had a pervasive effect on lifestyles in the country.

Historical Events	Related Literary Works in *WLAIT 5*
1898 Loss of Spanish-American War ends Spanish empire in the New World—Cuba gains independence and Guam, Puerto Rico, and the Philippines are lost to the United States; loss leads to earnest struggle by intellectuals to define Spain *Meditations on Quixote* by Jos Ortega y Gasset	
1902-1931 Reign of Alfonso XIII	
1909 General strike in Catalonia leads to church-burning and rioting in Barcelona; brutal government repression follows	
1910s-30s Rise of anarchist and fascist movements in Spain	*Bohemian Lights* by Ramón María del Valle-Inclán
1912 Spain establishes a protectorate over northwest Morocco	
1914 Catalonia receives grant of partial autonomy	
1914-18 Spain declares neutrality in World War I	
1917 General strike leads to crackdown by army	
1918-23 Period of labor unrest in Spain results in deaths of an estimated 1,500 people; post-World War I economic depression	
1921 Spanish army attempts to suppress dissidents in Morocco; 15,000 Spanish soldiers are massacred	
1923-30 Military dictatorship of General Primo de Rivera is supported by Alfonso XIII	
1925-27 Spanish and French forces unite to defeat Moroccan leader Abd el-Krim	
1929-39 Stock market crash in America, followed by global economic depression	*Poet in New York* by Federico García Lorca
1930 General Primo de Rivera is forced to resign	
1931 Alfonso XIII goes into voluntary exile; majority republican vote leads to proclamation of Second Republic, featuring democratic, reformist government	
1931-36 Under Second Republic, women gain new rights, including the vote; have little time to exercise them before fall of Republic; large swath of population remains conservative	*The Back Room* by Carmen Martín Gaite; *The House of Bernarda Alba* by Federico García Lorca
1933 José Antonio Primo de Rivera founds Falange party, modeled on fascist party in Italy	
1933-36 Right-wing politicians return to power under Second Republic, undo new reforms	
1934 Army suppresses armed revolts in Catalonia and Asturias	
1936 Left-wing factions unite and form Popular Front, win decisive majority in general elections	
1936-39 Spanish Civil War—right-wing generals attempt coup, resulting in three years of civil war; armed by Germany's Adolf Hitler and Italy's Benito Mussolini, right-wing camp of Nationalist forces under Spain's Francisco Franco and others emerge victorious; 500,000 to 1,000,000 perish, making this the bloodiest of Spain's many civil wars	*Requiem for a Spanish Peasant* by Ramón Sender; *Marks of Identity* by Juan Goytisolo; *Nada* by Carmen Laforet; *The Family of Pascual Duarte* by Camilo José Cela
1937 German planes bomb Guernica; Picasso displays his famous war painting *Guernica* in the Paris World Fair; May Crisis in Barcelona triggers open fighting between anarchists and communists	
1939-45 Spain remains officially neutral during World War II, but Franco sends troops and raw materials to Axis powers	

Historical Events	Related Literary Works in *WLAIT 5*
1939-75 Dictatorship of General Francisco Franco	*The Back Room* by Carmen Martín Gaite; *Marks of Identity* by Juan Goytisolo; *Time of Silence* by Luis Martín Santos
1940s Spain suffers post-Civil War economic depression	*Nada* by Carmen Laforet; *Time of Silence* by Luis Martín-Santos
1948-53 During the Cold War, Spain becomes an ally of the United States and NATO, whose attitude to Franco consequently softens	*Marks of Identity* by Juan Goytisolo
1954-73 Period of dramatic growth for Spanish economy, largely due to burgeoning tourist industry promoted by Franco regime. Spaniards come in contact with millions of tourists from the democratic West	
1955 Spain is admitted to the United Nations	
1956 Spanish protectorate in Morocco is abolished	
1959-90s Formation of ETA (Euskadi ta Askatasuna), a Basque separatist organization that practices terrorism; ETA stages car bombings during the 1980s and 1990s	
1962 Spain requests admission to European Common Market; series of strikes sweeps Spain, protesting working conditions	
1969 Franco proclaims Prince Juan Carlos, grandson of Alfonso XIII, Spain's future king and head of state; Juan Carlos's father, Juan de Borbón, is bypassed; interrupts the legitimate line of Spanish monarchs	
1975 Five anti-Francoist militants are executed; Franco dies; Juan Carlos I becomes king	*The Back Room* by Carmen Martín Gaite
1976 The Law of Political Reform establishes democracy in Spain, after being endorsed by almost 95 percent of voters	
1977 Spain holds first free elections in 40 years; the center-right founds a government under leadership of Adolfo Suarez; the Spanish Communist Party is legalized; negotiations begin for membership in European Economic Community (EEC)	
1978 National referendum approves new democratic constitution guaranteeing civil liberties and regional autonomy: ETA attacks on security forces lead to more than 50 deaths	
1979-80 The Basques and Catalans receive wide degree of autonomy; Spain becomes quasi-federal state of 17 Autonomous Communities	
1981 Parliament is held hostage during an attempted military coup that is thwarted by King Juan Carlos, who thereby earns widespread popular support.	
1982 Spain joins North Atlantic Treaty Organization (NATO); Socialists win landslide election victory; leader Felipe González becomes prime minister	
1984 Felipe González takes stand against terrorism and approves federal budget that grants large sums for modernization of armed forces and for education	
1986 Spain and Portugal join European Economic community	
1992 Olympic Games are held in Barcelona; World Expo-92 is held in Seville	
1996 Center-right Popular Party wins majority of seats in Cortes; leader José María Aznár becomes prime minister.	
1997 Mass protests against continued terrorism in the Basque country	
1999 Spain joins NATO military action against Serbia	

Historical Events	Related Literary Works in *WLAIT 5*
2000 Popular Party wins election with overall majority; José María Aznár is sworn in for second term as prime minister	
2002 Spain adopts Eurodollar as its currency and abandons the Spanish peseta	

INTELLECTUAL AND ARTISTIC MOVEMENTS: FROM THE RENAISSANCE TO LATE-TWENTIETH-CENTURY LITERARY CURRENTS

Like many European nations, Spain experienced a cultural rebirth during the Renaissance, largely a sixteenth-century phenomenon on the peninsula. The study of Latin and other classical languages led to the founding of Alcalá University in 1508 and the development of a multilingual Bible in Spain, milestones achieved by a small minority of scholars. The Renaissance paralleled Spain's pre-eminence as a world empire. Spearheaded by Castile, the growth of this empire led to the diffusion of the Castilian language, which became generally known as the language of Spain. As the century progressed, arts and letters flourished in Spain, flowering from roughly the mid-sixteenth to the mid-seventeenth century, an epoch regarded as Spain's literary Golden Age. The early part of this epoch saw the gold imported from the colonies put to artistic use, the precious metal inspiring magnificent architectural feats as well as works in the decorative arts. Also stimulating vigorous artistic activity was all the Continental travel inspired by military and political efforts. Encouraged by the expansion of the Spanish empire, this travel lent an international as well as a native dimension to many of the artistic works. Censorship meanwhile became an enduring reality in Spanish art and letters, the Inquisition continuing to regard it as a necessary restraint on potentially dangerous cultural influences. At times cunningly, the Spanish arts reached unparalleled heights despite the restraint. New intellectual and artistic movements surfaced in Spain as elsewhere in Europe and in the Americas. Emerging during and enduring beyond the Golden Age was the Baroque movement, followed by the Enlightenment, Romanticism, *costumbrismo,* realism, naturalism, modernism, social realism, and other twentieth-century literary currents. Spain's final loss of its overseas empire in the Spanish-American War at the close of the nineteenth century motivated pensive reaction in Spain that greatly affected the course of twentieth-century literature. Generations of intellectuals pondered the trajectory of their nation's political and social evolution, struggling to make sense of it in a way that would allow them to define Spanish identity. Of particular note are the Generations of 1898 and of 1927, which became the definitive voices for the twentieth century. Members of the two generations attempted to reclaim and reassert Spain's literary heritage, even as they extended it through impressive works of their own.

Historical Events	Related Literary Works in *WLAIT 5*
c. 1450-70 Spanish scholars study in Italy, return to Spain with high regard for Latin literature and Renaissance thought; Italians teach at the University of Salamanca	
1472 First printed book (*Sinodal*) using movable type issued in Segovia	
1499 *La Celestina* appears in print; will become second most renown work, after *Don Quixote,* in Castilian literature.	*La Celestina* by Fernando de Rojas

Historical Events	Related Literary Works in *WLAIT 5*
1514-1614 Life span of the Spanish painter El Greco; born in Crete, he came to Toledo in 1577	
1520s Spanish thinkers influenced by teachings of Dutch reformer Desiderius Erasmus, who criticizes church corruption and advocates a return to primitive Christianity	
1543 Publication of *Las obras de Boscán y algunas de Garcilaso de la Vega,* a collection of poetry by Juan Boscán and Garcilaso de la Vega, which revolutionizes Castilian verse, reorienting, Italianizing, and refining lyric poetry.	
1554 Publication of first picaresque novel in Spain *Lazarillo de Tormes*	
c. 1550-1650 Spanish Golden Age spawns literary giants in poetry, drama, and the novel	"The Dark Night" and Other Poems by Saint John of the Cross; *Interior Castle* by Saint Teresa of Avila; *Don Quixote* by Miguel de Cervantes; *Fuente Ovejuna* by Lope de Vega; *Life Is a Dream* by Pedro Calderón de la Barca; *The Swindler* by Francisco de Quevedo
1550-1700 Rise and heyday of Baroque movement in Spain, featuring irregularity, the inner life, and complexity of elements	*Life Is a Dream* by Pedro Calderón de la Barca
1599-1660 Life and career of Spanish painter Diego Rodríguez de Velázquez; known for portraits of daily life; his techniques and themes lead to impressionism in the 1800s	
1605 and 1615 Publication of Parts 1 and 2 of Miguel de Cervantes's *Don Quixote,* the first modern novel in world literature	*Don Quixote* by Miguel de Cervantes
1700-1720 Decline of the Baroque movement in literature; writings by imitators of the genre	
1700s-1800s The Enlightenment reaches Spain, but never becomes as widespread or powerful as in France or England	"An Essay on Woman" by Benito Jerónimo Feijóo y Montenegro; *The Maiden's Consent* by Leandro Fernández de Moratín
1746-1828 Life and career of Francisco José de Goya, who becomes fashionable portrait painter, inside and outside the court of Charles IV	
1819 Opening of Prado Museum	
1830s-50s Influenced by trends in Europe, Spanish novelists, dramatists, and poets establish their own Romantic movement, featuring individualism, emotionalism, and a re-exploration of Spain's Golden Age; heyday of *costumbrismo* literature, which focuses on ways of life in various areas of Spain	"The Old-Fashioned Castilian" by Mariano José de Larra; *Don Juan Tenorio* by José Zorrilla; *The Student of Salamanca* by José de Espronceda; *The Sea Gull* by Fernán Caballero
1830s-80s Period of technological development and modernization in Spain—steam power, postage stamps, the decimal system, telegraphs, and railways are all introduced	*La Regenta* by Leopoldo Alas ("Clarín"); *The House of Ulloa* by Emilia Pardo Bazán
late 1850s-80s Second wave of Romanticism in Spain, often referred to as post-Romanticism	*The Infinite Passion* by Gustavo Adolfo Bécquer; *Beside the River Sar* by Rosalía de Castro
1860 Census records population of 15.6 million; 178,934 women, in contrast to 6,346 men, are reported as living in poverty	*Fortunata and Jacinta* by Benito Pérez Galdós
c. 1868-1890 Realist and naturalist movements in Spanish literature	*Fortunata and Jacinta* by Benito Pérez Galdós; *La Regenta* by "Clarín"
1877-1900 Population of Madrid increases dramatically; in 1900, reaches one million	*The Quest* by Pío Baroja
1880s-1900s Bohemian lifestyle gains momentum through association with literary movement of "modernismo," concerned in its initial stage with art for art's sake	*Bohemian Lights* by Ramón María del Valle-Inclán
1881-1973 Life span of Pablo Ruiz Picasso, who revolutionizes painting by helping to invent cubism in 1907	

	Historical Events	Related Literary Works in *WLAIT 5*
1890-1910	Influenced by European and Latin American writers, modernist movement develops; celebrates creativity, individualism, and subjectivity; Catalan writer Joan Maragall (1860-911) and Portuguese writer Fernando Pessoa (1888-1935) join ranks of foremost modernists	*Fields of Castile* by Antonio Machado
1893-1983	Life span of Catalan painter Joan Miró, a surrealist painter of infantile dream-visions	
c. 1895-1915	Late naturalist movement	
1898-	Loss of the Spanish-American War; emergence of Generation	
early 1900s	of 1898—a group of young Spanish writers and intellectuals who expound on the identity and destiny of Spain and greatly influence younger writers	*Bohemian Lights* by Ramón María del Valle-Inclán; *Fields of Castile* by Antonio Machado; *The Quest* by Pío Baroja; *Mist* by Miguel de Unamuno; *Meditations on Quixote* by José Ortega y Gasset
1900s-1960s	Existentialist movement begins to develop in response to realist movement and acquires new momentum in the 1960s	*Mist* by Miguel de Unamuno; *Time of Silence* by Luis Martín-Santos
1904-89	Life span of Spanish painter Salvador Dalí, a surrealist painter of symbolic psychological dream-visions	
1927-30s	Generation of 1927—a group of young Spanish poets—progressive, middle-class, residents of 1920s and 1930s Madrid—come of age; expatriate community develops after many members of the Generation of '27 go abroad to escape political turmoil in Spain.	*Poet in New York* by Federico García Lorca; *The House of Bernarda Alba* by Federico García Lorca
late 1940s-60s	Social-realist novels center on small details of daily life; literature tries to fill in vacuum created by censorship of press	*The Family of Pascual Duarte* by Camilo José Cela; *Time of Silence* by Luis Martín-Santos
1960s-	Mid- to late-twentieth century literary currents show increased concern for experimentation in form and content	*The Back Room* by Carmen Martín Gaite; *Marks of Identity* by Juan Goytisolo

PORTUGAL: INVASION OF THE ROMANS TO POST-COLONIAL REPARATIONS

In many respects, Portugal's development as a nation paralleled that of its neighbor, Spain. The same ancient peoples settled there, Christianity became both countries' recognized faith, and the invading Muslims set their stamp on Portugal as well as Spain. The two nations themselves maintained an uneasy relationship across the centuries. Gaining its independence from León and Castile in the twelfth century, Portugal went on to distinguish itself independently of Spain as the foremost navigational explorer of Europe, the power that opened the Eastern Hemisphere to trade and exchange with the Western Hemisphere. Portugal's empire grew, including commercial ports that stretched from Brazil in the Americas to Ceuta, Africa; Calicut, India; and Macao, China. In 1580, after amassing this enviable empire, Portugal was united with Spain but broke free in 1640, and, except for a brief period during the Napoleonic Wars, has remained independent ever since. The nineteenth and twentieth centuries saw internal strife in the form of civil wars and a repressive dictatorship that lasted nearly five decades. Before the end of the twentieth century, the dictatorship had collapsed. Today Portugal is a democratic republic. Unlike other European countries, it held fast to its overseas colonies in the post-World War II era, fighting protracted wars in Africa that contributed greatly to bringing down the Portuguese dictatorship. Contributing also to its collapse was a national literature that, in keeping with tradition, challenged societal norms. The literature features a series of artistic movements that overlap in time and are linked to developments abroad and at home.

Historical Events	Related Literary Works in *WLAIT 5*
194-93 B.C.E. Lusitanians begin armed struggle against the Romans; Viriatus leads a successful defense that ensues for decades	
100s B.C.E. Portugal becomes part of the Roman Empire	
82 B.C.E. Sertorius leads a native uprising against Rome in Lusitania	
19 B.C.E. Romans pacify Lusitania	
409 C.E. Suevi, Vandals, and Alans occupy western Iberia	
711 Muslims invade Iberian Peninsula	
844 Viking attacks begin	
868 Christians resettle Oporto	
1054 Christian reconquest of Seia, Viseu, Lamego, and Tarouca	
1064 Definitive Christian reconquest of Coimbra	
1097 Alfonso VI, king of León, Castile, Galicia, and Portugal, marries his daughter Tarasia to Henri of Burgundy, with Portugal as her dowry	
1109 Henri of Burgundy frees Portugal from feudal dependence on León	
1128 Afonso Henriques begins his reign in Portugal; battle of São Mamede	
1139 Battle of Ourique; Afonso Henriques takes the title "king"	
1143 Portugal becomes an independent nation; beginning of the Burgundian dynasty's nine kings; establishment of Cistercian Order and construction of the royal convent of Alcobaça, the final resting place of Burgundian royalty	*Message* by Fernando Pessoa
1147-1217 Reconquest of Santarém and Lisbon	
1165 Reconquest of Évora	
1200s-1300s First collections of Portuguese-Galician verse called *cantigas*	
1211 First Cortes (parliament) convened at Coimbra	
1249 Under Afonso III (1246-79); Christians conquer Algarve from Muslims; Reconquest in Portugal is completed under Afonso's reign	
1254 Leiria Parliament is convened; representatives of the lower class participate for the first time	
1261-1325 Reign of King Dinis; a gifted poet and ruler, Dinis establishes Portuguese as official language, organizes Military Order of Christ (continuation of the Knights Templar), institutes agrarian reform and coastal forestation, fosters urban renewal, and sponsors international fairs	
1290 Apex of medieval Portugal; first Portuguese University is founded under King Dinis	
1297 Frontier is established between Portugal and Castile (Alcanises Treaty)	
1347-52 Portuguese population diminishes considerably due to the "black plague" and the increase in cereal prices	
1355 Murder of Inês de Castro and consequent revolt of Prince Pedro against his father, King Afonso IV; civil war ensues	
1357 Pedro assumes the throne, has the body of Inês disinterred and her corpse crowned as his queen, and marries her; dies in 1367, after which the tombs of Inês and Pedro at Alcobaça become a national treasure	

	Historical Events	Related Literary Works in *WLAIT 5*
1369-81	Series of wars between Portugal and Castile	
1385	Election of King John I and beginning of the Avis dynasty, which sees eight monarchs ascend the throne; King John's queen will be Philippa of Lancaster, England; their son, Henry the Navigator, will begin the Age of Discovery	
1386	Alliance with England, the world's oldest treaty still in force	
1400s-1500s	Renaissance in Portugal; Sá de Miranda (1481-1558) introduces new poetic styles; Crown sponsors studies abroad by Portuguese; João de Barros and Diogo de Couto chronicle voyages of exploration	*The India Play* by Gil Vicente
1415-1600s	Portuguese Age of Expansion and Discovery	*The India Play* by Gil Vicente; *The Lusiads* by Luis de Camões; *Message* by Fernando Pessoa
1427-32	Estimated discovery of the first of the nine Azorean islands settled by Portugal during its explorations of a sea route to India	*Stormy Isles* by Vitorino Nemésio
1438	Prince Henry the Navigator (1394-1460) sponsors maritime explorations and voyages of discovery	*The Lusiads* by Luis de Camões; *Message* by Fernando Pessoa
1467-70	Heroic paintings at Cathedral of St. Vincent (Lisbon) by premier artist Nuno Gonçalves, depict St. Vincent, royal court (including Henry the Navigator), clerics, fishermen, businessmen, and other members of society	
1495	First printed book in Portuguese—a translation of *Vita Christi* by Ludolfo de Saxónia	
1476	King Afonso of Portugal and Princess Juana of Castile engage in war of succession over Castilian throne with rival claimants Isabella and Ferdinand	*Fuente Ovejuna* by Lope de Vega
1487-88	Bartolomeu Dias rounds the Cape of Good Hope (Africa's southernmost cape) and opens up the way for the charting of Africa's East Coast	
1495	Accession of King Manuel (1495-1521), during whose reign Portugal extends its overseas empire in Africa, Arabia, India, Asia, and America; Manueline decorative art—Portugal's foremost art period—features such monuments as imposing monastery of Jerónimos and tower of Belém	
1496	Order to expel Jews from Portugal issued by King Manuel, but not carried out.	
1497-98	Vasco da Gama discovers sea route to India, arriving at Calicut, India	*The India Play* by Gil Vicente; *The Lusiads* by Luis de Camões; *Message* by Fernando Pessoa
1500	Pedro Álvares Cabral claims Brazil for Portugal	
1506	Anti-Jewish riots in Lisbon	
1519	Ferdinand de Magellan (Fernão de Magalhães), the Portuguese navigator, begins the world's first voyage of circumnavigation under the sponsorship of Spain	
1524	Vasco da Gama is sent back to India as viceroy	
1529	Treaty of Zaragoza gives the Moluccas to the Portuguese	
1531-36	King João II asks the Pope to establish Inquisition in Portugal; Inquisition is inaugurated five years later	*Baltasar and Blimunda* by José Saramago
1534	Portuguese occupy Diu in India	
1536	Portuguese Inquisition is established after the Spanish model; ends in 1821.	
1537	João III reforms Lisbon's university and transfers it to Coimbra	
1540	Catholic Church introduces censorship; Jesuits arrive in Portugal	

Historical Events		Related Literary Works in *WLAIT 5*
1543	Private Portuguese traders reach Japan	
1557	Portuguese attain commercial rights to Macao at mouth of the Pearl River, China	
1578	Portugal's King Sebastian is killed in North Africa; beginning of the messianic phenomenon called Sebastianism, which holds that the king did not die, but was enchanted and will return in triumph	"By the Rivers of Babylon" by Jorge de Sena; *The Lusiads* by Luis de Camões; *Message* by Fernando Pessoa
1580	Union of Spain and Portugal under Philip II, who claimed the vacant throne as the rightful heir through his Portuguese mother and grandfather King Manuel; beginning of so-called 60 year "Babylonian Captivity"	
1580s-1650s	Portugal competes with the Netherlands for territorial holdings in Africa and the New World	
1607	Portugal loses the Moluccas to the Dutch	
1615	Portuguese conquest of Maranhão, Brazil	
1640	Portugal declares its independence from Spain, which does not recognize it until 1668; beginning of the Bragança Dynasty, Portugal's last, which saw the reign of 13 monarchs, including two queens	
1640-1700s	Growth of a commercial bourgeoisie due to Brazilian colonization and trade in sugar, tobacco, and gold; essays promote Portuguese mercantilism, warn against excessive reliance on Brazil; Baroque and anti-Castilian literature flourishes; King João V turns to foreigners and foreign-educated Portuguese for cartography, medicine, engineering, and the arts	*Baltasar and Blimunda* by José Saramago
1644	*Trovas,* or nationalist messianic verses, of Bandarra the Prophet are published	
1648	Portugal reconquers Luanda, a port in Angola, from the Dutch	
1654	Portugal recovers northern Brazil from the Dutch	
1668	Spain recognizes Portugal's independence	
1693	Gold is discovered in Brazil in such quantities that it produces 80 percent of the world's gold supply in the 1700s, catapulting Portugal back into world prominence	
1711-30s	Portugal's second major art period, Joanine, named after King João V; he constructs the Basilica and Palace of Mafra to fulfill a vow made in honor of his queen's presenting him with an heir; although Pope calls King João "The Most Faithful," his blatant immorality is mirrored throughout the upper classes	*Baltasar and Blimunda* by José Saramago
1729	Diamonds are discovered in Minas Gerais, Brazil	
1752	Creation of Mozambique as a Portuguese captaincy—captain-general becomes first Portuguese administrator of area	
1755	Earthquake and fire destroys three-fourths of Lisbon, leading to massive reconstruction of city in Neoclassical style; it is widely held that the destruction is a just punishment from God; José I is the new king, but his prime minister, the Marquês de Pombal, is the power behind the throne	
1756	Pombal becomes chief minister; successfully curbs the power of the nobility, dismantles the Inquisition, expels the Jesuits, institutes far-reaching reforms	
1759	Expulsion of Jesuits from Portugal and its colonies	
1761	Slavery is abolished in mainland Portugal; elimination of slavery for Brazilian Indians.	

Historical Events		Related Literary Works in *WLAIT 5*
1769	Portugal abandons Mazagão, the country's last post in Morocco	
1772	Educational reforms in Portugal promote growing secularization	
1773	Abolition of mandatory registration of New Christians (former Jews or descendants of converts)	
1792	Domingos António Sequeira, Portugal's foremost painter next to Nuno Gonçalves, begins his long career with the monumental "Allegory of the Casa Pia"	
1807-11	French forces invade Portugal, touching off Peninsular Wars; the Portuguese royal family departs to Brazil along with 15,000 courtiers and the national treasury and library; kingdom's capital is transferred to Rio de Janeiro, the first and only time a European monarchy rules from one of its colonies	*Doomed Love* by Camilo Castelo Branco
1811-50s	After expulsion of French and conclusion of Peninsular Wars, Portuguese society remains in a state of social, economic, and political flux for decades to come	
1820	Revolt, modeled on the democratic Spanish revolution of 1812, ends British occupation of Portugal and leads to the drafting of a democratic constitution and recognition of Brazilian independence; Inquisition is abolished in Portugal	
1821	King João VI returns to Portugal from Brazil	
1822	Brazil declares independence but Portugal does not recognize it until 1825; Portuguese constitution is suspended	*Travels in My Homeland* by Almeida Garrett
1825	Publication of *Camões* by Almeida Garret initiates Romanticism in Portuguese literature	*Travels in My Homeland* by Almeida Garrett
1826	Constitutional Charter is granted by King Pedro IV; Pedro IV abdicates throne of Portugal in favor of his daughter Maria	
1830	After the European liberal revolution of 1830, Portugal again attempts fundamental political reform, expelling a royal pretender with absolutist aspirations, confiscating Crown lands, and dissolving the monasteries	
1831	Emperor Pedro I of Brazil (who is also Pedro IV of Portugal) abdicates the throne of Brazil in favor of his five-year-old son, Pedro II; returns to Portugal to remove his younger brother Miguel from and install his daughter Maria II on Portuguese throne	
1832-47	Rivalry in royal family between former Pedro IV and his brother Miguel leads to civil wars in Portugal; Miguel is exiled; war ends with the convention of Gramido; Portugal ultimately emerges as political democracy	
1834	Treaty of Évora Monte ends fighting between the Absolutists and Liberals	
1834-53	Reign of Maria II	
1837-68	Publication of *Panorama,* the first magazine devoted to Romantic letters	
1846	Vanguard of women, who were to be known by the name of Maria da Fonte, lead peasant rebellion in north, which is suppressed; Bank of Portugal is founded	
1850s-1918	Portugal consolidates control in areas of Africa	
1854	Slavery is abolished in Portuguese colonies	
1856	First railroad track is laid in Portugal; telegraph is installed	

Historical Events		Related Literary Works in *WLAIT 5*
1863	Decree changes inheritance laws, allows daughters to inherit from their parents	
1867	Abolition of death penalty in Portugal; first Civil Code improves situation of women in terms of the rights of the spouse, children, property and its administration	
1870s-90s	Late Romantic era writers ("Generation of the 1870s") denounce Portugal's political conservatism but compromise after British Ultimatum of 1890, calling selves *vencidos da vida*, ("the defeated by life"); initiation of realist genre in the arts, featuring gifted painters José Malhoa and Columbano	*The Maias* by Eça de Queirós
1870	Abolition of death penalty in colonies	
1876	Beginnings of Republican and Progressive parties in Portugal	
1880s	Portugal enters period of economic crisis—problems in textile industry, decline in wine exportation; active debate among politicians, economists, and thinkers on how to solve the nation's problems	
1887	Portuguese Macao recognized by China	
1890	British Ultimatum leads to Portugal's abandoning territory linking Angola to Mozambique in Africa; government starts setting up secondary schools for girls amidst controversy	
1891	Republican revolt in Oporto	
1908	Carlos I and eldest son are assassinated in Lisbon	
1910	Portugal is established as a republic after Manuel II abdicates, ending the monarchy; the writer Teófilo Braga becomes first president of the interim government; church and state are separated	
1911	Republican constitution is promulgated; Manuel d' Arriaga is first president; compulsory schooling for children between 7 and 11 is established	
1915	Manuel d'Arriaga resigns, Pimenta de Castro becomes dictator; publication of literary journal, *Orpheu,* initiates modernist movement in literature, introduces Portuguese public to poetics of European avant-guard; pre-eminent poet Fernando Pessoa (1888-1935), contributes to journal *Orpheu*; modernist writer and artist Almada Negreiros collaborates on journal	*Message* by Fernando Pessoa
1916	Portugal enters World War I on side of Allies	
1921	Portuguese Communist Party is established; leading political figures are murdered	
1922	Gago Coutinho and Sacadura Cabral complete the first flight across the South Atlantic Ocean	
1925	Portuguese complete colonial occupation of inland Angola and Mozambique	
1926-27	Military revolt and dictatorship; revolts against dictatorship in Oporto and Lisbon; new literary journal, *Presença* (1927-40), begins vigorous century-long activity	
1928	As Minister of Finance, António de Oliveira Salazar begins his rise to power; he will ultimately rule as dictator for 40 years	
1931	Recognition of right to vote for women with university degrees or secondary-school qualifications	
1932	António de Oliveira Salazar becomes prime minister, consolidates his powers on the way to becoming dictator	

Historical Events	Related Literary Works in *WLAIT 5*
1933-74 The New State is founded under the dictatorship of António Oliveira Salazar, adopting a new constitution that excludes women from rights of citizenship	*New Portuguese Letters* by Maria Isabel Barreno, Maria Teresa Horta, and Maria Velho da Costa (The Three Marias); *Ballad of Dogs' Beach* by José Cardoso Pires
1939 Portugal signs Treaty of Friendship and Peace with Franco's Spain	
1939-45 Portugal is neutral during Second World War	
late 1930s-60s Neo-realist movement in literature gives rise to anti-dictatorship poetry and prose	
1942 Portuguese loss of Indonesian island of Timor to Japanese; island is recovered after World War II	
1943 Portuguese come to secret accord with Allies for an air base in Azores	
1946 Failure of military revolt; Neo-realism in literature; surrealism begins to flourish in the arts as well; Mário Cessarini de Vasconcelos is leading painter	
1947 Labor leaders and army officers are deported to Cape Verde Islands	
1949 Portugal and 11 other nations form a military alliance, the North Atlantic Treaty Organization (NATO)	
1955 Portugal enters the United Nations	
1956 Establishment of the Calouste Gulbenkian Foundation, which will found libraries, museums, theaters, hospitals, orchestras, choruses, and journals and subsidize scholarships for research	
1958 Humberto Delgado runs for presidency; Admiral Américo Tomas wins elections	
1959-60 Military coup against Salazar fails; captain Almeida Santos, implicated in the rebellion, suffers political assassination	*Ballad of Dogs' Beach* by José Cardoso Pires
1960s Rebellions against Portuguese rule erupt in African colonies; Goa, Damão, and Diu are occupied by Indian forces in December of 1961; Portuguese immigrate in waves to America and European countries	
1961-74 Angola wages war for independence from Portugal	*South of Nowhere* by António Lobo Antunes
1963 Rebellion in Portuguese Guinea	
1964-74 Colonial war for independence in Portuguese colony of Mozambique	*The Murmuring Coast* by Lídia Jorge
1968 Marcello Caetano replaces Salazar after latter suffers a stroke	
1970s Postmodern-style literature questions official historical "truths," incorporates perspectives of the traditionally silenced on events of present and past, often accompanied by metafictional reflections on language, subjectivity, desire, and history	*Baltasar and Blimunda* by José Saramago; *The Murmuring Coast* by Lídia Jorge; *New Portuguese Letters* by Maria Isabel Barreno, Maria Teresa Horta and Maria Velho da Costa (The Three Marias); *South of Nowhere* by António Lobo Antunes
1972 The publication of *New Portuguese Letters* leads to prosecution of the Three Marias, and an international solidarity campaign on their behalf	
1973 Guinea-Bissau declares independence	
1974 Portuguese dictatorship (Estado Novo) is overthrown by revolution	
1975 Nearly all remaining colonies (including all in Africa) gain independence	
1976 Portugal holds its first free general election in over 30 years; Ramalho Eanes is elected president	

Historical Events	Related Literary Works in *WLAIT 5*
1979 Conservative Democratic Alliance, under leadership of Francisco Sá Carneiro, wins majority in Portuguese Assembly	
1980 Eanes is re-elected president; Sá Carneiro is killed in a plane crash	
1981 Francisco Pinto Balsemão becomes prime minister	
1986 Portugal joins the European Economic Community, an organization that becomes the basis of the European Union; Mário Soares succeeds Eanes as president	
1989 Revision of constitution: Marxist philosophy and rhetoric are purged from document	
1991 Soares is re-elected as president	
1992 Portugal signs Maastricht European Accord	
1995 President Jorge Sampaio and Prime Minister António Guterres take office	
1998 International Exposition (Expo '98) held in Lisbon	
1999 Macao reverts to China after nearly 500 years of Portuguese rule	
1999-2000 Portugal and Indonesia resume full diplomatic relations—severed since 1975 when Indonesia occupied former Portuguese colony East Timor; East Timor votes for independence from Indonesia	
2000 Portugal pledges annual $75,000,000 for reconstruction of East Timor, which will become eighth country whose official language is Portuguese	

Contents by Title

Contents by Title

Contents by Author

Contents by Author

Text and Image Credits

y Otros Textos Medievales, by Don Juan Manuel. —Fifteenth-century castle of Peñafiel looming above a small town, photograph by Mike Hammer. Reproduced by permission. —De Sena, Jorge, photograph. Property of Frederick G. Williams. Courtesy of Mecia de Sena. —Bust of Luis Vaz de Camões, sculpture by Raul Xavier, commissioned by the University of California at Berkeley, 1937, appearing in "Camoniana Californiana: Commemmorating the Quadricentennial of the Death of Luis Vaz de Camões," Proceedings of the Colloquium held at the University of California, Santa Barbara, April 25 and 26, 1980. Edited by Maria de Lourdes Belchior and Enrique Martinez-Lopez.—"Entrance into Granada," detail from the choir stalls in the Cathedral of Toledo, Spain, lithograph by Bachiller, photograph. The Art Archive/Bibliothhque des Arts Dicoratifs Paris/Dagli Orti. Reproduced by permission. —Pármeno and Sempronio killing Celestina and throwing themselves out of a window as authorities approach (top); executioner slitting the throats of Pármeno and Sempronio as authorities look on (bottom), woodcuts. From the 1514 Valencia edition of *La Celestina.* —St. John of the Cross, hands folded as if in prayer, halo of light surrounding his head, illustration. From *San Juan de la Cruz,* by José Luis L. Aranguren. Ediciones Jucar, 1973. — Saint John of the Cross sitting at a desk with a book in his hands, illustration. From *San Juan de la Cruz* by José Luis L. Aranguren. Ediciones Jucar, 1793. © Ediciones Jucar, 1973. —Two couples, caption reading "Dos parejas nobles," illustration. From *Tres Novelas Amorosas y Ejemplares y tres Desengan,* by María de Zayas Sotomay. Copyright © Editorial Castalia, S.A., 1989. — Convent of Las Duenas, Salamanca, Spain, photograph by Ruggero Vanni. © Vanni Archive/Corbis. Reproduced by permission.

Zorrilla y Moral, José, drawing. © Archivo Iconografico, S.A./Corbis-Bettmann. Reproduced by permission. —*Don Juan Tenorio,* costumes, photograph. Arte Publico Press Archives, University of Houston. Reproduced by permission. —Cervantes Saavedra, Miguel de. From *The History of That Ingenious Gentleman Don Quixote de la Mancha.* Translated by Burton Raffel. W.W. Norton, 1995. —Lithgow, John (on horseback), as Don Quixote, riding with Bob Hoskins (on donkey), as Sancho Panza, in a scene from the television movie "Don Quixote," photograph. AP/Wide World Photos. Reproduced by permission. —Branco, Camilo Castelo, 1876, drawing. —Title page from *Doomed [Fatal] Love: A Family Memoir (Amor de Perdicao),* by Camillo Castello Branco. —Feijóo y Montenegro, Benito Jerónimo, bronze bust after his death mask, photograph. Private collection, Santiago de Compostela, Spain. From "Simposio Sombre el Padre Feijóo y Su Siglo. Cuadernos de la Catedra Feijóo." Ovideo, Spain: Universidad de Oviedo, 1966. —Title page from *Universal Theater of Criticism,* by Benito Jerónimo Feijóo. —Cela, Camilo Jose, photograph by Isabel Steva Hernandez (Colita). © Colita/Corbis-Bettmann. Reproduced by permission. —Residents flee through the war-littered streets in Lerida in the region of Catalonia in northeastern Spain during the Spanish Civil War, on April 13, 1938, photograph. AP/Wide World Photos. Reproduced by permission. —Machado, Antonio, photograph. From the frontispiece of "Poesia completas," 1917, used in *Antonio Machado: Fragmentos de Biografia Espiritual,* by Juan José Coy, 1997. © Juan José Coy. © 1997, de esta edicion: Junta de Castilla y Leon. Consejeria de Educacion y Cultura. — "Self Portrait," drawing by Benito Pérez Galdós, left profile, shows just his head and collar, c. 1892. Casa Museo Pérez Galdós. Reproduced by permission. —Juanito Santa Cruz (bending over and touching a woman who looks startled), and his friend Villalonga, characters from *Fortunata and Jacinta,* drawing by Benito Pérez Galdós, c. 1867. Casa Museo Pérez Galdós. Reproduced by permission. —"Death to Narváez: Let every student follow me!" drawing of the Marqués de la Florida rousing anti-government sentiment before the massacre of the Eve of Saint Daniel on April 10, 1865, c. 1867, by Benito Pérez Galdós. Casa Museo Pérez Galdós. Reproduced by permission. —The owner of the Cafe Universal in Madrid and a waiter carrying a tray, c. 1867, drawing by Benito Pérez Galdós. Casa Museo Pérez Galdós. Reproduced by permission. —Caricature of Spanish Queen Isabella II, drawing by Benito Pérez Galdós. Actions by her government caused the Eve of Saint Daniel protests; she was deposed in September, 1868, and exiled to France, c. 1867. Casa Museo Pérez Galdós. Reproduced by permission. —"Fernando León y Castillo," drawing by Benito Pérez Galdós, c. 1867; this friend was the real-life model for Zalamero, a friend of Juanito Santa Cruz in *Fortunata and Jacinta,* by Pérez Galdós. Casa Museo Pérez Galdós. Reproduced by permission. —De Vega, Lope, illustration. Arte Público Press Archives, University of Houston. Reproduced by permission. —Scene from a theatrical production of Lope de Vega's play *Fuente Ovejuna,* photo-

The Back
Room

by
Carmen Martín Gaite

Carmen Martín Gaite was born in Salamanca, Spain, on December 8, 1925, "right in the middle of Primo de Rivera's dictatorship" (Martín Gaite, p. 129). As she describes in her autobiographical novel, *The Back Room*, she came of age during the Spanish Civil War under the regime of Francisco Franco. Martín Gaite studied at the University of Salamanca and at the University of Madrid, completing a doctoral thesis in Romance Philology. In 1954 she penned her first novel, *The Spa*, for which she won the Café Gijón Prize, and in 1957 she published *Between the Blinds*, which focuses on a girl growing up in Franco's Spain. After completing four more novels, Martín Gaite looked again at Franco's impact in her masterpiece, *The Back Room*. A postmodern classic that melds magical realism with historical events, *The Back Room* reveals the conscious and unconscious influences of Franco's dictatorship on the author's life and writing. A *kunstleroman* (novel of the development of an artist), the novel probes the many influences—including Hollywood, war, Golden Age literature, fantastic literature, and romance novels—that contributed to Martín Gaite's development as a writer and even explores how she derives the very novel we are reading. Triggered by Franco's death, the novel serves as both a personal psychological investigation and a social history of the repressive government's impact on an emerging artist.

Events in History at the Time of the Novel

The first autarky and the Second Republic. In the 1920s, when Carmen Martín Gaite was born,

---

> ### THE LITERARY WORK
>
> A novel set in Spain in 1975, reflecting on events from the Spanish Civil War (1936-39) to Franco's death (1975); published in Spanish (as *El cuarto de atrás*) in 1978; in English in 1983.
>
> ### SYNOPSIS
>
> Upon the dictator Francisco Franco's death, a female novelist recalls her life and experiences under the fascist regime.

Spain was still a largely agrarian nation just beginning to industrialize. A recent defeat in the Spanish American War (1898), which signified (at least symbolically) the death of the colonial empire, prompted a major ideological debate over how to restore Spain's former glory or at least bring the country into the twentieth century. The remedy imposed by dictator General Miguel Primo de Rivera was a system of autarky—an authoritarian, self-reliant government. Spain became a corporate, tightly controlled state like Mussolini's Italy. The press was censored, civil rights were suspended, and industry was nationalized. Though his tenure was relatively short (1923-30), Primo de Rivera's model of government and precedent as a dictator had profound, long-term implications. Soon both would be adopted by another, more tenacious general whose rule would greatly transform Spanish society—and Martín Gaite's life.

Carmen Martín Gaite

Primo de Rivera's exit gave birth to the Second Republic. The liberal parties of the left were voted into the Cortes (parliament) and ushered in a series of democratic reforms. The Constitution of 1931 granted women the right to vote, and the government promised to redistribute land and wealth among the majority of Spaniards who comprised the lower classes. Highly opposed to the power and wealth of the Catholic Church, the second prime minister, Manuel Azaña, publicly denounced it and declared, "Spain is no longer a Catholic country!" (Azaña in Pierson, p.

138). The government stopped state funding of the Church, converted the country to a system of secular public rather than private Catholic education, and legalized abortion and divorce.

Though the liberals had won a majority in the elections, Spain remained virtually split between two extremes: the far left and the far right. The Church and conservatives, who continued to have strong adherents, were greatly outraged by the new government's reforms. They had less to fear than one might suspect, however, for the Second Republic proved to be far more competent at passing reforms than implementing them. This frustrated the republic's supporters. In short, economic and social changes were too weak and slow for the left, too radical and rapid for the right, so that tensions mounted on both sides. These tensions resulted in a general strike by the left in 1934, poorly organized except in Asturias, where the miners effectively led the workers, only to suffer brutal repression at the hands of the army. The left, crushed in the strike, rebounded to win the general election in 1936, with Azaña becoming president of the republic. Positions polarized to the breaking point, impatience grew, and within five years the government of the left was attacked in a coup d'état by the right and the country found itself in the throes of a bloody civil war.

Spanish Civil War—Republicans vs. Nationalists. In broad terms the Spanish Civil War (1936-39) was a fight between Republicans and Nationalists; between the liberal left and the conservative right. Republicans included antifascists, Anarchists, Socialists, Communists, Libertarians, artists, intellectuals, much of the lower classes, atheists, and non-Catholics. Nationalists consisted largely of strong supporters of the Catholic Church and most clergy, the military, the landed classes and nobility, fascists, Falangists, and Carlists (the extreme Catholic right).

With World War II looming, Adolf Hitler and Benito Mussolini saw an advantage in allying themselves with Spain's Nationalist leader Generalissimo Francisco Franco. He had gained a reputation as a tough military man by fighting campaigns in Morocco on behalf of Spain, and he espoused the familiar fascist rhetoric of the Axis powers. In the summer of 1936, the Army of Africa conducted an uprising in Morocco, touching off uprisings by garrisons throughout Spain the next day. The military coup failed, however, and a full-scale civil war erupted between Republicans (those fighting to maintain the republic) and Nationalists (those fighting to reimpose a conservative, centralized, autocratic government). Mussolini furnished bombers to airlift the Army of Africa over to mainland Spain, beginning a generous program of military aid that would provide the Nationalists with 100,000 Italian troops (Carr, p. 255). While Germany likewise came to the aid of the Nationalists with troops and equipment, the Soviet Union supplied weapons and advisors to the Republicans. As it progressed, the war became a "cause célèbre" of the left in the West, attracting some 40,000 foreign volunteers, who enlisted to fight with the Republicans.

THE ART OF WAR

The Spanish Civil War captured the hearts and imaginations of many of the world's leading writers, artists, and intellectuals and inspired the creation of some of the world's artistic masterpieces. Not only did it seem to be a classic struggle between the social classes—the haves versus the have-nots and dogma versus free expression, it also was unfolding in a location easily visible to Western eyes. The murder by Nationalists of world-renowned poet/playwright Federico García Lorca in 1936 no doubt inspired much of this sentiment. It made him a martyr, symbolizing the death of culture and the avant-garde in Europe, and rallying artists and intellectuals worldwide to the Republican cause. America's Ernest Hemingway (*For Whom the Bell Tolls*), England's George Orwell (*Homage to Catalonia*), and France's André Malraux (*L'Espoir—Man's Hope*) were among the Western writers who joined the Republicans and later immortalized their experiences in famous works. After Lorca's death, many of Spain's leading artists fled the country but continued to agitate for change and raise awareness abroad. When the Nazis bombed Guernica—the first time a city was destroyed by aerial bombardment in history—Pablo Picasso painted a masterpiece based on the tragedy. Martín Gaite falls into line with such artists, drawing inspiration from the struggle of the Republicans, attempting to capture and perhaps wrest meaning from the destruction and division.

For three years Spain remained fiercely divided and embattled in war. A "take no prisoners" attitude on both sides prevailed, leading to more deaths after capture than on the battlefield. Teachers, journalists, and labor leaders were executed by Nationalists (more than half of Spain's university professors were killed); meanwhile, clergy, landlords, and police were executed by

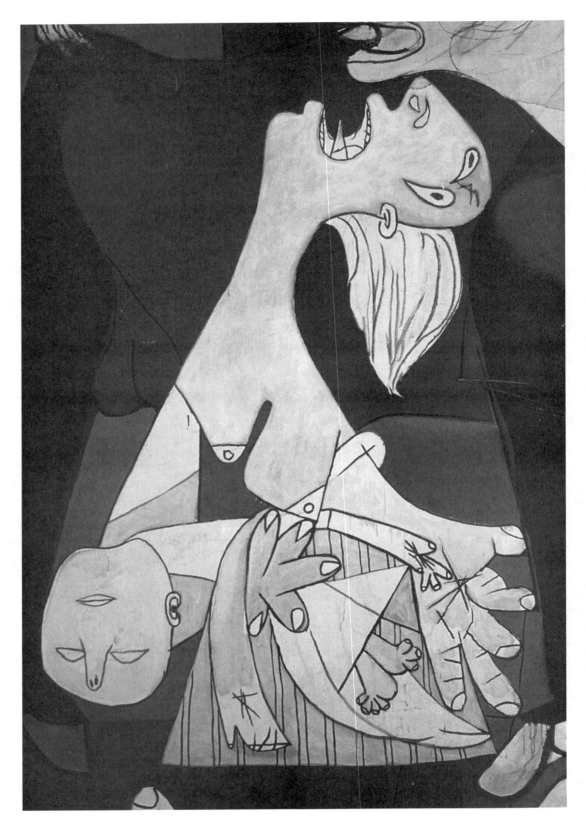

This detail from Pablo Picasso's *Guernica, 1937,* reveals a mother's agony at her child's death during the bombing of the city of Guernica.

Republicans. Estimates of the loss of life vary. While the government spoke of one million deaths, recent estimates place the total closer to 500,000 by fighting, bombardment, assassination, and execution. Not included are all of the deaths caused by starvation and disease. Another 200,000 deaths can be attributed to postwar (1939-43) executions and political killings (Beevor, p. 266). In the novel, Martín Gaite's uncle, a Socialist, was killed during the war, and after the Nationalist victory, she is warned by her family not to discuss it for fear they will be persecuted. As the novel details, the cost of war was far more than demographic loss. The repression and exile after the war of some 350,000, as well as the economic ruin, devastated the nation and particularly those, such as Martín Gaite's protagonist's family in the novel, who had sided with Republicans during the war. More than half the housing in Spain was destroyed; industry was left in ruins; and agriculture was largely suspended for three years in many parts of the country.

Blackest Spain. It has been called "one of the blackest periods in Spanish history" (Graham, p. 27). While there was comparable violence on both sides during the Civil War, the atrocities committed after the war's end by the Franco regime cast a dark, lingering shadow over his government and the Nationalist movement. According to the Spanish Foreign Office, approximately 10,000 Spaniards associated with the Republican movement were executed in the first 5 months after the war (Carr, p. 266). Unofficial estimates place the number of executions from 1939 to 1940 much higher, at 200,000-300,000 with an additional 250,000 imprisoned (Szulc, p. 200). Moreover, the regime continued to practice these tactics for the next 20-25 years, executing political prisoners almost daily. Periodically the government declared amnesties and announced that no prisoners remained, but within a few years it would again invoke the same deadly tactics. Franco put his supporters on alert against all subversives—that is, anyone who had backed the republic or who objected to the new government. "Serious passivity" toward the republic, he said, had been a crime in itself, and his regime enacted a law against it, retroactive to 1934. "Peace is not a comfortable and cowardly repose in the face of history" it was announced on state radio the day of the Nationalist victory. "The blood of those who fell for the Fatherland does not allow for forgetfulness, sterility or treachery. . . . Spain is still at war against all internal and external enemies" (Franco in Carr, p. 265). In the novel, Martín

Gaite is impressed by her best friend who, despite these serious threats, remains defiant:

> She never lowered her head when she said that her parents, who were schoolteachers, were in prison because they were Reds. She looked straight ahead, proudly, afraid of nothing.
> (Martín Gaite, *Back Room*, p. 52)

Personally terrified of the Franco regime, Martín Gaite recalls being afraid of everything during this time, the memory of the biting cold winter mixing with the phrases: "don't breathe a word about this," "beware of that," "don't tell anyone they've killed Uncle Joaquín" (*Back Room*, p. 52).

"THE FALANGE"

The Falange was founded by José Antonio Primo de Rivera, son of the dictator, based on the "spirit of sacrifice and service, an ascetic and military way of life" (Gilmour, pp. 11-12). A charismatic and widely respected leader—even by the left— he espoused anticapitalist economic theories. José Antonio believed that Spain ought to be a totalitarian state and that it needed to return to the Golden Age model in order to regain power and prestige. His Falange naturally aligned with the right, for both groups had the same philosophy as to what constituted "the true nature of Spain" (Gilmour, p. 12). In their view, true Spanish identity was founded on "sixteenth-century Spanish Catholicism . . . incarnating the Catholic ideal of our Military Monarchy" (José Pemartín in Enders, p. 55). They felt the Enlightenment and liberal ideas of the nineteenth century had led to Spain's downfall and set out to return Spain to the sixteenth century. During the free elections of the Second Republic, the nation demonstrated that it was not anxious to relive the past, for the Falangists did not win a single seat in the Cortes. But when Franco came to power, the party became the only legal political party and served, along with the Catholic Church, to provide ideological justification and political organization for the Franco regime. The Falange's founder, José Antonio Primo de Rivera, who died for his beliefs in prison during the Civil War, meanwhile became a cult figure. Drawing on his popularity, Franco invoked José Antonio's image to rally support for the Falange.

The pillars of Franco's new autocratic government were the army, the Church, the National Movement (the Falange), and civilian bureaucracy; its enemies were anyone or anything that threatened them. The government inculcated its ideology through education, psychological programming, and media propaganda. Franco's system of autarky, or self-sufficiency, led to three levels of deprivation: financial, intellectual, and personal. His motto "death to intelligence" was taken literally as school children were taught that the civil war had been "a war of independence against foreign ideas"; that Franco had saved Spain from the "red revolution" and "freed [it] from the poison distilled by envy" (Graham and Labanyi, p. 208; Gilmour, p. 9). No dissent was tolerated, the press was tightly censored, and the Catholic Church was restored to prominence. Franco believed that Spain had to resist corruptive outside influences, such as democracy and capitalism; on the strength of this belief, he implemented a stifling policy of state intervention and protectionism, becoming a totalitarian dictator such as Spain had never seen before:

> The man and his regime, in true totalitarian fashion, are one and inseparable. He is the Commander-in-Chief of all armed forces. He is the Chief of the Government. He is the Leader of the Party . . . the only Party. *His* parliament, the Cortes, boasts only one incontestable right: to approve his decrees.
>
> (Hughes in Crow, p. 352)

In the novel, Martín Gaite's protagonist recalls that during these years, "we were surrounded by ignorance and repression" and allowed only "those inadequate textbooks that blocked out learning" (Martín Gaite in Enders, p. 156).

Rationale and rationing. Shortly after the Civil War, World War II erupted but, reeling economically and militarily from its own three-year internal conflict, Spain was in no position to join either the Axis powers or the Allies. Though Franco had received aid from both Germany and Italy, he remained neutral or at least "non-belligerent" during the war, hedging his bets first in favor of the Axis powers when it looked as though they would win, then in favor of the Allies when their victory was assured (Pierson, p. 159). He did, however, take action on behalf of the Axis powers, facilitating passage of the German Army through Spain to North Africa and lending aid in other "non-belligerent" ways.

During World War II, shortages of food, work, and supplies of all kinds became critical. As evidenced in the novel, poverty, already common in Spain, became even more widespread and rationing of all essentials began. When the war ended, the rationing continued, for Spain found herself cut off from the world. After their defeat of Adolf Hitler and Benito Mussolini, the Western Allied governments took a dim view of Franco's continued fascist dictatorship, as well as his Axis-leaning non-belligerence policy during the war, and excluded Spain from the Marshall Plan of economic reparation. This, coupled with Franco's protectionist trade policy, left the country with no funding to rebuild war-ravaged Spain and with few trading partners outside South America.

While Franco remained cut off from trade, income levels plummeted below those of 1936, inflation soared, and the value of the peseta dropped 20 percent. Neglected fields lay fallow, livestock died, and the infrastructure remained ruined from war and lack of maintenance. Foreign investors were scared away by Franco's policy of non-dependence on foreign imports or credit and "conditions in Spain went from bad to desperate" (Pierson, p. 159). Shantytowns sprung up outside the cities. By 1949 prices had climbed seven times higher than before the Civil War, and the black market flourished. Corruption within the official agencies charged with providing rations ran rampant and was actually condoned by the government as a way to further punish subversives. As shown in the novel, government officials sold the daily staples they were supposed to be rationing: the black market they created became such a prevalent part of society that it figures in the childhood songs and games of Martín Gaite's protagonist and her friends. *Estraperlo* had been the name of a game of roulette but after the war it came to mean the black market. "It became something sordid and depressing. . . . Those secretly permitted under-the-counter dealings in contraband goods that raised the price of everything and made it hard to get rice, oil, coal, and potatoes were no laughing matter," Martín Gaite recalls (*Back Room*, p. 131).

Re-education, banning, and brainwashing. Under the Franco regime, education was once again intertwined with the Catholic Church, as the caudillo (patriarch) believed he was fighting the war for Christianity against communism. With more than half of the university professors killed during and after the Civil War and tens of thousands of schoolteachers imprisoned or killed for being Republican sympathizers, schools and universities relied on clergy to teach, and "education was subordinated to the needs of the regime: loyal Christian pupils were preferred to independent, inquisitive minds" (Graham, p. 38). The state worked hard to indoctrinate children in the military, ultra-patriotic values of Franco's regime, even creating for them little cut-out dolls that featured a young Franco holding a rifle in one hand and giving the fascist salute with the other. The textbooks used by Spain's new teachers were biased, often racist tracts that praised loyal Catholic Spaniards and denounced foreigners and independent-minded "bad Spaniards." "The cultural bias and educational mediocrity arising from Franco's Civil War victory was arguably the most lasting and damaging scar left by the conflict" (Graham, p. 39).

Did a book meet with government disapproval? If so, it was banned. After the war's end, Franco sealed the borders of the country; all bookstores were searched, and all foreign books—except the works of Fascists—were burned, along with all "liberal" works in Castilian. The Castilian language (what we call Spanish today—Franco imposed the title of "Spanish" on Castilian) became the only variety of Spanish allowed—Basques, Catalonians, and Galicians were forbidden to write in or speak their native tongues in public. All citizens were required to make the official fascist salute of outstretched right hand that meant "for the Empire towards God" and were encouraged to think of themselves as a "different" race. Franco made a concerted effort to keep modern culture and outside influences from seeping into the country, exploiting his countrymen's long-held "Spanish pride" to keep them isolated (Pierson, p. 12). Poets, writers, and dramatists went into exile, while artists such as Salvador Dalí and Pablo Picasso fled to Paris and New York to continue their work in freedom. Martín Gaite, though allowed to publish novels in Spain, would and could not openly write her critical account of the Franco regime until after Franco's death.

A woman's place is in the home. Under the left-controlled Second Republic, women gained significant rights, such as the right to vote (in the 1931 constitution). Their shift in status resulted in Republican women's fighting side-by-side with men in the Civil War. But when Franco came to power they were once again relegated to "the back room." Franco reinstated the Civil Code of 1889, which declared (Article 57) that a husband must protect his wife and a wife must obey her husband. Legally she needed his permission for every act; otherwise she could be fined or jailed. Married women could not sell or mortgage property, accept an inheritance, rent an apartment, or take a job without their husband's written permission; nor could they travel or take their children out of the country without the husband's consent. Under Franco, women were perpetual minors. His regime enforced strict dress codes and moral codes of conduct for women; a double standard of sexuality—encouraged in men, prohibited in women—flourished. Marriage again became an indissoluble institution, and although adultery was grounds for separation for both men and women, only women could be prosecuted and sentenced up to as many as six years in prison for such an offense. In separation, the husband was automatically awarded custody of the children and penalties for prostitution, abortion, and illegitimate children applied only to women. Education for girls, though free and mandatory until age 14, was separate from boys when possible; secondary education was open to young women but not a widely accepted option for them until the 1950s. The attitude was a throwback to an earlier generation, the generation, for example, of Martín Gaite's mother, who did not pursue her studies because "it wasn't the custom in those days for girls to prepare for a career, so the thought never even crossed her mind" (*Back Room*, p. 87). The regime negated the progress made under the Second Republic, which had begun establishing equal rights for men and women, though the Republic was of such short duration that in practice women's situation did not really improve.

In the mid-to-late twentieth century the women's liberation movement was gaining strength throughout the West. Spain, however, remained out of the loop. In 1940 women made up 14 percent of the working population, by 1970 it had risen to just 25 percent. Franco, as in other matters, applied the "Spain is different" rationale to women's issues and rewarded them for staying home and having children (Graham, p. 44). Laws passed by his regime went so far as to make it illegal for married women to work except as domestic servants. *Familias numerosas* were given discounts on public transportation, government subsidies, and higher salaries for the husband's work, and they could not be evicted. Each year Franco personally awarded the *familias numerosas* of the year a medal. It was not uncommon therefore for women to have 12, 15, 20 children—even upper-class families who had no need for the monetary rewards averaged six kids.

Under Franco, women were required to contribute two years of social service. They performed this with The Women's Section of the Falange, which taught women domestic skills and politically indoctrinated them. Franco's regime stressed the unselfish heroism of wives and mothers and "the importance of their silent and obscure labor as pillars of the Christian home and family" (*Back Room*, p. 89). The ideal woman was one who embodied "happiness and activity" as exemplified by Queen Isabel and the romantic heroines of Carmen de Icaza's novels (*Back Room*, p. 89). Emulating Isabel, Queen of Castile (reigned 1474-1504), girls were taught to fulfill their mission as Spanish women:

CONDITIONING WOMEN IN THE FRANCO REGIME

Under the Franco regime, all women had to perform mandatory social service, as directed by the Sección Femenina, or Women's Section of the Falange. This society indoctrinated in women the idea that Catholic values—and therefore Spanish values—began with the family. Women must first and foremost be good wives and mothers and "maintain the happiness of the home" (Gómez in Enders, p. 55). The goal of women's education was "to preserve their honesty and chastity" and promote the idea that because "a woman by nature is feebler and weaker than any other animal," she must sacrifice and suffer in order to redeem herself (Gómez in Enders, pp. 56-57). (This last teaching adheres to the Original Sin idea that Eve's weakness caused mankind to be cast out from paradise so women must suffer and sacrifice to make amends.) To be a nun was as viable and respectable a role as wife and mother in Franco's Spain. On the other hand, it was widely understood that to become a spinster was not only anti-Catholic but anti-Spanish. In stark contrast to the co- and equal education under the Second Republic, the educational system under Franco deemed that "there was no need to educate both sexes in equal terms" and that co-education was in fact dangerous given women's wanton nature (Gómez in Enders, p. 58). The feminine virtues of piety, purity, submissiveness, and domesticity were mandated, and any woman who deviated from the official path was "condemned to life as a sinner" (Gómez in Enders, p. 59).

We would learn to make the sign of the cross on our children's foreheads, to air a room, to make use of every last scrap of cardboard and meat, to remove stains, to knit mufflers and wash window curtains, to smile at our husband when he came home in a bad mood, to tell him that *tanto monta tanto manda Isabel como Fernando* [the famous historical motto of Ferdinand and Isabella that they ruled as co-equals],

that domestic economy helps to safeguard the national economy and that garlic is excellent for the bronchial tubes.

(*Back Room*, p. 92)

With few or no models in Golden Age literature, Queen Isabel became the female ideal. She was *the* symbol of unselfishness and fortitude, the model held up for women such as Martín Gaite to emulate because of her qualities of strength and sacrifice for her man and country. Romance novels that told of unhappy heiresses locked up in gothic mansions awaiting rescue from a dark prince also impacted Martín Gaite, particularly since she read them for her college major. Carmencita Franco, the dictator's daughter, seemed to fit the parameters. She was the same age as Martín Gaite and her protagonist, may have at least briefly lived in Salamanca like them, and even had the same name. Martín Gaite imagined the daughter to be one of these romantic heroines "trapped in a prison and under an evil spell" (*Back Room*, p. 59).

However, over the years, through cracks of the censored walls of Spain, some Western influences and some vastly different—if equally unrealistic—female role models seeped into Spain too. The Hollywood films of Deanna Durbin and reports of her starkly American behavior: roller skating to school and eating lemon ice cream seemed to Martín Gaite's protagonist to be "the very image of freedom" (*Back Room*, p. 60). Along with other girls of her generation she collected pictures of these "intangible idols possessed of a mysterious, remote radiance" and dreamed of roles Spanish women could play that differed from the ones to which they were consigned (*Back Room*, p. 60).

Political changes. In 1953, when the United States was at war with North Korea and fighting the more overarching Cold War against the Soviet Union as well, U.S. officials made a deal with Franco to establish military bases in Spain. This immediately reconnected Spain to the outside world and, along with a $625 million aid package, jump-started the Spanish economy. It would be a few more years before the economy saw a truly dynamic change. When Franco opened the country to foreign investment beginning in 1957, rural-to-urban migration quickened, and Spain transitioned into an industrial- and service-oriented rather than an agrarian society. Spain was readmitted to the United Nations and over the next two decades would crawl out of the economic abyss. Opus Dei technocrats replaced Franco's inept ministers and at long last began the process of industrialization. As Martín Gaite's protagonist does in the novel, Spaniards moved to the cities en masse and foreign firms set up subsidiaries. While government-controlled industries still dominated the marketplace, the influx of foreign businesses and investment, as well as a major influx of tourists, transformed Spain's economy and society. A middle class was firmly established by the 1960s, with 79 percent of Spaniards working in either the service sectors or in industry. Literacy rates, albeit based just on the ability to sign one's name, rose from 40 percent in 1920 to 92 percent in 1970, and university students began to agitate for change (Graham, p. 60). Though Franco cracked down harshly against protests, he saw that change was inevitable and decreed that the constitutional monarchy would be restored upon his death. Censorship decreased but state brutality against political protestors increased, particularly against the ETA (a Basque separatist organization, a terrorist group itself).

Ill and losing his grip on power, Franco died in 1975. His funeral, held on November 23, was witnessed by hundreds of thousands—some certainly to pay respects to the man who brought them so long a period of peace, but many to make certain he had truly passed away. A pivotal event in the lives of Martín Gaite and her contemporaries, Franco's funeral prompted her writing of *The Back Room*. Suddenly at the moment of Franco's burial, "time unfroze. . . . The man responsible for checking its flow and presiding over it had disappeared" (*Back Room*, p. 137).

The Novel in Focus

Plot summary. "Experience cannot be communicated without bonds of silence, concealment, distance" (Georges Bataille in *Back Room*, p. 1). As this opening quote suggests, from a distance, *The Back Room* embarks on an introspective quest to define an artist's development under the repressive Franco regime. Prompted by his death and funeral to search the "back room" of her memory, Martín Gaite's protagonist explores hidden, forbidden feelings and events that can only now come openly to light. In a complex weaving of dreams, memories, and narrative, the novel creates an elaborate conversation that conjures childhood experiences, including war, rationing, censorship, and Spanish and Francoist social mores. Its protagonist probes literary genres and describes how myriad influences have forged her style, formed her development, and ultimately shaped the novel we are reading.

The story begins and ends in the same place. Martín Gaite's protagonist is in bed, discussing her semiconscious state before she falls asleep. Memories, visions, and literary inventions flood her mind; they dance and mix and intertwine. She recalls her childhood; she dreams of romance novels; and she leaves us unsure about which events are past or present, real or imagined. Unable to rest, she scans the room and starts rummaging through a sewing basket. The contents spill out and each item triggers a new memory, one event leading to the next. She finds an old love letter buried in the basket and conjures the beach where her heroine met her lover, the barefoot man. Her mind wanders back and forth between personal memories and the plot of the "fantastic" romance novel she is writing as she drifts off to sleep. "I want to see you, I want to see you" she says with her eyes closed but has no idea whom she is addressing (*Back Room*, p. 18). In fact, she seems to be summoning herself—her hidden identity—wondering how she developed into the woman and artist she is today. The protagonist is awakened by a phone call. It is midnight and a man wants to come up. He says he is there for the interview, but she cannot recall this man or making the appointment. Not wanting to look foolish, she tells him to come up and quickly gets dressed.

The man comes into her apartment. He has black hair and eyes, and a black hat, which he places on the table next to her typewriter. "A page already begun is peeking out of the top of the typewriter and I read it out of the corner of my eye: "'The barefoot man has now disappeared from sight.' When did I write that?" (*Back Room*, p. 24). She cannot remember writing the page and does not recognize this man, but begins an extended conversation with him nonetheless.

As a storm brews outside, the two discuss fantastic literature, her education, and her novels. She recalls the first time she was "possessed by literature" and the beginning of her writing career (*Back Room*, p. 44). "Ambiguity is the key to fantastic literature," the man in black says. "Not knowing whether what one has seen is true or false, never finding out" (*Back Room*, p. 47). As the man in black says this, we realize that he is speaking of the novel we are reading. We don't know who the characters are at this point nor what is true or false. And we never actually find out.

As the two continue to talk, the protagonist recalls the Civil War and the bombing of her hometown, Salamanca. The protagonist discusses how the war shattered her illusions of romance yet all seemed unreal to her as a child. During a break in the conversation, Martín Gaite's protagonist goes to the kitchen for some tea. She sees the old furniture from the back room of the house in which she grew up and the sight triggers a wave of memories. A song, popular during her youth, plays in her mind, the chorus urging, "Come to Cunigan soon . . . you'll find it's marvelous, magic, unique, really magnificent" (*Back Room*, p. 74). Cunigan was a place she dreamed of escaping to, though she still doesn't know if it is real or not. But the back room *was* a place to which she knew she could escape to—in every sense. First, they had a back room in their house where her mother would sit and read, and where she and her sister would play. "I also imagine it's the attic of one's brain, a sort of secret place full of a vague jumble of all sorts of miscellaneous junk, separated from the cleaner and more orderly anterooms of the mind by a curtain that is occasionally pulled back" (*Back Room*, p. 87). As is happening to her right now, memories that live in the back room emerge only when the curtain is "pulled back."

When she returns to the living room, the man in black is at her writing desk, gazing at a picture she normally keeps in her bedroom. She is greatly annoyed, as she thinks he's been in her room. He insists, however, that he found it on the table and as she ponders the possibility that she moved it herself, she notices that the pile of papers next to the typewriter has grown in volume.

Appropriately enough, the two begin discussing time, as in the game of "red light, green light." An analogy of Spain under Franco's regime, players can only advance when the leader of the game has his back turned—if he turns around and catches players moving, they must go back to the starting line. But most silently advance, instantly freezing when the leader whirls around. The protagonist then takes a pill the man in black offers her from a box he leaves on her table. Like a hallucinogenic drug, the pill elicits yet more repressed memories. The protagonist reflects deeply on the war and its aftermath, a period of time once frozen, now in the process of thawing.

A phone call interrupts the conversation. It is for Alejandro, the man in black, from his jealous lover. She is calling because she believes the protagonist is Alejandro's long-time lover, the one with whom he has exchanged a mountain of love letters. At first the protagonist thinks the woman, Carola, is crazy for she still feels that the man in black is a stranger. As Carola describes the love letters, the protagonist realizes they are related to the one she found in the sewing basket, and we realize that this is the storyline of her fantastic romance novel.

By the end of the conversation, the protagonist develops a deep affection for Carola. She wants Carola to retrieve the love letters so the protagonist can determine if she wrote them. But that is impossible because they are locked away in another room. The protagonist hangs up reluctantly and resumes her conversation with the man in black. She tells him about her childhood best friend and their imaginary land of Bergai. Then suddenly a gust of wind blows through the window and scatters the papers of her novel about the room. She is amazed at how many there are. Though she is growing sleepier, she implores the man in black to stay while she rests. He covers her with a shawl, and she falls asleep.

When she wakes, she is back in her bed, and her daughter is kissing her on the forehead. She has just returned from a party and the man in black is not there, though there are two glasses in the living room and the box of pills she thinks that he brought are still there. The protagonist kisses her daughter good night, hops back in bed, and picks up the pile of papers that had been on the table. There are 182 of them and on the first page is written: THE BACK ROOM.

The back room of memory. The back room is a "kingdom where nothing is forbidden," a safe place where the protagonist could retreat to as a child and stash prohibited ideas and dreams (*Back Room*, p. 190). It is also a literal place in the house, which served as a food storage room during the war. Finally, it is a metaphor for the realm of memories kept in the recesses of her mind as an adult. The novel represents the opening of the door to the back room and the spilling of contents that the author has forgotten ever existed. Employing postmodern techniques, she peels the layers of her own understanding through an extended conversation with a stranger and this becomes the novel. Unaware that she is writing a novel, she keeps its existence hidden from herself just as the back room and its contents have been hidden all these years until she reaches the end and realizes what has been created.

Franco's death in 1975 prompted a torrent of literary output stemming from repressed memories and viewpoints not allowed to come to the fore until his regime ended. In the heavily censored, tightly controlled environment of Franco's Spain, where individual expression made you a "bad Spaniard," subversive thoughts and queries were deeply buried out of fear. Individuals born at the start of his 36-year dictatorship, like Martín Gaite, had to keep those thoughts under wraps for the majority of their lives. When Franco was buried, the memories were finally dug up, the back doors opened, and lifetimes of experience poured out. "The book came to me in fact the very morning of [Franco's] funeral," her protagonist explains to the man in black (*Back Room*, p. 127). "You may have noticed how many memoirs have come out since Franco's death," she says. "It's a real epidemic now" (*Back Room*, p. 127). Among them were those published by the many "moles"—men with Republican backgrounds who had lived in hiding, in some cases, for 40 years and emerged after Franco's death from secret "back rooms"—attics, basements, and holes beneath floors.

Not wanting to write another straightforward, "boring" memoir, Carmen Martín Gaite constructs a fantastic account of the process of writing the novel and coming to terms with her repressed memories and hidden dreams during the course of it. As if in therapy with a mysterious stranger, she reminisces and realizes what a profound effect Franco has had on her life. Before Franco, people enjoyed debating politics publicly. Discussions were passionate, heated, and "it didn't appear to be a monotonous game, but rather one with lots of variety" (*Back Room*, p. 129). People "talked about whatever they liked," but when Franco came to power all that changed dramatically, as the protagonist recalls (*Back Room*, p. 132):

> From the beginning it was clear that he was the one and only, that his power was indisputable and omnipresent, that he had managed to insinuate himself into all the houses, schools, movie theatres, and cafes, and do away with spontaneity and variety, arouse a religious, uniform fear, stifle conversations and laughter so that no one's voice rang out any louder than anyone else's.
>
> (*Back Room*, p. 132)

When Franco dies, Martín Gaite's protagonist cannot believe it. Many citizens celebrate loudly, some weep, but the protagonist remains unmoved. All the years of his regime come tumbling down on her. At this moment, the back door swings wide open and she utters thoughts and observations that she has kept in the recesses of her mind for her entire life.

As the novel illustrates, Franco had paralyzed time during his tenure. Martín Gaite realizes while writing that those years of her life—the bulk of

it—"felt like a homogenous block" (*Back Room*, p. 133). She could not differentiate the war years from the postwar years and had buried her apprehensions and secret thoughts, her spontaneity and the unhindered processes of her mind so deeply that it took this extended conversation, the writing of the novel, to begin to extract them. Locked away in the back room of her brain, they poured out only when the curtain was parted, when it was finally safe to revisit them and even acknowledge that region of her soul. The novel delves into the depths of the protagonist's experience in a stream-of-consciousness, dreamlike fashion, examining the minutiae, the underlying and often overlooked details of life. In the end, she realizes that Franco's funeral is actually happening and is about to radically change reality for everyone in Spain. The novel, she knows, is the back room of her mind—the catharsis that novelist and nation begin to undergo the day Franco dies.

FROM DICTATORSHIP TO DEMOCRACY

Transition to democracy happened remarkably quickly in Spain. Just three years after Franco's death, his regime had given way to a government based on universal suffrage, but the shift did not happen without resistance, centered in the army. It must be remembered that Franco lasted for 40 years in Spain because he had many supporters. Not until a couple decades after the novel appeared, in the 1990s, when the democracy achieved very tangible economic gains, would there be a clear majority in its favor.

Postmodernism in the arts. After World War II, when Martín Gaite was a young college student, the postmodernist movement in the arts and literature emerged in Europe. Postmodern writing insists that there is not one universal truth but many. As in *The Back Room*, identities are not fixed and there is as much emphasis on the unsaid as the said. For example, when Martín Gaite is searching her memory for "facts" about Franco, she realizes it is the intangibles, "the crumbs, not the little white pebbles" that she is seeking (*Back Room*, p. 138). This is a postmodernist concept: emphasizing the writing between the lines, the details that normally get glanced over or lost.

A main characteristic of postmodernism is playfulness. Martín Gaite consciously chooses to write about a man who imposed empirical order, who structured every thought and dictated every behavior in a postmodern, anti-empirical style. Like the early-twentieth-century British novelist Virginia Woolf, who was not a postmodernist, Martín Gaite employs stream-of-consciousness writing to peel the layers of understanding so that she can come to terms with thoughts, memories, and feelings that have been locked away in "the back room" for 36 years. The postmodern movement allowed writers like Martín Gaite to revisit tragedy and challenge the dogmas of a highly polarized, politicized era without applying their own dogmatic theory. The movement itself is the antithesis of a totalitarian, black-and-white view of the world and enables artists to visit historical events through a host of vehicles and view them from myriad perspectives.

Sources and literary context. *The Back Room* is based on Martín Gaite's personal life experiences. She uses her own name as the protagonist's and names the novels she has written, such as *The Spa*, as her protagonist's work. Because it is a probing of literary genres—part romance, part fantastic—as well as a *bildungsroman*, or novel of personal maturation, she considers naming it Romantic Rituals in Eighteenth-Century Spain, a title echoing that of her nonfiction bestseller *Usos amorosos del dieciocho en España* (Customs of Love in Eighteenth-Century Spain), which was a spin-off of her doctoral dissertation. She discusses personal experiences of the Civil War—the bombings, Franco's Falangist headquarters in Salamanca, where she grew up, and her feelings about Carmencita Franco, whom she encountered frequently as a girl since Carmencita was often in the news. Also she incorporates her personal expertise in romance literature into the fabric of the novel, as well as her desire to write a fantastic novel, which *The Back Room* becomes. In the novel itself, Martín Gaite references Todorov's book, *The Fantastic: A Structural Approach,* as an instructional guide, as well as the literature of Lewis Carroll (the novel is dedicated to him), Miguel de Cervantes, Daniel Defoe, and Carmen de Icaza; the Hollywood films of Deanna Durbin, the songs of Conchita Piquet, and popular poems and jingles of the 1940s.

Reviews. Hailed as Martín Gaite's "undisputed masterpiece" *The Back Room* won Spain's prestigious National Prize for Literature in 1978 (Buck, p. 791). Upon publication, the novel was praised in *El Mundo* for being excellently plotted and written with "perfect simplicity," while other critics singled it out for skillfully managing "to weave together the author's reminiscences of her childhood, the literature of the fantastic, and sentimental romance" (Buck, p. 79). In the *New York Times Book Review,* Patricia O'Connor described the novel as "an exquisite creation, elegant, smart, and sad—a remarkable story" (O'Connor, p. 34). Critic Debra Castillo applauded Martín Gaite for mingling reality and fantasy: "Apparent polarities [of] memory, forgetfulness, history and literature, true and false, reality and fantasy . . . are suddenly, ambiguously, flung together in a celebration of riches" (Castillo in Brown, p. 86). The novel, concludes Joan Lipman Brown, exhibits Martín Gaite's "mastery of multiple techniques, skill as a social observer, and astute depictions of the lives of women" (Brown, p. 86).

—Diane Renée

For More Information

Beevor, Antony. *The Spanish Civil War.* New York: Peter Bedrick, 1982.

Brown, Joan Lipman. *Secrets From the Back Room.* Mississippi: University of Mississippi, 1987.

Buck, Claire. *Bloomsburg Guide to Women's Literature.* New York: Prentice Hall, 1992.

Carr, Raymond, ed. *Spain: A History.* Oxford: Oxford University Press, 2000.

Crow, John A. *Spain: The Root and the Flower.* New York: Harper and Row, 1975.

Enders, Victoria Lorée, ed. *Constructing Spanish Womanhood.* Albany: State University of New York Press, 1999.

Giles, David T. *Modern Spanish Culture.* Cambridge: Cambridge University Press, 2000.

Gilmour, David. *The Transformation of Spain.* London: Quartet, 1985.

Graham, Helen, and Jo Labanyi, eds. *Spanish Cultural Studies.* Oxford: Oxford University Press, 1995.

Graham, Robert. *Spain: A Nation Comes of Age.* New York: St. Martin's Press, 1984.

Martín Gaite, Carmen. *The Back Room.* San Francisco: City Lights Books, 2000.

O'Connor, Patricia. Review of *The Back Room*, by Carmen Martín Gaite. *New York Times Book Review,* 28 June 1987, 34.

Pierson, Peter. *The History of Spain.* London: Greenwood Press, 1999.

Szulc, Tad. *Portrait of Spain.* New York: New York Times Company, 1972.

Ballad of Dogs' Beach

by

José Cardoso Pires

Born in São João do Peso, in central Portugal on February 2, 1925, José Cardoso Pires moved to Lisbon with his family while he was still a child. He completed his secondary education there and went on to study mathematics at the Faculdade de Ciências (1943-45). During this period, Cardoso Pires became a member of a leftist-leaning party, the Movement of Democratic Unity, and after its extinction he joined the Portuguese Communist Party, which he abandoned in 1974, two days after the Portuguese Revolution, in order to experience the country in its bourgeois freedom. However, he remained a staunch defender of Marxist ideology until his death on October 26, 1998. A half century earlier, during the 1940s, Cardoso Pires published his first short story as well as many essays in literary magazines and *Os Caminheiros e Outros Contos* (1949; Travelers and Other Stories), his first book. After the publication of his controversial (because of the subject matter) second volume of short stories, *Histórias de Amor* (1952; Love Stories), the author is briefly detailed by the PIDE, the Portuguese secret police. Many other literary works followed, bringing the author great critical acclaim and commercial success, including *O Anjo Ancorado* (1958; The Anchored Angel), *O Hóspede de Job* (1963; Job's Guest), and *O Delfim* (1968; The Dauphin). Winning renown as one of the greatest Portuguese narrators of the twentieth century, Cardoso Pires remained faithful not only to his Marxist ideology but also to his desire to write fiction that reflected upon Portugal and the Portuguese. This

THE LITERARY WORK

A novel set in Lisbon and also in and around the nearby town of Vereda in late 1959 and also 1960; published in Portuguese (as *Balada da Praia dos Cães*) in 1982, in English in 1986.

SYNOPSIS

Inspector Elias Santana investigates the murder of Major Luís Dantas Castro in April 1960, a few months after his involvement in an abortive military coup against the fascist dictator Oliveira Salazar. The investigation not only reconstructs events leading up to the assassination but also unmasks the political, social, and moral degradation endemic to both Portugal's fascist regime and its opposition parties.

is certainly true in *Ballad of Dogs' Beach*, a novel that reflects deeply about the climate of repression, the abuse of power, and the lack of freedom prevalent during the almost 50 years that the fascist dictatorship lasted in the country.

Events in History at the Time the Novel Takes Place

From the microcosm to the macrocosm. *Ballad of Dogs' Beach* fictionalizes real events that occurred in late 1959 and in 1960. To be more precise, the work is inspired by the 1960 political

José Cardoso Pires

murder of captain Almeida Santos, an individual
who had been implicated a few months before in
an abortive military coup against the fascist dictatorship of António de Oliveira Salazar. In the
novel, the name of captain Almeida Santos has
been changed to that of major Luís Dantas Castro. Major Castro is killed by his companions,
Filomena or Mena (the Major's lover), an architect (Fontenova), and an army corporal (Barroca)
after several months of isolation in the Vereda
house where they all took refuge after the three
escaped from the Forte da Graça, Elvas, where
they had been imprisoned for their participation
in the attempted military coup. Their plan was
to carry out another coup, but isolation, the climate of fear in the house, and the fact that all
four individuals were suspicious of each other's
movements and had to depend on outsiders to
carry out the intended coup created the oppressive conditions that led to the assassination of the
Major by the others. After Major Castro is murdered, the others bury him in Mastro Beach,
whose name is changed to Dogs' Beach for two
reasons: a dog discovers the body and the secret
police whose Portuguese acronym, PIDE, stands
for International Police for the Defense of the
State, are known as dogs. The secret police, it was
said, had the capacity to trace or track down any
enemy of the Portuguese State and could smell,
at any distance, all suspicious activities through
their very keen sense of smell, just like dogs.

The author uses a real event for a long dissertation on the general situation in Portugal. He
focuses on political intrigue, the climate of fear,
censorship, moral and social degradation, oppression and repression, abuse of power, and
conspiracy theories to impart an objective image
of the fascist period during the dictatorship of
Salazar (1932-68). The Portuguese subtitle of the
novel means "Dissertation on a Crime," which indicates that the author is researching a particular issue: a crime. However, he is not really researching the assassination of Major Dantas
Castro; in effect, he is researching a different type
of abomination, the political and ideological
crime committed by some Portuguese for repressive ends of denying freedom of expression
to the citizens of the country. The events surrounding the political murder of the Major serve
as a paradigm for the situation of the country as
a whole. In other words, the author is investigating much more than a murder of an opposition figure; in reality, he is investigating the
murder of a whole country and its citizens. Accordingly, the situation, the conditions, the social, political and ideological climate described
in *Ballad of Dogs' Beach* bear a great resemblance
to the real situation and conditions present in
Portugal in the late 1950s and early 1960s.

**António de Oliveira Salazar, dictator of Por-
tugal.** A late 1950s and early 1960s travel poster
in English from TAP (better known nowadays as
Air Portugal), created to attract tourists to Portugal, used the following slogan: "Portugal, Europe's best-kept secret. Fly TAP." In a sense, such
a slogan was emblematic of the Portuguese society of that era. Closed to foreign influences, the
society was controlled and repressed by several
paramilitary associations as well as the secret police. At the helm was an austere, tough-minded
dictator, António de Oliveira Salazar, who governed with an iron hand, ready to punish all
forms of dissidence and any apparent attack on
the sanctity of a fascist state built on policies that
were in essence anti-liberal, anti-communist, and
anti-democratic.

The emergence of authoritarian rule in Portugal dates to 1926, when a military coup put an
end to parliamentary rule in the country. The
military takeover enjoyed, at least initially, widespread popular support due to the instability and
chaos of most economic, political, financial, and
social institutions and also the inefficient bureaucracy prevalent during the period of the First
Portuguese Republic (1910-26). Salazar did not
really come into the picture until 1928, when he

was asked to become finance minister to improve the country's economic situation. Within a short period of time, Salazar had put the country's finances in order and as a result many Portuguese thought that he possessed messiah-like qualities that would extend to the political sphere. Several measures taken by the finance minister, a conservative technocrat and a professor of political economy from the University of Coimbra, led to a balancing of the books and to the accumulation of fiscal surpluses that would last until the 1960s. As Salazar's power grew, he began to exert more and more influence over the affairs and the direction of the government. In 1932 he was appointed Premier, becoming the first civilian Premier since the military takeover in 1926. Salazar would be *de facto* leader of the country until 1968 when the chair he was sitting on collapsed and he was knocked into a coma from which he never recovered. He eventually died in the summer of 1970. Marcelo Caetano took over the reigns of power, but he himself was knocked off this pedestal by the military during the Revolution of April 25, 1974. He had shown intransigence in dealings with the freedom fighters battling for independence in Portugal's African colonies and had grown estranged from the majority of officers in the army, who were tired of waging what they believed to be unwinnable wars in Africa.

The overseas empire. Salazar governed with a heavy hand, surrounding himself with many paramilitary organizations and other associations that controlled all aspects of Portuguese life and, in the process, denied basic freedoms to most citizens in the country. On the surface, the country seemed to run smoothly without dissent; tightly controlled, the press did not report internal friction. Yet there was plenty of turmoil in Portugal, especially during the 1950s and early '60s when the mythic image of Salazar as savior no longer held sway over the country's citizens. Much of this turmoil was brought about by Portugal's continued defense of its colonial heritage and its need to hold onto the colonies "whose agricultural and mineral resources were a strong factor in Portugal's financial strength after World War II" (Herr, p. 9). The constitution of 1932, which had created the Estado Novo (New State), a corporative and authoritarian type of system where political realities were subordinated to socioeconomic priorities, declared that it was the state's function to promote the moral unity and establish the juridical order of the nation. Salazar's intention in creating a new constitution

António de Oliveira Salazar, premier of Portugul from 1932 to 1968.

was to regenerate Portugal through a well-ordered economy. An appendix, the Colonial Act of 1930, also authored by Salazar, was attached to the political constitution and approved by Portuguese voters in 1933. Article 2 of this Colonial Act proclaimed that it was of the organic essence of the Portuguese nation to carry out the historic function of possessing and colonizing overseas dominions and civilizing the indigenous populations contained therein. In the 1950s and '60s, the state modified the Colonial Act in view of the decolonization being undertaken by other colonial empires, but the modifications failed to change the basic direction taken by the New State. The word *colonies* was changed to *overseas provinces*; the focus shifted to a full-scale integration and assimilation of indigenous Africans; the Africans gained a form of citizenship, albeit a discriminatory citizenship, since their rights as citizens were less than those for white Portuguese; and the government declared that Portugal was a multiracial, multicultural, and multicontinental nation. However, these changes were mostly cosmetic, for external consumption, given the changing international climate regarding colonialism. The colonial status of Portuguese Africa was being debated at the United Nations, the eastern countries, especially Russia and China, were arming freedom fighters in the Portuguese colonies, and the old allies, such as the

United States and Great Britain, had begun to question the continued colonial presence of Portugal in Africa. In spite of all these challenges, Portugal held firm to its economic interests in Africa and to its commitment to develop the colonies in order to safeguard those economic interests. The colonies, believed its statesmen, existed for the benefit of Portugal and not vice-versa; anything that happened in the colonies would take place on Portuguese terms.

The indigenous populations in the Portuguese colonies did not buy into the rhetorical propaganda of the New State. They knew they were considered inferior by whites and that they were being exploited in the name of a suspect civilizing mission, which, far from acknowledging their own traditions, sought to impose Portuguese Christian civilization. The idea that Portugal was the last defender of Western civilization in their area did not hold much sway over the African peoples either, and armed unrest began in earnest in 1961. Although there had been many signs that the empire was already crumbling, the launching of armed revolts in Angola, Mozambique, and Guinea-Bissau in the early 1960s signified that Portugal as a colonial empire would not be able to hold on much longer to its overseas possessions. Armed insurrection was the beginning of the end, an end that finally came in 1975 with the official independence of five African countries.

As noted, the empire had been striking back at Portugal for quite some time. Many of the modifications to the Colonial Act of 1930, made in the 1940s, 1950s, and 1960s, responded to pressures placed upon Portugal by indigenous populations clamoring for greater autonomy and eventual self-determination at a time when France and Britain were already freeing their colonies. Whatever measures Portugal took to ameliorate the colonial status of its colonized peoples in Africa, they amounted to much too little too late. Uprisings were occurring everywhere, especially in São Tomé (1953) and Guinea-Bissau (1959) in Africa. Other actions, such as strikes, were also taking place. During the 1950s, many nationalist movements aimed at reasserting the authority of indigenous cultures began to appear. However, the first real challenge to the empire came from India in 1961 when Indian troops invaded Goa and seized the colony from the Portuguese. More embarrassing for the nation was the fact that Portuguese troops did not really put up much of a fight to defend the possession from the invading Indian forces.

Other serious threats to the Portuguese colonial empire began to be posed by nationalist forces in Africa. In early 1961, "perhaps 200 armed Africans attacked the prisons where MPLA prisoners were held, and other targets of strategic significance in Luanda" (Robinson, p. 109). A white backlash followed the attack, and also organized massacres occurred. A few months later in Angola, a war of liberation broke out that would last until 1974 and soon afterwards other colonies, following Angola's example, also erupted into revolt against the imperial power.

Turmoil on the home front. If in the overseas colonies Portugal was involved in bloody campaigns to retain its empire, back at home, even in the 1950s, there were already major signs of dissolution of Salazar's New State. Although isolated revolutionary activities involving the Communist Party and the military had occurred since the New State was created, these activities increased considerably during the 1950s and even more so during the 1960s with the outbreak of the colonial wars. Indeed, "internal resistance was more or less continuous throughout the dictatorship, manifested mainly in attempted military coups, democratic electoral movements, and labour unrest" (Kayman, p. 31). Although the Portuguese corporatist apparatus enjoyed strong support from Western allies, which allowed Portugal to become a founding member of NATO and gave tacit political support to the regime's defense of its colonial patrimony mainly because of its anti-communist stance, the New State had to deal more and more with internal resistance that eventually lead to its disintegration in April 1974.

Salazar had "instituted an 'organic' vision of society and tried with a certain perseverance to use all the ideological and social control instruments within his reach to bring it about: administration, corporatism, school system, state propaganda, local elites, and the Church" (Herr, p. 100). The strategy limited the autonomy of the economic elite and kept its members in line. However, the Portuguese were becoming restive with a government to which they initially lent strong support because it had regenerated the Portuguese economy. The government no longer enjoyed such support because the economy had not kept pace with the rest of Europe, and people were tired of simply rubber stamping the official candidates put forth by the regime's only permitted political party, the National Union. There was no economic or political movement in the country. There was only economic stagnation and the concentration of wealth in a few hands.

Refusing to industrialize, Portugal had also remained mainly an agricultural country, at least until the 1960s, when Portuguese investors began to diversify into heavy industry, and when foreign investors began to pour capital into the country.

Given the concentration of political and economic power in a few hands, no large bourgeois class had developed to carry out counter-revolutionary activities against the New State. Most of these activities were generated by military officers, who occasionally would revolt against the government. This changed during the 1950s and the '60s, with the staging of a number of popular demonstrations against the government, many strikes to demand better living wages and better working conditions, and other political actions on university campuses and in factories. Many of these were instigated and/or organized by the Communist Party, the only organized opposition party at the time. The regime responded by imprisoning, exiling, and otherwise punishing the demonstrators and strikers, making an example of them to others who may have wanted to follow in their footsteps. The military, as mentioned above, carried out several attempts to overthrow the government. The most serious was in 1961, when General Júlio Botelho de Moniz, the Defense Minister, in conjunction with other military figures, conspired unsuccessfully to overthrow Salazar in order to liberalize the country and to resolve through negotiations the conflicts that were just arising in Portuguese Africa. Moniz was arrested, other conspirators were detained and Salazar took over the Ministry of Defense. In reality, this was the last important attempt at a coup d'état until the 1974 Revolution.

Two other episodes that served to call into question the authority and the very legitimacy of the New State and its leader Oliveira Salazar need to be mentioned. The first refers to the 1958 elections and the second to the hijack of the Portuguese liner *Santa Maria* by Captain Henrique Galvão in 1961. In 1958 Humberto Delgado ran as an opposition candidate against the National Union's hand-picked candidate, the future President of Portugal, Admiral Américo Tomás. Although Delgado was an extremely popular candidate, customary electoral fraud assured the election of the government candidate. He protested the election and asked for the resignation of Américo Tomás to no avail, and a coup, which had been planned in expectation of electoral fraud, did not materialize. However, the government learned its lesson well. Salazar "put

an end to the threat of a constitutional coup provoked by popular presidential campaigns by altering the Constitution: in the future, the President would be chosen by an electoral college, which he would be able to control through the National Union" (Kayman, p. 41). Another episode that inspired additional pressure for the overthrow of fascism was the hijack of the ocean liner *Santa Maria* on January 23, 1961, the date of the inauguration of John F. Kennedy as President of the United States. The mastermind behind the whole operation, Henrique Galvão, chose this particular date for several reasons: to obtain maximum international exposure for his action, to publicize his report on the colonies (calling for a political solution to the unrest in Africa), and to humiliate Salazar. The many activities and actions against both fascism and the ensuing colonial wars should be regarded as an expression of general discontent on the part of the Portuguese that culminated with the military takeover of the government in 1974.

The Novel in Focus

Plot summary. *Ballad of Dogs' Beach* begins with a medical report of an unknown man's body found by a scavenger dog in the sand dunes of Praia do Mastro, approximately 100 meters from the road, on April 3, 1960. Most of the report focuses on the state of the male body and the extensive damage done to it by the several bullets that had perforated it. There are also references on the report to the age, sex, and height of the individual. Indeed, the picture that one gets from reading the report is that the crime was unusually violent. It is not until a few pages later that the reader finds out that the victim is an ex-army officer, Major Luís Dantas Castro, a man who had participated in an abortive military coup the previous year, but who had been at liberty since December 1959 when he escaped from prison.

Ironically, the body was found close to an Air Portugal "popular travel-poster in English: PORTUGAL, EUROPE'S BEST KEPT SECRET. FLY TAP" (*Ballad of Dog's Beach*, Pires, p. 3). The poster sets the stage for the investigation that follows, with Elias Santana from the Criminal Investigation Department in charge. His purpose is not to find out who the perpetrators of the crime were, since the three are identified at the very beginning of the novel. They include Lieutenant Fontenova (an architect) and Corporal Barroca, two military men who were also involved in the attempted coup and had escaped from prison with the Major. The third perpetrator, the Major's lover Filomena (Mena) joined the group later in their hideout in Vereda, the place where the three men had taken refuge after their escape from prison. Elias Santana's intention is to find out the whys and the wherefores of the political assassination of the Major since the hypothesis of a sex crime has already been discarded. The theory of a political assassination is doubtful too because the Major has been murdered by his supposed friends and political sympathizers, men who shared his political convictions. They are all sworn enemies of dictator António de Oliveira Salazar and his fascist regime. Things are never

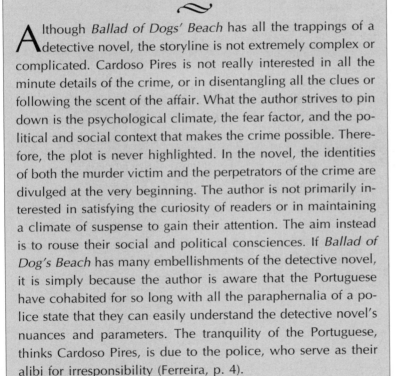

A DETECTIVE NOVEL?

Although *Ballad of Dogs' Beach* has all the trappings of a detective novel, the storyline is not extremely complex or complicated. Cardoso Pires is not really interested in all the minute details of the crime, or in disentangling all the clues or following the scent of the affair. What the author strives to pin down is the psychological climate, the fear factor, and the political and social context that makes the crime possible. Therefore, the plot is never highlighted. In the novel, the identities of both the murder victim and the perpetrators of the crime are divulged at the very beginning. The author is not primarily interested in satisfying the curiosity of readers or in maintaining a climate of suspense to gain their attention. The aim instead is to rouse their social and political consciences. If *Ballad of Dog's Beach* has many embellishments of the detective novel, it is simply because the author is aware that the Portuguese have cohabited for so long with all the paraphernalia of a police state that they can easily understand the detective novel's nuances and parameters. The tranquility of the Portuguese, thinks Cardoso Pires, is due to the police, who serve as their alibi for irresponsibility (Ferreira, p. 4).

what they seem to be. Like the travel poster that takes advantage of travelers' sense of curiosity about the unknown—about Portugal as a secret—to attract them to the country, the novel starts out trying to get readers' attention by playing on their sense of curiosity about the different possibilities and motivations behind the crime. As readers progress through the novel, they discover that appearances are deceiving. The real Portugal is indeed a well-kept secret, not

what it seems to be. On the surface, Portugal appears to operate on a stable foundation of political, economic, and social order; nationalism; morality; peacefulness; trust; unity; harmony; respect for the law and for others; sanctification of the nation and its rules; and the family as the basis for the state. The surface, however, masks a hellish interior fraught with criminality, fraud, abuse, fear, terror, repression, untrustworthiness, lies, censorship, corruption, political intrigue and deception, rampant sexuality, chaos, social degeneration, and general immorality. Heaven and hell seem to coexist in Portugal: heaven is the face it presents to the outside world and to its people; hell is the true reality of life in the country. This hellish dimension is the main focus of the novel. The author's intention is to show that beneath Portugal's apparently normal façade lies a pathological dimension that is hidden from the outside world but which the reader uncovers through the reading process.

Two broad, interwoven narrative strands can be identified in the novel. The first, based to a great extent on genuine newspaper articles, police communiqués, police interrogation reports and other documentation from the archives of both branches of the Portuguese police, the PIDE (International Police for the Defense of the State) and the GNR (the National Republican Guard), deals with the murder of Major Dantas Castro and all the events leading up to it, reconstructed mainly by Elias Santana's interrogations of Filomena/Mena. In other words, the first narrative strand is the murder story, which has a documentary feel to it, given its basis in real events of 1959 and 1960 in Portugal. The second narrative strand is essentially fictional. It focuses on the investigator Elias Santana; a human variety of the police attack dog, he will do anything to uncover every last sordid detail of the murder of Major Dantas Castro and those implicated in his murder. The novel follows Elias Santana on his many walks through Lisbon, especially his night strolls through the parks, streets, bars, nightclubs and cabarets of the capital, shares his keen observations of the multiple dimensions of a complex and decadent city, and discloses his unseemly behavior as he interrogates Filomena, his scheming, his perversity and immorality. Revealed too is his sickly and sleazy environment at home, where he keeps a lizard imprisoned in a cage as a pet and for which he scavenges the streets and parks of Lisbon to find nourishing insects. The second narrative strand provides ample and objective information about the social, political, and historical elements necessary to glean a full understanding of Portuguese society during the late 1950s and early '60s under the repressive dictatorship of Salazar. In reality, this may be considered a third narrative line, one that is inferred from, and grows out of the narrative focus on Elias Santana and his life.

After the initial appearance of the Major's body and the disclosure of the perpetrators of his murders, Elias Santana's mission is to piece together all the details of the events leading up to the murder and its aftermath, when the three murderers tried to flee the country and were apprehended. The first person to be apprehended was the Major's lover, Filomena. Consequently, most of the story is narrated from the perspective of Elias as he subjects the woman to a series of interrogations. These interrogations allow the inspector to pull all the different strands of the story together and come up with the evidence to prosecute the three criminals. He necessarily relies on her, since he does not have access to Barroca and Fontenova. PIDE is in charge of their case because of the political nature of the crime.

Elias believes that he can break down all of Filomena's defenses by invading her personal territory, including sleep. During his many interrogations, he moves his chair inch by inch towards her "[p]retext by pretext, question after question, until suddenly he was breathing 'police' all over her. Invasion of personal territory" (*Ballad*, p. 39). But, as Elias discovers, the closer he gets, the less she talks. He also learns that she is not interested in collaborating with the enemy, the government, and will not succumb to interrogation. She talks because she wants to escape from herself, not because she is forced to speak. Elias reaches this conclusion after he finishes his investigation. The two men and the woman kill the Major because the three want to reach freedom through the killing. The situation in their hideout had become constrictive and oppressive because of the Major's actions, especially his abuse and humiliation of the others and his frequent clandestine outings supposedly to organize a new coup against the fascist régime. The others were overcome by fear. More than fear of the Major, they feared themselves. However, it is the constant surveillance of the others by the Major, as well as his presence and insanity, that creates their internal fear. Consequently, they decide to murder the Major. All assume responsibility for the crime by taking turns shooting him. However, the two men are the ones who dispose of the body. They ride for miles along the coast with the corpse crammed in the back seat of their car until they finally de-

cided to bury it in Mastro Beach. The two men flee to southern Portugal, where they are finally apprehended by the police. They catch Mena in a hotel room in Lisbon, her suitcases packed, presumably for her flight from the country.

REAL-LIFE REACTION TO THE CRIME

In real life and in the novel, opposition groups were quick to accuse the government of committing a heinous political assassination. They also defended vehemently their comrade, the Major, considering him a brave man, someone who had become politicized because he resented the subservience exacted from people by the fascist regime. But in fact and fiction, this comrade is neither a man of honor nor a man of dignity. He is a bully who uses his power to humiliate others and to abuse them physically as well as psychologically; as such, he is representative of many other authority figures in the Salazar regime. The fear of his three companions in Vereda house was real. They feared for themselves and, ultimately, they feared fear itself. The Major had become impotent both in his sexual life and also his political life, his actions in both cases not producing the expected results. Consequently, he had resorted to humiliation, abuse, and even torture of those he considered his subordinates in order to compensate for his lack of potency. Since he had become impotent he had been torturing Filomena by marking her body with cigarette burns. The skin on her backside, from waist to neck, "was patterned with the silver-grey raised scars of cigarette-burns. They were neat, and they were numerous—scales in a fishbone pattern the length of her spine" (*Ballad*, pp. 154-55). Maybe fear, in addition to impotency, played an important role in the Major's actions too. Impotency too can be seen as a root cause for the behavior of his three companions. As Fontenova claims in a conversation he had with the author in 1980, a conversation that appears in an appendix to the novel, fear is extremely "constricting, since one's equilibrium is shattered and one is no longer in balance with one's external circumstances. Worst of all, this rupture will eventually make our reasoning entirely defensive; or for me it did. The reasoning of fear will undermine normal values until fear brings one to the point of murder." (*Ballad*, p. 180)

Novel as metaphor for Portugal. Elias Santana combines his suppositions, inquiries, assumptions, deductions, conjectures, and interrogations with his personal fantasies to piece together the puzzle (murder) and solve all the mysteries surrounding the supposed political assassination of Major Dantas Castro, including the role that his companions play in the episode, as well as the manner by which they carry out the murder and bury the Major in the beach. In the process, the detective elucidates a much larger crime, that of the authoritarian state against its own people. There is a piece of the mystery missing from his investigation, a piece that the reader can easily retrieve through the reading of the novel in order to solve the mystery and make sense out of the novel: it is the history of a nation apparently at peace but really in political turmoil. The violent murder provides a medium by which the novel exposes the conditions under which the Portuguese were living in the 1950s and 1960s, a condition unbeknownst even to some in Portugal, who were not aware of the extent to which the government would resort to repressive measures, even violence, to silence internal or external dissidence. The surveillance going on all the time in the novel, the watchfulness of Elias Santana as he wanders through Lisbon, his looking through a peephole to spy on Mena's moves, the torturous cigarette burns inflicted on her by the Major—all these details point to practices characteristic of the regime behind the scenes of the image projected to the world and Portugal's own population. Likewise, the opposition would employ tactics similar to those used by the fascist régime. Coincidentally, the discourse of both the authoritarian dictatorship and the opposition were modeled on similar structures of order and top-down hierarchy. Questioning authority was not a sin that could ever be forgiven by either the government or the opposition.

The views expressed above can easily be inferred from Cardoso Pires's narrative. In addition to the climate of fear and repression, there are many signs throughout the novel that indicate the country is morally and socially polluted. Reading the novel, one gets the impression that Portugal is a wasteland, a country without values intent on debasing its citizens and depriving them of their dignity. In a sense, the lizard in the glass cage that Elias Santana keeps at home and that depends on the insect scavenging instincts of the inspector for its survival is an appropriate metaphor for the country and its citizens. Elias regulates the temperature of the cage, just as the regime monitors the people, its caged animals, manipulating them to keep them in order, feeding them not with real nourishment or solutions to problems but with the equivalent of insects,

with palliatives to forestall dissent. Among these palliatives are small increases in salary, semiannual banquets, and, sponsored by newspapers, the marriages of St. Anthony—marriages paid for by the daily newspaper *Diário de Notícias*, which would sponsor weddings and honeymoons of 200 to 300 couples annually on the condition that the brides are virgins and are poor. The conditions in the country had reduced the Portuguese to the status of animals during the dark period of fascism. The fact that the novel ends with three empty cages passing by Elias late in the evening, three "circus-vans, with no animals in them, only the keepers sprawling half-awake as they traversed deserted streets in the small hours, faces between bars and legs struck out" (Pires, p. 177) is an indication that Portugal is just a big cage that encloses all of its citizens in a climate of state terror experienced by most Portuguese during the period of fascism. Juxtaposed to the image of the caged men is another allusion to Portugal as Europe's best-kept secret in a perfect ending to the novel. However, with *Ballad of Dogs' Beach* the secret is finally out. Portugal in the 1950s and 1960s, as the novel suggests, is a country whose leaders, including the victim himself, Major Dantas Castro, are "intent on hiding their weakness and impotence behind a facade of control and domination" (Sapega, p. 179).

Sources and literary context. Although *Ballad of Dogs' Beach* is based on real events, the author made many modifications to convey more precisely the social and political climate of the period. Many of the actual details were deliberately eliminated because the author deemed them too shocking to be part of his narrative. He felt quite strongly that if he had included certain documents, people would not believe that they were true. Consequently, he focused on the climate of fear, anxiety, lies, corruption, perversion, cages, and animals to portray Portugal as aptly as possible during the late 1950s and early '60s.

Ballad of Dogs' Beach fits neatly into the postrevolutionary narrative of Portugal. Many of these narratives use as their literary sources real facts and events from Portuguese history. After almost 50 years of fascism, replete with all the historical distortions and reinventions that are the hallmark of fascist discourse, Portuguese writers have felt a need to revisit their history in order to better understand the country and its people. The historical period that Cardoso Pires portrays diverges radically from the official history of the fascist period. It is a redefinition and an unmasking of the ideas and symbols of the fascist period, with the objective of exposing certain power structures that in the name of the state had systematically terrorized, abused, and repressed the citizens of the country. José Cardoso Pires, as many other contemporary Portuguese writers have done in the past two decades, uses history to present readers with alternative and contradictory evidence that confronts official historical discourse, in the process providing a more complete, less distorted vision of Portugal. The reconstruction of the past has in fact become one of the main currents of Portuguese post-revolutionary narrative. José Cardoso Pires, especially in *Ballad of Dogs' Beach* and *Alexandra Alpha*, engages extensively in the revision and redefinition of Portuguese history.

Cardoso Pires has been associated with the later phase of the Neorealist movement in Portugal. Neorealism had its heyday during the 1940s and '50s when the movement tried to serve as a revolutionary factor in Portuguese life through its production of artistic works directed at ending repression, classism, alienation, oppression, exploitation, and censorship. The initial Neorealist works attempted to portray, in almost documentary form, life under the fascist régime, but as the movement matured in the late 1950s and '60s, its initial dogmatism was replaced by a preoccupation with innovative aesthetic solutions that stressed psychological and historical rather than sociological elements. The novels of writers such as Cardoso Pires, Fernando Namora, and Carlos de Oliveira are excellent examples of this maturation process. With the advent of the Revolution and finally the establishment of a parliamentary democracy in Portugal, the fascist period would continue to be fertile ground for writers. Since 1974, many literary texts have dealt with this bleak period of Portuguese history including José Saramago's *The Year of the Death of Ricardo Reis* and "The Chair," Mário Cláudio's *Tocata para Dois Clarins*, Teolinda Gersão's *Paisagem com Mar e Mulher ao Fundo*, and António Lobo Antunes's *Fado Alexandrino*. However, unlike the Neorealist strain, these works focused mainly on uncovering the destructive and alienating tendencies of the myth-ridden word of fascism by exposing truths about, for example, the regime's use, misuse, and abuse of past national glory.

Events in History at the Time the Novel Was Written

From dictatorship to post-Revolutionary turmoil. In 1982, when *Ballad of Dogs' Beach* was

published, Portugal was on its way, after a shaky interim, to becoming a stable Western European parliamentary democracy. Years of turmoil during and after the Revolution (1974-76) ended in the firm establishment of a representative, pluralistic government, which remains in place today. The transition from authoritarianism to parliamentary democracy was far from easy, though. In a short span of eight years, Portugal shifted from an anti-communist, anti-Soviet position to a non-aligned, third-world position during the revolutionary period, back again to a pro-European stance. This last phase would be followed by the integration of Portugal into the European Community in 1986 and its full incorporation into the Western European democracies.

Back on April 25, 1974, when the armed forces marched into Lisbon and put an end to the almost 50 years of the Oliveira Salazar and Marcelo Caetano fascist dictatorship, their action caught many by surprise. Although the revolution succeeded without bloodshed, it created conditions that caused years of political and social instability. The military set out to revolutionize government and the economy in conjunction with the Communist Party, aiming but failing to turn Portugal into a government of the proletariat.

Political and social developments after the Revolution of the Carnations (as the 1974 Revolution would be called), occurred in reaction to the dictatorial Salazar years. The revolutionary leaders found a country that was by far the poorest in Western Europe. The country suffered from paltry medical services, widespread illiteracy, an abysmal health system, and public institutions plagued by corruption and nepotism. So dismal were the political and economic conditions that most of the labor surplus went abroad to work in countries such as France, Germany, the United States, and Canada, beginning in earnest in the 1960s. The turmoil brought about by the Revolution only exacerbated problems in the economic arena.

First there was a drastic redistribution of wealth through the nationalization of commerce and big business, an action strongly supported by the Communist Party. Agrarian reform also occurred, and at a rapid rate, especially in the communist stronghold of Alentejo where lands were confiscated from absentee landowners and given to workers' cooperatives. These measures were supported by the military's revolutionaries, who had organized themselves into the Movement of the Armed Forces (MFA), and by Prime

Minister Vasco Gonçalves. But some dissidents within the MFA were not happy with the leftward drift of the country and after several incidents, including mass rallies to demonstrate the country's opposition to a worker's state, the prime minister resigned (August 29, 1975). The influence of the radical left waned after the Gonçalves resignation, but stable civilian democratic rule still seemed to elude the country. Then came the events of November 25, 1975, which further halted the leftward drift. The so-called "group of nine," a dissident group of officers who disagreed with the radical leftist turn in the country, had lately gained the upper hand in the direction of the government. Opposed to the group were some revolutionary paratroopers, who, on November 25, attacked several air bases and demanded the dismissal of their commanders. A countercoup forced the paratroopers to surrender. In the end, Portugal would not become a worker's state and the Communists, a minority party, would not able to take the reigns of power. The November 25 episode confirmed the phasing out of the military from politics in Portugal.

From the end of the revolutionary period to 1982. Although at the time it was not perceived as a turning point in the democratization of Portugal, the events of November 25, 1975, changed radically its political and economic landscape. The military, through the Council of the Revolution, still exerted considerable clout over the affairs of the state, but its role diminished with the passage of time until in 1982 the Council was abolished altogether. Parliamentary elections had taken place in 1975, a new constitution had taken effect in 1976, and there was no longer any valid reason for the military to serve as the guarantor of democracy by exercising its power to invalidate unconstitutional acts.

The turn away from the revolutionary agenda during this period meant that some of the "excesses" of the revolutionary days would eventually be dismantled, especially those related to nationalizing businesses and agrarian reform. After 1977 there was a gradual restoration of private property. Some estates that had been illegally seized were returned to their owners; some enterprises were also privatized, but the majority still remained property of the state. Economic hardship continued, however. The aftermath of the Portuguese Revolution can be characterized as a period not only of turmoil but also of economic stagnation, hardship, and inflation. Bureaucracy grew excessively between 1975-1980, and corruption and nepotism continued. There

were many gains, such as freedom of the press, free elections, right to free association, freedom to strike, and the end of the colonial wars, but far from improving, life worsened for many Portuguese during the economic crisis of the late 1970s. Thousands emigrated for work, a situation that would diminish only after Portugal was accepted into the European Community in 1986 and the country received financial aid to use "largely for highways and public works that [would] provide the infrastructure for a modern economy" (Herr, p. 18).

By the end of the 1970s, a great number of intellectuals who initially welcomed the Revolution had grown disillusioned with it. They felt deceived, believing that a fraud had been perpetrated on the Portuguese people. They even opposed Portugal's becoming more integrated into Western Europe, seeing this as a potential loss of identity and the uniqueness of Portuguese culture. To many intellectuals, the rapprochement with Europe signified the institutionalization of a bourgeois society with bourgeois values and a market economy. They did not believe the Revolution radicalized the institutions of the country; on the contrary, they thought, most of the changes were cosmetic and ultimately self-serving. Bourgeois society had returned with a vengeance by the end of the 1970s, and these Portuguese intellectuals felt foolish for putting out too much hope for radical change in Portuguese society. In their view, the Revolution had simply been an exercise in opportunism. Among the intellectuals who felt deceived by the evolution of events surrounding the Revolution and its aftermath was José Cardoso Pires.

Reviews. *Ballad of Dogs' Beach* has been well received both in Portugal and abroad. It won the APE (Portuguese Association of Writers) Fiction Prize in 1982. The selection committee unanimously considered that the novel had established the standard by which all other novels (about 50) that were competing for the Prize ought to be judged (Alves, p. 6). The novel immediately became a bestseller in Portugal and was subsequently translated into many different languages. Maria Alzira Seixo refers to the work as one of the best-written novels of recent times; it channels passion, she says, between political fury and the drunkenness of a criminal investigation, condensing this passion into an exemplary textual serenity (Seixo, p. 56). Writing in *Hispania*, Helena Kaufman ascribes an effectiveness to the novel, maintaining that it forces the reader to plunge into the darkness of Salazar's fascist regime (Kaufman, p. 670). Finally, Maria Lúcia Lepecki compliments Cardoso Pires for confronting admirably the recent historical space of his country in *Ballad of Dogs' Beach,* adding that readers, through the creative process of a dissertation, are coerced into investigating and reconstructing a crime, a society, and a country and its people (Lepecki, p. 92).

—José N. Ornelas

For More Information

Alves, Clara Ferreira. "Balada de Cardoso Pires Premiada a Cinco Vozes." *Jornal de Letras: Artes e Ideias* 2, no. 56 (April 12-25, 1983): 6.

Ferreira, António Mega. "Entrevista com José Cardoso Pires." *Jornal de Letras: Artes e Ideias* 2, no. 47 (December 7-20, 1982): 3.

Herr, Richard, ed. *The New Portugal: Democracy and Europe.* Berkeley: University of California at Berkeley, 1992.

Kaufman, Helena. "A Sociedade Portuguesa sobre Investigação em *Balada da Praia dos Cães* de José Cardoso Pires e *Adeus, Princesa* de Clara Pinto Correia." *Hispania* 76, no. 4 (1993): 664-71.

Kayman, Martin. *Revolution and Counter-Revolution in Portugal.* London: Merlin, 1987.

Lepecki, Maria Lúcia. "Review of *Balada da Praia dos Cães.*" *Colóquio: Letras* 77 (1984): 92.

Ornelas, José N. "*Balada da Praia dos Cães* de José Cardoso Pires: Entre a História e a Ficção." In *Selected Proceedings: The Thirty-Fifth Annual Mountain Interstate Foreign Language Conference.* Ed. Ramón Hernández-Rubio. Greenville: Furman University Press, 1987.

Pires, José Cardoso. *Ballad of Dogs' Beach.* London: J. M. Dent and Sons, 1986.

Robinson, Richard. *Contemporary Portugal: A History.* London: George Allen and Unwin, 1979.

Sapega, Elen. "No Longer Alone and Proud: Notes on the Rediscovery of the Nation in Contemporary Portuguese Fiction." In *After the Revolution: Twenty Years of Portuguese Literature, 1974-1994.* Eds. Helena Kaufman, and Anna Klobucka. Lewisburg: Bucknell University Press, 1997.

Seixo, Maria Alzira. *A Palavra do Romance: Ensaios de Genologia e Análise.* Lisboa: Livros Horizonte, 1986.

Baltasar and Blimunda

by

José Saramago

José Saramago was born in 1922 in Azinhaga, in the Ribatejo province of Portugal, but his family moved to Lisbon when he was still a child. His parents were not wealthy, so he completed his secondary education in a vocational school, where he trained to become a mechanic. He nonetheless found time to read widely, and, after working only briefly as a mechanic, progressed through a variety of newspaper jobs, from clerical worker, to production assistant, proofreader, and newspaper columnist. Ultimately, after the democratic Revolution of 1974 that deposed Portugal's right-wing dictatorship, Saramago became adjunct editor of the major Lisbon newspaper *Diário de Notícias*. Meanwhile, his literary career began unspectacularly, including one early novel, two collections of verse, and four volumes of journalistic writing, none of which attracted much attention. It was only after being dismissed from his job at the *Diário de Notícias* in 1975, in the wake of a counter-revolutionary coup, that Saramago took up his writing career in earnest. He produced a collection of short stories and a second novel, before writing a third, critically acclaimed novel—*Levantado do Chão* (1980; Raised from the Soil). Similar acclaim and greater commercial success followed for subsequent novels, including *Memorial do Convento* (1982; *Baltasar and Blimunda*, 1987 and 1998), the work that launched him on a series of critical and commercial triumphs. Saramago's well-publicized loyalty to the Portuguese Communist Party and his outspoken views relating to politics and current affairs have led to his being

THE LITERARY WORK

A novel set in Lisbon and around Mafra, in central Portugal, in the first half of the eighteenth century; published in Portuguese (as *Memorial do Convento*) in 1982, in English in 1987 and (in a revised translation) in 1998.

SYNOPSIS

Baltasar and Blimunda, an ordinary couple, become involved in the plan of King João V of Portugal to build a great convent and palace at Mafra, and in the construction of a flying machine designed by the eccentric Father Bartolomeu Lourenço de Gusmão. Baltasar's ultimate fate is determined by the Inquisition, probably for reasons connected with his involvement in the project to build the flying machine.

viewed by many as a controversial figure. Works such as his rewriting of the gospel story in *O Evangelho Segundo Jesus Cristo* (1991; *The Gospel According to Jesus Christ*, 1993) provoked heated debate, in which government ministers condemned his work, contributing to his subsequent emigration to Spain. Despite the outcry, acclaim for Saramago's writing continued, culminating in his winning the Nobel Prize for Literature in 1998. Written in his characteristic multivocal, oral style, *Baltasar and Blimunda* epitomizes the powerful mix of social conscience and fantasy typical of his fiction. The novel allows the ordinary

José Saramago

citizen to take center stage in an age that usually gave such prominence only to royalty, clergy, and nobility.

Events in History at the Time the Novel Takes Place

All that glittered was not gold. Early-eighteenth-century Portugal was an imperial power at the peak of its prestige but already in decline in terms of influence on the international stage. The discovery of gold and diamonds in Brazil in the late seventeenth century, along with imports of luxury goods from the wide-ranging Portuguese trading posts in Africa and Asia, permitted the court of King João V to display fabulous wealth, rivaling that of the French court of Louis XIV in its opulence and sophistication. Major European cultural figures, such as the Italian composer Domenico Scarlatti and the German architect Johann Friedrich Ludwig (who both appear in fictional form in *Baltasar and Blimunda*) were invited by the Court to Lisbon from overseas, and they did much to enrich Portuguese cultural life. Portugal also saw the completion of several major projects during this period, including the magnificent baroque University Library at Coimbra, and the convent and palace of Mafra, which

is the pretext for the fictional setting of Saramago's novel. All the glitter and magnificence were deceptive, however.

The splendor and wealth masked Portugal's rapid decline as a world power. Although the country had recovered from 60 years of Spanish domination (1580-1640) to regain its role as a seat of empire in Africa, Asia, and America, its strength was relative: Britain, Holland, and France were now the major colonial and trading powers in Europe. Also, the 1703 Treaty of Methuen, in which Portugal permitted the import of English woolens in return for a preferential duty by England on Portuguese wines, proved more favorable to the British than to the Portuguese. Throughout the reign of João V, Portugal generally imported goods from Britain worth approximately three times the value of exports to that country. In addition, the dependence of the Portuguese economy on the export of one product—port wine—to the British market made the economic health of the country dangerously dependent on the needs and interests of this dominant trading partner.

Meanwhile the Portuguese came to rely on the wealth of Brazil in a way that did little to aid long-term development of Portugal's national economy. Colonial gold was used to import luxury goods from overseas rather than to invest in the development of domestic industrial production. As a result, Portugal tended to export raw materials and to depend on foreign markets for manufactured goods, to the detriment of the underlying economic health of the nation.

In the political sphere, the resources at the country's disposal enabled the king to avoid summoning the Cortes (parliament) throughout his reign, so he was able to impose his own will on the country virtually unchallenged. Whereas the new powers emerging in Northern Europe (primarily Britain, Holland, and France) benefited from the dynamism born of a spirit of philosophical inquiry, freedom of speech, and increasing democracy, Portugal remained a country institutionally rooted in the past. Not only did the king enjoy absolute power as monarch, he continued to be viewed as an expression of God's will on earth, precluding any separation of the powers of church and state. The prevailing view saw the monarchy as the head of a corporatist state, conceived along lines similar to those of Thomas Hobbes's *Leviathan* (1651), with each social element having its individual function within an organic whole. As societal head, the king thus had the uncontestable right to make decisions on behalf of the nation as a whole.

Though the sovereign had ultimate authority, the Church wielded considerable influence on civil society, especially in the era of the Inquisition (1536-1821). The Inquisition, a tribunal to suppress deviation from the teachings of the Roman Catholic Church, possessed the powers to condemn ordinary citizens for loosely defined offenses such as heresy, witchcraft, and observance of Judaic practices. H. V. Livermore writes that

> Confession and denunciation were required in cases of keeping the Sabbath on Saturday or Friday, fasting for Ramadan, praying shoeless, bathing the whole body, refusal to consume bacon or wine, the denial of hell, paradise, mass, absolution, the virgin birth or the articles of faith, and bigamy, witchcraft or the unauthorized possession of the Bible in Portuguese.
> (Livermore, p. 147)

The powers of the Inquisition would be severely curtailed by the Marquês de Pombal in the eighteenth century, but only in the second half of the century, after the novel takes place.

In the novel, Blimunda's mother, Sebastiana de Jesus, a converted Jewess, is sent into exile in Africa for claiming to have mysterious visions, while Baltasar is eventually executed for unspecified offences, probably linked to his second flight in Bartolomeu's flying machine. The total number of victims executed by the Holy Office probably was not as high as many might think. Oliveira Marques gives the total number burned at the stake between 1648 and 1747 as 146 (Marques, p. 312). Still, the influence that the Inquisition exerted, directly and indirectly, over life in Portugal was considerable, so that the "twin forces of piety and bigotry" continued to prevail in the country into the latter half of the eighteenth century (Birmingham, p. 78). Its victims included notable figures such as the playwright António José da Silva, whose execution for Judaic tendencies in 1739 is reported alongside Baltasar's in Saramago's novel.

The convent of Mafra. This giant building, which comprises a church, a monastery for 300 monks, and a royal palace and gardens, was constructed in fulfillment of a vow made by King João V in 1711 to build a new monastery for the Franciscan order if his Queen, D. Maria Ana of Austria, would bear him an heir. The massive project took nearly 20 years to construct and required the use of forced-labor chain gangs brought in from all over the country. This is presented in the novel as leading to the neglect and even the willful destruction of valuable agricultural land:

Convent and palace of Mafra, constructed during the reign of King João V.

> They left early, meeting up with other men along the route, whom Baltasar recognised as neighbours also helping to build the convent, which might explain why the surrounding fields have been abandoned, the old folks and the women cannot cultivate the land on their own.
>
> On a small plot of land situated behind the convent walls lying to the east, the friar in charge of the kitchen-garden attached to the hospice had planted fruit trees and laid out beds with a variety of produce and borders of flowers, the mere beginnings of a fully established orchard and kitchen-garden. All of this would be destroyed.
> (Saramago, *Baltasar and Blimunda*,
> pp. 197, 270)

These quotations illustrate the consequences not only of the building project of Mafra, but also of a general national agricultural policy of the period, which neglected useful developments in favor of short-term profit. Thus, reports Oliveira Marques, the wine industry (which enjoyed an unprecedented boom at the time, due largely to exports to Britain) was allowed to extend its vineyards to clearly unsuitable land, and this led to a decline in staples needed for domestic consumption, such as wheat (Marques, p. 281).

The grandeur and huge scale of the building project were clearly designed to invite favorable comparisons with other major construction projects by other monarchs (such as Philip II's monastery and palace at El Escorial, built near Madrid between 1563 and 1584, and Louis XIV's royal palace at Versailles, outside Paris, built between 1660 and 1685). To the modern eye, this seems like economic foolishness at best and cruel negligence of the kingdom's real interests at worst. Contemporary expectations of kings, however, were that they should spare no expense

and even the lucky ones (such as Baltasar's father in the novel) who possessed their own land might find themselves required to give it up for the good of the crown with no guarantee of compensation (*Baltasar and Blimunda*, p. 100). Ironically the one major construction project clearly undertaken for the public good, the Free Waters Aqueduct in Lisbon, was paid for by the common people themselves, with taxes being levied on staples such as wine, olive oil, and meat in order to finance the scheme (Carvalho in Levenson, p. 40).

THE MIGHT OF THE BEDBUG'S BITE

～

On nights when the King visits the Queen, the bedbugs come out at a much later hour because of the heaving of the mattress, for they are insects who enjoy peace and quiet and prefer to discover their victims asleep. In the King's bed, too, there are yet more bedbugs waiting for their share of blood, for His Majesty's blood tastes no better or worse than that of the other inhabitants of the city, whether blue or otherwise.

(*Baltasar and Blimunda*, p. 8)

These bugs recall Saramago's short story "The Chair," which features a succession of woodworms that gnaw away at the legs of a chair, eventually leading it to collapse. The story is clearly based on the accident suffered by the Portuguese dictator Salazar in 1968, when a chair collapsed under him, leading to his incapacitation for office and thus to the eventual fall of his regime, the New State, in 1974. The analogy sheds new light on the frequent likening in *Baltasar and Blimunda* of the workers at Mafra to ants. These "ants" can be seen not merely as unquestioning lackeys of the king, but as potential instruments of far-reaching change. Likewise, the bedbugs gnawing at the bodies of the king and queen under their eiderdown may be seen as signaling the fall of the monarchy and loss of its accompanying privileges.

The Novel in Focus

Plot summary. *Baltasar and Blimunda* opens at the court of King João V in Lisbon in 1711, presenting the reader with an irreverent portrait of the pomp and circumstance surrounding all royal activities, most notably the sexual coupling of the king with his queen, D. Maria Ana of Austria, who he hopes will bear him an heir to the throne. The bedbugs that afflict the royal couple as they lie beneath the blankets suggest the moral degeneracy of the monarchy.

The opening chapter concludes with the king's being persuaded by a representative of the Franciscan order to vow to build a convent for the order if his wish to have an heir is fulfilled, although the narrative slyly suggests that the king is a victim of ecclesiastical manipulation in that the queen's confessor may already be aware of her pregnancy and have informed the Franciscans of that fact in advance. Subsequent chapters set the scene for the major events of the novel by depicting (with some exuberant color) the realities of life for ordinary citizens in Lisbon in the early eighteenth century: the corruption and hypocrisy of the clergy; prostitution, crime, and disease; the popular entertainments provided by bullfights, religious processions, and, more sinisterly, the burning of heretics at the stake; and the miserable lot of average citizens such as Sebastiana Maria de Jesus, publicly humiliated by the Inquisition at an *auto-da-fe* (an exemplary public punishment). Also miserable is the lot of Baltasar Seven Suns, a soldier returning from fighting for his country in the War of the Spanish Succession, having lost a hand in battle, and now facing an uncertain future with no guarantee of employment.

On his return to Lisbon, Baltasar meets the mysterious Blimunda (Sebastiana's daughter), who has inexplicable powers to see inside people and things, and Father Bartolomeu Lourenço, an unorthodox priest intent on fulfilling his dream

in increasing their own prestige. Meanwhile, ordinary citizens, such as Baltasar and Blimunda, were essentially pawns of those with greater power in a society that still preserved many of the structures of feudalism: individual progress was dependent on patronage; soldiers were recruited by force from the ranks of the peasantry, and then discarded when no longer required by the Crown, as happens to Baltasar in the novel (*Baltasar and Blimunda*, pp. 26-27); people were removed from their homes or moved to different locations at the behest of their social superiors;

THE WAR OF THE SPANISH SUCCESSION

This scruffy-looking fellow with his rattling sword and ill-assorted clothes, even though barefoot, has the air of a solider, and his name is Baltasar Mateus, otherwise known as Sete-Sóis or Seven Suns. He was dismissed from the army where he was of no further use once his left hand was amputated at the wrist after being shattered by gunfire at Jerez de los Caballeros, in the ambitious campaign we fought last October with eleven thousand men, only to end with the loss of two hundred of our soldiers and the rout of the survivors, who were pursued by the Spanish cavalry dispatched from Badajoz. . . . Sete-Sóis, maimed and bedraggled, travelled the main highway to Lisbon, deprived of his left hand, part of which had remained in Spain and part in Portugal, and all because of a strategic war to decide who was to occupy the Spanish throne, an Austrian Charles or a French Philip, but no one Portuguese, whether unimpaired or one-handed, intact or mutilated.

(*Baltasar and Blimunda*, pp. 26-27)

This war, which lasted from 1702 to 1713, was caused by the death of King Carlos II of Spain in 1700, who did not leave any heirs to the throne. The principal contenders were Philip, Duc d'Anjou, supported by the King of France, and Archduke Charles of Austria, supported by Britain and also by Portugal. Although Philip was the one to eventually become King Philip V of Spain, Britain succeeded in winning important concessions in the war, including sovereignty over Gibraltar and Philip's renunciation of all claims to the throne of France, which helped avert French hegemony in Europe. It is striking in this passage from the novel that the focus is not on these great matters of historical importance, but rather on the way that participation in this war affected Baltasar, an ordinary man called up to serve the strategic needs of his monarch and abandoned by the Crown when he has ceased to be of use to it. Historian Russell-Wood sums up Portugal's involvement in the war: "The country had been ravaged . . . and the treasury was depleted," realities that lead the reader of *Baltasar and Blimunda* to credit all of Baltasar's achievements to the man himself, and not to his royal master (Russell-Wood in Levenson, p. 20).

of building a flying machine (known as the *Passarola*, or "big bird"). The attraction between Baltasar and Blimunda is immediately obvious; Bartolomeu oversees a ceremonial union of the two lovers, which is very pointedly not a Christian marriage and, in its simplicity and sincerity, contrasts vividly with the rituals and expenditure surrounding an arranged royal marriage later in the novel (*Baltasar and Blimunda*, pp. 46-47 and 304-05). Subsequently Baltasar and Blimunda help Bartolomeu build his flying machine (powered by the wills of ordinary people, which are captured from their bodies and stored in a glass jar by Blimunda before these people die). The three characters take one exhilarating but uncontrolled flight in the machine before it comes to earth, after which Bartolomeu flees to Spain, never to reap-

pear in the novel. The two other characters lovingly look after his flying machine while Baltasar also works on a number of projects connected with the construction of the convent at Mafra.

The consecration of the convent takes place on the king's forty-first birthday in 1730, nearly 20 years after the opening of the text. Even as the consecration takes place, however, a more significant event occurs in terms of the novel's development. Baltasar accidentally sets off the *Passarola* and is carried away by it to be seen again only in 1739, when Blimunda (who has spent nine years searching for him all over Portugal) finds him, just as he is being executed by the Inquisition for unspecified crimes. At the close of the novel Blimunda summons Baltasar's will from his dying body to be with her: "The last man to be burned has his left hand missing. Perhaps because of his blackened beard, a miraculous transformation caused by the soot, he looks much younger. And there is a dark cloud in the centre of his body. Then Blimunda said, Come. The will of Baltasar Sete-Sóis broke free from his body, but did not ascend to the stars, for it belonged to the earth and to Blimunda" (*Baltasar and Blimunda*, p. 343). By this action Blimunda asserts the significance of the popular over the powerful but wealthy king, who is but a shadowy figure beside the more memorable characters of Baltasar and Blimunda.

Bartolomeu Lourenço de Gusmão and his flying machine.

> My friend João Elvas has just told me that you are known as the Flying Man, tell me, Father, why have they given you such a nickname, Baltasar asked him (*Baltasar and Blimunda*, p. 2).

> They call me the Flying Man because I have flown . . . you yourself did not invent that hook you are wearing [a reference to the hook placed on the stump of Baltasar's left arm after the loss of his left hand in battle], someone had to discover the need for such an implement and hit on the idea of combining iron and leather in order to make it practical, and the same is true for those ships on the river, at one time sails had not been invented, and before that there were no oars, and before that no helm, and just as man, who inhabits the earth, found it necessary to become a sailor, so he will find it necessary to become a flier.
> (*Baltasar and Blimunda*, pp. 52-53)

The figure of Bartolomeu Lourenço de Gusmão, who becomes one of the main characters in the novel, is based on a genuine historical personality. Born in Santos, Brazil, in 1685, simply as Bartolomeu Lourenço (the additional surname is believed to have been adopted to honor a protector of the family's interests), this exceptional scholar first came to Portugal in 1701 and was highly regarded, both as a preacher and as a far-sighted inventor. In 1709 he gave a demonstration at the royal court in Lisbon of a prototype of his projected flying machine (based on a theory he described in a surviving document). There is, however, no strong evidence to suggest that he ever succeeded in building a machine big enough to transport a human being, in spite of later reports of a flight carried out from the castle in Lisbon to the nearby Terreiro do Paço. In 1724, accompanied by his younger brother João Alvares de Santa Maria, Bartolomeu fled Portugal on short notice, traveling under an assumed name to Spain, where he died in Toledo in November 1724. His brother subsequently testified to the Inquisition that Bartolomeu had adopted Judaism in preference to Christianity:

> The poor youth declared that his brother had tenaciously instilled in him the belief that he, Bartolomeu, was the Messiah, the Redeemer foretold by the Old Testament, since the redemption promised to the Jews by Holy Scripture had still not been fulfilled. If he did not undertake the work of Redemption, God would call him severely to account. . . . He was waiting only for the completion of 'a flying construction which he was building,' and with the aid of this machine he would control all the kingdoms of the world and, if necessary, he would 'subjugate and destroy their kingdoms' in order to establish a single world empire in which the Jews would reign over all others, and he would reign over them as their King
> (From testimony given to the Inquisition by João Alvares de Santa Maria in 1724, in Taunay, "Novidades do maior vulto sobre o Padre Voador," p. 2).

The evidence available does not make it easy to judge the reliability of these accounts of Bartolomeu's alleged insanity, heresy, and megalomania, which gives Saramago free rein to exploit the uncertainty regarding certain areas of this character's biography for creative purposes. The character of Bartolomeu thus becomes the principal representative of the unorthodox in the novel, through his refusal to conform to the expectations of a rigidly hierarchical society, an example followed by Blimunda at the end of the text, when she walks the length and breadth of Portugal, encouraging others to think for themselves and to reject "truths" propagated on the strength of institutional power alone (*Baltasar and Blimunda,* pp. 339-40).

Saramago's fictional development of Father Bartolomeu Lourenço de Gusmão and his flying machine bridges the gap that separates court from commoner. The priest's choice to involve Baltasar and Blimunda in his creative project elevates them to a status of greater inherent nobility than the court upon which he has effectively turned his back. Also the *Passarola* becomes a symbol of the freedom lacked by ordinary people in the eighteenth century. The notion of flight in the novel points to the infinite capacity of the human mind, will, and spirit to seek new possibilities of thought and self-expression, a capacity that was repressed in the eighteenth century by a combination of the Inquisition (which required absolute Catholic orthodoxy) and the power of the king to treat his kingdom as his own possession, without any consideration for the needs or wishes of ordinary citizens.

Sources and literary context. In spite of the prominent element of fantasy in his novel, Saramago makes extensive use of historically documented sources. Comparisons of the novel with biographical works on the priest Bartolomeu Lourenço de Gusmão reveal a considerable reliance on sources such as eighteenth-century sermons (including those of Gusmão himself, as well as those of the later Brazilian preacher Frei Francisco Xavier de Santa Rita Bastos), on the priest's own account of his plans for the *Passarola,* on records of life at the court of King João V, and even on the journal of an eighteenth-century French visitor to Portugal, who recorded the unusual visual faculties of a woman who almost certainly is the model (in this respect) for the figure of Blimunda in the novel.

Saramago's novel resembles works of the Neorealist movement that dominated Portuguese literature in the 1940s and early 1950s. Like these works, *Baltasar and Blimunda* focuses on the miserable experiences of the downtrodden poor in an authoritarian society that denies them any voice to express their feelings or alter their living and working conditions. Also like these works, Saramago's novel includes a detailed depiction of everyday realities and a progressive worldview, whose ideal is the bringing about of a more equal society for all. Such an approach had been adopted more directly by Saramago in his previous novel, *Levantado do Chão* (1980; Raised from the Soil), which ends in celebration of the 1974 Revolution and of the dawning land reform on the southern large estates, events that inaugurated a new era of democracy in Portugal.

The insertion of *Baltasar and Blimunda* into this literary context can obscure as much as it clarifies however, for the novel clearly diverges from Neorealist practices: in its exercise of the imagination (illustrated, for example, by the powering of the *Passarola* by the human wills captured by Blimunda); in its creation of unrealistic situations (the dialogues between the commoner João Elvas and the nobleman who reveals to him the details of a royal procession to the Spanish border, the disrespectful letter written by Baltasar to the king, etc.); and in the depiction of ordinary people, not as mere victims of unjust circumstance but as actors with the potential to effect radical change in their own circumstances if they become aware of the power that lies within their grasp.

Some commentators have placed Saramago in the magical realist tradition of such Latin-American writers as Gabriel García Márquez, a claim not entirely without validity, given plot developments that locate the novel firmly in the realm of the imagination as opposed to that of strict historical fact. What has perhaps been understated, however, is the author's debt to the concept of New History (as formulated by writers such as the French historian Georges Duby), that is, of history written from the perspective of the ordinary men and women whose experiences are marginalized by traditional accounts. Also understated is Saramago's debt to the concept of the dialogic novel in the tradition of the Russian literary critic Mikhail Bakhtin, that is, the novel that seeks to represent not one purportedly authoritative account of events, but a variety of perspectives, all of them being of equal validity and reliability. Both of these traditions emphasize the potential of the human voice and of the multiplicity of perspectives on life that have shaped the course of human history. Thus, instead of centering on the events at the royal court, which form the focus of its opening chapter, Saramago's novel gradually diverts attention to the ordinary characters, who tell their own versions of history as they go about their daily business, the clearest example of this being the various workers who have been engaged to transport a giant stone from Pêro Pinheiro to Mafra:

> My name is Julião Mau-Tempo, I'm a native of Alentejo, and I came to work here in Mafra because of the famine that scourges my province, I don't know how anyone has survived there, for if we hadn't grown accustomed to eating grass and acorns, I'll bet everyone would be dead by now. . . . I came to Mafra because my parish priest assured us from the pulpit that anyone who came here would soon be a servant of the King . . . he also assured us that no one in the King's service goes hungry . . . well, I soon discovered that I had been misinformed . . . and if I haven't died from hunger, it's because I spend everything I earn on food, I'm as shabbily dressed as I ever was, as for becoming one of the King's servants, I live in hope of seeing my sovereign's face before I finally pine away after all these years of separation from my family.
>
> (*Baltasar and Blimunda*, pp. 220-221)

Gathering round the campfire at night, in a quasi-Brechtian dramatic format, each worker presents himself to the reader before telling his own story, thus validating his life and experience and elevating him to a status of equality with the

BROADENING THE HISTORICAL FOCUS

Saramago's novels are almost always marked by an intrusive narrative style that inserts interjections, seemingly casual reflections on events, humorous incongruities, and other apparently incidental remarks. Frequently these remarks place the events described in a broader historical context, leading the reader to reflect on periods other than those in which the novel takes place. For example,

> News reached Mafra sporadically that Lisbon was suffering the tremors of an earthquake. . . . Had the previous earthquake been more severe and the number of dead greater, the same measures would have been taken to bury the dead, and take care of the living, a sound piece of advice should any such calamity ever happen again, but spare us, oh Lord.
>
> (*Baltasar and Blimunda*, pp. 206-07)

The earthquake alluded to here is not the great Lisbon earthquake of November 1, 1755, whose shock waves (both literal and metaphorical) were felt all over Europe, leading thinkers such as the French philosopher Voltaire to question the notion of a beneficent God as the unquestioned moral foundation for the universe. The reference here is to an earlier, smaller earthquake that occurred in October 1724. At the end of the passage there is an allusion to the notion of God's saving us from further catastrophes of this kind; it satirizes the passivity of the nation's successive governments, which have chosen to leave important matters to chance rather than attempting to foresee difficulties and face challenges before they become emergencies. It was widely believed after the 1755 earthquake that better city planning, improved sanitation, and more solid construction could have averted a large number of the deaths suffered in Lisbon. The sense that this reference to the 1724 earthquake is intended as satirical criticism is reinforced by Saramago's adaptation here of the pragmatic speech attributed to the Marquês de Pombal after the 1755 earthquake, in which he encouraged his fellow citizens to bury the dead and take care of the living. Pombal is generally credited with the revolutionary safer redesign of the central part of Lisbon in the aftermath of the disaster, and the clear implication of Saramago's repetition of his words in relation to the 1724 quake is that the later, greater quake need not have been as disastrous as it was. Pombal was dismissed on the succession to the throne of Queen Maria I and King Pedro III in 1777. No longer preoccupied with modernization, but rather with the entrenchment of power and privilege, Portugal returned to unenlightened absolutist rule. This brief allusion contains an implicit warning to Saramago's readers to be on guard against complacency in the protection of democratic freedoms.

aristocratic figures who are more commonly the focus of historical discourse. The extract printed above is one of seven successive narratives of the same type presented at this point in the novel, each one reinforcing the image of a poor, exploited workforce, which has been hoodwinked into serving the interests of its real enemies, the twin forces of Church and State. (The fictional Julião Mau-Tempo in the excerpt above is clearly an ancestor of the twentieth-century Mau-Tempo family, whose struggle for emancipation is de-

picted in Saramago's earlier novel *Levantado do Chão* of 1980.)

Not only does this strategy achieve equalization of commoner and royal, by foregrounding the commoner for a change, it also invites readers to reconsider their understanding of history in general and to see it not as an immutable, objective reality but as a collation of narratives shaped according to the needs and interests of its narrators at different periods. Saramago is thereby taking part in a broader tendency towards experimentation with the art of storytelling and preoccupation with recollections of the past, reflected in the works of other Portuguese writers such as Lídia Jorge and António Lobo Antunes (see **The Murmuring Coast** and **South of Nowhere**, also in *WLAIT 5: Spanish and Portuguese Literatures and Their Times*) and internationally by figures such as Britain's Salman Rushdie and Spain's Juan Goytisolo (see **Marks of Identity**, also in *WLAIT 5: Spanish and Portuguese Literatures and Their Times*).

Events in History at the Time the Novel Was Written

From sovereignty to dictatorship—pertinent parallels. By 1982 Portugal was a parliamentary democracy beginning to develop the full-scale integration into Western European patterns of life that are readily visible today. At the same time, however, it was still adapting to life after the fall in 1974 of the long-term right-wing dictatorship of António Salazar and Marcello Caetano. This dictatorship had defined twentieth-century Portuguese history, invoking an introverted, economically austere, and socially conservative model of a pious society dedicated to following the will of its father figure (Salazar), with a certain degree of connivance from the Roman Catholic hierarchy (even if, at a popular level, the social and political attitudes of the Church were more mixed than this broad generalization might suggest). As a result, the country entering a new era of democracy in 1974 had one of the highest illiteracy records in Europe, and rights and benefits that are today taken for granted in the West had still to be secured: women were regarded almost as the property of their husbands or fathers; material standards of living were the lowest in Western Europe; and there was no freedom of political or trade-union association. These unpleasant realities were further reinforced by strict censorship of the press and the media in general, which reproduced only officially sanctioned opinions.

One of the major reasons for the eventual fall of the dictatorship was Portugal's colonial rule in Africa. Portugal was the first and the last of the major European colonial powers in the continent, and, even after other imperial rulers such as France and Britain had relinquished these roles, Portugal continued to adopt a self-appointed and ultimately unsustainable role as importer of European civilization to Africa. This led to a long war of attrition against pro-independence guer-

rilla movements in Africa, a campaign sometimes referred to as "Portugal's Vietnam," from 1961 until 1974, when it was the difficulty in maintaining discipline and morale in the armed forces that played a major part in bringing down the dictatorship at home. The hierarchical model of Portuguese society before 1974 was not totally dissimilar to the one of the absolute monarch depicted in *Baltasar and Blimunda*: the self-importance of the eighteenth-century monarchy resembles Salazar's self-appointed role as the Father of the Nation in the twentieth century, and both of these stances provide a stark contrast to the underlying loss of Portugal's real position of influence in the world. The king's excessive reliance on Brazil in the novel forms a parallel with Portugal's increasingly desperate attempts to cling to power in Africa 200 years later.

In addition, the moral hypocrisy of a corrupt Church allied to a fanatical Inquisition and a government intent on imposing its will by decree rather than consent inevitably reminds one of the brutal methods and severe repression exercised by the notorious PIDE secret police under Portugal's twentieth-century dictatorship. Similarly, a parallel can be drawn between the dependence of the figure of D. João V on income from overseas in the novel and Portugal's economic reliance on its African colonies in the twentieth century.

From dictatorship to capitalist democracy. At the time the novel was written, some eight years after the Revolution, Portugal was seeking a new role for itself as a post-imperialist state. After a period in which it seemed likely that Portuguese society might be remodeled along explicitly socialist lines (banks were nationalized and many large agricultural estates were taken into collective ownership in the immediate aftermath of the Revolution), the country moved towards a more conventional Western European pattern of market capitalism combined with elements of social democracy. Property that had been appropriated after the Revolution was largely returned to private hands, and the country sought membership in the European Economic Community (now the European Union), a goal finally achieved in 1986. While this state of affairs, with its concomitant social liberties and Portugal's subsequent economic and social development, are indisputably preferable to the circumstances pertaining before the Revolution, for many commentators, including Saramago, the country missed an opportunity to create a new model of participatory democracy. Instead, Saramago

FLOWERS, MUSIC, AND REVOLUTION

The chest is no longer there, they have loaded it into the Passarola, what else do we need, the knapsacks, some food, and the harpsichord, what is to be done with the harpsichord, let it stay here, these are selfish thoughts, which one must try to comprehend and forgive, such is their anxiety that all three of them fail to reflect that if the harpsichord is left behind, the ecclesiastical and secular authorities are likely to become even more suspicious, why and for what purpose is a harpsichord in a coach-house, . . . an instrument so delicate that even being transported on the shoulders of porters was enough to put the keys out of tune. . . .

(*Baltasar and Blimunda*, p. 182)

This passage describes the hurried preparations made for flight in the *Passarola* by Baltasar, Blimunda, and Bartolomeu, after the priest announces that the Inquisition is in hot pursuit of him. The harpsichord was brought to the coach-house at São Sebastião da Pedreira, just outside Lisbon, by Scarlatti so that he may play for the would-be aviators as they construct their craft in secret. Shortly after this incident the composer himself disposes of the instrument down a well (*Baltasar and Blimunda*, p. 185).

The significance of the odd presence of this harpsichord lies in the clever verbal association that it permits Saramago to make, linking the *Passarola* with the 1974 Revolution of the Carnations (*cravos*) through Scarlatti's instrument (which is also known as a *cravo* in Portuguese). Repeatedly in the text the composer's music is said to have a liberating influence on others, just as the flying machine permits the three protagonists to escape from the clutches of the Inquisition at this moment. Even if Scarlatti feels obliged to conceal his harpsichord for the present, it remains underground, and significantly his music recurs again later in the text (*Baltasar and Blimunda,* p. 305). The point is thus made that institutions such as the Inquisition may postpone the achievement of liberation, but they cannot prevent it: the freedom of thought sought by Bartolomeu and denied him by the Inquisition and the freedom of action denied to ordinary people by poverty and oppressive government are ideals that must be lovingly cherished, just as Baltasar and Blimunda look after the *Passarola* even after Bartolomeu's death.

perceives the danger of a new authoritarianism in which the citizen willingly cedes his or her right to determine the circumstances surrounding individual life to a new power: that of corporate capitalism, as satirized in Saramago's most recent novel, *A Caverna* (2000, The Cave). One needs to keep in mind when reading *Baltasar and Blimunda* its author's belief that the conscientious citizen should be constantly aiming for an increase in personal empowerment, consistent with a responsible awareness of the needs of others. This is perhaps the real significance of the thwarted flight of the *Passarola* in the novel.

Reception. *Baltasar and Blimunda* was generally received with enthusiasm, both in Portugal and in English-speaking countries. There were some dissonant voices, but it is perhaps significant that in both linguistic environments, these were marked by misapprehensions as to the author's aims in writing the novel. Paul Stuewe, who describes the novel as "a mildly diverting curiosity rather than deeply compelling fiction" appears to have read the novel in the expectation of a work directly comparable to those of García Márquez (Stuewe, p. 30). He might also have taken a kinder view of the novel if the translation (as originally drafted by Giovanni Pontiero) had not been substantially altered at the insistence of the publishers, whose attempts to make the novel more palatable to an English-speaking audience removed the very element of multivocal discourse within the text that contributes so strongly to its appeal. The resulting text is a very bland read in comparison to the original Portuguese or to the 1998 English edition, which restored Pontiero's original version. On the other hand, even with the flawed 1987 translation, Irving Howe recognized the work as a "full-bodied novel," in which "harsh realism" is interwoven with pages of "lyric fantasy" (Howe, p. 7). Clare Ferros (who had clearly read the work in both languages) perceived that it was the novel's "very unorthodoxy" that made it difficult to categorize but also declared it to be "impressive in its scope, innovative in style, and powerful in its implications" (Ferros, p. 244).

In Portugal itself, Álvaro Pina effectively dismissed the novel as a failed attempt to embellish the Neorealist tradition with what he saw as gratuitous effects (Pina, pp. 83-84). But the vast majority of critics quickly recognized the important development in contemporary Portuguese prose-fiction represented by *Baltasar and Blimunda*, with various writers hailing the work as being genuinely innovative and inventive, qualities that would subsequently be confirmed by the author's later works.

—David Frier

This article was written during a period of research leave funded by the British Arts and Humanities Research Board, whose support for his work the writer gratefully acknowledges.

Birmingham, David. *A Concise History of Portugal.* Cambridge: Cambridge University Press, 1993.

Ferros, Clare. Review of *Baltasar and Blimunda,* by José Saramago. *Portuguese Studies* 4 (1988): 204-07.

Frier, David G. "Padre Bartolomeu Lourenço de Gusmão: Inspiration for *Memorial do Convento*?" (forthcoming). *Romance Quarterly* 49 (2002).

Howe, Irving, "Fueling the Passarola." *New York Times,* 1 November 1987, Sec. 7, 7.

Levenson, Jay A., ed. *The Age of the Baroque in Portugal.* New Haven: Yale University Press, and Washington D.C.: National Gallery of Art, 1993.

Livermore, H. V. *A New History of Portugal.* 2d ed. Cambridge: Cambridge University Press, 1976.

Marques, A. H. de Oliveira. *História de Portugal.* 3 vols. Vol. 2: *Do Renascimento às Revoluções Liberais.* 10th ed. Lisbon: Palas Editores, 1984.

Pina, Álvaro. Review of *Memorial do Convento. Colóquio: Letras* 76 (November 1983): 83-84.

Saramago, José. *Baltasar and Blimunda.* Trans. Giovanni Pontiero. London: The Harvill Press, 1998.

———. "The Chair." Trans. Giovanni Pontiero. Eds. Mike Gerrard and Thomas McCarthy. *Passport to Portugal.* Huntingdon: Passport and Serpent's Tail, 1994.

Stuewe, Paul. Review of *Baltasar and Blimunda* by José Saramago. *Quill and Quire* 53, no. 10 (October 1987): 30.

Taunay, Affonso de E. "Novidades do maior vulto sobre o Padre Voador." *Jornal do Commêrcio* (Rio de Janeiro), 25 April 1948, 2.

Beside the River Sar

by
Rosalía de Castro

Rosalía de Castro was born in 1837 in the northwestern region of Spain known as Galicia, where she lived much of her life. As the child of an unwed mother, she resided for most of her youth with various members of her extended family until she was finally reunited with her mother in 1852 in Santiago de Compostela, the city of her birth. One of her first collections of poetry, *To My Mother,* was written and published privately in response to her mother's death in 1862. Though her formal education—she studied French, drawing, music, and acting—was limited, Castro showed an aptitude for writing in her early years. After moving to Madrid at the age of 19, she published her first collection of poetry, *The Flower.* During her brief period of residence in Madrid, she also married the young Galician writer and critic Manuel Murguía, an admirer of her work who would later be instrumental in its publication and, perhaps more importantly, in its promotion after her death. The couple returned to Galicia to raise six children, the youngest of whom died in infancy. It was from her home in Galicia, amid considerable poverty and domestic hardship (most scholars agree the marriage was not a particularly happy one for either spouse) that Castro completed most of her writing, which includes five novels and five collections of poetry, as well as several shorter pieces. She wrote two of her poetry collections, *Galician Songs* (1863) and *New Leaves* (1880) in *Gallego,* the native language of the region, rather than in Castilian Spanish, as part of a general revival of the Galician cultural heritage that was taking place in the latter half of the nine-

THE LITERARY WORK

A collection of poems set primarily in the Galician countryside of northwestern Spain; published in Spanish (as *En las orillas del Sar*) in 1884, in English in 1937.

SYNOPSIS

In a series of intimate, lyrical poems, the author explores personal experiences, the regional landscape, and character and identity in the Galician countryside, as well as larger questions of religion, spirituality, and social injustice.

teenth century. In 1884, one year before the poet's death, she published *Beside the River Sar,* a loose collection of poems written over a considerable time span. Most of them untitled, the poems represent her intimate, lyrical reflections on themes ranging from the beauty and power of nature, to religion, justice, reality and illusion, and death. Though the content stems from personal reflections, the poems reflect shifting cultural attitudes, especially to religion and politics, as well as longstanding regional tensions in late-nineteenth-century Spain.

Events in History at the Time of the Poems

Revolution, republic and restoration. Rosalía de Castro's published writings cover a relatively short span of time, roughly three decades, but they correspond chronologically to several events of major importance in Spanish history. While Castro does not generally comment directly on political events and concerns in *Beside the River Sar*, it is important to consider the general political and cultural climate of Spain at the time of its publication, since the broad-ranging results of political and cultural reform of the era colored and shaped her experiences, perspective, and artistic vision.

The nineteenth century in Spain was the scene of ongoing tensions between conflicting political ideologies. While the nation was slow to adopt the democratic ideals that took root in other parts of Europe and in America in the late eighteenth century, by the early nineteenth century Spain began moving toward the idea of a constitutional monarchy, one that would grant governmental representation to the populace without completely dismantling the monarchical system. In Spain the movement toward a constitutional government began during the War of Independence against revolutionary France (1808-14), but such a system of government was not actually possible until 1833, when Ferdinand VII died and his young daughter, Isabella II, ascended to the throne. Even then, the constitutional monarchy was achieved at considerable cost. Upon Isabella's succession to the throne, the first of several civil wars known as the Carlist Wars (named for the arch-conservative, absolutist faction that initiated them) broke out in opposition to her legitimacy as her father's successor. Isabella brought to power a liberal government controlled by prominent generals in the Spanish Army. The government under their control proved relatively unstable: in Isabella's 45 years as queen, six different constitutions were drafted. Meanwhile, liberal reforms included a rather aggressive program of weakening the longstanding power of the Catholic Church in Spain, largely through the appropriation and redistribution of land and property owned by the Church.

Isabella's reign was brought to an end by the Glorious Revolution of 1868, led by various prominent military figures such as General Juan Prim. Isabella was exiled to France, and the rebels replaced her with Amadeo of Savoy, the son of the Italian king. After a brief rule, Amadeo abdicated, unable to control the political tensions and intrigues that still plagued the nation. His abdication set the stage for a short-lived experiment in secular, democratic government known as the First Republic (1873-74). Unstable from its in-

ception (in only 22 months there were four different presidents), and facing fierce opposition both from another Carlist War and from rising anarchist activity in the South, this government was ultimately brought down by the powerful military in an effort to restore order to the nation.

With the end of the First Republic in 1874, the Bourbon monarchy came back into power under Isabella II's son, Alfonso XII. The country returned to constitutional monarchy, albeit in a more moderate form than the one that existed under his mother's reign. While the new government did ostensibly restore a semblance of order to a divided society, it did not put a stop to the many underlying tensions that had intensified over the course of decades. Although Rosalía de Castro did not examine specific political events in her poetry, it is important to recognize that the political atmosphere within which she lived and wrote was one of both promise and disillusionment, of shifting ideologies, and of relative uncertainty. The instability of the central government invigorated alternative political movements and also intensified regional cultural identities, as reflected in many of the poems in *Beside the River Sar*.

Liberalism, secularization, and Krausism. In the wake of far-reaching political and cultural change, Spain as a nation saw a general shift in the nineteenth century toward a more liberal and secular society than had been the traditional norm. The liberal reforms of several decades created a plurality of political voices and ideologies in what became a reestablished social order. An important and influential element in the latter half of the nineteenth century was the introduction of the liberal philosophy of Krausism, imported into Spain by the influential Madrid scholar Julián Sanz del Río, who became acquainted with the doctrines of the German philosopher Karl Christian Friedrich Krause while studying in Germany on a government scholarship. The main thrust of Krausist doctrine, as interpreted by Sanz del Río, is that man is meant to be a harmonious compound of nature and spirit and thus should strive to achieve maximum harmony within himself and with the rest of humanity. The philosophy is often referred to as a form of "pantheistic idealism," stemming from its view that the world and all it contains exists *within*, rather than apart from, the "higher synthesis" known as God (Lipp, p. 25). Stressing moral perfection through a rational knowledge of God, Krausism can be considered "less a question of ideas than of an attitude toward life," from which "emerged a lay spiritualism with rigid principles and a faith in education which fired the men of the First Republic" (Vilar, p. 81). By the 1880s, the Krausists had initiated a program of educational reform far different from the traditional system controlled by the Catholic Church, encompassing "projects, excursions, co-education, a passion for nature study and a preference for biology and sociology" (Vilar, p. 82). The rational character of Krausism provided "a religious alternative to catholicism [sic]" (Hennessy, p. 79), suggesting that "faith that is blind and rejects reason can only lead to the degradation of the human spirit" (Lipp, p. 24). This philosophy was met with much resistance from conservative Catholics in Spain, who saw the new philosophical system as a threat to their traditional authority in Spanish society. Indeed, Krausism is representative of widespread anticlerical sentiment among late-nineteenth-century Spanish liberals. Another expression of this sentiment can be found, for example, in the writings of Benito Pérez Galdós. His novel *Doña Perfecta* (1876) alludes to the repressive and intolerant nature of the Catholic Church in the face of liberal reforms. Though the Church regained much of its authority during the Bourbon Restoration, these anticlerical trends were hard to reverse.

Krausism also advocated "political, social and intellectual freedoms"; its followers were opposed to "the intervention of the church in civic affairs" and "the excessive power of the state, to the extent that it threatened the autonomy of the individual" (Lipp, p. 24). Most importantly, the movement offered a sense of "open-mindedness . . . essential to Spain's political and cultural rejuvenation" and unseen prior to this era (Lipp, p. 42).

In general, the traditionally conservative and religious character of Spanish society began to shift toward a more progressive and secular one in the late nineteenth century:

> Catholic control over Spanish thought progressively lost strength over the course of the century. The abolition of the Inquisition, the disentailment of Church lands, the increasing—though still far from total—secularization of education, the growing calls for religious tolerance and separation of church and state, the intellectual prestige of the liberal Krausist movement as well as the religious indifference of the urban working class reflect a breakdown of religious unity.
>
> (Bretz, pp. 3-4)

In the face of these significant sociocultural changes it is not surprising that many of Castro's poems in *Beside the River Sar* exhibit a sense of disillusionment with systems of "justice," both human and divine, secular and spiritual. Such is the case in the following brief poem from *Beside the River Sar*:

> Human justice! I search for you
>   only to find
> that you are a glorious "promise"
> which is always denied by "deeds."
> In anguish, I ask myself
> if divine justice even exists
> since sin takes but a moment
>   and horrid penance
>   lasts as long as Hell.
>   (Castro, *Poems*, p. 183)

Continuation of regional diversity and tensions. Conflicting tendencies of centralization and regional autonomy have been part of the Spanish cultural scene since the unification process was begun by the "Catholic Kings," Ferdinand and Isabella, who married in 1469. It was a point of conflict under the Enlightened Despotism of the Bourbon monarchs of the eighteenth century as well, a system that required further centralization of authority for the sake of instituting social reforms and creating a better quality of life for the general populace. The regions of Cataluña, the Basque Country, and Rosalía de Castro's native Galicia, with strong regional identities and their own languages, have repeatedly asserted their claims to autonomy over the course of Spanish history. This tendency was felt strongly in the era in which Castro did her writing. As one literary historian asserts, "In a period of increased political awareness in many areas of society in the late eighteenth and early nineteenth centuries in Spain, the concern for the rights of previously unrepresented groups became an important part of the new political climate" (Stevens, p. 28). While Galician regionalism had a stronger political component in the first half of the century (in 1846 there was even an armed uprising against government troops stationed there), by the latter half, it had become a more cultural and literary phenomenon. As noted earlier, two of Rosalía de Castro's major collections of poetry were written in her native Galician language rather than Spanish. *Beside the River Sar*, though written in Spanish, still contains an inherently strong regional flavor and connection to the landscapes and customs of Galicia. Castro's first English translator, S. Griswold Morley, suggests that "more than Spanish she was Galician," and that the Celtic influence of Galician culture left its descendants with "a passive, melancholy outlook on existence, greatly at variance with the

robust Castilian spirit" (Morley in Castro, *Beside the River Sar,* p. ix). The poet's tone in *Beside the River Sar* often evokes her close connection to her homeland, as evidenced in these lines from the title poem of the collection:

> Dear native land, as fertile and as fair
>   Now as it was of yore!
> When I behold how sadly gleams our fatal
>   star
>   As by the river Sar
> My end draws near, I feel devouring thirst,
> Unquenchable, soul-stifling, and the accursed
> Vain hunger after righteousness that breaks
>   the mind
> When our weak cries for help are lost upon
> An angry tempest wind.
>
>   (*Sar,* p. 13)

A LAND OF CELTIC TRADITIONS

Galicia is a rather unique region of Spain. Situated on the northwestern Atlantic coast of the Iberian Peninsula, its landscape is lush and green, and its rolling hills and valleys present a sharp contrast to the country's central plateau. In its early history, before the birth of Christ, Galicia, unlike other regions of Spain, was inhabited by Celts, and to this day one can visit remnants of ancient Celtic villages along its coastline and hear traces of this heritage in the folk music, which, to name one such trace, relies heavily on the bagpipe (*la gaita*).

Post-Romanticism. Rosalía de Castro is generally considered to be a post-Romantic poet. This is a label that is applied in order to distinguish her from an earlier generation of Spanish Romantic poets, best represented by José de Espronceda (1810-42), who tended to write in a more exalted, passionate tone and created memorable, highly subversive characters (in the vein of British poet Lord Byron). Examples are Espronceda's unyielding, self-indulgent pirate and the arrogant, womanizing "student" of Salamanca, their purpose being to explore the often dark and libertine character of the Romantic vision, which stressed the liberty of the individual over the demands of social order, and encouraged the uninhibited exploration of the diversity of human emotions and the internal reality of the individual. Poets like Castro began to write in a more lyrical and understated tone, though she continued to emphasize the individual self and to feature the full range of her intimate and of-

ten unusual emotional experiences. "Simple they are and brief" she says of her poems, but such simplicity can be deceptive (Castro, p. 3). Two of Castro's contemporary translators suggest that her poetic style consists of a "personal, intimate, and suggestive lyricism which is imbued with melancholy and yearning" while her first translator credits her with "utiliz[ing] rare lines and combinations of lines" and "divest[ing] herself of the traditional Hispanic magniloquence" (Aldaz and Gantt in Castro, *Poems,* p. 6; Morley in *Sar,* p. ix). In other words, Castro was divesting herself of a prevailing emphasis on pre-established, often erudite poetic forms and structures and a preference for the grandiose over the mundane that characterize much of Spain's poetic tradition. Through her rhythmic experimentation and intimate, understated use of the language, Castro forged an innovative style within the Spanish poetic tradition.

The Poems in Focus

Contents overview. The poems in *Beside the River Sar,* written over the course of Rosalía's career and published collectively in 1884, are thematically diverse. The collection contains "long poems and short," many of which are untitled, as though, as the critic Jacinto Octavio Picón suggested, "the author wished to conceal the causes that inspired them" (Picón in *Sar,* p. XIII). In general, the various poems share the common context of the poet's intimate experiences as they are played out against the background of the Galician landscape and the ever-present symbols of nature: the sun and moon, forests, hills, and rivers. The title poem is placed early in the collection, setting the tone for many of the themes that the various poetic speakers will explore throughout the texts: the love of one's native land, nostalgia for lost youth, a sense of disillusionment and suffering, and the consciousness of mortality. The first and last poems of the collection seem to have been strategically placed in the published version, though not necessarily by Castro herself. S. Griswold Morley suggests that the opening poem "with its moving reminiscences of the old days and the old spirit, was done as a prologue to the volume" (Morley in *Sar,* p. xiv). The final short text, which begins with the lines "Nothing but doubt and terror are my fate, / O Divine Christ, when I depart from thee; / But when upon the cross I meditate, / I am resigned to bear my Calvary" (*Sar,* p. 141), seems to suggest the resignation of a woman suf-

Valley of the Sar

fering the final stages of terminal illness and coming to terms with her mortality. But the placement of this final text was likely determined by Castro's husband, Luis Murguía, so that it does not necessarily reflect an evolution in the poet's vision over the course of the poems.

Contents summary—nature poems. The representation of nature and the thoughtful analysis of the poet's changing relationship with nature are recurring motifs in the poems of *Beside the River Sar*. Indeed, the title of the collection itself suggests the important role that elements of nature will play in many of the poems. In the most positive cases, nature is a source of comfort, idealized and celebrated, which creates a feeling of community and completion within the poet who observes its power. In the poem beginning with the lines "Along the highway's ancient line / Is here a pine-grove and there a spring," we encounter this idealized vision. It describes a nature in which all things seem to be connected and in perfect balance. From amid the pine-grove gushes a spring, which then divides

---

POET OF TWO LANGUAGES

While Rosalía de Castro's novels were written in Spanish, *Beside the River Sar* is her only major collection of poetry written in Spain's official national language. (Two other minor collections, *The Flower* and *To My Mother*, were also written in Spanish.) Her other poetry collections were written in Gallego, the regional language of Galicia, which draws on the forms and rhythms of its oral traditions.

Galicia's language, which resembles Portuguese, has an illustrious history dating back to the Middle Ages. Medieval lyrics, among them those of Alfonso el Sabio, were written in Galician-Portuguese, probably the earliest literary language of the Iberian Peninsula. By the fifteenth century, however, Castilian had become the dominant literary language of Spain, and Galician was relegated to everyday usage, surviving in purely oral form.

(Aldaz and Gantt in Castro, *Poems*, pp. 2-3)

At the time of their publication, Rosalía's Galician collections were the first full-length texts in Galician to be printed in several centuries.

"into limpid brooks / That feed the forest's flowery nooks" (*Sar*, p. 43). These brooks meet in the River Sar, "the stream / Which, like a child in a placid dream, / Reflects the azure of the skies / Before it hides in ferneries" (*Sar*, p. 45). The scene then shifts to a nearby "deep wood of oak" where "silence spreads her all-embracing wings" over the "country dwelling and the humble home" (*Sar*, p. 45). The poem, reflecting upon these varied elements, concludes with a meditation on the beauty and power of nature and its effect upon the human spirit: "There always, when my spirits I evoke, / Or call them, they answer me and come" (*Sar*, p. 45).

This vision of nature as a balanced system of which the human being feels an integral part evokes precisely the type of pantheism advocated by the Krausists in Spain and similarly embraced by the American Transcendentalist poets like Ralph Waldo Emerson and Henry David Thoreau, in which spirituality and the presence of God is felt in all aspects of creation, and most notably in the system of nature. This creates the desire on the part of the individual to feel the sense of connection and communion with the natural world. In another of Castro's poems, which begins "Towering up, / Tall, taller yet," she expresses this desire in the most literal terms:

The traveler, short of breath and weary,
Who sees the steep pitch of the pathway
That still remains for him to conquer,
    Checks at the hill
And wishes he might be translated
    Into a bird or brook,
    Into a tree or rock.

(*Sar*, p. 17)

In Castro's poetry, nature also reflects her intimate connection to her native Galicia. In this sense it serves both an abstract and a rather concrete political function; the exploration of the Galician landscape is a way of reaffirming her loyalty and pride in the region of her birth. The somewhat lengthy title poem to the collection places the poet firmly within the context of the region, with specific references to the landscape and various places found there (La Torre, La Presa, and Trabanca, for example), which she evokes with a sometimes passionate tone: "O my Padrón! / My Iria Flavia!" (*Sar*, p. 11).

In spite of Castro's strong connection to the land and its affirmative effect upon her sense of regional identity, this relationship also becomes a source of nostalgia and melancholy for the poet. As she continues her evocation of Padrón and Iria Flavia, two villages in the province of La Coruña, where she lived much of her life, she sees amidst their beauty that "the warm flow of life has gone, / The sap of youth that once I drew / Out of your lavish bosom" (*Sar*, p. 11). The landscape, intimately connected to the course of the poet's own life, becomes a reminder of the passage of time and her impending mortality. Similarly, as she hears the "distant mill-sluice roar" and envisions the pool that lies close to it, she now sees that pool "where once I thought to drink / The healthful nectar of my hope" as "Lethe's water," a reference to the mythological river of forgetfulness leading to Hades (*Sar*, p. 11). Thus, nature plays a dual role in the text, both reaffirming the poet's regional identity and reminding her of the themes of nostalgia and mortality that will run through many of the poems in the collection.

In another poem, titled "To the Moon," Castro again combines abstract nature with the real social and economic context of her native land, contrasting the indifference of the moon as it passes over the land with the passionate hopes of those who watch it from below and "[s]olicit [its] clean light, to give / Redemption from their ills" (*Sar*, p. 113). As she addresses the moon, she uses the poem to comment on both the beauty and the misfortunes of Galicia:

> You go your way to light a happier land
>   Than our enchanted soil,
> Though none more fair exists on any hand
>   Or of more fecund toil.
>
> No other land like mine did God create
>   For freshness and for flower;
> Only he gave her, too, a saddened fate,
>   Beauty's eternal dower.
>
> (*Sar*, p. 117)

For the poet, the moon's indifference to her people's suffering is made more unsettling by the fact that the Galicians' Celtic ancestors once worshiped it. Still, the poem ends on a hopeful note, praying that eventually, upon its return to the land, the moon might "find here not weeping, as before, / But plenty everywhere; / And may the absent have returned once more / To crowd the village green and city square" (*Sar*, p. 117).

Contents summary—poems on science and religion. In various poems in *Beside the River Sar*, Castro displays a sense of distrust and disillusionment with two of humanity's great institutions and sources of knowledge: science and religion. This is in many ways a stance influenced by the Romanticism that characterized much of the first half of the nineteenth century, a movement that rejected the rational, scientific mentality of eighteenth-century Neoclassicism in favor of a more subjective, innovative and spontaneous approach to art. The Romantics consciously explored the irrational and intangible aspects of human existence, rejecting science and logic in favor of emotion, sensuality and alternative forms of spirituality. In the case of organized religion, Castro generally displays a conflicted rather than outright critical stance. While she does not fully reject her faith or the existence of God, her poetry clearly questions the bases of traditional Catholicism and looks for spirituality through alternative means. (Other Romantic

voices, as in José de Espronceda's "Song of the Pirate," worship no God; committing himself instead to his own complete freedom, Espronceda's voice firmly rejects traditional religious institutions and practices.) One should bear in mind here, however, that the societal constraints placed upon a woman writer of Castro's era most likely influenced her more cautious approach to controversial subject matter. What writers like Espronceda addressed more directly, Castro addressed by means of silences and subtexts within her poetry. Her personal exploration of religious themes, both complex and somewhat inconsistent, is also indicative of a more generalized weakening of traditional Catholicism in the face of liberal reforms and modernization in late-nineteenth-century Spain. Like the Krausists, she does not necessarily reject religion or a belief in God, but she clearly looks for alternative modes of understanding this phenomenon rather than accepting traditional dogmatic approaches.

In the poem that begins "A glowworm scatters flashes through the moss," Castro expresses doubt and disillusionment with both science and religion. The poem challenges science's power to supply effective answers to the questions of human existence: "Man's thought—we call it science!—peers and pries / Into the soundless dark. But it is vain: / When all is done, we still are ignorant / Of what things reach an end, and what remain" (*Sar*, p. 21).

The poet's stance on religion and traditional spirituality is even more strongly critical, and more complex. As the poem's speaker kneels in a church "before an image rudely carved," she ponders the great question of existence: "What are we? What is death?" (*Sar*, pp. 21, 22, 23). When in response she hears only the sound of a tolling bell, she becomes saddened and desperate, and appeals to God for an answer: "What horrible agony! Thou, only Thou, / O God, canst see and understand me now" (*Sar*, p. 23). She begs him to restore the faith that she has lost, which she refers to here (as well as in other poems) as a "blessed blindfold," which shields her from the alternative vision of eternity as a "plain of endless void" (*Sar*, p. 23).

Still, as the poem progresses, the speaker receives no satisfactory response. The bell continues to toll, and the lips to which she appeals, presumably on a statue of Christ, remain mute: "He lets my humbled heart remain engulfed / In darkness, —He, the Redeemer, the divine" (*Sar*, p. 23). Meanwhile, the architectural elements of the church, the "somber arch of stone" and the "vacant nave" provide no further comfort (*Sar*, p. 23). Thus she is led to conclude that

> The world is empty, Heaven untenanted,
> My soul is sick, and trodden in the dust
> The holy altar where I used to breathe
> My simple vows of ecstasy and trust.
> My Deity, shattered in a thousand bits,
> Has fallen to chasms where I cannot see.
> I rush to seek Him, and my groping meets
> A solitary vast vacuity.
>
> (*Sar*, pp. 23-25)

Yet, in spite of the intensity of criticism and disillusionment in the previous stanzas, the poem's final stanza suggests some sense of resolution and comfort. For the first time, an element of the speaker's surroundings, in this case the marble angel statues that "gazed down in sorrow," offer her some comfort and hope, as well as a piece of advice: "But well remember this: No insolent cry / To Heaven makes its way / From one whose heart adores material things / Who makes an idol out of Adam's clay" (*Sar*, p. 25). In other words, traditionally prescribed forms of spirituality and worship, specifically those based on a seemingly empty sense of materialism common to the bourgeois mentality of the late nineteenth century, do not bring satisfaction or existential security. Faith and spirituality are to be found somewhere outside the rules and practices of traditional religion, a point that reflects the weakening of the Catholic Church's authority in late-nineteenth-century Spain. The speaker's faith seems at least temporarily restored, however, by the notion that faith and spirituality can indeed be found, though one must look beyond organized religion.

In the longer poem titled "Saint Scholastica," Castro recounts a similar situation of desolation and doubt as she visits the Cathedral of Santiago de Compostela on a rainy and melancholy April afternoon. By the third of the poem's four sections, the poem's speaker has left the site of the Cathedral, which she earlier envisioned "tumbling down, / Towers and all, in ruins on my head" (*Sar*, p. 93), full of despair and uncertainty, concluding that

> There is no after-life! Heaven is so lofty
> And we so low, that earth which gave us forth
> Will draw us surely back into her sod.
> Why strive and struggle, when man is an ungrateful
> Beast of the field, and victory is void?
> For Hell will triumph, though there be a God.
>
> (*Sar*, p. 95)

Again, as in the earlier poem, there is a moment of resolution following the moment of despair. Here, the speaker moves from the site of the Cathedral to a small, empty church nearby; her "woman's soul responds / And thrills to it as to the joy of motherhood" (*Sar*, p. 97). In the quiet atmosphere, in the glow of a seemingly miraculous light, she notes the statues of an angel and a saint, "[r]inged with a mellow nimbus by the westering sun" (*Sar*, p. 99). The speaker's outlook changes drastically:

> Once more I felt the fire that flashes and creates
> Unrevealed yearnings, passionate nameless loves that strike
> Out of the soul, as from an aeolian harp the wind
> Its most sonorous notes, its sweetest melodies.
> I fell upon my knees, I prayed and blessed the One
> Who is all Beauty; and as I turned my trembling head
> Before Him, my soul burst forth in an exalted cry:
> "Poetry and art exist; then Heaven exists, and God!"
>
> (*Sar*, pp. 99-101)

Here the poet suggests once again that traditional modes of connecting with the divine are insufficient; she finds faith and comfort in human, earthly forms of art that ultimately testify to the greatness of God.

In other instances, as in the poem beginning with the lines "Thirsting, upon the beach the sand receives / The white-hot kisses of the noonday sun," Castro explores a more earthly alternative to traditional Christian spirituality that seems to be influenced by the type of pantheism advocated by the Krausist movement that gained popularity in nineteenth-century Spain. The speaker of this poem identifies with the sand on the beach and its relationship to the sea, seeing them as both suffering the "endless punishment of Tantalus," that is, yearning for something that is just barely out of reach (*Sar*, p. 33). Just as she hopes that one day the sea will "[t]ransgress the line of its mysterious bound" to quench the sand's "inextinguishable thirst," the speaker hopes too that "after all these years / Of breathless striving toward a hopeless goal, / My soul may cool its ardent thirst at last / Where seraphs drink of the eternal soul" (*Sar*, p. 33). The poem evokes a universal order in which human beings and elements of nature are subsumed within the essence of a higher power, and suggests that human beings can attain greater knowledge of that higher power through contemplation and understanding of nature. Furthermore, its conclusion represents an unusual combination of both natural and supernatural, religious imagery that suggests once again that the poet looks outside the boundaries of traditional Catholic spirituality for the promise of comfort and existential security, even if she doesn't find it immediately or easily.

Contents summary—poems contemplating rural poverty and emigration. A number of poems in *Beside the River Sar* evince sadness, nostalgia, and suffering felt by the poetic speaker and brought about by the widespread absence of loved ones who have been forced by extreme poverty to seek a better life in a foreign land, usually in the Americas. This emigration in considerable numbers was a significant reality for the region of Galicia throughout the nineteenth and into the early twentieth century. The poems characterize the trend as a rather devastating loss for the region, a source of sadness and, to a certain degree, shame and betrayal.

In "Return!," the speaker comments on the injustice of the poverty that forces unfortunate citizens, in Castro's poetry generally represented by men, to leave their native land in search of better economic circumstances, but also insists on the importance of their returning to their roots as soon it becomes possible: "Always tears come into my eyes, God knows, / For men who quit their native land to earn; / But deeper pity fills my heart for those / Who care not to return" (*Sar*, p. 59). The speaker recognizes that extreme conditions may leave one "[f]or whom your harried country has no place" with no other choice but to emigrate, but also reminds the émigrè that a "poor stark body never rests so sound / In foreign soil as in its native ground" (*Sar*, p. 59).

In two poems in the collection, the unfortunate effects of mass emigration are conveyed specifically through the perspective of the female, as both mother and wife. One of these begins with the lines "In their prison of hawthorn and roses / My children, poor darlings, are singing at play"; the speaker writes of her children's desire to escape the poverty and misfortune of their lives: "'All are leaving!' they cry, 'and we only, we only, / Must stay here forever in these ugly places! / Why must we stay, mother? Why don't you carry us / Where we may see other skies, other faces?'" (*Sar*, p. 49). She understands the children's desire, sympathizes with their suffering, but ultimately concludes (as in other instances)

that escape through emigration is not the best solution, that it is a false hope. In the pessimistic view of the speaker, poverty and injustice will follow her children, as it will all émigrés, throughout their lives. She ponders silently: "What spot / Is there on earth, poor captives, where my hand / Could lead you, and the same chains bind you not?" (*Sar*, p. 49). Ultimately, she concludes that oppression and exploitation

---

A DEBILITATING RESPONSE TO POVERTY

Castro's poems are of particular interest as a type of historical document evoking a very real experience at the time *Beside the River Sar* was published. While they reflect the Romantic preference for lyricism and the subjective expression of feelings and experiences, they bring these artistic tendencies to bear upon a situation of social import for the poet and her fellow Galicians. As a traditionally rural and relatively poor region of Spain, Galicia lost many of its residents to emigration in the latter half of the nineteenth century as the nation made a slow transition toward a more industrial economy. A study published in 1909 laments the emigration, "that terrible wound that is exhausting Galicia." Highlighted in the study are a tradition of economic stagnation, misuse of resources, lack of effective agriculture techniques, overpopulation, unequal distribution of wealth, and a system of excessive taxation, all of which resulted in mass emigration not only to other parts of Spain and to Portugal, but also to the Americas. Ricardo Mella, a political activist and anarchist of the late nineteenth century cited statistics in 1885 (only a year after *Beside the River Sar* was published) "to the effect that twenty thousand Gallegans emigrated annually to South America" (Meakin, p. 172). This situation was a harsh economic and political reality for the entire region. Despite its strong sense of regional identity, Galicia in the latter half of the nineteenth century was a population facing economic hardship and a loss of morale, realities that find their way into many of the poems in *Beside the River Sar*.

---

of the poor at the hands of the privileged is an inescapable aspect of the human condition: "My mother-love, dear children, cannot shield / Your hearts from man, the enemy of man" (*Sar*, p. 49). In another poem that begins with the lines "It was the final night, / The night of sad farewells," the poet tells the tale of a wife who watches as her husband leaves her and their children behind, "[a]s a servant leaves a hard taskmaster . . . [w]ith an emotion close akin to joy," to seek better opportunities in a foreign land (*Sar*, p. 55). The husband leaves with a great sense of optimism: "In our new fatherland we shall not lack / . . . . The coarse bread which our fatherland denied" (*Sar*, p. 55). The children "smile, well-pleased," and the wife "[h]olds the unshaken hope / That he will soon return / To take her with him, and she is consoled" (*Sar*, p. 55). But in the poem's second part, Castro again suggests the bitter effects of the mass emigration of those who leave their homeland without regard for those left behind: "As by slow sickness, today a hundred souls / Tomorrow a hundred more, sail outward-bound, / Till count is lost" (*Sar*, p. 55). Ultimately, using the metaphorical image of doves that flee in fear of the fox or the hawk, the poet once again suggests that leaving the homeland is not the solution, but will only lead to further unhappiness: "For when they rest their wings from the long flight / They find upon that distant, hard-won plain / The ripe fruit parched, and overhead they spy / An eagle wheeling slowly in the sky" (*Sar*, p. 56). The overall sadness felt in the face of mass emigration leads in some instances to a sense of ambivalence, detachment, or even bitterness on the part of the female who has been left behind.

Sources and literary context. Given the personal and intimate nature of the poems in *Beside the River Sar*, it is fair to say that much of the collection was inspired by events and experiences in the author's life. Many of these experiences were of an unfortunate nature. Certainly the repeated motifs of illness and poverty found throughout the collection are references to her life with Murguía and their six children. Castro herself suffered from poor physical health for a long time, and died prematurely of cancer at the age of 48. Her ill health inspired poems like the one beginning with the lines "The ailing woman felt her forces ebb / With summer, and knew her time was imminent" (*Sar*, p. 127). The death of her youngest son, an infant, prompted her to write the poem beginning with the lines "Mild was the air / And still the day," which recounts a mother's pain as she watches her child pass away: "He left this world, and peace was in his heart; / I watched his going, and mine was torn apart" (*Sar*, p. 19). Her poem in praise of nature that begins "Tall, taller still" was also composed in response to her son's death.

Morley suggests that the "prison of hawthorn and roses" to which Castro refers in the poem describing her children's dream of escaping their condition of poverty, refers to the family's last home in la Matanza (*Sar*, p. 149). Alberto Machado da Rosa further suggests that the "lost love" Castro evokes in poems like the one beginning with the words "I wish, dear heart, sweet mistress of my will," was a fellow Galician poet, Aurelio Aguirre, who drowned tragically at the age of 24. While this may be the case, it is not an opinion shared by all scholars of her poetry.

Rosalía read and was influenced by such Romantic writers as Heinrich Heine, Edgar Allen Poe, Byron and E. T. A. Hoffman, and she is often likened to her Peninsular contemporary the poet Gustavo Adolfo Bécquer (see **The Infinite Passion,** also in *WLAIT 5: Spanish and Portuguese Literatures and Their Times*). In spite of these connections and influences, Rosalía de Castro is generally viewed as an innovator, a great precursor to Modernist poets like Nicaragua's Rubén Darío. Shelley Stevens suggests that "[a]lthough she was clearly attracted to the introspective mode most dramatically represented by Byron, her strength as a poet, as she herself realized, lay with the popular poetic forms (Stevens, p. 35). Her simple, almost conversational language and the incorporation of the style and rhythms of popular Galician poetry made Castro an influential figure in Peninsular letters, even if this was not recognized until after she died. In an essay written after her death, Murguía cites another, unnamed young writer who praised Castro for her poetic innovation, referring to her as "a young writer of our times" who became the precursor of a "movement she began simply and instinctively, without any intention of starting a school, simply because, as a great musician, she was allowed to break with the old forms and to enlarge the domain of Spanish metrics" (Murguía in Castro, *Poems*, p. 7). The stylistic simplicity highlighted by these critics of Castro's work, however, does not negate her importance as an innovator or the unorthodox nature of her writing. Though based on traditional forms, Castro's poetry challenges stylistic patterns as well as ideological concerns of the late nineteenth century.

Reception. It is somewhat of a challenge to discuss the immediate critical reception of *Beside the River Sar*, largely because the collection, like its author, was initially marginalized from the mainstream of literary culture in Spain in the late nineteenth century. There is a general consensus among scholars of Spanish literature that Castro's reputation grew slowly, and that while she was an almost immediate success in her native region of Galicia, and particularly when she began publishing poetry in Galician, she was generally either ignored or harshly criticized by the literary establishment of the time, which had its center in Madrid. Emilia Pardo Bazán, an influential novelist of the period who was also a native of Galicia (see *House of Ulloa,* also in *WLAIT 5: Spanish and Portuguese Literatures and Their Times*), was particularly critical of Castro, referring to her poetry as "sickly complaints" (Pardo Bazán in Stevens, p. 34).

Shelley Stevens argues that the first wave of criticism regarding Castro's work, shortly after her death, was primarily headed by her husband and other members of the Royal Galician Academy. These writers, she suggests, paint her as the "embodiment of the Galician soul and as a symbol of virtue and saintliness. They mention pain and suffering only in the context of a selfless martyrdom" (Stevens, p. 23).

In an essay titled "Rosalía de Castro," the Spanish writer Azorín "complains about the exclusion of her poetry from anthologies and the unmerited critical neglect of her work" (Aldaz and Gantt in *Poems,* p. 7). It was primarily due to the attention paid to her by Spanish writers of subsequent decades, such as Azorín, Unamuno, and Antonio Machado, that Rosalía de Castro would become firmly established in the canon of Spanish Peninsular literature. More recently, a number of scholars such as Shelley Stevens, Susan Kirkpatrick, and Catherine Davies have examined Castro's poetry in light of contemporary feminist theory in an attempt to revise the image created by earlier critics, mostly male, of the poet as a modest and abnegated female writer. These studies generally see Castro as a strong figure working within but ultimately transcending the societal constraints placed upon women writers of her time.
—James Wojtaszek

For More Information

Bretz, Mary Lee. *Voices, Silences and Echoes: A Theory of the Essay and the Critical Reception of Naturalism in Spain.* London: Tamesis, 1992.

Castro, Rosalía de. *Beside the River Sar.* Trans. S. Griswold Morley. Berkeley: University of California Press, 1937.

———. *Poems.* Ed. and trans. Anna-Marie Aldaz, Barbara N. Gantt, and Anne C. Bromley. Albany: State University of New York Press, 1991.

Dever, Aileen. *The Radical Insufficiency of Human Life: The Poetry of R. de Castro and J. A. Silva.* London: McFarland, 2000.

Hennessy, C. A. M. *The Federal Republic in Spain.* Oxford: Clarendon, 1962.

Kirkpatrick, Susan. *Las Románticas: Women Writers and Subjectivity in Spain, 1835-1850.* Berkeley: University of California Press, 1989.

Kulp-Hill, Kathleen. *Rosalía de Castro.* Boston: Twayne, 1977.

Lipp, Solomon. *Francisco Giner de los Ríos: A Spanish Socrates.* Waterloo, Ontario, Canada: Wilfred Laurier University Press, 1985.

Meakin, Annette M. B. *Galicia: The Switzerland of Spain.* London: Methuen, 1909.

Smith, Angel. *Historical Dictionary of Spain.* Lanham, Md.: Scarecrow Press, 1996.

Stevens, Shelley. *Rosalía de Castro and the Galician Revival.* London: Tamesis, 1986.

Vilar, Pierre. *Spain: A Brief History.* Trans. by Brian Tate. Oxford: Pergamon, 1967.

Bohemian Lights

by
Ramón María del Valle-Inclán

Spanish writer Ramón María del Valle-Inclán was born in Villanueva de Arosa, in the northeastern region of Galicia in 1868, the same year that a liberal military rebellion overthrew Queen Isabel II. In 1892, before finishing his studies in law, Valle-Inclán moved to Mexico. When he returned to Spain a year later, he lived a bohemian life in Madrid. He resided in old guest houses and practically never left the cafés, going out at night and sleeping during the day. His behavior at the time showed contempt for the rational world of the bourgeoisie. He changed his appearance substantially, letting his beard and hair grow. He wore large tortoise-shell-rimmed glasses and very loose clothing, like a frock coat. People would stare and sometimes make fun of him. Occasionally he lost his temper, but never his arrogant attitude. With his high-pitched voice and a lisp, he monopolized attention, making up stories about himself or others and reacting violently to interruptions. Yet he impressed those who knew him well as a kind, shy man. A dispute with a journalist in 1899 led to his left wrist being injured; gangrene set in, and his arm had to be amputated. He had by this time already published stories in magazines and his first book–*Femeninas* (*Seis historias amorosas*) (1895; Of Women: Six Amorous Stories). In 1902 Valle-Inclán published *Autumn Sonata,* the first of a series of four novels relating the memories of the Marquis of Bradomín, a qualified type of Don Juan character, who unlike Don Juan is ugly, sentimental, and religious. Subsequent years saw the publication of *Sonata de estío* (1903;

THE LITERARY WORK

A play set in post-World War I Madrid; published in 1920 in the literary magazine *España*; in Spanish (as *Luces de bohemia*) in 1924; in English in 1969.

SYNOPSIS

Max Estrella, a poor, blind, has-been poet, wanders through Madrid on the last night of his life. In the process, he encounters injustice, affront, and misery, his story becoming a grotesque parable of the impossibility of living in a deformed, oppressive, and absurd Spain.

Summer Sonata), *Sonata de primavera* (1904; Spring Sonata) and *Sonata de invierno,* (1905, Winter Sonata). The series exalts a decadent world tinged with an aura of legend and mystery, replete with adventure and courtships. The fiction joins disparate elements like religion and sex in prose that relates incidents with exquisite elegance and daring immorality. In World War I he worked as a correspondent on the French front. After the war, Valle-Inclán returned to Spain, which in 1919 experienced tremendous civil unrest in Barcelona and the imposition of martial law in Madrid. Both of these events profoundly changed his view of the world and his literary style. The following year Valle-Inclán produced *Bohemian Lights,* his first *Esperpento* (the term means "scarecrow," or, in fiction, a grotesque deformation of reality).

Ramón María del Valle-Inclán (portrait by Spanish painter Juan de Echevarría that appeared on the cover of *Estampa,* January 11, 1936).

Events in History at the Time of the Play

The Restoration of the monarchy and the "Turno Pacífico." Perhaps more than any other of Valle-Inclán's works, *Bohemian Lights* sets out to reconcile the grotesque in literature with the pathetic in historic reality. The last years of the reign of Isabel II (1833-68) were plagued by the inefficiency of the government, except when General Leopold O'Donnell and General Ramón María Narváez were in charge. Even they were unable to stop the advances of progressive liberalism against the queen. When the two generals died, other army officers rebelled. In 1868 General Juan Prim overthrew the government and forced the queen and Prince Alfonso to leave Spain. The ensuing period was characterized by intense revolutionary activity and by intransigence in both the liberal and conservative political parties.

The "glorious revolution" not only deposed Isabel; it also produced the most progressive constitution ever in the history of Spain, granting power exclusively to the parliament and recognizing freedom of religion as well as the legitimacy of civil marriage. From 1868 to 1870 General Franciso Serrano served as head of the provisional government; General Juan Prim became prime minister in 1869, after the constitution had been generated. Prim had the difficult

decision of choosing a new king once Serrano's term ended. He convinced parliament to accept Amadeo of Savoy, son of the king of Italy. Most political parties were opposed to his decision. The supporters of Prince Alfonso, the Carlists, favored the brother of King Fernando VII, Carlos, and the Republicans were against any kind of monarchy. So fierce was the opposition that it became impossible for Prim to govern. The radicals committed murders and other excesses daily. The Carlists, offended by the change in government, began a new war. In 1873, after only three years, Amadeo renounced his rights to the throne.

After the royal family left, parliament convened in a national assembly and by a large majority proclaimed the First Spanish Republic. The main difficulty lay in the diverse conceptions of nationhood held by the different liberal parties. Citizens argued about the implementation of a federalist or centralized republic. How much power would be left to the provinces, and how much would rest in the capitol? The federalism of Francisco Pi y Margall, first president of the republic, degenerated into extreme localism. Cities like Granada, Málaga, and Valencia declared their independence from Madrid. The third Republican president in four months, Nicolás Salmerón, suppressed federalism because it was damaging national unity. He furthermore demanded dictatorial powers to control the workers' and Carlists' uprisings. In September 1873, Salmerón was replaced by Emilio Castelar; a moderate who governed without regard for parliament, he was accused of distancing himself from republicanism. Castelar's opponents forced him to resign, and General Manuel Pavía dissolved the National Assembly by force. Once again General Serrano assumed control; he became provisional prime minister. Serrano had at this point to contend with armed conflicts, which soured the people on the whole idea of the Republic. The population leaned toward the political party of Prince Alfonso, headed by Antonio Cánovas del Castillo, who favored the restoration of the monarchy.

In 1874, impatient with the electoral process and lacking confidence in the government, General Arsenio Martínez Campos raised an army in Sagunto and proclaimed the restoration of the monarchy in the name of King Alfonso XII. Alfonso's reign proved highly unstable. He ended the Third Carlist War and introduced the Constitution of 1876, which recognized Catholicism as Spain's official religion but showed religious tolerance. Legal authority was vested in the par-

In a mass demonstration in Barcelona, workers hold a banner with the words *Solidaridad Obrera,* meaning "workers' solidarity."

liament and the king. The military stopped their coup d'états, or *pronunciamientos.* Of paramount importance to the new system was the idea of *turno pacífico*—the periodic rotation of power between the two accepted political parties, the conservatives and the liberals. The government was headed first by the conservative Cánovas. He spent his "turn" working on the creation of an opposition party, led by Práxedes Mateo Sagasta, who governed for two years. *The turno pacífico* operated on a corrupt electoral process; results were manipulated and the victory was granted systematically to each party every two years. After the king died of tuberculosis, the peaceful alternation of government continued until Alfonso XIII reached adulthood. Meanwhile, in 1898, after years of disastrous administration and José

Martí's revolutionary uprising in Cuba, and its defeat in the Spanish-American War, Spain lost its last colonies.

The end of the nineteenth century did not mark any ideological shift for Spain. Its old institutions—the Church, the military, and the monarchy—maintained the status quo. However, as more and more Spanish peasants migrated to the cities for work, they came into contact with each other and with socialist ideas filtering into Spain from nearby France and other areas of Europe. These ideas led to realizations about past and present oppression that polarized the population into conservative and liberal wings. Tensions increased between the factions, finally exploding into the Spanish Civil War of 1936-39.

In terms of shifting ideologies, the Spanish Civil War can be regarded as the real start of the Spanish twentieth century. The genuine turn of the century had actually seen a landmark event, but it proved to be of little consequence. In 1902, 16-year-old Prince Alfonso XIII became king of Spain. The instability of the period, however, continued. In fact, so unstable was it that on his wedding day in 1906, there was an assassination attempt on his life. Spain was riddled with unrest: Catalan nationalism, Carlist activity, republicanism, the growth of anarchism and communism.

THE TRAGIC WEEK

Although there had been prior isolated bombings, Spanish anarchism saw a drift toward terrorism beginning in the 1890s. The week of July 26 to 31, 1909, saw rioting and destruction in Barcelona, the main city in the region of Catalonia. After a problem in Morocco, the Spanish government had decided to mobilize Catalan army reserves. An antiwar protest ensued, killing 104 civilians, 3 priests, and 8 policemen, the reason for the label "The Tragic Week." Martial law lasted for months, banning all public gatherings. The infamous "Ley de fugas," or Escape Law, was enacted, whereby prisoners would be shot in prison and then reported to have attempted escape. Although in subsequent years leading anarchists spoke against violence, anarchist terrorism would not totally disappear from the scene.

So radically did the liberal and conservative politicians differ that it became impossible for them to agree on mutually acceptable reforms. The conservative Antonio Maura governed from 1907 to 1909. His proposed reforms failed to satisfy the left, or the Catalan separatists. After an indigenous revolt in the Spanish colony of Morocco, he called up military reserve troops in Catalonia's main city, Barcelona, which angered residents there. They staged a general strike, which was quelled by the army. Francisco Ferrer, an anarchist leader thought to be the responsible instigator, was captured and later executed by firing squad. Violence in Barcelona (the "Tragic Week" of July 26-31, 1909) had international repercussions that caused Maura's fall from power as head of Spain. José Canalejas, an anticlerical liberal, governed from 1910 to 1912, showing a benevolence towards the workers that

infuriated the conservatives without quite satisfying the radicals. He was assassinated by an anarchist. Calm prevailed for a time during World War I. Then prices started to rise, which led to social chaos and workers' strikes. An uncontrollable revolutionary spirit emerged. Amidst this profound unrest, in 1923, General Primo de Rivera staged an army uprising on a new *pronunciamiento*. With the permission of the king, Rivera suspended the constitution and proclaimed himself dictator, ending the 50 years of sham parliamentary democracy of *turno pacífico*.

The rise of anarchism. Scenes Two, Six, and Eleven of *Bohemian Lights* were inserted in the book format in 1924 as modifications of the original manuscript after the turbulent political events that occurred in Spain in the 1920s. Valle-Inclán adopted a committed or *engagé* position and a much more revolutionary attitude than in 1920, when installments of the play first appeared in a magazine. He had at this point been mainly concerned with renovating literary style. Like other Spanish modernists, his interest at that time lay not in confronting conditions in the world; rather, he had evaded them by focusing exclusively on artistic matters. In the 1920s, however, Valle-Inclán virulently opposed Primo de Rivera's dictatorship, beginning to move dramatically to the left (in the 1930s he even joined the Communist Party and advocated for Spain a dictatorship like that of Vladimir Lenin in Russia). The addition of three scenes in the play dealing with anarchist activity and police repression are a direct result of Valle-Inclán's new position.

At the end of the nineteenth century Spain was an underdeveloped, backward, agrarian society. While the rest of Europe was becoming increasingly urbanized, the peasantry still clearly comprised a large majority in Spanish society. Society in general was characterized by an absolute monarchy in power, a demanding liberal bourgeoisie, a stagnant nobility, a savagely exploited urban working class, and a land-hungry peasantry. Spain's agrarian predominance in an age of continental industrialism was almost unique. Country dwellers still outnumbered the urban population by 10 percent. The only truly industrial cities in Spain were Barcelona and Bilbao. By 1922, the number of city dwellers nearly equaled that of country dwellers. Agriculture continued to account for 37 percent of the workforce, but industrial employment rose to 21 percent. Short of land, 20,000 peasants left Andalusia annually to make the trek north. They had no choice but to compete for jobs in industry.

Management-worker strife led to violence in the growing urban areas. Between 1918 and 1923, around 1,500 people perished as victims of labor unrest in Spain. In 1936, the year the Spanish Civil War began, the CNT (Confederación Nacional del Trabajo), at 1.5 million members, was the largest workers' union in the world. Roughly a million Spaniards were anarchosyndicalists, proponents of direct action to bring industry and government under the control of the labor unions.

Anarchy literally means without authority. Most people associate it with disorder and terrorism. However these are not intrinsic features of anarchism, which has been attributed to the drive of the oppressed to assert the spirit of freedom and equality. Spanish anarchism placed a strong emphasis on a libertarian lifestyle, one that valued spontaneity, passion, and initiative from the common people. Spanish anarchism originated in 1868 with the arrival of Italian anarchist Giuseppe Fanelli, a supporter of Russia's Michael Bakunin. Fanelli's intentions were to gain adherents to the First International, a workers organization established a few years earlier. His proselytization produced the Alianza de la Democracia Social, a group that preached anarchism and published the newspaper *La Federación*. Thousands of Spanish anarchists abandoned smoking and drinking. Parents often gave their children names like *Libertaria* (Liberty) or *Emancipación* (Emancipation) or exchanged their own names for those of anarchist heroes. They disdained the accumulation of money, and sought not power but its dissolution. If power were attained, intellectual anarchists warned, it would only lead the anarchists to become part of the establishment they sought to overthrow. Many anarchists became proficient in a common language called Esperanto, hoping that after the revolution there would be no language or cultural barriers among nations and people.

The origins of bohemian culture. "We must escape from this Bohemian life!" (Valle-Inclán, *Bohemian Lights*, p. 147). Bohemianism and anarchism are two aspects of counterculture society invoked by Valle-Inclán. Common to both movements is an antibourgeois sentiment. The name itself is taken from the French, who as early as the fifteenth century applied the term to the gypsies, thinking they came from or through Bohemia, a region of the Czech Republic. Over time, the French began using the term more generally, attaching it to wanderers, adventurers, and people who lead unconventional lives (particu-larly artists). Literature played a fundamental part in the development of a bohemian mindset. The political tumult of early-nineteenth-century Europe demanded an artistic revolution. Art had to more closely resemble life, which led innovators to conclude that it needed to break with the narrow rules of classical art. Classical tragedy was artificial, impersonal, and aristocratic. After the French Revolution, artists considered classicism inappropriate to the existing social conditions. In any case, thought the innovators, individual liberty ought to be included into form as well as the content of art and literature. Some of the proposed innovations were truly radical. In 1827 France's Victor Hugo produced the play *Cromwell*, in which he demanded freedom from the restrictions of the traditional style.

His writings were taken seriously by all the young struggling writers in Paris, who felt a great desire for liberty after reading the play. Later on, Hugo produced the play *Hernani*. Censorship had prohibited one of his plays from being performed before. To make sure it wouldn't happen again, Hugo assembled a crowd of supporters on opening night, February 25, 1830, so that authorities could not prevent the performance. It was a historic moment, the date when the new drama would shake off old, restrictive norms of classicism. Friends and foes of the Romantics were going to be in attendance. Hugo invited the young bohemian artists of Paris to act as *claqueurs*, the salaried applauders. Wearing absurd, incongruous, unfashionable styles, the young audience was allowed into the auditorium three hours before the play started. They made themselves at home, discussing the work about to be performed and eating and singing. When the bourgeois audience arrived, they were distraught by the damage, and by the absurd-looking young people already there. The forces of absolutism and liberalism clashed for the first time at this performance. Every violation of the rules was hissed by the classicists and applauded by the Romanticists. But as the play progressed and its beauty became manifest, the opposition weakened, and even converted. Romanticism had triumphed in France. *Hernani* had an initial run of 100 performances. The young men who helped foment the "scandalous" event later on became the bohemians, although that name would not be applied to them for a few more years. Victor Hugo's later masterpiece contributed to the development of the type. The 1862 novel *Les Misérables* was not primarily about bohemianism or student life, but Hugo, while trying to impart a global view of French society in the 1820s and '30s, included the bohemian lifestyle. The novel dealt with the outcasts, the underdogs, rejects, and rebels against society, along with the poor and the wretched.

The bohemian was usually a young bourgeois man who had grown somewhat disillusioned. He generally felt guilty about the privileges of his increasingly powerful class, acquired at the expense of exploiting workers and nature. Some of these young men left their comfortable homes to become artists and writers and to protest the new bourgeois society; they functioned as a sort of intellectual proletariat.

Parisian writer Henri Murger was one of the pioneers of bohemianism. When he was young, Murger lived with a group of friends who called themselves the Water-Drinkers because they couldn't afford much else. They shared an attic in the Latin Quarter, and though they experienced extreme poverty, they refused to undertake any commercially related activity. From his own life, Murger wrote *Scènes de la Vie de Bohème* about the bohemian lifestyle in Paris. Most of the stories concern efforts to raise money to fight hunger while pursuing love and fame. In the long run, these efforts made a difference. The movement proved to be one of vital importance.

The contributions of bohemianism must not be underestimated. Before the French Revolution of 1789, art was simply considered a trade, and confined mostly to certain families of artists. An artist was a kind of civil servant. First, he depended on finding a patron, which meant that he could not choose the subject of his work. Romanticism changed that type of art, and converted it into the lifestyle that we today associate it with. The Romantic writers began to be associated with sculptors and painters, making the profession more respectable, although still a little outlandish. The Romantic movement was the springboard for the bohemians and their carefree, art-for-art's-sake attitude. Novels that dealt with bohemia such as *Les Misérables*, *Scènes de la Vie de Bohème*, and *Trilby* were bestsellers; and for a long time everyone seemed to be fascinated with bohemianism and the freedom of student life.

In Spain too, the bohemian lifestyle began with the Romantic movement. Here too it constituted a protest against capitalism. Spanish writers like José de Espronceda and Mariano José de Larra had expressed their contempt about the mercantilism of the literary profession. The consolidation of a literary market in Spain, and the

professionalization of the Spanish writer was tied to the rising of the post-Romantic realist novel, considered the bourgeois genre par excellence because it featured bourgeois characters and catered to bourgeois buyers. Toward the end of the nineteenth century Spanish bohemia attained a more precise definition by becoming identified with the literary Hispanic movement called *modernismo*. Modernismo was an elitist, art-for-art's-sake movement, concerned with artistic independence, not with the materialist preoccupations of realism. Inevitably, this antibourgeois literary anarchism condemned the proud modernist writers to poverty.

At the turn of the twentieth century, amateur writers streamed into Madrid from the provinces, increasing the already flooded market and reducing the possibility of making a living as a professional writer. This circumstance, coupled with the extremely low percentage of readers and Spain's high rate of illiteracy (71.5 percent in 1887), placed a modernist writer at a great disadvantage. Not willing to play by the rules of the market made other modernist writers the only possible public for the modernist writer's literature. True bohemian writers, such as Valle-Inclán or Alejandro Sawa, endured a hard existence. Sawa died on March 3, 1909, and with him much of the ideal of the Spanish bohemia, which in Valle-Inclán's view would deteriorate into two equally unprincipled groups: 1) writers who sold out and accommodated to the mainstream market, or; 2) parasites and spongers. In *Bohemian Lights,* Valle-Inclán exposes these two groups and distances himself from them. By this time, Spanish modernism and the genuine group of bohemian writers had ceased to exist.

The Novel in Focus

Plot summary. The action in *Bohemian Lights* consists of a series of comic and absurd incidents that happen in one night, the last in the life of bohemian journalist and poet Max Estrella, who, realizing that he is unable to support his family, leaves for the street. He encounters all sort of low-life individuals, gets drunk, is arrested and mistreated, and ends up in jail. His personal odyssey unfolds against a background of Spanish reality. Max witnesses a child's shooting and an anarchist prisoner's death before a firing squad, victim of the infamous "Ley de fugas." After his release from jail, Max proposes to interpret Spanish reality from a different perspective: as if one were looking into a concave mirror. The resulting image would be comic, deformed, and ridiculous. In Max's view, the dismal reality of his life and of Spanish society demands a new kind of artistic approach: "The tragic sense of Spanish life can only be rendered through an aesthetic that is systematically deformed" because "Spain is a grotesque deformation of European civilization" (*Bohemian Lights*, pp. 160-61). Valle-Inclán transforms the work into a tragic and grotesque parable of the impossibility of living in an unjust, oppressive and absurd country. Spain, according to the play, has no place for purity, honesty and noble art. Max Estrella dies at dawn, overwhelmed by cold and alcohol, but also by the pathetic state of surrounding society.

Scene 1 is a portrait of Spanish bohemia. After losing his job in journalism, Max suggests they all (he and his family) commit suicide. He is blind and a true bohemian: poor, sick, sporting a long beard, living in an attic, and worried about how to obtain money. He shows comradeship for Don Latino even though Don Latino, who is a drunkard and an insensitive sponge, has cheated him of some money in the sale of some books. Max goes out to try to demand some more money for the books, advised by Don Latino, whom he animalizes as his dog. Scene 2 begins with the description of the bookseller's shop, where a literary gathering is taking place, including a cat, a parrot, a dog, and the bookseller (a parody of Spanish culture). Max is refused more money and heads to a tavern. The first reference to anarchist activity occurs on his way to the tavern: "A group of armed policemen pass by with a man in handcuffs" (*Bohemian Lights*, p. 102). At the end of the scene a boy asks the bookseller for melodramatic literature, a subgenre that many bohemians, including an early Valle-Inclán, had reluctantly to undertake sometimes to survive. Scene 3 begins in the tavern, where we discover that "Her Ladyship the Tango Tart" has been looking for Max. He spends some of his scant money on a lottery ticket and on prostitutes (the origin of his blindness is venereal). He owes the prostitute some money and pays her with the ticket. She leaves. Max pawns his cape to get back the ticket, but she is already gone to join in the tumult of a worker's strike. Scene 4 starts with comic references to the police, who walk in manner described as "epic trotting," and the altercations on the street (*Bohemian Lights*, p. 103). Max and Don Latino find the girl who has the ticket, and they all end up talking about politics, arguing for a revolution. Modernist writers appear. The play describes them disparagingly: they are "the key

figures of the Modernista Parnassus, a group of second-rate writers" (*Bohemian Lights*, p. 115). The police shows up and Max is taken to jail for causing a public disturbance and shouting anarchist slogans. In perhaps the play's best example of *esperpentism*, Scene 5 features Max being hauled to jail:

> MAX: I took the liberty of detaining these officers of the law! They were out getting sloshed in some disreputable joint so I asked them to accompany me here.
> SLICK-BACK SERAFÍN: Watch what you say, Sir.
> MAX: I'm not at fault, Mr. Policeman.
> SLICK-BACK SERAFÍN: Inspector.
> MAX: It's all the same.
> SLICK-BACK SERAFÍN: Your name, please?
> MAX: My name is Máximo Estrella, my pseudonym Manque Max. I have the honour of not being a member of the Academy.
> SLICK-BACK SERAFÍN: You're going too far. Constables, why was this man arrested?
> A POLICEMAN: For causing a public disturbance and shouting communist slogans. He's had a bit too much to drink!
> SLICK-BACK SERAFÍN: Your profession?
> MAX: Temporarily unemployed.
> SLICK-BACK SERAFÍN: Where have you worked?
> MAX: Nowhere.
> SLICK-BACK SERAFÍN: But you have worked?
> MAX: Free men and singing birds do not work. Yet am I not humiliated, abused, imprisoned, searched, and interrogated?
> SLICK-BACK SERAFÍN: What's your address?
> MAX. This needs to be written in italics. A palace, on the corner of Calle San Cosme.
> A SHORT CONSTABLE: You mean a tenement block. Before we were married my wife rented a poky room in that same building.
> MAX: Wherever I choose to live is a palace.
> A SHORT CONSTABLE: I wouldn't know.
> MAX: Because you bureaucratic arseholes don't know a thing, not even how to dream!
> (*Bohemian Lights*, pp. 122-23)

In Scene 6, one of the 1924 additions to the play, Max talks to a fellow prisoner. The prisoner, a Catalan worker and anarchist, says, "They are going to kill me" (*Bohemian Lights*, p. 129). He wonders what the press will print about it tomorrow, and Max observes that it will print whatever the authorities tell it to. "Are you crying?" his fellow prisoner asks (*Bohemian Lights*, p. 129). Max responds, "yes," he is filled with helplessness and fury. The comic tone of the play resumes in Scenes 7-10. The dialog dips into caustic criticism to describe different sectors of Spanish society: journalists, politicians, writers, and the marginal, ignorant classes. In Scene 11, the last of those inserted in 1924, the play sounds a humorless, sour note again, protesting social repression. The scene starts out relating the effects of the latest street riot. There is broken glass everywhere, and a poor woman is crying over the death of her child, shot in the head. A later revelation discloses that the anarchist prisoner with whom Max was jailed has been shot for supposedly trying to escape. Max is infuriated:

> Latino, I can't even scream any more. . . . The rage inside here is killing me! My mouth is filled with poison. That dead man knew what was coming. . . . And yet he did not fear death. Torture was his only fear. . . . During these wretched times the legacy of the Inquisition still clouds the history of Spain. Our life is a Dantesque Inferno of shame and anger. I am dying of hunger and yet I am content, content at not having played a part in this tragic masquerade.
>
> (*Bohemian Lights*, p. 159)

In Scene 12, Max describes the aesthetic theory of Valle-Inclán's *esperpento* and ends with the esperpentic death of Max. Don Latino chides the dying Max for twitching, who supposedly dead, in a comic-tragic moment, comes back at Don Latino with the rejoinder that dead people cannot talk. The next scene describes Max's wake. It is a shocking moment characterized by an inappropriate mix of the occasion's pain (centered in Max's wife and daughter), and the comical attitude of the rest of the characters. The drunk Don Latino recites a parody of a prayer, but also makes some very serious comments. The height of impertinence occurs when the pompous writer Basilio Soulinake tries to convince the gathered that Max is not dead. Methods of checking his vital signs, such as putting a mirror to his mouth or matches under his fingernails, are discussed. Scene 14 includes the Marquis of Bradomín, the protagonist from Valle-Inclán's *Sonatas*. After attending Max's funeral, he philosophizes with the Nicaraguan poet Rubén Darío about death, making biographical references to Valle-Inclán himself and discrediting *Hamlet* as an *esperpento*. From the last scene, we learn that by the cruel irony of destiny the lottery ticket is a winner, but because it was taken by Don Latino, it has not reached the heirs, who commit suicide. The scene ends with Don Latino's showing up in the tavern with the money from the ticket. All the characters fight for the winnings, an incident that demonstrates why both anarchists and bohemians were revered groups by Valle-Inclán: they pursued pure ideals and despised money.

Esperpentism: Aesthetic deformation of reality as criticism of Spanish society. According to Valle-Inclán, there are three ways for an author to see life and the characters in a work of art: from below, as heroes of Greek tragedies; at the same level, like brothers, as in the characters in Shakespeare's plays; or from above, as puppets, like Quevedo. From this last perspective springs forth *esperpento*, an extravagant mix of tragedy and farce that emerges because of the impossibility of conceiving a true tragedy out of the Spanish historical circumstances.

Valle-Inclán is concerned with the backwardness, the oppression, the inequity, and most especially the apathy of Spanish society. His play, for example, features a scene in which characters are annoyed about wasting time in their workday because the protagonist is lying dead at their door; to Valle-Inclán, such a reaction is patently absurd. In keeping with this perception, he attempts to portray a deformed reality (*esperpento*) in this groundbreaking drama. By portraying such a reality, he stages an aesthetic protest against conditions in Spain, one that reflects both his own radicalization and the growing force of anarchosyndicalists in politics.

Mixing tragedy and farce, Valle-Inclán's theatrical instructions are sometimes impossible to represent: "A mouse sticks his prying snout through a hole" (*Bohemian Lights*, p. 100). *Esperpento* is a deformation or distortion of the Spanish reality that shows how absurd it is for an artist to live in Spain. The play itself explains the theory:

> MAX: The tragic sense of Spanish life can only be rendered through an aesthetic that is systematically deformed.
> DON LATINO: Rubbish! Don't be so pompous!
> MAX: Spain is a grotesque deformation of European civilization. . . . Distortion ceases to be distortion when subjected to a perfect mathematic. My present aesthetic approach consists in the transformation of all classical norms with the mathematics of a concave mirror.
>
> (*Bohemian Lights*, pp. 160-61)

This distorted vision of reality is accentuated in the play by making the main character get drunk or by degrading characters into animals, things, or puppets: "Don Latino de Hispalis: my dog" (*Bohemian Lights*, p. 144). In his *esperpentic* style, Valle-Inclán includes some special ingredients that add up to a criticism of society. For example, he invokes caustic, ironic humor when he makes one of his characters in the already religious-dominated country of Spain remark that "If Spain were capable of such religious standards, she'd be saved" (*Bohemian Lights*, p. 103). Irony becomes parody through the use of pompous, affected language, sometimes peppered with literary sentences from famous authors such as Rubén Darío, Espronceda, Victor Hugo, and Dante. A type of burlesque taunting is achieved through the exaggerated use of Madrid's slang, or of customary and administrative expressions used by public servants and police officers.

The play achieves its absurd sense of the grotesque by evoking anxious, distressing feelings as much as comical ones. Perhaps the most pathetic and saddest moments of a drama are achieved when comical anecdotes are interpolated in very depressing situations, in the presence of death, for example. Precisely, Valle-Inclán uses repeated references to death to increase the aura of sadness, as when Max says: "We could commit collective suicide" (*Bohemian Lights*, p. 95). This feeling of helplessness accompanies him throughout the play: "I've come here to shake your hand for the last time" (*Bohemian Lights*, p. 146). However, the play is not a tragedy. The author, to distance the spectator or reader from this conception, inserts a gradient of contrasts between the painful and the comical. During Max's wake, as the funeral service coachman arrives to take Max's coffin, Basilio Soulinake intervenes with impertinent pedantry trying to convince the widow that the deceased was not really dead, and one could prove it by burning the dead man's fingers. The macabre scene accentuates the family's pain. His family does not want to believe that Max is dead; for a while the family doubts and ignores the stench coming from the body. In *Bohemian Lights*, Valle-Inclán selects the most painful and at the same time ridiculous elements of his contemporary society and integrates them into his profile of the life of a bohemian poet. The strategy achieves two objectives, one local, the other universal: it allows his play to criticize the Spanish society and to offer commentary on the human condition.

Sources and literary context. Valle-Inclán is sometimes included in the Generation of 1898, a group of writers who primarily centered their works on the topic of Spain. The writers belonging to this generation felt its history, its decadence, and the problems of its time with deep intensity, agony, and pessimism. Each of them reacted quite differently, adopting a very personal style, and diagnosing the illnesses of their country. Valle-Inclán's style has been split into two periods. The first one, characterized as modernist, deals mainly with stylistic renovation. His work in this period excludes him from the Generation of 1898, which was explicitly concerned above all with the problems of Spain. Contrarily the writing of his second period fits the Generation's focus as it critiques contemporary Spain, going so far as to hopelessly condemn Spanish reality. Some of the characters are reportedly inspired by actual people. The real Alejandro Sawa becomes Max. Valle-Inclán himself inspires the character the Marquis of Bradomín, but also aspects of Max. The real-life journalist Julio Burell inspires the Home Secretary in the play, the writer Ciro Bayo becomes the fictional Don Gay, the real-life journalist Gregorio Pueyo inspires Zarathustra, and the writers Dorio Gádex and Rubén Darío play themselves. The play's anarchist prisoner is most certainly based on the genuine anarchist Mateo Morral, while the play's anarchist journalist Basilio Soulinake is modeled on the Russian anarchist and writer Ernest Bark.

Reviews. The Madrid magazine *España* published *Luces de bohemia: Esperpento* in successive issues from July 31 to October 23 of 1920. This was the first time that Valle-Inclán used the word *esperpento* to refer to one of his works. In 1924, just a year after General Primo de Rivera had overthrown the constitutional government, *Luces de bohemia* was published in book format by Cervantina Editorial, including four new Scenes that explicitly addressed the contemporary political situation. *Bohemian Lights* was never staged while the author was alive, partly because of the difficulties in portraying such scenes as the bookseller's literary discussion with a parrot, a cat, and a dog. Another reason lay in Valle-Inclán's objection to the control on authors by theater owners. Much later, the play gained international success when it was staged by prestigious director Jean Vilar in 1963, at the "Théâtre National Populaire" in Paris. It first appeared on stage in Spain in 1969 under the direction of José Tamayo.

—Benito Gómez-Madrid

For More Information

Cardona, Rodolfo, and Anthony N. Zahareas. *Visión del esperpento: Teoría y práctica en los esperpentos de Valle-Inclán*. Madrid: Castalia, 1970.

Easton, Malcolm. *Artists and Writers in Paris: The Bohemian Idea, 1803-1867*. London: Edward Arnold, 1964.

The Book of Count Lucanor and Patronio

by
Don Juan Manuel

Born in Escalona in the province of Toledo in 1282, Juan Manuel lived through one of the most turbulent periods in the history of Castile, the largest of the medieval Spanish kingdoms. His father was the Infante (Prince) Manuel, youngest son of King Fernando III of Castile, and brother of King Alfonso X, which made Don Juan Manuel a member of the Castilian royal family. Engaging in conventional aristocratic activities, Juan Manuel became deeply involved in the wars and political intrigues of his times. Less conventionally, he was also a prolific writer. A man deeply concerned about his own status and rank, Don Juan Manuel wrote works that provide a vivid glimpse into the values held dear by the aristocratic culture of fourteenth-century Castile. He claimed to have written more than a dozen books and treatises, eight of which survive. Critics are divided about the exact dates and chronology of Don Juan Manuel's works. His titles range from the dry *Crónica abreviada* (c. 1325, Brief Chronicle), to the chivalric *Libro del cauallero et del escudero* (c. 1326, Book of the Knight and the Squire), and *Libro de la caça* (c. 1326, Book of the Hunt). The *Libro de los enxiemplos del conde Lucanor et de Patronio* (Book of Examples of Count Lucanor and Patronio), better known as the *Conde Lucanor*, is generally considered his crowning achievement. Completed in 1335, it can best be described as a collection of *exempla* (brief moralizing stories), although in its longer versions the work also contains sections of proverbs and a religious treatise. Its stories are held together by a *frame*, a larger narrative into

THE LITERARY WORK

A collection of short narratives set in Spain and the Mediterranean world in the late Middle Ages; written in 1335; published in Spanish (as *El Conde Lucanor*) in 1575, in English in 1868.

SYNOPSIS

Featured here are two short stories that, like the rest of the tales in the collection, end with an instructive moral. In "What Happened to a Young Man Who Married a Strong and Wild Woman," a young Muslim husband tames his too-independent wife; in "What Happened to a Lying Beguine," a heretic woman attempts to destroy a happy marriage.

which the short tales are imbedded. In the frame, a counselor, Patronio, applies the morals of the stories to the count's own life, by extension teaching other nobles how to behave in fourteenth-century Castile.

Events in History at the Time of the Novel

Illegitimate rule? Ever since Alfonso X (reigned 1252-84), also known as "The Wise," the political situation in Castile had been deteriorating. Alfonso may have been wise, and he was indisputably a great patron of literature and learning, but historians agree that he was not a good administrator. His policies eventually led his alienated second son, Sancho, to rebel against him. Sancho later became king Sancho IV, ruling from 1284 to 1295. He died young, however, leaving his nine-year-old son to rule as Fernando IV. Fernando, in turn, died in 1312, leaving his one-year-old son Alfonso XI to rule in the care of regents. By the time Alfonso XI came of age in 1325, the kingdom had passed through two lengthy periods of unrest. Tension and chaos reigned as powerful nobles jockeyed to be among the *tutores*, or regents, who ruled in the young king's name. When the young king reached his majority, he faced the task of regaining royal prestige and power from the unruly nobles, including Juan Manuel himself.

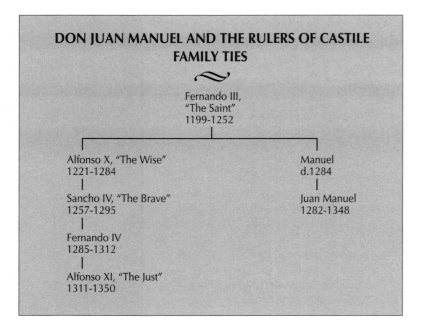

DON JUAN MANUEL AND THE RULERS OF CASTILE FAMILY TIES

Fernando III,
"The Saint"
1199-1252

Alfonso X, "The Wise"
1221-1284

Sancho IV, "The Brave"
1257-1295

Fernando IV
1285-1312

Alfonso XI, "The Just"
1311-1350

Manuel
d.1284

Juan Manuel
1282-1348

Juan Manuel's life was marked by violence from an early age. His father died in 1284, and his mother, Beatriz of Savoy, in 1290. By the age of 12 he had already nominally commanded a frontier skirmish in Murcia, although in reality he did not see battle himself, "for they did not dare place me in such great danger since I was so young" (Juan Manuel in Blecua, p. 10; trans. M. Hammer). Early on, he insinuated himself into the intrigues of the kingdom, and by 1319 he had been made one of the three regents who would share power in the waning years of the minority of Alfonso XI. After Alfonso came of age in 1325, he immediately showed a gift for political intrigue in his own right. Alfonso tried to

neutralize Juan Manuel, first by becoming betrothed to the nobleman's daughter Constanza, and then by holding the girl hostage once she was in his power. Reacting violently to this outrage, Juan Manuel spent much of the next decade in open rebellion against the king. He severed his ties with Castile, allied himself with Aragon, and even sought an alliance with the Muslim king of Granada.

Juan Manuel was deeply concerned about protecting and enhancing his own power. This preoccupation shows up in his writings, in which he emphasizes his own status as a powerful noble and carefully separates himself and his aristocratic class from the rest of society. As far as Juan Manuel was concerned, none of the kings from Alfonso X through Alfonso XI were worthy of praise. Their unworthiness contrasted starkly with Juan Manuel's feelings about himself.

His position as perpetual second fiddle rankled Juan Manuel deeply, and his bitterness shows in many of his works. In *Libro de la armas* (Book of Arms, written after 1337), for example, Juan Manuel glorifies his own family while simultaneously denigrating the ruling house. The work suggests it was Juan Manuel's deeply held and not-too-secret belief that if things had gone right he himself would have been king. Juan Manuel claims that his father, the Infante Manuel, had been the favorite son of Fernando III, had ruled as de-facto king of Murcia, and had distinguished himself as the only one of his children that Fernando III saw fit to bless. To Juan Manuel, this made the Infante Manuel the moral, if not the actual, heir of Fernando III. In support of this last point, the book relates an interview that allegedly took place between the 12-year-old Juan Manuel and his cousin, the dying king Sancho IV, who had succeeded his father, Alfonso X, to the throne of Castile. Sancho confesses to the boy that he himself had never been blessed by his father, Alfonso X. In like manner, Alfonso X had never been blessed by his predecessor, Fernando III. Thus, in Juan Manuel's *Libro de las armas*, Sancho IV all but confesses the illegitimacy of his entire line.

Literacy. Ironically this politically turbulent time was one of medieval Spain's richest in terms of cultural production. On the rise, literacy was no longer the exclusive province of clerics. From at least the twelfth century, shifts in reading patterns had been having an effect on lay spirituality and education in Europe. Cathedral schools gave way to universities and more books began to be produced to meet the needs of a larger public. New forms of book production, and the book itself, were taking shape. Meanwhile, a growing number of better-educated lay readers, better educated than ever before, had an impact on spiritual concerns. Lay people began to take a serious interest in their own salvation. Popular forms of heresy sprang up, many of them connected to literacy (described in the following section, "Preaching and exempla"). In hard numbers, the extent of lay literacy during this period—especially in Spain—is difficult to pinpoint. The word 'literate' itself does not always refer to the mere ability to read and write. During the Middle Ages, a literate person was one who could read and write Latin. Conversely, an illiterate person could *not* read Latin. "Calling a person unlettered, *illiteratus, idiota,* did not necessarily mean that he or she could not read or write but rather that he or she did not know Latin, the language which was always learned through reading and writing" (Ong, p. 7). However, by this time, Latin had become an artificial language that one learned at school and through books. The language of everyday speech—of business and of the court—was the vernacular, Castilian. Naturally literature began to be written in the vernacular too. Thus, people who were unable to read Latin could function on both the written and spoken levels in the vernacular.

As noted, Juan Manuel grew up during the reign of Sancho IV, whose court culture owed much to Sancho's father, Alfonso X. The reign of Alfonso X had seen some very significant advances in Spanish literary culture.

> Alfonso's reign is rightly regarded as the beginning of a flourishing prose literature in Castilian: under the King's patronage and active direction a vast corpus of historical, legal, scientific and other works was translated or adapted from Arabic or Latin into Castilian prose.
>
> (Deyermond, p. 158)

Himself a poet, Alfonso had sponsored the production of an enormous collection of religious lyrics called the *Cantigas de Santa Maria* (Songs of Saint Mary, written in Galician, which for a time acted as the preferred language of poetry in Spain), and had hosted troubadour poets from around Europe. More significantly for the development of Spanish literature, Alfonso made Castilian the official language of his court, sponsoring the composition of vernacular chronicles, scientific treatises, and other literature.

However, the fact that higher numbers of people than before could now read and write does not mean that the total number of literate people was very large. Some estimates suggest that up to 80 percent of the population of Castile remained illiterate through the end of the seventeenth century (Lawrance, p. 87). Writing was a skill practiced by scribes, and even an author like Juan Manuel most likely did most of his writing by dictation. As a rule, people had their books read *to* them, instead of doing the reading themselves. There was, nevertheless a distinct number of people—mostly noble—who could read and write and who actively participated in the literate culture of Alfonso X, and later, of his son and successor Sancho IV.

Juan Manuel, who grew up during Sancho's reign, would have been influenced by the court's culture. The years following the reign of Alfonso X used to be viewed as a time of cultural stagnation in Castile. At second glance, however, the court of Sancho IV was not a cultural wasteland. A great many literary works that may have influenced Don Juan Manuel were produced during the reigns of Sancho IV and then his son, Fernando IV, including the *Lucidario* (Lucidaire), a scientific and theological treatise framed by a dialogue between a scholar and his student, and the *Libro del cauallero Zifar* (Book of the Knight Zifar), an early chivalric romance that included many exempla and philosophical maxims.

Preaching and exempla. The new lay literacy that began to burgeon in the twelfth and thirteenth centuries coincided with new forms of heresy—a disturbing trend. Addressing it was high on the agenda of the Fourth Lateran Council. Convened by Pope Innocent III in 1215, this council was primarily concerned with reforming the Church and finding a way to win the Holy Land back from the Muslims. The presumed connection between lay literacy and heresy has long been a topic of critical debate. The same forces that contributed to the rise of vernacular literature also led to people's wishing to read and interpret holy writ for themselves. This, in turn, coincided with unorthodox ideas—such as the various Apostolic Poverty movements, which insisted that true Christians, like Christ's apostles, must live in poverty. Seen as destabilizing, these movements were viewed with suspicion. Among the well-known heresies singled out by the council was the Cathari faith, a dualist religion that espoused competing good and evil principles and was popular in southern France.

Facsimile of a manuscript page from the *Códice de Puñonrostro,* one of five medieval manuscripts containing versions of *The Count Lucanor.*

The policies promulgated by the Fourth Lateran Council, partly in response to the realities of new lay spirituality and heresy, contributed to the revival of an old form of didactic literature—the exemplum. The council increased the emphasis on lay spiritual development, advancing, for example, the policy that all Christians must confess and attend mass at least once a year. To make sure the laity would receive proper instruction for their religious activities, bishops were told to authorize others to preach at the parish level. The church also authorized the formation of new religious orders to combat virulent forms of heresy. Members of the new Dominican order—known too as the Order of Preachers—became the frontline soldiers in the war against heresy. As this new emphasis on pastoral care and preaching took hold, it quickly became obvious that the best way to teach the untutored the intricate rules and doctrines connected to their salvation or damnation was to tell them stories. Into popular vogue came the exemplum, a brief story or narrative designed to illustrate a moral point. There is no single all-encompassing definition for *exemplum* in the Middle Ages. The term refers to stories, maxims, proverbs, or the modern concept of "example." Conventionally the term is used to describe short, didactic narratives, usually meant to be included in sermons by preachers.

Exempla had been used for centuries prior to the Middle Ages. Gregory the Great (540?-604) extolled them as the perfect way to teach gospel truths to illiterate people. Long before Gregory, however, the Romans and the Greeks had used exempla. Jesus himself taught in parables, a form of exemplum. Now, with the advent of the preaching orders, examples took on a new importance. Preachers culled their tales from a vast body of anecdotes, fables, myths, legends, and tales of saints' lives, as well as stories imported from the east. Thousands of these little stories were collected and copied into manuals, then diffused all over Europe.

Many of the tales were priestly adaptations of popular legends, making them an intriguing meld of clerical and popular culture. "The stories told as exempla often transmitted oral and folkloric memories, helping to bridge the intellectual gap between the leaders of the church and its humblest members," one critic writes (Taylor, p. 67). Exempla dealt with all aspects of life, from the mundane to the supernatural. They demonstrated God's ready willingness to reward virtue or punish sin; they also vividly showed the active role the Devil tried to take in influencing human affairs. One exemplum that appears in several Dominican collections shows how the Devil—frustrated at his inability to break up a virtuous marriage—enlists the aid of a deceitful old woman who succeeds where the Devil had failed. In its early forms this story illustrated the danger presented by lying tongues; but by the time Juan Manuel adapted it for *The Book of Count Lucanor and Patronio,* it had become a warning against religious hypocrisy and heresy, specifically against the perceived hypocrisy of the Beguines, members of a lay order for women. Preachers used such stories to spice up dull sermons, keep their congregations interested, and wake up those who dozed off. Above all, the exemplum served to make the message comprehensible to the lay audience.

Reconquest and *convivencia*. Other significant changes that would impact the development of prose narrative were also going on at this time. In about the twelfth century, Western Europe had begun tentatively reaching out to the rest of the world. Through crusades and trade, Western Europe was finding points of contact with the East. Among other things, eastern story collections found their way into Europe by way of these points of contact. One important nexus for this cross-cultural pollination was Spain itself.

Spain had always been in a somewhat different position than the rest of Europe in relation to eastern cultures. The Muslim invasion of Spain in 711 had placed Spanish Christians in very close—and often uncomfortable—contact with Muslims. The Muslim city of Córdoba in southern Spain was the largest, most important and most advanced city in Europe during the ninth and tenth centuries—a potent symbol of wealth and learning. Jewish culture also had an influence. Jewish intellectuals, in fact, occupied important positions in both Christian and Muslim society. This close contact among Muslim, Jewish, and Christian peoples is often referred to as *convivencia*, literally, "living together." The term *convivencia* implies peaceful, friendly co-existence, in contrast to the other term used to describe Christian/Muslim relations at this time: Reconquest. Neither term is entirely accurate. The co-existence implied by *convivencia* was not necessarily peaceful, but the traditional belief that Christian Spain engaged in an 800-year ideological crusade to win their land back from the Muslims is also erroneous. Christians did claim significant chunks of Muslim land over the years, but the wars were not always ideologically motivated—at least not at first. Over time, the Reconquest began to take on the trappings of a Crusade, but Christian warlords did not hesitate to ally themselves with Muslims against Christian enemies, if circumstances demanded it. As already mentioned, Juan Manuel himself attempted an alliance with the Muslim king of

Granada during his estrangement from the Castilian king Alfonso XI.

Although both *Reconquest* and *convivencia* are inaccurate, both terms are useful in describing the political realities of medieval Spain. Behind these terms stands the fact that Christian, Muslim, and Jewish cultures co-existed in close proximity, and this close contact could not help but provide for a great deal of mutual influence. Muslim and Jewish cultural trends affected the development of Castilian lyric poetry and storytelling. A great many stories of eastern extraction found their way into Europe and were written down, first in Latin and then in the vernacular. Among these was the *Disciplina Clericalis* (Scholar's Guide), a collection of stories written by Pedro Alfonso shortly after 1100. Pedro was an Aragonese Jew who converted to Christianity in 1106. His book, which combined exempla and maxims, was hugely popular—more than 60 manuscripts are still extant. Like other books showing an eastern influence, Pedro Alfonso's stories are imbedded in a variety of "frames" where an older man—a teacher or father—counsels a younger man, who is his student or son. Later, during the reign of Alfonso X, other eastern story collections, such as *Calila e Dimna* (*Kalilah and Dimnah*, translated c. 1251), and the *Libro de los engaños de las mujeres* (*Book of the Wiles of Women*, also known as *Sendebar*, translated c. 1253) made their way into the Castilian vernacular. Alfonso X also sponsored a school of translators in Toledo, the conduit through which many works of eastern science and medicine found their way from Arabic and Hebrew into Latin and then the vernacular languages of Europe.

The Short Stories in Focus

Plot summary. *The Book of Count Lucanor and Patronio* is a collection of exempla and proverbs, wrapped in a frame that presents it to the reader as a cohesive unit. In each of the 50-odd examples that make up Part One of *The Book of Count Lucanor and Patronio*, Patronio counsels his patron, the count, first narrating a story and then applying that story to the count's situation by interpreting it with a maxim or moral. This is followed by an injunction, or a direct invitation to the count to incorporate the message into his own life. Finally, Don Juan Manuel finishes off each chapter by summing up the moral in a brief rhyming couplet.

One of the better-known stories bears a passing resemblance to William Shakespeare's *The

Taming of the Shrew* (c. 1594), although it was written more than two centuries before the Shakespearean play. In "What Happened to a Young Man Who Married a Strong and Ill-Tempered Woman," a young Muslim man marries the worst woman in town, against the advice of everyone including the woman's own father. His friends and family literally fear for his life if he goes through with his wedding plans. On their wedding night, as the young couple sits alone at dinner together, he turns to a pet dog nearby and demands that it fetch him some water. The dog, obviously, does not comply, whereupon the husband takes out his sword and cuts it to pieces. Next he turns to a cat, and the same thing happens. Finally he asks his horse, and when the animal does not comply he shrieks "What, Sir Horse, do you think that because you are the only horse I have that I will spare you if you do not do as I say?" (Juan Manuel, *The Book of Count Lucanor and Patronio,* p. 139). He ends up killing the horse, then turns to his frightened wife and politely asks her to get him some water. She complies. The strong and ill-tempered woman has been broken. When it becomes apparent that the young man has succeeded in taming the girl, his father-in-law attempts to cow his own wife in a similar way, by killing a rooster. She laughs scornfully and tells him she knows him too well for that to work on her: "Well now, Mr. So-and-So, you are a little late. It wouldn't matter to me now if you killed even a hundred horses. You should have begun sooner, for now we know each other" (*Count Lucanor,* p. 140). Patronio applies the moral—which is that men must establish control at the outset of marriage, before it is too late—to more than just marriage relations. "I advise you in all your dealing with others, always to let them know what you expect of them," he tells the count (*Count Lucanor,* p. 141). It is easier to be tough and consistent from the very beginning than try to rectify laxity by growing tough later.

In a second domestic tale, "What Happened to a Lying Beguine," (translated as "What Happened to a Woman of Sham Piety"), a Beguine woman makes a pact with the Devil to infiltrate and ruin a happy marriage. Beguines were lay religious women who took certain vows, but were allowed to keep their own property and live in their own homes rather than a convent. By Juan Manuel's time they had become suspected of heresy and the author often uses the word "beguina" as a synonym for hypocrite. Using flattery and deceit, the Beguine convinces the married couple that she is an old servant of the wife's family. Once inside the household, she gains the confidence of the wife and uses that confidence to sow doubt. The Beguine tells the wife that the husband is being unfaithful to her:

> I am terribly grieved for I have heard that your husband is much more interested in another woman than in you. I beg you to be nice to him and please him so much that he will not like the other woman as much as he does you, for more harm can come to you through this than from anything else.
>
> (*Count Lucanor*, p. 154)

Distressed, the wife wonders how to get her husband back. Meanwhile, the Beguine tells the husband that the wife suspects he is having an affair. This saddens him and immediately the relationship feels the strain. As things deteriorate from bad to worse, the Beguine finally tells the wife that to get her husband back the Beguine will have to make a magic potion containing one of her husband's hairs. She convinces the wife to lull her husband to sleep on her lap and then cut a hair from his throat. Meanwhile she tells the husband that his jealous wife plans to kill him in his sleep. That night the husband pretends to fall asleep on his wife's lap and silently waits while his wife takes out her knife. As soon as he feels the blade on his neck, he grabs it from his wife and cuts her throat. This violent act leads to a spiral of retribution that first involves relatives and then the entire village in an orgy of death. When her role in the calamity is discovered, the Beguine herself is "put . . . to death in a cruel manner" (*Count Lucanor*, p. 156). The moral that Patronio relates to Lucanor is to beware of lying, religious hypocrites, who are evil and deceitful. Then so that the count might know these hypocrites, Patronio repeats the biblical injunction: By their fruits ye shall know them. Beyond such tales, two of the surviving medieval and renaissance manuscripts that contain *The Book of Count Lucanor and Patronio* include three sections of proverbs and a treatise on various aspects of religious belief, including baptism and the Eucharist.

Reading the frame. "Framed narratives" are stories within stories that feature a character inside a text who narrates a story to another character inside that text. The frame filters the inner story to readers through a fictional storyteller and audience. In the most sophisticated framed stories, the frame itself is a story, with its own plot; the telling of the inner narratives enhances and ad-

vances the plot of the frame. Perhaps the best example of this is *The Thousand and One Nights*, where the life of Scheherazade hangs in the balance, each story she tells winning her another night's reprieve from death. She tells stories as a way to save her life; they become her act of salvation.

While less complexly layered, *The Book of Count Lucanor and Patronio* also narrates its stories through a frame, in this case that of a nobleman who seeks guidance from his trusted advisor. Juan Manuel tells each story through the frame of a nobleman seeking counsel from his trusted advisor. Some critics have suggested that this frame is merely a device to legitimize the stories, which are, at heart, merely entertaining. Many of the stories certainly do seem frivolous, and the morals attached to them do not appear very weighty. But despite their entertainment value, the ethical component to the stories cannot be dismissed. Juan Manuel himself, in his prologue to *The Book of Count Lucanor and Patronio*, said his reason for writing the book was to help men "accomplish in this world such deeds as would be advantageous to their honor, their possessions, and their stations, and so that they would adhere to the career in which they could save their souls" (*Count Lucanor*, p. 39). He wanted to help aristocrats like himself improve their rank, property, or reputation by knowing whom to trust, how to marry and, perhaps most importantly, how to profit from good advice. To make this advice more palatable, he wrote it in the form of stories, like doctors who tend to a person's ailing liver by mixing into their medicine "sugar or honey or something sweet" that the person swallows "because of the pleasure the liver gets from sweet things" (*Count Lucanor*, p. 41). The stories are the sweet sugar that makes the hard medicine of exemplary doctrine easier to endure. Even entertaining stories in the Middle Ages pointed toward an ethical choice by the reader. Active, attentive readers needed to be constantly on the lookout for behaviors that they could either praise or blame. In each story discussed above, the frame has Patronio interpret the tale for his patron's benefit, then tell him how to act. Each tale ends with the narrator stating that the count considered the advice good, followed it and profited from it. When readers see that Lucanor acts on Patronio's advice, they recognize that they are being given a model for how they should act as well. "The Conde and Patronio are there to add to the exemplum material a series of exemplary applications" (Dagenais, p. 75). The purpose of the frame, then, is to unite the readers—most likely aristocrats, like Don Juan Manuel—with the count so that they will also apply the exemplum in their separate lives.

The fifteenth-century manuscripts of *The Book of Count Lucanor and Patronio* reveal where readers a century after Don Juan Manuel underlined or otherwise highlighted what were to them the important passages. More often than not, these highlighted passages contain the moral to the story—the ethical information that the reader understands to be the point of the whole exercise. Two sixteenth-century manuscripts, in fact, leave out the narrative entirely and only give a recap of the morals that Juan Manuel had written in verse at the end of each story.

Sources and literary context. As a framed collection, *The Book of Count Lucanor and Patronio* bears a marked similarity to the framed collections that originated in the East and gradually took root in Western Europe, such as *Kalilah and Dimnah,* which probably originated in India as early as 300 B.C.E. and gradually moved west before being translated from Arabic into Castilian. Beyond the similar frame structures, many of the stories in *The Book of Count Lucanor and Patronio* have parallels in these eastern books. "What Happened to a Young Man Who Married a Strong and Wild Woman," is one of several *Count Lucanor* tales set in a Muslim context, strongly suggesting an Eastern origin. While there are no direct sources for the story, critics suggest that it likely came from Persia. One critic

has also found a parallel in an early French fabliau, "De la Dame qui fut corriegée" (Ayerbe-Chaux, pp. 154-157). In both the Persian and the French versions a husband tames his wife on their wedding night by killing one or more animals.

Other stories, like "What Happened to a Lying Beguine," appear to originate in the Dominican exempla collections, although these earlier versions of the story do not identify the woman as a Beguine. Juan Manuel had a close relationship with the Dominicans—even founding a monastery at Peñafiel—and the order's active interest in suppressing heresy could very well have influenced Juan Manuel's own hostility toward non-orthodox groups, including the Beguines. In fact, alternate versions of *The Book of Count Lucanor and Patronio* describe the antagonist as an evil old woman or a pilgrim rather than a Beguine. Ultimately it does not matter which term is the "correct" one. Since all three terms denote members of suspect, marginal groups, the essence of the story does not change. It makes sense, however, for Juan Manuel to have intentionally used "Beguine," since he had close ties with the Dominicans, and his thinking was heavily influenced by the order.

In general, *The Book of Count Lucanor and Patronio* appears to draw its inspiration from this vast pool of eastern and western exemplary literature available in the Middle Ages. While very few stories in the book can be matched up with direct sources, there are striking parallels not only to other earlier or contemporary story collections but also to Dominican preacher's manuals, such as the exempla of Etienne de Bourbon. Critics have pointed out that by its very nature as a framed collection, *The Book of Count Lucanor and Patronio* reflects the influence of a vast tradition of framed tales that extended from Asia to Western Europe. The collection was written more than a decade before the *Decameron* (1349-53) and a half century before the *Canterbury Tales* (1478). "Indeed, the *Conde Lucanor*, the *Decameron* and the *Canterbury Tales* constitute the trilogy of fourteenth-century framed narratives which all explicitly reflect back on a vast tradition, their own histories" (Menocal, p. 478). In other words, they are stories about the act of telling stories, designed specifically to draw the reader or listener in and make them a part of a continuing chain of transmission and interpretation.

Composition and reception. In his prologue to Part 2 of *The Book of Count Lucanor and Patronio,* Don Juan Manuel notes that he had writ-

The fifteenth-century castle of Peñafiel looms above the town where Juan Manuel deposited his master copy of *The Count Lucanor*.

ten the exempla and morals of the first part to appeal to an uneducated audience (i.e., one that did not know Latin). However, one of his readers apparently thought they were a little *too* easy to understand. Juan Manuel's good friend Don Jaime de Jérica apparently preferred literature that was subtle, obscure, and a little challenging. This gave the author an excuse to write the less-easy-to-understand material that follows in the last four parts of the book. We do not know exactly how Jaime de Jérica read the book. Juan Manuel may have sent him a copy, which Don Jaime then read, or he may have listened as someone else read the book aloud to him. Paul Zumthor insists that almost all medieval literature would have been received this last way: "Every medieval 'literary' text, whatever its mode of composition and transmission, was designed to be communicated aloud to the individuals who constituted its audience" (Zumthor, p. 67).

However it occurred, *The Book of Count Lucanor and Patronio* did circulate, as Juan Manuel fully expected it would. In his prologue, Juan Manuel mentions that he has prepared a master copy of his works and deposited it at the Dominican convent that he had established in Peñafiel. He did this, he says, because he knows that when books are copied by hand, mistakes

inevitably creep into the secondary copy. Therefore, if any readers take issue with what they have read, he asks that they consult first with his master copy before laying the blame on him. Juan Manuel was well aware of the realities of manuscript culture.

Mistakes and alterations certainly did creep in. The work survives today in five primary manuscripts, four from the fifteenth century, and one from the sixteenth century. Every manuscript of *The Book of Count Lucanor and Patronio* is—to a greater or lesser degree—different from every other. In addition to the five primary manuscripts remaining today, there were a handful of manuscripts that we know about that have since disappeared. The monastery of Guadalupe had a copy, as did Queen Isabel the Catholic. In addition, the sixteenth-century editor of the *Count Lucanor* had three copies from which he worked. This sixteenth-century edition, in turn, influenced other writers during the Spanish renaissance, most notably the dramatists Lope de Vega and Pedro Calderon de la Barca (see **Fuente Ovejuna** and **Life Is a Dream,** also in *WLAIT 5: Spanish and Portuguese Literatures and Their Times*). Both of these dramatists would write plays based on episodes from Juan Manuel's book.

—Michael Hammer

For More Information

The Book of Count Lucanor and Patronio

Ayerbe-Chaux, Reinaldo. "*El Conde Lucanor.*" In *Materia tradicional y originalidad creadora*. Madrid: Porrúa, 1975.

Blecua, José Manuel. "Introducción." In *El Conde Lucanor*. Madrid: Castalia, 1969.

Cacho Blecua, Juan Manuel, and Maria Jesus Lacarra. "Introducción." *Calila e Dimna*. Madrid: Castalia, 1984.

Dagenais, John. *The Ethics of Reading in Manuscript Culture: Glossing the "Libro de Buen Amor."* Princeton: Princeton University Press, 1994.

Deyermond, Alan. "The *Libro de los engaños*: Its Social and Literary Context." In *The Spirit of the Court*. Ed. Glyn S. Burgess and Robert Taylor. Woodbridge, Suffolk: D. S. Brewer, 1985.

Juan Manuel, Don. *The Book of Count Lucanor and Patronio: A Translation of Don Juan Manuel's El Conde Lucanor*. Lexington: University Press of Kentucky, 1977.

———. *El Conde Lucanor*. Ed. José Manuel Blecua. Madrid: Castalia, 1969.

Lawrance, J. N. H. "The Spread of Lay Literacy in Late Medieval Castile." *Bulletin of Hispanic Studies* 62 (1985): 79-94.

Menocal, María Rosa. "Life Itself: Storytelling as the Tradition of Openness in the *Conde Lucanor*." In *Oral Tradition and Hispanic Literature: Essays in Honor of Samuel G. Armistead*. New York: Garland, 1995.

Ong, Walter J. "Orality, Literacy, and Medieval Textualization." *New Literary History: A Journal of Theory and Interpretation* 16 (1984-85): 1-12.

Ríos, Mazcarelle, Manuel. *Diccionario de los Reyes de España*. Vol. 1. Madrid: Alderabán, 1998.

Sturcken, H. Tracy. *Don Juan Manuel*. New York: Twayne, 1974.

Taylor, Larissa. *Soldiers of Christ: Preaching in Late Medieval and Reformation France*. New York: Oxford University Press, 1992.

Zumthor, Paul. "The Text and the Voice." *New Literary History* 16 (1984-85): 67-92.

"By the Rivers of Babylon"

by

Jorge de Sena

Jorge de Sena (1919-78), poet, short fiction writer, novelist, playwright, critic, essayist, translator, biographer, and cultural historian, is one of Portugal's preeminent men of letters. Formally trained in both the sciences and humanities, he became the leading scholar on Portugal's two major poets, Luis de Camões and Fernando Pessoa (see **The Lusiads** and **Message,** respectively; also in *WLAIT 5: Spanish and Portuguese Literatures and Their Times*). Sena emigrated from Portugal in 1959 to escape the fascist Salazar regime. Moving to Brazil, he became a professor at the State University of São Paulo, Araraquara. In 1965, after becoming a Brazilian citizen, Sena emigrated once again, this time to escape the military dictatorship in Brazil. Moving to the United States, he continued his academic career, first at the University of Wisconsin and then at the University of California, Santa Barbara, with his status as Portugal's preeminent poet remaining intact throughout these changes. At his death in 1978 Jorge de Sena was regarded by many not only as Portugal's number one living poet but as the equal of Camões and Pessoa. All three spent part of their lives in exile, with Sena often using Camões's persona as a foil for his own thoughts and feelings, and a conduit for attacking evil in humanity and its institutions. In "By the Rivers of Babylon" Sena portrays an infirm Camões who has the capacity to castigate his countrymen for their shortcomings, but who instead focuses his poetic gifts on the sorrow he feels for the impending "death" or "exile" of his coun-

THE LITERARY WORK

A short story set in Lisbon near the end of the sixteenth century; written in exile in Brazil, published in Portuguese as ("Super Flumina Babylonis") in 1966; in English in 1989.

SYNOPSIS

The great Portuguese poet Luís de Camões is now old and poor, infirm and impotent, but his genius allows for one more creative burst: a poem on the theme of exile inspired by biblical Psalm 137.

try, which will come about with Portugal's takeover by Spain, the so-called Babylonian Captivity.

Events in History at the Time the Short Story Takes Place

Portuguese Age of Expansion. Portugal was Europe's first great maritime empire, one that at its peak in the sixteenth century, virtually girdled the earth. Beginning in 1415, with the capture of the Moorish garrison in Ceuta on the African coast, the growth of a Portuguese empire advanced precipitously with Portugal's discovery of a sea route to the East in 1498. During the fifteenth and early sixteenth century, Portugal would discover more than two-thirds of the world, opening up vast new vistas for Europe.

Jorge de Sena

As heirs of a long accumulation of technical skills achieved in the late Middle Ages and of Arabic and Jewish contributions in the form of astrolabes and maps, the Portuguese had developed a maritime technology that allowed them to roam the seas freely. This expertise coupled with superior Portuguese firepower led to the rise of the empire. For much of four centuries (1400s-1700s), the Portuguese held a monopoly on the commercial coastal trade of Africa, Arabia, Persia, India, Indonesia, Malaysia, China, Japan, and half of South America. Never had there been such a far-flung empire. Like the Italian city of Venice before it, Lisbon became a global seaport, drawing would-be profiteers from all over the earth.

Because of the voyages of discovery and conquest, the disparate ethnic and racial branches of the human family were brought together for the first time. Portugal became the ambassador of the West to these new lands, and served, in like fashion, as the interpreter of the newfound Eastern cultures to Europe. People, goods, flora, and fauna were exchanged between continents, with Lisbon serving as Europe's center of commerce and power, innovation and wealth, disease and corruption.

Discovering the sea route to India. The Portuguese developed and expanded their maritime technology and voyages of discovery over some 80 years (from 1415 to 1492, when Columbus discovered America for Spain), virtually without competition from any other country. Until 1492, Spain was still involved in the type of warfare that merely resulted in an exchange of real estate among European powers. In the Treaty of Alcáçovas, contracted with the Spanish kingdom of Castile and ratified by the Pope in 1479, Portugal agreed to forfeit its claim to the Canary Islands in exchange for any lands it might conquer outside Europe. A line was drawn east and west through the Canaries. Everything south of the line would belong to Portugal if conquered; everything north would belong to Spain on the same basis.

Having systematically sailed south along the west coast of Africa, Portugal was finally prepared to round the continent and sail northeast to India. The historic voyage was set for 1487. A party under Pero de Covilhã was dispatched to India by land to welcome the ships. Bartolomeu Dias led the fleet that was to have arrived by sea. Covilhã reached his destination; Dias did not. After rounding the Cape of Good Hope, his crew mutinied, thinking that worse conditions lay ahead, Dias was forced to return to Lisbon.

It was at this point that Christopher Columbus, who had married a Portuguese and had lived and worked in Portugal for years, proposed that India could be more easily reached by traveling west. His plans were turned down by King John II and his advisors as "nonsense," most probably because his calculations of the distance it would take to reach the goal was far short of what Portugal had already calculated on the basis of much experience. Four years later Spain became the second nation to fully enter into the Age of Discovery, taking advantage of Portugal's vast store of knowledge, equipment, and experience in the person of Columbus. Spain contracted the maverick explorer to undertake the proposed voyage, a last-ditch effort on the part of the Spanish to beat the Portuguese to India. Spain was feeling emboldened at the time, having just conquered Granada, the last remaining Moorish kingdom in the Iberian peninsula. The year was 1492.

When Columbus returned with the news that he had reached "India," not realizing that he had in fact reached the Americas, Portugal despaired. It recovered quickly, however, when it realized that according to its treaty with Spain, the land belonged to Portugal. A new accord was then hammered out by the two monarchies known as the Treaty of Tordesillas (1494), which held that lands south of the line running east and west

PORTUGUESE MARITIME TECHNOLOGY

The numerous Portuguese contributions to maritime technology can be grouped into three major categories: (1) the sailing ships (first the caravel and then the nau, which was larger than the Spanish galleon) and their abilities to travel against currents and winds (tacking); (2) the navigational techniques developed once the seamen freed their crafts from coastal sailing (astronavigation); and (3) the amassing of oceanographic information (winds, currents, meridians), together with its preservation (cartography, maps, charts, chapbooks, and the like). The first of the ships, the caravel, boasted a wide hull that displaced little water and three masts on which were hoisted triangular or lateen sails; such a sail allowed great mobility for tacking (it could form an angle of more than 50 degrees with the direction of the wind). In its smallest, early version, the caravel carried as much as 50 tons and operated with the help of a 20-man crew. Much larger, the later versions were referred to as floating cities and operated with upwards of 800 crewmen. All these cargo ships were armed and so could double as warships when needed. The legacy of fear engendered by a Portuguese warship with its colors flying, ready to do battle, survives in the name given to one of the most colorful and deadly of jellyfishes: the Portuguese Man of War.

through the Canary Islands would belong to Portugal, as long as they fell east of a new line running north and south 370 leagues west of the Cape Verde Islands, thus giving Portugal claim to Brazil, which was yet to be discovered. Lands on the west of that line would belong to Spain. Columbus died thinking he had reached the outer islands of "India," and only set foot on his discovery, the South American continent, during his third voyage. Meanwhile, Portugal's Vasco da Gama reached the real India in 1498, winning control of the coveted spice trade for his country and scoring a significant triumph in what was to become a century-and-a-half of Portuguese discovery and acquisition:

- **1415** Ceuta (Morocco), North Africa, claimed; lost in 1668 to Spain
- **1419** Madeira Islands (Atlantic Ocean) claimed; continues to be Portuguese
- **1427** Azores Islands (Atlantic Ocean) claimed; continues to be Portuguese
- **1444** Guinea-Bissau (West Africa) claimed; retained until its independence in 1975
- **1456** Cape Verde Islands (West Africa) claimed; retained until its independence in 1975
- **1471** Tangiers (Morocco), North Africa claimed; lost in 1665 to Arab kingdom
- **1472** St. Thomas and Prince Islands (West Africa) claimed; retained until its independence in 1975
- **1482** Angola (southern Africa) claimed; retained until its independence in 1975

- **1488** Cape of Good Hope (South Africa) reached
- **1498** India reached
- **1500** Brazil claimed; retained until its independence in 1822
- **1507** Mozambique (East Africa) claimed; retained until its independence in 1975
- **1507** Hormuz (Iran) claimed; lost in 1622 to Great Britain
- **1510** Goa (India) claimed; lost in 1961 to India
- **1511** Malacca (Malaysia) claimed; lost in 1641 to Holland
- **1514** China reached
- **1518** Colombo (Sri Lanka) claimed; lost in 1656 to Holland
- **1521** Timor (Indonesia) claimed; retained until independence in 1976
- **1534** Bombay (India) claimed; lost in 1665 to Great Britain
- **1542** Japan reached
- **1557** Macao claimed; lost in 1999 to China

Administration of the overseas empire. According to Charles R. Boxer, the Portuguese empire was "a commercial and maritime empire cast in a military and ecclesiastical mold" (Boxer, *Four Centuries of Portuguese Expansion*, p. 18). Individuals involved in the empire served either the Crown or the Church. But Portugal usually did not attempt to conquer existing nations or peoples, only to maintain a commercial monopoly. To this end, the Portuguese established naval supremacy in the Indian Ocean with three key

PORTUGESE AUTHORS IN THE AGE OF EXPANSION

Portugal produced a generation of writers to match the greatness of its political and maritime achievements. They included scientists such as Garcia da Orta (1501-68), who catalogued and described the medicinal and nutritional properties of new plants, and religious writers such as Samuel Usque (b. 1510) known for his *Consolation of the Tribulations of Israel*) and Frei Tomé de Jesus (1529-82) who wrote *The Acts of Jesus*. There were also numerous gifted historians to record the events, chief among them Gaspar Correia (1495-1561), who wrote *The Conquest of India*, João de Barros (1496-1570), author of *The Conquest of Asia*, and Diogo do Couto (1542-1616), author of *The Conquest by Decades*.

Among the literary greats were poets Sá de Miranda (1481-1558), Diego Bernardes (1530-1605), and the master Luís Vaz de Camões (1525?-80), who wrote the national epic poem, **The Lusiads** (also in *WLAIT 5: Spanish and Portuguese Literatures and Their Times*), about the discovery of the sea route to India. Playwrights included António Ferreira (1528-69), whose major work is *Castro,* and Gil Vicente (1465?-1537?), who wrote *The Ship of Hell* and **The India Play** (also in *WLAIT 5: Spanish and Portuguese Literatures and Their Times*). Novelists fell into three distinct genres: the chivalric, represented by Francisco de Morais's (c. 1500-72) *Palmerim of England*, the sentimental, by Bernardim Ribeiro's (1482?-1552?) *Child and Young Woman*, and the pastoral, by Jorge de Montemor's (1520-61) *Diana*. The major travel book, *The Peregrination*, was written by Fernão Mendes Pinto (1510-83). The genre of shipwreck literature was represented in the collection *Tragic History of the Sea* (narratives dated from 1552-1602, but only published in volumes in 1735 and 1736).

It has often been observed that the three major works of literary art to come out of the Portuguese Age of Expansion seem to focus on different aspects of the same enterprise: the discovery of the sea route to India, followed by the widespread conquest and domination in Africa, Arabia, India, Asia, Indonesia, and America. Camões's epic speaks of triumph and glorification; Pinto's travel book satirizes the undertaking by questioning the basic premises of conquest and forced religious conversion; while the shipwreck literature delves into the dark side of the adventure, and the cost in terms of human misery, due principally to greed.

strongholds: Goa in India, Ormuz in Persia, and Malacca in Malaysia. Once these were secured from Muslim traders, the Indian Ocean became a "Portuguese sea," safeguarded by fortresses established all around its perimeters from Africa to Asia, with these fortresses serving as commercial ports. Some were maintained by a military garrison; others were established by treaty or an alliance with the indigenous monarchs. In either case, Portuguese ships, with their superior maneuverability and cannon power, policed the entire area. Wherever possible, the Portuguese preferred to establish themselves on the coastal islands. Some ports became Europeanized cities, such as those on the Atlantic islands of Madeira and the Azores, or on the African islands of Cape

Verde, São Tomé and Príncipe, and Mozambique Island. Goa, the capital of Portugal's eastern empire, grew so wealthy that it rivaled Lisbon. Portuguese sovereignty would be retained here until December of 1961, when the territory, along with Daman and Diu, became part of India. Other important cities included Macao in China, whose return to Chinese sovereignty would occur even later, in December of 1999.

Portugal's "Babylonian Captivity." As early as the rule of King Manuel (1495-1511), Portugal attempted the policy of conquering European nations peacefully by marrying its princes and princesses into various ruling houses, especially Spain's. The plan ultimately backfired, when young King Sebastian was killed and his military forces were overwhelmed and defeated by a Muslim army at Alcácer Quibir, North Africa, in 1578. Having no issue, the throne passed to the dead king's grand uncle, Cardinal Henrique, who not unexpectedly left the throne vacant at his death in 1580. It was then that Philip II of Spain claimed the throne with the threat of military force and on the legal basis of his Portuguese heritage: his mother was Portuguese (Cardinal Henrique's sister), as was his grandfather, King Manuel, and his wife. Along with these strategies, Philip used persuasion to gain favor with the Portuguese nobles: he promised he would pay Portugal's war debt to the Muslim army and ransom Portuguese prisoners; he promised that no Spaniard would govern in Portugal's territories, and that no Portuguese would fight in any purely Spanish conflicts. Together the strategies succeeded. Philip II of Spain was acclaimed Philip I of Portugal, which ushered in the period of the union of the two crowns, the so-called Babylonian Captivity of Portugal under Spanish rule. To many, including Camões, the "Captivity" had a depressing finality about it that spelled the death of their country.

Luís Vaz de Camões (1525?-80) is now recognized as the greatest poet of the Portuguese language. As noted, he penned the national epic, *The Lusiads* (1572), which chronicles the entire panorama of Portuguese history framed within the Vasco da Gama voyage of discovery to India in 1498. As with the British playwright William Shakespeare, almost nothing definite is known about the details of Camões's life. Apparently he was a poor member of a noble family. As a young man he served in North Africa, where he lost an eye fighting against the Moors; he also spent time in Goa, Mozambique, Vietnam, and possibly Macau. These and a few more details have been gleaned from the half-dozen or so surviving contemporary documents that refer to Camões.

Besides not being accorded in life the recognition and acclaim that was commensurate with the greatness of Camões's poetic genius, some of his lyric verses would be attributed to his contemporary, Diogo Bernardes, as well as to others. The final injustice suffered by the poet who acquainted the West with the wonders of the tropics and Asia (he is considered the first European of imagination and genius to visit these lands [Bacon, p. xxviii]), came when Spain's Philip II was enthroned as King of Portugal in 1580. Heartbroken, Camões wrote that he would die with his country.

Bust of Luís de Camões, 1937, by Raul Xavier.

Everything which the man who wrote *The Lusiads* believed in went down with the headstrong, handsome, sub-normal young King. For Philip II of Spain could and did support his claim to the throne against two helpless native competitors when the old Cardinal Henry, Dom Sebastião's successor, died early in 1580. The fragment of a letter, which expresses absolute desolation of spirit, appears to be the latest surviving relic from the pen of Camões. It has been quoted many times. . . . "I loved my country so much that I shall die with her." The Poet did not delay long. A few months later, as Philip's armies advanced to take away Portuguese liberty for sixty years, Camões died, poverty struck, according to every testimony, and certainly heart-broken, on June 10, 1580.
(Bacon, p. xxix)

The Short Story in Focus

Plot summary. "By the Rivers of Babylon" centers on the creative process. The protagonist is an infirm and impotent Camões near the end of his life. The great national poet lives with his widowed mother in an upstairs apartment in Lisbon, barely scraping by on occasional writing commissions, dealing with subjects that do not inspire him. He also receives an irregularly paid stipend from the government, presumably for his epic poem *The Lusiads* and for his many years of service to the crown in Portugal's overseas empire. His dreams of fame and fortune have failed to materialize and his health is broken. An advanced case of syphilis may be affecting his mind as well as his body. Only with difficulty does he move about on crutches.

SYPHILIS: THE SCOURGE DISEASE OF THE AGE OF DISCOVERY

No one can say for sure where the venereal disease known as syphilis originated, but it is widely held to have come from the Americas. Historians have determined that syphilis was transmitted sexually through indiscriminate sexual contacts between European men and indigenous women. "The spread of syphilis to various regions of the world has been attributed by some historians to Portuguese sailors, settlers, and merchants. Medical accounts of syphilis appear in countries such as China, Japan, and India only after the arrival of the Portuguese" (Guider, p. 41). Until the discovery of penicillin and other "wonder drugs" in the first part of the twentieth century, there was no way to arrest the increasingly severe effects of this spirochete-caused disease on the body. Syphilis first produces a hard chancre, which forms at the site of the initial infection; the second stage involves pus-filled eruptions over the skin anywhere on the body, together with changes in the blood; the third and final stage is characterized by the disease's invasion into and debilitation of every system of the body, including the brain. If, after being discovered, the disease is left unchecked, it leads to an agonizing death. While there is no evidence that the real Camões ever had syphilis, it is perfectly plausible that he did, since the poet lived abroad and speaks in his poetry of multiple lovers. The affliction was apparently named during Camões's lifetime, after a 1530 poem in Latin by Girolamo Fracastoro, whose hero, the shepherd Syphilus, was the first to suffer the disease.

The sexually transmitted disease is a constant and painful reminder of his promiscuous past. His life is made all the more intolerable by his insensitive, unappreciative mother, who complains incessantly about her own misfortunes, nags him about his writing, and berates him for his former dissolute life; he feels shame each time she changes his soiled bandages.

When the story begins Camões is just returning home from his weekly visit with the friars,

his one source of enjoyment. It is not primarily his concern with death, judgment, and the afterlife that draws him to them, but the priests are the only educated people he has access to with whom he can converse on the wide range of subjects that interest him. He has difficulty climbing the stairs; he is slow, and it is painful. Any sustenance received from speaking with the brothers is erased by the difficulty of getting back to his room. This day his mother is not there to greet him, so for a time he is spared her chatter, complaints, and reminders. When she returns, she starts in on the demands, the overdue commissioned poems, the translations, and the literary favors she promised her friends. She reminds him how he started out as a strong, handsome, well-loved boy with a bright future; but he took up with bad women, became involved in a brawl, and had been forced to go abroad to India. As usual, he is not listening, or only partially listening as he eats his supper.

Increasingly, Camões's mind wanders, he recollects bits and pieces of his existence: former loves, distant lands, temptations, poems. He thinks about his years spent in exile separated from home and country and muses on what might have been. He had sought love, glory, wealth, and recognition. In the end, however, his genius was not recognized, nor was he recompensed; and he did not acquire wealth nor did he find love. Indeed, he had forfeited his health to sexual affairs and to the many physical trials he had had to endure, which included shipwreck, exposure, disease, and war. It was destiny, he concedes, together with his own errors, and his ardent love for women (the first line of one of his most famous sonnets—"Erros meus, má fortuna, amor ardente" [My errors, evil fortune, ardent love]) that produced his sorry plight (Williams, "The Poetry of Portugal," p. 64). He accepts his condition as the natural consequence of poor choices and bad luck, but feels terribly disappointed.

Camões broods about his sins and about having given in to the temptations of the devil; he is confident, however, that he will be saved: "They were not temptations for his soul, which God would never allow to be lost." ("By the Rivers of Babylon," p. 142). He ponders about God having become incarnate, a concept the poet can relate to, for he has created bodies for his thoughts and ideas. He believes that giving form to a poem is the supreme act of incarnation, greater than that of a woman giving birth, different too than even that of divinity's incarnation:

To feel pregnant with a poem, to feel oneself made fertile by a glimpse of lightning, and to be a man—this was as much as one could know. It is not known by the woman who gives birth, for it is their lot to give birth, at times without having loved. It is not known by the man who wants to have sons, for he can make them without love. But the poet who has practiced love even at the cost of his own flesh, who has written poems even though the spirit thinks poetry a small thing, this one, yes, this one knows what manner of thing is the Incarnation. But he merely knows it. He has not lived the Incarnation, it is the Incarnation that has lived him.

("By the Rivers of Babylon," p. 146)

While Camões thinks about these and other weighty issues, his mother drones on about mundane matters. Finally, with her usual admonitions, she excuses herself and retires for the night:

Be careful with the lamp, don't waste too much oil, for it costs an arm and a leg, and you know I'm afraid of fires and you might fall asleep there at the table, it wouldn't be the first time, and the lamp could set fire to your papers, to the house, may God help us and Saint Barbara protect us.

("By the Rivers of Babylon," p. 153)

Camões's current impotence refers not only to his sexuality, but to his creative powers. We read that he is "dried of love, weak in enthusiasm, disbelieving in his homeland, devoid even of the joy of writing verses. His verses now had abandoned him" ("By the Rivers of Babylon," p. 143). On this night, however, his inspiration returns and in one burst of creative genius we see Camões begin to compose one of his most famous works, "Babel and Zion," a long, seven-syllable poem, rhyming *abbab*, which revisits the very thoughts Sena's fictive Camões had been pondering that evening: his life's tortured course, exile, temptations, the poetic gift, a desire to return not just to a glorious Portugal, but to the heavenly city from whence he came:

It would be 365 lines, as many as the days of the year, like a via sacra of life, 73 stanzas of 5 lines each. . . .
He rose, impelled by a yearning that took his breath away, a dizziness that multiplied in the tiny light of the lamp. A wave of joy flooded over him, in anguished jolts. . . .
All atremble but with a firm hand, he began to write. . . . By the rivers that flow from Babylon to Zion I found myself seated. . . . He scratched it out, desperate. And began again. By the rivers

that run past Babylon I found myself and there sat weeping for memory of Zion and all that befell me. . . .
And he wrote on into the night.

("By the Rivers of Babylon," pp. 154-55)

Camões as a symbol of the fading glory of Portugal. Camões has traditionally been portrayed as the virile soldier-poet singing the triumphs and glories of Portugal in his national epic, *The Lusiads*. He had lived the adventure himself; he represented the nation's soul.

In contrast to this heroic persona, Sena's account portrays Camões as an ordinary human being (although with an extraordinary poetic gift), afflicted by the vicissitudes common to old age: poor health, loneliness, and doubts. The Portugal that Camões knew and praised in his epic would soon give way to an ignominious end: the Babylonian captivity by Spain. Both Portugal and Camões would die in 1580. In the story, Camões is inspired by his gift once more, to sing not of triumph and glory, but of sorrow and lament, presaging the nation's fall. The poem expands on Psalm 137, which recounts that while in captivity, the Jews wept by the rivers of Babylon, and because of sorrow, could not bear to sing the songs of Zion:

By the rivers of Babylon,
there we sat down, yea, we wept, when we remembered Zion.
We hanged our harps upon the willows in the midst thereof.
For there they that carried us away captive required of us a song;
and they that wasted us required of us mirth, saying,
Sing us one of the songs of Zion.
How shall we sing the Lord's song in a strange land?

(King James Version, Psalm 137:1-4)

In his poem "Babel and Zion," Camões is to Portugal what the psalmist was to Judah in 600 B.C.E., a singer of lamentation.

Sôbolos rios que vão
Por Babilónia, me achei,
Onde sentado chorei
As lembranças de Sião
E quanto nela passei.

By the rivers running fast
Through Babylon, I found me, where
I sat and wept, yea, with despair
For memories of Zion's past
And all that once befell me there.

(Rodrigues and Vieira, p. 50, trans. F. Williams)

Although the Psalm ends on a note of grisly despair, "Happy shall he be, that taketh and dasheth thy little ones against the stones" (Psalm 137:9), Camões ends his poem on a note of hope for those who may one day leave Babel and reach Zion:

> Ditoso quem se partir
> Para ti, terra excelente,
> Tão justo e tão penitente
> Que, depois de a ti subir,
> Lá descanse eternamente!
>
> He who departs blessed will be
> And seeks thee, land most excellent,
> So just so true and penitent
> Who, after climbing up to thee,
> There rests eternally content!
> (Rodrigues and Vieira, p. 50, trans. F. Williams)

Camões may likewise be speaking prophetically about Portugal's future. Certainly the theme of restoration of empire and glory, led by the messianic figure of the "enchanted" or hidden (not dead) King Sebastian, would become an important theme for Portuguese writers for centuries to come.

In addition to the parallels between ancient Judah's demise and Portugal's (both known as Babylonian captivities), and the identification of the exiled psalmist (speaking on behalf of the Jews) with Camões, who speaks on behalf of Portugal, we have the voice of author Jorge de Sena, a modern exile who, like Camões, bemoaned the lack of recognition for his poetic genius, the apparent plagiarism of his ideas, and the silent treatment or attacks in reviews of his works.

Sena writes about this infuriating unprofessional conduct by his contemporaries toward his own works in many of his prefaces and postscripts, but his most artistic as well as outspoken rendering on the subject comes in a poem in which the author's voice is masked behind the persona of Camões:

> **"Camões Addresses His Contemporaries"**
> You may well rob me of everything:
> ideas, words, images,
> as also metaphors, themes, motifs,
> symbols . . .
>
> . . .
>
> And later you may well not credit me,
> but suppress me, ignore me and even acclaim
> other more fortunate thieves.
> (Williams, *The Poetry of Jorge de Sena,* p. 136)

Sources and literary context. Although Camões is never identified by name in this fictional story, Jorge de Sena's "By the Rivers of Babylon" is not merely a flight of imaginary fancy, but is in fact based on or derived from the extant documents known about the life of Camões. So that the reader would not miss the historical and biographical references found woven throughout the story, Sena, in the notes in the back of the Portuguese editions, listed all known and creditable documents, and carefully explained what information or inferences of the poet's life were gleaned from each one. Sena was very interested in the topic of realism in literature. He devoted considerable time and space to writing about it. He believed in Erich Auerbach's contention (expressed in Mimesis) that realism has always been a part of writing since the Bible, and is not limited to the literary period called realism, which flowered in the second half of the nineteenth century. Sena also believed that an author's biography plays an important role in fiction writing.

In the short story under consideration, the details from the documents are historical; their inclusion and arrangement into the inner thoughts of Camões and monologues by his mother are fictional. Sena would argue that a purely historical approach would be dry and incomplete. Likewise, a purely fictional story, although perhaps more interesting, would ultimately not satisfy, since it would bear no relationship to the real Camões. But the combination of history and fiction, or historical fiction as it is called, provides the most satisfying of all narratives. Hence, the documents provide the facts of the outward actions and movements of the protagonist, while Sena provides the inward, hidden thoughts that no person could know. As noted by British novelist E. M. Forster (author of *Passage to India* and *Howard's End*), historical fiction presents the whole character—the inside as well as the outside:

> In daily life we never understand each other, neither complete clairvoyance nor complete confessional exists. We know each other approximately, by external signs, and these serve well enough as a basis for society and even for intimacy. But people in a novel can be understood completely by the reader, if the novelist wishes; their inner as well as their outer life can be exposed. And this is why they often seem more definite than characters in history, or even our own friends; we have been told all about them that can be told.
> (Forster, p. 47)

Events in History at the Time the Short Story Was Written

The military dictatorship in Brazil. Sena had fled Portugal and the fascist Salazar dictatorship for Brazil in 1959. The overthrow of the Brazilian government by a military dictatorship in 1964, two years before the publication of his short story, led to his flight to the United States the next year, for he did not wish to risk living under yet another authoritarian government. The dictatorship brought to an end a short-lived (20-year) interlude of democracy in the post-World War II era, which bore witness to the peaceful election and transfer of power to four presidents: Gaspar Dutra in 1946, Getúlio Vargas in 1951, Juscelino Kubitschek in 1956, and Jânio Quadros in 1961. For the second time in little more than five years, Sena and his family would pull up stakes and start over in a new land. Once again he had seen the demise of a nation's freedom, not through external conquest by a foreign power (as in Camões's day), but by a closed, and heavy-handed domestic dictatorship. There is an unsettling commonality, not only between Portugal's and Brazil's domestic dictatorships, but between them and the domination of Portugal by Spain in Camões's day. In each case, there is a kind of death: domestic society was crippled and individual freedom quashed by the imposition of stifling controls.

Reviews. Sena said, referring to his story "Super flumina Babylonis" ("By the Rivers of Babylon") and his novella *O Físico Prodigioso* (1977; The Wondrous Physician), that they "both are without doubt the best that I have ever written or will ever write" (trans. F. Williams; see Preface to *Os Grão Capitães*, p. 14). This self-assessment was confirmed when *By the Rivers of Babylon and Other Stories* came out in English. Reviewing the volume in *World Literature Today*, George Monteiro declared that "[the stories] introduce to English-language readers a formidable writer." Sena is "one whose name must be added to the rolls of the twentieth-century fiction writers who matter now and will still matter a century from now" (Monteiro, p. 289). The volume likewise received praise from Jonathan Keates in the *London Times Literary Supplement*, and from Amy Boaz in the *New York Times*. Boaz singled out the short story in question. Apart from what it conveys about exile or Camões or Sena, in her view, the tale imparts universal truths about the experience of composition: "To read the last tale of the collection, 'By the Rivers of Babylon,' is to

behold the agony and exaltation of the writer" (Boaz, p. 48).

—Frederick G. Williams

For More Information

Bacon, Leonard. "Introduction." *The Lusiads of Luis de Camões.* New York: The Hispanic Society of America, 1950.

Boaz, Amy. Review of *By the Rivers of Babylon: And Other Stories*, by Jorge de Sena. *New York Times Book Review*, 24 September 1989, 48.

Boxer, C. R. *Four Centuries of Portuguese Expansion, 1415-1825, A Succinct Survey.* Berkeley: University of California Press, 1972.

———. *The Tragic History of the Sea.* New York: Kraus, 1986.

Diffie, Bailey W., and George D. Winius. *Foundations of the Portuguese Empire, 1415-1580.* Minneapolis: University of Minnesota Press, 1977.

Forster, E. M. *Aspects of the Novel.* New York: Harcourt, Brace & World, 1954.

Guider, Margaret Eletta. *Daughters of Rahab: Prostitution and the Church of Liberation in Brazil,* Harvard Theological Studies 40. Minneapolis: Fortress Press, 1995.

Keates, Jonathan. "Moments of Contemplation—By the Rivers of Babylon by Jorge de Sena." *London Times Literary Supplement,* 27 September 1991, 26.

Monteiro, George. "Jorge de Sena: *By the Rivers of Babylon and Other Stories.*" *World Literature Today* 64, no. 2 (spring 1990): 289.

Pinto, Fernão Mendes. *The Travels of Mendes Pinto [Peregrination].* Trans. Rebecca D. Catz. Chicago: The University of Chicago Press, 1989.

Rodrigues, José Maria and Vieira, and E. Afonso Lopes. *Lírica de Camões.* Coimbra: Imprensa da Universidade, 1932.

Sena, Jorge de. *By the Rivers of Babylon And Other Stories.* Trans. Daphne Patai et al. New Brunswick: Rutgers University Press, 1989.

———. "Prefácio (1971)" in *Os Grão-Capitães: uma sequência de contos.* Lisbon: Edições 70, 1976.

Williams, Frederick G. *The Poetry of Jorge de Sena: A Bilingual Selection.* Santa Barbara: Jorge de Sena Center for Portuguese Studies, University of California, Santa Barbara, and Mudborn Press, 1980.

———. "The Poetry of Portugal: A Bilingual Selection of Poems from the Thirteenth Through the Twentieth Centuries." Santa Barbara: Department of Spanish and Portuguese, University of California, Santa Barbara, 1998.

La Celestina: Tragicomedy of Calisto and Melibea

by

Fernando de Rojas

Fernando de Rojas (d. 1541), the principal author of *La Celestina*, was born sometime in the fifteenth century in the town of Puebla de Montalbán near Toledo, Spain. As far as we know, *La Celestina* is the only book that Rojas ever wrote, and few details of his life have ever come to light. What is known is that he was a lawyer by trade educated at the prestigious University of Salamanca and that he belonged to a noble family of Conversos, or Jews who adopted Christianity. The genesis of *The Celestina* also carries with it an air of mystery. According to Rojas, he came across the first act, entitled *The Comedy of Calisto and Melibea,* while in Salamanca. This first act had supposedly been penned by an anonymous author. Rojas found himself so enchanted with the work that he decided to expand and complete it during a two-week vacation from practicing law. From the nucleus first act was born a drama about two young lovers who take a popular ideal of love in Rojas's era to an extreme that bears tragic consequences for themselves and those around them.

Events in History at the Time of the Play

The conflictive age. *The Tragicomedy of Calisto and Melibea* was born during a period of alteration, change, and ultimately, disharmony in Spain—one that the great scholar Américo Castro dubbed "the conflictive age." If we take the date of the first known edition of *La Celestina* (1499) as our vantage point, less than a decade had passed since the landmark year of 1492.

THE LITERARY WORK

A play set in Spain at the end of the fifteenth century; published in Spanish (as *Tragicomedia de Calisto y Melibea*) in 1499; in English (as *The Spanish Bawd*) in 1631.

SYNOPSIS

Having been rejected by Melibea, the daughter of a local nobleman, Calisto enlists the aid of the local witch and procuress Celestina in hopes of seducing the damsel.

Christopher Columbus's historic voyage to the Americas that year marked the encounter that launched sustained contact between two vastly different worlds. The implications of his "discovery," however, were largely unknown to the inhabitants of the Iberian Peninsula until many years later. Two other events of 1492 would profoundly alter the nature of Spanish society and shape the lives of Spain's people in a much more immediate way for the years to come: the capture of Granada and the expulsion of the Spanish Jews.

The capture of Granada and the expulsion of the Jews. The capture of Granada and the surrender of the city by its last Moorish king, Boabdil (or Muhammad XI), took place on January 2, 1492, capping off the long process that was known as the "Reconquest," the gradual military subjugation by the Christian kingdoms of those

Detail by Rodrigo Alman of the choir stalls of the cathedral of Toledo, illustrating the conquest of Granada.

areas of the peninsula that had been under Muslim domination since the eighth century. Granada was the last stronghold of Muslim power on the Iberian Peninsula, a power that had been steadily shrinking throughout the previous centuries. With the capitulation of Granada, Spain would no longer be a territory divided between Christian and Muslim kingdoms, but a union of kingdoms under the Catholic monarchs Ferdinand and Isabella, one that was free to expand its territories beyond the geographical limits of the peninsula.

Political unity, however, did not imply social unity. Less than three months after Granada's fall, on March 31, 1492, the edict of the expulsion of the Jews was promulgated. Prior to that point, Spain had been a multi-religious culture made up of Christians, Muslims, and Jews. With the edict, all Spanish citizens of Jewish ancestry who had not converted to Christianity were given a choice: either accept baptism or leave immediately. Some chose to convert and remained, while possibly as many as 50,000 abandoned Spain for places such as Portugal, North Africa, or Italy (Kamen, p. 42). Those who stayed behind suffered the fate of being objects of suspicion as to the sincerity of their conversion, an allegation leveled at the family of Fernando de Rojas. Spain's Muslim inhabitants, while not forced to

convert, would also become the center of much controversy and struggle in the years following 1492.

With these two events, several centuries of tense coexistence and struggle between the three main social groups of the peninsula—Christians, Jews, and Muslims—had finally been resolved in favor of one of them. Yet despite the project of incorporation of the diverse elements under one polity that Ferdinand and Isabella initiated, these actions by no means resulted in a harmonious and uniform nation. Instead, Spanish society contended against itself on multiple levels. Conversos (the group to which Fernando de Rojas belonged) not only lived under continual suspicion of insincere conversion but also under the suspicion of being subversives who practiced Judaism in secret. Tensions were aggravated by many Conversos' holding positions of power and influence in society, which won them the resentment of other Spaniards. Other conflicts involved the Mudejars (Spanish Muslims in conquered territories), who refused to be assimilated. So did the Moriscos (Christians of Moorish descent), a situation that would end in their expulsion little more than a century later. Still other conflicts included a Castilian agricultural class that resented the intellectuals and the rising merchant class. The newly united monarchy was meanwhile in perpetual struggle with long established noble families for control of lands under their dominion. Through the Inquisition, the tribunal established to suppress deviation from the teachings of the Roman Catholic Church, a sector of ecclesiastical authority fought against radical sects and sought to unmask those who secretly practiced Judaism. In short, *La Celestina* was born in a time of turmoil, a period of often internalized strife reflected in the opening lines of the play's prologue: "The great sage Heraclitus states . . . that all things are the result of conflict and contention" (Rojas, *La Celestina*, p. 15).

Marriage and love. If there is one central theme that can be found in *La Celestina*, it most certainly is love. Fernando de Rojas, in the introductory epistle "The Author to a Friend of His," says that one of the reasons he felt it was necessary to write *La Celestina* was "because of the multitude of youths and gallants in love" that abounded in the Spain of his time, and in particular for his unnamed friend whom he had witnessed in his youth "caught up by love and cruelly wounded by it for lack of defenses against the fires of passion" (*La Celestina*, p. 10).

Because of its theme and tragic ending, *La Celestina* has often invited comparison with Shakespeare's *Romeo and Juliet* (first performed a century later in 1595). There are, however, fundamental differences in the way love is approached in Rojas's tragedy. Indeed *La Celestina* is not a tale of two lovers threatened by hostile forces conspiring to keep them apart, such as the warring families found in the Verona of *Romeo and Juliet*. Rather, Calisto and Melibea came from noble families with no grudge between them, so there is no apparent impediment to the young suitor's asking for and receiving the hand of the damsel. Nor is there any secret marriage on the part of the lovers that would have legitimized it in the eyes of the Church, for it seems that neither of the two was interested in marriage. Calisto and Melibea are focused instead on a desperate, all-consuming worship of the other. For Rojas, such an attitude is idolatrous, and as such would make a mockery out of marriage, whose purpose was the building of a family, a view that both of the lovers recognize. Hence Melibea explains to her servant Lucrecia, "I want no husband, I do not care to sully the bonds of matrimony nor to follow the marital steps of another man, as I find in books that I have read that there are many women who have done this, and they were more discreet than I and of higher rank and station" (*La Celestina*, p. 199).

Medieval and Renaissance culture distinguished between different types of love, though as a rule physical love was divided into two categories: licit and lascivious. The type of bodily love that was considered licit, and therefore sanctioned by the Church, was that which found its expression within the bonds of matrimony and was centered on bringing children into the world. Any other physical passion was deemed to be unhealthy and a violation of God's design: a rupture of divine law and an offense against family honor. There was, however, another kind of love that became very accepted in elite circles and that seemed to straddle the dividing line between the lawful and the illicit, the spiritual and the sensual; scholars have generally referred to this other variety as "courtly love."

While it is difficult to pinpoint the exact origins of courtly love, suffice it to say that its influence spread throughout Europe, thanks to the popularity of the troubadour poetry that flourished in Provence, in southern France, during the twelfth century. In short, courtly love was an application of the highly ritualized rules of chivalry to relationships between men and women, and the name "courtly" was applied to it because this sort of behavior evolved in the courts of European royalty. By the time *La Celestina* was written, this practice had acquired certain standard characteristics. At its foundation was the ideal of the lover who aspired only to please a beloved whom he idealized to the point of adoration. Courtly love thus demanded that the gallant—a knight or other nobleman—undergo tribulations so as to merit the attention of the woman, of whom he considered himself to be totally unworthy. This ritual took place outside the bonds of marriage, and the woman was normally meant to be unattainable, more often than not the wife of another nobleman, who, if her admirer were successful, would grant him some token of her recognition, perhaps a kerchief or an article of clothing. Ideally, such a gift would then suffice as a sign of the chaste love between the two, with no other physical expression necessary, though in practice this was often not the case.

The custom of courtly love was widely embraced as an ideal by elite classes, in large part because of its portrayal in popular knightly fiction. At the same time, though in principle courtly love was not meant to lead to physical consummation, it was often criticized for being impossible to achieve in practice and for leading to adultery. This criticism had already found its way into literature, perhaps most notably in the

Italian poet Dante Alighieri's *Inferno* (1307-14), a book widely read in the Spain of Fernando de Rojas.

In Dante's *Inferno* the desires of two lovers, Paolo and Francesca, are excited by reading the legend of the love affair between England's Sir Lancelot and Queen Guinevere. They give in to a passion whose flames have been fanned by the chivalric romance, then die at the hands of Francesca's husband who catches them in the act of adultery. Like Calisto and Melibea, Dante's lovers are condemned because they die unrepentant for their sins, which Dante refers to as having "lost the good of the intellect" (*Inferno*, 3.18); similarly, Rojas's lovers are condemned because they have abandoned themselves to "runaway desires, uncontrolled by reason" (*La Celestina*, p. 124). Rojas's drama resembles the *Inferno* in that it is a warning regarding the excesses to which a concept of love reduced to desire and fantasy could lead: Calisto's suffering, Melibea's gift to him of her girdle, and their idealization of each other in some ways also follow the pattern laid down by the popular ideal of courtly love. Nevertheless, it would be simplistic to assume that Rojas merely wished to write an attack on courtly love (the term is never mentioned in *La Celestina*). Rather, like Dante, the author cautions against a love attuned not to God's will and the eternal good, but rather to the momentary satisfaction of the lovers.

In *La Celestina*, Rojas portrays both his male and female characters as universally corrupt and conniving; they resort to sordid tactics in the name of love. His play attempts to discredit the myth of the humble and chaste suitor and the idealized woman common to the popular literature of his time. By deglamorizing his protagonists and portraying the tragic outcome of their passion, the author of *La Celestina* seeks to demonstrate the falsity of the ideal that such literature presented to young people who read it. Thus, Rojas not only weaves a tale containing many of the hallmarks of courtly love, but also warns against its excesses and its dangers.

The Play in Focus

Plot summary. *La Celestina* is written in the form of a play in 16 acts, the first of which is considerably longer than the 15 that follow, and represents the original anonymous work that Rojas expanded upon.

The drama begins when Calisto enters a garden in pursuit of a falcon. There he meets Me-

libea and immediately becomes infatuated with her. He begins to flatter the girl and is rebuked by her. In the next scene, Calisto calls his servant Sempronio and bids him prepare the bedroom into which he hurriedly takes refuge. Calisto is obsessed by his meeting with Melibea, an obsession that scandalizes Sempronio, who protests that his master is not acting as a Christian by allowing the thought of Melibea and his frustration at her rejection to consume him. Calisto then responds with one of the most unforgettable lines of the whole drama: "I'm a Melibean! Melibea is the one whom I worship, the one in whom I believe, the one whom I love" (*La Celestina*, p. 24). After trying to deter Calisto from giving in to his obsession with Melibea, Sempronio begins to waver when Calisto offers to bribe him into helping him obtain Melibea. Eventually Sempronio's greed gets the better of him (though he makes the excuse that he does not wish to see his master in desperation), and he recommends the services of Celestina: an old hag schooled in the black arts and in prostitution. Calisto accepts the offer eagerly and sends Sempronio on his way to find Celestina. When he arrives, Sempronio's lover, Elicia, a prostitute who works for Celestina, is catering to a client. Celestina is there, however, and instructs Elicia to hide her client and to shower Sempronio with false affection so that he will not suspect anything. The ruse works, and the hypocritical Sempronio brings Celestina to Calisto's house. Pármeno, another servant of Calisto, opens the door and recognizes the old woman, who had been a friend of his mother. Pármeno warns Calisto against the malignancy of the old woman, but she overcomes Pármeno's opposition by offering him the love of one of her girls, Areúsa. Celestina then offers to help Calisto ensnare Melibea. With the deal made, she returns home to conjure the spirits of the underworld to aid in her endeavor.

When she goes on her errand to the house of Melibea, Celestina is greeted by the servant Lucrecia, a cousin of Elicia, and manages to reach Melibea and her mother, Alisa, under the charade of selling bread. The cautious mother, Alisa, is called away unexpectedly and Celestina is left alone with the young noblewoman. Appealing to Melibea's compassionate nature, Celestina tells her that she is there at the request of an ill person who can be saved by Melibea. Upon hearing it revealed that the sick man is Calisto, Melibea hurls a chain of invectives at Celestina, but the old woman is much too sly to let herself be defeated so easily. She invents a story that Calisto has a severe toothache and merely wishes to have Melibea write a prayer for him and to send him her sash, which is said "to have touched the holy relics in Rome and Jerusalem" (*La Celestina*, p. 76). Celestina's deception overcomes the girl's protestations, and not only does Melibea agree to send her girdle to Calisto, but she invites the procuress to come back in secret the next day so that she may collect the prayer without being noticed by Melibea's mother. The stage has now been set for the tragedy to unfold.

With her objective achieved, Celestina returns to Calisto's house and finds Sempronio there. In speaking with her, Sempronio's greed and jealousy are ignited when he begins to realize that Celestina is being paid well for her services and that he himself will not be receiving the remuneration he thinks he deserves. Both he and Pármeno conspire to take advantage of Calisto's distraction and embezzle his wealth. Calisto, oblivious to everything but his infatuation with Melibea, is elated at Celestina's success and urges her to carry on with her scheme.

Celestina returns to Melibea's house, where the maiden, who confesses to the old woman that she was smitten with Calisto from the first moment she saw him, struggles between her passion and her conscience, her desire for Calisto, and her knowledge that theirs is an affair that will bring neither honor nor happiness to her family. She nevertheless agrees to a secret rendezvous the following evening. Celestina returns to Calisto with the news, and he pays her with the gold chain that he wears around his neck. Upon learning of this reward, Sempronio and Pármeno decide to demand from Celestina a share of the payment.

When the two lovers finally meet again, Melibea feigns an attempt at dissuading Calisto from his infatuation. His protestations, however, convince her to set another tryst for the following night. In the meantime, Calisto's two servants approach Celestina to coerce her into sharing her profits with them. She tries to outwit them, but succeeds only in provoking the two men into killing her, which initiates a chain of deaths that will blight the rest of the story.

The next day Calisto awakens to discover that Pármeno and Sempronio have been executed for the murder of Celestina. He nevertheless decides to go through with meeting Melibea, and brings two other servants, Tristán and Sosia, with him. Upon climbing the walls of Melibea's garden, he finally attains the love he has been seeking and returns home.

Pármeno and Sempronio kill Celestina and then throw themselves from the window as justice approaches; their throats are cut by the executioner. Woodcut from the 1514 Valencia edition of the novel.

What Calisto does not know, however, is that Celestina's prostitutes Elicia and Areúsa have decided to punish him for the murder of Celestina and have persuaded a bully named Centurio to be the instrument of their revenge. Centurio, not sure he can carry out his charge, engages a friend to make some noise that will frighten Calisto's servants the next time the lovers meet.

In each other's arms again the following night, Calisto and Melibea are interrupted by the shouts of Calisto's servants. The young suitor decides to come to their aid, but in his haste Calisto falls from the ladder by which he entered Melibea's home and he dies. Melibea, crazed and in desperation, climbs to the top of a tower on her property, and after having confessed to her father, Pleberio, the affair she has hidden from him, throws herself down. The story ends with Pleberio uttering a long and sorrowful soliloquy in mourning for his daughter and against the illicit passion that caused her death.

Magic, religion, and unbelief. The figure that binds together the plot of the *Tragicomedy of Calisto and Melibea* is Celestina: a go-between, a procuress of prostitutes, and a sorceress. Indeed, Celestina's use of the black arts is an integral part of the story that expedites the consummation of the two young lovers' passionate impulses. She makes her living in part by conjuring spirits and using spells to bring the desires of her clients to fruition. It is this talent that brings her celebrity and also places her on the margins of society. While *La Celestina* is a work of fiction, magic and sorcery were acknowledged as realities during the time that the work was written. Otis Green, in his *Spain and the Western Tradition*, notes that the practice of lovers seeking out sorceresses to satisfy their desires was known and condemned by the Church (Green, p. 116). Indeed, one of the responsibilities of the Spanish Inquisition was to find and prosecute those involved in the exercise of magic.

MAGIC AND SORCERY AT THE TIME OF *LA CELESTINA*

Just as belief in God was universal in the Middle Ages and the Renaissance, so was the belief in evil spirits. Though it is not clear how widespread the use of sorcery was, the practice of resorting to spells and the aid of demonic powers in an attempt to achieve one's desires was recognized to exist and was condemned repeatedly by civil and ecclesiastical authorities. Celestina, though herself a fictional character, is modeled after witches of whom Fernando de Rojas most likely knew. Thanks to records from the Inquisition of Toledo, we know that during Rojas's time there were thought to be in use a large number of spells and incantations for the secret conquest of a lover, spells that often made use of herbs, potions, animal or human body parts, wax figurines, or amulets. Those accused of using or trafficking in such spells could be put on trial for heresy or apostasy—hence Celestina's fear at being caught by the authorities while she carries out her charges. At a special conference in 1526, after the time of the play, Spain's inquisitors would conclude that witchcraft was "little more than a delusion" and persecution for witchcraft would diminish in Spain (Kamen, p. 186). By the time the play was written, the Inquisition had outlawed persecution for witchcraft and authorities were trying only to squelch minor superstitions and the use of love potions and spells.

Nevertheless, within the plot of *La Celestina*, magic serves not as a source of tension in the plot, but rather as an expedient. The true source of dramatic tension lies elsewhere: "I believe in her as God, I confess her as God, and I do not believe that there is any higher power in heaven, even though she dwells among us here below" (*La Celestina*, p. 26). This cry of adoration that Calisto utters regarding Melibea encapsulates one of the central struggles of *La Celestina* and its times: that between religion and unbelief.

Two mindsets help explain common attitudes toward religion in the age in which *La Celestina* was born: the medieval mentality and that of Renaissance humanism. In early-sixteenth-century Spain, while the outlook of the European Middle Ages still took precedence, the ideals of the Renaissance that had been born in Italy were beginning to exert an ever stronger presence.

In terms of its worldview, the Middle Ages saw religiosity as coinciding with all aspects of life. People considered God to be the center of all activity, a world view that explains dramatically contradictory phenomena: the exaltation of man as brother, for example, and the attempt to bend his will by violence (the Inquisition). God, according to the medieval world view, had to do with everything. A reader during the time of the publication of *La Celestina* would not be shocked to read that Calisto goes into a church and calls upon St. Mary Magdalene to help him seduce Melibea, even though he or she would probably note the contradiction inherent to the action. On the other hand, the fact that Sempronio deems his master's worship of Melibea and consequent denial of Christ to be scandalous is in keeping with the tenor of the time, in which "there is not an object or an action, however trivial, that is not constantly correlated with Christ or salvation" (Huizinga, p. 151).

Yet the Spain of 1499 was also a Spain that had begun to see the influence of the Renaissance. In the fifteenth century, the winds of this new way of viewing the world began to blow through Spain and inspire its lettered classes. Whereas for the medieval person the goal of one's life was to aspire to heaven, under the influence of newly rediscovered classical texts, Renaissance humanists began to aspire to fame and honor in earthly endeavors such as art, warfare, and learning. They attempted also to harmonize conflicting ideals such as those of the pagan antiquity with Christianity. The humanists looked for inspiration to the pre-Christian writers of classical Greece and Rome. With their appreciation of Greek and Roman art came a new admiration for the beauty of the human form and a glorification of youth as its exaltation. At the same time, life on earth began to be seen as a series of opportunities for glory and pleasure, and its brevity as an experience of bitterness. "Gather from your joyful springtime," wrote Garcilaso de la Vega (1503-36) in Sonnet 23, "the sweet fruit, before fierce time / covers its lovely summit with snow" (Garcilaso in Rivers, pp. 37-38; trans. D. Bacich). Hence, though society in general retained a strong religious spirit, a split began to be regarded between earthly and spiritual matters. Heaven and eternity began to be felt as distant ideals that had less and less to do with the glory to be achieved on this earth. Melibea herself echoes this tension between the present and eternity when speaking of her desire for Calisto: "When I think of him I am happy, when I see him I rejoice, when I hear his voice I am glorified. . . . I have no other regret than the time that I wasted when I did not enjoy him, when I did not know him—after I have come to know myself" (*La Celestina*, p. 199).

Sources and literary context. Though the *Tragicomedy of Calisto and Melibea* is striking in its originality, scholars such as María Rosa Lida de Malkiel have pointed out some main antecedents to the play: Greco-Roman comedies, medieval theater, and the humanistic comedies of Italy.

To begin with, Rojas himself tells us that he considers the anonymous first act to be a "Terencian work," thus revealing something about its literary ancestry. Terence was one of the masters of Roman comedy in antiquity, together with Plautus, and both of them wrote plays from which certain external characteristics of *La Celestina* were drawn. Roman comedies, however, though they often dwelt on matters of love in developing their plots, almost never deemed it a topic worthy of serious consideration. *Elegiac comedies*, another source of inspiration that Rojas probably drew on, were works usually in Latin and popular around the twelfth century, with less complex plots and a less uniform structure than their classical counterparts. What really set elegiac theater apart from classical Roman comedy and brought it closer to what Rojas would eventually do with *La Celestina* was its serious treatment of love. Most elegiac comedies centered on a story of illicit love, a struggle between passion and duty, often with a courtly ideal at its base, features that would reappear in *La Celestina*. In addition to elegiac comedies, the medieval world also produced mystery plays, or *autos sacramentales* as they were known in Spain. Usually the autos narrated biblical episodes such as the Flight into Egypt or the Slaughter of the Holy Innocents, or else told morality stories with the help of allegorical figures, personifications of

abstract concepts such as Virtue or Vice. Such works were extremely popular with audiences in Spain at least until the end of the seventeenth century, and often were written by famous authors such as Calderón de la Barca. *La Celestina*'s didactic purpose in warning against the perils of passion unguided by reason and faith inherits this tradition of teaching through theater.

TRAGEDY OR COMEDY?

In the European Middle Ages *comedy* meant simply a story with a happy ending and not necessarily a work meant to be amusing (think of Dante's *Divine Comedy*). *Tragedy* generally referred to the story of someone of high estate brought down to desolation as a consequence of personal actions. Such a conception differed from the classical idea of tragedy, whereby the great (either gods or heroes), whether prompted by ignorance, by their own will, or by outside circumstances, were destroyed by an inescapable fate. Fernando de Rojas decided to label his work a *tragic-comedy* because the first act dealt with the pleasure of the protagonists, while the drama ultimately ended in sadness.

Humanistic comedy, another form of theater with which Rojas was familiar, first appeared in Italy in the fourteenth century and soon spread to Spain. Like elegiac theater, humanistic comedy treated love quite seriously, but prided itself on more complicated plots, on the richness and diversity of its settings, and on its rejection of formulaic structures.

A careful reading of *La Celestina* reveals that Fernando de Rojas drew on a vast reservoir of dramatic tradition in order to create the tragicomedy: stock characters from Roman comedy, serious treatment of the tension between passion and reason from elegiac theater, moral admonition from the mystery plays, realism as well as variety in the number of different settings and locations from the humanistic comedies.

Composition and reception. A complex piece of theater, *La Celestina* was never, according to María Rosa Lida de Malkiel, meant to be presented on stage. "It was written for recitation," explains Lida de Malkiel, "as can be inferred from the Prologue and from a stanza that urges that it be read expressively, modulating the voice to set off the differences of emotion and of character"

(Lida de Malkiel, p. 67). Nevertheless, from the moment of its appearance, *La Celestina* proved extremely popular, as shown by the number of its reprintings and translations as well as the numerous imitations it spawned. Many writers in the sixteenth and seventeenth centuries, including Miguel de Cervantes and Lope de Vega (see **Don Quixote** and **Fuente Ovejuna,** also in *WLAIT 5: Spanish and Portuguese Literatures and Their Times*), praised it both for its artistic merit as well as its didactic value. Indeed, Rojas did not hide the fact that his intention was to follow the dictum laid down by the Roman author Horace: to teach while giving delight. In the verses that accompany the prologue to *La Celestina*, Rojas compares his work to a bitter pill, which in order to be made easier to swallow, is coated in sugar, thereby causing the body to recover its health. In other words, whereas the plot, the characters, and their intrigues captivate the reader, the tragic end illustrates the bitter lesson—an ideal love that makes an idol, or object of worship, out of another mortal can only lead to dire consequences.

Nevertheless, the work was not without its critics, who reproached its author for giving too much delight while not teaching enough. Some, such as Juan Luis Vives, while recognizing that the tragic end of the protagonists represents a condemnation of their excessive passion, reprimanded Rojas for being frivolous by portraying their lasciviousness with too much zeal. Others criticized the play for not balancing its representation of vice with a sufficient representation of virtue, charging that the very youths it was meant to instruct focused on its titillating aspects to the exclusion of its moral lessons. Such a charge points to the extreme popularity that *La Celestina* had achieved by the end of the sixteenth century. In fact, the ambivalent opinions that many in Castile held regarding *La Celestina* were exemplified by its eventual censorship by the Inquisition in 1640. While not deeming the book deserving of outright prohibition, the Inquisition expunged several of its passages that were considered dangerous for impressionable readers. Specifically it expunged those passages in which Calisto pronounces himself a "Melibean," rejecting Christ and his church—ironically Rojas had used these passages to warn against the extremes to which the courtly ideal could lead.

—Damian Bacich

For More Information

Castro, Américo. *The Spaniards: An Introduction to Their History.* Trans. Willard F. King and Selma Margaretten. Berkeley: University of California Press, 1971.

Culianu, Ioan. *Eros and Magic in the Renaissance.* Chicago: University of Chicago, 1984.

Dante Alighieri. *The Divine Comedy: Cantica I Inferno.* Trans. Dorothy Sayers. London: Penguin, 1955.

Gilman, Steven. *The Spain of Fernando de Rojas: The Intellectual and Social Landscape of La Celestina.* Princeton: Princeton University Press, 1972.

Green, Otis H. *Spain and the Western Tradition: The Castilian Mind in Literature from* El Cid *to* Calderón. Madison: University of Wisconsin Press, 1968.

Huizinga, Johan. *The Waning of the Middle Ages.* New York: Anchor, 1954.

Kamen, Henry. *Spain 1469-1714: A Society of Conflict.* 2d ed. London: Longman, 1991.

Lewis, C. S. *The Allegory of Love: A Study in Medieval Tradition.* London: Oxford, 1938.

Lida de Malkiel, María Rosa. *Two Spanish Masterpieces: The Book of Good Love and The Celestina.* Urbana: University of Illinois Press, 1961.

MacKay, Angus. *Spain in the Middle Ages: From Frontier to Empire, 1000-1500.* London: Macmillan, 1977.

Rivers, Elias, ed. *Renaissance and Baroque Poetry of Spain.* New York: Dell, 1966.

Rojas, Fernando de. *La Celestina: Tragicomedy of Calisto and Melibea.* Trans. Wallace Woolsey. New York: Las Americas Publishing Company, 1969.

"The Dark Night" and Other Poems

by
Saint John of the Cross

Juan de Yepes y Alvarez, Saint John of the Cross's original name, was born in 1542 in Fontiveros, a village in the heartland of Castile, between Avila and Salamanca. A few years after his birth, his father, Gonzalo de Yepes, who barely made a living as a weaver, died of a lingering illness, leaving a widow and three sons in deeper poverty. For many years to come, Juan's mother, Catalina Alvarez, worked at the loom to support her family. During his adolescence the family moved in 1551 to Medina del Campo, a larger, somewhat prosperous town nearby. Juan was apprenticed, in turns, to a painter, carpenter, and tailor, and was soon returned as useless by all of them. He then volunteered his services at a hospital—el Hospital de las Bubas—where advanced cases of syphilis were treated free of charge. Most of his days were spent under rigorous schedules, but he got time off to pursue his first real education at a newly founded Jesuit school. Evidently an exceptionally good student, he learned Latin well, and remained at the school until he reached 21. Upon leaving, he was offered the chaplaincy of the hospital, but instead chose to take vows and lead a solitary life as a Carmelite friar under the name Fray Juan de San Matías. In 1564 Fray Juan went to the University of Salamanca, where he remained for four years, during which he had a momentous meeting. In 1567 Juan de San Matías met Teresa de Jesús (1515-82), then beginning her mission to reform the Carmelite order. Teresa asked the young friar for his help and Juan took vows in 1568, changing his name to

THE LITERARY WORK

Four poems set in Spain in the late 1500s; published in Spanish (as "El Ascenso al Monte Carmelo," "Noche oscura," Cántico Espiritual," and "¡Oh Llama de amor viva!") in 1618; in English in 1864.

SYNOPSIS

The four poems—"The Ascent of Mount Carmel," "The Dark Night," "The Spiritual Canticle," and "Oh Living Flame of Love!"—are a religious allegory of love through the mystical union between the soul of the poet and God.

Juan de la Cruz. During his career in the order, Juan wrote three poems considered matchless in mystical literature—"The Dark Night," "The Spiritual Canticle," and "Oh Living Flame of Love!" He penned prose as well, including commentaries on these three poems, and adapted songs into religious verse. In terms of quantity, Juan's output was limited; altogether he is thought to have composed fewer than 1,000 lines. All his works, moreover, concern one topic—the soul's journey toward perfect union with God. The poems, however, remains open to more mundane interpretations too. This artfulness lies in their wording, a product of both an extraordinary imagination and a tumultuous spiritual epoch.

Saint John of the Cross

Events in History at the Time the Poems Take Place

The Reformation. By the beginning of the sixteenth century, the Catholic Church, modeled on the bureaucratic structure of the Holy Roman Empire, had become extremely powerful but internally corrupt. From early in the twelfth century onward there were calls for reform. Between 1215 and 1545 nine Church councils were held devoted primarily to Church reform. The councils, despite their conciliatory intent, all failed to reach significant accord. Members of the clergy found themselves unable to live in keeping with Church doctrine because of an overemphasis on ceremonies and ritual.

In the first half of the sixteenth century, western Europe experienced a wide range of social, artistic, and geopolitical changes that can be traced back to a conflict within the Catholic Church. The basic conflict became known as the Protestant Reformation, and the Catholic response as the Counter Reformation. Igniting the conflict, in 1517 a German Augustinian friar named Martin Luther (1483-1546) posted on the door of All Saints Church in Wittenberg, Germany, a list of grievances, called the Ninety-five

Theses, against the Roman Catholic Church. So began the Reformation movement.

The Ninety-Five Theses were centered around a call to eliminate the sale of indulgences, absolution of part of the temporal penalty for a sin in exchange for money. Fulfilling the penalty was part of a sacrament—the sacrament of penance. Indulgences would be granted on the authority of the pope and made accessible to the people through his agents. Outraged, the Church demanded that Luther retract a number of his protests. He refused, whereupon the authorities summoned him to an imperial diet, or general assembly, in Augsburg in 1518. There normally would have been swift retribution for his crime, but the election of a new emperor, Charles V (1500-58), slowed the justice system. In the interim, Luther used his time to plan a complete reform program for the church. His proposals included:

1. National, rather than Roman, control of church finances
2. Permission for the clergy to marry
3. A series of sacramental reforms that would reduce the sacraments to Baptism, a reformed Mass, and the Holy Eucharist

Within the Roman Catholic Church, a series of powerful popes, including Leo X and Paul III, responded to the demand for reforms in various ways. Mendicant orders, such as the Jesuits, sprang into existence to reinforce the basic Catholic doctrine, while the Church, as it then existed, continued to receive support from major European monarchies, though England, for one, balked at the control and broke from it. Ultimately the Reformation created a mostly north-south split in Europe. In general, countries in the northern part of different regions became Protestant while those in the southern part remained Catholic.

The Reformation and art. Protestant reformers rejected the use of visual arts in the church, unleashing a wave of iconoclastic demonstrations in the North. Stained glass windows were broken, images of the saints were destroyed, and pipe organs removed from churches. In response to the iconoclasm, the Catholic churches promoted an exuberant style of art and architecture known as the baroque, which flowered in ideological opposition to Protestant severity. Not until the Neoclassical movement of the eighteenth century would there be an effective attempt to resolve this dichotomy. The theatrical designs of Saint Peter's in Rome became a triumphant symbol of the Roman Catholic Church's belief in itself and its history. In contrast, the plain churches of the north stood as staunch reminders of Protestant beliefs.

Due to the recent invention of the printing press (credited to Johannes Gutenberg around 1450), Luther's reforms spread quickly through Europe, attracting much support. Luther, however, was condemned as a heretic by Pope Leo X in the Edict of Worms (1521). Forced to escape, he had to live for a year in hiding, but his reforms nevertheless took root. The split in the Roman Church proved irreconcilable.

Europe divided. The Low Countries, which are today called Belgium and the Netherlands, had long been under the rule of the Spanish Habsburgs. In 1517 Luther's reforms would split the Low Countries. The southern part, Belgium, would remain strongly Catholic while the northern part, the Netherlands, adopted Protestant reforms, with the region's Dutch Calvinists rebelling against the Catholic Habsburg rule.

Although the Catholic's Holy Roman Empire would not dissolve until 1806, German states (Bradenburg, Prussia, Silesia, Saxony) were irrevocably separated from the influence of Rome. The princes in the northern German states protected Luther from both the pope and the Holy Roman emperor, meanwhile gaining political power by assuming many of the privileges once reserved for the church. In 1555, the Peace of Augsburg temporarily reconciled the Protestant north and the Catholic south in the German states, and the conflict moved west into the monarchies of Spain and France.

The Spanish Habsburgs and the French Valois came to an uneasy truce in 1559. The two monarchies were strongly Catholic, and both realized that only together could they hope to quell any Protestant uprisings. Their accord interrupted a string of Protestant-related threats to the hegemony of the Catholic monarchs. Once the Reformation was underway, the common people perceived it as a means of social empowerment. The peasant class sensed the potential for gaining secular freedoms through the movement. Raging through Germany, the Peasants War (1524-25) was a response to Luther's urgings for democratic reform in the Church and a reaction to an unbalanced social system in which nobles and the Church did not pay taxes while others did. Luther, initially sympathetic to the peasants, grew appalled by the war and angrily addressed the warring faction in his pamphlet, *Against the Thieving and Murderous Gangs of Peasants*. To Luther the sectarian groups represented an at-

tempt not at spiritual elevation, but at an easy redemption, that is, absolution without punishment. The social revolt had unfortunate consequences for Luther's reformation. The reformers objected to the humanist view that human beings might be brought to higher spirituality through education and innate ability. Instead the Reformers subscribed to the concept of man's embodiment of original sin and his incontestable need for redemption and the Grace of God.

Luther's Protestantism by and large cleaned up the Church of the decadent accouterments that had characterized Christianity in western and central Europe, but as time passed the uglier specter of an ill-tempered iconoclasm began to emerge. Reformers more extreme than Luther started to make further demands for change. Among these reformers was the scholar Ulrich Zwingli in Switzerland. Moving beyond the usual objections to the discrepancies between biblical teachings and Church practice, Zwingli wanted all ritual abolished from the Catholic Church. No imagery was acceptable to him, not the crucifix, the bishop's crozier, the chalice of the holy wine, clerical vestments, nor organ music.

Counter Reformation. The response of the Roman Catholic Church to the reformers' demands was the Counter Reformation. Founded by Ignatius of Loyola in 1534, the Jesuits aggressively led a campaign to support Catholic doctrine. Members of the order acted behind the scenes in the Catholic monarchies, exercising a strong influence in political spheres. Jesuit priests often served as confessors to major political leaders, for instance. Such Counter Reformation forces generally upheld papal authority and ensured that canonization and veneration of saints remained a cornerstone of celebratory ritual. Though they objected to overemphasis on ceremony and ritual, they also encouraged the visual grandeur of churches, and generously financed it to the end.

Holy Roman Emperor Charles V (1500-58) prompted the papal curia, or central administration governing the Church, to convene to resolve internal disputes, and after many delays a council did convene in Trent in December of 1545. The council addressed three basic issues. First, they clarified doctrinal points of discussion in order to quiet internal disputes. Second, they decided to definitively solve the problem of ecclesiastical abuses among the clergy. The third issue concerned the initiation of a crusade against the infidels. Pope Paul III (1468-1549) hoped to get widespread approval to condemn the Protestant heresy, and thereby gain support for a suppression of the reformers by force. In the end, the Council of Trent withheld this support, instead reasserting papal authority and simply presenting a united front against the Protestants. The Church had at last proved itself capable of action, and of reinforcing its version of the orthodox faith.

In the second half of the sixteenth century the theological conflict became a political power struggle. By the death of Martin Luther in 1546 and of John Calvin in 1564, the major developments of the Reformation were over. The Protestant movement had split into a number of sectarian churches, and no more great Protestant reformers would come to the fore. Ignatius of Loyola died in 1556 and the Council of Trent ended in 1563, events that brought the Counter Reformation to a theological halt. But all the tumult stirred responses in clergy and lay people alike. In response to the religious fervor, there was in Spain an explosion of spiritual writers, among them the greatest mystical poets of the Western tradition. Spanish mysticism peaked during the spread of the Renaissance (the sixteenth century in Spain). Evidence of this mysticism can be found in the masterpieces of Saint John's contemporaries: Fray Luis de Granada, Beato Orozco, Juan de Avila, Malón de Echaide, Fray Luis de León, and Santa Teresa (see *The Interior Castle*, also in *WLAIT 5: Spanish and Portuguese Literatures and Their Times*).

CARMELITE REFORM

St. Teresa strove to restore the austerity and contemplative character of basic life in the Carmelite order, that is the order of Our Lady of Mount Carmel. A major element of Teresa's reform was her emphasis on internal devotion as opposed to external ritual. In 1562 she founded a small convent in Avila, where a strict discipline of prayers, solitude, poverty, and contemplation were to be observed. In spite of difficulties of all kinds, she succeeded in establishing not only nunneries but also a number of friaries of this stricter observance. Observers of her reforms wore sandals in place of shoes and stockings, which led to their being called the Discalced or Barefoot Carmelites, a label that distinguished them from the older branch of the order.

Spanish mysticism. The word "mystical" derives from Greek mystery religions, which were characterized by initiation rites at the threshold to the inner knowledge of the divine. Through these rites, the adherent sought admission to a secret.

> I understand it [mysticism] to be the expression of the innate tendency of the human spirit towards complete harmony with the transcendental order; whatever be the theological formula under which that order is understood. This tendency, in great mystics, gradually captures the whole field of consciousness; it dominates their life and, in the experience called "mystic union," attains its end.
>
> (Underhill, p. xxi)

Saint John was a mystical poet in that his poems were written as a result of mystical knowledge.

To summarize briefly, according to Catholic theology, the soul may reach union with God when an individual goes through three basic stages: 1. *vía purgativa;* 2. *vía iluminativa;* and 3. *vía unitiva.* In the first, purgative stage, the body is regarded as the prison of the soul, and the individual escapes the limitation of human senses through discipline and will. Through the annihilation of the self, the soul attempts to reach the place of origin, which is next to God. In the second, illuminative stage, the soul sees and feels the presence of God. Finally, in the third stage, union, the soul becomes one with God—it moves towards God as God moves towards it. Conceived of as the *esposa,* or bride, the soul is consumed in perfect love as it joins in spiritual matrimony with the Beloved–*esposo,* or husband. Searching as well as physical and emotional pain characterize these three steps, until by journeying through the great light of faith, the soul rises into ecstasy, union, and oblivion. A fourth stage is sometimes added, consisting of the peace and beatitude that follow the union.

In the Iberian Peninsula, the best-known ascetics/mystics were important writers as well as religious figures. A tradition of mystical poetry in Spain harks back to the Middle Ages, when the most prominent and influential poet was Raimundo Lulio (1233-1315), known as the "Illuminated Doctor." He penned a famous poem, "Cántico del amigo y del amado" (Canticle of Friend and Lover), which parallels Saint John's work in both diction and thought. Lulio was a missionary among the Moors of Spain and North Africa, to whom he preached in Arabic. His Spanish verse and prose show the rich sensual imagery of Arabic poetry, which also surfaces in the writing of Saint John. An example of the Arab influence is the absence of the verb in a series of images:

My Beloved the mountains,
The valleys' solitary groves,
Strange islands
The resounding rivers
The wind whistling love's songs,

The calm night,
At the time of the rising dawn
Silent music,
Sounding solitude
The supper that kindles love and warms
("Spiritual Canticle," stanzas 13-14,
trans. J. Aladro)

Lulio was one of the main ties between Islamic and Christian mysticism in the Iberian Peninsula. In her study of Spanish mystic poetry entitled *San Juan de la Cruz y el Islam*, Luce López-Baralt maintains that, beyond Lulio, there were strong affinities between Spanish and Arabic mystics, in the invocation of colors in their poems, for instance, and of sensuality.

Saint John at work

The Poems in Focus

Contents summary. The corpus of Saint John of the Cross's poetry is relatively modest, yet with only a few poems he reaches the zenith of poetic possibility and expression. The four poems "The Ascent of Mount Carmel," "The Dark Night," "The Spiritual Canticle," and "The Living Flame of Love" are a religious allegory of love achieved through mystical experience between the soul of the poet and God. Saint John's poetry describes his personal journey and the union leading to this mystical experience. In his poetry he does not engage in intellectual attempts to define the nature of God; rather, he addresses God as a person, loved and loving. By humanizing God, Saint John seeks to teach and demonstrate the reality of his presence on earth and to bring about the divinization of the human individual. The final result is transformation, marriage, in which the human becomes divine insofar as possible in this life, a height that requires faith and contemplation. Saint John's poetry and spiritual practice are inseparable.

The Ascent of Mount Carmel. The stanzas of this poem describe the way to climb to the top of this mountain. The mountain itself is the highest state of perfection, the place where the union between the soul and God transpires. Saint John of the Cross used the metaphor of the climber to represent the poet's journey to the top of the moun-

tain in pursuit of the divine light of perfect union with the love of God.

The Dark Night. In these stanzas, Saint John of the Cross deals with the exchange of love between the soul and its bridegroom God, treating certain aspects and effects of prayer. Saint John wrote the poem in response to a request from Mother Ana de Jesus, prioress of the Discalced Carmelite nuns of St. Joseph's in Granada, 1584. In the poem, the dark night is a metaphor for sufferings and trials, as much spiritual as temporal, and for those who through this experience may reach the high state of perfection. The poem teaches the individual how to journey through the dark night.

The Spiritual Canticle. Also dedicated to Ana de Jesus, this poem has as its subtext the Old Testament's book *Song of Songs*, which centers on the mystical wisdom that comes from love. The point is that the songs need not be understood clearly in order to produce positive results and sharpen the soul. The process works in the manner of faith, through which the poet loves God without understanding Him. In other words, one of the fundamental steps in the soul's attaining the height of perfection is to believe the state exists without verifiable evidence, to rely instead on love and faith.

The Living Flame of Love. Written by Saint John of the Cross at the request of Doña Ana de

Peñalosa, the stanzas deal with the most intimate and select union and transformation of the soul in God. The speaker in the poem is the soul, already transformed into God's bride and consumed in perfect love with him. She now shares the inner quality of the fire of love. Not only is she joined to Him in this fire, but this fire makes a living flame in her.

THE LIVING FLAME OF LOVE: SONGS OF THE SOUL IN INTIMATE UNION WITH GOD'S LOVE

O living flame of love
That tenderly wounds my soul
In its deepest center! Since
Now you are not oppressive,
Now Consummate! If it be your will:
Tear through the veil of this sweet encounter!

O cautery that heals!
O consummating wound!
O soothing hand! O touch so fine and light
That savours of eternity
And satisfies all dues
Slaying, you have converted death to life

O lamps of fire, whose light
Streams in the cavernous soul:
Through mighty hollows, dazzled from above
Once blind in a blank night
Visiting splendor rolls
Lavishing warmth and brilliance on their love

How tame and loving
Your memory rises in my breast
Where secretly only you live
And in your fragrant breathing
Full of goodness and grace
How delicately in love you make me feel!

(trans. J. Aladro)

Generalizing the personal mystical experience. Saint John's poetry brought the mystical experience to his Spanish readers in keeping with the general stages characteristic of Catholic theology. His poetry, however, always departs from this second stage in the process (*via iluminativa*). Also it never talks directly about the suffering and pain that one endures.

On a dark night,
Anxious, by love inflamed,
—O joyous chance!—
I left not seen or discovered,
My house at last completely quiet.
　　("Dark Night," stanza 1, trans. J. Aladro)

In "The Dark Night," we can identify the confinements of the "house" with the incarceration of the soul in the human body. Searching and pain characterize the steps, as well as travel through the great light of faith and rising into ecstasy, union, and oblivion.

In the next stage (*via unitiva*), the soul becomes one with God; the poet's soul, or "Lover," is consumed in perfect love as it joins in spiritual matrimony with the "Beloved":

O night! O guide!
O night more loving than dawn!
O night that joined
Lover with beloved,
Beloved in the lover transformed!
　　("Dark Night," stanza 5, trans. J. Aladro)

In the fourth stage, peace and beatitude follow the union:

I lose myself and remain,
With my face on the beloved inclined;
All has come to rest,
I abandon all my cares
There, among the lilies, to die.
　　("Dark Night" stanza 8, trans. J. Aladro)

Few other poets in Western thought traveled so thoroughly through the bright and nocturnal spaces, or shared in this way the profoundly metaphysical labyrinths of their experience of love.

Sources and literary context. Formally, Saint John's poetry derives from four poetic traditions: the Italian, the Spanish, the biblical, and Arabic. Dámaso Alonso is the major critic of Saint John's poetry, and he is the one who brought out most clearly the important aspects of the four traditions as sources. In his *La poesía de San Juan de la Cruz* (The Poetry of Saint John de la Cruz), Dámaso Alonso traces in detail the origin of many of Saint John's poems.

The Italian influence in Saint John's work came to him through Garcilaso de la Vega (1501?–36), who, with Juan Boscán (1487?–1542), was the first known poet to write Castilian poetry in a variety of Italian forms. The *Lira*, which Saint John uses in his three central poems "Noche oscura," "Cántico Espiritual," and "¡Oh Llama de amor viva!" first appeared in Spanish in Garcilaso's poem "A la flor de Gnido" (To the Flower of Gnido). But Dámaso Alonso convincingly demonstrates that, while Saint John knew the work of Garcilaso, his immediate source was another Spanish poet, an intermediary by the name of Sebastián de Córdoba. In 1575 Sebastián de Córdoba published a volume entitled "Obras de Boscán y Garcilaso trasladadas a materias cristianas y religiosas" (Works of Boscán and Garcilaso Transformed into Christian and Religious Materials). In the volume, the author attempts to recast the poetry of Garcilaso and Boscan and link them to the concept "a lo divino" (the divine).

Spanish precedents for Saint John's poems can be found in relation to form and theme. Their most obvious popular Castilian quality is in the use of *romance* (ballad) meters and *estribillos* (refrains). The *Romances*, composed in a fixed meter of octosyllables with assonance in alternate lines, are short simple poems, usually by unknown poets for an unlearned audience. They were publicly recited or sung to provide entertainment or disseminate news of recent events. Like other contemporary poets, such as Lope de Vega, Góngora, and Gil Vicente, Saint John wrote verse that diverged from that of popular poems and thus made them his own.

The third major influence on the poetry of Saint John is the Old Testament. The biblical poetry depicted in the Vulgate appears in the form of pastoral images throughout Saint John's work, not only in his poems, and prose, but also in letters. *Cántico Espiritual* is an imitation and interpretation in Spanish of the *Song of Songs* or *Songs of Solomon*. This text from the Old Testament, a fragmentary collection of songs in the form of dialogue, has enough cohesion to be called a wedding idyll or ceremonial drama. From a very early period, this dramatic love poem was being interpreted in terms of the love between God and man. Saint John also uses it this way, adding to his version an allegorical meaning while retaining the original freshness. "Spiritual Canticle" has a paradoxical quality about it, of overall aesthetic coherence yet arbitrariness in the sequence of events. Saint John's version resembles the biblical *Song of Songs* in this respect. So completely does Saint John sustain unity of tone that no stanza jars. Concurrently the degree of diversity and number of gaps in the poem suggest that it may derive from this biblical folk song.

Another important source for Saint John's mystical-literary writing was León Hebreo's extraordinarily popular book *Dialoghi d'amore*, 1535, published first in Italian and then in Spanish. In his book, León Hebreo, a Spanish Jew who was exiled to Naples, proposes a philosophy of love as a means of obtaining union with God. The book is Neo-Platonic in nature, and reflects, in addition to biblical language, the thoughts and lexicon of Ben Gabirol, Maimonides, and the Jewish mystical writings known as the *Cabala*.

OUT OF DOCTRINAL ORDER

In terms of logical sequence, "Spiritual Canticle" is one of the poorest examples of order. Saint John himself appears to have perceived this, and so to have written the poem in at least two versions, one in the manuscript of Sanlúcar de Barrameda and another in that of Jaén. In the second, Jaén version, Saint John strives to correct the incoherence in order to achieve doctrinal order and also adds an extra stanza. The consensus of his critics is that the first version is superior. Be that as it may, in both the first and second redactions, the poet has succeeded in reproducing a unified yet fragmentary song, and in doing so has remained faithful to the biblical *Song of Songs*. Saint John states in the prologue of his poem that he wrote it "under the influence of abundant mystical intelligence [knowledge]." One can assume that it was not a similar "mystical intelligence" in the author or authors of the *Song of Songs* that led to its present fragmentary state. The artistic effect is the same. It should be remembered, though, that early Christian writers could justify the inclusion of this collection of impassioned Jewish folk songs only as an allegory of the love of Christ for his Church, or in Saint John's poetry of the *esposo* (husband-Christ) for his *esposa* (bride-Church-soul).

Events in History at the Time the Poems Were Written

Church career and imprisonment. Because Saint John's poetry is intimately connected with his personal experience, it is important to have a grounding in events of his life connected to his writing of the poems. During his first assignment as a Carmelite friar, Juan de la Cruz lived in a small, poor farmhouse converted into a hermitage. This humble home, which he shared with a few monks, was situated in Duruelo, only a few miles from Fontiveros and Juan's birthplace. Next he moved to Pastrama, near Alcalá de

Henares, becoming a master of novices and then to Alcalá, where he worked as a teacher in a Carmelite college.

In 1572 Teresa brought Juan to the unreformed Carmelite convent of Encarnación at Avila. During her stay there, she and Juan de la Cruz, who served as confessor and spiritual director, won over the majority of the nuns to the reform movement. An election among the nuns was held to determine the new prioress, and Teresa, who a few years before had held this office, was certain to be re-elected. The Provincial of the Carmelite order, there to supervise the election, threatened to excommunicate those who supported Teresa. In her letters, Teresa describes the subsequent course of events: the defiant nuns elected Teresa, whereupon the Provincial intervened, excommunicating and cursing the nuns who had voted for the reform candidate. He quickly burned their ballots, declared the election void, and appointed his own candidate. The sequel to the election occurred on the night of December 3, 1577, when an anti-reform group broke into the house where Fray Juan de la Cruz was living and hauled him off to a dark prison in the Carmelite Priory in Toledo. Fray Juan was Teresa's spiritual accomplice, reasoned the Carmelite authorities in Spain, and they intended, at any price, to stop the spread of the reform movement.

Juan de la Cruz's unlit cell was actually a small cupboard, not high enough for him to stand erect. He was taken each day to the refectory, where he received bread, water, and sardine scraps that he had to eat on the floor, like a dog. Then he was subjected to the circular discipline: while he knelt on the ground, the monks walked around him, singeing his bare back with their leather whips. At first a daily occurrence, the whippings were later restricted to Fridays, but with such zeal was he tortured that his shoulders remained crippled for the rest of his life. Saint John suffered other torments, too. For most of the six months of his incarceration, he received no change of clothing and remained infested with lice. He had dysentery from the food and suspected he was being poisoned.

At one point, a new jailer was appointed who proved to be far more generous than his predecessor. During this time of greater kindness, Juan wrote from 17 to 30 stanzas of "Cántico Espiritual" ("Spiritual Canticle") and completed "La Fonte" ("The Fountain") and probably "Noche Oscura" ("The Dark Night"), which, with its refrain *aunque es de noche* (although it is night), speaks of his faith amid darkness. The poem "Noche Oscura" is a love poem, an allegory of mystical union, despite and perhaps nurtured by his abysmal situation.

A key experience during this time of affliction and suffering finally made him resolve to escape. In August 1578 he had a vision:

> On the eve of the Assumption of the Virgin the Prior of the Convent entered his cell, and after kicking him brutally and [be]rating him for his disobedience, promised to release him if he would abandon the Reform and return to the mitigated rule. Juan replied that he could not break his vows, but asked if he might be allowed to say mass on the following day, as it was the feast of the Virgin. The Prior angrily refused and went out. But that night Our Lady appeared to Juan in a dream. Filling his cell with light, she commanded him to escape, promising her assistance.
>
> (Brenan, p. 266)

A few days after this incident, Saint John prepared himself for this venture, which takes on legendary, almost romantic proportions in biographical studies. After prying loose the hinges of his cell door in the middle of the night, he stepped over the bodies of some sleeping friars without notice. Then he lowered himself from a balcony to the city wall by means of a rope made from strips of his own blankets and clothing. From the wall, he jumped into a courtyard, which was enclosed by other high walls. The miracle recounts that he managed to scale these walls with the Virgin's help, to at last find himself free in the streets of Toledo.

Poetic beginnings. Saint John took refuge in a convent of the Discalced Carmelites. Already on this first day of his escape, while still recovering from his trials, Juan rushed to give poetic voice to his most recent experience. He dictated part of his poetry, which he had not been able to write down in his cell and so had committed to memory. It was too dangerous, however, for him to remain in Toledo so he left for a small hermitage in Andalusia, called El Calvario, by the upper waters of the Guadalquivir River. Saint John spent six months in El Calvario, and they would prove the happiest time in his life. From the darkest pit he had risen to the clear beauty of the Andalusian landscape. Here in the solitude of open land, his career as a poet became fixed. During this grand, creative period he appears to have completed the corpus of his poetry, except for the last stanzas of "The Spiritual Canticle" (which he finished in Baeza and revised later in Granada), and "Oh Living Flame of Love!" (also written in Granada). He was then 37.

Following this brief period of recovery at El Calvario, Saint John was sent to the city of Baeza in 1579 to direct a newly formed Carmelite college. These were less happy years, filled with new responsibilities and struggles. In his letters he records that he felt uneasy among the city crowds, so different from his desert retreat. He consoled himself by making frequent trips to nearby Beas de Segura, a convent of Castilian nuns founded a few years before by Teresa.

From Baeza, Saint John was sent in 1582 to Granada, where he became Prior of a new monastery, El Convento de los Mártires. The monastery sat on the hill of the Alhambra and looked out over the white Sierra Nevada Mountains, thus offering one of the most extraordinary views in Spain. Saint John speaks of the land's beauty in commentaries and poems. Subsequently, after 1585, his life became much more complex and demanding due to further political appointments. Saint John was named Vicar Provincial for Andalusia, in which position he had to journey all over southern Spain. A few years later, in 1588 he was made Prior in Segovia. It was during this time that he gave himself to meditation, arriving at the summit of his spiritual life. By his own testimony, found in both commentaries and poetry, he experienced mystical union with God during his stay in Granada and in Segovia.

Adversity renewed. Meanwhile, the Carmelite reformers had triumphed, at least insofar as Pope Gregory XIII recognized them as a separate organization entitled to elect their own Provincial. Renewed trouble and internal disorder erupted with the election of Nicolás Doria as the Provincial, in lieu of Teresa's and Saint John's protector, Gracián. After Teresa died in 1582, Ana de Jesús, her successor and a close friend to Saint John, was imprisoned. Other followers of Teresa and Saint John were exiled to remote convents. As for Saint John himself, he attempted to intervene in a controversial dispute in Ana de Jesús's convent in Madrid. He supported the rights of the nuns to use the secret ballot and govern themselves democratically, in accord with a recent brief from the Pope in 1580. The debate on behalf of the liberty to vote led to Juan's mistreatment much like his earlier struggle in Avila, which had led to his imprisonment in Toledo. As a consequence of his involvement in the present affair, Juan was stripped of all office and exiled to La Peñuela, a desert house in

Andalusia. Evidence was collected against him, some of it ridiculous, such as a false accusation by a nun in Málaga claiming that she had been kissed by Saint John through the grille of her window. At Beas de Segura, which used to be his favorite convent to visit, the nuns destroyed all papers and letters from him, for fear of being implicated along with the heretic monk. There was a move to expel him from the Carmelite order, and only his sickness spared him this last ignominy. Suffering fever and ulcers on the legs, he went to nearby Ubeda for medical care, where the Prior refused to give him the barest necessities. Treated with vengeful hostility, he suffered insults and humiliation. As the ulcers spread, his health declined and his body literally rotted away. Saint John died at midnight on December 14, 1591.

Juan's death set the town of Ubeda in a panic because of a popular belief that he was a saint. Though it was cold and raining, crowds entered the convent that night to tear off parts of his clothing, bandages, and even ulcerous flesh. He was buried in Ubeda, but Segovia claimed the corpse of its native son and finally, after nine months, a royal warrant was obtained and his corpse dug up at night. According to accepted legend, his body had not decayed and gave off a sweet aroma, which many cite as proof of his saintliness. So strong was the desire to possess something of the saint that parts of his body were cut off, embalmed, and kept as relics. He was deprived of a leg, which was left behind at Ubeda, an arm in Madrid, and fingers in various holy places. After his body reached Segovia, a counterappeal came to Rome from Ubeda and his remaining limbs were cut off and sent back there. It was the ultimate paradox of a life marked by torture and misery, a pitiful bodily death marked by scorn and exile and finally macabre disfigurement as eager admirers fought over his remains. During his lifetime, Saint John had sought, within the confines of a small cell, to see through the darkness and become entranced by beauty, to give himself entirely to the individual quest for light and love. Pope Clement X blessed him almost a hundred years after his death in 1675. A half century later, in 1726, Pope Benedict XIII canonized Saint John and exactly two centuries after that, in 1926, Pius XI declared him a Doctor of the Catholic Church.

Reception. The first editions of Saint John of the Cross's poetry were published in Alcalá, 1618 (without "The Spiritual Canticle"); in Barcelona, 1619 (without "The Spiritual Canticle"); in Paris,

1622; in Brussels, 1627; and in Madrid, 1627. The second edition was not published until 1703 in Seville. Never intended for popular consumption, Saint John's writings did not receive a popularly enthusiastic reception. Saint John's poetry has rather been fare for subsequent poets. He influenced French Symbolists, such as Arthur Rimbaud and Stéphane Mallarmé, as well as the Spanish poets Juan Ramón Jiménez, Jorge Guillén, and Pedro Salinas, and the Mexican Nobel Laureate Octavio Paz. His influence has extended to English poets as well, including T.S. Eliot, whose verse "East Coker" is a tribute to Saint John of the Cross's "The Ascent of Mount Carmel." In contrast to many of these poets, who searched for the ineffable essence of poetry, Saint John fixated his talents on finding the essence of God.

—Jorge Aladro

For More Information

Allison Peers, E. *Studies of The Spanish Mystics.* London: Macmillan, 1951.

Alonso, Dámaso. *La Poesía de San Juan de La Cruz.* Madrid: Aguilar, 1966.

Brenan, Gerald. "Studies in Genius-II: St. John of the Cross, His Life and Poetry." *Horizon* (May 1947).

Guillén, Jorge. *Language and Poetry.* Cambridge: Harvard University Press, 1961.

John of the Cross, Saint. *The Poems of Saint John of the Cross.* Trans. Willis Barnstone. Bloomington: Indiana University Press, 1972.

López-Baralt, Luce. *San Juan de la Cruz y el Islam.* Madrid: Hiperión, 1990.

Underhill, Evelyn. *Mysticism.* New York: Doubleday, 1990.

Wilson, Margaret. *San Juan de la Cruz. A Critical Guide.* London: Grant and Cutler, 1975.

The Disenchantments of Love

by

María de Zayas y Sotomayor

María de Zayas y Sotomayor is thought to have been born in Madrid on September 12, 1590, at the end of the reign of Phillip II (1555-98) when Spain, once the most powerful country in the world, began its decline. Her parents, Doña María de Barasa and Don Fernando de Zayas y Sotomayor belonged to the middle nobility. Don Fernando received the honor of "Caballero del Hábito de Santiago" (Order of Knights of Santiago—patron saint of Spain) in 1628. He served under the famous Count Lemos, viceroy to Naples from 1610 to 1616 and protector of writers such as Lope de Vega, Francisco de Quevedo, and Miguel de Cervantes. It is believed that Zayas's family traveled around Spain and Italy with the viceroy and his entourage. There is little information about Zayas; it is not known if she ever married or entered a convent, nor is there certainty about the year of her death. However, it is known that Zayas took active part in the literary circles of Madrid between 1621 and 1637. Important writers such as Lope de Vega in his *Laurel de Apolo* (1630), a book praising living poets of his time; Pérez de Montalbán in his *Para todos* (1633), a chronicle of literary life in Spain; and Alonso Castillo Solózarno, author of the novellas *Tardes entertenidas* (1629, Entertaining Afternoons), praised her abilities as a prose writer and a poet. Because of her *ingenio* (ingenuity) and daring, Zayas was called the Tenth Muse and a Sybil, a woman ahead of her times. She began her writing career by composing poems but then switched to prose for which she became better

known. In her first volume of novellas, *Aventuras amorosas y ejemplares* (1637; *The Enchantments of Love: Amorous and Exemplary Novels,* 1990), men and women recount tales of courtly love, that is, love among the nobles of Madrid. Her second volume, *Parte Segunda del soiree, y entretenimiento honesto (Desengaños amorosos)* (1647; *The Disenchantments of Love,* 1997) features women alone telling such tales. More pessimistic and sensationalist than the first volume, it highlights the danger of romance to women in seventeenth-century Spain.

Events in History at the Time of the Novellas

Imperial decline, cultural soul-searching. The historical period during which her stories take

Zayas cautions women against romantic relationships with the nobles of Madrid in *The
Disenchantments of Love.*

place and in which María de Zayas lived and
wrote is the same: the first half of the seventeenth
century, during the kingships of Phillip III
(1598-1621) and Phillip IV (1621-65). The era
was one of decadence and tumult in the Spanish
kingdom, on which the "sun never set" since its
empire spread from Roussillon (France), to
Naples, Sicily, Milan, and Sardinia (Italy), to Holland, Belgium, the Cape Verde Islands, the
Philippines, and the Spanish colonies in America from California to Tierra del Fuego.

Spain under the two king Phillips faced innumerable problems because these two monarchs, who were father and son, and of Austrian
heritage, had little interest in the politics of governing such a complex empire. Weak rulers,
they left the everyday business of government to
their favorites, the Duke of Lerma and the Duke
of Olivares. Spain itself suffered a host of problems: tax increases, a reduction in the price of
gold and silver, emigration to America that de-
populated the countryside, an increase in urban
population that exacerbated crime and led to
housing shortages, four plagues that destroyed
one quarter of the population, and the 1609 expulsion of the Moriscos, the remaining Arab
population in Spain, ostensibly converts to
Christianity. The Moriscos had no choice but to
comply with the expulsion, which led to a short-

age of farmers and artisans. All these events exacerbated hunger and misery within Spain.

Aside from its internal problems, Spain had
to cope with the uprising of Cataluña in 1640,
the war in Flanders and its independence from
Spain (1648), the Thirty Years War and concluding treaty of Westphalia (1648) by which
Spain lost its supremacy in Europe, and the independence of Portugal (acknowledged in 1668).
All the political and economic decadence not
only caused uncertainty and agitation in the population but also stimulated an intensely critical
atmosphere in which the nation's problems were
analyzed and studied with a profound desire to
overcome them, or at least to make everyone conscious of the issues that needed to be resolved.

Fertile intellectual era. The intellectuals of
Spain worked in what was later defined as the
Spanish Baroque, a period of artistic endeavor
characterized by duality, the struggle between
antagonist forces, disenchantment, pessimism,
and the idea that the world is a deceptive place.
Unlike the Renaissance ideal, which strove to
closely represent reality, Baroque works were full
of intellectual mystery; in a sense, Baroque art
was the art of the unfinished. In Spanish literature, a distinguishing trait of the Baroque was *desengaño* (disillusionment), the sudden realization
that what one sees or believes is not necessarily

UPRISING OF CATALONIA

In 1640 the region of Catalonia, in northwest Spain, began a revolt in reaction to the presence and unruly behavior of Spanish troops in the region. Since 1626, the Catalonians had refused to cooperate with the central government, not furnishing money or soldiers to help Spain's kings in their never-ending European wars. Now, in May 1640, peasants attacked Spanish troops in the north Catalan countryside; by June they had moved into the city of Barcelona. There they mobilized farm laborers into a revolutionary mob that seized the city and murdered royal officials, including the Spanish viceroy. Havoc followed. Poor peasants rose against their overlords, workers took over town streets, and gangs of bandits riddled the countryside. Uniting their forces with those of France, Spain's enemy at that time, the Catalan rebels drove out the Spanish troops. Subsequently Catalonia became a French protectorate, with some rebels growing more resentful of France than they had been of Spain. In 1651-52 the Spanish army retook Barcelona. The Spanish crown afterward promised to preserve Catalonian laws. In the end, the revolt accomplished little beyond years of suffering for the Catalonians and a weakening of the power of the Spanish Crown.

real or true. From this came the view that the world is irrational, a place in which the unjust govern the just and evil triumphs over good.

Baroque artists played with intertwined but conflicting ideas, or, more exactly they played with reality and fantasy in their creations and with individual control and the forces of destiny. In a society without many religious or political options, artistic expression provided the only real outlet for new ideas. Artistic experiment was generally permissible in Spain, as long as the experiment had nothing to do with the Church or the government. This was the age of the Counter Reformation. In 1478, Spain had introduced the Inquisition, a tribunal to seek out and suppress deviation from the teachings of the Catholic Church. The power of this tribunal intensified during the mid-sixteenth century in what is now known as the Counter Reformation (or Catholic Reformation), in which the Catholic nations banded together to combat the influence of Martin Luther's Protestant teachings.

María de Zayas was aware of the complexity of her century. Part of the nobility herself, she took care not to criticize the Church or the government. She did attack her society for its treatment of women, but she had no interest in attacking the privileges of her social class. In fact, her works do not concern themselves with economic or political issues. Her stories are set in a certain place and time, but only as part of a literary device popular in her day. Authors often

used such details to convince readers that their narratives were based on real events. This helped them to combat the common charges leveled by moralists, who claimed that fiction was detrimental because it merely entertained and did not educate. The primary tenet of the Baroque—that art needed to both delight and educate—grew out of these claims and out of the Counter-Reformation concern for the orthodox practice of the Catholic faith. This minimum of historical detail also allowed Zayas to praise the monarchy through her stories, as did other Baroque intellectuals. Zayas glorified the past, especially the reign of the Catholic monarchs Isabel and Fernando more than a hundred years earlier; for Zayas, theirs was a time to emulate because men were patriotic and chivalrous to women, while her contemporaries were not. In *The Disenchantments of Love* only two historical dates are given: 1619 (the trip of Phillip III to Portugal) in "The Ravages of Vice," and 1640 (the uprising of Cataluña) in "Slave to her Own Lover."

The Novellas in Focus

Plot overview. The ten novellas of *The Disenchantments of Love* can be best understood after reading Zayas's first set of novellas *The Enchantments of Love.* Published ten years apart, the two sets of stories share the same frame tale and are best understood as part of one collection. The use of the frame gave the author the opportunity

PHILLIP III VISITS PORTUGAL

In 1619 King Phillip III decided to travel to Portugal, then part of Spain. Portugal had become part of Spain in 1581, when Phillip II inherited the Portuguese crown because King Sebastian of Portugal died in an exploration to the North African Coast in 1578. Phillip II acquired the rights to the throne because, along with the unfortunate Sebastian, he was one of the grandchildren of the Portuguese King Don Manuel. In Phillip III's time, Portugal was a troubled part of the empire because of its aspirations for independence. He wanted to visit in order to keep the nobles happy, to reinforce his rights to the crown, and finally to celebrate the crowning of the future king, his son Phillip, as heir to the vast Spanish Empire. When Phillip III and his entourage reached Portugal, the people welcomed the king and prince, and treated them with pomp and hospitality. Unfortunately the Spanish king had to hurry home due to political problems in Madrid. On his way back, the 43-year-old king fell ill and died, whereupon his son inherited his declining empire. After the death of the king in 1620, it would take four decades for Spain to recognize Portugal's independence. Recognition finally came in 1668, after nearly 100 years of dominance over Portugal by its Spanish neighbor.

to air her ideas about women's role in society, about love and marriage, about the concept of honor, and about the violence perpetrated against females. The violence portrayed in Zayas's stories (poison, legs broken, murder, stabbing, bleeding to death, starvation, blindness) can also be found in the *comedia* (drama), prose, fiction, and even in the tabloids of the day. Over 30 women are beaten, strangled, tortured, stabbed, raped, or poisoned in Zayas's work, but all this violence should not be read as a realistic representation of the situation of women in the period. An exhaustive history of domestic violence has yet to be written, but we do know that the historical record shows few cases of wife-murder for the time. While this does not mean that women were not abused in their homes, it does make us question those who have read Zayas as a realist or *costumbrista* (a chronicler of her times). It is clear, though, that Zayas uses an aesthetic of violence to articulate an early modern feminist agenda that includes, among other things, a call for women's access to education and arms, and a plea for greater access to legal and social justice (see Vollendorf). Through graphic violence, her stories call attention to the unfair treatment women are suffering at the hands of men and to their need to prepare their bodies and minds to survive in a patriarchal society.

In *The Disenchantments of Love,* as in its precursor, the *Enchantments of Love,* the main character in the frame story is Lisis, an aristocrat from Madrid. She has reunited a group of friends for a *soiree* (a private party that took several days and in which guests recited poetry or told tales). In the *Enchantments of Love,* Lisis is suffering because her love interest, Don Juan, is no longer showering attention on her; he has shifted his amorous interest to her cousin Lizarda. In this first collection, men and women are telling tales, with the men speaking about how women trick them, and the women declaring themselves more faithful and caring than the males. Six of the stories end with a happy marriage, and three with the main character entering a convent. One focuses on the vice of avarice. At the close of this first collection, Lisis announces that she will marry Don Diego. However, she is still in love with Don Juan, and her doubts about her decision upset her so intensely that she grows ill.

Published ten years later, *The Disenchantments of Love* concerns itself with "men's cruelty and tyranny" and with those who insist on keeping women "cloistered and not giving us teachers" (Zayas, *The Disenchantments of Love,* p. 1). In the second collection's frame story, Lisis, her mother, her cousin, her gentlemen callers and other friends reappear. This time the *soiree,* or private party, is held to celebrate Lisis's recovery from her year-long illness and her upcoming wedding. At this soiree, only women can tell tales, the stories have to be true, and they must transmit a lesson for women to disenchant them from the dangers of falling in love and guiding their lives according to their naive ideas of romance.

The stories are told on three consecutive nights—four stories on the first night, four on the second, and two on the third. They take place in different countries (Spain, Italy, Portugal, Holland, Germany, Hungary, and Algiers), presenting variations on a common theme: violence against women by the males in their lives (father, brother, husband, father-in-law, and lover). The titles of the stories give a hint of the storylines and calamities that might befall women: *His Wife's Executioner, Innocence Punished, Love for the Sake of Conquest, Marriage Abroad: Portent of Doom, Traitor to His Own Blood,* and *Triumph Over Persecution.* It should be noted that when Zayas published *The Disenchantments of Love,* she titled only the first novella "Slave to her Own Lover"; the rest were just numbered; it was not until the Barcelona edition of 1734 that the rest were given titles which pertained to the storylines and resembled the titles in her first collection.

Plot summary. Of the ten stories of *The Disenchantments of Love,* the first and last are intertwined: "Slave to Her Own Lover" and "The Ravages of Vice." Lisis and her slave Zelima narrate these stories, demonstrating the depth of "sisterly" love, even in the case of a master and her slave. Zelima is in reality Doña Isabel, a Christian aristocrat from Murcia, who became a slave to follow the man who had first raped her. She agrees to the arrangement in hopes that he will marry her, which is the only action that will restore her honor. But after many incidents—disguising herself and serving as a Moorish slave, traveling to Italy, being a prisoner in Algiers, and finally returning home after six years—Zelima/Isabel learns that her unfaithful lover has no intention of marrying her. He is in love with the Algerian woman who helped them escape homeward. Luis, Zelima's one-time servant and aspiring lover, kills Manuel. Zelima has learned her lesson; her rapist only pretended to care for her while buying time to find a way out of his verbal promise to marry her. (At the time, a verbal promise was so serious that on the strength of one, a man could be forced to marry.) Meanwhile, Zelima/Isabel has been the cause of her father's death and her mother's eternal sorrow. Having violated all the morals her family taught her, she realizes the only decent and safe course for her to follow is to enter a convent. Luckily Zelima has hidden some jewelry that will pro-

vide her with enough money for the dowry needed to enter the convent. Lisis, feeling sorry for Zelima's misfortunes, frees her and offers to add money to her dowry.

RICH WOMAN'S REFUGE

Upper-class women had two options in the 1600s: marriage or the convent. Unfortunately there were not enough beds in the convents due to the high demand for monastic life (20 percent of the population belonged to the clergy). Convents found it especially difficult to support themselves at this point because of the limitations imposed on them; municipalities preferred male religious orders since they provided schooling and religious services, while the convents did not. Only later would their nuns provide services as nurses or teachers, so the convents had to depend for sustenance on rent from properties, gifts from the community and Crown, and the dowries brought in by the novices. To enter the religious life, a woman generally had to bring in a dowry, and its amount often determined her status in the convent. If the dowry was high, the woman became a mother and if it was small or nonexistent, a sister. Sometimes, to improve its income, a convent allowed a rich woman, regardless of her marital status, to live there indefinitely as long as she paid a fee. The trend resulted in dramatic changes in convent life because these rich women demanded comfortable apartments with enough space to keep servants or slaves and receive visitors. In larger society, the trend met with disapproval. The women, thought many, had a harmful effect, weakening not only convent rules but also faith.

Lisis's story, "The Ravages of Vice," concerns the evils of passion. A young Portuguese woman falls in love with her brother-in-law and becomes his mistress for four years, but wants to elevate herself to wife. With the aid of a servant, a plot is set in motion by which the husband will be led to believe that his wife is having an affair with a young servant. The husband, crazed with jealousy, kills not only his wife and the innocent young servant, but also all the pages, servants, and slaves in the house. He even tries to kill his lover, but she survives because one of the slaves places herself between the killer and his lover. After recovering, the protagonist decides to enter a convent as retribution for her sins. Back in the frame story, Lisis announces that she too has

Convent of Las Duenas in Salamanca, Spain.

decided to enter a religious order as a laywoman, not because she has suffered or been mistreated like many of the women in the tales told in her soiree, but because she is smart enough to avoid being a victim. The convent is the only place where women are safe in these tales. Also, the convent provides a female community in which women can exchange sisterly love without being plagued by an outside world where they compete and struggle for the love of men. Lisis has learned that men are women's worst enemies. So touching is her decision that everyone cries, but the main narrative voice—perhaps the authorial voice—assures us that Lisis's end "is not tragic but rather the happiest one you can imagine for, although courted and desired by many, she didn't subject herself to anyone" (*Disenchantments*, p. 405). The tales end with a plea from the main narrator: "I beg the ladies to mend their forward ways if they wish to be respected by men, and I beg the gentlemen to act like gentlemen by honoring women as is proper for them" (*Disenchantments*, p. 404). The narrator nurtures hopes of returning to an alleged golden age when men treated women with kindness and humans were not each other's worst enemy.

Slavery. Slavery in Spain existed from the times of the ancient Romans through the Middle Ages, but its nature was different at first. In ancient times, people became slaves because they were prisoners of war, or part of an inheritance or business exchange. The use of human beings as an important element of the overall economic spectrum did not begin until the close of the fifteenth century, when Europeans explored West Africa's coasts and also ventured to the Americas.

Before the sixteenth century, the Spanish slave population consisted mainly of Moriscos and Muslims (many of them casualties of the Reconquest). A minority were of Spanish origin. Numerous Christian lords owned Muslim slaves, using them as household servants or field laborers. The Reconquest took place in stages from the middle of the eighth to the end of the fifteenth centuries, producing so many slaves that even ordinary people came to own them. In the medieval era, it was thought prudent to treat one's slaves well and even to free them after loyal service. Owners could liberate their slaves orally before witnesses or through a written will or charter of liberty (*carta ingenuitatis*). Often the ex-slaves continued to labor for and remain under the protection of their former owners. When the Spaniards began establishing sugar plantations in Africa and in America in the fifteenth century, African slaves became highly profitable and attention in Spain shifted away from the Moorish and to the African bondsman. By 1565, 7.4 percent of the population in Seville consisted of slaves, most of them Africans. To Spaniards, as to other Europeans, Africans appeared to be an ideal solution to the demand for labor. They seemed stronger and less likely to escape, and were easier to acquire than Moors or *guanches* (slaves from the Canary Islands). The appearance of the Africans in bondage reinvigorated slavery in Spain itself, remarked one observer in 1655, around the time Zayas's stories take place: "The American trade has given new life to the institution of slavery in this country" (Kamen, p. 110). Zelima, the female slave in Zayas's story, is of European heritage but pretends to be a Morisca.

Sources and literary context. After Cervantes (1547-1616), María de Zayas is considered the most popular author of short novels of the Baroque. When Cervantes published his *Exemplary Novels* (1613), he was opening the door to a new genre already popular in Italy: novellas with a moral teaching, modeled after *The Decameron* (1496) by Boccaccio. Cervantes, father of the modern novel for his creation of **Don Quixote** (1605 and 1615; also in *WLAIT 5: Spanish and Portuguese Literatures and Their Times*) published his collection of novellas in 1613. Literature had not yet become the prosperous business that it would two decades later, around 1630, when the novella with moral teachings reached its peak. Cervantes's stories demanded a sophisticated reader, one who was familiar with the literary heritage of the Renaissance and the classics. But by the time Zayas started writing her short novels, the genre had become less serious and more popular; now it was being geared to readers interested in complicated stories full of action and exciting love plots. Many intellectuals of the seventeenth century did not consider such books serious literature, but this did not discourage writers from publishing amorous novellas that met with an enthusiastic reception among the general populous. Works such as Lope de Vega's *Novels to Marcia Leonarda* (1624), Juan Pérez de Montalbán's *Sucesos y prodigios de amor en ocho novelas* (1629, Wonders and Events of Love in Eight Novels) and Alonso Castillo Solórzano's *Tardes entretenidas* (1625, Entertaining Afternoons) were sources of inspiration for María de Zayas. In later centuries, such novellas would be defined as *novelas cortesanas* (courtly tales) because the main characters are rich urban dwellers with a great deal of free time to pursue love and play amorous games. The intention of these novellas was to entertain, and occasionally, to moralize. They immersed readers in a world ruled by passion and emotion. Between 1625 and 1634, Spain suffered a ban on the publication of novels and volumes of plays because the Church believed they did not teach sound morals. Perhaps for this reason, Zayas decided to call her novellas something different. She named the stories in her first collection *maravillas* (wonders), and in her second collection *desengaños*. In the end, Zayas did not face any problems publishing her short novels, because the censors saw in them a moral lesson to be learned by those who did not control their instincts or feelings.

Despite what may have been an effort to distance her stories from previous ones, Zayas's novellas presented many of the innovations of the novellas of her time: a great deal of action, sometimes started in medias res; many trips; direct discourse; a minimum of geographic descriptions, and interesting dialogue, all in a style dominated by *conceptismo* (use of complicated expressions, ideas, and conceptual games) and *culteranismo* (use of sophisticated language and references to the Greco-Roman classics). In regard to style, Zayas's novellas have an oral quality about them, suggesting that perhaps they were meant to be read aloud. She also has a rhetorically polished baroque style that, in combination with her fascinating portrayal of violence, makes her one of the most complex and engaging authors to emerge from this Golden Age of Spanish literature.

In regard to content, Zayas's stories tackled daring subjects: rapes, murders, male homosexuality, cross-dressing, lesbianism, the issues of race, cultural differences, and psychological and physical torture, and even the use of magic and the supernatural. Her innovation lay as well in the deep psychological insight into gender relations. Finally, Zayas's stories end differently from other novellas of the day in that hers do not finish happily, especially those in her second collection. The endings are in tune with her overall aim—to raise questions about the mistreatment of women. Why are they pursued, attacked, even killed? Why are women so desired one moment and despised the next? As a good daughter of the Baroque, Zayas was fighting a corrupt world in which women faced many obstacles. Her writings strove to make people aware of the problems, in the interest of seeing if women's lives could be improved.

The aristocratic setting of Zayas's tales mirrors the custom of literary salons and gatherings of the time. In the tradition of the *novela cortesana,* her characters tell tales aimed at entertaining and educating each other and, by implication, the external readers. Writing in the tradition not only of the Spanish authors named above but also of the Italian story writer Boccaccio (1313-75) and the French story writer Marguerite de Navarre (1492-1549), Zayas adapted the genre of the novella to fit her pro-woman didactic agenda.

While Zayas was innovative, then, she at the same time continued to develop existing traditions in world literature. Her novellas, for all their inventiveness, fall into line with and further develop already established traditions:

> Zaya's collection of tales is at the same time unique and highly conventional, both in its overall structure and narrative content. She draws on a tradition of familiar tales and narrative motifs, recombining, reworking, and augmenting them with stories partly or wholly of her own invention. Elements of her stories can be traced at least as far back as [the Arabic tale] *Kalilah et Dimnah* and the [Latin] *Disciplina clericalis* of Petrus Alfonsi
>
> (Greer, p. 37)

Publication and impact. By the first half of the seventeenth century, there were more than 50 printing shops in Spain, at least 25 of them in Madrid. Spain was the most powerful country

TO THE READER

It took a great deal of determination for a woman to become a writer in Zayas's time. Educated at home, women would have to wait two more centuries before they could attend university in Spain. Zayas had free time to educate herself because she belonged to the nobility. Like many other noble women of her time, she took an interest in the arts. Mostly these women showed interest in poetry and the theater. In *saraos,* soirees, women as well as men would exhibit their skills in poetry, singing, and dancing. It was acceptable for a female to demonstrate her intellectual abilities and wit in private. But she ought never, thought aristocratic society, behave this way in public or for profit. This is not to say that women did not achieve intellectual prowess. There were many learned nuns at the time, such as Sor Marcela de San Félix, daughter to the playwright Lope de Vega (see **Fuente Ovejuna,** also in *WLAIT 5: Spanish and Portuguese Literatures and Their Times*). A few uncloistered women, such as Ana Caro de Mallén and Mariana de Carvajal, managed to publish their works in the public book market. In general, however, women were not integrated into the intellectual life in Spain as they were in some other European countries, such as France and Italy. Aware of the difficulties anyone of her gender faced in pursuing literary success, Zayas addressed this very obstacle in her preface to this first volume.

> Oh my reader, no doubt it will amaze you that a woman has the nerve, not only to write a book but actually to publish it, for publication is the crucible in which the purity of genius is tested; until writing is set in letters of lead, it has no real value. Our senses are so easily deceived that fragile sight often sees as pure gold what, by the light of the fire, is simply a piece of polished brass. Who can doubt, I repeat, that there will be many who will attribute to folly my audacity in publishing my scribbles because I'm a woman, and women, in the opinion of some fools, are unfit beings. If only out of common courtesy, however, people shouldn't take my book as an oddity or condemn it as foolish.
>
> (Zayas, *The Enchantments of Love,* p. 1)

in the world at the time, with colonies in various reaches of the globe. Consequently its literature was read, translated, and imitated. Works by male writers, such as Miguel de Cervantes, Lope de Vega, and Francisco de Quevedo were influenced by and often influenced the rest of Europe. Female writers, on the other hand, were mostly relegated to the religious sphere. Few ventured, as María de Zayas did, into an industry in which men were the writers and owners of the printing presses. Literature had by then become a big business, one in which women had not yet succeeded, although they were avid consumers, especially of novels and novellas. At the same time, when Zayas wrote and published her volumes of novellas, competition was fierce. There were many writers of courtly tales, which by 1630 had become a good source of income for authors. In view of her gender and the competi-

tion, Zayas seems to have realized that she had to be different and daring, and that she could attract readers by writing shocking, dramatic tales. Meanwhile, Zayas had to keep in mind the censors of the Inquisition (established in 1478), the famous writers of her day, and her reputation as a lady. Since her society frowned on female authors unless they wrote religious books, she protected herself by having her stories teach a moral lesson while other aspects of them sustained interest. Her strategy—bizarre stories with twisted plots, featuring violence against women and torrid love affairs—succeeded. Zayas's novellas became bestsellers in her own day. Between 1637 and 1814, more than 20 editions appeared, with the two collections published together after 1659. Zayas's popularity peaked in the eighteenth century, after which her novellas were almost forgotten in the nineteenth. In the twentieth century, they would begin to again attract attention, but now as objects of intense study rather than popular bestsellers.

—Margarita M. Lezcano

For More Information

Alcalde, Pilar. "Estrategias temáticas y narrativas en María de Zayas." Ph.D. diss., University of Southern California, 1998.

Brownlee, Marina S. *The Cultural Labyrinth of María de Zayas*. Philadelphia: University of Pennsylvania Press, 2000.

Cuadros, Evangelina Rodríguez, ed. *Novelas amorosoas de diversos ingenios del siglo XVII*. Madrid: Castalia, 1986.

Greer, Margaret Rich. *María de Zayas Tells Baroque Tales of Love and the Cruelty of Men*. University Park: Pennsylvania State University Press, 2000.

Kamen, Henry. *Spain 1469-1714*. 2d ed. London: Longman, 1991.

Vollendorf, Lisa. *Reclaiming the Body: María de Zayas's Early Modern Feminism*. Chapel Hill: University of North Carolina Press, 2001.

Williamsen, Amy R., and Judith A. Whitenack, eds. *María de Zayas: The Dynamics of Discourse*. Cranbury, N.J.: Associate University Press, 1995.

Zayas y Sotomayor, María. *Desengaños amorosos*. Ed. Alicia Yllera. Madrid: Cátedra, 1983.

———. *The Disenchantments of Love*. Trans. Patsy Boyer. Albany: State University Press, 1997.

———. *The Enchantments of Love: Amorous and Exemplary Novels*. Trans. Patsy Boyer. Berkley: University of California Press, 1990.

Don Juan Tenorio

by
José Zorrilla

Born in Valladolid, Spain on February 21, 1817, José Zorrilla y Moral was educated at the Real Seminario de Nobles—a Jesuit school—and later at the universities of Toledo and Valladolid. Though Zorrilla's father hoped his son would become a lawyer, Zorrilla left his studies and went to Madrid to pursue a career as a poet. In 1837 he became an overnight success after his dramatic recital of an elegy at the funeral of the essayist and satirist Mariano José de Larra. Witnesses claimed that Zorrilla actually leaped into the grave and stood on the coffin to deliver his reading. His first volume of verse, *Poesias* (1837), garnered him immediate acclaim and recognition as one of the primary voices in Spain's Romantic movement. Between 1839 and 1849, Zorrilla composed 40 plays, including *Don Juan Tenorio* (1844), a version that parodies the old Don Juan legend. Although Zorrilla would later disparage *Don Juan Tenorio* as an unsuccessful youthful experiment, the play's lyricism, colorful characters, and engrossing plot have made it a popular favorite, still performed in Spanish theaters each year on All Saints' Day during the first week of November. The play's rendition of the legendary Don Juan furthermore casts him in a modified mold, one emblematic of his Romantic age.

Events in History at the Time the Play Takes Place

The transformation of Don Juan. Over 200 years elapsed between Don Juan's first onstage

> ### THE LITERARY WORK
>
> A romantic drama set in Seville in the years 1545 to 1550; performed and published in 1844 (as *Don Juan Tenorio: drama religioso fantástico en dos partes*); translated into English in 1944.
>
> ### SYNOPSIS
>
> A young Spaniard leads a life of debauchery but ultimately receives salvation through the love of a pure woman.

appearance—in Tirso de Molina's **The Trickster of Seville and the Stone Guest** (1630; also in *WLAIT 5: Spanish and Portuguese Literatures and Their Times*)—and his portrayal in Zorrilla's *Don Juan Tenorio* (1844). During those intervening years, the Don Juan legend had become widely known throughout Europe and yielded many different literary incarnations. Tirso had apparently developed his cunning libertine from various songs and ballads, and possibly from real life as well; at least one scholar suspects Don Juan to have been modeled on Don Pedro Téllez Girón, a dissolute nobleman who may have been related to Tirso.

Whatever his antecedents, however, the figure of Don Juan captured the imagination of succeeding generations of poets, dramatists, and even composers, each of whom brought their own unique perspective to the character. This was especially true of artists from other European

José Zorrilla

nations. In *Dom Juan ou le festin de pierre* (1665), written by the French dramatist Jean-Baptiste Molière, Tirso's dashing trickster became more intellectual and sophisticated, less a man of action than a calculating seducer. The Austrian composer Wolfgang Amadeus Mozart tried a dif-

ferent approach in his opera *Don Giovanni* (1787); his character combines the wit and cynicism of Molière's Don Juan with the passion and daring of Tirso's.

Other versions strayed even further from Tirso's interpretation and made Don Juan a figure of fun rather than a menace. When the story grew popular in Italy among the *comedia dell'arte* (troupes of masked ensemble actors), the legend's comic aspects began to overshadow the religious and moral themes. Don Juan became a common subject for lighter forms of entertainment—puppet shows, farces, and even pantomimes (the precursor to modern musicals). In England, on a somewhat more serious note, eighteenth-century theatergoers enjoyed such productions as *Don John; or the Libertine Destroyed* (Drury Lane; 1782), and *Don Juan; or the Libertine Destroyed: A Tragic Pantomimical Ballet* (Royalty Theatre; 1788). George Gordon, Lord Byron, the British Romantic poet, was probably well acquainted with the Don Juan of pantomimes when he wrote his own comic masterpiece, *Don Juan*—pronounced "joo-un"—from 1816 to 1824. Witty, bawdy, and irreverent, Byron's mock epic did not even attempt to take the traditional legend seriously.

Nonetheless, the nineteenth century also saw a resurgence of more serious treatments of the Don Juan story, especially after the Romantic movement took hold in Germany, Britain, France, and Spain. More attention was paid to Don Juan's individuality and motivations, to the desires and frustrations underlying his libertine behavior. German author August Heinrich Hoffman depicts Don Juan as continually disappointed in his quest for the ideal woman, and this repeated failure as fueling his resentment against God and his fellow man. José Zorrilla's bold stroke in *Don Juan Tenorio* was to return the character to his origins as a ruthless trickster, as he was in Tirso's play, but also to make him susceptible to true love, willing—however briefly—to redeem himself for love's sake, and, at the last, capable of repenting and being saved through love, as none of his precursors had been.

Don Juan's Seville. The setting of *Don Juan Tenorio*—sixteenth-century Seville—enhances the play's passionate, colorful atmosphere. Situated on the Guadalquivir River, the port city of Seville enjoyed a period of great prosperity after the discovery of the New World in 1492. Successful trade with the Americas established Seville as one of Europe's most prominent centers of commerce; indeed, much of daily life in Seville was regulated by the arrival and departure of transatlantic trade ships. During the sixteenth and seventeenth centuries, people from diverse professions—actors, artists, missionaries, navigators, adventurers—converged upon the city, transforming it into a cultural and intellectual as well as a commercial

capital of the world. Between 1533 and 1594, the population of Seville more than doubled: from 41,224 to 90,000 inhabitants (Ruiz, p. 57).

One idiosyncrasy of Renaissance Seville was its lack of a social and stable upper middle class. The *hidalgos*—minor nobility—who formed an important component of other Spanish cities, such as Madrid, hardly existed in Andalusia, the region where Seville is located. In Seville, businessmen and entrepreneurs who may have begun in the middle class tended to succumb, after making their fortunes, to what historian Marcelin Defourneaux describes as "the snobbish longing for ennoblement. . . . These merchants, wishing to climb up the social ladder, could buy titles or public appointments, such as becoming 'one of the Twenty-four' (a municipal magistrate), which considerably enhanced their social status" (Defourneaux, p. 83). Seville did, however, contain several great aristocratic families, whose wealth was usually derived from the vast domains they held in the lower Guadalquivir regions. Some of these families were so wealthy that they built palaces in Seville. The Tenorios in Zorrilla's play are just such a family; Don Diego owns a palace that, on his deathbed, he orders razed to the ground because of the misdeeds of his son, Don Juan.

Defourneaux contends that the city's vast prosperity created "a very particular Sevillean mentality" among its wealthier citizens (Defourneaux, p. 84). The rapidity with which fortunes in trade could be made—and lost—fostered "a sudden desire to enjoy the pleasures and refinements which wealth could provide and a certain detachment in regard to money, which should not be hoarded but spent. Thus the whole of the social life of Seville reflected a certain *insouciance* combined with a taste for ostentation" (Defourneaux, p. 85). Seville's richest inhabitants built palatial houses, dressed splendidly, and dined sumptuously. And Seville's public festivals—religious and secular—were magnificent to the point of, as Defourneaux suggests, ostentation. In Zorrilla's play, Don Juan Tenorio demonstrates that he is a true son of Seville, at least in matters of money. The young libertine thinks nothing of bribing Doña Inés's *duenna* (chaperone) and Doña Ana's maid with purses of gold in exchange for access to their mistresses. Nor has he any difficulty in finding and hiring bravos (hired thugs) to detain his rivals or help him abduct Doña Inés from her convent.

Carnival season. The first four acts of *Don Juan Tenorio* take place in a single night during carnival season of the year 1545, the period of feasting and celebration in Roman Catholic countries that immediately precedes Lent. Derived from the medieval Latin phrase "carnem levare" (take away the meat), carnival appears to have originated in Italy during the fifteenth century, becoming popular in France and Spain in the sixteenth century. Some scholars contend that carnival may have its roots in pagan festivals such as Saturnalia in ancient Rome (the festival of the god Saturn a period of unrestrained revelry in December). Certainly, like Saturnalia, carnival celebrated rejuvenation in the natural world—the end of winter and the beginning of spring—and did so with feasts, dances, and often the exchange of gifts among celebrants. Carnival festivities were to some extent sanctioned by the Roman Catholic Church. Although overindulgence was frowned upon, popes even became patrons of carnival at times; during his tenure (1464-71), Pope Paul II ordered various races to be held in Rome and introduced masked balls.

The start and duration of carnival season varied among nations and localities. For many countries, however, carnival commenced on Quinquagésima Sunday (the Sunday before Lent—which began on Ash Wednesday—and 40 days before Easter). In Spain at the time of *Don Juan Tenorio*, carnival festivities would have likely ceased by Ash Wednesday. Zorrilla's choice to set his play during the brief carnival season adds an element of local color—in the form of the masked revelers who avidly discuss and observe Don Juan's escapades—and enhances the hectic atmosphere as Don Juan scrambles to outwit his many opponents at both love and intrigue. Moreover, the sensual excesses of carnival season provide a marked contrast to the religious austerity of Doña Inés, the novice nun whose innocence improbably captivates Don Juan and leads him to contemplate redemption.

The Play in Focus

Plot summary. One night during carnival season, a masked Don Juan Tenorio arrives at the Hostería del Laurel (Laurel Tavern). The young gallant writes a mysterious letter, commanding his servant, Marcos Ciutti, to deliver it to a certain "Doña Inés" and bring back a reply. Meanwhile, more masked revelers converge upon the Laurel Tavern; many are Don Juan's own friends and acquaintances, eager to learn the result of a wager made a year ago between Don Juan and another gallant, Don Luis Mejía. Also among the throng, however, are Don Gonzalo de Ulloa—*comendador mayor* (a high-ranking official) of the order of Calatrava—and Don Diego Tenorio. Each has his own reasons for attempting to discern Don Juan's true character.

The hour of reckoning (8:00 P.M.) arrives: it is revealed that Don Juan and Don Luis wagered which of them could do more harm in 12 months. Before an avid audience, the two men meet, unmask, and regale each other with tales of their misdeeds during the past year, which include seductions, abandonments, brawls, duels, killings, and thefts. When they compare written records, Don Juan is revealed as the victor. His list of sexual conquests, however, lacks two kinds of women: a nun and the bride of a friend. Don Juan boasts that he can manage to attain both in 6 days and informs his rival that the bride in question will be none other than Doña Ana de Pantoja, whom Don Luis intends to marry the next day. Incensed, Don Luis warns Don Juan that the stake in this wager will be life, but Don Juan readily accepts the terms.

Just then, an outraged Don Gonzalo and Don Diego confront the younger men. Don Gonzalo reveals himself as the father of convent-bred Doña Inés—Don Juan's prospective bride—and declares he would rather see his daughter dead than married to such a scoundrel. Don Diego, Don Juan's own father, likewise expresses his disgust and publicly disowns his son. Don Juan openly defies both men, vowing to live his life to please only himself.

In an attempt to forestall Don Juan's seduction of Doña Ana, Don Luis lodges an accusation that results in his rival's arrest by the night watch. However, Don Juan has employed similar tactics so that Don Luis is arrested by another night patrol. Freed with the help of his friends, Don Luis hurries to Doña Ana's house to warn her. She agrees to let her betrothed into the house at ten o'clock, so that he can prevent an entrance by Don Juan. But Don Juan, also freed from custody, overhears their conversation and plots to impersonate Don Luis to gain access to the house and Doña Ana. Encountering Don Luis in the street, Don Juan has his own men bind, gag, and carry off his rival, then bribes Doña Ana's maid to give him the key to the house at ten o'clock that night.

Don Juan's other scheme—to abduct Doña Inés from her convent—also progresses. Meeting with Doña Inés's *duenna*, Brígida, whom he has bribed to deliver a letter to the young woman, Don Juan learns from her that the innocent Doña Inés already loves him, without ever having seen him. Entrusting Don Juan with a key to the convent garden, Brígida reveals the location of Doña Inés's cell before taking her leave.

At the Convent of the Calatrava Order, the Abbess praises Doña Inés for her piety and longs for the day when the girl will take her final vows as a nun. Alone, however, Inés confesses that her religious vocation, once so strong, has withered because of her newfound passion for Don Juan. Brígida, the girl's *duenna*, arrives at their shared cell and quickly directs Inés's attention to Don Juan's letter, hidden in a book of hours. On reading her suitor's impassioned verses, Doña Inés is so overcome by love that she swoons at the sight of Don Juan entering her cell at nine o'clock that night. Pleased with his success, Don Juan easily carries off the unconscious girl, accompanied by a fearful Brígida, from the convent. Shortly after their flight, Don Gonzalo arrives at the convent to make certain that his daughter remains cloistered, but discovers that she has already been kidnaped by Don Juan, and rides to her rescue.

Midnight finds Brígida and Doña Inés safely lodged in Don Juan's country house beside the Guadalquivir River on the outskirts of Seville. When Inés awakens, Brígida tells her the convent was on fire and Don Juan saved them. Not entirely convinced, Doña Inés prepares to flee the house but is prevented by the arrival of Don Juan, returned from his seduction of Doña Ana. Doña Inés pleads for her release but Don Juan assures her of her safety and makes a persuasive and impassioned declaration of love. Overwhelmed, Inés then confesses that she loves Don Juan and cannot live without him. Genuinely moved by her devotion, Don Juan vows to redeem himself so that Don Gonzalo will consent to their marriage.

Don Juan's noble intentions are thwarted, however, by the arrivals of Don Luis and Don Gonzalo, both determined to avenge the dishonor done to their loved ones. Refusing to believe Don Juan's supplications, Don Gonzalo will not grant him Inés's hand in marriage and furthermore accuses him of cowardice. Don Luis inflames the situation by taunting Don Juan. Enraged by their combined insults, Don Juan shoots Don Gonzalo and runs his sword through Don Luis, then leaps into the river to escape the police pounding at his door. Emerging from her chamber, Doña Inés discovers her father's corpse and is devastated to learn that Don Juan killed him. But the prospect of Don Juan's being punished for his crimes dismays her too.

Five years after the events of that night, as the second part of the play begins, a sculptor adds

Pedro de Pool
Don Juan Tenorio

Sergio Doré, Jr.
Don Luis Mejía

Aurora Collazo
Doña Inés

Actors from *Don Juan Tenorio,* which is performed throughout Spain on All Saint's Day.

the finishing touches to a pantheon of statues. He is interrupted at his labors by a masked man who claims to have been away from Spain for several years and who seeks to know the story behind the pantheon. The sculptor reveals that, on his deathbed, Don Diego Tenorio ordered his palace razed and a cemetery built for the victims of his wicked son, Don Juan. Warming to his theme, the sculptor displays to the stranger all of his statues, including that of Doña Inés, who died in her convent after Don Juan abandoned her. The masked man gives the sculptor a purse of gold to reward him for the beauty of his labors, then reveals himself as Don Juan and orders the sculptor to leave the grounds.

Kneeling before Doña Inés's monument in this midsummer night, Don Juan recalls his lost love and near-redemption, and prays wistfully to her spirit to ask God's mercy for him. Suddenly, the statue disappears and Don Juan finds himself speaking to the ghost of Doña Inés, who tells him she has made a bargain with God either to bring Don Juan's soul back to heaven with her or to be damned with him for all eternity. The choice is to be Don Juan's, however—and he must decide by dawn.

After Inés's spirit departs, Don Juan questions what he has seen and heard, although her statue is still missing. He also expresses doubt that his years of sin and depravity could ever be forgiven by God. Sensing that the pantheon statues have turned towards him, Don Juan shouts his defiance at them, attracting the attention of two passers-by—Don Rafael de Avellaneda and Captain Centellas—who are drinking companions from his days in Seville. The three men renew their acquaintance. Don Juan invites his friends to dine with him, then brashly extends the same invitation to the statue of Don Gonzalo, announcing that only his late enemy's presence at his table will convince him of an afterlife. Avellaneda and Centellas express unease at such fool-hardiness, but Don Juan declares that the dead do not frighten him.

While drinking and dining at Don Juan's house, the trio hear increasingly loud knocks upon the doors. After Don Juan bolts the door, the statue of Don Gonzalo comes through the door without opening it. Avellaneda and Centellas faint, leaving Don Juan alone with his one-time enemy, who informs Don Juan that he will die the next day and that the fate of his soul hangs in the balance. Don Gonzalo then invites Don Juan to come and make his choice to repent or be damned beside Don Gonzalo's tomb, subsequently disappearing through the wall. Still plagued by doubts, Don Juan attempts to dismiss Don Gonzalo's visitation as trickery, even after Doña Inés's shade reappears to plead with him once more. Rousing his unconscious friends, Don Juan accuses them of staging the visitation; they, in turn, accuse him of drugging them, and challenges to a duel are issued. Captain Centellas kills Don Juan outside his new home (as explained by the statue of Doña Ines's father, the Comendador Don Gonzalo).

Early the next morning, Don Juan returns to the cemetery, where the statues of Inés and Don Gonzalo are both missing. His knock upon Don Gonzalo's tomb transforms it into a banquet table that horribly mimics his own of the previous night. Snakes, bones, and ashes are served as dishes, goblets burn with fire, and ghostly guests sit around the table. Don Gonzalo's statue again attempts to tell Don Juan of the power of repentance, but the young man remains skeptical, even after learning that his earthly form was slain in the duel with his friends and is now being prepared for burial. As the funeral procession approaches the cemetery, Don Gonzalo takes hold of Don Juan's hand through trickery, then prepares to drag him off to hell. Frantic, Don Juan finally prays for divine forgiveness, stretching out his free hand to heaven.

The tomb of Doña Inés opens and her shade emerges to take his outstretched hand. Don Gonzalo and the other phantoms vanish as Inés's shade assures Don Juan of his salvation. They sink together onto a bed of flowers scattered by angels, and their joined souls—in the form of flames—mount to heaven as the play ends.

Faith and skepticism. Although Zorrilla's Don Juan is as reckless and bold as the Don Juan first presented in Tirso de Molina's *The Trickster of Seville*, ultimately both interpretations are very much the products of their times. Nowhere is this perhaps more obvious than in the character's differing philosophies.

Hedonistic and confident to the point of hubris, Tirso's Don Juan does not engage in self-analysis or reflection; rather, he lives entirely in the moment, never considering the future or the consequences of his misdeeds. By contrast, Zorrilla's Don Juan resembles other Romantic figures, such as Byron's Childe Harold and Manfred, in his brooding sensibility, self-scrutiny, and ongoing conflict between his higher and lower impulses. In a moment of introspection, Zorrilla's Don Juan admits to sharing the priests' belief "that there's a fallen angel / Lives in each man. My heart is like a cloister, / Wherein the man I might have been, the man I might / Still be, is shut away from sun and liberty" (Zorrilla, *Don Juan Tenorio*, p. 74). Nonetheless, he feels impelled to continue his libertine ways: "I bear a fire within me / That calls for victims, that unless I feed it, / Makes me a walking hell; sin's my religion, / Ill-deeds my sacraments, myself the priest. / What's law to me whose only law's desire?" (*Don Juan Tenorio*, p. 74).

Don Juan's sense of isolation is heightened by his failure to redeem himself through the love of Doña Inés. As he sees it, if salvation does not come through her, it will probably not come at all. The failure contributes to his skepticism—his ongoing doubt and need to challenge accepted beliefs, especially with regard to religion. This is another trait that sets him apart from his literary precursor. Tirso's Don Juan is not a skeptic, an unbeliever, or a heretic; indeed, he believes in God and arrogantly trusts that he will escape damnation for his wicked deeds by confessing his sins and receiving absolution while on his deathbed. Zorrilla's Don Juan, however, not only doubts his own salvation but the very existence of an afterlife, cynically declaring,

All that we are is here. We are not born
But as the brutes are; and like brutes we
    perish,
Crumble and rot; the rest is windy talk,
And traps of crafty priests that work men's
    fears
Of a hereafter, sell them dear salvation
By masses, candles, bulls, and trips to Rome.
                        (*Don Juan Tenorio*, p. 172)

Even after Don Juan receives proof of the existence of an afterlife by means of the animation of Don Gonzalo's statue, the young Spaniard continues to doubt divine mercy and his ability to earn it. Although the statue exhorts, "Repentance yet can change a soul's direction; / And heaven's grace gives you one moment more," a defiant, despairing Don Juan asks, "How shall one moment weigh the balance down / Against the weight of thirty years of sin? / . . . Shall God receive him who rejected God?" (*Don Juan Tenorio*, pp. 208-209). Don Juan's skepticism, mingled with his self-doubt, hinders his ability to place his faith in a higher authority or to embrace the concepts of grace and repentance. Not until damnation has literally taken him by the hand can Zorrilla's Don Juan beg for the mercy that he doubts so thoroughly could ever be accorded to him.

While the skepticism of Zorrilla's Don Juan is in keeping with the Romantic emphasis on the individual and his particular sentiments, it is worth noting that skepticism as a philosophy may have existed as early as 1000-600 B.C.E. Modern skepticism can be said to date from the sixteenth century as voyages of exploration, scientific discoveries, and religious movements such as the Reformation radically changed the entire world view of Western Europe. Significantly, Zorrilla sets *Don Juan Tenorio* not during the medieval era of Tirso's *The Trickster of Seville* but during the mid-sixteenth century—1545 to 1550, to be precise—in the midst of these dramatic historical changes. Thus, it could be argued that Don Juan's skepticism is as much the product of the play's setting as of the dramatist's Romanticism, or of Zorrilla's faith in the Virgin Mary, who, as the Mother of Jesus, can intercede on behalf of a sinner's salvation. Doña Inés fulfils such a role in *Don Juan Tenorio*.

Sources and literary context. According to Zorrilla's autobiography, *Don Juan Tenorio* was written at the request of a theater-owner friend facing bankruptcy, and the play took only 20 days to complete. In all probability, Zorrilla was already familiar with his country's popular folk-hero; indeed, only Don Quixote might be said to exceed Don Juan in familiarity to Spanish audiences. A variety of prior treatments of the story would also have been available, including Tirso de Molina's **The Trickster of Seville** (1630; also in *WLAIT 5: Spanish and Portugese Literatures and Their Times*) and Antonio de Zamora's *No hay plazo que no se cumpla ni deuda que no se pague* (1722; There is no term that does not expire nor debt that is not paid). The latter work, while less famous than Tirso's, might well have had the more immediate influence on Zorrilla's play. Literary scholar L. L. McClelland noted Zamora's embellishments to Tirso's starker play:

DON JUAN AND THE GRACE OF GOD

*T*he *Modern Catholic Dictionary* defines *grace* as "the supernatural gift that God, of his free benevolence, bestows on rational creatures for their eternal salvation" (Hardon, p. 236) "Grace" can *only* be bestowed freely by God—it cannot be claimed, coerced, or demanded. *Repentance* means "voluntary sorrow [for having committed an offense against God] . . . together with the resolve to amend one's conduct by taking the necessary means to avoid the occasions of sin" (Hardon, p. 463). Both "grace" and "repentance" play pivotal roles in Zorrilla's play: the proud Don Juan cannot bring himself to believe in the former, nor, at first, can he humble himself to express the latter. His last-minute act of contrition, however—together with Inés's love—earns him the gift of God's grace and allows his soul to be saved.

[T]he amount of sword-play is trebled; hidings and masqueradings occur more frequently; a new company of students provides riotous entertainment; all of which interrupts the powerful, sweeping movement of the original and turns it into a mixture of cloak-and-sword play and comedy of magic. Don Juan himself is not allowed to rest on the laurels of his former ill-gained victories. He must pursue his wicked ways more deliberately. He must kill more and deceive more, mock more and defy more.
                        (McClelland, p. 202)

Certainly, in terms of tone and atmosphere, *Don Juan Tenorio* resembles Zamora's play more closely than Tirso's, employing such elaborate touches as the fiery goblets at the feast held by the dead and stage directions that call for various ghosts to walk through walls or disappear through trap doors. Moreover, Zamora apparently ends his play with a hint of possible redemption for its swaggering anti-hero, an idea Zorrilla adopts and brings to full fruition.

Whatever the extent of these influences, *Don Juan Tenorio* emerges as both derivative and innovative. It contains elements of *capa-y-espada* (cape and sword) comedies, religious parables, swashbuckling romance, and supernatural fantasy. Zorrilla himself described *Don Juan Tenorio* as a *drama religioso-fantástico*, humorously noting that the seven-act drama violated every canon of the theater (*Don Juan Tenorio*, p. xi). Some nineteenth- and twentieth-century commentators pronounced *Don Juan Tenorio* poorly constructed and overly sentimental, yet few could deny that Zorrilla had written a colorful and engrossing work featuring a generous, passionate Don Juan with whom audiences could fully sympathize.

Events in History at the Time the Play Was Written

The Romantic Movement in Spain. During the absolutist regime of Ferdinand VII (1814-33), many Spanish liberals were exiled to England and France where they came into contact with the intellectual and aesthetic movement known as Romanticism, which the émigrés helped popularize upon their return to Spain in the 1830s. European Romanticism had begun in the late eighteenth century as a reaction against Neoclassicism, which emphasized the ideals and standards of classical Greece and Rome. Plays and poems of the Neoclassical period were judged according to how well they adhered to established verse or dramatic forms or how faithfully they upheld the classical dramatic unities of time, space, and action. Intellect and reason were the guiding forces in the Neoclassical movement.

By contrast, Romanticism emphasized elements that Neoclassicism disdained, such as imagination, emotion, and the importance of the individual as opposed to society. Proponents of the new movement altered their entire criteria of aesthetic evaluation, concentrating on the emotions infused into and evoked by the artist's work. Between them, England and Germany produced many dominant figures in Romanticism, including poets William Wordsworth, Lord Byron, and Heinrich Heine and composers Richard Wagner and Ludwig Von Beethoven. Spain too yielded many talented authors—Mariano José de Larra; José de Espronceda; Ángel de Saavedra, Duque de Rivas; and José Zorrilla. More renowned nationally than internationally, they emerged during that

comparatively brief period from 1833 to 1850, when Spanish Romanticism was at its height.

Salient traits of Spanish Romanticism included exaltation of the individual; the pursuit of political, artistic, and personal freedom; the choice of exotic and antique settings; and the rediscovery of the nation's traditional myths and heroes. Spanish Romantics embraced their past, reexploring medieval poetry and Golden Age drama but integrating their own perspectives as well. In *Don Juan Tenorio*, Zorrilla resurrects the traditional folk-hero made famous in medieval ballads and Tirso de Molina's *The Trickster of Seville*; however, the sensibility that infuses the play is Zorrilla's own. In Zorrilla's hands, Don Juan emerges a quintessential Romantic figure: a proud, passionate, flamboyant individual who scorns human and divine authority alike but who is not immune to the pure love that becomes his ultimate salvation.

Reception. Premiering on March 28, 1844, *Don Juan Tenorio* enjoyed moderate first-night success and remains a popular favorite with Spanish audiences today. Later, in his autobiography, Zorrilla scoffed at the play as "the greatest nonsense ever written" and pointed out how it violated all the canons of the theater (*Don Juan Tenorio*, p. xi). Nonetheless, Zorilla's best claim to enduring fame probably rests in his authorship of *Don Juan Tenorio*.

After Zorrilla's death on January 23, 1893, many critics and reviewers passed judgement on the play. While some disagreed about Zorrilla's technical skills as a dramatist, nearly all agreed that *Don Juan Tenorio*—whatever flaws it might possess—was an undeniably engrossing work and its author's best claim to immortality. In *Poet Lore*, Fanny Hale Gardiner noted Don Juan Tenorio's resounding popular success: "Fifty years of unabated applause for what was the work of twenty days to a young man of twenty-seven years, seems an incontrovertible verdict for genius and renown. It is probably safe to predict for it another fifty years of the same popularity" (Gardiner in Harris and Fitzgerald, p. 523). Gardiner was especially impressed by Zorrilla's transformation of his source material, proclaiming, "Although Zorrilla has simply resurrected and rehabilitated a mass of old legend, his work has thrown all other versions into the shade. . . . Don Juan Tenorio is the most important of his poetic productions, the greatest of his legends, and it encloses all his poetic personality" (Gardiner in Harris and Fitzgerald, p. 523-24). In *Poetry Review*, Ella Crosby Heath subjected Zorrilla to a more critical analysis, remarking, "His work is often lacking in unity, and weak in construction, but when the foundations were laid, and the structure indicated, as in the national legends, his facility of execution and his felicity of phrase gave the theme new life and fresh beauty" (Heath in Harris and Fitzgerald, p. 524). Summing up the enduring appeal of Zorrilla's best-known play, Heath wrote:

> Don Juan Tenorio, Zorrilla's supreme claim to immortality, is one of the most surprising plays ever penned. Only a Spaniard could have written it, and only in Spain can it be entirely understood and appreciated. It begins on a spirited note of brilliant comedy which develops into a farcical but equally brilliant flippancy; it passes from comedy to romantic and tragic drama.
>
> (Heath in Harris and Fitzgerald, p. 524)

—Pamela S. Loy

For More Information

Carr, Raymond, ed. *Spain: A History*. Oxford: Oxford University Press, 2000.

Defourneaux, Marcelin. *Daily Life in Spain in the Golden Age*. Trans. Newton Branch. London: George Allen and Unwin, 1970.

Hardon, John A., S. J. *Modern Catholic Dictionary*. Garden City: Doubleday, 1980.

Harris, Laurie Lanzen, and Sheila Fitzgerald, eds. *Nineteenth-Century Literature Criticim*. Vol. 6. Detroit: Gale Research, 1984.

Kamen, Henry. *Spain 1469-1714*. London: Longman's, 1983.

McClelland, I. L. *The Origins of the Romantic Movement in Spain*. Liverpool: University of Liverpool Press, 1975.

Ortiz, Antonio Domínguez. *The Golden Age of Spain 1516-1659*. Trans. James Casey. New York: Basic Books, 1971.

Rosenberg, John R. *The Black Butterfly: Concepts of Spanish Romanticism*. University: Romance Monographs, 1998.

Ruiz, Teofilo F. *Spanish Society 1400-1600*. London: Longman's Press, 2001.

Silver, Philip W. *Ruin and Restitution: Reinterpreting Romanticism in Spain*. Nashville: Vanderbilt University Press, 1997.

Zorrilla, José. *Don Juan Tenorio*. Trans. Walter Owen. Buenos Aires: Walter Owen, 1944.

Don Quixote

by

Miguel de Cervantes Saavedra

M iguel de Cervantes Saavedra was born in 1547 in the university town of Alcalá de Henares, Spain, to a struggling barber-surgeon's family. Unable to afford enrollment in the university, Cervantes acquired a different sort of education by joining the military. He served with distinction against the Turks in the battle of Lepanto (1571; in Greece), permanently losing the use of his left hand in the process. On the voyage home, he and his brother were captured by Barbary Coast pirates and imprisoned for five years in Algeria. After being ransomed, Cervantes returned to Spain to find the country in economic peril and his job prospects slim. He applied for posts in Spain's overseas colonies but, unable to secure one, took a job as a tax collector; when his accounts failed to balance, the job landed him in the Royal Prison of Seville. Cervantes has hinted that the seeds of *Don Quixote* (spelled *Don Quijote* in modern Spanish) took root during this imprisonment. At age 58, Cervantes experienced his first literary success by publishing Part 1 of this novel. He went on to write numerous poems, plays, and fictional works, most notably the *Exemplary Tales* in 1613 and Part 2 of *Don Quixote* in 1615. A parody of the chivalric romances popular in Cervantes's day, *Don Quixote* informs as it entertains. The work is considered the first modern novel because of how its central characters interact and because of its general reflections on life in Counter-Reformation Spain.

THE LITERARY WORK

A novel set in Spain in the late 1500s and early 1600s; Part 1 published in Spanish (as *El ingenioso hidalgo Don Quixote de la Mancha*) in 1605, in English in 1612; Part 2 in Spanish (as *Segunda parte del ingenioso cavallero Don Quixote de la Mancha*) in 1615, in English in 1620.

SYNOPSIS

After reading too many popular tales of chivalry, an idealistic, imaginative middle-aged gentleman goes mad, remakes himself as a knight, and, in imitation of his favorite fictional heroes, embarks on a series of adventures with his "squire," an illiterate peasant.

Events in History at the Time of the Novel

Spain's Golden Age—imperial pre-eminence. Cervantes was born 50 years into Spain's ascension as a global empire. The nation rapidly achieved the rank of a world power after the union through marriage of Queen Isabella I of Castile and King Ferdinand of Aragon in 1469. In 1492 Columbus's discovery of the New World gave Spain footholds in both Americas, lands occupied by indigenous peoples, whom Spain proceeded to conquer and colonize. Shortly

Miguel de Cervantes Saaverda

thereafter, through war and marriage, Spain gained control of most of Western Europe, including much of Italy, Germany, the Netherlands, and Austria. The breadth of Spain's achievement was awe-inspiring, prompting King Ferdinand to claim in 1514, "the crown of Spain has not for over seven hundred years been as great or resplendent as it now is" (Ferdinand in Kamen, p. 9). The "seven hundred years" harks back to Spain's 1492 reconquest of the last of the Muslim hold-outs in Granada, after more than seven centuries of widespread Muslim rule. Also in 1492 the "Catholic Monarchs" Isabella and Ferdinand called for the expulsion or forced conversion of all Jews.

Isabella and Ferdinand pursued a policy of Catholicizing all the subjects within their vast domain. They used a tribunal of priests, the Holy Inquisition, to test the purity of the religious faith of their converted subjects. Their successor and grandson Charles I of Castile (reigned 1516-56), also known as Charles V of the Holy Roman Empire, held grander ambitions for the achievement of a universal monarchy or united "Christendom" under Spain's direction. This conception of a Holy Roman Empire, a Christian version of the ancient Roman Empire, enjoyed favor among the Spanish nobility, the Spanish Catholic Church, and Spanish humanists with their esteem for classical learning. (Humanists favored a revival of Greek

and Roman letters and an individualistic, critical bent that would manifest itself in art.) Spain's achievements, indeed astounding, gave rise to an intense pride, which "revealed itself in a feeling of theological, and sometimes even of racial, superiority over others" (Kamen, pp. 193-94).

Whether or not Charles I himself sought world domination is debatable; however, his enemies—the French and the Ottoman Turks—took the threat seriously and became Spain's chief rivals for power in Europe, embarking on a series of wars through the next century. Meanwhile, northern Europe saw the onset of movements to reform Christianity. The Dutch humanist Desiderius Erasmus proposed disciplining the Catholic Church from within; reforms proposed by the German monk Martin Luther amounted to a disciplining from without, initiating in 1517 the Reformation, which divided Latin Christendom into Protestant and Catholic factions. Spain, for its part, continued to be a staunchly Catholic nation. But by 1550 its clergy was showing the same excesses common elsewhere in Europe: priests were notoriously absent from parishes; churchmen kept concubines and became famous for their illiteracy and ignorance. Such failings, along with the Reformation, led to the Counter-Reformation, a militant movement to reform the Church from within while opposing the Protestants and Erasmus. This militancy gave rise to some of the most unforgettable works of Spanish culture as well as to some of its most forgettable.

Spain's Golden Age—literary pre-eminence. *Don Quixote* is only one of the products of Spanish cultural pre-eminence from about 1550 to 1650. The era saw Spain produce some of the finest literature, thought, and painting in world history. The spread of Castilian, carried into the far reaches of the empire, as Spain's dominant language, was one of the main developments, but, in the words of one historian, "this does not mean that the 'Golden Age' was exclusively a Castilian achievement. On the contrary, the development of creativity occurred only because there was a positive response to multiple internal and external influences—Arabic, Jewish, Italian, Flemish, American—that stimulated all corners of the peninsula" (Kamen, p. 193). Cervantes himself spoke of his Spain as the "common mother of all nations" (Cervantes in Kamen, p. 193). The country was ripe for cultural exchange and creativity, and its artists rose to the occasion, producing unparalleled works.

Spain reached a summit of its Golden Age in the poetry and prose of Saint Teresa of Avila and

Saint John of the Cross (see **Interior Castle** and **"Dark Night" and Other Poems,** also in *WLAIT 5: Spanish and Portuguese Literatures and Their Times*). Saint John (1542-91), often described as the finest lyric poet to emerge in Europe, wrote about the human soul's quest for union with God. Much of the same mystic symbolism surfaces in the religious painting of El Greco (1541-1614). Another pre-eminent Golden-Age poet, Garcilaso de la Vega (1503?-1536) revolutionized Spanish verse, his posthumously published verse (1543) setting standards of refinement for subsequent lyric poets: Lope de Vega, Francisco de Quevedo, and Luis de Góngora. Also a playwright, Lope established a new way of writing theater in Spanish—a three-act play that mixes comic and tragic elements. Astoundingly prolific, he said he wrote 1,000 plays, (less than 400 are extant); not Lope, though, but his successor Pedro Calderón de la Barca, would write the most widely read play written in Spanish, the philosophical drama **Life Is a Dream** (also in *WLAIT 5: Spanish and Portuguese Literatures and Their Times*). Calderón was court playwright for King Philip IV. Philip's court painter, Diego Velázquez, reached new heights in his medium, representing distant vision with short brushstrokes (as in his *The Maids-in-Waiting*), anticipating nineteenth-century impressionism. Like Cervantes in *Don Quixote*, Velázquez also used his art to debunk heroic myth, satirizing, for example, the debauchery of military life in his own times in his painting *Mars*; which depicts the Roman war-god Mars as an aging, mustachioed soldier, sitting helmeted but otherwise unclothed on a bed after he has presumably enjoyed erotic relations with Venus.

Plight of the hidalgo. The era's ardent Catholicism, a legacy of the medieval Crusades (holy wars for Christian territory) and of the centuries of Reconquest, inspired a new chivalric spirit during the Golden Age. Much like medieval knights, Spain's armed forces in Europe and conquistadores in the New World thought of themselves as "soldiers of God," their numerous victories and seeming invincibility reinforcing this image of themselves. Men such as Hernán Cortés, conqueror of Mexico, captured the imaginations of those around them as the knights-errant of the sixteenth and seventeenth centuries. There was the possibility of wealth in the New World too. Many hidalgos (low-ranking members of the nobility who were often impoverished but nevertheless expected to keep up the appearances befitting their rank) sought to improve their fortunes as conquistadors in the New World. As already men-

tioned, Cervantes, who was himself an hidalgo, sought a post overseas, albeit unsuccessfully.

Whereas it had been possible in the Middle Ages for hidalgos to earn their fortune and glory by serving as knights in Europe, it was virtually impossible by the end of the 1500s. Most of Europe had already been conquered; and though Spain's empire spanned the oceans, the country itself remained poor, offering soldiers low pay and little or no opportunity to fight as part of a private force for booty, as the medieval knights had. On the other hand, the New World offered similar opportunities. "The pioneers in America were not nobles but dispossessed Spaniards of all conditions, many of them soldiers and sailors un-

---

FROM MEDIEVAL KNIGHTS TO GOLDEN AGE HIDALGOS

Medieval knights fought as commissioned soldiers for specific kingdoms and lords, and later, during the Crusades, for the Catholic Church. They would be rewarded with spoils from victory, as well as land and noble titles, which elevated their status. A hidalgo in the sixteenth-century, Don Quixote had no such opportunity. Properly speaking, *hidalgos* refers to those Spaniards who have the status of nobles but no specific rank. They comprised the lowest category of the nobility. Don Quixote's sole assets consisted of his status as an "old Christian" and "non-taxpayer." While higher-ranking nobles received palace appointments and tax revenues, hidalgos were entitled to neither, and like the lower classes, could no longer augment their fortunes or elevate their status by becoming knights, as in the Middle Ages. In a word, the hidalgo in Spain became obsolete. Those who did not join the conquistadores found themselves stricken with the "subtle hunger of the hidalgo," working in Spain at jobs they detested or aimlessly idling their lives away (Defourneaux, p. 41).

---

employed after the wars in Granada and Italy had come to an end, others young and hardy men of limited means, including many hidalgos and illiterate laborers who looked to America to better their fortunes" (Kamen, p. 91). To conquer the unknown, risking all to serve God and their king and to grow rich in the process became the credo of the conquistadores, who combined a spirit of militant Catholicism with personal aspirations, "their heads filled with fantastic notions, their courage spurred by noble examples of the great heroes of chivalry" (Schulte, p. 69).

The problem with novels of chivalry. From where did hidalgos get such fantastic notions?—in no small part, from the romances of chivalry. Throughout most of the sixteenth century, these works were bestsellers—*Amadís de Gaula* (1508; Amadis of Gaul) by Garci Ordóñez de Montalvo set the standard. A romance in four volumes, the

---

PRINTING AND THE NEW READER

~

Poor literature proliferated after the 1450 invention of the printing press by the German Johann Gutenberg. Before Gutenberg's time, manuscripts were reproduced by hand, a slow, painstaking process. As a result, books were rare and costly, and only a small fraction of the population—mainly clergy—could read or write. Moreover, most books were written in Latin—the universal language of educated Europe, but one unknown to most Europeans. With the advent of the printing press, the cost of books dropped precipitously and literacy rose dramatically. Despite the rise, the number of Spaniards who actually could have read the first part of *Don Quixote* in 1605 was probably no greater than 20 percent. But, even Spaniards who never learned to read were affected by the printing revolution. As the number of readers grew, the literate villager read aloud to neighbors. Scenes such as the one in *Don Quixote* that features a priest reading "The Story of Ill-Advised Curiosity" (otherwise called "The Tale of Foolish Curiosity") to guests at an inn, were undoubtedly common in Spain at this time. The result was a new audience, less educated and of a lower class than before, traits that had a great effect on the types of texts produced. By the late 1500s, more European books were being published in Castilian Spanish and other dialects than in Latin. Also books accessible to those with limited reading skills began to outnumber complex, scholarly texts. Curious new readers snatched up miscellanies of proverbs and practical tidbits as well as longer prose fiction. In addition to chivalric romances, pastoral romances such as Jorge de Montemayor's *Diana* (1559), a favorite of Don Quixote's, became bestsellers.

---

work describes the adventures of a knight who personifies the chivalric code—single-minded devotion to one woman, loyalty to one's superior, fanatic hatred of the infidel, absorption in the pursuit of idealistic justice, and defense of the oppressed. So successful was *Amadís de Gaula*

that its publication generated many other novels of chivalry, which carried its elements to excess. The adventures conveyed no universal truth and strayed far from any consideration of verisimilitude. It is against these inferior chivalric romances that Cervantes directs his satire. Don Quixote reads so many bad chivalric novels that he loses his sanity and decides to restore chivalric ideals to a world gone amuck. As he pursues his quest, the story becomes a parody of the romance of chivalry, meanwhile conveying universal truths in a lifelike context.

Cervantes censures bad chivalric novels for their immorality, poor style, untruthfulness, and absurdities. The purpose of art, says a priest to Don Quixote, is to teach and delight at the same time, but the mediocre novels of chivalry do neither. The style of many of these novels is so obscure that they offer negative examples to writers and readers. The chivalric novels of the real-life writer Feliciano de Silva (1492?-1558?), a favorite of Don Quixote, are a frequent butt of Cervantes's satire, which parodies their turgid style and overly complex sentences: "The heavens on high divinely drop your divinity down on you, the stars themselves bringing you strength, thus making you deserving of the high deserts which your immensity deserves" (Cervantes, *Don Quijote*, p. 9). "Specializing in obfuscation, the authors of inferior chivalry novels also confuse history with fiction. They do not know how to sustain the illusion that things are really happening, precisely because they have no clear purpose" (Riley, pp. 47-48). Cervantes reflects this confusion when his protagonist, grown mad from reading bad chivalric novels, believes fantastic characters like King Arthur and the Knights of the Round Table to be as real as Spanish historical figures like El Cid. Finally, bad chivalric novels were associated with immorality. They typically displayed excessive violence, eroticism, and sentimentality. The innkeeper in *Don Quixote* admires the hero of the novel *Felixmarte de Hircania* for slicing five giants in half like bags of beans; the chambermaid Maritornes, for her part, enjoys the sentimental eroticism of ladies embracing their knightly loves under orange trees while their *duennas,* spinster guardians, keep watch, filled with envy and anxiety.

The Novel in Focus

Plot summary. The first part of *Don Quixote* opens with Cervantes's prologue, in which the author encourages readers to probe the novel for deeper meaning, indicating that he has written an entirely different type of chivalric tale. Using the device of a friend who rescues him from his writer's block, Cervantes mocks the literary convention of writing flowery prologues, that of quoting ad nauseam every famous writer and philosopher from antiquity. His friend says he need not "because the whole tale is an attack on chivalry, which Aristotle never heard of, and St. Basil never mentioned, and Cicero never ran across" (*Don Quijote*, p. 6).

Chapter 1 sets up the parody of contemporary romances of chivalry. It opens with an introduction to a middle-aged country gentleman, Mr. Quixana (or Quijada, Quesada, or Quejana), who spends his idle hours—which are many because he is a hidalgo without much means or occupation—enraptured in chivalric prose. He marvels at the "pearl-like" wisdom of authors such as Feliciano de Silva who write such eloquent sentences as, "The ability to reason the unreason which has afflicted my reason saps my ability to reason, so that I complain with good reason of your infinite loveliness" (*Don Quijote*, p. 9). Trying to decipher the meaning of such prose causes poor Mr. Quixana to lose his sanity, for "even Aristotle couldn't have comprehended if he'd come back to life for just that purpose" (*Don Quijote*, p. 10). Further, intoxicated by the fantastic exploits and seeming valor of the knightly existence—particularly as compared to his own empty life—he remakes himself as a knight and sets forth to "right every manner of wrong" and "cover himself with eternal fame and glory" (*Don Quijote*, p. 10).

Naming himself "Don Quixote," a name apparently based on a word denoting a piece of armor for the thigh, he dusts off his great-grandfather's suit of armor—rusted and in a state of disrepair—dons it, and mounts his trusty steed, a poor workhorse that he renames "Rocinante," which means "old horse before," because "an old horse was exactly what it had been, before, while now it had risen to be first and foremost among all the horses in the world" (*Don Quijote*, p. 11). Here Don Quixote's idealistic qualities come to the fore, as does his vivid imagination. The world transforms itself in his mind's eye. An old horse becomes the first and foremost in all the world, and he, Don Quixote de la Mancha, the noblest and most esteemed knight-errant straight out of the pages of *Amadís de Gaula*. His transformation nearly complete, Don Quixote invents Dulcinea del Toboso, a noble lady whose honor he will preserve and fight his battles for (for "a knight-

errant without love entanglements would be like a tree without leaves or fruit" [*Don Quijote*, p. 12]). She is the transformation of a peasant woman with whom he has been secretly in love but has never addressed. In honor of Dulcinea, he embarks on his first chivalric expedition.

Don Quixote mistakes a decrepit country inn for a castle, two prostitutes for virtuous ladies, and a roguish innkeeper for a great lord. He requests the "lord" to dub him a knight in accord with the rituals performed in the novels of chivalry he has read, so that he may properly go about his knightly deeds. Amused by his madness, the innkeeper agrees to the ceremony and the ladies treat him kindly.

Upon leaving the inn, our hero performs his first knightly act, rescuing a servant he perceives to be blameless from a master's beating. However, as soon as Don Quixote leaves, the master resumes the beating more savagely than before and fires the servant without pay, revealing the harmfulness of misguided acts of chivalry. After this, Don Quixote is beaten up by a mule driver who dares insult the honor of Dulcinea del Toboso. Luckily, he is rescued by a fellow villager and returned home.

When the knight Don Quixote sets out again, it is with his newfound "squire," Sancho Panza—a peasant who speaks in prattling language and proverbs. With Sancho by his side, the knight fights windmills that he perceives to be giants, frees a chain gang of prisoners, who then rob him and his squire, and engages in similar adventures in the name of chivalry, doing more harm than good. In a series of elegant speeches, he makes the purpose of his adventures clear: to restore justice and virtue to the world by battling the forces of evil, thereby gaining fame and fortune. Sancho's motives are initially slightly less admirable. He clings to the hope that Don Quixote will make good on the promise to grant Sancho his own island to rule.

Interspersed between the adventures of the knight and squire are intercalated novels in the guise of stories told by characters they meet, including miniature pastoral romances and the tale of a soldier held captive in Muslim North Africa (autobiographical, this tale contains information based on Cervantes's own captivity in Algeria). The intercalated novels offer Cervantes the opportunity to experiment with different narrative possibilities suggested by the misadventures of his mad hero. Don Quixote's comical situation sometimes is given a serious variation in an intercalated novel. For instance, what if a madman had been driven mad because of an actual love, as opposed to a feigned chivalric love (as in Don Quixote's case)? Then there would be the intercalated novel of Cardenio of Part 1, Chapter 27.

While Don Quixote and Sancho listen to these stories and continue their exploits, the knight's village friends—the priest and the barber—devise a plan to rescue Quixote from his chivalrous hallucinations and bring him home. In disguise, they convince Don Quixote that he is enchanted and enclose him in a cage. After being released from the cage, Don Quixote is beaten to near death—this time after attacking a religious procession whose statue of the Virgin Mary he takes to be an enchanted damsel in distress. Barely able to move, he is placed on a cart and wheeled home, ending his second round of exploits.

Throughout Part 1 of *Don Quixote*, the narrator reminds us that the author's story is based on a translation of Don Quixote's original history, written by a Moor, Cide Hamete Benengeli. Cervantes purposely identifies the historian as a Moor because as an outsider hardly given to being overly sympathetic to a Christian knight, the Moor may well stray from the truthful portrayal of Don Quixote's adventures! Thus the reader must extrapolate the truth between Cide Hamete's lines.

In the final pages of Part 1, it is implied that, after recuperating from his injuries, Don Quixote engages in further adventures. Because the author can find no records of these adventures, however, this part must end with a series of poetic epitaphs found in a lead box discovered in the ruins of an ancient hermitage. These epitaphs, written in mock-epic language to parody romances of chivalry, mourn the deaths of Don Quixote, Dulcinea, Don Quixote's horse, Rocinante, and Sancho. The one for the damsel reads in part: "She whose fat and flabby face you see, / tubby-breasted, looking down her nose so, is Dulcinea . . . / whose love inspired the great knight Don Quixote" (*Don Quijote,* p. 344).

In Part 2, however, these characters return to life. After a prologue in which Cervantes scolds Alonso Fernández de Avellaneda, the author of an apocryphal sequel to *Don Quixote*, he picks up the action of the story only a few weeks after Don Quixote has returned home. There he is confronted by a neighbor, Sansón Carrasco, who has recently returned from the university, where he read Part 1 of *Don Quixote*. Carrasco explains to a pleased Don Quixote that his adventures are famous all over Europe. (This is in fact true at the point that Part 2 was written, ten years

after Part 1). Inspired by this news, Don Quixote and Sancho soon set out again to right more wrongs.

Their first adventure is an encounter with the Knight of the Mirrors, who challenges Don Quixote to a duel on the condition that, if Don Quixote loses, he will comply with any honorable requests the winner may have. However, Don Quixote soundly defeats the Knight of the Mirrors, who turns out to be Sansón Carrasco in disguise. Though Carrasco's intention was to lure Don Quixote back home again and keep him safe from more potentially harmful adventures, the neighbor gives up his plan for the time being and instead, noting the pain in his ribs, vows revenge.

After this victory, Don Quixote proudly resumes his exploits, which include an attack on puppets during a puppet-play. Since the play deals with a chivalric theme, he gets swept up into the illusion and thinks the puppets real. He embarks on a host of adventures, during which it slowly dawns on Don Quixote that he is not the hero he has deceived himself into believing. Disenchantment sets in during Chapter 10, which follows Don Quixote as he goes to the village of Toboso to greet his lady Dulcinea. When he commands Sancho to fetch her, his squire, hard-pressed to find a nonexistent lady, invents a chivalric fiction, though on a cruder, simpler plane than his master. To the credulous Don Quixote, he identifies an approaching peasant woman as Dulcinea. Don Quixote, shocked at this woman's coarse appearance, believes the enchanters have changed Dulcinea's form.

Chapter 23 marks the beginning of Don Quixote's disillusionment with his own efforts to be a knight errant. He descends into Montesinos's Cave—a symbol, perhaps, of his own unconscious. There he has a vision of Lady Belerma, figure of a chivalric tradition belonging to the legend of Charlemagne. She languishes, like his own Dulcinea, under an enchantment, for Belerma is a victim of the magician Merlin. Don Quixote also sees the enchanted Dulcinea in the cave, but, when one of her maidens asks him for a loan, he in unable to supply the cash his lady needs—a symbolic reference to his own impotence and inability to "disenchant" Dulcinea. In succeeding adventures he continues to harbor doubts about himself, about his efficacy as a hero, and about seeing the world as a place for chivalric adventure at all.

Meanwhile, Sancho Panza gradually undergoes a contrary development. His fantasy begins to run away with him. In Chapter 41, some pranksters set him and Don Quixote blindfolded on a hobbyhorse, and tell them they are flying through the air. While Don Quixote could swear they were still on the ground, Sancho has what amounts to a mystical experience, imagining himself playing in the constellation of the Pleiades (the Seven Sisters).

A series of elaborate pranks played on Don Quixote and Sancho comprise the middle section of Part 2, where knight and squire are taken in by a country duke and duchess. These nobles, who have read Part 1 of *Don Quixote,* fritter away their leisure to make life imitate art. They play along with the hero's fantasy and, for their own amusement, carry it even further. The duke and duchess grant Sancho an island to govern, as if to fulfill the chivalric promise Don Quixote made to his squire in Part 1. Sancho plays his part as governor very seriously. By now he is accustomed to living in the framework of the chivalric novel. Within that framework, Sancho uses common sense to administer justice. He "decreed such wonderful things that, to this very day, his laws are still observed there, and are known as *The Great Governor Sancho Panza's Legal System*" (*Don Quijote,* p. 623). (According to Howard Mancing, Sancho Panza occupies stage center here, as in all of Part 2. "He speaks more often [than Don Quixote] and more confidently directs the action to a greater degree"; the chapters devoted to his governership form the apex of his mental and psychological evolution [Mancing, p. 390].)

Don Quixote's faith in himself as a hero meanwhile continues to deteriorate. During a visit to Barcelona, the knight meets his downfall. He gets defeated in a joust by the Knight of the White Moon—a vengeful Sansón Carrasco in disguise. Under the terms of the agreement he had accepted before fighting Carrasco, he must renounce knighthood and return home for a year. The sacrifice proves too great: Don Quixote falls ill, and on his deathbed gives up knighthood forever. He explains that he is once again in his "right mind"—no longer Don Quixote but Alonso Quijano—and declares to Sancho: "Forgive me, my friend, for having made you seem as mad as I was, by making you fall into the same error into which I had fallen, namely, that there were, and still are, knights errant in the world" (*Don Quijote,* p. 731). Sancho, by now a thorough convert to the ideology of Don Quixote, begs him to revert to his old idealistic self and resume his mission to right the world's wrongs:

John Lithgow as Don Quixote and Bob Hoskins as Sancho Paza in the 2000 Turner Network Television rendition of *Don Quixote.*

"Don't die . . . but take my advice and live a long, long time because the worst madness a man can fall into, in this life, is to let himself die, for no real reason" (*Don Quijote,* p. 731). But it is too late. Don Quixote has reverted back to "sanity" and dies, the implication being that it is now up to Sancho—and us, Cervantes's "new readers"—to pick up where he left off.

The place of idealism. Role reversal takes place in *Don Quixote* on a scale previously unseen in any novel. Sancho Panza becomes quixoticized, caught up in the pursuit of impossible goals. Don Quixote grows to be ever more like Sancho Panza. Herein lies the great conscious innovation of the first modern novel: environment has impact on character change as the novelist explores in detail the meaning of life in general. This is the ultimate consequence of Cervantes's application of Aristotle's twin truths: it is a psychological fact—a historical truth—that Don Quixote's madness is "contagious," that ideals pass from one individual to another in ever widening circles; at the same time, it is a poetic truth that ideals should not last forever, lest society stagnate. The age of chivalry has disappeared, says this novel to its readers. The attitude of idealism, on the other hand, should last forever. The trick is to adopt attainable ideals. In Part 2 (Chapter 20), for example, the poor man Basilio adopts a reachable goal: scheming to marry the maiden Quiteria for love, he outwits her fiancé, the rich Camacho. Basilio feigns death, insisting that Quiteria marry him before he begs God's forgiveness for his sins in his final hour. "For someone as badly wounded as this young man," Sancho Panza murmured, "he certainly talks a lot" (*Don Quijote*, p. 461). Quiteria, who loves Basilio, gladly acquiesces, and the two get married at the very wedding intended for her and Camacho, her ideal suitor winning out over the practical choice.

HIDDEN MEANINGS—THE CRITICAL BENT

Woven through Don Quixote are various critiques of early-seventeenth-century Spanish society. For instance, there is implicit criticism of the excessive leisure characteristic of the high aristocracy in Cervantes's day. In the novel, the duke and duchess play enormous practical jokes on an unsuspecting Don Quixote, concocting a surrogate damsel in distress (Altisidora) instead of his own Dulcinea, when they could be occupying themselves with something far more worthwhile. Sancho Panza, to take another example, has a friend Ricote, who is a Morisco, or christianized Moor. Ricote, who disguises himself as a German because the Moriscos were expelled from Spain in 1609, lives bereft, longing for his Spanish homeland, suffering mistreatment even in North Africa, where Muslims abound. Through Ricote, the novel finds fault with the 1609 expulsion, bringing its initial readers face-to-face with the consequences of Spain's recent action.

Sources and literary context. Spain's Golden Age featured works that spanned a number of genres—pastoral romance, mystic poetry, cloak-and-dagger drama, picaresque novel. Reflecting the variety, *Don Quixote* contains elements of multiple genres. It is most obviously a parody of the chivalric romance of knightly misadventures written in a grandiose style. But it also includes stories of lovelorn unfortunates wandering the wilderness, in imitation of the pastoral romance, whose characters reject material concerns and escape to the countryside to commune with nature and lament their unrequited love. The novel is likewise a treasury of proverbs, sonnets, quotes from scripture, and debates about the nature of high quality literature. In one incident, for example, Don Quixote encounters a poor young man plodding off to war, which allows the novel, in the guise of his song, to include a contemporary Spanish literary form, a four-line folk-type verse known as the *seguidillas*.

> I'm taking my nothing
> off to war,
> but if I had anything
> I wouldn't go far.
>
> (*Don Quijote*, p. 478)

From the picaresque novel, *Don Quixote* borrows down-to-earth (sometimes slapstick) humor and characters such as the galley prisoner Ginés de Pasamonte. An often cynical response to romance literature, such novels focused on wretched antiheroes, usually poor young men forced to cheat and lie to survive in a cruel world (see **Lazarillo de Tormes,** also in *WLAIT 5: Spanish and Portuguese Literatures and Their Times*).

Although Cervantes relied on others before him for ideas about style, events, and form, the main characters in *Don Quixote* seem to be his own. Cervantes is consistently praised for his close attention to detail in portraying people from every corner of Spanish society. He gained keen insight into the lives of his fellow Spaniards—students, priests, dukes, soldiers, innkeepers, and peasants—from his wanderings. Many of his characters represent stages in Cervantes's life. He was, at various times, a student, a cardinal's assistant, a soldier, a captive in Algiers, a purveyor of food for the Spanish Armada, a prisoner, a tax collector, and, of course, a writer. Some of these jobs required frequent travel, which allowed Cervantes to form opinions not only about different classes of Spanish people, but about the different regions in which they lived. When Don Quixote battles a Basque, dines with a Barcelona gentleman, or discusses literature with the canon of Toledo, Cervantes draws on his own extensive knowledge of Spanish culture to render an authentic word-picture. Other fundamental sources on which Cervantes drew follow:

Some Sources of Ideas in Don Quixote
Poetics by Aristotle.
Greek idea of universal (poetic) truth and historical truth.
Philosophia antigua poética by Alonso López Pinciano (1596; *Ancient Poetic Philosophy*).
Harmonization of Aristotle's Poetics *with contemporary Italian literature to preserve Greek aesthetics in light of innovations.*
Ars Poetica by Horace (1800s-1700s B.C.E.; *Art of Poetry*).
Idea that the purpose of art is to delight and instruct.

Amadís de Gaula by *Garci Ordóñez de Montalvo (1508; Amadis of Gaul).*
Romance of chivalry whose hero, gathering super-human strength from fidelity to his beloved, is emulated by Don Quixote in a number of adventures (e.g., the penance performed in Sierra Morena). Also contains a governor of an island (like the one promised to Sancho).

Amadís de Grecia by *Feliciano de Silva (1530; Amadis of Greece).*
Continuation of Amadís de Gaula, *written in the convoluted style continually parodied by Cervantes; exemplifies only one of many mediocre chivalric novelists criticized in* Don Quixote.

Tirant lo Blanch by *Joanot Martorell (1490; Tirant the White Knight).*
One of the few chivalric novels respected by Cervantes for its veracity. It contains episodes with historical grounding and autobiographical elements, as does Don Quixote.

Examen de ingenios para las ciencias by Juan Huarte de San Juan (1575: Examination of Men's Wits).
Very influential on *Don Quixote,* the treatise newly applies the ancient notion of four humors, analyzing personalities based on combinations of four body liquids—blood, lymph, black bile, yellow bile; contains ideas for compensating for strengths and weaknesses of each personality type.

Dialoghi d'amore by León Hebreo (c. 1502; Dialogues of Love).
A main source of Cervantes's ideas on love and beauty.

Don Quijote de la Mancha by Alonso Fernández de Avellaneda (1614).
A false continuation of Cervantes's first part; influenced the final adventures in Part 2.

Orlando il Furioso by Ludovico Ariosto (1516; Roland the Furious).
Greatest Italian epic poem, affects the intercalated novel "The Curious Impertinent" as well as Don Quixote's penance in Sierra Morena.

Diana by Jorge de Montemayor (1559).
Pastoral novel, affects the story of Grisostomo and Marcela in Part 1 as well as other pastoral episodes in *Don Quixote.*

Reception. First published in 1605, *Don Quixote* (Part 1) met with immediate popular and critical success. It was in such high demand that six new editions were issued in the next four years, and foreign editions began to be released as well. Cervantes's instant celebrity helped him procure a generous patron, the Count of Lemos, whose financial assistance allowed him to finish the writing of Part 2 and several other works. If imitation is the sincerest form of flattery, then Cervantes must have felt dubiously flattered by the publication, only several months before Part 2, of the false sequel to Part 1 by a still unknown author, who used the pseudonym Alonso Fernández de Avellaneda. The reception to Cervantes's Part 2 was as enthusiastic as that to Part 1. Four hundred years later, in today's world, *Don Quixote* is unanimously hailed as the greatest literary work in the Castilian language. Apart from its innovation of character change, it covers many of the loftiest themes known to humankind—liberty, poverty, fame, virtue, immortality, envy, work and leisure, and love—coverage of which usually appears in dialogues between Don Quixote and Sancho.

DON QUIXOTE AND SANCHO PANZA ON LOVE

SANCHO PANZA: I can't imagine what this girl saw in you, your grace, to overpower and conquer her like that: I mean, what particularly choice part, what special charm, what display of wit, what feature of your face—which one of these, or what mixture of them all, made her fall in love with you? Because, truthfully, I often stop and look your grace over, from the point of your shoes to the very last hair on your head, and I see more things to frighten than to fire up love. . . .

DON QUIXOTE: Remember, Sancho, . . . that there are two kinds of love: there's spiritual love, and then there's bodily love; spiritual love walks, and shows itself, in the mind, in virtue, in honorable behavior, in generosity, and in good breeding, and these are all qualities that can occur and be found in an ugly man . . . a good man only has to be something other than a monster, to be well loved.

(Don Quijote, p. 653)

Although the novel has survived in Hispanic tradition as a model for a variety of writing styles, whether of elevated oratory, of pastoral love soliloquy, or of picaresque adventure narrative, Cervantes's dialogue is so lively that much of it remains today in the form of expressions that have passed into current Castilian speech, in the same way that Shakespeare's lines have entered present-day English. Examples of expressions from Cervantes used in Spanish today are, "Paciencia y barajar," (Be patient and deal the cards while you wait [Cervantes, *Don Quijote de la Mancha,* p. 735; trans. N. Orringer]) and "Peor es menearlo" (When in an embarrassing situation, it is "worse to rub it in," from [*Don Quijote de la Mancha*, p. 188; trans. N. Orringer].) Yet a fourth manifestation of the high quality of *Don Quixote* lies in its impact on world arts. As Mancing notes, the novel has inspired classical music (Germany's Richard Strauss), ballet music (Austria's Léon Minkus), and painting (Spain's Salvador Dali). Finally the success of Don Quijote resounds in its impact on some of the world's foremost writers, from Spain's Benito Pérez Galdos to England's Henry Fielding, France's Gustave Flaubert, Russia's Fyodor Dostoyevsky, Argentina's Jorge Luis Borges, and America's Joyce Carol Oates. One of the founders of the English novel, Henry Fielding, pays deference in *Joseph Andrews* (1742) to his Spanish model: "Written in Imitation of the Manner of Cervantes"; Fielding's *Joseph Andrews* was furthermore reviewed in comparison to the Spanish original: "'The remarkable thing about this work is that just as *Don Quixote* is the picture of Spanish customs, the work at hand is the picture of English customs" (Paulson, pp. ix-x). This was already more than a century after the Spanish novel's initial release, yet it was but the beginning. As the 1700s wore on, the novel would be much imitated by English writers, and German Romantics would begin to see profound philosophical implications in the work. *Don Quixote* had, in short, revolutionized world literature.

—Nelson Orringer and Diane Renée

For More Information

Cervantes, Miguel de. *Don Quijote: The History of that Ingenious Gentleman Don Quijote de la Mancha.* Trans. Burton Raffel. New York: Norton, 1995.

———. *Don Quijote de la Mancha.* Ed. Martín de Riquer. Barcelona: Editorial Juventud, 1955.

Defourneaux, Marcelin. *Daily Life in Spain in the Golden Age.* Stanford, Calif.: Stanford University Press, 1979.

Elliot, J. H. *Imperial Spain: 1469-1716.* New York: Penguin, 1963.

Gies, Frances. *The Knight in History.* New York: Harper and Row, 1984.

Goodman, David. *Spanish Naval Power, 1589-1665: Reconstruction and Defeat.* Cambridge: Cambridge University Press, 1997.

Jones, R. O. *A Literary History of Spain: The Golden Age: Prose and Poetry, The Sixteenth and Seventeenth Centuries.* New York: Barnes and Noble, 1971.

Kamen, Henry. *Spain 1469-1714: A Society of Conflict.* London: Longman, 1991.

Mancing, Howard. "Cervantes Saavedra, Miguel de." In *Dictionary of the Literature of the Iberian Peninsula*, A-K. Westport, Conn.: Greenwood Press, 1993.

McKendrick, Melveena. *Cervantes.* Boston: Little, Brown, 1980.

Paulson, Ronald. *Don Quixote in England: The Aesthetics of Laughter.* Baltimore: Johns Hopkins University Press, 1998.

Riley, E.C. *Teoria de la novela en Cervantes.* Trans. Carlos Sahagún. Madrid: Taurus, 1966.

Schulte, Henry F. *The Spanish Press.* Chicago: University of Illinois Press, 1968.

Doomed Love
(A Family Memoir)

by

Camilo Castelo Branco

THE LITERARY WORK

A novel set in northern Portugal in the first decade of the nineteenth century; published in Portuguese (as *Amor de Perdição*) in 1862, in English in 2000.

SYNOPSIS

The fates of a pair of star-crossed lovers unfold against the outdated views of an aristocratic society whose heyday has passed. In a fresh twist to this *Romeo and Juliet*-type tale, the hero relies on an intelligent, strong-willed peasant girl who helps him endure his tragic circumstances to the death.

Born in Lisbon in 1825, Camilo Castelo Branco was the illegitimate son of a lesser aristocrat from northern Portugal. At age 10, after both his parents died, he was sent north to live with relatives. The boy received an education from country priests, under whose guidance he studied Portuguese, French, and classical and ecclesiastical literatures, meanwhile coming to know a segment of the population that would later furnish material for his stories. In early adulthood, Castelo Branco moved to Oporto, where he insinuated himself into the city's bohemian and literary circles and found a ready outlet in journalism for his early political essays and for his fiction in serial form. From about 1848 to 1886, he wrote prolifically in a wide range of genres: poetry, drama, the short story, literary criticism, history, genealogy, translation, and the novel, the genre that would win him renown as one of the country's most popular writers. Meanwhile, his personal life became as public as his writing. Well before his move to Oporto, Castelo Branco became embroiled in a series of love affairs (including a short-lived marriage at the age of 16) that shaped both his life and reputation. Most notorious was his love for Ana Plácido, wife of a well-known businessman. The relationship led to the 1860 arrest of the transgressors on charges of adultery and, more happily, to *Doomed Love (A Family Memoir)*, which Castelo Branco wrote in jail. Exonerated and released after a year, the lovers remained together, only to suffer many more trials—the mental deterioration of a son, the deaths of other children, and the author's increasing blindness. In 1890 a despairing Castelo Branco committed suicide, bringing to an abrupt halt his vigorous post-prison outpouring of prose, poetry, plays, and novels. Despite the release of subsequent fiction (e.g., *The Fall of an Angel* (1866) and *Tales from the Minho Region* (1875-77), *Doomed Love* remains Castelo Branco's best-known work. The novel straddles transitional periods in Portuguese society and literature. Its story unfolds as a new money-oriented upper class gains ground over the hereditary aristocracy and as constitutional government starts taking precedence over the monarchy. At the time of publication, Romanticism had begun to give way to realism, with both literary movements resonating in Castelo Branco's novel.

Camilo Castelo Branco

Events in History at the Time the Novel Takes Place

The marquis of Pombal and the dawn of modernization. The earthquake that devastated three quarters of Lisbon in 1755 destroyed more than a physical space. It served as a catalyst for another transformation that, for some, would be equally devastating. Along with the rebuilding of the city came social, political and economic reforms, with repercussions that resounded well into the nineteenth century. Portugal had been plagued for some time by a faltering economy, one that was overly dependent on gold, diamonds, and other imports from Brazil and Portugal's other colonies. On the throne was an ineffectual monarch, José I (1750-77), a king ill equipped to deal with the daunting challenge of addressing a financial situation that demanded restructuring the economy to ground it more firmly in domestic wealth. Fortunately for Portugal, the 1755 earthquake brought to the fore a leader poised to take on the problematic economy as well as a city in ruins. He was José I's most trusted and able minister, Sebastião José de Carvalho e Melo, the future marquis of Pombal.

Most immediately, Pombal faced the task of rebuilding the devastated city. He planned not to just restore the now nonexistent infrastructure but to create an entirely new Lisbon. To this end, Pombal enlisted the aid of prominent architects to work out the details of his vision. The result was a graceful, efficient urban space, one well suited to the managed society that he also envisioned and that would be the focus of his life for the next two decades.

The marquis of Pombal was well traveled and well read in economic theory. He understood the social realities of his country, its centuries-old trade relations with England, the power of the nobility and the clergy, and the poverty of the lower class, and he resolved to bring the country more into line with a more modernized Europe. Pombal abolished slavery and ended the long-institutionalized persecution of the Jews, with a view toward incorporating the group into a more productive economic scheme. He centralized and developed commerce and industry to promote the growth of the middle class and of a new profit- and merit-based aristocracy. Also he defused potential opposition to change by mercilessly undercutting the traditional loci of power, the nobility and the clergy, imprisoning, exiling, and even executing many of the former and attacking the clergy through the abolition of its most powerful arm, the Jesuit order. Meanwhile, Pombal shrewdly ensured ideological support for his new society, reorganizing education to better emphasize modern philosophy, science, and mathematics. Some of his reforms proved short-lived, however, because of a reversal in fortune; upon the death of José I in 1777 and the accession of Maria I to the throne, the marquis was deposed and the old society resumed. This inaugurated a pattern that was to continue through the nineteenth century, with conservative and liberal governments assuming control in Portugal, one after the other. The main difference from the pre-Pombal era was the presence of a now firmly established middle class and a new aristocracy; both would continue to grow (and claim power), providing the domestic economic base that Pombal had sought.

The reign of Maria I (1777-1816). The accession of Maria I to the throne did not entirely negate the notion of reform. There was a reversal of policy, but only in certain regards: Pombal's political prisoners were released, and those exiled under his tenure were permitted to return. Many of Pombal's old enemies regained positions in the government, and Pombal himself was put on trial. Found guilty of the abuse of power, he was banished permanently to his country estate. The devout queen allowed the Church to regain influence, but she stopped short of embracing the Jesuits. Economically, her reign did away with Pombal's commercial and industrial monopolies and allowed business to respond to market demand. The upper middle class grew stronger, and the most powerful among them were accepted into the titled nobility, but the nobility itself lost a privilege. In 1790 Portugal modified its judicial system, abolishing the separate seigneurial justice that had given the nobility special legal privilege. Reform continued in education too, making it more relevant to a changing socioeconomic reality. Also communications improved; a road was built between Lisbon and Oporto, the country's two largest cities. Stagecoach service began on the road in 1798, a sorely needed improvement, since until then travel between the two cities had been undertaken almost exclusively by sea.

Meanwhile, the monarch suffered a grave setback. Maria I's reign was prematurely shortened by a decline in her mental powers. The death of her husband in 1786 threw her into a profound depression from which she never entirely recovered. She was declared incompetent to rule in 1792, and her son, the future João VI, assumed her duties as monarch. It was under his guidance that the country progressed so noticeably. The final years of the eighteenth century witnessed the new entrepreneurs extending their reach from the city into the rural areas to the north and south of Lisbon. "The indigenous trading class had grown to 80,000 strong and had begun to invest in neglected lands in the Estremadura and Alentejo provinces. . . . Craftsmen began to prosper . . . [without] being predominantly tied to aristocratic and religious patrons" (Birmingham, p. 94). João was officially declared regent in 1799.

The Napoleonic invasion and its aftermath.
Under the regency of João VI, Portugal did all that it could to remain free of the turmoil created in Europe in the wake of the French Revolution and its ideology. But Portugal fell victim to that turmoil when France and England became embroiled in open warfare. In 1807 Portugal failed to close its ports to England as expeditiously as Napoleon demanded, and the French invaded the country. The royal family, along with others positioned to do so, fled to Brazil, literally sailing out of Lisbon just as the invaders entered the city. A regency made up of five people under the leadership of the marquis of Abrantes was left behind to govern, but it soon fell to the French occupation forces, which set up a new government under the leadership of the French general and France's former ambassador to Portugal, Andoche Junot. French troops proceeded to devastate the countryside and antagonize the Portuguese to the point of rebellion. A resistance movement, organized in Oporto and throughout the North, stood ready when the British came to the rescue under the command of the future duke of Wellington. Wellington defeated the French in a series of battles, the most notable in 1811 near Torres Vedras, a strategically significant rural town, well protected by a series of fortresses manned by the Portuguese. The French were routed and pursued by Wellington into Spain and eventually back to France.

The French invasions and occupation (1807-11) had lingering consequences for the country. Not only did the looting and costly warfare destroy agricultural, industrial, and cultural resources in Portugal, but the royal family had remained in Brazil because of the French at a time when an independence movement was gaining strength in that colony:

> Four years of war had left the country in poor condition. . . . [Portugal became] both an English protectorate and a Brazilian colony. The government was in Rio; in Portugal there was only a regency. . . . The regency kept intact the old methods of governing, showing no disposition whatsoever to adjust to modern ideas. A ferocious persecution of all liberals took place. Throughout the country discontent against the king, the English, and the regency were accompanied by a deplorable economic and financial situation. Revolutionary ferment was everywhere and would soon lead to open rebellion.
> (Marques, p. 87)

Upper- versus lower-class standards for women.
The experience of women in early-nineteenth-century Portugal varied from class to class. However, the law of the land, the *Ordenações Filipinas* (1603; Philipine Laws), in effect until the Civil Code of 1867, did not distinguish among the classes in most respects. Book Four, Article 88, for example, asserts a father's prerogative in arranging a daughter's marriage. According to this article, if a daughter under the age of 25 sleeps with a man or marries without her father's consent, or, if she has no father, without her mother's consent, her family will disinherit her. This will happen, says the law, unless she weds a well-known man and has married better and more honorably than her father or mother would be able to marry her, in which case she will not be disinherited. Men are likewise regu-

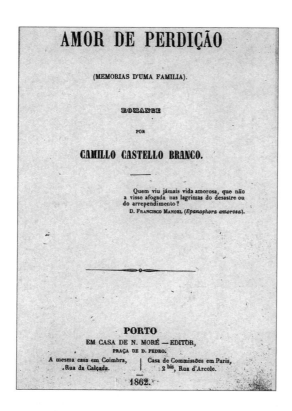

Title page from the first edition of *Doomed Love,* published in 1862.

lated in this respect. Book Five, Article 22, states that a man who gets married without due permission to a widow under the age of 25 and in the custody of her father, mother, grandfather, or guardian will forfeit all his property (to the custodial party) and be exiled to Africa for a year. These laws pertained regardless of social class. On the other hand, social class figures in the case of adultery. Book Five, Article 25, sets death as the penalty for adultery for either a male or a female transgressor unless the adulterer is of a higher class than the woman's husband, especially if the adulterer is of the aristocracy and the husband is a peasant. In these cases, the matter is to be submitted to the king for adjudication.

Class differences manifested themselves not so much in law but in custom. Personal letters and travel accounts show that, up to the early eighteenth century, upper-class Portuguese women were more cloistered in the home than in the cloisters themselves, as families sought to impede heterosexual contacts that might imperil valuable marital alliances. Indeed it was a matter debated openly by the aristocracy. According to a letter dated 1708 (Lopes, p. 49), the Count of Ericeira headed a group that argued for a more open society; the Count of Vimioso championed the old

order. The posture of the reactionary element is best understood in relation to the decline of the nobility and the rise of the wealthy bourgeoisie. Both for the most part chose to perpetuate women's seclusion as an emblem of status. For the nobility it was an assertion that they were holding fast to the status quo; for the *nouveaux riches* it was an indication that they had achieved equal footing with the old guard.

There is some evidence in travelers' accounts that the newcomers were even more rigid than the old nobility. Some set up chapels in their own houses so that women would not even have to leave home to worship. In either case—that of the nobility or that of the nouveaux riches— women were virtually prisoners in their own homes until society slowly relaxed its hold. In the latter half of the eighteenth century, Brazilian gold created unprecedented affluence. The desire to display that affluence in the home gave impetus to a change in women's daily lives as they became an integral part of that display. Though it can be argued that women remained commodities in the service of their family's social and political status, the change nevertheless benefitted them. Now to be shown off in addition to being advantageously married off, young women were encouraged by their families to become better educated, if only to develop the conversational and musical skills needed to dazzle their privileged guests.

The situation of lower-class women differed considerably, largely because of their need to work. Whether in rural or urban settings, work required mobility and, more often than not, exposure to a broader public than the immediate household. These working women were subject to the same laws as the economically privileged, and they generally lived and raised their children within the bounds of traditional matrimony. But statistics indicate that there was a certain amount of deviance from the norm. Birth records for 1860, for example, reveal that 18.8 percent of births in the country were illegitimate; by 1862, the figure had risen to 20.3 percent (Serrão, pp. 174, 180). Since upper- and middle-class women were so carefully guarded, it follows that the largest share of the rise can probably be attributed to relationships involving lower-class women. Society seems to have been more tolerant of their transgressions. The reasons for the rise in those transgressions, however, is not easy to establish. Certainly it cannot be casually attributed to a greater acceptance of love matches as the basis for family units.

The Novel in Focus

Plot summary. Camilo Castelo Branco begins his novel with an introduction that makes the following declaration:

> Leafing through the old record books of the prison in Oporto, in a volume listing prisoners incarcerated between 1803 and 1805, I read the following: Simão António Botelho, who attested that such was his name, that he was single, a student at the University of Coimbra, a native of the city of Lisbon and a resident at the time of his imprisonment of the city of Vizeu, son of Domingos José Correia Botelho and Rita Preciosa Caldeirão Castelo Branco. . . . In the left margin of this entry is written: He went to India, March 17, 1807.
>
> (Branco, *Doomed Love,* p. 23)

The author uses this information, along with family lore, to attach a semblance of truth to a fictional account of his young uncle's tragic love.

The first chapter paints a satirical portrait of Simão Botelho's (and the author's own) family, members of the old hereditary aristocracy whose antiquated sense of honor will thwart the happiness and fulfillment of the young lovers. The family patriarch, Simão's paternal grandfather, is a member of the lesser nobility from the northern mountain province of Tras-os-Montes. Allegedly well regarded by Pombal, he is depicted nonetheless in images that speak more of decadence than of progressive vitality:

> Before getting into her husband's ancestral litter [Rita Preciosa] asked, with the most feigned seriousness, if it was not risky to travel in that antique. Fernão Botelho assured his daughter-in-law that his litter was not yet a hundred years old and the horses no more than thirty.
>
> (*Doomed Love,* pp. 26-27)

Fernão Botelho's son and Simão's father, Domingos José Correia Botelho de Mesquita e Meneses, reads for the law in Lisbon and becomes a less-than-impressive magistrate known at Maria I's court as the "wind-bag doctor." His mother is a woman whose high-sounding name, Rita Teresa Margarida Preciosa da Veiga Caldeirão Castelo Branco, belies the reality of her condition: she lacks a dowry. A haughty and attractive lady-in-waiting to Maria I, Rita Preciosa is the daughter of one horse captain, the granddaughter of another. She descends from a general who "died fried in a cauldron" in some unknown Moorish land, "in truth a rather burning glory but so lofty that the fried general's descendants came to call themselves Caldeirões (Caul-

drons)" (*Doomed Love,* p. 26). Domingos José and Rita Preciosa become the parents of three daughters and two sons, the younger of the two being Simão Botelho. They reside in the small but distinguished ancient city of Viseu.

In 1801 Simão is 15 years old, arrogant, irreverent with respect to his ancestry, and given to unbridled delinquent behavior. At the time the story begins, he is a student in the humanities at the University of Coimbra, where political unrest is rampant. The students there are "sympathetic to confused theories of freedom," affected only vaguely by the French Revolution, and rancorous towards England (*Doomed Love,* p. 31). In Simão's view, "Portugal should regenerate itself in a baptism of blood to ensure that the hydra of tyrants would never again raise a single one of its heads under the club of the popular Hercules" (*Doomed Love,* p. 32). He sacrifices a school year to his advocacy of violent change, including regicide, until the authorities send him home. After three months in Viseu, Simão undergoes a remarkable transformation that ends in his forsaking all violence and seeking only solitude and serenity. The explanation for the about-face is that Simão Botelho has found love. "That is the magic word, the explanation for the apparently absurd change at the age of sixteen" (*Doomed Love,* p. 33). He showers his love on the attractive young Teresa de Albuquerque, 15-year-old daughter of next-door neighbor Tadeu de Albuquerque. Like Simão's family, the latter is a member of the rural aristocracy and, unfortunately for the lovers, a man who despises the magistrate, Simão's father, "because of litigation in which Domingos Botelho had passed sentence against him" (*Doomed Love,* p. 33). The stage is set for a tragic love story in the tradition of William Shakespeare's *Romeo and Juliet.*

Teresa's father discovers the girl's secret relationship with Simão and, enraged, takes immediate steps to destroy it. His first solution is marriage to another. She will become the wife of his nephew Baltasar Coutinho, the master of an estate in Castro-d'Aire and a man whose nobility is parallel to Teresa's in her father's eyes. But Teresa, who has a mind of her own, rejects Baltasar's proposal. Next Albuquerque threatens her with the convent, the common repository for recalcitrant daughters in the nineteenth century. Teresa prefers this alternative, and without mentioning Baltasar Coutinho, she informs Simão of her predicament in the first of many letters that will henceforth be the lovers' sole means of communication. "My father says that he is going to shut me in a convent because of you. . . . Don't you forget me" (*Doomed Love*, p. 34). An elderly beggar woman serves as their go-between.

Simão returns to the university, a model student now, unrecognizable as the former delinquent and terrorist. "He studied feverishly like one who was already setting the bases for future renown and for the position he merited, sufficient to support a wife in comfort" (*Doomed Love*, p. 34).

THE EARLY-NINETEENTH-CENTURY CONVENT

While convents are by definition communities of women devoted to the service of God and have functioned in that capacity throughout Portuguese history, they have also been used by the country's paternalistic society to exercise control over women. Up to the early nineteenth century, upper class women unable to marry advantageously were sent to the convent. Women would also be secluded in convents for thwarting their father's plans for them and for perceived political rebellion. Unsurprisingly, these women, cloistered for reasons other than religious fervor, chose, within limits, to cultivate secular activities: theatrical performances, poetry readings and concerts, and musical events. They were even known to entertain suitors at the convents' gates. In Spain, where a similar situation existed, such suitors became known as *galanes de monjas* (suitors of nuns). In Portugal they were called *freiráticos*. The first of the two convents in *Doomed Love* is a satirical recreation of the lax atmosphere found in some of the convents in Castelo Branco's day.

Albuquerque presses his plans for Teresa's marriage. When the girl finally informs Simão of this, his tranquility now shattered, he leaves the university to visit her in secret and to confront the threat to their love. Fearing discovery, he arranges to stay with a blacksmith, João da Cruz, outside the city and in time accepts the aid of this blacksmith and his brother-in-law in the dangerous enterprise. Simão finds a soul mate in the blacksmith's beautiful daughter Mariana, who comes to love him selflessly, asking no more than to be by his side. When he is wounded in an ambush by Baltasar Coutinho's servants, who are then killed by the blacksmith, Mariana nurses him and, despite her own feelings, serves eventually as an intermediary between Simão and

Teresa. In the meantime, in the face of Teresa's continued recalcitrance, Albuquerque follows through on his threat to banish her to a convent.

Albuquerque decides to put distance between the lovers and to thwart any plans they might have for a reunion by transferring his daughter to a convent in Oporto (not insignificantly a convent with a Mother Superior who happens to be a relative). On the day of her projected departure for Oporto, at the door of the convent and in her presence, an altercation breaks out between her two suitors. Simão kills Baltasar Coutinho, then makes no attempt to flee. The authorities arrest Simão and charge him with murder. His magistrate father, to preserve his own honor and because he too opposes the lovers' union, refuses to help his son. Simão in turn, also for reasons of honor, refuses even the meager help his mother offers him and repudiates his family forever. Ironically both lovers end up in Oporto, Teresa languishing in the convent and Simão in prison. Mariana follows Simão to the city and nurtures him in prison, as she had in her own home. (At that time, prisoners were forced to provide for their own needs: food, clothing, and furnishings.) The three remain in Oporto for a couple of years, the two lovers finding some measure of spiritual and emotional solace in their faith and in the letters they continue to exchange. Finally Simão's case is resolved. He is saved from the gallows but, in keeping with a common practice of the time, exiled for ten years to Goa, Portugal's colony in India. As Simão sails off into exile with Mariana still at his side, all the principles find liberation in death—Teresa by wasting away from an at least partly psychosomatic illness; Simão by fever, and Mariana by faithful suicide.

Class distinctions, personal worth. In this otherwise traditional story of tragic love, Camilo Castelo Branco inserts an element that not only adds dimension to his exploration of love but highlights, by contrast, the perversity and decadence of the upper class. In many respects, the blacksmith João da Cruz and his daughter Mariana serve as an illuminating counterpoint to the two aristocratic families—Tadeu de Albuquerque and his daughter, and Domingos Botelho and his son. Without idealizing the blacksmith (he has apparent defects), the novel creates in João da Cruz a vigorous, principled man of valor and intelligence, who understands the distinctions between right and wrong and acts on the basis of loyalty, honor, and love. His allegiance to Simão, at first an act of gratitude to the magistrate Domingos Botelho for having saved him from the gallows once, is wholly transferred to the son in recognition of the younger man's greater merit. Also the blacksmith's love for his daughter and devotion to his wife's memory are limitless. Unlike the two aristocratic fathers who willingly sacrifice family to a senseless and effete hereditary honor, João da Cruz gambles his very life in the service of love, personal honor, and right. He is fully aware, for example, of the danger posed by the enmity of Baltasar Coutinho, who had previously attempted to engage him to kill Simão. Simão Botelho, for whom honor and valor are also important, finds in João da Cruz the model father he never had.

João da Cruz's daughter, Mariana, is one of the most complex and memorable of Castelo Branco's characters. Like her father, a person of intelligence and vitality, she gives direction to his life as well as her own. She is also a woman of striking beauty (some say more beautiful than Teresa), yet does not let this affect her sense of place. The peasant girl knows full well her role in the social order. She is aware that because of her class her love for Simão can never be consummated in marriage (people of whatever economic means normally married within their class) and will never carry equal weight to that of Teresa's in Simão's eyes. Still, she devotes her life to a platonic relationship with him. Her love demands no more or less than the opportunity to do so. Simão, even in his delirium, recognizes her, along with Teresa, as the ultimate sustaining force in his life.

By juxtaposing the two classes in this fashion—the decadent and pretentious remnants of an old aristocracy against the vibrant and productive energy of the common folk—the author challenges what remains of a traditional value system. His position anticipates in some measure the one that will be taken in the following decade by the Generation of 1870.

Sources and literary context. The scholar Jacinto do Prado Coelho remarks that authorial claims to historical truth are liberally dispersed throughout the author's work. However, he questions the veracity of those claims and wonders whether they might not be simply a convention common in Romantic fiction. More exactly, Prado Coelho provides information on *Doomed Love* that confirms the historicity of some of the novel's details but challenges others. Domingos Botelho, for example, as historical documentation reveals, was a man of even worse character than the author suggests. Simão Botelho was indeed imprisoned in the same jail

that later held the author, but there is no evidence that there was a love story behind the real Simão's imprisonment. There is evidence that, contrary to his fate in the novel, he reached the Indian port of Goa in November 1807. There is no known documentation to support the existence of Teresa and Mariana or of their respective fathers.

The historical foundations of Camilo Castelo Branco's fiction may be approached from a direction more fruitful than documented models of character and plot. Its elements are steeped in material drawn from the reality of northern Portugal. The novelist employs "figures, dramas, cases, happenings, tied to the old world of first-borns, of commanders, of litters, of powdered wigs, the world of petty lords or of liberals bound by ignorance or pride, abbots more or less educated but rooted in archaic customs, connoisseurs of the heart and the life of their sheep" (Eduardo Lourenço in *Doomed Love,* p. xiii). It is primarily in the overall recreation of this way of life that *Doomed Love* can claim to be drawn from history.

The individuals who comprise the society that Castelo Branco recreates emanate from a variety of sources. The robust and determined peasants are drawn not descriptively but dramatically through word and deed. It is in fact their language, with its colloquial expressions, proverbs, and terms common to the religious experience of their class, that makes João da Cruz and Mariana so vivid and lifelike to the Portuguese reader. For the aristocratic figures, Castelo Branco employs a technique more consonant with his intended ideological and institutional satire, a single-minded ridiculing distortion often verging on caricature. For Simão and Teresa, the author reserves a third register: the lyrical written expression of their anguished love. Castelo Branco's novel is not simply a product of the author's youthful observations; it is also informed by the literary and aesthetic currents of his day.

When Castelo Branco began to write, the last vestiges of eighteenth-century Neoclassicism were still in place but would soon be edged out by the Romanticism that reached Portugal from England and other continental European countries in the 1820s and 1830s. The new aesthetic was characterized in part by an interest in the past, recent or distant, and even more by a cult of the individual. The latter manifested itself in political anarchy and in the critique of institutions but also in a sentimentalism and a lyricism with a degree of intensity heretofore unseen. The preferred literary genres were the historical novel and theater, social and political theory, and historiography. Journalism also experienced an unprecedented growth in response to an increasing readership, literate but literarily unsophisticated. The principal representatives of the new movement in Portugal were Almeida Garrett (1799-1854; see **Travels in My Homeland,** also in *WLAIT 5: Spanish and Portuguese Literatures and Their Times*) and Alexandre Herculano (1810-77), the first a moderate liberal, the second a champion of the new aristocracy who described himself as liberal but antidemocratic. Herculano was the primary theorist of Romanticism in Portugal, notably in articles appearing in the journals *Repositório Literário* and *Panorama* between 1834 and 1840. A second wave of Romantics included Camilo Castelo Branco and António Feliciano Castilho (1800-1875), a writer whose Romanticism retained a Neoclassical overlay. Castilho became the center of an admiring group of younger writers.

By the mid-1860s, another literary movement was coming into focus under the leadership of two young writers at the University of Coimbra: the poets Antero Quental and Teófilo Braga (Braga would later, on two occasions, be President of Portugal). The Romantic veteran Castilho took it upon himself to publicly censure the younger men, to which Quental responded with the pamphlet *Good Sense and Good Taste* (1865), in which he defined the new writers' mission: they would be the conduits of revolutionary thought, militant but with a moral conscience. It was the beginning of a debate that would last for years and would follow the group to Lisbon. Here, joined by other gifted writers and intellectuals (Eça de Queirós, Jaime Batalha Reis, Oliveira Martins, Ramalho Ortigão, and Guerra Junqueiro), the innovators would gain distinction as the Generation of 1870, the group that inaugurated realism. The Generation organized a series of lectures to be presented at the Lisbon Casino in 1871. Delivering one of the lectures, Eça de Queirós, author of **The Maias** (also in *WLAIT 5: Spanish and Portuguese Literatures and Their Times*), discussed realism as the new expression in art. Officials outlawed the series of lectures before it could be completed, fearing a subversive intent, but the ideas unleashed were not so easily squelched. Eça de Queirós's lecture "Realism as the New Expression in Art" became the foundation for the next major literary movement.

Castelo Branco, who defended Castilho in the debate with the younger writers, wrote his own works primarily under the influence of Romanticism. However, he was not altogether impervious to the realist aesthetic. *Doomed Love* is clearly a Romantic piece. Romanticism governs its exploration of ideal love, its fatalism and preoccupation with death, the nature of its characters, and even the novel's diction in the lovers' letters to each other. Teresa, the quintessential image of Romantic purity, shares with Simão Botelho an anguished love and welcomes the death that becomes for both of them not only the price of rebellion but a liberation and transcendence. Similarly, the lower-class characters João da Cruz and his daughter Mariana might be construed as part of a Romantic idealization of the common folk. Yet Castelo Branco does not idealize them. They are flesh and blood human beings, as real as the concerns with money, food, and social practices he disperses through the novel, which link him to the realist aesthetic in Portuguese literature at the time.

Events in History at the Time the Novel Was Written

Mid-century political turmoil. After the expulsion of the French from the Iberian Peninsula in 1811, Portuguese history remained tumultuous throughout the first half of the nineteenth century. The old regime, says David Birmingham, came to an end in three phases in Portugal:

> • A revolt in 1820 . . . led to the ending of the British occupation, the drafting of a democratic constitution and the reluctant recognition of Brazilian independence.
> • Ten years later, following the European liberal revolution of 1830, Portugal made a second attempt at fundamental political reform, expelled a royal pretender with absolutist aspirations, confiscated the crown lands and dissolved the monasteries.
> • Finally in 1851, in the wake of the 1848 revolution in Europe, a parliamentary regime was established. . . . Thereafter Portugal once again embarked on a modest programme of industrialisation and was brought into closer contact with Europe by the railway age.
> (Birmingham, p. 103)

The anticipation and consequences of Brazilian independence added to the economic stagnation and unrest already created by the peninsular war against Napoleon, cutting off a major source of Portugal's revenues. There was an obvious need for socioeconomic and political change; the catalyst finally arrived in the form of an uprising in Oporto on August 24, 1820, that soon spread south to Lisbon. The revolt came to an end a month later, on September 28, and its liberal leaders set about reorganizing the country. John VI returned from Brazil with his court in 1821 (leaving his son Pedro behind as regent), but even before he arrived the liberals had begun to achieve their goal, driving out the British occupiers and regaining independence after years of foreign occupation. In time they held an election for an assembly that would draw up plans for a constitutional government in a liberalized Portugal. Adopted in 1822, the constitution established a hereditary monarchy responsible to a unicameral parliament to be elected by all literate males. João VI swore to uphold the constitution but his wife, the calculating Carlota-Joaquina, refused to do so and was banished to a convent near Lisbon. João VI's son, Prince Miguel, the queen's favorite, also refused to swear allegiance and was sent into exile. In the face of this inauspicious beginning and lacking the support of a strong middle class able to sustain a constitutional government in opposition to the old aristocratic interests targeted in *Doomed Love,* the constitution failed. Illiteracy was still too widespread and industrial development too moderate to produce a solid power base among the masses. The constitution lost João VI's support, and he abolished it in 1823.

Civil war. The next significant event in this tumultuous century was the civil war brought on by João VI's death in 1826. Dom Pedro, the rightful heir to the crown, was now emperor of an independent Brazil. Rather than reuniting the two countries, Pedro chose to abdicate the Portuguese crown in favor of his seven-year-old daughter, Maria. She would marry Prince Miguel, who would serve as regent until she came of age. Pedro submitted to Portugal a Constitutional Charter, like that of Brazil, on which to base the new government. But after Miguel swore allegiance to the Charter, he promptly nullified it, dissolving the Chamber of Deputies. On her way from Brazil to Portugal at the time, the young Maria found herself rerouted to England for her own safety. Miguel assumed power as head of an absolutist government persecuting the liberals, winning support from the old order and having himself declared king. Many liberals fled to the Azores, where they began to organize a countercoup. In the interest of mounting it, they summoned Pedro from Brazil. Pedro abdicated his Brazilian throne in favor of his son and reasserted his legitimacy as king of Portugal, reestablishing the

Charter of 1826 (the foundation of constitutional monarchy in Portugal), and supporting his daughter's claim to Portugal's throne. From the Azores, the liberals invaded the mainland at Oporto in 1832. With help from England, they beat off Miguel's forces in the North and then, instead of continuing south to Lisbon as the miguelistas expected, they moved north on Lisbon from the southernmost region of the Algarve. They received assistance from an uprising in Lisbon itself, the war ending with the Treaty of Evoramonte in 1834. Maria II, brought from England to join her father in Lisbon, restored the Charter, and ejected Miguel's supporters. To pay off the civil war debt, the new government abolished all monasteries and convents, confiscated their properties, and sold them to Pedro's supporters. The middle and peasant classes benefitted little from the change, a failing that would prompt the next revolt, the Septembrist revolt of 1836.

The reigns of Maria II and her immediate successors. In sad economic straits and with a political leadership splintered into three distinct ideological groups—the royal absolutists, the conservatives, and the progressives—Portugal remained unstable. Several revolutions followed: the Septembrist revolt of 1836, which restored the constitution (revised in 1838); the restoration of the Charter of 1826 in 1842, followed by a period of fiscal, judicial, and educational reform; and finally, in 1846, the unprecedented Maria da Fonte revolution, begun by the women of northern Portugal. Women had become a powerful economic and political force in the Minho region, having had to manage household property and agriculture in the absence of their emigrating husbands. In 1846, they found themselves in opposition to what they perceived as the intrusion of government into local affairs when it established a land registry program.

Despite the upheaval, much was accomplished during Maria's reign. Libraries and museums were opened to receive books and artworks from the closed monasteries. Civil registries for births, marriages, and deaths replaced the ecclesiastical ones. Most importantly, under the direction of the well-educated and well-traveled engineer António Maria de Fontes Pereira de Melo, the regime initiated an important public works program in 1851. Some of its achievements were a modern postal system, a telegraph system, roads, bridges, and railroads. Portugal now had an infrastructure in place for modernization based on the free movement of people and goods throughout the country.

Maria II died in childbirth at the age of 34, leaving eight children. The oldest, Pedro V, was 16 when he became king in 1853. He and two brothers died of typhoid fever in 1861, whereupon a surviving brother, 23-year-old Luis I, took over the monarchy and reigned until 1889. Despite these trials, the brother benefitted from a new stability associated with 1) the modernization of the infrastructure and of education, which led to the expansion of the middle class and 2) a new system of government based on the alternation of conservative and liberal parties in power. Camilo Castelo Branco, a resident of the politically active North, participated in these social and political movements, serving as a journalist and pamphleteer as well as a novelist. As suggested, he did not join the Generation of 1870 in their support for modernization. Instead, Castelo Branco made the fading old world the subject of his fiction, meanwhile acknowledging the dawning of the emerging new world, even dedicating *Doomed Love* to the engineer of modernization, Fontes Pereira de Melo.

Reception. In the preface to the second edition of *Doomed Love* (1863), Castelo Branco testifies to the unanticipated success of the work:

> This book . . . had a reception greater than that accorded all its brothers. I had doubts because it was sad with no moments of laughter. . . . In honor and praise of the people who admired the book, I must confess with pleasure that I thought ill of them. I do not approve of their judgment but critical writings agreed with the majority.
> (*Doomed Love*, p. 21)

The author's response to the book's success was obviously ambivalent. While he did not share his readers' judgment of the quality of that work, he did value their praise. In the preface to the fifth edition (1879), with the new realism now in full swing in Portuguese literature, the author speaks again of the book's "phenomenal and extra-Portuguese success" and criticizes it as a "Romantic novel, declamatory, and with lyric blunders and perverse ideas that verge on the excesses of sentimentalism. . . . I will never cease to criticize this novel," he states (*Doomed Love*, p. 19).

It was not just the unsophisticated public that responded so enthusiastically; it is significant that although the members of the Generation of 1870 rejected the Romantic postures of Castelo Branco's generation, they did not reject the author's novels. Indeed, they, like the bulk of Castelo Branco's readers since the author's day,

referred to him simply and admiringly as Camilo. No more was necessary as an identifier. Since Camilo's death, *Doomed Love* has been frequently republished and adapted into both film and opera; it has inspired Portuguese novelists from Aquilino Ribeiro to Miguel Torga and Agustina Bessa-Luís. Perhaps the greatest tribute of all, however, came from outside Portugal, from Spain's Miguel de Unamuno (see **Mist,** also in *WLAIT 5: Spanish and Portuguese Literatures and Their Times*), who deemed *Doomed Love* "the most intense and most profound love story ever written in the Iberian Peninsula" (Unamuno, p. 19).

—Alice Clemente

For More Information

Anderson, James M. *The History of Portugal.* Westport, Connecticut: Greenwood Press, 2000.

Birmingham, David. *A Concise History of Portugal.* Cambridge: Cambridge University Press, 1993.

Branco, Camilo Castelo. *Doomed Love (A Family Memoir).* Trans. Alice R. Clemente. Providence, R.I.: Gávea Brown, 2000.

Cabral, Alexandre. *Dicionário de Camilo Castelo Branco.* Lisbon: Caminho, 1988.

Coelho, Jacinto do Prado. *Introdução ao Estudo da Novela Camiliana.* 2 vols. Lisbon: Imprensa Nacional—Casa da Moeda, 1982.

In Memoriam: Camilo. Centenário da Morte. Oporto: Comissão Nacional das Comemorações Camilianas, 1992.

Lopes, Maria Antónia. *Mulheres, Espaço e Sociabilidade. A Transformação dos papéis femininos em Portugal à luz de fontes literárias (segunda metade do século XVIII).* Lisbon: Livros Horizonte, 1989.

Lourenço, Eduardo. "Situação de Camilo," in *O Canto do Signo—Existência e Literatura (1957-1993).* Lisbon: Editorial Presença, 1993.

Marques, A. H. de Oliveira. *History of Portuguese Culture.* Lisbon: Imprensa Nacional—Casa da Moeda, 1991.

Proceedings of the Camilo Castelo Branco International Colloquium. Ed. João Camilo dos Santos. Santa Barbara, Calif.: Center for Portuguese Studies, University of California, 1995.

Saraiva, José Hermano. *Portugal: a Companion History.* Manchester: Carcanet Press, 1997.

Serrão, Joel. *Fontes de Demografia Portuguesa— 1800-1862.* Lisbon: Livros Horizonte, 1973.

Unamuno, Miguel de. *Por tierras de Portugal y de España.* Buenos Aires: Col. Austral, Espasa Calpe Argentina, 1944.

Vicente, Ana. *As Mulheress Portuguesas Vistas por Viajantes Estrangeiros (Séculos XVIII, XIX e XX).* Lisbon: Gótica, 2001.

"An Essay on Woman, or, Physiological and Historical Defense of the Fair Sex"

by
Benito Jerónimo Feijóo y Montenegro

Benito Jerónimo Feijóo y Montenegro (also spelled Feijoo, without the accent) was born on October 8, 1676, in Casdemiro, a village in the bishopric of Orense, province of Galicia, Spain. The eldest son of ten children born to Antonio Feijóo y Sanjurjo and María de Puga Sandoval Novoa—both of noble descent—Benito renounced his claims to succeed to the family estate in order to devote his life to a religious career. At age 14 he entered the Benedictine order at the monastery of St. Julian of Samos, then continued his religious and academic education at several colleges, belonging to orders in Galicia and León and later at the University of Salamanca. He was educated in the era's scholastic system, which he subsequently campaigned to change. Beginning his doctoral work at the Monastery of San Vicente, Oviedo, in 1709, Feijóo spent the rest of his life in this town, writing all his works here and teaching theology at the University of Oviedo. The proximity of Oviedo to the seaport of Gijón exposed Feijóo to intellectual currents of the day, allowing him to obtain recently published foreign books and treatises and newly invented instruments. In 1734, due to poor health, he retired from teaching and devoted the rest of his life to his writing. Between 1726 and 1740, Feijóo published the eight volumes of his major work *Teatro crítico universal* (Universal Theater of Criticism) and from 1742 to 1760, the five volumes of *Cartas eruditas* (Intellectual Letters). Together these sets of articles comprise an encyclopedic array of human knowledge as capsulized by Feijóo. "An Essay on Woman" is Essay 16 of

THE LITERARY WORK

An essay set in the early eighteenth century for a Spanish audience; published in Spanish (as "Defensa de las mujeres") in 1726 and revised in 1740; published in English in 1765.

SYNOPSIS

Taking a radically unique stand for its day, the essay defends the intellectual faculties of women and their right to be educated in the same subjects as men.

Volume 1 in the *Teatro Crítico Universal*. Feijóo continued his life of study and meditation until he was stricken by an attack that left him paralyzed and unable to hear or speak. He died in Oviedo on September 26, 1764, leaving behind among other riveting tracts for their time his revolutionary treatise on women, which anticipates a similarly revolutionary essay by England's Mary Wollstonecraft (*A Vindication of the Rights of Woman*, 1792) by 66 years.

Events in History at the Time of the Essay

The Enlightenment in Spain. At the close of the seventeenth century, Spain's Habsburg king, Carlos II, remained without direct descendants. This situation set the stage for the Bourbons' ascension to the Spanish throne, beginning with

Bust in bronze of Benito Jerónimo Feijóo, by Francisco Asorey.

French king Louis XIV's grandson, Felipe V, and Spain entered an era of "Frenchification," during which it fell under the influence of French ideas and customs.

Like the French, the Spaniards opened their intellectual and social life to the effects of the European Enlightenment. The seeds of this movement appeared first in Holland in the seventeenth century, spreading later to England, where it found two notable representatives in John Locke (1633-1704) and Isaac Newton (1645-1727). But it was in France that the movement flourished, through the writings of the philosophers Voltaire, Jean Jacques Rousseau, and Denis Diderot, and through the publication of the *Encyclopaedia* of arts, sciences and trades. From these works came the enunciation of radical ideas for the time, celebrating individual thought and attacking the heretofore uncontested authority of the Church and other established institutions. At the heart of the movement was the desire to educate the masses in new discoveries and scientific advancements, or, more generally, to improve the human condition.

Enlightenment thought in Spain was never as strong or widespread as in France. In Spain, the movement restricted itself mainly to intellectuals and groups of politicians close to the royal court, especially under Carlos III. For the first time, with the introduction into Spain of the reforms advocated by the defenders of the Enlightenment, a rift occurred between the existing religious, political, and cultural traditions of the nation and its political and administrative regime. This division led to a confrontation between major sectors of the population (especially the uneducated groups) and the nobles and intellectuals who defended the new doctrines.

More exactly, the king pitted himself against the Catholic Church. During the Enlightenment, the Spanish Bourbons—Felipe V (1700-46), Fernando VI (1746-59), Carlos III (1759-78), and Carlos IV (1778-1808)—set out to establish political absolutism in the Peninsula, and to centralize administration of the old Spanish empire—namely the Spanish possessions in the Americas and the Philippines, and the kingdom of the Two Sicilies in Italy. This policy gave unlimited power and control to the king, leading to a series of major changes that clashed with the Catholic Church's upper clergy. Until then the king had relied on the Church's advice for almost every matter. But now, the king, rather than the Pope, started appointing ecclesiastical dignitaries, and he furthermore reduced the number of religious institutions and decreased his regime's pecuniary contribution to the clergy. The king did not implement these policies without resistance from the Church. The Inquisition, the tribunal to suppress deviation from the teachings of the Roman Catholic Church, took some time to collect itself as a counterforce, distracted by the setback it suffered as the object of the Enlightenment's attacks, but it soon recovered its authority and became the mouthpiece of the Catholic Church, confronting the absolute power of the king. Despite this resistance, the Bourbons invoked reforms that improved the nation's economy, promoting industry and commerce, at the same time reinvigorating agriculture and livestock. Also, while Spain continued being a class-conscious land, the new administration supported the enterprises of the middle class and founded economic societies to educate its people.

The Enlightenment's commitment to education, in particular to the sciences, resulted in the creation of a series of cultural institutions: the Royal Academies of the Spanish Language (1713), of Medicine (1735), of History (1738), and of Fine Arts (1752); the National Library of Madrid (1712); and the Astronomic Observatory of Cádiz (1753). In the realm of the arts, the

Baroque—characterized by a complexity of design, a profusion of ornaments, and an emphasis on grandeur and mystery—dominated the first part of the eighteenth century, but soon shared the aesthetic domain with the rococo—characterized by excessive refinement, asymmetrical designs, curves and countercurves, gold and pastel colors. On the heels of the rococo came the Neoclassic styles, a reaction to the frivolity of the rococo that resurrected the ancient models of the Greeks and Romans, regarding their civilizations as the cradles of reason, philosophy and democracy.

Neoclassicism in Spain manifested itself not only in the visual arts but also in literature, particularly in drama and poetry. In poetry, for example, the obscurantism, colorful language, and sublime emotions that characterized the Renaissance (middle of the fifteenth century through the sixteenth century) and the Baroque and late Baroque (seventeenth century through the first half of the eighteenth century) were replaced by the simple language and didacticism of Neoclassicism (second half of the eighteenth century). Neoclassic writers in eighteenth-century Spain adopted as their guiding tenet Horace's famous quotation: *Omne tulit punctum qui miscuit utile dulci/lectorem delectando paritarque monendo* ("He has won every vote who has blended profit and pleasure, at once delighting and instructing the reader"—Horace, lines 343-44).

The *Teatro crítico universal* and the Age of Reason. The eighteenth century gave rise to thinkers who contested and contradicted ancient, established theories, their doubts and abstract thoughts leading to a larger number of new findings than before. Moreover, these new findings influenced the middle and lower classes for the first time in history; results of scientific experiments reached ordinary citizens, thanks to the spread of information through new maritime and terrestrial trade routes, through the growing number of publishing houses in Europe, and through the advent of journalism. With this gain came a concomitant loss. The ordinary citizen did not stay in as close touch with his local environment, that is, with traditional knowledge and custom.

Before the teachings of French philosopher René Descartes (1596-1650), the acceptance of new theories was controlled by the Church and based not on reason or direct observation and experimentation but on theological dogmatic criteria—the Bible and the works of the fathers of the Church, such as St. Augustine and St. Thomas

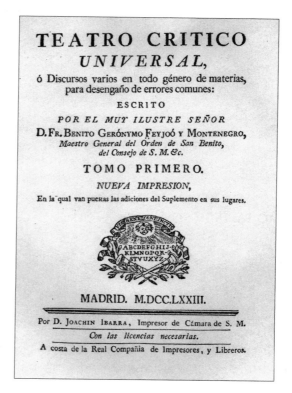

TEATRO CRITICO
UNIVERSAL,
ó Discursos varios en todo género de materias, para desengaño de errores comunes:

ESCRITO

POR EL MUY ILUSTRE SEÑOR

D. Fr. Benito Gerónymo Feyjoó y Montenegro,
*Maestro General del Orden de San Benito,
del Consejo de S. M. &c.*

TOMO PRIMERO.

NUEVA IMPRESION,

En la qual van puestas las adiciones del Suplemento en sus lugares.

MADRID. M.DCC.LXXIII.

Por D. Joachin Ibarra, Impresor de Cámara de S. M.

Con las licencias necesarias.

A costa de la Real Compañia de Impresores, y Libreros.

Title page from a collection of Feijóo's essays.

Aquinas. The Enlightenment's new discoveries—the telescope, thermometer, microscope—were, however, geared toward evidence collecting and empirical truth, and led to challenges against the currently authorized theories of the Church. Two famous examples of Church dogmatism were the forced retraction of Galileo Galilei (1564-1642), who systematized Copernicus's theory of the sun as the center of the universe (and not the earth, as the Church assessed), and the Church's condemnation of the Spanish Michael Servetus (1511?-53), who was burned alive for his discovery of the circulation of the blood—a fact denied by the Catholic and Protestant Churches. The Enlightenment's empiricism conflicted with scholasticism—the existing method of teaching at the Church-dominated university system. Scholasticism favored the deductive approach based on Aristotelian syllogisms (e.g., "legumes are edible; legumes are vegetables; therefore vegetables are edible"). Empiricism, in contrast, favored an inductive approach, to which the scholastic-minded academic authorities reacted negatively.

Descartes' theories furthermore conflicted with more than those of just the traditionally educated. They clashed as well with the *vulgo* (the "common herd"), an expression used by Feijóo to designate not a social class but rather the mentally inactive members of any social group, whether learned or not. In his view, the *vulgo* uncritically accepted anything that appealed to their thirst for sensationalism, especially unnatural phenomena, which led them to favor superstition over empirical truth.

Feijóo wrote the *Teatro crítico universal* (*Universal Theater of Criticism*) to let the *vulgo* know they were behind the times, and to help them

---

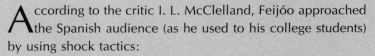

FEIJÓO TAKES THE OFFENSIVE

According to the critic I. L. McClelland, Feijóo approached the Spanish audience (as he used to his college students) by using shock tactics:

On at least the natural plane, many of your ideas about yourselves, other people, and the world in general are basically wrong. This is partly because you are too lazy or too stupid to observe and think for yourselves; partly because new evidence about the universe has come to light. I am passing it on to you. Some of this evidence, as you will realize if you use your brains at all, gives a clear explanation of things not understood before. Some of it merely proves that in certain fields we have everything to learn. Some of it, as it stands—the Copernican theory for example—seems to contradict even the unassailable authority of the Bible, and this is a field in which we must suspend our own judgment and wait for the pronouncement of the Church. But, as presumably thinking beings, we must know about such evidence, even if we hesitate to interpret it; for we must be able to understand the mind even of the heretic, not only in order to convert him, but because, outside religion, he is as likely as we are, and more likely than most of you, to arrive at truths about nature. What I demand of you, therefore, is a willingness to learn and to go on learning. For the time when explanations of all things could be thought of as final and conclusive has gone for ever. I invite you all, without much hope of cooperation from you all, to accompany me into the unfamiliarity of the unencompassed.

(I. L. McClelland, p. 44)

---

eradicate old ways of thinking and erroneous assumptions and superstitions. In the "Prologue to the Reader," he acknowledges that a relatively large audience will disagree with most of his arguments but nevertheless hopes to instill doubts by advancing reasons that may change those attitudes. Given his intended audience, Feijóo wrote not in Latin—as was expected from a

member of the Church and according to this type of work—but in Spanish so as to reach every member of the *vulgo*.

The eight volumes of *Teatro crítico universal* are divided into 118 discourses of variable length on a diversity of subjects: art, astronomy, economics, geography, history, political science, philosophy and metaphysics, philology, physics, mathematics, natural history, literature, aesthetics, Christian morals, medicine, superstitions, and more. The vast, multifaceted encyclopedic work is not organized in any orderly fashion; it makes no pretense to be a scientific treatise, aiming only to provide information and a commentary on anything that could become a subject of curiosity within the cultural or everyday world.

Feminism at the dawn of the eighteenth century. At the beginning of the eighteenth century the situation of women in Spanish society had not changed much from ancient times. Men went out into the public sphere in pursuit of political and commercial activities, while women remained guarded in the private sphere, and limited in their education to the acquisition of skills useful around the house.

During the baroque period, (seventeenth to early eighteenth century) philosophers showed an interest in educating women or at least in discussing the consequences of their education. Their interest built on the earlier activism of Erasmus of Rotterdam (1469-1536), foremost representative of Christian Humanism in Europe, who attempted to change the misogynist attitude inherited from the Middle Ages. Erasmus advanced new rules to transform women's perception of themselves and their role in society. Two of his followers were the Spanish scholars Luis Vives (1492?-1540?) and Juan Huarte de San Juan (1530-92), who promoted women's education but addressed it in different ways. In the *Examination of Men's Wit* (1575, published in English in 1596), Juan Huarte de San Juan—referred to as the "father" of differential psychology—discussed a type of education based on an individual's skills and capabilities and related to professions and particular courses of study. He insisted that women's education needed to be reduced to what was necessary for them to run a household; in spite of their good memory and fluency, argued Juan Huarte de San Juan, their overall mental inferiority prevented them from attaining any sort of intellectual depth. On the other hand, Juan Vives, the forefather of modern psychology and author of *On the Education of a*

Christian Woman (1523), defended the organic unity of pedagogy and supported popular education. He felt that women should not be excluded from this popular education, though perhaps they required a different kind of schooling because of their different functions in life. Echoing and extending this tack, Spain's Fray Luis de León (1527-91) in The Perfect Housewife (1583) established a clear sexual division of work. De León declared that while women were worthy of an elementary education, their place was in the house, cooking, cleaning, and spinning.

Despite the educational restrictions reinforced by such views, several women scored personal victories during the Baroque era not only in their intellectual achievements but also in the polemic about the separate natures of the sexes. There were two aspects to the feminist issue during this period: access to education and freedom to choose a husband. The novelist María de Zayas (1590-1661?) was a conservative feminist who advocated the education of women, though she always focused on the aristocratic class and supported the patriarchal system (see **The Disenchantments of Love,** also in *WLAIT 5: Spanish and Portuguese Literatures and Their Times).* Maintaining that souls have no sex, she contended that men's denial of women's rights to education stemmed from a fear of competition. A main concern for Zayas, aside from women's education, was the defense of their honor and reputation, and to this end, she depicted them in stories that provided rational explanation for their behavior in relation to men. In México, then part of Spain's empire, Sor Juana de la Cruz (1648-95) echoed Zayas's concerns, and in her philosophic satire "Foolish Men Who Accuse [Women]" condemned men who spoke ill of women while at the same time demanding their favors. In her two polemic writings, "Letter worthy of Athena" and "Reply to Sor Filotea," Sor Juana defended her own desire for broader knowledge and access to culture at a time when women were expected to shun intellectual pursuits. Feijóo's "Essay on Woman" includes Sor Juana among the women who distinguished themselves in literature in Spain, praising her for "the sublimity, force, and erudition of her poems," saying that any tribute to her would be "superfluous" and that "perhaps not one equals her in variety and extent of knowledge" (Feijóo, "An Essay on Woman," pp. 156-57). Yet he chastised her in a religious matter, siding with Father Vieyra, whose opinions Sor Juana had refuted in her "Letter worthy of Athena." At issue was their understanding of a phrase attributed to Christ just before he died: "A new commandment I give unto you: that you love one another as I have loved."

> Her criticism on Father Vieyra's sermons, shows the poignancy of her wit; but it must be allowed not to come up to that of the matchless Jesuit, whom she attacks; and is it anything strange that a woman should be inferior to that man, whom no preacher has hitherto equaled for sublimity of thought, solidity of argument, and a perspicuous force of expression?
>
> ("Essay of Woman," p. 157)

In general, the Enlightenment promoted women's education and the right to equal education for both sexes. Descartes theorized that the intellect, being independent of the body, was the same in both sexes and Feijóo denounced society for not acting on such theories to improve women's rights during his era. His "Essay on Woman" is just such a denunciation. The importance of Sor Juana, on one side of the Atlantic, and of Father Feijóo, on the other, lay in their claiming vindication for "all" women, rather than one individual and in their making not some abstract philosophical generalization but a comment on the behavior of their times.

The Essay in Focus

Contents overview. The title of the essay, "Defense of Women," and Feijóo's words in Section 5, "I being only a council, must not take on myself to act the judge," indicate the legal character of this work ("An Essay on Woman," p. 43). The "defense" aims to vindicate women from past injustices in society and to substantiate the claim for women's right to an equal education, in keeping with the Enlightenment's prescription for an educated society. The essay is divided into 24 sections, arranged according to the five-part division of the rhetorical style of speech attached to the Roman statesmen Cicero and Quintilian. In Section 1, the introduction (or *exordium*), Feijóo prepares his readers for the nature of the subject he will discuss: the vindication of women from a series of erroneous charges that have been historically attributed to them. In Sections 2 through 23 he clarifies his position (the *narratio*) and presents the arguments that establish his case (the *argumentatio*), summing them up in Section 24, (the *peroratio*).

Contents summary. Section 1 elaborates on how the argument will progress, from the moral and physical aspects of women's being to their intellectual abilities.

In the moral part of their composition, say those unnatural railers, women are all vice, and their physical part is full of imperfections.

("Essay on Woman," p. 4)

Many will scarce allow that the sex affords one single good woman; and in those whose outward deportment speaks a constellation of virtues within, it is construed design and hypocrisy. . . . ("She may seem a prude, and affect the austerity of a Sabine dame, but it is all a mask.")

("Essay on Woman," p. 10)

I am far from denying that great crimes have been committed by women; but . . . let him who would have all women good, set about converting all men. Nature has implanted modesty in them, as a fence against all the batteries of appetite; and it is very seldom that the first breach in this fence is made from within the place. As for some passages in the scriptures, which seem to bear hard against the women, they are undoubtedly to be understood only of the wicked and perverse.

("Essay on Woman," p. 13)

Here, methinks, adversaries rise up on all sides, and stun me with that common, but senseless clamor, that women are the cause of all evil; and in proof of it, the very populace are continually roaring out, "Caba ruined Spain and, Eve the world." [Florinda (a.k.a. Caba) was raped by the last Visigoth king Rodrigo, and she revealed the rape to her father, Count Julian, who was stationed in Spanish North Africa at the time. To avenge his daughter, the count instigated the Moorish invasion of Spain in 711, which led to eight centuries of Moorish domination. Historically Caba has thus been blamed for the fall of Spain to the Moors.]

("Essay on Woman," p. 16)

In Section 2, (the *narratio*, or explanation), Feijóo attacks the theory that women comprise the defective sex, and the idea that their existence is "fortuitous and foreign from nature's intent" ("Essay on Woman," p. 23). He furthermore discredits the belief that at the resurrection women will be perfected by a sex change.

To proceed from the moral to the physical part, as more immediately relative to our present purpose, the preference of the robust sex to the delicate, sex is accounted, beyond all question, as self-evident. Great numbers make no scruple to call a woman an imperfect, and even monstrous animal; and affirm, that nature, in generation, always intends a male, and that it is only from mistake or deficiency either of the matter or the faculty, that a woman is produced. Excellent philosophers truly! So nature intends

its own destruction, as without the concurrence of both sexes, the species cannot be maintained; and human nature would, in this its capital operation, fail as often as it hits, the number of both sexes being in all countries very nearly equal. . . .

("Essay on Woman," pp. 20-21)

From the same physical error of reviling woman, as an imperfect creature, sprung another theological error, combated by St. Augustine, in his *City of God*, Book 22, Chap. 17. And of which, the partisans, take upon them to say, that at the universal resurrection, this imperfect work, will be rendered perfect, by a change of sex; all the women, becoming men, grace being then to complete that work, which nature had left, only as it were, rough hewn.

("Essay on Woman," p. 26)

In Section 3, Feijóo discusses men's physical superiority, to which he contrasts women's beauty, gentleness, and candor. He demonstrates that the character of these physical qualities varies depending on their use; in one case they may be seen as a vice; in the other, as a virtue.

Section 4 discusses another positive quality associated with women, modesty, "the strong redoubt, covering the whole castle of the soul, against the batteries of vice" ("Essay on Woman," p. 38). In Section 5, Feijóo contends that granting separate positive qualities to both sexes still does not give men the advantage, since the masculine type "is counterpoised, by many women being eminent for those endowments on which men value themselves" ("Essay on Woman," pp. 44-45).

The endowments, which I have on evident grounds, attributed to women, balance, and perhaps surpass the qualities which distinguish men, but, who shall decide this process? Were it my province, my verdict would be very concise, that the qualities, in which women excel, tend to make them better in themselves, and the talents, in which men are superior, make them better, that is, more useful to the public; but, I being only a council, must not take on myself to act the judge; so for the present, the cause must remain undecided.

("Essay on Woman," pp. 42-44)

In Sections 6 and 7, Feijóo introduces a catalog of meritorious women to inductively demonstrate women's aptitude by furnishing examples of those who have excelled in political acumen and in courage in various countries and ages (e.g., England's Queen Elizabeth, Spain's Queen Isabella, France's Joan d'Arc, and Italy's heroine Blanca de Rossi). Finally, in Section 8,

Feijóo discusses "a point on which men sport their wit, as that in which the weakness of women, mostly betrays itself: the keeping of secrets" ("Essay on Woman," p. 77). Here, also by example, he proves that women do keep secrets "with invincible firmness" ("Essay on Woman," Section 8, p. 80). Bringing the argument to a close, he contests the basic charge, substantiating his view:

> Some persons, I make no doubt, will charge this parallel, between women and men, with flattery [from me to women]; but I refer [these persons] to Seneca, whose stoicism, so far from flattering, spared no pardon; yet, he puts women absolutely on a level with men, for any valuable talents and qualities. His words are these: *Quis autem dicat naturam malique cum mulieribus ingeniis egisse, et virtutes illarum in arctum retraxisse? Par illis, mihi crede, vigor, par ad honesta (libeat) facultas est. Laborem, doloromque ex equo si consuevere patiuntur* (in *Consol. Ad Marciam*). ("Who will say that nature has not dealt kindly with women, bestowing on them, but a very slender share of virtue. No; they have an equal strength of mind, equal disposition and ability for virtue and decorous actions; and with a little use, bear toil and pain, as well as we.")
> ("Essay on Woman," pp. 85-86)

At the center of the controversy over women is the question of their intellectual aptitude. Feijóo analyzes this subject in depth (sections 9 through 15), and systematically overturns religious and scientific arguments that discredit women's talents.

> To talk thus contemptuously of women, denotes a superficial man. Seeing female knowledge to be in general limited to those domestic employments in which they have been trained up; they from thence infer (though without knowing, that they do infer, as being unacquainted with reflection) that they are not capable of anything farther; whereas, every smatterer in logic, knows, that the absence of the act does not imply the absence of the power; and thus, if women do not know more, is no conclusive argument, against their having a talent for greater employments.
> ("Essay on Woman," pp. 90-91)

Feijóo's essay challenges a theory of the French philosopher Nicolas Malebranche about women's "softness of the brain," wherein their discernment of sensible things is superior than men, but absurd in abstract matters ("Essay on Woman," p. 93). According to Feijóo, this "failing" must be attributed to difference of application and practice.

> A woman of very clear intellects, has her thoughts taken up all day, about her domestic concerns, without hearing any discourse of a superior nature, or, if any edifying subject is introduced, hears it only superficially. Her husband, though greatly her inferior in natural endowments, is often in company with learned ecclesiastics, or expert politicians, in whose conversation, he acquires [a] variety of knowledge, becomes acquainted with the course and conduct of public affairs, and of many other important particulars.
> ("Essay on Woman," p. 97)

Feijóo moves on to the body, discussing jokingly in Section 12 the theory that equates mental aptitude to the amount of substance and temperature of the brain. He quotes the opinion of several philosophers who agree "that the greater the quantity of brain, the greater share of reason; which they infer from the observation that man has, in proportion, more brain than any other animal" ("Essay on Woman," p. 111). Feijóo wonders if the quantity of brain would cause any difference in the degree of understanding and if this quantitative difference would apply in the same manner to large-frame and small-frame males. (Not surprisingly, he feels obliged to the subscribers of this theory, "he having his share both of height and bulk" ["Essay on Woman," p. 112].) Another theory of his day posits the inferiority of women's intellect, attributing this inferiority to a difference of temperature—men are hot and dry while women are cold and moist. Tackling this theory, Feijóo proves its absurdity through deductive logic and through examples. He concludes rather comically: "Let not moisture any longer labor under the unjust reproach of being incompatible with wit; and be it allowed as a certain truth, that no such argument can afford any satisfactory proof that women are inferior in reason and understanding to men" ("Essay on Woman," p. 137).

In Sections 16 through 22, Feijóo once again catalogs examples of meritorious women (e.g., the Spanish philologist and polyglot Louisa Sigea, the French poetess Magdalena Scuderi, the Italian writer Dorothea Bucca, and the German child prodigy Anna Marra Schurman, who excelled in the liberal arts and the sciences). His goal in this case is to prove that "female intellects are equally capable of the most abstruse sciences, as those of men: this is indeed the best way for convincing the generality, all examples weighing more with them than reasons, which it is not given to all to comprehend" ("An Essay on Woman," pp. 148-49). Because he fears that his praise of women's intellectual gifts may shift around prejudice in society, he warns women not to exhibit discriminatory behavior towards men: "My opinion therefore is against all declamation about an inequality in the capacities of either sex" ("Essay on Woman," p. 201).

In his closing argument, Section 23, Feijóo contends that God's command about the superiority of men over women was meant to prevent social anarchy, not to establish intellectual advantages for one sex over the other.

> Some imagine all the premises to be at once overthrown by this single reply: if women are equal to men in understanding and an aptitude for sciences, and political and domestic government, how comes it that God invested man with the dominion and superiority over woman; which he plainly does by this decree in the third chapter of the Genesis [3:16] *Sub viri potestate eris* ("thou shalt be under the power of thy husband") . . . I answer, first, the precise sense of that text cannot be certainly known, by reason of the difference of the [Bible] versions.
> ("Essay on Woman," pp. 211-12)

> Secondly, the domestic subjection of women may be affirmed to have been merely a penalty for the breach of God's injunction, and thus would not have taken place in the state of innocence, at least, the text says nothing to the contrary: or rather, had woman been originally subject to man in the state of innocence, the all-wise and gracious Creator of both would not have omitted making this subordination known at the formation of Eve. Thus it was not on account of any superior understanding in man that such authority was conferred on him, but because woman had led the way in the transgression. Thirdly, even had God originally invested man with an authoritative superiority over women, that does not absolutely conclude for man's intellectual superiority: the reason is, that though both be equal in talents and understanding, the decorum and tranquility of the house and family required subordination, as otherwise it would have frequently been a scene of clamor and confusion.
> ("Essay on Woman," pp. 212-14)

Section 24 consists of the *peroratio* or conclusion, and in it Feijóo reaches a harmonious balance between rationalism and his own religious convictions. Equality among sexes, says Feijóo, will increase self-esteem, strengthen the bond of matrimony and reduce carnal sins.

> I shall conclude this discourse with an exception, which may be raised against the whole tenor of it; which is, to promote a persuasion, that both sexes are equal in intellectual qualities, is so far from being of any public advantage, that it may rather occasion many mischiefs, as fomenting the pride and presumption of women. This difficulty may be removed only by saying, that in everything, which comes under the cognizance of reason, it is of use to display truth, and explode error.
> ("Essay on Woman," p. 216)

> But I claim a still greater merit; the maxim which we have corroborated, so far from tending to any moral evil, may bring about much good. Let it be considered how many men this imaginary superiority of talents has prompted to undertake criminal conquests on the other sex.
> ("Essay on Woman," p. 218)

> Another very interesting consideration is, that any woman yields the more easily to the man whom she fancies to be greatly her superior. A man finds little reluctancy to serve another of higher birth, but where that circumstance is equal, servitude goes sorely against the grain. It is the very same in our case. If a woman is so far mistaken as to think man of a much more noble sex, and that as for herself, she is but an imperfect animal, a kind of inferior being, she will think it no shame to submit to him. . . . I have not yet displayed all the moral benefit, which would accrue from men and women being cured of their mistake, with regard to the disparity of the sexes. It is my real belief, that this mistake is of infinite prejudice to the marriage bed. Here some may imagine, I am running into a strange paradox, yet, it is an evident truth, as a little attention will show.
> ("Essay on Woman," pp. 220-22)

> In such a situation, how shall the most discrete, the most resolute woman act? How resist two impulses, directed to one and the same end, one impelling her, the other gently drawing her? [the despotic behavior of the husband and the gallant approach of a prospective lover]. Without the powerful support of Heaven, fall she must; and if she falls, who can deny, but that it was by the hand of her own husband. Had he not treated her with contempt, all the blandishments of the gallant, would not have prevailed against her. The rigor of the one, enforced the complaisance of the other. Such are the evils which frequently spring from that mean opinion of the other sex, which married men so often harbor and delight in exemplifying. Would these but throw aside such false maxims, their wives would spurn at every temptation to infidelity.
> ("Essay on Woman," pp. 226-27)

Feijóo's *vulgo* and the common error. Feijóo's *Teatro crítico universal* is intended to critically examine everyday customs, national conventions, and the beliefs embedded in people's minds. He did not take upon himself the task of creating a new vision of the world or establishing new trends in philosophy: as noted, he intended only to upset old common *errors* and superstitions, and to remove habits of thinking in Spain as well as abroad.

In referring to the mass of the people as *vulgo,* with the inclusive meaning he bestows on the term, Feijóo continues a tradition from the Spanish Golden Age. Werner Bahner explains that in the sixteenth century the word *vulgo* was not limited to ordinary people (Bahner, p. 90). The novel **Don Quixote** (also in *WLAIT 5: Spanish and Portuguese Literatures and Their Times*), for example, says that all of those who are ignorant can and must join the *vulgo*: "And you must not think, sir, that when I speak of the 'ignorant mob' I am referring only to humble working people, for all those who know nothing of poetry, whether they be lords or princes, can and should be thus classified" (Cervantes, p. 430). Bahner himself says "vulgo are those people who have not reached the ideological foundations of the century of the lights," and who instead of relying on reason, blindly accept the decrees of the "authorities" (Bahner, pp. 91, 93; trans. J. Grinstein). For Feijóo, the *vulgo,* consists not only of the mass of ordinary people but also of many erudites—a large number of writers, academicians, and clergymen as well as members of the upper classes. In his view, knowledge is not equated solely with erudition; it needs to be accompanied by discernment and wisdom.

Spanish tradition endorses beliefs such as the "people's voice is the voice of God," meaning that something must be true if it is believed by such a large crowd. Feijóo disagrees, and to this would reply "the value of opinions are measured by weight [quality] and not by the number of believers" ("Voice of the People," *Teatro crítico universal,* vol. 1, p. 1). By correcting and instructing the *vulgo,* Feijóo does not aim to eliminate this group but to rectify the deeply rooted common errors—superstitions, absurd traditions, and irrational customs. In keeping with the didacticism that is characteristic of the Enlightenment, he campaigns to rectify their mistaken notions, or *errors,* which he defines as "any opinion [he] believe[s] to be false" ("Prologue to the Reader," *Teatro crítico universal,* vol. 1, p. lxxiii).

The subject of the supernatural was a main source of *errors* in Feijóo's time. Ghosts, demons, witches, and angels figured in many pagan and Christian oral traditions. A man of religion, Feijóo does not assail dogmas or principles of the Catholic Church, which in the eighteenth century held a monopoly on interpretation of all non-natural phenomena. However, he criticizes the lower clergy for encouraging and perpetuating wonder tales that he describes as superstitions—alleged miracles not investigated enough by authorities of the Church. Some common errors identified by Feijóo follow:

Errors Born of Marvel Tales, Alleged Miracles, and Popular Traditions

- Women have smaller brains than men, thus less intellectual capabilities

- Women are imperfect human creatures; by being upgraded to manhood during the Final Judgement, they will attain perfection

- Jews have tails (demoniac personification)

- Jews kill one out of every five patients because they hated Christians

- Goblins exist in Oviedo in spite of contrary evidence

- Witches and demonically-possessed individuals exist who are agents of supernatural forces

- The Bull of St. Mark is a living miracle (the tradition holds that a wild bull docilely participates in the rites of the Mass on the feast of St. Mark, before returning to the wilderness)

- The Bell of Vellilla is a living miracle (since the Moorish invasion, it has rung by itself before disasters or propitious events)

- The flowers of St. Louis are a living miracle (during the Mass on the feast of this saint, the walls appear every year to be covered by small white flowers [which are in fact insect eggs])

Errors Born of Medical Ignorance

- Surgery is nonacademic technology

- Menstrual discharge is poisonous

- Bleeding and purging are recommended for almost every ailment

- Stages of an illness can be correlated with the seven phases of the moon (a week), and the crisis can be plotted on the seventh day or a multiple of seven

Sources and literary context. Feijóo's first 50 years were spent in religious practices, lecturing on Ecclesiastical history and Canonic law at the university, and avidly reading the ancient and *avant-garde* authors in Latin or in the original language. In his writings, Feijóo acknowledges a great debt to his vast array of readings by quoting the sources of his arguments, unless their authors were censured by the Inquisition. He cites the ancient pagan philosophers and classical authors as well as the sacred scriptures and the writings of the Fathers of the Church. Among the Spaniards, the already mentioned Luis Vives proved to be the greatest influence on Feijóo's thoughts in relation to the Enlightenment. Also influential were numerous foreign writers, philosophers, and scientists—records have identified 354 of them, from Corneille, Descartes, and Montaigne, to Montesquieu, Rousseau, Erasmus, Voltaire, and Bacon.

Francis Bacon was particularly influential on Feijóo's thought because of a general intellectual skepticism that led him to test the word of the authorities, his insistence on systematic and analytical experiment, and his conception of knowledge as a complex system of relationships. Bacon's draft of a dictionary of arts and sciences and suggestion for a "Calendar of doubts and problems" accompanied by another "Calendar of popular errors" helped inspire the goal as well as the selection of topics and polemic style of Feijóo's *Teatro crítico universal*. Feijóo also drew inspiration from two very important French journals: the *Mémoires de Trévoux* (Memoranda for the History of the Arts and Sciences), and the *Journal des Savants* (Savants' Journal). The first one, published by French Jesuits from Trévoux from 1701 to 1762, reported new findings and theories—especially in medicine and public health—from a variety of cultural settings and countries. The *Journal des Savants*, published in Paris from 1665 to 1792, was a scholarly critical review, covering culture and scientific matters, and Feijóo quoted it frequently in his essays. Mostly the *Teatro crítico universal* resembles these journals, in its character as a "Calendar of popular errors," adapted in Feijóo's case to local Spanish conditions and reflective of an academic rigor characteristic of its author alone. In relation to the specific article, "An Essay on Woman," while France distinguished itself as the cradle of the Enlightenment, it did not produce a voice like Feijóo's to vindicate women's rights at the time. On the contrary, as years passed French thinkers promoted separation of the sexes. Rousseau, in *Emile or On Education* (1762), stated that inequality between the sexes was imperative, and designed distinct educational models for them. Similarly Voltaire, in *Dictionary of Philosophy* (1764), declared that men were the superior sex, informing his readers that the arts and all important aspects of culture were invented by men.

Reception. The publication of the first two volumes of *Teatro crítico universal* took Spain by storm, with Feijóo's strong arguments in regard to the ordinary Spaniard's attitude towards new knowledge, as well as his advocacy of rationalism and experimental science, provoking academic and nonacademic reaction. A long polemic began between admirers and detractors, coming to an end only after the intervention of the Spanish king Fernando VI, who issued a decree in 1750 forbidding further attacks on Feijóo's books. Published between 1726 and 1742 were 97 works defending or attacking Feijo's ideas—books, letters, notes, and apologies, some under very provocative titles, such as *Intellectual combat* [...] and *Anti-theater of Criticism*. The particular article "An Essay on Woman" was the subject of ten of those 97 polemic works, only four of these ten supporting Feijóo's standpoint. Dr. Martín Martínez defended Feijóo in his *Carta defensiva* (Letter in Defense [of Feijóo's "Essay on Woman"]: "His sixteenth essay to make amends to women is fair and well elaborated. As a professor of anatomy, I can state that [the body's] organization does not differentiate in both sexes thoughts, and since they [the thoughts] emanate from the same organ in both men and women, I do believe that their attitude towards science has to be the same." (Martínez, p. 231; trans. J. B. Grinstein). Feijóo's critics included those who portrayed him as a detractor of Spanish values and a follower of foreign theories and fashions.

Fifteen editions of *Teatro crítico universal* were printed between 1725 and 1787, and close to half a million copies of all of Feijóo's works were sold before his death in 1764 (Alborg, p. 147). They were translated into French, Italian, Portuguese, English, and German during the century, and indexes and dictionaries appeared to facilitate the reading of his works. As a believer in the constant evolution of knowledge, Feijóo modified some of his opinions and presented new theories and information. Volume 9 was titled "Suplemento" (Supplement). In it he included additions and clarifications to the previous eight volumes, as well as some of his responses to attacks by other scholars and Churchmen. Future editions did not include the ninth volume, since the new information was added as footnotes (our English version) or endnotes (most Spanish versions).

The English took strong interest in *Teatro crítico universal*, publishing John Brett's translation of the entire work in London in 1780 under the title *Essays, or, discourses*. Earlier and later they also published translations of different sets of the essays (in 1739, 1751, 1779, and 1800). Essay No. 16 appeared several times under various titles: "An essay on woman, or, physiological and historical defense of the fair sex" (London, 1765, 1770, 1779); "An essay on the learning, genius, and abilities, of the fair-sex, proving them not inferior to man, from a variety of examples, extracted from ancient and modern history" (London, 1774); and "Three essays or discourses on the following subjects, a defense or vindication of the women, church music, a comparison between ancient and modern music," (London, 1778). The translation being used for this entry, "An Essay on Woman. A Defense of Women" (London, 1774) reflects Feijóo's influence. The translator added some pages to Section 21 of the original work, including examples of meritorious Englishwomen because "Father Feijóo having for reasons best known to himself thought fit to pass over the females of these islands, I take the liberty of inserting three or four, in commemoration of a few out of many, after the example of my original" ("Essay on Woman," p. 192). Among the names added were Constantia Grierson, Lady Jane Grey, the countesses of Derby and Winchelsea, and a Mrs. Macauley.

After 1787 the interest in Feijóo's works declined, largely due to the hostility expressed by Romanticism towards the Enlightenment era. Only a few abridged versions were published in the nineteenth and twentieth centuries, but still the polemic continued. In the nineteenth century, Marcelino Menéndez y Pelayo doubted the validity of Feijóo's attribution of common errors to the *vulgo*, blaming it on the arrogance of a Benedictine monk who simply wanted to vaunt his own vast knowledge.

Impact. What impact did Feijóo's "An Essay on Woman" have in Spain? His essay set out to prove women's ability to be trained in any field, including the military or medicine, and, though the essay became a *cause célèbre,* it did not instigate any major change in Spanish society. In fact, the rest of the seventeenth century would be witness to theatrical works that ridiculed women's desire for change, in plays attended by the *vulgo* whom Feijóo had set out to educate. However, there were a few exceptions to this generalized attitude. Gaspar Melchor de Jovellanos (1744-1811), a politician, promoted the idea of women's access to the work force in his "Report on the free practice of the profes-

sions" (1785)—he was referring to trades and not liberal professions. The dramatist Leandro Fernández de Moratín (1760-1828) wrote plays championing the right of young women to choose their own husbands (e.g., **Maiden's Consent,** also in *WLAIT 5: Spanish and Portuguese Literatures and Their Times*), though he did not favor equal access to education (as shown in his *La comedia nueva* [The New Comedy]). María Rosa de Gálvez (1768-1806), the major Neoclassic Spanish female dramatist, vigorously criticized the patriarchal system and defended women's access to education and free will to choose a husband or stay single (in her *La Delirante* [The Delirious Lady] and *La familia a la moda* [Family à la mode]).

In the second half of the nineteenth century and on the bicentennial of Feijóo's birth, the importance of "Essay on Woman" was acknowledged by the feminist movement, mainly represented by the lawyer and writer Concepción Arenal (1820-93) and the novelist Emilia Pardo Bazán (1852-1921; see **House of Ulloa,** also in *WLAIT 5: Spanish and Portuguese Literatures and Their Times*). During much of the twentieth century, however, the Spanish feminist movement foundered, frustrated in its design to modernize society, which caused the "Essay"'s demise as an ideological work. The resurgence of the movement in the 1970's brought renewed attention to many seminal works of the European Enlightenment. In 1997, "Essay on Woman" was reedited in Barcelona by the distinguished feminist writer Victoria Sau, who in the Introduction discusses the essay as a major landmark of feminist history.

—Julia Bordiga Grinstein

For More Information

Alborg, Juan Luis. *Historia de la literatura Española.* 5th ed. Vol. 3 of *Siglo 18.* Madrid: Gredos, 1985.

Bahner, Werner. "El vulgo y las luces en la obra de Feijóo." *Actas del Tercer Congreso Internacional de Hispanistas* (1968): 89-96.

Cervantes Saavedra, Miguel de. *The History of that Ingenious Gentleman Don Quijote de la Mancha.* Trans. Burton Raffel. New York: Norton, 1996.

Feijóo y Montenegro, Benito Jerónimo. *Teatro crítico universal.* 9 vols. Madrid: Imprenta Real de la Gaceta, 1765.

———. "An Essay on Woman." In *El teatro crítico.* London: Bingley, 1774.

Horace. *The art of poetry: an epistle to the Pisos. Epistola ad Pisones, De arte poetica.* Trans. George Colman. New York: AMS Press, 1976.

The Family of Pascual Duarte

by

Camilo José Cela

Camilo José Cela Trulock was born in 1916 in the seacoast village of Iria Flavia in Galicia, which sits in the northwestern corner of Spain. His father's job as a customs official required frequent moves by the family, making coastal Galicia and Madrid the poles of the young Cela's life. Further disrupting Cela's pre-university education was his misconduct at different schools and his first bout with tuberculosis in 1931. Cela's university career in Madrid as a student of medicine came to an abrupt halt because of the Spanish Civil War (1936-39), in which he suffered a shrapnel wound while serving with the Nationalist forces. By 1940 Cela was hard at work on *The Family of Pascual Duarte*, his writing interrupted by a recurrence of tuberculosis in 1941. Undaunted, Cela not only finished this first novel but went on to publish more, including *La colmena* (1951; *The Hive*, 1953). He published as well collections of stories, essays, poetry, and travel literature; in this last genre, his most renowned work is *Viaje a la Alcarria* (1948; *Journey to the Alcarria: Travels Though the Spanish Countryside*, 1964). Despite occasional problems with government censors, by the early 1950s Cela was earning his living as a writer of fiction and nonfiction. His 1957 induction into the Spanish Royal Academy of the Language, and his 1989 award of the Nobel Prize for Literature signify, respectively, Cela's national and international recognition. In *The Family of Pascual Duarte*, Cela sets a career-long pattern of centering his fictions around the lives and points of view of people he identifies as losers in soci-

---

THE LITERARY WORK

A novel set in the impoverished Estremadura region of west central Spain from the 1880s to 1942; published in Spanish (as *La familia de Pascual Duarte*) in 1942; in English in 1946.

SYNOPSIS

From prison the 55-year-old agricultural laborer Pascual Duarte narrates his life, especially the events that led to his two jail terms for two homicides, and to his execution in 1937 for a third murder, that of the local nobleman.

---

ety. Success for these characters, including Pascual Duarte, amounts to achieving self-knowledge and becoming reconciled to one's lot in life.

Events in History at the Time the Novel Takes Place

Revolution, the Restoration and the oligarchy. Between the September 1868 Revolution, which led to the expulsion of Queen Isabella II from her throne, and the 1875 Restoration of the monarchy, in the person of Isabella's son Alfonso XII, Spain experimented with democracy. In fact, it experimented with several kinds of democracy, including the antimonarchical, wholly elected government of the First Republic. But monarchically inspired civil war in the north

Camilo José Cela

and democratically inspired armed autonomy movements in the south weakened the Republic, produced a coup d'etat in 1874, and led a year later to the restoration of constitutional monarchy under Alfonso.

Cela has his protagonist Pascual Duarte born in the early 1880s, a period in which Spain op-

erated under the post-restoration political compromise between the conservatives of Antonio Cánovas del Castillo and the liberals of Práxedes Mateo Sagasta. The compromise aimed theoretically at re-establishing social and political order by better balancing the needs and demands of the upper and lower classes. In practice the

Restoration witnessed the increasing domination of Spanish society by the oligarchy (formed by the traditional landed aristocracy, the new industrial and financial elite, and the leaderships of the Catholic Church and the military).

Segments of this group made a mockery of parliamentary rule by widespread election fixing. Extremely powerful provincial bosses–*caciques*– used the economic clout of the oligarchy to field pliable candidates to the Spanish parliament (the Cortes), to buy votes for those candidates, and to suppress opponents. Liberal and conservative professional politicians, mainly from the upper middle classes, took turns administering the parliamentary system. Their power-sharing arrangement—called the *turno pacífico* (the pacific turn)—protected the oligarchs' interests and improved the economic position of the politicians. The shortcomings and failures of this system became especially apparent in the 1890s to the working classes—agricultural laborers of the great estates in Andalusia, industrial workers of the coal and iron regions in Asturias and the Basque Country, and factory workers in Catalonia. Solutions to these problems included demands for higher wages and shorter working hours.

Violence and radicalization of Spanish society. Spain's government, as indicated, was in alliance with its oligarchy. At the end of the nineteenth century and the beginning of the twentieth, many events both placed the working classes in opposition to this alliance, and revealed the government's inability to manage well the country's affairs. Among the more spectacular of these events were

- The prosecution of colonial wars in Morocco in northwestern Africa in 1893 and in Cuba in 1895 to protect the mining, agricultural, and mercantile interests of the oligarchy

- The August 1897 assassination by an anarchist of Prime Minister Antonio Cánovas del Castillo, the architect of the Restoration and the *turno pacífico*

- The loss of the 1898 Spanish-American War, in which more than 50,000 Spanish working-class soldiers and sailors died from tropical illnesses and in battles they were not equipped or led to win

- Renewed colonial misadventures in Morocco, including military disasters (most notably in 1909 and 1921), which led to more than 11,500 Spanish deaths on the battlefields, and to bloody riots, assassinations, and executions at home

The middle classes and the oligarchy, who constituted no more than 30 percent of the Spanish population, could buy their sons out of the draft that funneled soldiers and sailors to the above-named wars and adventures. The working classes enjoyed no such alternative. Instead they saw their sons fall to disease or become cannon fodder to protect the colonial plantations, mines, and markets so important to the monied interests of the country. Even Spain's neutrality in World War I, which boosted Spanish agricultural and industrial production to supply the demand of the warring powers, benefitted the upper classes much more than the laboring ones.

Unfortunately for the oligarchy, however, with increased production came notable increases in the number, concentration, and radicalization of organized Spanish workers. Within about a decade Pablo Iglesias's Socialist trade union, the UGT (General Union of Workers) climbed from only 3,000 members (1908) to 200,000 (1920) (Thomas, p. 25). The more radically inclined CNT (National Confederation of Labor) rose from 50,000 members in the early 1870s to 1.5 million in the 1930s (Thomas, pp. 40-41). Meanwhile, by 1936, the year the Civil War began, as many as 30,000 super-radical workers, judging the CNT too willing to compromise with the government, had become active in the secret society known as the FAI (Federation of Iberian Anarchists). Bomb throwers and assassins, its members were deadly terrorists.

The reign of the constitutional monarch Alfonso XIII (1886-1941) began in 1902 when he entered his majority. Not surprisingly the young, inexperienced king had no particular success in helping to create a new agenda to alter either the already well-established pattern of governmental incompetence, corruption, and criminal malfeasance, or the working classes' escalating violent responses. General Miguel Primo de Rivera's coup d'etat of September 1923 was welcomed by a tired, divided country. The general, popular for his successes in reasserting Spanish dominance in Morocco following the 1921 massacre of 10,000 Spanish soldiers there, ushered in a prosperous, peaceful period of nearly six years. Regrettably, however, the Primo de Rivera dictatorship did nothing to advance the political development of the country. Instead the regime contented itself with creating the simulacrum of a parliamentary monarchy headed by the inept Alfonso XIII, who fell into a pattern of accepting and condoning Primo de Rivera's unconstitutional measures. As a result the fundamental issues of socioeconomic justice in Spain festered, making radical left-wing political alternatives attractive to the laboring masses.

The Second Republic and the Civil War. Faced by the need to re-establish effective parliamentary rule and to rehabilitate the tarnished image of Alfonso XIII, the post-Primo de Rivera government called for national elections in April 1931. Contrary to government hopes and expectations, the vote became a negative reaction to constitutional monarchy and to Alfonso, who had cooperated with the dictator Primo de Rivera. On April 14 the Second Republic was

---

THE REBELLION OF THE MASSES

A decade before Cela's *The Family of Pascual Duarte* appeared, another Spanish writer, José Ortega y Gasset, tackled the issue of violence in his study *The Rebellion of the Masses* (1930). Ortega, the scion of an important Madrid newspaper family, analyzes societal problems, including violence. He condemns all, regardless of socioeconomic class and position, who do not have a holistic vision of history and society yet pretend to be competent in directing contemporary political life. At home and abroad he observed the contention among capitalists, fascists, and communists that flourished between the two world wars. He concluded that the agenda of each of these groups was too narrow, too self-interested, too uninformed to merit any of them the leadership of the peoples and nations of the world. Concretely Ortega proposed that European society be directed by skilled, altruistic politicians who would be advised by broadly humanistic historians, scientists, writers, and philosophers.

---

proclaimed and Alfonso went into an exile from which he never returned.

The Second Republic had a tall order to fill. It contended with mounting mutually exclusive demands from the political left and right. Especially significant were the growth and militancy of the centralizing Communist Party, guided and supported by the Soviet Union, and growing autonomy movements in nearly all regions of Spain. In villages, towns, and cities, as Ernest Hemingway records in *For Whom the Bell Tolls*, old personal wrongs and grievances fueled class hatreds. On the left were peasants, workers, intellectuals, and labor leaders. On the right were politicians,

priests, military officers, and wealthy individuals. Both sides singled out for assassination opponents in the enemy camp. In February 1936 the last parliamentary elections of the Second Republic were held. They were won by the Popular Front, a coalition of socialists, communists, Catalonian separatists, and republicans. But already in January military officers, including General Francisco Franco, and the oligarchical financial elite had begun plotting the overthrow of this coalition and the Republic in general. So it is not surprising that the level of societal violence rose tremendously. Between February and June 1936, there were 269 murders, 1,287 injured and wounded, 160 churches destroyed and 231 damaged, 69 right-wing political headquarters wrecked and 312 damaged, 113 general strikes and 228 partial ones, and 10 newspaper offices sacked and 33 others attacked (Bertrand and Petri, p. 382). The specific event that triggered Franco's July 18, 1936, rebellion was the assassination of José Calvo Sotello, a very prominent monarchist representative to parliament. In the early hours of July 14 he was taken from his Madrid residence by leftist militants on the police force and killed in the street by them; then his body was dumped in a local cemetery. These militants were, for their part, revenging a drive-by assassination earlier that evening of a Communist policeman by young, upper-class gunmen. Punctuating this panorama of violent chaos was a Popular Front measure of special relevance to the background of *The Family of Pascual Duarte*. In late March, 3,000 small, medium, and large estates, mostly in Estremadura, were divided up among as many as 75,000 peasants. While the novel does not even allude to this policy in Spain or around Pascual Duarte's village, the historically aware reader understands that Pascual's murder of the Count of Torremejía, the local large land owner, probably took place in later March, shortly after the Popular Front's appropriations and redistributions of Estremaduran lands.

The Novel in Focus

Plot overview. *The Family of Pascual Duarte* begins with a "Preliminary Note by the Transcriber," a person whose identity we never learn. In the middle of 1939, the transcriber found, in a pharmacy of the small city of Almendralejo in Estremadura, an "original manuscript" that "was almost unreadable, for the writing was rough and the pages were unnumbered and in no consecutive order" (Cela, *The Family of Pascual Duarte*,

p. 3). The pages comprise the handwritten narrative of one Pascual Duarte. Despite acknowledging that he has cut certain crude passages, the "transcriber" affirms that he has "not corrected or added a thing" (*Family*, p. 4). He justifies publishing the manuscript on grounds that the reader's conduct should be the exact opposite of Pascual Duarte's.

Two other documents follow: a letter dated February 15, 1937, written by Duarte from Badajoz Prison in Estremadura to a pharmacist in the nearby city of Mérida; and an extract from the pharmacist's will dated May 11, 1937. The pharmacist was a friend of the Count of Torremejía, the last man whom Pascual Duarte murdered. The manuscript as a whole begins with his short dedication to the Count, "who, at the moment when [Duarte] came to kill him, called him Pascualillo, and smiled" (*Family*, p. 11). In conjunction with this dedication, the letter to the pharmacist shows that Pascual feels remorse for the killing, and that he wants someone who knew the Count to understand his killer and to forgive the crime. The pharmacist's will shows that, though filled with revulsion by Pascual's story, he decided the manuscript should survive him and have a future independent of him.

From the January 1942 materials at the end of the novel—more words from the transcriber and letters from a prison chaplain and a guard—the reader learns details of Pascual Duarte's last days. The materials review his religious conversion, his initial acceptance of his fate, and his subsequent recalcitrance—he ultimately had to be dragged kicking and screaming to the place of execution by garrote.

Contained between these framing sections, there are, in the Kerrigan translation cited here (done in collaboration with Cela), 18 unnumbered, chapter-like divisions of Pascual Duarte's first-person narrative.

Plot summary. Pascual Duarte's handwritten materials recapitulate the principal persons and events in his life as an agricultural laborer. Pascual was born and lived in a house owned by his family, but, in a region of estates, without appreciable land for the Duarte family to cultivate. He writes about his parents, siblings, animals, spouses, friends, enemies, and victims on the one hand; his period spent in Madrid and La Coruña, his incarcerations, and his thoughts on the other hand. In the initial paragraph of section four, Pascual explains to the pharmacist, his designated addressee, the lack of a systematic thread in his writing:

Residents flee through war-littered streets during the Spanish Civil War.

> You will know how to forgive me the lack of order in this narrative. Following the footsteps of the people involved rather than the order of events, I jump from beginning to end and from the end back to the beginning. Like a grasshopper being swatted. But I can't seem to do it any other way. I tell the story as it comes to me and don't stop to make a novel of it.
>
> (*Family*, p. 39)

Despite the literary sophistication suggested by this apology, Pascual's education, which he owed to the insistence of his otherwise abusive, sometimes jailed father, was limited. By age 12, around 1894, at his mother's bidding, seconded by his own inclination, he stopped studying. He had by then learned the basic skills: "how to read and write, and to add and subtract" (*Family*, p. 27). Although Pascual never explicitly states how he earned his living while in his home village, a web of indirect references indicate that he worked for the large landowner the Count of Torremejía, and that his hunting, fishing, and care of a few domesticated animals supplemented his cash income as an agricultural laborer.

Pascual's memoirs, again despite his apology about their randomness, have a generally chronological structure. He does, in keeping with the apology, present successions of people and events and intervals of time between them rather than a start-to-finish narrative. But the information he gives, in conjunction with dates from the framing sections, allows a reader to organize easily Pascual's life in time. He was born in 1882 to an authoritarian Portuguese father, who was a smuggler, and an uncaring Spanish mother in a small village six miles east of Almendralejo. The family house, small and dark with a dirt floor, was situated a few hundred yards outside a village, just beyond its cemetery. The Count lived in the principal residence on the village square. While Pascual's family house seems to pass down through the maternal line, the men were the

THE FAMILY OF PASCUAL DUARTE ON CELLULOID

In 1976 the Spanish director Ricardo Franco (1950-98) released his film version of *The Family of Pascual Duarte*. Whereas Cela's novel avoids all direct and most indirect historical and political references to the Spain of 1936, the filmmaker stresses them. He creates scenes that do not exist in the novel: Pascual's father as a left-wing political sympathizer; politically motivated shootings and arson in and around Pascual's village; and Pascual shotgunning the Count. The film further contextualizes this last scene by having it occur just as the nobleman is about to leave his estate for the city because the countryside is too dangerous for big landowners. Franco's movie thus becomes a fairly realistic recreation of the period, especially when Pascual is taken off to prison by soldiers, not police. It is commonly known that Cela does not like Franco's restructuring of his novel. Cela intentionally left out such direct ties to history in the novel. By making the actions and conflicts of Pascual's memoirs ambiguous in their sociohistorical references, Cela universalizes issues of the individual, society, and violence, rather than limiting them to the Spain of the Civil War period. Pascual Duarte's extended family is humankind.

breadwinners. When Duarte or his father were home, money was apparently never a problem for the family. Nonetheless, life in the house was extremely contentious because of Duarte's parents' bitter relations, and the boy learned it was best to keep out of sight. His sister, the future runaway and sometimes prostitute Rosario, was born about 1887. As an infant she was a unique source of joy for Pascual and his father. Throughout their lives, even when separated by geography, the bordello, or jail, Pascual and Rosario maintained an abiding love for each other. In

1902, at a time when Pascual had had the luck to complete (exceptionally for the period) an uneventful military service, the birth of his second sibling, the mentally and physically deficient Mario, preceded by two days the horrible death from rabies of Pascual's father. Although Pascual cared for Mario, despite guessing him to be the offspring of his mother's lover Don Rafael, he did not intervene during the years of mistreatment and abuse of the child by its heartless mother and Don Rafael. Pascual mentions that Mario's ears were eaten off one day by a family pig, and that on another day Don Rafael kicked the child senseless and left him bleeding from the ears. This much amused his mother. When Mario fell into an oil vat and died at age nine, Pascual viewed it as a release from a life that was very hard even for the strong. While lingering at his brother's grave after a burial service, Pascual encountered a local woman named Lola. She was attracted to Pascual, and when he failed to take advantage of their isolation, she mocked his manhood and he responded by forcibly taking her right there on the freshly turned earth of Mario's plot. Lola then conceded Pascual was a man and confessed her love for him.

At this point there is a break in the narration. Pascual states that for the preceding 15 days he has written nothing. He has been busy with his lawyer and has been moved to another prison. He has also reread what he has written. From his new cell, which he likes much better than his old one, he can see the outdoors: countryside, butterflies, mules and teamsters, women and children. He muses about his writing, his life, what was and what could have been.

Resuming his narrative, Pascual explains that when Lola was eight months pregnant they were married in the local church and, by horse, took their wedding trip of about 20 miles to Mérida. Pascual recalls it as the happiest time of his life. When passing through the village on their return, Pascual was persuaded to stay and drink with his friends while Lola continued alone on Pascual's mare to the house. When some words were exchanged between Pascual and another man, Pascual sliced him several times with his knife and went home. There he learned that the mare had thrown Lola and that she miscarried. Filled still with drink and rage, Pascual went out and stabbed the mare to death. Lola's second pregnancy produced a son who filled her and Pascual with joy. Pascual remembered that, given his customary bad luck, he was very apprehensive about the child's welfare. His fears proved well-founded. At age 11 months, around 1915, Pascual junior died from the effects "of an ill wind, a treacherous and evil draft" (*Family*, p. 88). Pascual thought both his mother and wife blamed him for the infant's death and felt a growing hatred for his mother, who seemed to be the origin of all that was wrong in his life. One day in the fields, while resting from hunting with his dog Chispa, Chispa sat looking at him. Feeling that even the dog was blaming him, he killed her with his shotgun. This made Pascual understand that, because of the hate he had, he must leave home or he would deal with his mother as he had with Chispa.

Here there is a second break in Duarte's narration. A month has passed since Pascual wrote about his hate. The day before taking up his pen again, he confessed his sins to the same prison chaplain who communicated with the transcriber in 1942. Pascual now dwells on what might have been had he known before his crimes his present sense of peace. He also discusses the difficulties of writing and his fear that he may be executed before he finishes his story.

The narration proper resumes with Duarte fleeing his home in the dead of night. Having decided to go to America, he took all the family money and boarded a train bound for Madrid. There he lodged in the house of a laborer for two weeks. After taking in the sights and noting how Madrilenians could become very angry, say things that would provoke a knife fight back home, and yet not fight, Pascual went to the Galician seaport of La Coruña. Learning that he did not have half the necessary fare for passage to America, he remained in La Coruña for 18 months, first working at odd jobs, then settling in as a bouncer at a house of prostitution.

When overcome by homesickness, Pascual returned to his village, probably in early 1918. His mother received him very coldly. Life had been difficult for her and his wife Lola in his absence. The mother, it seems, had facilitated relations between Lola and Stretch, Rosario's debaucher and pimp, and Pascual's archenemy. Lola informed Pascual that she was pregnant. When he obliged her to tell him by whom, she confessed that Stretch was her lover and then appeared to drop dead from fright. Pascual immediately searched for Stretch, but learned from Rosario that he had fled upon Pascual's return. Tired of prostitution and with Stretch gone, Rosario came back home to be with Pascual. A period of contented tranquillity in the Duarte home ensued. In retrospect, though, Pascual observes that an old pattern in

his life was reemerging: just as things seemed to be looking up for him, the influence of "my unlucky star, that evil star which seemed bent on destroying me" reasserted itself (*Family*, p. 125). This time his ill fate was signaled by Stretch's reappearance, first in town, then, coming to fetch Rosario at the Duarte home. In their new meeting Stretch demonstrated so much arrogance and disdain for Pascual that Pascual smashed him with a stool, crushing Stretch's shoulder bones. Despite being seriously wounded, Stretch, who had mistaken Pascual's previous restraint towards him as cowardice, could not remain quiet. He taunted Pascual, promising to shoot him when he recovered and mocking him for not being able to take care of his women. At that point Pascual crushed and killed Stretch like a bug underfoot.

Around 1921, after serving a jail term shortened to three years for good behavior, Pascual returned home. At his sister's urging, he married Esperanza, a family friend who had always loved him from a distance. Pascual was happy with Esperanza, but within two months his mother's evil presence was preying upon his mind. Pascual wondered why he came back home when the only remedy for what he felt towards his mother was putting distance between them. While writing his memoirs 15 years later, he attributed that return to his habitual unlucky star. In any case, Pascual was soon plotting his mother's death. On the night of February 12, 1922, he entered her room. Filled with conflicting emotions, he watched her sleeping for a long time. Just as he decided he could not kill her and was leaving the room, he made a noise that woke her. He then felt impelled to kill her. After a fierce struggle, he stabbed her in the throat and was covered by her spurting blood. Running out of the house, he bumped into Esperanza and kept on going. Once free in the fields, he recalled, in the final words of his narration, "I could breathe . . ." (*Family*, p. 158).

From the framing materials mentioned above, the reader understands that Pascual spent most of the time between 1922 and 1936 in prison. Knowledge of the history of the period indicates the following: Pascual was probably included in the amnesty of February 1936 that freed mainly political prisoners from jail; he may have killed the Count around the time in late March when the Popular Front government divided Estremaduran estates among agricultural workers; and he was probably taken prisoner for the murder of the Count sometime after August 7, when nearby Almendralejo was occupied by General Franco's Nationalist forces. The framing materials suggest Pascual was executed in late February 1937 for the murder of the Count.

At the root of the problem. In the first section of his narrative, Pascual tells how he used to fish for eels in a foul-smelling stream behind his house. His wife commented "that the eels were so fat because they ate the same" as the Count of Torremejía, "only a day later" (*Family*, p. 19). On the day Pascual is specifically remembering, he noticed Almendralejo in the distance. He suddenly realized that no one there "knew or cared that I had been fishing, that I was watching the

---

THE FEBRUARY 1936 AMNESTY

Following the failure of a right wing, Catholic government to bring order to national life, the Spanish parliament was dissolved in January 1936 and the ensuing February parliamentary elections brought the leftist Popular Front to power. One of this government's first actions, implemented in some areas before explicit governmental authorization, was the amnesty of some 30,000 political prisoners in jail throughout Spain. Most of them had been imprisoned in the aftermath of the bloody repression by General Franco of a 1934 Communist rebellion of miners in the Asturias mining region of north-central Spain. If common criminals such as Pascual Duarte, then jailed for matricide, happened to be in the prisons of regions where leftist sentiment was high, they were also liberated and, given the societal chaos of spring 1936, remained free.

---

lights in their houses come on, that I was guessing what they said"; and, he then observed: "The inhabitants of cities live with their backs to the truth," that they are unmindful of country people (*Family*, p. 19).

In his own way Pascual is experiencing what Ortega y Gasset called "particularism" in his book *Invertebrate Spain*, a work published first in 1921, just about the time Pascual and his wife come to the realizations noted above. For Ortega, particularism meant that individual social groups lost their identity as parts of the larger society and that all groups thereby lost an understanding of how members of other groups felt and thought. When Cela's novel has the heedless Count let his sewage flow into the small stream, or has Pascual comment on the indifference of city people

to country people, it makes particularism a concern. For Ortega, Spain was great when a common spirit and purpose infused the country during the centuries of the Reconquest from the Moors and the century of the discovery, conquest, and colonization of the Americas. It began its decadence, continuing still in Ortega's early twentieth century, with the advent of particularism, which Ortega traces as far back as 1580.

When Duarte and his wife experience the particularistic isolation dividing the landed noble and the peasant, the city and the country, Cela incorporates into his novel a fundamental analyses of the Spanish national situation that culminated in the Civil War. This said it must also be observed that Cela, partly because of censorship, partly because of his view of how fiction relates to society, does not make Pascual Duarte the kind of typical, representative character found in nineteenth-century realist novels. Although Pascual Duarte lives specifically between 1882 and 1937, the Ortegan particularism he observes and lives is centuries old. He and his story are something like allegorical representations of the Spanish condition. The violence that characterizes this one man is a reaction to particularism and also symbolic in that it is a national characteristic. For Ortega the most negative aspect of particularism is its encouragement of violence by individuals and groups who have lost the socially learned preference and talent for conversation and mediation as ways to resolve problems.

Sources and literary context. The dominant prewar Spanish literature was vanguardist, embarking, as did Picasso in painting, on all manner of post-realist and post-naturalist experimentation. Miguel de Unamuno and Ortega y Gasset were the principal intellectual leaders of Spain at the time (see **Mist** and **Meditations on Quixote**, also in *WLAIT 5: Spanish and Portuguese Literatures and Their Times*). In Madrid, as a student and disciple of the poet Pedro Salinas, Cela participated fully in the cultural life of the country. His hospitalizations for tuberculosis in 1931 and 1941 and convalescence from shrapnel wounds in 1937 allowed him to read voluminously, particularly in the complete works of Spanish classics published by the Biblioteca de Autores Españoles (Library of Spanish Authors). Following a chance wartime stay in Estremadura and Almendralejo, the setting for much of *The Family of Pascual Duarte*, Cela, influenced by that reading and the prewar intellectual ferment in Madrid, began to incorporate into his writing the human and social observations he made.

Certain elements of the traditional picaresque first-person narrative and others of ballads of bandits and evildoers, were placed in the frame of a found manuscript, a strategy established by Cervantes in **Don Quixote** (also in *WLAIT 5: Spanish and Portuguese Literatures and Their Times*). But while the discoverer of the Don Quixote materials must have them translated from the Arabic for his Spanish reader, the transcriber of the Pascual Duarte materials finds and organizes a narrative whose original version, he claims, was so chaotic as to have been unreadable. For his part, Pascual offers artistically self-conscious comments on his work as autobiographer and about his fear that he might be executed before he can finish his tale. The strategy recalls from *Don Quixote* the knight's criticisms of how his squire Sancho Panza tells a story. Finally, Cela's novel includes a multiplication of perspectives on Pascual Duarte that again derives from Cervantes's practice in *Don Quixote* and that philosophically echoes Ortega's 1925 essay titled "The Historic Sense of Einstein's Theory." When Pascal famously begins his tale with the words "I am not, sir, a bad person, though in all truth I am not lacking in reasons for being one," the transcriber, the pharmacist, Duarte himself, and implicitly the Count have already given opinions about Duarte that make those words problematic (*Family*, p. 13). And after Duarte's memoirs conclude, the transcriber, the prison guard, and the chaplain give more versions of Pascual's life. This structuring may be read as an Ortegan experiment in truth seeking. The philosopher held that truth results from the discovery and reconciliation of all relevant, individual points of view. Cela's novel presents many characters, from both the framing sections and from Pascual's narrative proper, who opine on the actions and motivations of the protagonist. While each character has his opinion of Pascual Duarte, only the reader can take equally into account all viewpoints in the effort to determine as truly as possible the meaning of Duarte and *The Family of Pascual Duarte*.

Events in History at the Time the Novel Was Written

Postwar violence—the national scene. In 1940, when Cela began reading to his friends fragments of what was to become *The Family of Pascual Duarte*, Spain was still reeling from the effects of the Civil War. Its population stood at 25.8 million. The best studies calculate that dur-ing the three years of civil war and the following year of repression 500,000 Spaniards—mostly males in their productive years—were killed or exiled; another 74,000 became political prisoners (Tamames, pp. 170-71). Furthermore, the economy was in ruins. At war's end, towns and villages in the most bitterly contested zones had between 60 percent and 100 percent of their buildings destroyed (Tamames, p. 171). And as the nation began rebuilding, its agricultural and industrial production were 21.2 percent and 31 percent lower, respectively, than in 1935 (Tamames, p. 172).

In this panorama of terror, destruction, and death, the triumphant leader of the so-called Nationalist rebellion that began the Civil War in 1936, General Franco, had one principal aim: the consolidation of dictatorial military and political control by him over Spain. On the domestic front this meant snuffing out pockets of guerrilla resistance to his rule from die-hard Republicans. It also meant the legitimatization of his position by strengthening his ties to the Catholic Church and to the Falange party, the most harmless, from his viewpoint, of the prewar right-wing political groups. In the international arena his position was delicate. Although he was the declared ally of Hitler and Mussolini, and had received vital aid from them during the Civil War, Franco had little interest in the world war that was beginning as Spain's war was ending. Hence, even though he and most Spaniards believed until late 1942 to early 1943 that the Axis would win, Franco only made one significant contribution to the fascist cause. In 1941 he sent the Blue Division, composed largely of former Nationalist soldiers whose personal loyalty to Franco was doubtful, to aid the Germans on the Russian front. For the rest of the war Franco maintained active diplomatic relations with the Allies, and, aided by luck, Spain's peripheral position in Europe, and his own cunning, remained in control of Spain.

Postwar violence—the individual story. The primary reality for the average Spaniard in the period of the writing of *The Family of Pascual Duarte* was to survive the peace. This meant public adherence to the political and religious orthodoxy over which Franco presided and, in the private sphere, the securing of food, clothing, medicine, and shelter for self and family. For those tainted by previous personal or familial activities associated with the left-wing political parties of the Republic and its armed forces, the post-Civil War period was a daily life-and-death struggle. While those who were considered truly serious risks to the Franco regime were jailed or executed (at the rate of 200 per month between March 1939 and January 1940), low-risk dissidents, as well as their families and those of the executed and jailed, were subjected to persecution and ostracism, which lasted into the 1950s. Taken from them were their national identification cards and as a result many individuals lost their legal identity and could have no dealings through the judicial or bureaucratic systems. The confiscation of their passports meant that they could not easily or legally emigrate from Spain either. Finally, professionals had their degrees and/or licenses to practice taken away. The unremitting and very public mistreatment of this sector of the population constantly reminded the citizenry of the costs of resisting the regime. In many cases, those singled out as pariahs survived only through the charity of family members and friends whose loyalty was not questioned and who could function in the reduced economy of the period.

The literary environment. This climate of fear and terror carried over into the literary field. Arbitrary censorship and great concern about reprisals for any written indication of ideology or criticism contrary to the Franco regime were ever present. Hence, when Cela asked the prestigious, 70-year-old novelist Pío Baroja (see **The Quest,** also in *WLAIT 5: Spanish and Portuguese Literatures and their Times*) to write an introduction for the first edition of *The Family of Pascual Duarte*, Baroja refused. Having read the novel in manuscript, he considered it too morally problematic to endorse personally by providing a prologue for it. This refusal was partially vindicated by the publication history of the novel. Even though censors allowed it to be published in December 1942, eleven months later they confiscated the second printing of the novel. In 1946 the censors again allowed the novel to be published in Spain. Nothing in Cela's book had changed, just the delicate, ever-shifting, terror-inspiring equation of what the Franco dictatorship allowed and what it did not. Two statements by Cela add significant nuances to this point. In the framing materials at the beginning of *The Family of Pascual Duarte*, Cela has the transcriber justify the publication of Pascual's memoirs for their negative moral: "Do you see what he does? Well, it's just the opposite of what he should do" (*Family*, p. 4). Eighteen years later, in a prologue for an American school edition of the novel, Cela repeated the negative moral of the story, but play-ing on the word "pedagogical" added that its moral was not "very pedagogical from the perspective of typical pedagogy" (Cela, "Palabras ocasionales," p. x). Here Cela, who had to earn his living in 1960 while still under the watchful eye of Franco's censors, hints that Pascual's violent behavior is more complicated than Franco's Spain of 1942 or 1960 can or wants to contemplate. The fact is that Pascual Duarte's violence is not idiosyncratic. Tremendous violence typified Spain during all of his life and the entire nineteenth century (the 1808-14 War of Independence from the French, three Spanish civil wars between 1835 and 1875, and the Spanish-American and Caribbean wars of independence). That being the case, despite his unexemplary life, one must ask: why should Pascual Duarte and his violence be surprising or be singled out for condemnation? It is clear that the fundamental constants of Spanish national life for this whole period were injustice, violence, and blood. On the eve of his execution, Pascual looked back on his life and said he would have lived differently if he had known earlier what he had come to learn. As World War II raged in Europe and Asia and the threat and exercise of repressive terror kept order at home, Cela offered Pascual Duarte's story as an allegory about violence in Spain and all warring places. In 1942, as well as in 1960, when Cela added his prologue for the American edition, and in the present, the novel's central question is the same—why all the violence? It gives one pause to consider that if Pascual had it all to do over again, he would live his life differently.

Reception. *The Family of Pascual Duarte* is, after *Don Quixote*, the most frequently published Spanish book. From its publication late in December 1942, the novel was received as the rebirth of the literarily serious Spanish novel after three years of war and three more years of repression. When the 1946 Spanish edition was allowed by censors, it was accompanied by the unofficial protection of a prologue by Gregorio Marañon (1887-1960), a politically untouchable world-class Spanish endocrinologist, literary essayist, and eminent public figure. In literary terms Marañon's enthusiastic endorsement of the novel was especially important because of his personal friendships with three generations of Spanish writers represented by Benito Pérez Galdós, Pío Baroja, and Cela.

From a contemporary perspective earlier critical tendencies to categorize *The Family of Pascual Duarte* as a novel of European existentialism and as the prototype of a Spanish literary movement called *tremendismo* (whose thematic emphasis is on brutality, want, and violence) are arguable. Cela has consistently rejected such labels for his fiction. Although he has tended to be evasive in discussing his creations, it is clear that he sees more correspondence between his work and that of Cervantes, the picaresque novel, and Ortega's writing, than with those of existentialists such as Jean-Paul Sartre or Albert Camus, or with any group of Spanish contemporaries with whom he supposedly shared a community of technical and thematic concerns. In any case, *The Family of Pascual Duarte* remains today one of Cela's best and most enduring novels. Comments upon it figure importantly in the citations for both his 1989 Nobel Prize for Literature and his 1996 Cervantes Prize, awarded annually to a prominent author writing in Spanish.

—Stephen Miller

For More Information

Bertrand, Louis, and Charles Petrie. *The History of Spain*. 2d ed. London: Dawsons of Pall Mall, 1969.

Carr, Raymond. *Modern Spain 1875-1980*. Oxford: Clarendon Press, 1980.

Cela, Camilo José. *The Family of Pascual Duarte*. Trans. and intro. Anthony Kerrigan. Boston: Little, Brown, 1964.

———. "Palabras ocasionales," *La familia de Pascual Duarte*. Ed. Harold L. Boudreau and John W. Kronik. Englewood Cliffs, N.J.: Prentice-Hall, 1961.

Charlebois, Lucile C. *Understanding Camilo José Cela*. Columbia: University of South Carolina, 1998.

Kerr, Sarah. "Shock Treatment." *New York Review of Books* 39, no. 16, 8 October 1992, 35-39.

Kirsner, Robert. *The Novels and Travels of Camilo José Cela*. Madrid: Chapel Hill, University of North Carolina Press, 1963.

Miller, Stephen. "The Artistic Experimentation of Camilo José Cela: An Interview of the Writer in Texas on August 16, 1992." *South Central Review* 10, no. 1 (1993): 12-21.

Pérez, Janet. *Camilo José Cela Revisted*. New York: Twayne, 2000.

Spires, Robert. "Systematic Doubt: The Moral Art of La familia de Pascual Duarte." *Hispanic Review* 40 (1972): 283-302.

Tamames, Ramón. *La República. La era de Franco*. Vol. 7 of *Historia de España*. Ed. Miguel Artola. Madrid: Alianza Editorial, 1986.

Thomas, Hugh. *The Spanish Civil War*. New York: Harper Colophon, 1963.

Fields of Castile

by
Antonio Machado

Born in Seville, Spain, on July 26, 1875, Antonio Machado y Ruiz would come to be regarded as one of the finest poets of his generation and one of the most important Spanish writers of the twentieth century. The Machado family moved to Madrid when Antonio was eight, and he later attended the Institución Libre de Enseñanza (Free Institution of Learning) there. Machado married Leonor Izquierdo in 1909. He went on to labor briefly as a translator in Paris, France, and more permanently as a French teacher in various parts of Spain. Written in Soria, Spain, *Campos de Castilla*, his third book of poetry, was published the same year his young wife died of tuberculosis. Shaken by his wife's death, Machado moved to Baeza, where he composed an additional section published in a revised edition of this third book in 1917. Literary critics agree that *Campos de Castilla* represents a transition from the poetic intimacy of Machado's earlier collection, *Soledades* (1903; Solitudes) to the poetry of the objective, external world. Machado would publish a corpus that in its entirety included several collections of poetry and numerous dramas and essays. In his later career, he delved into metaphysical and philosophical poetry and aphorisms in the tradition of Spain's distinguished medieval writer of proverbs, Rabbi Shem Tov, producing works such as *Juan de Mairena: Sentencias, donaires, apuntes y recuerdos de un profesor apócrifo* (1936; Juan de Mairena: Proverbs, Witty Commentaries, Notes, and Memoires of a Counterfeit Professor). Machado participated in the Civil War on the

> ### THE LITERARY WORK
> A collection of poems based upon the poet's reflections on the landscape of Castile, Spain. First published in Spanish (as *Campos de Castilla*) in 1912; revised in 1917; selected poems published in English in 1959.
>
> ### SYNOPSIS
> The poet explores his inner self, the destiny and identity of Spain, and the fundamental question of life as he observes and comments on the landscapes of Castile.

side of the anti-Francoist forces, and after their defeat escaped into exile across the French border. On February 22 he died of pneumonia and other complications, leaving behind poetry that evokes his love for Spain and its traditions as well as the pain and isolation of the human experience.

Events in History at the Time of the Poems

Historical background—Castile. The bulk of Castile sits in the middle of Spain and is predominantly formed by a high mesa of arid, rocky terrain. Today the once-powerful kingdom is separated into two autonomous regions: Castile-León and Castile-La Mancha. The capital of Spain, Madrid, has traditionally been the most

Antonio Machado

kingdoms, especially Portugal, Navarre, and Aragon. The fall of Toledo, a major defeat for the Moors, helped cement Castile as the dominant Christian kingdom of Spain. The Christians put their bitter infighting on hold in 1212, when thousands of soldiers banded together to march against al-Andalus, as the Moorish territory on the peninsula was called. In the battle of Las Navas de Tolosa, the Christians soundly routed the Muslim forces, and Castile claimed the territory as its own. During the thirteenth century, it captured the rest of the Moorish lands on the peninsula except for 1) the kingdom of Granada, which would remain an independent Muslim enclave for more than two centuries; 2) the province of Valencia and the Balearic Islands, which Aragon reconquered; and 3) the southern half of present-day Portugal, which the Portuguese kingdom would regain a few decades later when it expelled the Moors in 1249. For the next two centuries, the political configuration of the peninsula experienced little change.

The catalyst for change came in 1469, in a marriage between two heirs to their respective thrones, Isabel of Castile and Fernando of Aragon. In due course the heirs became the monarchs of their domains. With the quasi-unification of Castile and Aragon by the now king and queen in 1479 (the two kingdoms never merged into one but kept their separate identities), Castile solidified its position as the most important region in the peninsula due to the fact that it was by far the largest geographically and the most populated. In addition, it had a strong army and efficient political leadership under Isabel. Fernando and Isabel waged war on the Moorish kingdom of Granada, which finally fell in 1492 and was absorbed by Castile. At this point, there was no doubt as to Castile's hegemony on the peninsula. The kingdom would soon lead the way in maritime discoveries and conquests in the Americas and in imperial victories in Europe, thereby confirming and augmenting its status. The global prominence would not last, however, and even the hegemony within the peninsula would dwindle somewhat. At the end of 1580, Spain had managed to incorporate Portugal into its fold in a union between the two countries that dissolved in 1668, after decades of Portuguese wars of independence and liberation.

By the late 1600s, Spain, with Castile still its most powerful province, had begun to fade as a global power, and by the eighteenth century it figured as only a second-rate player in European politics. At home the picture looked brighter.

important city in Castile. Other cities of note are Toledo, Segovia, Ciudad Real, Cuenca, Avila, Valladolid, Burgos, León, and Soria. The latter, a central focus of *Fields of Castile*, is located in the northeast of the autonomous region Castile-León.

Castile came into existence as a kingdom in 1035 when Sancho III of Navarre crowned his son Fernando I ruler of the former county of Castile, which had been created in the eighth century as a buffer zone by the Christian kingdom of Asturias to protect itself against the Muslim Moors to the south. Fernando proceeded to defeat the king of León, Vermudo III, in battle in 1037, thereby becoming the monarch of a new and powerful Christian kingdom, Castile-León. He would remain the reigning monarch until his death in 1065 (the realm would eventually absorb other kingdoms and counties and ultimately take the name Castile).

With a fanatical religious fervor, a growing economic base from which to draw, and the largest population of any Christian kingdom on the Iberian peninsula, Castile succeeded in pushing south over the next four and a half centuries, gaining victory after victory over the Muslims during the Reconquest. Meanwhile, Castile engaged in constant warfare with other Christian

With the reign of Felipe V from 1700-46, Castile at last consolidated its power in Spain and forced Aragon and Valencia to give up their quasi-independent status and use its language and laws in official matters; thus, the regions of Spain were united in an uneasy arrangement. By the nineteenth century, Castile was one of several provinces in the nation, but it retained its position of superiority because of its history and because its largest city, Madrid, was also Spain's capital. The ensuing century witnessed political chaos and economic stagnation. Nineteenth-century politics tore at the nation, dividing it into "two Spains," one half liberal and the other half conservative. In the twentieth century, through the times in which Machado's poems were composed and translated, Madrid, along with peripheral regions of Spain, would play a dynamic role in the nation's modernization. Along with the rest of Spain, Castile would endure two separate periods of dictatorship before the nation finally adopted a democratic form of government after the fascist dictator Francisco Franco died in 1975.

The Spanish-American War. In 1912, when *Campos de Castilla* was first published, Castile was the most powerful of the Spanish provinces. Its geographic extension, however, had shrunk greatly since it was a kingdom composed of the areas now known as the autonomous regions of Castile-León, Castile-La Mancha, Andalusia, Murcia, La Rioja, the Basque Nation, Asturias, Cantabria, Extremadura, and Galicia. By 1912 the province consisted only of Old Castile and New Castile, composed of Castile-León and Castile-La Mancha, respectively.

Spain in 1912 was a country in crisis. It had just lost the rest of its overseas colonies (Cuba, Puerto Rico, the Philippines, and Guam) to the Americans in the Spanish-American War. The war sprang from the United States' concerns over the presence of Spanish troops in Cuba following a year-long revolt by Cubans, who wanted complete independence. In the eyes of U.S. politicians, Spain's domination of Cuba constituted a threat to the possibility of U.S. expansion in Latin America. The American government sent the battleship *Maine* to Cuba allegedly to protect American interests on the island. On February 15, 1898, the ship blew up, and Spain was immediately blamed for the incident (although later investigation identified the true cause as spontaneous combustion of fuel). Spain was not ready for war. The country had an ill-equipped navy, including few seaworthy battleships, and its finances were poorly managed. The war erupted

in May 1898 in the Philippines when American naval forces sank several Spanish ships in Manila Bay. Then, in one of the worst military defeats in modern history, Americans destroyed the Spanish navy at Santiago de Cuba, after which Teddy Roosevelt and his men rushed up San Juan Hill to declare victory. After three months of fighting, Spain surrendered. At the end of the year, the Treaty of Paris was signed, stripping Spain of the rest of her colonies and reducing it to a third-rate power. The decadence that had characterized Spain for two centuries reached its lowest point in 1898. Spaniards immediately began to agonize over what caused a nation that 300 years earlier had been the most powerful in the world to plummet to such a low depth.

Generation of 1898. The agony of Spain's defeat in the Spanish-American War echoed in the field of arts and letters under the tutelage of the *Generación del 98* (Generation of 1898), a group of young Spanish writers and intellectuals who expounded on the identity and destiny of Spain. Their key message was that Spain was a country in crisis: where had Spain gone wrong? How could the nation's problems be resolved? The Generation of 1898 mused about the humiliating military defeat at the hands of the Americans and reacted against the political incompetence and corruption that were undermining Spain's progress. They criticized as well the social and cultural norms of the nation, especially those of the dominant class.

Antonio Machado was a central figure in this artistic group. Along with the other members of the Generation of '98, Machado fought against the conservative faction in Spain and adopted a liberal ideological position similar to that of other contemporary European writers. He, like the others, believed passionately that Spain needed to be liberalized and modernized to align it with other European countries. The focus on bourgeois life, so common in realism, was abandoned by these writers, replaced by an obsessive preoccupation with the Spanish spirit and identity. The Generation of '98 adopted a more innocent idealism that recalled Romanticism. However, mixed with this idealism was anxiety and doubt over religious, moral, and patriarchal values.

The first fundamental worry the intellectuals of '98 all had in common concerned the identity of Spain in the modern world. Again they asked themselves, what had happened to the nation and where was it heading? What was it about Spain that had once made it so powerful and prosperous? How could that be recaptured? The second worry had to do with the very nature of life itself. The Generation of '98 pondered the question of existence, faith, and time. In their philosophical approach to these issues, they exhibited a tremendous curiosity about the metaphysical aspect of the human experience.

In attempting to tackle the identity question, the Generation of 1898 utilized words to create vivid images of native landscapes, which they felt contained the spirit of the nation and its people.

BARREN LAND, BARREN GOVERNMENT— THE REIGN OF ALFONSO XIII

Crowned king of Spain in 1902, Alfonso XIII inherited a very messy social and political reality. During his reign, which lasted through the writings of *Fields of Castile* until 1931, there were a total of 33 different parliamentary governments. Both parliament and the constitution limited Alfonso's powers. Still, anarchism and socialism were on the rise, and the two movements put increasing pressure on Alfonso XIII to step down. After another humiliating defeat of the Spanish military, this time by Berber forces in Morocco in 1921, the parliament investigated how the king could have permitted such a calamity to take place. The investigation was a disgrace to the king and, more importantly, it undermined his powers as a monarch. In 1923 General Primo de Rivera led a successful uprising in favor of the king. For all intents and purposes, the general proceeded to run the government dictatorially, eliminating the parliament. When Spaniards voted overwhelmingly for a republican form of government in April 1931, Alfonso XIII abdicated and went into exile. He would never rule Spain again.

The majority of these thinkers expressed an emotional connection to the Castilian countryside, which they found to be somber and austere. They did not, however, perceive this landscape in an objective manner, but rather in a subjective and idealistic way. The writers, including Machado, attempted to capture and reflect the reality of the dry topography and, through it, the soul of Castile and its people. Machado's writing describes the relationship between the barren Castilian land and the past and present of Spain: "The [river] Duero crosses the oaken heart / of Iberia and Castile. / Miserable Castile, triumphant yesterday, clad in its rags, disdaining the unknown way" (Machado, "The Banks of the

Duero," (*Fields of Castile* in *Dream Below the Sun*, p. 49). The desolate countryside that the poet witnesses is matched by the decadence of Spanish life, as opposed to Castile's successful history. Tradition, landscape, time, and identity are all constant themes throughout his poetry.

The Poems in Focus

Content summary. In the fundamental 1912 edition Machado observes the land and its people, especially in and around Soria, and from that springs poetry preoccupied with the destiny of Spain, the character of Spaniards, and the problematic experience of human existence. In 1917 Machado released a complete collection of poetry, *Poesías completas*, which included an updated version of *Fields of Castile*. The 1917 edition contained about 60 new poems, most of which he wrote after his wife died when he resided in Baeza (in Andalusia).

"A orillas del Duero" ("The Banks of the Duero"). In this poem, the poet describes a somber and harsh Castilian landscape as he walks along the banks of the River Duero on a sunny, hot July afternoon. He presents realistic, factual information about the land that he surveys: "I discerned a sharp peak beyond far fields, / and a round hill like an embroidered shield, / and scarlet slopes over the grayish soil. . ." ("Banks," *Fields of Castile*, p. 47). Next to the dry and rocky terrain, the river Duero snakes its way around the town of Soria. Machado emphasizes the Duero in his description of the landscape because to him it symbolizes the fluidity of life as it constantly moves across the land, forever pushing its way out to the ocean. The ocean, to Machado, is a metaphor for death because it is the final destination of rivers (life) and because it represents a seemingly infinite, dark, lonely void. (Machado borrowed the river and ocean symbols from Jorge Manrique [1440?-79], the most renowned medieval Spanish poet of the late fifteenth century and one of Machado's favorites.)

Around the beginning of the third stanza, Machado shifts his attention away from merely describing the landscape to tying it to the past and present of the Spanish nation. We begin to understand that the panorama that he views interests him primarily for the people who live in it and are shaped by it. He compares the decadence and bleak landscape of today with the glorious past of Spain: "The mother formerly a source of captains / is now a stepmother of lowly urchins. / Castile no longer is that generous state

The River Duero and surrounding lands of Soria.

/ of Myo Cid who rode with haughty gait"
("Banks," *Fields of Castile*, p. 49). Emotion and
subjectivity creep into the poem in these descriptions, and from them we can sense the deep
passion that Machado had for his homeland.

He finishes the poem by turning the reader's
attention back to what he observes and hears as
he walks along: the setting of the sun, church
bells ringing, and an inn standing alone on the
road amidst the fields. Machado seems to indicate that, even in this austere natural environment, there is a sort of beauty that warms the
soul of the observer and reminds him of the
greatness that has come from the land, a greatness perhaps to be repeated again soon.

"Campos de Soria" ("Fields of Soria").
Machado again discusses the decadence of Spain

in this poem as he attempts to objectify the reality that he experiences. The work consists of
nine sections. The first part describes the cold
and arid land of Soria. We witness what the observer does as if we were looking through a camera. Soria is experiencing its first signs of spring,
and the daisies stand out against the ash-colored
hills. In the second stanza, the poetic voice offers the first hint of subjectivity in the verse "The
land lies unrevived, the fields dream" ("Fields of
Soria," *Fields of Castile,* p. 57). The Sorian fields
are personified: like humans, they dream, perhaps about the impending sunny days when they
will be covered by a blanket of vegetation.

In the second section, it is the observer who
dreams: the landscape that he describes—a small
orchard, arable land, rocky slopes—are the stuff

of a child's imagination. In other words, the images that he sees are being recreated in his mind as an "innocent vision of Arcadia" (Terry, p. 34).

The third part of the poem encompasses the whole of the landscape. It is summer and one can see sunflowers dancing on the rolling fields, which are crossed by roads that hide travelers riding on brown donkeys. These people are "little figures" in the distance which "stain the gold linen of the sunset" ("Fields of Soria," *Fields of Castile,* p. 59). Although humans are clearly an essential part of the landscape, they are dwarfed and made to seem insignificant by the limitlessness and beauty of the earth.

Section four returns to the country inhabitants who cut a silhouette against the Sorian sky. It is autumn now, and two oxen plow a knoll as a man plods behind them and a woman plants seeds in the furrows. A baby's basket hangs from the yoke. Machado emphasizes the parallel between humans and nature: there is a close connection between them concerning new life. One form of life depends on the other for its very existence. The recurring chore of plowing and planting crops underscores the idea of repetition and monotony in human life.

The next part ushers in winter by describing a snowy scene. The tone is desolate and sad, describing a solitary scene in which a family sits around a fire and stares out the windows at the snow. It impedes them from being with others and reminds them of a lost family member who was trapped in a snowstorm and buried in the sierra. A little girl dreams of the spring days when she can frolic with her friends in the green fields below azure skies. The highway nearby and the surrounding countryside are deserted.

The sixth part of the poem describes Soria as "cold," "pure," and "dead" ("Fields of Soria," *Fields of Castile,* pp. 58-60). Machado characterizes the city this way in terms of the season, but also in relation to its present decadence vis-à-vis its colorful past. It is a ghost of a city now, standing to remind us of its triumphant history. The poet captures the moment of observation in the verses "Cold Soria! The courthouse bell strikes one" ("Fields of Soria," *Fields of Castile,* p. 61). The telling of time crystallizes the picture for the reader. The observer is a solitary figure looking upon the city in the dead of night and seeing it by moonlight. We feel a certain sense of melancholy both about the city and the observer, for both seem isolated in space and time.

The feeling of melancholy that the sixth part's words evoke resonates in the seventh section as well. Machado opens it by listing off what he sees: silver hills, white roads, poplars by the river, and bald peaks. However, halfway through this part, there is a sudden subjective commentary: "Sorian afternoons, mystical and warlike, / today I feel a sadness for you, deep / in the heart, a sadness / that is love" ("Fields of Soria," *Fields of Castile,* p. 61). Although the observer experiences sadness about Soria, it is not a negative emotion. On the contrary, he equates it with love. In other words, he has come to accept Soria for what it is: although desolate, decadent, and isolated, he loves it nonetheless and sees a deep beauty in it.

The poetic voice focuses on the poplar trees he sees on the river's banks in part eight. The rustling sound of their dry leaves adds to the sounds of the river. On their trunks, lovers have scratched their names and the dates when they were there. The speaker then refers to the trees as poplars of love. He witnesses and narrates what he sees in the present, but he also talks of the nightingales that yesterday filled the trees' branches and of the wind's lyres that the trees will be tomorrow. He captures the past, present, and future by utilizing the flow of the river and the presence of the poplars as symbols of continuity. Finally, he speaks directly to the poplars, telling them that he captures them in his heart as he goes along his journey. In essence, he has internalized the landscape that he is witnessing. Even though he may leave the banks of the Duero, he will always carry the spirit and emotion of what he has seen inside him.

In the final part, from the poplar trees, the speaker expands the view to the fields of Soria, saying that he will carry them in his heart as well. He asks if the country and town scenes that he has witnessed have reached his soul or if they were there all along. By saying this, the speaker seems to imply that what he witnesses is already a part of himself, and in a dreamlike state he is only retelling what he already knows. He concludes the poem by wishing that Spain's sun fill the hearty people of Soria with happiness, light, and wealth.

"A un olmo seco" ("To a Dry Elm"). In this poem, Machado reflects on the passage of time and the idea of hope in spring's eternal rebirth. The speaker describes an old, dry elm that has been split in two by lightning but which, after the rains of April and the sun of May, continues to sprout green leaves. The speaker directs his words at the elm, saying that before the tree is cut down or falls over and is washed to sea, he wants "to note / the grace of your greening leaf" ("To a Dry Elm," *Fields of Castile*, p. 63). The poem, however, is not simply about the fact that the elm is old and decaying. Rather, the elm is seen clearly in relation to past, present, and future. The opening lines demonstrate the elm's past: "The elm. One hundred years on the hill / lapped by the Duero!" ("Dry Elm," *Fields of Castile*, p. 63). We have an idea of its longevity from these words, which emphasize a past but also a present existence. The present is the moment at which the speaker observes and describes the elm. It is a very transient moment marked by surprise and sadness at seeing the elm in its present condition. The future is captured by what the speaker doesn't want to happen to the tree: being cut down or swept away by the river. The old elm is seen by the poet as a dynamic entity changing with time and the elements. Machado concludes the poem on a sentimental note: "My heart also waits hoping / —toward the light and toward life— / for another miracle of spring" ("Dry Elm," *Fields of Castile*, p. 63). These last lines make us question what the whole poem is about. The subject is not so much the dying tree as the hopes and sadness that the tree brings out in the observer. Machado wrote the poem when his wife Leonor was very ill, and the sadness and hope he felt about the situation permeates his message. By expressing his desire to see the elm bloom the next spring, Machado intimates that he hopes to enjoy another spring with Leonor, although he knows sooner or later she will die.

Searching for Spain's identity in Castilian landscapes. The Spanish landscapes and nature that Machado observed over the course of a lifetime inspired him to write some of the finest poetry ever created in the Spanish language. They also inspired him to express his profound admiration and love for Spain. However, they reminded him as well of the decadence and problems that existed in the country at the time. Although a native of Andalusia, Machado wrote most of his poems in this collection about Castile because, like for many other Generation of 1898 writers, it epitomized the rich language, tradition, history, and power of Spain: in short, Castile was the center of the nation in that it had forged Spain and had given it its most lasting significance. In the Castilian people and landscape, Machado saw Spain at its most authentic and representative. By observing nature within the Castilian context, Machado strove to better understand those who populated the land. In al-

most all of his poems, Machado includes the inhabitants of the Castilian countryside in his observations of the landscape. In studying both of these, the poet attempted to come to grips with Spanish identity: what Spain was, why it existed, and who its inhabitants were. The land and the nature therein that he observes are symbolic in his poetry of the people who inhabit it and of life in general: in his poetry, the ocean represents death; the river is symbolic of life; trees stand for

---

MACHADO'S CONNECTION TO EUROPEAN AND LATIN AMERICAN WRITERS

In 1899 Machado made his first trip to Paris to work alongside his brother as translator for the publishing house Garnier. In 1902 Machado found himself in Paris again, this time to work as an official at the Guatemalan consulate. It is during this second stay that Machado met the already famous modernist writer Rubén Darío. His next visit occurred in 1911, when he won a scholarship to study French language and literature at the Collège de France. His residencies in France's capital city—and one of the world's cultural capitals—allowed him to meet writers of great stature and to keep abreast of literary styles and trends. In essence, Machado took back to Spain a deeper understanding of what was occurring in the European and Latin American Modernist movement, and he reflected that influence in his own poetic works by, among other things, creating musical verse and colorful imagery. He would afterward take advantage of his French language skills, honed during his stays in Paris, to develop a career as instructor of French at various institutes in Spain. Although Machado admired France, he wanted Spain to take its own lead in the development of ideas and cultural products. To generate such authenticity, he wrote about his own nation and people, giving the ideas he learned in Paris a uniquely Spanish twist.

---

continuity, life, and rebirth; routine farmers' chores underscore the monotony of life; the seasons signal birth and infancy (spring) to youth (summer) to middle age (autumn) to old age and death (winter). When Machado observes nature, he records a complex cyclical relationship between humanity and earth, time and space, spirit and material. Although humanity and nature are governed by universal laws of entropy, the poet nonetheless offers hope of a bright tomorrow and of a new Spain. He seems to say that what he observes is not as external as it at first appears: the landscape of Spain is as internal to Spaniards as their very thoughts and dreams. Perhaps what Spaniards see in their landscape is what has already been created in their collective imagination.

Machado's preoccupation with Spain and its character and destiny is mirrored in the other writers of the Generation of '98. At the turn of the twentieth century, they experienced and wrote about a Spain that was entering into a new realm of existence, one for which it was not altogether prepared. The moment of patriotic crisis that these writers expressed was shared by most Spaniards. Spain entered its post-colonial phase with a new identity that it found hard to accept: as a small, weak European country being eclipsed by stronger countries around the world. What Machado and the other members of the Generation of 1898 learned, however, is that the beauty in one's nation, in nature, in oneself, and in life in general is what one chooses to see. Machado found beauty and strength in the barren and dry landscapes of Castile because he accepted nature for what it was, and he found resilient and hopeful inhabitants who looked forward to rising with the sun the next day.

Sources and literary context. One of Machado's earliest influences was Francisco Giner de los Ríos, his teacher at The Institution of Free Learning and a friend of his father's. One idea that Machado took away from his studies at the institute and one that he employed throughout his poetry was that humans must learn to appreciate nature and work to establish a peaceful coexistence with it instead of trying to destroy it. In its depiction of the Spanish countryside, *Fields of Castile* effects an ingenious interplay between reality and meditation. Machado succeeds in freezing time and space to capture a nostalgic vision of a simpler, if more solitary, Spain that allows for this interplay. There is a balance between what Machado observes in the external world and the metaphors he creates from those details for the speaker's emotions. Delving further into the individual, his poetry assumes that human identity cannot be separated from dream and memory, an idea representative of Machado's work. In sum, the poet portrays the Castilian landscapes he so carefully records as mirrors onto his soul and conscience: what he observes is not so important for its own sake as for what it reveals about himself, man in general, and the human experience. Another early influence was that of Henri Bergson, a French philosopher and professor under whom Machado studied at the Collège de France in Paris. Bergson's ideology argued that humans can use their intuition to obtain true knowledge once they liberate themselves from the constraints of traditional conceptions of time and space. We see this ideology resonating throughout *Fields of Castile*. One of his central concerns is the fleeting passage of time and the representation by poetry of the fluid aspect of experience: the future turning quickly into the present and the present sliding into the past. In addition, Machado constantly reminds us of the specific space in which he finds himself in his poetry by minutely detailing his surroundings and bringing our attention to the objects or people he observes.

The modernist writers of the era, especially Spaniards, influenced *Fields of Castile* to some degree, although by the time he wrote this work Machado was moving away from modernism. His brother Manuel, an accomplished writer himself; Azorín, who influenced Machado with his book *Castilla*; Juan Ramón Jiménez, considered one of the fathers of Spanish modernism; Miguel de Unamuno, for whom Machado wrote one of his "Elogios" ("Praises"); and the Nicaraguan Rubén Darío, the foremost modernist writer of the Spanish tongue, helped shape Machado's ideas and style.

The death of his wife Leonor moved Machado to write several poems, most of which he included in the revised edition of 1917. These were known as the Baeza poems because of his residency in this small Andalusian town after Leonor died. Some of these are very personal in nature and recall his earlier works *Solitudes* and *Solitudes, Galleries, and Other Poems.*

The language of *Fields of Castile* has been described as austere, in keeping with the Castile environment. It also has been described as concise, colorful, and mellifluous. Often it reflects Machado's thoughts and emotions, revealing the poet's solitary and contemplative nature. The poems' style is popular, with an emphasis on assonant rhyme and a preponderance of natural metaphors to conjure up substantive issues of human experience. Verbs and adverbs tend to dominate the verses in *Fields of Castile*, lending them a dynamic quality that, combined with the melancholic tone of most of the poems, stamps Machado's indelible mark upon it.

Reviews. *Fields of Castile* was a popular and critical success when first published in 1912, enough so for Machado to release the updated version in 1917. The poet's overall artistic achievement is evidenced by the fact that just a decade after the publication of the 1917 version, Machado was voted in as a member of the Real Academia Española (Royal Spanish Academy). He was heralded as a Republican patriot by liberal intellectuals. Machado's prestige reached its apex in the late 1940s and 1950s when the Generation of 1936, representing a younger group of Spanish poets, paid homage to him in an issue of the literary review *Cuadernos Hispanoamericanos* (Hispanoamerican Notes) published in Madrid in 1949. Outside Spain, exiled Spanish poets who fled the fascist Franco regime paid homage to him as well. Gabriel Pradal-Rodríguez wrote an important study of Machado's life and work as part of an homage to Machado in an issue of the New York literary journal *Revista Hispánica Moderna* (Modern Hispanic Review) in 1949. The subsequent generation of Spanish poets, coming of age in the 1950s, regarded Machado as their primary poetic inspiration, and his impact proved enduring thereafter. Today he is celebrated as one of the greatest Spanish poets of all time both inside and outside of Spain.

—Mehl Penrose

For More Information

Albornoz, Aurora de. *Poesías de guerra de Antonio Machado*. San Juan: Ediciones Asomante, 1961.

Cano, José Luis. *Antonio Machado. Su vida, su obra*. Madrid: Ministerio de Educación y Ciencia, 1976.

Cernuda, Luis. *Estudios sobre poesía española contemporánea*. Madrid: Guadarrama, 1972.

Glendinning, Nigel. "The Philosophy of Henri Bergson in the Poetry of Antonio Machado." *Revue de Littérature Comparée* (*Review of Comparative Literature*) 36 (1962): 50-70.

Grant, Helen. "Antonio Machado and *La tierra de Alvargonzález*." *Atlante* 2 (1954): 139-58.

Machado, Antonio. *Antonio Machado. Selected Poems*. Trans. Alan Trueblood. Cambridge, Mass.: Harvard University Press, 1982.

———. *Antonio Machado. Solitudes, Galleries and other poems*. Trans. Richard L. Predmore. Durham, N.C.: Duke University, 1987.

———. *Campos de Castilla*. Trans. Arthur Terry. London: Grant and Cutler/Tamesis, 1973.

———. *Castilian Ilexes. Versions from Antonio Machado, 1875-1939*. Trans. C.H. Tomlinson and H. Gifford. London: Oxford University Press, 1963.

———. *Fields of Castile*. In *The Dream Below the Sun: Selected Poems of Antonio Machado*. Trans. Willis Barnstone. Trumansburg, N.Y.: The Crossing Press, 1981.

Young, H.T. *The Victorious Expression. A Study of Four Contemporary Spanish Poets*. Madison: The University of Wisconsin Press, 1964.

Fortunata and Jacinta: Two Stories of Married Women

by

Benito Pérez Galdós

Born in Las Palmas on Grand Canary Island, Benito Pérez Galdós (1843-1920) left his home in 1862 to study law in Madrid. Once there, he abandoned the university in short order, preferring instead to study Spain's people and national life in its capital city and becoming active in the daily and periodical press. In this environment, Galdós experienced firsthand the increasingly authoritarian government of the Bourbon Queen Isabella II (1830-1904), including the closure of a newspaper for which he worked as a reporter. The action of *Fortunata and Jacinta* recreates the Madrid of Galdos's early years there as student and then writer. It coincides also with the revolutionary period that culminated in the queen's expulsion from Spain in 1868, and records the failure to consolidate a post-Bourbon government in Spain, the growing anarchy of this era, and the 1875 Restoration of the throne to the exiled Isabella's son, Alfonso XII. Also, the fickle protagonist Juanito Santa Cruz vacillates between dalliance and domesticity in a way that mirrors Spain's vacillation between revolutionary experiments and a return to monarchical legitimacy.

Events in History at the Time the Novel Takes Place

The fight for democracy in nineteenth-century Spain. Following the failure of the last Habsburg king of Spain to produce an heir, Spain's monarchy was entrusted to the Bourbon family in 1700. After the turn of the following century, the weak

> ## THE LITERARY WORK
>
> A novel set in Madrid from 1865 to 1876; published in Spanish (as *Fortunata y Jacinta. Dos Historias de Casadas*) in 1886-87; in English in 1973 and 1986.
>
> ## SYNOPSIS
>
> Both the lower-class Fortunata and the middle-class Jacinta are unhappily married and in love with Jacinta's husband, the idle, rich Juanito Santa Cruz. On her deathbed, having come to identify with Jacinta during their five-year rivalry, Fortunata entrusts her and Juanito's newborn to the childless Jacinta.

king Charles IV abdicated the throne in favor of his son Ferdinand VII, who, however, was forced to remain in France under the custody of Napoleon from 1808 until 1814. These six years saw the Spanish War of Independence from France imitated in the New World by the early years of the Spanish American fight for independence from Spain. On the Iberian Peninsula, the leaderless populace, sometimes aided by the regular military—in Bailén, Zaragoza, and Gerona, for example—waged a guerrilla war against the French best known today through Francisco José de Goya's 85 etchings *Disasters of War* and his paintings *The Battle of May 2, 1808* and *The Execution of the Rebels on May 3, 1808*. Of key importance during this period was the

Benito Pérez Galdós, self-portrait c. 1892.

formulation of the 1812 Constitution of Cadiz, the first document of modern Spanish democracy. The constitution proposed a one-house legislature, giving lawmaking power to it and only a suspensive veto to the crown, thereby transferring authority from the monarch to the people. Though the constitution never would become a legal governing document, it did serve as an ideological rallying point around which Spanish liberals resisted Ferdinand VII's absolutism following his return to Spain and until his death in 1833.

Between 1834 and 1876 there were three civil conflicts known in Spain as the Carlist Wars. They pitted the constitutionalists, who supported the succession of Ferdinand's infant daughter, Isabella, against the increasingly minority absolutists, who wanted Ferdinand's brother, Charles, and his descendants to occupy the throne as Charles (Carlos) V, VI, and VII. *Fortunata and Jacinta* occurs between April 1865 and April 1876, a period that coincides with the one leading up to and including the last Carlist War (1872-76). The first page of the novel places its male protagonist, the then-student Juanito Santa Cruz, at the April 10, 1865, beating and imprisonment of perhaps 200 demonstrators and the killing of as many as 30 more by the mounted troops of Prime Minister General Ramón María Narváez's government. This action, known as the Massacre of the Eve of Saint Daniel, signals his-

torically the beginning of the revolutionary process that led to the September 1868 expulsion of Queen Isabella II from Spain. The fateful protest—organized by Galdós's Canary Island friend Luis Fernández Benítez de Lugo, Marqués de la Florida—had received government authorization. But on the actual day of the demonstration, the numbers of university students, laborers, and other protesters caused the nervous, repressive government to cancel its authorization at the last moment and then to attack those who rallied. At issue was a series of government dismissals from university posts. Victims of these dismissals were professors who had either criticized Isabella's public actions or supported the right to criticize them, perhaps most notably Professor Emilio Castelar, one of four presidents of the First Republic (1873-74).

Other important events of this period include the June 1866 uprisings of the artillery sergeants of Saint Gil barracks in Madrid, the most visible aspect of a failed attempt at armed revolution against the queen and her government by dissident military officers under Generals Francisco Serrano and Juan Prim. There was a public execution of the captured artillery sergeants in July, after which key opposition groups, united in their democratic ideals, met in Ostend, Belgium. The groups declared their purposes: dethrone Isabella II; create universal male suffrage; and elect a constituent assembly to decide between monarchical or republican government in Spain.

When General Narváez died in late April 1868, Isabella lost her last military strongman. By the summer of 1868 her general capriciousness and scandalous conduct had helped undermine her former popular appeal, fanning the flames of opposition to her government's undemocratic policies. Liberal generals exiled in France and the Canary Islands returned to Spain at summer's end to stage what became the September Revolution of 1868. The great military victory of the revolution, whose combined casualty count was more than 1,800 dead and wounded, occurred September 28-29, 1868, at the Battle of Alcolea in southern Spain. Confirmation of the victory came in early October with the unopposed entrances into Madrid of Serrano's army from the south and of Prim's army from Valencia and Barcelona.

The time between the September Revolution and the Restoration of the Bourbons on January 9, 1875, called the Liberal Sexenary by Spanish historians, may be divided into three periods. Between October 1868 and December 1870 the liberal Constitution of 1869 was drafted to include the vote for all males 25 and older; freedom of religion, instruction, the press, and of association; and the advisability of a constitutional monarchy. This last item led to the parliamentary election of Amadeus, son of Victor Emmanuel II of Italy, as king of Spain. But the December 1870 assassination of Prim, this king's principal and strongest supporter, crippled the monarchy at its inception. The second period, the brief two years of Amadeus's reign, amounted to an unending series of internal and colonial problems. These included

- The beginning of the third Carlist war in northern Spain
- The continuation of the first Cuban war of independence
- The organization and first radicalization of agricultural and industrial workers in eastern and southern Spain
- A very serious attempted assassination of Amadeus
- Armed insurrections in northwestern and southern Spain for these regions to obtain legal political autonomy from Madrid

When Amadeus realized that the national problems represented by these events were truly beyond his ability to resolve, he abdicated (February 11, 1873). The third period of the Sexenary saw the founding of the First Republic in Spain, the first attempt to govern Spain with no monarchical component. But this new form of government, in a country lacking practical democratic experience and questioning the legitimacy of its government's authority, augmented the problems faced by Amadeus. Within two years Emilio Castelar, the fourth and last president of the republic, operated more as a dictator than as the president elected by the representative parliament. Hence there was no real opposition to the coup d'etat of January 3, 1874, led by General Manuel Pavía y Lacy.

Following the year-long regency of General Francisco Serrano y Domínguez, the Bourbon monarchy was restored to Spain in the person of Isabella's son Alfonso XII. He returned to Spain on January 9, 1875, and in June of 1876 a new Constitution was drafted. It represented a compromise between the two principal governing forces in Spain until the Spanish-American War of 1898 created a new crisis in national life. During the compromise, the conservative Cánovas de Castillo and the liberal Sagasta alternated with each other as prime minister, allowing for the observance of the forms of representative constitutional monarchy. From the vantage point of the conflict-weary forces, the alternating system had two vital components. It assured civilian control over governmental affairs in the wake of too-frequent military interventions into national life from the 1830s until the present. Secondly it oversaw an equitable distribution of economic and political spoils for the oligarchy—a mix of the traditional landed aristocracy and the new self-made, monied aristocracy—regardless of which party ran the government. The political factions renewed support for this strategy after Alfonso XII died (November 25, 1885), when they faced, given the posthumous birth of the infant who would become Alfonso XIII, the prospect of a long regency by the king's Austrian widow, María Cristina of Habsburg.

Class formation and structure. Although the political, demographic, and economic effects of the Industrial Revolution took longer to appear and were less far reaching in Spain than in England, Germany, France, and other European countries, all post-Ferdinand VII governments tried to make Spain more like their progressive neighbors. Most significant in this effort was the continuation and augmentation, especially after Ferdinand VII's death, of the disentailment of great landholdings, begun timidly in 1769 under Ferdinand's grandfather, the enlightened despot Charles III. While the lands of religious orders were especially targeted, leading to dissolution for many and to the adherence of the clergy and country people to the Carlist cause, by the last third of the nineteenth century, most of the entailed religious and governmental, including royal, holdings had been nationalized and sold at auction. By taking lands from so-called "dead hands" and trying to place them in those of the active, profit-oriented middle and upper classes, liberal governments hoped to achieve two aims: create generally increasing economic activity and, through infusions of full-price cash and mortgage payments for the auctioned lands, establish a more solvent basis for the national treasury. While this attempt proved successful in a macro sense, increasing food production for a population that soared from 12.3 million at Ferdinand's death to 16.6 million by the end of the Third Carlist War, the rural lower classes continued to be landless. At the same time Madrid, Spain's largest city with a population that approached 400,000, was benefitting from the disentailment-inspired demolition or remodeling of church properties both within the urban center and just outside the former walls of the city. With the growth of Madrid as the governmental and administrative center of Spain, an increasing number of bureaucrats and professionals created larger middle classes. From their ranks emerged the individuals who became large urban property owners, speculators in government securities, and players in the stock market. Galdós's study in *Fortunata and Jacinta* of the Santa Cruz family, as well as of families related to them by blood, marriage, and friendship, provides multiple case histories of this process of class formation. In the three generations of the Santa Cruz family upon which Galdós concentrates, the progression from middle class to high bourgeoisie to new monied aristocracy is clear. By the time he was writing *Fortunata and Jacinta*, the most successful historical equivalents of his fictionalized families were becoming commercial, financial, and industrial dynasties. As happened elsewhere in Europe, the new monied aristocracy became heedless of the lower and middle classes. Through business, political, and marital alliances it either supplanted fallen members of the old aristocracy, ruined by high city living and mismanagement of their rural estates, or shared wealth and influence with nobles who retained their old positions.

Together the old and new aristocracies formed less than 2 percent of the Spanish population while the middle classes consisted of less than 20 percent so that the lower classes formed the vast majority. Centered in Madrid, Barcelona, Valencia, and Seville, the middle classes consisted of professionals, bureaucrats, military officers, secular priests, and small businessmen and property holders. Their earliest leaders were born two generations before Galdós and received their practical democratic education in periods of political exile during the worst times of Ferdinand VII. They observed firsthand the highly unfavorable contrast between backward Spain and the advanced political and economic progress of England and France. This led them to advocate Spanish modernization through constitutional government and better, higher-level education for ever larger contingents of society. Despite this laudable goal, roughly four of five Spaniards were either wage-earners and their families or members of the lower classes for whom each day was a struggle for subsistence. In the mid-to-late 1800s less than 5 percent of the lower classes could read and write, so prospects for a better life for those people were remote. For his part, the middle-class Galdós became in his day perhaps the most forceful apologist for a democratic Spain based on talent, education, and work.

The status of women. In the mid-to-late 1800s the dependent situation of women was especially conspicuous in the growing middle-class sector of urban society. Educated to be wives and mothers, the overwhelming majority of Spanish women who lived in urban communities lacked the skills needed to earn their own living. As in the early-nineteenth-century Spain of Goya and Fernández de Moratín and the England of Jane Austen, survival for most women of all social classes meant marriage to an economically well-situated male (see Moratín's **Maiden's Consent,** also in WLAIT 5: *Spanish and Portuguese Literatures and Their Times*). This often meant marriage to an older man selected by the woman's parents or guardians. The woman's lot demanded subordination to her husband and father, and involved, if she was fertile, numerous pregnancies. Other defining characteristics of nineteenth-century women were low literacy rates and no direct political or economic power. According to Spain's 1860 census, which recorded a population of 15.6 million, women made a paltry showing in the urban work force and had to settle for farmhand status in the countryside, where millions of females worked the soil side-by-side with their fathers, brothers, husbands, and children. Of the approximately 648,000 women employed for wages, two-thirds served as domestics, 7,800 taught at the primary level, and the rest labored in light industries dedicated to the production of such items as textiles, cigars, and confectionaries. Yet virtually no woman so employed could support herself. Whether as a domestic servant, a nun in a convent (there were about 19,000 Spanish nuns in 1860), or a daughter or wife in her parents' or husband's home, women depended on someone else to provide their shelter. When all else failed, younger women, such as the novel's Fortunata, prostituted themselves as kept women or streetwalkers or in bordellos, while older women begged in the streets. Many of these unfortunate women originally served as domestics, but after being discovered as the sexual object of one or more of the family's males and being blackballed by the dominant females, the former servants resorted to prostitution, seeing it as their only economic alternative. The 1860 Spanish census contains a category *pobres de solemnidad* ("the solemnly poor"). People in this group were able-bodied but without jobs or resources. The breakdown by gender of its membership makes the starkness of the female

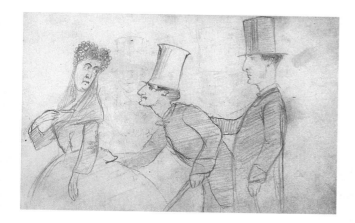

In sketchbooks such as his 1867 *Atlas zoológico,* Galdós drew well-known historical persons, places, and events, as well as portraits and action pictures. Some of the drawings in the *Atlas* would later have textual significance in *Fortunata and Jacinta* and other Galdosian novels set in 1860-70s Madrid. **Top Left:** The womanizing Juanito Santa Cruz— Fortunata's love/Jacinta's husband—and his friend Villalonga. **Middle Left:** Galdós portrays his friend the young Marqués de la Florida rousing anti-government sentiment before the massacre of the Eve of Saint Daniel on April 10, 1865. **Bottom Left:** Many scenes of *Fortunata and Jacinta* occur in cafés, such as the Café Universal, rendered here with its owner and a waiter. **Top Right:** Actions by Queen Isabella II and her government gave occasion to the Eve of Saint Daniel protests. Galdós provides this caricature of the queen, deposed in September 1868 and exiled to France. **Bottom Right:** Galdós's lifelong friend Fernando León y Castillo. The future cabinet secretary and ambassador to France was the real-life model for Zalamero, a serious-minded friend of the novel's Juanito Santa Cruz.

economic condition abundantly clear. While 6,346 men were classified *pobres de solemnidad*, 178,934 women were so labeled. A simple mathematical calculation could justify the assertion that woman were 29 times worse off economically than men.

The Novel in Focus

Plot summary. *Fortunata and Jacinta* is divided into four volumes of about 190 pages each. The novel begins with the aforementioned 1865 Massacre of the Eve of Saint Daniel. Introduced in

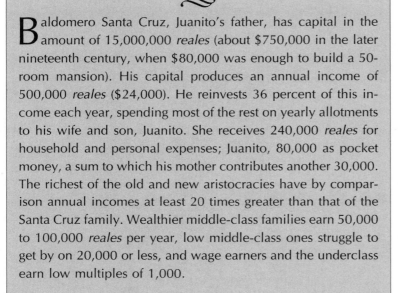

WEALTH, INCOME, AND WAGES—A RELATIVE AFFAIR

Baldomero Santa Cruz, Juanito's father, has capital in the amount of 15,000,000 *reales* (about $750,000 in the later nineteenth century, when $80,000 was enough to build a 50-room mansion). His capital produces an annual income of 500,000 *reales* ($24,000). He reinvests 36 percent of this income each year, spending most of the rest on yearly allotments to his wife and son, Juanito. She receives 240,000 *reales* for household and personal expenses; Juanito, 80,000 as pocket money, a sum to which his mother contributes another 30,000. The richest of the old and new aristocracies have by comparison annual incomes at least 20 times greater than that of the Santa Cruz family. Wealthier middle-class families earn 50,000 to 100,000 *reales* per year, low middle-class ones struggle to get by on 20,000 or less, and wage earners and the underclass earn low multiples of 1,000.

relation to this incident are the male protagonist, Juanito Santa Cruz, an only son, and his two university chums, Villalonga and Zalamero. The narrator's characterization of Juanito's expedient release from jail indicates at the outset that the Santa Cruz family is a rich and influential force of the upper bourgeoisie. The description that follows details Juanito's subsequent lapse into apolitical idleness, which demonstrates the shallowness of his Saint Daniel Eve liberalism. More generally, these details illustrate how the novel embeds the personal storyline into broader Spanish history, establishing parallels between public events and the private, novelistic action.

The first volume details the formation of the Santa Cruz family fortune, which springs from the Madrilenian cloth trade of the first half of the

nineteenth century. The business grew under the guiding hand of Juanito's father, who passed it on to hardworking middle-class nephews. This left the father free to enjoy his position as an urban landlord and, with dinner-table access to inside information, to speculate successfully in the stock market and in government bonds. One December day in 1869, his idle son Juanito, known also as the Dauphin, has nothing else to do and goes to the heart of old Madrid, the Plaza Mayor, to inquire after the health of an esteemed family dependent, Estupiñá. Climbing some stairs, he meets the striking 18-year-old Fortunata drinking raw egg from its shell. This experience introduces Juanito to the deliciously vulgar, vital world of the urban poor, which soon finds him promising marriage to Fortunata. When he tires of her, ignorant of her pregnant condition, Juanito acts on his watchful mother's suggestion and marries his first cousin, the middle-class Jacinta, in May 1871.

Two years into her childless marriage to an unfaithful husband, Jacinta learns of the possible presence in Madrid of Juanito's child by Fortunata. With the help of Guillermina Pacheco, a family friend who has dedicated her life to the urban poor and who is then constructing an asylum for abandoned and orphaned children, Jacinta arranges to buy the child she thinks to be Juanito's by Fortunata through her uncle José Izquierdo. When Jacinta's actions become known to the family, Juanito explains that his illegitimate child died. Furthermore, Izquierdo, without Fortunata's knowledge and aided by the former writer of sensational novels *Ido del Sagrario*, has tricked Jacinta with a "novel" about the illegitimate child.

The child Jacinta has acquired, who is about the same age Fortunata's child by Juanito would have been, is actually the offspring of Izquierdo's dead stepdaughter. In the end, the hapless youngster becomes one more orphan under Guillermina's care. The last incident of Volume 1 begins with a visit to the Santa Cruz household from Villalonga. His ostensible purpose is to report on Pavía's coup d'état, which ends the First Spanish Republic. But the suspicious Jacinta soon understands that Villalonga is reporting to Juanito on a more beautiful Fortunata, newly returned to Madrid after a long absence as the kept woman of an arms dealer. The volume ends with Juanito catching pneumonia after wintry days spent searching in vain for Fortunata.

The second volume introduces the Rubín family of the childless widow and usurer Aunt Lupe and her three orphaned nephews: the 28-year-old, café dwelling, sometimes salesman, sometimes Carlist conspirator Juan Pablo; his 25-year-old brother Nicholas, a gluttonous priest active with the Carlists; and the 19-year-old malformed, sickly pharmacy student Maximiliano. Maximiliano meets Fortunata at the apartment of a fellow student, Olmedo (her old lover Juanito is on the verge of death about this same time). Fortunata has recently begun street-walking, and, until she can amass some money, stays at Olmedo's on the strength of an old friendship with his live-in girlfriend. While Maxi is instantly taken by Fortunata, she pays him no more heed than she would a fly. Nonetheless, Maxi makes it his project to redeem Fortunata from the streets and convinces his family to aid in her moral and cultural education. Even though the family sees the obvious contrast between Fortunata's health and physical appeal and Maxi's lack of both, they support him, acknowledging how much brighter and more competent he has become since taking an interest in Fortunata. He begins by setting her up in her own apartment and giving her lessons in reading and writing. He then sends her to the Micaelas, a convent for the reform of fallen women.

At the convent, Fortunata spends much time with the daughter of a sometime employee of Maxi's Aunt Lupe, the drunken Mauricia la Dura. Not only does Mauricia confirm Fortunata's belief that Fortunata is Juanito's true wife, but for the first time Fortunata sees Jacinta, who comes to the Micaelas to do charitable work. After Fortunata finishes her term at the convent, she and Maxi marry. But on their wedding night, returning to their new apartment, Maxi falls victim to impotence and an excruciating migraine and takes sleep-inducing drugs. The newlyweds' unfaithful servant then informs Fortunata that Juanito Santa Cruz is her recently installed next-door neighbor. Although Fortunata resists Juanito at first, her enduring love for him leads to their reconciliation and to her betrayal of Maxi. When confronted by the Rubín family for her infidelity, Fortunata flees from them.

The third volume contains the restoration of domestic order in the marriages between Jacinta and Juanito, and Fortunata and Maxi, as well as the Restoration of the Bourbon dynasty as a constitutional monarchy in Spain, when Alfonso XII assumes the Spanish throne. At the same time, Maxi's brother Juan Pablo Rubín, advised and aided by an old and influential friend, the retired Colonel Evaristo Feijoo, abandons the Carlist

cause and becomes a provincial governor under Alfonso. Meanwhile, Juanito, again bored with Fortunata, returns to Jacinta, and Feijoo, long aware of Fortunata and her history through Juan Pablo, begins a liaison with her. When their life together causes a precipitate decline in his health, Feijoo, also friendly with Aunt Lupe, arranges for a reconciliation between Fortunata and Maxi. One of Feijoo's parting gifts to Fortunata is "a course in practical philosophy," during which he preaches to her the necessity of keeping up

LITERATURE BECOMING LIFE

Early in his career, Ido del Sagrario (whose name translates to something like "Off-His-Rocker") wrote cheap, melodramatic novels in which dukes and duchesses had torrid romances producing spurious offspring. Those loves and children had incredible complications, with rags-to-riches outcomes for passion's innocent byproducts being the most popular plot line. Just as Jacinta falls victim to Ido's "novel" about Fortunata's first child, other principle Galdosian characters also try to live as if their lives were a novel. Most notable among these is Isidora Rufete, the protagonist of *The Disinherited Lady* (1881). Isadora's institutionalized, insane father and his crazy old cousin Santiago Quijano-Quijada convince her that she is the illegitimate granddaughter of the rich marchioness of Aránsis. Isidora, whose family hails from Don Quixote's home territory of La Mancha, ruins her life trying to convince the marchioness that she is her dead daughter's love child (see **Don Quixote**, also in *WLAIT 5: Spanish and Portuguese Literatures and Their Times*). For his part Ido, after a hard day in the streets, often explodes into his miserable apartment screaming and yelling, looking to kill the count whom he imagines he will discover making love to his withered, selfless wife.

appearances, of having a husband, of avoiding the temptation of Juanito but of learning to live an outwardly respectable, duplicitous life should she not be able to control that love.

The novel's subtitle—*Two Stories of Married Women*—finds special relevance in the fourth and final volume. The volume offers a marked counterpoint to Fortunata and Jacinta's dependency on men who are unworthy of their women morally or physically, and of Fortunata and Jacinta's consequent humiliations and sufferings. The two married women now have a common bond—the youngish, childless widow Aurora Samaniego Moreno, a rival to them both in Juanito's affections. Aurora's mother, one of the Dauphin's mother's dearest friends, resolved to educate her daughters in a trade that would allow them to earn their living should this prove necessary. Aurora attained her education through hands-on experience in France in the occupations of accounting and through marriage to a Frenchman, whose retail business in linens, lace, and intimate apparel she helped run. Returning to Madrid, the talented Aurora became successful in business and gained personal independence. Her daily life rested on the kind of awareness of the world that Feijoo had tried in vain to teach Fortunata. Guided by this understanding, Aurora manages to live well on her own terms. Meanwhile, Fortunata is now pregnant with his second child, and Jacinta again bores him, so Juanito turns to Aurora. They go from being family acquaintances to becoming lovers.

Shortly after delivering her child, Fortunata learns about Aurora. The discovery fills her with rage, having come by now to consider herself *and* Jacinta as the legitimate spouses of Juanito. As Fortunata sees it, she can accept Jacinta's legal rights to Juanito and assert simultaneously her rights to him by natural law. But Aurora's liaison with Juanito affronts Jacinta's goodness and her own motherhood. In the name of their unique status as a kind of dual wife whose rights to Juanito are being usurped by Aurora, Fortunata leaves her apartment, finds Aurora, and beats her. The violence causes postpartum hemorrhaging, which ends Fortunata's life in April 1876. She carries her identification with Jacinta, her alter ego, to its logical conclusion by willing her son to the childless wife. Buried the same day as the much-mourned Feijoo, Fortunata's funeral is scantily attended, with no one from the Santa Cruz family appearing. But Fortunata's son displaces Juanito as the center of Santa Cruz family life. Fortunata's husband, Maxi Rubín, is committed to an insane asylum, but he does not care. Unhindered by his weak body, the asylum's walls, or society, Maxi lives the ideal life of the unbounded mind.

Classless womanhood. The chapter "The Honeymoon," in Volume 1, chronicles the wedding trip of Juanito and Jacinta to various points in Spain. Jacinta observes firsthand the onerous life of working-class women in industrial Barcelona and learns from Juanito how he seduced the innocent, lower-class Fortunata by promising marriage to her. While visiting a textile factory, Jacinta suddenly has genuine insight into the lives of working-class women. She comprehends that the young women who work there "earn a measly salary that's not even enough to live on" (Pérez Galdós, *Fortunata and Jacinta*, p. 63). Given this experience she sees why any one of them would let herself be seduced by a smooth talker promising an easier life: "it's not that they're evil; it's that the time comes when they say, 'It's better to be a bad girl than a good machine'" (*Fortunata and Jacinta*, p. 63). Toward the end of the trip, after unaccustomed drinking leaves Juanito inebriated, and he adds details concerning how shabbily he treated Fortunata, including his heedless abandonment of her when she was pregnant with their first child, Jacinta exclaims: "Poor women! They always get the worst of it" (*Fortunata and Jacinta*, p. 78). Trying to save face, Juanito explains that "There are two worlds, the one you *can* see and the one you *can't* see" (*Fortunata and Jacinta*, p. 78). He then explains how "Differences in education and background always establish a great difference in conduct in human relations," stressing that this is not a religious, but a more basic social reality (*Fortunata and Jacinta*, p. 78). By the end of the novel, Jacinta has experienced and seen so much of Juanito's double-dealing that she understands that she and Fortunata belong to much the same world—one in which Juanito does as he pleases; they both are in their own ways "poor women."

By the same token, one can extend Jacinta's conclusion about poor, exploited women to general observations about how the high bourgeoisie exploits unrepentantly the 98 percent of Spanish society that does not belong to the old or new aristocracy. Recall that it was Maxi, his middle-class family, and even old Feijoo who tried to make Fortunata literate and to impart to her the religious and social instruction that would facilitate her ascent to a new, higher place in society as Maxi's wife. In contrast, Juanito and the Santa Cruz family simply exploited Fortunata's body, first for sexual pleasure and then as the source of an heir. It is sobering to consider that everything in the novel, and in Spanish social history of the time, indicates that this child will be "educated" in the same way as Juanito and that he will live much as Juanito did.

Literary context and sources. Galdós gained distinction as the most prominent and prolific Spanish realist and the last major novelist of European realism. He, however, viewed himself as the product of three main literary traditions: Western literature and art since the Greeks, with

Shakespeare being the dominant non-Hispanic writer; Spanish literature from the Golden Age to his present; and the European historical novel and novel of manners of Sir Walter Scott, Charles Dickens, and Honoré de Balzac.

In respect to Spanish literary tradition, Galdós divided it into earlier and later epochs. The earlier was formed basically by the picaresque novel and Cervantes. The later, into which he placed himself, included the eighteenth-century dramatists Ramón de la Cruz and Leandro Fernández de Moratín; Ramón de Mesonero Romanos, writer of prose sketches of earlier nineteenth-century Madrid; and Ventura Ruiz Aguilera, poet, short-story writer, editor, novelist and dramatist. In his realist manifesto of 1870, "Observations on the Contemporary Novel in Spain," a review on three volumes of stories by Aguilera, Galdós laid out a strategy for the creation of a contemporary national novel comparable to that of Balzac and Dickens. Citing the practice of the best Spanish writers and painters of the past in recreating their times, he concluded that anyone who would write such novels in the 1870s must study the persons, places, and conflicts of Spanish society as represented in the strivings of the urban middle classes for a better individual and societal life. He viewed this group as the most active social force in all European countries and hence as the most worthy and important of literary subjects. Galdós hoped that by exposing to Spanish society urban-middle-class vices and virtues, the former would be corrected; the latter cultivated; and socioeconomic progress for Spain would be assured.

A 1981 study of Galdós and the European novel by Stephen Gilman traces an intertextual dialogue between Galdós and other authors. *Fortunata and Jacinta* harks back, argues this study, to two Spanish novels, **Don Quixote** and **La Regenta,** (also in *WLAIT 5: Spanish and Portuguese Literatures and Their Times*) and one French one (Gustave Flaubert's *Madame Bovary*). All three construct an alternative reality for protagonists whose diversely limited horizons cause them to substitute readerly experience for active, worldly lives. In Galdos's novel, before meeting Fortunata, only reading awakened the dull, poorly formed, impotent Maxi to a dreamy world of beauty and ideals that he tried to reform into the reality of life as Fortunata's husband. For her part, Fortunata conjures a similarly dreamy "reality," embarking on a Quixote-like project of becoming as legitimate a spouse to Juanito as his wife Jacinta.

Events in History at the Time the Novel Was Written

Galdós—Restoration politician. In November 1885, shortly after Galdós began writing *Fortunata and Jacinta,* King Alfonso XII died and a new prime minister, the liberal Sagasta, took power from the conservative Cánovas del Castillo. A half-year later, on May 17, 1886, Sagasta presented Alfonso's posthumous son as the future king of Spain to 300 persons, including select members of Spanish society, of the government,

and of the international diplomatic corps. Galdós was part of the seven-member parliamentary delegation that attended the ceremony. This presence of Galdós is important. To begin with, he was a *diputado,* or a member of parliament only because Sagasta had been attracted to him by virtue of Galdós's high visibility as a popular, nationally known liberal writer. Considering that Galdós's prestige could only enhance his new government, Sagasta had intermediaries approach Galdós, and then, in April 1886, had him elected as the *diputado* from Guayamas, Puerto Rico, a place in which Galdós had never set foot. Although it remains problematic today that Galdós, who would later become a founder of the Republican-Socialist Coalition, let himself be used this way, the experience provided him with an inside look at the maneuvers of Spanish political life. Galdós's daily legislative activities taught him much about Spanish politics and how upper-class families, such as the Santa Cruces, gained power through their wealth. Such families doubted at first whether the queen mother María Cristina, a woman born and raised outside Spain, could as regent carry out two main functions: select and retain ministers to advance programs of legislation in the bicameral parliament; and consolidate the legitimizing authority that

---

GALDÓS AND HIS LOVERS

All biographers and editors of his correspondence agree that the never-married Galdós had hundreds of lovers during his life, many from the working-classes but also from the higher classes such as the novelist, the Countess Emilia Pardo Bazán. While it seems that some of his upper-class companions may have been influential in the direct writing of his later works, his relations with lower-class women probably served to help him in the creation of such characters as Fortunata. Galdós keenly understood that such women as the orphaned Fortunata, once they left the scant protection of relatives, had very hard lives. The alternative to a poor marriage was to be a kept woman, a prostitute, and probably to suffer an early death. In this context it is noteworthy that among the provisions the old retired colonel Evaristo Feijoo, Fortunata's most altruistic lover, made for her when he felt death coming was to give her a Singer sewing machine. It so happened that it was Galdós's custom to give Singers to the working-class lover he was leaving for another. In the cottage industry of sewing at home, the machine assured better than subsistence wages for one person.

---

her husband Alfonso XII had re-established with the 1875 Restoration. As *diputado,* Galdós helped create the power behind the throne in Restoration Spain. The oligarchy, dissembling in back of the Constitution and a weak monarchy, divided Spain into dozens of fiefdoms over which so-called conservatives and liberals ruled, obtaining benefits for important constituents while also securing personal benefits. The local power in these areas was vested in men called *caciques*. In the 1890s Galdós's friend Fernando León y Castillo, the model in *Fortunata and Jacinta* for Juanito Santa Cruz's friend Zalamero, was considered the *cacique* of the Canary Islands.

Reviews. Virtually all Spanish nineteenth-century authors complained of the lack of professional criticism in response to novels. Galdós was no exception, though his novels did become a primary subject of the two most important Spanish critics of his time: Manuel de la Revilla and Leopoldo Alas, otherwise known as "Clarín." Following the publication of his own *The Regent's Wife* (1884-85), Alas focused on his own creative work, so his review of *Fortunata and Jacinta* is laudatory but perfunctory. A much lesser known critic, Pedro Muñoz Peña, published in 1888 an 88-page pamphlet dedicated to *Fortunata and Jacinta*, praising it greatly, without the benefit of the important audience Revilla and Alas enjoyed. In 1930 a three-act stage version of the novel met with success, and in 1980 Spanish Television (TVE) became the lead producer of a highly celebrated, ten-hour adaptation screened throughout Europe and the Spanish-speaking world.

The delay until 1973 of the first translation of *Fortunata and Jacinta* into English caused a late Anglo-American reception. But in 1978, during the so-called "boom era" of the Spanish American novel, C. P. Snow surprised the English-speaking literary world by announcing that a star as bright as Balzac, Dickens, or Fyodor Dostoevsky had been missing from its literary skies because of poor luck, few translations, and simple ignorance. Snow recognized *Fortunata and Jacinta* not only as Galdós's masterwork, but also as one of the best novels of all time and as the most profound study of women's personalities ever written. He marveled at Galdós's mastery of technique that allowed for such easy comprehension of hundreds of characters and scores of intertwined lives set in all the socioeconomic classes of Madrid. In touch with Pedro Ortiz-Armengol, Galdós's most exhaustive and profound biographer in Spanish, Snow shared much information about Galdós's personal life and how it impacted on his literature. Particularly significant in this regard was the insight into women which the never-married Galdós had gained during 50 years of long- and short-term relationships with women of all social classes.

—Stephen Miller

For More Information

Becker, George J. "Benito Pérez Galdós." In *Master European Realists of the Nineteenth Century*. New York: Frederick Ungar, 1982.

Berkowitz, H. Chonon. *Pérez Galdós: Spanish Liberal Crusader*. Madison: University of Wisconsin Press, 1948.

Bly, Peter A. *Galdós's Novel of the Historical Imagination: A Study of the Contemporary Novels.* Liverpool: Francis Cairns, 1983.

Carr, Raymond. *Spain, 1808-1939.* Oxford: Clarendon, 1966.

———. *Modern Spain 1875-1980.* Oxford: Clarendon, 1980.

Gilman, Stephen. *Galdós and the Art of the European Novel: 1867-1887.* Princeton: Princeton University Press, 1981.

Miller, Stephen. *Galdós gráfico (1861-1907): orígenes, técnicas y límites del sociomimetismo.* Las Palmas, Spain: Colección Galdós/Ediciones del Cabildo Insular de Gran Canaria, 2001.

Pattison, Walter T. *Benito Pérez Galdós.* Boston: Twayne, 1975.

Pérez Galdós, Benito. *Fortunata and Jacinta: Two Stories of Married Women.* Trans. Agnes Moncy Gullón. Athens: University of Georgia Press, 1986.

———. *Atlas zoológico.* Edición e introduccion de Stephen Miller. Las Palmas, Spain: Colección Galdós/Ediciones del Cabildo Insular de Gran Canaria, 2001.

Ribbans, Geoffrey. *Pérez Galdós: "Fortunata y Jacinta."* London: Grant & Cutler, 1977.

Rodgers, Eamonn. *From Enlightenment to Realism: The Novels of Galdós 1870-1887.* Dublin: Jack Hade, 1987.

Snow, C. P. "Galdós." In *The Realists: Portraits of Eight Novelists: Stendhal, Balzac, Dickens, Dostoevsky, Tolstoy, Galdós, Henry James, Proust.* London: Macmillan, 1978.

Turner, Harriet S. *Benito Pérez Galdós: "Fortunata and Jacinta."* Cambridge: Cambridge University Press, 1992.

Fuente Ovejuna

by
Lope de Vega

Lope Félix de Vega Carpio was born in Madrid, Spain, in 1562 and educated at the University of Alcalá de Henares. In 1583 he became involved in the theater world, writing several plays for his mistress Elena Osorio, an actress and the daughter of an actor-manager. The love affair ended badly in 1587, after which Lope vented his feelings in writing. He circulated scurrilous verses about Elena and her family that resulted in his being convicted of malicious libel and exiled from Madrid for eight years and from Castile for two years. During his banishment, Lope married Isabel De Urbina by proxy. In 1588 he sailed with the Spanish Armada in its ill-fated attack on England, then took up residence with his bride in Valencia, where his career as a professional playwright began in earnest. After his exile from the region of Castile ended, Lope moved to Toledo, then to Alba de Torres, entering the service of the Duke of Alba, the first of many noblemen he would serve until deciding to become a priest in 1613. Until his death in 1635, however, Lope conducted numerous romantic liaisons and, according to modern scholars, composed an estimated 340 plays. Two notable plays among others in his corpus are *El Caballero de Olmedo*, the story of a young nobleman who rides to and fro from Olmedo to Medina to court a girl, though warned that if he continues he will meet with an unhappy fate, and *Peribáñez y el Comendador de Ocaña*, a play on country life that includes a villainous nobleman and a king who champions the commoner. *Fuente Ovejuna* (The Sheep-Well; also spelled

---

> **THE LITERARY WORK**
>
> A play set in a small town in Cordoba, Spain, in the year 1476; published in Spanish (as *Fuente Ovejuna*) in 1619; in English in 1959.
>
> **SYNOPSIS**
>
> The citizens of Fuente Ovejuna rise up against and kill their tyrannical overlord.

Fuenteovejuna) is noted for its stirring depiction of history and its critique of the abuses of political power.

Events in History at the Time the Play Takes Place

The war of Castilian succession. The ongoing conflict over the throne of Castile forms the historical background in *Fuente Ovejuna*. In December 1474 Enrique IV of Castile died after declaring his 13-year-old daughter Juana his rightful heir. His death sparked a war of succession that would last until 1479. There were two main contenders for the throne: Juana, whose legitimacy was doubtful (her detractors claimed she was actually fathered by Don Beltrán de la Cueva, her mother's favorite at court); the second contender was Isabel (Isabella), Enrique's younger half-sister. A third contender, Fernando (Ferdinand), the king of Sicily and prince of Aragon, who was Enrique's cousin and Isabel's

Lope de Vega

their own gain. Historian Felipe Fernández-Armesto describes the ensuing conflict:

> [It was] a war without fronts, with rebellions and counter rebellions spread across Castile like pinheads in a map, but there were to be three main theaters of conflict: one in the north, where Afonso was poised to invade and where the [Portuguese] Duke of Arevalo was stirring up insurgency; another in the centre where the Marquess of Villena was most active; and a last in the South, where the Count of Uruena sought to exploit divisions among the monarchs' supporters.
> (Fernández-Armesto, pp. 16-17)

In March 1476—about a month before the events in *Fuente Ovejuna* take place—the contest yielded an important victory for Isabel and Ferdinand: Castilian forces cut off the supplies of the Portuguese troops, then defeated them conclusively at the Battle of Toro. The triumph consolidated Isabel's position as heir to the throne and increased her contingent of supporters. After Isabel produced a healthy male heir in 1476, opposition to her claim grew even weaker. In September 1479, the treaty of Alcacovas-Toledo ended the war: on behalf of himself and Juana, Afonso V renounced all rights and claims to the Castilian throne. The betrothal between Afonso and Juana was dissolved, Juana was sent to the convent of Santa Clara at Coimbra, and Isabel became the undisputed Queen of Castile.

The Military Order of Calatrava. The involvement of Castile's three major religious-military orders further complicated the war of succession. Established in the twelfth century, the monastic knightly orders of Santiago, Calatrava, and Alcantara were created to defend the Christian states of Spain against the Muslims. The intention was for these orders to embody the religious and secular ideals of chivalry; however, over the years, the orders became distracted by mundane, materialistic concerns. They acquired great wealth and power, with which they were reluctant to part. Many nobles eagerly sought inclusion in the orders. Members were subject only to the authority of their grand masters—the heads of the orders—and officials, and, as religious knights, they enjoyed clerical as well as aristocratic privileges, such as the right to hold land. During the war of succession and the early years of her reign, Queen Isabel increasingly came to see the orders as a threat to her authority.

At the time that *Fuente Ovejuna* takes place, the Grand Mastership of the Military Order of Calatrava was held by Don Rodrigo Téllez Girón, 17 years old and the illegitimate son of the pre-

husband, was not really a claimant in his own right but rather through his wife, Isabel.

In fact, Isabel was considered to have the strongest legal claim—unlike Juana, she was unquestionably legitimate and, unlike Fernando, she was Castilian born and bred. Moreover, at the time of the king's death, Isabel was conveniently situated in Segovia, a city not far to the north of Madrid, the city in which Enrique died. Within hours of receiving the news, Isabel had her succession proclaimed; next, she secured the royal treasure, and, a few days later, assumed the crown. After Isabel was proclaimed Queen, the Castilian Cortes (parliament) met in Segovia and swore allegiance to her; accepting these developments, Fernando hurried to Castile, quickly establishing his own position as king consort. Meanwhile, despite the rumors of her illegitimacy, Enrique's daughter, Juana, had acquired supporters and a powerful ally in her uncle Afonso V, King of Portugal, who betrothed himself to her in early 1475. In May 1475, Juana issued her own claim to the throne of Castile. The Spanish nobility found itself divided: while the people of Segovia completely supported Isabel's claim, several highborn families of Castile opposed it, and a few nobles, like the Marquess of Villena, played both sides against each other for vious Grand Master, Don Pedro Girón. Don Pedro had, in fact, been selected by Enrique IV of Castile as a husband for Isabel, then the Infanta (princess). After receiving a papal dispensation that allowed him to put aside the monastic vow of chastity he had taken, Don Pedro set out in 1466 to claim his bride but fell ill on the journey and died. Before his death, Don Pedro had chosen his eight-year-old son Rodrigo as his successor as Grand Master of Calatrava. Until 1474, however, the real chief of the order was Don Juan Pacheco, Rodrigo's uncle and the Marquess of Villena, whom Pope Paul II designated to be coadjutor. Don Juan Pacheco would serve as head of the order until Rodrigo came of age.

During the war of succession, the Girón family, one of the most powerful and influential in Castile, favored Juana's claim to the throne. In 1476, acting on the advice of his brother and cousin, Don Rodrigo Téllez Girón and several of his knights attacked and seized Ciudad Real, which occupied an important strategic position between Castile and Portugal. His triumph was short-lived: Fernando and Isabel's forces quickly recaptured Ciudad Real. Eventually, Don Rodrigo was reconciled with Fernando and Isabel, who excused his conduct because of his extreme youth and the undue influence exerted on him by his family, especially his late uncle, Villena. Don Rodrigo raised no more rebellions but served his sovereigns loyally until his death in battle at Loja in 1482. Although Don Rodrigo's attack on Ciudad Real is the more minor of the two subplots in *Fuente Ovejuna*, Lope effectively depicts the young Master of Calatrava's ambition, familial pride, and ultimate repentance of his rash actions. Lope does, however, take a liberty with one of the powerful members of the Order of Calatrava, the *comendador mayor* Fernán Gómez de Guzmán. (A *comendador mayor* was second only to the Grand Master of a military order.) To make Fernán Gómez, who was also overlord of Fuente Ovejuna, more villainous, Lope has *him*, rather than the Giróns, persuade Don Rodrigo to attack Ciudad Real.

The Fuente Ovejuna uprising. Like many of Lope's historical plays, *Fuente Ovejuna* is based on an actual event: a peasant rebellion in April 1476 that resulted in the death of a feudal overlord. Even before the uprising, however, the real Fuente Ovejuna—a town situated in the province of Córdoba with a population of less than 1,000 inhabitants—had an unusual history. In 1460 Fuente Ovejuna became a bone of contention between Córdoba and Don Pedro Girón, who was the Grand Master of Calatrava at the time. As a

reward for Girón's loyalty to the Castilian throne, Enrique IV conferred upon him in perpetuity the towns of Fuente Ovejuna and Bélmez. The citizens of Córdoba, however, opposed Girón's claims to the lands and petitioned the crown for their return. In time, after much haggling on all sides, Enrique IV annulled the grants of Fuente Ovejuna and Bélmez to Pedro Girón, who, by this time, held the more desirable towns of Osuna and Cazalla. Córdoba thus received the right

to recover by arms the places that had been taken from it; violence proved unnecessary, because Fuente Ovejuna and Bélmez had never became disaffected from Córdoba.

Civil dissension between the two citizens Alfonso de Aguilar and Don Diego Fernández de Córdoba over control of Córdoba, however, created a distraction that Fernán Gómez, *comendador* mayor of the Order of Calatrava, exploited. In 1468, taking advantage of the distraction, he employed the force of arms to seize Fuente Ovejuna for himself and his military order. Subsequently, on April 22, 1476, a crowd of about 1,000 peasants stormed the *comendador mayor*'s residence, overcame his guards after a long night of fighting, forced their way inside, and slew the *comendador mayor* when he confronted them. The mutilated corpse of Fernán Gómez was thrown out the window, suffering further indignities at the hands of the crowd. Investigation of the incident by an emissary of the royal authorities failed to establish individual guilt—under interrogation, townspeople reportedly said only that Fuente Ovejuna had killed Fernán Gómez. Ultimately no one was punished for the crime. Control over Fuente Ovejuna reverted to the Order of Calatrava. The pope blamed Córdoba for the uprising, thinking it may have instigated the resistance, so he refused to reward the Córdobans with Fuente Ovejuna.

What did Fernán Gómez do to suffer such a fate? History presents conflicting portrayals of his character and rule. A chronicle by Francisco de Rades y Andrada's (*Chrónica de las tres Ordenes y Cavallerias de Santiago, Calatrava y Alcantara* [1572])—to which Lope de Vega faithfully adhered—depicted the *comendador mayor* as a cruel, brutal tyrant who oppressed the citizens of Fuente Ovejuna economically and pursued the townswomen ruthlessly. This unflattering depiction was echoed in Sebastian de Covarrubias Horozco's *Emblemas morales* (1610) and *Tesoro de la lengua castellana* (1611). Literary scholar Claude E. Anibal, however, cites other fifteenth-century writers, including historian Alonso Fernández de Palencia (1423-92) and Pedro Tafur, who praised Fernán Gómez's military prowess, noble character, and love of culture and refinement. Evaluating his conduct as overlord of Fuente Ovejuna, Anibal argues that

> The Comendador must be judged by the standards of his time. Probably he did not abuse the recognized rights of any feudal baron, and certainly he was no worse than the Giróns, the Pachecos, or many another fellow nobles of this cruel and loose epoch. Indeed contemporary testimony recognizes in him an unusually high degree of respectability. He seems in any case to have been the victim not so much of his own extortion and vices, as of a political situation for which he himself was in no way responsible.
>
> (Anibal, p. 704)

The "political situation" to which Anibal refers was the continuing hostility between the Order

of Calatrava and Córdoba, which resented the order's continuing possession of its towns, including Fuente Ovejuna. Anibal advances the theory—also voiced by historian Don Rafael Ramírez de Arellano in 1901—that the Fuente Ovejuna rebellion was encouraged, even fomented, by Córdobans eager to reclaim their former property. Indeed, less than a week after Fernán Gómez's death, Córdoban representatives reportedly arrived in Fuente Ovejuna to take possession of the town. The Order of Calatrava, in turn, protested the removal of Fuente Ovejuna from its jurisdiction. Ultimately, a papal bull of Pope Innocent VIII awarded Fuente Ovejuna to Calatrava and implied that Cordobans had instigated the rebellion. Various public officials and inhabitants of Córdoba were excommunicated and subjected to other ecclesiastical sentences for their occupation of Fuente Ovejuna after the rebellion. None of these issues is addressed in Lope's play. It ends after King Fernando pardons the former rebels; stopping the narration of the story here is perhaps partly responsible for the play's becoming one of Lope's best-known works outside of Spain.

Vassals and overlords. Feudalism—a land-holding system based upon the "fief," valuable property held by vassals in trust for their overlord in exchange for certain services—did not really exist in the kingdom of Castile in the fifteenth century. Muslim invasions in the earlier Middle Ages had eroded the foundations of a feudal baronage, and Christian resettlement in the Duero Valley was, at least initially, carried out by small settlers who were not dependent on any powerful lord. These settlers developed into a society of small proprietors who learned to defend themselves and their frontier holdings from attacks by the Moors. Historian Henry Kamen explains:

> The authority and lands of the king of Castile advanced during the great Reconquest campaigns, but there was little need for contracts between the crown and the warrior nobles, since these could be rewarded directly from the conquests without having to depend on the crown for reward. The great independent Military Orders—of Santiago, Calatrava and Alcántara—carved out huge territories for themselves in the frontier lands of New Castile. The "fief," which created a bond of dependence between warriors and their prince, and which is the institution most commonly associated with "feudalism," was consequently very rare in Castile.
>
> (Kamen, p. 11)

Later in the Middle Ages, as the Reconquest progressed and the frontier advanced southward, the society of small proprietors was replaced by one of warlords who controlled large areas of land and of settlers who accepted the warlords' protections as "vassals."

The peasantry represented a large segment of this new society during the time that *Fuente Ovejuna* takes place, with relationships between peasants and those socially above that varied depending on the geographical region. In central Spain, which included the kingdoms of Old and New Castile, peasants could hold or even own small pieces of land and have a share of the communal lands in their villages. However, on the Castilian plains, large domains were often owned or held by ecclesiastical and lay lords; peasants rented lands from these lords—sometimes through long-term leases—and paid them dues in the form of rent. What remained constant was the relationship between peasant and lord, as historian Teofilo F. Ruiz explains:

> There were no peasants without lords; even well-to-do farmers were never released from their obligations, rental dues, and debts of allegiance to the lord of their lands. The lord could be distant and benign, or close-by and horrible. The lord could be the king, usually the most favourable arrangement, or a neighbouring monastery or cathedral chapter. Thus masters and peasants were enmeshed in complex networks of reciprocity.
>
> (Ruiz, p. 49)

The complexities of the lord-peasant relationship are reflected in Lope's play. The population of Fuente Ovejuna consists of people from various walks of life: laborers, farmers, and students, for example. All, however, are accountable to their overlord, Fernán Gómez, who knows that he may dispose of their lives as he chooses. When the Master of Calatrava asks Commander Fernán Gómez if he can provide soldiers from Fuente Ovejuna for the campaign to take Ciudad Real, the latter replies that his vassals, "if they are obliged, / They'll fight as fiercely as lions" even though they are "humble people, more used to fields / And ploughshares than battles" (Vega, *Fuente Ovejuna*, pp. 6-7). The consciousness on both sides of the contract between vassals and overlord renders the townspeople's ultimate decision to rebel against Fernán Gómez for his abuses of power all the more startling.

The Play in Focus

Plot summary. The play opens with Fernán Gómez, Grand Commander of the Military Order of Calatrava and overlord of Fuente Ovejuna, visiting his superior, Rodrigo Téllez Girón, the 17-year-old Master of Calatrava. The two men discuss the ongoing war between Aragon and Portugal over the throne of Castile. Fernán Gómez reminds the Master that the Girón family always supported the Portuguese claim, then urges the younger man to assemble the knights of Calatrava and capture the strategically placed town of Ciudad Real. The Master agrees to the plan, Fernán Gómez promises him some soldiers to support his efforts, and the two men leave for Ciudad Real.

In Fuente Ovejuna, two young peasant women, Laurencia and Pascuala, express relief that Fernán Gómez, their overlord, has left for battle. They then discuss his pursuit of the local women, including Laurencia herself, who has continually rebuffed his advances. Three of Fuente Ovejuna's young men—Mengo, Barrildo, and Frondoso—enter and begin to banter with the two women about the nature of love, Frondoso revealing his growing attraction to the witty Laurencia. Just then, Flores, one of Fernán Gómez's servants, interrupts the conversation with news of the battle: under Girón's leadership, the knights of Calatrava have successfully taken Ciudad Real.

On his victorious return to Fuente Ovejuna, Fernán Gómez receives a warm welcome and gifts of food and drink from the town magistrates, including Esteban, Laurencia's father. The victorious *comendador mayor* uses the occasion of his celebration to renew his pursuit of Laurencia, who still rebuffs him. Elsewhere, King Fernando of Aragon and his wife Queen Isabel learn of Ciudad Real's capture and dispatch troops of their own to try to reclaim the town.

Back in Fuente Ovejuna, Frondoso woos Laurencia, but their courtship is interrupted by the appearance of Fernán Gómez, who is out hunting. Spying Laurencia, he seizes her, but Frondoso picks up a crossbow and threatens to shoot him unless he releases the girl. Furious, Fernán Gómez obeys but vows revenge on the insolent peasant. Relations between the *comendador mayor* and the citizens of Fuente Ovejuna further deteriorate at a town meeting to discuss the grain harvest. Several men rebuke Fernán Gómez for his pursuit of the town's women, but he belittles their concerns and continues to plot, with his servants Flores and Ortuño, assignations with several local beauties.

A newly arrived soldier informs the *comendador mayor* that troops from Aragon have laid siege to Ciudad Real and exhorts him to join the

Scene from a 1970 production of *Fuente Ovejuna* at New York's Columbia University.

other knights of Calatrava to prevent them from losing the town. Fernán Gómez quickly assembles his men and prepares to ride; before he departs, he orders Flores and Ortuño to capture Jacinta, a local married woman, and bring her to him. Jacinta flees for protection to Mengo, one of her relatives, but ultimately, she is abducted and Mengo receives a savage whipping from Fernán Gómez's men for trying to defend her. The townspeople are outraged to learn of this attack but feel powerless to stand against their overlord. Meanwhile, Frondoso and Laurencia have fallen in love and received the consents of their parents to marry. But Fernán Gómez, returning to Fuente Ovejuna after Calatrava's defeat at Ciudad Real, interrupts their wedding. Using the crossbow incident as the cause, he orders Fron-

doso's arrest and imprisonment, then carries off Laurencia to his house.

In the wake of this catastrophe, the men of Fuente Ovejuna hurriedly call a secret meeting to discuss their wrongs at the *comendador mayor*'s hands and what they should do to retaliate. The sudden appearance of Laurencia, escaped from her captors (who had unsuccessfully tried to rape her), interrupts the meeting. Bloodied and disheveled from her ordeal, Laurencia berates the men of Fuente Ovejuna for failing to protect their women from Fernán Gómez and bitterly informs them that her husband, Frondoso, is to be hanged without trial. Shamed into action, the men vow to take up arms and kill their tyrannical overlord, while Laurencia rallies the women of Fuente Ovejuna to the same cause.

Fernán Gómez and his men prepare to hang Frondoso from the battlements when the townspeople storm Fernán Gómez's residence. The townspeople kill him, then pursue his followers, Flores and Ortuño. Later, a wounded Flores escapes to Córdoba, where King Fernando and Queen Isabel are staying, and informs them of Fernán Gómez's brutal murder by his vassals. King Fernando vows that the culprits will be punished and sends a magistrate to Fuente Ovejuna to investigate the crime.

On learning of the magistrate's arrival, the townspeople all agree to form a united front and maintain that the community of Fuente Ovejuna murdered the *comendador mayor*. During the interrogations and torture that follow, all the townspeople assert that Fuente Ovejuna killed Fernán Gómez. Thwarted by the citizens' continued defiance and the overall lack of evidence to convict anyone, the magistrate at last informs King Fernando that everyone in Fuente Ovejuna must be either pardoned or put to death. Several of the town's inhabitants, including Frondoso, Laurencia, Esteban, and Mengo, appear before the king to plead their case, revealing Fernán Gómez's many cruelties and injustices towards them. King Fernando ultimately decides to pardon the rebels, since they have sworn to be loyal to his cause, but informs them that their crime was serious nonetheless and a new *comendador mayor* must be appointed. The citizens of Fuente Ovejuna thank the king for his mercy and submit to his authority.

Honor among peasants. Since the fifth century and the advent of the Visigoths, honor—the respect and esteem accorded to one who was virtuous, worthy, or of noble standing—had been an important concept in Spain, all the more so because honor could easily be lost or compromised. A man could lose others' respect and esteem by being called a liar, by having his face struck, by having his beard pulled, or by being humiliated by the sexual misconduct of his wife or daughter. According to medieval law, such a man was socially dead until his honor was restored; he could seek redress legally (in the courts) or he could kill those who had offended his honor. Indeed, the law usually recognized a Spaniard's right to avenge a dishonor done to a family member, even to the point of condoning a cuckolded husband's murder of an unfaithful wife and her lover. Furthermore, public dishonor required public vengeance, while private dishonor required that vengeance, if executed, be concealed. Throughout the Middle Ages in Spain,

as in the rest of Europe, honor was considered a prerogative of the nobility, while commoners were believed to be without honor. By the late sixteenth century, however, many Spanish intellectuals had come to realize that all men, regardless of birth or station, deserved respect. Honor became increasingly associated with nobility of spirit rather than noble birth.

This shift in the meaning of honor fuels much of the hostility between Fernán Gómez and the townspeople in *Fuente Ovejuna*. From the beginning of the play, Fernán Gómez reveals his preoccupation with the outward marks of deference and respect he feels are due him, rebuking the Master of Calatrava for keeping him waiting during a visit: "My love and background led / Me to expect much more respect / From you, Master of Calatrava, / Towards your most obedient servant and / Commander" (*Fuente Ovejuna*, p. 4). The *comendador mayor* behaves still more harshly towards those he considers his inferiors, such as Frondoso, who aims his crossbow at Fernán Gómez for accosting the peasant maid Laurencia: "I shall take / Revenge on him for this, both for / The insult and the interruption. / I should have tackled him. That I / Did not adds further to my sense of shame!" (*Fuente Ovejuna*, p. 26). Fernán Gómez inextricably associates honor with noble birth and high social standing; it never occurs to him that his seductions of the local women compromise their honor or that of their families or that his own honor is besmirched by his lustful pursuits.

The townspeople, however, bring that point home to Fernán Gómez at a town council meeting. Hearing the *comendador mayor* mention his pursuit of Laurencia, Esteban, the girl's father, rebukes him for speaking so freely and reminds him that "there are people of great worth / In Fuente Ovejuna" (*Fuente Ovejuna*, p. 31). When Fernán Gómez mocks Esteban as "an eloquent peasant," an alderman warns him: "To speak of us like that / Is to deny us honour" (*Fuente Ovejuna*, p. 31). The *comendador mayor* responds even more scornfully, "You believe / You have honour? You'll be claiming next / You are knights of Calatrava!" (*Fuente Ovejuna*, p. 31). The meeting ultimately dissolves in mutual recriminations, Fernán Gómez fuming over the insolence of his vassals, the townspeople expressing similar outrage over his arrogance and tyranny. The tensions resulting from conflicting and incompatible concepts of honor set the stage for the violent reckoning between Fernán Gómez and the townspeople in the play's final act.

Significantly, despite his sympathetic depiction of the Fuente Ovejunans, Lope does not present their rebellion as the best or even the correct solution to their woes. Indeed, in avenging their honor, the townspeople display a degree of mob fury that is every bit as savage and brutal as Fernán Gómez's attacks on them. Literary scholar Robin Carter contends that

> The pattern we are meant to see is one of disorder and tyranny among the villagers bringing the Comendador's evil home to roost, their mass behaviour being a reflection of, as well as the result of, the Comendador's behaviour. . . . The motif of "Fuenteovejuna lo hizo"[Fuenteovejuna did it] in the torture scene emphasizes the fact that the villagers' act was a crime, that all of them did take part, and that the whole village is indeed guilty.
>
> (Carter in Fox, p. 138)

While King Fernando may tacitly acknowledge the abuses committed against the townspeople's honor and persons, he also makes it clear that they are pardoned only because their individual guilt cannot be proved and because they are willing to swear their loyalty to him. The former rebels receive forgiveness but not validation.

Sources and literary context. Lope drew from several historical sources to provide the context of his play, chiefly Francisco de Rades y Andrada's *Chrónica de las tres Ordenes y Cavallerias de Santiago, Calatrava y Alcántara* (1572), Sebastian de Covarrubias Horozco's *Emblemas morales* (1610), and *Tesoro de la lengua castellana* (1611). All three supplied accounts of the incident at Fuente Ovejuna, though Lope appears to have leaned most heavily on Rades's *Chrónica* for his information. But while historical sources mention the real-life figures of Fernán Gómez, the Master of Calatrava, King Fernando, and Queen Isabel, the townspeople in Lope's play—virtuous Laurencia, brave Frondoso, comic Mengo—appear to be his own invention. Indeed, portraying the townspeople as distinct individuals allowed Lope to emphasize Fuente Ovejuna as a community.

Overall, Lope's salient traits as a dramatist include his consistent use of the three-act play (over the four- and five-act form), his preference for verse over prose, his avoidance of tragic endings in favor of tragicomic ones, and his integration of songs, stories, and customs gleaned from common people into his works. Such qualities made Lope a hugely popular playwright, much admired and imitated. One dramatic innovation initiated by Lope was "putting royalty on the stage," making such historical figures as

Pedro the Cruel, King Fernando, and Queen Isabel as flesh-and-blood characters in his plays (Hayes, p. 68). But Lope was equally adept at depicting the countless types of common people who made up the masses.

Many of Lope's plays belong to the tradition of the *comedia de la capa y espada* (cloak-and-dagger plays): light comedies featuring characters from the lower nobility, engaged in plots focused on love and jealousy. By contrast, *Fuente Ovejuna* is most accurately described as a "historical" play, despite the romantic subplot between Frondoso and Laurencia, and Fernán Gómez's jealous, lustful pursuit of Laurencia. *Fuente Ovejuna* can also be termed a *comedia villanesca*, a play featuring peasant characters that dramatizes the relationship between peasants and the nobility, or even in some cases, between peasants and royalty.

Events in History at the Time the Play Was Written

Spain in decline. Towards the end of the sixteenth century, Spain coped with serious challenges to its economic as well as to its military and political power. Silver bullion, mined from its American colonies, was spent in several ways. Spain used it to help pay for its troops in the Netherlands and Italy, to help support Spanish forces in Germany (the forces of Charles I of Spain, also known as Charles V, the Holy Roman Emperor), and to help maintain conspicuous consumption among wealthy Spaniards at home. The vast quantity of imported wealth contributed to inflation in Spain itself, an economic phenomenon occurring elsewhere in Europe too. Taxes rose, as did the price of Spanish goods until they were too expensive to compete in international markets. Spanish industry gradually declined and even agriculture suffered, after an increasing number of country people relocated to the cities. Plague and emigration reduced the overall population of Spain, which decreased from 8 million in the early sixteenth century to 7 million by the mid-seventeenth century (Solsten and Meditz, p. 20).

Spain also suffered from a decline in the quality of its rulers. On his deathbed, Philip II—who reigned from 1556-98—lamented, "God, who has given me so many kingdoms, has not granted me a son fit to govern them" (Philip II in Grunfeld, p. 116). As Philip II grimly prophesied, neither Philip III (reigned 1598-1621) nor Philip IV (reigned 1621-65) provided Spain with a clear direction: "The vigor and zeal of the Catholic [M]on-archs, inherited by Charles V and Philip II, had played itself out and disintegrated into apathy and incompetence" (McKendrick, p. 125). Philip III and Philip IV demonstrated their ineffective leadership by handing over the reins of government to their favorites, the duke of Lerma and the count-duke of Olivares, respectively. The final monarch of the Spanish Habsburg dynasty, Charles II (reigned 1665-1700) was even worse than his two predecessors: sickly, incompetent, and, as a result of generations of inbreeding, half-mad.

Ironically, Spain's political and economic eclipse formed a dramatic contrast to its successes in the arts during that same period. The seventeenth century witnessed the appearance of such masterpieces as Miguel de Cervantes's **Don Quixote** (1605, 1615; also in *WLAIT 5: Spanish and Portuguese Literatures and Their Times*) and Lope de Vega's *Fuente Ovejuna* (1612-14). Indeed, one may contend that Lope—whose career spanned the reigns of Philip III and Philip IV—intended *Fuente Ovejuna* to impart a lesson for kings and ministers. Unlike the ineffectual Philip III, Fernando and Isabel, as presented in Lope's play, are model rulers, attempting to bring peace, justice, and order to their war-torn realm. They are depicted as closely involved in the lives of their subjects, thus instilling great loyalty.

Reception and impact. Throughout his long career, Lope de Vega reigned supreme as Spain's leading—and most prolific—popular dramatist. Lope boasted that he had written 1,500 plays, as well as several novels, stories, and verse epics. Miguel de Cervantes, author of *Don Quixote*, called Lope "one of nature's marvels" and "the reigning monarch of the stage" (Cervantes in Gerstinger, p. 103). In the theatre world, he was often referred to as "El Fénix de España" (The Phoenix of Spain). His works inspired numerous admirers, imitators, and younger dramatists cast in the same mold, including Tirso de Molina and Pedro Calderón de la Barca (see **The Trickster of Seville and the Stone Guest** and **Life Is a Dream,** also in *WLAIT 5: Spanish and Portuguese Literatures and Their Times*). During his lifetime, a customary expression in Spain to describe something good and praiseworthy was "Es de Lope" (It's by Lope).

Despite the great fame Lope enjoyed in his lifetime and in his own nation, his work did not become widely known outside Spain until the twentieth century. Even today only a handful of his plays are performed; *Fuente Ovejuna,* however, is one of those plays, becoming a particular favorite in such countries as France, Germany,

and Russia. Modern productions of *Fuente Ovejuna* have often emphasized the timelessness of the story by altering the play's staging or outcome. For example, some productions in the former Soviet Union presented the peasant uprising as the triumphant overthrow of tyranny, downplaying the final scenes in which the rebels submit to King Fernando's authority. In the 1930s,

---

LOPE'S PRESCRIPTION FOR SUCCESS

In 1609 Lope challenged his detractors, who preferred Aristotelian to popular drama, by presenting a verse treatise *Arte nuevo de hacer comedias* (The New Art of Play Writing) before a Madrid literary society. In this treatise, he set down his formula for popular success, arguing that, while he had known the classic rules of drama since he was ten years old, he chose to ignore them because "the man who attempts to write according to rules known to so few people will fail financially. . . . I keep my eye on the box office, and because the common man pays the piper, I pipe the tune he likes" (Lope de Vega in Hayes, p. 78). Lope's formula to please the "common man" included choosing the subject carefully; mixing the comic and tragic; keeping a tight unity of action, disregarding strict replication of time and place if they presented dramatic obstacles; and dividing the play into three acts, reserving the suspense until the middle of the last one to maintain the audience's interest. It was a formula he usually exploited throughout his career, whether writing in a serious or a lighter vein. The formula affected not only Lope's works, but those of a number of Spanish dramatists in the country as well. In fact, Lope has been hailed as the founder of Spain's national theater.

> He establishes the definitive form of the play: three acts in polymetric verse. He is inspired mainly by the great themes of Spanish history, by folk poetry, and by national legends, which he presents without regard for Aristotelian unities. He creates the comic sidekick, the *gracioso*, who becomes essential in almost all plays of the time.
>
> (Bleiberg, Ihrie, and Pérez, p. 1672)

---

the Spanish dramatist Federico García Lorca directed a production with his student company (*La Barraca*), which set the play in the twentieth rather than the fifteenth century, thus highlighting its revolutionary character.

Fuente Ovejuna has also been performed in the United States. In 1970, the Theatre Arts Division of Columbia University made its debut with a creditable performance of *Fuente Ovejuna*. George Gent, reviewing the production for the *New York Times*, wrote that "its traditional form and contemporary ambiance are precisely right for the young players" (Gent in Gerstinger, p. 116). Dr. Bernard Beckerman, director of the Theatre Arts Division's production, explained the company's unusual choice of vehicle: "'Fuente Ovejuna' is a classic play with contemporary relevance in that it was one of the first to depict a community of workers and peasants as capable of courage and resolution" (Beckerman in Gerstinger, p. 116).

—Pamela S. Loy

For More Information

Anibal, Claude E. "The Historical Elements of Lope de Vega's *Fuente Ovejuna.*" In *PMLA* (September 1934): 657-718.

Bleiberg, Germán, Marueen Ihrie, and Janet Pérez. *Dictionary of the Literature of the Iberian Peninsula.* Vol. 2. Westport, Conn.: Greenwood Press, 1993.

Defourneaux, Marcelin. *Daily Life in Spain in the Golden Age.* Trans. Newton Branch. London: George Allen and Unwin, 1970.

Fernández-Armesto, Felipe. *Ferdinand and Isabella.* London: Weidenfeld and Nicolson, 1975.

Fox, Dian. *Refiguring the Hero: From Peasant to Noble in Lope de Vega and Calderon.* University Park: Pennsylvania State University Press, 1991.

Gerstinger, Heinz. *Lope de Vega and Spanish Drama.* Trans. Samuel R. Rosenbaum. New York: Frederick Ungar, 1974.

Grunfeld, Frederic V. *The Kings of Spain.* Chicago: Stonehenge Press, 1982.

Hayes, Francis C. *Lope de Vega.* New York: Twayne, 1967.

Kamen, Henry. *Spain 1469-1714: A Society of Conflict.* London: Longman, 1991.

McKendrick, Melveena. *The Horizon Concise History of Spain.* New York: American Heritage, 1972.

Ruiz, Teofilo F. *Spanish Society 1400-1600.* Harlow, England: Pearson Education, 2001.

Solsten, Eric, and Sandra W. Meditz, eds. *Spain: A Country Study.* Washington, D.C.: Federal Research Division, 1990.

Vega Carpio, Lope Félix de. *Fuente Ovejuna.* In *Three Major Plays.* Trans. Gwynne Edwards. Oxford: Oxford University Press, 1999.

The House of Bernarda Alba

by
Federico García Lorca

Federico García Lorca (1898-1936) was born in the Andalusian town of Fuente Vaqueros, but spent much of his youth in the nearby city of Granada. Many years later, he would be executed by a Falangist firing squad in that city during the early weeks of the Spanish Civil War. Lorca studied law at the University of Granada, but in 1919 he moved to Madrid to pursue his passion for art and literature. Although in the early 1920s he published both drama and poetry, it was not until he linked Spanish folklore with surrealist imagery in his collection of poems *Gypsy Ballads* (1928) that he earned national recognition. His theater during the 1920s alternated between comedy and avant-garde experimentation in works such as *The Shoemaker's Prodigious Wife* (1926) and *Once Five Years Pass* (written in 1929 and 1930). In the 1930s, however, Lorca began to focus more intensely on tragedy and wrote his three most important dramatic works: *Blood Wedding* (1933), *Yerma* (1934), and *The House of Bernarda Alba* (1936). The three plays as a whole, but *Bernarda Alba* in particular, portray the tragedy of individual oppression in rural Spain with an extraordinary blend of lyrical passion and social detail, both hallmarks of Lorca's drama.

Events in History at the Time of the Play

The concept of "two Spains" resurfaces. In 1898, the year of Lorca's birth, the United States and Spain went to war. At first glance, this brief conflict between the two countries would appear

THE LITERARY WORK

A play set in rural Spain during the early twentieth century; written in Spanish (as *La casa de Bernarda Alba*) in 1936; first performed in 1945; published in English in 1947.

SYNOPSIS

A tyrannical mother compels her five daughters to live confined within their house during the period of mourning for their deceased father. Repressed passions produce rebellion and tragedy in the household, which in the end remains bound to the firm authority of Bernarda Alba.

to offer only a minor rupture within the flow of Spanish history. After all, the war lasted only a few months and the death toll was small on both sides. Yet the symbolic drama of Spain's defeat weighed heavily upon the national community. Although many factors came to a head in 1898 to bring about the Spanish loss—for example, Cuba's desire for independence from Spain, the United States government's growing confidence in its imperial power, economic and political turmoil in Spain—the moment became a national disgrace that shook Spanish pride to its very core. No longer able to sustain even the appearance of a world power, Spain seemed bereft of historical will. For much of the nineteenth century, it had drifted in and out of political chaos. Liberal and conservative factionalism formed the center of

Federico García Lorca

his office in January of 1930, Spanish politics again plunged into chaos, with no national consensus or respected political leader to inspire hope that the nation could be unified. Nonetheless, the proponents of democracy had won their long fight for change, even if their victory seemed perilously fragile. In April of 1931, when national elections were held for the first time in several decades, the second Spanish Republic was born.

Yet once again, matters took a turn for the worse. With wide swings in the outcome of national elections in 1931, 1933, and 1936 between right- and left-wing political parties, the Republic proved unable to provide economic stability or national unity. Individual liberties that seemed guaranteed by the basic premise of a democratic republic fell victim to the powerful agendas of political factionalism. Liberal dominance in the elections of 1931 and 1936, with a conservative victory in 1933, stood all hope of continuity on its head. As each new government proposed radical policy changes to appease their diverse constituencies, the country grew increasingly polarized. The old concept of "two Spains," a nation sharply divided between traditionalists and progressives, with large political followings in each camp, not only intensified anxiety throughout Spain but loomed as an unresolvable dilemma. By 1936 conservative forces supporting the church, monarchy, and military stood firmly aligned against the trade unionists, anarchists, and social democrats. Peaceful reconciliation seemed distant and improbable. On July 18 of that year, General Francisco Franco Bahamonde led a military uprising against the Republican government. The civil war had begun.

Lorca and his times. Lorca came of age during these years of turmoil in Spain, and their influence on his personal, artistic, and political views is substantial. It would be inaccurate to claim for Lorca the role of political activist. Throughout his life, he refused to join a political party, despite intense pressure from his leftist friends, and he generally avoided election campaigns and endorsements of political candidates. Nonetheless, Lorca often attended rallies, offered broad support for progressive causes, and embraced the liberal policies of the Republican government elected in 1931. He became a prominent signatory on documents promulgated by the Communist Party in support of Spanish workers, and often spoke on the important role of art in bringing about social justice. In the later years of his life, Lorca even joined with other writers to honor the Communist poet Rafael Alberti, and

ongoing tensions between tradition-bound supporters of the Church, military, and monarchy on the one hand, and progressive forces advancing democracy, secularization, and working-class power on the other. With the stark defeat of their forces by the United States at the dawn of a new century, and with no agreement at home on what path the nation should follow in the future, the country seemed hopelessly trapped in divisiveness and defeatism.

Unfortunately for Spain, circumstances were not about to improve. King Alfonso XIII ruled under a constitutional monarchy from 1902 to 1923, but his government managed to lead the nation only deeper into turmoil. His inability to control the internal political conflicts within the central government in Madrid, persistent labor strife with the emergent labor unions, and prolonged fighting of the Spanish army in the Moroccan wars, gradually led to Alfonso's fall from influence and eventually from power. In 1923, with the support of the military and conservative factions within the government, General Miguel Primo de Rivera proclaimed himself head of state. His rule was to last seven years and proved in the end to be as ineffective as King Alfonso's. Although discontent among the liberal and professional classes in Spain undermined Primo de Rivera's government from the beginning, economic turmoil and the financial crisis of 1929 led to his downfall. When the general resigned he paid homage to the controversial Galician writer Ramón del Valle Inclán, a long-time proponent of Republican politics. In short, over the course of his adult life, and in particular during the Republican period of the 1930s, Lorca lent visible support to the liberal factions of the "two Spains." Above all, he drew upon his celebrity to endorse policies and concepts that clashed with the traditional, orthodox elements of Spanish culture set on preserving the ways of the past. In *The House of Bernarda Alba* this clash emerges with tragic consequences as the young Adela longs for individual freedom while Bernarda, her mother, enforces the behavioral codes of a conservative Spain linked to custom and convention.

Lorca's commitment to liberal politics in Spain remained firm throughout his life. Yet what inspired deeper and more personal passion in the writer transcended the local and peculiarly Spanish. The brutality of fighting in World War I had forever tainted the myths of heroism and the nobility of warfare, and like many writers of the time, Lorca decried what he perceived as inhuman destruction carried out in the name of nationalism. These antiwar sentiments continued to shape his view of violence later in life. Even as Spain spiraled toward civil conflict in 1935, and Lorca continued to embrace Republican causes, he refused to endorse violence to achieve nationalist goals fashioned by partisan politics. As he noted in an interview with the newspaper *El Sol* in 1935, "I am a brother to everyone, and I loathe the man who sacrifices himself for an abstract nationalist ideal" (Lorca in Stainton, p. 435).

Lorca thus came to define his commitment to human dignity and freedom in the broadest sense. His exposure to other cultures when he traveled to New York and South America in the late 1920s and early 1930s intensified his awareness of the often harsh obstacles to personal freedom faced by others outside his homeland. In New York especially, Lorca witnessed at close range both the anguish and pride of African Americans long repressed by white society. His collection of poems, **Poet in New York** (also in *WLAIT 5: Spanish and Portuguese Literatures and Their Times*), which vividly portrays African-American culture with surrealistic and symbolic power, underscores his commitment to social justice. His stay in New York proved also to be a liberating experience for him personally, above all because it helped to bolster his willingness to live more openly with his homosexual desire. When he returned to Spain in 1930, his concerns turned more inward,

to his own alienation in a culture that often seemed to deny him the possibility for personal fulfillment. In the plays that would follow, including *Bernarda Alba*, Lorca portrays, if at times obliquely, the repressive elements of Spanish society that made life disconcerting and even perilous for him as a homosexual and Republican sympathizer: a rigid family structure, class stratification, an honor code rife with hypocrisy, sexual oppression (most strikingly for women), and a moral and social order rooted in Catholic dogma and aristocratic tradition.

Early in his career, Lorca was often referred to as the poet of Andalusia or the poet of the gypsy spirit (he began to write his gypsy ballads in 1924 and published them in book form in 1928). As he matured and grew more secure in his writing through the 1920s, however, Lorca's interests broadened, and he became fully immersed in the emergent tenets of the European avant-garde.

THE "TWO SPAINS"

The idea of Spain divided into two nations—not geographically, but politically and culturally—began to emerge in the late eighteenth century. One Spain was liberal, progressive, and secular in cultural matters, with an increasing interest in liberal democratic principles. The other Spain, conservative, Catholic, and traditionalist, linked the uniqueness of Spanish culture to an imperial time when the church, military, and monarchy gave firm shape to the political and cultural concept of the nation. The conflict between the two Spains persisted throughout the nineteenth and early twentieth centuries, causing political turmoil and economic instability. The roots of the civil war in Spain from 1936 to 1939, won by the conservatives, thus are deeply entrenched in Spanish society and help to explain the violence and bitterness of the conflict that brought Francisco Franco to power.

Lorca, of course, did not stand alone among his contemporaries in his interest in exploring innovative and experimental forms of writing, particularly in poetry. Spanish authors such as Rafael Alberti, Jorge Guillén, Dámaso Alonso, Pedro Salinas, Gerardo Diego, and Vicente Aleixandre (winner of the Nobel Prize for literature in 1977) shared with Lorca a desire to experiment with poetry through the play of language. Most importantly, they focused on the creation of new metaphors as they sought to perfect poetic images that would enable language to detach itself from reference to the real world. Much of their poetry during the 1920s and early 1930s was inspired by the baroque Spanish poet Luis de Góngora (1561-1627), to whom Lorca and his fellow poets paid homage in 1927 on the tricentennial of his death (hence the name "Generation of 1927" that is often used to link these poets to a single aesthetic movement). Góngora's work opened to Lorca and his generation new ways in which difficult syntax, esoteric language, and chaotic structuring could lift poetry above the world and allow it to stand alone. Not only did Lorca and his friends embrace such a purpose, but they viewed it as essential for the development of new forms of writing.

Lorca also sought to incorporate innovative techniques into his theater. He developed a keen interest in the dreamlike imagery of surrealism and lauded the experimental drama of his time— from the grotesque *esperpentos* of Ramón del Valle Inclán in Spain (see **Bohemian Lights,** also in *WLAIT 5: Spanish and Portuguese Literatures and Their Times*) to the metadramatic inversions of fiction and reality of Luigi Pirandello in Italy. In works such as *Once Five Years Pass* (1931) and *The Audience* (left incomplete in manuscript form in 1931), Lorca experimented with the fragmentation of time and space and the distortion of traditional character to such an extreme that he knew even as he wrote these plays that the Spanish public was not prepared for them. He in fact viewed the two works, and later his unfinished *The Dream of Life* (1935), as unperformable.

Yet Lorca remained an independent thinker, and in important ways he stood apart from his avant-garde friends. What distinguished him above all from many poets of his cohort was not only that he had become an accomplished dramatist, but that he seemed unable to embrace fully elitist writing that sought to isolate itself from social engagement. In other words, while he was drawn to the aesthetic tenets of ultraism, surrealism, and cubism, they seemed to him insufficient for defining the role that literature could play in the larger scheme of life and community. With the exception of Rafael Alberti, whose strong allegiance to the Communist Party sharply influenced the radical commitment of his writing to party politics, Lorca showed an interest in linking societal and aesthetic issues that stood among the most fervent of the Spanish avant-garde. Lorca himself recognized, as he told

friends on several occasions, that even in his most experimental drama, he struck a psychological and social depth that revealed the recurrent obsessions of his life and writing: failed love, fear of death, repressed desire and sexuality, and social injustice. These are the very issues that surface in *Bernarda Alba,* and they ally it closely with Lorca's theater as a whole.

The social value that Lorca attached to theater was at times almost abstract in nature (for example, he believed theater capable of transforming the cultural spirit of Spain). At other times, however, Lorca argued that theater could serve as a concrete vehicle for the representation of inequality and social oppression. The depth of Lorca's commitment to the potency of theater moved to the fore in the 1930s in two important and somewhat diverse ways. First, he was impressed by the power of drama to ennoble the spirit and deepen the sensibility of humanity. In 1931, when the new Republican government set out to reduce the nation's high rate of illiteracy, Lorca not only vigorously supported government programs to educate Spanish youth about literature and art, but volunteered to participate as a music teacher.

As fate and government policy would have it, however, Lorca took on a much more ambitious project: the formation of a traveling theater company called La Barraca, which was to be funded by the government and directed by Lorca. The company's goal was to rescue Spanish theater from growing indifference among the public and to place it firmly at the center of the cultural consciousness of people across the nation. Lorca himself was motivated by his belief that the public performance of dramatic works not only brought a shared heritage into the cultural spotlight, but also helped to forge national identity through connections with the classical works of Spanish drama. Over the course of four years under Lorca's directorship (1931-34), La Barraca barnstormed the nation and offered almost 200 free performances of classical Spanish plays. It was for Lorca one of the most satisfying periods of his life, for it allowed him to indulge his passion for directing and performing while nurturing his growing sense of social commitment to the Spanish masses.

The second manifestation of Lorca's interest in the social reach of theater grows directly from his writing rather than his directing. During the years of his association with La Barraca, Lorca began to envision more concretely the ways in which he might represent social despair through tragedy. Although his insistence on the lyrical and poetic essence of drama precluded the possibility that his theater would offer a narrow reflection of everyday life, he clearly viewed drama as a way of challenging deeply entrenched injustices of Spanish society. He asserted on many occasions during the 1930s his belief that writers should embrace social causes precisely because they have a unique relationship with the public. As he observed in an interview in 1935, the writer "must set aside his bouquet of white lilies and sink to his waist in the mud" (Lorca in Stainton, p. 435). In other words, writers must expose the ills of culture through their art and inspire the public to seek change. Importantly, this change must occur not only through the implied call to action when injustice diminishes social well being, but through a more transcendent heightening of public tolerance for difference and individual freedom. It is in fact precisely this concern with individual freedom and desire, frequently constrained by societal tradition and dogma in Spain, that lies at the heart of Lorca's tragic dramas and that gives compelling resonance to *The House of Bernarda Alba*.

The Play in Focus

Plot summary. Lorca viewed *The House of Bernarda Alba* as the least lyrical and most realistic of his plays. The work is set in a rural Spanish village during the intense heat of summer, with all of the on-stage action located in the "house" of Bernarda Alba. The historical time of the play remains vague, but is set sometime during the early decades of the twentieth century. At the beginning of Act I, Bernarda and her five daughters (ranging in age from 20 to 39) have just returned home from the funeral of Bernarda's husband when Bernarda announces what will shape both the plot and eventual tragedy of the play:

> For the eight years of mourning, not a breath of air will get in this house from the street. We'll act as if we'd sealed up doors and windows with bricks. That's what happened in my father's house—and in my grandfather's house. Meantime, you can all start embroidering your hope-chest linens.
>
> (García Lorca, *The House of Bernarda Alba*, p. 164)

Bernarda's insistence on the closure of the house and strict adherence to the traditions of mourning create anger and rebellion among the daughters, but there is little they can do to re-

sist. Bernarda rules the house with tyrannical authority and imposes her rigid code of conduct with severity. Among the wealthiest people in town, Bernarda closely ties the proper behavior of her daughters during the period of mourning to their elevated standing in the social and economic hierarchy. The daughters are thus forced to live as if in a convent, deprived of normal social contact and the freedom to pursue their passions. To make matters worse, they share the house with Bernarda's demented mother, María Josefa, who is generally locked in her room but who on occasion moves about the house proclaiming her desire "to get married to a beautiful manly man from the shore of the sea" (*House*, p. 175). María Josefa appears in the play only a few times, but her presence in the house cruelly underscores the daughters' repressed sexuality in

the present and offers a haunting glimpse of what awaits them in the future.

A "manly man" does in fact live in the local village, a young bachelor named Pepe who has been given the hand of Bernarda's unattractive eldest daughter, Angustias. While the marriage arrangement conforms with village tradition and will provide Pepe with Angustias's inherited wealth, his passion has led him to the youngest of the daughters, the 20-year-old Adela. Not only does the spirited Adela seek to break from her cloistered existence, she also is eager to pursue her desire for Pepe, despite her sister's engagement to him. As we learn later in the play, Adela sneaks from the house at night to meet the young man and carries on a secret affair with him even as plans for Angustias's wedding move ahead.

Bernarda and her family continue to observe the rituals of mourning, the silence and oppression of their lives feeding the growing tensions among them. Isolated within the thick walls of the house, the daughters dutifully embroider sheets for Angustias's trousseau. They talk among themselves about their older sister and her handsome young fiancé, and exchange local gossip from the village that manages to penetrate the imposed silence of the household. The women

HONOR—THE PERENNIAL CONCERN

The concept of honor in Spain has long shaped social behavior. While not reducible to a simple and fixed set of rules, honor can be viewed within two broad categories: as human virtue and dignity held in the eyes of God (intrinsic honor); as reputation and standing perceived through the eyes of society (extrinsic honor). In classical Spanish theater, these dual concepts of honor often helped to determine the plot and prescribe the outcome of a play. The restoration of honor was essential to the resolution of conflict and to the eventual imposition of social justice. In *The House of Bernarda Alba*, Lorca is concerned only with the powerful force of extrinsic honor in the small towns of rural Spain. Honor was most often linked in these towns to public appearance, which in turn frequently depended upon the proper conduct of women to sustain family dignity. The social code of honor is closely tied to sexual morality, most often to public knowledge and appearance rather than to private thoughts or actions. It is precisely the hypocrisy of honor based on reputation rather than virtue that Lorca condemns, for in his view this hypocrisy stifles individual freedom and inevitably turns human desire into tragedy.

yearn for a return to the social gatherings of their town and bemoan their state as women not permitted to make their own decisions. "To be born a woman is the worst possible punishment," exclaims Amelia, a third daughter, as she sews— no freedom to enter and leave as they wish, no opportunity to escape their tedious confinement in the heavy summer heat (*House*, p. 185). Bernarda reigns over the household and observes every detail of her daughters' lives. Above all, she seeks to maintain the honor of her house, an honor rooted in the public perception of her daughters' behavior and sustained by Bernarda's insistence on the appearance of absolute order.

Because little happens to disrupt the routine of daily life in the house, small tensions grow large among the sisters, and Bernarda's presence becomes ever more tyrannical. When Angustias's picture of Pepe seems to have been stolen, she furiously accuses her sisters (Martirio, a fourth daughter, turns out to be the culprit). Yet Bernarda shows less concern for the anguish of Angustias and the reasons for the theft than for the potential gossip that might arise among the neighbors if they were to learn of the incident. She contemptuously berates her children and scorns their behavior: "What scandal is this in my house in the heat's heavy silence? The neighbors must have their ears glued to the walls" (*House*, p. 188). As the second act comes to a close and the conflict of the play is firmly established between desire and repression, events from outside the house heighten the emotional rawness of the daughters. News has spread among the villagers that a poor young girl has killed her baby born out of wedlock and is about to be beaten by her neighbors. When the daughters learn of the incident, their reactions range from horror to sympathy. For her part, Bernarda harbors no doubt about the severity of the offense and the requisite punishment. She rails against indecency, warning her daughters of the consequences of immorality. As Adela listens in horror, Bernarda cries out for the girl's death: "Let whoever loses her decency pay for it. . . . Kill her! Kill her!" (*House*, p. 195).

In the final act of the play, the repressed passion of the sisters' confinement breaks free with a destructive fury that even Bernarda can barely control. Adela's liaisons with Pepe are finally discovered, but the young woman no longer cares. She vows to be Pepe's mistress even if he marries Angustias, and she challenges her sisters and her mother to prevent her from pursuing her desire. When Bernarda takes after Pepe with a shotgun, Martirio runs to tell Adela that Pepe has been killed, though she knows that Pepe has managed to escape. In despair, Adela enters her room and hangs herself. The tension of the house is suddenly deflated; pity, it appears, will replace hatred and hostility. When Bernarda discovers the body of her daughter, she briefly loses her composure and sobs as a bereaved mother. However, social propriety quickly replaces bereavement, and Bernarda reasserts her authority over the order of the house. She will not allow Adela's actions to stain the family honor and demands that the illusion of respectability conceal the reality of Adela's transgressions.

Scene from a 1986 production of *House of Bernarda Alba* at London's Lyric Theatre.

Cut her down! My daughter died a virgin. Take her to another room and dress her as though she were a virgin. No one will say anything about this! She died a virgin. . . . We'll drown ourselves in a sea of mourning. She, the youngest daughter of Bernarda Alba, died a virgin.

(*House*, p. 211)

Bernarda's vigilance over her house will continue unabated, as the end of the play signals a return to the beginning. Once again the space of Bernarda's house will enclose the honor and respectability of her family; once again Bernarda will impose her harsh authority. Her final words in the play, which are identical to those uttered at the beginning, close tightly the circle of oppression: "Silence, silence, I said. Silence" (*House*, p. 211). In this tragedy of tradition and honor, order is maintained and silence once again returns to the house. However, it is a silence born not of sympathy but of tyranny, and thus offers despair rather than comfort to those condemned to endure it.

The social culture of Bernarda Alba. During the time when he was writing *The House of Bernarda Alba* in the spring and summer of 1936, Lorca told friends that the only topics he wished to explore in his theater were social and sexual ones. To be sure, his own homosexuality by now had become widely known, but hardly accepted. Spanish culture did not encourage feelings of se-

curity among homosexuals, and by no means was Lorca able to live free of derision. In 1935 he affirmed the need for "a true revolution, a new morality, a morality of unfettered liberty," and he viewed the theater as a compelling space for the enactment of this revolution (Lorca in Gilmour, p. 152). Hence it seems certain that the sexual oppression and fear that Lorca experienced throughout his life plays at least some role in the development of his characters in *Bernarda Alba*, especially the young Adela. But it also is clear that when the play is placed in the larger context of social chaos, political tensions, and the strict traditions of a Catholic and conservative Spain—all critical factors that shape Lorca's formation as a writer—*Bernarda Alba* stands as a microcosm of Spanish society about to erupt into civil war.

Spanish Republicanism of the 1930s firmly embraced principles ensuring that individual freedom superseded institutional coercion. Although idealistic and perhaps even utopian, the concept of individual freedom—not only freedom to develop as an individual, but freedom from the imposition of rigid moral codes and traditions—gained Lorca's enthusiastic support. In 1931, for example, he attended the legislative debate in Parliament on the role of religion in Spanish life, a debate that produced some of the early and most controversial Republican laws separating state and church. Five years later, with the country still harshly divided over this separation, the character of Bernarda comes to embody for Lorca the conservatives' tight hold on the status quo: narrow-minded and reactionary Catholic morality, as well as the moneyed and politically connected class of prewar Spain intent on preserving their traditional standing and power. Lorca sensed, and rightfully so, that the ideological and social beliefs of the ruling class (which Bernarda Alba embodies explicitly through her economic position in the town, and implicitly through the rule over her own house) were aimed at maintaining stability at the cost of freedom. While Bernarda herself is an extreme example of conservative Spain, her central role in the work brings fully into view the repressive social forces that Lorca so ardently opposed.

In each of the three plays of his trilogy on rural life in Andalusia, Lorca explores the overflow of passion checked by unyielding social restrictions. Codes of honor, of morality, and of class and gender interactions emerge as decisive obstacles to personal desire and eventually doom characters to a tragic destiny. While destiny can be a slippery term, often viewed as the consequence of known and unknown forces against which individuals strain to fulfill desire, in *Bernarda Alba* Lorca offers definable social and material causes for the tragic outcome of his work. Adela recognizes, for example, that her passion is frustrated by the imposed social time of mourning. Bernarda locks her daughters into a temporal chasm from which escape seems impossible. When this time is folded into the confined space of the house, the daughters' destiny is literally sealed. Hence the "house of Bernarda Alba" does not stand outside of social structures as a space where laws and moral codes diverge from those of society at large. To the contrary, Bernarda's house merely objectifies Spanish society and foretells the impending and inevitable tragedy of Spain as a nation. For Lorca, the tragedy of *Bernarda Alba*, as well as the larger tragedy of Spain, lies squarely in its excessive dependence on the wrong-minded moral authority of the church, on social codes that limit individual freedom, and on a political system that bolsters tyranny to forestall progress. As the dictator of her home, Bernarda imposes moral law on her family and embraces the codes that restrict society as a whole. Those who transgress (a young girl who is a complete stranger or Bernarda's own daughter) must be punished so that order will be maintained and tradition upheld.

The trap of tragedy is thus fully set in *Bernarda Alba* when those who seek freedom clash with social circumstance. The young Adela, who more than any of the daughters pursues her desire and passion in conflict with social conformity, emerges as the most revolutionary character of Lorca's theater. Her willingness to defy her mother (and thus to defy all that Bernarda represents in the context of Republican Spain), and her urgency to pursue a destiny that she forges for herself, hints at Lorca's own journey through the minefield of social rigidity. Yet it is clear that Adela's revolutionary fervor is bound to fail when pitted against her powerful mother. Adela thus becomes one of Lorca's most tragic characters—the only one, in fact, who takes her own life. She hangs herself not just because she believes Pepe to be dead, but because she perceives no exit from the daunting pressure of prescribed conduct. The imposed time of mourning, the enclosed space of her house, and the tyranny of her mother all coalesce to deny Adela the opportunity for either the planned or spontaneous expression of her desire and thus of her freedom.

Of course, if the tragedy of *Bernarda Alba* derived only from the frustrated love affair of a young woman with her sister's fiancé, the play would be melodrama rather than tragedy. Much to his credit, Lorca seemed fully to know the difference. Hence he grounds Adela's personal struggle in a larger struggle between social prescription and individual freedom within the context of a Spain about to come apart at the seams for the very same reasons. At the root of Lorca's view of tragedy lies tyranny against the individual, and at the core of tyranny in *Bernarda Alba* lies the oppression of Spanish society.

Sources and literary context. The main characters of *Bernarda Alba* grow only partly from Lorca's prodigious imagination. He based the figure of Bernarda on a woman named Frasquita Alba, who lived with her five daughters and son near Lorca's cousins in the town of Asquerosa in Southern Spain. Lorca had not known the Alba family well, but during his time in Asquerosa (where he lived for a time with his family) he was able to observe many aspects of small-town life. He drew upon these observations of people and customs for the names and mannerisms of the Alba family depicted in his play. Lorca insisted to friends that Frasquita Alba ruled harshly over her household and that she had forced her children to endure a lengthy period of mourning. In reality, her death in 1924 preceded her husband's, she had a son in addition to her five daughters, and by all accounts she was not the tyrant that Lorca depicted in his play. Lorca's mother had urged him to change the name of Alba, for she feared it would embarrass people in the village, but Lorca refused.

Bernarda Alba has generally been viewed as the third work of Lorca's trilogy on the tragedy of life in rural Andalusia. He had proclaimed on a number of occasions in the early 1930s that dramatists should explore the tragic elements of drama, and his trilogy illustrates his own views on how tragedy can be used to explore social injustice. *Blood Wedding* (1933), first of the three works, is based loosely on a newspaper article that Lorca had read many years before about a wedding in the southern town of Almería. The play portrays the fatal conflict between social conduct and desire when, rather than remain with her husband, a bride flees with her lover immediately after the wedding. *Yerma*, second work of the trilogy, once again explores the tension between desire and social repression when Yerma, a lonely housewife trapped in a loveless marriage, is unable to conceive a child with her husband. Yerma eventually strangles her husband, thus forever denying herself the opportunity to bear children.

Lorca had announced to friends as early as 1933 that he had formulated a mental outline of the third work of the trilogy, which was to be called *The Destruction of Sodom* (a work he sometimes also referred to as *The Daughters of Lot*). However, it is clear that Lorca never completed such a play, and no manuscript of it has been found. It seems most likely, especially in retrospect, that he decided to write *Bernarda Alba* as the third play. The thematic similarity with the two previous works, the same rural environment, and the female protagonists of the plays all point to their logical grouping as a trilogy.

Reviews. Lorca had planned to premier *The House of Bernarda Alba* in the fall of 1936 in Madrid, with famed Spanish actress Margarita Xirgu playing the role of Bernarda. The outbreak of civil war in Spain and Lorca's execution shortly thereafter forced postponement of the performance. Not until 1945, in Buenos Aires, Argentina, did the play finally reach the stage. As Lorca had hoped, Margarita Xirgu played the title character. Argentine reviews of the play were favorable, linking it to classic Spanish dramas by Lope de Vega and Calderón de la Barca (see **Fuente Ovejuna** and **Life Is a Dream,** also in *WLAIT 5: Spanish and Portuguese Literatures and*

Their Times). One critic noted that within the trilogy of Lorca's plays, "the tragic inspiration of García Lorca reaches its summit in this work" (Klein, p. 21). *The House of Bernarda Alba* appeared on American television in 1960 (starring Anne Revere as Bernarda and Suzanne Pleshette as Adela). This was four years before its premiere in Spain. The *New York Times* offered praise for the play, comparing its representation of grief and anguish with the later works of American playwright Tennessee Williams. *The House of Bernarda Alba* opened in Madrid in 1964 to positive reviews, despite the antipathy of the Francoist government toward Lorca and his role in Republican Spain. The theater critic of the conservative newspaper *ABC* praised the play, calling it "very probably one of the greatest works in Spanish dramatic literature of the twentieth century" (Klein, p. 22). Nearly all of the reviews in Spain related the play to classical Spanish theater of the seventeenth century and pointed to the powerful treatment of honor, resentment, and envy at the root of Lorca's tragic vision of life in a tradition-bound society.

—David K. Herzberger

For More Information

Carr, Raymond. *Modern Spain: 1875-1980.* Oxford: Oxford University Press, 1980.

Corbin, John. "Lorca's *Casa.*" *Modern Language Review* 95 (2000): 712-727.

Edwards, Gwynne. *Lorca: The Theatre Beneath the Sand.* London: Marion Boyars, 1980.

García Lorca, Federico. *The House of Bernarda Alba.* In *Three Tragedies.* Trans. James Graham-Luján and Richard L. O'Connell. New York: New Directions, 1955.

Gibson, Ian. *Federico García Lorca: A Life.* London: Faber, 1989.

Gilmour, John. "The Cross of Pain and Death: Religion in the Rural Tragedies." In *Essays in Honour of J.M. Aguirre.* Ed. Robert Havard. New York: St. Martin's Press, 1992.

Klein, Dennis. *Blood Wedding, Yerma, and The House of Bernarda Alba, García Lorca's Tragic Trilogy.* Boston: Twayne, 1991.

Newton, Candelas. *Understanding Federico García Lorca.* Columbia: University Press of South Carolina, 1995.

Morris, C. Brian. *García Lorca: La casa de Bernarda Alba.* London: Grant & Cutler, 1990.

Soufas, C. Christopher. *Audience and Authority in the Modernist Theater of Federico García Lorca.* Tuscaloosa: University Press of Alabama, 1996.

Stainton, Leslie. *Lorca: A Dream of Life.* New York: Farrar, Straus, Giroux, 1999.

The House of Ulloa

by

Emilia Pardo Bazán

Born in La Coruña in northwest Spain in 1852, the countess Emilia Pardo Bazán is one of the main exponents of the nineteenth-century Spanish narrative. Her father's political activism gave Pardo Bazán the opportunity to acquire firsthand knowledge of the Spanish political arena from a very young age. In 1869 José Pardo Bazán was elected representative to the parliament, and the family moved to Madrid in central Spain, spending winters in the capital and summers in their home province. The grown Emilia Pardo Bazán led an unconventional private life for her era. At 16, she married José Quiroga Pérez Pinal, a young aristocrat. The couple had three children, but the marriage proved unhappy and Pardo Bazán took several lovers. The publication of her letters to another renowned Spanish writer, Pérez Galdós (see **Fortunata and Jacinta**, also in *WLAIT 5: Spanish and Portuguese Literatures and Their Times*), reveals their passionate romance. Pardo Bazán meanwhile continued her professional pursuits. Over the years, she spent considerable time traveling outside Spain to other European countries, such as France, where she became acquainted with current philosophical and literary theories. Particularly impressed by Emile Zola's use of naturalism, she published *La cuestión palpitante* (The Burning Question), a book of essays that shared her views on the movement as applied to Spain.

Altogether, her writings would include 19 novels, numerous short stories, and nonfiction works on French and Russian literature. For two

<table>
<tr><td>

THE LITERARY WORK

A novel set in the countryside of Galicia (in northwest Spain) on the eve of the liberal revolution of 1868; published in Spain (as *Los pazos de Ulloa*) in 1886, in English (as *The Son of the Bondwoman*) in 1907.

SYNOPSIS

A young priest educated in the small city of Santiago is appointed to the decaying house of the marquis of Ulloa, where he struggles against the forces of nature and the moral decay, brutality, and ignorance of the countryside.

</td></tr>
</table>

years (1891-1893) Pardo Bazán published her own magazine, *El nuevo teatro crítico,* which included historical sketches as well as stories, essays, and literary criticism. Her contemporaries viewed her with some skepticism because of her gender, but most of them regarded Pardo Bazán with respect, as evidenced by the fact that she became the first woman admitted into the male-dominated intellectual scene of the time. Through her fiction, she portrayed slices of Spanish life. Pardo Bazán laced her best-known work, *House of Ulloa,* with rural characters and customs typical of rural Galicia, pitting what she portrays as an overpowering natural environment against civilized morality in late 1860s Spain.

Emilia Pardo Bazán

Events in History at the Time of the Novel

Carlist Wars and Isabel the II. For much of the nineteenth century, Spain suffered great instability. Continuous wars, *levantamientos* (upris-
ings), and revolutions created a scene of chaos
and uncertainty that diminished citizens' faith in
and respect for whatever government happened
to be in power. In 1833 the Bourbon king Fer-

dinand VII, whose reign was marked by tyranny and brutality, died without a male descendent. Before his death, in order to ensure that his only daughter would succeed him as monarch, the king abrogated the Ley Sálica, a 1715 Bourbon law forbidding female inheritance of the throne. When Ferdinand died, his daughter Isabel was duly proclaimed queen, but since she was still a minor, her mother, María Cristina, ruled as regent. Discord quickly erupted under her rule. Challenging the legitimacy of Isabel's succession was Ferdinand's brother, Don Carlos, who was also proclaimed reigning monarch and was supported by the conservative provincial upper classes. The dynastic quarrel resulted in three civil wars (1833-40, 1846-48, and 1872-76). All three were lost by the Carlists (supporters of Don Carlos). At stake was far more than just who controlled the throne. More than a dispute over succession, Carlism has been described as a counterrevolutionary movement bent on perpetuating the privileges of the Catholic Church and rural upper class.

Unsurprisingly, in view of the controversy over the ascension to the throne, not only María Cristina's regency but also Isabel's later reign was marked by instability and political decay. Isabel aggravated the situation by leading a scandalous personal life that exacerbated the instability and damaged her reputation as queen. In a 45-year period, Spain experienced 15 *levantamientos,* and six constitutions. The final reaction to all this chaos was a liberal revolution in 1868 that forced the queen into exile in France.

Pardo Bazán had very close contact with the Carlists. Her husband was a fervent militant of the party, and for a while she sympathized with its cause, until her ideology became more liberal—though it never did become democratic. In 1888, during a trip to Italy, she met Don Carlos himself in his palace in Venice, then wrote a chronicle about this meeting for the newspaper *El Imperial.* Carlism surfaces as well in her novel *The House of Ulloa,* when a main character, the marquis Don Pedro Moscoso, loses his bid for office as a Carlist candidate opposed to the liberals who are in power.

The "Gloriosa" and the First Republic. *The House of Ulloa* takes place on the eve of Isabel II's overthrow by the 1868 liberal revolution, an event known as La Gloriosa (The Glorious). Orchestrated by the Progressive Party, the revolution was, according to some historians, led by a couple of smooth-talking "politicians"—General Francisco Serrano and Don Juan Prim. Serrano

and Prim, argue these historians, invoked an extremely liberal discourse just to gain popular support; they had no plans to implement radical changes. In any case, there was a notable change in electoral rights: the new provisional government, headed by Serrano, established universal suffrage for males over 25 years old.

On June 6, 1869, Serrano and Prim took charge of the new government, which inherited a number of problems. An agricultural crisis, aggravated by a very dry season, blighted the economy, and unemployment soared, creating unrest among the lower classes. (The agricultural crisis stemmed from a liberal attempt to transfer ownership of the land to those who worked it; the attempt backfired, ending in the peasants having to pay rent to a different landlord.) At the same time, insurrections in the colonies of Puerto Rico and Cuba demanded the new government's immediate attention in the forms of manpower and funds. Also during the summer of 1869, Carlists from Catalonia, in northeast Spain, led a minor uprising. All of these problems, along with the government's inability to satisfy two popular requests—the abolition of military service and of the *puestas y consumos* (tax on commerce)—caused unrest among the lower classes.

In 1870 the Cortes (parliament) approved the candidacy of Amadeo of Savoy, from the Italian royal family, as the new king of Spain. The decision caused fresh uprisings by the Carlists, who naturally felt Carlos, not Amadeo, should have been chosen. Only two years into Amadeo's reign, the newly appointed king resigned, overwhelmed by the complicated political scene: Prim had been murdered the day of the new king's arrival; the Carlists continued to pose a threat; the Cuban conflict had not been resolved by the prior government; various liberal factions perpetuated the political friction in Spain, and the Republican party was demanding more power.

In 1873, upon Amadeo's resignation, the Cortes established the first Spanish republic (on February 12, 1873), but it did not last long, due in part to internal friction in the Republican Party. Within two years, the republic had four liberal presidents. Anarchic revolts became so common that in 1874, General Manuel Pavía proclaimed a dictatorship in order to restore the monarchy, making Isabel II's son, Alfonso XII, the king.

Many critics consider Pardo Bazán a liberal writer, especially in her defense of women's rights. Politically, however, she welcomed neither the revolution of 1868 nor the republic, since she did not believe that the lower classes,

The House of Ulloa as it stands today in Galicia, Spain. Originally constructed in the sixteenth century, the house was commissioned by María de Ulloa and Xoana de Hungría.

largely illiterate at the time, were ready for a social revolution. Actually her outlook did not differ from that of many liberals at the time; it was quite common for liberals of her day to be politically moderate.

In the nineteenth century, Galicia's population was mainly rural and, again, illiterate. By 1887 more than 85 percent of Galicians lived and worked in small agricultural holdings, usually limited to supplying the family's needs, and rented from landowners. Literacy statistics for the region and era are difficult to ascertain, but even 50 years later, in 1927, as much as 98 percent of the women and 65 percent of the men in Galicia could not read and write (Romero, p. 396). Modernization had not reached late nineteenth-century Galicia either; in fact the region's agricultural equipment had improved very little since the Middle Ages. Industrial and financial developments were likewise inadequate. Though in the eighteenth century Galicia's manufacturing production was similar to that of the rest of Spain, by the end of the nineteenth century, it had fallen drastically behind. This situation was due, in part, to the late arrival of the railroad to the region.

Those with some measure of power in Galicia at the time were *hidalgos* (noblemen), divided into three categories:

- Educated professionals such as doctors or attorneys
- Abbots and bishops (usually born into noble families)
- Heirs of houses and states with noble titles, who usually depended on an administrator or majordomo to manage the land and deal with the peasants that had rented it

All of them suffered the consequences of backwardness in Galicia's economy. Meanwhile, the small bourgeoisie in Galician cities were gaining some power in the countryside. Since they owned the little commerce there was in the region, they had the means by which to buy up available lands.

Caciquismo. The word *cacique*, which referred originally to an Indian chief, stems from an indigenous American language. In Spanish, the word retains its connotation of social and political power, referring to the system in which local representatives of the central political parties coerce citizens into voting for those parties. This system reached its peak in the nineteenth century, with an elaborate network of caciques at different levels. Despite the constitution, an oligarchy of individuals from different political parties controlled government. These politicians had representatives, or caciques, in every province, who controlled lesser, local caciques, usually men with money, social prestige, or power.

The caciques coerced citizens to give their vote to a certain political party in exchange for protection or other benefits. Those who did not co-operate might be jailed, blamed for a crime they did not commit, or impoverished by arbitrary taxes or fees imposed by local authorities. Driven by a desire for material acquisition and power and privileges, the lesser caciques followed no political ideology. It became common for them to switch parties, in deference to who was in office at the time and what benefits he had to offer.

Many nineteenth-century Spanish writers criticized the abuses exercised by caciques as proof of the inefficiency of a constitutional system that failed to implement the law. In a story called *El cacique,* Leopoldo Alas (Clarín), one of the most important Spanish realist writers and a contemporary of Pardo Bazán, ridicules the protagonist who has reached an important position in Madrid through the exercise of *caciquismo* in his own hometown (see Clarín's **La Regenta,** also in *WLAIT 5: Spanish and Portuguese Literatures and Their Times*). Another formidable personage of the day, journalist, sketch artist, writer, and politician Alfonso Rodríguez Castelao, launched a lifelong attack on the system, analyzing and criticizing it in writings and caricatures. Pardo Bazán herself dedicated considerable attention to the topic. In the article "La España de ayer y de hoy," (The Spain of Yesterday and Today) she describes it as follows: "It is a machine with many wheels, which catch us up in their cogs; the machine is set in motion in Madrid; the spring is in the minister's office and its action affects every single Spaniard who, although certainly unaware of the mechanism, finds himself forced to vote and act just as the omnipotent *cacique,* the name given to the little tyrants of local politics, bids him" (Pardo Bazán in Henn, *The Early Pardo Bazán,* p. 131). The dynamic described above is clearly portrayed in the second half of *The House of Ulloa.* When Moscoso, the marquis, runs for political office, the reader witnesses the actions of the two local *caciques*: Barbacana (the Carlist party) and Trampeta (the Liberal party). The abuses range from fraud, to ballot tampering, to murder when supporters of Barbacana kill Moscoso's head servant, Primitivo, for having betrayed them. In real life, this system of political corruption did not subside until the twentieth century, when it finally disappeared during the period leading up to the Civil War of 1936 and Franco's subsequent dictatorship.

Social status of women. In *The House of Ulloa,* Pedro Moscoso shows a strong preference for having a son rather than a daughter, showing the same prejudice that society in his day did towards women. In the nineteenth century all women were considered second-class citizens. They had no right to vote and their access to higher education was limited. By 1870 only 9 percent of the female population could read, in contrast to about 40 percent of the male population (Rodríguez, p. 39).

The social class into which women were born determined their role in society. Whether rural or urban, lower-class women generally enjoyed the most freedom, since they were expected to go out into the world to contribute to the family income. Their participation in the workforce implied a certain economic independence and mobility that wealthier women lacked. At the same time, these lower-class women were relegated to the worst jobs for only menial salaries. Those who failed to find work in the farmfields or the new urban industries usually resorted to becoming servants, a position that made them vulnerable to physical and/or sexual abuse by the house master.

Meanwhile, females in noble and rich bourgeoisie families had to settle for spending time on frivolous activities. Unless self-taught, like Pardo Bazán, the average woman acquired an education only in a few "ornamental" skills—a smattering of French, some piano playing, and needlework. Her main worries were reduced to fashion, gossip, or daily outings, while her main aspiration, in accord with societal precepts of the day, consisted of finding a husband.

Middle-class young women found themselves in the worst position. Their fortunes were not large enough to allow for the frivolous living appropriate to the upper class, yet society conditioned them to pretend they did not have to work, and they learned the lesson well, for many of them would rather starve or live in misery than do so. Their only objective was to attract a man from a higher class, who could ease their economic stress and improve the family fortune. Since marriages were arranged by the bride's parents, whose interests lay more in financial stability than in their daughter's happiness, it was common for both parties to have love affairs on the side. Sometimes parents failed to find their daughter a suitable husband, the most unenviable of all positions. Far from gaining freedom, such women had no choice but to remain under their father's or a brother's protection.

Much of the analysis and testimony concerning the status of women in this period was voiced by intellectuals. Emilia Pardo Bazán distinguished herself as one of the strongest feminist voices of her time, and certainly the one who commanded the most authority among her male peers. She knew of and sympathized with the ideas of earlier authors who had denounced the repression of women, not just in Spain but also in other countries. Two such authors were the eighteenth-century Spanish writers Benito Jerónimo Feijóo and Leandro Fernández de Moratín (see **Essay on Woman** and **The Maiden's Consent,** also in *WLAIT 5: Spanish and Portuguese Literatures and Their Times*). Another writer who impressed Pardo Bazán was the nineteenth-century feminist Concepción Arenal (an activist too, Arenal became one of the few females of the era to serve in an official capacity, as inspector of women's prisons in Galicia in 1868, the very year that *House of Ulloa* takes place). Pardo Bazán also read the British writer John Stuart Mill's *The Subjection of Women* (1869; La Esclavitud Femenina) and immediately had it translated into Spanish.

Pardo Bazán's own writings on the topic of feminism are numerous. Probably the most elaborate is a study entitled *The Women in Spain* published in 1889, in which she affirms that women enjoyed better conditions before the eighteenth century because they at least had more access to education. In fact, she believed that educating women would correct most of the errors connected to their social status. They would become more moral because by knowing the real world they would not be easily misled by men. And education could lead to economic independence, which would free women from so strong a need for husbands that they entered inappropriate marriages.

In her lifetime, Pardo Bazán had the fortune to witness advances in women's rights to education. The major one was brought about by the *Institución Libre de Enseñanza* (Free Institution of Teaching), a lay school found in 1876 by Francisco Giner de los Ríos and based on pedagogical techniques espoused by the Germans Karl Kristian Friedrich Krause (1781-1832) and Henry Ahrens (1808-74). The school, which educated most of the intellectuals of the next few generations, opened its doors to women, giving them the same opportunity as men.

Through her fiction, Pardo Bazán explores the social status of women of every class. In *The House of Ulloa*, Sabel, the marquis's servant and mistress, represents the lower rural class. Of a strong and healthy physical nature, Sabel's character contrasts with that of the weak and sensitive Nucha, the marquis's cousin from the city of Santiago who becomes his wife. Although she belongs to a noble family, Nucha and her three sisters suffer conditions similar to those of the middle class, due to the economic decay of the nobility. Aware of their need to marry a good "catch," their father resolves not to let his nephew, the marquis, leave the city until he has married one of the four cousins. Nucha's sisters meanwhile spend their afternoon outings trying to attract the notice of young men of their class.

Aside from detailing women's role and prospects in society, the novel denounces the violence and abuse perpetrated against them. It likewise calls attention to their potential to change the situation and the intimidation felt by males when women step out of their traditional role.

In a period when feminist movements in Europe and the United States were gaining strength, Pardo Bazán did not demand the right to vote but worked to legitimize her position as an intellectual in a society that still resented intelligent women. She broke new ground for women, joining the *Ateneo,* the cultural center of Spain where intellectuals of the time met to debate, inform, teach and share the current philosophical and intellectual tendencies. In her own words "my work to open the doors to feminism has only been of a personal nature; giving an example of doing everything I can of what is forbidden to women. I have had the pleasure of being the first member of the Ateneo; the first president of the literature section; the first and only woman that has been a professor of the *Escuela de Estudios Superiores*, right at the *Ateneo*; the first member of the *Real Sociedad Económica Matritense de los Amigos del País* and other appointments. There is no doubt, that if many women followed my example, feminism in Spain would be a fact" (Pardo Bazán in Clemessy, p. 591). Despite her activism, the Spanish writer encountered numerous obstacles. Many critics believe that one of Pardo Bazán's main regrets was not being accepted as a member of the *Real Academia de la Lengua Española* (Royal Academy of the Spanish Language), the institution created in the eighteenth century as the highest authority on issues related to the Spanish language. She also had to contend with overt criticism whenever she introduced a new intellectual tendency or idea in her writing.

The Novel in Focus

Plot summary. A young man rides a horse through the countryside of Orense, a province in

Galicia, on his way to the House of Ulloa. The weak, feminized ways of the young rider contrast sharply with the harsh landscape and its inhabitants. Asking for directions from locals, he receives ambiguous answers that introduce him to an inhospitable environment, whose residents are resistant to foreigners.

The reader learns the identity of the mysterious traveler when he encounters three other men returning from a hunting expedition. The hunters are Pedro Moscoso (marquis of Ulloa), a strong man about 30 years of age, his majordomo Primitivo, and the old abbot of Ulloa. The traveler is Julián Álvarez, a recently ordained priest sent from the city of Santiago by the marquis's uncle to help with the administration of the marquis's house and to look after the soul of his nephew.

The very night of his arrival at the House of Ulloa, the chaplain Julián witnesses several incidents that shock his innocent sensibilities. The three men seem very fond of wine and to Julián's surprise, the abbot does not leave until he has become quite drunk, a condition that will impede him from conducting mass the next day. Furthermore, in an attempt to ridicule the young chaplain's intolerance for alcohol (he can't handle his liquor), the hosts ply the three-year-old son of the house servant Sabel with wine until he passes out.

It does not take Julián long to perceive the dangerously decaying economic and moral conditions of the house. All of the family archives and written records are stored in a humid, dirty, unorganized room, many already destroyed and others very hard to decipher or classify. Don Pedro Moscoso, the marquis, seems unconcerned about his lack of control of the house's finances; in fact, he confesses to Julián that he has become completely dependent upon Primitivo's fraudulent administration of his estate, and even though he is aware of the fact that his majordomo embezzles the manor's income, Primitivo's power among the local folk is such that the marquis has no recourse against him. Spiritual life seems nonexistent in the area; hunting represents the main concern of both the nobles and clergymen.

Julián's unconventional personality, so alien to the area, earns him some enemies. First, the ever-hostile Primitivo, who does not welcome the chaplain's meddling in the house's records, tries without success to have his daughter seduce the newcomer. Second, Julián's fellow clergymen, accustomed to enjoying lively pleasures such as eating, hunting, and gossiping, resent his criticisms and take offense at his quiet shyness. For his part,

the moment Julián discovers from a neighboring priest what everyone in the area already knows: that Sabel, Primitivo's daughter, is not only mistress to the marquis but also the mother of his illegitimate son, Perucho, Julián decides to leave the house.

Upon the chaplain's announcement of his departure, a new opportunity for salvation arises. Julián proposes that the marquis accompany him to visit the marquis's uncle and cousins in Santiago. Moscoso, the marquis, agrees to the trip and even contemplates the possibility of finding

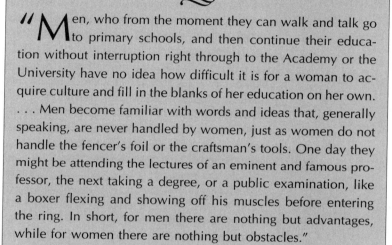

PARDO BAZÁN ON SEXUAL INEQUITY

"Men, who from the moment they can walk and talk go to primary schools, and then continue their education without interruption right through to the Academy or the University have no idea how difficult it is for a woman to acquire culture and fill in the blanks of her education on her own. . . . Men become familiar with words and ideas that, generally speaking, are never handled by women, just as women do not handle the fencer's foil or the craftsman's tools. One day they might be attending the lectures of an eminent and famous professor, the next taking a degree, or a public examination, like a boxer flexing and showing off his muscles before entering the ring. In short, for men there are nothing but advantages, while for women there are nothing but obstacles."

From "Notes Towards an Autobiography," published as a prologue to the second edition of *The House of Ulloa*

(Pardo Bazán, *House of Ulloa*, p. 13)

a wife in the city. Needless to say, the idea does not thrill Primitivo who, on the day of the departure, does everything in his power to obstruct it. He injures the horse and the donkeys, refuses to guide the couple on foot, and is later discovered by the marquis pointing his pistol at Julián from a hiding place on the trail. Clearly Primitivo is a menace to anyone who dares challenge his status in the House of Ulloa.

In Santiago, Moscoso encounters a welcoming uncle and four young cousins: Rita, the oldest and prettiest, is outgoing and flirtatious; Manolita is also attractive and outgoing; Carmen, has a more melancholic nature; and Nucha, the youngest and most serious, is excessively thin and cross-eyed. Moscoso immediately feels attracted to Rita, but has doubts about her purity due to her playful character. According to his criterion, only a clean and pure woman deserves to be the mother of his heir. Following Julián's advice, and to everyone's surprise, Moscoso decides to ask for Nucha's hand, willing to forfeit beauty for purity.

After a few months, the newly married couple travels to the Ulloa manor. On the way, Nucha announces that she is pregnant. Moscoso does not hide his excitement about the upcoming birth of an heir; he treats his wife with love and care during the months of pregnancy. Nucha endures a long, hard labor, and after more than two days of agonizing pain, gives birth, to her husband's dismay, to a girl. From this moment, life reverts to the way it was before the marquis's trip to Santiago: Sabel resumes her position as the master's mistress, and Moscoso spends most of his time hunting. He completely ignores his wife and daughter.

It takes Nucha several months to regain some strength. Her life revolves around her daughter, but she feels more and more intimidated by the House of Ulloa and its inhabitants, especially as her suspicions about Perucho's real father grow stronger. Julián, who has become very close to Nucha, fears for his friend's life, suffering such severe emotional imbalance that he hallucinates:

> He noticed her air of dejection, the black rings around her eyes, her frequent sighs . . . and he drew the obvious conclusion. There were other symptoms also, which set his imagination running and gave him great cause of concern.
> (*House of Ulloa*, p. 221)

Primitivo and Barbacana, a local *cacique*, convince the marquis to run for the Carlist party in the upcoming elections. He accepts not because of his political ideology, but because he feels flattered by the attention he receives. In order to finance the campaign, Moscoso must borrow money from Primitivo, who ironically amassed it by stealing from the manor's income. After many irregularities in the election, Trampeta, the other *cacique*, and his liberal party win, thanks, in part, to Primitivo, who has betrayed his master to gain control of his possessions as a form of repaying the loan. Before he can enjoy his triumph, however, Primitivo is brutally murdered by Barbacana's supporters.

After he loses the election, the marquis grows more ill tempered and physically abuses his wife. Nucha cannot take the abuse any longer, especially because she fears for her daughter's life, so she asks Julián to help her flee to her father's. As they plan the escape in church, Moscoso, alerted by his son, Perucho, under the instructions of Primitivo, catches them. Julián is accused of having an affair with Nucha, forced to leave the manor, and sent to a mountain village for ten years. Six months after he has been in this isolated area, he receives the announcement of Nucha's death.

After ten years in exile, Julián is again appointed to the House of Ulloa. Nothing has changed in the manor, but the last scene features a curious sight: a young girl in rags and a young man well dressed—Manolita (Nucha's daughter) and Perucho.

Countryside vs. city. The first scene of *The House of Ulloa* portrays a young man traveling through an inhospitable countryside to which he is not accustomed. Throughout the novel the opposition between countryside (where the manor is located) and city is blatant. The novel portrays rural characters as undisciplined people in a primitive state, heeding their natural instincts to the point that their rudeness and backwardness likens them to an animal. The introduction of Perucho in the novel offers an excellent example:

> As if the dogs also understood their right to be served before anyone else, they rose from their dark corner and began to sniff, wag their tails and yawn hungrily. At first Julián thought there was one dog more than before, but as they came into the light around the fire he realized that what he had at first taken for another dog was in fact a three- or four-year-old boy whose long brown jacket and white burlap breeches resembled at a distance the patched coats of the dogs—with which the child seemed to live in perfect harmony and fraternity.
> (*House of Ulloa*, p. 33)

Their health, though, is much better than that of city people. On occasions, the novel contrasts the strong Sabel to the weak Nucha, and the hearty marquis to Julián's sensitivity. The city—as suggested by such comparisons—promotes progress, hygiene, self-restraint, and civilization in general, but does not allow a person to cultivate his or her body.

This contrast mimics the actual political and social scene of the second half of the nineteenth century. The feudal-like system that had persisted in Galicia's rural areas was shaken by political and economic forces. Traditionally, a noble landowner, such as the marquis of the novel, rented land to the peasants in exchange for money or a part of the crops. The lord of the land exercised power over his tenants, who respected and feared him. As the nobles suffered economic decay, their power decreased considerably. This situation worsened with the *desamortización* (disentailment) laws promulgated in Spain by the liberal party; these laws confiscated land and buildings owned by the church and the municipalities and sold them in public auctions in order to collect money to finance different conflicts such as the Carlists and the Cuban uprisings. The lands were purchased by economically stable families, mostly members of the growing bourgeoisie, who by now mingled with Spain's nobility. Money began to take priority over tradition and the inheritance of a title; many noble families were forced to swallow their pride and marry their daughters into bourgeois families in order to remain solvent. In order to preserve tradition and class distinctions, the conservative Carlist party aimed to abolish the *desarmortización* laws. The Carlists therefore became identified with provincial and rural Spain.

The city, open to new liberal ideas, threatened the stability of the countryside. In fact, the laws changing landownership in Spain had been dictated from its capital city, Madrid. The liberals considered the country antiquated and frozen in time, full of inhabitants that failed to keep pace with the progress made in other European countries. At best, the differences created tensions between residents of cities and the countryside in mid-to-late nineteenth-century Spain. In *The House of Ulloa*, Moscoso feels uncomfortable and intimidated when he visits the city of Santiago; the same happens when Nucha and Julián enter the alien environment of rural Orense.

Sources and literary context. Most critics see *The House of Ulloa* as the finest example of Pardo Bazán's naturalist techniques. In 1883, three years before its appearance, her series of essays *La cuestión palpitante* (1882-83; *The Burning Question*) revealed her reaction to the French novelist Émile Zola's naturalism (the movement in literature based on the notion that all human behavior results from one's heredity and environment). The main fault Pardo Bazán sees in Zola's philosophy is that his variety of naturalism presumes the absence of free will, thereby denying a basic premise of Catholicism. The Spanish naturalism defended in *La cuestión palpitante* modifies Zola's insistently scientific approach, positing that human spirit can overpower heredity and environment.

Pardo Bazan's discussion of naturalism comes in a period of transition in Spanish literature. Most authors had already stepped away from the Romanticism of the beginning of the century and into realism in order to serve as objective witnesses to life in their time. Zola's theories and use of the scientific and experimental novel opened the door to new narrative techniques in Spain. Spanish writers focused more directly on lower-class characters and settings than ever before, portraying human misery and lowly instincts in graphic fashion. In fact, some authors were already incorporating some of those techniques in their works. The commotion caused by *La cuestión palpitante* responds probably more to the fact that the author is a woman than to the nature and innovation of the discussion. In any event, upon the publication of Pardo Bazán's ideas about naturalism, the Spanish intellectual community engaged in vigorous debate. On the other end of the spectrum, her primary opponent, the novelist Juan Valera, argues that literature should not aspire to disclose any truth but rather to simply entertain.

There is no doubt that many naturalistic traits appear in some of Pardo Bazán's novels, especially in *The House of Ulloa*. Her reputation as the main exponent of Spanish naturalism and one of the finest Spanish writers of the nineteenth century rests not on these traits, however. Rather, it is the debate stirred by her writings and by the social issues they address that has helped canonize her in these ways.

Apart from the influence of Zola's naturalistic techniques, there are no recognized sources for the novel other than the author's own personal experience. In the *Autobiographical Sketches* published as a preface to the second edition of the novel, Pardo Bazán mentions many other readings that have influenced her; however, none of them had a direct tangible effect on the novel. It is clear that the action takes place in the region of Carballido, where the author used to spend considerable time. She therefore had firsthand knowledge of the landscape and inhabitants. There is in fact a manor in Galicia with the name of *Pazo de Ulloa*.

Pardo Bazán had explored similar topics in her portrayal of a decaying rural noble house in the short novel *Bucólica* in 1884. She herself has discussed the importance of this novel as a writing exercise prior to the composition of *The House of Ulloa*. It, in turn, would be followed up by a sequel, *La madre naturaleza* (*Mother Nature*), published the following year and based on the lives of Perucho and Manolita 15 years after the ending of the first novel.

Events in History at the Time the Novel Was Written

Restoration (Alfonso XII and XIII). In 1874, in light of the failure of the first republic and after General Pavia's *levantamiento* (uprising), Alfonso XII, son of Queen Isabel, was brought back from exile in France and proclaimed king of Spain.

Upon his arrival, the new king tried to solve the nation's major problems. He joined his troops against the Carlists and they finally triumphed in 1876, forcing Carlos María, grandson of the original Carlist contender, into exile in France. Now released to attend to other problems, Spanish troops were sent to Cuba to calm the revolts there.

Alfonso XII ruled with more stability than his predecessors until 1885, when he died of tuberculosis before turning 30. María Cristina, his pregnant wife, became the regent and the next year she gave birth to a male, Alfonso XIII. Politically this period became known as the *Turno Pacífico*, an allusion to the peaceful alternation of power between the liberals and conservatives.

The strategy resulted in free rein for the *caciques*, who did not need to fear political accountability and therefore could exercise their power as they wished. No doubt the tumultuous year Spain was experiencing when *The House of Ulloa* was written, with the death of one king and birth of another, reminded Pardo Bazán of the period of uncertainty in which the novel takes place, that of the 1868 revolution. By incorporating local *caciques* in the novel, she manages to criticize their actions in the past and present.

Reviews. The publication of a second edition, containing the autobiographic prologue *Apuntes autobiográficos*, of *The House of Ulloa* only a few months after its initial release proves its tremendous success. Most of the criticism was also favorable. The contemporary author José María de Pereda, for instance, in a letter to Benito Pérez Galdós, author of **Fortunata and Jacinta** (also in *WLAIT 5: Spanish and Portuguese Literatures and Their Times*), says "I find *The House of Ulloa* to be the best novel of Pardo Bazán, with chapters of unquestionable beauty" (Pereda in Clemessy, p. 241).

In the same letter, Pereda expresses his satisfaction at not having found any traces of naturalism in the novel. Clarín, author of **La Regenta** (also in *WLAIT 5: Spanish and Portuguese Literatures and Their Times*), agrees with Pereda in his praise of the novel. However, Clarín disagrees about the absence of naturalism, even comparing Julián to the abbot Mouret, one of Zola's characters.

House of Ulloa has been reedited continuously since it first appeared and translated into more than ten languages. The two most recent English translations, of Paul O'Prey and Lucía Graves (1990) and Roser Caminals-Heath (1992) received highly positive reviews. The critics celebrated not only the excellence of the translations, but also their inclusion of the *Autobiographical Sketches* published in the second edition of the novel but absent in recent Spanish editions.

—María P. Tajes

For More Information

Bretz, Mary Lee. "Masculine and Feminine Chronotopes in Los pazos de Ulloa." *Letras Peninsulares* 2 (spring 1989): 45-54.

———. *Voices, Silences and Echoes: A Theory of the Essay and the Critical Reception of Naturalism in Spain.* London: Tamesis, 1992.

Clemessy, Nelly. *Emilia Pardo Bazán como novelista.* Trans. Irene Gambra. Madrid: Fundación Universitaria Española, 1981.

Fowler Brown, Donald. *The Catholic Naturalism of Pardo Bazán.* Chapel Hill: The University of North Carolina Press, 1957.

Henn, David. "A Priest in the Land of Wolves." *Times Literary Supplement,* 18 January 1991, 12.

———. *The Early Pardo Bazán.* Trowbridge: Redwood Burn, 1988.

Pardo Bazán, Emilia. *The House of Ulloa.* Trans. Paul O'Prey and Lucia Graves. London: Penguin, 1990.

———. *Obras completas.* Madrid: Aguilar, 1973.

Pierson, Peter. *The History of Spain.* Connecticut: Greenwood Press, 1999.

Pozzi, G. Review of *The House of Ulloa. Choice* 30, no. 1 (spring 1992): 122.

Ramos Oliveira, A. *Politics, Economics and Men of Modern Spain 1808-1946.* London: Victor Gollancz, 1946.

Rodríguez, Adna Rosa. *La cuestión feminista en los ensayos de Emilia Pardo Bazán.* Sada: Ediciós do Castro, 1991.

Romero Masiá, Ana. *Galicia. CC.SS. Xeografía e historia.* La Coruña: Bahía, 1997.

The India Play

by
Gil Vicente

THE LITERARY WORK

A farcical play set in early sixteenth-century Lisbon; published in Portuguese (as *Auto da Índia*) in 1509 or 1510; in English in 1997.

SYNOPSIS

Enclosed in her home in the company of a maid, a young woman playfully exploits adulterous courtships after her husband sets sail for India in search of fame and fortune.

Gil Vicente is considered the founder of the Portuguese theater as well as the greatest dramatist in the Iberian Peninsula before Spain's Lope de Vega. He is thought to have been born sometime between 1460 and 1470 in Lisbon, Portugal, and to have been put to rest in Évora, Portugal, sometime before 1537. It is known that Vicente first came to Évora as a goldsmith for the court during the 1490 wedding of Crown Prince Afonso of Portugal to Princess Isabel of Castile. Vicente himself wed twice: to Branca Bezerra and, after her death, to Melícia Rodrigues. He had five children in all—two sons by Branca (Gaspar and Belchior) and two daughters and a son by Melicia (Valéria, Paula, and Luís). Although Vicente's educational background remains a mystery, the philosophical and theological knowledge exhibited in his plays indicates some formal instruction. He was a musician, a poet, and an actor, as well as a writer, and he held a seat on the Lisbon Town Council. Vicente's oratory skills earned him respect, as attested to by a sermon on tolerance in which he reprimanded monks in Santarém for maintaining that faithlessness among the "New Christians" (converted Jews) had angered God into striking the Portuguese with the earthquake of 1531. Insisting that it was a natural phenomenon, not a sign of divine displeasure, Vicente's sermon prevented a pogrom. In his career as a dramatist Vicente wrote more than 40 plays, some in Portuguese, some in Spanish, and some in a mix of the two languages. His career began at court the day after the 1502 birth of Prince João (the future João III), with the play *Monólogo do Vaqueiro* (The Herdsman's Monologue, also known as The Visitation Play). He would write three more works (*The Castilian Pastoral Play, The Play of the Magi,* and *The Play of Saint Martin*), then take a five-year hiatus before penning the farce *The India Play*. Farce was a genre distinguishable from *comedia,* a term used for the longer, more developed theater, be it serious or humorous. A transitional dramatist, bridging the medieval and Renaissance eras, Vicente, along with Spanish playwright Torres Naharro, would go on to forge Iberian *comedia*. Still in the genre of farce, *The India Play* nevertheless entails some serious commentary. The play elucidates bourgeois domestic relations at a time in which men were increasingly being called to expansionist adventures; in the process, it ties the domestic to the national scene in early-sixteenth-century Portugal.

Events in History at the Time the Play Takes Place

A frenzy of exploration and trade. The *India Play* was performed in 1509 in honor of King Manuel's mother, Dona Leonor, after Portugal had already pioneered the way to the riches of the Orient. In 1498 Vasco da Gama had rounded the Cape of Good Hope at the tip of Africa to reach India, becoming the first to connect Europe to Asia by sea. Vicente's farce dramatizes the consequences of this breakthrough voyage of exploration to India and of Portugal's subsequent presence in the East. The farce emphasizes the private, human side of the public enterprise by adopting the point of view of a commoner residing in the busy port city of Lisbon.

The work involved in what was to become the Portuguese empire building spanned much of the fifteenth century, with *The India Play* opening on the heels of close to a hundred years of vigorous activity on the part of the Portuguese:

1415 The Portuguese conquer Ceuta in North Africa.

1427 Diogo de Silves is believed to have reached the Azores.

1469 Pedro Escobar and João de Santarém reach Mina in Northern Africa; the Portuguese conquer Arzila and Tangier.

1472 João Corte-Real reaches Greenland.

1482 Diogo Cão reaches the south of Guinea and lodges for the Portuguese the first *padrão* (standard column) in the mouth of the Zaire River in Africa.

1492 Dom João II allows Jews expelled from Spain into Portugal.

1494 The Tordesillas Treaty divides areas of dominion in the west Atlantic Ocean between Spain and Portugal at a line 370 leagues west of the Cape Verde Islands, attempting to create monopolies in what would later be recognized as international waters.

1496 King Manuel I orders the expulsion from Portugal of all Jews who are not willing to convert to Christianity.

1497-98 Vasco da Gama sets sail for the East from Restelo Beach in Lisbon, eventually reaching Calicut, in India.

1499 King Manuel adopts the title *Senhor da conquista, navegação e comércio de Etiópia, Arábia, Pérsia e Índia* (Lord of conquest, navigation and commerce in Ethiopia, Arabia, Persia, and India).

1500 Pedro Álvares Cabral reaches Brazil.

1505 Hunger epidemic in Lisbon; Dom Francisco de Albuquerque takes the cities of Quiloa and Mombaça in Eastern Africa.

1506 Tristão da Cunha reaches the archipelago in the south Atlantic Ocean known today as Tristan da Cunha.

1507 Afonso de Albuquerque takes the city of Ormuz (now part of Iran); outbreak of the plague and hunger in Lisbon.

1509 King Manuel regulates the India House (Casa da Índia); a repository for imported goods, it stands in Lisbon next to his residence, the Palace by the River Tejo.

1508 Tristão da Cunha returns to Lisbon with ships laden with spices and jewels.

Lisbon had thus become quite the cosmopolitan city by Gil Vicente's day and would continue to qualify as such in the following decades. In his 1554 *Urbis Olisiponis Descriptio* (Description of the City of Lisbon), a sort of humanist guide to Lisbon, Damião de Góis points to the seemingly limitless riches coming from the East that were stored in the India House:

> [The India House is] executed in marvelous style and replete with the abundant spoils and plundering from many nations and peoples. Because it is there where the business affairs with India are handled, our people have named it the India House. In my opinion, it might sooner be called an opulent emporium, due to its aromas, pearls, rubies, emeralds, and other precious stones brought to us from India year after year; or perhaps a grand depository of gold and silver. . . . There stand . . . innumerable compartments arranged with an artful cleverness, overflowing with such a great abundance of those treasures that—word of honor!—it would surpass one's capacity to believe, if they did not leap before the eyes of all, and if we could not touch them with our own hands.
>
> (Góis, pp. 29-30)

King Manuel financed much of the overseas venture with capital from foreign bankers (Genovese, Florentine, and German), who were quick to sponsor the Portuguese enterprise. Ironically this sealed the empire's fate, prompting Portugal to become a wholesaler of sorts and severely limiting how much the country itself could benefit: "Portugal's poverty prevented the consumption of these exotic cargoes at home, and it was in the port of Antwerp that these riches found distribution into the markets of northern Europe" (Ruth in Góis, p. xv).

Regardless of these financial considerations, Portugal gained distinction in Europe as the first to open up new avenues of contact and exchange among very distant peoples. Gold, slaves, and pepper from Africa; ivory, cinnamon, and other spices from East Asia; and sugar from islands in the Atlantic and later from Brazil would pour into European markets via Portugal. Their receptiveness, in turn, fueled the frenzy for further Portuguese exploration.

The epoch of the *India Play* is framed in particular by the celebrated expedition of Portuguese navigator Tristão da Cunha (c. 1460-1514). In 1506 Tristão da Cunha embarked with 15 vessels from Lisbon to East Asia, he himself on the *Graça*. During his most significant voyage, Tristão da Cunha discovered three volcanic islands in the South Atlantic, one of which received his name. After taking control of the city of Socotra off Arabia in hopes of establishing a monopoly over the Red Sea, the navigator went on to India in the pursuit of Eastern riches. At this point, Afonso de Albuquerque detached part of the fleet.

A nobleman, Albuquerque fought to secure Portugal's presence in the East. He masterminded a strategy of establishing bases in the region, not just to ensure access to commercial goods but to protect Portugal's pathway to Europe and, also, to safeguard Portuguese operations from Muslim attacks. The center of Portuguese activity was to be an island off southwest India, an area defensible by land or sea. Establishing it as a capital, Albuquerque conquered this island—Goa—in 1510, shortly after *The India Play* was first performed. He would go on to plan the planting of permanent garrisons, naval reserves, and even shipbuilding enterprises in the East so that Portuguese forces could survive the onslaughts of their foes. Thus, it is at the brink of the consolidation of the empire that *The India Play* is set.

Meanwhile, Tristão da Cunha continued voyaging to the East himself. In 1513 he was sent by King Manuel on a renowned diplomatic mission to the papal court in Rome. During the festivities celebrating the election of Pope Leo X, the charismatic Tristão da Cunha appeared dressed in a hat "entirely covered with large pearls" and exhibited the finest riches from the East, including papal regalia (Góis in Dos Passos, p. 268):

All these vestments were woven with gold thread and so covered with precious stones and pearls that only in a few places could you see the cloth of gold. . . . In certain places the fabric appeared as if painted in gold and silk with the face of our Savior and of the saints and apostles all outlined with pearl and those gems we call raw rubies, not worked or polished, but used

just as they came from the places where they were found in their natural splendor.
(Góis in Dos Passos, p. 268)

The most bizarre sight in this opulent display was yet to come. Along with these first gems from the East, the Portuguese mission paraded to the eminent crowd an elephant, a then bizarre spectacle that mesmerized the onlookers:

The pope viewed the scene from a window in a lower story of the Castle of Sant'Angelo. The elephant made three curtseys, and, filling his trunk with water in a trough placed there for the purpose, shot a stream so high above where the pope was that it landed on a number of cardinals looking out from the upper stories.
(Dos Passos, pp. 267-68)

CINNAMON

One of the reasons for the European competition for the East was to monopolize the spice trade. Cinnamon was so important a commodity in the sixteenth century that Gil Vicente mentions it as a symbol of India itself. The wife's comments on it as she complains about her husband having abandoned her for India:

In an evil hour did I
kneed and bake biscuits
for him to take his damned
cinnamon to the devil.

(Vicente, *The India Play*, verses 28-31)

Used as a mouthwash, cinnamon was also considered a sort of panacea that alleviated (among many other ailments) problems of the stomach, kidneys, and even the heart. Probably the Europeans also knew of its aphrodisiac qualities. More than just for culinary and medical uses, the competition for eastern spices becomes a metaphor for "other," European cravings: "It is as if the magnetism of the East, the spell it cast, inspired Europeans to create or recreate an East that would accord with what the West wanted it to be: mysterious, wonderful, bizarre and perhaps even immoral" (Cuddon, p. 664).

The presentation was so successful that King Dom Manuel sent the pope another shipload of treasures in 1517, including Dom Manuel's very own rhinoceros, the same one that painter Albrecht Dürer made famous in his well-known engraving of 1515. Dom Manuel was often seen

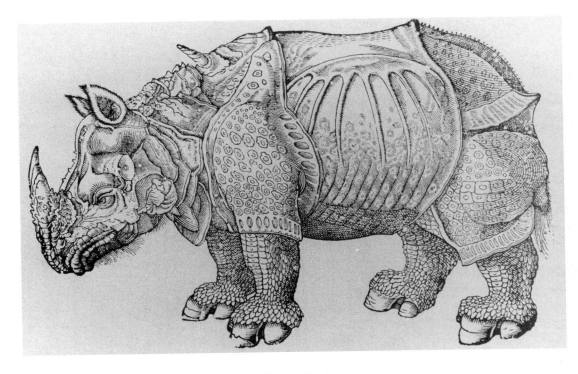

King Manuel's rhinoceros, made famous in this sketch by Albrecht Dürer.

strolling down *Rua Nova* in Lisbon with exotic animals in tow—typically four elephants, a rhinoceros, and a leopard. He was Europe's first Christian king to own such a prestigious menagerie.

These promotional displays of the Portuguese had a connection to religion. More exactly, King Dom Manuel nurtured a messianic ambition to bring an end to Islam and establish an alliance with a legendary Christian King of Ethiopia (Prester John) in East Africa. This ambition complemented the commercial and military interests of the Portuguese Crown. But there were objections from a significant faction of the population: the landed nobility opposed military activities that would consume the kingdom's resources in areas other than the familiar military ground of North Africa. The debate between this nobility and those who favored energetic exploitation of the eastern markets is echoed later in the sixteenth century in the epic poem **The Lusiads** (also in *WLAIT 5: Spanish and Portuguese Literatures and Their Times*). In the epic, a "venerable" old man, watching Vasco da Gama's fleet take its leave at Restelo Beach, condemns the moral decline such colonial ventures produce:

> You ignore the enemy at the gate,
> In search for another so far away,
> Unpeopling the ancient kingdom,

Leaving it vulnerable and bereft!
You are lured by the dangers of the unknown,
So history will flatter you, as
"Seigneurs" (or titles yet more copious),
India's, Persia's, Arabia's Ethiopia's!
>   (Camões, 4.101)

These lines are a direct indictment of the military's extended overseas ventures and, more specifically, of King Manuel's "messianic" design. In *The Lusiads*, this *"venerable old man . . . with a wisdom only experience could impart"* warns the adventurers: *"you promote separation and adultery"* (Camões, 4.94, 95, 96). His warning echoes a message advanced some 60 years earlier in Vicente's *The India Play*, which contains one of the first known criticisms of overseas expansion.

Women in early-modern Portugal. In *The India Play*, the maid—an *accomplice-voyeuse* (facilitator and voyeur)—is implicated as much as her mistress in the promiscuous game of adultery that takes center stage, since she agrees from the very beginning to serve as a go-between (Ferreira, "Intersecting Historical Performances," p. 107). Her mistress, Constance, promises the maid a reward for her service and for her silence: "I'll give you a silk cap," to which the maid greedily responds: "Or, when he gets back / give me something he's brought you" (*The India Play*, verses 49-51). Thus, both women stand to lose—or gain, as the case may be—in their dangerous, but playful pastime.

However playful, Constance, it should be noted, also has good cause for her flirtatious behavior. She toys with her suitors partly in self-defense, in case her husband fails to return. Her game nevertheless is a perilous one. It was not uncommon during this era for an adulteress to be penalized with death if the wronged husband chose such a penalty. "[A]mong many nations, as the Italians, Spaniards, and Turks, it is counted a capital crime in the wife to tread awry" (Sommerville, p. 144). In the best case, a husband might decide to retain his spouse, albeit in a confined situation that was perhaps worse than death, for he could kill her at a moment's notice. Mário Fiúza recalls an anonymous Portuguese collection of sixteenth-century sayings that registers the following observation: "My lady, I pray thee, please betray me so that I can forever more rule over you" (Fiúza, p. 40; trans. R. Garay).

Vicente's play draws a parallel between domestic and national squabbles. His protagonist, Constance, pretends to be the virtuous wife. At the end of her duplicitous ruse, one realizes that she is guarding her personal India or material subsistence. She shows a resilience, an aptitude for tactics of survival, that would do her country proud were she a soldier in the East or a trader in the international European market:

> Constance's two seducers—an eloquent, arrogant Spaniard who sells vinegar, and an enamored Portuguese . . . who is now without work—attempt to rip off the profits from India by seeking to occupy an 'available' body-space—woman/home. . . . Yet, Constance is no mute, passive body-space for anyone's possession; in control of her situation she confronts each pretender with his own ultimate aim while clearly setting her own conditions of acceptance . . . she keeps them both at bay so as not to lose the possible gains that each may bring her.
>
> (Ferreira, "Intersecting Historical Performances," pp. 106-07)

This strong, self-willed woman struggles, within the limits of the era, for control of her passions and life. In reality, such a struggle was not easy, given the prevailing double standard in sexual behavior. It was an era in which, notes historian Margaret Sommerville, "a wife's infidelity undermined her husband's status far more than his did hers. A husband almost automatically obtained a separation for his wife's adultery, but a wife who attempted to sue for a separation solely on grounds of her husband's adultery—

without also being able to prove cruelty or desertion—was unlikely to have success" (Sommerville, pp. 141-42). Part of the reasoning for this double standard lay in the more injurious effect on society of a wife's infidelity. Only her promiscuity caused a breakdown of matrimonial obligations, by making a male care for a child not his own. This, of course, had economic ramifications: "Infidelity by either party was thought to involve 'filthiness and falseness,' but only a wife's transferred her husband's 'estate to strangers and other men's children'" (Sommerville, p. 148). On the other hand, some early modern thinkers placed the responsibility for a wife's infidelity directly on the men.

THE INDIA PLAY AND THE LUSIADS—LITERARY COUNTERPOINT

Although *The India Play* (c. 1510) and *The Lusiads* (1572) agree on the imperial project's promoting separation and adultery, the thrust of these two literary works diverge. *The Lusiads* emphasizes the historical imperative of Portuguese national history, invoking timeless images of mythological pageantry and depicting the dauntless qualities of national heroes. *The India Play*, by contrast, dramatizes antiheroic pranks in the domestic setting of a family home. The same can be said for the depiction of the Muslim "other." Whereas *The Lusiads* portrays the easterner as cunning and therefore untrustworthy, the situation of the protagonist Constance in *The India Play* reflects another aspect of European contact with the East. She expresses jealousy over her husband's possible relations with the "beautiful Indian women," a menace to domestic accord (*The India Play*, verse 487).

A number of treatises on marriage were published by contemporary thinkers in Spain and Portugal in the sixteenth and seventeenth centuries (e.g., F. Osuna, *Norte de los estados en que se da reglas de bivir a los mancebos . . .*, 1531; A Young Man's Precepts for Moral Living . . .). In a world governed by forced separation, especially in maritime nations such as Portugal and Spain, such thinkers as F. Osuna accused men of abandoning their wives in a sea of temptations. Especially the young and beautiful women were placed in temptations' way by the absence of their husbands (P. Luján, *Coloquios matrimoniales . . .*, 1550; Matrimonial Dialgues . . .). In

Casamento perfeito (1630; Perfect Marriage), Diogo de Paiva Andrada notes a further very real danger to marital unions in these separations: ships made their way home laden with "riches" other than the variety expected: some carried into port exotic female slaves for sexual purposes (Andrada in Pacheco, p. 54).

The Play in Focus

Plot overview. *The India Play* is a comic spoof on the consequences of abandoning the homeland in search of newfound riches in the Far East. With adultery as its main subject, the play follows closely the slapstick tradition of medieval farce. The play unfolds as one complete action without the multi-act divisions typical of most modern theater, yet it has definite sections. There are three dramatic movements–*exposition* of the narrative material, in which the precipitating circumstances are related; the *conflict,* which begins as soon as Constance's husband has left for India; and the *denouement,* or resolution, which turns out not to be a solution at all. Dramatically the three parts correspond to 1) conversations about the awaited departure of Constance's husband for India; 2) the adulterous amusements of Constance; 3) her husband's return from India.

In brief, a woman (ironically named *Constance*) laments the departure of her husband for the East, but, as the audience quickly learns, her sorrow is feigned. As soon as her husband's ship is on its way, a Castilian suitor appears to woo the hypocritical wife. This suitor's departure is followed by the arrival of yet another suitor, the lowly Portuguese squire Lemos, who is made to believe that the Castilian is Constance's brother. The burlesque encounters between the wife and each of her lovesick suitors are frequently interrupted by the maid. In one such instance, she announces that the ship that carried Constance's husband to the East has just returned to Lisbon. Her suitors escape by the skin of their teeth, after which Constance, greeting her husband with her typical hypocrisy, insists that she has been the model of a virtuous wife and scolds her husband for leaving her heartbroken and alone.

Plot summary. As the play opens, the maid speculates about Constance's grief, "is it because the fleet has left?" to which Constance retorts "would that make me shed tears?" (*India Play,* verses 2, 4). When the maid leaves the stage to confirm that the husband is in fact on his way to India, Constance invokes Saint Anthony, the patron saint of marriages, and goes to sleep. Shortly

thereafter, she brings to the fore more reasons for her subsequent actions. "They leave here in May, / when the new blood begins to rise. / Do you think that is fair?" (*The India Play,* verses 91-93). This reflects an historical event, going on year after year. Tristão da Cunha's expedition, which Constance's husband presumably joined, left in fact for India in April 1506. The second part of the play develops Constance's betrayal, or adultery. First, she receives a braggart Castilian, Juan Zamora, who woos her in the most ornate rhetorical style. Although his flirtatious discourse fails to move Constance, she promises to see him that evening, at "nine o'clock and no later, / and throw a little pebble / a teeny-weeny stone / at the garden window" (*The India Play,* vv. 184-87). In her tête-à-tête with Juan Zamora, Constance informs him that her husband left two days ago, whereupon the Castilian observes:

> Then to the devil let him go,
> the accursed wretch!
> What more India could there be,
> what more precious stones than you?
> What more things of beauty
> than both of you to be together?
>> (*The India Play,* verses 129-134)

To this rebuke, Juan adds that in abandoning family and home, the Portuguese are fulfilling a divine plan that will work to his (and, one can extrapolate, to his country's) advantage.

> But as Gospel-truth is this:
> God has made India
> only so that we two
> could go through this together;
> and, solely for my happiness
> to partake of this joy
> God had India discovered,
> and there's nothing else to say,
> by God's holy mother!
>> (*The India Play,* verses 144-52)

The Castilian, who remains outside the home during the scene, is made to leave so that a second suitor, Lemos, may enter.

Constance's maid, a perceptive witness to the situation, muses on her mistress's hypocrisy: "How many wiles, how many deceits / can my mistress perform! / One in the street, the other in bed!" (*The India Play,* verses 353-55). Lemos, Constance's "forsaken lover," a typical poverty-stricken Portuguese squire, arrives to make the most of the situation in the absence of Constance's husband (*The India Play,* verse 209). Although his part in the play is small compared to Juan's, his character traits reveal even more elements of a society in decay. With biting satire, the play exposes his pretentious behavior in comic scenes that exploit the impoverished squire's fraudulent sense of largesse. He asks the maid to buy expensive foods and wine for supper but is unwilling to pay the price: "Are you only giving me a farthing?" asks the maid (*The India Play,* verse 282).

Like the Castilian, Lemos makes use of the courtly love rhetoric and Petrarchan imagery that was already becoming obsolete in Vicente's day. The Portuguese suitor continuously exaggerates Constance's social position, making her superior to others of her own social standing. He hopes through verbal and gestural flattery to seduce Constance. No fool, Constance observes his grandiose posturing when first he enters her sphere: "Jesus! What a bow / By any chance, am I a queen?", to which he answers: "But you are my Empress" (*The India Play,* verses 225-26, 227). As noted by Ana Paula Ferreira in "Performing Inconstancies," the suitor reflects a type in Portuguese society of the era; in contrast to the Spaniard, he illustrates the parasite at home, a menace to society.

In the third and final part of the dramatic movement, Constance's diversions with the two suitors are arrested by the news of her husband's arrival: "Oh, ma'am, I'm frightened to death! / Our master's here today!" The news elicits a curse from Constance to the maid: "you wicked excommunicate" (*The India Play,* verses 385, 386, 388). Upon her husband's arrival, Constance's adulterous behavior naturally comes to a halt. Her immediate reaction is one of disgust ("Jesus! How black you are, and tanned! / I don't love you, I don't love you"; but her anger subsides after her husband's reply: "And I do love you, for I hope / you've been a prudent woman" (*The India Play,* vv. 420-21). The remark tames the shrewd but inconstant Constance, who knows full well the fatal consequences associated with adultery in her society.

Gil Vicente's dramaturgy in the age of humanism. Gil Vicente is considered a transitional figure in Portuguese literature, straddling the eras of the Middle Ages and the Renaissance. Displaying characteristics typical of medieval drama, his plays invoke religious themes and strategies—for example, the use of allegorical figures to personify abstract ideas and human virtues and vices. At the same time, Vicente's plays pave the way for humanism, a Renaissance movement that featured individualism as well as a social critical bent and a heightened focus on secular concerns. The humanists exalted a person's rela-

Title page of the first (1562) edition of Gil Vicente's works.

tionship to God, individual free will, and human superiority over the forces of nature. Many of Vicente's plays prompt the audience to ponder the new humanist ideals. Certainly *The India Play* presents a critical view of the Portuguese business-driven involvement in the East. The play advances an iconoclastic, nonheroic view of the maritime adventure. Challenging the religious motives for the enterprise, *The India Play* brings to the fore the designs for profit that hide behind and propel the costly explorations of markets in the East.

Stylistically, Vicente was able to preserve elements of the medieval farce while finding ways to accommodate and expand upon the new Renaissance experimentation. His theatrical innovations point the way to those principles of drama that will not only define the Portuguese national theater, but will also typify the structure of the *comedia* throughout the Iberian Peninsula. *The India Play* exhibits some characteristics typical of medieval theater (for example, its a-temporal logic is based on non-Aristotelian notions of time that see no need for unity in this regard). Yet *The India Play* also displays classic, Aristotelian parts of a dramatic work (exposition, conflict, and denouement). Vicente's farce furthermore features characters that are more rounded than the allegorical, medieval fare, even, to some extent, psychologically conceived. The depiction of women in particular exhibits an acute sense of their individualism based on observation of their passions and reactions vis-à-vis longstanding notions of female subservience. In this regard, his famous *Farsa de Inês Pereira* (1923) is a notable example of women's active agency first brought to the fore in *The India Play*.

Sources and literary context. *The India Play* makes use of one of the most important moments in Portuguese (and Western) history: the discovery and colonization of the Eastern world. Within this register of real events, Vicente's farce reflects actual social consequences. The character of the "husband" is not only a copy of the many stereotypical cuckolded husbands of medieval narratives but also a depiction of the many men of various classes who set out for the East, often in search of a better future for themselves and their families. The anxieties associated with his absence in the play reflect genuine concerns.

More than just a social document of these ventures abroad and their repercussions in sixteenth-century Lisbon, *The India Play* is also the first play by a Portuguese playwright that achieves a truly dramatic design, representing an organic action with an intrigue that contains three distinct dramatic movements. In this respect, *The India Play* may be considered the first genuinely dramatic play in Portuguese theatrical history. Drawing on some existing genres, Vicente culls from the medieval tradition of the Galician-Portuguese "Cantigas d'escarnio e mal dizer," a type of song that spoofed people and social circumstances (in the vein of the French fabliau). In *The India Play*, he ties notions about the evils of women, present in this Galician-Portuguese genre, to the context of early-sixteenth-century overseas expansion. Of all Vicente's works, *The India Play* is in fact the only one that ties adultery to overseas expansion. It is now known that Gil Vicente inherited particular theatrical motifs from Portugal's Henrique da Mota and the *Cancioneiro* tradition, or court/festival entertainment tradition. Armed with these motifs, he became the first to endow them with techniques that gave dramatic form to such semi-theatrical genres. One of the subjects inherited by Vicente is that of marriage and adultery.

To be properly understood, *The India Play*'s concern with marriage needs to be considered in the context of its relation to Spanish Golden Age drama. As noted, the concept of *comedia*, or theater, differed from farce, a short, highly satirical and hence light genre. Vicente wrote on the cusp of the Golden Age, the era of literary preeminence that began to dawn in the Iberian Peninsula in the early 1500s, then flourished between 1550-1650. In Spanish Golden Age *comedia,* the central unifying motif of marriage sanctioned the union between man and woman; it was also the means by which Gil Vicente, his contemporaries, and later dramatists resolved levels of conflict. The *farce* diverged from the *comedia* in that it usually satirized marriage, focusing on its precariousness, often attributed to adultery. Whether matrimony is presented seriously (as in *comedia*) or humorously (as in *farce*), both forms exhibited a didactic intent.

Vicente introduced a further innovation that appears in *The India Play*. Its scenic apparatus includes a complexity unknown in the peninsula before Vicente. Within a scene, action takes place inside the home and outside the home, and the home itself has two levels. This same complexity would surface later in the *comedia* of the Spanish Golden Age playwrights, which *The India Play* precedes.

Reception. The immediate response to the *India Play* is unknown today. However, it is known that Vicente himself later rejected the entire genre of farce, offering the king instead more elegant theater, the new *comedia,* which aimed to incorporate a sound sense of mirth with serious intent and excellent diction. Good examples of this later focus may be found in Vicente's tragicomedies *Dom Duardos* (1522) and *Amadis de Gaula* (1523).

Vicente's works would be rediscovered in the nineteenth century by the writer, poet, and dramatist Almeida Garrett (see **Travels in My Homeland,** also in *WLAIT 5: Spanish and Portuguese Literatures and Their Times*). Garrett hailed Vicente as the founder of Portuguese theater, setting out himself to revitalize it with a Romantic play invoking this founder (*Um Auto de Gil Vicente,* 1838; A Play by Gil Vicente). Since then, Vicente has remained a popular playwright in Portugal and the rest of the Iberian Peninsula. His notoriety has extended to other parts of the European continent as well and to Latin America too. In twentieth-century Britain, A. R. Milburn described Vicente as "the greatest [dramatist] in Europe before Shakespeare" (Milburn in Thorly, p. 800). Back in Portugal, *The India Play* gained particular importance after the Revolution of April 1974, which deposed the dictatorship and ultimately brought the Portuguese empire to an end. The work became part of the official Portuguese high-school curriculum, and in the 1980s, of all Vicente's plays, proved to be the most frequently performed by student, amateur, and professional groups. Not coincidentally, the Portuguese empire, now a historical phantom, was gaining new critical and nostalgic contours at the time (Ferreira, "Intersecting Historical Performances," p. 101).

—René Garay

For More Information

Camões, Luíz Vaz de. *The Lusiads*. Trans. Landeg White. Oxford: Oxford University Press, 1997.

Cuddon, J. A. *The Penguin Dictionary of Literary Terms and Literary Theory*. New York: Penguin, 1992.

Dias, Ana Paula. *Para Uma Leitura de* Auto da Índia *de Gil Vicente*. Lisbon: Editorial Presença, 1997.

Dos Passos, John. *The Portugal Story: Three Centuries of Exploration and Discovery*. New York: Doubleday, 1969.

Ferreira, Ana Paula. "Intersecting Historical Performances: Gil Vicente's *Auto da India*." GESTOS 9, no. 17 (1994) 99-113.

———. "Performing Inconstancies: Gil Vicente's *Auto da Índia*." Paper presented at the International Conference, "Staging Brazilian and Portuguese Theater." Yale University, Nov. 11, 2000.

Fiúza, Mário, ed. *Auto da Índia*. Porto: Porto Editora, 1979.

Garay, René. *Gil Vicente and the Development of the Comedia*. Chapel Hill: University of North Carolina Press, 1988.

Góis, Damião de. *Lisbon in the Renaissance, a New Translation of the Urbis Olisiponis Descriptio*. Trans. Jeff Ruth. New York: Italica Press, 1996.

Pacheco, José. *O Sexo Por Cá*. Lisboa: Livros Horizonte, 2000.

Parker, Jack Horace. *Gil Vicente*. New York: Twayne, 1967.

Sommerville, Margaret R. *Sex and Subjection. Attitudes to Women in Early-Modern Society*. London: Arnold, 1995.

Thorly, Anthony. *Penguin Companion to European Literature*. New York: McGraw, 1969.

Vicente, Gil. *The India Play* ("Auto da Índia"). In *Three Discovery Plays*. Trans. Anthony Lappin. Warminster, England: Aris & Phillips, 1997.

The Infinite Passion (Rimas)

by

Gustavo Adolfo Bécquer

orn in Seville in 1836, Gustavo Adolfo Bécquer was the son of painter José Dominguez Bécquer, who died when Gustavo was five. Orphaned at an early age, he was raised by his godmother, a pious woman who apparently hoped he would be a merchant but nonetheless provided him with a good education. At 17, Bécquer boarded a train to Madrid in pursuit of a literary career. He founded various publications, but all of them failed. Despite these setbacks, Bécquer managed to eke out an existence as a freelance journalist and translator. Between 1860-68, he contributed poems and stories to the newspaper *El Contemporáneo* and worked as a government censor. In 1868 Bécquer produced an edition of his best pieces, collected under the title *Book of the Sparrows* (Libro de los gorriones), purchased by the Prime Minister González Bravo (sometimes written "Brabo") but then lost when the Prime Minister's house was raided during the Revolution of 1868. Plagued by ill health and an unsuccessful marriage to his physician's daughter, Bécquer separated from his wife in 1868 and, with his two young children, set up house in Toledo with his older brother Valeriano Bécquer, a painter. During this period, Bécquer became editor of *La Ilustración de Madrid* and rewrote his own lost poems, relying partly on memory, partly on rough drafts and previously published versions. Despite these achievements, poverty and illness took their toll on him as well as his brother: Valeriano Bécquer died in September 1870, Gustavo Adolfo Bécquer three months later. Before his passing, he asked his friend Ferrán to burn

some of his writings, primarily letters, probably because he felt they would dishonor him. Bécquer had led something of a double life, contributing articles to the satiric newspaper *Gil Blas* under a pseudonym, a common practice during his day. His authorship of these articles was revealed only after his death. Their satiric nature is far different from that of the lyrical pieces most often associated with Bécquer. In 1871, Bécquer's friends published a collection of his writings in two volumes. The *Rimas*, a series of over 70 poems, are perhaps his best-known work, owing to their delicate treatment of timeless themes—love, longing, the nature of poetry itself—and the simple, musical lyricism that was Bécquer's particular contribution to Spanish literature. Aside from his poetry, he composed over two dozen legends

THE LITERARY WORK

Poems set in mid-1800s Spain; written in the late 1850s to early 1860s; published in Spanish (as *Rimas* [lyrics]) in 1871; in English in 1924.

SYNOPSIS

In a series of lyric poems, the speaker explores love, longing, disillusionment, and death, as well as the nature of poetry and the role of poet. The verse represents an unsatisfying search for the ideal, often closely tied to the search for romantic love.

Gustavo Adolfo Bécquer

(*leyendas*) based on medieval lore and other sources. His works are replete with a range of emotions, an apropos quality in the production of a pre-eminent figure of Spanish Romanticism.

Events in History at the Time of the Poems

The rise of Romanticism. Throughout the first half of the nineteenth century, most of Europe was dominated by a philosophical and aesthetic movement that became known as Romanticism. While no single, authoritative definition of the term is likely to be formulated, Romanticism as an aesthetic project is associated with such characteristics as imagination, emotion, spirituality, intuition, sentimentality, and subjectivity. Philosophically, the movement represents a fundamental shift in the perception of the self, as well as its relationship to external experience, meaning its relationship to nature, God, and the universe. This shift can be viewed largely as a rejection of eighteenth-century Enlightenment thought—which privileged reason as the road to happiness and human progress. In contrast, the Romantics favored subjective experience and the exploration of the irrational.

During the eighteenth century, intellectuals and artists had subscribed to the neoclassical school of thought, which emphasized the ideals and standards of ancient Greece and Rome. Poems and plays were judged by reference to their forms, their mastery of rhyme and meter, and their adherence to classical dramatic unities. Intellect and reason held sway over imagination and emotion.

The Neoclassicism of eighteenth-century Europe represented a mind-set in which the human being was seen as part of a well-ordered universe, overseen by a deity whose existence had been reaffirmed by Cartesian logic. This philosophical sense of hierarchy and structure influenced the aesthetic principles of the era. The advent of Romanticism, however, reversed those standards, making the emotions the central criteria for evaluating a literary work.

> Does the work evoke an overwhelming emotion of terror or of joy? Does it communicate the writer's deepest passions and desires. Thus, the cleverness and sophistication of the well-balanced and reflective intellectual—the writer par excellence of the Age of Reason—give way to the wild and impassioned lyrics of the disordered, suffering, emotional genius.
>
> (Stamm, p. 128)

In short, the Romantic's rejection of a sense of reason and order, valued in the eighteenth century, generated a shift in perceptions about literature and its central role in the human experience.

As an aesthetic and philosophical influence, Romanticism originated in England—through the works of William Wordsworth, Samuel Taylor Coleridge, Lord Byron, Percy Bysshe Shelley, and John Keats—and in Germany, where the main representatives included composers Richard Wagner and Ludwig von Beethoven and writers such as Johann Goethe and Heinrich Heine. By degrees, Romanticism reached France, Italy, and Spain, where it was most directly influenced by German models.

Romanticism in Spain. Spanish Romanticism is generally viewed as consisting of two distinct waves. In the first wave, roughly spanning the 1830s to the 1850s, writers such as Mariano José de Larra and José de Espronceda figure prominently. The second phase of Spanish Romanticism, often called Post-Romanticism, is characterized by writers such as Gaspar Núñez de Arce, Gustavo Adolfo Bécquer and the Galician poet Rosalía de Castro. (See ***Beside the River Sar,*** also in *WLAIT 5: Spanish and Portuguese Literatures and Their Times*.)

The first wave of the movement contained a strong political element, a direct response to conditions marked by the repressive government of

Ferdinand VII. In the Spanish War of Independence (1808-14), the Spaniards ousted Joseph Bonaparte, who had been placed on the Spanish throne through the influence of Napoleon. During the war, Ferdinand VII, the legitimate Bourbon heir to the throne, lived in exile in France. Upon his return to Spain, the king promptly reversed the liberal democratic reforms that had been achieved during the course of the war, most notably the creation of the nation's first constitution, and imposed a government based on traditional notions of monarchy and conservative Catholicism.

The liberal-traditional controversy affected romanticism, some of whose practitioners called for "a regenerative and revolutionary romanticism which proclaimed liberalism in politics and advocated Europeanizing Spain. They asserted that traditionalism was the basic cause of the nation's decadence" (Díaz-Plaja, p. 244). Issues of national identity and political freedom dominated the first wave of Spanish Romanticism. Consequently, in this phase, the emphasis on creative powers and imaginative faculties typical of Romanticism in other cultures is less prominent, though not totally absent. The Spanish poet José de Espronceda, for one, overtly celebrates the freedom of the individual in works like "The Song of the Pirate," and both he and the essayist Larra explore themes of human subjectivity in a rather innovative way.

Bécquer, a figure of the second wave of Spanish Romanticism, represents a different approach to literature. His poems are emotional, visionary, and highly subjective, written with a simple lyricism that is in sharp contrast to the energetic and exorbitant tone of first-phase Romantic writers like Espronceda. In general, Post-Romanticism features a more introspective exploration and expression of the self, of the diverse and often intangible emotional experiences of which the human being is capable. Post-Romantic texts are written in a more subdued tone, using simple language that often explores complex emotions and concepts. These characteristics surface in the poetry of Bécquer. He was in these ways an innovative voice in Spanish literature, as well as a precursor to modern modes of thinking and writing in Spain and elsewhere.

Isabella II and the Revolution of 1868. Although Bécquer's poetry ignores the social and political events of the time to concentrate on an individual's dreams and emotions, contemporary politics did, in fact, have a significant impact on the fate of Bécquer's writings. Since 1833, Spain

had been ruled by Queen Isabella II, who had acceded to the throne at the age of three. Isabella's mother, Maria Cristina of Naples, and General Baldamero Espartero governed successively as regents until the young queen came of age in 1843.

THE EVOLVING CONCEPT OF THE SELF

While the individual or "self" plays a prominent role in Romantic and Post-Romantic poetry, it also becomes a problematic element for the writer of the period. In the eighteenth-century Enlightenment view, largely influenced by the French philosopher René Descartes, the self is presumed to be the basis for one's experience of reality. It is privileged as the source of reason and certainty in the world. Though commonly explored and exalted in Romantic and Post-Romantic writing, the self is not necessarily viewed with the same sense of certainty shown in the Enlightenment. By the early nineteenth century, the German philosopher G. W. F. Hegel had initiated a shift in the concept of the self. Hegel spoke about its active interrelationship to the world, introducing terms like "empathy" and "praxis," which placed the self in a dynamic of action and interaction with external reality.

> The self only becomes self through action. That which is externalized is then internalized, and the self that becomes itself in interaction with other selves and in the projection onto the world of its inwardness reintegrates that which flowed out to reach its next stage of development. No longer abstract thinker, detached observer, patched-together identity, grammatical fiction, or prerequisite of any possible experience, this self unfolds, acts, creates, develops, struggles, and finally identifies with the results of its actions, creations, developments and struggles.
>
> (Levin, p. 45)

Hegel's approach leads to a more dynamic and problematic view of the self, a view visible in the often paradoxical and pessimistic images of the poet in Bécquer's verse. By the late nineteenth century, the rise of positivism, a more pragmatic view of a person as a rational entity capable of resolving social problems through scientific reason, would reassert the integrity and certainty of the self. But the concept would later be probed anew by many twentieth-century artists and thinkers.

Political unrest and a series of uprisings marred the years of Isabella's personal rule (1843-68). Dominating her government were military

Isabella II

politicians—particularly, General Ramón Maria Narváez and General Leopoldo O'Donnell; it changed hands approximately 60 times during her reign, each time exacerbating the nation's political instability. Meanwhile, liberal opposition to the authoritarian policies of the royal regime continued to grow, especially in light of Isabella's obstinate refusal to admit progressive parties to power. Foolish decisions in her personal life also undermined Isabella's popularity with her subjects. Although she had married her cousin Don Francisco de Asís, heir to the duke of Cadiz, in 1846, the royal couple set up separate households and the promiscuous Isabella had many indiscreet love affairs, mostly with army officers. Paradoxically, she at the same time fell under the influence of religious fanatics, including Sor Patrocinio, a nun, and Father Antonio Claret, a Catalan evangelical.

Between 1863 and 1866, student demonstrations and clashes with the soldiers flared up throughout Spain, and in June 1866, a full-scale attempt at mutiny—at the San Gil Barracks near the royal palace in Madrid—led to bloody street fighting and the loss of over 200 out of an estimated 500 mutineers. An additional 76 were executed by firing squad. The deaths of O'Donnell in 1867 and Narvaez in 1868 left Isabella without a strong military ally, on top of which the administration of her new prime minister, Luis

González Bravo, was plagued from the outset by economic problems. Attempting to balance the budget, González Bravo reduced military expenditures, alienating both the army and navy, and posted the more political generals to distant sites in the Canary and the Balearic Islands. In defiance of these policies, liberal military forces and progressive political parties banded together against the monarchy. Led by General Francisco Serrano and General Juan Prim, rebel troops defeated the government's army and in September 1868 they marched into Madrid, where the overthrow of the Bourbon monarchy was proclaimed. Receiving the news at San Sebastian, Isabella fled with her family to France, where she lived in exile until her death in 1904.

While none of these events are chronicled in Bécquer's *Rimas*, the poet's life was nonetheless significantly affected by these shifts in political power. Appointed as a censor of novels—a position obtained for him by his friend and patron, prime minister González Bravo—during Isabella's reign, Bécquer afterward found himself without a position and, consequently, without income. Even more significantly, Bécquer lost the first manuscript of his poems, which González Bravo had purchased, when the prime minister's house was ransacked during the Revolution of 1868. As noted, the poet reconstructed his lost poems based on memory and on earlier manuscripts. Eventually, after his death, his friends would arrange and publish the version of the *Rimas* that exists today.

Bécquer's observance of the goings-on at Isabella II's court, and the unstable and hypocritical nature of her government, may have affected his often pessimistic, skeptical attitude toward love and the search for the ideal. In 1986 an anonymous party offered some watercolors to Madrid's National Library—erotic watercolors of 1868-69. Attached to the pseudonym "SEM," the watercolors have been attributed to the Bécquer brothers. The pictures satirize Queen Isabella, her indiscreet love affairs, and prominent personages in her court. Caricatured are the king, Sor Patrocinio, Father Claret, and Bécquer's own benefactor, González Bravo, as well as the Carlists, among others. In certain images, the queen and her family are depicted in a ridiculous vein, either as circus performers or dancing the Can-Can. In many of the prints, there are rather graphic pictures of the queen having sexual relations with government ministers and religious figures, and of the king sprouting horns (a sign that he has been cuckolded) or being sodomized by Father Claret. While sexual iconography, anticlericalism, and antimonarchical sentiments were somewhat common in Europe around 1860, these views were expressed with somewhat more hesitancy in Spain, given its cultural and, at times, official censorship. The prints attributed to SEM, indicative of their authors' liberal politics and scandalous enough to merit publication under a pseudonym, provide useful insight into the nature of the conflict between liberalism and conservatism that dominated much of nineteenth-century Spanish politics. They meanwhile broaden a reader's perspective on the sociopolitical context within which Bécquer composed his *Rimas*.

The evolution of nineteenth-century society. By the latter half of the nineteenth century, Spanish society was undergoing significant change. Most notably, the period saw increasing industrialization and urbanization, which led to considerable migration and subsequent population growth in cities such as Madrid. The growth of cities in this period naturally had important effects on social relations, cultural production, and the general collective consciousness of the times. According to the historian Eric Lampard, this general trend in population growth led to "a higher degree of segregation of work, residence, class, occupation, and ethnicity than had existed in the early modern cities or colonial towns" (Lampard in Ugarte, p. 13). On one hand, the changing urban environment fostered the sense of alienation and desperation commonly associated with the modern city, which sometimes leads to suicide. On the other hand, it fostered, at least in the artistic sphere, the exaltation and exploration of the individual—often marginalized and rebellious, sensual and self-absorbed—central to Romanticism and, in the case of Bécquer, to Post-Romanticism. In Spain, this heightened sense of individuality relates as well to the continued growth of liberal politics and democratic ideals in the last half of the nineteenth century, albeit in the face of strong resistance from conservative political groups.

The growth of the cities created both new problems and new opportunities. In the arena of public health, sanitation was generally poor and outbreaks of tuberculosis and venereal diseases became more common; Bécquer himself would contract syphilis. Alcohol and drug addiction grew. A need for escapism led to a rise in the consumption not only of minor stimulants like tea and coffee, but also to an increased consumption of liquor and opium. At the same time, the growing urban population led to the creation of new communities, such as the bohemian artistic community to which Bécquer belonged. It also created a growing population of readers, a

CARLISM

Dynastic conflicts had surrounded the 1843 accession of the child-queen Isabella II, who was the eldest daughter of Ferdinand VII and Maria Cristina of Naples. The king's younger brother, Don Carlos Maria Isidro, disputed his niece's claim on the basis of the Salic law—passed by Philip V in 1713—that barred women from the throne. Although female inheritance had been reinstated in 1789 by the Cortes (Spanish parliament), Charles IV, who was king at that time, had not published that new law. Thus, most Spaniards continued to regard the Salic law as the law of the land until 1830, when the 1789 decree was finally made public. Taking issue with the timing, Don Carlos insisted that this decree was put into effect only to prevent him from claiming the throne. In 1833, he declared himself Charles V; his supporters became known as Carlists. Adherents to the Carlist cause included staunch Catholics—many of whom inhabited the Basque and Navarrese regions of northern Spain—and political conservatives who feared the small but present liberal element in King Ferdinand's courts. During the early years of the First Carlist War (1833-38), the Carlists enjoyed several military victories and established their own state, which extended from Galicia on the west to Catalonia on the east and as far south as lower Aragon. Rejection by the Spanish propertied classes, which had profited from liberal confiscation of Church lands, weakened the Carlist cause, however. The revolt failed to spread beyond the north and a truce, the Convention of Vergara, was established in 1838. Peasant unrest after the marriage of Isabella II fueled the Second Carlist War in 1848, but the uprising was quelled a year later. Not until Isabella II was deposed in 1868 did the Carlist movement become fully reactivated. The Third Carlist War (1870-76), growing out of uprisings in the Basque provinces, Navarre, and parts of Catalonia, contributed to the collapse of Spain's first republic and the restoration of Isabella's son, Alfonso XII, to the throne in 1874. Two years later, the king mounted a large-scale offensive against the Carlists that prompted many of them to flee to France.

phenomenon that gave rise to a more extensive and rapid system of print journalism. This development, in turn, allowed writers like Bécquer to be both "artists" in the traditional sense and professionals who could make a more pragmatic living at the craft.

The Poems in Focus

Contents summary. It has been argued that Bécquer's 76 *rimas* form a loosely woven narrative. Certainly, the speaker's situation and state of mind undergo a series of changes from the first to the last poem. However, it is important to keep in mind that the ordering of the poems in the collection was done by Bécquer's friends after his death and does not necessarily represent the order in which the poems were written or the order in which the poet had placed them. It is more accurate to view the succession of poems as a reflection of the friends' vision of the Romantic trajectory—from discovery of the ideal, to loss, to despair. In this sense, the collection can be regarded as a reflection of Romanticism's general vision of life rather than an attempt by the poet to construct a linear narrative of his experience. At the same time, the *rimas* also seem to convey the complex process of self-exploration typical of the Romantic poet, through which the self occupies a series of diverse positions and perspectives and becomes more multifaceted and problematic. This is an indicator of Bécquer's incipient modernity in terms of the poetic process. Robert Havard suggests that one of the defining contributions of Bécquer's poetry is his "modern reflexivity," that is, his "acute awareness of his medium, and with it, his vocational urge as a poet to discover himself—his own Self—within that medium, his will to unearth meaning by virtue of his activity as a poet" (Havard, p. 3). Rima 2 conveys the poetic speaker's sense of unsettled subjectivity, concluding with these lines: "Such am I, by chance / In the world, unknowing / Whence come I, nor whither / My steps are going" (Becquer, *The Infinite Passion,* 2.17-20)

Throughout the collection, the poetic voice of the *rimas* is consumed with an ecstatic yearning to create poetry, to "[w]rite it in words that were at the same time / Sighing and laughter, color and notes" (*Infinite Passion,* 1.7-8). The speaker's love of poetry and the creative process affect his perceptions of nature and fuel his dreams of a poetic muse who generally takes the form of an imaginary woman: "'What is poesy?' you ask me, gazing / Into mine eyes with your eyes blue. / What is poesy? And do you truly ask me? / Poesy . . . are you" (*Infinite Passion,* 21.1-4).

Other poems in the collection represent more directly the relationships of flesh-and-blood human beings, often ultimately leaving the speaker to brood bitterly over the end of a romance and his lingering devotion to a woman he now sees as unworthy. In the well-known Rima 53, the speaker turns from passions of the mind to passions of the flesh, specifically the unhappy resolution of his romance with an unnamed woman. The speaker evokes the cyclical changes of the natural world in his bittersweet farewell to his beloved, describing how once again swallows will nest on her balcony and honeysuckle bloom in her garden. But the particular swallows and blossoms that witnessed the course of their love affair are, like her love for *him*, gone forever. The poetic speaker assures the one who has left him that she will never again be loved in the same way as he has loved her:

From Rima 53
Burning words of love will come
    Again full oft within thine ears to sound;
Perchance thy heart will even be aroused
    From its sleep profound;
But mute and prostrate and absorbed,
    As God is worshipped in His holy fane,
As I have loved thee . . . undeceive thyself:
    Thou wilt not be thus loved again!
                (*Infinite Passion*, 53.17-24)

At other moments, the poetic voice reflects upon the nature of death, speculating upon the loneliness of the dead and the possibility of an afterlife. After beholding the sculpted effigy of a beautiful woman on a tomb, he finds consolation in contemplating his own eventual death: "Oh, what love is serene as that of death! / What sleep so tranquil as the sepulcher!" (*Infinite Passion,* 76.43-44).

The nature of poetry and the role of the poet. Havard suggests that "[n]ot until Bécquer had poetry been the subject of poetry, at least not so conspicuously and at least not in Spain" (Havard, p. 2). Likening him to the sixteenth-century mystic San Juan de la Cruz (see **"Dark Night" and Other Poems**, also in *WLAIT 5: Spanish and Portuguese Literatures and Their Times*), Havard sees Bécquer as "a modern secular visionary" who "struggles openly and tormentedly with what in his first *rima* he calls 'el rebelde, mezquino idioma' ('the rebellious, mean language')" (Havard, p. 2). This exploration of the nature of poetry and the role of the poet becomes a central theme in Bécquer's *Rimas*.

In Rima 7, the speaker, on beholding a dusty, abandoned musical instrument, imagines the songs imprisoned in its strings, waiting to be freed by the touch of "the master." He compares the silent lute to the dormant poetic imagination, which—like the dead Biblical figure Lazarus—must be awakened by a greater power, a divine hand or voice, implying that this is one of the important functions of the poet.

Rima 7

In a shadowy nook of the chamber,
   All covered with dust and mute—
Forgotten, perhaps by its master—
   Was seen the lute.

What tones in its strings were sleeping,
   As birds in the branches sleep,
Awaiting the master's snowy hand
   Its chords to sweep.

How oft, I thought, thus sleepeth
   In the soul's depths genius' worth,
Like Lazarus waiting for a voice
   To say, "Come forth!"

        (*Infinite Passion*, 7.1-12)

However, the relationship of the poet to the poem is not necessarily as simple as that of the master to his creation; it is not just an exercise in form or technique. Rima 4, another well-known piece from the collection, proclaims in its first stanza that "There may be no poets, but forever / Poesy will be" (*Infinite Passion*, 4.3-4). Again beginning with the image of the lute, suggesting the musical and intangible nature of poetry, the speaker suggests that the instrument will never be silenced, that poetry exists as a force of nature, independent of the creative hand of the poet. The poem goes on to enumerate a series of elements of human experience that, even in the absence of the poet, would still be the source of poetry.

The poetic speaker begins by evoking a series of natural elements: waves, sunlight, clouds, breezes, and aromas, suggesting these as basic elements of poetry. The speaker then goes on to invoke one of the fundamental tenets of the Romantic vision—the rejection of scientific reason in favor of the irrational and intangible, a powerful source of poetry in itself:

From Rima 4

As long as by science the well of life
   Has not been found,
And in seas or in heavens an abyss remains
   That men cannot sound;

While ignorant whither, but forward yet,
   Goes humanity;
As long as one mystery remains for man,
   Poesy will be!

        (*Infinite Passion*, 4.13-20)

Finally, in Romantic fashion, the poem delves into the realm of emotional experiences such as joy, sorrow, hope, and memory, and suggests their importance to the nature of poetry: "As long as the heart and head battle still, Poesy will be!" (*Infinite Passion*, 4.27-28). Ultimately it is the experience of love and sensuality that marks the inspiration of true poetry:

As long as eyes mirror the tender gaze
   Of other eyes;
As long as a sighing mouth still responds
   To a mouth that sighs;

As long as two souls in a kiss can feel
   One unity;
As long as one beautiful woman is. . .
   Poesy will be!

        (*Infinite Passion*, 4.29-36)

Woman—the elusive ideal. Women figure prominently in Bécquer's *Rimas*. Indeed, even from the first poem of the collection, which ostensibly addresses the mystery of poetry, the presence of a female other can be felt, since the poet ultimately intends to share the poem with her: "Vain the essay: no characters are there / That can contain it; —scarcely, O my own! / Clasping thy hands in my hands might I, / Hearing it, sing it to thee alone" (*Infinite Passion*, 1.9-12). The writing of poetry seems inextricably linked to the idea of woman, whether she be the one to which the poetic voice is addressed, the muse who inspires it, or the metaphorical representation of the ideal to which poetry aspires.

In nineteenth-century bourgeois culture, the ideal woman tended to be very feminine, devoted to her husband and children, skilled at running her household, and, above all, chaste. During Bécquer's lifetime, women from most social classes married young—in their late teens to early 20s—and settled into lives of tranquil domesticity. Romanticism challenged this dutiful female image with a second, less respectable ideal: the woman who placed passion and love above social acceptance. Such a woman was more a literary figure than a reality, more the exception than the rule.

It is perhaps indicative of Bécquer's airy Romanticism that the "ideal woman" in his poems is not a sweet domestic dove but a distant, often unattainable fantasy, not unlike those in the love poems of the Italian masters Petrarch and Dante Alighieri. The ongoing conflict between the ideal and the real fuels much of the interaction between the poetic voice and the female figures in Bécquer's *Rimas*.

The Infinite Passion (Rimas)

The nature of the female figures in the *Rimas*, and their relationships to the poetic speaker, vary widely throughout the collection. There are certainly a number of poems in which the speaker evokes the concrete romantic relationship, as in the case of the previously cited Rima 53, in which the speaker laments the loss of what was presumably a meaningful love. In Rima 55, he suggests a more fleeting interaction, which takes place amid an orgy, and the female figure is referred to as simply his "darling for the day" (Infinite Passion, 55.9). Rima 41 evokes a turbulent, unsuccessful emotional relationship that also hints at its sexual nature by means of phallic symbolism: "Thou wert the hurricane; I the lofty tower / That did defy its power: / Needs must thou spend thyself or shiver me! . . . / It could not be!" (*Infinite Passion,* 41.1-4).

In many cases in Bécquer's *Rimas*, however, the speaker yearns not after any flesh-and-blood woman but after an elusive, intangible fantasy that somehow unites his love of poetry, his appreciation of nature, and his awareness of feminine charms. This fusion of woman with nature and poetry is in fact characteristic of Romantic literature. In the famous Rima 11, the speaker rejects first a woman of passion and then a woman of tenderness, in favor of a misty phantasm who baldly warns him, "I cannot love thee":

Rima 11

"I am dark-tinted and ardent as fire,
    I am the symbol of fervency;
My heart runneth over with joyous desire.
    Searchest thou for me?"—*No; not for thee.*

"Pale is my brow and golden my tresses;
    Endless felicity I can bestow;
I guard a treasure of rare tendernesses.
    Callest thou for me?"—*Not for thee; no.*

"I am a dream, I am an impossible
    Fantasy hollow of luster and gloom;
I am impalpable, I am intangible;
    I cannot love thee."—*Oh, come thou; come!*
                              (*Infinite Passion* 11.1-12)

The sentiments expressed in Rima 11 are reinforced in Rima 15 when the speaker describes his eternal pursuit of that bodiless ideal: "You, airy shadow, who, when I endeavor / Only to touch you, disappear ever / Like unto flame, like unto sound, / Like unto mist, like the murmur profound / Of the lake blue" (*Infinite Passion,* 15.7-11).

In Rima 27, the speaker's preference for the ideal woman over the real one is manifested through his desire to keep his beloved in a state of slumber: "Awake, I tremble to behold thee, / But I am bold to gaze on thee, asleep; / So, spirit of my spirit, whilst thou slumb'rest / My watch o'er thee I keep" (*Infinite Passion*, 27.1-4). Throughout the poem, though the speaker finds beauty in his beloved in both her dreaming and wakened states, he invariably prefers her in the former, repeating the command "Sleep!" at the close of each stanza. This is reaffirmed in the concluding stanza as well: "Already at the balcony have I drawn / The curtains, to keep / Without the dawning's wearying splendor, / Lest it awake thee" (*Infinite Passion*, 27. 36-39)

There are moments, however, when the ideal woman reveals herself as flawed, and the speaker reacts cynically at the recognition that there is a sometimes enormous distance between the ideal and the real, as in Rima 34. The speaker notes that the woman he observes "has light, and color, and perfume, / And line has she; / And form, engenderer of desires; expression, / The everlasting fount of poesy" (*Infinite Passion*, 34.13-16). However, his concluding comment, with its derogatory tone, reveals a recognition that the ideal is unattainable and artificial: "But she is stupid? . . . Bah! While, silent, she keeps / The secret, always / To me what she holds silent will be worth / More than all that anyone else can say" (*Infinite Passion,* 34.17-20).

At other moments further disillusionment sets in. In Rima 39, the speaker admits that he is aware that the female he idealizes is flawed, even as he ruefully accepts his continuing devotion to her:

Rima 39

Why tell me so? I know it: she is fickle,
    Capricious, she is arrogant and vain;
Before true feeling from her heart would
        spring,
    Water would gush forth from the sterile
        plain.
I know there is no fiber that responds
    To love within her heart, a serpent's lair:
That she is an inanimate statue . . . but . . .
    She is so fair!
                              (*Infinite Passion* 39.1-8)

In various poems placed near the end of the collection, thoughts of death and the afterlife preoccupy the poetic speaker. Ultimately, he undergoes an epiphany when he beholds the statue of "a lovely woman— / A marvel of the chisel" lying on a Gothic tomb: "Quickened in my spirit / The thirst for infinity / And all the yearnings of this life for death, / To which the centuries but an instant be" (*Infinite Passion,* 76.33-36). The speaker thus finds a full range of

BÉCQUER IN LOVE

~

The prominence of the theme of love and the intense subjectivity in Bécquer's poems lead to inevitable speculation on the poet's own love life. Bécquer's biographers are sharply divided on this issue but most agree that, while living in Madrid, Bécquer fell in love with Julia Espín y Guillén. Daughter of the orchestra director at the Teatro Real and herself a successful opera singer, she may be the inspiration for his poems. The exact details of their relationship are unknown. One account relates that Bécquer often visited Julia's residence but she openly rebuffed him; another maintains that Bécquer met Julia socially only a few times and was content merely to worship her from afar, like a medieval courtly lover. Certainly, Julia's elevated social position (she was from a well-known family in social circles of the time) may have intimidated Bécquer, discouraging him from declaring his feelings in any direct fashion. Whatever the circumstances, Bécquer's love remained unrequited. Julia eventually married an influential politician.

Not much more is known about Casta Esteban y Navarro, whom Bécquer married in 1861. From the province of Soria, she was the daughter of a country physician, a specialist in venereal diseases who had treated Bécquer in the past. (As noted earlier, Bécquer suffered from syphilis.) The marriage was apparently unhappy from the start, and the couple parted in 1868, Bécquer taking their two children with him. His wife, who seems to have had an affair, was pregnant with a third child; though recognized as Bécquer's, the baby remained with her. Explanations for the failure of Bécquer's marriage vary. Some sources argue that Casta did not understand Bécquer's sensitive nature. Others trace the marital strife to friction between Casta and Bécquer's beloved brother, Valeriano, who lived with the family. A third set speaks of Casta as an unfaithful wife, referring to the claims of Bécquer's daughter Julia that her father was jealous of a former suitor of Casta's, Esteban, whom Casta did marry shortly after Bécquer's death. Whatever the explanation, all sources concur on the unhappiness of the marriage. How greatly this affected the content of his *Rimas* is matter of conjecture. Though not necessarily autobiographical, his own bittersweet loves no doubt influenced his poetic depiction of unhappiness in love.

emotional and subjective experience in the course of the *Rimas*—from loving the intangible, to desiring the physical, and, finally, to yearning after the infinite, all three of which are represented by women.

Sources and literary context. Many scholars and biographers have attempted to discern whether a particular woman provided Bécquer with the inspiration for some of the verse in *Rimas*. These specialists disagree as to what extent Bécquer's own romantic experiences may have shaped those of the poetic speaker of his *Rimas*. While it is likely that Julia Espín y Guillén or even Casta, Bécquer's own wife, provided some of the inspiration for the unhappy romantic threads in *Rimas*, his own words suggest that the often cruel beloved who spurns the speaker's

love is equally a product of his imagination. According to Bécquer, the women in his imaginative universe are a complex mix of the real and the ideal:

> It costs me labor to determine what things I have dreamed and what things have happened to me. My affections are divided between the phantasms of my imagination and real personalities. My memory confuses the names and dates of women and days that have died or passed away with the days and women that have never existed save in my mind.
>
> (Bécquer, *Legends, Tales, and Poems*, p. xxxv)

The question of poetic influences on Bécquer's work poses another conundrum. Since none of Bécquer's contemporaries or precursors in his native Spain appear to have written in the same poetic vein, he is often compared with other continental Romantics, such as the German poet Heinrich Heine and the French poet Alfred de Musset. It is unclear whether Bécquer read the works of either poet, although Heine's verses, at least, had started appearing in Spanish in 1857.

BÉCQUER ON POETRY

Like many Romantics, Bécquer formulated distinct ideas about poetry and poetry's purpose. In a *prologo* (prologue) to a collection of poems by his friend Augusto Ferrán y Forniés, Bécquer wrote about two kinds of poetry: "There is a poetry which is magnificent and sonorous, the offspring of meditation and art, which adorns itself with all the pomp of language, moves along with a cadenced majesty. . . ." (*Legends, Tales, and Poems*, p. xxxvi). He then described the second kind of poetry: it is "natural, rapid, terse," and "springs from the soul as an electric spark, which strikes our feelings with a word, and flees away" (*Legends, Tales, and Poems*, p. xxxvi).

> Bare of artificiality, free within a free form, it awakens by the aid of one kindred idea the thousand others that sleep in the bottomless ocean of fancy. The first [kind of poetry] has an acknowledged value; it is the poetry of everybody. The second lacks any absolute standard of measurement; it takes the proportions of the imagination that it impresses; it may be called the poetry of poets.
>
> (*Legends, Tales, and Poems*, p. xxxvi)

According to Bécquer, his friend's poetry belongs to this second category. The description, which reflects Bécquer's own Post-Romantic, pre-modernist aesthetic, can also be applied to his own verse—famous for its elegant simplicity and naturalness of expression.

However much scholars diverge on the subject of Bécquer's love life or literary influences, all agree about his importance to the second phase of Spain's Romantic movement. Bécquer's most enduring contributions to Post-Romanticism are represented by his simple but beautiful language; his delicate, dreamlike imagery; and his willingness to create and explore different kinds of poetry. Literary scholars Richard E. Chandler and Kessel Schwartz observe that Bécquer's poetry "has risen in popularity and esteem with twentieth century poets and critics. . . . Many now feel that his poetry although slight in quantity, is the greatest poetry of the century, principally because of his ability to foresee and to predict, in a sense, the modern schools of poetry" (Chandler and Schwartz, p. 352).

Impact. The fame that eluded Bécquer in life was bestowed upon him posthumously, thanks in large part to friends who collected his work for publication. One such friend, Ramón Rodríguez Correa, was especially influential; his prologue to the first edition of Bécquer's works provided most of the known facts regarding the poet's life. According to literary scholar Everett Ward Olmsted, the collection of Bécquer's works in 1871 apparently "caused a marked effect, and their author was placed by popular edict in the front rank of contemporary writers" (Olmsted in Bécquer, *Legends, Tales, and Poems*, p. xxix). Within seven years of Bécquer's death, four editions of his work had been published, all of which found an eager readership not only in Spain but in other countries as well. By the 1920s, some 400 editions of Bécquer's *Rimas* alone had been published in Spanish, two of those editions in the United States.

Nineteenth-century literary scholars found much to commend in Bécquer's work. P. Francisco Blanco García marveled at how different Bécquer's poetic sensibility was from those of his Spanish literary compatriots, wondering, "How could a Seville poet, a lover of pictorial and sculptural marvels, so withdraw from the outer form as to embrace the pure idea, with that melancholy subjectivism as common in the gloomy regions bathed by the Spree [River, in Germany] as it is unknown on the banks of the Darro and Guadalquivir [Rivers, in southern Spain]?" (Blanco García in Bécquer, *Legends, Tales, and Poems*, p. xxxiv). Written by Mrs. Humphrey Ward for *Macmillan's Magazine* in 1883, another early assessment praises Bécquer for the uniqueness of his poetic voice:

> His literary importance indeed is just beginning to be understood. Of Gustavo Bécquer we may almost say that in a generation of rhymers he alone was a poet.
>
> (Ward in Bécquer, *Legends, Tales, and Poems*, p. xxxiv)

—James Wojtaszek and Pamela S. Loy

For More Information

Bécquer, Gustavo Adolfo. *The Infinite Passion*. Trans. Young Allison. Chicago: Walter M. Hill, 1924.
———. *Legends, Tales, and Poems*. Boston: Ginn, 1907.
Bécquer, Valeriano, and Gustavo Adolfo Bécquer.

SEM: *Los Borbones en pelota*. Madrid: Ediciones El Museo Universal, 1991.

Bynum, B. Bryant. *The Romantic Imagination in the Works of Gustavo Adolfo Bécquer*. Chapel Hill: North Carolina Studies in the Romance Languages and Literatures, 1993.

Chandler, Richard E., and Kessel Schwartz. *A New History of Spanish Literature*. Baton Rouge: Louisiana State University Press, 1961.

Clinkscales, Orline. *Bécquer in Mexico, Central America and the Caribbean Countries*. Madrid: Editorial Hispanonorteamericana, 1970.

Díaz-Plaja, Guillermo. *A History of Spanish Literature*. New York: New York University Press, 1971.

Guillén, Jorge. *Language and Poetry: Some Poets of Spain*. Cambridge: Harvard University Press, 1961.

Havard, Robert G. *From Romanticism to Surrealism: Seven Spanish Poets*. Totowa, N.J.: Barnes and Noble, 1988.

King, Edmund L. *Gustavo Adolfo Bécquer: From Painter to Poet*. Mexico: Editorial Porrua, S. A., 1953.

Levin, Jerome D. *Theories of the Self*. New York: Hemisphere, 1992.

Stamm, James R. *A Short History of Spanish Literature*. New York: New York University Press, 1979.

Ugarte, Michael. *Madrid 1900: The Capital as Cradle of Literature and Culture*. University Park, Penn.: Penn State University Press, 1996.

The Infinite Passion (Rimas)

The Interior Castle

by
St. Teresa of Avila

Teresa de Cepeda y Ahumada (1515-82) was born into an aristocratic family in the city of Avila, about 50 miles northwest of Madrid. In 1535, at age twenty, she entered the Carmelite convent of the Incarnation at Avila, taking the monastic name Teresa of Jesus (only after her canonization in 1622 would she be known as "Teresa of Avila"). Like other Carmelites in the sixteenth century, the nuns at the Incarnation observed a "mitigated" or softened version of the order's original rule, and for two decades Teresa lived an accordingly relaxed and materially comfortable existence. In 1555, however, she experienced a religious awakening that called her towards a more ascetic and meditative life. By 1562 she had secured Pope Pius IV's approval to open the first convent of the Carmelite Reform, in which she hoped principles of humility and poverty would be more rigorously observed. By the late 1570s Teresa had founded further Reform Carmelite convents, but great controversy often surrounded her work. Central to that work was the idea of mental prayer, which Teresa believed could establish a close personal link between the individual and God. Teresa explored this idea in her many writings, which include letters, poems, and scriptural commentary as well as four longer prose works: the autobiographical *Life* (written in 1562); *The Way of Perfection* (written in 1564); *The Book of the Foundations* (written in 1573 and describing her struggles to found convents); and finally *The Interior Castle* (written in 1577), widely considered to be the most vivid and fully realized

THE LITERARY WORK

A religious allegory exploring techniques of mystical prayer; published in Spanish in 1588 (as *Las Moradas del Castillo Interior*), in English in 1852.

SYNOPSIS

The author likens the soul to a castle that contains seven groups of *moradas,* or dwelling places, each group representing a stage in the journey towards spiritual union with God, which occurs in the seventh or central ring.

account of this influential mystic's spiritual method.

Events in History at the Time of the Allegory

Catholicism in Golden Age Spain. During the sixteenth and early seventeenth centuries the Spanish reached heights of imperial and cultural splendor from which they dominated Europe and much of the world. The lifetime of the woman later known as St. Teresa of Avila spanned roughly the first half—that is from the accession of King Charles I of Spain in 1516 to the death of his son, King Philip II, in 1598—of this so-called Golden Age. While Spain's cultural achievements continued well into the seventeenth century, Spanish military and economic

St. Teresa of Avila

strength began to decline before Philip II's death, so that Teresa can be said to have lived during the age in which Spanish power reached its peak.

The driving force behind Spain's dynamic expansion was its militant adherence to the Catholic faith, forged during the long Reconquest of Spain from the Muslims. Muslim Arabs and North Africans (called Moors) had conquered Spain in the eighth century, and Jews had settled there in their wake, adding to a preexisting Jewish population. The vigorous Moorish culture that resulted blended Islamic, Jewish, and Christian influences, making medieval Spain the most culturally diverse of European lands. Since the Moorish conquest, however, Spain's Christian kingdoms had waged a long and successful struggle to reconquer the peninsula, a campaign that had taken on the character of a holy war. The Reconquest was concluded by Charles I's grandparents, King Ferdinand and Queen Isabella, who captured the last Moorish stronghold, the southern city of Granada, in 1492.

As they had reconquered Moorish territory, Spain's Christian rulers had also energetically sought to convert their new Muslim and Jewish subjects to Christianity. Muslims and Jews who refused to convert were ultimately expelled from Spain. In 1492, for example, the same year that

Granada was captured, Ferdinand and Isabella also expelled Spain's remaining Jewish population, amounting to some 170,000 people. Under threat of expulsion, many Muslims and Jews had indeed become Christians: Muslims who converted and their descendants were called Moriscos; Jews who converted and their descendants were called Conversos. In the 1940s historians discovered that Teresa's father, Alonso Sánchez de Cepeda, was from a Converso family, for Teresa's paternal grandfather was a Jew from Toledo who converted to Christianity during the reign of Ferdinand and Isabella.

Known as the Catholic Monarchs for their strict piety, Ferdinand and Isabella were gravely concerned about their subjects' religious purity. They were aware that many Moriscos and Conversos had become Christian in name only, accepting baptism but secretly continuing to observe their original faiths. With the Pope's blessing, the Catholic Monarchs established a special branch of the Church known as the Spanish Inquisition, with broad powers (which eventually included censorship) to ensure that Moriscos and Conversos worshipped according to Catholic standards. Throughout Spain's Golden Age, both Moriscos and Conversos were subject to continuing persecution by such institutions as the Inquisition, whose methods ranged from interrogation to confiscation of property, torture, and execution by fire. In 1485 the Inquisition in Toledo, suspecting the Sánchez family of Jewish practices, subjected all of them—including Teresa's father, then five years old—to an examination that culminated in a humiliating procession of penance through the city's streets, during which they were taunted by their fellow Toledans. Historians believe that it was to escape such persecution that the family moved to Avila in 1493, where Teresa's grandfather reestablished his successful garment manufacturing business.

Reformation and Counter-Reformation. Starting in 1517, when Teresa was two years old, the European world underwent a major religious upheaval that would extend throughout Teresa's lifetime and beyond, and in which Teresa herself would play an important part. For centuries complaints had been raised against corruption and abuses within the Catholic Church, but numerous reform movements had resulted in little change. In October 1517, however, a reforming German monk named Martin Luther set in motion a train of events that would result in a momentous division, as former Catholics split away from the Catholic Church and formed what would become the various Protestant churches. Europe could no longer be considered a Catholic continent. Protestantism grew strongest in northern lands such as England, the Netherlands, and the German principalities, where it provided a rallying point for rulers eager to defy Habsburg and Papal authority.

At around the same time an answering Counter-Reformation arose within the Catholic Church, as Catholic leaders attempted to address the Church's problems without abandoning Catholicism itself. Catholicism remained strong in Spain, which now became the leader of the Catholic world, in France, Spain's rival for leadership despite a sizeable Protestant minority, and in Italy. In the past, historians have viewed Spain's leadership of the Catholic Counter-Reformation as primarily repressive and authoritarian in nature. For example, after the Reformation the Spanish Inquisition turned its main attention from Moriscos and Conversos to Protestants, whom they called *luteranos* (indiscriminately lumping all Protestants together as Lutherans). Thousands of real or suspected *luteranos* were burned in the Inquisition's *autos-da-fe* or "acts of faith," mass public executions by fire usually attended by large, enthusiastic crowds. Both Spaniards and foreigners in Spain could be subjected to the Inquisition's feared interrogations and punishments.

More recent scholarship, however, has also recognized a balancing creativity in Spain's leadership of the Counter-Reformation. In the 1530s, for example, the Spanish priest St. Ignatius Loyola (1491-1556; canonized, 1622) founded the exclusively male religious order known as the Society of Jesus, or Jesuits. Unlike other religious orders, many of which accepted primarily wealthy or aristocratic novices, the Jesuits took new members based on scholastic aptitude and general merit, a socially egalitarian approach that would later inspire Teresa in her reform of the Carmelites. Bound by an oath of obedience to the Pope, and working under the centralized command of a general in Rome, this dedicated and highly organized company of priests recognized no local church authorities. Ignatius, the Jesuits' first general, founded many schools and colleges in Spain, and made the Jesuits into primarily a teaching order.

Combining spiritual discipline, classical education, rigorous training, and intensive foreign missionary activity, the Jesuits became a leading arm of the Catholic Counter-Reformation.

The Jesuits were only one example of what amounted to an outbreak of religious fervor in sixteenth-century Spain, resulting in a spate of monastic and other religious foundations. While the Jesuits were certainly concerned with prayer and spiritual matters, their training tended to focus on academic learning and subtle nuances of doctrine and theology. Many Spaniards sought a more direct religious experience, wishing to establish a personal and mystical connection with

LIMPIEZA DE SANGRE AND LA HONRA

Spanish society in the Golden Age deemed it honorable to come from a family without any Moorish or Jewish ancestors, a principle called *limpieza de sangre* or "purity of blood." Real or, if necessary, false genealogies could be bought, and Spanish aristocrats often went to great trouble in this way to proclaim their Christian "purity," a crucial component of one's all-important honor (*la honra*). In reality, however, like the future St. Teresa, many Spanish aristocrats were descended from wealthy Jews who had converted to Christianity decades or even centuries earlier. Fewer noble families had ancestors who married Moriscos. Laws often restricted important positions in the Catholic Church to so-called "Old Christians," excluding those suspected of Converso or Morisco ancestry.

The rejection of such considerations in deciding whom to admit to her convents was an important element of Teresa's Carmelite Reform, one that historians suggest may have had origins in Teresa's own Converso background. In *The Interior Castle*, as in her other writings, Teresa seems to oppose such prejudices, if always in veiled terms. For example, she writes that in the outer rooms of the castle "souls are still absorbed in the world and engulfed in their pleasures and vanities, with their honors and pretenses" (St. Teresa of Avila, *Interior Castle*, p. 293). Critics have seen this and similar passages as referring to such pervasive social preoccupations as *limpieza de sangre* and *honra*.

the divine. Starting in the early 1500s, groups of mystics called *alumbrados* or "illuminated ones" began appearing in Spanish towns and cities. Meeting informally in private homes, the *alumbrados* often belonged to various established Catholic religious orders—some might be monks or nuns, others priests. They shared a belief that the individual could be "illuminated" by the Holy

A nun belonging to the order of Carmelites, at prayer in her cell.

Spirit so that he or she could understand Christian Scripture without the benefit of rigorous academic training.

Appearing as early as 1509, the first *alumbrados* predated the Protestant Reformation by nearly a decade, and historians believe that their movement arose independently, although from impulses similar to those that motivated many Protestants. At first Spanish authorities tolerated them, but after the Reformation the Inquisition targeted the *alumbrados* as dangerous heretics, in effect *luteranos* who shared the Protestant belief that God and humans could commune without the intermediary of the Church. Issuing its first edict against the movement in 1525, the Inquisition persecuted a number of *alumbrado* leaders, several of them women, sentencing them to be publicly whipped and then imprisoned for life.

Despite the success of such measures in breaking up the groups, accusations of *alumbradismo* resurfaced periodically in succeeding years, reaching another peak in southern Spain in the 1560s and 1570s, when the Inquisition published further edicts banning *alumbrado* beliefs and practices (in 1568 and 1574).

This second wave of persecution occurred in response to a phenomenon that had little in common with the original *alumbrados*, other than the fact that many of the persecuted worshippers again were women. The groups in southern Spain were, in fact, mostly women. They were engaged in ecstatic prayer under the direction of a male leader, and the alleged *alumbrados* were this time charged with sexual misconduct rather than heresy. In 1577, the same year in which she later wrote *The Interior Castle*,

Teresa herself faced similar charges (see below). In *The Interior Castle* and other writings, Teresa takes great pains to forestall any such accusations of *alumbradismo* against herself, repeatedly and explicitly praising accepted Catholic virtues such as chastity and distancing herself from any heretical beliefs that could be associated with the movement.

Women in the Church and society. The Catholic Church has based its exclusion of women from the priesthood largely on several passages in the New Testament. Most important are those attributed to St. Paul, who tells Christian men, "Let your women keep silence in the churches; for it is not permitted unto them to speak, but they are commanded to be under obedience" (1 Corinthians 14:34; Authorized King James Version). Again, Paul enjoins Christians, "Let the woman learn in silence with all subjection," claiming that the example of Eve—who was deceived by the serpent, in contrast to Adam, who was not—justifies the Church's not permitting "a woman to teach, nor to usurp authority over the man" (1 Timothy 2:11-12). Furthermore, Paul implies elsewhere, the feminine disposition is likewise especially susceptible to deception by false prophets, who easily beguile "silly women laden with sins, led away with various lusts, ever learning, and never able to come to a knowledge of the truth" (2 Timothy 3:6-7).

While the official structure of the Catholic priesthood has always been shut off to women religious figures, who have therefore had only the unofficial venue of the convent in which to follow their calling, this doctrine of so-called "Pauline silence" has been interpreted with varying degrees of strictness at various times. The late medieval period, for example, saw a flowering of female mystics, many recognized as Catholic saints, who wrote highly influential accounts of their visions and other inner experiences. Examples from the fourteenth century include the Italian mystic St. Catherine of Siena, who was illiterate but dictated her widely read works, and the English Mother Julian of Norwich, whose revelations depicted Christ as a nurturing Mother.

By the time of the Renaissance in the late fifteenth century, humanists like the Dutch scholar Desiderius Erasmus (c. 1466-1536) rejected the assumption that women were spiritually inferior to men, denying as well that special education was necessary to understand Christian Scripture. Erasmus advocated ideas that were taken up by the Protestants during his lifetime, such as translating Scripture into the vernacular to make it accessible to all, but he himself remained a Catholic. His influential writings were embraced in Spain before the Reformation by Cardinal Ximénez Cisneros, Spain's leading Catholic official, who oversaw the translation into Spanish of works by a number of mystics, both men and women. In general, Cisneros supported a greater role for women in the Church. He established religious education for nuns and promoted Spanish women mystics, such as his contemporary María de Santo Domingo, whom Cisneros successfully defended when the Pope's investigators arrived to ascertain the validity of her visions.

MYSTICISM AND OUTSIDERS

Some historians have noted that, like Teresa, a high proportion of Spanish mystics have come from Converso backgrounds. For example, another saint from sixteenth-century Avila, St. John of Avila, was also a Converso, as was Teresa's younger colleague St. John of the Cross, who followed Teresa's reform of Carmelite convents with corresponding reforms of Carmelite monasteries. These historians speculate that the Conversos' status as outsiders in Spanish society helped foster an especially strong, internalized faith that sought a deeper expression than the externalized rituals common in Catholic practice. Historians have also attributed similar motives to the many women mystics active in such movements as that of the alumbrados. *The Interior Castle* explores the landscape of this internalized faith. Ironically, an emphasis on internal faith often provoked suspicion from Catholic institutions such as the Spanish Inquisition, for the Church had reacted to similar impulses among the Protestants by enforcing an even greater reliance on ritual. Supporters of this increased ritualization were among Teresa's strongest opponents in the controversies surrounding her reforms.

Cisneros died in 1517, the same year that the Reformation began, and his successors effected a backlash against his liberal policies. The persecution of the *alumbrados* mentioned above was part of the reaction that followed Cisneros's death, as was a general diminution of the role of women in the Catholic Church. It was during this extended backlash that Teresa lived, worked, and wrote. The backlash can be seen as part of Spain's complex response to the Reformation, for while the Catholic Church did attempt to reform abuses within its institutions as part of the Counter-Reformation, at the same time the Inquisition strove to censor humanist and Erasmian influences as dangerously close to Protestantism.

However, the decreased participation of women in the Church can also be seen as more truly reflecting the values of a conservative society, one that traditionally shut women of Teresa's class out of public life, strictly cloistering them in either the home or the convent. Middle- and upper-class girls in Spain were carefully watched over by their parents until marriage, when the husband replaced the parents as the guardian of a woman's honor. Girls were expected to marry in their teens. Teresa's mother, for example, Beatriz de Ahumada, had married at 15 (Alonso Sánchez, whose first wife had died, was 29 when he married Teresa's mother).

REFORM AND CONTROVERSY

A major element of Teresa's Carmelite reform was her emphasis on internal devotion as opposed to external ritual, as exemplified by her demands for her nuns to practice mental prayer. This and other similar practices left her potentially vulnerable to charges of *luteranismo* (Protestantism), charges that she is careful to forestall in her writings. For example, throughout *The Interior Castle* she calls for mental prayer along with vocal prayer rather than instead of it. Still, her reforms stirred constant controversy during her lifetime, and she was always in danger of persecution by institutions such as the Spanish Inquisition.

If a girl did not marry, as Teresa had not by the advanced age of 20, her parents would likely decide to place her in a convent, and she would become a nun. The convent generally demanded a substantial dowry or cash payment as an entrance fee, which her father would pay, just as he would pay a dowry to her husband if she married. Often her social life would continue in the convent, where the nuns would usually be segregated by class, with the wealthier sisters enjoying special comforts and privileges. Starting in the 1560s, Teresa's reforms would abolish such practices in the convents she founded, for Teresa insisted that her convents be cloistered and subsist on charitable donation, and that life there be based on internal religious devotion rather than on social connections, class, or wealth.

The Allegory in Focus

Contents summary. Teresa dedicates *The Interior Castle* to her sisters of the Carmelite Reform, otherwise known as the Discalced or Unshod Carmelites (to distinguish themselves from the other Carmelites, as well as to symbolize their poverty and humility, the Discalced Carmelites wore only sandals, not shoes). In a brief Prologue she explains that she has been ordered by her superiors to write about her techniques of prayer. Because for several months she has felt ill and has had difficulty concentrating, she prays for help performing the task.

In the first chapter she records that, when she prayed for assistance in writing, an image came into her mind of the soul as a beautiful castle of diamond or crystal, with many *moradas* or dwelling places, "just as there are many dwelling places in heaven" (*Interior Castle*, p. 283). Accordingly, the book is divided into seven sections corresponding to the seven groups of dwelling places she perceives in the soul. The first or outer dwelling places represent the least spiritually enlightened state, and the seventh or central ones represent the dwelling place of God, the King who rules the castle. These seven sections fall into two larger parts, with the first part (dwelling places one through three) covering normal human spiritual experience, and the second part (dwelling places four through seven) covering mystical, less accessible aspects of spiritual development.

• *The First Dwelling Places.* The first step is to enter the castle, for many souls are content to admire the castle's beautiful walls from the outside or to stay in the outer courtyard. The soul, by entering the castle, enters itself, and "the door of entry to this castle is prayer and reflection" (*Interior Castle*, p. 286). Souls that do not pray are like bodies that are crippled and paralyzed. Souls that have entered the first dwelling places, however, see only a little of the glowing light that emanates from the King's inner chambers. The first room represents self-knowledge, which in turn leads to all-important humility. Yet the devil puts many temptations in these first rooms, and the soul must be determined in pushing on to explore further and not succumbing to pleasurable distractions.

• *The Second Dwelling Places.* These rooms are for souls who have begun to practice prayer, and who now are called upon to make even greater efforts and face greater afflictions from the devil. Those souls must persevere, and "shouldn't be thinking about consolations at this beginning stage" (*Interior Castle*, p. 300).

• *The Third Dwelling Places.* Souls that have progressed to these rooms have achieved a disciplined life in general accordance with Christian principles. Yet they continue to cling to worldly pleasures such as wealth and honor, and risk complacently turning away from further effort. They rarely achieve a real depth or selflessness in their prayer and reflections.

• *The Fourth Dwelling Places.* "Supernatural experiences begin here," Teresa writes of the highly beautiful rooms of the fourth dwelling places, but such experiences "are something most difficult to explain" (*Interior Castle*, p. 316). She emphasizes a basic difference, that between active prayer achieved by human will (as in the previous rooms), and passive or quiet prayer in which the individual lets go of the intellect and surrenders to the peace of God's love. At this early stage of mystical development, the individual practices both active (or natural) and passive (or supernatural) prayer. The former is like filling a water trough through man-made aqueducts, while the latter is like filling it from underneath through a bubbling spring.

• *The Fifth Dwelling Places.* The souls who make it this far have mastered pure passive prayer, which is "not some kind of dreamy state" but a meditative yet delightful union with God in which the soul seems separated from the body (*Interior Castle*, p. 337). Here, in *The Interior Castle*'s most famous image, Teresa employs the analogy of a silkworm to illustrate how the soul ends its life of worldly attachments, emerging from its cocoon in God's dwelling place to find new life in Christ as a small white butterfly. In another analogy, she compares the remaining stages of spiritual development to the process of courtship, engagement, and marriage. Two people first find out if they are compatible, then if so they get to know each other more deeply, and finally they cement their love in a perfect union.

• *The Sixth Dwelling Places.* Where the other dwelling places are described in sections of from one to four short chapters each, Teresa's description of the sixth dwelling places fills eleven chapters, making this the longest section in *The Interior Castle*. Teresa expands on the metaphor of marriage, stressing that the soul must possess courage to be joined in its spiritual union with God. This courage, which comes from God after mental and vocal prayer, helps the soul through many external and internal trials, such as adversity from others, the praise and flattery attendant on success, illnesses, and inner fears and doubts.

To the soul that withstands these trials God shows secrets, revelations, and visions, and the soul begins to understand divine mysteries. Some of the visions are intellectual (sustained revelations taking place in the mind), others she calls imaginative (comparatively fleeting sensory impressions). Yet the soul must reach a further state in which it is able to put aside its wonder at divine things and recollect instead that Christ was human as well as divine. The soul must perceive that all blessings come from God through the fully divine yet fully human Christ. Teresa stresses that theological discussion about Christ is different from the experiential reality of mystical union with Him.

• *The Seventh Dwelling Places.* The prayers and visions of the fifth and sixth dwelling places, Teresa tells us, join the soul to God "by making it blind and deaf" with delight, so that the soul does not perceive the true nature of the union: "In this seventh dwelling place the union comes about in a different way: our good God now desires to remove the scales from the soul's eyes and let it see and understand . . . the favor He grants it" (*Interior Castle*, p. 430). Where earlier revelations concerned God and then Christ, the intellectual visions now granted to the soul bring a deep and intuitive understanding of the Holy Trinity (God the Father, Christ the Son, and the Holy Spirit). The soul grasps that "these Persons are distinct," yet "through an admirable knowledge the soul understands as a most profound truth that all three Persons are one substance and one power and one knowledge and one God alone" (*Interior Castle*, p. 430). After revisiting the metaphor of marriage to illustrate the mystical union between God and the soul, Teresa concludes by exhorting her sisters to remember that "the Lord doesn't look so much at the greatness of our works as at the love with which they are done" (*Interior Castle*, p. 450).

Teresa's rhetorical subservience. Teresa begins *The Interior Castle*'s Prologue with the following statement: "Not many things that I have been ordered to do under obedience have been as difficult for me as this present task of writing about prayer" (*Interior Castle*, p. 281). To a Catholic reader, the phrase "under obedience," would recall St. Paul's well-known pronouncement (quoted above) concerning feminine silence and subservience in the Church. Throughout the rest of the book that follows, in different ways Teresa will continually reiterate the point that she is writing with some reluctance on orders from her (male) Carmelite superiors. For example, only a few lines later, near the end of the Prologue, Teresa writes:

> In all that I say I submit to the opinion of the ones who ordered me to write, for they are persons of great learning. If I should say something that isn't in conformity with what the holy Roman Catholic Church holds, it will be through ignorance and not through malice.
>
> (*Interior Castle*, p. 282)

Here Teresa links the idea that she is writing under orders with the idea that she, a woman, is herself ignorant. Several pages into the text, she then explicitly reinforces the connection between her ignorance and her femininity: "Learned and wise men know about these things very well, but everything is necessary for our womanly dullness of mind" (*Interior Castle*, p. 290). This point, too, is one that she will continually reiterate in different ways throughout the remainder of the book.

While they exemplify Carmelite ideals of obedience and humility, Teresa's repeated disavowals of intent and her conspicuous self-deprecation can also be seen as a protective strategy for a woman who wrote at a time when the penalties for incautious religious pronouncements could (and often did) include arrest, torture, and death. While both men and women risked such punishments, the dangers for women were particularly high, owing to the traditional strictures on women in the Catholic Church at large and in Spanish society in particular. In light of this very real threat, critic Alison Weber has found a similarly defensive role in *The Interior Castle* for several aspects of Teresa's style, including her consistent vagueness and avowed uncertainty when referring to Christian Scripture (scriptural commentary, which fell under the rubric of teaching, was an especially restricted field for women).

Similarly, Weber notes, Teresa frequently laments her own incompetence and disorganization, leaving it to God to see that she gets things right. "Since this work is for my Sisters, the disorder won't matter much," she says disarmingly (*Interior Castle*, p. 354). As Weber observes, such disclaimers, it could be hoped, might serve to deflect the potentially hostile gaze of the Inquisition: "the depreciatory statements about women in this work must be understood as part of a strategy that carves out an area of 'insignificant' discourse unworthy of male scrutiny" (Weber, p. 103). In Golden Age Spain, women knew, male scrutiny could be fatal.

Sources and literary context. Teresa's courage in writing *The Interior Castle* is underscored by the fact that even as she accepted the assignment, a previous work, her *Life*, was being held and examined by the Inquisition. Indeed, Friar Gracián, her friend, supporter, and Carmelite superior, originally asked her to write the book that became *The Interior Castle* precisely because the earlier work was unavailable, and he wished her to provide the nuns the same assistance in prayer that they might otherwise have found in the relevant parts of the *Life*.

Although the meditative techniques described in *The Interior Castle* were Teresa's own, critical studies have shown that she drew on a wide range of sources for literary inspiration, including both secular and religious works. As a girl, she had avidly read chivalric romances, and much of her language—for example, the conception and description of the castle, romantic images of love and union, as well as martial images of battles and victories—may reflect this early literary interest. However, the religious fervor of the sixteenth century saw an explosion of mystical writings, and the metaphor of a castle was a common one in describing the soul and spirituality. For example, a major literary influence on Teresa was the Spanish Franciscan monk and mystic Francisco de Osuna, who had used that very metaphor in his popular *Third Spiritual ABC*. Teresa's copy of that work survives, with just such a passage marked by crosses in the margin.

Composition and impact. *The Interior Castle* was composed in two month-long spurts of writing in the summer and fall of 1577. It was an especially turbulent year for the 62-year-old Teresa and her Discalced Carmelites, who were no strangers to controversy in the best of times. Earlier that year, a disgruntled nun at the new Discalced Carmelite convent in the important city of Seville had denounced both Teresa and Friar Gracián to the Inquisition for *alumbradismo* and licentious behavior. The Inquisition rapidly dismissed the charges, but only after subjecting Teresa, who was acting as the convent's prioress (head) at the time, to a stringent examination. Political struggles with the Calced (Shod or unreformed) Carmelites were going badly, and the Carmelites' superior general had withdrawn his support for her reforms, forbidding further foundations and ordering Teresa to sequester herself in the order's Toledo convent. That same year, Nicolás Ormaneto, a Papal envoy and her main supporter at the Vatican, died, and was replaced by an official who was hostile to Teresa. In that year, too, her protégé and fellow Carmelite reformer, John of the Cross, was jailed in a Calced monastery, also in Toledo. On top of it all, as she complains in *The Interior Castle*, a number of health problems added to her difficulties in concentrating.

Yet the resulting work has been widely recognized as Teresa's masterpiece. Leading scholars today rank her, along with St. John of the Cross, as one of the two pillars of Spanish mysticism, as well as a defining voice of the Catholic Counter-Reformation. *The Interior Castle* was published along with her other works in 1588, six years after its author's death, and its detailed, authentic descriptions of her approach to spirituality was instrumental in facilitating her canonization by the Catholic Church in 1622. The original copy in Teresa's hand, bound in red leather, is treasured by the nuns of the Discalced Carmelite convent in Seville, who keep it in a castle-shaped reliquary to preserve this relic of their founding saint.

—Colin Wells

For More Information

Ahlgren, Gillian T. W. *Teresa of Avila and the Politics of Sanctity*. Ithaca: Cornell University Press, 1996.

Bilinkoff, Jodi. *The Avila of Saint Teresa: Religious Reform in a Sixteenth-Century City*. Ithaca: Cornell University Press, 1989.

Clissold, Stephen. *St. Teresa of Avila*. New York: Seabury, 1982.

Defourneaux, Marcelin. *Daily Life in Spain in the Golden Age*. Trans. Newton Branch. Stanford: Stanford University Press, 1979.

Dominguez Ortiz, Antonio. *The Golden Age of Spain 1516-1659*. Trans. James Casey. London: Weidenfeld and Nicolson, 1971.

Frohlich, Mary. *The Intersubjectivity of the Mystic: A Study of Teresa of Avila's* Interior Castle. Atlanta: Scholars Press, 1994.

Slade, Carol. *St. Teresa of Avila: Author of a Heroic Life*. Berkeley: University of California Press, 1995.

Lynch, John. *Spain Under the Habsburgs*. Vol. 1 of *Empire and Absolutism 1516-1598*. Oxford: Blackwell, 1965.

Teresa of Avila, Saint. *The Interior Castle*. In *The Collected Works of St. Teresa of Avila*. Vol. 2. Trans. Kieran Kavanaugh and Otilio Rodriguez. Washington, D.C.: Institute of Carmelite Studies, 1980.

Weber, Alison. *Teresa of Avila and the Rhetoric of Femininity*. Princeton: Princeton University Press, 1990.

Wilson, Katharina M., ed. *Women Writers of the Renaissance and Reformation*. Athens, Ga.: University of Georgia Press, 1987.

Lazarillo de Tormes

as translated by
Michael Alpert

Published anonymously in 1554, *Lazarillo de Tormes* (*Lazarillo* is the diminutive, meaning "little Lázaro") enjoyed immediate popularity and was quickly reprinted by a number of publishers. However, no writer ever took credit for the novel, and not until the early seventeenth century was anyone put forward as the author. The first claim was made in 1605, on behalf of Juan de Ortega, a monk of the Order of St. Jerome, and appeared in a work on the history of that monastic order. Ortega was said to have written the tale while a student in the Castilian city of Salamanca. Ortega's authorship, however, has been discounted by modern scholars. A more credible claim was made in 1607, when a catalogue listing Spanish writers attributed "the pleasant little book, entitled *Lazarillo de Tormes*" to Diego Hurtado de Mendoza (1503-75), an accomplished statesman, historian, and poet from one of Spain's most illustrious families (Chandler, p. 194). While, on balance, most modern scholars doubt Mendoza's authorship, his remains the only name commonly attached to the book, and the question is unlikely to be settled one way or the other. Beyond doubt, however, is the originality and lasting influence of *Lazarillo de Tormes*, which literary historians view as founding a new genre of literature, the picaresque novel—that is, the novel that features a *pícaro* or rogue as its central character.

Events in History at the Time of the Novel

The dawn of Spain's Golden Age. During the early sixteenth century, Spain embarked on a period of imperial expansion and cultural vitality

---

THE LITERARY WORK

A short novel set in the Spanish kingdom of Castile in the first half of the sixteenth century; published in Spanish (as *La Vida de Lazarillo de Tormes y de sus fortunas y adversidades*) in 1554, in English in 1568.

SYNOPSIS

Lázaro de Tormes, a young rogue or *pícaro*, tells his life story, recounting his service to a number of masters and relating how he has finally secured a comfortable position as town-crier in the Castilian city of Toledo.

that lasted about 150 years, into the late seventeenth century. Later known as the Golden Age of Spain, this remarkable era is generally reckoned to have begun in 1516 with the accession of King Charles I of Spain. Several fortunate circumstances combined to favor the Spanish at the outset of their Golden Age—although it should be stressed that the very concept of a Spanish identity had not yet firmly taken hold. Instead, the Spanish peninsula had traditionally consisted of separate and often competing kingdoms. Only after the fortuitous marriage of Charles's maternal grandparents, King Ferdinand of Aragon and Queen Isabella of Castile, had the largest and most powerful two Spanish kingdoms been ruled in tandem, creating the basis for a unified Spanish state. *Lazarillo de Tormes* takes place entirely within Castile, the largest and most populous

The expulsion of the Jews from Spain.

kingdom, and the one that would take the leading role in the newly unified Spain of the Golden Age.

Their royal power strengthened by their own marriage alliance, Ferdinand and Isabella arranged a second fortuitous marriage, one that ultimately brought much of Western Europe under the rule of their grandson, King Charles I. In 1496 their daughter Joanna married Philip I, the son and heir of the powerful Habsburg ruler Maximilian I, emperor of the Holy Roman Empire; when Philip predeceased his father and Joanna's mental illness made her unfit to rule, their son Charles, born in 1500, was left as the heir of both dynasties. He inherited his Spanish titles on Ferdinand's death in 1516 (including territory in Italy conquered by Ferdinand), and his Habsburg titles on Maximilian's death in 1519, becoming Charles V, emperor of the Holy Roman Empire (including Austria, the Netherlands, and Germany). Along with his royal titles, Spain's teenaged king—"our victorious Emperor" as Lázaro calls him at the end of the novel—also inherited Spain's increasingly lucrative empire in the Americas, which the Genoese explorer Christopher Columbus had discovered in 1492 while in the employ of Ferdinand and Isabella (*Lazarillo de Tormes*, p. 79).

Moriscos and Conversos. Ferdinand and Isabella had further enhanced Spain's solidarity and its self-image—among the Catholic majority, at any rate—by taking the offensive against the peninsula's largest two non-Christian minorities, its Muslims and Jews. Since medieval times large numbers of Muslims and Jews had lived in Spain, making it the most culturally diverse of all European lands. Muslim Arabs and North Africans—called Moors—had conquered the peninsula in the eighth century, and Jews had settled there in their wake, adding to the pre-existing Jewish population. The vigorous Moorish culture that resulted blended Islamic, Jewish, and Christian influences. Since the Moorish conquest, however, Spain's Christian kingdoms, led by Castile, had waged a long and successful struggle to reconquer the peninsula, a campaign that had taken on the character of a holy war.

By the fourteenth century, only the southern city of Granada remained in Moorish hands. Ferdinand and Isabella finally conquered it in 1492, and both they and their successors would press the attack to Moorish island outposts in the Mediterranean and even into North Africa. Commanding the siege of Granada was the grandfather of Diego Hurtado de Mendoza, the man alleged to have written *Lazarillo de Tormes*. In the novel, Lázaro's father is killed while serving in one of the subsequent campaigns against the Muslims. Having reconquered Moorish territory, Spain's Christian rulers energetically sought to convert their Muslim and Jewish subjects to Christianity. Under threat of expulsion from Spain, many did indeed become Christians: Muslims who converted and their descendants were called Moriscos; Jews who converted and their descendants were called Conversos. After Lázaro's father is killed, his mother becomes the concubine of a Moorish stablehand who is a Morisco. It has furthermore been suggested that the unknown author of the novel itself may have been a Converso or a Jew.

Known as the Catholic Monarchs for their strict piety, Ferdinand and Isabella were gravely concerned about their subjects' religious purity. They were aware that many Moriscos and Conversos had become Christian in name only, accepting baptism but secretly continuing to observe their original faiths. With the Pope's blessing, the Catholic Monarchs had established a special court known as the Spanish Inquisition, with broad powers (which eventually included censorship) to ensure that the Moriscos and Conversos worshipped according to Catholic standards. Muslims and Jews who refused to convert were ultimately expelled from Spain. In 1492, for example, the same year that Columbus discovered America and that Granada was captured, Ferdinand and Isabella also expelled Spain's remaining Jewish population, amounting to some 170,000 people.

Throughout Spain's Golden Age, both Moriscos and Conversos were subject to continuing persecution by such institutions as the Inquisition, whose methods ranged from confiscation of property to torture and execution by fire. Moriscos in particular made up an underclass in Spain's Catholic society, generally serving in the most menial positions, for as one modern historian writes, "no one believed in the sincerity of their conversion" (Domínguez Ortiz, p. 162). These social outcasts were routinely punished more harshly for common crimes than Christians would be for the same crimes. In the novel Lázaro's Morisco "stepfather," Zaide, works in a stable (*Lazarillo de Tormes*, p. 26). After stealing food and supplies from his employer to help support the household, Zaide is both "whipped and basted with hot fat," while Lázaro's mother receives "the usual hundred lashes"—though it is unclear whether her culpability lies in the crime or in taking up with a Morisco in the first place (*Lazarillo de Tormes*, p. 26). Lázaro says that the stable owner's investigation was prompted when he heard about the relationship, suggesting that cohabitation between a Morisco and a Christian could by itself automatically excite suspicion or hostility.

Germanías and *comuneros*. Charles V had been raised in the Netherlands, arriving in Spain for the first time in 1517 to claim his inheritance as the king of Aragon and Castile. Spaniards at first perceived him as a foreigner, and many resented his ostentatious retinue of Netherlanders, who

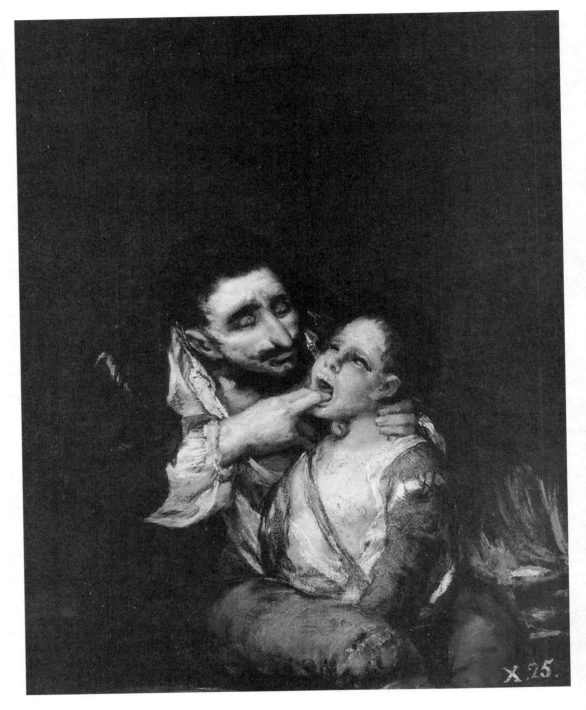

Francisco José de Goya's 1808-10 painting, *El Lazarillo de Tormes*. The main character, Lázaro, is restrained by his blind master, who accuses Lázaro of stealing food from him.

took the most desirable offices in Charles's government. In the early years of his reign, Charles was forced to overcome two extensive rebellions, one in Aragon and the other in Castile. The Aragonese rebellion broke out in 1519, in the Valencia region of southern Aragon. Led by the Germanías, or Christian brotherhoods (associations of tradesmen who opposed the Aragonese nobles), it was suppressed in 1521 by troops under the command of Charles's aristocratic viceroy in Valencia, Diego Hurtado de Mendoza, a cousin of the alleged author of *Lazarillo de Tormes*. Sporadic resistance in the countryside around Valencia continued until 1524.

While the Germanías' revolt grew out of class conflicts between the tradesmen and the nobles, the Castilian rebellion was a more direct political challenge to the king himself. Called the *comunero* movement, it began in May 1520, after Charles left Spain to claim his Habsburg inheritance following Maximilian's death. Led by Toledo, Castile's most important urban center, the Castilian cities rejected the authority of the king's officers (called *corregidores*) and demanded recognition instead as self-governing republics or *comunidades*. Only when Charles won the support of the Castilian nobles, many of whom had earlier sided with the rebel *comuneros*, was he able to quash the revolt. Toledo held out until October 1521, and its resistance represented the last opposition in Castile to Charles's rule.

Over the course of the novel, Lázaro, born in a small village near the city of Salamanca (site of Spain's leading university), gradually progresses to Toledo, and the novel concludes there in "the same year as our victorious Emperor entered this famous city of Toledo and held his Parliament there" (*Lazarillo de Tormes*, p. 19). Charles chose Toledo as his imperial capital, and critics observe that Lázaro's humble arrival in Toledo parodies the Emperor's more majestic entrance into the imperial city, though they disagree on the date of the latter. Some scholars believe this passage refers to the Cortes, or parliament, held after Charles's entry into the city in April 1525, when, several years after stamping out the two revolts, the Emperor returned from defeating a French army in Italy. Alternatively, others argue that it refers to the Cortes held in Toledo in 1538-39, three years after Charles's victory over the Muslims in a successful raid on the North African port of Tunis.

Historians have also disagreed on the nature of the revolts, particularly that of the *comuneros*, which was a complex political movement involving disparate and ultimately conflicting elements. Historians do agree, however, on the significance of the movement's failure, which resulted in a much stronger monarchy in Castile. In Aragon, by contrast, the monarch's power remained weaker compared with that of the nobles. Castile's shift toward monarchical absolutism contributed to its central role in Spain's Golden Age empire, for that empire was based on the monarch's power and prestige, which it also in turn enhanced.

Imperial riches, persistent poverty. The Spanish did not conceive of their empire as a source of raw materials to be used in industrial manu-

facture, as, for example, the British would later see their colonies in North America. Spain remained primarily an importer of manufactured goods and an exporter of raw materials. Instead of a spur to industry, the Spanish saw the Americas as essentially a treasure trove from which the Spanish crown—and the nobles, who relied on lucrative royal appointments to overseas positions—might make easy and unlimited withdrawals. Pearls, emeralds, luxury dyes, and above all gold and silver were the chief cargoes of the Spanish ships that plied the Atlantic. At first, gold predominated, but in the 1540s the Spanish de-

NOBLES, CLERICS, AND PEASANTS: THE THREE ESTATES

Like the rest of Europe, Spanish society in the Middle Ages was divided (in theory at least) into a rigid hierarchy of three levels. At the top were the nobles or aristocracy, then the clerics or church officials. These two classes owned virtually all the land. At the bottom were the peasants who worked the land and paid rent to their landlords. Traditionally, these social classes are known as the "three estates." As illustrated by the character of the *hidalgo*, or country squire, in *Lazarillo de Tormes*, each estate had its own upper and lower levels; the novel's poor but proud *hidalgo* is a low-level aristocrat who jealously guards his honor and social rank. As trade expanded throughout Europe during the early Renaissance, a fourth group, the newly wealthy merchants, jostled for influence with the nobles, who despised the merchants as their social inferiors.

veloped rich new silver mines at Potosí, Peru (in 1545), and Zacatecas, Mexico (in 1546). Silver soon surpassed gold as the main cargo of the treasure ships, particularly after the advent of new refining techniques in the 1570s. Between 1500 and 1650, Spanish ships transported around 16,000 tons of silver, as compared with about 181 tons of gold (Elliott, p. 19).

Imperial wealth meant little to most Spaniards, however, who took no share in it. Instead, the bulk of the cash flowed rapidly out of Spain, either to foreign merchants for imported manufactured goods, or to the German and other bankers who financed Spain's continual and expensive wars against enemies such as France. For the majority of Spaniards there was no "Golden Age" at all, but an often bitter daily struggle to survive that absorbed virtually all of their attention. Poverty in Spain was persistent and widespread. Furthermore, historians have generally agreed that poverty's effects were worsened rather than ameliorated by the influx of American treasure, which helped drive prices up by creating an increase in the cash supply without a corresponding increase in production.

LIFE-CYCLE SERVICE

Like Lázaro's family, the poorest families in Golden Age Spain commonly arranged for one or more children to leave home as domestic or private servants for a period of time before beginning their adult lives. Historians call this phenomenon life-cycle service. Most rural life-cycle servants worked for better-off peasant families in a nearby village, but many also worked for merchants, artisans, or priests (in the novel, Lázaro's masters include a blind beggar, a priest, a *hidalgo*, and a monk). In poorer villages, however, often only the priest had a servant. Life-cycle service most commonly began at around age 12, which is about the age that Lázaro leaves home in the novel, but documentary evidence records some children leaving home as young as 7 and others as old as 20. Treatment also varied widely, although historian David E. Vassberg suggests that "social pressures in a small village community might have prevented employers from being excessively abusive or unfair to their charges" (Vassberg, p. 91). Lázaro's harsh treatment by several of his masters contrasts sharply with this picture, but may simply reflect the anonymous author's desire to entertain his readers.

From 1500 to 1550, prices in Spain more than doubled, while between 1520 and 1550—roughly the period of time covered by the novel—real wages fell by 20 percent (Lynch, pp. 126-27). At the same time the gap between rich and poor widened dramatically, as the rich got richer and the poor got poorer. These trends would continue throughout the Golden Age (though at slower rates than in the time of the novel), in an inflationary spiral that historians have called "the price revolution" (Lynch, p. 121). *Lazarillo de Tormes* clearly and colorfully illustrates the oppressive effects of this price revolution, for nearly all the characters portrayed in the novel—from Lázaro's parents, to several of his employers, to Lázaro himself—are dirt poor. Those of Lázaro's masters who are not themselves

poverty stricken turn out to be ludicrously stingy. Indeed, throughout the story Lázaro's major preoccupation is his constantly gnawing hunger, and much of the book's humor comes from the ingenious tricks he devises to obtain food, often at the expense of one of his miserly masters. As one critic notes of *Lazarillo de Tormes*, while other novels followed it in the picaresque tradition, "it alone makes us stare at poverty" (Dunn, p. 294).

The Novella in Focus

Plot summary. *Lazarillo de Tormes* runs to just over 50 pages in the English translation featured here. In a brief prologue Lázaro addresses the narrative to *Vuestra Merced* (translated as "Your Honour" or "Your Grace"), an unnamed noble who, it appears, has solicited information about Lázaro for an unspecified reason: "Your Honour has written to me to ask me to tell him my story in some detail, so I think I'd better start at the beginning, not in the middle, so that you may know all about me" (*Lazarillo de Tormes*, p. 24). Lázaro continues that the accident of noble birth means little, concluding the prologue by declaring "how much more worthy are those who have endured misfortune but have triumphed by dint of hard work and determination" (*Lazarillo de Tormes*, p. 24).

The narrative itself is divided into seven *tratados* or chapters, which vary in length from about 15 pages to a single paragraph. Critics have observed that the first three chapters are longer and more fully fleshed out than the following ones, which may consist partly of an outline meant to be filled in later. Chapter One begins with an account of Lázaro's background: the son of a miller, he was born in his father's mill on the river Tormes, from which he takes his surname, and raised in the nearby village of Tejares, near Salamanca. When Lázaro is eight, his father is caught bleeding wheat from the sacks that neighboring farmers have brought to be milled into flour, and as part of his sentence, he is sent on an expedition against the Moors, where he is killed. Working as a cook and a washerwoman before becoming a mistress, the boy's mother begins a relationship with a Morisco named Zaide, and the two have a child. When Zaide is arrested for stealing to help feed Lázaro and his half-brother, as part of their mother's sentence the court forbids her to go near him. To escape gossip she goes to work at a nearby inn, taking her children with her. Lázaro runs errands for guests at the inn, until one of the guests, a blind man, offers to take the boy on as a servant and guide. Lázaro and his mother bid each other a tearful farewell, and the boy embarks on his new life with the blind man.

After a brief stay in Salamanca, Lázaro and the blind man, who makes his living by begging and offering to pray on behalf of passers-by in exchange for cash, set out on the road for Toledo. (A blind man's prayers were believed to be especially effective.) As they cross a bridge outside Salamanca, they encounter the stone figure of a bull. In one of the novel's most famous episodes, the blind man tells Lázaro to put his ear up close to the bull and he will hear a noise inside. Lázaro does so—and the blind man hits him hard on the head, slamming his head into the stone. "You silly little nitwit! You'll have to learn that a blind man's boy has got to be sharper than a needle," the man says, cackling (*Lazarillo de Tormes*, p. 27). Though his head hurts for days, Lázaro feels as if his eyes have been opened. The blind man, Lázaro says, is himself "sharp as a needle," for he knows "hundreds of prayers off by heart," and makes "more in one month than a hundred blind men usually do in a whole year" (*Lazarillo de Tormes*, p. 28). Yet despite the blind man's steady income, he is tight-fisted and gives Lázaro barely enough food to survive on. Taking the lesson of the bull to heart, he quickly learns to fend for himself: "It's a fact that if I hadn't used all my cunning and the tricks I knew, I would have died from hunger more than once" (*Lazarillo de Tormes*, p. 28).

For example, Lázaro learns to unpick the threads of the bag in which the blind man keeps the food, to help himself from it, and then to sew the bag back up. He and the blind man conduct an escalating contest over the blind man's wine jug, as the blind man foils Lázaro's progressively more devious techniques for sneaking wine out of the jug. Finally, as Lázaro worms his way under the jug to catch the stream from a hole he has drilled in it, the blind man suddenly lifts the heavy clay jug and with great violence lets it fall—ostensibly by accident but actually with deliberate intent—onto the boy's mouth, knocking him out, lacerating his head and face, and breaking several of his teeth. After recovering from his injuries, Lázaro decides to leave the blind man after exacting revenge. They continue to wrangle over food, having a heated altercation over a sausage, and the blind man beats the boy. The next day, when they need to cross a broad open stream, Lázaro positions the blind man right in

front of a solid post, facing it. He then tells the blind man to jump as hard as he can, and the blind man crashes into the post and falls to the ground with his head split open. Only then does Lázaro leave the old blind man.

The following day Lázaro reaches Maqueda, a town northwest of Toledo, where, as he says, "for my sins I fell in with a priest" (*Lazarillo de Tormes*, p. 38). He becomes the priest's servant, but to his dismay his new master turns out to be even more parsimonious than his old one. The priest keeps all the bread offerings collected at the church in a locked chest in his house. There is nothing else to eat in the house, except for a string of onions; Lázaro's ration is one onion every four days. By contrast, the priest himself eats very well, sending Lázaro to buy meat for his lunch and dinner every day. Occasionally he gives Lázaro a crust of bread or some well-gnawed bones from his plate. Only when the priest conducts funerals does Lázaro eat well, at the feasts held after the ceremonies. Lázaro prays to God to forgive him for wishing that people would die more often.

One day a tinker (an itinerant metalworker who mends household utensils) comes to the door. Pretending that he has lost his master's key, Lázaro gets the tinker to make a key to the bread chest, paying him with one of the votive loaves. When the priest becomes suspicious, Lázaro makes it look as if mice have gotten into the chest. Again he and his master engage in an escalating contest over food, as the priest struggles to mouseproof the chest while Lázaro maintains false mouseholes in it to give his story credibility. In a complex and humorous series of incidents, the escalation once again results in Lázaro's being clubbed violently in the face, when, in the dark, the priest mistakes him for a snake that he believes has been stealing food from the traps. (The priest hears a snakelike whistle made by Lázaro because of the key in his mouth.) After Lázaro recovers from his wounds, the priest dismisses him, crossing himself and saying he can't match the boy's craftiness. He could only have been a blind man's boy, such boys being known for their slyness.

Chapter Three opens with Lázaro's arrival in Toledo, where he meets his next master, a proud, kindly, and well-dressed *hidalgo,* or country squire, who comes from a notorious Jewish ghetto but masks this fact as he does others in his life. After happily agreeing to be the *hidalgo*'s servant, Lázaro walks with him through the city's market, thinking that the man is about to do his shopping or stop for a tasty lunch. As the day progresses and the *hidalgo* buys no food, Lázaro assumes they will eat when they get home. When they arrive at the *hidalgo's* house in the early

---

PRIESTS AND ANTICLERICALISM

Though a devoutly Catholic people, by the sixteenth century a select group of Spaniards, like others throughout Europe at the time, had begun to resent what they perceived as the excesses of a corrupt and oppressive Catholic Church. Called anticlericalism, such resentment is reflected in the appearance of hypocritical priests in many of the folktales that influenced *Lazarillo de Tormes*. The anticlerical bent reflects a larger movement in Spain at the time, Erasmianism, named after the Dutch reformer Erasmus. Erasmus criticized church corruption, defended personal faith, and championed a return to primitive Christianity. His teachings influenced a number of Spanish thinkers in the 1520s. "In the churches, in the convents, even in the inns and on the highways," everyone was reading Erasmus in Spanish, though much of the clergy remained hostile to his ideas (Kamen, p. 122). Centers of Spanish Erasmianism flowered in Barcelona, Zaragoza, and Valencia. The movement's heyday in Spain was short-lived, though. Erasmianism dwindled, then was crushed in the 1530s; as religious positions in Europe became polarized, Castile adopted a reactionary stance to Erasmus and to followers such as the philosopher Juan Luis Vives. Born of Converso parents who practiced Judaism in secret, Vives lived in exile in the Netherlands. His father was arrested by the Inquisition for Judaizing and burned alive in 1524, while his dead mother's bones were dug up and burned postmortem. The next decade the Inquisition would quash Erasmianism in Spain, concluding by then that it threatened the orthodoxy of the Catholic religion. The Inquisition identified Erasmus with the upstart Martin Luther, instigator of the Protestant Reformation that was leaving its mark elsewhere in Europe at the time. This is not to say that no reform movements existed in Spain at all. In the late fifteenth century, a Cardinal Francisco Jiménez de Cisneros had begun a movement of cleaning up the Church, and reform efforts would continue in sixteenth-century Spain. There, as well as in other Catholic countries, the Counter-Reformation attempted to remedy clerical abuses without abandoning Catholicism.

---

afternoon, however, the *hidalgo* says that he has eaten early and won't eat again until supper. Lázaro produces a few pieces of bread that he has begged from strangers, and only then does he realize that his new master is ravenously hungry.

In fact, as Lázaro gradually comes to understand, the *hidalgo's* proud manner cloaks poverty that is as dire as Lázaro's own:

> Who would not be deceived by his demeanour and his smart cloak and jacket, and who would think that that noble gentleman spent all day yesterday without taking a bite of food except that crumb of bread that his servant Lázaro had carried for a day and a half under his shirt and where it couldn't have kept very clean, and today, when he washed his hands and his face and didn't have a towel, he used his shirt-tail?
> (*Lazarillo de Tormes*, p. 54)

Lázaro feels sorry for the *hidalgo* and grows fond of him, feeding the *hidalgo* with what he begs on the streets, even when it means going hungry himself. All the while, the *hidalgo* keeps up the pretense of plenty, offering frequent platitudes on the virtues of eating lightly, and holding a straw in his mouth as if picking his teeth after a full meal. "There's only one thing I had against him," Lázaro says: "I wished he wasn't quite so vain and would come down to earth and face the facts a little more" (*Lazarillo de Tormes*, p. 58).

Lázaro learns that the *hidalgo* has a country estate that could supply him with an honorable income if it were in better repair. The reason he left was to avoid taking his hat off first to a neighbor of higher social rank than himself. He had done so many times, but thought the other man should take his hat off first occasionally as well. After Lázaro has been with the *hidalgo* for about ten days, the *hidalgo* flees town to escape his creditors, leaving Lázaro to explain as best he can to the city constable, who arrives to put a lien on the *hidalgo's* property because of his debts.

In its single paragraph, Chapter Four recounts Lázaro's brief service with a friar, whom he leaves after a week because of all the running around the friar makes him do. The paragraph hints at the friar's being a homosexual. Chapter Five covers Lázaro's employment with his fifth master, a *buldero* or pardoner, a man who sells papal indulgences (which Catholics believed would prevent God from punishing them in this world or in purgatory for their sins). The *buldero* knows "some really clever tricks" to get people to buy his indulgences (*Lazarillo de Tormes*, p. 67). For example, in one village, he stages a loud public fight with an accomplice, after which he asks God to strike down whichever of them was in the wrong. When the accomplice falls to the ground in a fit, people rush to buy the *buldero's* pardons.

Lázaro stays with the *buldero* for four months, happy that he has finally found a master who feeds him enough.

Chapter Six consists of only a few paragraphs but spans four years, in which Lázaro, "a well set up young man by now," works first for an artist who paints tambourines. He next works for another priest, selling drinking water that he carries around the city on a donkey, the priest here serving more as a small businessman more than as a leader of the faith (*Lazarillo de Tormes*, p. 76). Lázaro quits this profitable job as soon as he can afford some decent clothes, however. The last chapter, a few pages long, briefly sketches the events leading to Lázaro's current position as town crier. His duties include making "public announcements of the wines that are to be sold in town, and of the auctions and lost property. I also accompany criminals being punished for their misdeeds and shout out their crimes" (*Lazarillo de Tormes*, p. 77). He makes a comfortable living, and has married a woman who works as a maid for the priest of a nearby church. The priest in fact arranged the marriage—for his own convenience. While Lázaro enjoys the priest's frequent and generous gifts of food, he has decided to ignore the gossip that his wife is the priest's concubine, and "as a result, . . . there is peace at home" (*Lazarillo de Tormes*, p. 79). Lázaro concludes his tale by saying, "I will inform Your Honour of my future in due course" (*Lazarillo de Tormes*, p. 79).

Spoil over toil. "I came down to this city hoping to find a good position," the proud *hidalgo* tells Lázaro (*Lazarillo de Tormes*, p. 62). Though claiming that it is simply "bad luck" that he can't find a decent employer, he unwittingly reveals that employment itself, and not the particular behavior of any employer, inevitably entails intolerable blows to his pride: "I'm often asked to be the right-hand man of minor noblemen, but it's very difficult working with them because you're no longer a man, just a thing they use. If you don't do what they want then it's 'Good-bye to you'" (*Lazarillo de Tormes*, p. 63). Doing "what they want," however, defines employment: in the end the *hidalgo* would rather go hungry than humble himself to work. Significantly the *hidalgo* also links his independence to his manhood and to his all-important honor, which he says is "all that decent men have left today" (*Lazarillo de Tormes*, p. 62). He herein reflects the tenor of a time in which Castilians were so obsessed with honor that they would even purchase false genealogies.

Historians have long found *Lazarillo de Tormes*'s *hidalgo* to symbolize the social attitudes that led to Spain's rapid commercial eclipse in the seventeenth century by nations such as the Netherlands and Britain. As historian John Lynch observes, the mania for noble status "produced a contempt for trade and a restless anxiety to join the aristocracy which were ruinous for Spain and her people. . . . The starving *hidalgo* of *Lazarillo de Tormes* was, indeed, a symbol of a real situation" (Lynch, p. 106). Religion, given the Christian injunction against usury, reinforced this contempt for trade. Nobles generally conceived of the desire for lucre, that is, money or profits, as beneath them. Even successful merchants often wished to leave business as soon as possible and invest instead in land, which was viewed as the only honorable source of wealth. As Lynch notes, "the odium attached to manual work and to business" was reflected in a contemporary phrase, *el deshonor de trabajo*, or "'the dishonor of work'" (Lynch, p. 106). Spanish tradition thus militated against the emergence of a commercial middle class, by suppressing the trade and industry upon which such a class might be based.

These issues can be linked to larger pictures, both of the novel as a whole and of Spain's world empire. Historians have stressed the central role that the *hidalgo* class played in building the empire, which was based on the same preference for spoils over industry that prevailed within Spain. Preferring to live by his wits rather than by toil, Lázaro himself reflects this approach. Scholars today see such attitudes as a primary cause not just of Spain's internal economic decay, but also of its imperial decline at the end of the Golden Age.

Sources and literary context. Unlike previous literary prose tales popular in Spain, *Lazarillo de Tormes* focuses not on a courtly aristocratic hero but on a poor commoner who lives by his wits. It furthermore depicts his adventures with a humor and grittiness lacking in the flowery chivalric romances of early Renaissance Spain. For this reason, the novel is credited with bringing a new degree of realism to Spanish literature, for the world depicted in the romances was one of idealistic knights errant, gentle damsels, and impossibly educated shepherds who sing ornate, poetic songs.

Yet the author of *Lazarillo de Tormes* did draw on an old and well-established body of common folk tales and popular dramas. The name Lázaro was a typical poor boy's name in medieval Spanish folklore, and many of the novel's characters are common stereotypes from such lore. For example, thieving millers, flim-flamming pardoners, and miserly priests appear in folk stories across Western Europe, as well as in other literary works, such as the *Decameron* (1349-53) by Italian writer Giovanni Boccaccio. The gluttonous, hypocritical priest and the blind beggar engaged in a contest of wits with his boy is also commonly featured in various European folktales. Within Spain itself, the penniless squire with his airs and concealed hunger was already a recognizable stereotype, though after 1554 to be forever identified with the novel's unforgettable portrait. Some of Lázaro's own literary ancestors go as far back as the wily, conniving characters of the Latin comic playwright Plautus (third century B.C.E.), and of the Latin novels *Satyricon* by Petronius (first century C.E.) and *The Golden Ass* by Apuleius (second century C.E.).

Publication and reception. Though scholars suspect there may have been an earlier edition, *Lazarillo de Tormes* was published in four editions in 1554: in Burgos, Spain; in Alcalá, Spain; in Medina del Campo, Spain; and in Antwerp, Belgium. The story's immediate popularity is confirmed both by its rapid translation into the major European languages, and by the appearance of a sequel in 1555: *La Segunda Parte de Lazarillo de Tormes*. This *Second Part of Lazarillo de Tormes* was, like the original, published anonymously, and is considered the work of a different and lesser writer. Many other sequels and imitations followed in its wake.

In 1573 a *castigado*, or expurgated version, of the original work appeared, with parts of the story censored by the Inquisition, although the literary historian Frank Wadleigh Chandler (writing in the late nineteenth century) attests that "the emendations of the Inquisition were not as considerable as might have been expected" (Chandler, p. 192). Philip II, son of Charles V, ordered the *castigado* to be printed because, despite being banned by the Inquisition in 1559 (the first year it put out a list of forbidden books), the novel had continued to be widely read. The *castigado*'s introduction offers the earliest critical commentary on the story, calling it "so lively and faithful a representation of what it describes with such wit and grace that in its way it is estimable

and has always been relished by all," and going on to reveal that "although prohibited in these realms, it has been commonly read and printed abroad" (in Chandler, p. 192).

Lazarillo de Tormes's impact on subsequent Spanish literature is generally held to be second only to Cervantes's masterpiece *Don Quixote* (Part I, 1605; Part II, 1615). Picaresque novels that followed in its footsteps range from its immediate successors, Mateo Alemán's *Guzmán de Alfarache* (1599) and Francisco de Quevedo's *El Buscón* (*The Swindler*; 1626), to many later works, including Henry Fielding's *Tom Jones* (1749). *Lazarillo de Tormes* even contributed to the Spanish language, for soon after the novel's publication the word *lazarillo* entered Castilian, the major dialect of Spanish, as the common word for a blind man's guide.

—Colin Wells

For More Information

Chandler, Frank Wadleigh. *Romances of Roguery*. New York: Lenox Hill, 1974.

Domínquez Ortiz, Antonio. *The Golden Age of Spain 1516-1659*. Trans. James Casey. New York: Basic Books, 1971.

Dunn, Peter. *Spanish Picaresque Fiction: A New Literary History*. Ithaca: Cornell University Press, 1993.

Elliott, J. H. *Spain and Its World 1500-1700*. New Haven: Yale University Press, 1989.

Ife, B. W. *Reading and Fiction in Golden-Age Spain: A Platonist Critique and Some Picaresque Replies*. Cambridge: Cambridge University Press, 1985.

Kamen, Henry. *Spain 1469-1714*. London: Longman, 1991.

Lazarillo de Tormes. In *Two Spanish Picaresque Novels: Lazarillo de Tormes and The Swindler*. Trans. Michael Alpert. Harmondsworth: Penguin, 1969.

Lynch, John. *Spain Under the Habsburgs*. Vol. 1, *Empire and Absolutism 1516-1598*. Oxford: Blackwell, 1965.

Rico, Francisco. *The Spanish Picaresque Novel and the Point of View*. Trans. Charles Davis and Harry Sieber. Cambridge: Cambridge Univerity Press, 1984.

Vassberg, David E. *The Village and the Outside World in Golden Age Castile: Mobility and Migration in Everyday Rural Life*. Cambridge: Cambridge University Press, 1999.

Libro de Buen Amor (The Book of Good Love)

by

Juan Ruíz, Archpriest of Hita

Like a number of medieval authors, Juan Ruíz emerged into the modern era solely between the covers of his book. Apart from what he says about himself in *Libro de Buen Amor* (the title is variously translated as *The Book of Good Love* and *The Book of True Love*), we know nothing whatsoever about him; there are no contemporary witnesses or reactions to his work (apart from a fragment in Portuguese translation), and no document from his lifetime has come to light that refers to him. Nevertheless, a number of facts (or at least strong possibilities) can be deduced or inferred from the few clues available. Given the frequent allusions to matters of judicial procedure and church law in the *Libro de Buen Amor*, there is no reason to doubt that he is telling the truth when he identifies himself in the poem as an archpriest. (Archpriests in fourteenth-century Spain were "ecclesiastical administrators and judges with power of correction over the entire archipresbyterate—a fairly large area surrounding the town of Hita" [Kelly, p. 8].) We also know more or less when the *Libro de Buen Amor* was written; internal evidence indicates that it must have been composed after 1338, and one of three surviving manuscripts of the work bears a scribal date of 1389. Since most scholars agree that the work shows signs of having been revised and augmented a number of times, we can assume that the author was working on it during this period. None of the three manuscripts is in the author's hand; they are all probably several stages removed from any original copy. The work itself is by turns fervently pi-

> ## THE LITERARY WORK
>
> A poem about various types of love set in mid-fourteenth-century Spain; first published in 1790.
>
> ## SYNOPSIS
>
> A Spanish archpriest narrates his amorous pursuit of a number of women; in the process, the narrator (who adopts several personas) and other characters digress frequently, telling fables, describing allegorical episodes, and uttering lengthy prayers.

ous and exuberantly profane. A diverse work, *Libro de Buen Amor* is not about any one thing, but the "good love" in the title, used ambiguously, reflects the preoccupation with love in all its varieties that pervaded medieval Spain.

Events in History at the Time of the Narrative

Spain in the fourteenth century. The history of medieval Spain has always stood apart from the history of medieval Europe in general, primarily because of the factor of Islam. While other regions of Europe had periodic brushes with Islamic aggression during the heady days of its explosive initial expansion throughout the Mediterranean region, only in Spain (and to a lesser extent Sicily) did Islamic society take root. The Moors (as

Spanish Muslims were called) conquered virtually the entire Iberian peninsula in the early eighth century, and Christian Spain did not completely reconquer the domain until 1492. During the intervening centuries an unusually cosmopolitan (by western European standards, at any rate) society developed, one in which Christians, Muslims, and Jews lived under successive Christian and Muslim regimes that, for the most part, allowed their subjects a degree of freedom of worship and association not found elsewhere in medieval Europe. Conflict was constant and often bitter, but nevertheless the three groups forged relationships that allowed them to influence each other's art, literature, laws, and customs.

The Christian reconquest of Spain began in earnest in the late eleventh century. By the fourteenth century the only region still under Muslim hegemony was Granada, a small kingdom in the south. Many Muslims saw no reason to move as long as their lives and property were not threatened, so they remained in the reconquered regions and were tolerated by Christian Spain as long as they obeyed the law and paid their taxes. For the most part, Jews likewise retained the rights they had enjoyed under Muslim rule, so they tended to remain as well. Thus, to Juan Ruiz, Muslims and Jews were part of everyday experience, a situation inconceivable to (say) the average fourteenth-century Englishman. For him, Muslims were a far-off and poorly understood threat; Jews a renegade and hostile people whom his country had expelled in 1290. On one hand, medieval Spain was very much a part of the larger European community; intermarriage with European aristocracy, an active mercantile class with overseas interests, and the fact that the Church was essentially its own supranational state all combined to bring Spain into the mainstream of European political, cultural, and religious life. On the other hand, it possessed a more socially diverse character than many other European kingdoms. The question of to what extent this cultural and religious diversity influenced Spain is still a subject of considerable debate. It seems unlikely that centuries of Islamic occupation would have no cultural and social impact, but it must also be recognized that medieval Christian Spain did manage to maintain its sense of identity as a part of western Christendom despite this occupation—and this sense of identity often included regarding non-Christians as dangerous aliens. Fourteenth-century Spain had not yet expelled its Jews and Muslims, but waves of intolerance and outright persecution were common.

Medieval Spanish literary culture. The same problem that confronts students of medieval Spanish history exists in the realm of literary studies as well. Was medieval Spanish literature simply a subset of the larger European literary culture, or did it have a unique quality, derived from non-Christian Spanish elements? For much of the mid-twentieth century, this question was at the heart of critical debate about the *Libro de Buen Amor*. In a long chapter of his seminal work *España en su Historia* (1948), Américo Castro applied his general thesis about Spanish culture to the work of Juan Ruiz, arguing that in both form and content the *Libro de Buen Amor* is dependent upon Islamic models—specifically, upon the eleventh-century *The Dove's Neck Ring* of Ibn Hazm. Castro is certainly right in noting that Jewish and Muslim literature circulating in Spain in the fourteenth century exhibited many of the qualities to be found in the *Libro de Buen Amor*—a mix of religious piety and eroticism, a blend of prose and verse, the use of fables to make thematic and narrative points, and so forth. However, these qualities appear in the Latin and vernacular literature of western Europe as well, and it is only to this body of writing that Ruiz refers specifically.

Like England's Geoffrey Chaucer (c.1340-1400), Ruiz shows considerable familiarity with the work of the Roman poet Ovid and his medieval imitators on the subject of love, and he also makes use of the collection of beast-fables attributed to "Aesop," which circulated throughout Europe in various forms. The *Libro de Buen Amor* is a collection of tales contained within a larger narrative framework, and so are the *Canterbury Tales* of Chaucer and the *Decameron* of the Italian poet Boccaccio (1313-75). Furthermore, the *Roman de la Rose* of Guillaume de Lorris and Jean de Meun (completed c. 1275) was an immensely popular long poem on the subject of love, containing many short tales within the narrative proper. Like the *Libro de Buen Amor*, the *Roman de la Rose* focuses on a lover in pursuit of physical gratification, though Ruiz shows far less of the pervasive misogyny than the *Roman de la Rose* and other thirteenth- and fourteenth-century works on love. Setting the *Libro de Buen Amor* against this larger background makes obvious the kinship between its main thematic, stylistic, and structural qualities and those of other European works. For instance, Ruiz follows a venerable tradition in western medieval literature in his use of allegory, featuring characters who are simply personified abstractions, such as "Lord Flesh" and

"Sir Love." Not characters in the modern sense, these figures act out the human impulses that their names indicate, usually for some overarching didactic purpose. Thus, the battle between Sir Flesh and Lady Lent is not meant to be taken as a literal battle between two realistic characters, but as an allegory of the warring impulses of appetite and abstinence in the human soul.

A quality of the *Libro de Buen Amor* that has given some readers pause is the seeming lack of tension between its religious and erotic material. The prayers and sermons are sincere and fervent, and the expressions of sexual longing unashamed in their unrestrained libidinousness. How is this to be read? The answer is not entirely clear, but two factors should be remembered. First, the literary culture of the fourteenth century permitted such incongruity; it appears in the works of Chaucer, Boccaccio, and others, many of whom were churchmen of unimpeachable sanctity. Sermon literature that heaped condemnation upon the erotic impulse was readily available, but literature celebrating physical love also had an audience, one that did not seem to find sensuality threatening or morally dangerous. This audience (composed largely of the nobility, the wealthy merchant class, and members of the clergy and court bureaucracy) appreciated the fine sensibilities exhibited by the grand lovers of courtly romance, and seemed to do so in a manner to some degree divorced from the Christian sexual morality. Second, as Ruiz periodically reminds his readers, there are many ways to profit from literature; one must not necessarily model one's behavior on that of literary characters. One can simply enjoy the poetic art; one can laugh at the follies of impassioned lovers; and one can take the portrayal of illicit sexuality as a negative example—a helpfully detailed account of the path to be avoided. With this last interpretative mode in mind, countless medieval authors composed *exempla*, that is, short narratives (often featured within sermons), to illustrate a moral point. Whether an illustration of virtue or vice, an *exemplum* sought to point the way clearly to the path of wisdom and morality. Collections of *exempla* were quite common in literary and ecclesiastical circles in Ruiz's day; an important example is **The Book of Count Lucanor and Patronio** (c. 1335), written by Don Juan Manuel (also in *WLAIT 5: Spanish and Portuguese Literatures and Their Times*).

The Church and the law. The Church occupied a role so central to the lives of medieval Spaniards that it is difficult to provide something analogous

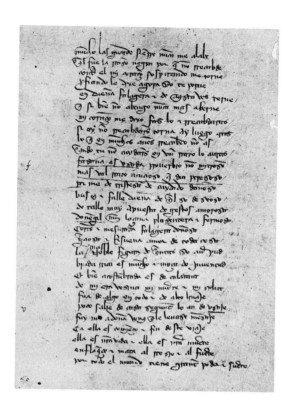

Manuscript page from a 1389 edition of *Libro de Buen Amor.*

in the modern world. A great many individuals joined religious orders, and the church exercised full legal sway over basic aspects of peoples' lives. There were two legal systems in play at the time. Civil law, promulgated by the monarch, covered such secular matters as rights of property, treason, the coining of money, and so forth. Canon law, the law of the church, went far beyond regulating the behavior of churchmen and women. All Christian citizens were subject to its power. The cases of those in holy orders were adjudicated solely in its courts, and laypeople appeared there regularly too, to be judged on matters that the Church considered under its purview. Any issue relating to the sacraments was a matter for the canon-law courts. The sacrament of marriage, for example, was a common locus of legal wrangling; since questions of inheritance often hinged on whether or not a marriage was valid, the law of the Church was powerful indeed. Sexual offenses were also punished in canon-law courts, since illicit sex was considered an offense to the sacrament of marriage. Despite the separate legal systems, the Crown exercised a great deal of power over the Church in fourteenth-century Spain, with the king naming the officials in its canon-law courts.

The *Libro de Buen Amor* is intimately concerned with legal matters, both civil and canon. It contains a full-fledged trial episode that, however humorous (the litigants and judge are animals, and the offense is chicken-stealing by a fox), conforms strictly to the standards of legal procedure. Juan Ruiz himself is in the legal profession; he identifies himself as an archpriest, that is, a priest responsible for seeing to it that the Church's law is kept within the geographical area to which he has been assigned. He is not a pastor with a church and parishioners—his job is to identify malefactors and see them brought to justice. The question of why he would choose to write a long poem featuring an archpriest named Juan Ruiz who vigorously (and illegally) seeks partners in fornication cannot be finally answered, but the incongruity of such a scenario would have been readily apparent to his readers. As if to emphasize the point, the narrator's pursuit of the nun Lady Garoza is a case study in what an archpriest should *not* be doing. Medieval handbooks on penance customarily organized sexual sins in order of seriousness, with simple fornication between unmarried laypeople being the least sinful. Generally the most sinful was sex between a priest and a nun—more so than between a priest and a married woman—because nuns were considered to be brides of Christ. In the case of the narrator and Lady Garoza, the fact that the priest was an archpriest (whose job was to enforce the law, not break it) made his attempt a virtual worst-case scenario.

The narrative voice. The narrative "I" in *The Book of Good Love* is usually (but not always) an archpriest of Hita named Juan Ruiz. At the outset, it should be noted that this person should not be identified with Juan Ruiz, the author of *The Book of Good Love*. Like many other medieval authors (such as Chaucer and Dante), Ruiz inserts a fictive version of himself into his poetry, a strategy that imparts an air of credibility to his narrative. This fictive persona is a subject of the story just like the other characters, and his knowledge, unlike the author's, is limited. Further complicating the issue in this poem is the fact that the "I" who tells the story does not maintain the same character throughout. Sometimes he is prayerful and pious. At other times he is sexually predatory and seemingly indifferent to moral norms. At one point he is a different person altogether, a layman by the name of Don Melón, who marries (an impossibility for an archpriest). This ever-shifting narrator must simply be accepted as part of how the story is told; at various points throughout the story, the "I" may refer to the protagonist, the narrator, the author, or even simply a representative of man in general. This shifting "I," sometimes called a composite "I," can be compared to an author's use of the pronoun "he" in a story with reference to a number of different persons. The composite "I" serves also as a literary device, indicating that a number of sometimes overlapping characters speak with one voice. Ruiz, like many medieval authors, uses the composite "I" as a literary device rather than simply as a pronoun indicating the authorial or narrative self.

The Poem in Focus

Plot summary. The *Libro de Buen Amor* has no plot, at least not in any sense that the word "plot" is now generally understood. It does tell a story (in fact it tells many stories), but in a manner that most twenty-first-century readers would find strange. Essentially it is a collection of poems assembled into a book. Some poems are prayers, many are beast-fables, and a number have little evident relation to the overall story being told—that of the narrator's episodic quest for sexual partners. Yet each individual poem has a role to play, and the reader should not be disconcerted by seemingly disjointed narrative leaps.

The book begins with a prayer; the speaker (who identifies himself as an archpriest) begs God and the Virgin Mary to free him from prison and protect him from the lies of his enemies. Nothing more is said of imprisonment in the poem (apart from a probably nonauthorial statement at the very end, which claims that the *Libro de Buen Amor* was composed by Juan Ruiz while imprisoned by the archbishop of Toledo), and it is unclear whether a literal or metaphorical prison is meant (i.e., the soul's imprisonment by sin). The latter is certainly possible, for after the conclusion of the prayer, the speaker goes on to discuss at some length (in prose, with regular quotations from the Bible) the nature of true wisdom, which consists of fearing God, following the commandments, and avoiding evil. It is in accordance with this, says the speaker, that he has written "this little piece of writing":

> And I composed this new book in which are written down some of the methods and arts and deceitful, cunning tricks of foolish love of the world, which some people practice in order to sin.
>
> Reading and heeding which, a man or woman with true understanding, who wishes to be saved, will choose and act upon it.

And he will be able to say with the Psalmist: *I have chosen the way of truth, et cetera.*

On the other hand, those of little understanding will not be lost, for . . . in discovering that their most clever, deceitful practices, which they use to sin and to deceive women, are made public, they will arouse their memory and not despise [besmirch] their reputation. . . . However, inasmuch as it is human to sin, if anyone should wish (which I do not advise) to have a taste of this worldly love, here they will find some models for doing so.

(Ruiz, *Libro de Buen Amor*, p. 27)

Thus, by writing about wicked love, the speaker intends to make the idea of good love more plain, and to make wicked love readily avoidable by those seeking to be virtuous. The book also has a practical side:

And I composed this book also to give people a lesson and example in counting verses and rhyming and composing poetry; for the songs and rhymes and lyrics and ballads and poems, which I have made here, are completely according to the rules this art requires.

(*Libro de Buen Amor*, p. 28)

Turning back to verse, the speaker directs another prayer to God, in which he identifies himself as Juan Ruiz, archpriest of Hita, and his book as the *Libro de Buen Amor*, and begs his reader to consider it carefully; there is also a great deal of pious wisdom hidden beneath the seemingly foolish exterior.

After several more prayers and an extended discussion of how the meaning of a text lies more with what the reader brings to it than with the content set down in words, the narrative proper begins. In a brief section entitled "How the Archpriest Fell in Love," the speaker describes having fallen in love with a beautiful and accomplished lady. Unable to approach her himself, he sends a go-between with a message of love. What follows sets a pattern that will be repeated throughout the *Libro de Buen Amor*; the object of the speaker's love responds by telling a story (usually a fable on the Aesopian model), the "moral" of which serves as her reply to the speaker's overture. In this case, the lady is aware that the go-between is experienced at convincing young women to succumb to love's allure, and so maintains her guard. She tells a story about a lion who was ill; all the other beasts came to pay their respects to their sick lord. The King of Beasts soon recovered, and his subjects planned a celebratory feast. A bull was slaughtered, and the wolf was chosen to carve and serve. Feigning concern for

the lion's health, the wolf kept the carcass for himself, and served the lion the bull's entrails, explaining that this was all the lion's delicate constitution could probably handle. The lion was very hungry and, angered at the wolf's duplicity, struck him a blow across the head, severely injuring him. Now the fox was ordered to serve, and she acted much more wisely, giving the lion the lion's share. In response to the lion's wonderment at her perfectly judicious division of the bull, the fox replied that she had learned her lesson from the fate of the wolf. Concluding her narrative, the lady threatened the go-between with the same fate as the wolf if she did not learn her lesson, as did the fox; no more messages of love, she commanded. The speaker's rebuff and discomfiture was the subject of gossip far and wide, and his misery knew no bounds until another woman, Dame Cross (he was not so ambitious this time—she was the wife of a baker), found a place in his heart. His friend Ferránd García now served as go-between, but proved faithless, and obtained Dame Cross's love for himself.

After a brief period of introspection, during which the speaker meditates on astrology (he was born under the sign of Venus, and so must forever seek the love of women) and the fact that love encourages delusional behavior, he falls in love again, this time with a noblewoman of surpassing beauty, grace, and virtue. In hopes of winning her, he sends her love poems, but she rejects them and him out of hand, exclaiming, "I won't lose my reward in God and his paradise / For sinful love" (*Libro de Buen Amor*, p. 67). Her refusal is accompanied by a story, concerning a faithful guard-dog. One day a thief enters the house, and, when confronted by the dog, offers him a loaf of bread secretly poisoned with arsenic. The dog is not tempted, and replies:

For this small hunk of food, which my big
    jaws tonight may seize on,
I'll not give up the meat and bread that every
    day I feed on.
If I ate your foul food, I would soon choke to
    death, I reason.
You'd steal what I am here to guard and I'd
    commit great treason.

(*Libro de Buen Amor*, p. 67)

With this brief allegory, the lady perfectly expresses the moral foundation for her refusal of the speaker's offer of love. She likens the dog to herself, the dog's master to God, the thief to the speaker, and her chastity to the valuable goods in the house. Faithfulness is not only its own reward, but it brings the promise of much greater rewards in the future, and the temporary pleasure of the loaf of bread (i.e., illicit love) is soon gone and is mortally harmful.

At this point, the speaker is visited by Love himself—the very personification of his own amatory impulse. With a sudden outpouring of hatred, the speaker assails Love at great length as a liar, a cheat, a rogue. The speaker even accuses Love of being responsible for each of the seven deadly sins: pride, avarice, lust, envy, gluttony, wrath, and sloth are all rooted in covetousness, and all stem ultimately from Love. The crafty and duplicitous appeal of Love is illustrated by the speaker with a story about a lawsuit involving a wolf, a fox, and the judge Sir Monkey. This story, also a satirical portrait of lawyers, is presented as an actual courtroom event, in which the rules of judicial procedure are carefully observed. The wolf catches the fox stealing a rooster from Sir Billygoat, and hypocritically brings a legal action against her (he, of course, is guilty of the same crime). Wolf and fox are represented by counsel (greyhound and sheepdog, respectively), and a lengthy trial ensues. Despite the efforts of the two lawyers, Sir Monkey, a just and competent judge, recognizes that both parties to the action are poultry thieves, and renders a just verdict. The point of the story is that language can easily be used to pervert truth and justice, and this is how Love manages to convince people that wrong is right.

Love does not take this attack lying down. He does not so much dispute the accuracy of the speaker's charges, but implies that the only reason the speaker is upset is because he has been unsuccessful in love. Stop slandering me and listen, Love says, and I can show you the way to obtain any woman you desire. Love's advice is eminently practical—there is no moral dimension to it. There are many ways to obtain the love of a woman, and Love recounts them all, cheerfully indifferent to the fact that he is giving instruction in the art of lying and deception. Most important, he counsels, is to use a go-between, ideally an old woman who knows how to appeal to a young woman's vanity:

> Try one of these old crones: the use of herbs
> they have refined;
> They go from house to house and pose as
> midwives—of a kind.
> With pots of fancy makeup, soft face powder
> and bright rouge,
> They case an evil eye on girls and really make
> them blind. . . .
> These convent-trotters manage many deeds in
> secret done.
>
> (*Libro de Buen Amor*, p. 131)

A "convent-trotter" (*trotaconventos* in the original Spanish), it seems, refers to a woman who knows her way around convents, which housed potentially (though illicitly) available nuns and the young women they educated. The idea of the convent-trotter is an important one for much of the rest of the *Libro de Buen Amor*; such a character in fact serves as the speaker's go-between for an extended period. She is simply referred to as Convent-trotter throughout, though we learn that her name is Uracca.

Convinced by Love's arguments, the speaker (who now is seemingly no longer the archpriest of Hita, but Don Melón, a lawyer and layman) proclaims his allegiance to Venus (the goddess of sex), and selects a go-between to approach his new love, Lady Plum. The task is formidable. Lady Plum is a widowed aristocrat, far above the speaker's station, and has already spurned his advances. Convent-trotter is nevertheless confident they will prevail:

> I'll go now to the house where your good
> neighbor lives,
> And tell her such sweet charms and such a
> honeyed balm I'll spread,
> That your deep wound will soon be cured by
> my shrewd medicine.
> . . . . . .
> I have this lady whom you named beneath
> my thumb, you see.
> No man in all the world can ever have her,
> save through me.
>
> (*Libro de Buen Amor*, pp. 189 and 191)

Her confidence is well-placed, for after a bit of persuasion (Convent-trotter tells a story about a bustard and a swallow, and the wary Lady Plum responds with a fable of her own), the Lady is brought around, and Don Melón obtains her love—and marries her.

The archpriest returns as speaker of the narrative, and his pursuit of love resumes. Convent-trotter continues to be of good service, at least until he takes her for granted and makes jokes at her expense. In revenge, she spoils his prospects with a lady to whom he has been sending love poetry and makes him beg her forgiveness. She will serve him, she promises, but he must treat her with respect ("don't apply cheap names or any ugly word to me. / Call me True Love and I will give you my true loyalty" [*Libro de Buen Amor*, p. 239]). This he promises to do. In fact, he names his book after her ("From love of that old woman and to speak in simple truth, / I called my book *True Love* and her the same" [*Libro de Buen Amor*, p. 239]). Thus, in a sense, the *Libro de Buen Amor* is the book of Convent-trotter.

The narrator then takes a journey that leads through a mountain pass. Here (and again on his return trip) he meets a succession of mountain girls, strong and lusty cowherds who compel him (he is unwilling, because they are frighteningly ugly) to have sex with them. Bruised and shaken from this experience, he attends a vigil in honor of the Virgin Mary at a shrine, and offers two long, heartfelt prayers in the form of poetic meditations on the passion of Jesus.

There follows an extended allegorical episode in which the narrator has little role to play other than telling the story. The episode involves Lent—the period of fasting and moral reflection that lasts from Ash Wednesday until Easter Sunday—and its never-ending conflict with appetite and the celebratory impulse. Since it is an allegory, the reader naturally encounters a host of personifications. Sir Shrove-Tuesday (the French would call him Sir Mardi Gras) is a guest at the speaker's house a week before Lent is to begin, when threatening letters arrive from Lady Fast. She accuses Lord Flesh of misbehavior and commands the speaker to summon him to battle in seven day's time. Fearing his frivolity will soon come to an end, the speaker does as directed, and on the appointed day Lord Flesh arrives equipped for combat. His army consists of opulent dishes of food, and the night before battle is engaged he and his forces glut themselves into insensibility. In the morning (i.e., on Ash Wednesday) Lady Fast makes short work of Lord Flesh, wounding him with the more abstemious fare of fast-days, such as leek soup and fish. After being fettered and handed over to Lady Fast, he is forced to confess his sins and submit to her strict dietary regimen. He nevertheless escapes, and seeks out his Jewish friends, who, not being bound to Lenten observance, have plenty of the meat he craves. In any event, Lent is soon over, and Sir Love and Lord Flesh (who seems none the worse for his experience) together celebrate the Easter season.

It is in the midst of these Easter festivities that the narrator again turns his thoughts to Love. He sends for his faithful Convent-trotter, who agrees to help him find feminine companionship. After several leads do not pan out, she advises him to set his sights on a nun, for they are safe and discreet:

> Friend, now listen to me for a trice.
> Make love to some young nun, believe me, this is good advice.

> She can't get married later or let what she does be known;
> You'll have a love of long duration, more than may suffice!

(*Libro de Buen Amor*, p. 333)

She goes on to explain that she knows the nuns' world very well, having lived in a convent as a serving-woman for ten years.

ROYAL PROTECTION FOR ARISTOCRATIC NUNS

The following letter (*c.* 1404) from King Enrique III of Castile concerns Teresa de Ayala and Maria de Ayala, two nuns of noble blood who planned to journey outside their convent. The king warns all his subjects, on their peril, to treat them honorably.

I, by the grace of God, King of Castile . . . Greetings and grace. You are all hereby notified that doña Teresa de Ayala, prioress of the monastery of Santo Domingo el Real de Toledo, and doña Maria, her daughter, are traveling through various parts of my kingdom. I therefore order you all and each one of you to receive them, and any persons who may be with them, whenever and at whatever places of yours they may appear. You are to welcome them and provide them with decent lodgings, not unsuitable inns. You are to supply them with food and anything else they may require, for which they have money to pay. See to it that no one is permitted either to harm them or to attempt to injure or disturb them in any way. And let anyone who does, or tries to do so, be punished in a manner appropriate to the evil deed intended. . . . Let no one of you do them any harm whatsoever, on penalty of my curse, and that of God. . . . I, the King

(Constable, pp. 302-303)

With an attractive prospect already in mind, she visits the place of her former employment, sits down with the nun Lady Garoza, a noble-woman whom she formerly served, and immediately states her business:

> Since I left you I've been in service with a fine archpriest,
> A young man, bold, high-spirited; I live now by his aid.
> And so that he might court you, I enflame his mind each day—
> My lady, do not make him shy of your convent, or afraid.

(*Libro de Buen Amor*, p. 337)

A woman of intelligence and virtue, Lady Garoza will have nothing to do with Convent-trotter's proposal. She responds by telling a story of a farmer who charitably nurses a near-frozen snake back to health, and is squeezed to death for his pains. Just so, exclaims Lady Garoza, has Convent-trotter been to her; she took Convent-trotter into the convent when she was poor and despised, and how she returns to repay this kindness by tempting her to mortal sin! Convent-trotter is unfazed; she responds with a story about a greyhound who, after a long and productive life as a hunting dog, grows old and feeble, and is beaten and despised by the master he had served so well. This goes on at considerable length; in all, five stories are told by each, until Lady Garoza finally agrees to see the narrator. They meet at mass, and the narrator is transported with desire:

> Though in a way it be adultery against our
>   Lord
> When any gallant lover commits sin with a
>   good nun,
> Oh God, I wish that I myself might be that
>   sinner now!
> How gladly I'd do sweet penance once that
>   sweet sin had been done!
>   (*Libro de Buen Amor*, p. 373)

Their love becomes mutual, and they embark upon an intense, but seemingly chaste, love affair. Though the language is a bit obscure, the implication is that the narrator has at last found "true" (in the sense of "godly") love, in the person of a nun who will not submit to his carnal appetite but instead prays for him and encourages him in virtue. He is devastated when, two months later, she dies. His newfound virtue is evidently soon forgotten, for he summons Convent-trotter to find him a concubine to help assuage his grief. She approaches a Muslim girl, but is rebuffed when the girl pretends to speak only Arabic. This is Convent-trotter's last adventure; she dies, and the narrator embarks on a long tirade against death: "Oh, Death, may you be dead, just dead and wretched and in shame! / For you have killed my go-between! Would you had killed me first!" (*Libro de Buen Amor*, p. 379). In a paroxysm of grief, the narrator continues in this vein at great length. He ends by praising her memory, imagining her in heaven, and composing her epitaph. Seemingly still in a contemplative mood, the narrator then lectures his audience on the nature of Christian moral duty. Death took away Uracca, and it will take us all away as well; woe betide the sinner who dies in a state of sin! The world, the flesh and the devil all conspire to realize our damnation, and so energetic spiritual warfare must forever be waged against this unholy trinity. The hour of our death cannot be known; therefore we must avoid sin at all times, as if each moment were our last.

By now the reader will not be surprised to learn that the narrator's piety is short-lived. Indeed he follows this sermon with an account of the pleasing qualities of small women, and a brief description of his replacement go-between, Sir Ferret. A low-born scoundrel, Sir Ferret has none of Convent-trotter's skill, and only succeeds in repelling the women he attempts to entice. With this, the narrative portion of the *Libro de Buen Amor* comes to a close, and the narrator encourages his readers to respect and value his book; it contains, he says, much fine poetry, as well as wisdom and sanctity, and he requests that his readers pray for him.

The rest of the work consists primarily of prayers to and about the Virgin Mary, though there are also poems narrated by blind men and poor students seeking alms. It concludes with a short narrative about the clerics of Talavera, who are told by their archbishop that they must put away their concubines, on penalty of excommunication. They are outraged and plan an energetic appeal.

The many faces of love. "Love" was as multifaceted an idea in medieval Spain as it is now, in that *amor* could refer to anything from the love of God towards his creatures to the services sold by a prostitute to her customers, and everything in between. The ambiguity of the word was convenient for poets, who wrote about love as much as anything else in the Middle Ages, and were evidently quite interested in exploring its various shades of meaning. For Juan Ruiz, the narrator's quest for love is something all men experience, though perhaps not quite to the same degree of variety. God, of course, is the source and embodiment of infinite, perfect love; all loves other than divine fall short somehow. Even sinful love, though, is not unrelated to the love of God; through misdirected affection, the sinner seeks comfort and happiness in a place where it cannot be found, with someone who cannot provide it. This love, even if achieved, is but a pale reflection of the love God can provide, and only temporarily eases the longing that only God can address. In his more temperate moments, the narrator of the *Libro de Buen Amor* realizes this, as in the Lady Garoza episode; here, his sexual goal is not met, but her charitable love and holiness leave him far more satisfied than if she had submitted to his lust.

Even apart from the idea of God, human love in the *Libro de Buen Amor* is complex. The women pursued by the narrator come from many walks of life, and his love for them consequently takes different forms. At one extreme is the love he experiences with the girls of the mountains; they force themselves upon him, and the resulting activity is semi-bestial and wholly without refinement. He feels no physical relief, only relief at escaping their clutches. This evidences a preference on his part for the polished and cultured love to be found with women of the upper classes, and indeed it is to such women that his most ardent addresses (usually in poetic form) are tendered; these are the lovers that fire his soul, that make him feel noble and significant. Ideas of love in the Middle Ages support him in this; love was thought of as an ennobling emotion, one that could impel lovers to feats of knightly bravery and heroic virtue. The standard example can be found in the Arthurian legends (well-known in Spanish literary culture since the twelfth century), in the character of Lancelot. His love for Guinevere was adulterous, to be sure, but it nevertheless helped make him the best knight in the world. Alongside Iberian adaptations of Arthurian material (many of the classic stories involving Arthur, Lancelot, and Guinevere were translated into Castilian, Catalan, and Portuguese in the thirteenth and fourteenth centuries), readers in Ruiz's day also had a chivalric romance of authentically Spanish origin. *El Libro de Cauallero Zifar* (The Book of the Knight Cifar) is a prose romance of the early fourteenth century, featuring a full-fledged romantic hero (Cifar) who pursues the love of noble women, and performs deeds of great valor in the process. It is probably due to the influence of such models that Juan Ruiz is careful to note the social class of each woman that his narrator is pursuing, because it in many ways determines the quality of his love.

Sources and literary context. The sources of the *Libro de Buen Amor* fall into two categories: secular and religious. Probably the most important secular source text is the *Pamphilus*, a twelfth-century Latin play that was extremely popular and widely disseminated throughout Europe. In it, the title character (the name means "all love" or "wholly in love") falls in love with Galathea, and after being advised by Venus and assisted by a crafty bawd, attains his desire. The seduction episode involving Lady Plum in

Libro de Buen Amor is directly modeled on the *Pamphilus*, with Venus appearing in both narratives. The role of Don Melón echoes that of Pamphilus, Lady Plum owes much to Galathea, and Convent-trotter takes on the character of the bawd. The endings, however, are different—in the *Pamphilus*, Galathea is raped, and regrets having listened to the bawd, while in the Lady Plum episode, the two lovers are happily married. *Pamphilus* presents love in the unsentimental, even cynical manner characteristic of the Roman poet Ovid. (Ovid too has an "old woman" character in his poetry [Dipsas in *Amores*], and he as well as his medieval imitators probably also influenced Ruiz directly.)

As shown, the influence of the beast-fable tradition is evident throughout the *Libro de Buen Amor*; the characters use these animal stories to argue with each other, and their morals are applied to the human issues being debated. Also, Ruiz is clearly familiar with Spanish vernacular poetic traditions; the poems involving the narrator's adventures with mountain girls represent a fairly widespread genre in medieval Spain. Usually humorous, these poems (called *serranilla*) tell of a man's journey into the mountains, whereupon he is waylaid by a wild shepherdess or cowherd and compelled to provide sexual favors.

The influence of religious texts upon the *Libro de Buen Amor* is more difficult to pin down, probably because religious motifs were generally commonplace, appearing in many different sources. Nevertheless, certain statements can be made with confidence. The author, whether or not he was actually an archpriest named Juan Ruiz, was clearly familiar with the texts of canon law. These laws were circulated in standard collections, usually accompanied by explanatory glosses, and an educated canon lawyer would also be familiar with standard commentaries on the laws. One such commentary, the *Novella* of John Andreae, is quoted in the *Libro de Buen Amor*. Scriptural texts of course appear with some regularity, and in the narrator's more pious moments, he explains moral and religious doctrine in a manner wholly consistent with the dictates of standard fourteenth-century sermon manuals. His evident devotion to the Virgin Mary is also characteristic of his time; the later Middle Ages saw a huge upsurge in the veneration of the mother of Jesus, and the many prayers in honor of Mary contained in the *Libro de Buen Amor* express the basic elements of this veneration perfectly. Mary is the intercessor, the sinless human intermediary between man's sinfulness and God's avenging justice who can effect salvation for those sufficiently devoted to her. She is also the perfect model of human behavior. Christ's own perfection is a behavior model, but his divinity poses an insurmountable barrier. Mary, on the other hand, is fully human; she understands human frailty, and (like a good mother) is more ready to forgive than judge.

Reception. The *Libro de Buen Amor* was first published in 1790. Its editor, Tomás Antonio Sánchez, was somewhat troubled by the work's racier passages, which prompted him "to justify its publication as a document for the study of historical Spanish grammar, medieval customs, and metric forms, and to suppress those less morally enlightening passages which did not readily lend themselves to such research" (Seidenspinner-Núñez, p. 1). Much modern criticism of the work has devoted itself to answering the questions raised by Sánchez's bowdlerizing; how serious is it? How can a reader profit from the religious material in the face of such ribaldry? If the ribaldry was the purpose of the work, why dampen the reader's enjoyment with moralization? These questions show no signs of being answered definitively as of yet, but several approaches to them should be considered.

One answer is to see the work as fundamentally satirical, either in the service of conventional morality (as posited by the scholar Amador de los Ríos) or countercultural iconoclasm (the view of Menéndez Pidal). However, most modern critics see such approaches as too simplistic. The *Libro de Buen Amor* possesses many voices: some satirical, some fervently religious, some cynical, and some starry-eyed with love. Each voice seems sincere, and many critics regard it as unreasonable to expect a unified voice from a work that so clearly does not mean to provide one. An important contribution to the recognition of this multivoiced quality was made by the great scholar of medieval French literature Felix Lecoy in 1938. Later critics were more inclined to see the *Libro de Buen Amor* as a legitimate artistic whole, in spite of its many voices and segmented structure.

—Matthew Brosamer

For More Information

Amador de los Ríos, José. *Historica critica de la literatura española.* Vol. 4. 1863. Reprint, Madrid: Gredos, 1969.

Castro, Américo. *España en su Historia.* Buenos Aires: Losada, 1948.

Constable, Olivia Remie. *Medieval Iberia: Readings from Christian, Muslim, and Jewish Sources.* Philadelphia: University of Pennsylvania Press, 1997.

Elliott, Alison Goddard, ed. and trans. *Seven Medieval Latin Comedies.* New York: Garland, 1984.

Gybbon-Moneypenny, G. B., ed. *"Libro de Buen Amor" Studies.* London: Tamesis, 1970.

Kelly, Henry Ansgar. *Canon Law and the Archpriest of Hita.* Binghamton: Medieval and Renaissance Texts and Studies, 1984.

Lecoy, Félix. *Recherches sur le "LBA" de Juan Ruiz, Archiprêtre de Hita.* Farnborough: Gregg International, 1974.

Menéndez Pidal, Ramón. *Poesia juglaresca y origines de las literatura romanicas: Problemas de historia literaria y cultural.* Madrid: Instituto de Estudios Politicos, 1957.

O'Callaghan, Joseph. *A History of Medieval Spain.* Ithaca: Cornell University Press, 1975.

Ruiz, Juan. *The Book of True Love.* Ed. and trans. Saralyn R. Daly and Anthony N. Zahareas. University Park: Pennsylvania State University Press, 1978.

Seidenspinner-Núñez, Dayle. *The Allegory of Good Love: Parodic Perspectivism in the "Libro de Buen Amor."* Berkeley: University of California Press, 1981.

Spitzer, Leo. "Note on the Poetic and the Empirical 'I' in Medieval Authors." In *Traditio.* New York: Fordham University Press, 1946.

Life Is a Dream

by
Pedro Calderón de la Barca

Pedro Calderón de la Barca (1600-81) shared with Lope de Vega the distinction of being one of Spain's two most celebrated playwrights during its Golden Age (1550-1650). He was the third of six children born to Diego Calderón and Ana María de Henao. Educated at the Jesuit Colegio Imperial, Calderón studied logic and rhetoric at the University of Alcalá (1614-15) and canon law at the University of Salamanca (1615-21). He served in Spanish campaigns in Italy and the Netherlands, and also became embroiled in personal disputes. In 1621 Calderón and two brothers faced murder charges for having killed an adversary in an argument. A couple of years later Calderón staged his first play *Love, Honor, and Power* (1623) in the royal palace. King Philip IV, extremely devoted to Calderón, gave him a royal pension, encouraged him to write ever new plays, and offered him funds for their lavish production and performance. In the 1630s, the king named Calderón director of all plays produced in the royal palace. He proceeded to pen many of his best-known works in the 1630s, including *The Devotion to the Cross* (1633?), *Life Is a Dream* (1636), *The Constant Prince* (1636), and *The Physician of His Own Honor* (1637). In 1640, after being named to the military Order of Santiago, Calderón fought as part of this Order against the rebellious Catalans, suffering wounds in battle. Calderón never married, but in the early 1640s, like his father, whose marriage to his mother was one of convenience rather than a love match, he had an illegitimate son. His writing in this decade consisted of religious plays,

> ### THE LITERARY WORK
>
> A philosophical drama set during an unspecified time in Poland; published in Spanish (as *La vida es sueño*) in 1636, in English in 1853.
>
> ### SYNOPSIS
>
> A prince, imprisoned since birth to thwart an astrologer's prediction of his future rebellion, learns self-mastery: at first lacking self-control, he gains it when he realizes the illusory nature of human pursuits.

the only kind permitted in Spain from 1644 through 1649. Ordained in 1651, Calderón displayed a genuine vocation to the priesthood. In 1663 Philip IV appointed Calderón honorary court chaplain. From his ordination to the year of his death, Calderón wrote plays. Of the 120 that have survived, 80 belong to the religious genre of *autos sacramentales*, allegorical plays that celebrate Corpus Christi, the festival honoring the Eucharist (the sacrament through which, when the priest pronounces the words of consecration ["This is my body," etc.], the wafer and wine taken by a worshiper are transformed into the body and blood of Christ). His other plays include tragedies, histories, comedies, and philosophical plays. Calderón's most renowned work, the philosophical play *Life Is a Dream*, addresses the religious issue of free will in the context of life in early-seventeenth-century Spain.

Pedro Calderón de la Barca

Events in History at the Time of the Play

The Spanish Baroque (1550-1700). Writing in the last decades of Spain's Golden Age, Calderón epitomizes Baroque style, dominant in seventeenth-century Spanish culture—architecture, sculpture, painting, music, and literature. Baroque works, unlike those based upon classical models, are often described as "irregular," as well as ornate, dynamic, exaggerated, and deeply concerned with expressions of the "inner life." The Baroque takes Renaissance themes like nature, the relationship between life and death, and human character and explores them in more complex ways. Renaissance painters, for example, would present subjects in clear daylight while Baroque painters tended towards chiaroscuro, dramatically highlighting the subject against a dark background. According to Pedro Laín Entralgo, the Baroque contains four formal features: dynamism, subordination of parts, a preference for the infinite and the infinitesimally small, and layers of complication (Laín Entralgo in Orringer, p. 146). The Renaissance artist or writer sought clarity and simplicity, harmonizing all objects to this end. But the Baroque writer or artist preferred to complicate the composition, subordinating one object to the other in a rational way, relying on the perception of the audience to order the elements into the appropriate hierarchy.

In Spain, great Baroque writers include the poet Luis de Góngora, father of *culteranismo,* or sensuous experimentation in poetry rearranging the syntax of Spanish in almost incomprehensible ways, in imitation of Latin, a language in which word order is less important because the case endings of nouns and adjectives make the meaning clear. Francisco de Quevedo achieves a similar level of complexity through the literature of conceits (sometimes called *conceptismo*)—the witty juxtaposition of ideas, images, and metaphors to express concepts (see **The Swindler,** also in *WLAIT 5: Spanish and Portuguese Literatures and Their Times*). Calderón, using both *culteranismo* and the literature of conceits in his Baroque drama, achieved the pinnacle with his *Life Is a Dream.* The play has no fewer than three parallel plots—a son's pursuit of his father's throne, a noblewoman's pursuit of her honor, and her former lover's pursuit of the throne for himself through marriage. These three plots are intricately interwoven in a play that includes particularly Spanish dimensions of the Baroque.

Like Baroque works elsewhere, those in Spain were concerned with issues such as hierarchy, rationality, and willpower. But Baroque works in Spain also showed an extra introspective dimension born of the dissolution of its political and religious empire. As the seventeenth century wore on, the country would acquire an increasing awareness of its powerlessness in the face of the rise of Protestantism in northern Europe. This sense of weakness appears even within the Iberian Peninsula. There had been an effort to consolidate all Peninsular regions under a centralized Spanish administration that saw progress in 1580, with Spain bringing Portugal into its fold, but the undertaking was short-lived. In 1640 Portugal broke away from Spain and gained independence. Though in vain, Catalonia sought sovereignty as well, testing Spain's strength through a long, consuming civil war. Alongside all this internal disunity, Spain suffered defeat in Europe. Protestant Holland achieved independence from Spain in 1648 (the Peace of Westphalia); a weakened Spain then felt forced to ally itself to its archenemy France through marriage between their sovereigns. Afterwards, Spain took an isolationist stance, clinging tenaciously to its traditional Catholicism, losing its taste for worldly ambitions. This attitude of disenchantment with the pursuit of power, wealth, beauty, and love in this world, as if awakening to their short-lived, dreamlike quality, became known in Spanish society as *desengaño,* literally, "undeceit" (i.e., disillusionment) in appearances. Certainly undeceit lies at the heart of the philosophy of *Life Is a Dream.*

Human destiny, free will, and astrology. The beginning of the sixteenth century saw the founding of Protestantism by Martin Luther. His attempts to reform the practices of the Catholic Church, beginning in 1517, resulted in the founding of the Protestant Church. Some of those who remained in the Catholic camp were distraught themselves about current practices, such as the frequent absence of priests from their districts, their keeping of concubines, and their widespread illiteracy. Their dismay gave rise to a movement to reform the Catholic Church from within, known as the Counter-Reformation.

All of this religious upheaval resulted in the tackling of fundamental questions about life, death, and salvation. Protestants, like Martin Luther, believed in the doctrine of predestination—the belief that God has predestined certain humans to receive God's grace (necessary for salvation) while withholding this grace from others. Various Catholic leaders in Spain vigorously disagreed with such a belief. The priest Luis de Molina argued that God and the human being act simultaneously to assure all people grace; salvation, he taught, depends on a sinner's willingness to receive grace. Molina's idea generated controversy between two powerful religious orders in Spain, the Jesuits and the Dominicans. The Jesuits agreed with Molina's notions of free will; the Dominicans did not. Since Calderón had received his education from the Jesuits, he seems to have concurred with Molina on the issue of free will.

Life Is a Dream broaches the conflict, present in the theology of the times, between free will and predestination, handing the victory to free will. Calderón's philosophy is this: the human being lives under the influence of nature, comprised of four elements (as identified by the ancient Greek thinker Empedocles): earth, air, fire, and water. The influence of these elements is manifested in the stars, which supposedly control human destiny. The study of the impact of the constellations on human destiny constitutes astrology. According to a famous dictum of Catholic theology, however, the stars incline people to certain behaviors but do not determine those behaviors (*Astra inclinant, non necessitant*). Human beings have free will and reason, which distinguish them from animals, enabling them to display the four cardinal virtues of prudence, justice, temperance, and fortitude. In this way they can rise above the influence of nature (including animalistic passions). This ability, in turn, enables them to understand that earthly pursuits are ephemeral. Life is in essence a dream, and a mortal's pursuits on earth should be directed to good deeds that will merit God's grace and salvation after death.

In *Life Is a Dream,* King Basilio confesses at the start of the play that he has placed too much faith in astrology. Heeding closely astrological predictions that he would one day have a rebel child who would topple him from his throne, Basilio has reared his son, Segismundo, in a prison tower. Through a combination of circumstances, Segismundo adopts a different attitude from that of his father, concluding that man can master his astrological destiny through reason and willpower. He even comes to regard life as a dream and all worldly ambitions as vain.

> ## THE *AUTOS SACRAMENTALES*
>
>
>
> The *autos sacramentales* were breathtaking displays. Full of scenery, costumes, and music, the spectacles were performed in Spain during the Corpus Christi feasts. On these days there was a procession led by a dragon-like serpent ridden by a woman, followed by folk dancers, child singers, candle bearers, priests with the Holy Eucharist under a canopy and then the actors of the *autos sacramentales.* Calderón himself defines this genre in an *auto* called *The Second Wife* (1648): "What are they?" asks a ploughman. "Sermons," answers a shepherd. "Set to verse . . . matters / Of Sacred Theology / Which my reason cannot manage / To explain or comprehend" (Calderón in Sullivan, p. 23).

The theme of honor in Spanish drama. While the main plot of *Life Is a Dream* focuses on the conflict between fate and free will, the subplot of Rosaura's attempts to avenge her dishonor has attracted considerable attention. Loss of honor and the attempt to regain it were recurring themes in Golden Age drama. Lope de Vega, in his verse treatise *New Art of Playwrighting,* remarked that cases of honor being called into question put the minds of Spanish theatergoers in a state of suspense. "Honor," in this case, means the opinion that one has of oneself, conditioned by the opinion that society holds of that person. The notion entered Spain in the fifth century with the Visigoths, a Germanic people who brought with them a feudal-like system, characterized by "private oaths of fidelity" to a lord, dependent land tenures, and the like; in the end, feudalism failed to develop fully in Spain but varieties of it surfaced and influenced life there, especially from the ninth century, when it became a main facet of life in northern Europe (O'Callaghan, pp. 165-67).

The system revolved around a lord and vassals who received land from him in exchange for their service and allegiance, beginning with the chief lord, the king. The arrangement between a lord and his vassals who were nobles conferred honor upon those vassals if the lord respected their rights. In the Middle Ages, a noble who suffered insult or injury from someone else forfeited others' esteem and became a social outcast unless he managed to erase the affront either by seeking legal redress in the courts or by punishing the offenders with his own hand. Sexual misconduct by a man's wife, daughter, or other female relative became the most shameful dishonor and called for the harshest punishment of all. Women themselves were usually subject to punishment even if they were mere victims, not consenting participants, as in rape, kidnapping, seduction, and slander. Because women's shame compromised their families, they were commonly banished, even killed, after their disgrace became public knowledge; apparently only blood shed by both the seduced and seducer would eradicate the stigma of sexual dishonor.

Dishonor through real or even only suspected sexual misconduct provides plots for many Golden Age dramas. Using aristocratic characters, cloak-and-dagger dramas spun intricate plots around love, intrigue, and honor. The problems in these plays could be happily resolved with reunions between estranged lovers, family reconciliations, and multiple weddings. Lope de Vega and Calderón both wrote a number of comedies in this genre. Both playwrights also examined the darker side of honor in tragedies. Calderón wrote at least four notable honor tragedies: *For a Secret Insult, a Secret Vengeance; The Painter of His Own Dishonor; The Physician of His Own Honor;* and *Jealousy, the Greatest Monster.* In all but one, notes Everett Hesse, "a guiltless person perishes . . . because of the breath of scandal, egoism, and a frenzied imagination which invents the circumstances of guilt" (Hesse, p. 104). In *The Physician of His Own Honor*, a faithful wife is bled to death on her own

husband's orders simply because she has been compromised by a meeting with a former suitor. The honor subplot in *Life Is a Dream*, though it ends much more happily, nevertheless has the driving power of the subject as treated in honor tragedy.

The Play in Focus

Plot summary. At the start of Calderón's three-act drama, Rosaura—a noblewoman from Muscovy (present-day Moscow)—comes on stage disguised as a man. She and her servant, Clarín, are traveling in the wild mountains of Poland, when they stumble upon a tower-prison where a young man, Segismundo, lies in chains. Rosaura overhears the Polish prince Segismundo, who soliloquizes about his unhappy fate: birds, beasts, and fish are lowlier creatures than he, yet they enjoy the freedom that escapes him. Rosaura approaches the young man, who greets her eagerly. Their conversation is interrupted by the appearance of Clotaldo, Segismundo's jailer and tutor and the king's right-hand man. Clotaldo sets out to arrest Rosaura and Clarín for discovering Segismundo's hiding place, since it is a state secret. However, Rosaura reveals that she has come to Poland seeking to avenge a grievance. She yields up her sword to Clotaldo, and he recognizes it as one that he himself left behind with a mistress many years ago, which leads him to believe that Rosaura, the intruder, is his own illegitimate "son" (since she is in disguise). Yet he feels duty bound to arrest the intruder out of loyalty to his lord, the king.

At the Polish court, Astolfo, Duke of Muscovy, and Estrella, nephew and niece of King Basilio, disagree about which of them has the better right to the throne. Though they are rivals, Astolfo is also courting Estrella to consolidate his claim to the Polish throne, believing that it will grow that much stronger if they wed. The two assume that their uncle's only son, Segismundo, is dead. King Basilio brings the argument to a halt by revealing that Segismundo is in fact alive. Dire astrological readings and terrible portents at his birth convinced the king to imprison his infant offspring in a mountain tower.

Now full of remorse for having believed in the stars, Basilio decides to bring Segismundo to court to see if he exercises the self-control one needs in order to rule. Clotaldo begs for the life of Rosaura, still in disguise, and Basilio allows her to be set free. Segismundo's imprisonment, in any case, is no longer a state secret.

Still at court, Estrella and Astolfo continue having differences. It disconcerts her that he wears around his neck the portrait of another woman (Rosaura) whom he secretly loves but feels he cannot marry because her social status is beneath his. In this same act, Rosaura reveals to Clotaldo that the powerful Astolfo is precisely the one who dishonored her. Astolfo, Clotaldo realizes, must eventually become his enemy, since the dishonor of a child is the dishonor of its father.

At the start of Act 2, Basilio informs Clotaldo of his plan to drug Segismundo and bring him to the palace to see whether he behaves tyrannically or justly. If tyrannically, he will drug the prince anew and return him to his prison, duping him into believing that he merely dreamed his visit to the palace. Envisioning disaster, Clotaldo disapproves of the plan, but being the loyal vassal he is, he proceeds as directed. A drugged Segismundo is brought to the palace, clad in fine raiment instead of his original animal skins.

Learning of his true identity, the young man soon confirms Basilio's worst fears. He brawls with the servants, quarrels with Astolfo, and makes improper advances towards Estrella and Rosaura, who by now has abandoned her original male disguise and taken on another, as a lady-in-waiting to Estrella. Segismundo furthermore explodes at Clotaldo and Basilio for his years of imprisonment. Calling Basilio "a tyrant over my *free will*," the young prince rages, "I'm free of any obligation toward / Thee; rather can I call thee to account / To me for all the time thou didst deprive / Me of my freedom, life, and honor" (Calderón de la Barca, *Life Is a Dream*, p. 45; emphasis added). To explain the injustice, Basilio relays the dire portents at the prince's birth, but this hardly mollifies him.

Meanwhile, Rosaura finally comes face-to-face with her offender, Astolfo. Serving in her capacity as lady-in-waiting to Estrella, Rosaura goes to retrieve the portrait of the woman that Astolfo wears on his breast. Astolfo at once recognizes her as the subject of the portrait, but she denies this, insisting that she is only Estrella's lady-in-waiting. She takes the portrait but withholds it from Estrella, not wanting her identity to be discovered. It is a small victory, though; without the aid of another, she cannot achieve her ultimate goal of recovering her honor. She needs the help of a powerful noble, someone as formidable as Segismundo. And he, drugged by Basilio's servants, is no longer around. Transported back to the tower, he awakens once again in his familiar prison.

In chains once again, Segismundo undergoes a change of heart. He recalls that during his stay in the royal palace, Basilio and Clotaldo warned him that his sudden rise to power might be only a dream. After his jailer, Clotaldo, confirms that Segismundo has been dreaming, the prince realizes that all life is a dream. But Clotaldo advises him that the merit of doing good deeds is never lost, even when they are done in dreams. Accordingly, in probably the most famous soliloquy in the Spanish language, Segismundo resolves to repress his previous unruliness and regard all earthly ambitions as mere dreams.

> What is life? A frenzy.
> What is life? An illusion,
> A shadow, a fiction,
> And the greatest good is paltry:
> Since all life is a dream,
> And dreams are also dreams
> (Calderón de la Barca, *La vida sueño*, 2.1195-1200; trans. N. Orringer)

In Act 3, incensed that King Basilio has named Astolfo, the Muscovite duke, his successor, the Polish people release Prince Segismundo from his tower-prison and proclaim him their ruler. Throughout the act, Segismundo vacillates between thinking he is dreaming and living for the present moment. When conceiving of life as a dream, he performs good deeds; when living for the present, he behaves selfishly. On the threshold of battle with Basilio's army, he meets Rosaura, dressed as a woman warrior. She offers herself as an ally to Segismundo against Basilio and Astolfo, her old enemy. In a final soliloquy, Segismundo vacillates between violating Rosaura and helping her regain her honor. He decides to help her because life is a dream and good conduct becomes a prince.

The Polish people defeat the forces of Basilio, who surrenders to Segismundo, expecting that the astrological prophecy will be fulfilled and his son will seize the throne from him. After reproaching Basilio for keeping him in prison, Segismundo prefers to show the virtue of a perfect prince and submit to his father's will. The son has acquired enough self-mastery to forgive his father for having deprived him of a normal childhood. Basilio, impressed by this self-restraint, cedes his throne to Segismundo, whose first act as Poland's ruler is to command Astolfo to marry Rosaura, thereby restoring her honor. Any compunctions Astolfo may have about the match are relieved by Clotaldo's revelation: Rosaura is his daughter, and

Scene from a 1983 Royal Shakespeare Company production of *Life is a Dream* at The Other Place in Stratford-Upon-Avon, England.

since he belongs to the high nobility, Astolfo will not be marrying beneath his station.

Aware of Estrella's aspiration to the Polish throne, Segismundo offers his own hand to her in marriage. A model prince, he sacrifices his love for Rosaura to the prudence of a powerful political alliance with Estrella. Before the curtain comes down, Segismundo confesses that his teacher for performing good deeds has been a dream!

Undeceit. The idea of *desengaño*, undeceit, lies at the heart of *Life Is a Dream*. In the soliloquy that ends Act 2, Segismundo puts it succinctly when he says, "All life is a dream, / And dreams are also dreams." This outlook on life—regarding success in politics, in love, in self-beautification, or in business as transitory and therefore dreamlike—appears not only in Calderón's best-known play but also in other plays he wrote; in the drama, prose, and poetry of his contemporaries, and even in painting. For Calderón, life is not only as insubstantial as a dream but as unreal as play-acting. Like *Measure for Measure* by his near-contemporary William Shakespeare (1564-1616), Calderón's *Life Is a Dream* offers a vision of the world as a theater, a game of deceptive appear-

ances, in which the human moves about as an actor on stage. Segismundo dreams this while in a narcotic stupor as Basilio's servants carry him back to his tower-prison after his disastrous palace visit: "May my valor without equal / Come out on the ample stage / Of the great world theater: / so that my vengeance is suitable, / may it see Prince Segismundo / triumph over his father (*La vida sueño,* 2.1085-90, trans. N. Orringer). Of course, he utters this hope before the notion of undeceit begins to dawn on him.

Calderón's most beloved *auto sacramental, The Great World Theater* (written 1675), relates the issue of undeceit to the Eucharist. The *auto* views existence as a fiction in which God lends all worldly goods as props to actors who play their parts to deserve salvation at the end of the production. If they perform well, they pass on to the true life of heaven, where Christ awaits at the Eucharistic banquet table. If they perform badly, they go to hell. Two characters in the *auto* achieve immediate salvation: the nun, portrayed as Discretion (or the cloistered life), and the innocent Pauper. Others—the Farmer (daily labor), Beauty, and the King (political power)—must spend time in purgatory before rising to Christ's table. Another—The Rich Man (greed)—must suffer the flames of hell, for he has not yet learned the lesson of undeceit.

Calderón's martyr play *The Constant Prince* (1636) relates undeceit to the renunciation of power. A historical play with a saintly ending, *The Constant Prince* begins where *Life Is a Dream* leaves off. Unlike its predecessor, which features a human beast who develops through undeceit into a perfect prince, *The Constant Prince* centers on a perfect prince who evolves into a Christian martyr. In Act 1, Don Fernando, Prince of Portugal, shows constancy as a Christian warrior prince against the military superiority of the Moorish King of Fez. In Act 2, he renounces any privileges to which he is entitled as an honored prisoner of war, then refuses to be ransomed in exchange for the Christian city of Ceuta. In Act 3, he perishes, poor and starving, for his faith. In the course of the play, a curious relationship develops between Don Fernando and the Moorish princess Fénix, who lives in the palace where he serves her father as a slave. Afflicted by a vague melancholy, she, herself a beauty, tries in vain to console herself with beautiful objects—nostalgic songs or garden flowers. The Constant Prince, reduced to hideous slave, recites to Fénix the famous "Sonnet of the Flowers," which display pomp and joy in the morning, only to become objects of pity by afternoon and die at night. Likewise, human fortunes are made and lost in a single day, so of what value to Fénix is her beauty?

Playwrights other than Calderón—for instance, Tirso de Molina in **The Trickster of Seville** (also in *WLAIT 5: Spanish and Portuguese Literatures and Their Times*)—have cultivated the issue of undeceit in their works too. Poets too concerned themselves with the issue, which manifested itself in verse such as the following sonnet by Góngora:

Sonnet 156

While trying to compete against your hair,
Gold polished in the sunshine gleams in vain,
While scornful in the middle of the plain
Your brow of white looks at the lily fair,
While your two lips are followed by more
    eyes
Than follow in the spring the first carnation,
And while you show with haughty jubilation
That graceful neck of crystal that you prize,
Enjoy your neck, your hair, your lip and
    brow
Before what was your golden youth till now,
Which gold, lily, carnation, and crystal
    brought,
Not only turns to silver or crushed petals,
but one day even you and the whole lot
turn into earth, to smoke, to dust, to naught.
                    (Góngora, p. 163; trans. N. Orringer)

In Baltasar Gracián's three-part allegorical novel *The Critick* (1651, later translated as *The Faultfinder*), undeceit proves useful as a stratagem for penetrating appearances to get at the underlying reality of deceit and immorality that threaten the individual as a person throughout life. Critilo and his son Andrenio journey through seventeenth-century Europe to seek Felisinda, Critilo's wife and Andrenio's mother. In the process, they must avoid many allegorized traps and pitfalls that will impede their journey. Undeceit helps them stay steadily on course, while enabling the author to satirize many aspects of corrupt Baroque culture in Gracián's time.

Finally, paintings of the era centered on undeceit, as reflected by canvasses in the Prado Museum in Madrid. Diego Velázquez, for instance, like Calderón, a member of Philip IV's court, painted *Venus before a Mirror*, in which the smooth flesh tones of a nude, lying on her side with her back to the spectator, seem to convey the impression of blossoming youth or early maturity, while the mirror held by Cupid and vaguely reflecting her face sends back the image of a woman past her prime.

Sources and literary context. Arguably, Calderón's most immediate source for *Life Is a Dream* was a play he himself coauthored with Antonio Coello, *Yerros de naturaleza y aciertos de fortuna—Nature's Errors Redeemed by Fortune*—perhaps a few years before he wrote *Life Is a Dream*. In this earlier work, twin heirs—a brother and sister—vie for their late father's throne, and a second pair of siblings, Rosaura and Segismundo, becomes involved. At one point, the male twin, Polidoro, is imprisoned in a tower for compromising Rosaura's honor.

MASTERPIECE REVISITED

Calderón so highly valued the lesson of *Life Is a Dream* that around 1677 he reworked it under the same title into an *auto sacramental*. In this version, the characters are transformed into allegorical figures: Basilio, the king, becomes God; Segismundo, the rebellious prince, represents Man; Wisdom and the Dream itself are personified as they impart to Man the lesson that mortal life is ephemeral, while life eternal comes only after death.

Less immediately, *Life Is a Dream* almost certainly owes its existence to a happy marriage of Western and Eastern sources. Calderón has devised in it a tragedy with a happy ending, a drama that moves from adverse to prosperous fortune—one of the two kinds of tragedy that Aristotle distinguishes in his *Poetics*. *Life Is a Dream* has so much in common with Sophocles's tragedy *Oedipus the King* that Calderón likely had it in mind while composing his own great work. Before the start of the ancient Greek tragedy, Prince Oedipus's father, King Laïus, tries to thwart a prophecy that his son will one day kill him (thereby usurping his throne). Laïus has baby Oedipus thrown onto a mountain. Oedipus, secretly saved by his mother Jocasta, once he has grown up, (unknowingly) kills his father in self-defense, thereby realizing the prophecy. In *Life Is a Dream*, Segismundo likewise has the opportunity to kill his father in self-defense. However, instead of fulfilling the prophecy, he spares his father's life and, in a reversal of *Oedipus the King*, places himself at his father's mercy. A Christian prince, he behaves according to the four cardinal virtues—justice, temperance, prudence, and fortitude—prized by Counter-Reformation Spain, not by the values of ancient Greece.

Calderón synthesizes with the Oedipus myth several Eastern tales that link imprisonment with conversion. In one such tale, an Indian potentate secludes his newborn, Josephat, in the mountains after astrologers foretell that the boy will convert to Christianity; the prophecy is anyhow fulfilled when the holy hermit Barlaam finds Josephat and converts him. Calderón might have been acquainted with any number of versions of the original story as well as Lope de Vega's version, *Barlán y Josafá*.

Another source for *Life Is a Dream* may have been a tale from the *Arabian Nights*, in which a man, Abu Hassan, receives an opiate, awakes in a palace, and enjoys royal privileges for a day. The man is later drugged anew and returned home; upon awakening, he believes his stay in the palace to have been just a dream.

As noted, Calderón's drama emerged in an era replete with literature that deals with undeceit. His play furthermore evokes comparisons with other Golden Age works dealing with dreams, the process of self-discovery, and the conflict between appearance and reality, such as the five satirical narratives by Quevedo, *Sueños*, "Dreams."

Reception. *Life Is a Dream,* along with Calderón's other drama, inspired some talented imitators in the Golden Age (e.g., Alvaro Cubillo de Aragón [1596?-1661] and Juan Claudio de la Hoz y Mota [1622-1714]). The first half of the eighteenth century gave rise to mediocre imitations of Calderón, and later in the century German Romanticism discovered Spanish Golden Age theater. Encouraged by the great German writer Goethe, Johann Dieterich Gries (1775-1842) translated all of Calderón's plays into German. Some nineteenth-century Spanish critics, well-read in the German Romantics, took issue with their uncritical comparisons of Calderón to Shakespeare. The Spanish critic Marcelino Menéndez Pelayo (1856-1912), for one, faulted the play for lack of character development, observing that there was too brusque a transition from Segismundo as slave to his passions to Segismundo the perfect prince. Menéndez Pelayo also dismissed the subplot of Rosaura's search for her honor as irrelevant and parasitic. The suggestion here is that it feeds off the praiseworthy main plot, contributing little to the play (Sloman, p. 90). The turn-of-the-twentieth-century writer Miguel de Unamuno echoed Menéndez Pelayo in deeming Calderón the archetypal Spanish playwright, with characteristic strengths and defects.

His plots, said Unamuno, displayed excessive poverty and simplicity, including parasitic episodes that hindered rather than advanced the main action. Among other drawbacks, Calderón's drama does not, said both Menéndez Pelayo and Unamuno, combine two or more plots the way Shakespeare's does (Unamuno, p. 818). Unamuno added that while Shakespeare's *Hamlet* embodies humankind as deeply as Segismundo does, he outshines him by his more lifelike characterization. Later Spanish and English critics took issue with these points. Spain's José Ortega y Gasset preferred Calderón's works to Shakespeare's, on the grounds that Shakespeare's are better read than seen, whereas Calderón's are better seen than read, and theater should be a spectacle. "It is fitting to imagine a delightful presentation of *Life Is a Dream*," writes Ortega, "by stressing as much as there lies in the theme which would be useful for a ballet or pantomime. In this presentation what is important would be the scenery, the costumes, the rhythm of the movements" (Ortega y Gasset, p. 325; trans. N. Orringer). Outside Spain, at Cambridge University, the literary scholar Edward M. Wilson countered the view that Calderón creates only an abstract symbol in a character like Segismundo. Spain's critic Menéndez Pelayo, Wilson argued, stresses too greatly characterization and overlooks many fine Calderón plays with exciting plots, careful plot structure, elaborate diction, and a sound variety of stock characters. Beginning a trend, Wilson refuted the contention that Segismundo passes too rapidly from human beast to perfect prince and that the Rosaura subplot has little to do with the main plot (Wilson in Wardropper, p. 66). Subsequent criticism confirms this British position.

—Nelson Orringer and Pamela S. Loy

For More Information

Armas, Frederick A. de, *The Prince in the Tower: Perceptions of La vida es sueño*. Lewisburg: Bucknell University Press, 1993.

Calderón de la Barca, Pedro. *Life Is a Dream*. Trans. William E. Colford. Woodbury: Barron's Educational Series, 1958.

———. *La vida es sueño. El alcalde de Zalamea*. Ed. Augusto Cortina. Madrid: Espasa-Calpe, 1964.

Góngora, Luis de. "Soneto CLXVI." In *Renaissance and Baroque Poetry of Spain*. Ed. Elias L. Rivers. 2d ed. Prospect Heights, Ill.: Waveland Press, 1988.

Hesse, Everett W. *Calderón de la Barca*. New York: Twayne, 1967.

Kamen, Henry. *Spain 1469-1714*. London: Longman's Press, 1983.

O'Callaghan, Joseph. *A History of Medieval Spain*. Ithaca: Cornell University Press, 1975.

Orringer, Nelson R. "The Human Body in Spanish Renaissance and Baroque Poetry: Testing Laín Entralgo's Theories." In *Studies in Honor of Elias Rivers*. Ed. Bruno M. Damiani and Ruth El Saffar. Potomac, Md.: Scripta Humanistica, 1989.

Ortega y Gasset, José. "Elogio del 'Murciélago.'" In *Obras completas*. Vol. 2. Madrid: Revista de Occidente, 1963.

Parker, Alexander A. *The Mind and Art of Calderón*. Cambridge: Cambridge University Press, 1988.

Sloman, A. E. "The Structure of Calderón's La vida es sueño." In *Critical Essays on the Theatre of Calderón*. Ed. Bruce Wardropper. New York: New York University Press, 1965.

Spitzer, Leo. *Representative Essays*. Stanford: Stanford University Press, 1988.

Sullivan, Henry. *Calderón in the German Lands and the Low Countries: His Reception and Influence, 1654-1980*. Cambridge: Cambridge University Press, 1983.

Trudeau, Lawrence J., ed. *Drama Criticism*. Vol. 3. Detroit: Gale Research, 1991.

Unamuno, Miguel de. *Obras completas*. Madrid: Escelicer, 1966.

Wardropper, Bruce W., ed. *Critical Essays on the Theater of Calderón*. New York: New York University Press, 1965.

The Lusiads

by
Luís de Camões

In bold Renaissance fashion, Luís de Camões (1524?-80) fashioned himself into a scholar, a poet, and a soldier. The following description is found in an anonymous early-seventeenth-century memoir: "That famous poet Luís de Camões—who, speaking in absolutes, was the prince of them all—was a tall man with broad shoulders and reddish hair. His face was freckled and he was blind in one eye. He was a man of sharp mind, clear judgement and rare wit. He was well-read in the humanities, well-versed in the sciences, skilled at arms, and valiant of spirit" (Lund, p. 170).

Of his otherwise undocumented soldiering, we know that he lost the use of that one eye in Ceuta. Yet if he was ready to defend his own honor or that of others with his sword, it would be his pen that would most indelibly mark history. He was born to a Portuguese family of minor nobility. There is no record of his having officially attended the University of Coimbra. But he had friends and relatives in high places, and in Coimbra he acquired a solid grounding in classical literature just 50 years after the Portuguese reached India. Vasco da Gama's singular voyage around the Cape of Good Hope, up the East Coast of Africa, and across the Indian Ocean to Calicut, India, is the event that a number of historians have seen as the defining moment of the beginning of modernity. It shrank the globe, thereafter yoking Asia inseparably with western Europe. It pulled commerce out of the Mediterranean Sea to the Atlantic Ocean. Camões would apotheosize the event in his epic poem. Although

THE LITERARY WORK

An epic poem set in Portugal, Africa, and India and at sea between 1139 to the mid-1500s; published in Portuguese (as *Os Lusíadas*) in 1572, in English in 1655.

SYNOPSIS

Portugal's national epic poem, *The Lusiads* celebrates the Portuguese nation and its discovery of the sea route to India, including a recapitulation of the entire history of Portugal and a competition between Roman gods to promote or foil the expedition.

also penning lyric poems and plays (such as the comedy *El-rei Seleuco* [King Seleucas]), he would forever be linked to the aforementioned epic, winning still unsurpassed renown by skillfully memorializing a grand moment in Portuguese history in a way that reflected the humanist tendencies of his era.

Events in History at the Time of the Poem

Henry the Navigator. Portugal is a tiny country squeezed onto the Iberian Peninsula between Spain and the Atlantic Ocean. Its curiosity as well as its economic considerations have caused Portugal to look seaward from as early as the end of the thirteenth century. Among other interests, Portugal wanted to find Prester John, a mythical

Luís de Camões

about 1420 to 1460 he sent dozens of small armadas further and further down the coast of Africa, convinced that sooner or later he would find a southeast passage to the Orient. In 1441 Antão Gonçalves, who had been commissioned by Henry the Navigator to explore the African coast, first brought African slaves into Portugal. Henry subsequently commissioned him to continue his exploration, charging him to seek information about Prester John and about India. By 1488, when Bartolomeu Dias returned to Lisbon, having rounded what was then called the Cape of Storms at the southern tip of Africa, confidence in finding a route to India approached certainty. It was at this point that King John II renamed the tip of Africa the Cape of Good Hope.

Christians and Moors. The Christians had fought the Moors for centuries. In retaliation for the 711 Moorish invasion of Europe, the Christians mounted a Reconquest of the Iberian peninsula that was pursued from the eighth through the fifteenth centuries. Although Portugal had driven the Moors from its territory by the end of the thirteenth century (under the reign of Alfonso III, 1246-79) it was not until 1492 that they were expelled from neighboring Granada in Spain. Over the years up to the time of Camões, Portugal had both initiated crusades and taken part in campaigns led by Christian allies against the Moors. If Spain's Ferdinand and Isabella were known as the Catholic monarchs, Portugal was considered a no less able and willing defender of the faith. It is not surprising, therefore, that Camões made a significant part of his storyline the age-old conflict between Christians and Moors, even though the Portuguese had driven the Muslims out of the country more than 200 years earlier. In the 1497 voyage to India, da Gama's four ships did in fact contend periodically with Moorish hostilities when seamen went ashore for provisions and exploration along the African coast en route to India. The menace was magnified in Camões's epic. For a hero in a Christian epic to attain a legendary degree of glory, there had to be an equally legendary "evil" to vanquish. The anti-Christian Moors of the sixteenth century easily filled that role.

At the poem's mythological level, the Roman goddess Venus represents positive, Christian interests; the Roman god Bacchus, adversary of the Portuguese, represents the dark side, the evil of religious "infidelity" and its stratagems. Bacchus and a number of Moorish princes do what they can to impede the Christian missionary zeal omnipresent in Vasco da Gama's voyage.

Christian leader thought to be living anywhere from northeastern Africa to Asia. Establishing contact with such a mysterious Christian leader had long intrigued most of Europe, for he would be an important ally in the Christian crusade against the infidel.

In actual practice, Portuguese overseas expansion dates from at least 1415, when King John I attacked and conquered Ceuta on the northwest coast of Africa. The new possession would be as important as a symbol of the Portuguese presence in Africa as it was as a trading post. King John's renowned son Henry the Navigator (1394-1460) had participated in the conquest of Ceuta. Although he did not personally do much sailing, Henry showed avid interest in the theory and practice of navigation, especially during the last 20 years of his life from atop the Sagres promontory in southern Portugal. Gradually he fastened on to the idea of finding a sea route to India. Much of his work was carried out in secrecy. Henry engineered a number of navigational improvements including the construction of a sleeker, faster ship known as the caravel. The caravel proved valuable for its ability to sail to windward, making longer voyages possible. Henry also promoted exploration. From

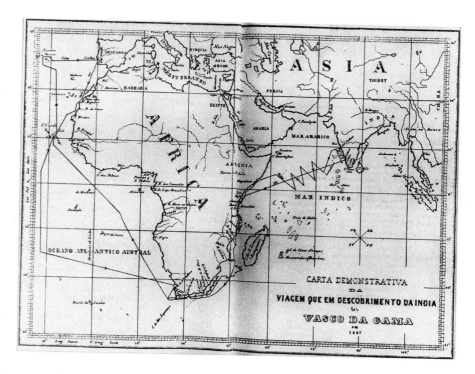

Map of the route Vasco da Gama took from Lisbon to India in 1497, according to the diary of his pilot.

One must remember that fifteenth-century evangelical zeal often took the form of a crusade. Crusaders were much more Christian soldiers than preachers. They used their swords more readily than their Bibles. This form of evangelization sometimes became a "just war" against infidels. The idea was to eliminate resistance, even by bloodshed, establish the Church, and evangelize the inhabitants. Before King John I became fully committed to attacking Ceuta in Africa, he required his best theologians and ecclesiastical lawyers to furnish official guarantees (e.g., documents) that such a move would be "in the service of God," otherwise there would be no attack. When that was done, Ceuta was conquered, a church was built, and a more docile kind of missionary work was turned over to the Franciscans.

Prince Henry the Navigator was imbued by the spirit of crusade. He was the treasurer of the religious-military Order of Christ on the Iberian Peninsula, founded in 1319 by Portugal's King Dinis. An initiative blessed by the Pope, it was put together using the knights, properties and wealth of the just-then defunct Knights Templar. Vasco da Gama was also a knight of the Order of Christ. He pointed his tiny fleet, whose sails bore large red crosses symbolic of his order, toward India with that same sober spirit of crusade.

Renaissance. Having originated in Italy, excitement about this rebirth of classical learning was pervasive in Europe by the end of the fifteenth century. The Renaissance proved to be especially significant in two ways. First, it rediscovered a wealth of knowledge by republishing key philosophical, historical, and literary texts of antiquity. Secondly, it placed high value on curiosity and the pursuit of new knowledge. Portugal, which had established its University of Coimbra in 1290, responded favorably to the fertile thought of this period. From a maritime point of view, it led the world in this new age of discoveries. From an intellectual point of view, it followed the lead of Germany's Johann Gutenberg, establishing presses and a book trade well before the sixteenth century. Henry the Navigator became the epitome of the direction in new science: pragmatic application of theory. The Portuguese discoveries led to significant advances in astronomy, biology, botany, pharmacology, meteorology, mathematics, physics, and, of course, navigation, geography, and cartography. Garcia da Orta, for example, who traveled widely in the far reaches of the new Portuguese empire, published in 1563 his *Coloquios dos Simples*, a treatise on drugs and medicines used in India, mixed with natural philosophy and based on firsthand observation. It was translated many times during the sixteenth century. At odds with

A HUMANIST EPIC

Renaissance humanism—usually traceable to the fourteenth-century Italian poet Petrarch (in whose work, incidentally, Camões found inspiration for many of his own lyric poems)—had reached the Iberian Peninsula by the fifteenth century. Its adherents were scholars who avidly searched private and monastic archives for the Greek and Latin classics. The diffusion of the movement was greatly enhanced by the rediscovery and adoption of classical Latin and by the invention of moveable type which made classical texts available to the increasingly literate public. Humanists found in man the measure of existence and embraced any attitude that exalted his relationship to God. They discovered in the texts of antiquity—in the epics of Homer and Virgil, for example—the human qualities and virtues that most appropriately defined this Renaissance man. Humanists used the human portraits that emerged from these texts to plumb the vastness of man's potential. Reflecting upon the epic event of Vasco da Gama's voyage, Camões infused it with a mythological significance not only befitting the event but also exemplary of the new European literary movements for which the rebirth of classical learning had been the springboard:

> *The Lusiads* is in many ways the epic of Humanism. The new vision and the new values which came with the revival of learning found in Camões a poet singularly fitted to sing of them. He is a Humanist even in his contradictions, in his association of a Pagan mythology with a Christian outlook, in his conflicting feelings about war and empire, in his love of home and his desire for adventure, in his appreciation of pleasure and his desire for adventure.
>
> (Bowra, p. 138)

much of the wisdom of conventional doctors and pharmacologists, Garcia da Orta—precisely because of his apparent challenge to the status quo of medicinal science—was tried and condemned by the Roman Catholic Inquisition in Goa, India. Interestingly, one of the few poems other than *The Lusiads* published by Camões during his lifetime appears as congratulatory verse in the prefatory pages of Orta's book.

Renaissance humanists immersed themselves in the mythologies of classical antiquity. Imagine the excitement of these early scholars, totally absorbed in their own learned discoveries amidst ancient archives, as they gradually filled in the genealogical details of these families of major and minor gods, thereby providing a wealth of material that Renaissance poets would use to their own advantage. In this way Camões found Adamastor ideally suited to his needs of anthropomorphizing the Cape of Storms—arguably the sea-gate to the Orient through which Portugal had to pass. Adamastor was one of the mythological giants, a son of Tellus. One version asserts that he was turned into the promontory cape as punishment for having fought with the giants against the gods. In his poem, Camões sets him up as a mythological interlocutor whose own age-old geographical authority attests to the fact that no one has ever before entered his watery domain.

The momentous voyage. On July 8, 1497, da Gama and his crew departed Portugal from a suburb of Lisbon known as Restelo in four ships (the *S. Gabriel*, the *S. Raphael*, the *Berrio*, and a large supply vessel). After brief contact and minor skirmishes with aboriginal people along the southwest coast of Africa, they successfully rounded the Cape of Good Hope and made their way north along the southeast coast of Africa. Scurvy and other illnesses began to take their toll. So did the inevitable shock of opposing cultures. The Sultan of Mozambique presented the first real armed challenge to da Gama and his men. But disaster was averted and the Portuguese sailed further north. On April 7, 1498, they arrived in Mombasa, where they were told that other Christians lived. Delighted, they anticipated going ashore to hear Mass. Instead, 100 men armed with cutlasses unsuccessfully tried to board da Gama's ship. The next day was Palm Sunday. The King of Mombasa sent pseudo-Christians bearing gifts and might well have lured da Gama's fleet into the harbor to possible destruction had it not been for an accidental bumping of ships. Fearing their plan had been detected, the Muslim pilots jumped into the sea, inadvertently providing a providential forewarning. Again da Gama escaped.

Seven days later, da Gama's fleet arrived in Malindi to a much more hospitable reception, perhaps due to the fact that fame of their military prowess had preceded them. Another theory is that the local sultan hoped that the establishment of an alliance with a distant king might mitigate the fealty he owed to Kilwa. In any case, the encounter was a friendlier one. In Malindi the Portuguese finally obtained the pilot who would guide them across the Indian Ocean to Calicut.

On May 20, 1498, da Gama's fleet anchored off the shore of Calicut. Here they would stay for three months. Not just da Gama, but the whole Portuguese nation had fulfilled the mission for which it had seemed destined. But establishing a toehold in India's most important west coast trading center was neither immediate nor easy. The *zamorin* (ruler) who governed Calicut lived with his Brahmin courtiers in a palace outside the city. The entire export trade was in the hands of the Muslim merchants who looked on the arrival of da Gama and his Christians as a serious threat. There was a standoff of sorts. After a symbolic march through town, accompanied by drums, trumpets, and the firing of guns, da Gama managed to meet with the *zamorin* and explain the purpose of his visit. The parties met in what was most probably a Hindu temple. The Portuguese, who still hoped to find Christians and thought they saw everywhere analogies with their faith, felt sure that the religions in India were some sort of less orthodox evolution of primitive Christianity. Edgar Prestage even surmises that the Portuguese interpreted cries of "Krishna, Krishna!"—the second element of their Trinity—to be "Christ, Christ!" (Prestage, p. 260). Da Gama's own diary is careful to point out "these [Brahman priests] wore some threads passing over the left shoulder and under the right arm, in the same manner as our deacons wear the stole. They threw holy water over us" (da Gama in Ravenstein, p. 30).

After hard bargaining from equally skeptical parties, da Gama finally obtained a letter from the *zamorin* addressed to King Manuel requiring coral, silver and gold, and scarlet cloth in exchange for spices and precious stones. A stone pillar brought by da Gama and symbolic of this tentative agreement was erected in Calicut. In late August, da Gama set sail for Lisbon in adverse weather with relatively small stores of cinnamon, cloves, ginger, nutmeg, pepper, and precious stones. Because da Gama did not produce great quantities of spices upon his return to Lisbon, popular sentiment was unsure that he had even been there. But King Manuel was sure. In fact, he was so convinced of da Gama's success that he soon began sending word to the crowns of Europe of the Portuguese discovery. Just two days after da Gama's return, he fired off a missive to the Queen of Castile announcing Portugal's feat. He sent letters to Rome, as well, seeking thereby to obtain papal recognition of Portuguese pre-eminence in India. He gave to Vasco da Gama the village of Sines with all of its revenues and rights, a substantial annual royal stipend, and bestowed on his brave captain the title of *Dom*, or Lord. In the words of K. G. Jayne, "the quest for Christians and spices had been accomplished, and Portugal was mistress of the sea-route to India" (Jayne, p. 59).

The Poem In Focus

Plot overview. *The Lusiads* is divided into ten cantos. From Olympus, Jupiter looks down upon Vasco da Gama's tiny fleet cutting through uncharted seas to discover the sea road to India. Jupiter calls a council of the gods to discuss the implications and problems of this unique Portuguese voyage that promises a vast new eastern horizon to the commercial and missionary interests of western Europe in the face of the rapidly waning Middle Ages. The two most audible voices in that council are those of Venus and Bacchus. Venus, goddess of Rome, champions the Portuguese; Bacchus, god of the Orient, embodies resistance to the Lusitanian endeavor. First named Cape of Storms in 1488 by Portuguese explorer Bartolomeu Dias, the southernmost tip of Africa has been renamed Cape of Good Hope by Portugal's King John II in optimistic anticipation of his country's successful quest up the east coast of Africa and across the Indian Ocean to Calicut. Da Gama survives the vicissitudes of an 11-month sea voyage down the west coast of Africa, around the Cape of Good Hope. As

PORTUGUESE PRE-EMINENCE: FROM PROPHECY TO REALITY

1139 Afonso Henriques wins Battle of Ourique; sees vision of Christ, who promises sponsorship of kingdom

1141 Afonso Henriques is acclaimed Portugal's first king

1290 University of Coimbra is established

1300s Portuguese plant pine forest of Leiria (source of future ship lumber)

1415 King John I conquers African city of Ceuta

1438 Henry the Navigator moves to southern Portugal; continues to commission exploratory expeditions down African coast

1488 Bartholomeu Dias rounds Cape of Good Hope

1492 Columbus seeks India sailing west; denied Portuguese sponsorship, he sails from Spain, landing on territory he believes to be India

1495 King John II dies; Manuel I becomes king and gains the epithet "the Fortunate" because discovery of sea route to India happens during his reign

1498 Vasco da Gama discovers sea route to India; arrives at Calicut, India

1500-30 Portugal enjoys a monopoly of spice trade

1524 Camões is born

1536 Inquisition is established in Portugal

1553 Camões begins bureaucratic work in the Orient

1560s Camões writes *The Lusiads*

1570 Camões publishes *The Lusiads,* commemorating discovery of sea route to India

integral to the poem as his triumph over all the adversity that he encounters en route during an ultimately successful voyage is the mythical competition between Bacchus and Venus, a conflict full of symbolic meaning interwoven through the ten cantos of the poem.

Plot summary. Commissioned by King Manuel I, Vasco da Gama and his crew set sail in 1497 with the express purpose of finding India by sea. Just prior to their departure, a voice of warning is heard from "The Old Man of Restelo," who rises from the shore. An anonymous yet experienced and venerable man, he personifies popular Portuguese concern that the quest for India may be too dangerous and inevitably disastrous. Soberly yet rhetorically, he asks if a conquest nearer to Portugal—perhaps in North Africa where there were also Moors and riches for the taking—might not be a wiser course. After all, Ceuta was already Portuguese. He reminds da

Gama and his crew of the tragic results that befell Prometheus and Icarus, who thought through heroic undertakings to rob, respectively, fire and flight from the gods. He warns against the reckless seduction of Fame and Fortune.

Paying little heed to the old man's advice, the tiny armada sets sail and retraces the 1488 route of Bartolomeu Dias. As they approach the Cape of Good Hope, da Gama comes "face to face" with the mythological giant Adamastor. Stories, warnings, and prophecies are exchanged. As the Portuguese expedition proceeds where no man has gone before, it does so knowing that it has overcome the natural obstacles of the southern cape; it has beaten Adamastor. As it moves north along the east coast of Africa, Vasco da Gama's armada encounters problems in Mombasa, but a warmer reception in Malindi.

Faithful to epic tradition, Camões begins with a proposition: he will celebrate the heroes of Portugal together with its navigation and discoveries. Then he asks the nymphs of the River Tagus for inspiration, and dedicates his poem to Portugal's King Sebastian. Periodically throughout the cantos, Camões invokes the poetic power and influence of the epic muse of classical mythology Caliope. Also faithful to epic tradition, Camões begins his narration *in media res*, in the middle of his story, with Vasco da Gama already moving up the east coast of Africa. In the first canto the mythological protagonists Bacchus and Venus appear. At a council on Olympus, and in the presence of Jupiter, Venus gives reasons for regarding the Portuguese highly; and Bacchus makes his opposition to them known.

Venus is a good choice for Portugal's advocate before Jupiter on several counts. Camões uses her convincing voice to articulate important parallels between Renaissance Portugal and ancient Italy. As she draws these parallels, she enhances the reader's expectation that the supreme god Jupiter will bless the voyage of Vasco da Gama, even as he blessed the journey of Aeneas from Troy in ancient times. Lisbon bears comparison with Rome. Portugal was once part of the Roman empire (218 B.C.E.–c. 450 C.E.). Like Rome, Lisbon is set on seven hills. Venus reminds Jupiter that of all the modern inheritors of ancient Latin, Portugal has developed a language—Portuguese—that most closely resembles the original source. Likewise, Vasco da Gama has shown more fearless, noble courage in the face of unknown maritime dangers as he attempts to penetrate "seas no other nation had braved" than anyone since Aeneas (Camões, *The Lusiads*, 5.37.3). Her advocacy before the Olympian father is based on heroic logic and nostalgia.

Bacchus is an excellent adversary. Traditionally the god of Asia, now being approached by Christian Portuguese, he is also a forebear of Lusus, the mythical ancestor of the Lusitanians, or Portuguese (hence *The Lusiads*), in the genealogy of Roman mythological gods. Bacchus is very jealous of the prestige he has accrued in the Orient and is of course resistant to the threat of intrusion by anyone—especially by his own descendants!

Both Venus and Bacchus intervene in the navigation of the Portuguese, alternately helping and impeding the voyage. Da Gama and his men meanwhile regard their deliverance from peril as blessings from their Christian God. These two main narrative threads—that of da Gama's voyage and that of the Olympian gods' intercession on behalf of him and his sailors—progress in a parallel fashion. Aware of what the Portuguese are doing, the gods intercede from time to time,

Venus assisting them with favorable winds, Bacchus trying to thwart their advance. Meanwhile, the Roman Catholic Portuguese sail toward their destination, trusting in their Christian god, knowing nothing of Venus or Bacchus.

In Canto 2, da Gama has his first serious conflict. Historically, this was a conflict with the Moors. Poetically, Camões alleges the collusion of Bacchus in the treachery that threatens the captain, and provides fuller portraits of Jupiter and Venus. The Portuguese journey continues to a more favorable reception in Malindi. In Cantos 3 and 4, da Gama tells the king of Malindi the history of Portugal from pre-Roman beginnings to the mid-fourteenth-century tragic murder of Inês de Castro, the Castilian mistress of Pedro, heir to the Portuguese throne.

It is not until the crucial fifth canto—halfway through the voyage to India, and, symbolically, halfway through the poem—that these narratives intersect. As the Portuguese prepare to round the cape, the rocky tip of the African continent, personified in the craggy personage of the giant Adamastor, speaks thunderingly to da Gama, delivering both a recognition and a warning. The somewhat reluctant recognition is that this brave Portuguese captain and his tiny band are the first ever to enter Adamastor's waters, learning "secrets and mysteries of the deep, / Where no human, however noble / Or immortal his worth, should trespass" (*Lusiads*, 5.42.2-4). This is tantamount to an Olympian confession of defeat and an important anticipation of da Gama's navigational success.

Adamastor's warning, however, is the promise that from those myriad brave captains who inevitably follow da Gama on successive voyages, shall be extracted the payment of unimaginably tragic shipwrecks and maritime disasters. (Historically this proved to be the case. The poet Camões had the benefit of 60 post-da Gama years of hindsight, all carefully chronicled by historians Diogo do Couto [a personal friend of the poet], João de Barros, Garcia de Resende, and others. In fact, for several hundred years, about 20 percent of the ships that sailed annually to India never made it back to Lisbon, resulting in a collection of narratives cumulatively known as the "tragic maritime history of Portugal.")

Cantos 6-8 relate the tales of the Portuguese arrival in Calicut, the wonders of India, and da Gama's narrow escape from the treachery of the Muslim merchants by payment of ransom. This event inspires the poet to meditate on the evils of money and gold.

The second time that da Gama's crew interacts with the Olympians is in Canto 9. Victorious Vasco da Gama, having established commercial relations (albeit tenuous ones) with India, is sailing once again on the high seas, returning to Lisbon and the glory that there awaits him. But Venus, who has often intervened on da Gama's behalf during the Portuguese voyage, prepares her own reward for him and his sailors. She has arranged for them to find and sail for an Isle of Love that she causes to appear before them in the middle of the ocean—a kind of garden of delights, on which numerous maidens and comely sea nymphs await, each for her Portuguese sailor. This maritime rest and recuperation is the poet's imaginative and propitious reward for the Portuguese maritime discovery. Included in the narration of the amorous and sensual celebrations on the Isle of Love are prophetic visions of the Portuguese future in the Orient voiced by an attending sea nymph. Through prophecy, the poem praises the post-da Gama efforts of Portuguese governors and military.

This encounter on the Isle of Love achieves two aims. Most obviously it immortalizes the Portuguese sailors, conjoining them with the gods. That same conjugation, however, serves to mortalize the pagan gods. By linking the mythological gods to Christianity, the Isle of Love raises the issue of an allegorical key that Camões seemed obligated to include in his poem. (The next section treats the problem of allegory.)

By the end of Canto 10, the reader has reviewed the history of Portugal, followed Vasco da Gama on his trip around Africa, appreciated the peculiarities of the sea as recounted from the poet's own experience, read the poet's warnings to the Portuguese about their tendencies to stray from the moral high ground, and experienced the intercession of Olympic deities, including a vision of the Ptolemaic cosmos that the goddess Tethys shares with da Gama on the Isle of Love. The reader has also been apprised of the poet's warnings to the Portuguese, about the perils and uncertainties of life. "Where may frail humanity shelter," wonders the poet at the end of Canto One; "Briefly, in some secure port, / Where the bright heavens cease to vent their rage / On such insects on so small a stage?" (*Lusiads*, 1.106.5-8). Canto 6 draws to a close with a meditation on the true value of glory: "So the heart develops a callous / Honourable contempt for titles / And wealth, rank, and money . . . So one's judgement grows enlightened, . . . Studying, as from

a great height / Mankind's pettiness and confusion; / Such a person . . . [w]ill rise (as he must) to a great position, / But reluctantly, and not through ambition" (*Lusiads*, 6.98.5-7, 6.99.1-8). The poet concludes the eighth canto with a lamentation on the omnipotence of gold: "Gold conquers the strongest citadels, / Turns friends into traitors and liars; / Persuades the noblest to acts of infamy" (*Lusiads*, 8.98.1-3). Thus, the poet fleshes out a simple storyline, producing by its conclusion a tapestry of narrative threads—skirmishes with indigenous peoples, national historical exploits, descriptions of sea life as well as life at sea, and meditations on moral and ethical questions—all made salient by expectation and the fulfillment of expectation, prophecy and the fulfillment of prophecy, commitment and the fulfillment of commitment.

Pagan mythology in a Christian epic. It has been established that the plot of *The Lusiads* is a simple one. Like the astronaut Neil Armstrong, who climbed into his rocket ship, flew to the moon, and returned, Vasco da Gama boarded his boat, sailed to India, and returned to Lisbon. Both were firsts in their day. The story is one of sailing from point A (Lisbon) to point B (India), laying claim for the Portuguese, and returning to point A. But imagine the preparation and the support needed for such a quest. Vasco da Gama does not know where point B is when he sets sail. Da Gama ventured forth into the unknown armed with far less support than a Neil Armstrong, who had the benefit of "mission control" back home. Da Gama left armed only with the cumulative knowledge of Henry the Navigator and company, adding to it the groundbreaking science that he and his pilots gathered even as they sailed. Herein lie the mystery and the eventual thrill of his maritime discovery.

But for Camões, the poet, there *had* to be a mission control, some *deus ex machina*, or larger-than-life poetic apparatus, to help explain da Gama's otherworldly certitude, and his unfailing ability to overcome the obstacles encountered on his voyage. So Camões created Jupiter and Venus to look after Vasco da Gama and his sailors. In spite of his own Christian anchor, and in spite of the Inquisition looking over his shoulder, Camões availed himself of traditional mythological figures to illustrate, and thereby elevate, the da Gama voyage to the mythic proportions that aptly conveyed its place in Portuguese history. The recourse to myth was, moreover, highly appropriate to his European times. Camões was, after all, a Renaissance man.

PRINCIPAL CONTENT OF THE TEN CANTOS OF *THE LUSIADS*

1 Camões proposes to write the Vasco da Gama voyage. He invokes the epic muses. He dedicates the poem to King Sebastian of Portugal. Narrative begins *in media res* (in the middle of the action), with da Gama in the Indian Ocean. First council of the gods. Camões's own meditation on the transitory nature of life.

2 Conflict between Venus and Bacchus. Venus advocates Portuguese cause to Jupiter, who prophesies da Gama's success. Da Gama arrives at Melinde, Africa.

3 Da Gama tells the history of Portugal to the King of Melinde, focusing on its kings and heroes.

4 Recitation of Portuguese history continues. Da Gama's dreams of Portuguese presence in Asia. Old man of Restelo warns of dangers of pride and power.

5 Flashback to Lisbon. Da Gama's departure. Details of the sea voyage. Encounter with Adamastor. Camões meditates on dearth of worthy poets (like Virgil and Homer) in the world.

6 Bacchus strategizes with Neptune. Second council of gods. Storm at sea. Da Gama prays for deliverance and is delivered by Venus. Da Gama thanks God. Camões meditates on true meaning of glory.

7 Arrival at Calicut; Portuguese introduction to Indian customs and culture.

8 Recounting of Portuguese heroes. Bacchus seeks to undo Portuguese victory. Camões reflects bitterly on omnipotence of gold.

9 Isle of Love is given to Portuguese as reward for exploits.

10 Celebration banquet continues with Portuguese and sea nymphs. Da Gama envisions universe and future. Camões exhorts King Sebastian to do great things.

Did the poet himself ever see his interlacing of mythology in a Christian poem as a dilemma? He is a poet writing in a country very concerned with questions of orthodoxy, newly articulated by the doctrines of the Counter Reformation that flowed from the Council of Trent (1455-63). This is precisely when he is writing his poem. Yet he is also a poet equally committed to the exhilarating possibilities of model classical texts that had re-emerged during the impetus of Renaissance humanism, the postmedieval movement noted for a revival of classical learning, an individualistic and critical tenor, and a gravitation from religious to secular concerns. So how was he to justify a mythological apparatus in a Christian epic without offending the literary and doctrinal censors of the Inquisition?

Camões, as many of his Mediterranean literary peers had done, chose to view mythological deities in allegorical terms. That is, they saw all of pagan mythology as a sort of allegory, prepara-tory to the advent of Christianity, where the Olympian deities and their intrigues were but prefigurations of God, His angels, the intermediary saints of Roman Catholicism, and Satan and his underworld legions. Still, Camões's manuscript had to run the inquisitorial gauntlet despite having already been licensed by the king. Apparently one of the censors thought that Camões needed to provide some sort of key for the less-prepared reader who might be led astray. This "key" is provided in two places in the poem. The first seems a bit more awkward than the second, apparently inserted by the poet under some duress, in order for his text to receive the imprimatur of the Holy Inquisition. The second key may have been the only one that he intended to include.

The first is inserted after the sensual Isle of Love victory celebration offered the Portuguese by Venus in Canto 9. In stanza 91 the poet lists all the pagan gods that he has so ingeniously woven into his poem—Jupiter, Mercury, Mars, Venus, Pallas, Ceres, Juno, Diana, and so on. "All," he writes, "served only symbolically to enhance the superhuman achievements of the Portuguese. For, as everyone knows, they were never more than inventions of the human imagination" (Bowra, p. 117). As Bowra suggests, "th[is] explanation is worse than an anticlimax; if we treat it seriously, it spoils much of the poem" (Bowra, p. 117). It is like cold water thrown on an epic fire. Was the poet instructed to include such an explanation by the inquisitors who read his manuscript? Perhaps, under the obligation of the Inquisition to explain the gods, he writes his denial in this coarse and rather transparent fashion so that his readers can easily see *why* it is there.

"Camões' real explanation," continues Bowra, "is more profound and more satisfying. It is that his divinities are symbols for different activities of one supreme God, subordinate powers to whom various special functions are allotted"—"'the patronage of the seven spheres / Which by the highest Pow'r to them was giv'n'" (Bowra and *The Lusiads* in Bowra, p. 118). The heretical question of attributing blessings or evils experienced by da Gama to mythological figures instead of to God and the devil would be revisited. In 1640, a year after his monumental commentary on *The Lusiads* was published, Manuel de Faria e Sousa was called upon by the Inquisition to address the question of the pagan gods. In a thorough and masterful treatise, he offered numerous "proofs" of what he considered to be Camões's obvious use of allegory. The treatise identified Jupiter as an allegory for Christ—the same Christ who presented himself to the first king of Portugal at the Battle of Ourique, and was now "choosing Portugal to take His doctrine to India" (Faria e Sousa, p. 3; trans. C. Lund). According to Faria e Sousa, Bacchus was the Devil trying to impede the mission. Venus was the embodiment of militant religious doctrine as well as a "Marian" advocate before God of the righteous desires of man. Mars was equated with St. James, and Mercury with one of the good angels. Faria e Sousa's eloquent response to the Inquisition, written in 15 days, was successful. *The Lusiads* would face no more serious Inquisitorial challenges.

Sources and literary context. In the tradition of Homer's *Iliad* and *Odyssey,* followed by Virgil's *Aeniad,* Camões relays the epic tale of the founding of a Portuguese empire and, in Camões's case, the tale is certifiably true. In his invocation of the epic muse, Camões asks only for sufficient inspiration to be able to give full

and adequate treatment to this one story. Though Camões himself believed his epic matter to be far superior to that of the *Aeniad,* he is not at all hesitant to recognize his debt to Virgil in whom most of the epic poets of the Renaissance found inspiration. In the first canto, Camões includes all the formulaic constituent parts of an epic poem. He begins with a proposition, telling the reader what he will celebrate. Lest there be any doubt about the model he has chosen to follow, his very first line paraphrases Virgil's familiar line *Arma virumque cano* ("Arms and the man I sing"): "Arms are my theme, and those matchless heroes, / Who from Portugal's far western shores" to the eastern boundary of the known world ventured (*Lusiads,* 1.1-2). Camões thereby acclaims the excellence and prestige of his classical model, even as he sets out to improve upon it. How, he wants to know in Canto 5, can the monstrous Scylla and Charybdis, set down by Virgil's fanciful imagination, even begin to compare to the real dangers of contrary winds and ship-dashing currents ever present in navigating around the Cape of Storms at the southern most tip of Africa, in the rigors of high seas navigation, or in the monsoon hurricanes of the Indian Ocean? The tale he tells, says canto 1, is greater than any imagined adventure ever written. Although the details of da Gama's voyage had already appeared in many historical narratives, it was Camões's epic poetry that would immortalize the importance of the feat.

During his life, Camões produced a rich lyric poetry, writing in the new styles of the Renaissance (sonnets, canzones, sestinas, odes, elegies) that had so recently been brought to Portugal directly from Italy by Sá de Miranda in 1525. He loved the traditional redondilla as well: based in part on his own life, his *Babel and Zion* is a beautifully composed, Platonically inspired, allegorical redondilla, written during his sojourn in the Orient (probably in the 1560s) in which the poet affirms his own Christian beliefs. Camões uses his lyric poems as autobiographical entries in a kind of lifelong diary of his own repeated misfortunes. In them he expresses the constant reversal of fortune that characterized his life from Lisbon to China and back again. His writings suggest that Camões suffered poverty, unrequited love, and disappointment in his political ambitions and in his aspirations for literary recognition. An admirer of the Italian poets, he shows a Petrarchan love of antithesis in his verse. Camões's lyric poems were first published posthumously in 1595. Although questions of authorship for a number of these poems have not yet been completely sorted out, it is clear that his poems rank among the finest in Renaissance Europe. But if Camões stood in the company of few as a lyrical poet, he was unique as a sixteenth-century epic poet. The many personal themes of his lyrics (e.g., tragic love, political deception, poverty, and belief in Christ) find resonance in *The Lusiads*.

Events in History at the Time the Poem Was Written

Camões and the demise of Portugal. Exactly when Camões began to formulate the ideas for his national epic poem is not clear. He had grown up in a Portugal that during his own formative years was one of the richest and most prestigious countries in Europe. His country had enjoyed economic good fortune from the spice trade that it monopolized for several decades. Camões, the Renaissance scholar, gradually became aware of his own gifts and powers as Camões, the poet. No doubt, the challenge of writing his country's recent impressive achievement beckoned.

By the mid-sixteenth century in Portugal and Spain, young noblemen launched their personal careers by serving their king in one of the proliferating bureaucratic offices of their respective colonial empires. In 1553 Camões left for India to serve his Crown—perhaps very willing, as well, to distance himself from one Gonçalo Borges, whom he had wounded in a duel. With a head full of Virgilian poetic structures, he set sail on his odyssey, driven at times by his own spirit of adventure, and at times by the political whims of commanders in the growing kingdom's far-flung outposts. He experienced the same long sea voyages—replete with the same thrills, natural wonders, and hardships that Vasco da Gama had experienced—as he went first to India, then on to Macau, China (a territory that Portugal has only just now relinquished), and back to Lisbon by way of Africa.

Even in his own lifetime, Camões began to see the empire that had been born of da Gama's voyage begin to crumble. The sudden influx of wealth had a profound impact on Portuguese society. Investments and speculation increased. The middle class surged. The phrase "waiting for one's ship to come in [from India]" perhaps was first uttered by Lisbon merchants. The Dutch and English began operating in the Orient, whittling away at Portuguese hegemony, well before Camões's poem was published.

Much of this change is documented in Garcia de Resende's *Miscellanea*, first published in 1545. This book was possibly known to the poet and may have served to help Camões find proper expression in his own moralistic considerations with which he periodically ends his cantos. The *Miscellanea* is an artful yet astute synthesis of the cultural and moral evolution of Portugal from about 1500-30. The vision of its text is tempered by the maturity of a man who was writing in his late fifties, intuitively contrasting his vision of his contemporary Portugal with that of the Portugal he knew when he was thirty. It is a text in which Resende asks repeatedly, is this the Portugal he knew before Vasco da Gama brought home his first pepper from India? Written in verse, it catalogues the changes, disclosing a "variety of stories, customs, events and things that happened in his time" (Resende, p. 335). Due largely to the sudden influx of wealth, Portugal sees no end of new novelties. The *Miscellanea* lists the new fruits, vegetables, animals—imagine, trained elephants!—clothing, jewelry, religions, and philosophies, that sprung up in Lisbon as a result of Vasco da Gama's voyage. But it is principally on the moral front that Resende's observations, shared by many reflective men in Portugal, may have helped Camões: there is now a Catholic Church persecuted "more by Christians than by Moors"—the wealthy have servants who have servants; there is an increase in lying, cheating, skulduggery; sloth abounds; waste increases. Where are the good old days? Many of Resende's concerns find echoes in Camões's meditative sections of *The Lusiads*.

Royal and general reception. Little documentation survives about the initial reception accorded to *The Lusiads* in 1572. The question of its influence on King Sebastian is occasionally raised by critics. According to one tradition, Camões himself read his poem to the king. In any event, the king knew about the poem, for he had granted his royal license to have it printed. Though its Camonian exhortation for the king to achieve great deeds may have helped dispel any hesitation in his resolve to carry out his own Christian crusade against the Moors in north Africa, *The Lusiads* cannot be blamed for Sebastian's ill-fated campaign of 1578. Camões, along with the majority of the Portuguese nation, watched the rag-tag formation of the royal army during the previous year. Then they were horrified and devastated when news of the Portuguese defeat reached Lisbon. Unmarried, King Sebastian had left no heir to the kingdom. His uncle,

Cardinal Henrique, took the throne but died in 1579, when Camões was ill. The poet, who with the majority of the country now saw Phillip II of Spain poised to claim the Portuguese throne, wrote to a friend "I came back to Portugal not only to die in my country, but with her" (Hart, p. 212). He was right. By 1580 Phillip II held the Portuguese crown and Camões had died.

The Lusiads, on the other hand, gained stature and endured. Before Camões's death, King Sebastian, in part as a favor to Don Manuel de Portugal, who had befriended the poet, granted an insignificantly small annual pension (the equivalent of $150, according to Burton) to Camões. This three-year "reward" was renewed twice before the poet died. Ever after, despite the fact that it may not have been an immediately resounding success, Camões's epic has really never ceased to grow in importance and popularity as literature.

During the decade or so following the publication of the first edition of *The Lusiads*, three more Spanish translations appeared (two in 1580, one in 1591). Perhaps when Portugal lost its sovereignty to Spain in 1580, political reasons prompted the publication of the early Spanish translations. After all, the story of Portugal, told so eloquently by Camões in Portuguese, should also be available in Spanish. Phillip II of Spain had just doubled his empire, annexing to it the vast possessions that Portugal had acquired largely due to da Gama's voyage. Perhaps these first extramural translations appeared just because *The Lusiads* was a great epic poem that needed to be known in other tongues. With equal logic, political motivation may be read into the many editions printed in Portuguese during the seventeenth century, some in anticipation of the restoration of Portuguese sovereignty in 1640, some in celebration of it. The poem's impact was great too. In the wake of Camões's masterwork, more than 50 distinct epic poems appeared in Portuguese from the end of the sixteenth century to the middle of the nineteenth century. One of the poems that helped Almeida Garrett inaugurate the Romantic movement in Portugal was entitled, fittingly, "Camões." The Portuguese romantics loved the story of Inês de Castro—cruelly murdered by King Afonso IV, the father of her lover—so passionately told by Camões in Canto 3.

In 1974, as the socialist revolution that toppled 40 years of dictatorship claimed victory in Portugal, Camões and his epic were threatened by radical students who saw in his work a quintessential capitalism that they considered antithetical to their cause. But the Portuguese love and appreciation for its national poet survived the momentary ideological crisis and the bard is still required reading in the curriculum.

Outside the Iberian peninsula, *The Lusiads* would be translated into almost every western European language, experiencing an ever-growing popularity in the eighteenth and nineteenth centuries. England's William Wordsworth had praise for the poet. His correspondence suggests that he knew *The Lusiads* through a 1776 translation by William Julius Mickles. Brian Head traced Camonian influence in Melville's prose and poetry, where he found allusions to the Isle of Love, Adamastor, and storms at sea. Head quotes the character Jack Chase in Melville's novel *White Jacket*: "Camoens! White-Jacket, Camoens! Did you ever read him? *The Lusiad*, I mean? It's the man-of-war epic of the world, my lad. Give me Gama for a Commodore, say I—Noble Gama!" (Melville in Head, p. 47).

—Christopher C. Lund

For More Information

Belchior, Maria de Lourdes, and Enrique Martínez-López, eds. *Camoniana Californiana*. Santa Barbara: Jorge de Sena Center for Portuguese Studies, University of California, Santa Barbara, 1985.

Bowra, Cecil Maurice. *From Virgil to Milton*. New York: St. Martin's Press, 1972.

Camões, Luís Vaz de. *The Lusiads*. Trans. Landeg White. Oxford: Oxford University Press, 1997.

Faria e Sousa, Manuel de. *Información en favor de Manuel de Faria i Sousa sobre la acusación que se hizo en el Tribunal del santo oficio de Lisboa, a los comentarios que escrivió a las Lusiadas del poeta Luis de Camoens*. [Madrid?: privately printed, 1640?].

Hart, Henry Hersch. *Luis de Camoens and the Epic of the Lusiads*. Norman: University of Oklahoma Press, 1962.

Head, Brian. "Camões and Melville." *Revista Camoniana* I (1964): 36-77.

Jayne, K. G. *Vasco da Gama and His Successors 1460-1580*. London: Methuen & Co., 1910.

Lund, Christopher C., ed. *Anedotas Portuguesas*. Coimbra: Livraria Almedina, 1980.

Prestage, Edgar. *The Portuguese Pioneers*. New York: Barnes and Noble, 1967.

Ravenstein, E. G., trans. *Vasco da Gama's First Voyage*. In *Portuguese Voyages 1498-1663*. Ed. Charles David Ley. London: J. M. Dent & Sons, 1947.

Resende, Garcia de. *Crónica de dom João II e Miscelânea*. Lisboa: Imprensa Nacional-Casa da Moeda, 1973.

The Maias

by

Eça de Queirós

José Maria Eça de Queirós (1845-1900) has been acclaimed Portugal's greatest nineteenth-century novelist and one of the most outstanding writers of the Portuguese language of all time. Born out of wedlock in Póvoa de Varzim, a small fishing town in northern Portugal, Eça de Queirós never lived with his parents (who would officially acknowledge him only at the time of his own wedding in 1886) but was raised by his father's family until he attended a boarding school in Oporto, Portugal's second largest city. Subsequently he studied law at the prestigious Coimbra University, where he became deeply interested in literature and intrigued by sociopolitical reformist ideas. He practiced law briefly, then traveled to the Orient, and finally pursued a diplomatic career that resulted in his living abroad in Cuba, England, and France until his death in 1900. While still a student in Portugal, Eça worked closely with his French teacher and lifelong friend Ramalho Ortigão and produced a monthly journal *As Farpas (The Barbs)*—the first platform for his ironic strain of realism. Continuing to spice his writing with a honed social satire, Eça published his first novel, *The Sin of Father Amaro*, in 1875. Its depiction of a relationship between a priest and a parishioner impressed readers as a vivid attack on the power of the Church in Portugal, winning the novelist immediate attention. His next novel, *Cousin Bazilio* (1878), portrays a perverse love affair between first cousins in a context of marital boredom that lambastes bourgeois society of the time; and his subsequent novel, *The Relic* (1887), like-

THE LITERARY WORK

A novel set in Lisbon, Portugal, from the early 1820s to 1887; published in Portuguese (as *Os Maias*) in 1888, in English in 1965.

SYNOPSIS

Against a backdrop of political, social, and moral turmoil, the novel depicts the declining fortune of the Maia family over three generations. The story focuses particularly on an incestuous romance in the last of these generations.

wise focuses on the degeneracy of bourgeois society. In *The Maias*, Eça's fourth and longest novel, written over a space of eight years, Eça portrays a Portuguese aristocratic family in a way that mirrors the global and domestic fate of Portugal itself at the time.

Events in History at the Time of the Novel

From global to domestic decline. The action of *The Maias* spans the 1820s to the late 1880s, a tumultuous period for Portugal at both an international and domestic level. On an international front, this period was deeply marked by several major political and economic defeats that the public attributed to government incompetence and viewed as shameful acts of failure. The

José Maria Eça de Queirós

French invasion was followed by British governance and commercial domination in Portugal, and Brazil's declaration of independence from Portugal in 1822 showed Portugal to be a country at the mercy of foreign policies and interests, unable to defend its own rights. Once it became apparent that Brazil's independence would not be reversed, Portugal sought other avenues for economic prosperity in order to regain public confidence and repair its badly damaged national pride. In the 1830s the prospect of an African empire came to the forefront of political and national debate. The imperial ambition consisted of linking the large Portuguese colonies in the eastern and western regions of Africa, Mozambique and Angola, respectively, by annexing present-day Zimbabwe. A general European scramble for control of African territories ensued as the century wore on, which, until the mid-1880s, followed no general policy: "Each country with colonial ambitions . . . tried to subdue as much territory as it could, either in 'vacant' lands or at the expense of others. Historical rights, true or false, were often invoked to justify an act of conquest or its counter-defense" (Marques, p. 107). This was certainly Portugal's argument at first, given its lack of manpower and economic and military resources. However, the historical rights argument was superseded by new policies enacted at the first European partition conference

held in Berlin in 1884-85, which decided that occupation in African territory would henceforth require effective occupation and governance. In order to secure the inland territories between Mozambique and Angola, Portugal would have to dispatch troops and civil officials to those areas, an impossible mission due to the lack of funds and manpower. Yet the Portuguese did not concede defeat immediately, attempting to organize expeditions and to effectively occupy these inland African territories. An ultimatum from England in 1890, however, accompanied by the threat of war, ultimately forced the Portuguese to abandon this imperial dream, once again humiliating them at home.

On a domestic level, the years encompassed in *The Maias* were marked by revolutions, unstable rule, civil war, and over 40 different governments. The successive three Maia generations (Afonso, Pedro, and Carlos) correspond respectively to the constitutional struggle and the liberal war years of the 1820s and 1830s, the era of liberal idealization and political limbo of the 1840s, and the Age of Regeneration (also known as the birth of Portuguese capitalism) that began in 1851. In the 1820s several major events dominated Portuguese politics, beginning in the first year of the decade with the Oporto revolution that led to the end of British occupation (an occupation resulting from the Napoleonic invasion of 1807, whereby the French ruled Lisbon for several months before being driven out by the British). The Oporto revolution was mainly concerned with reestablishing Portuguese independence and with the growth of social and economic liberalism. One of the momentous events of the first decade of the revolt was the drafting and proclamation of a democratic constitution in 1821-22.

During the French and British occupations of the early part of the nineteenth century, King John VI and the rest of the Portuguese royal family had fled to Brazil. In 1821, after the Oporto revolution, King John returned to Lisbon, leaving Brazil in the hands of his son, Pedro I. Brazil declared independence from Portugal in 1822, designating the son, Pedro, its emperor. After King John VI's death in 1826 Pedro supported his young daughter's claim to the Portuguese throne and nominated his brother Miguel as acting regent. Miguel, however, claimed the crown for himself, sparking a conflict that split the country into strident camps. The monarchists (or absolutists) led by Prince Miguel squared off against Pedro's liberals, who proposed a compromise constitution "charter" modeled on the Brazilian constitution.

This fratricidal conflict ensnares the characters in *The Maias,* pitting Afonso da Maia, a liberal, against his father, Caetano, a Miguelist supporter. Yet, when Afonso stands in need of financial aid, he turns to his father and a reconciliation ensues, a symbolic reference to the corrosion of liberal ideals by materialistic aspirations in internal politics in Portugal. Afonso's experience in the novel is reflective of real-life developments in another respect too. The actual conflicts between monarchists and liberals lasted intermittently for 31 years, during which opponents to those in power sought exile abroad, as Afonso does in the novel when he escapes twice to England.

Two political figures worthy of mention stand out in this agitated political context: António Bernardo da Costa Cabral (governor of Lisbon and twice leader of a right-wing reform government, 1842-46, 1849-51) and Field Marshal João Carlos Saldanha (a leading military figure in the Portuguese Revolution, and appointed premier in 1846-48 and 1851-56). Costa Cabral (whom Pedro da Maia teaches his parrot to insult in the novel) sought to carry out a modernizing regime based on urban and commercial interests, emphasizing order through a regime of repression and violence. In 1846 he was evicted from office due to the unpopularity of his measures, in particular a taxation increase and a prohibition against burials inside churches that provoked an uprising known as "Maria by the Fountain," because of the significant participation of women in the incident. Following a period of failed governments, Costa Cabral returned to power, first in alliance with Saldanha (from 1847 to 1849) and then reassuming total control as prime minister (in mid-1849). Stepping down from government, Saldanha became the leader of the opposition and revolted once again in 1851; supported by a military uprising in Oporto, he managed to evict Costa Cabral from office, ushering in the Age of Regeneration in Portugal.

Like Costa Cabral, Saldanha aimed to modernize the country. However, his government's measures earned popular support by representing a strong yet flexible coalition of moderates, rightists, and leftists. Saldanha chose highly skilled personalities as part of his cabinet, among them the poet and writer Almeida Garrett (Secretary of Foreign Affairs 1852; see *Travels in My Homeland,* also in *WLAIT 5: Spanish and Portuguese Literatures and Their Times*) and the politician Fontes Pereira de Melo (Secretary of Finance, Secretary of Public Works, and Prime Minister 1851-86), whose well-developed policies for modernization drastically improved Portugal's transportation and communication systems. The Regeneration entailed dramatic public works projects, including the establishment of a modern postal system, the electric telegraph, an expanded road system, and the railway system.

In opposition to the Regenerators rose a new group, the Historicals, later known as the Progressives, who rotated power peacefully with the Regenerators for almost 50 years. "Both were loose coalitions based on personal loyalties and local interests. Liberal and conservative labels were worn lightly. Ideological differences were of far less importance than personal or factional ones. When a party in government found it difficult to discharge its offices, the monarch [switched allegiance] and offered power to the other" (Gallagher, p. 15). Thus, from 1851 until the fall of the monarchy in 1910, governments ruled as long as possible, then transferred the reins of power to the opposition.

The beginning of the 1870s saw tumult in European politics on the whole, with the unification of Germany and Italy, the Franco-Prussian war, civil strife in France itself, and a new phase of political evolution in Portugal. As politics abroad alarmed the government at home, groups of intellectuals began to organize themselves around common ideals. It was apparent that Portugal was entering a phase wherein newly formed political parties boasting separate ideologies would emerge. In *The Maias,* the 1870s correspond to a new lease on life for the ancestral Lisbon home of the Maia family, who will relocate to Lisbon in 1875.

Portugal in general was contending with a considerable economic obstacle at the time. By the 1880s it was evident that the country was lagging behind much of western Europe in industrial development. Memories of the glorious imperial expansion era prompted the country to look nostalgically to the successes and heroes of the past, a tendency that came to the forefront in 1880 with the tercentennial celebration of the death of Camões, Portugal's most patriotic poet (see *The Lusiads,* also in *WLAIT 5: Spanish and Portuguese Literatures and Their Times*). "Portugal underwent a veritable paroxysm of civic pride and messianic hopes for a new day—the tercentenary year marking the death of Camões himself. Civic enthusiasm and patriotic fervor were at their height" (Coleman, p. 187). The need to regain an optimistic outlook as a nation and to rekindle hopes for a brighter future was manifested in the erection of an obelisk on the main Lisbon boulevard in 1886, commemorating the Portuguese restoration of independence from Spain in 1640. These events are paralleled in *The Maias* by the apparent success of Carlos da Maia, followed by a tragic coming to terms with reality. In real-life, sobering events put the brakes on national optimism. At the end of the 1880s Portugal entered a period of crisis tied to developments such as a decline in wine exports and in the textile industry. During these crucial years, historians, politicians, economists, and writers debated the future of the nation and the potential avenues that would raise Portugal from underdevelopment and economic and cultural dependence to a modernized state. This is the period portrayed at the conclusion of *The Maias*.

Portugal in relation to Europe—an identity crisis. In part because of its geographic location, Portugal has remained culturally and economically on the periphery of Europe. Turning predominantly towards the sea, Portugal established an identity for itself in relation to far-off lands rather than the neighboring states of continental Europe. But in the nineteenth century, given the decline of its seaborne empire, Portugal began to measure itself in relation to the rest of Europe. People modified their habits, adopting various European ways. On a cultural and political level, Portugal became dominated by French influences.

The import of French literature and ideas was quickened by an extraordinary revolution in the intellectual life of Portugal: the opening of the first railway line between Paris and Coimbra in 1864, facilitating the introduction of packing-cases of books. The writers of the time desired more fully to join Europe in order to "escape from the stifling provincialism into which Portuguese literature had sunk in the mid-nineteenth century" (Hemmings, p. 313). The consensus among the leading intellectuals of the day was that Portugal needed to undergo a national revival of its own and that for this to happen social conditions and education would have to improve in ways that could be culled from modernized nations abroad. While such a revival was a longer-term process than blindly imitating foreign trends, the intellectuals deemed it a far better alternative. Writers in Eça de Queirós's generation perceived their mission to be two-fold: to rescue Portugal from an identity crisis accompanied by general malaise and backwardness, on the one hand, and to connect Portugal intellectually to the rest of Europe, on the other.

With this aim in mind, Eça and several of his contemporaries rallied together as the "Generation of 1870." The group had four leading members: a poet (Antero de Quental), an essayist (Teófilo Braga), a historian (Oliveira Martins), and a novelist (Eça de Queirós himself). The monthly satirical journal *As Farpas* provided a forum through which the group disseminated its ideas throughout Portugal from 1871 to 1883. It furthermore planned a series of lectures in the Casino at Lisbon (commonly referred to as the "Casino Lectures," or "Democratic conferences"). Motivated by the desire to react against Portuguese indifference, by acute sensitivity to Portuguese decadence, and by opposition towards the government in power, the group sought to discuss new avenues for Portugal. It focused its sights on social reform, questions of national identity, and religious and educational issues. However, the initiative was short-lived; perceived as a daring social and political attack on the existing order, the lectures were cut short by the government, which put a stop to them in 1871. In *The Maias* it is this ambiance that Eça vividly and ironically portrays. His is a country in danger of losing its national identity, being invaded by French cultural artifacts, even as it longs to re-embrace a more authentic Portugal. In Eça's view, the elite are bringing on the danger by their blind, unthinking adoption of French habits, as reflected in a satirical passage from the concluding pages of his narrative.

> This simple shape of boot explained the whole of contemporary Portugal. . . . Having cast off her old character, the wretched country had decided to turn modern; but having no originality or energy or ability to create a character of its own, it had ordered models from abroad—models of ideas and trousers and customs, laws, art, culinary and otherwise.
>
> (Eça de Queirós, *The Maias*, p. 621)

Even the French political scene had repercussions in Portugal, where developments were closely followed. *The Maias* illustrates this preoccupation through discussions centered on the Second and Third French Republics and the establishment of the Commune (a 72-day period in 1871 when radicals organized Paris into a self-governing city, wanting France to change into a decentralized federation of free municipal units). The novel's discussions center also on the real-life French political leader Léon Gambetta. Gambetta, one of the founders of the Third Republic, has been viewed as "a symbol of a corrupted ideal—the hero of the Commune turned into a demagogic windbag, a bourgeois politician only interested in the support of the proletariat to the extent that he can exploit it" (Gledson, p. 152). Recent histories actually describe him as a more laudable sort. "He was [in fact] a man who liked to remark, that 'politics is the art of the possible,' and who accepted the label 'Opportunist' to illustrate his belief that each advance must await the opportune moment" (Wright, p. 224). Whatever the true nature of his character, for Eça, Gambetta embodies both the ideal of republican rule and the forces that undermine it.

The Lisbon elite at the end of the nineteenth century. *The Maias* can be set apart from Eça's previous novels in that it portrays the lifestyle of the elite social class of Lisbon rather than the rural middle class and bourgeois middle class depicted in *The Sin of Father Amaro* and *Cousin Bazilio*, respectively. The pastimes of Lisbon's upper class revolved around activities that predominantly enabled its members to "see and to be seen." Within Lisbon, one of the most popular activities was promenading along Lisbon's central enclosed avenue, the Passeio Público ("the public walkway"), on Thursdays and Sundays. As in other social venues, appearance was everything, and wearing the latest fashion (ranging from a certain color of gloves to cashmere jackets or the distinguishing eye-glass) or boasting a spotless carriage (usually the open, backwards-facing dog-cart) were distinct indicators of social status. Following the promenades, it was customary for the elite to attend private evening parties, usually accompanied by musical entertainment or dancing, where drinking gin and imported wine was the norm in contrast to the domestically produced Oporto wine, the variety consumed by the lower social classes.

For a trip away from the capital, it was considered most prestigious to spend the day in Sintra, a bucolic haven situated 40 miles northwest of Lisbon in a beautiful scenic environment. Traditionally, since the reign of King John I (1385-1433), the royal family took up its summer residence in Sintra, conferring social elegance to a town flanked by lush mountains, abounding in palaces, and overlooked by a majestic Moorish castle. The chic hotels and restaurants were tailor-made for special romantic getaways of nineteenth-century aristocrats.

Another forum for Lisbon's elite were evenings at Lisbon's São Carlos theater and opera house, founded in 1793. It provided prestigious entertainment and a privileged mingling area for Lisbon high society, with the royal family making appearances. These evenings at the opera or theater were often considered the indoor equivalent of the Passeio Público; the spectacle happened mostly amongst the audience, whose members would eye one another and only secondarily the stage.

IMMORAL ENCOUNTER

The protagonist of *The Maias* brings back a far less innocent souvenir from France than fashionable clothing. His female companion, Maria Eduarda, it turns out, was a courtesan. The nineteenth century was one of accelerated urban development, which makes it unsurprising that there was an imbalance in the ratio of men to women in the capital cities such as Paris, France, where Castro Gomes meets Maria Eduarda, "a woman who would have offered herself naked to any man in Paris who had a thousand francs in his pocket!" (*The Maias,* p. 427). High-class Paris prostitutes catered largely to foreign aristocrats. For foreigners, or provincials visiting the capital for a few days or weeks, such female company became something of a rite, promoted by conditions of the era. Other features of the era were newly created wealth tied to industry, declining Church influence, and growing sensitivity to individual liberties and free-thinking, all of which helped make the last three decades of the nineteenth century a golden age in prostitution.

In 1874 the creation of the hippodrome, a horse-show arena in Lisbon, offered yet another alternative for social gatherings, constituting a valiant effort at cosmopolitanism, even at the price of foreign imitation. At first it was thought that the horse races would replace to a degree the traditional Portuguese bullfight; however, proving not to be very popular, the hippodrome was torn down in 1883.

Other than engaging in such local activities, being well traveled set Lisbon's elite apart from the less privileged classes. From Lisbon the most popular destinations were the metropolises of England, France, and Italy, where the elite would spend months and even years. As vividly portrayed in *The Maias,* most prominently in relation to France and England, the knowledge of foreign cultures, languages, and customs was an important part of the education of the upper class, which was often achieved or assisted by governesses and private teachers from abroad.

The Novel in Focus

Plot summary. Most of *The Maias* is situated within a relatively short time frame, the 14 months that fall between the end of 1875 and the beginning of 1877. In the autumn of 1875 Afonso da Maia, the patriarch of the Maia dynasty, leaves his rural home in the Douro hills to install himself in Lisbon in a family home known as Ramalhete. Ramalhete has been empty for years, under the stewardship of old Vilaça, who believed that the "walls of Ramalhete had always been fatal to the Maias" (*The Maias*, p. 9). Afonso, who at his age loved the peace and quiet of his country abode, nonetheless saw fit to live in the capital to better receive his grandson, Carlos Eduardo da Maia, after his graduation. The grandson, accustomed to metropolitan life and driven by dreams of his future as a doctor and medical researcher, would most likely not want to live in the small Douro town of Santa Olávia.

At this point in the novel, the storyline moves back in time to establish the main events affecting the Maia family since the beginning of the nineteenth century. The flashback brings Afonso da Maia's family from the period of the Portuguese liberal revolutions of the 1820s to the end of 1875 and the beginning of the main plot.

Belonging to the generation that entered adulthood before the liberal revolution of 1820 and the proclamation of the Constitution in 1822, Afonso da Maia enthusiastically supports the liberal cause. His enthusiasm persists though his father, Caetano da Maia, expels him from the family home of Benfica to the family estate in the Douro, regarding his son as "the most ferocious Jacobin in Portugal" (*The Maias*, p. 14). After a brief stay in Santa Olávia, Afonso seeks his father's blessing before departing to England where his liberal fervor dwindles and he becomes engrossed in English society of the day. When his father dies suddenly, Afonso returns to Lisbon for the funeral and meets his bride-to-be, Dona Maria Eduarda Runa, whom he soon marries. A son is born, Pedro da Maia. Disillusioned by the state of affairs in Lisbon under the reign of Dom Miguel, Afonso sets off for England once again, this time with his wife and child. They remain there until his wife, ill and failing rapidly, begs him to return to Lisbon, where she dies.

Pedro, Afonso's only son, resembles his mother both physically and temperamentally. A small, nervous child, "he developed slowly, without curiosity, indifferent to toys, animals, flowers and books. No strong desire ever seemed to move that half-somnolent and passive soul" (*The Maias*, p. 20). A grown Pedro drowns his mother's memory in brothels and taverns before burying himself in religion. He later becomes involved with Maria Monforte, daughter of a rich Azorean who had formerly been the captain of a brig that had transported cargoes of slaves to Brazil, Havana, and New Orleans. Needless to say this amorous relationship does not meet with Afonso da Maia's approval, so Pedro and Maria elope. They depart for Italy and Paris, and upon their return to Lisbon, a gulf still divides Pedro and his father, even after Pedro's daughter Maria Eduarda and his son Carlos Eduardo are born. In the end, Pedro seems to have endured his father's wrath all for naught, for his marriage collapses. Maria Monforte flees with an Italian prince, Tancredo, taking her daughter with her, whereupon Pedro commits suicide, leaving his son, Carlos, to his father. Afonso, grieved by the misfortune and dishonor that has befallen the Maia family, dedicates himself to his grandson's upbringing and education. Carlos da Maia receives an English education, very different from the one Afonso had seen his wife insist upon giving their son Pedro. Carlos goes on to study medicine in Coimbra and, after traveling throughout Europe, returns to Lisbon to live with his grandfather. It is the end of 1875.

Afonso da Maia and Carlos are elite members of Lisbon society. Afonso is full of hopes for his grandson's future, and Carlos is driven by ideas and projects. He arrives in Lisbon to establish his medical practice, open a laboratory for scientific investigation, and write medical articles and a book, or, as he states, to "embark on a career that will be a glory to the nation!" (*The Maias*, p. 87). Yet nothing comes of his aspirations. Carlos instead indulges in a life of luxury and pleasure, entailing *soirées* at Ramalhete, evenings at the S. Carlos opera, dinners at the Hotel Central, and a love affair with the "enticing . . . enchantingly well-made" Countess de Gouvarinho, the wife of a diplomat, who turns out to be insatiable and far too demanding (*The Maias*, p. 122). He, in short, becomes lost in the mediocre high society of Lisbon. Then one day, in the Hotel Central, Carlos spots a beautiful woman, Maria Eduarda, the wife of a rich Brazilian, Castro Gomes. He grows infatuated with this unknown beauty and attends her sick child. Later, through the sickness of Miss Sarah, the Gomes's governess, Carlos appears again. First as the family doctor, then as a friend, he becomes a regular of the household's inner circle while Castro Gomes is absent in Brazil.

Carlos and Madame Castro Gomes have an affair, provoking bitter jealousy in Carlos's peer, the condescending Damaso Salcede, and frustration in Carlos's mistress Countess de Gouvarinho. Maria Eduarda, who fully reciprocates Carlos's love, agrees to spend the summer in the "Hideaway," a country house in the outskirts of Lisbon, at Olivais, where Carlos arranges for her to live. However, Castro Gomes soon dispels Carlos's misconceptions about Maria Eduarda. He returns to Portugal and, having been informed of Carlos's relationship with Maria Eduarda in an anonymous letter written by Damaso, informs Carlos that Maria Eduarda is not his wife, but "just a woman [he] paid" (*The Maias*, p. 426). This episode leaves Carlos dumbfounded, but facing the truth of Maria Eduarda's past ends up consolidating their relationship. They discuss marriage. "Now they would not have to hide a guilty love but enjoy instead the tranquility of a legitimate happiness" (*The Maias*, p. 445).

Carlos and Maria Eduarda's destinies are once again upset when Guimarães, one of Damaso's uncles, comes on the scene. A Parisian reporter, Guimarães had formerly known Carlos da Maia's mother, Maria Monforte, in Paris. It is Guimarães who reveals to Carlos's close friend João da Ega that Maria Eduarda is Carlos da Maia's sister, leaving Ega speechless, "staring at him in horror and a terrible pallor covering his face" as he faced "the monstrous certainty that Carlos was the lover of his [own] sister!" (*The Maias*, pp. 545, 549). Ega entrusts the Maia steward Vilaça with truth-shattering documents to prove this, then reveals the whole story to Carlos and his grandfather Afonso. Carlos intends to end his relationship with Maria Eduarda, whom he now knows is his sister, but, unable to resist her, he ends up consciously committing incest, albeit with feelings of "physical nausea" (*The Maias*, p. 589). "[Carlos] was human and weak, and unable to stop being swept along by that violent impulse of love and desire which drove him before it like a tempest!" (*The Maias*, p. 587). Afonso da Maia, informed of his grandchildren's fraternal incest, dies of grief. Ega then leaves the Maria Monforte documents with Maria Eduarda, along with part of the inheritance that, as a Maia, is rightfully hers. Maria Eduarda leaves for Paris, and Carlos sets off with Ega for America and Japan. It is the beginning of 1877.

A year later Ega appears in Lisbon. Carlos, still badly shaken, has installed himself in Paris "in a magnificent apartment in the Champs-Élysées, living the life of an artistic Renaissance prince" (*The*

Maias*, p. 609). Ten years later he encounters Ega in Lisbon, and informs him that Maria Eduarda will be married to a Frenchman in Orléans. Ega and Carlos take stock of the past and the present, discussing Portugal and her ills. Laughing at their former dreams and illusions and the Portuguese attempts at modernization, they conclude that all efforts, both on a personal and collective level, are ultimately pointless. Short of a miracle or a catastrophe, in *The Maias*—as in the majority of Eça's work—there is no concrete solution to this deep-felt state of despair, which translates into the author's own pessimism towards Portugal at the end of the nineteenth century.

Alongside the main protagonists of the novel, *The Maias* presents a crowded gallery of characters, representative figures of Portugal of that time. Included are the following: the Count de Gouvarinho, a narrow-minded, rhetorical politician; Miss Sarah, the Gomes's English governess, who lives a double life of English Puritanism by day and libertine ardors after dark; the Jewish banker Cohen, whose wife Rachel is João da Ega's lover and the great romantic passion of his life; the ultra-romantic poet Alencar; the sad Eusèbiozinho, product of a religious, provincial education, considered a prodigy child in his youth; the shallow, solemn and ridiculous Finnish minister Steinbroken; the corrupt journalist Palma Cavalhão; and Cruges, the unappreciated maestro and intimate of the Maia circle. Set apart from this group is João da Ega, Carlos's confident, whose councils and witty comments accompany Carlos through the years. João da Ega's impertinent denunciation of the ills of the country, and the mediocrity of the men that represent it, is commonly thought to be a reflection of the novelist's own views.

Incest in nineteenth-century Portugal. The incest motif can be traced back to classical Greek literature (for example, Sophocles' *Oedipus*) or the Bible. In *The Maias* the theme of incest brings a tragic dimension to the novel in the Oedipus tradition, projecting passions and problems that cannot be easily solved or destroyed. The societal taboo involves two innocent siblings who did not foresee their blood relationship. Ultimately, once their consanguinity is revealed, Carlos's incapacity to refrain from committing incest transforms what was ignorance to a conscious perversion and then a deadly act: Carlos degrades himself, defiles his sister, and provokes his grandfather's death. Yet, other than Afonso's sudden death, neither Carlos nor Maria Eduarda are punished, but go their separate ways to live

THE IBERIAN SOLUTION

The death of the Portuguese King Sebastian in the battle of Alcácer Quibir (1578) in northern Africa opened the way to Iberian union: from 1580 to 1640 Spain and Portugal were united for the first time under the same sovereign, King Philip II of Spain. After the restoration of Portuguese independence in 1640, Spain was considered the dangerous neighbor and remained a permanent, though often dormant, threat to Portugal's nationhood. During the nineteenth century the discussion of an Iberian union resurfaced following the unifications of Italy in 1859-60 and Germany in 1871 and during the years 1873-75 when the Spanish Crown was in limbo until it was solidified under Alfonso XII. "For many Portuguese intellectuals, including a great number of Republicans, the dream of an Iberian Union had a strong appeal, as a remedy for the backwardness of both countries and the dawn of a new era for the united 'Spaniards.' They defended of course a sort of federation with Spain (or even a confederation of several states dismembered from Spain) which might preserve Portugal's cultural and political identity" (Marques, pp. 71-72). This debate comes to the forefront in *The Maias* as the protagonists discuss possible solutions to Portugal's current state of degeneracy. "On that night Ega was incorrigible, and now he uttered another enormity. 'Portugal doesn't need reform, Cohen! What Portugal needs is a Spanish invasion!' Alencar, who was an old-fashioned patriot, became indignant. . . . But Ega was speaking in earnestness and was full of reason. Obviously, he said, invasion would not involve absolute loss of independence" (*The Maias*, p. 150).

comfortable lives of idle luxury, not as outcasts but as well-accepted members of society. This pseudo-happy ending minimizes the tragic impact that the incest has upon the protagonists. However, though there is apparently little damage on the surface, pessimism undergirds the close of the novel, a pessimism tied to the unpredictable forces to which humanity is subject. There is a disheartening focus on the incapacity of humankind to control its destiny, exemplified by the destruction of happiness once thought untouchable.

In Eça de Queirós's work, the incest theme is also present in two other novels that merit mention, *Cousin Bazilio* and *A Tragédia da Rua das Flores* (The Tragedy of the Street of Flowers). The matrimonial state was considered the cornerstone of respectable middle-class society in nineteenth-century Europe, and the bourgeoisie's deepest anxieties were roused by anything that could constitute a threat to its stability. Posing such a threat, incest exposes these anxieties. Eça's vivid depiction of incestuous relationships likewise points to the degeneration of the family in late-nineteenth-century Portuguese society, a degeneration that points to the decreasing influence of the Church, the greater mobility of the population due to improved infrastructures, and the increasing role of women in society, who were no longer as strictly confined to the stereotype of wife and mother. Finally, incest points to the sterility of nineteenth-century Portuguese life. Carlos, the last man of the Maia lineage, personifies the decline of society, the loss of dignity, hope, and identity. Just as the Maia clan will have no future issue, Eça foresees dismal days for the future of Portugal if it remains on its present course. His vision is one of decadence and corruption, with emphasis on the repulsive aspects of life, in the interest of change. To this end, the Portuguese aristocracy provides an ideal backdrop for his condemnation of a society guided not by reason but by sentimental impulses, and of a country in desperate need of social, institutional, and educational reforms.

Sources. Within Portuguese literature, *The Maias* is strongly acclaimed as one of the great masterpieces of the nineteenth century, a testament of realism artistically projecting customs of Portuguese society interspersed with ultra-sentimental episodes. Though Eça de Queirós traveled extensively and lived many years outside Portugal, he never lost contact with his homeland and it remains central to the great majority of his work.

The circumstances of Eça's childhood and adolescence are frequently thought to have deeply influenced his writing. Though he is nowadays most commonly known by his first surname, "Eça," which was his mother's maiden name, his birth certificate reads "mother unknown." Moreover Eça's mother refused for over 40 years to acknowledge her first-born son, even after she married Eça de Queirós's father, with whom she had four more children. Eça's work rarely features a stable, happy family unit. What predominates are abnormal relationships (or the lack of relationships) between parents and children. As previously mentioned, the incest motif is representative of this lack of normality. In his youth, Eça apparently wanted to marry a cousin with whom he was raised, and he probably projects this desire into his work.

Resemblances between *The Maias* and Eça's adulthood can also be conjectured. At the end of the novel, Carlos da Maia and João da Ega discuss lost illusions. Eça himself, along with the other members of the "Generation 1870," wanted Portugal to experience a profound transformation but hope waned and dreams were abandoned. Perceiving all efforts to be in vain, the "Generation 1870" formed the group "Vencidos da vida" ("Life's defeated") at the end of 1887 and the beginning of 1888, when *The Maias* was first published.

As noted, the protagonist João da Ega is often referred to as the author incarnate, and in relation to one episode in particular the parallel certainly seems to ring true. While Eça de Queirós was serving as District Administrator in Leiria, Portugal (1870-71), he was invited on February 21, 1871, Shrove Tuesday, to a masked ball at the house of the Barons de Salgueiro. Towards the end of the evening, the Administrator was caught committing a social taboo in one of the darker rooms of the home by kissing an already attached woman very similar to Rachel Cohen in the novel. As a result, Eça was told to leave the masked ball. In *The Maias* it is João da Ega, dressed as Mephistopheles, who is shown the door at a masked ball given in honor of Rachel Cohen's birthday, an episode that explicitly recalls that of Eça's life.

Literary context. In the early-to-mid nineteenth century European writers developed a new literary genre, realism, in response to the one in vogue at the time, Romanticism. Offended by the disguised eroticism of idealized Romantic litera-

In *The Maias,* João da Ega has an illicit encounter with a woman at a masked ball, while dressed as Mephistopheles, an incident that mirrors one in Eça de Queirós's own life.

ture and the corrupting effect of such fiction on the bored, poorly educated women of their class, realist writers sought to portray characters illustrative of social trends and institutions, aiming primarily "to tell the truth." Though writing mainly in England and then France, Eça de Queirós distinguished himself as the foremost realist writer of Portuguese literature in his time. His intent was to faithfully depict modern life, with all its negative attributes, so it would serve as a guidepost to future action.

Eça's mission was to give literary expression to customs of Portuguese society, and to general human passions. He dreamed of creating his own "Comedy of Human Life," a project paralleling the French writer Honoré de Balzac's lifetime endeavor, *The Human Comedy* (some 90 novels about human life and society). In Eça's case, the plan was for the series to consist of intertwined novels representing aspects of nineteenth-century Portuguese society. Though he never completed the project, his works would indeed capture slices of Portuguese society. *The Maias* was appropriately subtitled "Episodes of romantic life." Though the subtitle is lost in the

English translations, it was highly important to Eça, who insisted his editor print it on the cover of the novel. In *The Maias* the slice of life depicted is that of the waning aristocracy and the rising bourgeoisie, both corrupted by material ideals and driven by ambitions of power.

EÇA ON THE POWER OF LITERATURE

In order to use the past as a means of education, we want to produce a photograph, I almost said a caricature of the old bourgeois world, sentimental, devoted, catholic, explorative, aristocratic. . . . An art that has this aim is a powerful aid of revolutionary science.

(Queirós, *Uma Campanha Alegre*, p. 68;
trans. K. Bishop Sanchez)

Eça wrote at a time when realism's literary offspring, naturalism, was widespread in Europe. Naturalism aimed to faithfully represent reality with emphasis on the accidental, physiological dimensions of characters, who were viewed either as more or as less fortunate victims of their heredity and environment. Eça introduced naturalism into Portugal, a genre adopted by writers of the 1880s and 1890s, such as Abel Botelho and Júlio Lourenço Pinto. Eça's earlier novels are considered his most naturalist works. Traces of naturalism surface in *The Maias*, but his absence from Portugal prevented direct "scientific" observation of the social milieu, and Eça moved progressively away from a naturalist style of writing.

Reviews. When the novel came out in 1888 it was immediately the focus of critical attention, mostly due to the incestuous relationship that Eça so blatantly developed. The novel was both praised and condemned, as portrayed by several key articles published in the newspapers of the time. An article by Fialho de Almeida, one of Eça's contemporaries and himself a writer of short stories and chronicles, was published in the Portuguese newspaper *Repórter* on July 20, 1888, vividly attacking the violence of some of *The Maias*'s portraits, referring to all the men as grotesque rogues and the women as shameless. He accuses Eça de Queirós of having produced a book that could well have been written by a foreigner unfamiliar with Portuguese society, merely judging Portuguese life from the outside

through hotel scenes, newspaper articles, social gatherings, etc. This article merited a prompt reply from Eça in a letter written from Bristol dated August 8. Later that same month the literary critic Mariano Pina wrote a summary of the book's impact on contemporary readers and critics for the newspaper *A Ilustração*. According to this article, the main faults were the length of the novel, some 990 pages that could well have been condensed into 300 pages, and the impression that several of the characters were repeats from Eça's former novels. Following this critical synthesis, Mariano Pina defends the novel, deserving the following response from Eça "Excellent article on *The Maias*, full of good humor and irony. Je vous en serre la main?" (Matos, p. 573). The year following the novel's publication, the Portuguese poet Bulhão Pato, indignant after recognizing himself in the character of the ultra-romantic poet Alencar, published a flamboyant satire against Eça ("*O Grande Maia*"), to which Eça responded with characteristic irony. But Eça had his champions too. Mariano Pina asserted that *The Maias* once again proves Eça on par with the great European modernists: contrary to the opinion of several critics, its portrayal of Portuguese society is far from monotonous or short-sighted and Eça's unparalleled style combined with his command of the Portuguese language contributes to the novel's strength.

—Kathryn Bishop Sanchez

For More Information

Birmingham, David. *A Concise History of Portugal*. Cambridge: Cambridge University Press, 1993.

Coleman, Alexander. *Eça de Queirós and European Realism*. New York University Press: New York, 1980.

Corbin, Alain. *Women for Hire: Prostitution and Sexuality in France after 1850*. Trans. Alan Sheridan. Cambridge, Mass.: Harvard University Press, 1990.

Demetz, Peter. "Eça de Queirós as a Literary Critic." *Comparative Literature* 19 (1967): 289-307.

Gallagher, Tom. *Portugal, a Twentieth-Century Interpretation*. Manchester: Manchester University Press, 1983.

Givens, Terryl L. "*Os Maias*: Incest, Dilettantes, and the Ethics of Realism." *Hispanofila* 100 (1990): 53-65.

Gledson, John. "The Meanings of *Os Maias*: The Role of Gambetta." *Bulletin of Hispanic Studies*. Special Homage Volume (1992): (147-54).

Hemmings, F. W. J. ed. *The Age of Realism*. Harmondsworth, England: Penguin, 1974.

Macedo, Helder. "Introduction." *The Maias*, by Eça de Queirós. J. M. Dent & Sons: London, 1986.

Marques, A. H. de Oliveira. *History of Portugal.* 2d ed. Vol. 2. New York: Columbia University Press, 1976.

Matos, A. Campos, ed. *Dicionário de Eça de Queiróz.* 2d ed. Lisboa: Caminho, 1993.

Overton, Bill. "Church and State: Eça de Queirós, Alas, Galdós." In *The Novel of Female Adultery: Love and Gender in Continental European Fiction, 1830-1900.* Macmillan: London, 1996.

Queirós, Eça de. *The Maias.* Trans. Patricia Mc-Gowan Pinheiro and Ann Stevens. London: Penguin Books, 1998.

———. *Uma Campanha Alegre.* Porto: Lello & Irmão, 1966.

Wright, Gordon. *France in Modern Times.* New York: Norton, 1987.

The Maiden's Consent

by

Leandro Fernández de Moratín

Leandro Fernández de Moratín was born in 1760 in Madrid. His father was Nicolás Fernández de Moratín (1737-80), a pre-eminent literary figure of eighteenth-century Spain. Although the younger Moratín did not attend university, he followed his father, uncle, and grandfather in working as a jeweler. Writing in his spare time, Leandro began attracting favorable attention in the 1770s. He traveled in 1787 to Paris as the secretary of the Count of Cabarrús, a diplomat in the service of the Spanish king, Charles III (1716-88). Upon his return from Paris, Moratín wrote a musical version of the first of his five extant plays, *El barón* (The Baron), in which he already treats his favorite theme of unequal marriages between affluent, aged men and very young women of little means. After staging the metacritical play *La comedia nueva* (The New Comedy) in which he satirized the bad theater of his time, Moratín received a pension from the royal minister Manuel de Godoy. He began travels through Europe in Paris, where he witnessed with revulsion the Reign of Terror in the months before the execution of Louis XVI in the French Revolution. He then spent a year in London and gained sufficient command of English to be able to execute the first translation of Shakespeare's *Hamlet* into Spanish. After residing in Italy between 1793 and 1796, he returned to Spain and secured a government position as Secretary of the Interpretation of Languages. Literature continued to occupy him and in 1799 he became the Director of the Group for the Management and Re-

THE LITERARY WORK

A play set in an inn in Alcalá de Henares, outside of Madrid, in the mid-1790s; performed and published in Spanish (as *El sí de las niñas*) in 1806, in English in 1962.

SYNOPSIS

The 59-year-old rich, respectable Don Diego wants to marry the poor 16-year-old Doña Francisca, but only if she will freely accept him. While her family promotes the marriage as a socially acceptable and financial necessity, Doña Francisca already loves a young officer, who turns out to be Don Diego's nephew, Don Carlos.

form of Theaters. Following the May 1808 outbreak of the War of Independence of Spain from Napoleonic France, Moratín chose to continue in government service under Napoleon's brother King Joseph I Bonaparte of Spain. With the final triumph of the Spanish over the French in 1814, Moratín's position, that of an *afrancesado* or Frenchified person and sympathizer, made life in Spain problematic for him. Despite some bright moments for him there in coming years, his life became more French than Spanish until he died in Paris in 1828. His burial in Paris between the graves of Molière and Jean de La Fontaine, two fundamental French authors, indicates the classic status that the author of *The Maiden's Consent* had achieved only a generation

Leandro Fernández de Moratín

after the play's premiere. Like the French authors, Moratín humorously showed society how necessary it was to re-examine important but incorrect assumptions about relationships between men and women.

Events in History at the Time of the Play

The Enlightenment and the old regime. The basic tension of late-eighteenth-century Europe is sociopolitical; there was conflict between the practical pro-democratic, anti-authoritarian principles of Enlightenment philosophy and the contradiction to that thought offered by the absolutist monarchies and courts of the Old Regime. Following the American Revolution of 1776-83 and, more particularly, the French Revolution of 1789, no one could ignore the contradiction. The Enlightenment oriented humankind toward striving for happiness in this world based on the exercise of human virtue informed by the observation of natural processes and the reasoned learning derived therefrom. Old Regime absolutism depended upon a worldview in which earthly religious and secular hierarchies were accepted as the human extension of a divine plan. The reign of the Bourbon King Charles IV of

Spain, between 1788 and 1808, coincided with the crisis of Old Regime absolutism in Spain. For the enlightened Moratín, these were his most productive years.

The crisis of the Old Regime in Spain. In the clearest possible fashion the personal and public life of Spain's Charles IV, his queen María Luisa of Parma, and other members and friends of the royal family, particularly the prime minister Godoy, demonstrated all the evils of the Old Regime and, unlike the reign of the preceding King Charles III, very few of its positive points. To begin with, the royal couple gave rise to scandal. Similar to the proposed marital match in *The Maiden's Consent*, the marriage of Charles and María Luisa was arranged. Even though that was the normal practice in pairing royals, and despite the fact that Charles and María Luisa differed very little in age, there were many reports, including one integrated by Benito Pérez Galdós into his 1873 historical novel, *The Court of Carlos IV*, of María Luisa's affairs. It is thought that two of her children, royals by birth, were in fact not by Charles IV, but by her alleged lover, prime minister Godoy, a man 16 years her junior and to whom all knew her to be attracted from 1788 onwards. Hence on an elemental level, the broad theme of arranged marriages and their ills was a normal part of then contemporary society, as were the accompanying Bourbon familial complications which spilled over into national life. For example, faced by the ever increasing authority of Godoy in court, in 1807 the crown prince Fernando conspired, unsuccessfully, to kill his mother, dethrone his father, and, on the way to his kingship, dispose of Godoy.

In properly international and domestic affairs, Charles IV ruled no more competently than in his own family. As one of the reigning monarchs of the Bourbon dynasty, his foreign policy was broadly dynastic: preservation of the life of his cousin, the French King Louis XVI, following the French Revolution. Then, when Louis was guillotined in January 1793, Charles took measures to try to reverse the Revolution. This, however, led to a disastrous war between March 1793 and July 1795 between Spain and the French revolutionary armies and resulted in the French occupation and control of much of northeastern Spain. Between this period and that of the Spanish War of Independence from the French (1808-14)—known in English historiography as the Peninsular Wars because of English intervention there on the side of Spain and Portugal—Spain alternated in fighting with or against the French

THE LEGACY OF MORATÍN

In the historical novel, *The Court of Charles IV,* Pérez Galdós dramatically revealed his aesthetic allegiance to Moratín by making the premiere of *The Maiden's Consent* part of the action of his novel. In fine metaliterary tradition, Galdós had Gabriel Araceli, his first-person narrator/protagonist, explain and approve of the exemplary nature of Moratín's aesthetics as demonstrated in this play. When Araceli comments upon and praises Moratín's simple, pure Spanish and his recreation of representative middle-class persons confronting and resolving problems typical of their time and place, he is also setting forth key parts of Galdós's own aesthetics. At the beginning of the twenty-first century *The Maiden's Consent* is considered as classic a work of Spanish theater as Lope de Vega's **Fuente Ovejuna** and Calderón de la Barca's **Life is a Dream** (also in *WLAIT 5: Spanish and Portuguese Literatures and Their Times*). It continues to be staged frequently in Spain by both amateurs and professional companies, and new editions of the play multiply.

and in fighting with or against the English. When allied with France, as in 1779-83, 1796-1801, and 1804-08, Spain's general goal was to combat the pressure of English privateers and naval forces on Spain's monopolistic commerce with its American colonies. When allied with the English, as in 1793-95 and 1809-14, Spain's intent was to defend itself from France. From the French perspective, alliance with the Spanish was beneficial because of the impressive Spanish fleet, which King Ferdinand VI had begun to build up tremendously in the 1750s to use in naval operations against the British. From the British perspective, alliance with Spain was beneficial because the British wanted to prevent French control of Portuguese and Spanish ports along the Atlantic and Mediterranean. The build-up of Spanish armed forces in the 1750s had in fact been designed to assure Spanish neutrality in wars between France and England, and to retain effective control over the New World colonies. But Charles IV broke that neutrality in order to defend Bourbon family interests, a violation that worked to the detriment of Spain's domestic and colonial concerns. The colonies' role was to provide cheap raw materials to Spain and to offer a captive market for the manufactured goods of that country. But in the wake of such naval defeats as that of the combined French-Spanish fleet by the English under Admiral Horatio Nelson at Trafalgar in 1805, imports of such colonial products as cacao, sugar, and tobacco were reduced to less than 1 percent of their prewar quantities, gold and silver ships ceased to arrive in Cadiz, and Catalonian bankruptcies mounted,

especially in the textile industry. All these developments contributed to economic depression and bankruptcy of the national treasury. Charles IV's national policy of this period was self-interested, since he aimed to prevent the spread to Spain of revolutionary ideas that could lead to the same fate for the Spanish Bourbons as that of the French branch of the family.

Although Moratín does not specifically state the historic time in which the ten hours of the action of *The Maiden's Consent* transpire, references to the military history and present duties of Don Diego's nephew, a serving lieutenant colonel in the Spanish army, point to sometime after the 1793-95 war with France, but before that army is engaged in any action more important than monitoring the 1795 Basilea Treaty, which left France in control of northeastern Spain and the non-noble Godoy with the royal title Prince of Peace. In the ensuing brief period of relative calm in Spain, Moratín's Don Carlos can take leaves of absence from his post at the strategic, but not frontline stronghold of Zaragoza.

The *afrancesados*. On the cultural level, the reigns of Charles III and IV in Spain were dominated by the contention between those who supported and opposed the wholesale importation of French models to supplant national customs and traditions. Those who favored the "Frenchification" of Spanish life, the so-called *afrancesados,* were active throughout the eighteenth century in following French practice in creating cultural institutions. Taking their cue from

THE *CORTEJO*

The eighteenth-century Spanish *cortejo* was a practice probably imported from Italy, but with precedents in France. In a time of arranged and often unequal marriages, it organized in the upper and upper-middle classes a kind of service to married women by unmarried, younger men called *petimetres*. These men constituted a kind of court in which the woman, neglected by a complaisant older or otherwise occupied husband, was queen. They assisted her in grooming, dressing, and diverting herself. While some such relations were platonic, moralists of the period, particularly clerics, viewed the *cortejo* as tantamount to socially sanctioned adultery. When Don Carlos warns Don Diego about the consequences of his marrying Doña Francisca, who loves Don Carlos, he specifically invokes her high morality to indicate that she would not engage in anything like a *cortejo*. But Don Diego understands well that that would be a risk. The relation between Queen María Luisa de Parma and Manuel de Godoy seems to have been a *cortejo* sanctioned by Charles IV. Needless to say the *cortejo* was abhorrent to Spanish traditionalists. Yet in her 1972 study *Usos amorosos del dieciocho en España* (Customs of Love in Eighteenth-Century Spain), the highly regarded novelist Carmen Martín Gaite defended the *cortejo*. Despite all its negative aspects, she argued that it not only fulfilled real female needs but also helped lay the ground for the principle of equality between the needs of men and women and their satisfaction.

French models, the *afrancesados* gave rise in Madrid to the Royal Academies of Language (1714), History (1736), Art (1752), and what became the national library; in larger Spanish cities such as Barcelona, Valencia, and Seville, royal societies of letters, economics, and sciences prospered. The males of the Moratín family worked in one such organization—the Royal Jewelers—and the eminent painter and etcher Francisco Goya labored first as a cartoonist for the Royal Factory of Tapestries and, beginning in 1786, as painter of the Royal Court and then of the Royal Chamber. But this cultural activity had a negative side for Spanish traditionalists. While this Enlightenment cultivation of the higher pursuits of humankind might have been harmless in itself, it became identified with its royal and aristocratic sponsors. The worldly ways in manners and morals of this elite was viewed as bad enough, but the fact that it threatened to spread widely through the upper classes caused scandal and conflict in a society dominated by the austere, other-worldly orientation of Spanish Catholicism. Only for a minority of Spaniards, those most influenced by the life of the Bourbon court, did the morally liberal, intellectually probing view of life emanating from Paris seem superior to received national ways and customs.

These problems were accentuated by the influence of the Italian wives of the early-eighteenth-century monarchs Philip V (María Luisa Gabriela of Savoy and Isabella Farnese) and Charles IV (María Luisa of Parma), and by the Italian residence of the most enlightened of Spanish kings, Charles III, son of Isabella Farnese and himself King of the Two Sicilies from 1734 until he ascended in 1759 to the Spanish throne upon the death of his half-brother Ferdinand VI. In literature imitators of the exhausted Spanish baroque literature of the latter sixteenth century contended with those such as Moratín who looked elsewhere for models—to the classic literature of Greece and Rome, the Spanish Golden Age, and the France of Louis XIV through XVI. Hence while the Bourbon court paved the way for cultural progress in Spain, it was a way that the Spanish Church, the more independent, traditional nobility, and the common people viewed as the negation of essential Spanish values. This equation was greatly complicated by the French Revolution. The very Bourbons who had been responsible for the liberalization of Spanish thought and society were obliged to renounce the logical consequences of that process as they observed its practical outcomes develop in France, that is, the rise of the lower classes at the expense of the aristocracy and monarchy. The liberal nobles finally decided that Enlightenment thought led to a new conclusion: government must serve the people, not people serve the government. By this time, however, it was too late to reverse the democratization process. Spanish traditionalists, who favored royal absolutism, came to the same decision earlier than the French. But even as these Spaniards felt vindicated in their rejection of Bourbon liberalism, the most astute among them observed that democratization was a force in Spain too.

As previously noted, the Spanish fleet, along with its French allies, met with destruction at Trafalgar in 1805. This defeat occurred under French commanders that Charles IV and Godoy foisted on the Spanish navy. As a result, the king, his minister, and Queen María Luisa came to symbolize all that was wrong with French-dominated Spain. Within three years the Spanish nation, without guidance or assistance from the Bourbons, perhaps most conspicuously without the new king Ferdinand VII, who let himself be placed in 1808 under house arrest in France by Napoleon, began the War of Independence. Following the conclusion of the war, enlightened *afrancesados* found themselves in the most difficult of positions. During the war they had drafted and signed Spain's first, but ill-fated, democratic document, the Constitution of Cadiz in 1812. This document of constitutional monarchy included, for reasons very hard to comprehend in light of Ferdinand's conduct before and during the war, a preamble pledging loyalty to him. Yet upon his return, Ferdinand wanted to revive Old Regime absolutism and to that end persecuted the *afrancesados*. His victims included those who had been politically active in drafting and defending the Constitution, along with those such as Moratín, who had simply continued in government service under Joseph Bonaparte. Not until Ferdinand's death in 1833, five years after Moratín and Goya had died in exile, could the surviving *afrancesados* return to Spain in complete safety, and could a new generation of similarly minded thinkers and writers, represented by the Duke of Rivas and Mariano José de Larra (see **"The Old-Fashioned Castilian,"** also in *WLAIT 5: Spanish and Portuguese Literatures and Their Times*), resume Moratín and Goya's practice of criticizing the ills of Spanish society through their art.

The Play in Focus

Plot summary. The action of the play occurs in the mid 1790s, between 7:00 P.M. on one day and 5:00 A.M. on the next in Alcalá, located 21 miles east of or about a day's stage ride from Madrid (today it forms part of metropolitan Madrid). Summer heat and mosquitoes plague the second-floor common area of an uncomfortable inn in Alcalá de Henares from which access to four numbered rooms is gained. The main characters are 59-year-old Don Diego, a prosperous, well-known, and respected gentleman; his 25-year-old nephew, the lieutenant-colonel Don Carlos, known during much of the play to some of the characters as Don Felix; Doña Francisca, the 16-year-old poor but respectable intended bride of Don Diego; and her mother Doña Irene, a poor widow in her sixties.

Act 1 opens with a conversation between Don Diego and his servant Simon. They are travelling incognito, in the context of the Madrilenian master stressing the need for protecting their disguise, and the servant's perplexity at this behavior. The two men converse at cross-purposes concerning plans for a marriage. Don Diego is praising Doña Francisca, of whom he has much news through her mother Doña Irene. He is especially happy that she has been raised far from the distractions and temptations of the world. Doña Francisca has been receiving her education at a convent in Guadalajara, 37 miles northeast of Madrid, where her aunt is a nun. As Don Diego discourses on the considerations of age and economic position that some might consider impediments to the planned marriage, Simon struggles with confused thoughts. Assuming that Don Diego is arranging the marriage of Doña Francisca to his nephew Don Carlos, the servant does not understand his master's scruples. As the conversation continues the spectator learns that Don Carlos is an accomplished mathematician, a decorated war hero, and a lieutenant colonel serving in the Spanish army. Suddenly the characters and spectators perceive the misunderstanding: Don Diego wants the young woman for himself, not for his nephew! Moreover, Don Diego, who is the guardian and financial supporter of his orphaned nephew, expresses displeasure with Don Carlos because, in his opinion, his nephew has recently been spending too much money and time first in Madrid and then in Guadalajara, rather than at his post in Zaragoza, 212 miles northeast of Madrid.

Que Sacrificio! by Francisco José de Goya, depicting a young woman forced to enter into an unwanted marriage with a rich, old man.

In the next scene Doña Francisca and her mother, Doña Irene, enter from the street where they have been visiting with friends and relations. Doña Irene, in her early sixties, thrice widowed and mother to one surviving child out of the 22 born to her, states that everyone considers the proposed match between Don Diego and her daughter a fine one, but Don Diego comments that it is much more important that Doña Francisca finds it so. In a long conversation in which her daughter is mainly mute, Doña Irene narrates the family history. The spectator learns that Doña Francisca is, in the rough English equivalent, a gentlewoman whose family has fallen on hard times, but that she has all the same received the best of educations while in Guadalajara in her aunt's convent. With this ground covered, the three parties leave the common area, but return momentarily.

Now on the scene are Doña Irene and Francisca's servant Rita and one Calamocha. The latter is Don Carlos's servant and has become friendly with Rita in Guadalajara during the courtship of Doña Francisca and the officer known to her as Don Felix (in reality Don Carlos). Calamocha and Don Carlos have just ridden all the way from Zaragoza, via Guadalajara, after receiving a letter from Doña Francisca telling the news of her arranged marriage to an elderly suitor and trip to Madrid. Rita explains her young mistress's hope: that the officer known to her as Don Felix can resolve the problem; in the meantime she is bound by filial obedience to follow her mother's commands. The act ends with Rita and Doña Francisca discussing these developments.

Act 2 occurs as night falls. The first scenes are between Doña Irene and her daughter. Before a passive, apparently docile Doña Francisca, the mother rehearses the economic benefits that will grace their lives through marriage to Don Diego. She also admonishes Francisca about the obedience a child owes to a parent, and stresses the need for her to act well with Don Diego. When he arrives on the scene, a serious conversation develops between him and Doña Irene, with Francisca exhibiting the passivity that characterizes her when with her elders. At issue is Don Diego's abiding concern that the young woman enter the marriage freely. Don Diego cogently explains the natural reasons why a young woman might not want to marry an older man. He specifically discounts obedience to a parent being sufficient grounds for marriage. He indicates also that it is precisely Doña Francisca's convent education and removal from the world that make it possible that she might willingly enter into a relationship in which friendship more than passion would prevail. Doña Irene concurs with this view and, by means of leading questions, has her daughter agree to it. When the older people leave the scene, Francisca is joined by Rita, who informs her of the arrival of Don Felix (Don Carlos), and then is joined by the young officer himself. Francisca explains the situation and her obligations to her mother. As a person raised in the same milieu, Don Carlos immediately grasps the situation and even grants the probable good intentions of Francisca's elderly suitor. Yet he thinks his wealthy uncle in Madrid, to where all are to go on the morrow, will sponsor his and Francisca's marriage to each other. When she returns to her room, Don Carlos and Calamocha recognize Don Diego's servant Simon coming into the common area in the growing darkness. For his part, Simon recognizes Don Felix as Don Carlos, Don Diego's nephew. While all three men are trying to understand one another's presence at the inn, Don Diego arrives. He is very displeased to find his nephew there and not at his post in Zaragoza. As they talk, a crestfallen Don Carlos realizes that his uncle is his rival for Doña Francisca. Becoming passive, following the same principle of filial obedience as she, Carlos unhesitatingly agrees to obey his uncle and return immediately to Zaragoza. In the next scene Simon, who knows nothing of the relationship between Francisca and Carlos, mentions to Doña Francisca what just happened between his master and the man she knows as Don Felix. Not yet realizing that Don Felix and Don Diego's nephew, Don Carlos, are the same person, Francisca is filled with confusion and a sense of betrayal: she only knows that the man in whom she has placed her hope and trust is abandoning her.

Act 3 extends the action into the dawn. Off-scene Don Carlos returns to the inn, performs in the street a short serenade to gain Francisca's attention, and then throws from horseback a letter up through the window of the common area. Unfortunately the serenade has also awakened Don Diego and Simon. In the confusion of the dark and several people emerging from their rooms and bumping into things, Don Diego, not Doña Francisca, recovers the letter meant for her. Hence Don Diego learns that Don Carlos passed himself off as Don Felix in Guadalajara, so Don Diego would not find out he was dawdling there, and of Don Carlos's resolve to make no further pretensions to Doña Francisca. Apprised of these new circumstances, Don Diego is filled with anger, disappointment, and sadness. But as his reason gains control over these emotions, he acknowledges that, as Simon perceived in Act 1, the natural and reasonable relationship is the one between the two young people, not the one he was both trying to conceal while in Alcalá and at the same

DOÑA IRENE AND MRS. BENNET

The emphasis placed on the economically-successful marriage of Francisca by Doña Irene is very similar in its urgency and motivation to that of Mrs. Bennet in Jane Austen's *Pride and Prejudice* (1813), written just a few years after Moratín's play. While both Doña Irene and Mrs. Bennet are portrayed as grasping, imperious ninnies by Moratín and Austen, and actors in stage and film versions reinforce those characterizations, any feminist consciousness must re-examine those women and their portrayals. Both Moratín and Austen, in the works in question, as well as in other writings by them, make it abundantly clear that survival for their middle-class female protagonists lies in marriage to a man of means. Failing such, their future will be like that of the poorly married, thrice-widowed Doña Irene: a constant battle with poverty and all its degradations and deprivations. Mrs. Bennet and, for that matter, the Bennet daughters' friend Charlotte Lucas, chastened by such battles in the lives of others, prudently, if not romantically, take measures to avoid that fate themselves. Like Doña Francisca and Don Carlos, Elizabeth and Jane in *Pride and Prejudice* are simply and exceptionally lucky in making love matches that are also either very or spectacularly successful in economic terms. Resolutions of this kind to the conflicts in the novel and in *The Maiden's Consent* demonstrate the distance between Moratín and Austen's sensibility and the realism and naturalism demonstrated in the less happy portrayals of relationships in subsequent nineteenth-century literary works.

time intending to consummate in Madrid. It is in this frame of mind that Don Diego has his nephew brought back to the inn, and learns from him the innocent history of how his love for Doña Francisca began at a social function in Guadalajara and mutually grew. Doña Francisca then is informed of who Don Felix really is, and, as Doña Irene sees her and her daughter's chance for security slipping from her grasp, Don Diego announces that he will bless and finance the union of Doña Francisca and his nephew. Having condemned the educational system that made Francisca so passive and obedient as to falsely say she wanted to marry him, Don Diego will find the consolation of his old age in the family Francisca and Carlos will form.

When reason reigns. In Act 3, Don Carlos, under questioning from his uncle, gives the history of his love for Doña Francisca. When Don Diego asks him if he understands that circumstances now require him to yield in this competition, Carlos agrees. Don Diego, sinking temporarily to the authoritarian level occupied by Doña Irene, tries to bolster his situation by citing the agreement of Doña Francisca's family to the match, the issue of the filial obedience she owes to her mother, and her own spoken consent to the older

suitor. Don Carlos responds by distinguishing between Doña Francisca's words and her heart:

> You'll hold your wedding whenever it suits you; she will always behave in a manner that befits her honor and her virtue; but I am the first, the only object of her love—I am now and I always will be. . . . She'll call you her husband; but if once or many times you surprise her, and see her beautiful eyes bathed in tears, she'll be shedding them for me. . . . Never ask her the reason for her moods of sadness . . . I, I will be the cause. . . . The sighs she'll try in vain to suppress will be loving messages addressed to an absent sweetheart.
>
> (Fernández de Moratín, *The Maiden's Consent*, pp. 95-96)

Don Diego grows enraged. But Don Carlos, to the surprise of his uncle, who expects an equally passionate response from him, moves to exit the common area and to demonstrate his own filial obedience by returning to Zaragoza. He also indicates that it will be a long time before his uncle again sees him. In answer to Don Diego's question, Why? Don Carlos speaks of rumors of war and indicates that he plans to repeat the heroics of his past, to be always the first officer to lead his men into the breech. This plan, which is tantamount to one of suicide, brings the horrified Don Diego back to reason and to acknowledging to himself the truth of his nephew's reasoning about Doña Francisca's disquietude if she were to marry him. Consequently Don Diego moves to resolve reasonably and happily the problems and conflicts of the play.

The scene indicates at least three lessons being taught by Moratín, the Enlightenment *afrancesado* and neoclassical dramatist bound by a dual obligation to please and to teach through his art. The first lesson concerns the question of socioeconomic class distinctions and practical wisdom. As happens in the best Spanish plays of contemporary manners by Tomás de Iriarte, Moratín's lesser-known dramatic predecessor and peer, it is the servants, specifically Simon in *The Maiden's Consent,* who immediately understand the path of conduct that reason recommends and that their masters either do not follow (in Iriarte) or follow only after a significant delay (in Moratín). Simon, it will be remembered, alerts both Don Diego and the audience from the first scene of *The Maiden's Consent* that his master's conduct goes against nature and therefore reason. But, as Don Carlos explains and the audience understands, the social system and economic realities grant to Don Diego the authority to be the arbiter of the conflict and to expect his judgments to be accepted. Nonetheless, from the viewpoint of the play, it is not reasonable for him to use his power to crush Francisca and his nephew. The specific moral here is that the gift of reason is not limited to those at the apex of the socioeconomic system, and that, if those who are at the apex fail to be reasonable, great harm must ensue.

There was a second, sociopolitical lesson, in times of democratic revolutions in America and France, and of the more or less moralizing allegories of France's La Fontaine, Britain's Jonathan Swift, and Spain's Félix María Samaniego. Don Carlos's warning to his uncle is also a threat. The rich and powerful of the Old Regime of absolute monarchy and hereditary nobility have the run of society, but the human heart—nature—will not allow them to enjoy the spoils that fall to them as their birthright if they trample the emotions and needs of their familial and social dependants. In this context it is especially revealing that the old Don Diego, a representation of the Spanish establishment, needs, during those bellicose times, the heroics of the young military men of Don Carlos's generation to protect his possessions and position. The question the play implicitly poses is: how long will the young and economically subjugated support and defend those above them if they will have to continue tolerating abuse and injustice?

The final lesson of *The Maiden's Consent* is, then, the final resolution taken by Don Diego. When he does succeed in controlling the inflamed passions of the threat posed to his own love by the Francisca-Carlos relationship, he is acting reasonably, in accord with the realities of biology and human experience. At the end of the play, Don Diego has one request: that the first-born child of the soon-to-be married young couple be figuratively his. Seeing this child in his mind's eye, Don Diego, who has become sublime in his self-denial, imagines: "And when I hold him in my arms, I'll be able to say: he owes his life to me, this innocent child; as long as his parents live, as long as they're happy, I'll have been the cause of it" (*Maiden's Consent,* p. 106). In this last scene of the play, Moratín is suggesting the widespread social and human benefits that will flow to all if those above regard and treat correctly those below.

Literary context and sources. *The Maiden's Consent* is Moratín's last dramatic work. Structured by the three unities of action, place, and time, the play revolves around the single question of who will marry Doña Francisca in one 24-hour period and at one location (the inn at Acalá). The play furthermore unfolds in a straightforward type of Spanish language. Though humorous, it is also a didactically oriented criticism of customs governing marriage and the education of young women. Altogether these components have led to its being considered the most perfect work of neoclassical drama informed by Enlightenment thought in Spain.

The theme of the unequal marriage between youth and age has a rich tradition. The precedents probably best known to Moratín included: Cervantes's exemplary novel *The Jealous Estremaduran*; several comedies by Molière, especially *The School for Wives*; and, Marivaux's *La Mère confident* (The Confident Mother) and *L'Ecole de mères* (The School for Mothers). Among Moratín's contemporaneous countrymen, Francisco Goya also took up the theme in, for example, his 1787 tapestry cartoon "The Wedding" and plates 2, 5, 14, 15 and 75 in *Los Caprichos* of 1799. Moratín also had direct experience in relation to unequal marriages. In the 1780s he loved and was loved by Sabina Conti y Bernascone, but her family, not seeing great prospects in the jeweler with literary ambitions, married her to a wealthy uncle twice her age. In the next two decades Moratín penned at least five plays, four being extant, about older, wealthy men wanting, with the blessing of society, to marry young, poor, or less well-to-do women. Generations after Moratín such important Spanish realist novelists as Pedro Antonio de Alarcón, Juan Valera, Benito Pérez Galdós, Leopoldo Alas, José Palacio Valdés, and Emilia Pardo Bazán continued to observe such relationships and transform them into significant elements of characterization and plot (see *Fortunata and Jacinta, La Regenta,* and *House of Ulloa,* also in WLAIT 5: *Spanish and Portuguese Literatures and Their Times*).

The difference between these realistic uses of the old man-young woman theme and Moratín's in *The Maiden's Consent* derives from his direct experience of the Enlightenment. Along with his friends Goya and Iriarte, Moratín was very familiar with and impressed by the graphic, moralizing representations of such distinguished English satirists as William Hogarth and James Gillray. He must also have become familiar, during his European travels of the 1790s, with Gotthold Ephraim Lessing's plays of the 1770s, which centered on the middle class, and with his theatrical parable of religious tolerance *Nathan the Wise*. Like all the writers named here, Moratín embraced the neoclassical aesthetic of the Enlightenment: *prodesse et delectare,* the creation of a pleasing drawing, painting, poem, or play to provide the moral lesson of reason conquering passion for the greatest societal and individual good. Just as Goya believed that "The Dream of Reason Produces Monsters" (plate 43 of *Los Caprichos*), Moratín focused his simple plot on Don Diego awakening from unreasonable reveries about the very young, healthy, attractive Doña Francisca unnaturally preferring to marry a man two generations older than she. In Act 2, as the enormity of the proposed marriage becomes more real to him, Don Diego, while conversing with the talkative Doña Irene and the reserved Doña Francisca, corrects Doña Irene's evaluation of the role of feelings in her daughter's decision making. He explains that "at her age the passions are livelier and more overruling than at our age, and while her reasoning is still imperfect and feeble, the impulses of the heart are all the more violent" (*Maiden's Consent,* p. 49). The play shows Don Diego coming to particular terms with this general principle of human nature. When Don Diego understands that his nephew and Francisca love each other

with the lively passion of youth, he, as an enlightened person must do three things: admit to himself that their love is the more natural and hence reasonable pattern in life; recognize that his age militates against his inspiring this kind of love; and desist in his pretensions to Francisca, yielding to the love between her and Carlos. He, in adopting these reasoned stances, rejects the domestic version of the absolutist, authoritarian hierarchical ordering of people and society maintained by the Roman Catholic Church in Spain. Don Diego's fight to prevent the dominance of his passions over his reason brings into focus the heart of the play, reflecting the prominence given to reason in Enlightenment thought. As a reasonable man, Don Diego must first understand the natural ages and relations of human life. Then he must consistently act with reason. When Don Diego succeeds in governing himself and then calmly surveys the situation, his solution to the problems and conflicts of the play is straightforward and positive for him and his nephew, as well as for Doña Francisca and her mother. Implicitly, but all the same very clearly rejected is the traditional version of the absolutist hierarchical order found in the received dictates of the Roman Catholic Church in the religious sphere, and of the monarchy and nobility in the civil order. These powerful creations of the medieval period have seen their day and must now yield, as the thought of the Enlightenment puts into practice the new insights gained from the study of nature and the reasoned analysis of human relations and institutions. From a broadly cultural viewpoint *The Maiden's Consent,* as well as Iriarte's plays of contemporary manners, constitutes a presentation and critique of vices and negative practices in Spanish society, and provides examples of the kind of reasoned conduct that would better that society.

Reception. Nearly two centuries after the premiere of *The Maiden's Consent,* it can be judged the single most influential play of the Spanish stage. The then-contemporary markers of its success included an unusually long run following its premiere; simultaneous productions of the play in other parts of Spain; and four printings of its text version in 1806. Despite the long War of Independence, Moratín's association with the hated Godoy, and his subsequent ostracism as an *afrancesado,* the force of Moratín's literary achievements became clear during the last years of the life of Ferdinand VII, when the Royal Academy of History published a four-volume edition

GODOY, MORATÍN, AND GOYA

While Manuel de Godoy is generally denigrated in Spanish history, his protection of such Enlightenment artists as Moratín and Goya reveal a certain positive dimension to him and the Bourbon system. From 1792 until 1808 the middle-class Moratín enjoyed a combination of government pensions and jobs that enabled him to pursue his education abroad and to continue his literary activity. In addition, Godoy's protection shielded Moratín from attacks on him by Spanish traditionalists, who saw dangerous social and religious criticism in *The Maiden's Consent*. Similarly, in 1799, when the anti-clerical satires included in *Los Caprichos* attracted the ire of the Inquisition, Godoy intervened to protect Goya. Then, in 1803, Godoy arranged for Charles IV, who in any case thought well of Goya, to buy out the numerous warehoused copies of *Los Caprichos*, lest Goya continue to be deprived of income from the edition.

(1830-31) of Moratín's theatrical and other works. All subsequent principal Spanish authors from Ramón de Mesonero Romanos and José María Larra through Benito Pérez Galdós praised *The Maiden's Consent* both as a satisfying night of theater and as a literary model to be followed. In 1857 Ventura de la Vega, who viewed himself as a disciple of Moratín and who is considered one of the principle Spanish dramatists of the nineteenth century, was responsible for the very public rehabilitation of Moratín; through de la Vega's efforts, Moratín's remains were returned to Madrid.

—Stephen Miller

For More Information

Aguilar Piñal, F[rancisco]. *Introducción al Siglo XVIII*. Vol. 25 of *Historia de la literatura española*. Ed. R[icardo] de la Fuente. Madrid: Ediciones Júcar, 1991.

Cook, John A. *Neo-Classic Drama in Spain*. Dallas: Southern Methodist University Press, 1959.

Dowling, John. *Leandro Fernández de Moratín*. New York: Twayne, 1971.

Fernández de Moratín, Leandro. *The Maiden's Consent*. Trans. Harriet de Onís. Great Neck, N.Y.: Barron's Educational Series, 1962.

Glendinning, Nigel. *The Eighteenth Century*. Vol. 4 of *A Literary History of Spain*. Ed. R. O. Jones. London: Ernest Benn, 1972.

Goya, Francisco. *Los Caprichos*. Ed. Philip Hofer. New York: Dover Publications, 1969.

Herr, Richard. *The Eighteenth Century Revolution in Spain*. Princeton: Princeton University Press, 1958.

Martín Gaite, Carmen. *Usos amorosos del dieciocho en España*. Madrid: Editorial Anagrama, 1987.

Tomlinson, Janis A. *Goya in the Twilight of Enlightenment*. New Haven: Yale University Press, 1992.

Marks of Identity

by
Juan Goytisolo

Juan Goytisolo was born January 5, 1931, to a bourgeois family in Barcelona. The infant Goytisolo became quickly acquainted with tragedy when his mother was killed by anti-Franco forces in a bombing raid during the Civil War (1936-39). Goytisolo came of age during Franco's rise to power and attended conservative Catholic schools, followed by the University of Barcelona and University of Madrid (1948-52). His literary career began with the publication of *Juegos de Manos* (The Young Assassins) in 1954, which earned him critical acclaim and a reputation as a voice of the "restless generation" (Jones, p. 235). An outspoken critic of the Franco dictatorship, Goytisolo believed writing should have social implications, and he used his novels to raise consciousness and challenge the status quo. He, however, grew increasingly frustrated by the repressive climate and extreme censorship in Spain, emigrating to Paris in 1957 to pursue his literary and journalism career with greater freedom. Goytisolo worked as a photographer for Agence France Presse and penned realist novels and politically oriented travelogues until he abandoned the realist style and began experimenting with form. *Marks of Identity* is the initial volume in his Mendiola Trilogy (the remaining two are *Count Julian,* 1974, and *Juan the Landless,* 1977). It is also his first novel to employ nontraditional literary styles and experiment with technique. A complex, introspective work, it won international praise both for its scope and content, daring to take on controversial issues such as the short-comings of anti-

> ## THE LITERARY WORK
>
> A novel set in Spain and France, recalling events from 1936 to 1963; published in Spanish as *Senas de Identidad* in 1966; in English in 1969.
>
> ## SYNOPSIS
>
> An experimental novel that traces the national, cultural, and individual development of Spain and a Spanish ex-patriot in the twentieth century.

Francoists and the "selling out" of Spain by the bourgeoisie. With *Marks of Identity* Goytisolo seeks to unmask his own as well as Spain's identity as both have developed since 1898, exploding myths and manifestos of the left and the right in the process.

Events in History at the Time of the Novel

Past glory, present disaster. The loss of Spain's remaining colonies (Cuba, Puerto Rico, and the Philippines) in 1898 after nearly four centuries of imperial rule gave rise to nationwide soul searching. The so-called "Disaster of 1898" was not a sudden nor an unforeseen calamity, for Spain's Golden Age had long past and the country had been in decline since the seventeenth century. But this final loss of power and prestige was

Juan Goytisolo

a blow to the nation's ego. "The loss of the remaining Spanish colonies happened just when the great European powers—among which Spaniards naturally considered themselves—were carving up the world, and their victories or defeats were interpreted in terms of racial and national superiority or inferiority" (Junco in Gies, p. 75). Spaniards felt they had been embarrassed, had "staged a pathetic show of incompetence in front of the whole world" and immediately set out to discern the causes, re-evaluate, and recreate their national identity (Junco in Gies, p. 75).

Politicians, writers, and thinkers of the Generation of 1898 searched for answers, trying to understand how Spain had gone from a world leader to an impoverished, defeated nation just as her European neighbors were on the rise. Spaniards revisited history—to the era of Ferdinand and Isabella (c. 1492) when Spain dominated Europe and was conquering the Americas—in an effort to restore Spain to her former glory. Many reasoned that Spain had lost her way; that she had been corrupted by foreign influences and kings, such as the Enlightenment, the Bourbons, and the Hapsburgs. They argued that in order to regain power and prestige Spain had to return to the successful fifteenth-century model: a strong centralized state with Catholicism as its moral and educational foundation. The regions that comprised modern Spain—Asturias, Galicia,

León, the Basque Province, Navarre, Aragon, Catalonia, Castile, Estramadura, Valencia, Murica, and Andalusia—maintained longstanding distinctions. Reformers asserted that Spain's fragmentation into regions that maintained separate customs was detrimental to national unity and that homogenization and emulating the model of Castile (the seat of Philip II's sixteenth-century empire and already a thriving urban center) would be the key to modernization. Contrary to what Goytisolo is arguing for in *Marks of Identity*, these men favored stasis rather than progress, maintained the need for social hierarchy, and feared democracy. Essentially elitist, many of the Generation of 1898 held the Golden Age Castilian imperialist as the ideal and not only discounted the contributions of the Moors, Jews, and Protestants but blamed them for Spain's decline. When Francisco Franco came to power nearly 40 years later, he would use the ideology of the Generation of 1898 to his advantage, to cement his power and further his own agenda.

Civil War. When the democratically elected Second Republic was attacked in a coup d'état in 1936, civil war erupted in Spain. In broad terms, it sprung from a power struggle over differing models of progress: democratization vs. centralization; creating a new Spanish identity vs. returning to the Golden Age imperial model. "Spaniards had come to conceive of national politics as a Manichean struggle between the 'true' Spain and the 'anti-Spain'; at stake was the identity of the nation itself, threatened less by external rivals than by the enemy within" (Boyd in Gies, p. 86; *Manichean* refers to a dualistic philosophy taught by Persian philosopher Manes). Nationalists (the land-owning elite, military, monarchists, and conservatives who wanted a centralized government) and Republicans (the lower, landless classes, workers, students, and intellectuals who wanted a republic) fought over the "two Spains" in a brutal, three-year conflict that tore the nation apart. At stake was land reform, regional autonomy, and representative government on the one hand and maintaining the social hierarchy, the feudal system, and State control on the other. Supporting the Republicans became a cause célèbre among the world's intellectuals and social activists, many of whom joined the Republicans in combat. But without aid from Europe or the United States as the Nationalists were receiving from Germany and Italy, the Republicans eventually lost the war and a new and even more brutal battle began.

GENERATION GAP

The Generacion del '98 (Generation of 1898) was a group of novelists, poets, essayists, and thinkers who, in light of the Spanish-American War defeat of that year, set out to define the essential qualities or "soul" of Spain in order to help plot the course for a better future. Named by José Martínez Ruiz (a.k.a. Azorín), the disparate group proclaimed a cultural rebirth for Spain after the defeat. They engaged in a common quest to solve Spain's problems, discover her "true" identity, and plot her next course, aiming in the process to shake Spaniards out of their apathy and restore national pride. In many ways, Goytisolo's novel seeks to do the same, or at least to relaunch a type of national soul-searching. But it argues for revolutionary, radical change, and, in direct opposition to the Generation of 1898, asserts that the identity of Spain needs to be broad and all-inclusive, taking into consideration all its multicultural, religious, and racial components. Part of a generation born amidst another national calamity, the Civil War, Goytisolo represents a later, mid-century generation, whose members distinguished themselves for "their reaction against social, political, religious, and moral conformity" (Jones, p. 28).

With the Nationalist victory in 1939, General Franco was swept into power and immediately established himself as Spain's absolute ruler. The question over Spain's future identity was answered definitively, and those who had or continued to oppose his viewpoint were imprisoned or executed. The total number of deaths that can be attributed to the war remains open to question. While the government spoke of one million deaths, recent estimates place the total closer to 500,000, by battle, bombing, assassination, and execution. Executions and political killings from 1939-43 have been estimated at 200,000, the peak prison population at 213,000 (Beevor, p. 266). From mid-January to early February 1939, a half million refugees fled to France; some 60,000 "failed to make the border in time and were rounded up by the Nationalists," the "gaunt, shivering masses" becoming subjects of postwar reprisals (Beevor, p. 250). In the novel, though Alvaro (like Goytisolo) is just a child during the war, he realizes that the "terrors and frights of the war" and its aftermath have deeply affected his life (Goytisolo, *Marks of Identity*, p. 43). Fear and violence rooted in this conflict continue to haunt him and the nation, to the extent that they have not only blighted Alvaro's (and Goytisolo's) personal existence but had also become part of the national identity.

The shaping of a national identity. In 1939 Franco proclaimed that he had been ordained by God to save Spain from atheists and communists (those fighting for the republic in the civil war) and that his war victory had confirmed it. Convinced that Spain's downfall had come as a result of emulating other Europeans and adopting ideas of the Enlightenment, he established a totalitarian dictatorship closed to outside influence. Franco enacted the Law of Political Responsibilities (1939, retroactive to 1934) and the Law for the Suppression of Masonry and Communism (1940) condemning to death or prison those whom he termed "bad Spaniards." He outlawed sedition, which included any anti-Christian or anti-Franco activity (including before and during the Civil War), and deemed that traditional Spanish identity was rooted in the Golden Age, Catholicism, and a hierarchical social order with one supreme authority: Franco.

To perpetuate his ideology and eliminate opposition, Franco created a climate of fear and repression. He divided the nation into the victors and the vanquished, rewarding the victors and severely repressing the vanquished. His regime imprisoned and executed Republicans and sympathizers, devastating, in particular, the intellectual community. The regime closed newspapers, censored the press, and persecuted all whom it considered threatening to the stability of the government, including teachers, artists, and politicians (particularly socialists, communists, and anarchists). By 1940, 270,714 anti-Francoists were political prisoners and those who were not jailed or executed either concealed their beliefs or went into exile abroad.

> Spain was thus deprived of many of her bravest and most capable sons, driven by defeat to foreign lands . . . the demographic loss due to the war and its consequences must be assessed at nearly 1,500,000 inhabitants; for a country with a population of 26,000,000 this meant a deep gash that bled it white.
>
> (Gallo, p. 70)

Media mind control. Franco used the Church, the media, and carefully selected fragments of history to legitimize his rule, further his objectives, and forge a national identity. He picked and chose the historical data he allowed to be taught, taking examples from the Golden Age of the conquistadores, Ferdinand and Isabella, the Counter-Reformation, and the Re-conquest (when Spain defeated the Moors) to prove his claims that Spain was successful when she rejected other European influences and forged her own path. He basically erased the entire nineteenth century from textbooks, as well as the Second Republic democracy, and insisted that Spain, like Sleeping Beauty, had been a sedated princess who was only awakened from her poisoned slumber when Franco came to her rescue in 1939. "The providential mission of the Nationalist 'Crusade' was to restore the spiritual and political unity of the imperial Golden Age and thereby rescue the nation from the humiliation and moral debasement to which it had been condemned by 'bad Spaniards' and their foreign allies" (Boyd in Gies, p. 94).

Franco used the Catholic Church structure and Christian concept of Original Sin to justify hierarchy within the social order and to warrant his dogged persecution of those who opposed his rule. For example, he insisted that atonement for past sins (such as fighting for the Republic) could be made only through obedience to authority. The Catholic maxim of "expiation through suffering" was used to condone the regime's use of anti-Francoists as unpaid laborers. Sacrifices had to be made for the betterment of the State, the Franco regime insisted, and "only those 'capable of loving the Fatherland, of working and struggling for it, of adding their grain of sand to the common effort' would be tolerated" (Graham and Labanyi, p. 176). Those who profited from the suffering and unpaid labor were the State and bourgeois business people whose industrial base was built on the backs of the poor and powerless masses. The complicity by the bourgeoisie

in Franco's national exploitation earns total condemnation from Goytisolo in the novel. He sees their profiting from un- and low-paid labor as the ultimate "anti-Spanish" act.

As in all dictatorships, censorship was a key ingredient to maintaining control. Franco's 1938 Press Law established the media to be "at the service of the state" and stated (ironically), "All Spaniards may express their ideas freely provided they do not contravene the fundamental principles of the state" (Graham and Labanyi, p. 209). In other words, citizens were free to agree with Franco and support his platforms. All written and artistic material was censored, from romance novels to restaurant menus, with an average 500 books per month passed through committees that eliminated anything that "offended Catholic dogma, morality, the Church, the regime, and its associates" (Graham and Labanyi, p. 209). Books were publicly burned and double versions of films were made: heavily censored for Spain, uncut for export (this to give false testimony to the outside world of Franco's support of the arts and tolerance of dissent). As evidenced in the novel, opposition voices were silenced and the Nationalist cry, "Death to Intelligence!" epitomized what Franco wanted: a sedate, unthinking, and obedient populace willing to conform to his notion of national identity (Graham and Labyani, p. 208).

Political and cultural autarky. The 1940s were known as the "years of hunger" in Spain for myriad reasons. First, there was drastic poverty and physical starvation due to the ravages of war, drought, and economic isolation from the rest of Europe and the United States. The system of autarky deemed that Spain be entirely self-sufficient—that is, pursue a policy of economic independence with trade and price protection for national industries. After World War II that policy was reinforced by the Western Allies who excluded Spain from the Marshall Plan and cut off all diplomatic and trade ties because of Franco's dictatorship and ties to the Axis powers. Thus Spain was deprived of all potential trading partners except in South America and forced to solely provide all daily essentials for her overwhelmingly rural, poor population, which the country could not.

On a second level, there was extreme cultural and intellectual deprivation during these years, as Franco re-painted history and attempted to "white-wash" the citizenry. Centuries of Moorish rule and Jewish presence were denied, as were any varying viewpoints, and, again, the Golden

FRANCO THE FILM STAR

In 1942 Franco formed the official film company, NO-DO, which made news reels and documentaries that ran at obligatory screenings in all the nation's cinemas. He personally appeared in 900 productions, typically touting his regime's tremendous achievements, i.e., opening factories, building cheap housing for the working class, or heralding his favorite professional soccer team, Real Madrid. When he finally allowed the topic of the civil war to be broached in 1959, it was depicted by NO-DO as *El camino de la paz* (The path to peace)—a film in which he insisted the war had been necessary to restore peace, order, and morality destroyed by the wanton chaos of the Second Republic (Graham and Labanyi, p. 202). Pure propaganda, NO-DO films and documentaries also showed segments of the outside world that served the regime's purposes. They depicted strikes in France and Britain, starvation in Russia and China, and routinely rallied around one theme: the evil of communism. NO-DO also produced films on the glory of the Crusades, women's sacred duty as wife and mother, the glorious defeat of the Moors by the great Catholic kings, and expulsion of the Jews. The movies reinforced Franco's chauvinistic and racist viewpoints and promoted his definition of the ideal Spaniard and the "true" character of the country. Goytisolo's novel is a direct attack on the NO-DO film monopoly and its forced definition of the Spanish people. Alvaro is making his own documentary on the reality of Spanish life—unearthing characteristics, events, and influences the regime would never acknowledge or allow—and the author himself is documenting the history and hypocrisy the regime would never tolerate to be publicized.

Age model was promoted as the only acceptable Spanish identity. The regime decreed that "Spanish national identity and purpose had crystallized in sixteenth-century Castile with the fusion of the 'Catholic-ideal' and the 'military monarchy'" (Gies, p. 93). Franco cleverly veiled his propaganda in popular songs and entertainment: "The reinforcement of national-patriotic values was . . . pursued via forms of mass commercial culture, such as musical comedies and popular song, which promoted the superiority and wholesomeness of all things Hispanic" (Graham and Labyani, p. 237). He made Castilian the official Spanish language, outlawing all regional dialects, such as Galician, Catalonian, and Basque, even though 25 percent of the population spoke these languages (Gies, p. 93). Franco's autocratic system sought to homogenize the country, rewarding those who played the "good Spaniard" (spoke Castilian Spanish and worked diligently for the regime) and severely punishing those who clung to regional customs, asked for better working conditions, or in any way questioned their role.

A great beneficiary of the system, the Church initially overwhelmingly endorsed Franco's policies. Officials considered Franco's campaign "an ideological war in defense of national culture and tradition" and condoned his brand of fascism as "the religion of religion" (Gies, p. 93). They were put in charge of education and "Catholic control of schooling and intellectual production was used to inculcate an exclusionary view of national history and identity that denied legitimacy to the entire national tradition of progressive thought" (Gies, p. 94). In sharp contrast to the regime's autocratic brainwashing, Goytisolo's novel is committed to investigating Spain's hidden history, culture, and identities, such as her African and Arab roots, in order to re-nourish culture-starved Spain. His novel is providing intellectual and cultural sustenance for a country that was denied such food for thought.

1950s Rapprochement. In the 1950s, a *rapprochement* occurred between Spain and the European and U.S. governments who had previously frozen relations with Franco. When the Western Alliance dissolved and the Korean and

Workers clean up the rubble from war-damaged
buildings in Madrid.

Cold wars ensued, Franco used his historic anti-communist stance to curry favor with his European neighbors, and with the United States in particular. Appealing to McCarthyites by campaigning under the slogan "Christians over Communists," Franco won global support to the extent that the United Nations voted to resume diplomatic relations with Spain. Two weeks later, on November 16, 1950, the United States granted a $625 million loan to Spain and laid plans to establish a U.S. military presence there. In 1952 UNESCO voted to include Spain in its ranks and in 1955 the United Nations followed suit. The major coup for Franco was a deal with the United States in 1953 to allow three American military air bases and one naval base in exchange for economic and military aid. Spain at once became "the sentry of the West" guarding against "Red encroachment in the heartland of Christian civilization" (Gies, p. 99).

With political acceptance came economic liberalization. Spain's economy was in trouble at the time, experiencing soaring inflation that diminished the value of wages, "which were as little as 35 percent of their pre-Civil War level" (Carr, p. 268). Though illegal, a rash of strikes spread through Spain. In 1957 Franco unhappily assembled some new economic advisors, technocrats who aimed to relax economic restric-

tions. To this end, the government invoked the Stabilization Plan of 1959, which eliminated price protections, and lifted import restrictions and limits on foreign investment. In short, the autarky was "freed up" and Spain's economy—and society—began to radically transform.

"Miraculous" change: 1959-63. Primarily agrarian into the 1950s, Spain urbanized and industrialized at a breakneck pace beginning in 1960. Dubbed the "Spanish miracle," the economic, social, and physical transformation of the country was astounding. Spain's Gross Domestic Product rose at 7.2 percent annually as 70 percent of the population moved to cities and earned their living in factories, offices, or in the service sector, leaving, by 1975, just 29 percent of the people to continue to farm. Wages rose to an average $2,246 per year from $300 and consumerism became the national pastime. Because the modernization was strictly economic, with little social liberalization, Spaniards exercised the only freedom and power they had: purchasing power. The so-called "culture of evasion" encouraged them to buy television sets and to attend (state-produced or heavily censored) films and soccer games (Boyd in Gies, p. 100).

Though certainly all Spaniards benefitted from the "economic miracle," clearly the top strata of society reaped the greatest rewards. Illiteracy was eradicated by 1970 (though this is highly suspect given that the ability to sign one's name was considered proof of literacy) but secondary school remained a privilege of the upper classes. Corruption remained rampant and poverty continued to grip the masses. "The gap was wide" between business ownership and workers and "the domination of private interests ensured that policy was geared to dividends rather than socioeconomic benefit and public service" (Graham, p. 81). By the 1960s the middle class climbed toward 20 percent of the population, but this percentage still lagged far behind the rest of Europe and there remained a vast disparity of wealth. Due in large part to unplanned growth and uncontrolled economic development "social contrasts were intensified—the rich grew richer, the poor poorer" as prices rose and the purchasing power of consumers declined to below what it had been during the Second Republic (Gallo, p. 207). Still, Franco touted his economic achievements, pointing to the "Spanish miracle" as proof that his totalitarian regime was good for Spain. He had brought "twenty-five years of peace and social order along the magnificent and broad path of industry and

COLLECTIVE BOURGEOISIE GUILT

It is no coincidence that the bulk of anti-Franco writers of the so-called Generation Mid-Century were born into the bourgeoisie. Goytisolo's parents were landowners and his mother was killed by Republicans. Some have suggested that the Generation's anti-Franco writing stems from a collective guilt, because as members of the Nationalists or at least of the middle/upper classes, their families were given special privileges once Franco came to power. While disease and misery plagued the bulk of the population, it was the anti-Francoist (former Republicans) who bore the brunt of the suffering. Imprisoned and forced into labor camps, the lower classes also received fewer rations. In the novel Alvaro recalls the "poor children reduced to eating a scanty ration of four ounces of daily bread while the fortunate possessors of a third-class ration card would get a pound" (*Marks*, p. 25). Though all were deprived, Alvaro feels guilty because he, like Goytisolo, was of the fortunate, bourgeois class favored by Franco with higher rations. The postwar atmosphere of extreme poverty and continued differentiation between classes (Nationalists and Republicans), as Alvaro's recollections demonstrate, prevented the wounds of the Civil War from healing, accentuated the disparity of wealth, and demoralized the lower classes who had to adjust not only to the loss of the war and their voice but also to that of any chance at social or economic reform. This continued division of the victors and the vanquished may have created in writers such as Goytisolo a "class guilt" that led to activism as adults (Graham and Labanyi, p. 246).

progress," said the official spokesman, an assertion the novel questions (*Marks*, p. 307).

Tourism. Ironically the man who previously declared "the breezes of foreign shores are corrupting Spain" began actively encouraging both tourism and foreign investment in the 1950s (Carr, p. 270). When Spain became "the sentinel of the West," European—and in particular American—culture began impacting Spanish society and the nation's identity (Preston, p. 594). The country was suddenly overrun by "Frenchmen, Swiss, Belgians, Dutchmen, Germans, Englishmen, Scandinavians who were coming to see bullfights; drink Manzanilla; lie in the sun like saurians; eat pizza and hot dogs in garish cafes" (*Marks*, p. 129). Critics of this trend, such as Goytisolo, accused the bourgeois and aspiring middle class of selling out to Franco and tourism; some even insisting that "the foreign presence was little short of colonial exploitation" (Graham, p. 69). By 1959, 14 million people per year were visiting Spain and bringing in nearly $1 billion annually. Goytisolo and others viewed the relationship between the tourism industry and Franco's regime as "incestuous" and fueled by greed—further evidence of the fading cultural

dignity of Spain. In the novel Alvaro daydreams about "a real Spain, about fellow countrymen raised to the dignity of people with a human existence maintained in the face of the voracious enemies of life" (*Marks*, p. 114). For Alvaro (and Goytisolo), Franco and capitalist exploitation are these enemies of life.

Franco's concept of tourism, while benefitting the tour operators and related businesses, tended to keep the poor impoverished, as their "rustic" lifestyle made for picturesque vignettes. "Life in Spain was easy for the tourist, hard for the Spaniard" and there was "much that the tourist never saw in Spain," such as police harassment of students, demonstrations and strikes, and the stark reality that Spain had one of the lowest standards of living in Europe. Far from the carefree paradise the travel brochures depicted, "living in Spain meant, for a Spaniard, working harder for less food" (Gallo, p. 252). As Goytisolo depicts in the novel, a little white-washing of the walls was done to cover the dirt but no substantive change, aid, or land reform was provided for the peasants. "The darkness hides the picturesque poverty of the place and the lights from the fair weakly illuminate a livid and disconsolate countryside,"

Alvaro observes (*Marks*, p. 111). Tourism may have been Spain's "best propaganda," allowing foreigners to "appreciate the social peace, the public order" but those living in Spain and those like Alvaro who looked below the surface knew better (*Marks*, p. 249).

Layers of exile. During the Civil War and its aftermath, anti-Francoists fled Spain en masse to avoid imprisonment and slaughter. Initially, the exiles—including socialists, communists, regional autonomists, and anarchists—fled to Paris, New York, and South America and established anti-Franco movements abroad. They were received by legitimate European and U.S. government representatives who were opposed to Franco and his fascist dictatorship. These officials bolstered hope for the ousting of Franco and the re-establishment of a Spanish republic. Particularly during WWII, anti-Francoists were convinced the Allies would militarily depose Franco as they had Hitler and Mussolini. But when that didn't occur, and then a decade later Franco gained world acceptance, many anti-Francoists abandoned the cause or returned to Spain.

The anti-Franco movement suffered not only from lack of western aid but from disunity. In the novel, for example, Alvaro finds division within the exile community in Paris—even a "geological strata" that ranks exiles in terms of tenure and importance (*Marks*, p. 204). Not only did exiles and expatriates have differing ideologies but they were of different generations and backgrounds. Those that left Spain in 1939 were revered as the true exiles while those that left, as both Alvaro and Goytisolo do, in the 1950s were seen as expatriates. In exile, this "generation gap" contributed to the stratification within the community and its lack of definitive leadership. It also stigmatised expatriates like Alvaro (and Goytisolo) who unlike the Civil War exiles chose to leave Spain and were thus considered traitors who broke ranks, "a know-it-all in mourning and a mendacious pimp" (*Marks*, p. 7).

The Novel in Focus

Plot summary. In a series of interior monologues, parodies of official jargon, extracts from police reports, political speeches, and free verse, Juan Goytisolo relates his character's search for identity after 10 years of self-imposed exile. It is 1963—the year marking Franco's so-called "25 years of peace." Alvaro Mendiola is returning to Barcelona for three days from Paris after a heart attack. Disillusioned and confronting his own mortality, the journalist is searching for clues in his homeland, and among his family and his friends; he is tracing events chosen and accidental to see how they have shaped his life, marked his identity.

The novel opens with fragmented quotes from newspaper articles citing the way Spanish society perceives him: "an affected little big shot from Paris" coming back to Spain to find fault with the nation (*Marks*, p. 6). He knows that he is largely disrespected by Spaniards because of his expatriation. Clearly ill at ease with his role, he is trying to figure out how both he and Spain have evolved to this point.

On a previous trip to Spain in 1958 Alvaro filmed a documentary on emigration. He now recalls the trip as other memories also begin to surface. Visiting his childhood home, he recalls his youth and the Civil War. The Republican defeat in the war and the disappearance of his father spring to mind as he tries to piece together details about his father's death that he has never known. He realizes that in 1939 everything changed—not only for the nation but inside himself—and that the end of the war marked the beginning of what became a life pattern for him of breaking and dispossession. "He knew that everything, including himself, was not definitive and lasting as he had confidently believed until then, having based his opinion on the continuity of his universe that had been reconstituted after the terrors and frights of the war, but that it was changeable, precarious, governed by a biological cycle against which will and virtue were powerless" (*Marks*, p. 43).

Alvaro is outside Barcelona with his wife, Dolores, when his friends Ricardo and Artigas stop by with two Danish girls. They drink and reminisce, and the foreign girls' presence prompts speculation on the effects of tourism on contemporary Spain. He ponders the tragedy of the "the people who died uselessly between 1936 and 1939" in order that Spain would become "a fertile and rich nursery of climbing vines and sausages" to feed the appetites of foreign tourists (*Marks*, p. 129). Clearly, he finds the development contemptible.

Alvaro recalls his university days, meeting his friends, becoming aware of class differences, and coming of age. He fondly recalls the influence of Professor Ayuso—a social reformer who strongly impacted Alvaro's life. He also recollects Ayuso's death. "The rebellion of your youth had returned intact and, as you thought about Professor

RAVAGES OF EXILE

Examining himself, Alvaro ponders, "Today's adult was hard to recognize, suspended as you were in an uncertain present, lacking a past as well as a future, with that desolate and intimate certainty of knowing that you had come back not because things had changed and your expatriation had had meaning, but because little by little you had exhausted your reserves of patience, and, in a word, you were afraid of dying" (*Marks*, p. 10). Like Alvaro and so many expatriates and exiles caught between two worlds—between hope and reality—Goytisolo tries to find meaning in his accident of birth and self-imposed exile. Through a "laughable decree of fate" he was born into the post-Civil War Spanish bourgeoisie—"a promiscuous and hollow order from which you tried to escape, confident, like so many others, of a regenerating change and cathartic which, because of mysterious imponderables, had not come about" (*Marks*, p. 7). The cathartic experience that Goytisolo's character asserts would have come from the ousting of Franco has not occurred, and like thousands of others, he is contemplating "the ravages of exile on the soul of the exiled" (Schraibman in Gunton, p. 189). This novel is an attempt to reconcile events past and present, chosen and accidental, so that he may come to terms with his identity, heal the wounds of exile, and discover the purpose of his life.

Ayuso's posthumous fate, you felt like vomiting" (*Marks*, p. 63). The thought of school leads to recollections of religious epithets he was made to memorize as a child, after which he muses:

> Such a strange religion, your people's, you were thinking, and so strange what it tells—a god cheated by the fiasco of his own creation to such a degree that he feels obliged to descend to earth to correct and fulfill it; with the well-known results: was it not another obvious failure? What moral lesson can be deduced from a rocambolesque fable like that?
>
> (*Marks*, p. 64)

He is questioning all that he learned as a child—religious edicts, the lives of saints, and child martyrs—wondering how they have impacted his development. Disparate thoughts come and go, one on the heels of the next, as Alvaro delves deeper and deeper into his quest for truth and answers, into all that has gone into the shaping of his identity.

As he ponders, Alvaro recalls learning to love Barcelona and his first introduction to a liberated woman, Ana, his friend's mother. The streetcar strike of 1951 then springs to mind, along with the disillusionment he felt at Ayuso's death, which leads him to consider his father's death in La Mancha by anti-Franco forces. He envisions the scene and romanticizes the circumstances of his father's imprisonment and execution, sad that

they will never meet again and that he will never know what actually happened.

Next, the annual bull running that he films in 1958 and the violence of the La Graya peasant uprising before the civil war in 1936 merge—both images of struggle and brutality; of slow torturous death. "Violence engenders new violence," he realizes, "brutal images cross" (*Marks*, p. 123). More seemingly disparate yet equally brutal images cross, as he compares the "picturesque poverty" of Franco's New Spain tourism and the tragedy of the Civil War. This leads him to daydream about what would have happened if the Republicans had won in 1939. He passes from dreams to memories to wishes in an effort to make sense of it all, unsure what is fact and what is fiction: "You were still unable to reconstruct the incidents and imagine the situations, dive into the past and emerge in the present, pass from evocation to conjecture, shuffle the real in with what had been dreamed" (*Marks*, p. 91).

The next major section focuses on his friend Antonio's arrest. Alvaro feels guilty because he fears he abandoned his friends and the cause when he went into self-imposed exile while they stayed behind, continued to protest against Franco, and suffered arrest and imprisonment. He had a romantic life in Paris, fell in love, traveled the world, and feels he did little to bring about change in Spain. "With your friends caught up in the turmoil of politics, what were you doing?" he asks himself (*Marks*, p. 175).

Goytisolo illustrates the extreme police state Spain has become by relating the personal history of Alvaro's friend and fellow reformer, Antonio. Antonio discusses his jail-within-jail status living as a marked man in Franco's Spain, being constantly watched and monitored—"a free man in that vast and extensive prison" (*Marks*, p. 194). We see that this is not paranoia, as the proof of surveillance is documented in the police reports that Goytisolo intersperses within Antonio's narrative. Further, he notes that not only are the police watching but that the citizens themselves "had become changed into a grim and sleepy country of thirty-odd million non-uniformed police" (*Marks,* p. 190).

Alvaro next recalls his relationship with other exiles in Paris and the strata of that society-within-a-society. He conjures Madame Berger's café, where they congregated, and mocks the society they formed and magazines they planned but never published. He notes that Paris served as "a rock against which the successive waves of youthful Iberian enthusiasm broke and died" and realizes that in that sobering setting "he had lost his youth forever" (*Marks*, p. 215). He recalls meeting Dolores, their courtship over the years, her abortion (which symbolically coincided with the virtual break-up of the anti-Francoists at a conference in Geneva), and a brief homosexual affair. Though ambiguous, the affair harks back to an earlier passage where he alludes to being in love with a young man during his youth. Here Alvaro is delving into his personal life, trying to uncover his sexual identity as he begins to realize that his marriage is over.

The novel flips back and forth between events in Spain and France, indicating Alvaro's undefined role as a man caught between two worlds. Leafing through an old atlas, Alvaro recalls the aspirations of his youth and how at first his exile enabled his dreams to come to fruition. Outside Spain he was able to freely express himself—professionally, sexually, socially. Now, back in Spain, he tries to identify with the country he was born in but can't—"the city you were looking at, was it yours" he wonders (*Marks*, p. 338). He walks and searches—even quotes the tourist pamphlets—but he no longer recognizes his homeland:

> everything has been futile
> oh my country
> my birth among yours and the deep love that
> without your asking

> for years I have obstinately offered you
> let us part like good friends while there is still
> time

> (*Marks*, p. 350)

At 32 Alvaro is born again, "with no marks of identity," but remains unsure why events have occurred as they have in his life. He strives to uncover his identity from his personal history, his native country and adopted home, his family, friendships, and sexual relationships, but finds no marks there. He questions the purpose of his self-imposed exile, and, hence, the purpose of his life to this point. "Perhaps someone will understand later," he closes, "what order you tried to resist and what your crime was" (*Marks*, p. 352).

Identity of an expatriate. In the novel Alvaro seeks to define himself through his accident of birth as well as through the choices he has made. Born during the Civil War and raised under the repressive Franco regime, he left Spain to "bear Parisian witness to aspects of Spanish life that might serve to *épater le bourgeois*" (*Marks*, p. 5). But he feels he's failed in that quest and is experiencing a sense of both loss and guilt at having become an expatriate. Alvaro raises the question that so many of his generation faced: what can be the modern Spanish identity for those who rebel against the regime and, moreover, what can be the identity of an expatriate?

Full of optimism and firm in his convictions, Alvaro left Spain to change it from without. He went to Paris, joined the exile community, and embarked on ambitious projects designed to publicize "the truth" about Franco and oust his regime. But, as so many experienced, his projects either never came to fruition or affected no change. He listened to pseudo-intellectuals, one after the other, drone on about aiding the Spanish rebels as they sipped wine in cafés and did nothing; he attended conferences and meetings of exiles that systematically ended in disputes over leadership and ideologies; he belonged to the editorial board of several magazines "whose essential characteristic consisted in never having been published" (*Marks*, pp. 214-15). Out of these experiences, skepticism crept in and "as the roots of childhood and the land were broken, Alvaro could feel the forming on his skin of a scaly crust: the feeling of the uselessness of his exile and, simultaneously, the impossibility of his return" (*Marks*, p. 215). Both through the accident of his birth and the choices he made, Alvaro became a man with no identity—unfulfilled in his goals abroad and at the same time unable to resume life as he had known it before.

Though he realizes he cannot regain his lost innocence, Alvaro returns to Spain to come to terms with his life:

> Your efforts at reconstruction and synthesis had run up against a serious obstacle. Thanks to the documents and proofs stored away in folders, you were able to dust off in your memory happenings and incidents that in the past you might have considered lost and which . . . were able to shed light not only on your own biography, but also on certain obscure and revealing facets of life in Spain. . . . Your own adventures and those of your country had taken divergent directions: you went one way . . . your country and that group of friends who were persevering in their noble efforts to change it, paying with their persons the cost that from indifference or cowardice you had refused to pay, coming to their maturity at the price of indispensable mistakes, they were adults, with the concise tempering you did not have. . . . With an empty memory after ten years of exile, how could you reconstruct that lost unity without doing it mischief?
>
> (Marks, p. 133)

Alvaro desperately wants to reconnect on some level but knows that it is too late. Feeling the guilt of the expatriate, he fears that he was a coward for leaving, not a rebel as he had initially thought. The newspapers call him arrogant and question why he is compelled to paint a bad picture of his homeland and countrymen. Their reaction makes him question the worth even of his documentary (which he believed in); perhaps it served no purpose, or worse yet, offended those to whom he was appealing through it. This only adds to his sense of disillusionment.

In short, Alvaro is somewhat ashamed that he chose freedom while his friends stayed in Spain and fought the regime from within. They sacrificed themselves for the greater good while he traveled the world, pursuing his dream. But, in fact, what did they accomplish? Nothing changed and they are still living "in the middle of a vast and extensive prison" (Marks, p. 194). In essence, Marks of Identity accomplishes what Alvaro and his friends want to achieve: it raises awareness about what happened to the members of his generation, showing there were no optimal choices, none that were even good. There was only loss. Alvaro's loss of family, friends, country, and, more abstractly, identity, reflect the ravages and cost of rebellion and exile during his era. Though Alvaro meets up with Dolores, a fellow expatriate, and they cling together, each remains "an amputated branch of the native trunk, a plant growing in the air, expelled like so many others, now and always, by the jealous guardians of your century-old heritage" (Marks, p. 283). Alvaro declares to Dolores, "I was born with you. . . . You're my past. My marks of identity are false" (Marks, p. 279). Yet, Dolores is also rootless and ultimately cannot be the sole reference point from which Alvaro can define himself.

While Alvaro's self-imposed exile has left him rootless, his friends' rebellious activities have also severed their ties to mainstream society. They are under constant surveillance, to the point of being periodically jailed. They have no freedom. Their experiences are something Alvaro can only imagine and piece together from reports; there is now a permanent division between them, yet another reality ravaging Alvaro's soul. Comparing his activities to those of his friends, he realizes that neither has accomplished anything. His own exile has to this point accomplished nothing, yet he feels no compunction to return to Spain or rejoin his compatriots, even if he could. Alvaro emerges a man with no marks of identity—a homeless expatriate guilty, he feels, of a nameless crime for an unknown reason. His sense of futility and loss is the blame the novel lays on a regime and society that allowed—even forced—a generation to deny themselves, whether they stayed or left.

Sources and literary context. Goytisolo based Marks of Identity on personal experience and historical facts. He uses the real incidents of the Civil War and its aftermath, the tramway strike of 1951, student uprisings, and his adolescence in Barcelona, mixing the events with fictional characters based on himself and his friends who were part of the mid-twentieth-century generation of Spanish writers and activists. He incorporates into the novel his personal experience of exile, as well as his travels in Europe, Africa, and Cuba. Like Alvaro, Goytisolo took refuge in Paris, worked for Agence France Presse, and traveled the world. But Goytisolo left Spain in 1957 and Alvaro in 1952 and, unlike Goytisolo, Alvaro returns in 1963 to mock Franco's so-called, self-proclaimed "25 Years of Peace."

Marks of Identity has been called Goytisolo's "most personal novel" in respect to its emphasis on the police state of Franco's Spain and its scathing comments on the tourism industry and Western capitulation to Franco in the 1950s (Jones, p. 235). He likewise derides both the Generation of 1898 and contemporary reformers, both in Spain and abroad, for their failure to forge a coalition to defeat Franco or alter Spanish society. Also woven into the novel is his personal struggle with sexual identity as well as the death of a parent during the Civil War. Finally, Alvaro and Goytisolo share a similar Catholic and Barcelona education and their role as "that strange species of writer claimed by none and alien and hostile to groups and categories" (Jones, p. 235).

Reception. Some critics originally panned *Marks of Identity,* accusing the novel of having an imbalance between its themes and experience, and of confusing fact with fiction. It was also criticized for "imprecise use of language, replete with errors" which the author acknowledged resulted from excessive concern with "vital experiences" rather than creating a "truly harmonious work of fiction" (R. Schwartz in Gunton, p. 181).

The bulk of the literary community, however, acclaimed the novel for its controversial themes as well as experimental style. Goytisolo was praised in particular for his "courageous" denunciations of "anti-Franco émigrés, their empty talk, petty intrigues and political inefficiency" as well as for his willingness to take on such taboo subjects as homosexuality and the moral decay of Spanish society (R. Schwartz in Gunton, p. 181; K. Schwartz in Gunton, p. 182).

Upon the novel's publication, Goytisolo became a leading voice of his generation. Along with Luis Martín-Santos and Juan Benet, he was credited with creating a "new novel" and re-ordering "the full-length narrative, often destroying former models" in the process (Brown, p. 18). The novel is widely considered an example of "a startlingly new kind of Realism" with a political edge reminiscent of James Joyce (Gunton, p. 181). Joseph Schraibman, writing for *World Literature Today,* added, "There is little doubt that this [novel's] attempted dialogue has enriched the cultural background of younger Spaniards (and others)" (Schraibman in Gunton, pp. 189, 181).

Marks of Identity earned Goytisolo renown as a "pitiless satirist" and an outspoken critic of "the injustice, inequality or rigidity that exist[ed] in society" under Franco (Jones, p. 235, Brown, p. 16). It is considered a milestone in Spanish literature, a "thrilling, ironic, trenchantly pessimistic, brilliant novel" that has helped cement Goytisolo's status as "the best Spanish novelist of his generation" (Gunton, p. 181).

—Diane Renée

For More Information

Beevor, Antony. *The Spanish Civil War.* New York: Peter Bedrick, 1982.

Brown, Joan Lippman. *Secrets From The Back Room: The Fiction of Carmen Martín Gaite.* Mississippi: University of Mississippi, 1987.

Carr, Raymond, ed. *Spain: A History.* Oxford: Oxford University Press, 2000.

Gallo, Max. *Spain Under Franco.* New York: Dutton, 1969.

Gies, David T. *Modern Spanish Culture.* Cambridge: Cambridge University Press, 1999.

Gilmour, David. *The Transformation of Spain.* New York: Quarter Books, 1985.

Goytisolo, Juan. *Marks of Identity.* London: Serpent's Tail, 1990.

Graham, Helen, and Jo Labanyi, eds. *Spanish Cultural Studies.* Oxford: Oxford University Press, 1995.

Graham, Robert. *Spain: A Nation Comes of Age.* New York: St. Martin's Press, 1984.

Gunton, Susan, ed. *Contemporary Literary Criticism.* Vol. 23. Detroit: Gale, 1983.

Jones, Daniel, ed. *Contemporary Authors. New Revision Series.* Vol. 61. Detroit: Gale, 1998.

McKendrick, Melveena. *Horizon History of Spain.* New York: American Heritage, 1972.

Preston, Paul. *Franco.* New York: Basic, 1994.

Meditations on Quixote

by
José Ortega y Gasset

hilosopher, journalist, critic, and educator, José Ortega y Gasset (1883-1955) distinguished himself as one of the leading thinkers in early-twentieth-century Spain. Born in Madrid to two influential publishing families, he was educated in Spain and in Germany, where he pursued studies in philology and philosophy in Leipzig, Berlin, and Marburg. From 1910 to 1936 Ortega served as a professor of metaphysics at the University of Madrid, then went into voluntary exile before the outbreak of the Spanish Civil War (1936-39). He wrote prolifically, founding several journals, most notably *Revista de Occidente* (1923-36; Review of the West), which set out to introduce the best of current culture into Spain. Published nine years before his death, his *Obras completas* (1946; Complete Works) comprise 12 volumes of over 500 pages each. Of all his works, the one to reach the widest audience was his controversial *La rebelión de las masas* (1929; The Revolt of the Masses, 1932), a critique of moral and mental mediocrity in contemporary Europe. Using the method of a philosophical movement of the era, phenomenology, the book analyzes the decline of moral and mental meritocracy in Europe. Ortega had drawn earlier on this same philosophy to write *Meditations on Quixote*, his first major work. Published when Spain was at a cultural crossroads, the essays in this slender volume use phenomenology to explore Spanish identity.

> ## THE LITERARY WORK
>
> A two-part collection of essays set in Spain circa 1914; published in Spanish (as *Meditaciones del Quijote*) in 1914, in English in 1961.
>
> ## SYNOPSIS
>
> To bring Spain up to the height of its times, the essays argue that its idealistic, impressionistic worldview needs to be combined with a focus on the rational. They argue too that Cervantes's writing contains the key to Spain's problems, going on to show what makes his novel *Don Quixote* great.

Events in History at the Time of the Essays

Restoration and illusion. Early-twentieth-century Spain suffered an identity crisis that some say had been festering for 26 years, ever since the Restoration of the monarchy to the Spanish throne in 1874 (Orringer, "Redefining the Spanish Silver Age," p. 319). In general the nineteenth century had been immensely trying in Spain. The beginning of the century found the Spanish busily clinging to remnants of their own country as Napoleon's French army invaded and took charge of their land. Spain subsequently waged a successful war of independence (1808-13), then concerned itself with decades of political infighting and experimentation that led to

José Ortega y Gasset

Meditations on Quixote

the main political parties that had earlier fomented unrest and civil war—alternated peacefully in power, regulating affairs through *caciquismo*. Elections proceeded apace, calmly, or so it seemed on the surface; they in fact operated on a foundation of deep-seated corruption. Peaceful elections were crookedly fixed on a local level by party bosses, the *caciques*. Under their direction, votes, for example, were cast by nonexistent bodies, and corpses would emerge from their graves to vote.

The architect of the Restoration and the author of the Constitution of 1876 was the Conservative leader Antonio Cánovas. In *Meditations on Quixote* Ortega attacks Cánovas and the illusion that everything was functioning well in Spain. He suggests a link between the Restoration's cultural shallowness and a general blindness to the profound nature of Cervantes's novel. On the contrary, Ortega argues, during the Restoration Spanish culture had lost touch with its Golden Age masterpiece, **Don Quixote** (also in *WLAIT 5: Spanish and Portuguese Literatures and Their Times*).

> There has been a time in Spanish history when people refused to recognize the depth of *Don Quixote*. This period is known by the name of the Restoration. During that time the heart of Spain slowed down to the lowest number of beats per minute.
>
> (Ortega y Gasset, *Meditations on Quixote*, p. 70)

Ortega goes on to quote several paragraphs from a famous lecture he gave in 1914 entitled *Vieja y nueva política*, Old and New Politics. In this lecture, he sharply contrasts political and cultural figures of the Golden Age with those from the Restoration, condemning the latter as a mere "parade of phantoms" and Cánovas himself as "the impresario of that phantasmagoria" (*Meditations*, p. 71). Ortega sought in this lecture to gather those intellectuals devoted to reforming Spain into a new political party, the League of Political Education. Among those he hoped to attract were members of the Generation of 1898.

The Generation of 1898. Spain lost the last vestiges of empire after suffering a humiliating defeat by the United States in the brief Spanish-American War. It was no longer possible for even the most avid imperialists to maintain the illusion. Fighting had lasted for only a few months in 1898, but the decisive defeat galvanized the intellectual community and revealed the weakness of Spanish arms. The Treaty of Paris, which formally ended the war, stripped Spain of its final colonies, over which the

the toppling of its Bourbon monarch, the initiation of democratic government in the form of the First Republic, and then a restoration of the Bourbon monarchy with two houses of Parliament in imitation of the British system. In all the turmoil, Spain lost its imperial grip. One by one, its colonies in the Americas and elsewhere proclaimed independence, until by the last quarter of the nineteenth century, only Cuba, Puerto Rico, Guam, and the Philippine Islands remained under Spanish control. Determined to retain these vestiges of empire, Spain harshly repressed independence movements in both Cuba and the Philippines.

Though its empire had dwindled drastically, Spain continued to conceive of itself as a major world power. The illusion was kept in place by an orderly but corrupt political system—*caciquismo*—which replaced the chaotic factionalism that led to the removal of the monarch (Isabel II) by a military junta in 1868. The restoration of a monarch (Alfonso XII) in 1874 ushered in an era of peace, and in 1876 a new constitution proclaimed Spain a constitutional monarchy along British lines. The so-called constitutional monarchy belied reality, however. Beneath the constitutional veneer, for two decades, the Liberals and the Conservatives—

contest had arisen and where the fighting had largely taken place. In addition to marking the emergence of the United States as a world power and illustrating the decayed state of Spain's military, the war left Spain with the self-image of a weak and backward nation.

Even before the war, a number of Spanish intellectuals had begun opposing the corruption, artificiality, and political repression inherent in the *caciquismo* system. Led by the reforming politician Joaquín Costa, they called for the *regeneración,* or regeneration, of Spanish society. The regenerationists, as they were dubbed, promoted a rational approach to solving Spain's problems (chiefly widespread poverty and poor education). The largely political, rationalistic approach of these regenerationists influenced a new movement arising after the catastrophic events of 1898. Made up of writers and artists and encompassing diverse agendas rather than a cohesive program, this new movement became known as the Generation of 1898. Though its highly individual members shared some of the regenerationist goals, this 1898 group had more broadly cultural concerns, and many of its members questioned the usefulness of employing only rationalism to solve all of Spain's problems. Ortega, though much younger, identifies himself as part of this so-called Generation of 1898 at the start of *Meditations on Quixote.*

Some of the Generation of 1898's leading thinkers propounded ideas that bordered on the mystical. For example, the literary critic Azorín (the pseudonym of José Martínez Ruiz) focused on what he called the Spanish soul. A friend of Ortega's, Azorín was in fact one of the first to call the loose association of writers the Generation of 1898; later (1923-36) he contributed to Ortega's journal *Revista de Occidente* and Ortega mentions him by name in the *Meditations.* Another friend of Ortega's, Ramiro de Maeztu, a journalist and essayist, couched his examination of Spanish identity in terms of *raza,* or "race," a term that appears prominently in early editions of the *Meditations* as well. A third leading figure in the Generation of 1898 was Miguel de Unamuno, a philosopher and novelist some 20 years older than Ortega whose ideas strongly influenced the younger man's (see **Mist,** also in *WLAIT 5: Spanish and Portuguese Literatures and Their Times*). Unamuno stressed the conflict between faith and reason in thoughts about human existence. His philosophy led to Ortega's concept of *razón vital,* or vital reason, an idea elaborated in later writings but foreshadowed in *Meditations.* More

directly, Unamuno published works in 1905 (*The Life of Our Lord Don Quixote*) and 1913 (*The Tragic Sense of Life*) to which *The Mediations on Quixote* can be viewed as a response.

Early-twentieth-century search for Spanish identity. "I am myself plus my circumstance," writes Ortega in one of his most oft-quoted lines (*Meditations,* p. 45). The key circumstance in Ortega's time was the national soul-searching that the older and younger generations of Spanish intellectuals were undergoing, in hopes of reforming their country. These writers turned to the Spanish Middle Ages and to the Golden Age (1550-1650) in pursuit of the origins of the Spanish national character. As noted Unamuno turned to the Golden Age's **Don Quixote** (also in *WLAIT 5: Spanish and Portuguese Literatures and Their Times*). Continuing the discussion, he followed his *The Life of Our Lord Don Quixote* (1905) with another key text, *The Tragic Sense of Life* (1913), both of which preceded Ortega's essays. *Don Quixote,* argues Unamuno, is one of the finest works ever produced by Spain, and its hero's best claim to fame is his quest for personal immortality. Early-twentieth-century Spain, continues Unamuno, should follow suit; like Don Quixote, it should take up the idealistic standard and attempt to preach the pursuit of immortality to the rest of the world, putting its energy into that which defies or goes beyond reason. Unamuno goes on to prescribe the means for achieving immortality—creative endeavors and salvation. His views, it should be noted, reflect his own inner struggle between faith, which told him death was followed by salvation, and his reason, which said it was followed by nothingness.

In any case, Unamuno's advice was too vague for Ortega. The junior philosopher, younger than Unamuno by 20 years, skeptical about his own religious beliefs and eager to make a name for himself, countered Unamuno's argument about the significance of Don Quixote for turn-of-the-twentieth-century Spain. *Meditations on Quixote,* his counterargument, was inspired by personal as well as altruistic reasons. Ortega hoped not only to bring Unamuno over to his way of thinking but also to induce Unamuno to join his new political party, the League for Political Education. How did Ortega's view differ? Spain, he said, needs to imitate not the hero Quixote, but the author Cervantes, whose novel integrates idealism (the "knight" Don Quixote) with realism (his practical-minded "squire" Sancho Panza).

Unamuno was not the only intellectual whose allegiance Ortega sought. He tried especially to enlist other young men who belonged to his own 20-to-30-year-old age group, spelling out a political program for them in newspaper articles and speeches between 1907 and 1914. The first step was to identify the status quo in Spain as faulty; the second step, to reform Spain, to take action. As Ortega saw it, the older generation had failed to modernize Spain to the degree typical of England, France, and Germany. The Spanish were still woefully, painfully behind the times. His own generation needed to remedy the failure, but how? Not, thought Ortega, through Unamuno's prescription of preaching religious salvation, but through politics, which to Ortega meant education of the masses. The most educated strata of society needs to transmit to the masses ideals of "liberty, social justice, competence, and Europeanization" (Wohl, p. 130); it had to sidestep the established government and go directly to the villages to sow seeds of culture, technology, and social cooperation among the people. To this end, Ortega helped found a reform political party in 1913—the League for Political Education. Dedicated to social transformation, it was a liberal, left-of-center group that bore no connection to the established Liberal party, which to the new group's mind, was too consumed with individual interests. Ortega's group had every intention of bringing about social change without a military revolution.

> Where there was shouting, Ortega always insisted, there could not be science; and science, or rational discourse was and always remained for Ortega the central aim. "More light, more light," he cried with Goethe, against those, like Unamuno, who felt drawn toward murky spiritual depths.
>
> (Wohl, p. 134)

That his audience deemed his message important is signified by their regard for Ortega. By early 1914, after a half dozen years of speech-making and article writing, he had to some degree realized his ambition. Men of his own age were acknowledging him as their political and intellectual leader.

Unamuno's reception of Ortega was another story. In attempting to win his allegiance, Ortega maintained that they were not really at odds. Ortega reminded the older intellectual that, although presently focused on Don Quixote's idealism, years ago Unamuno himself had advocated combining idealism with attention to material reality (in a book of essays called *En torno al casticismo* [Concerning Racial Purity]). But, in this instance, Ortega's persuasive powers were used to little effect; Unamuno never went back to his earlier view.

In the interest of modernizing Spain—phenomenology. Ortega struck up friendships with many of the Generation of 1898's leading writers through his family's newspaper *El Imparcial*, which his father edited and which served as a major forum throughout the 1890s for criticism of the Restoration establishment. It was through his father's newspaper that Ortega met Unamuno, Maeztu, Azorín, and many others, including novelist Pío Baroja (mentioned affectionately in the *Meditations*) and poet Antonio Machado (see **The Quest** and **Fields of Castile,** also in WLAIT 5: *Spanish and Portuguese Literatures and Their Times*).

These disparate writers shared the desire to expose Spanish culture to recent European intellectual developments, from which, they felt, the Restoration had isolated it. Ortega became well acquainted with some of these developments when he received a government grant to study in Germany after earning his doctorate in philosophy in Madrid. Beginning in 1905, on and off for nearly a decade, Ortega pursued his studies at distinguished universities in Germany. His work exposed him to the latest ideas in philosophy, including the school of thought called phenomenology, recently founded by the German philosopher Edmund Husserl and others. Phenomenology would gain wide recognition in 1913, when Ortega was back in Spain.

Taking its name from the Greek word *phainomenon* or appearance, phenomenology represented a new way of studying existence. The philosophy attempts to apply rigorous scientific methods to philosophical statements about reality, while at the same time stressing the importance of intuition, from direct observation, in perceiving an object's essence. To analyze experience, taught phenomenology, one ought to leave out of consideration any prejudgments in order to arrive at universal truths. These universal truths encompass the experience being analyzed. The next step is to subtract everything that has to do with this experience but does not define it—everything unessential. After the subtraction process is complete, one has the essence of the experience and needs to describe it in all its aspects.

The question "What is a novel?" is a case in point. After one arrives at the universal truth that it is a literary genre, one subtracts all that does not define it—the epic, lyric poetry, tragedy, comedy. The subtraction continues until one arrives at the essence—a novel is a literary genre

DON QUIXOTE AND SPANISH IDENTITY

~

Almost since its publication in the early seventeenth century, Miguel de Cervantes's groundbreaking novel has been crucial to Spanish identity in two ways. On one level, the novel's hero depicts qualities considered characteristically Spanish by intellectuals like Unamuno:

- A heroic refusal to accept the limitations of everyday reality and mundane existence

- Fighting for a noble cause against overwhelming odds

- Privileging altruism and idealism (the character of Don Quixote) over materialism and realism (Sancho Panza)

On a broader scale, the novel has been a source of national pride. Spaniards have prized its incalculable impact on European culture, pointing to its international reputation as the first and most highly regarded modern novel, the first novel whose central characters change as a result of their environment (Don Quixote becomes more like the practical-minded Sancho Panza by the end; Sancho Panza, more like the idealistic Quixote). Europeans would continue to credit the novel with spawning the literary genre that rose to dominate European letters in the eighteenth century and thereafter. The novel became an object of intense contemplation in the atmosphere of defeat in Spain after its loss of the Spanish-American War of 1898. Measuring their decline against one of their greatest achievements, Spaniards struggled to understand the descent. They looked not only at Don Quixote's idealism, but also at the fumbling nature of his exploits. While continuing to regard the novel itself as a pinnacle achievement, they questioned the implications of an equation that meant viewing his defeats and naïvete as defining elements of Spanish identity.

portraying the struggle between everyday material reality and the ideal. This essence then needs to be described in all its aspects, meaning here in its stylistic aspects. But the key is to sever one's thought from preconceptions and old definitions to arrive at the essence of the novel around which these aspects converge.

Ortega's secondary intention—exposing Spain to this complex philosophy from Europe—explains the accessible and even lyrical style of his *Meditations*. He delivers the complex philosophy in a highly palatable text that strives to seduce his readers into adopting it. As Ortega himself writes in his introduction, the essays in the *Meditations* are "propelled by philosophical desires" but "they are not philosophy, which is a science. They are simply essays. The essay is science, minus the proof" (*Meditations*, p. 40).

The Essays in Focus

Contents summary. In the introductory essay "To the Reader," Ortega announces that his book

of essays will be the first of several such collections of "Meditations" on various subjects having to do with "Spanish 'circumstances' either directly or indirectly" (*Meditations*, p. 31). (No other "Meditations" were in fact published in subsequent editions.) His aims are modest, he writes: motivated by "intellectual love," his essays are meant to have no informative value whatsoever, but are intended merely to place "objects of all kinds . . . in such a position that the sun as it strikes them may give off innumerable reflections" (*Meditations*, pp. 31-32). Now, in the early 1900s, Spaniards are unable to view each other with appreciation for their individual identities or essences. Love impels him to share a philosophy that helps make these identities and the identity of Spain as a whole manifest.

Ortega stresses the role of love in inspiring this writing. While he suspects that "the inner dwelling of the Spaniards was long ago captured by hate," which always puts a "strong spring of steel" between us and the world, only love, he claims, "binds us to things" and "unites them to us" by making their existence indispensable to us (*Meditations*, pp. 32-33). Of the many kinds of love that exist, he will focus especially on "the eagerness to comprehend" (*Meditations*, p. 34). The desire to understand has a moral and even a religious value, and in this light, philosophy can be considered a "general science of love" in that it seeks to understand (*Meditations*, p. 38). The parts of the world it is possible to understand, says Ortega, are those parts that are closest to us, which comprise our circumstances. "Man reaches full capacity only when he acquires complete consciousness of his circumstances. Through them he communicates with the universe" (*Meditations*, p. 41). This communication is mutually beneficial. Thus, Ortega completes his famous line, "I am myself plus my circumstance" with "and if I do not save it, I do not save myself" (*Meditations*, p. 45). In other words, contemporary Spain is an integral part of Ortega, and if he does not help save it, he does not save himself.

EL ESCORIAL

In his introduction to the Preliminary Meditation, Ortega describes how the thoughts in the essays came to him during a visit to one of Spain's most impressive national monuments, the monastery at El Escorial, about 25 miles northwest of Madrid. The massive monastery was built from huge blocks of dark granite at the height of Spain's Golden Age by King Philip II, and nearly all Spain's monarchs since Philip II have been buried there. Like Cervantes's *Don Quixote*, El Escorial has symbolized for many the heights Spain did and could reach.

Ortega cautions that in his essays he will be focusing on *Don Quixote* as a literary work, not on Don Quixote as a character. Such a monumental book cannot be understood easily or directly, however. It cannot be stormed like a castle. "A work as great as *Quixote* must be taken as Jericho was taken," Ortega writes, referring to the ancient city captured by the Biblical Joshua: "In wide circles, our thoughts and our emotions must keep pressing in on it slowly, sounding in the air, as it were, imaginary trumpets" (*Meditations*, p. 52). The essay prepares the way for using phenomenology to get to the essence of *Don Quixote*, a goal invoked patriotically, for the good of Spain, since the writing of Cervantes, as a later

essay will assert, contains the key to Spain's potential: "If one day someone were to come and reveal to us the profile of Cervantes's style, it would suffice for us to prolong its lines over our other collective problems and we would awake to a new life" (*Meditations*, p. 107).

The body of Ortega's essays is divided into two sections, "Preliminary Meditation" (15 essays) and "First Meditation: A Short Treatise on the Novel" (20 essays). (As noted, Ortega planned at the time to write subsequent Meditations.) Both sections have a brief introduction. All the essays in the book are short, ranging in length from a single paragraph to a few pages, and each has a brief descriptive title highlighting its primary theme.

In general, the essays are thematically ordered, and one essay usually flows logically into the next. For example, in the first essay, "The Forest," Ortega considers the German proverb "You can't see the forest for the trees," which, he says, illustrates the principle that "depth is fatally condemned to become a surface if it wants to become visible" (*Meditations*, p. 59). We must, though, not insist on making depth visible. The next essay, "Depth and Surface," elaborates on this thought:

> Some men refuse to recognize the depth of something because they demand that the profound should manifest itself in the same way as the superficial. . . . They do not realize that to be hidden beneath the surface, merely appearing through it, throbbing beneath it, is essential to depth.
>
> (*Meditations*, p. 62)

To demand the profound to show itself in the same way as the superficial is to devalue the world. This is "a sin of the heart" because "it derives from a lack of love" for understanding the world and the objects, superficial or profound, in it (*Meditations*, p. 62). The allusion in these two essays is to Spain's being impressionistic, relying excessively on the senses; the pursuit of the forest, which is hidden, thus becomes a patriotic exercise.

In the next two essays, Ortega examines the nature of distance and discusses what the perception of distance adds to the dimension of depth. When we see only a surface but our perceptions tell us intuitively that depth lies beneath the surface, a phenomenon results that Ortega calls foreshortening. The fifth essay links the foregoing discussions to *Don Quixote*, describing Cervantes's masterpiece as "an ideal forest" and "the foreshortening book *par excellence*" (*Meditations*, pp. 70, 73). It is in this fifth essay, entitled

El Escorial

"The Restoration and Erudition," that Ortega characterizes Restoration culture as having lost the capacity to understand "anything really strong, excellent, whole, and profound," including *Don Quixote*, whose depth, "like all profundity, is very far from being obvious" (*Meditations*, pp. 72-73).

In succeeding essays in this first section, Ortega continues to probe the qualities and ambiguities of surfaces and depth as they relate to culture. In the context of European culture, which he says evolved out of the Latin culture of the ancient world after the arrival of Germanic peoples, he suggests that the newer Germanic culture is one of "profound realities"; the older Latin culture that mixed with it is one "of surfaces" (*Meditations*, p. 75). Under the Latin culture lies a deeper Mediterranean culture that Ortega characterizes as essentially sensuous and, again, impressionistic, living only for the moment, as opposed to Germanic culture, which is meditative and rational. Mediterraneans see clearly; Germans think clearly, writes Ortega. Both sorts of clarity are necessary and valid. Largely a Mediterranean people, the Spanish are impressionistic, which has made their culture nonprogressive: "Every Spanish genius has started all over again from chaos as if nothing had existed before" (*Meditations*, p. 94).

Ortega concludes this first section by suggesting not that Spaniards abandon their impressionism, but that they integrate it with Germanic rationality. By integrating Germanic idealism with Mediterranean sensualism, Spain can bring itself up to the height of its times. Any work of art that does not combine both, he argues, must in the end "produce only ambiguous values" (*Meditations*, p. 100). In fact, the facet that, above all, characterizes this quintessentially Spanish work of art is its ambiguity, for despite many attempts to explain the novel, no one can be really sure what it is trying to say:

> There is no book more potent in symbolic allusions to the universal meaning of life, and, yet, there is no book in which we find fewer anticipations, fewer clues for its own interpretation. For this reason Shakespeare would appear to be a thinker as compared with Cervantes. . . . In a greater or lesser degree Shakespeare always explains himself.
>
> (*Meditations*, p. 102)

Now ambiguity may be cloaking deeper meaning, or it may not. In the case of *Don Quixote*, it appears to be cloaking deeper, genuine ideas. The novel seems to Ortega to be integrating these genuine ideas with the surface sensations. The mystery lies in the purpose behind the ambiguity: "Is Cervantes making fun of something? And of what?" (*Meditations,* p. 101). That Cervantes does not explain himself may perhaps even be his "supreme gift," and since "it is doubtful that there are other truly profound Spanish books," Ortega finds "all the more reason for us to focus on *Quixote,* our great question: O God, what is Spain?" (*Meditations,* p. 102). Just as Don Quixote ignores the constraints of everyday, mundane reality, Spaniards themselves "must go against tradition, beyond tradition" in striving to fulfill the "very lofty promise" of what it means to be Spanish: "In one huge painful bonfire we ought to burn the inert traditional mask, the Spain that has been and then, among the well-sifted ashes, we shall find the iridescent gemlike Spain that could have been" (*Meditations,* p. 106). Yet although Cervantes represents "a Spanish plenitude . . . a word which we can brandish on every occasion as if it were a lance," only when someone comes along who is able to pin down his meaning exactly can this "new Spanish experiment be made in its purest form"; until then, his writings should be interpreted with caution, "lest we say something improper or extravagant in our effort to come too close to him" (*Meditations,* p. 107).

In his introduction to the second section, Ortega writes that because the "most external" aspect of *Don Quixote* is that it is a novel, and because it is generally considered both the first and the best novel, he will now consider the basic question, "what is a novel?" (*Meditations,* p. 111). He follows the phenomenological prescription, siphoning out all that is not definable as "novel" from all that is. After an essay describing the various literary genres, Ortega devotes an essay to Cervantes's other novels and several essays to the genre of epic poetry, which unlike the novel is generally set in a remote and idealized past. In an essay entitled "Helen and Madame Bovary," Ortega goes on to contrast epic subjects, such as the rape of Helen and subsequent epic war between the Greeks and Trojans, with novelistic subjects, like the adulterous affair of the young doctor's wife in the French novel *Madame Bovary* by Gustave Flaubert (1857). The epic figure, says Ortega, is a unique entity, not a type recognizable from daily life, like the novelistic character. Ortega goes on to point out that related to ancient epic poetry were the chivalric medieval romances, from which, in turn, novels evolved. In contrast to its two literary ancestors, epic poetry and chivalric romances, the novel relies more on how a story is told, on style or presentation, rather than the intrinsic interest of the plot or

characters. In the novel, not only characters but also plot tends to be more commonplace than the exceptional heroes and events in epics and romances. *Don Quixote* originates this emphasis on style over content and is therefore rightly viewed as the founding example of the modern novel.

Indeed, Ortega points out, Cervantes expressly "declares that he is writing his book against the books of chivalry" popular in Golden Age Spain (*Meditations,* p. 135). With the advent of the Renaissance and discovery of "the stern laws which govern the universe . . . adventures are impossible"; at the same time the inner world of the psychological has come to the fore, with the result that adventure itself is "reduced to the psychological" (*Meditations,* p. 138). *Don Quixote,* with its hero's absurd quest for adventure, which he finds only in his fevered imagination, encapsulates "this great new turn which culture takes" as it moves toward the modern (*Meditations,* p. 138).

In the next seven essays, Ortega draws further connections and contrasts between the novel and other literary genres. For example, in an essay entitled "Realistic Poetry" Ortega again stresses the representation of reality in literature, and explains how it can move us more than the reality itself (in both the novel and the realistic poem, commonplace events may, for example, be related in an unusual or interesting way). Other genres Ortega examines in this way include mime, lyric poetry, tragedy, comedy, and tragicomedy. In a brief essay entitled "The Hero," Ortega offers his interpretation of Don Quixote as "a man who wishes to reform reality," defining heroism as residing precisely in this "will to be oneself": "The hero's will is not that of his ancestors nor of his society, but his own" (*Meditations,* pp. 148-49). (Ortega positions himself here as a reformer of Spanish reality too, in his quest to bring its identity to the fore.) Spain, Ortega implies, can heroically choose its own identity, rather than allowing the past (that is, reality or tradition) to impose an identity on it.

In a final essay entitled "Flaubert, Cervantes, and Darwin," Ortega suggests that "every novel bears *Don Quixote* within it like an inner filigree," and praises Flaubert for realizing this. Ortega also praises the French novelist for understanding that "the novelistic art is a genre with critical intention and comic sinews" (*Meditations,* p. 163). Finally, Ortega laments recent scientific advances that he says have resulted in deterministic thought, in which free will has disappeared and "life is reduced to mere matter" (*Meditations,* p. 164). In particular, he protests the social impact made by the evolutionary theory of English naturalist Charles Darwin, a theory published in Darwin's *On the Origin of Species* (1859). As Ortega understands the theory, it shows life to be shaped by nothing more than passive adaptation to its environment, a lamentable development: "Darwin has swept heroes off the face of the earth" (*Meditations*, p. 164).

Spain and its circumstances. In the very first sentence of the *Meditations*, Ortega announces the work as "several essays on various subjects of no very great consequence to be published by a professor of philosophy *in partibus infidelium*," that is "in a land of infidels" (*Meditations*, p. 31). This Latin phrase suggests both how Ortega saw himself (as a philosopher) and how he saw most Spaniards (as ignorant of philosophy and possibly hostile to it). As the scholar Philip Silver puts it, Ortega was "a philosopher who . . . had placed his life at the service of a philosophically indigent country" (Silver, p. 3).

The nature of such service, Silver suggests, explains the seeming lack of complex philosophical content in the *Meditations*, which instead offers the reader an approachable and urbanely self-effacing authorial voice. Yet complex philosophical issues do (as Ortega might have said) throb beneath the placid surface of these readable essays, and the form of the book itself thus ironically parallels the surface/depth dichotomy with which much of its discussion is concerned. His discussion, while presented in everyday language and without the technical jargon used in some philosophical tracts, does in fact reflect real phenomenological thought. In Marburg, Germany, Ortega was a student of Herman Cohen, who is mentioned in the *Meditations on Quixote*. From Cohen, Ortega got the idea to take a given fact, such as "a man, a book, a picture, a landscape, an error, a sorrow" and "to carry it by the shortest route to its fullest [cultural] significance" (*Meditations*, p. 31). With this simple philosophical notion, he brings to the average reader the idea of focusing on appearance and ignoring preconceptions.

The *Meditations'* literary surface, especially its inquiry into the literary masterpiece that defines Spanishness, perfectly fits Ortega's purpose of bringing Spain up to date with the rest of Europe, which could not be achieved without addressing the nature of Spanish identity. By downplaying the philosophical nature of his inquiry, Ortega tailored his book to the circumstances that prevailed in Spain at the time he was writing. And in doing so, he once again played ironically with

his philosophy, one of whose tenets is the crucial role of circumstance in shaping identity.

Sources and literary context. Reflecting the dual nature of the content in *Meditations,* Ortega's sources for the essays fall into two broad categories, philosophical and literary. Of the numerous philosophical works that undoubtedly influenced his thought, those of Edmund Husserl must be counted as among the most important. Ortega would have read Husserl's major works before writing the *Meditations*, including *Logical Investigations* (1900; 1901) and *Ideas* (1913). In the latter book, scholars have traced an emphasis on the role of circumstance that, they suggest, influenced Ortega's own version of phenomenology. Ortega himself later famously claimed to have rejected phenomenology as soon as he encountered it; he referred to his own philosophy as "vital reason." Scholars, however, have suggested that what Ortega rejected was Husserl's return to the thought of Immanuel Kant, which became a very active area in philosophy and took off in several different directions. Ortega's own thought at the time of the essays, these scholars believe, was largely in line with phenomenological ideas as originally formulated.

Ortega credits some philosophers for the ideas in the essays, but not all by name. He refers specifically to those with whom any moderately educated Spaniard would have been familiar, such as the ancient Greeks Socrates, Plato, and Aristotle (fifth and fourth centuries B.C.E.), or the famous German Immanuel Kant (1724-1804). Ortega does not credit particular philosophers for the phenomenological ideas in the essays. However, they have since been identified:

Source	Idea Inspired
Hermann Cohen (1842-1918)	Applying *Don Quixote* to culture
Nicolai Hartmann (1882-1950)	Seeing truth as an unveiling of a reality
Wilhelm Schapp (1884-1969)	Contrasting a surface to a depth
Henri Bergson (1859-1941)	Positing theories of comedy and tragedy
Edmund Husserl (1859-1938)	Using phenomenology to evaluate essences of experience
Miguel de Unamuno (1864-1936)	Inspiring the writing of *Meditations on Quixote*
George Simmel (1858-1918)	Recognizing that a reformer is always foiled by reality

| Max Scheler (1874-1928) | Discussing the relationships of love, knowledge, and philosophy |

Of the essays' literary sources, most obvious is *Don Quixote* itself, a book that, as noted, was very much on the minds of Ortega's friends in the Generation of 1898 when Ortega wrote his essays. Ortega set out precisely to filter the novel through the thought of the above-named philosophers. He did so after not only Miguel de Unamuno had written his *The Life of Our Lord Don Quixote* but also after Azorín had used Cervantes's novel to explore Spanish themes in his 1905 *The Route of Don Quixote*. Ortega also makes references throughout his essays to books from Spanish and other European literatures. Most of these references are to the literature of ancient Greece in the interest of defining the genre of "novel." The essays refer especially to the epic poems the *Iliad* and *Odyssey* and also to tragic playwrights of fifth century Athens, such as Aeschylus and Sophocles.

Reception. *Meditations on Quixote* made very little impact among philosophers when published in 1914, although Ortega himself always considered it a favorite. The book enjoyed modest success among its intended audience, the reading public of Spain at the time, largely because of the essays' well-known literary subject and because Ortega (though not yet the national figure he would become) already commanded an expanding audience for his lectures and journalism. As the twentieth century wore on, in part due to Ortega's own growing recognition after the release of his seminal 1932 work *The Revolt of the Masses,* the slender volume enjoyed a growing reputation among philosophers. Ultimately

Meditations on Quixote came to be regarded as "a masterpiece" that is both "delightfully written" and philosophically "of capital importance" (Marías in Ortega y Gasset, p. 9).

—Nelson Orringer and Colin Wells

For More Information

Carr, Raymond. *Spain: 1808-1939.* Oxford: Oxford University Press, 1966.

Ceplecha, Christian. *The Historical Thought of José Ortega y Gasset.* Washington, D.C.: Catholic University Press, 1958.

Dobson, Andrew. *An Introduction to the Politics and Philosophy of José Ortega y Gasset.* Cambridge: Cambridge University Press, 1989.

Graham, John T. *A Pragmatist Philosophy of Life in Ortega y Gasset.* Columbia, Missouri: University of Missouri Press, 1994.

Marías, Julián. *José Ortega y Gasset: Circumstance and Vocation.* Trans. Frances M. López-Morillas. Norman, Oklahoma: University of Oklahoma Press, 1970.

McClintock, Robert. *Man and His Circumstances: Ortega as Educator.* New York: Teachers College Press, 1971.

Orringer, Nelson. "The Two Unamunos in 'Meditaciones del Quijote,'" *LA CHISPA Proceedings 1981.* New Orleans: Tulane University Press, 1983.

———. "Redefining the Spanish Silver Age and '98 Within It." *Anales de la literature Española contemporanea* 23, nos. 1-2 (1998).

Ortega y Gasset, José. *Meditations on Quixote.* Trans. Evelyn Rugg and Diego Marin; Introduction and Notes by Julián Marías. New York: Norton, 1961.

Silver, Philip W. *Ortega as Phenomenologist: The Genesis of* Meditations on Quixote. New York: Columbia University Press, 1978.

Wohl, Robert. *The Generation of 1914.* Cambridge, Mass.: Harvard University Press, 1979.

Message

by

Fernando Pessoa

Fernando Pessoa was born in Lisbon on June 13, 1888, and he died there in November 1935. When Pessoa was five years old, his father died, and his mother remarried two years later. Pessoa's stepfather was the Portuguese consul in Durban, South Africa, and after the boy and his mother moved there in 1896, he attended local schools and became fluent in English. Pessoa returned to the Portuguese capital in 1905, where he enrolled in the University of Lisbon, but two years later abandoned his studies in favor of a career as a commercial correspondent. He never returned to school and rarely ever left the area of greater Lisbon. Best known for writing poetry under the guise of four distinct literary personalities (heteronyms), Pessoa published only one complete book of poems during his lifetime—*Mensagem,* or *Message.* While his work was known only to a small group of friends and specialists at the time of his death, he is now considered one of the most important, complex voices in Portuguese poetry. In *Mensagem* the poet evokes key moments and figures of Portuguese history to trace the contours of a spiritual quest for identity that is both personal and collective.

Events in History at the Time the Poem Takes Place

The origins of the nation and the Reconquest. Portugal emerged as an independent nation at the beginning of the twelfth century when the first king, Afonso Henriques, successfully re-

THE LITERARY WORK

A group of 44 poems set mainly in Portugal, but also in Africa and India, from the twelfth to the sixteenth century; written 1913-34; published in Portuguese (as *Mensagem*) in 1934, in English in 1992.

SYNOPSIS

Featuring the motif of the semi-legendary King Sebastian, the poems revolve around key events and figures of Portuguese history and myth in relation to the nation's founding, the Reconquest, and the voyages of exploration.

belled against his mother, Theresia (called D. Tareja in *Message*), the illegitimate daughter of Alfonso VI, who ruled the Spanish kingdoms of León, Castile, Galicia, and the kingdom of Portugal. At that time, the Christian populations of the northern Iberian Peninsula were engaged in the Reconquest, a series of military campaigns to oust the Islamic rulers who controlled more than half the peninsula's territory. In his tenure as founder of Portugal's first dynasty, the House of Burgundy, Afonso Henriques managed to extend the nation's frontiers well to the south of Lisbon and, during the reign of his grandson, Afonso III (1246-79), the Reconquest was completed in Portugal. Immediately following this consolidation of national borders, Afonso III's son, Dinis, proclaimed Portuguese to be the national language, created a national university (in Lisbon,

THE HETERONYMS

Besides writing and publishing poems under his own name, Fernando Pessoa created a series of literary personae who also produced a significant body of work. Pessoa chose to call these personae "heteronyms" instead of pseudonyms because each had a personality that he considered different from his own. The poems attributed to Alberto Caeiro, Ricardo Reis, and Álvaro de Campos are written in styles unlike that used by Pessoa in the work that he signed under his own name. In addition, all these "poets" were given distinct biographies which, according to their creator, contributed to both their literary style and their personalities. The first to appear was Caeiro, who was considered the "master" by Pessoa and the others. Caeiro was a simple man, barely literate, who championed a poetry of the senses. Reis, on the other hand, cultivated a neo-classical verse style, while Campos was the author of long modernist odes, written in free verse, and of shorter, ironic poems filled with his existential doubts. Bernardo Soares, author of the *Livro do Desassossego* (*Book of Disquietude*) wrote exclusively in prose. For this reason and because, as Pessoa explained, Soares was not a different personality from his, but rather a mere mutilation of his personality, Pessoa considered him a "semi-heteronym" (see *Obras Completas*, vol. 2, p. 343). While Pessoa resorted to various explanations regarding the appearance and role of the heteronyms, it is evident that they were more than mere literary artifices, nor can they be understood in purely psychological terms. Generations of critics have debated the form and function of these personalities from a variety of linguistic and literary perspectives.

later moved to Coimbra), and established Lisbon as the capital. Dinis (reigned 1279-1325) also gained renown as a poet, one of the last to cultivate the medieval verse form of the *cantigas,* songs inspired by the troubadour culture.

The House of Burgundy's rule came to an end and the House of Avis was initiated in 1385 when João I (John I) proclaimed himself king after successfully rebelling against Leonor Teles, widow of King Ferdinand I. João married Phillipa of Lancaster, daughter of the British Duke John of Gaunt, thereby cementing a political alliance with England that would last until the present day. The couple had five sons (Duarte, Pedro, Henrique, João, and Fernando). Commonly referred to as the *ínclita geração* (the illustrious generation), they would become active participants in the first voyages of discovery. Duarte, in conjunction with his father, organized a military expedition to the Moroccan port of Ceuta, which the Portuguese forces attacked and successfully captured in 1415. Upon establishing a military presence and erecting a fortress there, the men returned to Portugal rich with booty and confident in the knowledge that they were helping to expand the Christian faith. While many immediately clamored to continue the campaigns in Morocco, King João I decided to forego any subsequent expeditions.

On the death of his father in 1433, Duarte assumed the throne; in 1437, he was persuaded to resume Portuguese crusades in North Africa. That year the Portuguese assailed Tangier in an attack that failed miserably—Duarte's brother Fernando was taken captive during this campaign and died in prison, earning the nickname *Infante Santo* (Sainted Prince). Once again, expeditions to Africa came to a halt. Upon Duarte's death in 1438, his brother Pedro, duke of Coimbra, assumed the role of regent after a brief civil war that pitted those in favor of continuing the incursions against the "infidel" in North Africa against those opposed to the endeavor. Under Pedro's leadership, the expeditions to Africa resumed.

Voyages of discovery. Of the remaining sons of João I, his namesake, João, left the slightest mark on history. Henrique, on the other hand, who was to become known as Henry the Navigator, is best remembered for his role in preparing the way for Portugal's overseas expansion and subsequent empire. Named Duke of Viseu and Master of the Order of Christ, Henrique was awarded the governership of Ceuta and the Algarve (the southernmost part of continental Portugal, a separate kingdom at the time). He also received rights to develop the recently discovered islands of Madeira and the Azores. In order to better exploit the wealth and potential of his possessions, Henrique established a center of learning in Sagres, at the far southwestern tip of Portugal. Surrounded by scholars and experts on foreign trade, he found himself in an excellent position to sponsor a series of sea voyages along the coast of West Africa. By the time of Henrique's death in 1460, Portuguese vessels had arrived to the south of the Geba River, in what is present-day Guinea-Bissau.

Ostensibly the motivations for these voyages were to extend the Reconquest, to spread the Christian faith, and hopefully to make contact with the mythic territory ruled over by the rich and powerful emperor-priest Prester John, a legendary Christian leader thought to be living anywhere from northeastern Africa to Asia. However, a subsidiary plan gradually took shape. It became increasingly clear that there were enormous profits to be made from these voyages of exploration. In addition to the great quantities of gold added to the nation's coffers, the expeditions yielded slaves (imported to Portugal and to the rest of Europe) and such precious commodities as red pepper, cotton, grain, and ivory. Moreover, as the Portuguese continued to chart new stretches of the coast, leaving behind *padrões* ("standards" or stone pillars topped by a cross), claiming the newly discovered territories for the Crown, a plan to reach the Indian Ocean by sea emerged. In 1485-86, during the reign of João II (grandson of Duarte), the navigator Diogo Cão charted the coast of Africa from Gabon to Namibia. Finally, in 1488, a fleet of three caravels, commanded by Bartolomeu Dias, rounded the southern tip at Cape of Good Hope. While Vasco da Gama's history-making voyage to India was not to occur for another ten years, Europe's understanding of science and geography were forever changed by Dias's feat.

In conjunction with the efforts to round the southern tip of Africa, King João II also chartered many expeditions to the west. By the mid-1480s, the king and his advisers had accepted the theory that the earth was a sphere. When he declined to subsidize Christopher Columbus's trip, believing correctly that the sea route to India via the east was much shorter, Columbus left Por-

Fernando Pessoa. Drawing by José de Almada Negreiros, a collaborator of Pessoa's in the magazine *Orpheu*.

tugal and sought support from the king and queen of neighboring Spain. Columbus had, however, lived and studied navigation and geography in Portugal, so upon his return from the New World, he stopped off in Lisbon to inform the Portuguese king of his success. This led to a series of negotiations with Castile and to the subsequent division of the globe on a line that ran north-south 370 leagues west of the Cape Verde Islands. According to the Treaty of Tordesillas (1494), lands to the west of that line would belong to Spain; those to the east, to Portugal.

João II did not live long enough to see his dream of sending a fleet to India fulfilled; it was during the reign of his successor, Manuel I, that Vasco da Gama would complete the trip, his ships returning to Europe loaded with valuable spices and with important knowledge about navigating the Indian Ocean. On the following voyage to India, led by Pedro Álvares Cabral, Brazil was discovered when Cabral's ships sailed far to the southwest, apparently in search of strong currents to propel them back around the Cape of Good Hope. According to the Treaty of Tordesillas, this new land also belonged to the king of Portugal, while the rest of South America would remain Spanish. Another Portuguese adventurer, nonetheless, played an important role in the discovery of Argentina and Chile—Fernão de Magalhães (Magellan). In service to the king of Spain at the time, he became the first to circumnavigate the globe as he searched for a western route to the Moluccas (Spice Islands of Indonesia).

During the decades after Vasco da Gama's voyage to India, the Portuguese Crown's main interest lay in Asia, a continent that was home to diverse cosmopolitan societies, many of whom were eager to trade with Europeans. Within a very short time, Portugal gained sea control of the entire Indian Ocean and, over the course of the following decades, it established commercial and military alliances in India, Malacca, China (Macau), and Japan. The administrative heart of the Eastern Empire was in India, whose territory of Goa received its first viceroy in 1505. It was, however, the second viceroy of India who would become known as "both the true founder of the Portuguese 'empire' in Asia and the best warrant of its permanence" (Oliveira Marques, p. 233). During the rule of this second viceroy, Afonso de Albuquerque (1509-1515), Portuguese authority was established from the Persian Gulf to the Straits of Malacca.

King Sebastian and the sebastianist myth. The central metaphor of *Message* is that of King Sebastian (who disappeared while in battle in North Africa) and the prophecy that the Fifth Empire of the world would be inaugurated upon his return. The real Sebastian had a brief, albeit dramatic, life. By 1557, when young Sebastian inherited the throne (he was just three at the time), Portugal controlled a commercial empire with holdings on three continents (Asia, Africa, and South America), commanding the respect and envy of other European nations who looked to them as a model for expansion. That is not to say there were no problems to solve. Much of the wealth from overseas trade was invested unwisely, and corruption ran rife. Moreover, religious intolerance soared until Portugal established its own Inquisition in 1537. Unfortunately, Portugal could not look to Sebastian to solve its problems. His death in 1578 would, in fact, bring Portugal face-to-face with the greatest obstacle it had ever confronted. When Sebastian disappeared in a battle against the Moors in Alcácer Quibir (Morocco) in the summer of 1578, he left no heirs (the young bachelor-king was said to abhor the idea of taking a wife). Two years later, in 1580, his great-uncle, King Felipe II of Spain, asserted his rights to the Portuguese

throne. The "Iberian Union," under which Spain and Portugal were governed by the same monarch, would last 80 years, until the restoration of Portuguese independence in 1640.

Sebastian's physical and intellectual weaknesses have been documented by many sources. Raised in a climate of religious fanaticism, he showed little interest in governing Portugal, instead recklessly dreaming of leading his army in a campaign to conquer Morocco. At a time when European expansion was moving swiftly into a modern, mercantilist phase, he acted on a misguided desire to revive the medieval ideology of Reconquest. Nevertheless, his loss was sorely felt, especially among Portugal's lower classes. While the aristocrats tended to support the post-Sebastian Habsburg rule, which assured them financial gain and political protection, the less privileged felt abandoned and decided to resist. Rumors began to circulate, alleging that the young king had not actually died in the battle. Since his corpse had never been definitively identified and no one would admit to having witnessed his death, a myth began to take shape that Sebastian had retired to some hidden land from whence he would soon return to save Portugal and restore independence.

This belief, called *sebastianismo*, became yet one more of many messianic prophesies that circulated in sixteenth-century Europe. In Portugal, the myth surrounding Sebastian's disappearance was quickly associated with earlier predictions circulated by a shoemaker named Bandarra during the reign of King João III. Bandarra had announced the arrival of a hidden king or savior (*o encoberto*) who would redeem humanity. At the same time, the sebastianist myth took on special meaning for the "new Christians" (Jews forced to convert by the Inquisition), who related the lost king's return to a belief in the so-called Fifth Empire of the Old Testament. (An apocalyptic prediction in the Book of Daniel, the Fifth Empire refers to the Greek nation's demise being followed by that of four kingdoms. From their ruins would arise a powerful king whose appearance would signal the end of history and a resurrection of the righteous and the wicked.) Eventually, the form of this savior began to be confused with that of the duke of Bragança who, as King João IV, would lead the nation after independence from Spain in 1640. Father António Vieira (1608-1697), a Jesuit priest who preached in both Brazil and Portugal, was one of the main exponents of a theory that João IV would succeed in founding a universal empire based on a purified "True Faith." Even after the death of the king, Vieira, who declared himself a prophet like those of the Old Testatment, continued to believe in the king's imminent resurrection. As one might expect, his declarations resulted in Vieria's having serious trouble with the Inquisition, the tribunal established to suppress deviation from teachings of the Catholic Church. He was confined to a monastery, then exiled to Rome. By the twentieth century, when Fernando Pessoa chose the sebastianist myth as the organizing metaphor for *Message*, clearly no one continued to believe in the return of the historical King Sebastian as savior of the Portuguese people. But for some, messianic sebastianist thought did still hold a certain imaginative power, and all Portuguese knew the story that the desired king (*o Desejado*) would appear, on a foggy morning, to save the nation from its torpor and decadence.

Sebastian I

The Poem in Focus

Contents overview. *Message* is divided into three parts–"Blazon," "Portuguese Sea," and "The Hidden One." As readers move through the poetry that comprises each part, it becomes clear that they are accompanying the poet on a journey that is both historical and spiritual. They are advancing toward a rebirth or regeneration that will occur once the signs are in place (that is, once the necessary prophecies have occurred) and the time is prepared for the return of King Sebastian.

"Blazon." The short poems that comprise the first part of *Message* correspond loosely to the various components in the Portuguese Royal Coat of Arms. They are arranged in five subsections, beginning with "The Fields." The two poems in this subsection define the background of the blazon, describing the Portuguese nation in physical and spiritual terms. In "The Castles," Europe is portrayed as a woman gazing out at the west, a space described as "the future of the past, / The face that stares is Portugal" (Pessoa, *Message, The Poems of Fernando Pessoa*, p. 161). The following poem, "The Five Shields," begins by affirming that "disaster's the price of glory" (*Message*, p. 161). The speaker goes on to celebrate these two opposite extremes, observing that life is short and that, to achieve Grace, one must be willing to risk lowliness and misfortune. While Sebastian is not specifically mentioned, the emphasis on extremes and on disaster evokes the

king's recklessness, a characteristic presented as fundamental for the attainment of grandeur.

The remaining four subsections in this first section correspond to the seven castles, the five shields, the crown, and the crest found on the coat of arms. Each poem in the "The Castles" subsection is directed to a mythic or historical figure: Ulysses, supposedly the founder of the city of Lisbon, is invoked, as is Viriato, the courageous Lusitanian warrior who dared to defy the Roman invaders. The other figures addressed all belong to Portugal's early history, and it is implied that their role is one of preparation for the glorious moment of expansion. Included are Count Henry, Queen Tareja, King Afonso Henriques, King Dinis (described as "planter of ships to come" [*Message*, p. 164]), King John I, and Phillipa of Lancaster. The five poems in "The Shields" subsection are spoken in the first person—four from the perspective of the sons of João I; the final one from that of Sebastian. In this first of many references to this king, we hear him praise his madness, for it alone can explain the degree of greatness he desired: "Which fate gives nobody" (*Message*, p. 166). Next come poems describing four national heroes whose deeds assured Portugal independence and imperial glory (Nun'Álvares Pereira, Prince Henrique, King John II, and Afonso de Albuquerque).

"Portuguese Sea." Twelve poems make up the second section of *Message*. In this section, the dangers and uncertainties of the Age of Discoveries are dramatized, first through a poem directed to Prince Henry the Navigator, followed by a more general appeal to the sea beyond the horizon. In the third poem, Diogo Cão claims the endless sea for the Portuguese, while the fourth poem decries the dangerous, mythical sea monster that inhabits the rocks along the Cape of Good Hope. The reference here is to the mythical Adamastor, a sea monster whose tragic prophecies alarm the Portuguese explorers in the Portuguese epic ***The Lusiads*** (also in *WLAIT 5: Spanish and Portuguese Literatures and Their Times*). From Adamastor, the section progresses to prominent real-life figures associated with the

---

ORGANIZING EPIGRAPHS

Introducing each part of the Portuguese version of *Message* is a Latin epigraph that evokes the general tenor of that section:

Salutation *Benedictus Dominus Deus Noster Qui Dedit Nobis Signum*—Blessed is the Lord Our God Who Gave the Sign to Us

   Epigraph to Part 1 *Bellum Sine Bello*—War Without War

   Part 2 *Possessio Maris*—Possession of the Sea

   Part 3 *Pax in Excelsis*—Peace in the Highest

   Valediction *Valete, Fratres*—Farewell, Brothers

---

voyages of discovery (Bartolomeu Dias, the Columbus brothers, Magellan, and Vasco da Gama). Then come several poems focusing on the loss of King Sebastian and on other prices paid in the name of Portuguese glory. The poet recognizes the tears shed by mothers, and future wives left behind. He concludes, however, that "Anything's worth it, / If the soul's not petty. / If you'd sail beyond the Cape / Sail you must beyond cares, past grief. / God gave perils to the sea and sheer depth, / But mirrored heaven there" (*Message*, p. 173). The eleventh poem, "The Last Ship," describes King Sebastian's departure, sailing into the sun "Alone, ill-omened, to anguished cries impending" (*Message*, p. 174). Here, in the final two stanzas, the speaker refers to himself as poet, using the first-person pronoun ("I") for the first time as he addresses the mad young king (previously the speaker made use of either a collective "we" or assumed the dramatized perspec-

tive of other historical figures). In preparation for the final part of *Message*, the speaker exclaims "The hour I do not know, but know there is an hour" (*Message*, p. 173). The closing poem of this section then comprises a prayer in which the poet asks: "And once again we'll go and vanquish Distance— / Of the ocean-sea or anything, so long as it is ours!" (*Message*, p. 174).

"The Hidden One." The third and final section of *Message*, "The Hidden One," includes 13 poems in three subsections. Each subsection corresponds to the necessary conditions for King Sebastian's return. The first subsection, "The Symbols," describes elements of sebastianist myth, such as the Fifth Empire. In the second subsection, "The Prophecies," after two poems that refer to historical figures who prophesied Sebastian's return (Bandarra and António Vieira), Pessoa includes an untitled poem, in the first person, that directly addresses the lost king, asking when he will redeem the poet, making him "more than the fitful sigh / Of some vast yearning God created?" (*Message*, p. 178). After this poem, in which he implicitly declares himself the third prophet of Sebastian's return, the poet ends the volume with five short poems in the subsection "Times" (in Portuguese, *Tempos* refers to both historical era and to weather conditions). Night, storm, calm, pre-dawn, and heavy fog—these times will lead to the much awaited misty day on which the king will arrive. There is a pessimistic assessment of contemporary Portugal ("All's uncertain, nears its end, / All's fragmented, nothing's whole. / O Portugal, today you are the fog"), followed by energetic exaltation. The way has been prepared for the longed-for personal and national redemption—"Comes the Hour!" (*Message*, p. 181).

Occultism and esoteric thought. Much of the structure and content of *Message* is informed by esoteric thought or occultist practice. The poem's tripartite organization, as well as the additional division of the third section into three subsections, draws upon the "three-step initiatory hierarchy to be found in many of the occultist sources that Pessoa knew, from Freemasonry to ritual magic to Theosophy" (Sousa, p. 142). In these rites, the initiate moves from an incipient state of ignorance through a phase of struggle in order to attain enough insight and knowledge to be able to carry on the journey on his own. Applying the three stages to *Message*, one can surmise that the readers occupy the role of the initiate, and it is the poet's responsibility to show them the way (through his or her portrayal of Portuguese history). Thus, the first section of *Message* recalls figures and moments of the early stages of Portugal's history that may be viewed as preparatory to the age of discovery. The second section ("Portuguese Sea") corresponds to the phase of struggle by invoking the vicissitudes of Empire. In the third and last section, the reader is finally granted access to the signs and prophecies that will allow recognition of spiritual truth and afford the possibility of regeneration, symbolized by the myth of King Sebastian and the Fifth Empire.

The sebastianist cult that infuses the poem and developed in Portugal in the sixteenth century had its roots in a wide variety of medieval philosophies and esoteric practices. Among these were the mystical prophecies regarding the appearance of a messiah that circulated in the New Christian communities of Portugal and the secret rites of the religious order of the Knights Templar, which was disbanded in 1312. As Pessoa himself was to explain in a letter written near the end of his life to the literary critic and poet Adolfo Casais Monteiro, the practices of the latter group became extinct or dormant in Portugal around 1888, but he was able to consult a manuscript containing the rituals of the first three steps of the Templar Order.

In his reply to Casais Monteiro, Pessoa also responded to a question as to whether he himself believed in occultism. While he categorically stated "I do not belong to any Iniatiatic Order" (*Obras Completas,* vol. 2, p. 345; trans. E. Sapega), he demonstrated a knowledge of great depth about occultist practices. Another biographical note written around the same time, however, contains contradictory information. There, he states that he is "initiated, by direct communication from Master to Disciple, in the three lower levels of the . . . Order of the Templars in Portugal" (*Obras Completas,* vol. 3, p. 1429; trans. E. Sapega).

In many regards, Pessoa's paradoxical statements in regard to his occultist beliefs and practices mirror other aspects of his literary project, such as the creation of the heteronyms. In this latter case, each "personality" can be seen as representing a different point of view or approach to representing the contradictions of existence. It is quite possible, therefore, that the "Pessoa" who wrote *Message* (as well as several other "occultist" poems) was an initiate, while an altogether different "Pessoa" wrote the letter to Casais Monteiro.

Sources and literary context. Pessoa is considered one of the founders of the modernist movement in Portugal. His early work was greatly influenced by symbolist poets (French and Portuguese), who experimented in writing "pure poetry" that attempted to transform everyday experience through the creation of a private language based on a poet's sensations. Pessoa's effort to celebrate the creative ethic of the Portuguese nation has roots in the poetic environment of the early years of the First Republic. Of influence, for example, was the poetry of Teixeira de Pascoaes; in Pascoaes's work, Pessoa recognized, with appreciation, an ability to resolve the dichotomy between the feeling and the idea by "finding in everything a beyond" (Pessoa, *Obras Completas,* vol. 2, p. 1176; trans. E. Sapega). Pessoa, however, demanded a greater level of complexity than he found in local poetry of his day and so he looked to the writing of such diverse practitioners as American poet Walt Whitman and French-Italian writer F. T. Marinetti.

The epic view of Portuguese history implicit in *Message* has led many of the poem's commentators to compare it to *The Lusiads* by Renaissance poet Luís de Camões. As Jacinto do Prado Coelho has pointed out, both *The Lusiads* and *Message* display a mystic, missionary concept of Portuguese history. While Pessoa's poems never make explicit reference to the Renaissance epic, many of them describe the same historical figures and events celebrated by Camões. *Message,* however, invokes a different notion of heroism, transferring the object of the poet's longing and hope to the realm of dream and utopia. Pessoa's work furthermore favors a lyric, metaphysical view of the nation's past rather than the descriptive, narrative elements typical of *The Lusiads.*

Other influences in *Message* include English poets and philosophers whose work Pessoa knew as the result of the British education he received as an adolescent in Durban, South Africa (including John Keats, John Milton, and Thomas Carlyle). Carlyle, in particular—with his theories of a society based on an aristocracy of heroes (in which the poet represents the most important hero of all)—seems to have played an important role in the composition of *Message.*

Events in History at the Time the Poem Was Written

Soul searching—Republican Portugal to the New State. By the late nineteenth century, when

Fernando Pessoa was born, King Sebastian's return clearly no longer represented a viable solution to the political, economic, and social problems that the Portuguese nation was facing. Still, many artists and intellectuals of the day felt a need to revive this and other nationalist mystical beliefs in the process of imagining a new role for Portugal within the concert of European nations. An interest in spiritualism and theosophy

---

ORPHEU

The first issue of *Orpheu*, an avant-garde magazine that was the brain child of Fernando Pessoa and fellow poet Mário de Sá-Carneiro, was published in March 1915. Its contents, which included a "static," one-act drama by Pessoa entitled *O Marinheiro* (The Mariner) and two poems by Pessoa's heteronym, Álvaro de Campos, caused a scandal in Lisbon's conservative artistic and literary circles. A second issue of *Orpheu* (also containing poems by Pessoa and Campos) came out in June of that same year, and a third issue was planned for 1916. Due to lack of funds and to Sá-Carneiro's tragic suicide, this final issue never went beyond the stage of page proofs. It is interesting to note, however, that it contained an early version of one of the poems in *Message* (originally titled "Gládio" [Sword], it would be given the name "D. Fernando, Infante of Portugal" in the 1934 volume). While *Orpheu* was not the first Portuguese magazine to publish Pessoa's poetry, its blend of irreverence and experimental artistic techniques made it a touchstone in the history of Portuguese modernism. In Pessoa's words, "There are only two interesting things in Portugal—the countryside and *Orpheu*. . . . *Orpheu* is the sum and synthesis of all modern literary movements; for that reason, it is more important to write about it than the countryside, which is only just the absence of the people who live in it" (Pessoa, *Páginas Íntimas*, pp. 146-47).

---

was widespread in Europe and the Americas at this time, constituting, in part, a reaction to the so-called positivist views espoused by writers of the naturalist school, who believed that scientific principles could be used to explain people's relationship to the world around them. The reaction against positivism bespoke a disillusionment with the possibility of a rational explanation for the universe. In Portugal this disillusionment was accompanied by an awareness of the nation's increasingly diminished role as an imperial power, a disillusionment that perhaps helps account for the resurgence of secret societies such as Freemasonry.

Though Portugal's political decline was hardly sudden, it advanced precipitously as the twentieth century approached. In 1890 support for the Portuguese monarchy suffered a severe blow in response to a British ultimatum. The ultimatum demanded that Portugal relinquish all territorial claims on the area of Africa roughly corresponding to present-day Zambia, Malawi, and Zimbabwe or face the possibility of a break in diplomatic relations with Britain and the use of force to the same end. Portugal had no alternative but to capitulate. In so doing, the nation's citizens found themselves acknowledging that Portugal's reduced presence in Africa was a direct consequence of its marginal position and military weakness in relation to other, more powerful European nations. In the literary sphere, poetry reflected the defeatism felt by the people as a whole, but the writers also set about examining the hidden, spiritual qualities that they believed made the Portuguese a distinct community that could boast not only a glorious past but also a singular emotional understanding of the world. Central to this inquiry was the elaboration of a theory of *saudade*, a uniquely Portuguese word that invokes a longing, both pleasurable and sorrowful, for someone or something no longer present. Writers in this vein became known as part of the Saudosista Movement; Pessoa's poem goes beyond their purview, invoking the longing by recalling national heroes of the past, then moving forward to a spiritual rebirth in the vision of an apocalyptic yet redemptive future.

Portugal's monarchy fell in 1910, to be replaced by a republic that was to last until 1926. The cornerstones of the new government were a strong colonial policy and the secularization of schools and other institutions previously controlled by the Catholic Church. It was during this period that Freemasonry, another esoteric system influencing Pessoa, gained in authority as it added new members, with some 100 lodges enrolling 4,000 participants. Many of the Republic's programs were never fully implemented due to the economic and political chaos that marked the period, however, and a right-wing military coup in 1926 put an end to the secular democratic experiment, also outlawing Freemasonry two years later.

The military coup of 1926 would lead directly to the creation of the Portuguese Estado

Novo (New State), the dictatorship headed by António de Oliveira Salazar. In 1928, Salazar arrived in Lisbon to assume the position of Finance Minister. Salazar acquired direct control over all other ministerial budgets, gaining a financial power that allowed him to quickly assert his influence in all spheres of government. As early as 1929, he was addressing the nation on matters that went well beyond finance (speaking on political and moral issues), and in 1933 a new conservative constitution was approved that institutionalized such corporative governmental structures as a single national party and government-controlled labor syndicates instead of labor unions.

While Salazar himself had previously been allied with right-wing Catholic political movements, he did not go so far as proclaiming Portugal a Catholic nation, and the Constitution of 1933 maintained the republic's separation of Church and state. Intolerance of non-Catholic practices increased, however, while the nationalist sentiments that had inspired the republic's proclamation were now tailored to suit the more conservative interests of the New State. Thus, in 1913 when Pessoa embarked on *Message,* he did so in a relatively open environment, conducive to personal and national introspection and experimentation. By the time he finished in 1934, Portugal had turned a corner, sending such introspection under cover.

Reviews. While many of the poems that comprise *Message* were written during the period of the First Republic, Pessoa did not organize them into a volume until one year before his death in 1935. He then entered his book in a competition for a literary prize that was sponsored by the government of the Portuguese New State, headed by António de Oliveira Salazar. According to the regulations for the contest, the award would go to the work that best communicated a sense of patriotic pride. *Message* did not win, but the Director of Propaganda, António Ferro, acknowledging the value of Pessoa's poem, decided to reward it anyway, and a "special" category was created. During the years immediately following its publication, *Message* was treated as a work inspired by a nationalist, even imperialist, sentiment, leading many critics who were closely associated with the regime to interpret it as a paean to Salazar's New State. During this time, therefore, the book was hailed by those who agreed with Salazar's politics, while it was often treated as mediocre by those in the opposition.

Later generations of critics came to recognize the poem's complexity, with critics such as António Quadros and Y. K. Centeno going to great lengths to document its relation to esoteric texts and practices. After the Portuguese revolution of 1974, it became possible to openly discuss and analyze Pessoa's politically satirical poems and several critical studies appeared that focused on his ambiguous relationship with the Estado Novo. Given the patriotic themes implicit in its treatment of history, the knowledge of the historical context in which it first appeared, and the hermetic view of personal and national experience behind its occultist approach to history, *Message* remains one of Pessoa's most controversial projects.

—Ellen W. Sapega

For More Information

Almeida, Onésimo Teotónio. "A ideologia da *Mensagem.*" In *Mensagem e Poemas esotéricos de Fernando Pessoa.* Ed. José Augusto Seabra. Paris: Signatário Acuerdo Archivos, 1993.

Blanco, José. "A *Mensagem* e a Crítica do seu Tempo." In *Fernando Pessoa no seu tempo.* Eds. Eduardo Lourenço and António Braz de Oliveira. Lisboa: Biblioteca Nacional de Lisboa, 1988.

Centeno, Y. K. "O pensamento esotérico de Fernando Pessoa." In *Mensagem e Poemas esotéricos de Fernando Pessoa.* Ed. José Augusto Seabra. Paris: Signatário Acuerdo Archivos, 1993.

Cirugião, António. *O "Olhar esfíngico" da "Mensagem."* Lisboa: Instituto de Língua e Cultura Portuguesa/Ministério da Educação, 1990.

Coelho, Jacinto do Prado. *Camões e Pessoa: Poetas da Utopia.* Lisboa: Europa América, 1983.

Oliveira Marques, A. H. de. *History of Portugal.* 2d ed. New York: Columbia University Press, 1976.

Pessoa, Fernando. *Obras Completas.* 3 vols. Porto: Lello & Irmão, 1986.

———. *Páginas Íntimas e de Auto-Interpretação.* Eds. Goerg Rudolf Lind and Jacinto Prado Coelho. Lisboa: Ática, 1966.

———. *Message.* In *The Poems of Fernando Pessoa.* Trans. Edwin Honig and Susan Brown. New York: Ecco, 1986.

Sadlier, Darlene. *An Introduction to Fernando Pessoa: Modernism and the Paradoxes of Authorship.* Gainesville: Florida University Press, 1998.

Seabra, José Augusto, ed. *Mensagem e Poemas esotéricos de Fernando Pessoa.* Paris: Signatário Acuerdo Archivos, 1993.

Sousa, Ronald. "Pessoa the Messenger." In *The Rediscoverers.* State College: Pennsylvania State University Press, 1981.

Mist

by
Miguel de Unamuno y Jugo

ited by many as the greatest intellectual Spain has ever produced, Miguel de Unamuno (1864-1936) made his mark in philosophy, poetry, fiction, drama, travel writing, autobiography, and journalism. Unamuno was born to a religious Roman Catholic household on September 29, 1864, in Bilbao, capital of the Basque region of Spain. He received his early education in Bilbao and his doctorate in philosophy and letters from the University of Madrid in 1884. Six years later he became chair of Greek language and literature at Spain's oldest university, the University of Salamanca. After being appointed rector of the university in 1901, he was abruptly dismissed in 1914 for reasons still unclear, and in 1924 he was exiled for opposing the military government of Primo de Rivera. He returned to Salamanca in 1930 to experience the repeat of his former fate. Unamuno was re-elected rector, then removed once again, in 1936, this time for denouncing General Francisco Franco's Falangists. Placed under house arrest, the by-now popular and controversial Unamuno died of a heart attack a few months later, on New Year's Eve, 1936. He attained distinction in literature as a major figure in the Generation of 1898 and for launching Spanish writing into the modern era. His outspoken presence in Spanish public life endeared him to Spaniards but not to the leaders he criticized, both in direct statements and in his novels, whose philosophical musings challenged the status quo of an autocratic Spain painfully undergoing a series of political upheavals. *Mist*, published just

> ## THE LITERARY WORK
>
> An experimental novel set in an indefinite place and time; published in Spanish (as *Niebla*) 1914; in English in 1928.
>
> ## SYNOPSIS
>
> Idle and wealthy Augusto Pérez falls in love with two women and speculates about the nature of love and the reality of fiction before being killed off by his creator, Miguel de Unamuno, who appears as a character in his own novel.

before his 1914 dismissal, tackles some of the themes whose frank exploration made Unamuno so popular and controversial, including the question of the Spanish national character, his interest in the conflict between reason and faith, and his passionate concern with immortality, life, and death.

Events in History at the Time the Novel Takes Place

Spanish political instability. While the novel—or *nivola*, as Unamuno reworks it—scrupulously avoids reference to a specific time or setting, Unamuno's own presence in it suggests that it takes place within his lifetime. References to a Spanish national character and the travel by the protagonist to Salamanca point to a setting in Spain.

Miguel de Unamuno y Jugo

Unamuno was born into a Spain in turmoil. Since the temporary establishment of a constitution and a parliament early in the century, Spanish Republicans had agitated for reform in the face of one absolutist monarch after another. During a civil war between urban progressives and the rural, deeply Catholic anticonstitutional conservatives known as Carlists, Queen Isabella II (ruled 1833-68) succeeded to the throne. She proved to be an incompetent, divisive ruler, and her reign ended with her subjects' deposing her in the "Glorious Revolution" of 1868. The struggle for power that ensued, combined with a revolt by the Spanish colony of Cuba, led to political anarchy, quashed only by the army's restoring absolutist rule in the person of Isabella's son. Before the accession of Alfonso to the throne, however, the Basque region would experience the 1874 siege of Bilbao as the rural traditionalists with a stronghold throughout the north of Spain fought progressive forces; a child at the time, Unamuno witnessed this cruel siege, whose violence had a profound effect on him.

With the restoration of the monarchy came two decades of political stability, leading to some economic prosperity in the long-depressed nation. A renewed Cuban insurrection resulted in the Spanish-American War in 1898. The Spanish loss of that colony as well as Puerto Rico, Guam, and the Philippines, combined with agri-

cultural depression and the end of the economic boom, all of which came to a head in 1898, prompted an intellectual and political reaction (see *Generación del 98* below). These losses constituted challenges to the Spanish sense of national identity that merged with internal, regional movements for self-determination, the rise of labor movements, and the resurgence of republican sentiment in the early twentieth century. Spain remained neutral in World War I, even experiencing economic benefits. But the regional agitation, labor disturbances, and colonial rebellion continued, citizens grew disenchanted with the parliamentary regime, and a military coup resulted, establishing Primo de Rivera as dictator of Spain in 1923. (While *Mist*'s original publication in 1914 precedes this coup and Unamuno's vociferous opposition to Primo de Rivera, a prologue he added to the 1935 or third edition of the novel connects its events to Spain's political history; although the novel's characters theorize about whether or not they really exist, they live with each rereading, through all three editions, and through reprintings thereafter, outlasting the oppressive dictatorships crippling twentieth-century Spain.)

Unamuno's hostility to the Primo de Rivera regime led to his exile, first in the Canary Islands, and then in France. He returned to Spain only in 1930, when Primo de Rivera's fiscal extravagances and tight control finally wore thin with the public. New elections called for the establishment of a Spanish republic in 1931. That same year, Alfonso, the king who had endorsed Primo de Rivera's rule, left Spain, prudently acknowledging his unpopularity as manifested in a Republican resurgence, labor movements, and a society whose faith in monarchy had been shaken by its king's compliance with the dictatorship. The new republic tackled the current problems; it quieted regional insurgencies by inaugurating home rule for the Basque region and autonomy for Catalonia, initiated public works projects, and balanced taxation to make it more equitable. But these vast and difficult reforms, along with the severing of ties between the Church and state and the restructuring of the age-old Church-based educational system, began to strain the ties holding the fragile republic together. By 1936, a narrow electoral victory by the left, strikes, peasant rebellion, and general unrest gave way to a conspiracy to overthrow the government. Civil War ensued, and Francisco Franco emerged as a leader of the Nationalist, or anti-Republican, forces. Unamuno publicly de-

UNIVERSITY OF SALAMANCA

Located about two hours to the northwest of Madrid, the city of Salamanca has a varied and often distinguished history. Its cityscape is marked by architectural ornaments in Roman, Romanesque, Renaissance, and Neoclassical styles, representing the thousands of years of history there. Central to the last millennium of this history is the university located in the center of town. Founded in 1218 under Alfonso IX, it began to resemble a modern university in 1254, when, under Alfonso X, grandson of the founder, three chairs in canon law and one each in grammar, arts, and physics were established. One of the four principal universities in Europe (along with Oxford, Bologna, and Paris), Salamanca was, in the late Middle Ages, a hotbed of intellectual activity, especially in philosophy. This engagement with philosophy continued during the age of Fray Luis de León, a poet and scholar with a long and distinguished tenure at the university interrupted by four years (1572-76) of imprisonment by the Inquisition for unorthodoxy. As Spain itself became marginalized in Europe, losing hold of its global empire and remaining unindustrialized, Salamanca's university suffered a drop in continental reputation. The university saw many of its buildings destroyed during Napoleon's retreat from Spain and claimed only 400 students by 1875. But with Unamuno's appointment to the chair in Greek literature, Salamanca rallied against its by-then backwater status. Unamuno's high profile in newspapers and his well-publicized dismissal and later exile for his political convictions contributed to the restoration of the university's prestige. Today, the town of nearly 200,000 boasts a thriving university, whose ancient and beautiful buildings are still being used for classes. Another claim to fame here is the distinctively arcaded Plaza Mayor, one of the best-known sites in Spain. In fact, tourism, along with agricultural trade, comprises the economic base of present-day Salamanca.

nounced Franco's forces, and for this was removed from his office at the university. In 1939, three years after Unamuno's death, Franco would secure power in an iron grip with which he would rule for nearly 40 years.

Generación del 98. Spain's loss of the Spanish American War in 1898 topped off decades of instability, prompting writers and thinkers to embark on a period of national self-examination. While Spain, as one of the nations at the forefront of overseas explorations and colonial expansion, had helped usher Europe into its imperial era, the nation had long since faded from international prominence. This was due in part to economic and political troubles, and in part to the majority's relation to a Spanish Catholicism that encouraged religious faith rather than intellectual skepticism. The Golden Age of Spanish drama long past, Spain's largely marginalized arts and letters paralleled its political position on the periphery of world affairs; intellectuals and

artists saw a link between the two declines and sought to reinvigorate the national culture.

The Generation of 1898 was never an organized school and its members, while concurring that Spain's cultural and military decline was catastrophic, often disagreed on the best path for Spain to follow. The call for regeneration came from novelists, poets, essayists, and thinkers of widely different styles and philosophies. Yet they shared a common goal. All of them searched earnestly for the way to forge a modernized Spain, yet one distant from the politics orchestrated by the professional politicians who were removed from the genuine populace.

The term "Generation of 1898" came into use at the movement's inception, but it was formalized and made permanent by the essayist Azorín, whose collected works, *Clásicos y modernos* (Classics and Moderns), appeared in 1913, one year before the initial publication of *Mist*. Other noted members of the group included philosopher and critic José Ortega y Gasset, novelists

Angel Ganivet, Pío Baroja, and Ramón María del Valle-Inclán, and poets Antonio Machado and Manuel Machado. The two poets were particular friends of Unamuno. Interested in foreign works as well as domestic roots, members of the Generation reconnected Spanish letters to the rest of European thought. Ortega y Gasset, like Unamuno, was particularly influenced by Continental philosophy. In his skilled hands, along with Unamuno's and Azorín's, the essay achieved distinction as a genre in the country. The entire movement was pivotal in galvanizing Spanish intellectuals at the time, and in imparting a sense of purpose to modern Spanish life.

Unamuno and philosophy. While Unamuno thought of himself foremost as a poet, he also produced a number of novels and philosophical treatises. All of his writing held true to his belief that everyday language could express deep thoughts effectively. The absence of a formal structure in his philosophical writings distinguishes Unamuno from many of his contemporaries; he is aware of and embraces paradox in such works as *Del sentimiento trágico de la vida en los hombres y en los pueblos* (1913; The Tragic Sense of Life). Beginning with the logical musings of Descartes, European thought had taken a direction that relied on reason. But after having seen the cruelty of humans in the Carlist Siege in 1874 and having suffered a spiritual crisis when his son was struck with meningitis in 1897, Unamuno did not believe that reason alone could lead humans to peace or understanding. Rather, like the Danish philosopher Søren Kierkegaard, Unamuno rejected the faith in human reason that underpinned most of nineteenth-century philosophy. Emphasizing instead the irrationality of belief and the impossibility of knowing, Unamuno repeatedly discussed the human desire for immortality and the way it conflicted with our knowledge of the certainty of death. The decision to act as though life has meaning is indeed what gives it meaning. In keeping with this, belief must come from personal decisions, not from social norms or expectations, which provide only the illusion of significance. With these concepts at the core of all of his writings, Unamuno is an advocate of individualism in the face of the pressure to conform. His rejection of highly systematic approaches to the human condition and of blind faith place him in the existentialist tradition. Coined in the World War II era, existentialism refers to a family of philosophies that would gain currency in France and elsewhere three decades

after Unamuno wrote his novel. They were philosophies of despair, though much in existential writing does not really fit this definition. A human being has no God-given or nature-given essence, taught the existential philosophers. Instead each being defines him or her self by his or her choices and actions. Preoccupied with similar issues of individualism, choices, and death, Unamuno's own perspective can be viewed as a precursor of this tradition.

The Novel in Focus

Plot overview and prologues. *Mist* "recounts the lamentable life and mysterious death" of Augusto Pérez (Unamuno, *Mist*, p. 3). A wealthy, orphaned idler, Augusto falls in love with two women, exchanging stories and speculating throughout about love and fiction with his friend Víctor. When both women leave and deceive him, Augusto seeks solace in philosophy, consulting the well-known writer and philosopher Miguel de Unamuno, who also happens to be Augusto's creator. Confronted with the suggestion that he might not exist, Augusto angrily suggests that he, the character, has created the author, before succumbing to the death Unamuno has planned for him.

Although this plot sounds relatively straightforward until its climactic final confrontation of author and character, Unamuno was reluctant to call it a novel. Rather, he invented the term *nivola*, which sounds like the Spanish word for novel, *novela*, but also suggests a new level, or *nivel*, of writing. Essentially, Unamuno's nivolas are more dialogue-based than novels, rely less on description, and engage with philosophical issues.

Mist opens with a prologue signed by one Víctor Goti, who will also appear as a character in the novel. The fact that Unamuno has authored this prologue himself is never disclosed, though hints do appear throughout it, as Goti explains some of Unamuno's aesthetic beliefs and defends him against critics. Referring repeatedly to his own lack of free will, Goti nonetheless contends that Augusto succeeds in committing suicide.

Goti's prologue is humorous in its pedantry as well as its apparent lack of irony. "Don Miguel de Unamuno insists on my writing a prologue to this book of his" (*Mist*, p. 3), Goti begins, a line that in retrospect becomes quite funny when we realize that as a creation of Unamuno's mind, Goti is obliged to do whatever Unamuno tells him. Goti praises Unamuno for

EXISTENTIALISM

While the philosophy of existentialism is best associated with later figures, notably mid-twentieth-century French novelist and philosopher Jean Paul Sartre, Unamuno provides a link between the movement and its nineteenth-century Danish predecessor, Søren Kierkegaard (1813-55). Unamuno learned Danish especially so that he could read Kierkegaard's works, which rejected belief in rationalistic systems of organization. Only through the process of existing could people find truth, taught Kierkegaard; religious faith could only be achieved through serious personal contemplation. In *Either/Or* and *Fear and Trembling*, Kierkegaard explores the idea that organized religion often fails to provide answers, a feeling Unamuno had in 1897 when he experienced a crisis of faith. Like Kierkegaard, Unamuno believed that belief was an intensely personal experience.

Unamuno's own explorations of the conflict between faith and reason and the idea that free will and self-determination were a fallacy presaged those of Europe at large. The often senseless massacres of World Wars I and II, alongside an increasingly mechanized daily life and the rise of totalitarianism, led many to question the nature of human existence and the relationship between choice and morality. In the 1940s, existentialism became a major force in European thought; existentialists believe that because all actions are a result of choice, humans have absolute freedom, which leads to a sense of dread at the overwhelming responsibility of living. Unamuno was not as optimistic about free will, but he shares with the existentialists the belief that humans must live as if human life has transcendent meaning although there can be no certainty that it does.

pages before abruptly declaring that contrary to what the novel says, Augusto Pérez committed suicide, and was not killed by the author who created him.

Goti's prologue is followed immediately by a "post-prologue" that Unamuno himself takes credit for, one that he feels compelled to write in response to Goti's assertions. In it, Unamuno takes issue with the question of a character's powers versus those of the author, as well as with Goti's value judgments about the nature of Augusto's passing. The voice in this post-prologue is of an author trying to retain control of his characters, including Víctor Goti.

A third preamble, which occurs only in later editions, is written more in what might be called Unamuno's "real" voice or persona. In this prologue to the text, Unamuno refers to the real life, biographical events that have occurred since publication of the first edition of *Mist*, including the coup of Primo de Rivera and the looming dominance of Franco. These events make his earlier treatment of the questions of authorial control and the boundaries between the real and fictional world seem startlingly prescient. Referring

to the characters in his fictions, Unamuno writes that "This world of mine . . . is more real to me than the world of leaders and politicians like Canóvas and Sagasta, and Primo de Rivera, and kings like Alfonso XIII" (*Mist*, p. 23). Part of the reason that the dream world is more real is that it is eternal, whereas eras and events in history pass. With these thoughts, Unamuno argues that fictional ideas can have very real consequences and that reality is often influenced by the written word, concluding that though the novel, or *nivola*, tells the story of Augusto's death, he is eternal, immortal.

These three preambles, whose very presence sets the tone for the novel as well as introducing several of its characters and spelling out its subject matter, cannot be separated from the rest of the novel, which now begins in earnest. The reader is introduced to Augusto Pérez, a wealthy young man whose father has been long dead but whose mother has only recently passed away. Shortly before her death, Augusto's mother enjoined him to marry. Augusto lives with two longtime servants, Domingo and Luduvina, in a comfortable house in an unnamed Spanish provincial

THE *NIVOLA*

In creating a new form that he called the "nivola," Unamuno sought to avoid setting, description, and authorial predetermination, all in order to free characters to become individuals. He goes so far as to allow his character Víctor, in *Mist*, to take credit for the new approach to creation. The scene in which Víctor explains to Augusto his aesthetic approach exemplifies the very *nivola* form that he describes:

[Víctor] "Well, you see, one day when I didn't really know what to do, but felt an urge to do something, a deep yearning, a gnawing of phantasy, it was then that I decided to write a novel. But I determined to write it as life itself, without knowing what will happen next. I sat down, took out paper and started by setting down the first thing that crossed my mind, without thinking what would happen next, without any plan. My fictional characters will create themselves by the way they act and talk, especially in the way they talk. Their personalities will develop gradually. And sometimes their personalities will be not to have any personality at all."

[Augusto] "Like mine."

[Víctor] "I don't know. We'll see. I'm simply letting myself be carried along."

[Augusto] "And are you using psychological techniques? Description?"

[Víctor] "Whatever comes out in the dialogue, especially the dialogue. . . "

[Augusto] "You start thinking you're leading the characters around with your own hand, when you suddenly discover that you're being led around by them instead. Often enough, it's the author who becomes the toy of his own creations . . . it won't be a novel."

[Víctor] "No, that's true . . . it will be a *nivola*. . . . Then no one can say I'm violating the rules of the novel form."

(*Mist*, pp. 128-30)

city. An earnest, thoughtful man, Augusto takes himself very seriously, his dramatic emotions often appearing humorous to the reader.

Plot summary. As the novel opens, Augusto plans to amble about town under his umbrella (there is a light rain, one of the many mists to which the title refers), his mind racing through whimsical philosophical thoughts about God and the imagination. Unable to decide which way to walk, he plans to follow the next dog that passes, but his eye is caught and mesmerized instead by a beautiful woman, whom he tails to her home. Bribing a concierge, Augusto learns that her name is Eugenia Domingo del Arco, that she teaches piano, and that she is single. He returns home to compose a passionate letter to her, then delivers it to her apartment, where he learns that Eugenia has been the recipient of many such letters. Next, he goes to play chess with his friend Víctor, to whom he confesses his love. Curiously,

Víctor knows Eugenia, as do Domingo and Luduvina, Augusto's servants. Their unexplained acquaintance with Eugenia may be the first hint that the reader has that although this seems to be a lighthearted comic novel, what is happening on the level of plot is secondary to Unamuno's interest in the nature of fiction. Further evidence of Unamuno's philosophical interests comes in Augusto's existential conversations with a dog he finds, Orfeo, in which he speculates about the nature of reality and dreams, what it means to be in love, and whether he has a soul.

Winning an invitation into Eugenia's home by saving her aunt's canary from a fall, Augusto finds himself a welcome suitor in the eyes of the young woman's guardians, a busybody aunt and anarchical, Esperanto-speaking uncle. This uncle provides continual comic relief, as when he links non-phonetic spelling to human repression: "And away with the *H! H* is the height of absurdity, of reaction, of authority, of the Middle Ages, of retrogression! Down with *H!*" (*Mist,* p. 71). When Eugenia herself arrives home, however, she is cold and distant. Curious but undeterred by her reaction, Augusto returns home.

Meanwhile, we learn that Eugenia has a lover named Mauricio, of whom her guardians disapprove because he has no job. When Eugenia urges him to find work so that they can marry and she can quit teaching those hateful piano lessons, Mauricio lazily promises to look for work.

In search of a confidante, Augusto seeks out Víctor. En route to their gentleman's club, he turns his head toward woman after woman, finding himself drawn to and in love with all of them. Suddenly Augusto is confronted by Víctor, who, tired of waiting for him at the club, has discovered the young philosopher wandering in the opposite direction. Víctor explains to Augusto that he is in love with the abstract idea of woman as a way of expressing his concrete love for Eugenia. Augusto's inner monologue turns over the question of whether he is really in love.

The next day he returns to Eugenia's home, only to be rebuffed even more firmly than before. Soon his eye is caught by the young washerwoman Rosario, who delivers the laundry. His amorous attentions to her are marred by his admission that he loves another. She is hurt but promises to visit again. Soon after, Eugenia arrives at Augusto's home, furious because Augusto has bought the mortgage to the home Eugenia has been working to pay off. While Augusto swears he meant the gesture as one of unconditional love, Eugenia takes it as an attempt to buy her, so she rejects his gift of the mortgage payment. This refusal leaves him in "A mist of nonexistence," from which he emerges to find himself in a church (*Mist,* p. 98). The encounter in the church is the first of a number in which an anecdote is related with tangential meaning to Augusto's own life. Here, Don Avito Carrascal (a character who first appears in Unamuno's novel *Love and Pedagogy*) tells of the woes of his son, "a fictive personage like himself" (*Mist,* p. 99). Unsure if he believes in prayer or not, Avito is experiencing a spiritual crisis. His wife is his only comfort; he advises Augusto to marry a woman who loves him.

Needing to clear his head, Augusto heads to his club for a game of chess. Víctor mentions his own early forced marriage to a woman whom both his family and she mistakenly believed he had impregnated. He and his wife at first despaired of ever having children, then rejoiced in the freedom and companionship of their life, and

Primo de Rivera

were now expecting a child. At this point neither of them wants the child, whose incipient arrival causes another rift between them. Víctor thus advises Augusto to marry only if he wishes to engage in such struggles.

After expressing her outrage to her aunt at what she perceives as Augusto's effort to buy her by paying the mortgage, Eugenia goes to see Mauricio, who is still unemployed. He confesses to being a born idler and suggests that she marry Augusto to ensure the lovers a steady income. After this remark, Eugenia storms away from him in a rage. Meanwhile, Augusto and Víctor again philosophize at the club. Víctor relates a final relevant story, that of a landlady who marries her mortally ill tenant in the hopes of collecting the widower's pension, which would have gone to waste had the man remained a bachelor. The tenant marries her because he can no longer afford rent. Ironically, he lives longer than either expects. Rating the story as better than fiction, Víctor confesses that he is writing a novel to distract himself from his wife's pregnancy. The novel that he describes, which had no clear plot, little description, and a preponderance of dialogue, very much resembles the one we are reading. Víctor calls it a "nivola," claiming credit for a term that Unamuno himself has invented. Hearing about this enterprise leads Augusto to question whether his own existence is merely as a part of God's dreams: "*And what is my life? A novel? Nivola? Just what is it? Everything that happens to me and everyone around me, is it reality or fiction? Perhaps this is all no more than God dreaming, or somebody else dreaming*" (*Mist*, p. 131). As he does throughout the novel, Augusto speculates that reality is not as clear-cut as our senses tell us. Rather, moments of mist, when things are suddenly hazy, are actually moments of insight.

Upon seeing the young washerwoman Rosario again, Augusto becomes very tender. He kisses her and strokes her hair, then stops suddenly when he feels "mist" closing in over him. Again he begins to question his own existence. A few days later, Eugenia's aunt arrives to let Augusto know that Eugenia has been crying and refusing food and is now ready to accept his gift, if it does indeed come without condition. He assures the aunt that it does. His love for Eugenia having waned, he is annoyed when she arrives to visit and hints that perhaps she would be open to a renewal of his amorous avowals. In the middle of their meeting, Rosario's arrival is announced. When he meets with her, the laundress proclaims her loyalty to him.

The next day at the social club, a Don Antonio tells Augusto a story: Antonio's wife had an affair with another man, and Antonio ends up falling in love with the other man's wife. Next Augusto hears from Víctor about the status of his marriage: the erstwhile dreaded child is now a welcome addition to his household. These further stories and his mixed feelings about Eugenia and Rosario prompt a confused Augusto to write a study of women. He begins his research with Rosario, first behaving amorously and then sending her away abruptly. Approaching Eugenia next, he is instead controlled by her, and soon the two are engaged.

While Augusto is now a welcome visitor in her home, Eugenia continues to act coolly towards him. Rosario never visits again. One day Eugenia informs Augusto that her old boyfriend Mauricio is bothering her and asking that her fiancé use his influence to secure a job for him somewhere far away. Mauricio appears at Augusto's house with thanks for the job and the news that he and Rosario will be leaving together. Though he longs for Rosario, Augusto goes ahead with his engagement, until one day he receives a letter from Eugenia informing him that she and Mauricio have gone off together, leaving Rosario behind. Conversations with Víctor, now an elated father, fail to restore Augusto's mood, and soon he resolves to kill himself. He travels to Salamanca to meet with Unamuno, having read an essay by the author with reference to suicide. As they talk, Unamuno reveals to him that he is a fictional creation incapable of deciding to kill himself. Augusto counters by suggesting that perhaps it is Unamuno himself who is not real. They argue, mutually condemning each other to death. Augusto sadly returns home, eats an enormous meal, and dies, leaving the reader unsure as to whether he or his author has willed the death.

Metafiction. Unamuno is not the first author to appear in his own work, but his argument with Augusto over who controls the character's destiny predates by over 50 years sustained Western experimentation with the hierarchy of narrative levels in the novel and the concurrent theorizing about the "Death of the author." Unamuno's interest in exploring the limitations of the novelistic form, as well as in stretching and poking fun at previous schools of writing, reveal him to be concerned with Augusto's fate at a very serious level despite the novel's light tone.

One of Unamuno's main targets is realism. The previous generation of Spanish writers, epitomized by Benito Pérez Galdós, were part of a larger Western movement towards realism in writing (see **Fortunata and Jacinta,** also in *WLAIT 5: Spanish and Portuguese Literatures and Their Times*). Naturalists, authors who extended realism to its limits, subscribed to the belief that authors should give an abundance of physical and psychological details. These intricate descriptions were necessary because a human's surroundings determine his personality and actions. Unamuno's own philosophical outlook on life made such a view untenable to him, so *Mist* avoids the broad historical sweep and attention to detail of realist and naturalist fiction; it is instead a novel that, as L. Livingstone has said, "eliminate[s] all externals, particularly settings and character descriptions, in order to focus on individual personalities" (Livingstone in Gale).

From the first events of the novel, Unamuno hints to readers that his *nivola* will depart from the sorts of descriptive, plot-driven novels that readers usually expect. The multiple prologues mock the traditional use of a prologue by a famous author to boost the reputation of a lesser-known writer: "It is only natural that a young beginner like myself, wishing to make himself known, should ask a veteran man of letters, not for a prologue by way of presentation, but for the opportunity to prologue one of the master's works," on the assumption that books are bought for the content of the main body, not the prologue (*Mist*, p. 3). Moreover, the attribution of the first prologue to a character from the novel begins the process of clouding the distinctions between fiction and reality, as well as calling attention to the fact that we are reading a work of fiction. Finally, the discussion by both Goti and Unamuno in their separate prologues of Augusto's death distances this novel from one in which plot resolution is one of the main goals.

Augusto's opening decision in the novel, that he will follow the first dog he sees, can be viewed, Gayana Jurkevich has suggested, as "a humorous debunking of the determinism prevalent in the naturalist canon" (Jurkevich, p. 62); that is, while Unamuno himself questions the existence of free will, he finds the naturalist belief in behavior shaped by one's immediate environment to be simplistic, so he parodies it. The utter lack of description throughout the novel—we never get a description of any of the characters, of any of the settings, or of any clothing, for example—also challenges the idea that fiction relies on such details for its verisimilitude.

The metafictional dimension of the novel calls to the reader's attention that it is the act of writing that makes a character live; Unamuno's final prologue reminds us that characters depend on the act of reading as well. Through revisiting an old novel, we make it contemporary: "they live and relive as they are dreamed by each dreamer" (*Mist*, p. 20). In this way, the immortal characters of a novel are at some level more alive than human beings with a contained life span. Unamuno writes that his fictional world "is more real to me than the world of leaders and politicians" (*Mist*, p. 23). The ability of a fictional world to survive and withstand a world marked by random acts and oppressive dictators (such as Primo de Rivera) reveals the political angle that can underpin the metafictive project: just as an author has total control over his or her characters, so a dictator can dominate the lives of his subjects. The capacity for self-determination, the very battle Augusto fights with Unamuno and that Unamuno himself fights in a Primo de Rivera-dominated Spain, is a *vital* concern in the outside world, and sometimes fiction is the only place where ideals live on.

Literary context. Writing in the rich intellectual context of the Generation of 1898, Unamuno reflects the contemporary concern of breaking with tradition while reinvigorating national pride. Spain has ample reason to be proud of its literary history, boasting many great authors who produced poems, plays, and fiction of high quality. Miguel de Cervantes's **Don Quixote**, often cited as the first novel, is a masterpiece of comedy, satire, adventure, and romance; Calderón de la Barca's **Life is a Dream** is a dramatic masterwork (both also in *WLAIT 5: Spanish and Portuguese Literatures and Their Times*). The Golden Age of Spanish drama in the sixteenth and seventeenth centuries and the towering presence in the nineteenth century of the aforementioned Pérez Galdós, a master of psychological realism, also offered the Generation of 1898 ample sources for pride. Along with the essayist Azorín, who helped coin the name "Generation of '98," Unamuno led the way in encouraging renewed interest in Spain's literary classics. Unamuno's work regularly engages with his predecessors, and most especially with Cervantes; the tone of *Mist*, ironic and satirical yet serious, resembles that of Cervantes's mock epic. Like Pérez Galdós, Unamuno acknowledges distinctively Spanish ideas like Don Quixote's foolish yet noble idealism and aspects of a unique Spanish national character, including religious devotion and a passion for conversation.

While Unamuno's literary peers in Spain are clearly important sources for his work, the development of literary modernism on the rest of the European continent is also relevant. Outside Spain, the nineteenth century's literary goal of a near-scientific depiction of reality, which reached its height in realism and naturalism, confronted its limitations in the face of a modern era of confused urban chaos and psychological complexity. This recognition of the limits of empirical logic dovetailed nicely with Unamuno's own rejection of pure reason during a personal spiritual crisis he underwent in 1897. Like Unamuno, many modernist artists and authors broke with the goal of a mimetic representation of reality, seeking instead to openly challenge existing forms of representation and subject matter. Unamuno's description of the *nivola* touches on modernist discontents with existing modes of narration, and his interest in the notion of authorship parallels and even predates a modernist obsession with artistic identity. *Six Characters in Search of an Author* (1921), by Italian dramatist Luigi Pirandello, similarly explores the presence of multiple layers of artifice and reality in the production of a play, while protagonist Stephen Dedalus, created by Irish novelist James Joyce, speculates on the role of the author in much the same way that Víctor Goti does in Unamuno's *nivola*.

Unamuno's literary experiment reaches even further into twentieth-century consciousness, anticipating the questioning of dreams and reality in the mid-twentieth-century metafiction of Argentina's Jorge Luis Borges. Moreover, Unamuno's existential concerns with the meaning of reality and the possibility of free will and choice resemble those of later writers influenced by existentialism, including France's Albert Camus and Jean Paul Sartre and Ireland's expatriate novelist and dramatist Samuel Beckett. Still later movements, such as the French "New Novel" of the 1960s, share Unamuno's interest in innovation, disrupting boundaries between narrator, author, and character and experimenting with narrative techniques like avoiding description or blurring temporal distinctions. In its concern with the relationship of character to author and its innovative narration, *Mist* stands alone at the beginning of a twentieth century in which these interests will become central.

Reviews. While *Mist* was not necessarily understood by critics (Unamuno intended to "unnerve" them with it) the novel was among the most popular of the author's works (*Mist*, p. 18). As he himself notes in his 1935 prologue, *Mist* had by then been translated into at least ten languages. A 1928 English translation received mixed reviews. While many reviewers recognized the value of the novel's philosophical conundrums, it was seen as "an ironic exercise in dialectic rather than a novel" (*The Nation* in Knight, p. 778).

Spain itself did not warm immediately to Unamuno's challenging and puzzling novel: "The initial reception of *Niebla* [*Mist*] suggests that reader expectations in general were not ready for Unamuno's radical modal violations" (Spires, p. 34). Indeed, early critical reception classified the work as an attack on the novel. Early literary critics focused largely on Unamuno's other, more conventional works. Only in the 1960s, with the arrival of the French New Novel and the growth of interest in existentialism and metafiction throughout literary criticism, did *Mist* at last became the focus of sustained critical attention.

—Mary McGlynn

For More Information

The Gale Group. "Miguel de Unamuno." *Contemporary Authors Online.* 12/8/99. http://www.flicklives.com (May 2001).

Johnson, Roberta. *Crossfire: Philosophy and the Novel in Spain, 1900-1934.* Lexington: University Press of Kentucky, 1993.

Jurkevich, Gayana. *The Illusive Self: Archetypal Approaches to the Novels of Miguel de Unamuno.* Columbia: University of Missouri Press, 1991.

Knight, Marion, et al. *The Book Review Digest: Twenty-Fourth Annual Cumulation, Books of 1928.* New York: H. W. Wilson, 1929.

Marías, Julian. *José Ortega y Gasset: Circumstance and Vocation.* Trans. Frances M. López-Morillas. Norman: University of Oklahoma Press, 1970.

Shaw, Donald Leslie. *The Generation of 1898 in Spain.* London: E. Benn, 1975.

Spires, Robert C. *Beyond the Metafictional Mode: Directions in the Modern Spanish Novel.* Lexington: University Press of Kentucky, 1984.

Unamuno, Miguel. *Mist.* In *Novela/Nivola.* Vol. 6 of *The Selected Works of Unamuno.* Trans. Anthony Kerrigan. Princeton: Princeton University Press, 1976.

The Murmuring Coast

by

Lídia Jorge

Lídia Jorge was born in 1946, in the Algarve, a region of Portugal that would provide the setting for her two first novels. After graduating from the University of Lisbon, Jorge spent two intervals in Africa, first in Angola in 1969-70 and then in Mozambique in 1972-74. Her literary career started auspiciously in 1980 with the publication of her first novel, the highly acclaimed *O Dia dos Prodígios* (The Day of Wonders). To date, her body of works consists of ten titles, including a collection of short stories and a play about the early-twentieth-century Republican feminist Adelaide Cabete, *A Maçon*, (1977; The Free Mason). Her novels, some of which adopt a collective point of view, some of which use a more intimate narrative voice, present a complex, multifaceted picture of contemporary Portugal, one that conveys variations between urban and rural realities, between different generations, and indeed between male and female experiences. In keeping with her interest in exploring a plurality of voices and perspectives, *The Murmuring Coast* juxtaposes a male-authored tale with its revision by a female commentator.

Events in History at the Time the Novel Takes Place

Women during the New State. For over 40 years, Portugal lived under a dictatorial regime, António Salazar's "New State," which would last from 1932 until reestablishment of democracy by the Carnations Revolution in 1974. The New State's ideology coalesced around the interlinked

THE LITERARY WORK

A novel set during the colonial war in Mozambique (1964-74); published in Portuguese (as *A Costa dos Murmúrios*) in 1988, in English in 1995.

SYNOPSIS

The novel opens with the short story "The Locusts," which centers on the wedding reception of Evita and Luís Alex in wartime Mozambique. There follows an extended commentary by Eva Lopo, the former Evita, on the short story. She evokes in greater detail events experienced 20 years previously and, in the process, questions the focus adopted in "The Locusts."

notions of "Deus, Pátria, Família" (God, Country, Family). As suggested by the slogan, the regime enlisted religion both to support traditional family values and to legitimize Salazar's nationalistic empire-building project in Africa.

Salazar's conservative outlook—he was a seminary-educated bachelor from a rural background—had a particularly adverse effect on women. The progressive Republican Constitution of the 1910s was replaced by the New State's 1933 constitution, which significantly reduced the rights of women. For instance, whereas the 1910 constitution made divorce available to men and women on equal footing, the new constitution outlawed

Lídia Jorge

divorce for all women married within the Church, that is, for the overwhelming majority of the female population. Salazar's repressive expectations of women, to be dutiful, dependent wives and mothers, were furthermore encoded in law, which, under the guise of equality, in effect subordinated women to men. Indeed, the 1933 Constitution (in)famously stated that everyone was equal before the law "except, as regards women, the differences resulting from their nature or from the interest of the family" (Guimarães, p. 19). In 1939, a new legal code declared that a husband could force his wife to return to the marriage if she had left him. Married women were curtailed in other ways too: until 1969, they could not get a passport to leave Portugal without their husband's permission, for instance. In sum, while valued as mothers, women were all too often confined to domesticity.

How did the female population react? From the late 1950s onwards, there was an ever-increasing gap between the progressive outlook of a minority of the more urban, middle-class, educated women on the one hand, and the limited expectations of rural and/or lower-class women on the other. It is certainly no coincidence that the 1972 release of an explosive new work, *New Portuguese Letters*, advocating women's rights, was written by three women who attended university in the late 1950s. It is a work (by Maria

Velho da Costa, Maria Isabel Barreno, and Maria Teresa Horta) that vividly captures the ignorance and oppression in which Salazar's regime maintained the uneducated masses, particularly women. Historically speaking, the silent majority's acceptance of traditional roles is tellingly encapsulated in the widespread popularity of "Casamentos de Sto António," or mass wedding ceremonies in honor of patron saint Anthony. These ceremonies took place yearly between 1958 and 1973, thanks to joint sponsorship by the government and the local business community, with eligibility being based on the bride's poverty and her virginity. In *The Murmuring Coast*, Salazar's active pursuit of pro-family policies, and concomitant indoctrination of women at the expense of their individual freedom, is relentlessly ridiculed. While "The Locusts" depicts as its central theme a traditional wedding, Lídia Jorge undermines its fairy-tale aura through the use of irony: not only is the protagonist Eva Lopo not a virgin, but she far from lives happily ever after with Luís Alex. In fact, his suicide brings the love story to an abrupt end, before she can bear him any children.

The dominant discourses of Portuguese colonialism. Salazar's nationalistic empire-building project in Africa had its roots at the turn of the century, when European powers engaging in a scramble for control of Africa were required to provide proof of effective occupation of their colonies. The consolidation of the Portuguese empire was undoubtedly central to the regime's rhetoric, which endeavored to construct an image of Portugal as a renewed world player.

At home, the dictatorship reappropriated the nation's cultural heritage to legitimize its expansionist politics in Africa. Fernando Pessoa's *Mensagem* (1934; ***Message,*** also in *WLAIT 5: Spanish and Portuguese Literatures and Their Times*), for example, was used and abused to justify colonial ideology, which subordinated the economic, social, and political interests of the colonies to those of the metropolis. A key text, *Mensagem* formulates the myth of a new empire led by the Portuguese. Schoolchildren were made to learn by heart the patriotic poems of *Mensagem*, a fact ridiculed in *The Murmuring Coast*, where some of Pessoa's most famous lines are deliberately misquoted. This happens most notably in a two-page description of the hotel's receptionist, the black Bernardo, who is perceived as a symbol of the civilizing mission bestowed upon the Portuguese by divine decree: "It was there in the last port, that

---

WOMEN'S TRAJECTORY FROM REPUBLIC TO NEW STATE: QUALIFIED FREEDOM TO CONFINEMENT

1910 New marriage laws say a woman is no longer obligated to obey her husband; divorce becomes legal in Portugal for men and women equally; women still cannot vote

1933 New constitution makes all citizens equal before the law, except for women, because of "differences inherent in their nature and the interest of the family"

1948 Government disbands National Council of Portuguese Women after it organized debates, discussions, and a large exhibition of books written by women

1967 A new civil code proclaims that the husband is head of the family with the power to make all decisions related to married life and children

1972 Publication of the book *Novas Cartas Portuguesas* (New Portuguese Letters) by Maria Velho da Costa, Maria Isabel Barreno and Maria Teresa Horta, a book that talks openly about women's sexual lives

1974 Revolution of April 25 overthrows dictatorship; democracy is established; Portugal abolishes all electoral restrictions based on gender

---

Bernardo had been found. . . . The road had been difficult but worthwhile" (Jorge, *The Murmuring Coast*, p. 84). The cracks in this civilizing mission are succinctly exposed when Bernardo is poisoned by methylated spirits, which, like countless other "uncivilized" blacks, he had mistaken for white wine.

Abroad, Salazar's colonial discourse was equally shrewd. In the aftermath of World War II, when England lost India, "the Jewel in the Crown," Portugal adjusted policies in its own empire. In 1951, for example, Portugal renamed its colonies "Overseas Provinces." Policymakers aimed to demonstrate to the outside world that African possessions such as Angola and Mozambique constituted an integral part of the national territory.

Colonial war in Mozambique. Throughout the 1960s, Portugal became involved in deeply damaging colonial wars in Africa. Rebellion broke out in Angola in early 1961, and by 1964 armed struggle had spread to Mozambique. The Portuguese government mounted intensive military campaigns, but the rebels continued to engage in heavy fighting throughout the decade and into the 1970s. It is thought that at the height of the war, Portuguese involvement was such that "a quarter of all men of military age were in uniform" (MacQueen, p. 76).

In the case of Mozambique, the liberation movement, FRELIMO (*Frente de Libertação Moçambicana*) suffered two serious, albeit temporary, setbacks. The first took place in February 1969, when FRELIMO's president, Eduardo Mondlane, was assassinated by a parcel bomb sent to his office. The second occurred when its liberated zones in the northern provinces were partially recaptured by the colonial army following a massive Portuguese campaign from May to August 1970. Led by Portugal's General Kaúlza de Arriaga, the campaign involved about 30,000 ground troops. By comparison, FRELIMO at the time claimed a total of about 10,000 fighters (MacQueen, p. 48).

These historical facts are echoed in the closing chapter of *The Murmuring Coast,* when a nameless Portuguese general announces the unqualified success of a Portuguese offensive in a press conference. It "had struck the principal enemy sanctuaries, captured weapons, ammunition, supplies, dismantled cultures by fire and bombardment" (*Murmuring Coast*, p. 243). The assassination of FRELIMO's president, Mondlane, is explicitly mentioned in the general's parting words: "The general recalled the bomb that had recently exploded in Mondlane's face" (*Murmuring Coast*, p. 249). This was adduced as a further proof that a definitive Portuguese victory was within sight. The novel, however, undermines the Portuguese general's grandiloquent discourse, by juxtaposing on either side of it a string of details that graphically illustrate the reality of the war: drunken men, a large-scale need for washing (both literal and metaphorical), and the

PORTUGUESE EXPANSIONISM AND *THE MURMURING COAST*

The dominant discourses of Portuguese expansionism are parodied and relentlessly ridiculed in *The Murmuring Coast* in an episode in which a blind captain travels through Portuguese Africa to deliver a lecture pompously entitled "Portugal D'aquém e D'além Mar é Eterno" (Portugal Within and Beyond Its Borders Is Eternal). The lecture reproduces all the clichés of the Establishment regarding the sacred integrity of the overseas provinces. The captain's blindness may indeed be a thinly veiled reference to the metaphorical "blindness" of Salazar, who in 1968 had been left disabled by a stroke, but who misguidedly continued to believe himself in charge of the nation until his death in 1970. Simultaneously, the lecturing captain may also act as an oblique reference to Marcelo Caetano who, upon assuming the mantle of leadership from Salazar, undertook a week-long tour of the colonies in April 1969 (in contrast to Salazar, who never set foot in Africa). Regrettably, Caetano's tour only strengthened his resolve to pursue his predecessor's policies on colonial war.

scathing perspective of Evita's husband—"It was a goddamned hell" (*Murmuring Coast,* p. 250).

In any case, the temporary military success of the Portuguese quickly evaporated. Not only did FRELIMO regain Cabo Delgado and Niassa, it was also able to maintain "an enlarged presence in Tete" (MacQueen, p. 47). The Portuguese responded by stepping up violence: "the colonial security forces adopted terrorist tactics learnt [second-hand] from Vietnam to burn down villages and round up peasants in security compounds" (Birmingham, p. 178). This culminated in the Wiriamu massacre in December 1972, an event alluded to in the novel as a horror waiting to happen in the wings of history, alongside others: "that will be the smell that will rise from Wiriamu, Juwau, Mucumbura" (*Murmuring Coast,* p. 265). Historians usually foreground Wiriamu as the one exemplary war atrocity perpetrated by the Portuguese on civilians, perhaps because it came to international attention fairly promptly through a report in *The Times* on July 10, 1973.

In fact, the reports of missionaries, on which *The Times* article was based, testify to repeated massacres on the part of the Portuguese army.

> The first report states that at about 2 P.M. on Saturday 16 December jets bombed the hamlets of Wiriyamu and Juwau. In the neighbouring village of Chawola the people saw the bombs dropping and the smoke rising and gathered in the centre of their village, terrified. They intended to flee but soldiers arrived and forced them to line up. They were told to clap their hands, and as they did so the troops opened

fire. The bodies were then covered with straw and burnt, during which time a few survivors managed to slip away.

> The second part of the report fills in what happened at the other two settlements. After the bombing, commandos arrived by helicopter, and proceeded to ransack Wiriyamu and Juwau and kill the inhabitants, exhibiting gross brutality—kicking children to death, beating people, burning them alive, tearing an unborn child from the womb, and raping young girls.
> (International, p. 19)

Furthermore, other reports of similar incidents continued to surface: "Portuguese soldiers kill another 19 innocent in Dak" "Women and children burnt and killed by the commandos in Mucumbura" and "Massacre in the chiefdom of Chief Gandali" (International, pp. 33, 34, 41).

In other words, by listing Wiriamu alongside that of several lesser-known massacres, Jorge succeeds in avoiding the historical textbook practice of discussing one representative war atrocity, which often results in the overshadowing of countless others. Moreover, the novel's central episode consists of a lengthy disclosure of hundreds of horrific secret photographs, which inscribe the violence inflicted on local populations by the Portuguese army, in a series of fictional campaigns endowed with grotesquely fictional names (such as Crazy Tiger, Ferocious Wolf, and so forth). The photographs do not depict any one historically documented massacre. Yet, despite their fictional status, they undoubtedly foreshadow the violence of each and every subsequent war killing, Wiriamu included.

The novel's divergence from the "truth" as depicted by historical analyses arguably makes the full-scale horror and human cost of the tragedy of war more immediate. But Jorge's preference for the fictional over the analytical mode can also be partly explained as a reaction to an essential feature of the New State: several decades of censorship. Indeed, for many years, every single newspaper published both in the metropolis and in the overseas colonies had to carry the stamp "*visto pela censura*" (seen by the censors). This ensured that the media was largely unable to voice political dissent, especially in connection with the colonial wars. The strategies of avoidance and cover-up used by the regime in connection with the war are wryly exposed to a devastating effect in the "The Locusts," where euphemisms are repeatedly used to deny that a war is taking place at all: "besides, this wasn't really a war but merely a rebellion being carried out by savages" (*Murmuring Coast,* p. 6). In such a climate, the Wiriamu massacre was promptly denied by official governmental sources and was not discussed in the Portuguese press of the time, nor were other breaches of human rights. Later, the official inquiry was shelved by Kaúlza de Arriaga, the very general implicated in the violence.

Yet, despite the stepping up of violence and succession of war atrocities, the Portuguese army did not manage to regain overall control of Mozambique. As a result, the officers' morale slowly disintegrated as the unwinnable war went on and on without definitive result.

The Novel in Focus

Plot summary. *The Murmuring Coast* opens with the short story "The Locusts," a highly stylized account of reality, whose veracity is later thrown into question by Eva's account. Several loosely connected events that in fact occurred over a period of two and a half months (as Eva Lopo subsequently discloses) are brought into focus through the wedding reception of Evita and Luís Alex, a Portuguese mathematician-turned-soldier. The wedding, which takes place in the Hotel Stella Maris, on a terrace overlooking the Indian Ocean, becomes a focal point around which all other action converges.

The tale starts with a fairy-tale framing of the newlyweds as they kiss, but immediately draws attention to the constructed nature of the event itself by introducing a photographer who makes the couple adopt several poses while he searches for the best angle to capture them on camera. The newlyweds leave in a car loaned to them by Luís Alex's superior in the army, initially introduced as simply "a hero." The couple subsequently returns to make love in the bathroom.

In the morning everyone congregates again on the terrace, but this time encounters a very different spectacle: that of countless black dead bodies washed ashore by the tide. The explanation for this puzzling fact is provided by the groom's superior, Jaime Forza Leal: the blacks mistook methylated spirits for white wine and, after consuming it, they died. As the blame for the deaths is squarely attributed to the blacks themselves, the initial stir soon dissolves.

The newlyweds, who have remained almost blissfully removed from the commotion, return to the terrace at nightfall, dancing to imaginary music. By this point, imagined visions of reality are shown to be more real to the gathered community than reality itself. As the lights switch on, everything turns green, thanks to an invasion of locusts. The locusts, which give the short story its title, illustrate how events are unavoidably colored or filtered, according to the lens used. In the story, the locusts cancel out all the red objects in the terrace, before obscuring everything. Red is the color of blood, violence, and war, while in Portugal green stands for hope, so the locusts might imply on a symbolic level the end of war and Portuguese victory. Yet such interpretation is thrown into doubt as the story draws to a close, to such an extent that it becomes difficult not to bear in mind instead the powerful symbolism of the locusts as a biblical curse.

Indeed, what follows is the rumor of a white body amongst those of the blacks, which prompts the arrival of a journalist. Luís Alex volunteers to deal with the intruder and a shot is heard. In an unexpected final twist, however, the tale ends with the appearance of the dead body of Luís Alex himself, who has committed suicide. Despite increasingly disturbing events culminating in the groom's suicide, the steadfast belief in a hidden harmony among the Portuguese, the driving force that holds the community and the story together, remains overtly unchallenged. Thus, even Luís Alex's untimely demise becomes transformed through poetic vision into a transcendental truth of ineffable beauty: "Everybody, including Evita, understood that an excess sense of harmony, happiness, and beauty can provoke suicide more than any other state of mind" (*Murmuring Coast,* p. 33).

African soldiers of the Mozambique Liberation Front.

If on one level language creates a cohesive, albeit increasingly ludicrous and incongruous vision of reality, an all-pervasive irony simultaneously renders the text unstable and deconstructs it. What is ultimately questioned is the patriarchal ideology of Salazar, a colonial-style ideology that poisons both marriages and the local population in the name of a greater cause. As such, the colonized point of view (be it that of blacks or women), although repeatedly silenced, cannot be indefinitely suppressed and is re-inscribed through highly symbolic details. In the tale, this is perhaps best encapsulated by the five-man band playing at the wedding, where the white lead man, intent on imitating a black voice, sings the highly meaningful lyrics "Please get out of here tonight," unwittingly articulating the perspective of the colonized.

Likewise, Eva Lopo's memory of events is instrumental in voicing an alternative point of view. In her lengthy commentary after reading the short story, a commentary that occupies the bulk of the novel, the events providing the "raw material" for the highly selective account of "The Locust" come to the fore. From the start, Eva (and by extension her creator, Lídia Jorge) challenges the belief in unity, universal harmony, and underlying pattern, dismissing it as a Renaissance and Enlightenment myth. In so doing, she calls into question the viability of a grand narrative modeled on earlier master narratives, such as the epic poem on the Portuguese discoveries, *The Lusiads* (also in *WLAIT 5: Spanish and Portuguese Literatures and Their Times*). Although in the course of her conversation Eva repeatedly tells the author of "The Locusts" that he was right to leave out a number of episodes, so as not to upset the overall coherence of his story, she gradually brings out omissions to such a devastating effect that her own disjointed picture displaces the original version.

Eva's oral account, which eschews rhetoric, gradually erodes any manmade illusions of order, control, or knowledge. In Chapter 2, the rhetoric of heroism is unmasked as a megalomaniac fallacy in a reference to the enormous war scar of Jaime Forza Leal, the ridiculously macho superior of Luís Alex: "when the Captain walked by in his transparent shirt, I thought I was looking at the last man of the century to see himself in his scar" (*Murmuring Coast*, p. 59). Instead, Eva focuses on the numerous women left behind in the Hotel Stella Maris, and their own private "fights" while their husbands are away on a "sacred" war mission. Furthermore, the two main war episodes that emerge from her narrative prove to be barbaric acts carried out against unsuspecting civilians.

The first consists of the above-mentioned death of countless blacks, following widespread consumption of methylated spirits mistaken for white wine. The conspiracy of silence surrounding countless casualties makes Eva, armed with incriminating evidence, seek out a mulatto journalist, Alvaro Sabino. But the latter drags his heels, and it is not until the death of a white pianist that newspapers take up the story. Against the backdrop of these absurd deaths, another type of violence is foregrounded through the hundreds of secret photographs shown to Evita by Helena, Forza Leal's wife, which provide disturbing evidence of the Portuguese army's killing of civilians.

The violence captured by the camera and orally confirmed by Góis, the invalid colleague of Luís Alex, is such that it shakes to its roots Evita's sense of identity, not to mention her relationship with her husband and the world at large. The chapters that follow question various dominant discourses, with Eva resolutely positioning herself as a dissident voice. She remembers a former history professor at the University of Lisbon and his dogmatic intransigence, as he verbally shot down any alternative points of view. Next comes a description of the previously mentioned lecture "Portugal Within and Beyond Its Borders Is Eternal," delivered by a blind captain. The wisdom he embodies is ironically challenged when he is prevented from making a proper conclusion by the sudden invasion of locusts. Finally, in the closing chapter, upon the return of soldiers from the front, the general gives a press conference, confidently predicting a Portuguese victory. The prediction is, however, questioned by Luís Alex, who states that: "It was a bluff" (*Murmuring Coast*, p. 250). In other words, megalomanic discourses of power and control are unmasked as grotesque delusions.

Meanwhile, yearning for like-minded souls, Eva spends most of her free time with her two potential allies: Helena and the journalist Alvaro Sabino, who becomes her lover. But although both appear to be against the dominant order, their behavior ultimately reinscribes the *status quo*. Helena remains subservient to her cruel husband, and Sabino departs for Europe, actions that prompt Eva into distancing herself from both of them.

As the novel draws to a close, the damage and mutilation caused by Salazar's imperial ideology and war policies are shown to be extensive and responsible for the almost schizophrenic split created within the main characters. Eva Lopo repeatedly dissociates herself from her former

name ("I was Evita"), showing that her two selves are not interchangeable. As for Luís Alex, whose nickname, like Evita's name, undergoes transformation as he changes from mathematician (Evariste Galois) to would-be hero (Luis Galex), we also witness the collapse of his sense of identity. On return from the front, his masculinity has been undermined at its core, to such an extent that he does not have sexual relations with Evita again, in sharp contrast with his sexual power in the short story. Once Luís Alex has lost faith in a heroic war, the only possible solution for him is death. Significantly, serious doubt is cast as to whether he commits a heroic suicide, as portrayed in "The Locusts," or as is retrospectively claimed by the journalist. According to Eva, at the end of the novel, Luís Alex prosaically loses his life in a car accident. Her version of events implies that his death was certainly not prompted by "an excess sense of harmony, happiness, and beauty," as suggested in the short story, but precisely by its opposite, because his belief in a unifying system has been shattered.

The problematization of history. *The Murmuring Coast* displays affinities with many other postrevolutionary works of fiction in its questioning of the traditional mode of writing history. Throughout the narrative, Eva Lopo is intent not so much on setting the record straight, since she in fact doubts whether it is ever possible to reach one definitive version of events, but on fleshing out the ghost story provided by the "The Locusts," thus offering at least an alternative version.

Eva provides this version in two ways. The first is by repeatedly drawing attention to the importance that traditional historiography places on the printed text (and/or images) to the exclusion, it is implied, of less coherent or reliable oral accounts such as her own. In that connection, her initial reaction to the disclosure of the gruesome photographs is extremely revealing. She wishes their destruction, for without tangible evidence, it would be as if nothing had happened.

> Ah, Library of Alexandria, so often set ablaze, how I admire you (said Eva Lopo)! The sublime knowledge of your yellowing, burned papyrus, transformed into curls of smoke, has written miles and miles of unawareness throughout the centuries.
>
> (*Murmuring Coast*, p. 132)

Yet, by the end of the novel, her very recalling and inscription of the scene in which Forza Leal and Luís Alex burn the incriminating photographs shows that Eva resolutely refuses to collude with their suppression of evidence, even though she realizes the fragility of her testimony.

Eva uncovers a further shortcoming of traditional historiography as she questions its artificial construction of a linear narrative, which depends on a potentially arbitrary selection of material. In fact, as a history student at the University of Lisbon, she had already revealed herself to be weary of manmade versions of history, with their reductive, linear view of time, which privileges the point of view of the dominant order. Her own concept of history highlights simultaneity: "in my concept of History there is room for the influence of invisible muscles" (*Murmuring Coast,* p. 203). Her own narrative details how, for instance, the public uproar over the death of the white pianist achieves press coverage, while the simultaneous miscarriage of one of the wives, who not only loses her child, but also ruptures her sphincter muscle in the process, elicits attention only from the other women in the Stella Maris.

By juxtaposing events in this way, Eva is drawing attention to the fact that historical accounts are fictional constructs; they organize, include, and exclude with an unspoken ideological bias. Her own narrative is an effort to offer an alternative point of view. By recovering the wound of the wife who miscarries from oblivion, Eva provides an ironic counterpoint to the "heroic" war scar of Forza Leal, firmly reinscribing not only women's roles into mainstream accounts, but also a woman-centered representation of reality. This culminates in the closing pages of the novel, where she provocatively contrasts her version of Luís Alex's death with both that of the journalist and that of the male narrator of "The Locusts," by reiterating "There was in fact a slight difference" (*Murmuring Coast,* p. 267). In her version of events, Luís Alex meets an inglorious end.

Eva's commentary can in many ways be equated to a counter-odyssey, insofar as it challenges predominantly male ways of writing history. In the *Odyssey,* the Greek hero Odysseus (credited in Portuguese mythology with the founding of the capital of Portugal's kingdom, Lisbon), journeys home to Ithaca from the Trojan war to recover his house and his own kingdom. Unlike him, Eva does not return 20 years later to her exact point of origin. But what she can and does do is challenge the Greek epic's stance and concomitant proclamation of the heroism of war, which the general so uncritically endorsed: "Let each man march to the front line,

whether he dies or whether he lives. Thus do war and battle kiss and whisper" [murmur in the original] (*Murmuring Coast,* p. 248). It is precisely because she does not collude with the prevailing patriarchal ideology, which ultimately can only afford the kiss of death, as demonstrated by Luís Alex's abrupt demise, that Eva survives the memory of the traumatic events in which she is involved. Her transgressive laughter in the closing lines of the novel signals her wry awareness of both the need to displace false memories and mutilating ideologies and, simultaneously, of the transient nature of all points of view: "the sounds separate themselves from the words, and of the sounds only murmurs remain, the final stage before erasure, said Eva Lopo, laughing. Handing back, annulling 'The Locusts'" (*Murmuring Coast,* p. 274).

Sources and literary context. After the Carnations Revolution of April 1974, Portugal witnessed a proliferation of writers intent on re-examining its recent history. Postrevolutionary fiction usually betrays the influence of postmodernist ideas and, as such, often rejects conventional representation, privileging instead fragmented and/or multiple voices as well as subjective points of view, which articulate alternative truths. One of the major distinguishing features of the postrevolutionary period is the monumental increase in women's fictional output. A notable precursor in the new trend was the appearance in 1972 of the **New Portuguese Letters** (also in *WLAIT 5: Spanish and Portuguese Literatures and Their Times*), which marked a watershed, both by challenging more conventional modes of writing fiction and by paving the way for subsequent female-authored texts.

As far as the re-examination of colonial war was concerned, the trend started with Lobo Antunes's damning account of the war in Angola, in **South of Nowhere** (1979; also in *WLAIT 5: Spanish and Portuguese Literatures and Their Times*). There followed female accounts such as Wanda Ramos's *Percursos* (1980; *Journeys*) and Joana Ruas's *Corpo Colonial* (1981; *Colonial Body*), as well as other male-authored texts such as João de Melo's *Autopsia de um Mar em Ruínas* (1984; Post-Mortem of a Sea in Ruins). Numerous other authors bring the more general issue of colonial war into their novels. An interesting example is to be found in Teolinda Gersão's *Paisagem com Mulher e Mar ao Fundo* (1982; Landscape with Woman and Sea in the Background), a work of fiction primarily concerned with challenging patriarchal discourse (in which dictator Oliveira Salazar features under the ominous guise of his initials O. S.).

Events in History at the Time the Novel Was Written

The Portuguese revolution, decolonization, and democracy. The Carnations Revolution in April 1974 was a military coup by the MFA (Movimento Forças Armadas), a movement led in Lisbon by the young captains who had fought in Africa. Following the re-establishment of democracy in Portugal, decolonization took place fairly swiftly, with all the African countries achieving their independence by the end of 1975. The final footnote to the end of Portugal colonialism occurred in 1999 when control of Macau reverted to China.

A byproduct of the return to democracy and ensuing African decolonization was the demobilisation of the troops and the simultaneous return of some half million Portuguese nationals (known as *retornados)* from the ex-empire. Their reabsorption into mainstream Portuguese society presented a considerable challenge and, in this connection, literature undoubtedly had an important role to play, helping to articulate experiences and cement the healing process.

From the late 1970s onward, Portugal's external policy became increasingly concerned with its links to Europe, a move that culminated in 1986 with Portuguese entry into the EEC (European Economic Community), at the same time as Spain. By then, Portuguese internal politics, which until the early 1980s had been characterized by a succession of minority governments, was achieving greater stability. Indeed, the leader of the center-right party PSD (Partido Social-Democrata), Cavaco e Silva, who had been in power since the end of 1985 in a minority government, was re-elected as prime minister in July 1987 with an overall majority in parliament. Significantly, the previous year, in 1986, the socialist Mário Soares was elected president, a fact widely interpreted by political commentators as an illustration of the country's endemic fear, following decades of an authoritarian regime, of giving too much power to a single political group. Only in the mid-1990s would there be for the first time a president and a prime minister of the same political persuasion.

Meanwhile, in Mozambique, fighting continued in the aftermath of the April Revolution until a cease-fire was finally negotiated and took effect from September 1974. The agreement stipulated that the country would become independent the following year, on June 25, 1975, when FRELIMO took power. But, far from ensuring political stability, independence led to renewed conflict as the country became embroiled in a prolonged and damaging civil war, which was to last until the early 1990s, leaving the country economically and structurally devastated.

Women after the Revolution. The Revolution brought about many significant changes for women, not least of all the right to equality, enshrined in the new constitution of 1976. Women were at last allowed to join the diplomatic service or pursue a career as magistrates (but interestingly, not as members of the armed forces until a decade later, in 1987). A further symbolic barrier was broken when in 1979 a woman, Maria de Lurdes Pintassilgo, briefly held the office of prime minister. But to this day, women's representation in the Portuguese parliament and local politics remains one of the lowest in Europe.

Furthermore, in the most backward, often illiterate sectors of society, women were and are still frequently perceived to be second-class citizens. Since 1975, the Comissão para a Condição Feminina, renamed Comissão para Igualdade dos Direitos da Mulher (the Women's Equal Rights Commission) in the early 1990S, has mounted a commendable effort to eradicate all forms of discrimination against women, fighting illiteracy and sexist stereotyping of women in advertising and school manuals. Also the commission has campaigned against problems such as prostitution (a theme tackled by Jorge in 1984 in *Notícia da Cidade Silvestre* (Echoes from the Wild City) and wife-battering (a theme developed in one of Jorge's most haunting short stories, "Marido," published in *Husband and Other Stories* (1997).

Reviews. The publication of *The Murmuring Coast* in 1988 was greeted with widespread acclaim. By then, Jorge had already been hailed as one of the most promising postrevolutionary writers, and her preceding three novels had received recognition for their thematic virtuosity and stylistic innovations in the form of several literary prizes: *O Dia dos Prodígios* (1980; The Day of Wonders) was awarded the Ricardo Malheiros prize; *O Cais das Merendas* (1982; Picnic Quay) and *Notícia da Cidade Silvestre* (1984; Echoes from the Wild City) both received the Cidade Lisboa prize. *The Murmuring Coast* has been unanimously considered Lídia Jorge's most remarkable work to date. It quickly achieved the status of a canonical work of fiction, selling over 50,000 copies in under one year, followed by numerous reprints (by 1992, the date of the publication of her next novel, it had been reprinted seven times) and translation into several languages. Like its predecessor, Lobo

Antunes's seminal novel, *South of Nowhere*, *The Murmuring Coast* was praised in the first instance for its powerful exorcism and revision of the traumatic effects of the colonial war. The attention of more recent scholars has since broadened to focus on the novel's far-reaching reflections on issues such as personal and collective identity, memory, history, language and representation itself. Indeed *The Murmuring Coast* is both a war novel and much more. In the words of a distinguished Portuguese reviewer at the time of publication, "Is *The Murmuring Coast* a bitter, nihilistic novel? Most certainly not. . . . *The Murmuring Coast* is above all else a magnificently planned and written work . . . recreating once more, out of the crushing denunciation of imperialism, colonialism, war, oppression, violence, sexism, the fragile, paradoxical dignity of human existence" (Santos, p. 67).

—Claudia Pazos-Alonso

For More Information

Birmingham, David. *A Concise History of Portugal.* Cambridge: Cambridge University Press, 1993.

Ferreira, Ana Paula. "Lídia Jorge's *A Costa dos Murmúrios*: History and the Postmodern She-Wolf." *RHM* 45 (1992): 268-278.

Guimarães, Elina. *Portuguese Women: Past and Present.* Lisbon: Comissão de condição feminina, 1978.

International Defense and Aid Fund. *Terror in Tete: A Documentary Report of Portuguese Atrocities in Tete District, Mozambique 1971-72.* London: International Defense and Aid Fund, 1973.

Portuguese Literary and Cultural Studies 2 (1999).

Jorge, Lídia. *The Murmuring Coast.* Trans. Natália Costa, and Ronald W. Sousa. Minneapolis: University of Minnesota Press, 1995.

Kaufman, Helena, and Anna Klobucka, eds. *After the Revolution: Twenty Years of Portuguese Literature.* London: Associated University Presses, 1997.

MacQueen, Norrie. *The Decolonization of Portuguese Africa: Metropolitan Revolution and the Dissolution of the Empire.* London: Longman, 1997.

Sadlier, Darlene. *The Question of How: Women Writers and the New Portuguese Literature.* New York: Greenwood, 1989.

Santos, Maria Irene Ramalho de Sousa. "Bondoso Caos: *A Costa dos Murmúrios* de Lídia Jorge." *Colóquio-Letras* 107 (1989): 64-67.

Vicente, Ana. *As Mulheres em Portugal na Transição do Milénio.* Lisbon: Multinova, 1998.

Nada

by
Carmen Laforet

Born in Barcelona in 1921, Carmen Laforet spent her childhood and adolescence in the Canary Islands (Las Palmas). After the death of her mother in 1934 and the Spanish Civil War (1936-39), she moved back to Barcelona and enrolled as a humanities student at the University of Barcelona. She studied later in Madrid but did not complete her university education. Focusing on her writing, Laforet wrote short stories and articles for local journals before composing *Nada*, her first novel and an instant success with critics and publishers. In 1945, the novel received the Premio Nadal, one of Spain's most prestigious literary prizes, accompanied by a cash award of 5,000 pesetas, a significant amount of money for the time. Laforet has gone on to write three other full-length novels (the most recent, *La insolación,* in 1963) and several short stories (anthologized in *La niña y otros relatos,* in 1970). Distinguished as the most notable of all Laforet's works, *Nada* reinvigorated Spanish prose through its rich descriptions, distinctive narrative style, and the psychological depth achieved in its portrayal of characters living in post-Civil War Spain.

Events in History at the Time of the Novel

A devastating war. The origins of the Spanish Civil War stem back to a long and entangled history of economic issues, Church-state relations, and regional separatism, among other problems. While these problems began in the early nine-

THE LITERARY WORK

A novel set in Barcelona in the early 1940s; published in Spanish (as *Nada*) in 1945; in English in 1958.

SYNOPSIS

A young woman who moves to Barcelona to attend the university and live with her extended family experiences a variety of challenges in her personal relationships as she searches for her own identity.

teenth century, the immediate political origins of the war can be traced to the years 1931 to 1936. The Second Republic was established in 1931 with a democratically elected *Cortes* (parliament), whose members ranged from Fascists and Spanish Catholic Party adherents, to moderate Republicans and Socialists, to the more extreme factions of the Second Republic, the Communists and Anarchists. Beginning to address Spain's nagging problems, the *Cortes* adopted a new constitution in 1931. Some of the new laws, however, alienated the Church and army and divided the middle classes, one of these laws being the separation of Church and state. There was a Catalan statute that allowed the region some political autonomy, but did not go far enough for Catalan politicians. One of the most difficult challenges of the period was providing economic relief, improved working standards, and more job

Carmen Laforet

opportunities for the poor in Andalusia, Spain's largest agricultural region.

By 1936 divisions had exacerbated sharply between Church conservatives and liberals; among landowners, the middle class and the working class; and between those who demanded local rights and advocates of central control by Castile. Gil Robles, leader of the Spanish Catholic Party (*Confederación Española de Derechas*) "recalled that the Government had had, since the elections in February [1936], exceptional powers, including press censorship and the suspension of all constitutional guarantees. Nevertheless, during those four months, 160 churches . . . had been burned to the ground, 269 political murders were committed, and 1,287 assaults of various kinds occurred. [Robles] also reported that there had been in this four month period 113 general strikes" (Thomas, p. 4). All the controversy finally, perhaps inevitably, erupted into a civil war that pitted the Nationalists (military men, Church conservatives, monarchists, and landowners), ultimately led by Francisco Franco, against the Republicans, or anti-Franco defenders of the Second Republic.

On December 23, 1938, Franco began his last military offensive, aiming to finish off the war. By this time, supplies on both sides were low, so

Franco obtained new German equipment and some Italian troops. Meanwhile, the anti-Franco forces suffered seemingly irremediable problems; their troops were depleted and no support from France or England was on the way. The Republican government moved from Valencia to Barcelona in October 1938, then conducted its final retreat in January 1939. Italian and Nationalist armies completed the takeover of Barcelona that month. Barcelonans had no heat, electricity, or dependable water supply. Most stores were closed, and lentils and bread were about the only food available to the people. For four days in January the city was again bombed by Italian pilots. On January 25, Nationalist and Italian troops began to occupy the city. The Republican government held its last meeting near the French border at Figueras. On February 6, Manual Azaña, president of the Republic, left for France. Prime Minister Juan Negrín and General Vicente Rojo followed three days later. Azaña resigned at the end of February. The Republican government was left without a president, and no willing successor. Franco's army had defeated the Republic and now began to restructure a society in dire need of recovery from the devastation of the war.

The family and the Civil War. In some cases, the Spanish Civil War divided family members along political lines, at times forcing siblings, cousins and other family members to oppose each other on the battlefield and at home. Two male characters in the novel, Juan and Román, have participated in the war, and while the narrator does not provide many details of their experiences, some of them can be reconstructed from the text. Román has spent time in a *cheka*, a communist prisoner-of-war camp centered in Madrid. A relative remarks that "he changed during the months he was in the 'cheka'; they tortured him there" (Laforet, *Nada*, p. 38). Spread throughout Madrid, such *chekas* were in fact known for their characteristic cruelty and torture.

From the novel we also learn that Juan spent many years in North Africa (Morocco), where he joined the army (this could have either been the Spanish Army of Africa or the Foreign Legion, which consisted largely of Spaniards). In the Civil War, however, he seems to have fought with the Republican army, since Román tried to convince him at one point to join the Nationalists. Juan ultimately heeded his brother's advice, going to Madrid and crossing over to the Nationalists, as Román had earlier. At this juncture, Román took Juan's wife, Gloria, back to Barcelona to live while Juan remained in Madrid. Román risked his life by returning to Barcelona, since anti-Franco forces there could have caught and killed him for switching sides.

Years of hunger: economy and survival in postwar Spain. Laforet situates her novel in the early 1940s, a postwar era marked by economic difficulty and the establishment of Francoist policies. In the novel the narrator makes several references to hunger and lack of food, observations that reflect real-life conditions at the time of the novel. There was such a dearth of material goods that the 1940s has been characterized as *los años de hambre* (years of hunger). For most Spaniards, the challenge was one of sheer survival in finding food and jobs. Electrical brownouts were common in the early evenings to save energy; gasoline was expensive and in short supply; people sold cigarettes (a delicacy for the protagonist in *Nada*) one at a time; and cities economized in their own separate ways. In Barcelona, city authorities kept the electricity on for just a few hours a day; in Madrid, they halted public transportation for 60 minutes in the morning and 90 minutes in the afternoon to conserve resources.

Before the Civil War, Spain had moved steadily towards becoming an industrial and urban society. Between 1925 and 1936, for example, coal production had increased by more than 1,500 tons. The progress was neither continuous nor pervasive—sometimes production levels dropped, especially in 1929 as a result of the North American stock market crash; at other times they increased. The war, however, halted any progress the Spanish economy was making. The national income during the 1940s and for much of the 1950s fell back to that of 1914. Considering the increase in population, observed París Eguilaz, a prominent economist under Franco's regime, the situation was actually worse: "the per capita income fell to nineteenth-century levels. That is, the Civil War had provoked an unprecedented economic recession" (Eguilaz in Carr, p. 155). Hardest hit was the agricultural sector, which was not to reachieve its 1929 level of production until 1958.

Barcelona in the early 1940s. Barcelona had been the center of Republican resistance in the Civil War and for some time the headquarters of the Second Republic government. The war largely demolished the city. Gloria, one of the female characters in *Nada*, recalls air raids that destroyed its environs. Throughout the war, Franco solicited military aid from Germany and Italy, and at one point, in March 1938, Mussolini him-

self ordered air raids on Barcelona. Italian pilots flying twin-engine seaplanes attacked at around 10:00 P.M. Making 18 raids in a 44-hour period, they killed 1,300 and injured some 2,000 others (Thomas, p. 523).

The major task after the war was to revive the city's infrastructure and economy. The average weekly wage of an industrial worker was 100 pesetas, and a kilo of beef cost 50 or 60 pesetas, a dozen eggs 30 and a kilo of rice 11 pesetas. As these statistics indicate, salaries could barely provide enough to feed a family. Another problem facing the city was how to accommodate the high number of migrants arriving in the early '40s. The lack of decent-paying jobs compounded the housing problem. Some 100,000 migrants are said to have arrived in Barcelona in the 1940s looking for opportunities they could not find elsewhere in Spain. Early in the decade Eduardo Moreno lamented the city's problems: "The housing shortage gave rise to a catastrophic situation which was not far from complete breakdown. The 1940s were characterized by subletting, shanty dwelling, couples condemned to eternal courtship by the shortage of flats for the young married, intergenerational conflict in the family home, and promiscuity" (Vázquez Montalbán, p. 155).

In addition to these economic problems, the people of Barcelona and the larger region of Catalonia faced a threat to their cultural survival in view of Franco's attempt to unify Spain by eliminating regional identities. Barcelona and other cities that comprise the Catalan region of Spain have maintained an independent cultural identity throughout peninsular history. Intending to forge a single Spanish entity, Franco called for the suppression of these autonomous regions in favor of a federal identity originating from Castile or, more exactly, Madrid. One of Franco's first measures was to ban public use of the Catalan language. In another example of what was viewed by many as cultural genocide, his regime ordered the restructuring of the prestigious Autonomous University of Barcelona. The failure of the novel to mention this restructuring and reaction to it is so conspicuous as to give rise to the thought that the novel may be purposely silent on this issue, perhaps because of censorship considerations. The novel mentions only Andrea's studies and social network at the university, when it is known that the drive to quash long-standing distinctiveness threatened the cultural identity of the city and that this elicited strong reaction.

The Falange and the woman's role in Franco's society. In October 1933, José Antonio Primo de

FROM THE OFFICIAL BULLETIN DISSOLVING THE AUTONOMOUS UNIVERSITY OF BARCELONA, FEBRUARY 3, 1939

Article 3. [The autonomous] University of Barcelona will cease under the established regime by the Decree of June 1, 1933 and will be governed by the regulations that govern other central universities of Spain.

Article 6. The professorate of the University of Barcelona who belonged to the general ranks of the University will be suspended of their employment and will be obligated to reinstate themselves according to the rules that are indicated in the Order of this same date. The other professors of the University named by the General Assembly of Cataluña are suspended and can be reinstated once their ideology and political and social situation has been determined with relation to the [Fascist] Movement.

Rivera united the various authoritarian nationalist parties to create the Spanish Falange, his intent being to bring about a social and economic revolution in Spain. The party grew rapidly in the early months of the Civil War, and in April 1937 it fused with the Carlist party (those loyal to the monarchy) to form the Traditional Spanish Falange (FET). During Franco's dictatorship, the Falange became the only recognized political party. It initiated and instituted many of the economic policies and practices implemented in the early 1940s, including the attempt to integrate all social classes through national syndicates or unions. The Falange strove for a hierarchical, authoritarian, and nationalistic state. It encouraged Catholic and patriotic values, insisting upon loyalty to Church and nation and, through the Falange's Women's Section, the traditional roles of wife and mother. The policy aimed to reverse a trend advanced by the Second Republic, whose parliament had, among other progressive steps, granted women the vote in 1931. To help effect the reversal, Pilar Primo de Rivera (sister to José Antonio) founded the Women's Section of the Falange and advised women to remain subordinate: "Do not pretend to be equal to men, because far from achieving what you want, men will detest you tremendously and you will not be able to have any influence on them" (Pilar Primo de Rivera in Enders and Radcliff, p. 62).

Her teachings coincided with Franco's goals. He conceived of the traditional family as the social foundation for his regime, the basis that would stabilize and justify his power. Supported by the Catholic Church, Franco championed a family structure based on an authoritarian male model that cast women in supporting roles.

The patriarchal family was seen as representing the corporate order of the state in microcosm. . . . The regime promoted an "ideal" image of womanhood as "eternal," passive, pious, pure, submissive woman-as-mother for whom self-denial was the only road to real fulfilment.
(Graham and Labanyi, p. 184)

Confined to the domestic sphere, women became subject to nineteenth-century conceptions of them as the angel of the home. Francoist ideology expected them to assume responsibility for the cooking, cleaning, and imparting to children religious (Catholic) values, patriotism, and respect for male authority.

The Women's Section of the Falange played a prominent role in promoting this Francoist ideology. Founded in 1934, the section aimed to educate women in their role in society. It featured teachers who provided schooling in home economics and the duties of motherhood while conditioning women to believe that men were the ones fit for the public world. Aside from its instructional functions, the Women's Section administered the social service program (*servicio social*), which required volunteer service of all women aged 17 to 35 for six months in schools, orphanages, hospitals, and kitchens. Thus, they ensured a state system of welfare while being educated in Falangist values. The section's permanent membership consisted largely of middle-class women, and its leaders had to be unmarried, in contradistinction to its role as an advocate of marriage. Aside from their other duties, members monitored couples to make sure that they did not use birth control and that they raised their children according to Catholic tenets.

Laforet's novel challenges Franco's patriarchal family model through its strong female characters and through Laforet's own status as a woman writer in postwar Spain—a woman who is not the domesticated type that Franco was trying to encourage. The novel's characters Andrea and Ena are both university students; Angustias and Gloria are employed outside the home. Within limits, then necessary in view of censorship laws, the novel reacts against Franco's model and illustrates postwar realities and possibilities in relation to women and work or a university education.

The Novel in Focus

The plot. *Nada* is a first-person narrative, from the perspective of Andrea, who serves also as the novel's protagonist. She bases the tale on her memories and experiences during a year spent with her mother's family and university friends in Barcelona just after the Civil War. Divided into three sections, her story transpires over the course of 12 months. Rather than a tight narrative thread, it unfolds as a series of events and episodes that Andrea experiences among her friends and family.

Part 1 opens with Andrea's late arrival in Barcelona by train. Because of a switch in the train schedule, no one is waiting for her at the station, but she seems not to mind. Andrea enjoys the freedom of being out at night, alone, in a large city. These sensations are cut short as her taxi arrives at her new home on Aribau Street, where she reunites with members of her mother's family, who live in a filthy, dilapidated house. The oppressive domestic environment will compel Andrea to seek freedom, happiness, and stability outside her new home. After brief introductions to her grandmother, she steps into the bathroom to wash up before bed. Andrea compares the room to a witch's house of smeared walls, chipped paint, and twisted faucets that suggest smiling madness. Throughout Part 1, she continues to describe the filth and oppression, meanwhile interacting with her relatives, characters governed either by unruly emotions or by tradition as they struggle to exist in ravaged postwar Barcelona. Her childhood memories of this place, which she visited when she was seven, clash violently with what she encounters now.

Andrea's mother's family displays a host of negative attributes. Juan and Román, Andrea's uncles, cater to their passions, vices, and laziness. During the Civil War, they initially fought on opposite sides, and now they evince an enduring animosity toward each other. Juan, an un-

successful artist, overestimates his talents as a painter and has difficulty selling any of his mediocre paintings. Envious of his brother Román's creative talents, Juan struggles to find other employment. From time to time, he lands menial work, jobs that do not take advantage of the skills he has to offer; Juan is chronically underemployed. His wife, Gloria, suffers physical and verbal abuse at the hands of both Juan and Román. The brothers met Gloria during the war, and both had romantic feelings for her. Román hurls continuous insults at Gloria in Juan's presence. Defiant in her own way, Gloria sneaks out of the house at night to earn money for Juan and their infant son by gambling at her sister's pub, located in the red-light district of Barcelona (*barrio chino*). Meanwhile, the unmarried Román ensnares women with his tan good looks. A shady character, he operated as a double agent during the Civil War and deals now on the black market, which takes him away from home for extended periods of time. Román has many talents but does not make any effort to develop them, perhaps because the job market is so poor. He was once a respected pianist and violinist.

On its female side, Andrea's kind, sensitive grandmother attempts to understand her children's behavior as a result of the war and dismal circumstances that came after it. The family also includes Aunt Angustias, an assertive female of the traditional type. In Angustias's view, a woman must either marry or enter a convent, as she does at the end of Part 1. According to some characters, however, she does so not strictly for honorable purposes but to conceal an affair with her employer, a supposition the novel does not completely deny or confirm. Angustias attempts first to indoctrinate Andrea, admonishing her to follow traditional, Catholic values. After Andrea arrives, Angustias takes charge of her upbringing. But Andrea never does adopt the values of her stern aunt, who neither understands nor loves her. Showing her own strain of defiance, Andrea breaks from her aunt's dominance when she begins to manage her own finances.

Part 2 begins as Andrea leaves her university friend Ena's house. Ena's family lives in a model, middle-class household, vastly different from the one Andrea occupies. Andrea, who notices the blonde heads and cheerful complexions of those seated at Ena's dinner table, compares her own family's dark faces with the light characteristics of Ena's brothers. "The contrast could not be clearer," according to one critic, "Aribau [Street] represents the degenerate counterpart, the demonic inversion

A man buys bread on the black market in 1940s Barcelona.

of the ideal family symbolized by Via Layetena [Ena's family]" (Jordan, p. 31). Ena's father, Luis, is handsome and generous; her mother, Margarita, who seems slightly out of place within this model family, plays the piano and sings beautifully. To Andrea, Ena's family represents temperance and beauty in contrast to the perversion and ugliness of her own family. Andrea readily accepts invitations to eat at Ena's. She also enjoys being with Ena and her boyfriend, Jaime, a 29-year-old man who shows little interest in business affairs but is honest and considerate in his relationship with Ena.

At certain points in the story, Andrea's relationship with Ena changes in ways that help Andrea learn about herself as well as her friend. The results are surprising. Andrea's world collides with Ena's in Part 3 when Andrea learns that there is a common bond between her uncle, Román, and Ena's mother, Margarita. Margarita tells Andrea about a romantic and strange affair she had with Román. Aware of this love of her mother's, Ena enters into a dangerous game with Román to avenge her mother of the damaging relationship. Her visits to Aribau leave Andrea embarrassed and confused; she tries to protect Ena from her dangerous uncle while Ena revels in her manipulation of Román, which perhaps has such an effect that it helps explain Román's death by suicide. Another contributing factor may have been that both Ena and Gloria had threatened to disclose Román's illegal business dealings.

A supplementary social world in which Andrea circulates is the bohemian loft of her artistic friends from the university. These friends invite her to spend afternoons with them while they discuss art and their aspirations to create great masterpieces that will shock the artistic world. Appreciating her differences, they approve of Andrea, and she basks in their attention.

During her year in Barcelona, Andrea experiences a few romantic encounters and gains a growing awareness of her own sexuality, which the novel portrays with a level of discomfort and misunderstanding appropriate when seen through the eyes of the inexperienced Andrea. She remains naive and suspicious about men, basing her understanding of male-female relationships on romantic notions of love. More than her romantic relationships, Andrea relishes her artistic male friends, who make no sexual demands on her. She relaxes around them, without feeling forced to occupy a role for which she is unprepared.

Andrea's many experiences during her year in Barcelona help her grow up. The title ironically suggests that she has gained nothing from a year that exposes her to anguish, death, love, and artistic creativity, all of which contribute to her maturation. Reminiscent of a fairy tale ending, the conclusion of the novel offers Andrea a new life full of opportunity. Faced with the decision of whether to stay in Barcelona or accept an offer to move to Madrid and work for Ena's father while finishing her studies, her choice promises Andrea the stability that has eluded her amidst the difficult circumstances at Aribau.

What *Nada* leaves out. The narration of *Nada* raises questions in the reader's mind about the characters and their activities. Many loose ends are left unresolved. What were Juan and Román actually doing in the war? What exactly was their relationship with Gloria? What happened to Andrea's grandfather? What are the details of Angustias's relationship with her boss, Jerónimo Sanz? On the one hand, these unresolved issues lend credibility to the narration. Andrea, an outsider for many years to the family's history, provides only the information she could possibly deduce from her current interaction with her various relatives. On the other hand, the ambiguities indicate the presence of censorship. Censorship in the immediate postwar period caused writers to remain overtly silent on issues that could threaten the stability of the Franco regime, such as the causes and effects of the Civil War. Literary historian Margaret E. W. Jones notes that "No accurate portrayal of the postwar Spanish cultural scene would be complete without mention of the type of censorship exercised during

this period" (Jones, p. 2). The scantness of details regarding Juan and Román's involvement in the war and their employment after it point to key details that may have intentionally been left out because they would have threatened Franco's military victory and undermined his power. In the immediate postwar years, what an author could or could not write became, in some ways, more important than what was written. In other words, the ambiguities and silences challenged censorship and Franco's definition of life in Spain as black and white, true and false. Censorship itself was not a black and white process in postwar Spain:

> Censorship of a novel did not mean that a work would be totally banned; there were many variations on the final verdict, which ran from total suppression to a request for changes or deletions; the censor might ban the book within Spain but allow it for export, authorize only a limited edition of the work, or even confiscate the book after publication. Evidence suggests that the most prevalent form of censorship was not the complete prohibition of a novel; most authors preferred to revise or cut the offending passage rather than not publish the work at all. Finally, Abellán [the scholar Manuel L. Abellán] notes still another, undocumented result of the censorship mentality: a type of self-regulation on the part of the author himself. This 'autocensura' [self-censorship] was actually a state of mind that was subconsciously responsible for determining the entire composition of the work, thus automatically passing over potentially offensive material.
>
> (Jones, p. 3)

Self-censorship forced a writer to leave out any challenging materials and resort to subversive techniques such as ambiguity and silence, which, unconsciously or consciously, allowed an author to testify to freedom-of-speech realities of the time. Though subtle, such techniques allowed an author to critique and challenge Franco's cultural imposition of his power.

Sources and literary context. Laforet's technique, themes, and other aspects of her work cannot be traced to a specific source or model, but the contents of *Nada* suggest a link between the story and the author's life. When interviewed, Laforet maintained that her novels are not autobiographical. However, like other novelists such as Ernest Hemingway and Marcel Proust, who fuse their fiction with details of their own life, Laforet's work indicates a similarity between fiction and real-life experience. Like her character Andrea, Laforet attended the University of Barcelona, moved to Madrid in 1942, and lived with her mother's family. She maintained a close friendship with her friend Linka and Linka's family in Madrid, just as Andrea does with Ena and Ena's family in the novel. Laforet enjoyed walking about Madrid alone after studying at the Ateneo, Madrid's literary club, just as Andrea does in Barcelona after studying at the university there.

Within the Spanish literary tradition, Laforet's novel along with Camilo Jose Cela's *La Familia de Pascual Duarte* (1942; **The Family of Pascual Duarte,** also in *WLAIT 5: Spanish and Portuguese Literatures and Their Times*) is an early example of *tremendismo*. In vogue in Spain in the 1940s, this type of literature featured seemingly unmotivated violence, emphasizing ugliness and horror and describing with pleasure some of the most sordid and repulsive aspects of human nature. The violence in *Nada* surfaces in details such as Juan's treatment of his wife and in larger events like Román's suicide. A trend not new to Spanish literature, *tremendismo* is rooted in the sixteenth-century picaresque narrative and manifested visually in the art of Francisco de Goya in the early nineteenth century.

Nada breaks with the stale literary culture of dime-store novels whose publication was encouraged by the Franco regime during the postwar period, offering an alternative to this escapist literature. Commenting on this kind of culture, historian Raymond Carr observes that "[Spaniards] were immersed in the culture of evasion: the music hall; . . . 'photo novels'; anodyne radio serials which enjoyed an extraordinary vogue; 'kiosk literature'; finally, TV" (Carr, p. 164). An example of kiosk literature would be novels by Marcel Antonio Lafuente Estefanía, which were cheap, short, and entertaining. Lafuente Estefanía wrote and sold more than 125 of this kind of book between 1945 and 1950, all dealing with some aspect of the North American West, sporting titles such as *Los batidores [rangers] de Texas, Camino de Santa Fe,* and *Los bandidos de Utah.* This last, an 80-page novel published the same year as *Nada,* sold for 3 pesetas. *Nada,* a 300-page novel, sold for 20 pesetas. Happily, despite its length and cost, it would become a bestseller in 1940s Spain.

Reviews. Readers and critics alike have praised *Nada* for its spontaneity, vitality, and psychological depth. Upon discovering that Laforet was only 22 when she wrote the book, contemporary reviewers were astonished. They falsely assumed that the book was written by a man or at least by an older woman. Critics initially lauded the novel for its youthfulness, originality, and alternating depiction of brutality and tenderness. Older, established writers such as Azorín praised it as a beautiful book, inviting the author to write more novels that allow the reader to think and feel. Less enthusiastic, the poet Juan Ramón Jiménez complained about the lack of a coherent plot. Other critics faulted Laforet for a lack of realism in the creation of her characters (Johnson, p. 26; Jordan p. 28). Despite such criticisms, this novel continues to captivate readers and critics intrigued with its ambiguity, poetic imagery, and psychological depth. Nadal Prize committee member Rafael Vázquez Zamora, remarked that the novel "had a tremendous 'impact' and stood out signally among the others presented by the contestants, thrust forward for its quality. It was undoubtedly an innovation in what was being written in Spain." (Zamora in Johnson, p. 25).

—David Wood

For More Information

Carr, Raymond. *Modern Spain 1875-1980.* Oxford: Oxford University Press, 1980.

Enders, Victoria Loreé, and Pamela Beth Radcliff, eds. *Constructing Spanish Womanhood: Female Identity in Modern Spain.* Albany: State University of New York, 1999.

Graham, Helen, and Jo Labanyi. *Spanish Cultural Studies: An Introduction.* Oxford: Oxford University Press, 1995.

Grugel, Jean, and Tim Rees. *Franco's Spain.* London: Arnold, 1997.

Hooper, John. *The New Spaniards.* London: Penguin Books, 1995.

Johnson, Roberta. *Carmen Laforet.* Boston: Twayne Publishers, 1981.

Jones, Margaret E. W. *The Contemporary Spanish Novel, 1939-1975.* Boston: Twayne Publishers, 1985.

Jordan, Barry. *Laforet: Nada.* Critical Guides to Spanish Texts. London: Grant & Cutler, 1993.

Laforet, Carmen. *Nada.* Trans. Glafyra Ennis. New York: Peter Lang, 1993.

Preston, Paul, ed. *Spain in Crisis. The Evolution and Decline of the Franco Régime.* London: Harvester Press, 1976.

————. *The Spanish Civil War.* London: Weidenfeld and Nicolson, 1986.

Thomas, Hugh. *The Spanish Civil War.* New York: Harper and Brothers, 1961.

Vázquez Montalbán, Manuel. *Barcelonas.* Trans. Andy Robinson. New York: Verso, 1990.

Wyden, Peter. *The Passionate War.* New York: Simon and Schuster, 1983.

New Portuguese Letters

by

Maria Isabel Barreno, Maria Teresa Horta, and Maria Velho da Costa (The Three Marias)

Maria Isabel Barreno (b. 1939), Maria Teresa Horta (b. 1937), and Maria Velho da Costa (b. 1938) were all born in Lisbon. Since all three names began the same way, the women came to be known collectively as "The Three Marias" when referred to in connection with their collaborative work. By the 1970s, they had already published individual works on women in contemporary Portugal. Maria Velho da Costa and Maria Isabel Barreno had both written novels (*Maina Mendes* [1969] and *Os outros legítimos superiores* [1970], respectively) that featured women defying traditional bourgeois patriarchal family structures. Maria Teresa Horta's early literary career focused more on poetry, specifically erotic verse expressing women's right to enjoy their sexuality, an assertion that also found its way into her collection of poems *Minha Senhora de Mim* (*Milady of Myself*), which was banned in 1971. It was this banning, in part, that inspired the three women to challenge the regime further by writing the collective work of protest *New Portuguese Letters*. The Three Marias produced their collaborative text according to specific ground rules, agreeing to meet twice a week and to exchange their pieces of writing. No one author would have the right to edit, censor, or rewrite the work of any of the others, and each piece was to be anonymous. In fact, the sequence in which the various pieces are organized is determined by their actual dates of composition. What emerged was a literary comparison of women's experiences of love and sexual relations in the seventeenth and twentieth

centuries, that brought to the forefront the exclusion and silencing of women under Portugal's New State and, more generally, throughout patriarchal history.

Events in History at the Time of the Satirical Work

A seventeenth-century nun. *New Portuguese Letters* is mostly a satirical reworking of the seventeenth-century text *Lettres Portugaises*, (1669; Portuguese Letters). The reworking shifts between two main time periods, the seventeenth and late twentieth centuries, with the love affair of the nun and French cavalier linking the periods. In order

Maria Theresa Horta, Maria Velho da Costa, and Maria Isabel Barreno at their trial in Lisbon.

to talk about their own twentieth-century lives as part of women's history, the Three Marias draw on a combination of myth, legend, and historical fact surrounding the figure of Sister Mariana Alcoforado (1640-1723), a real-life nun credited with authoring the seventeenth-century letters to the cavalier. Rather than engaging directly with the empirical scholarship surrounding the letters' authenticity and the nun's identity, the authors use Mariana as a vehicle to discuss women's invisibility and marginality in mainstream history. One of the Three Marias addresses the nun directly in this vein: "Would you ever have left a name for yourself, if your letters had not made their way to France? Today there are many who do not believe you ever lived the life you supposedly did, who maintain you never wrote the letters attributed to you: you are merely a stained-glass window, a forgotten myth" (Barrena, Horta, and Velho da Costa, *New Portuguese Letters*, p. 124).

In the original 1669 edition of the actual love letters, neither the nun nor her lover is identified by name. Subsequent editions published in the same year, however, named the cavalier as a real historical figure, Noël Bouton, the Chevalier de Chamilly (1635-1715) who was later to become the Marshall of France. The nun herself was not identified until over a hundred years after the first edition of the letters. In 1810 a French scholar,

Jean-François Boissonade, happened to discover a handwritten note in the margin to his first edition of the text, naming its author as Sister Mariana Alcoforado. A real historical figure who lived from 1640 to 1723, this Mariana was subsequently traced to a Franciscan order of nuns at the Royal Convent of our Lady of the Immaculate Conception in the Alentejan town of Beja. She entered the convent in 1656, was a professed nun by 1660, and remained there until she died in 1723, at the age of 83. Whether or not Mariana Alcoforado wrote the letters, her life in her convent community and in her family reveal much about the circumstances of cloistered women in the seventeenth century.

The convent in which the real Mariana Alcoforado lived was founded in 1467. Studies of her life indicate that she came from a large, Alentejan aristocratic family. Her father, Dom Francisco da Costa Alcoforado, placed at least one other daughter, Peregrina, in the same convent, and possibly a third, Caterina. Like Mariana in *New Portuguese Letters*, the real Mariana had a sister, Ana Maria, who married well with the help of a good dowry. Mariana also had an older brother, Baltasar, who would have wielded considerable power over his sisters, particularly in defending the family honor that was vested in the sexual purity of his female relations. This is reflected strongly both in *Portuguese Letters* and in *New*

Portuguese Letters, with Mariana fearing her family's reaction to her transgression far more than that of her religious superiors. In real convent life, the hierarchy of wealth and family status continued to exercise an influence within the religious environment through the distinction claimed by aristocratic nuns. Even in their religious lives, the nobility retained the title of Dona, as opposed to Soror or Sister.

Many nuns of this period possessed the education and the freedom to think, write, and pursue the arts, evidenced by the burgeoning of poetic and other literary works by nuns in Portugal during the late seventeenth and early eighteenth centuries. Famous religious contemporaries of the real Mariana Alcoforado were Sister Maria do Céu (1658-1753), Sister Madalena da Glória (1672-176?) and Sister Violante do Céu (1601-93). The last of these in particular was renowned for her poetry on profane as well as religious love themes. The pursuit of sexual relations among the religious during this period is indicated by the royal ordinances governing convents, designed to deter men from breaking into cloisters and to prevent nuns from acting as messengers or go-betweens. Both *Portuguese Letters* and *New Portuguese Letters* suggest that nuns themselves did in fact act as go-betweens, a role allotted to Dona Brites in both texts. The legal penalties for marauding men and complicit nuns, were, tellingly, tightened right after Portugal's War of Independence with Spain (1640-68). The desire and the opportunity for such incursions into convents would naturally increase with the influx of foreign soldiers into garrison towns, such as Beja, the site of Mariana's convent and a town very close to the frontier with Spain.

The Wars of Independence between Portugal and Spain began in 1640, when Portugal rebelled against the Spanish Habsburg dynasty, which had ruled Portugal since 1580. Spanish dominance came about when Spain successfully invaded Portugal, following the collapse of Portugal's ruling Avis dynasty after the death in 1578 of Portugal's boy king, Dom Sebastião, on an ill-considered crusade to North Africa. The Portuguese did not tolerate this "usurption" for long, particularly as their overseas empire fell under Spanish control, and the Portuguese naval fleet suffered severe losses in the defeat of the Spanish Armada in 1588, by Portugal's oldest ally, England. A Catalan insurrection against Spanish rule in 1640 encouraged sectors of the Portuguese nobility to do likewise, faced with the unacceptable choice of supporting the Spanish

in suppressing the Catalans. The 1640 rebellion restored a Portuguese monarchy under Dom João of Bragança, later to become King Dom João IV. War continued, however, until 1668, when Spain officially recognized Portugal's independence. In the quest for much needed French military reinforcements in these campaigns, Portugal courted the unreliable support of Cardinal Richelieu, who was intent on using Portugal's enmity with Spain only insofar as war with Spain furthered the strategic interests of France. It is known that the real Chevalier de Chamilly, on

whom, as noted, the lover in the *New Portuguese Letters* is modeled, came to Portugal serving in the Briquemault Cavalary regiment during the campaigns led by Count von Schomberg (1661-68). In *New Portuguese Letters,* de Chamilly's attitude towards Mariana purposely reflects Richelieu's attitude towards Portugal. The lover is less concerned about liberating the cloistered Mariana than about fulfilling his personal need for sexual conquest and gratification. The ongoing analogy between national and sexual identity is made explicit in *New Portuguese Letters*. One of the Marias asserts that Mariana was "born in a decadent era, . . . in the age of the Spain of the Philips, when Portugal had been castrated of its virility—of its independence and a king of the purest Portuguese stock, of our Portuguese blood" (*Letters*, p. 114).

Women in the twentieth-century New State. The twentieth-century backdrop for *New Portuguese Letters* is the "Estado Novo," or New State regime in Portugal (1933-74). The New State was largely the project of one man, António Oliveira Salazar, a former financial law lecturer at Coimbra University, who ruled Portugal as absolute dictator from 1933 until an accident incapacitated him in 1968. The reins passed to Marcelo Caetano, who ruled until the Revolution of April 25, 1974, put an end to the New State.

THE THREE MARIAS' TEXT IN THE CONTEXT OF THE PORTUGUESE NEW STATE 1933-74

1926 The Portuguese Republic is brought down by a military coup.

1933 A newly generated constitution establishes the New State under the dictatorship of António Oliveira Salazar.

1940 With the signing of a Concordat with the Vatican, Portugal reinforces Church power in the Portuguese state.

1961 The Angolan Insurrection marks the beginning of the colonial wars in Africa.

1968 Salazar is succeeded by Marcelo Caetano.

1972 The publication of *New Portuguese Letters* leads to prosecution of the Three Marias, and an international solidarity campaign on their behalf.

1974 The Revolution of April 25 ends the New State regime.

1975 The first English translation of *New Portuguese Letters* is published.

Salazar had risen to power in the 1920s following the overthrow of Portugal's republic during another insurrection, the military coup of 1926. In light of the 1930's global economic depression, Salazar's economic management skills served him well. His subsequent rise to power instigated an authoritarian dictatorship often described as Portugal's version of a fascist state, although his dictatorship lacked the mass popular movements attached to Adolf Hitler's Germany and Benito Mussolini's Italy. Nonetheless, the New State drew initial inspiration from Italian fascism, which influenced the formulation of Salazar's legal codes, and from Germany's Third

Reich, whose Gestapo provided the model for the PIDE, the New State's secret police.

Imperial Portugal. Portugal's imperial policy would ultimately prove to be the Achilles' heel of the regime. Salazar's Colonial Act, initially passed in 1930, and subsequently appended to his foundational 1933 Constitution, had ushered in a new age of economic interest in Portugal's colonies in Africa. Salazar's concept of empire envisioned Portugal as the center of a single united fatherland drawing together all of its overseas possessions under the dictates of "One State, One Race, One Faith and One Civilization" (Anderson, p. 112). As the 1933 Constitution stated, "the Overseas Territories of Portugal are given the generic name 'provinces'. . . they are an integral part of the Portuguese State" (Anderson, p. 108). This active revival of empire led to a considerable rise in white Portuguese settler migration to Angola and Mozambique in the 1940s and '50s. It was a trend that contravened the dominant thrust of the post-World War II era, which saw imperial powers contend with anticolonial independence movements that would lead to the dissolution of their empires. Great Britain, for one, granted sovereignty in stages to India, a process other British possessions would undergo as well in the next few decades. Portuguese ideology showed no such flexibility. However, unable wholly to resist the general tenor of the times, its colonial system began to reveal some instabilities. In 1961, the Portuguese enclaves in India—Goa, Daman, and Diu—were successfully invaded by India's own national army. That same year an armed insurrection in Angola marked the beginning of Portugal's colonial wars in Africa; similar uprisings followed elsewhere in Portuguese Africa—in Guinea Bissau and Cape Verde in 1963 and in Mozambique in 1964.

On April 25, 1974, Caetano's regime was finally overthrown by a bloodless coup led by a military elite opposed to the regime. The colonial war in Africa had fomented an increasingly disillusioned junior officer class, who formed the "Armed Forces Movement," inspired by the Marxist ideologies its members had been trained to combat. As a symbolic revolutionary gesture, the soldiers marched through the capital city with carnations in their rifles to suggest the peaceful nature of their action, inspiring the name "Carnations Revolution."

Censorship. One in every three Portuguese women and one in every five Portuguese men were illiterate according to surveys for 1974 (Kaplan, p. 182). During the Salazar/Caetano regime, censorship had combined with already high illiteracy rates to severely restrict the reading public, causing disillusionment among writers. Freedom of the press was muzzled. According to a decree passed in 1933, books and newspapers had to be submitted to a panel for censorship before they were published. The panel of censors consisted mainly of army officers. This stringent approach was somewhat relaxed during the Caetano period, and a change in the law meant that publishers, printers, and distributors, as well as authors were legally responsible for the content of the work they produced. This tended to reduce authors to the absurd practice of self-censorship. The outright banning and seizure of published books, as happened to *New Portuguese Letters*, was relatively rare by this time, so the case of the Three Marias, who were prosecuted along with their publisher, stood out as an extreme.

In this repressive climate, freedom of speech and defiance of censorship became acts of resistance for a new generation of politically committed, primarily communist writers who emerged in the 1940s and '50s. Together they created Portuguese Neorealism, their own variety of Neorealism, a literary movement occurring elsewhere in Europe that foregrounded the depiction of real-life conditions, events, and views. In the less-than-free society of fascist Portugal, Neorealism became noted especially for its use of allegorical subtexts and symbols. The movement's writers encoded and encrypted their political criticisms so as to evade the notorious "blue pencil" of the censors and reach the limited community of oppositional readers trained to decode the hidden messages. "The dawn," for example, came to symbolize the longed for coming of the revolution that would end the "dark night" of the New State. The literary activity of the Neorealist generation proved highly significant for keeping alive intellectual opposition to the New State. As the writer José Cardoso Pires (see **Ballad of Dog's Beach,** also in WLAIT 5: *Spanish and Portuguese Literatures and Their Times*) puts it in 1972, "for over forty years Portuguese writers have opposed Salazar's 'politics of the mind.'. . . This has earned them a permanent place on the blacklist of the unredeemed" (Cardoso Pires, p. 101).

In this climate of new feminist influences, continued literary and press censorship, and anticolonial war agitation, *New Portuguese Letters* articulated a protest that worked on several levels at once. Ostensibly it attacked the oppression of women within a family structure designed to act

as an instrument of state control. However, the book also makes this a pretext to undermine the extreme military machismo required by Portugal's anachronistic imperial nationhood in its pursuit of a colonial war. Finally, on a third level, it turns the constraint imposed by censorship into a virtue, preempting official attempts to restrict the range of meanings that could be communicated by focusing on the ability of multiple word play to create a profusion of meaning beyond the censors' control.

For this reason, the working of language is central to the Three Marias' narrative project. Their game of hide-and-seek with censorship constitutes a protest against the absurd effects of silencing dissent by censorship, with the text showing meaning to be more than the sum total of the written signs on a page. The satire engages in extensive punning, emphasizing meaning as connotative and ultimately indeterminate.

The Satirical Work in Focus

Plot summary. *New Portuguese Letters* rewrites the seventeenth-century love affair of Mariana Alcoforado, working from the assumption, implicit in the original text, that the nun has survived her desertion and despair through the therapeutic act of writing. As the history of the letters shows, the nun has also effectively taken her revenge on the cavalier in that the letters have become famous and created a scandal abroad. Taking up the twin themes of passion and revenge, the Three Marias meanwhile describe their own journey towards political affirmation, self-expression, and independence in their contemporary setting. To this end, they invent a whole cast of new characters, who engage in dialogue through letters. Many of these invented characters are direct descendants of the original Mariana Alcoforado and her family and social circle. The result resembles a kind of tapestry, but with a constantly shifting pattern that is difficult to pin down. As one of the Marias concludes, "we would never be able to follow the total pattern of the characters, of the situations, to the very end" (*Letters*, p. 301).

The one main thread that can be traced through the book is the story of the affair between Mariana and the cavalier. The reader is invited to use this to connect ideas and draw parallels between analogous situations at different times in history. Key themes, events, and characters are repeated throughout the book with significant variations. Mariana herself is reinvented in the seventeenth, eighteenth, and twentieth centuries, as a rebellious free thinker and writer, who eschews marriage and children in order to pursue learning.

Like her real-life counterpart, Mariana Alcoforado is presented in *New Portuguese Letters* as the daughter of landed Alentejo gentry who have sent her to become a nun to save their money for the dowry of the other sister, Maria. Mariana enters the cloister against her will; devoid of any religious vocation, she finds her new quarters tantamount to imprisonment. Her unattractive sister uses the dowry to buy herself a husband, the seemingly shy and timorous Count de C. Meanwhile, Mariana's best friend Joana de Vasconcelos corresponds clandestinely with Mariana in the convent, lamenting her own unhappy arranged marriage to a nobleman whom she does not love. She compares her lack of freedom to choose her fate with Mariana's enforced enclosure in the convent and becomes Mariana's only trusted link to the outside world. When French troops arrive in Beja to help the newly restored Portuguese monarchy fight for independence from Spain, it is Joana who unwittingly changes Mariana's life for good by introducing her to the handsome Chevalier de Chamilly, who has been moved to pity by the story of her fate. Joana subsequently facilitates their meetings and communications while one of the nuns, Dona Brites, is also aware of the liaison.

A passionate affair ensues between Mariana and the cavalier, one that leaves him drained of his youth, energy, and masculine prowess. Mariana uses him as much as he uses her. The affair signals the death of his confident selfhood as he remarks in his final letter to Mariana, "day by day myself was dying in your arms" (*Letters,* p. 95). Mariana miscarries the child she has conceived with the cavalier, achieving a dose of immortality not from biological reproduction but through literary fame. Her published letters create a scandal abroad. The cavalier finds that although he can leave the nun behind, he cannot so easily escape his colorful reputation.

In the next generation, it falls to Mariana's niece, also named Mariana, to "continue" her aunt's correspondence with the cavalier as a purely formal literary exercise, since by now both of the original lovers have died. The niece has read the cavalier's final letter to her aunt on her deathbed. Resentful at being the object of the nun's amorous writings, he too has now taken refuge in the life of the mind. "And my life henceforth," he writes, "will be spent solely in searching here on my estates for a place for a wisdom

that my heart will not gainsay, for feelings that my wisdom may accept as genuine. My becoming cloistered and shut up behind walls was your doing, Senhora" (*Letters,* p. 97).

The niece's reply to this letter, written in the first person, assuming her aunt's name and persona, provides a retort to the cavalier's criticism of Sister Mariana. Disparaging the male quest for immortality, she tells him, "it is the custom among males to find the horizon that will lead them to the absolute by playing with the lives of women" (*Letters,* p. 134). Comparing the blood of war with the blood shed by women who undergo abortion, she points out to the cavalier the unequal share of risk he has imposed on Mariana by violating her family honor.

The Mariana Alcoforado story is expanded upon through a series of flashbacks. These flashbacks disclose bastardization in the Alcoforado dynastic line and the hypocrisy of their supposed honor. It becomes clear that the cavalier has also made love to Mariana's best friend, Joana. Mariana's brother-in-law, the Count of C., emboldened by her humiliation, makes his own unsuccessful attempt to seduce the nun. Even Mariana's own mother, Dona Maria das Dores Alcoforado, has had an illicit relationship, which began against her will when her husband's longstanding enemy used her sexually in a vengeful attempt to sully her husband's honor. The result was an illegitimate daughter, Mariana, which explains why her mother hated her and has kept her away from her true father.

A similar story of love and revenge accounts for the mysterious death of Mariana's much-loved younger cousin, José Maria Pereira Alcoforado. As Mariana's only family ally, in turns a surrogate brother and putative son, José Maria never recovers from losing Mariana to the convent. He eventually hangs himself from a fig tree on the family estate, leaving behind a cryptic poem about the death of the fatherland. The poem refers obliquely to the end of the myths of Portuguese heroism embodied in the national epic poem, *The Lusiads* (also in *WLAIT 5: Spanish and Portuguese Literatures and Their Times*). However, a clearer and more personal motivation for his death surfaces later, when his former love, Mónica, commits suicide, leaving him a note in which she explains that she had merely used him to take revenge on the man she really loved. Male heroism is exposed as fragile and dependent on the love and fidelity of women to maintain its sense of power and purpose.

Alongside these intersecting storylines about Mariana and her family, the Three Marias explore contemporary social issues affecting women. Their sweep includes rape and incest, economic migration, women's confinement to the private sphere, domestic violence, illegal abortion, a schoolgirl questioning her convent school indoctrination by the New State, and the different penalties meted out by the Portuguese Penal Code to men and women who commit adultery.

The account reveals the assertion of women's self-worth under the patriarchal system to be impossible. The Three Marias therefore regard themselves as an alternative family group. As one of the Marias remarks, "we made each of ourselves the mother and the daughter of each of the others, and sisters determined to talk about precisely why we were orphans and suffering and destitute. A new family" (*Letters*, p. 107). From this new-found position of strength and solidarity, they criticize the false prospects for women's liberation held out by the sexual revolution. In relation to Portuguese society, this last subject prompts ironic commentary:

> Here in Portugal we are in the midst of the era of women's liberation: Women vote, women attend universities, women hold jobs: women drink, women smoke, women enter beauty contests; women wear mini-skirts, maxi-skirts, "hot-pants," Tampax; women say "I'm having my period" in front of men, women take "the pill".... [Nonetheless women in the anti-fascist struggle remain] the spoils today of warriors who pretend to be our comrades in the struggle, but who merely seek to mount us and be cavaliers of Marianas who are prisoners in other prisons, and nuns in different convents without realizing it.
>
> (*New Portuguese Letters*, p. 234)

The three refer to key moments in western humanist history only to reveal its partiality to men and irrelevance to women's life experiences. The text shows the lack of improvement in women's status, even during revolutionary periods such as the eighteenth-century Enlightenment era. Dona Maria Ana, an eighteenth-century descendant of Mariana's niece concludes that women's daily lives have changed remarkably little, even though:

> We are living in an age of civilization and enlightenment, men write scientific treatises and encyclopaedias, nations continually change and transform their political structure, the oppressed raise their voices, a king of France has been sent to the guillotine and his courtiers

along with him, the United States of America has gained its independence.
>
> (*New Portuguese Letters*, p. 151)

Scandal and national identity. Several publishers rejected *New Portuguese Letters*, fearing the controversy it would raise, and aware that the publishers of banned books were also legally liable to prosecution. Eventually, the Portuguese writer and critic Natália Correia, herself a previous victim of New State censorship, managed to get the book accepted by Estúdio Cor. It was an immediate bestseller but the regime banned it and arrested the Three Marias, prosecuting them for offending public morals and decency. During the two-year court case that ensued, the anonymity of each of their individual contributions enabled them to obstruct the prosecution's attempts at discovering who had written the specific passages on which the pornography case was constructed.

ONE OF THE "PORNOGRAPHIC" PASSAGES

This passage from a section entitled "The Father," satirically mimics the voyeurism of a rapist father who blames his daughter for being sexually alluring.

"She was perverse:
she lolled about on sofas, her arms drawn back, stretched out full-length, simply lying there, smooth and lithe, within reach, running her sharp-pointed tongue over her already wet lips. . . .

"She was perverse:
she would forgetfully leave the door ajar as she undressed, disclosing her soft belly, her thin shoulders, in tiny little motions, with secret sounds and pacts with childhood."

(*New Portuguese Letters*, p. 140)

Portugal's counter-regime writers supported the cause, comparing this book to other great works of European literature unjustly persecuted for obscenity such as D. H. Lawrence's *Lady Chatterley's Lover* and James Joyce's *Ulysses*. An international solidarity campaign, orchestrated by feminist movements worldwide, countered the suppression too, drawing negative world attention to the absence of free speech, oppression of women, and abuse of human rights in Portugal. The trial finally ended in May 1974, not with the Three Marias' acquittal but with their "official pardon," after the New State itself had collapsed in the April 25 Revolution.

The reasons for the prosecution of *New Portuguese Letters* in 1972 relate to its treatment of nationally and culturally controversial issues, as well as to its broaching of taboo subjects such as autoeroticism, incest, lesbianism, and rape. These inherently "private" issues are exposed in the text as everyday realities, as aspects of life that the repressive sexual ideology associated with the New State and its empire attempted to silence.

FROM A FIFTEENTH-CENTURY SONG OF MOCKERY AND SLANDER

"Oh! Ugly lady you sought to complain
Because in your praises, I have sung not a strain;
But now I do want to sing a refrain,
In which, notwithstanding, your praise I will tell;
You will see then how I would praise your name:
You ugly old lady, you who are stupid as well!"

(Fonseca, Fernando V. Peixoto da, p. 35; trans. H. Owen)

Refuting the idea that "woman is man's last colony," the Three Marias make writing both an end in itself, and a means to resist all forms of "colonial" occupation (*Letters,* p. 235). Breaking the mould of romantic love in western literature, *New Portuguese Letters* constitutes an attempt to reimagine heterosexual relations. Replacing passion itself with the act of writing about passion, Mariana finds her way out of the impasse of tragedy and death, enshrined in France's legendary lovers Abelard and Heloïse, or the Celtic lovers Tristan and Isolde, or England's Romeo and Juliet. Mariana writes a final letter to the cavalier, who is now prosaically married, bored and middle-aged. She tells him, "I wrote you letters of great love and great torment, Senhor, and after having had no commerce with you for so long, I began to love them and the act of writing about them more than I loved your image or the memory of you" (*Letters,* p. 272).

Sources and literary context. The most obvious influence on *New Portuguese Letters* is clearly the seventeenth-century *Portuguese Letters* originally published in French. As discussed above, for several centuries after their publication, the letters were considered by experts to be authen-

tic, and to have been authored by the real seventeenth-century Mariana Alcoforado. However, the evidence connecting the nun to the letters is inconclusive and no original manuscript in Portuguese has been found to date. Subsequent scholarship has tended to concur that *Portuguese Letters* was a skillful literary fake, written originally in French by Gabriel-Joseph de Lavergne de Guilleragues, who claimed to be their translator and then published them (Klobucka, pp. 2-21).

While the myth and history of Mariana are the Three Marias' main inspiration, their treatment of *Portuguese Letters* takes very substantial liberties with the original. *New Portuguese Letters* is, in many respects, the epitome of an anti-genre work. It combines the format of an epistolary novel with lyric poetry, social commentary resembling journalism, and a polyphonic alternation of voices in dialogue, which lends itself well to public reading and dramatization. Drawing on a wide range of literary influences and sources, the Marias invent their own "women's tradition," making particular use of lyric poetry and medieval Galician-Portuguese *cantigas de amigo*, or women's songs, to retell Mariana's story.

Their choice of the *cantiga* is especially significant since the medieval Galician-Portuguese *cantiga de amigo* was generally a female-voiced oral form, usually anonymous though some could be attributed to known female poets. In adapting these primarily anonymous medieval songs, the Marias reaffirm not the power implicit in individual authorship, but the collective power of the female voice in poetic dialogue and debate throughout history. Given the scandalous nature of Mariana's story, their intertextual echoes of satirical Galician-Portuguese songs such as the *cantigas de escárnio e maldizer* (songs of mockery and slander) is particularly fitting. These ribald songs, usually sung by men about women, exposed social and sexual scandals, permitting their singers the liberty of the jester.

Reception. The international solidarity campaign that surrounded the trial of the Three Marias helped make *New Portuguese Letters* one of the best known and most widely translated texts ever produced in Portugal. It also became a major source of reference and inspiration for international feminist movements. Although the response from feminists was very positive, the first English translation in 1975 received a mixed reception from reviewers in England and the United States, partly perhaps because the notoriety that preceded the translation had raised expectations of its capacity to shock. One of the most favorable and informative reviews in England came from fellow Portuguese writer Helder Macedo, who was able to contextualize the work for the English reader in relation to twentieth-century Portugal's resistance literature. A more ambivalent perspective came from Jane Kramer in the *New York Times Book Review*. Kramer claimed that the Three Marias were "as obsessed with love as poor Soror Mariana" acting like "female Norman Mailers" and "proud prisoners of sex" (Kramer, p. 1). One of the enduring strengths she finds in the book, however, concerns the Marias' witty recreation of the cavalier, "because love after all is a *folie à deux*, and the object of the new woman (is it not?) is to put an end to the folly and not the partner" (Kramer, p. 2)

New Portuguese Letters passed rapidly out of the limelight in postrevolutionary Portugal. The Three Marias themselves went on to build successful, independent literary careers. There was no new edition of *New Portuguese Letters* in the original Portuguese between 1980 and 1998, at which point it finally was republished and recognized as the widely influential text that it was for the boom generation of women writers in the 1980s. The contemporary Portuguese writer Lídia Jorge (see **Murmuring Coast**, also in *WLAIT 5: Spanish and Portuguese Literatures and Their Times*) once tellingly described it as women's "passport of equality in the domain of writing" (Jorge in Louro, p. 26). The passport is a fitting image for a text that permitted the mapping and traversing of new cultural spaces for generations of women constrained, like Penelope, wife of the ancient hero Ulysses, to wait at home.

—Hilary Owen

For More Information

Anderson, Perry. "Portugal and the End of Ultra-Colonialism—2." *New Left Review* 16 (July-August 1962): 88-123.

Barreno, Maria Isabel, Maria Teresa Horta, and Maria Velho da Costa. *New Portuguese Letters*. Trans. Helen R. Lane. Poetry trans. Faith Gillespie and Suzette Macedo. London: Readers International, 1994.

Cardoso Pires, José. "Changing a Nation's Way of Thinking: Censorship as a Technique." *Index on Censorship* (spring 1972): 93-106.

Cordeiro, Luciano. *Soror Mariana, a freira portuguesa.* Lisbon. Livraria Ferin, 1888.

Fonseca, António Belard da. *Mariana Alcoforado. A Freira de Beja e as "Lettres portugaises."* Lisbon: Portugal-Brasil, 1966.

Fonseca, Fernando V. Peixoto da, ed. *Cantigas de Escárnio e Maldizer dos Trovadores Galego-Portugueses.* Lisbon: Clássica Editora, 1971.

Guimarães, Elina. *Portuguese Women Past and Present.* Lisbon: Comissão da Condiçao Feminina, 1978.

Kaplan, Gisela. *Contemporary Western European Feminism.* Sydney: Allen and Unwin; London: UCL Press, 1992.

Klobucka, Anna. *The Portuguese Nun: The Formation of a National Myth.* Lewisburg: Bucknell University Press, 2000.

Kramer, Jane. "The Three Marias." *New York Times Book Review,* 2 February 1975, 1-2.

Lavergne, Gabriel de. *The Love Letters of a Portuguese Nun.* Trans. Guido Waldman. London: Harvill, 1996.

Louro. Regina. "A surpresa no feminino." *Expresso,* 5 February 1983, 26-27.

Macedo, Helder. "Teresa and Fátima and Isabel." *Times Literary Supplement,* 12 December 1975, 1484.

Owen, Hilary. *Portuguese Women's Writing 1972 to 1986. Reincarnations of a Revolution.* Lewiston: Edwin Mellen Press, 2000.

"The Old-Fashioned Castilian"

by

Mariano José de Larra

Born in Madrid on March 24, 1809, Mariano José de Larra would later gain renown under the pseudonym "Fígaro." One of the most critically acclaimed Spanish writers of the nineteenth century, he was only about 19 years old when he published his first newspaper series, *El Duende Satírico del Día* (The Satiric Goblin of the Day). His newspapers contained the best examples of the *artículo de costumbres*, or essay on social customs to date. Larra soon became known as an outspoken social and political critic, penning caustic literary essays that decried the nation's lack of a progressive social and political vision, the affluent classes' foppish imitation of everything French, and the modest classes' blind adherence to outdated Spanish traditions. "The Old-Fashioned Castilian" constituted the eighth issue in Larra's second self-published paper, *El Pobrecito Hablador* (The Poor Little Blabbermouth). It is one of the most representative of Larra's customs essays, painting a colorful portrait of a middle-class household steeped in traditional Spanish values. The essay indirectly critiques those who believed that the solution to all of Spain's ills could be found only in its own traditions and customs. Satirical and entertaining, it exposes distinct types of Spaniards in early-nineteenth-century society.

Events in History at the Time of the Essay

The reign of Fernando VII. By the time Larra wrote "The Old-Fashioned Castilian," the reign

---

THE LITERARY WORK

An anecdotal essay set in Madrid, published in December 1832 in the review *El Pobrecito Hablador* (The Poor Little Blabbermouth) as "El Castellano Viejo"; in English in 2001.

SYNOPSIS

In this social satire, a poet attends a birthday dinner given by a conservative, ardently patriotic member of the Spanish bourgeoisie, who attempts to appear more refined than he truly is.

---

of Fernando VII (1814-33) was coming to an end. The king suffered from failing health, his country from an era of crisis. Fernando had been in power since 1814, when he returned triumphantly from France to reclaim the Spanish throne for the Bourbon dynasty. French forces had been routed at Vitoria the year before in the final large-scale skirmish of Spain's War of Independence from France, which began on May 2, 1808, when common Spaniards rioted in the streets of Madrid to protest the presence of French troops. Altogether, on both sides of the conflict, there were hundreds of thousands of lives lost. Joseph Bonaparte, Napoleon's brother, who had ruled Spain since 1808 as King Joseph I, barely escaped execution as he fled back into France.

Fernando immediately made null and void the democratic Constitution of 1812, assuming

Mariano José de Larra

absolute power. The liberal surge that the French invasion had helped to foster was now hindered, but not halted. In 1820 a military uprising in Cádiz under the direction of Colonel Rafael de Riego handed Spain its first *pronunciamiento*, or change of government imposed by the military, forcing Fernando VII to allow the Spanish liberals to form a parliament and to reestablish the Constitution of 1812. Once the liberals were back in charge, they abolished the Inquisition, a tribunal to suppress deviation from the teachings of the Roman Catholic Church, and they made the Jesuits leave the country because of their ultra-conservative, iron-fisted grip on the country's educational system. During this period most of the Spanish American colonies declared independence. The attempt to instill democracy in Spain itself ended abruptly in April 1823, when Louis XVIII of France, with the support of the Holy Alliance, sent an army into Spain to restore Fernando's absolute authority. This time the common people of Spain did not rise up against France. They backed the French force's efforts to restore the Spanish crown because it represented Spanish tradition. The average Spaniard was very traditional, believing deeply in the king, the nation, and the Church. The general population did not support the liberals because they represented rapid change, a frightening prospect because it entailed the unknown.

Once restored to power, Fernando ruled Spain with an iron fist. He moved quickly against the liberals, executing, imprisoning, or exiling many of the leaders. He abolished freedom of the press and allowed the Jesuits to return. He did not, however, reestablish the Inquisition, well aware that the French would oppose such a move. Fernando's iron-fisted rule lasted until his death in 1833, ending a ten-year phase that has become known as the "ominous decade" (1823-33) because of the severe, official repression orchestrated by Fernando VII.

The *moderados* and the *progresistas*. Riego's 1820 coup d'état actually divided Spanish liberals into two camps: the *moderados*, or moderates, and the *exaltados* (later to be called the *progresistas*), or radicals. The *moderados* advocated slow, systemic change. They were principally men of means who saw a radical revolution as rocking the boat and perhaps spoiling what privileges they had. The *exaltados*, on the other hand, wanted to fight a revolution for the people. They tended to be urban liberals with less means and property than the *moderados*, and their calls for civil disorder made many Spaniards very nervous. The group for whom they were supposedly fighting, the Spanish masses, did not understand the radicals' objective, which was to overturn the existing sociopolitical system through revolution and retain the Constitution of 1812, with its unicameral democracy. Their extremist measures scared the majority of Spaniards. The common people clung to old-fashioned ways of thinking and doing things and vehemently opposed liberal actions. Their Catholic, conservative views supported an absolute monarchy despite the fact that the majority of them lived in miserable conditions. They certainly did not support the Constitution of 1812, which called for limited authority on the part of the crown and a democratic form of government with elected officials. Nor did they support the liberal coup d'état of 1820-23. When Fernando VII returned from France in 1814 and when he regained power in 1823, the average Spaniard was delighted. The Church played no small part in all of this. It aligned itself with the absolute monarchy and constantly decried the liberal position. Priests preached to their congregations that supporting the Constitution of 1812 might give them voting rights, but it would cost them their salvation (Herr, p. 203).

The First Carlist War. Before dying, Fernando VII had produced with his fourth wife, María Cristina, only one potential heir to the throne: his daughter Isabel, born in 1830. However, Fernando's brother Carlos, who was the other potential heir to the crown, challenged the legitimacy of Isabel's inheritance by invoking the Salic Law, which stated that a woman could not rule as monarch of Spain. What Carlos and his ultraconservative supporters, known as Carlists, did not know was that a special session of the parliament in 1789 had repealed the Salic Law (Williams, p. 153). Isabel, then, stood as rightful inheritor of the throne. Fernando VII published the revocation of the Salic Law, or Pragmatic Sanction, which had not yet been done, but Don Carlos refused to accept it or the validity of Isabel's claim as the next ruler of Spain. His fanatical backers refused as well, igniting a very dangerous spark in the Spanish political landscape. Carlists were the most reactionary segment of Spanish society, and for them, even Fernando VII was too lenient with liberals. They consisted predominantly of rural peasants, the clergy, and ultraconservative monarchists. Carlists believed in the divine right of royalty to have absolute power in the country's governance. They called for the exile of all *progresistas*, the abolition of public education and the army because the liberals maintained a strong presence in both, and the reinstatement of the Inquisition, considered essential to the salvation of the Catholic faith. The Carlists furthermore stood ready to place Don Carlos on the throne as soon as Fernando died.

Fernando VII's death in September 1833 plunged Spain into the First Carlist War, a civil war pitting liberals against reactionaries. It was a long, bloody, and costly conflict that raged on until 1839. More than a dynastic competition, it was, in essence, a fight for Spain's future, between mostly urban liberals, who sought to shove the nation into the modern era, and primarily rural traditionalists, who ardently tried to hold onto the past. Every segment of the country became embroiled in the conflict: rich and poor, city dweller and peasant man and woman.

Until Isabel II came of age in 1843, María Cristina served as queen-regent in charge of the government. She was bound by a constitution and a parliament and backed by both the moderate and extremist liberals. The liberals wanted to impose on the nation a centralized government that divided the old regions into uniform provinces on the French model. In 1834 a conservative constitution was introduced that granted limited suffrage and bourgeois property rights, and it was supported by both the *moderados* and the *progresistas*. However, even a new

constitution could not stabilize the government. Ministers came and went, aided by *pronunciamientos* by the military, in a tug-of-war between the moderates and progressives that would continue for years to come.

Fernando VII's death in 1833 opened the door for the return of the exiled liberals, most of whom had fled to England and France when he regained

THE BOURBON DYNASTY IN SPAIN

In 1814 Fernando VII inherited the crown of a relatively new royal line in Spain, the Bourbons. Fernando was only the fifth Bourbon king to rule the nation. The line started with his great-great-grandfather, Felipe V, also known as Philippe, Duke of Anjou, who was actually one-quarter Spanish Habsburg. Felipe V became king in 1700 at the age of 16 when the last Spanish Habsburg ruler, Carlos II, named him heir to the Spanish throne on his deathbed. Felipe's grandfather was Louis XIV of France, and because of him France was able to enjoy extraordinary influence in the affairs of the Spanish state. During the eighteenth century, the Bourbons set about making Spain more "European," modernizing and liberalizing the country. The monarchy encountered problems at the end of 1807, when French forces under Napoleon aided the Spanish army in subjugating Portugal. After Portugal was defeated, Napoleon's forces in Spain stayed on and new ones poured into the country. Carlos IV, king of Spain at the time, was ineffectual and let his wife, Queen María Luisa, and his favorite minister, Manuel Godoy (who was María Luisa's lover), run the government. Carlos's son Fernando VII was bitterly opposed to Godoy and his parents. His supporters incited a riot in March 1808 at the royal retreat in Aranjuez (near Madrid), scaring Carlos IV enough to abdicate in favor of Fernando, although he soon tried to make the abdication null and void because it was done under duress. None of this mattered, for Carlos, María Luisa, Godoy, and Fernando were quickly packed off to France by Napoleon. Fernando finally returned and took the throne as king of Spain in 1814, only to become one of the most reactionary and disliked Bourbon kings ever to rule.

control of the government in 1814. From these two advanced countries, they brought back cutting-edge social, political, and literary ideas that would influence generations to come. There was, however, a strong reaction by conservatives to

Ferdinand VII

these revolutionary ideas imported from abroad. They ardently believed that the ideas would corrupt the country and spoil its beloved traditions. The return of the exiles fueled the progressive, or extreme liberal, cause; they supported María Cristina and her daughter Isabel against the rising conservative backlash.

During this time of liberal control of the government, anti-clericalism grew to a hysterical level in Spain. By 1835, the Progressive minister Juan Alvarez de Mendizábal, appointed by María Cristina to head the government, had enacted a decree closing all religious orders. Later, Mendizábal launched a land-reform initiative that would redistribute land in a process called amortization. He had church property confiscated and offered for sale, despite outcries from the clerical community in Spain and from the Pope. Roughly a quarter of all church properties were auctioned off in the first two years of the program. The amortization plan failed miserably, however, because the intended beneficiaries of the land reform, the poor peasants, could not afford to pay for the properties. Instead, wealthy landlords, speculators, and other bourgeois types snatched up the land and further exacerbated the problem of land distribution. The intended agrarian reform was a flop.

To make matters worse, urban mobs rose up against the clergy, killing priests in the street, sacking and burning churches and monasteries, and defiling anyone who openly opposed their actions. Although Mendizábal and other Progressives were not enemies of Catholicism, Catholics forever linked the unruly mobs' actions to their political maneuvers. Consequently, a mighty wall went up between the Church and the liberal establishment.

The power struggle between the Progressives and the Moderates caused an intense instability in the governance of the nation. The two different factions of the liberal party did not come to power as a result of democratically held elections that abided by the tenets of a liberal constitutional government. On the contrary, Moderates and Progressives grabbed power through *pronunciamientos* or through appointment by María Cristina. The royal court usually appointed Moderate ministerial governments, causing even more friction between the two factions. In short, the military and the royal court abused their authority in a shameless power grab that would continue for several years after the publication of the essay.

The growth of the bourgeoisie. At the dawn of the nineteenth century, the middle class barely existed in Spain. An ascendant but tiny class of merchants, landowners, and professionals constituted the base of the bourgeoisie at that time. However, the majority of Spanish society was divided between the aristocrats, or lucky few who had money, power, and property, and the teeming masses, most of whom were poor, landless, and illiterate. The growth of the middle class in Europe has historically been closely tied to increased trade and industry. Because Spain's economy was predominantly agrarian well into the twentieth century, the bourgeoisie developed much more slowly here than in other European countries. Still the class had a great deal of impact on society. The small number of middle-class Spaniards belies their import in the progress of Spanish politics. The impetus behind the liberal political victories in 1812, 1820, and in the 1830s came mostly from the bourgeoisie. The conflict concerning absolute versus constitutional monarchy resulted in part from the middle class's rise to power.

The nobility, on the other hand, saw the handwriting on the wall. In terms of power and money, nobles were losing ground. The more industrialized and mercantilist Spain became, the less power the aristocracy had. In the newly emerging economy, the nobility's landed estates and titles meant less than they had in prior centuries. Money began to function as a key means to economic, social, and political success. Most of the Ancien Regime did not know how to compete in this new world order and so were eclipsed by those in the middle class (bankers, traders, manufacturers, and business owners) who did. The liberal, predominantly bourgeois regimes that controlled Spain for most of the nineteenth century forced the nobility to the political sidelines. Afterwards, as in the rest of Europe, the aristocrats would never regain power completely.

Just as the bourgeoisie constituted the main threat to the nobility, the *pueblo*, the masses, stood as an adversary of the middle class (as well as the nobility). Forming the overwhelming majority of the population, they were predominantly poor and illiterate, rural dwellers. During the Bourbon monarchy, the masses first became a serious threat to the more affluent classes and to royal authority in 1766, when Madrid crowds rioted for three days in reaction to food shortages and a ban on traditional capes and hats, which had been imposed by the secretary of finance, the Italian marquis of Esquilache, on the grounds that they concealed the identity of thugs. Riots over food shortages, as well as the cost of bread, spread to 70 other locales. After fleeing from Madrid to Aranjuez, the royal retreat, Carlos III was finally able to restore order, but not without granting concessions. The marquis of Esquilache fled to Italy. A second major threat posed by the masses occurred in 1808, when they took to the streets of Madrid and other cities in open revolt against the French invaders. The War of Independence was for them what the French Revolution was for common Frenchmen.

The Essay in Focus

Contents summary. Very few of Larra's essays have been translated into English, despite his landmark status in Spanish letters. Due to the lack of accessible translations, "The Old Castilian" has been newly rendered into English for *WLAIT 5: Spanish and Portuguese Literatures and Their Times* and placed immediately after this summary for easy reference.

One day the narrator, Fígaro, is out for a walk, collecting material for the articles that he writes for the newspaper. He loses himself in thought, mechanically moving his lips as he wanders, muttering soliloquies, head downcast, through the streets of Madrid. Now and again he looks up just in time to avert running head first into someone. *Madrileños* (residents of Madrid), realizes Fígaro, are not very understanding of poets and philosophers or their scatterbrained soliloquies. They dart mocking smiles his way and stare at him as they pass by.

Just as he thinks this, someone surprises him from behind by landing a huge hand on his shoulder. Before Fígaro can turn around, the person places his hands over the narrator's eyes in an attempt to play a joke. The man finally reveals himself to be a friend, Braulio, and invites Fígaro to his birthday dinner, which will occur the following day. Fígaro tries very politely to refuse the invitation, but Braulio insists, insinuating that if Fígaro doesn't attend the dinner, it will be because he thinks he's too good to attend such a lowly function. Fígaro reluctantly accepts.

He then describes Braulio in somewhat unflattering terms as a member of the middle class, holding a second-rate position and making a modest income. Braulio's patriotism borders on the fanatical; his social manners are overly polite and at times ridiculous.

The next day, as the fateful hour draws near, Fígaro dresses slowly, like a condemned criminal, and then he arrives at Braulio's house fashionably late. When he enters the drawing room, he notices several people with whom he is not familiar. He surmises, based on their sloppy fashion and insipid courtesies and conversations, that they must be fellow employees within the mediocre concern that employs Braulio.

Once the colleagues leave with their wives, children, dogs, and tasteless umbrellas and outfits, the guests are invited not to stand on ceremony but to have a seat. Fígaro notes that on days when Braulio and his wife don't have guests, they are quite content to eat dinner at a low, modest table that resembles a shoemaker's worktable. He observes that Braulio and his wife are putting on a big production to impress their company.

The dinner is a disaster. Fígaro is placed between a child who now and again flicks olive pits at others and a corpulent man who needs two chairs instead of the one he has. One guest insists on carving up the chicken and manages to launch it across the table and knock a container full of broth over onto Fígaro's shirt. A servant, after collecting the escaped fowl, spills grease from the sauce all over poor Fígaro's trousers as she attempts to carry the chicken off. She then bumps into another servant and dishes go crashing to the floor. Meanwhile, Braulio is constantly upbraiding his wife about the inferior quality of food and beverages. To top it all off, Braulio and the other guests insist that Fígaro recite some poetry. The poet is the only person of at least some social renown at the dinner and it is a triumph for Braulio's ego when Fígaro does finally recite some verses. For the other guests, who most likely do not frequent such social gatherings with members of the artistic community, it is as much entertainment as anything else. Fígaro surmises that the only way to avoid such disasters is to eat and serve oneself decently every day, not, as in Braulio's case, only when guests are around.

Managing at last to escape the fiasco, Fígaro is deliriously happy to breathe the fresh air out on the street once more. He asks God to spare him future dinner invitations hosted by old-fashioned Castilians. As he changes out of his stained clothes back home, he reflects that all men are not the same. Even those of the same country don't share the same refinement and customs. Fígaro ventures out once again, this time to happily rub shoulders with the more refined set of Madrid society. Those who are well bred, he ponders, are few and far between. They are lucky enough to have a good rearing that teaches them to pretend to like and respect one another even when they truly don't so as not to make each other uncomfortable. Other people (like Braulio's set) make each other uncomfortable in a grandiose manner, offending and mistreating each other, all the while perhaps truly caring about and respecting one another.

The essay in translation. Below find a translation of the essay under consideration, followed by discussion of its relevance to Larra's society and of the sources, literary context, and reception pertinent to this work.

The Old-Fashioned Castilian

At my age, very rarely do I like to alter the order of my way of doing things that I established quite some time ago. My reluctance to change is due to the fact that every time I have left the sanctity of my home and broken my routine, my false hopes have been dashed and I have later most sincerely regretted it. However, I am compelled to upset my normal schedule because of the old tradition of social conduct our parents adopted that deems rejection of certain dinner invitations impolite or, at the very least, an absurd affectation of refinement.

A few days ago I was wandering about the streets of Madrid looking for material to use in my articles. Absorbed in my thoughts, I surprised myself several times by laughing like a poor madman at my own ideas and moving my lips mechanically. A few stumbles now and again caused me to look up and reminded me that it's best not to be a poet or philosopher while walking the cobblestone streets of Madrid: more than a few maligned smiles, more than a few expressions of admiration from those who passed by made me realize that soliloquies should not be carried out in public. Many times I bumped into people as I turned a corner who were as distracted and walking as rapidly as I. These collisions underscored the fact that the distracted do not indeed have elastic bodies; nor are they glorious and impassive beings. In such spirits, imagine what I felt upon receiving a horrible slap from a huge hand connected (so I was soon to find out) to an enormous arm on one of my shoulders which, by the way, are nothing like Atlas's.

I didn't want whoever it was to think that I was unfamiliar with this energetic method of presenting oneself, nor did I want to reject the show of affection from the person who had undoubtedly believed that he would make me happy by practically crushing me, leaving me crumpled up for the rest of the day. I only tried to turn around to find out who could have been such a friend as to treat me so badly, but my old-fashioned Castilian is a man who doesn't know when to stop when he is in a joking mood. After all that, would you believe that he continued to demonstrate his confidence and affection for me? He put his hands over my eyes and grabbed me from behind:

"Who am I?" he yelled, exhilarated with the success of his oh-so-delicate and tasteless joke. "Who am I?"

"An animal," I was going to respond, but then I suddenly remembered who it might be, and instead said to him, "It's Braulio."

Upon hearing me, he removed his hands from my eyes, laughed, and held his sides. He caused everyone in the street to stare with curiosity, making a spectacle of both of us.

"Well, my friend! How did you know it was me?"

"Who could it be but you?"

"Are you just getting back from Vizcaya?"

"No, Braulio, I never went."

"Never went? Ah, come on—always the same joker. What do you expect? How happy I am that you're here! Did you know that tomorrow is my birthday?"

"Congratulations."

"There's no need for formalities between us; you already know that I am a frank and old-fashioned Castilian. I call a spade a spade. Therefore, I request that you do not congratulate me if you do not want to, but you are invited."

"To what?"

"To dine with me."

"It's not possible."

"I insist."

"I can't," I persisted, trembling.

"You can't?"

"Thank you, no."

"Thank you? Get out of here, friend. Just because I'm not the Duke of F. nor the Count of P."

Who can resist a surprise strategy like this? Who wants to appear to be arrogant?

"It's not that, it's just . . . "

"Well, if it's not that," he interrupted me, "I'll expect you at two o'clock. At my house we eat *a la española*: early. I have many people coming; we'll have the famous X., who will improvise marvelously for us. T. will sing a *rondeña* [A popular song from Ronda] to us after dinner with his natural grace, and in the evening J. will sing and play a little something."

His words consoled me a bit, and I had to capitulate. Anyone, I said to myself, can get through one bad day. To keep friends in this world, it's necessary to withstand their attentions now and again.

"Don't miss out, or I'll have a bone to pick with you."

"I'll make it," I replied with a very submissive voice and fallen spirits, like a fox who turns round and round in the trap in which he has let himself get caught.

"Okay then, see you tomorrow," and by way of farewell he gave me a hard pinch.

I watched him go like the farmer who watches the cloud move away from his planted field, and I remained there pondering how I could continue to let this hostile and unfortunate friendship exist.

My reader will probably have figured out, being as perspicacious as I believe him or her to be, that my friend Braulio is very far from belonging to what is called high and refined society, but he is not, at the same time, a man of inferior class. He is one of those employees of second-class rank who counts among his earnings and estate forty thousand *reales* of income. He wears a little ribbon tied to his buttonhole and a little cross at the corner of his lapel [indicating that he belongs to a minor social/religious order]. He is a person, in short, whose class, family, and creature comforts in no way kept him from receiving a more refined

upbringing and more polished and smooth manners. However, vanity has caught up with him like it has almost always with all or a great part of our middle class and all of our lower class. His patriotism is such that he will trade all the beauty of foreign countries for one eyesore of his own. This blindness makes him adopt all of the short-sighted views of such a thoughtless affection, so that he argues that there are no wines like Spanish wines, and he may be right. He defends the country by positing that there is no upbringing like a Spanish one, about which he very well might not be right. Instead of advocating the blissful purity of Madrid skies, he will say that our lower-class girls are the most charming in the whole wide world. He is a man who, in short, goes from one extreme to the other. His condition is more or less like that of a female relative of mine, who is crazy about humps only because she had a lover who had a fairly visible growth on each shoulder blade.

It would fall on deaf ears if I were to speak to him about polite social customs, mutual respect in public, urbane reservation, and the delicacy of address that establishes a beautiful harmony between men, whereby one says only that which aims to please and always keeps to oneself what might offend. On the contrary, he loves to tell the most humiliating truth to a vain individual, and when he resents someone, he says it to the person's face. Since he has thrown aside all restraints, he cannot understand why everyone doesn't know that formalities are simply a fulfillment of social obligation and lack sincerity. He calls urbanity hypocrisy, and decency he calls ridiculous affectation. To everything that is good, he applies a pejorative nickname. Refined language is, to him, little more than Greek: he believes that good breeding is reduced to saying "God keep you" upon entering a room and to add "excuse me" every time he moves; to ask everyone about his entire family and to bid farewell to every last person; all of which he would no more forget than he would a pact with the French. In sum, he is one of those men who do not know how to take leave unless they do it in concert with others; who humbly leave their hats, which they call 'their heads,' under a table; who, when they find themselves in society without their walking sticks, God forbid, would give anything not to have hands and arms, because in reality they don't know where to put them nor what to do with them in society.

Two o'clock arrived, and as I knew my Braulio as well as I did, it didn't seem appropriate to dress too elegantly for dinner; I'm sure that he would have been offended if he knew the truth. I did, however, put on a colored tailcoat with a white handkerchief, an indispensable thing in just such a situation and in such a house. I dressed as slowly as possible, like the condemned criminal who wishes he had one hundred more sins to confess in order to gain more time. The invitation was for two o'clock, and I entered the parlor at two-thirty.

I wish not to speak of the countless ceremonious guests who came and went in that house before the dinner hour, among whom were not a few fellow office employees with their wives and children, capes, umbrellas, galoshes, and dogs. I won't even mention the idiotic courtesies that they paid to the man of the hour, nor of the immense circle with which the motley collection of people adorned the parlor. They spoke about how the weather was going to change and that in winter it's usually colder than in the summer. But more to the point: the clock struck four, and we guests found ourselves alone with one another. Unfortunately for me, Mister X., who was supposed to entertain us so well and who was obviously all-too-knowledgeable about these kinds of invitations, had managed to become sick that morning. The famous Mr. T. was conveniently unable to get out of a prior commitment. The famous Miss J., who was going to sing and play for us so marvelously, was hoarse, and it surprised even her that anyone could understand a single word that she said. She also had an inflammation on one finger. So many dashed hopes!

"It looks like everybody who's going to eat is here!" exclaimed Don Braulio. "Let's sit down at the table, my dear."

"Just a moment," his wife replied to him almost in a whisper.

"With so many guests I've still got some things to finish up in there, and . . . "

"Okay, but look, it's almost four o'clock."

"We'll eat in just a bit."

It was five o'clock before we sat down to eat.

"Gentlemen," said our host when he saw us squirm uncomfortably in our respective seats, "I demand the utmost frankness from you; in my house there are no formalities. Ah, Fígaro! I want you to be completely comfortable. You are a poet, and besides, these gentlemen, who know how tight we are, won't be offended if I favor you; take off your tailcoat—you might stain it."

"Why would I stain it?" I asked, biting my lips.

"It doesn't matter; I will give you a jacket of mine. I regret that I don't have one for everybody."

"It's not necessary."

"Oh, yes, yes! My jacket, please! Take it, look at it. Hmmm, maybe it's a little big for you."

"But, Braulio, . . . "

"I insist; no need to stand on ceremony."

And with this he took off my tailcoat, like it or not, and I become buried in a requisite striped jacket, from which only my head and feet extend, and whose long sleeves probably wouldn't allow me to eat. I thanked him. After all, the man thought he was doing me a favor!

When my friend doesn't have guests at his house, he contents himself with a low table, little more than a shoemaker's work table, because he and his wife don't want for more, in his words. From that little table he makes the food rise to his mouth like water from a well, and after a long voyage it reaches his mouth, dripping all the while. To think that these people would have a regular table and be comfortable every day of the year is to think of the impossible. It is easy to imagine that the installation of such a large table for guests was indeed quite an event in that house. Thus, they believed the table could accommodate the fourteen of us when it could barely sit eight comfortably. We had to sit sideways, as if we were going to eat with our shoulders, and the guests' elbows established intimate relations among themselves with the most fraternal consideration in the world. In order to show their regard for me, they placed me between a five-year-old child, propped up on pillows that had to be adjusted every little bit because they constantly slid to this side or that, thanks to the natural energy level of the young diner. On my other side was one of those men who occupy the space of three and whose corpulence overflowed on all sides the one little chair on which he sat, as if he were seated on the point of a needle.

The napkins, indeed very new as they were props in disuse most days of the year, were unfolded in silence by these good gentlemen and placed in the buttonholes of their coats like gangplanks from their lapels down to the sauces.

"You'll have to excuse this meager meal, gentlemen!" exclaimed our host once seated. "I don't have to remind you that we are not in Genieys [the most elegant restaurant in Madrid at the time]," he continued, with a declaration he obviously felt necessary to make. If what he says is a lie, I said to myself, his comment would be quite an affectation; if true, how awkward to have to prepare your guests for a lousy meal!

Unfortunately it didn't take me long to figure out that there was more truth in Braulio's words than even he knew. The pleasantries with which we bored ourselves while passing platters of food around the table were interminable and in poor taste:

"Please, serve yourself."

"Could you pass me. . . ?"

"Of course."

"I shouldn't have that."

"Pass this to the lady of the house."

"It's okay to put it there."

"Excuse my reach."

"Thank you."

"Please, gentlemen, all these formalities aren't necessary!" exclaimed Braulio.

And he dipped in first with his own spoon. After the soup came a stew stocked with all the delicious ingredients typical of this troublesome yet tasty dish: some meat; vegetables; garbanzo beans; ham; chicken; bacon; and Extremaduran sausage. Next came a dish of veal prepared with thin strips of bacon (may the Lord condemn it), and then another, and others, and others, half brought from the local inn, half made in the kitchen by the regular servant, a Vizcayan helper hired for just this purpose, and the housewife, who on such occasions attends to everything and who, therefore, usually attends to nothing.

"Please pardon this dish," Braulio's wife said about the cooked pigeons. "They're a little burnt."

"But, honey . . . "

"Goodness, I stepped away for a moment, and you know how these servants are."

"Too bad this turkey wasn't cooked half an hour more! It was put on a little late."

"Don't you think this stew has a smoky flavor?"

"What do you want? One can't be on top of everything."

"Oh, it's excellent!" we exclaimed, leaving it on the plate. "Excellent!"

"This fish is spoiled."

"Well, they told me at the market that the fish had just arrived; the servant is such a brute!"

"Where's the wine from?"

"About that you are incorrect, because it's . . . "

"It's very bad."

These short exchanges were accompanied by countless furtive looks on the part of the husband to constantly warn his wife of some shortcoming, making us understand that both

of them were very informed about what is considered refined on such occasions. Of course, all of the inadequacies were a direct responsibility of the servants, who never do learn how to serve properly. But these shortcomings were repeated so often, and the looks served such little purpose, that the husband felt it necessary to resort to pinching and stepping on people's feet. Up until now Braulio's wife was able to withstand the badgering of her husband, but now her face became red and tears welled up in her eyes.

"*Señora*, don't feel bad about all that," said the person next to whom she was seated.

"Ah! I assure you that next time I will not do all this cooking here at home; you don't know what it is to have to do all this. Once again, Braulio, we will go to the inn and you won't have . . . "

"You, my lady, will do as . . . "

"Braulio! Braulio!"

An awesome storm was about to break out, although all of the guests competed in trying to placate the dispute, which was the result of an attempt to display an ultimate sense of sophistication. Braulio's obsession with this played no small part in it; nor did his expression about the uselessness of formalities, repeated again to us, which is what he calls being well-served and knowing how to eat. Is there anything more ridiculous than these people who want to pass as refined when they haven't the faintest clue about social customs, and in order to please you they force you to eat and drink and bar you from doing what you want? Why do some people only want to eat a bit more decently on their birthdays, instead of every day?

As if this weren't enough, the child on my left took olives from a plate of ham slices with tomato and flicked them, and one landed in my eye, with which I couldn't see well for the rest of the day. The corpulent gentleman on my right had taken the precaution of putting his olive pits and poultry bones on which he had gnawed next to my bread on the tablecloth. The guest across from me, who announced that he was quite the carver, had taken upon himself the autopsy of a castrated chicken, that is to say, a rooster—for we never found out which. Whether due to the advanced age of the victim or to the absolute lack of anatomical knowledge on the part of the victimizer, there seemed to be no joints on the bird.

"This chicken has no joints!" exclaimed the unhappy carver, sweating and struggling, digging more than carving. "How strange!" On one of his attacks, the fork slipped over the animal as if it had scales, and the chicken, violently discharged, seemed to want to take flight like during his happier times, and landed tranquilly on the tablecloth like on a perch at the henhouse.

The incident shocked everyone and the alarm reached its peak when a container full of broth, with which the flying chicken came into direct contact, spilled all over my very clean shirt. The carver got up quickly at this point in order to hunt down the fugitive chicken, and rushing to get to it, he knocked over a bottle to his right, which left its perpendicular position and spilled an abundant stream of Valdepeñas wine over the chicken and the tablecloth. The wine ran, the uproar increased, and the salt rained down over the wine, poured by everyone in an effort to save the tablecloth. To save the table, the guests inserted napkins underneath the tablecloth until a pile was heaped up. A very flustered servant took the chicken away in its sauce dish. When she passed by me she slightly dipped the dish and down poured an awful rain of grease, leaving eternal pearl-colored spots on my pants like dew upon the fields. The anguish and bewilderment of the servant knew no bounds. She left confused without being able to find a way to excuse herself. Upon turning around, she knocked into a male servant carrying a dozen clean plates and a tray full of wine goblets. The whole tray fell to the floor with the most horrendous crash and confusion.

"By Saint Peter!" shouted Braulio, a deathly pallid color spreading out over his features, while his wife's face became so red it looked like it was on fire. "But let's continue, gentlemen; this has been nothing," Braulio added, recovering his composure.

Oh, respectable houses where a modest stew and a final calamity constitute the daily happiness of a family; flee from the tumult of a birthday invitation! Only by eating and serving oneself well each day can one avoid similar catastrophes.

Could anything else go wrong? Good heavens! Yes, for unlucky me, yes. Doña Juana, the one with the black and yellow teeth, extended a small gift to me from her plate with her own fork, and it was a must to accept and eat it. The child enjoyed himself by throwing pits plucked out of cherries at the guests. Don Leandro made me try the exquisite Andalusian white wine, which I at first refused because he offered it from his own goblet that had indelible traces of his greasy lips upon it. My fat neighbor was now smoking non-stop and I played the flue for his chimney. At last, (oh, talk about the ultimate in mishaps!) the disorder and conversation grew; people's voices were hoarse now and they were asking for a poetry recital and there was no other poet there but Fígaro (me).

"You have to. You must recite something!" all clamored at this point.

"Give him a verse to get him started; we hope he says a couplet for each person here."

"I'll get him started: To don Braulio on this special day."

"Gentlemen, please!"

"We insist."

"I've never improvised."

"Don't be so timid!"

"I'll leave."

"Lock the door."

"You won't go from here without reciting something."

And I recited verses at last, and I spewed forth silly things, and they loved them, and the uproar grew, as did the smoke and the hell of it all.

I thanked the good Lord when I was able to escape the pandemonium. At last, I was able to breathe the fresh, clear air out on the street. No longer did I have to put up with dumb people, nor were there old-fashioned Castilians around.

"My Lord, I thank you!" I exclaimed, breathing like a deer who has just escaped a dozen hounds and who now barely hears their baying. "From now on I will not ask you for riches, nor for jobs, nor for honors. What I ask is that you free me from domestic banquets and birthday invitations; free me from these houses in which an invitation to dinner is a big deal, in which they only set the table decently when they have guests, in which they think they are pleasing you when they are mortifying you, in which people do nice little things for you like pass you food they've chewed on, in which they recite poetry, in which there are children, in which there are fat people, and in which the brutal frankness of old-fashioned Castilians reigns supreme. If I fall into the temptation of doing something like this again, I hope that I never eat any more roast beef; I hope steak disappears from the earth; that *timbales de macarrones* [flour dough filled with macaroni, chicken, meat, shrimp, etc.] are eliminated altogether; that there be no more turkeys in Perigueux nor pastries in Perigord; that the vineyards of Bordeaux dry up; that everyone except me drinks champagne's delicious foam."

Done with my mental supplication, I ran to my room to take off my shirt and pants, ruminating that all men aren't the same, since those of the same country, even perhaps of the same persuasion, can't possibly share the same customs, nor the same refinement, when they see things in such a different way. I dressed and tried to forget such an ill-fated day, making my way out among the scarce number of people who think, who live subject to the sweet yoke of good breeding, unencumbered and vast. At least they pretend to esteem and respect each other so as not to make themselves uncomfortable, while old-fashioned Castilians make an ostentatious display of making themselves uncomfortable and offending and mistreating one another, perhaps truly caring about and respecting each other all the while.

(trans. Mehl Penrose)

Costumbrismo. Fígaro's comments on the customs and habits of his friend, Braulio, and of Braulio's guests reveal the general intent of the essay. It satirizes the conservative, ardently patriotic bourgeoisie who try too hard to seem more refined and wealthy than they are. From their point of view, being perceived as traditionally Spanish, even if it means they must maintain flawed ways of thinking and behaving, is the best compliment one could pay them.

As a member of the middle class, Larra seems to be poking fun not only at the conservative members of the middle class, but also at himself. Larra was, in effect, laughing at himself for his own pretensions of grandeur, especially as they pertained to his writing career. His alter ego, Fígaro, also a bourgeois character, is shown to be smug in his conviction that he is somehow superior to the people with whom he dines. He is furthermore ridiculed in the story, when it reduces him to reciting idiotic verses for people whom he believes have no appreciation for refined art.

Larra's portrayal of the customs of his fellow Spaniards categorizes the essay as *costumbrista* but, as explained later, Larra gives it a satiric twist that other costumbristas did not include. *Costumbrismo*, a submovement of Romanticism, traditionally tends to seek out and describe local types, extolling their traditional Spanish virtues and manners. It started in Spain in response to the many published stories and diaries circulated elsewhere in Europe, mainly in France, England, and Germany, by non-Spanish travelers who wrote rather exaggerated depictions of Spaniards. Romantic writers north of the Pyrenees saw Spain as the perfect setting for their stories, considering the country much more traditional, even backward, in comparison to the advanced countries like France and England. One writer even stated that Africa began at the Pyrenees mountain range, which separates Spain from France. Travel writers, seeking to paint a verbal portrait of exotic Spain moved in their writings from region to region, capturing the local color of ordinary Spaniards, helping other Europeans get a better glimpse of life, albeit in an exaggerated form, on the Iberian peninsula.

Many Spanish Romantic writers took issue with this foreign picture of their country. They considered it inaccurate and took offense at its image of Spaniards as inferior and backward. Some of them, like Ramón Mesonero Romanos and Serafín Estébanez Calderón, retaliated with vivid, accurate descriptions, generating a few of the most illustrative examples of *costumbrismo*. Mesonero Romanos wrote about the people and customs of mostly middle-class Madrid, and Estébanez Calderón focused on the people and local color of Andalusia. Writings by both were very popular. It is clear from their essays that these writers approved of a traditional Spain, one free of foreign influence, a Spain that clung to and celebrated its customs of yore. However, the attempt of these writers to depict quaint and pure Spanish customs had the exact opposite effect than intended. Because Spanish society was so much more traditional than the advanced European countries, and because many sections of the country were very isolated, their depictions of Spaniards seemed to confirm what the foreign travel writers were saying about Spain. It was indeed an exotic country, full of colorful customs not found in other European countries. In the end, *costumbrismo* romanticized Spain to the rest of the world and even to Spaniards themselves.

The essay of customs and manners was already very much in vogue in France when Mesonero Romanos, Estébanez Calderón, and Larra began to create their own Spanish versions of it. France's Etienne de Jouy was achieving popular success at the time for his portrayal of French customs and manners. Each of the three Spanish authors considers Jouy a major influence on his own writing.

As much as Larra admired Jouy and the *costumbrismo* movement in general, he decided to take it in a new direction. Instead of describing traditional customs as vital for conserving the culture of Spain, Larra poked fun at many customs and lambasted what he considered a national penchant for regressive thinking. In essence, he turned the *costumbrista* essay into a satirical weapon, acerbically criticizing all that he saw in Spain as a hindrance to the nation's social and political development. One of his targets is the kind of Spaniard, like Braulio, who believes Spain is perfect the way it is and should never be changed. Larra took issue with this self-righteousness because he saw many egregious flaws in his nation's character. Having lived in France as a boy and having later traveled to France, England, and other parts of Europe, he was amazed by those countries' progressive vision. Larra, however, did not want to simply imitate foreign social, political and cultural models. As a matter of fact, he lampooned affluent Spaniards who slavishly imitated English and French fashion and ways of being simply because it was stylish to do so. He condemned poor Spanish imitations of foreign literary works, and he spoke out against producing French theatrical works translated into Spanish because the average Spaniard did not understand the foreign cultural context in which the plays were created. Larra sought instead to advance the country by bringing to the fore the best

---

JOUY

~

Unequivocally the leader of the modern "customs and manners" movement, the Frenchman Victor Joseph Etienne (1764-1846), whose pseudonym was Jouy, gained a popular following in France at the beginning of the nineteenth century. He wrote amusing descriptions of French people and their way of life in newspapers and magazines, in essence holding up a mirror to French society, especially the middle class. His work inspired many other writers in this genre, including Mariano José de Larra, Ramón Mesonero Romanos, and Serafín Estébanez Calderón, three of the greatest *costumbrista* writers of Spain. One of Jouy's most famous works was *L'Hermite de la Chausée d'Antin*, a collection of "customs and manners" essays.

Spanish ideas, or at least by adapting advanced ideas and models from the rest of Europe to Spanish cultural norms. Spaniards, he argued, were not ready for a Romantic writer such as Alexandre Dumas, famous in his native France for *Antony*, among other works. In a two-part review of *Antony*, Larra "combats what he sees as an extreme, exacerbated Romanticism, the kind in which the individual erects his own standards and norms without taking into consideration his fellow citizens, that is, society" (Schurlknight, p. 80). Larra believed that Spain was not developmentally ready for such avant-garde literary works, and therefore Romanticism in Spain had to be written by and for Spaniards.

Larra took a unique position in terms of the debate raging over Romanticism in Spain at the time. He clearly did not align himself completely with the exiled Spanish writers, who had returned from places like England and France with very progressive ideas. These writers saw Dumas and others like him as Romantic models, and they were ready to create literary works within that liberal vein. On the other hand, Larra refused to side with the conservative Romantics, such as Mesonero Romanos and Estébanez Calderón, because he firmly believed that in order to progress, Spain had to do more than look to its past. In his eyes, Spain needed to embrace the future and to prepare for it. He believed that his nation had to acknowledge its weak points and attempt to overcome them. It had to adapt the most forward-looking ideas coming out of Europe to a Spanish context, instead of simply adopting those ideas wholesale like many Spanish liberals advocated. Many returning exiles, for example, wanted to copy the political and economic systems they saw in France and England, which were advanced by any measure. Larra felt that it was imprudent to do so because Spain was not ready for such rapid change in so short a period of time. He believed in reforming, among other things, the Spanish political system with its constitutional monarchy instead of, as had happened in France, engaging in revolution that would oust the monarchy altogether. He wanted to incorporate the European democratic ideals that Spain could absorb at that moment in time and reject those that it couldn't. Larra argued that Spain also desperately needed to generate its own ideas in an attempt to create a stronger nation. As much as he liked the progressive attitudes of England and France, Spain would be no more than a follower unless it sought its own direction.

Sources and literary context. As a major *costumbrista* literary figure, Larra was inspired principally by Jouy, whom he read in French and whom he often quoted. His other major sources of literary inspiration from France were Mercier, a "customs and manners" writer, Pierre-Augustin Caron de Beaumarchais (who wrote *The Marriage of Figaro*; hence Larra's pseudonym, Fígaro) and the satirist Nicolas Boileau. Sources of literary inspiration on his own home ground included Spain's eighteenth-century authors José Cadalso, Tomás de Iriarte, and Baltasar Melchor Gaspar María de Jovellanos, and its Golden Age authors Francisco Gómez Quevedo, and Miguel de Cervantes Saavedra (see **The Swindler** and **Don Quixote,** also in *WLAIT 5: Spanish and Portuguese*

Literatures and Their Times). Of all his Spanish predecessors, the eighteenth-century authors probably influenced Larra the most. His works all contain at least a hint of the prior Enlightenment movement, which placed great importance on the use of reason and took a more or less didactic approach in conveying a text's message. Larra, however, was writing at the height of Romanticism (an aspect of which was the celebration of national customs), and for all intents and purposes is considered a Romantic writer.

"El Castellano Viejo" stands out because it is one of the best examples of social satire that Larra produced. It is also one of the best examples of *costumbrismo* itself due to its brilliant portrait of the conservative bourgeoisie. Because of Larra's sharp criticism of Spain and its people in essays such as this, his works are remembered as the finest examples of *costumbrismo* ever written, although they are certainly not the most typical or "pure" *costumbrista* sketches.

Reception. The Spanish public reacted well to "Old-Fashioned Castilian" as well as other articles by Larra, especially in Madrid. By the time he began writing for *La Revista Española* (*The Spanish Review,*) under the pseudonym Fígaro, Larra was quite well-known and was the best-paid journalist of his day. (As shown, in "The Old-Fashioned Castilian," Larra's narrator is also named Fígaro; Larra did not distinguish between the "writer" and narrator of his stories—they were the same.)

Larra's importance as a literary figure would only grow. The novelist Pérez Galdós (see **Fortunata and Jacinta,** also in *WLAIT 5: Spanish and Portuguese Literatures and Their Times*) was inspired by Larra in writing his realist novels, and the so-called Generation of 1898 writers saw him as one of their greatest sources of inspiration. His profound impact was due to his love of Spain and his earnest attempt to improve it, clearly evident in his texts, despite his severe criticism. Larra was a master at identifying the problems that afflicted Spain. He "described Spain as the country of *casi* (which means "almost" or "not

quite"). Something was always missing, from institutions recognized by "not quite" the whole nation to canals "not quite" finished and museums "not quite" arranged (Williams, p. 158). In the end, Larra took his own life—"what was picturesque [about Spain] for foreign romantics finally drove Larra to suicide" (Williams, p. 158). In his lifetime, he urged his readers to take up his calls for reform, and eventually those calls were heard, especially by the writers of the Generation of 1898. Just as Larra would have wished, Spain did march forward, slowly and painfully reinventing itself by way of its own ideas and resources.

—Mehl Penrose

For More Information

Alvarez Junco, José, and Adrian Shubert, eds. *Spanish History since 1808*. London: Arnold, 2000.

Herr, Richard. "Flow and Ebb: 1700-1833." In *Spain: A History*. Ed. Raymond Carr. Oxford, U.K.: Oxford University Press, 2000.

Kirkpatrick, Susan. "Spanish Romanticism and the Liberal Project: The Crisis of Mariano José de Larra." *Studies in Romanticism* 16 (1977): 451-71.

Martin, Gregorio C. *Hacia una revisión crítica de la biografía de Larra (nuevos documentos)*. Porto Alegre: Editora Meridional EMMA, 1975.

Montgomery, Clifford Marvin. "Early Costumbrista Writers in Spain, 1750-1830." Philadelphia, 1931.

Schurlknight, Donald E. *Spanish Romanticism in Context: Of Subversion, Contradiction and Politics (Espronceda, Larra, Rivas, Zorrilla)*. Lanham, Md.: University Press of America, 1998.

Shaw, Donald L. *A Literary History of Spain: The Nineteenth Century*. London: Ernest Benn, 1972.

Sherman, Alvin F., Jr. *Mariano José de Larra: A Directory of Historical Personages*. New York: Peter Lang, 1992.

Ullman, Pierre L. *Mariano de Larra and Spanish Political Rhetoric*. Madison: The University of Wisconsin Press, 1971.

Williams, Mark. *The Story of Spain*. Puebla Lucía, Spain: Mirador Publications, 1992.

Poem of
the Cid

Little is known about the author of the *Poem of the Cid*. Although the closing lines of the original manuscript claim that Per Abbat (Pedro Abad) wrote the poem, scholarly opinion is divided on whether he was its author, as "individualists" contend, or merely its copyist, as "traditionalists" maintain. Evidence suggests that whoever composed the *Poem of the Cid* was learned, familiar with legal documents and procedures, and probably conversant with French epic poetry. Some have suggested that the author was a monk, while another noted scholar has identified a Castilian lawyer as the most likely candidate for authorship. There has likewise been controversy about the origins and dating of the *Poem of the Cid*. The traditionalists place the poem's composition as early as 1140—just over 40 years after the death of the Cid—and argue that the transcribed poem was the culmination of several oral versions of the tale, transmitted by traveling minstrels and storytellers. While their view negates the idea of a single author, the most recent consensus is that it was composed by a single individual and, on the strength of this author's likely sources, places the composition in the late twelfth or early thirteenth century. The date of 1207 C.E., found in the manuscript, cannot be ruled out entirely. In any case, most scholars and historians seem to agree that the *Poem of the Cid* is the earliest extant epic poem in Spanish. Through the centuries, the poem's stirring depiction of the exploits of Christian heroes and warriors in Muslim Spain has possessed a timeless appeal. Recent scholarship on the poem fo-

---

THE LITERARY WORK

An epic poem set in Christian and Moorish Spain in the eleventh century; written in Spanish (as *Cantar de mio Cid*) in the late twelfth or early thirteenth century; published in English in 1808.

SYNOPSIS

Exiled from his homeland, a Spanish knight wins wealth, fame, and a royal pardon while fighting the Moors.

---

cuses on the disparity between the heroic Cid of legend and the more ambiguous Cid of history.

Events in History at the Time the Poem Takes Place

The Cid of history. The events in the *Poem of the Cid* are loosely based on the life and career of Rodrigo (Ruy) Díaz de Vivar, known as El Cid, a name derived from the Arabic title Al-Sayyid ("lord"), though it is unclear just when Rodrigo Díaz acquired that name. Born around 1043 in Vivar, Rodrigo Díaz was the son of a minor nobleman of Castile; on his mother's side, however, he was connected with the great landed aristocracy of Spain. Rodrigo Díaz was brought up at the court of Fernando I of Castile, in the household of the king's eldest son, who would later become Sancho II of Castile (reigned 1065-72).

Military commander Rodrigo Díaz de Vivar, known as El Cid, on whose life *Poem of My Cid* is based.

In 1060, young Rodrigo showed military prowess when he participated in a campaign against Aragon for control over the Muslim state of Saragossa. When Sancho acceded to the throne in 1065, he named the Cid, then 22 years old, as his standard-bearer or commander-in-chief of the royal troops.

The Cid's military talents were indispensable to King Sancho throughout his reign. In 1067 the Cid accompanied Sancho on another campaign against Saragossa, playing a pivotal role in the negotiations that made Muqtadir, the Saragossan king, a tributary of the Castilian crown. Next, Sancho set his sights on the territories of Galicia and León, which his father had bequeathed to Sancho's brothers, García and Alfonso, respectively. By 1071, García had been defeated, while Alfonso was deposed and exiled to Muslim Toledo. In 1072, however, the childless Sancho was killed at the siege of Zamora; Alfonso returned from exile to claim the thrones of Castile and León as Alfonso VI. The Cid, who had led many of Sancho's campaigns against Alfonso, found himself in an awkward position. Although he swore loyalty to Alfonso, he lost his position as standard-bearer. It went instead to Count García Ordóñez—the new king's favorite—and the two became bitter rivals.

King Alfonso attempted to win the allegiance of his brother Sancho's most powerful supporter:

in 1074, he arranged a marriage between the Cid and his own niece, Doña Jimena, daughter of the Count de Oviedo. The couple had two daughters, Cristina and María—who married into noble families of Navarre and Barcelona—and one son, Diego Rodríguez, who was killed in 1097, fighting the Almoravids. Despite the apparent success of the marriage, the Cid's position at Alfonso's court remained precarious: he had lost much of his old influence and was surrounded by rivals. In 1079, while on a mission to the Moorish king of Seville, the Cid clashed with García Ordóñez, who was participating in the king of Granada's invasion of Seville. The Cid's forces defeated the Granadine army at Cabra, and during the battle, the Cid captured García Ordóñez, to Alfonso's great displeasure. In 1081, after the Cid led an unauthorized raid on the Moorish kingdom of Toledo, which was under royal protection, the king exiled the Cid and confiscated his estates.

For nearly a decade, the exiled Cid fought as a mercenary in the service of the Moorish king of Saragossa. His experiences brought him both further renown as a general undefeated in battle and rich rewards from his appreciative Moorish masters. In 1087, after suffering his own defeat by the invading Almoravids at the battle of Sagrajas, Alfonso pardoned the Cid and recalled him from exile. The reconciliation was short-lived, however, and banishment was reimposed in 1089, after the Cid's enemies accused him of retaining part of a Moorish tribute for himself. The Cid returned to Saragossa and embarked on an independent campaign in the Levante (eastern region of Spain), targeting the rich Moorish kingdom of Valencia. His shrewd exploitation of the political situation—eliminating the influence of the counts of Barcelona and gradually tightening his own control over the region—and his military expertise paid off. After a siege that lasted from December 1093 to June 1094, the Cid took possession of Valencia; nominally, he held Valencia for Alfonso VI, but in actuality, he ruled as its lord until his death in 1099. In 1096, the Cid converted the great mosque of Valencia into a cathedral and appointed a French bishop to be in charge of the new jurisdiction. After the Cid's death, his widow, Jimena, retained control over Valencia until 1102, when she was driven out by Almoravid armies.

Although the *Poem of the Cid* mentions many of Rodrigo Díaz's triumphs, such as his conquest of Valencia, it also downplays or omits more ambivalent details, such as his earlier allegiance to

King Sancho and his service under the Moorish king of Saragossa. Similarly, the Cid himself is presented as a wholly heroic character: a peerless warrior who remains undefeated on the battlefield; a faithful vassal to an unworthy overlord; a devout Christian who ascribes all his victories to God; and, finally, a devoted husband and father. The faults and ambiguities of the historical Cid vanish, so that the perfect hero of legend may be created. The accuracy of this idealized figure is questionable; for example, it is unclear whether the Cid was truly a devout Christian, especially during his years living among Muslims in Saragossa.

The reign of Alfonso VI. The *Poem of the Cid* presents not only an idealized portrait of the Cid but an unsympathetic portrait of Alfonso VI (reigned 1072-1109), who is depicted as harsh, punitive, prejudiced against the Cid, and envious of the Cid's popularity and influence. While the relationship between the king and the Cid seems to have been uneasy at best, history shows that Alfonso VI was neither an ineffective nor an incapable ruler.

Family strife and armed conflict marked Alfonso's road to the Castilian throne. Alfonso, the second son in the royal family, was actually favored by his father, Ferdinand I, from whom he inherited the kingdom of León along with the tributes paid by the Muslim kingdom of Toledo. Alfonso's older brother, Sancho, inherited the kingdom of Castile and the tribute of Saragossa, while García, the youngest prince, inherited the kingdom of Galicia. Sancho, who envied his brothers their holdings, sought to capture them by force. In 1071, Sancho and Alfonso both despoiled García of Galicia; in 1072, Sancho defeated Alfonso at the battle of Golpejerra and forced him into exile in Toledo. That same year, the insatiable Sancho laid siege to his sister Urraca's lands in Zamora; during the siege, partisans of Alfonso and Urraca—who favored Alfonso and helped foment a rebellion against Sancho in León—assassinated the Castilian king.

Sancho's death—without issue—left Alfonso the logical heir to both León and Castile. Returning from exile, Alfonso quickly assumed both thrones and occupied Galicia as well (García remained in prison until his death). Legend claims that the Cid, Sancho's standard-bearer and commander-in-chief, along with other Castilian nobles, refused to take an oath of loyalty to the new king unless Alfonso swore by the Bible that he had not been involved in Sancho's death. While the exact veracity of this episode is un-

known, it might account for any lingering tension between Alfonso VI and his brother's erstwhile and powerful supporter.

Alfonso enjoyed notable military success in the early years of his reign, leading raids as far southward as Córdoba and Seville and seizing the Rioja and Basque provinces. By 1077, he was proclaiming himself *imperator totius Hispaniae* ("emperor of all Spain"). In 1085 Alfonso achieved perhaps his greatest triumph when, after a long siege and with the aid of foreign crusaders, he captured the Moorish kingdom of Toledo. Christian Spain thus regained one of the most important historical, strategic, and cultural centers of the Iberian peninsula, which had been in the possession of the Muslims since the eighth century. Meanwhile, Alfonso exacted heavy tributes from the Moorish kingdoms under his control in return for his protecting them from other enemies. The influx of Muslim gold financed Alfonso's military campaigns and endowed shrines, churches, and monasteries.

The later years of Alfonso's reign brought crushing defeats in battle by the invading Almoravid (Berber) tribes from North Africa. In 1087, after one such defeat at Zallaqa, Alfonso recalled the Cid, whom he had exiled in 1081 after the knight led an unauthorized raid on Toledo. During the 1090s Alfonso entrusted the recalled Cid with the defense of eastern Spain, a maneuver that proved mainly successful. Other battle fronts did not fair as well. The king's problems with the Almoravid continued. Between 1086 and 1109 Alfonso was mostly defeated by the Almoravids; in 1108, he lost his only son, Sancho, at the Battle of Uclés. Alfonso's daughter Urraca succeeded him on his death in 1109.

Moorish-Christian relations. The eighth century brought dramatic political, religious, and cultural changes to Spain, which had been largely under Visigothic control since 480 C.E. In 710, a contested election for a king ultimately led to the collapse of the Visigoths' empire. After the death of King Witiza, the Visigoth nobles chose not Witiza's son Achila but their own candidate, Rodrigo, as the next king, provoking Achila into rebellion. Achila had company. Apparently King Rodrigo's enemies invited Tariq ibn Ziyad, a Muslim chieftain from North Africa to aid them in Spain. Their invitation led to repercussions they probably never envisioned. In 711, Tariq landed with a force of 7,000 men at Algeciras Bay near a great rock the invaders called Jabal al Tariq (Mountain of Tariq) in honor of their leader (the name was later corrupted to Gibraltar). On

Title page from the 1546 edition of *Poem of the Cid*

the banks of the Guadalete River, near Jerez de la Frontera, the combined foes of Rodrigo's foes and the Muslim invaders defeated those of Rodrigo, who apparently drowned while fleeing the battlefield; his body was never recovered.

After the battle, Tariq chose not to return to North Africa. Instead, the chieftain called for reinforcements, made further alliances among Rodrigo's enemies, and advanced with his people further into the Iberian Peninsula. By 718, the Muslim invaders—called Moors because they had launched their invasion from Mauretania—had driven what remained of Spain's former rulers into the northern mountains, had established an Arab emirate over most of the country, and had incorporated most of southern Spain into the Islamic world. The Moors' advance might have continued northward into France and the rest of Europe, but they were beaten in 732 by Frankish forces led by Charles Martel at the Battle of Poitiers. The defeat forced the Moors back into Spain, where they remained.

Meanwhile, in the northern outpost of Asturias, the unconquered Christians mounted counterattacks against the invaders. They eventually reclaimed most of the territory of León and established a tenuous hold over Galicia and Navarre. During the tenth century, the rulers of León extended their control eastward along the northern bank of the Duero River; the region gained by this determined expansion was given the name Castile, because of the many castles built to protect the people who held and worked the land. For the next 200 years—up to the time of the *Poem of the Cid*—the Duero River marked the frontier between Christian Spain and "al-Andalus," as Muslim Spain was sometimes called.

Significantly, the Moors never established political unity over their domains in Spain, which included the kingdoms of Córdoba, Seville, Granada, and Valencia. Factionalism and revolts thwarted attempts—even by the powerful caliphate of Córdoba in Muslim Spain, established by Emir Abd-al-Rahman III in 929—to impose an undivided hegemony over al-Andalus. Financial strains incurred by expensive military campaigns undertaken to subdue their various enemies contributed to the collapse of the Córdoban caliphate in 1031. Thereafter, al-Andalus was never a single unified power; rather, Muslim Spain splintered into about 30 *taifas,* or factional states, each with its own ruler. Consequently, the Christian realms were able to recover still more territory during the eleventh century, although the rulers of the North spent as much time fighting each other as they did fighting the Muslims.

The relationship between Moors and Christians was often uneasy but not always hostile. Fierce military campaigns waged by each to acquire territory held by the other alternated with lengthy periods of peace, even amity. Moorish kings often sought aid from Christians to defend their *taifas* or to fight their Muslim rivals. The Cid, for example, spent several years while exiled from Christian Spain in the service of the king of Saragossa. Furthermore, there was little religious persecution at this point. The Moors generally tolerated Christianity, seeing parallels to their own faith in the Christians' belief in a single deity and reliance on a holy book. They tolerated Judaism too in al-Andalus; many Christians who inhabited Moorish Spain even converted to Islam. Others, known as Mozarabs ("arabized"), retained their Christian faith but adapted themselves to the Islamic lifestyle in other ways—developing a distinctive art and poetry, for example, creating a bridge between the two cultures. The *Poem of the Cid* explores both sides of the Moorish-Christian relationship: on one hand, the Cid and his men continually battle with the Moors over territory; on the other, the wealthy Moor Abengalbón who twice extends his hospitality to the Cid's family is presented as the Cid's friend, superior in courage and honor to the scheming Infantes (young princes) of Carrión who plot to rob and murder him.

CHRISTIANS AND JEWS IN MEDIEVAL SPAIN

The Cid deceives some Jewish moneylenders in the *Poem of the Cid* without remorse, intimating that they deserve such deception, reflecting a common antipathy of the era. Around the time the poem was written, in the mid-thirteenth century, there were 4-5 million Castilians, including perhaps 300,000 Muslims and Jews, though estimates vary widely (O'Callaghan, p. 464). The two minorities were treated quite differently, a reaction in part to their different roles in Christian society. The Cid shows far greater tolerance toward Muslims in the poem, as was actually the case in society at the time. Christians and Jews coexisted in medieval Spain, divided by suspicion and a deep-seated anti-Jewish hostility that harked back to ancient Spain. Under the rule of the Romans in the fourth century, the law discriminated against Spain's Jews, followed two centuries later, under the Visigoths, by similar laws formulated at the Council of Toledo (589), which forbade Jews to marry Christians, own Christian slaves, or hold official power over Christians. Over the years, other councils reiterated and extended these laws. In 1055, the Council of Coyanza forbade Christians to reside or take meals with Jews, and in 1081 Pope Gregory VII warned King Alfonso VI not to give Jews public authority over Christians. In fact, Spain's rulers ignored such warnings, employing Jews as physicians, scholars, army-supply coordinators, financial advisors, and tax collectors in the separate kingdoms. The Christian proscription against usury led to a dependence on Jews for moneylending too. To some extent, these tendencies isolated the Jews occupationally, and they were physically isolated by the areas in which they resided. Jews generally settled in a town, in a self-governing subcommunity, though some might live in other neighborhoods too. In Castile, above and beyond meeting their general tax obligations, they were obligated to pay 30 *dineros* a month "in memory of the death of our Lord Jesus Christ when the Jews put Him on the cross," a reference to the myth that Jews, not, as has since been proven, Romans, killed Christ (O'Callaghan, p. 464). Such myths, combined with other factors, prompted twelfth-century society to perpetuate the age-old antipathy, which would grow fiercer in subsequent centuries. Now, in the medieval era, the degree of anti-Jewish hostility varied from town to town and era to era in Christian and in Muslim Spain. Some towns invoked anti-Jewish laws; in other towns Jews enjoyed much the same rights as non-Jews. But in both regions Spanish Jews suffered a resentment rooted in the past and aggravated by their roles in the present that could erupt into deadly persecution, as when the Muslim town of Córdoba sacked and burned its Jewish quarter in 1135.

The Poem in Focus

Plot summary. The first *cantar*, or song, of the poem begins abruptly—scholars contend that an earlier part of the manuscript is missing. The Cid, exiled by King Alfonso VI of Castile, leaves his domain of Vivar, a village north of the Spanish city Burgos. Reaching Burgos with a company of loyal followers, the Cid finds every door shut against him. He learns from one of the citizens, a nine-year-old girl, that all who offer him aid will, by the king's command, forfeit their possessions, their eyes, their bodies, and their souls. The Cid rides out of the city with his men and sets up a camp by the river. Martín Antolínez, another citizen of Burgos, supplies the Cid's company with bread and wine from his own stores and asks to join them, a request that the Cid grants. Needing money to pay his men, the Cid successfully dupes two Jewish usurers, Raquel and Vidas, into lending him 600 marks in exchange for two coffers supposedly holding his riches, but really filled with sand.

The Cid and his men next ride to the monastery of San Pedro de Cardeña, where the Cid's wife, Doña Jimena, and his two young daughters, Doña Elvira and Doña Sol, have been ordered to remain; the family shares a bittersweet reunion and a tearful parting. Afterward, the Cid is pleased to see that 115 more knights have ridden out to join his company. By now, six of the nine days allowed the Cid for his leaving Christian Spain have elapsed, so the entire company depart from San Pedro after morning mass is said for them. During the last stage of his journey, the Cid dreams of the angel Gabriel who assures him that all will go well with him.

Once in exile, the Cid becomes a soldier of fortune, leading his men in battle against the Moors. He captures the Moorish town of Castejón, while his men conduct raids along the Henares Valley; the vast spoils gained in both campaigns are divided among the Cid and his men. Moving onward from Castejón, the Cid continues his conquest of Moorish territories, each time amassing more wealth, power, and fame. After taking the town of Alcócer and defeating a Moorish force sent from Valencia, the Cid sends his lieutenant Minava Álvar Fáñez bearing gifts, including 30 fine horses, to King Alfonso. The king, though pleased by the gifts and the reports of the Cid's prowess, does not repeal the Cid's decree of banishment. Meanwhile, the Cid leaves Alcócer for the Jalón valley, where he carries out successful raids, which soon provoke an attack on his forces by Count Ramón of Barcelona. The Cid defeats Count Ramón in battle and takes him prisoner; the humbled count is released only after he gives up all his property to the Cid.

During the course of his campaigns, the Cid approaches the Moorish city of Valencia; he eventually engages in battle and defeats the inhabitants, then lays siege to the city, which surrenders to him after 10 months. The king of Seville leads an army to take back Valencia, but the Cid's forces defeat those of Seville. The Cid establishes his authority over Valencia *and* over his men, some of whom are growing homesick for their own lands. Threatening all potential deserters with death, the Cid maintains control over his vassals.

On his master's orders, the Cid's minion, Minaya Álvar Fáñez, again travels to Castile bearing gifts. This time he presents King Alfonso with a gift of 100 horses and requests that the Cid's wife and daughters be permitted to join him in Valencia. Pleased by the gift and the news of the Cid's victory, King Alfonso grants this request. The Cid happily reunites with his family; soon after, he defeats the forces led by the Emir of Morocco. This victory gains him even greater fame and riches, including the emir's luxurious tent, which the Cid sends to King Alfonso, along with 200 horses. So touched is the king by this latest present that he finally pardons the Cid.

At a meeting on the banks of the Tagus river, King Alfonso and the Cid are reconciled. To do his vassal great honor, the king proposes to marry the Cid's daughters to Diego and Fernando González, the Infantes of Carrión, who had expressed interest in wedding the girls. Although the Cid has reservations about his daughters marrying so young, he agrees that the alliances would be very prestigious and consents to the king's proposal. The marriages take place in Valencia amid much rejoicing. Two years of happiness and prosperity follow.

One day, while the Cid is sleeping, one of his lions escapes from the menagerie. The Cid's vassals hurry to protect their lord from the lion; meanwhile, the *infantes* run and hide. Waking, the Cid easily recaptures the lion; he less easily tries to put an end to the mockery his vassals direct towards his cowardly sons-in-law. The *infantes* take offence and privately vow to avenge their dishonor.

Soon after, an army arrives from Morocco and a battle ensues. The Cid is once again victorious; he praises all who participated in the battle, including his sons-in-law. But, in contrast to their unknowing master, the Cid's vassals are aware that the *infantes* behaved as cravenly as ever, and the mockery of the princes resumes. Resentful and humiliated, the *infantes* hatch a scheme for revenge, telling the Cid that they wish to take their wives to visit their new lands in Carrión. The unsuspecting Cid bestows more wealth on the *infantes,* including two treasured swords, Tizón and Colada, and sends along an escort of his own men to accompany them. Almost as an afterthought, the Cid sends along his nephew, Félez Muñoz, charging him to take care of the Cid's daughters.

On the journey, the *infantes* further disgrace themselves by plotting to rob and murder their host, Abengalbón, a wealthy Moor who is the Cid's friend. Their scheme is foiled, however, by a display of arms on the part of Abengalbón and his men. Later, the princes set up their camp in a wild wood. The next morning, having sent on their escorts ahead of them, the *infantes* strip their wives of their fine clothes, whip them viciously, and leave them for dead. Riding away, the *infantes* justify their behavior by saying that the Cid's daughters were not their equals in status and that they had to avenge their dishonor. Meanwhile, Félez Muñoz, concerned for his cousins, doubles back into the forest and finds the badly beaten girls. Reviving them, he places them on his horse, and they ride to the town of San Esteban, where the girls are nursed back to health before returning to their father in Valencia.

News of the princes' wicked deeds spreads quickly. King Alfonso and the Cid are shocked and appalled, the former vowing to try the *infantes* in a court held in Toledo, the latter swearing to avenge his daughters' ill-treatment and marry them to far greater husbands. At the trial, the Cid demands the return of his two swords, then the return of his gold from his former sons-in-law. The *infantes* give back the swords but, having squandered the Cid's gold, they are forced to make up the amount in horses and property. Finally, the Cid demands satisfaction for the *infantes*' cruel, dishonorable treatment of his daughters. Three of the Cid's vassals then issue formal challenges to the *infantes* and their brother, Asur González. In the midst of these proceedings, ambassadors from Aragon and Navarre arrive in Toledo to ask for the Cid's daughters as brides for their future kings. King Alfonso and the Cid consent to the arrangement, delighted that Doña Elvira and Doña Sol will be queens and thus socially superior to their former husbands.

Meanwhile, the combat between the Cid's knights and the Carrións takes place the next day. Pedro Bermudez and Martín Antolínez, the new owners of the swords Tizón and Colada, easily defeat the *infantes,* just as Muno Gustioz defeats Asur. The Cid and his men return to Valencia, with all their honor restored, while the Carrións are forced to live with everlasting disgrace. Soon after, the Cid's daughters marry the princes of Aragon and Navarre, later becoming queens and mingling the Cid's line with that of the kings of Spain. The Cid's illustrious career ends with his death in Valencia on Whit Sunday.

Honor among nobles. From the very start of the *Poem of the Cid*, the hero is concerned with the loss of his honor and prestige. The Cid feels keenly not only the pain of parting from his homeland and family but the humiliation inherent in his sentence of exile: he is stripped of his lands in Castile, denied the king's favor, and shunned by the city of Burgos. Therefore, his spectacular military campaigns in Muslim Spain are not only undertaken as a means to support himself and his men financially but as a means to recover his honor.

An important concept in Spain since the fifth century, the term "honor" carried subtle, far-reaching implications. Material wealth and high social position were often associated with honor, but by no means did they represent the full sum of honor. Scholars and translators Peter Such and John Hodgkinson explain,

> The notion of honour, as it is represented in the *Poema*, does not relate to the intrinsic worth of an individual, but rather to his status among his fellows and the respect which he is granted by others. Honour furnished a theme which was to be of great importance in the Spanish literature of later centuries, but it is clear from the law codes of medieval Castile and León that conflicts of honour were already a very significant feature of the society of Christian Spain.
> (Such and Hodgkinson, p. 14)

The *Poem of the Cid* accurately reflects the times of its setting and composition by depicting the many ways in which honor could be gained or lost. Through his victories over the Moors and his vast acquisition of booty, the Cid garners fame and honor, reports of which are carried back to King Alfonso, along with rich gifts that further enhance the Cid's prestige. By the time the Cid reconciles with Alfonso, the knight is as rich in admiration as he is in material possessions. The advantageous marriages of his daughters, first to the Infantes of Carrión, then to future kings of Navarre and Aragon, bring the Cid still more honor.

Conversely, the outcome of the *infantes*' episode in the *Poem of the Cid* reveals how easily honor can be lost or compromised among nobles and soldiers. The *infantes* dishonor themselves through cowardice: first, by hiding when a lion escapes from the Cid's menagerie; secondly, by failing to distinguish themselves in battle against the Moroccan army. Resenting the resultant mockery by the Cid's men and fearing that news of their cowardice will spread, the *infantes* plot to avenge themselves by casting an even greater shame upon the Cid. The *infantes* beat and abandon their wives, thus expressing scorn of the, in their view, "lowly" match that King Alfonso had arranged.

Both Alfonso and the Cid perceive the insult to them through the injuries done to Elvira and Sol, and act quickly to avenge their own dishonor. According to medieval law, a dishonored man was socially dead until slights against him were avenged, either through legal redress in the courts or through the killing of those who had dishonored him. Significantly, the Cid opts for the former, appearing in his finest clothes at the court Alfonso has convened in Toledo, making the restoration of his family's honor—and wealth—as public as possible. The Cid's own men also avenge their commander's dishonor by challenging and defeating the Carrións on the field of battle. The affronts to the Cid, Elvira, and Sol are thus amply avenged, and the even more prestigious marriages of the girls to princes of Navarre and Aragon erase any lingering stain on the Cid's honor. The defeated *infantes* are meanwhile condemned to perpetual disgrace and dishonor. It is a reflection of the way women were regarded during the time in which the *Poem of the Cid* was composed that, while Elvira and Sol suffered unprovoked mistreatment, they are perceived as less important in themselves than as appendages to their father. Their injuries are an insult to the honor of their male relative.

BEARDS AND BOASTS

In the poem, it is a point of great pride with the Cid that his long, flowing beard has never been plucked by anyone. Indeed, such an assault on a man's beard, along with striking him in the face, was considered a mortal insult, one punishable by death! Before appearing in court, the Cid arrays himself in his finest clothes and ties up his beard with a ribbon, as a safeguard against even accidental pulling. Encountering his old rival Count García Ordóñez in the courtroom, the Cid taunts him with the memory of how, years before, "I took [the castle of] Cabra, and pulled you by the beard, / there was no young child who did not pluck his bit. / The piece which I plucked has not yet properly grown" (*Poem of the Cid*, ll. 3288-3290).

Sources and literary context. The primary sources for the *Poem of the Cid* were, in all probability, historical accounts of the Cid's life and career. A Latin poem, the *Carmen Campidoctoris* (c. 1093), mentions the Cid's exploits, as does a shorter Latin chronicle, the *Historia Roderici* (c. 1110). Other fragments of the Cid's story apparently exist in several chronicles, including *Primera Crónica General*. Some scholars have also seen resemblances between the *Poem of the Cid* and French epics, specifically the *Chanson de*

Roland. The problematic dating of the *Poem of the Cid*, however, makes that claim difficult to verify conclusively. Whatever its exact sources are, the *Poem of the Cid* appears to take some dramatic liberties with historical accounts: the Cid's career as a mercenary in the king of Saragossa's service is omitted, as is his second banishment from King Alfonso's domains in 1089. Moreover, the episode of the marriages of the Cid's daughters—Elvira and Sol, in the poem—to the Infantes of Carrión seems to be entirely fictitious. The real-life Cid's daughters—Cristina and María—in fact married well, to a prince of Navarre and a count of Barcelona.

Although the *Poem of the Cid* is held to be the oldest extant Spanish epic, it apparently had relatively little effect on later literature. Rather, *Mocedades de Roderigo*, a romance—written in the fourteenth or fifteenth century—relating the Cid's youthful deeds, eclipsed the epic the *Poem of the Cid* in popularity. This later version inspired fifteenth- and sixteenth-century ballads about the Cid. Nor is there any conclusive evidence that the *Poem of the Cid* was representative of a larger tradition of Spanish epic poetry. Indeed, literary scholar Colin Smith argues that the *Poem of the Cid* may actually have been the very *first* epic composed in Castilian, and "in consequence an innovatory and experimental work" (Smith, p. 1). Such and Hodgkinson likewise maintain that

> we must in general be wary of attributing to the Spanish epic an antiquity for which there is little firm evidence. It has been argued that the *Poema de Mio Cid* is the oldest of the Spanish epic poems and that it established a form for those which followed. Many scholars will prefer to emphasize the debt owed by the *Poema* itself to an established tradition; but two points should be clear: firstly, that the *Poema* cannot be taken as a representative work typical of the Spanish epic in general or of the literary creature of its age; secondly, that it is a work of exceptional quality, and this may well have ensured its survival, almost alone among the epic poems of medieval Spain.
>
> (Such and Hodgkinson, p. 6)

Events in History at the Time the Poem Was Written

The Reconquest during the twelfth century. The period during which the *Poem of the Cid* was most likely composed (1140s-1207) encompassed many political and social changes. Christian Spain's attempted reconquest of the peninsula progressed, though somewhat haphazardly, experiencing setbacks as well as advances. One notable victory was the Aragonese capture of the Moorish kingdom of Saragossa in 1118. Meanwhile, the power of the Almoravids began to wane in the mid-1100s but in 1146, the Almohads, another Islamic fundamentalist sect from North Africa, poured into Spain and quickly took over the government of al-Andalus. The Almohads were more intolerant and aggressive than the Almoravides; their arrival prompted thousands of Jews and Mozarabs to flee to comparative safety in the North.

Divisions among the kingdoms of Christian Spain prevented them from taking action against the new invaders for several years. In 1157, an unstable situation ensued when Alfonso VII died, dividing his realm between his two sons; Sancho III inherited Castile, while Fernando II inherited León. Sancho's three-year-old son succeeded him as Alfonso VIII in 1158, after his father's early death, leaving Castile open to possible threats from Fernando. The Leonese king backed his nephew's accession but annexed more territory for himself as compensation, repopulating his kingdom south of the Duero and pushing his frontiers southward beyond Badajoz.

Meanwhile, Alfonso VIII spent his years as an adult monarch fighting the Almohads and waging territorial disputes with his cousin Alfonso IX of León, who succeeded his father Fernando in 1188. The Almohads defeated the Castilians at the Battle of Alarcos in 1195, but in 1212, Alfonso's troops, allied with those of Pedro II of Aragon and Afonso II of Portugal, crushed the Almohads at Las Navas de Tolosa and opened al-Andalus to conquest. This victory was still five years away from the 1207 completion date of the *Poem of the Cid*'s manuscript. Nonetheless, the poem's accounts of the Cid's triumphs over the invaders might have provided encouragement and inspiration to a generation of Castilians waging an often disheartening battle against the forces of Islam.

Reception. The manuscript for the *Poem of the Cid* was rediscovered in Vivar, Spain, in 1596, and apparently circulated among scholars for many years. However, it was not until 1779 that Tomás Antonio Sánchez published it for "modern" readers.

The *Poem of the Cid* began to receive serious scholarly attention in the 1800s. It especially impressed the Spanish "generation of 1898"—an intellectual movement that opposed the restoration

of the monarchy, favored a political return to the origins of Spain, and regarded Castile as the soul of the nation. Ramón Menéndez Pidal, a noted medievalist scholar and a member of the Generation of 1898, published a three-volume edition

TOWNS AND COURTS

As the frontiers of Christian Spain expanded southwards, Spanish settlers, including Jews and Muslims, were increasingly encouraged by their regional governments to occupy the new territory, establishing homes and building towns. Settlers were granted special rights and privileges—called *fueros*—in hopes that they would become permanent colonists of the region. New towns and villages built on the Castilian border, for example, became relatively self-governing under councils that were elected by householders. Although kings or overlords had ultimate jurisdiction over the region, these communities enjoyed an unusual degree of autonomy. The number of *fueros* increased dramatically as the Reconquest gathered momentum, from 45 granted in the eleventh century to nearly 600 granted in the twelfth and thirteenth centuries. Hundreds of towns came into being, bringing a new element into political life, which until then had been dominated by land-rich nobles. Frustrated by the power and contentiousness of the nobility, several Spanish kings cultivated alliances with the townspeople. In 1188, Alfonso IX of León summoned an assembly to León that included clergy, nobles, and townspeople. People called it the *Cortes* (courts), the term used even today for the Spanish parliament. In 1250, Castile followed León's example and established their own *Cortes*. Providing a much-needed balance of power, the *Cortes* frequently spoke out for urban interests against the powerful landed nobility. Also, democratically elected town councils for both Castile and León came into being around 1220. Although the *Poem of the Cid* takes place nearly a century before the establishment of the *Cortes*, the third section of the poem may be said to anticipate this development, as well as the dawn of a more justice-minded age, when the Cid, a relatively minor noble, seeks redress for his daughters' beatings and abandonments by their royal husbands, the Infantes of Carrión, not on the battlefield but in the courtroom.

of the *Poem of the Cid* in 1908-11 and a pivotal study of the work, *La España del Cid*, in 1934. In his writings, Menéndez Pidal maintained that the *Poem of the Cid* was the "national epic of Spain" and should be studied as an accurate historical document (Menéndez Pidal in Lazzari, p. 61). Menéndez Pidal also supported the "traditionalist" argument that the epic in its final form represented the culmination of several oral versions circulated by folk poets and traveling performers.

The *Poem of the Cid* attracted favorable attention outside Spain as well. In 1814, the British poet and essayist Robert Southey admired the work and faulted the Spaniards for having "not yet discovered the high value of their metrical history of the Cid as a poem" (Southey in Ticknor, p. 25). American Hispanist scholar George Ticknor likewise praised the *Poem of the Cid* in his *History of Spanish Literature* (1849; 1879):

> The whole of [*Poem of the Cid*], therefore, deserves to be read, and to be read in the original; for it is there only that we can obtain the fresh impressions it is fitted to give us of the rude but heroic period it represents: of the simplicity of governments, and the loyalty and true-heartedness of the people; of the wide force of a primitive religious enthusiasm; of the picturesque state of manners and daily life in an age of trouble and confusion; and of the bold outlines of the national genius, which are often struck out where we should least think to find them. . . . It seems certain that, during the thousand years which elapsed between the time of the decay of Greek and Roman culture down to the appearance of the "Divina Commedia," no poetry was produced so original in its tone, or so full of natural feeling, graphic power, and energy.
>
> (Ticknor, pp. 24-25)
> —Pamela S. Loy

For More Information

Crow, John A. *Spain: The Root and the Flower*. New York: Harper and Row, 1963.

Fletcher, Richard. *Moorish Spain*. Berkeley: University of California Press, 1992.

———. *The Quest for El Cid*. New York: Alfred A. Knopf, 1990.

Freund, Scarlett, and Teofilo Ruiz. "Jews, Conversos, and the Inquisition in Spain, 1391-1492." In *Jewish-Christian Encounters over the Centuries*. Ed. Marvin Perry and Frederick M. Schweitzer. New York: Peter Lang, 1994.

Grunfeld, Frederic V. *The Kings of Spain*. Chicago: Stonehenge Press, 1982.

Lazzari, Marie, ed. *Epics for Students*. Detroit: Gale Research, 1997.

McKendrick, Melveena. *The Horizon Concise History of Spain*. New York: American Heritage, 1972.

O'Callaghan, Joseph F. *A History of Medieval Spain*. Ithaca: Cornell University Pres, 1975.

Pierson, Peter. *The History of Spain*. Westport: Greenwood Press, 1999.

Poem of the Cid. Trans. Peter Such and John Hodgkinson. Warminster: Aris & Phillips, 1987.

Read, Jan. *The Moors in Spain & Portugal*. Totowa: Bowman and Littlefield, 1975.

Smith, Colin. *The Making of the Poema de mio Cid*. Cambridge: Cambridge University Press, 1983.

Ticknor, George. *History of Spanish Literature*. Vol. 1. Boston: Houghton, Osgood, 1879.

Poet in
New York

by

Federico García Lorca

Both a playwright and a poet, Federico García Lorca would become the most internationally renowned Spanish writer of the twentieth century. He was born in 1898 in Fuente Vaqueros, a village in Andalusia near Granada, to Federico García Rodríguez, a wealthy landowner, and to Vicenta Lorca Romero, a schoolteacher. His mother instilled in him a love for music, dance, and literature. García Lorca attended the University of Granada, where he studied law, philosophy, and letters, and met two professors who greatly impacted his life as mentors: Martín Domínguez Berrueta and Fernando de los Ríos. After participating in cultural history tours organized by Domínguez Berrueta, Lorca wrote his first work, *Impresiones y paisajes* (Impressions and Landscapes) in 1918. It presents a prose account of the people and countryside that he observed on these trips. Fernando de los Ríos, a leading socialist figure, convinced both Lorca's parents that the youth should study in Madrid, and so in 1919 Lorca moved to the capital city to live in the Residencia de Estudiantes (a type of residential college) of the University of Madrid. A meeting place of young artists and writers, the Residencia brought Lorca into contact with Salvador Dalí, and the two developed a romantic relationship for a period of time. Lorca lived in the Residencia until 1928, during which time he wrote three books of poetry and several plays. In 1929 and 1930 he traveled to the United States and Cuba, returning to spend most of his time in Madrid, remaining a vital member of the literary and artistic community there. On August 19, 1936, right-wing gunmen in the countryside near

THE LITERARY WORK

A collection of 34 poems set predominantly in New York but also in Vermont and Cuba, in 1929 and 1930; published as a collection in Spanish (as *Poeta en Nueva York*) in 1940, in English in 1940.

SYNOPSIS

Reflecting the sense of isolation and depression felt by the poet at the time, the work denigrates modern, techno-industrial civilization as represented by a dehumanized, materialistic, hostile, chaotic New York City.

Granada executed Lorca because he was viewed as a liberal threat to the military regime. *Poet in New York* was his fourth collection, following *Libro de poemas* (1920; Book of Poems), *Canciones* (1927; Songs), and *Romancero gitano* (1928; Gypsy Ballads, 1953), with the latter two establishing Lorca as a writer of popular renown. *Poet in New York* offers a unique perspective on America's urban culture. Lorca's disorientation and isolation in New York strengthens his own feelings about his native Spain and about what it means to be Hispanic.

Events in History at the Time of the Poems

Personal and national depression. Lorca arrived in New York City in July 1929. During his

Federico García Lorca

verted into makeshift flats. Packed in damp, rat-ridden dungeons. Floors were of cracked concrete, and the walls were . . . rust-streaked. There were only slits for a window and a tin can in a corner was the only toilet." There was no heat in the winter, no air in the summer. . . . Death was a commonplace. . . . Most of the mortality . . . was from disease.

(Watkins and Hedgman in Watkins, pp. 62-64)

Harlem in the 1920s was the center of New York's African-American community. Thousands of children died yearly here from tuberculosis and pneumonia. According to a *New York Herald Tribune* article appearing in February 1930, unemployment was five times higher in Harlem than in the rest of the city. Harlem in the 1920s attracted almost 88,000 mostly penniless immigrants from the Caribbean, who crowded into an already densely populated area that was deteriorating daily. Criminals, prostitutes, and delinquents abounded in the neighborhood (C. Brian Morris, *América*, p. 26).

In 1929 conditions promised only to get worse. The top 0.1 percent of Americans earned as much as the bottom 42 percent. Many middle- and lower-class Americans lost their homes and farms, and middle-income Americans especially focused their energies on saving money instead of spending it. This caused less demand for goods and a concomitant increase in stores' and factories' inventories, which, in turn, led to a slowdown in industrial production and a rise in employee layoffs, with African Americans being the last hired and the first fired. A pervasive hopelessness filled the air as people went month after month without work, perhaps exacerbating Lorca's personal depression at the time.

Long a city of economic extremes, New York during the Depression was a city with a deeply intensified disparity. Wealthy New Yorkers would drive along in luxury automobiles while their poorest neighbors begged for food or stood in soup lines. By the late 1920s, the city had become highly industrialized, employing countless workers in manufacturing. Lorca's impression of New York—gray, natureless, cold—was formed in part by the economic shambles it was in, but also by the isolation and confusion he experienced being in a large, noisy, industrial American city. Contributing to his negative outlook of the city was his own emotional state: beginning in the summer of 1928, Lorca suffered an emotional crisis whose exact cause is only conjecture. He carried this depression with him throughout his trip to the United States, finding little relief

residence in the city he stayed in a room in John Jay Hall, a dormitory on the Columbia University campus. His plan was to study English at the university, but he withdrew from class after a week because he believed himself unable to learn the language. He stayed in New York until April 1930, when he was invited to lecture in Havana, Cuba.

Four months after García Lorca arrived in New York, Wall Street suffered its horrendous stock market crash, and soon the Great Depression was wreaking havoc on the U.S. economy. The Great Depression deprived millions of Americans jobs and rendered many people homeless. At the height of the Depression, the jobless composed a quarter of the total American labor force. Banks folded, factories sat idle, and companies laid off workers because of the economic downturn. The human suffering was enormous everywhere, but worst of all in the African American neighborhoods.

> For those among the urban black population the levels of poverty most had learned to endure fell to depths for which even long experience could not prepare them. In Chicago's . . . South Side . . . they lived 90,000 to the square mile . . . as compared to 20,000 to the square mile for the non-black population. . . . In New York City's Harlem, the situation was hardly better. More than ten thousand people . . . "lived in cellars and basements which had been con-

Followers of Marcus Garvey march at the annual convention of the Provisional Republic of Africa in Harlem.

in his new environment. New York was not the sunny, rural landscape Lorca was so accustomed to back in Andalusia. He spoke almost no English, which further isolated him. He immediately identified with the African Americans, though, in particular to their music: "What marvelous songs. . . . Only our Anadalusian cante jondo could be compared to them" (Lorca in Gibson, p. 255). The visit to New York was supposed to be a welcome escape from the pressures of his life in Spain. In a letter written on board the ship taking him to America, Lorca states: "I don't know why I left; I ask myself that a hundred times a day. I look at myself in the mirror of this narrow cabin and I don't recognize myself. I seem to be another Federico" (Lorca in Harris, p. 10; trans. M. Penrose). The confession is revealing: to some degree, Lorca seems to have been suffering from an identity crisis. Considering the state that Lorca and New York were in while he resided in the city, it is no wonder that his poetry paints such a negative vision of it, especially if one considers that it was his first time living abroad and he did not speak English.

Activism and artistic expression. Lorca lived in Harlem (while residing at Columbia University) and frequented its establishments. He befriended African American writer Nella Larsen, with whom he often visited local cabarets and

theaters. On the streets of Harlem, he would listen to jazz being played and witness the daily lives of thousands of local inhabitants. Meanwhile, bringing the disparity right into the neighborhood, whites came to attend Harlem clubs and parties and listen to jazz artists like Duke Ellington.

Because of Harlem's squalid conditions, social unrest became commonplace, especially during the depression. Harlem in the early 1900s was an area frequented by "soapbox" speakers, street-corner activists sharing political ideas and getting listeners to think about their lives in social and economic terms. Demonstrations and rallies attracted whites and blacks alike. The Jamaican immigrant Marcus Garvey, a key protest figure, started the "Back to Africa" movement that promoted the return of all African Americans to the continent from whence they originally came. Declaring himself provisional emperor of Africa, he put on ostentatious parades for his followers (Morris, *América*, p. 22). Garvey and other black nationalists urged African Americans to take control of their lives: "'Up you mighty race, you can accomplish what you will,' he thundered" (Nash, p. 797). By 1927, Garvey would be deported as an undesirable alien, but his message had registered, and he left behind other black leaders who would continue urging African Americans to take matters in their own hands and improve their working and living conditions. Meanwhile, the Depression set in and conditions worsened rather than improved, which led to Lorca's prediction of a human eruption in one of his poems. Only ten years earlier, in 1919 and the early 1920s, a rash of race riots had spread through cities across America, furnishing substantial precedent for the prediction.

Along with the activism, Harlem during the 1920s experienced a cultural and artistic rebirth called the Harlem Renaissance. Primarily a literary movement, it blossomed from the mid-1920s to the mid-1930s, during Lorca's stay there. Writers such as W. E. B. DuBois, Langston Hughes, Nella Larsen, Wallace Thurman, and Zora Neale Hurston propelled the Renaissance forward with works that shared with the mostly unknowing American public the black experience.

Cuba. Lorca resided in Havana from March until June of 1930, invited there by the Hispano-Cuban Institute to give lectures on his works. Times were dismal in this country too. Cuba suffered greatly in the worldwide Depression. The sugar industry, the mainstay of the economy, saw prices tumble to all-time lows. Thousands of Cubans lost their jobs and tens of thousands were chronically underemployed when sugar prices first fell in 1926. By the early 1930s, thousands more had become jobless. In search of work, many Cubans migrated from the countryside to the cities, only to discover that people there were being laid off in record numbers. Many of those who chose to stay in the countryside died of starvation. Protests erupted throughout the country, the protesters lodging demands for jobs, improved wages, and less severe working conditions. The president of Cuba at the time, Gerardo Machado, tried to suppress the protests with brute force, his early popularity beginning to plummet as moderate and radical leftist groups turned on him. Civil unrest continued unabated, and in 1932 Machado suspended the Constitution. A general strike ensued, followed by the opposition's takeover of the military. These two events forced Machado to resign the presidency in 1933.

Turmoil in Spain. Lorca returned to Spain in June 1930. He came back to a country in deep turmoil: Primo de Rivera's dictatorship had just ended and the era of the Second Republic had dawned. In 1923 Miguel Primo de Rivera, an Andalusian army general, had assumed power as "prime minister" (in fact dictator) after leading a successful coup on behalf of Alfonso XIII, the

king of Spain. All the king's ministers resigned, and Alfonso appointed Primo de Rivera as prime minister. However, refusing to abide by the constitution, Primo de Rivera failed to reconvene parliament, and Alfonso did nothing to stop him. After America's Wall Street disaster on October 29, 1929, the peseta lost much of its value overnight and the relatively prosperous economic times in Spain came to an abrupt end. Subsequently Primo de Rivera made a decision regarding military promotions that undermined the king's powers and contradicted what many army generals wanted. The aging dictator lost the support not only of the king but also of the only institution in Spain that could have kept him in power—the military. Under pressure from army generals, Alfonso, who had tried to save face for having given Primo de Rivera control over the government in the first place, finally dismissed the dictator in 1930.

Primo de Rivera's ousting, however, did not end the turmoil in Spain. It continued with the launching of the Second Republic in April 1931. The democratic government installed by the Second Republic experienced intense factional fighting between leftists and rightists. The Republic would last until the outbreak of civil war in 1936. In 1939 fascist general Francisco Franco declared victory; he would rule Spain with an iron fist for the next three and a half decades, quashing any chance of maintaining a republic.

As the Second Republic was being launched, Lorca set about publishing in magazines several of the poems written by him in the Americas. He often read these poems to friends at private gatherings; by the mid-1930s many of those in *The Poet in New York* collection had been circulated in print or in person through his readings. Like many of his intellectual and artistic friends, Lorca espoused a leftist ideology and supported liberal political groups. His involvement with Spain's left cost him his life when the Spanish Civil War broke out in 1936. Lorca's fame as a writer and intellectual made him a target for those who espoused rightist politics.

Generation of 1927. While Primo de Rivera was still a dictator, several young Spanish poets were coming of age and beginning to make a name for themselves. This group, which came to be called the *Generación del 27* (Generation of 1927), included the following members: Pedro Salinas, Jorge Guillén, Gerardo Diego, Vicente Aleixandre, Dámaso Alonso, Emilio Prados, Rafael Alberti, Luis Cernuda, Manuel Altolaguirre, and Federico García Lorca. In 1927 almost every member of the circle paid homage to and celebrated the life of the seventeenth-century Spanish poet Luis de Góngora on the tricentennial anniversary of his death by dedicating essays, books, conferences, and critical editions to him.

Taken from this occasion, the name Generation of 1927 came to designate the group of poets. Although they had very different personalities and writing styles, aside from the mutual friendship, members shared several common characteristics: (a) they showed a progressive bent; (b) they all resided in Madrid during the 1920s and 1930s; (c) the majority of them went into exile during or after the Civil War; (d) all were members of the bourgeoisie; and (e) in their work, one sees an attempt at perfection and reflection about language in an effort to extract from it all its expressive possibilities (Ramoneda, pp. 40-43).

The Spanish exile and expatriate community. Lorca voluntarily accompanied his mentor and friend, Fernando de los Ríos, who was exiled by the Primo de Rivera regime, to New York City. The company that Lorca kept while in the United States consisted mainly of other Spanish expatriates. These were people he had known for several years, including his mentor Fernando de los Ríos, the poet Dámaso Alonso, the painter Gabriel García Maroto, the dancer Argentinita, and the bullfighter Ignacio Sánchez Mejías.

Lorca, like practically all members of the Generation of 27, spent some time abroad. Most of the poets taught Spanish language and literature at universities. Salinas became a Spanish assistant instructor at the Sorbonne and at Cambridge University and taught at a couple of universities in the continental United States and at one in Puerto Rico. Guillén served as a Spanish assistant instructor at Oxford University and the Sorbonne and taught at several universities in the United States. Prados studied at the universities of Freiburg and Berlin. Cernuda was named Spanish assistant instructor at the University of Toulouse. Altolaguirre lived in London from 1933-35, where he established the journal *1616*. Alonso spent time teaching at the universities of Cambridge and Oxford and at several American universities. Of the ten members of this circle of poets, six went into exile during the Spanish Civil War or after it ended in 1939 (Salinas, Cernuda, Guillén, Altolaguirre, Prados, and Alberti) because they disagreed vehemently with the politics of Franco's fascist regime. Alonso, Diego, and Aleixandre stayed in Spain. Lorca, as mentioned earlier, was shot to death at the outset of the war. Their foreign visits and/or residencies allowed these writers to understand humanity at an international level, at the same time permitting them to look more objectively at their own nation.

LUIS DE GÓNGORA (1561-1627)

Born in Cordoba (in Andalusia) into an aristocratic family, Góngora would become Spain's most prominent Baroque poet. During his youth he became a clergyman, but he never took the vocation seriously, instead spending his time writing, gambling, or attending bullfights. Still, he was named chaplain to the court of Phillip III (1578-1621), a privileged position that allowed him to travel around Spain on ecclesiastic missions. His works, which include the long poems *Fábula de Polifemo y Galatea* (1612, Fable of Polyphemus and Galatea), *Soledades* (1613, *Solitude*), and over 100 ballads and 200 sonnets, display a flowery but elegant cultivated style that incorporates heavy usage of metaphors, hyperbatons, and hyperboles. For example, Góngora's clever use of metaphor comes to the fore in "Soneto CLXVI":

> While trying with your tresses to compete
> In vain the sun's rays shine on burnished gold;
> While with abundant scorn across the plain
> Does your white brow the lily's hue behold.
>
> (Góngora, trans. Alix Ingber)

The speaker compares the woman's hair to gold, against which the sun's rays cannot compete, and her brow to the white lily. By doing so, he evinces the beauty and perfection of his idol. Góngora often wrote of the search for beauty and absolute perfection in his sonnets. His hallmark lay in his ability to cultivate speech and to inject it with sophistication and beauty. His style, flowery and mellifluous, became known as *gongorismo* or *culteranismo* because of its recourse to cultivated subjects and images. Góngora died in 1627 after suffering a stroke the year before.

The Poems in Focus

Contents summary. *Poet in New York* contains ten sections. The first, labeled "Poems of Solitude at Columbia University," reflects the loneliness and isolation Lorca experienced in New York. He sees himself as a victim of the chaos of life and meditates on the innocence of his childhood.

Section Two, "The Blacks," and Section Three, "Streets and Dreams," are centered around the religious motifs of *Paradise Lost* and the *Dance of Death*. In "The Blacks," Lorca portrays the African American community as the innocent victims of white civilization who will rise up to seek vengeance. Blacks have come to symbolize confused humanity in a chaotic, ruthless world (del Río in García Lorea, p. xix). In "Streets and Dreams," Lorca presents a portrait of a modern, desolate city; the section opens with a poem titled "Dance of Death," in which a grotesque African mask comes to New York to preside over the dance. The participants in this dance are not the dead, but the living. Grief and death are ubiquitous, and the world is subjugated by power, greed, and lust. The fourth and fifth sections, "Poems from Lake Eden Mills" and "In the Farmer's Cabin, Country Near Newburg," represent Lorca's escape from the city to a charming rustic setting. The speaker changes his tone, softening his vision of the world and paralleling it to the beauty of the bucolic oasis in which he finds himself. In several poems, however, there is a subtle presence of death, which becomes the dominant theme in the next section, "Introduction to Death, Poems of Solitude in Vermont." The speaker's solitude now seems to be more meditative than emotional; his language and thoughts become more meaningful. The triumph of death is now not a tragic masquerade, but a universal, depersonalized force that is an essential part of life (del Río in García Lorea, p. xxii). In Section Seven, the speaker makes his "Return to the City." His head is clear now, and he quickly denounces the materialism and greed that he witnesses. In the next section, "Two Odes," he harshly protests life as it is lived in New York. In "Cry to Rome: From the Chrysler Building Tower," he blames modern urban civilization for the betrayal of the spirit of Christianity and he offers a prophetic vision of human slavery and war. In "Ode to Walt Whitman," the speaker decries what he sees as modern man's corruption of the ideals of humanity, democracy, and love that Whitman preached. The last two sections of the collection, "Flight from New York, Two Waltzes Toward Civilization" and "The Poet Arrives in Havana," describe the speaker's happy escape from New York toward "civilization," that is to say, the Hispanic world. Now life makes complete sense to him, and he portrays Cuban life in a positive, folkloric manner, inspired by songs and customs of the African Cubans.

Three of the 30 poems in *Poet in New York*—"The King of Harlem," "Dawn," and "The Black Son of Cuba"—can be viewed as representative of the overall work. The first two reflect the speaker's views of New York; the last one expresses joy and relief at being in a Spanish-speaking country once again.

"El rey de Harlem" ("The King of Harlem"). This poem comes from the second section of the book, "Los negros" ("The Blacks"). A surrealistic barrage of images, the poem begins with four stanzas that introduce a pent-up Harlem, full of despair and oppressed African Americans. It is a dark, primitive scene that expresses a tragic vision: "With a spoon / he gouged out the crocodile's eyes / and thumped on the monkey-rumps" "the little boys smashed little squirrels" (García Lorca, *Poet in New York*, p. 19). It hints at the potential of blacks to rise up and riot: "Eternity's spark still slept in the flint" (*Poet*, p. 19). These lines "represent the poet's vision of the world that he passively beholds, a world of violence and agony and stench his conscious mind receives" (Craige, p. 56).

The fifth through the seventh stanzas change the tone and direction of the poem. The speaker reacts to what s/he has seen, telling African Americans to address the injustice brought upon them by Caucasian society: "We must murder the yellow-haired hawkers of brandy / and the comrades of apple and sand;" "You Harlem! You Harlem! You Harlem! / No anguish to equal your thwarted vermilions, . . . / your hobbled, great king in the janitor's suit" (*Poet*, pp. 19-21). Instead of surrealistic imagery painting a picture of oppression, the speaker in these stanzas gives the call to arms to the African-American community in very clear language, promoting violence to achieve its aims, so that the king of Harlem can sing with his people and lead them out of subjugation by white society.

Stanzas Eight and Nine provide momentary relief from the emotion of the previous stanza. Again the speaker describes the moonless night and refers to whites drinking whiskey: "They drink silver whiskey within sight of volcanoes" (*Poet*, p. 21). This image forecasts the lava-blood that is about to flow down and engulf the European Americans. The volcano is central to Lorca's vision of the African civilization of Harlem, which is "boiling inside with the hot blood of outrage and sexual passion ready to erupt" (Craige, p. 57).

The tenth stanza repeats the opening lines of the poem and again builds to a climax, this time with the words *Blacks, Blacks, Blacks, Blacks*. The repetition forms a chant, preparing us for the coming of the blood, which is described in the next five stanzas. "Blood has no doors in your night, lying face up to the sky," the speaker says (*Poet*, p. 21). In other words, the blood pulsing underneath the skin of Blacks has no outlet and eventually will boil over and flood the earth: "Blood flows; and will flow / on the rooftops and sheds everywhere; . . . . / and explode in a low-yellow dawn of tobacco," that is to say, lava ash that the volcano emits (*Poet*, p. 23).

This explosion of emotion is followed in the next three stanzas by calm. African American cooks, the waiters and servants of whites, "those who would cleanse with their tongues / the millionaire's wounds" seek their king in the streets who would act as savior to deliver them from the oppression they experience at the hands of European civilization (*Poet*, p. 23). A south wind blows in the black mud, suggesting the primeval order of the world (Craige, p. 57).

There is another break to prepare the reader for the last stanzas, which express the triumph of the African American rebellion. The speaker commands blacks not to attempt to climb the impassable wall, which is growing and surrounding the city, to achieve freedom, but rather to "Seek out the great sun of the center" (*Poet*, p. 25), that is to say, to look for salvation in the natural world. Next, the speaker again chants "Blacks" to goad them on.

The final stanzas describe what will happen when blacks inherit the world after the city's destruction. The speaker urges them not to fear death, since it is an entirely natural phenomenon: "Never serpent or zebra or mule / That paled at death's imminence" (*Poet*, p. 25). Once the city is destroyed, African Americans will repossess the industrial and technological society that isolated and repressed them and reabsorb it into nature: "Black man, only then, only then, only then / can you kiss out your frenzy on bicycle-wheels / or pair off the microscopes in the caves of the squirrels" (*Poet*, p. 25). Finally, the speaker announces that s/he has heard the plight of the African Americans: "You Harlem in masquerade! / You Harlem, whom torsos of street-clothing menace! / Your murmur has come to me" (*Poet*, p. 25). These lines refer to Harlem as a center of nightlife for both blacks and whites. The menace of "torsos of street-clothing" suggests the crowds of elegantly dressed Caucasians who would arrive in Harlem nightly to drink in abandon at the many cabarets and bars (C. Brian Morris, "Cuando yo me muera," p. 27). The speaker views such an invasion as harmful to Harlem's survival, and he acknowledges the African-American disdain of such an unhealthy encroachment upon their neighborhood.

Lorca's poem foreshadows to some degree what would happen just four years after his departure. In 1934, in keeping with Lorca's prediction, a riot erupted in Harlem because of the economic distress caused by the Depression and increasing tensions between the black community and white storeowners. Lorca's sensitivity to Harlem, his intuition about its dynamics, and his status as an outside observer enabled him to write a poem with such prophetic vision. Lorca had a lifelong empathy for Gypsies in Spain that was translated in the New World to blacks, who, for him, represented "a tragic expression of the imprisonment of the blood force of life by the mechanical, depersonalized civilization which is New York City" (Craige, p. 55). Their isolation, marginalization, and oppression by Caucasians bespoke a grave injustice, one that could be fixed by blacks rising up and eliminating the causes of their horrific state.

"La aurora" ("Dawn"). From the section "Streets and Dreams," this poem portrays New York City as a modern, technological, industrial behemoth that poisons its inhabitants with its artificial environment. It is a city of skyscrapers and cement, steel and glass, compared to Lorca's native Andalusia, a beautiful rural region of olive and citrus groves with no large cities. Lorca blamed the modern urban conglomeration for the plight of the average New Yorker; he felt that it caused humans to lose sight of what is important and made them work endlessly for a blighted existence. No matter how hard they worked, the result was the same—this blighted existence.

In this poem, the dawn does not bring hope and light, but rather produces darkness and despair. These are the forces visited upon a technological and industrial mass of slaving and sleepless humanity.

The first two stanzas describe the dawn of New York as bearing "four pillars of slime / and a storm of black pigeons / that dabble dead water"; it moans on towering stairs, "seeking on ledges / pangs traced upon nard [tuberoses]" (*Poet*, p. 63). The traditionally positive symbols of pigeons/doves and water are negated with the words "black" and "dead."

In the third stanza the speaker compares the dawn with the Host of the Mass: "Dawn comes, there is no mouth to receive it, / for here neither morrow nor hope is possible" (García Lorca in Ramoneda, p. 209; trans. C. B. Morris). Instead of the Host of the Mass, a furious rabble of coins enter and devour abandoned children. This is a clear denunciation of the corrupting power of money, as represented by Wall Street, and materialism that the speaker saw in the city. It is also a criticism of a city that the speaker considered godless and without soul.

The fourth stanza indicates an awareness of death by the inhabitants of the city: they "know the truth in their bones" (*Poet*, p. 63). They also know that there will be no paradise or leafless passions, an allusion to freedom from sexual guilt in a return to Eden. The natural world and the hope that flickers is extinguished by a concrete jungle. New Yorkers recreate mechanically and labor without reward.

CUBAN *SON*

The *son* is an urban style of dance music that developed in Cuba in the first few decades of the twentieth century. It combined elements of Spanish folk music, such as the guitar, with those borrowed from the *rumba*, an Afro-Cuban style of dance music. Along with African rhythms, the *son* adapted call-and-response singing from the *rumba*.

The final stanza returns to the image of light, which has been buried by the grime and steel of New York. The lack of light signifies the unnatural and depressing character of New York. Insomniacs wander through the neighborhoods as if they had recently escaped a bloody shipwreck.

"Son de negros en Cuba" ("The Black Son of Cuba"). This poem, the concluding one in the collection, comes from the tenth section of *Poet in New York,* "The Poet Arrives in Havana." As its title indicates, the work was written soon after Lorca landed on the island. It reflects a *son*, or African-inspired Cuban dance rhythm. The speaker says that s/he will go to Santiago de Cuba in a car of black water when the moon is full. The moon for Lorca was emblematic of death, and the traditionally positive symbol of water is negated by the word "black." It seems that the vehicle of water is perhaps a hearse carrying the speaker to Santiago. "I'll go to Santiago" is the refrain of the poem and is repeated a total of 19 times, spaced evenly throughout the work

(*Poet*, p. 137). The refrain lends a musicality and harmonious rhythm to the poem, suggesting that it is to be sung rather than simply read. The eighth and tenth lines indicate a metamorphosis: "When palm would be stork" and "When banana [tree] goes jellyfish" (*Poet*, p. 137). The trees wish to change into animals of the air and ocean, thereby losing their terrestrial identity. Perhaps they are trying to escape as well, just like the speaker, or maybe they are trying to escape death (Harris, p. 67). Santiago could be seen as a refuge from death, that is, from modern urban civilization.

The twelfth and fourteenth verses refer to Cuban cigar boxes in a very oblique allusion to Lorca's childhood: "I'll go to Santiago / with the yellow-haired head of Fonseca / . . . With the Romeo-Juliet rose" (*Poet*, p. 137). The poet's father smoked Cuban cigars, and Federico liked to look at the pictures on the boxes as a child, some with the portrait of Manuel Deodoro da Fonseca, the leader of the Brazilian independence movement and the republic's first president from 1889-91, others with a picture of Romeo and Juliet, whose names serve as one of the most famous brand of cigars in the world. The boxes Lorca sees in Cuba remind him of his own childhood, full of fond memories and innocence.

Surrealism à la Lorca. The depression, isolation and confusion that Lorca experienced in New York resulted in a poetry that utilized dreamlike images to convey the poet's perspective on a modern industrial-technological city that he felt to be dehumanizing. *Poet in New York* represents a radical departure from Lorca's previous poetry, most notably, the *Gypsy Ballads*. The shift parallels Lorca's drastic change in living environment. Most critics refer to *Poet in New York* as a work influenced by surrealism, but not a true representation of it. While surrealist works typically express a flow of ideas in which the barriers between the conscious and subconscious are removed and very often the poem is an entity unto itself without making reference to outside reality, Lorca did not seek to combine conscious and subconscious experience in his poetry; nor did he agree that poetry should be divorced from a realistic context. He shied away from the term surrealism to describe some of his poetry, commenting instead that his poems contained pure emotion liberated from logical control without losing references to outside reality. However, surrealist influence shows up in the poet's employment of free association and symbolism unrestrained by logic. Indeed, it is the preponderance of positive and negative symbols that distinguish Lorca's poetry from that of others, and in *Poet in New York*, this system of symbols becomes very complex. Take, for example, the first three lines from "The Black 'Son' of Cuba:" "When a full moon rides over in Santiago de Cuba / I'll go to Santiago / in a hack of black water" (*Poet,* p. 137). In Lorca's poetry, the moon conjures up images of death. The "hack of black water" evokes logic-defying, negative images of a hearse made of black water. Instead of water giving life, its traditional role in poetry, it is taking it away, underscored by the symbolic use of the color black, long associated with evil and death. These images are all the more complex because we are not sure whether the speaker views Santiago as a place of refuge from death or as the stopping point of it.

Thus Lorca, like many other members of the Generation of 1927, frequently employed surrealist imagery in his poetry. However, he was not considered the leader of the surrealist movement in Spanish poetry. Indeed, in a letter written to his publisher, Lorca warns that *Poet in New York* is not surrealist. Two of his fellow countrymen, Juan Larrea, who moved to Paris in the 1920s and founded a surrealist literary magazine, and Rafael Alberti, were the first Spanish poets to adopt surrealist ideas and techniques to their works. In fact, Alberti probably experimented with surrealism more than any other member of the Generation of '27. Also, another Spanish poet, José María Hinojosa, moved to Paris in 1925 and eventually helped to disseminate the movement's ideas in Spain. Despite these contributions to surrealism, the movement never took hold in Spain like it did in France, and to some poets of the Generation of '27, it meant little (Ramoneda, p. 55).

Most of the Generation of '27 combined elements from the Spanish lyric tradition with those of the diverse movements occurring in literature in the first three decades of the twentieth century, such as Dadaism, surrealism, "ultraísmo," a movement which attempted to abolish sentimentalism and unnecessary ornamentation in poetry, and "creacionismo," an offshoot of "ultraísmo" started by the Chilean poet Vicente Huidobro that promulgated the idea that the poet is totally free to create, independently of any social or moral preoccupation. Several members of the Generation of '27 also incorporated Spanish folkloric forms into their poetry such as the Spanish ballad and the *cante jondo,* Andalusian songs of Gypsy origin that express deep passion about

some profound sentimental topic. Lorca, in fact, was the most spontaneous and the most original at weaving folkloric elements into his poetry.

Sources and literary context. As stated above, Lorca's principal inspiration in writing this collection of poems emanates from within. Lorca seems to have been in search of himself when he made the voyage to New York, but what he did not realize at the time is that he was leaving his own, personal natural world for an environment that suppressed all that was natural and life-affirming. His trip to Cuba and his return to Spain in 1930 were his reentry into what he considered a more natural world, free from the stress of modern urban life. Once back in a Hispanic environment, Lorca resumed his old life, becoming positive and focused about what he experienced.

The artists of the era who most influenced Lorca include Salvador Dalí and Luis Buñuel, with whom he had close personal relationships before leaving for New York. In the avant-garde magazine, *Gallo,* which he founded in 1928 and edited, Lorca acknowledged the influence of Pablo Picasso, Joan Miró, Jean Arp, Le Corbusier (Charles Edouard Jeanneret), Paul Eluard, Louis Aragon, Jean Cocteau, Igor Fyodorovich Stravinsky, André Breton, and many others. There is no doubt, then, that Lorca was a key player among the most avant-garde writers in Europe at the time he penned the poems that would later be collected together as *Poet in New York.* Their influence is apparent in the work, although Lorca did separate himself from the mainstream of surrealism, as noted above.

Reception. The critical and popular reception of the poems in *Poet in New York* was less than enthusiastic. Individual poems were first circulated in the early 1930s by publication in periodicals or through readings that Lorca would give to his friends. They were compared to Breton's and Eluard's surrealist poetry and were given minor critical attention as serious works of symbolic expression. Lorca's readers were confused by the sudden change in the poet's style, language, tone, and technique, and at first many felt that Lorca had made a wrong turn along his creative career path. Some critics felt that Lorca was attempting to escape his fame as a popular poet, while others believed that he was trying to compete with the Spanish surrealist poet Rafael Alberti. When the collection was finally published in 1940, surrealism had been accepted as an expression of the era's restlessness.

Lorca had been executed, the Spanish Civil War had ended, and fascism was spreading across the face of Europe. Readers and critics alike welcomed and appreciated *Poet in New York* to a degree unseen several years earlier. After Rolfe Humphries translated Lorca's work in late 1940, it was very favorably reviewed by Conrad Aiken in the *New Republic*. Aiken recognized Lorca as a "terribly acute critic of America" and praised the work's creative genius (del Río in García Lorea, p. x). Today *Poet in New York* is esteemed as perhaps the most complex, prophetic work in Lorca's oeuvre—prophetic in that it predicted the Harlem riots that would occur just a few years after Lorca left New York.

—Mehl Penrose

For More Information

Anderson, Reed. *Federico García Lorca*. London: Macmillan, 1984.

Craige, Betty Jean. *Lorca's Poet in New York: The Fall into Consciousness*. Lexington: The University Press of Kentucky, 1977.

García Lorca, Federico. *Poet in New York*. Trans. Ben Belitt. New York: Grove Press, 1983.

Gibson, Ian. *Federico García Lorca: A Life*. New York: Pantheon, 1989.

Góngora, Luis de. "Sonnet CLXVI." Trans. Alix Ingber. trans. *Golden Age Spanish Sonnets*. 2001. http://www.sonnets.spanish.sbc.edu (15 July 2001).

Harris, Derek. *Federico García Lorca: Poeta en Nueva York*. London: Grant and Cutler Ltd./Tamesis, 1978.

Morris, C. B. *América en un poeta: los viajes de Federico García Lorca al nuevo mundo y la repercusión de su obra en la literatura americana*. Seville: Universidad Internacional de Andalucía, 1999.

———. *Son of Andalusia: the Lyrical Landscapes of Federico García Lorca*. Nashville: Vanderbilt University Press, 1997.

———. *"Cuando yo me muera": Essays in Memory of Federico García Lorca*. Lanham, Md.: University Press of America, 1988.

Nash, Gary B., et al. *The American People: Creating a Nation and a Society*. Vol. 2. New York: Harper and Row, 1990.

Predmore, Richard L. *Lorca's New York Poetry: Social Injustice, Dark Love, Lost Faith*. Durham, N.C.: Duke University Press, 1980.

Ramoneda, Arturo, ed. *Antología poética de la generación del 27*. Madrid: Castalia, 1990.

Watkins, T. H. *The Hungary Years: A Narrative History of the Great Depression in America*. New York: Henry Holt, 1999.

Williams, Mark. *The Story of Spain*. Puebla Lucía, Spain: Mirador Publications S.L., 1992.

The Quest

by

Pío Baroja

THE LITERARY WORK

A novel set in Madrid around 1900; published in Spanish (as *La busca*) in 1904, in English in 1922.

SYNOPSIS

After his mother's death, Manuel Alcázar, a young Spanish boy, struggles to survive on the streets of Madrid.

Pío Baroja y Nessi (1872-1956), considered by some the most influential Spanish novelist of the twentieth century, was born in the Basque region of northern Spain and raised largely in Madrid, Spain's capital, where his family moved when he was seven and where he lived for most of his life. Baroja studied medicine, and worked briefly as a doctor before giving up this profession, first to run a bakery owned by his family and then to write. He published his first two books, a collection of short stories and a novel, *La casa de Aizgorri* (The House of Aizgorri) in 1900. A prolific writer, Baroja ultimately produced more than 100 books, including over 60 novels as well as volumes of memoirs and collections of short stories, essays, and poems. Among his best known works is a trilogy entitled *La lucha por la vida* (1904; *The Struggle for Life,* 1922-24), of which *The Quest* is the first part: *La busca* (1904; *The Quest*, 1922); *Mala hierba* (1904; *Weeds*, 1923); *Aurora roja* (1904; *Red Dawn*, 1924). Like *The Quest*, most of Baroja's individual novels form part of a series of connected works. Altogether Baroja wrote 11 trilogies, as well as a series of 22 novels and novellas *Memorias de un hombre de acción* (1913-35; Memoirs of a Man of Action) based on the life of a nineteenth-century Spanish adventurer to whom he was distantly related. Adventure features prominently among his more popular tales, including *Zalacaín el aventurero* (1909; Zalacaín the Adventurer), *César o nada* (1910; *Caesar or Nothing,* 1919), and (*Las inquietudes de Shanti Andía* (1911; *The Restlessness of Shanti Andia and Other Writings,* 1959). While Baroja's earliest works also contain elements of adventure, they focus as well on the characters' social and economic milieu. *The Quest*, for example, presents a gritty and often brutal picture of urban life in working-class Madrid, as the novel's main character, Manuel Alcázar, is buffeted by socio-economic forces beyond his control.

Events in History at the Time of the Novel

Spain after 1898. Spanish life in the early twentieth century was overshadowed by a national catastrophe at the very end of the nineteenth, when Spain suffered a humiliating military defeat by the United States and lost the remnants of its once mighty world empire. The actual fighting in the Spanish-American War lasted less than three months, from May to July 1898, but the decisive and one-sided outcome shocked the

Pío Baroja

Spanish public and revealed the weakness of Spanish arms. The Treaty of Paris that formally ended the war in December stripped Spain of the colonies over which the conflict had arisen: Cuba and Puerto Rico in the Caribbean Sea, and Guam and the Philippines in the Pacific Ocean. In addition to marking the emergence of the United States as a world power and illustrating the decayed state of Spain's military, the war left Spain with the self-image of a weak and backward nation. In the minds of many, Spain's perceived stagnation and backwardness contrasted especially sharply with America's forward-looking energy and drive. "What a country!" one of *The Quest*'s characters exclaims during a casual conversation about the United States: "That's what you call progress!" (Baroja, *Quest*, p. 131).

While the novel focuses primarily on the textures and difficulties of working-class life in Madrid, such passages offer vital clues to the larger context in which Baroja wrote. Baroja was one of a number of Spanish writers whose work was deeply influenced by the shock of the Spanish-American War. Known as the Generation of 1898, these philosophers, poets, essayists, and so forth varied widely in their outlooks. While Baroja himself rejected the idea that he was a member of any cohesive group, literary critics have persisted in labeling him as the Generation of 1898's leading novelist, citing some fundamental goals that he shared with this otherwise diverse group of writers. Chief among those shared goals was a desire to address Spain's social ills, which had long included widespread poverty and persistent political instability. In addition, Baroja and other members of the generation wished to bring Spanish culture more into step with the rest of the continent by exposing it to recent developments in European intellectual life. Baroja was especially affected by the ideas of two influential nineteenth-century figures, the English biologist Charles Darwin and the German philosopher Friedrich Nietzsche (see below).

Regeneración. By the early years of the twentieth century, the Generation of 1898's aspirations had been epitomized by the popular catchword *regeneración* or "regeneration," which became a key concept for those who wished to improve Spanish society. Like much about the man, Baroja's attitude to the Generation of 1898 and to *regeneración* was ambivalent and contradictory. For example, Baroja later denied membership in the Generation of 1898, yet he engaged in a brief creative association with the very man who coined that label, José Martínez Ruiz. Known by his pseudonym Azorín, Martínez Ruiz would soon become the leading Spanish literary critic of the day. In 1901, just a few years before Baroja wrote *The Quest*, Azorín, Baroja, and another writer named Ramiro de Maeztu formed a group called simply *los tres*, the Three. Dedicated to the regeneration of Spanish society through such vaguely defined means as educational and economic improvements, the group broke up shortly after being founded. Its brief existence, however, is echoed in the novel when Manuel and two of his idle ne'er-do-well friends form a gang of the same name, the Three. The gang's one escapade, a robbery, turns into a farce when the Three comically botch the job.

Historians have found the breakup of the real-life Three unsurprising, since each of the group's members held strongly nonconformist, individualistic ideas that at times approached anarchism. Each, scholars have observed, also favored discussion over concrete action, a propensity that some have seen as applying to the Generation of 1898 as a whole. Indeed, at times the writers of the movement themselves lamented their preference for words over deeds. For example, in his novel *La voluntad* (1902; Volition) Azorín agonizes over his inability to act, a paralysis of the will he sees as stemming from too much critical analysis. Azorín's novel also offers a portrait of Baroja in the character of Enrique Olaiz, a romantic who scorns the masses, exalts the gifted individual, and opposes any political system that relies on rigid dogma, whether it be socialism, democracy, or anarchism. Baroja's own political views resist easy categorization, but he has been described as a mild anarchist who ideally preferred a stateless society but had no desire to see his views translated into action.

As Azorín's novel *Volition* suggests, the writers of the Generation of 1898 grew acutely self-consciousness about what they perceived as a gulf between their discussions of Spain's ills and their lack of concrete action to remedy those ills. Reflecting this self-consciousness, in *The Quest* Baroja satirizes the advocates of regeneration with a comical depiction of a Madrid shoe shop grandiosely called "The Regeneration of Footwear." The shop is run by Manuel's uncle Ignacio, a cobbler and "a mild liberal" who enjoys discoursing about "the future of Spain and the reasons for national backwardness—a topic that appeals to most Spaniards, who consider themselves regenerators" (*Quest*, p. 60). Enjoying the sound of his own voice, Señor Ignacio "swelled with enthusiasm over these words about the national sovereignty" but stopped short of political action, limiting himself to talking about what "he'd certainly do if he had a say in the government" (*Quest*, pp. 60-61).

Working-class children and family life in Madrid. Overtly political content is less prominent in *The Quest* than is Baroja's vivid evocation of the sights, sounds, and smells of daily life in Madrid. Spain's capital since 1561, Madrid has been the nation's center not only politically and geographically but culturally as well. The city has long been divided into different *barrios*, or districts, each with its own style and flavor. These barrios have been further grouped into three categories—*altos* (high), *centrales* (middle), and *bajos* (low)—depending on the social rank of their inhabitants and on their position relative to the low-lying areas along the Manzanares River, which runs through the city. *The Quest* takes place largely in the *barrios bajos*, the poor districts near the river's edge. Here, at the time of the novel, the city's slums stretched southward towards the river along the *Calle de Toledo* (Toledo Street) from the *Plaza Mayor* (Main Square) near the city center.

The most dramatic change that occurred in Spanish city life over the course of the nineteenth century was a sharp rise in urban populations, not just in Madrid but in other cities as well. Like Manuel in the novel, peasants came to Madrid

and other cities in hope of economic opportunity. Madrid grew earlier and faster than other cities. Even in the middle of the nineteenth century, nearly half its population was born elsewhere because the capital attracted hopeful immigrants from throughout the Iberian peninsula. By the late nineteenth century, major cities such as Madrid, Barcelona, and Bilbao had begun undertaking *ensanches* or planned expansions. In 1900 Madrid's population stood at about one million; Barcelona and Bilbao both more than

doubled their populations between 1877 and 1900, with Barcelona's jumping from an estimated 250,000 to about 600,000 (Shubert, p. 48).

As the nation's capital, Madrid offered a large number of jobs in the government bureaucracy, which expanded in the second half of the nineteenth century. These jobs became highly popular, with competition for them growing exceedingly fierce, a phenomenon known as

A scene from El Rastro, the area in Madrid where a weekly flea market is held.

empleomanía. Other middle-class professions—law and medicine, primarily—also saw rapid growth in Madrid. However, Madrid was not an industrial city, (in contrast to Barcelona, for example). Therefore, working-class opportunities in Madrid fell largely into three categories: construction trades such as carpentry or plastering; retail shops or street stalls; and small manufacturing workshops owned by an artisan and staffed by a few apprentices, often family members. Examples from the novel include the vegetable stand of Señora Jacoba, Señor Ignacio's mother, and the shoe shop of Señor Ignacio himself, where Manuel works, though the restless boy lacks the commitment to be considered his uncle's apprentice.

The novel touches on a number of areas that defined working-class daily life in Madrid and other Spanish cities around the turn of the twentieth century. Most apparent to the reader of *The Quest* is the harsh existence of the novel's main character, fifteen-year-old Manuel. The economic necessity to help support their families meant that boys in working-class urban families received minimal schooling and took jobs at an early age, often as early as seven or eight years old. Social historian Adrian Shubert has recently drawn on five published autobiographies of working-class individuals—four men and one woman—who grew up in Spanish cities in the early 1900s, and

whose experiences were very close to those of Manuel in the novel. For example,

> Leandro Carro, the second son of a shoemaker with thirteen children, began work at the tender age of 7, as the errand boy in a household goods store and then, at 9, was apprenticed to an iron molder. Largo Caballero also began work at 7, passing rapidly through a variety of jobs before finding his métier as a plasterer.
>
> (Shubert, p. 138)

Boys generally began working earlier than girls, because more jobs were open to them and because they were expected to contribute more to supporting the family. Girls found work as domestic servants in wealthier households, but not until their mid-teens, the age at which both of Manuel's sisters find such work in the novel. When they were not in school or working, Shubert reports, children were often "left to their own devices, roaming the town and its surroundings and playing, boys and girls together, the same games, jumping onto passing freight cars, hanging from aerial trams and going into tunnels" (Shubert, p. 137). This account (based on the woman's autobiography among the five from which he drew) also bears a strong resemblance to Baroja's depiction of Manuel's adventures on the streets of Madrid in the novel.

Shubert's findings on family life likewise resemble Baroja's picture in the novel. While the family was a central feature of working-class life, the autobiographies Shubert cites suggest that working-class marriages were often rocky and that domestic violence was common. For example, Largo Caballero remembers "frequent quarrels between my parents, which usually ended with my father hitting my mother" (Caballero in Shubert, p. 139). "The break-up of a marriage," Shubert continues, "through separation or, probably more commonly, the death of one of the spouses, generally made a difficult economic situation even more desperate. The hardship facing a single parent was particularly intense if that parent was a mother" (Shubert, p. 139). In the novel, two of Manuel's aunts are beaten by their husbands, and Manuel's father was a brutal machinist who quarreled with his wife Petra constantly and often beat her. The father's death, two years before the novel opens, has forced Petra to give up their comfortable apartment, take a job as a servant in a Madrid boardinghouse, and send Manuel to live in the country with a relative.

The Novel in Focus

Plot summary. *The Quest* opens one evening in a middle-class neighborhood of Madrid, in the boardinghouse of Doña Casiana, where Petra, the maid, has finished her nightly scouring and fallen asleep in a chair, her mouth open. A scrawny woman with greyish skin, Petra breathes shallowly and with difficulty. She awakens as a clock in the hallway strikes and resumes her chores. A few minutes later noisy activity erupts at the brothel across the street, Isabella's brothel, and Petra chats with Doña Casiana, who wishes that she herself ran such an establishment: "That's what pays," she tells Petra over and over (*Quest*, p. 6).

Before her husband's death two years earlier, Petra herself had rented out rooms from her own home; afterward the loss of his income forced her to become a landlady's servant instead of a landlady, a change in social status that she accepts stoically. She arranged for her two daughters to become servants as well, and sent her two sons to live with her brother-in-law, a railway station manager in a small rural town. Now, however, she has received word that Manuel, her rebellious older son, is on his way into Madrid, and she wonders what has happened to upset her plans. As it turns out, nothing in particular has happened—Manuel simply got tired of living with his relatives, who prefer his gentle brother Juan to the lazy Manuel. Perhaps, her

brother-in-law writes, Manuel can become an apprentice and learn a trade in Madrid.

With some trouble Petra persuades Doña Casiana to let Manuel live in the boardinghouse, and the landlady agrees that Manuel can run errands and help serve meals. Manuel soon meets the colorful characters who rent rooms from

HOUSES OF GOOD AND ILL REPUTE

Boardinghouses like Doña Casiana's in *The Quest* were common in Madrid, where few people lived completely alone even if single. Instead, single men and women most commonly rented a room in a converted house or large apartment and, as in the novel, shared communal meals that were included in the rent. This respectable arrangement stood in contrast to the brothels (some 150 in Madrid) that were legal in Spain in the early twentieth century. Prostitutes were supposed to register with the state, although in practice many more did not (presumably the prostitutes whom Manuel encounters in the novel were of this second variety). In 1899, for example, five years before the novel was published, Madrid had some 2,000 registered prostitutes, while official estimates of unregistered prostitutes stood at some 7,000.

Doña Casiana, and who gossip incessantly about each other. They include:

- Don Telmo, an old man who carefully wipes all of his plates and glasses before eating from them.

- The Biscayan, a gigantic woman with thick fleshy features.

- Doña Violante, an elderly courtesan.

- Doña Violante's daughter Celia and granddaughter Irene, both of whom spend their days and nights trying to find a wealthy man to woo.

- The Superman, a blond, thin, and very serious young journalist.

- The Baroness, a mysterious woman reputed to be an adventuress, and her pretty young daughter Kate.

- A half-English student named Roberto Hasting y Nuñez, who believes with unshakeable conviction that he is the legitimate heir to a vast fortune that he plans to acquire by means of genealogical proof.

Again Petra's plans are frustrated. Her son Manuel loses his place at the boardinghouse when he gets into a fight with a salesman who is also one of the boarders. The boy goes to live with his uncle Ignacio, a cobbler, who has a shoe-repair shop in the slums of the *barrios bajos*, the poor district down near the Manzanares River, which flows through the city. Señor Ignacio's shoe-repair shop, *The Regeneration of Footwear*, competes with another similar establishment across the street with an equally grandiose name, *The Lion of the Shoemaker's Art*. Both shops are rundown, and the only sense in which Ignacio's shop regenerates footwear these days is by dismantling old shoes so the materials can be salvaged.

Manuel begins working alongside his cousins, a tough older boy named Leandro and his frail, roguish younger brother Vidal, who is about Manuel's age. Manuel meets the rest of his uncle's family: Ignacio's mother, Señora Jacoba, who has a stand where she sells vegetables; Ignacio's wife, a sour woman named Leandra; and Leandra's pretty, cheerful sister, Salomé. Salomé lives with her two children at Señora Jacoba's house, which is near Señor Ignacio's, and in which the family often gathers; Salomé's good-for-nothing husband helps himself to the money she makes by sewing, and he often beats her as well. Once, when Manuel and Vidal return to Señor Ignacio's, they hear Ignacio beating his own wife Leandra, and Manuel goes to spend that night at Señora Jacoba's. Manuel also meets Vidal's gang of friends, who call themselves the Pirates. Among them is a bragging bully nicknamed El Bizco, or Cross-eye. Vidal and many of the other boys their age have girlfriends, and El Bizco boasts to Manuel about his sexual conquests among the neighborhood girls, telling him that most of them are prostitutes, along with their mothers.

The huge and decrepit tenement building in which Ignacio's family lives has a number of nicknames in the neighborhood, but it is most commonly called *El Corralón*, or "the Big Yard," because of the great size of its main courtyard. The massive building is "a microcosm," its many inhabitants living in a state of abject poverty, without hope or dreams of any kind:

> It harbored men who were everything and yet nothing: half scholars, half smiths, half carpenters, half masons, half business men, half thieves. . . . They lived as if sunk in the shades of a deep slumber, unable to form any clear notion of their lives, without aspirations, aims, projects, anything.
>
> (*Quest*, p. 79)

As the weeks go by, Manuel becomes familiar with several of his new neighbors, including:

- *La Muerta*, the Death, a haggard old crone who begs in the main entrance.

- *El Corretor*, a proof-corrector, and his large family.

- Milagros, one of *El Corretor's* daughters, and the girlfriend of Leandro, Señor Ignacio's elder son.

- Señor Zurro, who owns a second-hand shop.

- Encarna, Zurro's daughter, who harbors a passion for Leandro and thus hates Milagros.

- Rebolledo, a dwarf who operates a portable barber stand.

- Perico, Rebolledo's talented son, an inventor and artist.

One day Roberto Hasting, the half-English student back at the boardinghouse, pays a visit to *The Regeneration of Footwear*, where Manuel is at work. Hasting was the only one of Doña Casiana's tenants who befriended Manuel, and who spoke up on Manuel's behalf after his fight with the salesman. Now Roberto wants the boy's help in searching the slums of the *barrios bajos* for two women who he says can assist him in his quest for the fortune that belongs to him by right. Manuel goes with Roberto to *La Doctrina*, an area across the Manzanares River where the city's ill and crippled beggars gather; they are cared for here by Catholic nuns and wealthy women volunteers. Later Roberto says that one of the women he seeks is a former circus acrobat, and the two continue the search in various taverns, as Roberto questions several exotic characters, including an old circus performer.

It is also in a series of dingy taverns that Manuel witnesses some of the ups and downs of Leandro's turbulent and tragic relationship with the pretty but unfaithful Milagros, who drops Leandro for a young man known as *Lechuguino*, the dude. Enraged and unstable, Leandro finally stabs Milagros, killing her before taking his own life. Manuel, finding that Milagros continued to wear a locket with Leandro's picture in it, is fascinated by the thought that Milagros probably loved Leandro the whole time.

The shock of Leandro's death ruins Señor Ignacio's health, and Manuel is sent back to Doña Casiana's. Petra arranges jobs for him, first as an errand boy in a grocery store and then as a baker's apprentice. Manuel hates both jobs, but especially loathes the difficult and grimy work at the bakery, where his responsibilities include stoking the fire and moistening the loaves as they emerge from the oven, tasks that leave him with dirty, burned hands. When he falls ill his mother nurses him back to health, but after recovering, he is again ejected from the boardinghouse when Doña Casiana catches him trying to seduce her niece. Out on the street, he runs into two of his *barrios bajos* companions, Vidal and El Bizco, who have been leading a life of petty thievery. Reluctantly—for he and El Bizco hate each other—Manuel lets Vidal press him into joining the other two in a gang they call the Three. Soon afterward, Manuel learns that Petra has fallen ill and is confined to her bed. Manuel attends her as she rapidly declines, and is with her when she dies shortly thereafter.

Grief-stricken and fearful, Manuel now has nowhere to go. He bids goodbye to Doña Casiana (who forgave him when her niece was discovered in the bedroom of another young man). He takes up with other homeless urchins on the street, sleeping in doorways, alleys, or hollows in the *Retiro*, the large park in central Madrid. For a while Manuel picks up odd jobs to sustain himself, but eventually he is forced to seek food at the María Cristina barracks, a charity establishment that serves the poor. There he encounters Roberto, who insists, "someday I'm going to be wealthy, and when I am I'll recall these hard times with pleasure" (*Quest*, p. 207). Roberto brings Manuel up to date on his quest for the fortune he considers rightfully his. Manuel suspects that Roberto is "a bit off his base," though he keeps his suspicions to himself (*Quest*, p. 208). Eventually Roberto produces a detailed family tree supporting his case, but Manuel remains unconvinced.

Manuel seeks out Vidal and El Bizco, and the Three embark on a series of shady adventures that leave Manuel feeling remorseful yet unsure of what other choices he has in life. In one episode, they break into a house but find little worth stealing; attacked by a guard dog, they barely escape, selling their scanty takings to a *trapero*, or trash dealer. After a period of living on the streets, Manuel meets another *trapero* who calls himself Señor Custodio, and who offers Manuel a job and board. Tired of sleeping in the rough outdoors and with winter approaching, Manuel accepts. He finds life at Señor Custodio's well run rubbish yard pleasant and interesting, particularly when he meets his employer's attractive daughter, Justa. The flirtatious girl only teases him, however, and he is heartbroken when she decides to marry the son of a butcher. When he encounters the ragged El Bizco on the street, Manuel refuses to reconstitute the defunct trio.

Attending a bullfight with Señor Custodio's family, including Justa and her suitor, Manuel is sickened by the spectacle. He picks a fight with the butcher's son, but is manhandled and humiliated by the other boy's friends. He passes that night walking the streets, and talks with two prostitutes he knew when he was keeping company with Vidal and El Bizco. As day breaks, Manuel struggles to make sense of his life. He decides that for some, life holds indolence, vice, and darkness, while for others it holds work, fatigue, and sunlight. The novel ends with Manuel's conclusion that he should belong to the "the folk who toil in the sun, not those who dally in the shadows" (*Quest*, p. 289).

TAVERN LIFE

While bullfights, circuses, and inexpensive theater were all popular entertainments among urban working-class Spaniards at the time of the novel, by far the greatest amount of leisure time was spent in the many taverns that could be found in virtually every neighborhood. These drinking establishments offered male companionship (though less respectable women frequented them as well), often accompanied by a game of cards. In the novel Manuel drinks in a tavern and plays *mus*, a popular card game in such settings.

The struggle for life. In describing *La Corrala*, the great building in which Senior Ignacio lives with his family, Baroja calls it "a seething world in little, as busy as an anthill . . . a microcosm" (*Quest*, p. 78). As the comparison of its inhabitants to ants suggests, the grinding poverty of this miniature world has reduced the men and women who live there to the level of animals:

> From time to time, like some gentle sunbeam amidst the gloom, the souls of these stultified, bestial men,—of these women embittered by harsh lives that held neither solace nor illusion,—would be penetrated by a romantic, disinterested feeling of tenderness that made them live like human beings for a while; but when the gust of sentimentalism had blown over, they would return to their moral inertia, as resigned and passive as ever.
>
> (*Quest*, p. 80)

In other words, poverty's dehumanizing effect on these people has been accomplished by stripping them of their feelings—not just any feelings, but the "disinterested" and tender feelings for others that, Baroja says, separate humans from nonhuman animals. The streets of Madrid are depicted as a similarly dehumanizing environment, in which the strong, driven by self-interest and lack of feelings, prey upon the weak, and in which anyone can fall victim to random, impersonal forces. By using such terms as "microcosm" in his description of *La Corrala*, Baroja implies that the larger world outside that of the novel works in a similar way.

Like the very title of the trilogy to which *The Quest* belongs, *The Struggle for Life*, this view of the world owes much to the influential ideas of English biologist Charles Darwin (1809-82), ideas that revolutionized virtually every area of intellectual endeavor in late-nineteenth-century Europe. In proposing a mechanism for biological evolution, Darwin suggested that all living beings are shaped by a harsh, impersonal, and unceasing competition for survival—and that humans have been shaped by such competition just like other animals. Published in his book *The Origin of Species* (1859), Darwin's conceptions of nature and humanity had a huge impact on European thought, because they were easily (if often misleadingly) carried over from biology into other areas, such as social theory, politics, art, and philosophy. Darwinian theory, for instance, was used to reinforce ideas about the positive moral value of work, part of the social fabric in prosperous industrial societies such as late-nineteenth-century Britain and the United States.

Baroja and other writers of the Generation of 1898 wished to expose Spanish society not only to Darwin's but also to other recent ideas that had recreated the European intellectual landscape by the late nineteenth century. However, Darwin's ideas may have seemed particularly relevant to Spain in the early twentieth century, a once powerful nation that had recently and catastrophically fallen victim to competitive forces in the Spanish-American War. Furthermore, the moralizing ending of *The Quest*—in which Manuel accepts the value of hard work—perhaps reflects the author's endorsement of a work ethic that Darwin's ideas reinforced, and that already existed in northern European countries like Britain. The novel's ending can be seen as suggesting that only by adopting such values will Spain be able to compete successfully in a harsh world and emerge from the "backwardness" that seemed to plague it in the early twentieth century. Otherwise, Baroja seems to hint, Spain risks a future of dehumanized idleness similar to that which has robbed *La Corrala*'s inhabitants of drive and ambition.

Sources and literary context. Baroja's own life in Madrid supplied the realistic details that bring the city to life in *The Quest*. Other experiences also contributed to the novel's authentic feel: for example, Baroja's familiarity with the daily routine of a bakery (he had run a bakery owned by his family) is reflected in the description of the bakery job that Manuel briefly holds. By the end of the trilogy Manuel has fully accepted the middle-class work ethic, which he first begins to grasp at the end of *The Quest*, and he achieves a modestly prosperous existence with a steady job. This overall structure recalls the paradigm of the Spanish picaresque novel, in which the adventures of a rogue or *picaro* typically end with his achieving a secure if not extravagant *bourgeois* existence. Manuel's avoidance of work—as well as the combination of humor and brutality in the descriptions of the hardships that arise from it—can be traced to this most popular of Spanish literary genres, the prototype of which was the influential anonymous novel **Lazarillo de Tormes** (1554; also in *WLAIT 5: Spanish and Portuguese Literatures and Their Times*).

Other literary influences include novels by England's Charles Dickens (1812-70), such as *Oliver Twist* (1837-38), which follows the adventures of a young urchin on the teeming streets of London. Also there are the realistic social novels of Russia's Fyodor Dostoyevsky (1821-81) and Maxim Gorky (1868-1936) and the gritty nineteenth-century French novels of the *bas fonds* (lower depths) that focus on urban poverty. Closer to home are the realistic novels of Spain's Pérez Galdós (see **Fortunata and Jacinta,** also in *WLAIT 5: Spanish and Portuguese Literatures and Their Times*). Nonfiction writings that influenced Baroja included those not only of Darwin but also of the German philosophers Arthur Schopenhauer (1788-1860) and his follower Friedrich Nietzsche (1844-1900), both of whom depicted humans as solitary strugglers in an indifferent world and stressed the role of the individual will in facing the trials of life. In *The Quest* there is the minor character of a journalist nicknamed the Superman. His nickname is a reference to the so-called superman of Nietzsche's philosophy, a hypothetical person of superior intellect and moral standards, whom humanity, according to Nietzsche, had the potential to evolve into. Critics have also seen a Nietzschean influence in the determined, self-disciplined, iron-willed Roberto Hasting, who reappears throughout the trilogy. Baroja himself named Darwin, Dickens, Schopenhauer, and Nietzsche as among his most important influences.

Reception. In keeping with Baroja's prodigious output, all three novels in the trilogy—*The Quest*, *Weeds* (*Mala hierba*), and *Red Dawn* (*Aurora rojo*)—were published in the same year, 1904. All three books enjoyed both popular and critical success with Spanish audiences. Critic Gregorio Marañon praised the trilogy for opening the eyes of Spain's middle class to the dire poverty that afflicted most Spaniards. The philosopher José Ortega y Gasset—strongly related to but of a later era than the Generation of 1898—lauded both Baroja's social conscience and the trilogy's realism, dubbing the author *el Homero de la canalla*, "the Homer of the rabble" (Ortega in Patt, p. 94; see **Meditations on Don Quixote** also in *WLAIT 5: Spanish and Portuguese Literatures and Their Times*). Baroja's work has generally been accorded less recognition among English-language critics than among those writing in Spanish; Spanish author Camilio José Cela (see **The Family of Pascual Duarte,** also in *WLAIT 5: Spanish and Portuguese Literatures and Their Times*) later

lamented the fact that Baroja never won the Nobel Prize for Literature. However, the leading twentieth-century American writers John Dos Passos (1896-1970) and Ernest Hemingway (1899-1961) both included Baroja among their most important influences. Hemingway, who admired Spanish culture in general and certainly enjoyed bullfights more than the novel's Manuel, visited the older writer in Madrid three weeks before Baroja's death in 1954. When asked to act as a pallbearer at Baroja's funeral, Hemingway declined, saying that he felt unworthy to do so.

—Colin Wells

For More Information

Baroja, Pío. *The Quest*. Trans. Isaac Goldberg. New York: Knopf, 1922.

Carr, Raymond. *Spain 1808-1939*. Oxford: Oxford University Press, 1966.

Eoff, Sherman H. *The Modern Spanish Novel*. New York: New York University Press, 1961.

Patt, Beatrice P. *Pío Baroja*. New York: Twayne, 1971.

Shubert, Adrian. *A Social History of Modern Spain*. London: Unwin Hyman, 1990.

La Regenta
(The Judge's Wife)

by
Leopoldo Alas ("Clarín")

Leopoldo Alas, better known by the pseudonym "Clarín," which he adopted in 1875, was born in Zamora, Spain, on April 25, 1852, but his ancestry and cultural preference tie him to the province of Asturias on the northern coast. From 1863 he lived in its capital city of Oviedo, leaving to spend summers at a small farm he inherited in the rural village of Guimarán (also the surname of a major character in *La Regenta,* or *The Judge's Wife*). Alas completed his undergraduate law degree at the University of Oviedo in 1871, then earned a Doctorate in Jurisprudence from the University of Madrid and became a professor in Roman Law at his hometown University of Oviedo in 1882. The position made it possible for him to marry and to begin writing his most important works. To supplement his meager salary as a college professor, Clarín wrote dozens of short stories and scores of newspaper articles, mostly book reviews. In his own day he was less well known for the two novels he also managed to write: *La Regenta* and *His Only Son* (*Su único hijo,* 1891). The former now ranks among the finest realist novels of nineteenth-century Spain. The latter, by contrast, shows a change, perhaps a decline, in Clarín's narrative artistry and creative energy. His fondness for gambling, his late-night habits of writing until dawn and his disorganized, crowded work schedule ruined the author's already poor physical and psychological health. He died before his fiftieth birthday, June 13, 1901, a sad and largely forgotten figure, unaware of the impact his one novel would have on Spanish

THE LITERARY WORK

A novel set in Vetusta (fictionalized version of Oviedo), a provincial town in northern Spain in 1877-80; published in Spanish (as *La Regenta*) in 1884-85, in English in 1894.

SYNOPSIS

Ana, a beautiful young woman, is coerced by her two aunts into marrying an old retired judge (*regente*). Pursued by a priest and by the local womanizer, she finds herself seduced by the latter and shunned by the Catholic Church.

letters a century after his passing. In *La Regenta,* Clarín evokes life in a provincial town during an age of tumultuous change in late-nineteenth-century Spain.

Events in History at the Time of the Novel

The politics of a hereditary monarchy. Whenever a king dies in a hereditary monarchy, his first-born offspring automatically inherits the throne. In Spain, as elsewhere in Europe, the normal order of things also dictated that the first-born male child—not the female—customarily became king. In fact, the Salic Law, instituted in 1713 under the Bourbon king Felipe V, forbade the ascension of a woman to the throne in Spain unless there were no eligible male heirs. Because

Leopoldo Alas ("Clarín")

the law did not have to be invoked for many years, it was largely forgotten. In the minds of many jurists, a more equitable rule of succession already existed dating from the time of King Alfonso the Wise (1221-84). The Law of Partidas stated that the crown is patrimonial in nature, meaning that a king will be succeeded by his eldest child, male or female and, in the event of his or her death prior to ascending the throne, that child's first-born child, would, in turn, be the next in line.

As Fernando VII lay dying in September of 1833, he was persuaded to declare the earlier Law of Partidas as the only legitimate mandate, thereby paving the way for his three-year-old daughter Isabel to inherit the crown upon reaching maturity. Opposition to the declaration came swiftly and vigorously from those who wanted Fernando's brother Carlos to become king. Isabel's partisans won the day. After the caretaking regency of her widowed mother, María Cristina, Isabel became queen in 1843, whereupon Carlos's supporters began a series of three bloody civil wars. Called the Carlist Wars, the three conflicts lasted half a century and ended with the defeat of his supporters—the pretenders to the throne—several years after the death of Carlos himself. By the beginning of the third

Carlist War (1872), his grandson, Carlos María, would have been king. Isabel's reign lasted until 1868, when the government and Spaniards in general became disenchanted with a queen whose marriage at sixteen years of age to her cousin, the homosexual Don Francisco de Asís had driven her into countless affairs with members of her administration, and whose politics had allowed the country to drift into social chaos and financial ruin. Isabel and Francisco finally separated in May of 1870 while in exile in France. (On a microcosmic level, the negative reaction experienced by the heroine of Clarín's novel echoes the reaction to Isabel's indiscretions in real life.) By 1868 labor unions had begun to exert a degree of force in society, the Catholic Church had extracted a settlement for the 1836 expropriation of their lands and buildings whereby priests and other church officials became part of the government payroll, and the overseas colonies, feeling the loosening of political dominance by Spain, were beginning to rebel. The crises became so constant and so severe that Isabel was finally deposed, peacefully, while summer vacationing on the northern coast. Unfazed, she simply went into exile in Paris until 1877, leaving Spain in the hands of a provisional government. Formed by a parliament and several military factions, this coalition issued a new constitution and eventually paved the way for a return to monarchical rule. Since no one wanted anything to do with Isabel or the Bourbons, her 13-year-old son Alfonso was passed over in favor of Prince Amadeo of Savoy, third son of King Victor Immanuel II of Italy. Though their lineage was in no way connected to the Spanish monarchy, General Juan Prim, who headed the government at the time, persuaded the constitutional Parliament to ratify his wish to bring new blood to the throne. This was done by a slim vote margin on November 16, 1870. The rule of this imported monarch lasted scarcely three years—from January 2, 1870, until February 11, 1873. Amadeo, officially Spain's fifteenth king, was unable to cope with the country's profound unrest. Left alone after his main supporter and prime minister, General Prim, was assassinated and despite his kind and agreeable nature, the new king failed to consolidate any power base from which to operate. Other difficulties—the simmering civil (Carlist) war, the opposition of the young prince Alfonso's party, a secessionist rebellion in the colony of Cuba, and the people's indifference to a foreigner as their ruler negated whatever chances for success Amadeo may have had. An assassination attempt on him and his wife on July 18, 1872 in broad daylight on one of Madrid's main avenues no doubt made him resign from this failed experiment and return to Italy, where he died in 1890.

Parliament accepted Amadeo's resignation and declared a new republic. What followed was a short period of anarchy during which the Carlists intensified the third of their campaigns for the throne (beginning December 1872), and other political and military groups vied for power. In the following 25-year period, Spain's two strongest parties, the conservatives and the liberals, disenfranchised all others (including the extreme right-wing Carlists) and made a pact whereby elections would be rigged so that each group could enjoy alternating periods at the helm. This political maneuvering, known as the *turno pacífico,* worked quite well, since each party was assured a turn in power.

Far from Madrid, in the provinces, where *La Regenta* takes place, most of this power was wielded by *caciques*, local political bosses, who could be anyone from a conservative aristocrat (such as the Marqués de Vegallana in Clarín's novel) to a moderate liberal (such as Alvaro Mesía, Vegallana's secret right-hand man and political ally). As Clarín implies by the two men's relationship in the novel, there was little or no difference between the two parties in charge of either the central or the local government in real life. Eventually, the head of the real life conservative group, moderate Antonio Cánovas del Castillo, persuaded his own party as well as the opposition to agree to restore the monarchy in order to further stabilize the country. Preparations were made to bring Isabel's son to power.

The Bourbon Restoration. As a preparatory move, the young Alfonso became a cadet at the British military academy of Sandhurst to learn not only the art of war but also the ways of governing, to develop an understanding of how a constitutional monarchy should run, and to meet other dynastic scions likely to become his peers in the capitals of Europe. On December 1, 1874, using the prince's birthday as a pretext, Cánovas engineered the "Sandhurst Manifesto," a strategic political document that spelled out in some detail the tenets of the monarchical restoration about to take place. A few weeks later, on December 29, a military uprising in favor of Alfonso proclaimed him king. His mother Isabel had long ago (1870) reconciled herself to renouncing the throne on his behalf. With nothing standing in the way, the new king triumphantly entered Madrid on January 14, 1875, as Alfonso XII. There followed a decade of relative tranquility (during which Clarín's novel takes place). The last Carlist pretender fled to neighboring France on February 27, 1876; the Cuban crisis entered into a long truce achieved through a peace accord on the strength of General Martínez Campos's victory on behalf of Spain in Zanjón, Cuba, on February 10, 1879; and Spain itself could boast of an orderly rotating form of government led alternately by the liberal Práxades Mateo Sagasta and by the conservative Cánovas del Castillo.

After the sudden death of his first wife and cousin Mercedes of Orleans, Alfonso married a Habsburg princess. He proved to be a conciliatory ruler, one interested in serving as king for all his subjects, regardless of their past loyalties. The well-liked monarch traveled widely throughout Spain and abroad, especially in France and Germany, though his health was weak and living conditions were, at best, unpredictable throughout Europe. Early in his reign, Alfonso contracted tuberculosis, an incurable disease at that time and one that he kept secret from everyone outside the palace circle. Alfonso continued to visit troubled parts of Spain—the southern provinces of Málaga and Granada, which were devastated by major earthquakes in 1884, and the area surrounding Aranjuez, where an outbreak of cholera claimed hundreds of victims in 1885. His own death would soon follow. That autumn, on November 26, 1885, unable to withstand the rigors of the Castilian climate, he succumbed to tuberculosis at the age of 28. Spain was stunned by the news of his premature death, never having been told of the king's ill health. Alfonso left behind a royal family—his queen María Cristina and their two daughters, María de las Mercedes and María Teresa. Five-and-a-half months after Alfonso's death, the widowed queen gave birth to a son. The birth insured an uninterrupted succession: the infant would become the future Alfonso XIII, grandfather of the current king of Spain Juan Carlos I. From the day of her husband's 1885 death until 1902, when her son took over as the new monarch, María Cristina de Habsburgo-Lorena continued to oversee the familiar alternating governments of Práxedes Mateo Sagasta and Antonio Cánovas del Castillo (until the Cánovas's assassination in 1897). A strong regent queen, her international influence was underscored by Queen Victoria's goodwill visit from England to Spain during her reign.

Social progress in nineteenth-century Spain. Despite the political intrigues and their ensuing

Cover of the 1884 edition of *La Regenta*.

turmoil, industrial advancements found their way into Spain and slowly helped to modernize what was then one of the most backward countries in Western Europe. Progress came haltingly in a two-steps-forward, one-step-backward fashion. In 1834, for example, after centuries of persecutions and public burnings, the Inquisition (the tribunal to suppress deviation from the teachings of the Roman Catholic Church) was formally dissolved. Its dissolution was followed by the creation of the Civil Guard in 1844, which inspired the same fears and engendered even greater abuses. If great wealth came to the industrialized regions of Catalonia and the Basque provinces, so did labor unrest, strikes, and sabotage, following the publication of Karl Marx and Friedrich Engles's *Communist Manifesto* (1847). If the Catholic Church's vast properties were expropriated and put up for public sale (Desamortización de Mendizábal, 1835), only the already powerful and wealthy were able to take advantage of the newly available lands, so the *latifundios* (enormous estates) were enlarged and the poor further disadvantaged. Yet the general population also experienced improvements in life. Most Spaniards came to enjoy the economic, health, and safety benefits of such innovations as the use of steam power in factories (in Barcelona in 1833) and the public lighting of streets in large cities (in the 1840s). This, in turn, promoted longer hours of commerce, stricter building codes, paved streets, the addition of sidewalks to separate traffic from pedestrians, and enough prosperity to warrant new storefronts with large windows to showcase merchandise. The July 1849 adoption of a uniform chart of weights and measures, based on the decimal system, further aided commerce and consumer confidence. The following year, the first postage stamp was issued, promoting long distance communication over land. In 1852 a faster means of bridging distances, the telegraph system began operating as a regular service. Transportation of people and freight progressed to the relatively inexpensive, rapid, safe, and regularly scheduled service of a small railroad inaugurated in 1848 between the cities of Barcelona and Mataró, and, by the 1880s, to a national network of railways that facilitated travel within the country and opened up Spain to foreign visitors and commerce. Foreign business was further aided by the passage in 1869 of a fairly comprehensive set of trade laws that encouraged the exportation of great quantities of minerals and other goods. Sales of copper, zinc, lead, and iron fostered a much-needed economic upturn following the severe 1866-68 recession that was largely responsible for Isabel II's overthrow. New construction of underground sewer systems, indoor plumbing, water reservoirs, and canals did away with human water bearers and encouraged better hygiene, particularly in crowded urban areas where, according to the 1860 census, many of Spain's 16 million people lived. This total, which had grown by 6 million since the beginning of the nine-

teenth century, included a large number of discontented workers who, in 1879, founded the Spanish Socialist Worker's Party to remedy labor grievances and settle disputes.

Of course, established factions of society ardently resisted change. The elite, comprised—in the novel—of the Judge, the marqués de Vegallana, Fermín de Pas, Alvaro Mesía and their hangers-on, constituted the most conservative element of Vetusta's society. Against their ruling status we begin to notice the growing economic forces of a) the nouveaux riches—individuals who make their money in business and commerce, b) the returning emigrants who have accumulated wealth abroad in the colonies and now seek preeminence, and finally c) the very large, menacing masses of salaried factory workers ready to strike and hold protests as a means of gaining higher wages, better working conditions and a more equitable distribution of capital. Examples of the three groups are sprinkled throughout *La Regenta*. Ana's walk through the new part of the city (Chapter IX), when the ill-dressed, coarse-mannered, and sweat-stained factory men and women leave their workplace in the evening, is portrayed as an encounter with an uncontrolled river of people whose intentions and aspirations run contrary to the status quo that Ana's husband and their friends seem determined to maintain.

LA REGENTA AND PROVINCIAL SPAIN

"Alas [Clarín] shows in vivid and telling detail the absurd, unchanging world of mediocrity, pretense, hypocrisy, boredom and quirkiness of decadent provincial society" in late-nineteenth-century Spain (Rutherford in Alas, p. 16).

The elite, as might be expected, resisted the elevation of average citizens that had been experienced in nearby France since the French Revolution there. Clarín reveals his suspicions of French customs and ways time and again in his writing, referring to them mostly with derision. In *La Regenta* one of the most visible instances is Alvaro's affected mode of dress. As a dandy, his clothes, his impeccable shirt-fronts, his cologne, his mannerisms of speech and his tastes in cheap popular literature are all imported from Paris, a city he knows only superficially.

Out of the social mainstream—provincial gentry and women. Most members of the nobility lived in and around the court city—initially Toledo and then Madrid—since the center of power, money, and influence always depended on the king's whereabouts. The minor aristocracy and landed gentry, however, preferred to live in the provinces. There the less powerful or wealthy families saw their resources diminish with each passing generation. Titles, such as count or marquis, meant only past glories but present financial ruin unless marriages of convenience could be arranged so that new money could be added to an impoverished lineage. In the case of Ana, the novel's heroine, her father, Don Carlos, married a penniless Italian seamstress for love and proceeded to squander his meager fortune on lost causes, so Ana is left with nothing but countless mortgages on the family's estates.

FREEDOM EDUCATION INSTITUTE

The Freedom Education Institute was founded by Francisco Giner de los Ríos (1839-1915) on May 31, 1876. Giner was a follower of the German idealist philosophers—mainly Karl Krause. His importance lies in assembling a small group of like-minded educators, whose teachings shaped the lives and writings of men such as the author of *La Regenta* and every generation of intellectuals in the last third of the nineteenth century. These instructors sought 1) an educational system free from political and religious coercion, 2) equal rights for all educators (men and women alike), 3) reforms to update scientific inquiry, and 4) the freedom to think, write, and research in the field of one's choice. They also championed a host of principles that would liberate students from the dogmatism and stagnation long prevalent in Spain. The institute's artists looked at their predecessor Francisco de Goya (1746-1828) as a wellspring of Spanish art. Among his best-remembered canvasses are the large oil representation of execution-style killings by Napoleon's troops firing upon unarmed peasants, which Goya himself witnessed near his house in the Madrid outskirts.

Women's status in late-nineteenth-century Spain changed very little from centuries past. Their places outside of marriage were the convent, the brothel, the agricultural field, or domestic service. With the onset of urban commerce, they slowly made their way into the workaday world as lowly clerks in fabric concerns, groceries, and flower shops, where they catered to other, more well-to-do women. In all cases, such working women would be supervised by male managers or owners. Women who married well might, depending on their husband's wishes, have servants and time for leisure. Few of them engaged in meaningful intellectual pursuits since, as of 1870, only 9 percent of all women could read.

In *La Regenta,* mindful of their niece's impoverished status as a result of her father's—that is, their brother's—bankruptcy at death, Ana's old spinster aunts, Anunciación and Agueda Ozores, oblige their orphaned charge to marry a respectable judge. That he, Don Víctor, is older does not much matter to either of them. He meets their requirements, for he is honorable, distinguished, and a member of Vetusta's upper class. In the end, however, the thirty-some-year age difference between Ana and the judge, with all of its attendant implications (differences in tastes, habits, and sexual and other needs), dooms them.

Culture in nineteenth-century Spain. The cultural highlights of the nineteenth century began with the reopening of the universities upon the death of Fernando VII, who had ordered their closure, the construction of the Prado Museum, filled largely with treasures imported from Italy and Flanders by Diego Velázquez (1599-1660), the inauguration of several lyceums and academies, among them Madrid's Ateneo in 1835, the Institución Libre de Enseñanza (The Freedom Education Institute) in 1839—which had the greatest impact on Spanish writers of the second half of the nineteenth century and well into the next one, including especially Clarín—and the Real Academia de Ciencias in 1847.

In the realm of literature, two great movements stand out, Romanticism (1835-44) and realism (1849-1902). To Romanticism belongs ***Don Juan Tenorio*** (1844; also in *WLAIT 5: Spanish and Portuguese Literatures and Their Times*), a play about a rakish young nobleman by José Zorrilla (1817-1893) that Clarín uses explicitly within the novel as the centerpiece and turning point of *La Regenta* (Chapter 16), itself realism's most formidable paradigm. Linking the two works of literature, Clarín fashions a superimposition of characters: Ana, who identifies herself with Zorrilla's Doña Inés and Alvaro with Don Juan. However, Alvaro himself, jaded by Zorrilla's play has no patience for either the playwright's idealism or Ana's sublimated imagination. The Romantic concept uniquely espoused by José Zorrilla that man's salvation is possible through the love of a woman was likewise dismissed by the realists, who saw life as a struggle rather than a choreographed dialectic of passion and betrayal.

The Novel in Focus

Plot summary. Although the action in *La Regenta* takes place in the late 1870s during the early stages of the Restoration Period (1875-1902), the work spans the larger part of the nineteenth century. Its 30 chapters are divided into two halves. Part 1, published in 1884, contains the initial 15 chapters and lasts three days, beginning in the early afternoon of October 2, 1877, and ending well into the evening of October 4. Part 2, published in 1885, spans a three-year period, its chronology based on the liturgical calendar whose dates correspond to well-known holy days in Catholic Spain.

The setting is a small provincial city that is located in the northern region of Asturias and functions as the religious center of an equally unimportant diocese in this remote area. As its name, Vetusta ("Ancient"), implies, nothing much has changed here throughout history. The cathedral, a mixture of gothic architecture and later additions, constitutes the symbolic, spiritual, and physical center of the daily lives of its inhabitants. Thus, appropriately, the novel begins and ends in this edifice.

Two days before the feast day of Saint Francis of Assisi, as the townspeople sleep off the effects of a typically heavy midday meal, we are introduced to the most formidable character of the novel as he plies his trade from his center of operations. He is Fermín de Pas, the canon and vicar-general of the cathedral, perched atop the highest steeple of the church, telescope in hand, spying on the faithful and the not-so-faithful Vetustenses before he is called to attend afternoon choir services along with other members of the church administration. Because only three days transpire in the first part of *La Regenta,* the narrative tempo is slow—not time but space, through abundant but rather static descriptions, fills the pages. The narrator dwells on the lives of the protagonists and the places where they thrive. Fermín's metiér is the cathedral and everything connected with it—the confessional, the vicarage (where he lives with his mother and with a lusty maid), the pulpit, the bishop's apartments, and the living rooms of his richest parishioners, where he wields influence and power. Though a priest, Fermín remains nonetheless a vigorous man, trapped, by the time we meet him, by his mother and his vestments in a life that has

ceased to offer further challenges or rewards. From the confessional, he controls wives and through them their husbands and lovers, and he also learns those secrets that no one else can know since he alone can connect all of the dots. Information gives him power. Fermín also derives much of his power from his mother Paula's influence over the bishop, a holy man whose only misfortune (ironically, his name is Fortunato) was a sexually weak moment with her, which he is being made to pay for all his life. Paula's ambitions for her son include making him rich, a goal she achieves by bankrupting all competitors in the sales of religious objects in Vetusta. With a simple (though secret) decree, every parish priest in the diocese is obliged to purchase everything from candles to missals in an establishment she owns as a silent partner, piously called "The Red Cross." In addition to his mother, the aristocracy is Fermín's ally in his fight for control of all of Vetusta, an uphill battle in those times when the urban factory workers and many of the *nouveaux riches* preferred a totally secular existence, free from the shackles of a dogmatic Church and a domineering aristocracy.

Fermín's telescope lingers on the figure of Ana Ozores, a member of Vetusta's impoverished aristocracy and the young wife of an old retired appellate court judge. Closer to Fermín's age, the judge's wife represents for Fermín the most desirable forbidden fruit. He begins to court Ana, ironically when he takes over as her confessor and spiritual advisor. Always careful not to let his passion show, Fermín tries to seduce her by means of dazzling religious challenges designed to prove to the other Vetustenses his sway over the most admired woman in the city. At first, Ana (scarred as a child by the sexual perversions of her father's housekeeper, Camila, and Camila's lover) accepts willingly the intellectual and spiritual ways of Fermín. One day, however, she realizes that his constant demands and intimate presence exceeds the realm of the spiritual and constitutes nothing less than the possessiveness of a jealous lover. Horrified at the thought of being a married woman pursued sexually by a man of the Church, Ana withdraws and the stage is set for the consummation of an adulterous affair with Vetusta's local womanizer, Alvaro Mesía.

Significant in the love triangle of Ana, Fermín, and Alvaro, is the absence of her own husband Víctor (another narrative irony) from this traditional structure. In *La Regenta,* it turns out, the wronged man is not the husband but instead the spiritual figure of Fermín. He has become, in his own eyes, Ana's true spouse due to Víctor's inability to function as her sexual partner, her friend, and her defender against the amorous assaults mounted by Alvaro. The thirty-some-year age difference between Ana and Víctor, combined with separate bedrooms and a childless marriage, the lack of common interests, and a provincial existence in which males dominate every facet of life, mean that the spiritual, intellectual, and physical longings of this beautiful, sensitive, and intelligent young woman cannot be fulfilled.

FROM SPANISH REALISM TO FRENCH NATURALISM

The realist aesthetic under which Clarín wrote *La Regenta* came very close to the naturalist credo of the French novelist Emile Zola (1840-1902), wherein man's instincts would always triumph over his spiritual desire for moral righteousness. The Credo holds that one's heredity, the milieu in which one is reared and the moment in which s/he lives determines that individual's conduct. In other words, given the right circumstances anyone can fall prey to immoral or unethical behavior and give in to passion or instinct.

When the novel begins, Ana and Víctor have already been married for eight years. In that time, they have begun to slowly drift apart as each has become more set in his/her ways: Victor hunts, goes to the theater every night, trains caged birds, and builds ineffectual animal traps. Ana, on the other hand, reads the works of the Spanish mystics such as Saint Teresa (see **Interior Castle**, also in *WLAIT 5: Spanish and Portuguese Literatures and Their Times*). Also Ana writes poetry and a diary, and goes for walks in the country with a traitorous maid. While the husband avoids any and all sorts of domestic contact, the wife hungers for spiritual stimulus and intellectual gratification to sublimate the emptiness and isolation to which she feels condemned.

Ana reaches her moment of crisis when she realizes Fermín's desire for her—a double sin since it threatens not only adultery but also sacrilege because it involves a priest's breaking his vow of chastity. Ana is repelled by the thought: "[she] felt something like hatred for a moment. 'What? Her own confessor was compromising her? . . . How horrible! How disgusting! A love affair with a priest!'" (Alas, *La Regenta,* p. 631). Weary of her marriage, her confessor, and an in-

different circle of jealous friends who would like to see her morally diminished, she spots Alvaro on his white horse a few days prior to the feast of All Saints (November 1st), when the romantic play by José Zorrilla, *Don Juan Tenorio*, is traditionally staged. Persuaded to attend the performance, Ana is transfixed by Zorrilla's lovers to the point that she identifies with the heroine Inés. The heroine harbors a chaste love for Don Juan, is abandoned by him, and dies. Ana's response to the play amazes her real seducer, who observes her from the opera box he shares with other members of Vetusta's minor aristocracy. A jaded rake, Alvaro is incapable of being moved by sentimental pleasures or Zorrilla's romantic rhetoric. He realizes that the time is ripe for him to make a daring move. The seduction scene takes place offstage, so to speak, outside the narration, between chapters 28 and 29, so that when the action resumes a couple of months later, Ana and Alvaro, now lovers, are having Christmas day dinner at the Judge's house in a strange and at the same time familiar setting. Though outwardly normal, the dining-room scene unfolds on several levels: Víctor worries that the maid Petra may betray his innocent flirting with her; Ana is upset with Petra because of her arrogant behavior of late; Petra conceals her duplicitous allegiance to Fermín, who has decided to hire her as a maid if she helps him wreak vengeance on the Judge (for his unconcerned cuckoldry) and his wife (for her infidelity to both); and Alvaro realizes that his age precludes the sexual prowess necessary to keep the maid silent with his attentions while also satisfying Ana as a lover.

Fermín, ever the devious manipulator, has the maid set Víctor's alarm clock ahead on the morning he goes hunting so that the unfortunate old man sees Alvaro leave his wife's bedroom through a back balcony. Fermín's revenge is truly complete when Alvaro kills Víctor in the ensuing duel and subsequently leaves Vetusta for Madrid where an old conquest awaits him. Ana is left alone, destitute with a widow's pension, and shunned by the society she herself had once disdained, which now hypocritically condemns her—not for her illicit affair, but for not having avoided the scandal that killed her husband and forced one of the city's most prominent figures to depart. "Vetusta the noble was scandalized, horrified. . . . Mesía's bullet, for which the judge's wife was to blame, broke the peaceful tradition of silent, well-mannered prudent crime. Many illustrious ladies . . . were known to be deceiving, or to have deceived, or to be about to deceive their respective husbands—but without any shooting!" (*La Regenta*, p. 706). The social order of this regimented society has been transgressed and no one is willing to forgive, least of all the two principal bastions of convention—the aristocracy and the Church. The novel ends, as it had begun three years earlier, in the cathedral as Fermín tends to his liturgical tasks; but when his eyes now rest upon Ana—who comes in search of forgiveness—they are so full of hatred that she falls to the stone floor faint with the fear that he's about to strike her.

A play within the novel. Chapter 16, which centers on *Don Juan Tenorio*, falls exactly in the middle of the novel. It is also the first chapter of the second volume of the work. Both factors indicate its primary importance in *La Regenta*. In his novel of love and betrayal, the author introduces a second level of meaning by introducing Zorrilla's play of evil redeemed by love as counterpoint to his own plot. José Zorrilla, though still alive at the time Clarín wrote his novel, had premiered his play on March 28, 1844, 30 years before the publication of *La Regenta*. The play had become successful beyond anyone's dreams, certainly beyond Zorrilla's, who signed away his author's copyright for a meaningless sum and now watched as others became wealthy while he struggled near poverty. Though no one can be absolutely sure why *Don Juan Tenorio*'s popularity grew to such proportions, the fact remains that Spanish theatergoers expected to see its annual staging on November 1 as an almost pagan celebration of All Saint's Day and the Day of the Dead (November 2). Perhaps its many fans saw in the characters of the libertine Don Juan (tireless lover, profligate gambler, invincible swordsman, repentant sinner) and the angelic Doña Inés a tale of love triumphant, where one woman's sacrifice tips the balance in the eyes of a merciful God to save a sinner from the fires of hell—a salvation that had not befallen the same character in the Friar Tirso de Molina's (1571-1648) original theological drama of the Golden Age **The Trickster of Seville and the Stone Guest** (1630; also in *WLAIT 5: Spanish and Portuguese Literatures and Their Times*). There, the protagonist had been made to pay for his sins by eternal damnation. In Zorrilla's "drama religioso-fantástico," as he subtitled it, Don Juan is redeemed by the love he feels for Doña Inés and her pact with the Almighty that he be given one last chance to repent for his sins.

Clarín's heroine, Ana, not only sympathizes with Zorrilla's innocent female figure, but actually identifies with her and even sees herself playing the role of someone who can save the sinner she recognizes as Alvaro. Ana's tearful and mesmerized state in the course of the performance astonishes even the jaded Alvaro. The novel's use of this romantic text, then, a) better profiles the innocent character of Ana and the skeptic one of Alvaro, and b) serves as a narrative stratagem that introduces the most important segment of the novel, the willing seduction of Ana, who mistakes sex for love at the hands of a womanizing, empty-headed male archetype.

> The judge's wife was happy as she fell [into her adulterous affair]: she could feel the dizziness of her fall in her stomach. And if on some mornings she awoke not to happy thoughts but to doleful ones . . . she soon cured herself with the new system of naturalistic metaphysics which she had at last unwittingly created for herself so as to satisfy her invincible desire to carry all events of her life into the regions of abstraction and generality.
>
> (*La Regenta*, p. 642)

Literary context. The nineteenth-century Spanish novel developed over a 50-year period, beginning with Fernán Caballero's **The Seagull** (1849; also in *WLAIT 5: Spanish and Portuguese Literatures and Their Times*) and ending with Vicente Blasco Ibáñez's *Reeds and Mud* (1902). Spanish literature of the second half of the century is dominated by the narrative, whether the short story or the novel. Although Benito Pérez Galdós (1843-1920), Clarín's friend and fellow author, wrote 34 novels—many more than Clarín—and is considered by many to be the greatest writer of Spanish realism, Clarín's *La Regenta* is almost universally acknowledged as the masterpiece of realist fiction in Spain. It appeared just before Galdós's own renowned four-volume **Fortunata and Jacinta** (1886-87; also in *WLAIT 5: Spanish and Portuguese Literatures and Their Times*), and Emilia Pardo Bazán's (1852-1921) **The House of Ulloa** (1886; also in *WLAIT 5: Spanish and Portuguese Literatures and Their Times*). That Clarín's novel is ranked so highly can perhaps be attributed to its sense of a complete, closed world where every possibility is exhausted in terms of character portrayal, situational complexities, theme development, historical context, and richness of psychological insight. The ironic perspective of its narrative and the daring nature of its main argument—the love triangle involving a married woman and a priest—undoubtedly add to its enduring appeal, as does the cloud cast upon the dominant role of the Catholic Church in nineteenth-century Spain.

Reception. Since Clarín was known primarily as a writer of short stories, book reviews, and newspaper columns, the publication of his first novel came as a surprise for many people. Among other writers, the reaction was both cautious and largely reserved. Only Galdós had much to say publicly, and this was many years after the original publication of *La Requenta* when Clarín asked Galdós to write a prologue to the second edition of *La Regenta*. Since Galdós knew that his friend was dying, the words are kind and full of admiration for Clarín's talents as a writer, but they are also carefully chosen due to the strong impact that the work had had on the larger popular audience.

IN SELF-DEFENSE

In his reply to the Bishop of Oviedo's denunciation of his novel, Clarín justifies the writing:

I believe that my novel is moral, because it is a satire of bad habits without alluding to anyone directly . . . . for example, no one can see even the remotest likeness between my bishop don Fortunato Camoirán and the present day bishop of Oviedo. . . . As far as the insults that have been heaped on me in your pastoral letter, I will overlook and forgive them because they come from your Grace, besides they do not injure me since I cannot demand satisfaction from a bishop. . . . But I hope that, according to the letter and the spirit of the Gospel, that you will rectify the false affirmations which I have pointed out.

(Cabezas, pp. 144-46; trans. R. Landeira)

In the prologue Galdós writes: "I would say that Fermín de Pas is more than a cleric, he represents the ecclesiastical state in all its greatness as well as with its failings, the gold of an immaculate spirituality falling onto the impure mud mire of our origins" (*La Regenta,* p. xvii). The Catholic Church, on the other hand, was neither muted nor cautious in its reaction to *La Regenta*. Monsignor Martínez Vigil, Bishop of Oviedo, where Clarín lived and taught, and the historical referent of Vetusta, took to the pulpit to denounce the novel—as did other priests—and to advise good Catholics not to read it. Sexual appetites in priests (Fermín is not the only cleric who falls victim to lust), adultery among the aristocracy, and fights to the death between husbands and lovers are top-

ics too destabilizing for the Church to tolerate. Clarín thought the condemnation so stinging and unjust that he himself replied to his bishop in a long letter published by the local newspapers, which subsequently has been reprinted in critical studies many times over.

Clarín's concern about the attacks upon his novel and his religious beliefs were not unfounded, as can be seen by the veritable disappearance of *La Regenta* from bookstores and libraries for decades. No paperback popular version of the work existed until 1962, and not until one decade later was a reliable critical edition available. Censorship during the Franco dictatorship (1939-1975) made it difficult—in other words, unprofitable—for publishers to reissue the novel by itself, so that the only way to access the work was to purchase it as part of a very expensive leather-bound volume of selected works, poorly printed in an ancient double column format full of typographical errors. Thankfully, homage volumes commemorating its centenary, several new critical editions, and two recent translations into English have since been published in acknowledgement of *La Regenta*'s status as one of Spain's pre-eminent realist masterpieces.

—Ricardo Landeira

For More Information

Alas, Leopoldo. *La Regenta.* Trans. John Rutherford. Middlesex: Penguin, 1984.

Brent, Albert. *Leopoldo Alas and "La Regenta."* Columbia: University of Missouri Studies, 1951.

Cabezas, José Antonio. *Clarín: El Provinciano Universal.* Madrid: Espasa-Calpe, 1936.

Durand, Frank. "Structural Unity in Leopoldo Alas' *La Regenta.*" *Hispanic Review* 31 (1963): 324-35.

Eoff, Sherman H. "In Quest of a God of Love." In *The Modern Spanish Novel.* New York: New York University Press, 1961.

Nimetz, Michael. "Eros and Ecclesia in Clarín's Vetusta." *Modern Language Notes* 86 (1971): 242-53.

Rice, Miriam Wagner. "The Meaning of Metaphor in *La Regenta.*" *Revista de Estudios Hispánicos* 11 (1977): 141-51.

Sánchez, Roberto G. "The Presence of Theater and 'The Consciousness of Theater' in Clarín's *La Regenta.*" *Hispanic Review* 37 (1969): 491-509.

Savaiano, Eugene. *An Historical Justification of the Anticlericalism of Galdós and Alas.* Wichita, Kans.: Wichita State University, 1952.

Valis, Noel Maureen. *The Decadent Vision in Leopoldo Alas.* Baton Rouge and London: Louisiana University Press, 1981.

Weber, Francis. "Ideology and Religious parody in the Novels of Leopoldo Alas." *Bulletin of Hispanic Studies* 43 (1966): 197-208.

Requiem for a Spanish Peasant

by
Ramón Sender

Ramón Sender was born in 1901 to a country at a crossroads. Three years earlier, Spain had suffered a humiliating defeat to the United States in the Spanish-American War, and a debate raged among Spanish intellectuals and politicians about how their country could become a modern state, able to compete with the developed nations of the world. As Sender became a young man, the debate began to focus on a few key domestic issues, among them land reform and the relationship between the Catholic Church and the state. Sender's childhood was spent in small villages in the rural province of Aragon, yet these national issues were quite relevant to his own life. He witnessed the injustices suffered by Aragon's landless peasants, later expressing his concern for these injustices in his journalism and fiction. Sender's writing was also influenced by his strict Catholic upbringing, which contributed to his critical view of the Church. Ultimately, the debate about Spain's future would erupt into the bloody Spanish Civil War. The victory of Francisco Franco's Nationalist forces drove Sender out of Spain, but could not drive the painful images of the war from his mind. Sender settled in the United States, only to write a number of novels based on his experiences in Spain, including *Cronica del Alba* (1942; *Chronicle of Dawn,* 1944) and *El rey y la reina* (1949; *The King and the Queen,* 1948). They were followed in 1953 by *Requiem for a Spanish Peasant*, which drew on his experiences in the Civil War to tell the story of a national tragedy on a local level.

THE LITERARY WORK

A short novel set in Spain from about 1910 to 1937; published in Spanish (as *Mosén Millán*) in 1953; in English in 1960.

SYNOPSIS

A priest remembers the life and death of a young man killed at the beginning of the Spanish Civil War.

Events in History at the Time the Novel Takes Place

A defeated nation. Spain suffered a traumatic loss in 1898; the once prodigious empire had to forfeit Cuba, Puerto Rico, and the Philippines, its last remaining colonies, because of its defeat to the United States in the Spanish-American War. What had once been a powerful empire spanning multiple continents was now a small country unable to compete with the modern armed forces of the United States. To many Spaniards, including the group of intellectuals known as the "Generation of '98," this defeat was a powerful symbol of more deeply seated problems. The country did not just need to modernize its military forces; it was suffering from political and economic crises as well.

Spain's present form of government, a constitutional monarchy, was supposed to protect the country's interests by requiring the throne to share its power with an elected parliament;

Ramón Sender

however, this structure did little to safeguard the rights of Spain's average citizens. Elections to the parliament were engineered by the king and by corrupt local leaders known as *caciques*, who often used threats of violence or promises of government jobs to garner the votes they needed to ensure victory for their party. At the turn of the century, one contingent of politicians and intellectuals believed that Spain should eliminate the constitutional monarchy and replace it with a truly democratic government that would protect the rights of all Spanish citizens. Another contingent argued that Spain had no need of a parliament and ought instead to rely on a strong, authoritarian ruler who could push though the changes necessary to modernize the country without threatening the power of the current elite, nobles, and wealthy landowners.

Not only did Spain suffer from a corrupt, outdated government, but it also limped along under an economy mired in the past. Still largely an agricultural nation at the turn of the century, Spain found itself unable to generate the wealth necessary to keep pace with the more industrialized economies of its British, German, and French neighbors. In much of rural Spain, especially the southern regions of Andalusia and Extremadura, a huge income disparity existed between landowners and farm laborers. A small fraction of landowners monopolized possession

of rural Spain, operating huge estates with the sweat of a multitude of hired landless laborers. Often, these laborers were hired on a daily basis with no job security, so that on average they worked only 200 days a year and lived in squalor for the remaining months. Even in regions like Aragon, where a comparatively higher percentage of the population owned land, too many peasants competed for too little fertile soil. In England, France, and Germany, children of farmers could cope with such conditions by moving to earn a living as factory workers, but in Spain, few factories existed at the turn of the century, so patriarchs divided the family farm into smaller and smaller portions as their families grew, exacerbating poverty. Conditions spiraled so that by the dawn of the twentieth century in Spain, some sort of land reform became inevitable.

Anarchism, communism, and socialism in Spain. In 1868, an Italian disciple of Russian thinker Mikhail Bakunin visited Spain and introduced its peasants to his philosophy of anarchism. As its base, anarchism is the theory that all forms of government should be eliminated, but Bakunin's brand of anarchism was tinged with more religious sentiments. Bakunin spoke of a universal day of revolution and salvation, when landless workers would become the equals of their landlords, all land would be shared, and people would live harmoniously, without selfishness or the need for government. Bakunin's ideas appealed to many rural Spaniards and eventually spread to the cities; by 1910 a uniquely Spanish brand of anarchism had evolved, and the anarcho-syndicalist union (CNT) was established. The CNT sought to replace the government with trade unions and collectives, which would allow all Spaniards to exchange goods and services in a fair, equitable way. In the service of this utopian vision, however, many anarchists supported the use of violence to help instigate the revolution. In fact, a CNT insurrection in 1933 resulted in the group's being banned by the government for three years. The CNT remained popular, though. When the group emerged from underground in 1936, CNT membership approached one million.

With the success of the Russian Revolution in 1917, more Spaniards became interested in fighting for dramatic social change. Spanish peasants of the late 1800s had not greeted the philosophy of Karl Marx, which forecasted a revolution sparked by the industrial working classes, with much enthusiasm. However, when Spaniards saw that such ideas could be applied to Russia, an essentially agricultural nation like their own, Spain's communist and socialist parties, both based on Marxism, took on new life. The development of industry in the provinces of Asturias, Catalonia, and the Basque Country in the early 1900s contributed to the growth of these parties, which, like the anarchists, supported the unionization of factories. By the mid-1930s, the Partido Comunista Español (Spanish Communist Party) counted about 30,000 members, and the more moderate Socialist Party, the Union General de Trabajadores, counted over one million. Sender himself showed an interest in communism, socialism, and anarchism during his young adulthood in Spain. After a trip to Moscow from late 1933 to early 1934, he wrote articles for the CNT newspaper *Workers' Solidarity*, and in the spring of 1936, in a Marxist literary review, he urged Spanish novelists to use their writing to improve the lot of the working class.

From dictatorship to republic. Ultimately both of the main voices in the debate over Spain's political structure would see their ideas realized within the first few decades of the twentieth century. Not only would Spain experiment with authoritarian rule, but it would also become a democratic republic. From 1918-21, a series of anarchist revolts among the landless peasants of the south and violent clashes in Barcelona between factory owners and laid-off workers had brought Spain's political and economic crises to a peak. When Spanish general Miguel Primo de Rivera staged a coup in 1923, many Spaniards, including King Alfonso XIII, welcomed him as dictator, suspecting that one powerful fist could lead Spain out of its miasma more effectively than dozens of corrupt, squabbling parliamentarians. Primo de Rivera, however, found it difficult to please all of his initial supporters. Some expected him to protect the interests of the Catholic Church and wealthy landowners and to squelch reform, while others hoped he would be an "iron surgeon," a leader who could singlehandedly modernize Spanish industry and infrastructure, reform the military and education systems, and improve the lives of rural and urban laborers so that all Spaniards lived in harmony (Joaquín Costa in Ribeiro de Meneses, p. 12). In his attempts to live up to both of these contradictory sets of expectations, Spain's new dictator turned many of his supporters against him, including King Alfonso. Soon Alfonso would come to regret Primo's fall, however. The dictator's replacement by another general, Dámaso Berenguer, did little to improve the public perception that a dic-

tatorship-monarchy was not solving Spain's problems. In 1931, after witnessing the broad national support for a republican government in municipal elections (an event mirrored in *Requiem for a Spanish Peasant* by Paco's election), the king fled the country. The monarchy and the dictatorship were no more; Spain was now a republic.

In its first incarnation, the new Republic had a leftist bent. Socialists and leftist Republicans controlled the parliament, with the leftist Republican Manuel Azaña serving as prime minister from 1931-33. Spain's new government wasted no time in establishing its ground rules. Within a few months, the country's leaders had drafted a new constitution that proclaimed a true

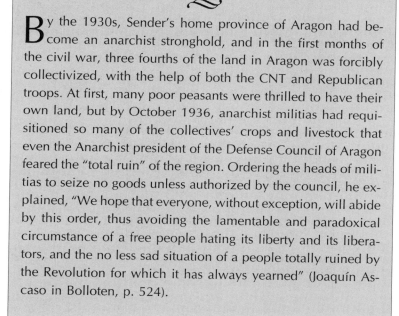

UTOPIAN IDEALS BREAK DOWN: ANARCHISM IN ARAGON

By the 1930s, Sender's home province of Aragon had become an anarchist stronghold, and in the first months of the civil war, three fourths of the land in Aragon was forcibly collectivized, with the help of both the CNT and Republican troops. At first, many poor peasants were thrilled to have their own land, but by October 1936, anarchist militias had requisitioned so many of the collectives' crops and livestock that even the Anarchist president of the Defense Council of Aragon feared the "total ruin" of the region. Ordering the heads of militias to seize no goods unless authorized by the council, he explained, "We hope that everyone, without exception, will abide by this order, thus avoiding the lamentable and paradoxical circumstance of a free people hating its liberty and its liberators, and the no less sad situation of a people totally ruined by the Revolution for which it has always yearned" (Joaquín Ascaso in Bolloten, p. 524).

democracy and put an end to corrupt *cacique* influence. It also declared "Spain is a republic of workers of all classes," and instituted widespread reforms to address the needs of the working class (Browne, p. 8). Agrarian reforms were the first, and according to some historians, the most revolutionary. Day laborers were protected with a mandated eight-hour workday and a law that landowners must hire farmhands within their own municipalities, a precautionary measure to avoid driving down wages. The Republic also encouraged collective bargaining among worker unions and employers, establishing an arbitration board to oversee the process. Finally, to fight

Republican soldiers reading from books provided by the Cultural Militias during the Spanish Civil War. A member of the Alliance of Intellectuals for the Defense of Democracy, Ramón Sender joined the Republican militia and championed intellectual and cultural growth during the war.

unemployment, the new government required that all arable land be cultivated, and to protect against eviction, it demanded that rents for farmland be frozen. These were only a few of the numerous social and economic reforms instituted in the first few years of the new Republic.

By 1934, though, the coalition that had been so effective at pushing through such sweeping reforms crumbled. Disagreements about the pace and scope of reform led to divisions within the left and opened the door for the right to take over the parliament until 1935, reversing many of the left's reforms. The shortcomings of both the left's and the right's rule were described in the following editorial:

From the June 6, 1936, Edition of the Moderate Republican Newspaper *El Sol*

Since the advent of the Republic, we have been oscillating dangerously between two extremes, particularly in the countryside. During the first biennium [1931-1933] agriculture was burdened with a ridiculous working day, and the wave of idleness and indiscipline through which it passed ended by ruining it. The farm laborers received high wages and worked as little as possible. . . . During the second biennium [1933-35] we fell into the other extreme. Within a few months wages declined sharply from ten and twelve pesetas a day to four, three,

and even two. Property took revenge on labor, and did not realize that it was piling up fuel for the social bonfire of the near future.

(Bolloten, p. 4)

Although the February 1936 elections returned Manuel Azaña to leadership, this time with a coalition of moderate republicans, socialists, and communists known as the Popular Front, the "social bonfire" had already been sparked. Frustrated by delayed land reforms and urged on by communist newspapers, landless peasants seized the estates of wealthy landowners for themselves. In the cities, strikes of angry workers demanding higher wages and shorter hours paralyzed the economy. Throughout the Republic political divisions led to multiple murders, such as those committed by the men from Madrid in *Requiem for a Spanish Peasant*. Meanwhile, many on the right, especially those in the military, became increasingly convinced that their country's crisis could not be solved without abolishing the Republic.

The changing relationship between Church and state. Part of the impetus for abolishing the Republic came from its transformation of Spain into a secular state. For centuries, Spain had been ruled by Catholic monarchs with close ties to the Church. Through these close ties, the Church acquired huge amounts of land, substantial political power, and financial backing. In the nineteenth century, however, liberal reformers began to place limits on the property and power of the Church. The government claimed and sold most of the Church's lands, but made them available only to those who could afford them, thus weakening even more the position of workers and strengthening that of the upper- and middle-class landowners. Instead of the Church, the king gained the right to appoint bishops and other clergy not affiliated with a specific religious order. Yet until 1931 Spain was still a Catholic state. All schools, from primary to university level, followed Catholic doctrine, and many were run by members of the clergy. Non-Catholic religious practices were allowed, but only in private. With the new Republican government, all of this changed. The Constitution abolished state financial support of the Church and established a secular education system. Freedom of religion was proclaimed, and divorce, considered a sin by the Catholic Church, was finally legalized.

While many Spaniards applauded such changes, they alienated a large number of middle-class Catholics who otherwise would have supported the Republic's reforms. To add insult to injury, when a small group of anticlerical Spaniards destroyed religious images in some 100 Church buildings during May of 1931, the Republican government ordered the police force not to intervene. Hard-line Catholics were outraged, and it did not take long for them to respond. Within a year of the Republic's founding, a coalition known as the Confederación Española de Derechas Autonomas (Spanish Confederation of Autonomous Right-wing Groups), or CEDA, was established to fight for conservative issues within the structure of the Republic. Others were convinced that only a return to the monarchy or another form of absolute rule could restore the power of the Church and reverse the moral decay they believed had already begun in their country. Some resentful Catholics had begun to join forces with army officers angered by the Republic's military reforms. One such officer, José Sanjurjo, had been demoted by Azaña from his position as head of the Civil Guard. With the support of about 5 percent of the army, he staged a coup in 1932; though it was unsuccessful, it served as a bitter omen of what lay in store for Spain within four years.

Civil war breaks out. In July of 1936, amidst the chaos of strikes, land seizures, and political assassinations, a military uprising against the Re-

public began, and with it, the Spanish Civil War. The rebellious military officials, who waged war in the name of "Nationalism," were joined by a coalition of anti-Republican forces—monarchists, fascists, and former CEDA members—who envisioned themselves rescuing Spain from the influence of godless foreign ideas like Marxism and restoring order and tradition to their troubled country. With extensive foreign aid from Portugal, Germany, and Italy, the Nationalists gradually took over the country from the Republicans, whose sole source of consistent foreign support was the Soviet Union. By spring of 1939, the war was over, and General Francisco Franco, leader of the victorious Nationalists, became the dictator of Spain.

CIVIL WAR BALLADS

In the eyes of many Spaniards, the Republicans came to represent progress and reform, but this did not mean that they rejected all of their country's traditions. In fact, during the Spanish Civil War, the Republican Army relied on one very old tradition, ballad singing. A ballad, known in Spain as a *romance*, is a song passed from generation to generation that tells a story—usually a tragic human drama that often changes with the times. At the peak of their popularity in Spain, the late 1400s to the late 1600s, ballads were as popular among royalty as peasantry. By the start of the Spanish Civil War, however, they had become a symbol of working-class solidarity, written and sung to inspire Republican troops and their supporters. Ballads praising the valiant fighting of Republican peasants were broadcast over Republican-controlled Radio Madrid, printed on flyers dropped out of airplanes, and blasted from loudspeakers across battlefields to the Nationalist forces on the other side. Franco's Nationalists apparently made no attempts to coopt the ballad for their own propaganda purposes. According to one literary historian, among Franco's supporters, "the romance was looked down upon as a lesser verse form suitable for ignorant people" (Hart in Smith, p. x).

The Novel in Focus

Plot summary. *Requiem for a Spanish Peasant* begins in 1937, a year after the start of the Spanish Civil War, in a rural Aragonese village near the Catalonian border. Mosén Millán, a priest, is waiting in his church sacristy for people to arrive for a requiem mass. The description in the first paragraph of the novel creates a vivid picture of the priest's still, fragile world of tradition and ritual:

> The parish priest, clad in the chasuble of Requiem services, sat in an armchair, head bowed, waiting. An odor of incense hovered in the sacristy. In a corner was a sheaf of live branches left over from Palm Sunday, its leaves so dry that they looked metallic. Whenever Mosén Millán passed nearby, he avoided brushing against them for they were ready to part from their stems and fall to the floor.
>
> (Sender, *Requiem for a Spanish Peasant,* p. 3)

As he bides his time silently, head bowed, his acolyte comes and goes, reporting that no one has entered the church yet. The acolyte then begins singing a ballad composed by the people of the town:

> There goes Paco del Molino
> Crying with a mournful sound;
> They've given him his sentence now,
> And marched him to the burial ground.
>
> (*Requiem,* p. 5)

Through this verse of the ballad (which the acolyte continues to sing throughout the novel), we learn that the mass is being held for Paco del Molino, a man the young acolyte remembers as a local hero. As Mosén Millán continues to wait, he thinks back to his first memory of Paco, the day he baptized the dead hero. This memory sparks a series of related flashbacks that tell the story of Paco's life.

Paco is born to a coarse, practical peasant with little interest in religion. He expects nothing more of Paco than that the boy "learn to pull up his breeches and make a good overseer for the farm hands," but Mosén Millán seeks a more religious future for Paco (*Requiem,* p. 19). The priest considers himself Paco's spiritual father, and thinking he might be able to win his family over to the Church, he befriends the boy, who comes to serve as the priest's acolyte. One day, Paco accompanies Mosén Millán to a cave near the village, where a dying man waits for the priest to perform last rites. Overwhelmed by the squalid conditions in which he finds the dying man, a farm laborer, and his wife, Paco asks the priest why no one from the village visits the couple or tries to help them. Mosén Millán compliments him on his compassion but warns him not to get involved: "The best thing he could do was to go straight home. When God permitted poverty and affliction, he said, it was for some purpose" (*Requiem,* p. 41).

Paco gradually drifts away from the priest in the years following this event, and when he reaches young adulthood, his father begins to share with him his concerns about the family's livelihood. Paco learns that his family rents their pasture land from an old duke who has never seen the village and who also collects rent from the farmers of five nearby villages. Protesting to his father that this system is unjust, Paco is told to ask Mosén Millán about it, since he is a friend of the Duke's administrator, Don Valeriano. Paco complies, telling the priest that something should be done to help the poor people in the village who live in wretchedness, but the priest's reply is as peremptory as his earlier response: "What wretchedness? . . . There's more misery in other places than there is here" (*Requiem,* p. 47).

As Paco continues to struggle with the injustice he has grown aware of, strange events begin to happen in the town. One night, the local police, enforcing a ban on evening serenades, arrest Paco and his friends in the midst of their songs, but Paco seizes their guns before they can bring him to jail. Although Paco returns the guns to the mayor the following day, this act earns him a reputation as a daredevil and rebel. Soon afterward, the village elects a group of young, nonreligious members to the municipal council. The group, which includes Paco, plans to seize the Duke's land. Then word reaches the village that the king of Spain has fled the country, and a new countrywide government, a Republic, is elected. Soon, with the help of an order from the Republic, Paco has seized the Duke's land for the village and begins to devise a plan to help the cave dwellers. But all at once Paco's progress is halted. The village police are called away and a group of rich young toughs from Madrid arrive, murdering councilmen and other villagers under cover of darkness. To protect his own life, Paco hides out in an abandoned house outside the village. Meanwhile the young toughs have seized control of the village and named Don Valeriano mayor; the Duke's lands have been returned to the Duke. Mosén Millán learns of Paco's whereabouts, and under pressure from the band of murderers, reveals his location to them, on the condition that they let him live. Of course, when they find Paco, they shoot him, but not until Mosén Millán has heard his final confession and administered his last rites.

Interspersed between the events in Paco's tragic story are descriptions of the priest's waiting to begin the requiem mass. As he waits, puzzled by the absence of any villagers in the church, the three wealthiest men of the village, including Don Valeriano, arrive and offer to pay for the mass; Mosén Millán refuses their money, reflecting bitterly to himself that they contributed to Paco's death. Paco's mule, which has been roaming freely through the village since his master's death, then bursts into the church mysteriously and gallops around it until he is coaxed out by the three men and the acolyte. Finally, convinced that no one else will arrive and troubled by his own guilty memories, Mosén Millán begins the requiem mass.

Trapped in the past. Ramon Sender wrote *Requiem for a Spanish Peasant* more than 15 years after the fictional action in the novel concludes, but the vividness of descriptions, such as that of the priest waiting in the first paragraph, sometimes makes it seem as if it were written in a time capsule. In one sense, it was, for Sender's access to Spain ended when he fled the country near the end of the war. The memories of Spain that he carried with him, from his childhood in Aragon to his days as a Republican soldier, come to an abrupt halt at the end of 1938. As an exile, Sender's vision of Spain was trapped in history, so it seems fitting that one of the central issues in the novel is Mosén Millán's inability to move beyond the past.

Like many of the Spaniards who rejected the religious and economic reforms of the Republic, Mosén Millán is a character heavily invested in the traditions of the past. As a priest, he is automatically entitled to a modicum of respect from his parishioners, as well as the harvest offerings that even Paco's nonreligious father donates to the Church. More crucially, he benefits from his close association with Don Valeriano, the duke's administrator—a symbol of the Catholic Church's traditional affiliation with the conservative elite. When the rich terrorists from Madrid make their rounds, Mosén Millán knows that both his status as a priest and his friendship with Don Valeriano will protect him from harm. Perhaps he is attached to tradition partly because of the security it offers.

Sender demonstrates the limits of such an attachment throughout the novel, however. When the king flees Spain and the villagers look to Mosén Millán for guidance during the transition, he simply ignores the king's departure, not even mentioning it in his homily. When the men from Madrid begin their reign of terror in the village, he is confused and disturbed, but is only able to articulate a concern about the unholy way in which his parishioners are being murdered. He complains to Don Valeriano that they were killed "without being given time for confession" (*Requiem*, p. 95).

Through the priest's actions in these scenes, the novel shows his passivity and inability to face the truth of his circumstances. Furthermore, it reinforces this critique in a more subtle way, through its very structure. There are two stories within *Requiem for a Spanish Peasant*. The novel begins with the story of Mosén Millán's waiting to perform the requiem mass, a story that ends virtually where it begins. In the 20 to 30 minutes that transpire during this story, the priest is seated almost the entire time and speaks very little, usually to ask his acolyte the same question: "Has anyone arrived for the mass?" Paco's story, which comprises the core of the novel, is a fast-paced drama full of action and emotion that spans about 25 years. By establishing such a dramatic contrast in pace and movement between the two stories, Sender injects Paco with life while draining the life out of Mosén Millán. The fact that Paco has been immortalized in a ballad that will likely be sung for generations, while Mosén Millán cannot find one honest parishioner to attend his requiem mass is Sender's final blow to the priest. In the minds of the villagers, Paco is not dead; the priest's religious ritual—an empty tradition of the past—is.

Sources and literary context. *Requiem for a Spanish Peasant* is clearly a novel that grew out of Sender's own experiences in Spain. It is set in an Aragonese village, much like the one in which Sender spent his childhood. Though Sender's father was not a farmer, like Paco's father, Sender's did work for a short time as a land administrator and may have served as a model for the character of Don Valeriano. Reputed to be a cold, distant man and a strict Catholic, Sender's father may also have inspired the critical treatment of Mosén Millán. Two important similarities exist between the plot of the novel and Sender's own life. As a young boy, Sender once accompanied a priest on his visit to a dying man in a cave dwelling, and he was profoundly shaken by the misery in which the cave dwellers lived; he later attributed the birth of his own social conscience to this event. Secondly, Sender's wife and brother were executed by Nationalist forces for sympathizing with the Republicans; their executions took place in October 1936, around the same time that Paco is killed in the novel. Perhaps *Requiem for a Spanish Peasant* was Sender's own literary requiem for these lost loved ones.

Like Sender's *Requiem*, many of the numerous novels set during the Spanish Civil War contain significant autobiographical threads. Some Spanish authors who chose to make their art resemble life so closely were part of a movement for "socially committed" literature. They may have been influenced by the 1905 call of Russian Marxist leader Vladimir Lenin for literature that clearly supported the cause of the working classes. Others were reacting against *The Dehumanization of Art*, a key 1925 work of aesthetic criticism by the Spanish intellectual José Ortega y Gasset. In this work, Ortega claims that art and literature should not be concerned with social reality—that quality art and literature are self-contained and have no transcendent meaning. In the 1930s, Sender clearly believed that he should be writing committed, not "dehumanized," literature. In a 1936 essay published just three months before the war broke out, he ridicules previous writers who

---

SOME SPANISH CIVIL WAR NOVELS

From the Republican Perspective
- *Campo cerrado*, by Max Aub (1943; Closed Camp)
- *La forja de un rebelde*, by Arturo Barea (1944; *The Clash* or *The Forging of a Rebel*, 1946)

From the Nationalist Perspective
- *Camisa azul*, by Felipe Ximénez de Sandoval (1939; Blue Shirt)
- *La fiel Infantería*, by Rafael García Serrano (1943; The Loyal Infantry)

---

focus on "trivialities of form" and fail to embrace the "life force" of the working class (Sender in Thomas, p. 95; trans. A. Weisz). It is unclear whether Sender continued to hold such strong views when he wrote *Requiem for a Spanish Peasant*. In any case, his creative use of narrative structure shows that innovative form and social realism are not mutually exclusive.

Events in History at the Time the Novel Was Written

Republican exodus. With the Nationalist victory in the Spanish Civil War came a mass exodus of Republican sympathizers from Spain. Between 400,000 and one million Spaniards left, many writers among them, the majority of them settling in France or in the Spanish-speaking coun-

tries of the Americas. Most left out of a well-founded fear that they would be imprisoned or even executed for their Republican sympathies. Others who had not been politically active knew that their freedom of expression would be stifled by Franco's harsh censorship laws. In Paris, Toulouse, Buenos Aires, and Mexico City, Spanish exiles founded literary and political journals to keep some sense of national consciousness alive. These writers sought to come to terms with the new challenges and opportunities of exile without succumbing to the despair of being *transterrados*, or "transplanted ones." In his essay "For Whom Do We Write?" the exiled novelist Francisco Ayala concludes that because exiled Spanish writers must adjust to writing for a new, broader audience, they should enlarge their scope as writers, moving beyond texts that focus on Spain's present situation and destiny. However, his mixed feelings about the success of such a response are evident in the conclusion to his essay: "For whom do we write? For everyone and for no one" (Ayala in Ugarte, p. 64). While some exiled writers were able to immerse themselves and their pens in the new cultures they joined, many were either unable or unwilling to leave the tragic past of the Spanish Civil War behind them. During the 25 years following the end of the war, at least 30 novels dealing with the war were published by Spanish writers using publishing houses in Mexico, Venezuela, and Argentina. Of course, none of these novels were available to readers in Franco's Spain. In 1966, however, with the relaxation of Spanish censorship laws, exile literature began to flood the country, much of it to wide acclaim.

Reception. Ramon Sender may have shared the fear of many exiled Spanish writers that they would lose their readership when they left home, but many of his works, including *Chronicle at Dawn* and *The Affable Hangman*, received international critical acclaim. However, the 1953 publication of *Mosén Millán*, the original title of *Requiem for a Spanish Peasant*, was slow to attract the attention of reviewers. It was not until the early 1960s, after the publication of the English translation, that reviews of Sender's short novel began to appear in international journals. Gradually American academics began to take notice of *Requiem*; One scholar of Spanish literature called it "a superbly written short novel" and praised its "straightforward" style and its "psychological realism" (King, p. 80). A teacher argued for its use in high school Spanish classes in the United States, claiming that it painted an excellent picture of Spanish civilization. The novel continued to grow in popularity and is now one of the most commonly studied novels of the Spanish Civil War, both in the United States and in Spain. At a recent conference on Sender in Aragon, the novel was praised for its effectiveness at bringing history to life for local students; though Sender himself would only return to Spain briefly before his death in 1982, it seems that his *Requiem for a Spanish Peasant* has returned to stay.

—Allison Weisz

For More Information

Bolloten, Burnett. *The Spanish Civil War: Revolution and Counterrevolution.* Chapel Hill: The University of North Carolina Press, 1991.

Browne, Harry. *Spain's Civil War.* 2d ed. London: Longman, 1996.

Compitello, Malcolm Alan. "*Requiem por un campesino español* and the Problematics of Exile." In *Homenaje a Ramon J. Sender.* Ed. Mary S. Vasquez. Newark, Delaware: Juan de la Cuesta, 1987.

Harding, Susan Friend. *Remaking Ibieca: Rural Life in Aragon under Franco.* Chapel Hill: University of North Carolina Press, 1984.

Jones, Margaret E. W. *The Contemporary Spanish Novel, 1939-1975.* Boston: Twayne, 1985.

Jordan, *Writing and Politics in Franco's Spain.* London: Routledge, 1990.

King, Charles L. *Ramon J. Sender.* New York: Twayne, 1974.

McDermott, Patricia. "*Requiem por un campesino español:* summa narrativa de Ramon J. Sender." In *El Lugar de Sender: Actas del I Congreso sobre Ramon J. Sender.* Ed. Juan Carlos Ara Torralba and Fermin Gil Encabo. Huesca: Instituto de Estudios Altoaragoneses and Zaragoza: Institucion Fernando el Catolico, 1997.

Ribeiro de Meneses, Filipe. *Franco and the Spanish Civil War.* London: Routledge, 2001.

Sanchez, Jose M. *The Spanish Civil War as Religious Tragedy.* Notre Dame, Indiana: University of Notre Dame Press, 1987.

Sender, Ramon. *Requiem for a Spanish Peasant.* Trans. Elinor Randall. New York: Las Americas, 1960.

Smith, Colin, ed. *Spanish Ballads.* Bristol: Bristol Classical Press, 1996.

Thomas, Gareth. *The Novel of the Spanish Civil War (1936-1975).* Cambridge: Cambridge University Press, 1990.

Ugarte, Michael. *Shifting Ground: Spanish Civil War Exile Literature.* Durham, N.C.: Duke University Press, 1989.

The Sea Gull

by

Fernán Caballero

Cecilia Böhl von Faber, known by her pen name Fernán Caballero, was born in 1796 in Morges, Vaud, Switzerland, to intellectual parents. Her father, Johann Nikolaus Böhl von Faber, was a German scholar and naturalized Spanish citizen whose writings introduced the theories of German Romanticism into Spain. Of Spanish and Irish heritage, her mother presided over literary gatherings. Caballero spent her early childhood in Cádiz, Spain, then moved to Germany, where for seven years she attended a French school. Upon her return to Cádiz at age 16, she beheld her country through the curious eyes of a foreigner, keenly noting Spanish habits, diversions, and speech patterns, observations that would stand her in good stead when she sat down to portray Spanish character types and customs, a hallmark of her writings. Widowed twice while still young, Caballero found herself in financial difficulty during her third marriage, a situation that compelled her to publish her many literary works. These include the novels *Clemencia* (1852) and *La familia de Alvareda* (1856) as well as collections of Andalucian folklore. Most notable today is *The Sea Gull,* which signaled the reawakening of the novel, a genre that had virtually been dormant in Spain since the Golden Age. Regarded as didactic, *The Sea Gull* places its tradition-oriented characters in a positive light and ridicules those who prefer liberal French ideas, at a time when Spanish society found itself at a crossroads between two divergent trends in its evolution.

THE LITERARY WORK

A novel set from 1836 to 1848 in Spain; written in French; serialized in Spanish in the Madrid newspaper *El Heraldo* in 1849; published in Spanish (as *La Gaviota*) in 1856, in English in 1867.

SYNOPSIS

In a Spain divided between conflicting currents of traditionalism and modernization, the daughter of a Spanish fisherman marries a German doctor and becomes an opera star, only to lose her voice after falling in love with a bullfighter.

Events in History at the Time of the Novel

A nation on the margins. In the early nineteenth century, Spain lagged behind various other European countries in terms of political, social, and economic progress. The military strength of countries such as France and Britain led to an expansion of their imperial power, as they established new colonies overseas. In contrast, Spain's international prestige suffered in the first part of the nineteenth century. Its military was in decline, and from 1808 to the 1830s, Spain lost most of its immense empire in the Americas. Its remaining colonial possessions were Cuba, Puerto Rico, and the Philippines. Cuba in particular assumed an integral role in the Spanish

Cecilia Böhl von Faber

economy, for the colony not only delivered tax revenues to the impoverished nation, but also provided a market for goods such as Castilian grain and flour. A pressing international problem for Spain in the 1840s was maintaining possession of Cuba, which the United States coveted both for the island's trade potential and for its strategic geographical location in the Caribbean. Spain kept a protective eye on Cuba. Aside from its economic value, the colony played a psychological role in that it was viewed as one of the last vestiges of Spain's past imperial glory.

Meanwhile, nearby France strongly influenced Spanish taste in fashion, literature, and music in the early-to-mid nineteenth century. In fact, French styles became highly popular in urban Spain. At one point *The Sea Gull* features a character, considered ridiculous by the narrator, who goes to great lengths to follow French fashion.

During the 1830s and ´40s, the time of *The Sea Gull*, the industrial revolution had not yet permeated Spain. Its economy remained almost exclusively agrarian. When French and British travelers—accustomed to factories and capitalist production in their countries—saw Spain's crumbling inns and medieval ruins, they felt as if they had returned to a past era. Noting the lack of even a railroad system, the visitors regarded Spain as tremendously backward. Many French regarded Spain as a land in transition between

Europe and Africa, a marginal space on the fringes of modern Europe. In fact, the French author Stendhal (Henri Beyle) went so far as to identify Spain with Africa: "It seems that I am going to go to Spain, that is to say, to Africa" (Stendhal in Hoffmann; trans. M. Tanenbaum, p. 81). This image the French had of Spain is reflected by a conversation in *The Sea Gull*; one of the aristocrats (who favors modernization in Spain) remarks, "How right the French are when they say Africa begins beyond the Pyrenees," to which another character replies, "They don't say it since they [now] occupy a part of the [African] coast. . . . It would be too flattering to us" to associate Spain with French holdings (Caballero, *The Sea Gull,* p. 240).

The Romantic country *par excellence*. The perceived backwardness of Spain was precisely the quality that most attracted the French Romantics. These intellectuals abhorred the greed and the conformity associated with the rise of the *bourgeoisie* (middle class) in their own country during the first part of the nineteenth century and nostalgically yearned for an age when courage and dignity reigned. In Spain, French Romantics such as Théophile Gautier and Prosper Mérimée admired marginal characters such as the Spanish gypsy, whose lifestyle they viewed as a courageous rejection of the mediocrity of society. Furthermore, the French Romantics, alienated from their own industrial cities, valued the bonds between people in agrarian Spain, mourning the disappearance of these ties in France's new capitalist system. There seemed to be less difference between social classes in Spain; the country came to represent a bygone age of harmony and heroism for which the French Romantics longed.

The pack animals and carts, broken-down roads, and traces of the ancient Moorish civilization that the French found in Spain offered fresh sources of inspiration for their writing, as did the castanets, folk dances, and characteristic clothing. An added attraction was the "ideal" Spanish woman, who captivated them with her dark hair, sensuality, and mystery. In fact, the country as a whole struck the French as exotic, a space that was alluring but also dangerous. Rumor had it that bandits roamed the countryside, particularly in the hot and distant South, which was regarded as the country's most exotic region, an area in which all of its characteristic elements could be found in abundance.

The Sea Gull is replete with the very elements that the Romantics found picturesque in Spain.

Guitar music, decaying edifices, and bullfights imbue the novel, which takes place mostly in the southernmost region of the nation, Andalusia. A preconception of the Spanish people as cruel is also a recurrent theme: the German doctor, for instance, is so sickened by a bullfight that he leaves the arena, wondering how anyone could enjoy the slaughter of innocent animals.

Absolutism and liberalism. In reality, Spain was not at all standing still at the time. Spain's King, Fernando VII (1784-1833), met with fierce opposition from liberals during his reign. Events outside and inside of Spain challenged the old system of political and economic oppression: the pivotal French Revolution of 1789; the Industrial Revolution in Britain; the Napoleonic invasion of Spain in 1808, when the emperor's brother Joseph Bonaparte replaced Fernando as king for five years and attempted to introduce economic reforms; and the Constitution of 1812, a blueprint for civil liberties composed by Spanish liberals but stifled for the time being with the return of Fernando in 1814. Influenced by these events, Spain's mercantile and commercial classes pressed their king for greater economic and political freedoms and were supported in their drive by the intellectuals, who wanted Spain to keep pace with the rest of Europe. But the despotic king opposed liberalization, as did Spain's two other bastions of wealth and power—the nobility and the Catholic Church. Tensions mounted. Fernando was forced to capitulate to the Spanish liberals in 1820, but he managed to reclaim absolute authority in 1823. As earlier, when he had returned to the throne in 1814, Fernando squashed his liberal foes, clamping down on innovative ideas and banning all foreign literature associated with liberalism. Thousands of liberals fled Spain in fear of persecution.

By the late 1820s, insurgence in the Latin American colonies had led to tremendous debt in Spain. Faced with the necessity of raising funds, Fernando decided to reach out to the conservative liberals, that is, to the wealthy commoners who desired a "bloodless, controlled transition to a liberal regime" (Smith, p. 6). Fernando's gestures towards compromise with the conservative liberals laid the foundation for the development of a more liberal society. Over the next decade the guilds were forced to relinquish their control of the different trades, which paved the way for greater openness in manufacturing and in selling goods. Also, the Church's holdings were assailed. In order to fill the country's coffers, certain municipal and Church lands were seized and sold on the open market, which made it possible for people who did not belong to the aristocracy to own land. Disentailment (*desamortización*), or the transformation of these lands into private property, began in 1836, after Fernando's death. In general, the nobility supported such liberal compromises, since they minimized the threat to its power. The compromises allowed the nobles to keep their lands and to maintain their political and social influence. Part of the so-called liberal revolution of the 1830s was a new constitution in 1837, which gave some power to Spain's parliament but left most of it with the reigning monarch.

THE PSEUDONYM OF CECILIA BÖHL VON FABER

Writing in the nineteenth century was typically regarded as an activity suitable solely for men, as it was suspected that literary involvement—even reading—could corrupt the moral principles of women. Perhaps influenced by her father, who did not endorse women's intellectual pursuits, Cecilia Böhl von Faber demonstrated a reluctance to flaunt this cultural taboo: although she penned her earliest work during her teenage marriage, she did not submit her manuscripts for publication (with the exception of a work published in Germany and a short story published in Spain under her initials "C. B."). It was only in the late 1840s, when her financial resources were dwindling (perhaps due to the carelessness of her third husband) that she decided to publish *The Sea Gull*, which had been composed several years earlier. Symptomatic of her ambivalence over whether a woman should have a literary career, Cecilia selected a pseudonym that was emphatically male: *caballero* means "gentleman." Moreover, the full name evokes traditional Spain, adding to the patriotic tone of the work. *Fernán* recalls epics and monarchs; *caballero* also means "knight." The pseudonym, then, allowed the writer to camouflage both her gender and her German heritage.

The First Carlist War (1833-40). In 1830 Fernando selected his newborn daughter Isabel (1830-1904) to be his successor, and his wife María Cristina of Naples to be regent until Isabel came of age. Fernando's absolutist brother, Carlos María Isidor de Borbón (1788-1855), had other ideas, though. Desiring the crown for himself, he argued that the Salic Law, imposed by the French in 1713, forbade passing the crown to a female. Fernando tried to repeal this law, decreeing that the manner of succession revert to Spanish custom, which allowed a woman as well as a man to ascend to the throne. The clergy, infuriated by Fernando's compromise with the liberals, sided with Carlos, supporting his claim to the crown.

When Fernando died in 1833, civil war broke out over the question of the royal succession. Supporting Isabel were the liberals, who favored modernization and a less powerful Catholic Church. Opposing her were Carlos's advocates—the "Carlists"—the Church, the artisans, and the peasants. The liberal reforms posed a threat to these groups. The artisans faced competition on account of the weakening of the guilds. Disentailment jeopardized the peasants' livelihood, depriving them of access to common lands, where they traditionally grazed their animals and grew food for themselves.

A bloody struggle ensued between liberal and anti-modern forces. Called the First Carlist War, it spread through much of northern Spain, lasting from 1833 to 1840. In retaliation for the violence initiated by the Carlists, the liberals not only seized ecclesiastic lands, but also dismantled most male religious orders. *The Sea Gull* dramatizes this upheaval through the recurring image of a disintegrating monastery that no longer has any religious function.

Ultimately the Carlists conceded defeat through the Vergara Pact of 1839, which signaled the imminent end of the war. But the Carlist movement did not disappear: opposition to economic modernization and cultural change in Spain would continue until the 1930s, most notably in the countryside, where some of the poorest members of society protested the results of the liberal revolution. Thus, the political struggle over whether to modernize persisted through the time of *The Sea Gull* and beyond—for roughly another hundred years. This struggle in fact initiates events *in The Sea Gull,* since the novel's male protagonist travels to Spain to serve as a doctor for the liberals in the Carlist War.

The countryside and the city. In the first part of the nineteenth century, the typical village in Spain had its own government, a council composed of male inhabitants of the village, which made and interpreted laws based on local customs. It was obligatory, for example, to give shelter to needy transients; it was also mandatory to attend funerals. Since their laws grew out of local traditions, villagers found the centralization and homogeneity propounded by the liberals to be antithetical to their way of life. Villagers feared the loss of their community identity, for the liberals aimed to form "municipalities out of formerly distinct villages" (Shubert, *A Social History of Modern Spain*, p. 191). After the liberal revolution of the 1830s, some villages ignored the new national laws that came from the central government, instead continuing to abide by the traditions in their own community. Indicative of the independent nature of the villages were certain idiosyncratic religious rituals, which seemingly had no connection to the official liturgy.

Although aristocrats possessed a great deal of land in outlying villages and towns, they generally lived in Madrid or in the provincial capitals. Rarely visiting their holdings, they leased them out to tenants for cultivation. In the large cities, the aristocrats tended to socialize in *tertulias,* salons in which intellectual discussions took place. As noted, the liberal revolution brought an increase in economic opportunities. From this increase in opportunities came the growth of new social classes, perhaps most notably of an urban elite whose status was based on wealth rather than birth. The old aristocrats refused to mingle with the newly wealthy, a practice that would change only in the late 1880s, when the two groups began to intermarry.

Change occurred elsewhere in society as well. After the liberal revolution, when government became more centralized, the number of civil servants in Spanish cities increased. They formed part of *las clases medias* (the middle class). Along with doctors, printers, and landlords, the civil servants generally earned enough income (at least 8000 *reales* a year as of 1845) to qualify for the vote. Also in the middle class were shopkeepers, barbers, and music teachers, who usually did not earn enough (or pay enough taxes) to vote. At the bottom of the scale, the working class toiled mostly in the fields as agricultural laborers. In the cities, a small working class provided labor for industries such as rope factories, or sold candy and other wares in the streets. Some of these workers were women. While middle- and upper-class women were expected to devote their lives to domestic affairs and eschew a public identity (unless their involvement in public life took the form of charitable duties), working-class women labored out of economic necessity. Likewise, while the sons of the elite attended Jesuit schools, many working-class children sought jobs at an early age in order to contribute to the family's income.

The Novel in Focus

Plot summary. *The Sea Gull* opens with a sea voyage to Spain in the year 1836. During the crossing, a Spanish duke named Don Carlos strikes up a friendship with an unemployed and homesick German doctor named Fritz Stein, who hopes to find work as a surgeon in the Spanish civil war in Navarre.

Two years later, Stein is wandering through the Andalucian countryside on his way to a seaport after being dismissed from the army for administering medical aid to a soldier on the opposite side (a Carlist). Delirious with fever, the doctor stumbles upon a dilapidated monastery whose inhabitants, an elderly woman named Aunt María and her family, nurse him back to health. Stein stays with the family and becomes acquainted with their folklore, proverbs, and superstitions. He also explores the nearby village of Villamar, where he encounters medieval Spanish relics.

One day the doctor is summoned to the seaside hut of an ailing 13-year-old girl and her doting father, a fisherman. The girl's name is María, but she is known as "Marisalada" (or, in one English translation, "Marysal"); the nickname, which means "salty María," implies a dry sense of humor, grace, and a liking for the sea. However, a boy in the monastery, Momo, tauntingly calls the girl *la Gaviota,* the Sea Gull, "Because she's got such long legs . . . because she's in the water as much as she's on land; because she sings and yells, and jumps from rock to rock, just like the rest of them" (*The Sea Gull*, p. 45). Under Stein's care, the Sea Gull recovers her health and becomes strong enough to sing again.

Struck by Marisalada's gorgeous voice, Stein offers to give her singing lessons. The urchin Momo warns that Marisalada is ungrateful and selfish (*la gaviota* implies a wild, shrewish woman). Nevertheless, Stein falls in love with his pupil, mistakenly supposing that her emotional singing indicates a compassionate heart. At the urging of the monastery's elderly Aunt María, who is determined to keep the gentle doctor in the village, Stein and Marisalada marry.

Three years later, Stein performs surgery on an injured hunter who turns out to be his old friend Don Carlos, the duke whom he met on his way to Spain. Amazed by Marisalada's voice, the duke insists that she and Stein share their respective skills with the world. The Sea Gull, enthralled with the promise of fame and fortune, welcomes the opportunity to leave the rustic village; her saddened husband, who has been content in the village, reluctantly acquiesces. While her father

sobs with grief, Marisalada departs with her husband and Don Carlos for Seville.

The next chapter takes place in a palace in Seville. The countess of Algar entertains guests who comment about the condition of Spain. Some discuss the exoticization of Spain and the influence of French culture on their own, while

---

BULLFIGHTING: FROM SPORT TO SYMBOL

The city of Seville, the setting for part of *The Sea Gull*, was famous in the nineteenth century for its *corridas de toros* (bullfights), an indigenous sport that came to symbolize Spain itself. Since the Middle Ages, bulls had played a role in certain rituals practiced by commoners, as well as in celebratory occasions at court, when nobles on horseback fought bulls to commemorate events such as royal weddings. Although aristocrats began developing specific rules for bullfighting in the sixteenth and seventeenth centuries, the sport languished at the beginning of the eighteenth century when the new Bourbon king of Spain, who was French, did not support it. Soon, though, commoners adopted the bullfighting guidelines developed by the nobility and began performing the sport at village and city festivals, attacking the bulls according to increasingly strict rules. A typical bullfight of the mid-eighteenth century consisted of a team of bullfighters, with apprentices who weakened the animal with lances and darts so that the matador, the expert, could deal the death blow. Over time, the matadors, who fought on foot, became the heroes of the spectacle and began to attain great wealth and national glory. By the start of the nineteenth century, the sport had grown into a lucrative business, with bullfights raising funds for religious, charitable, and political causes. The business attracted entrepreneurs, who leased newly built bullrings, purchased bulls especially bred to be aggressive, and hired bullfighters (*toreros*), most of whom came from the lower classes in Andalusia. Crowd control became a concern, for the fights were raucous affairs; rowdy spectators would pelt timid bulls and *toreros* with fruit and stones. Over the years, the bullfight would take on special significance for various writers, who came to regard it as a symbol of Spain's repudiation of the modern world.

---

one of them emulates French tastes with disastrous results. After reaching Seville, Marisalada creates a sensation there when she performs the lead in an Italian opera. Everyone is astounded

NORMA.   **9**

Coro. Casta diva che inargenti Queste sacre antiche piante, A noi volgi il bel sembiante Senza nube a senza vel. *Nor.* Fine al rito; e il sacro bosco Sia disgombro dai profani; Quando il Nume irato e fosco, Chiegga il sangue dei Romani— Dal Druidico delubro La mia voce tuonerà. *Tutti.* Tuoni! e alcun del popol empio Non isfugga al giusto scempio! E primier da noi percosso Il Proconsole cadrà. *Nor.* Sì, cadrà, punirlo io posso. (Ma punirlo il cor non sa.)	*Cho.* Queen of heaven, while thou'rt reigning Love upon us is remaining, Clad in pureness, and disdaining Grosser earth's nocturnal veil. *Nor.* All is ended, be now the forest Disencumber'd of aught mortal. When our god-head's thirsting anger Wills the lifeblood of the stranger, From our temple's awful portal My command then thunders forth. *All.* May it! this cause with glory bright'ning Shall in vengeance outsweep the lightning, And deliver, ere 'tis finish'd, Yon Proconsul to our wrath. *Nor.* My wrath would see him punish'd, (But to punish the soul is loth.)

AH, BELLO A ME RITORNO—THE BLOOM OF LIFE IS LYING. NORMA.

Tutti. Sei lento, si sei lento O giorno di vendetta; Ma irato il Dio t'affretta Che il Tebro condanno. *[Norma parte; e tutti in ordine la seguono.*	*Cho.* In slumb'ring preparation May war's glad declaration From stain'd page of creation Blot out these cursed foes! *[Exit Norma, the rest follow in procession.*

SCENA V.—*Entra* ADALGISA.	SCENE V.—*Enter* ADALGISA.
Adal. Sgombra è la sacra selva,— Compiuto il rito. Sospirar non vista Alfin poss' io, qui, dove a me s' offerse La prima volta quel fatal Romano Che mi rende rubella al tempio, al Dio. Fosse l' ultima almen!—Vano desio! Irresistibil forza Qui mi strascina: e di quel caro aspetto Il cor si pasce; e di sua cara voce L' aura che spira mi repete il suono. *[Corre a prostrarsi, sulla Pietra d' Irminsul.* Deh' proteggimi, o Dio! perduta io sono!	*Adal.* Grove, is thy only tenant Quivering moonlight? Pale and gently trembling As that mute watcher, here may my bosom utter A secret sighing for the fatal Roman Who has render'd it rebel to worthier religion. Would this sigh were the last! Empty expectance! Some most resistless magic Urgeth me hither and clothes his lov'd remembrance In brighter beauty; air echoes still his accents, Seeming infected with eloquent music. *[She advances and throws herself prostrate on the steps of the altar.* Protect me now, great power! lest I sink and am lost!

In *The Seagull*, Marisalada sings the aria "Casta Diva" from Bellini's opera *Norma*.

by her stunning voice. Infatuated with the young star, her patron, the (married) duke, composes love sonnets for her. She takes no interest in them, or him, for that matter, but a bullfighter named Pepe Vera captures her attention. He arranges a secret rendezvous with her.

Marisalada travels to Madrid, where she performs to even greater acclaim. Her voice is unparalleled in Spain. Back in the Andalusian countryside, her father, still depressed because of his daughter's departure, lies dying. The urchin Momo arrives in Madrid to fetch Marisalada and

Stein but returns without them, claiming that he saw the Sea Gull die a violent death before he fled the city in terror. Momo does not understand that what he saw was just an opera. The villagers mourn the deaths of Marisalada and her father.

One night Pepe Vera, the bullfighter, jealously grabs the Sea Gull, who by now has become his mistress, and forbids her from performing on stage. Although she catches a chill during their argument, Pepe forces her to go to a tavern with him anyhow. Stein meanwhile discovers his wife's adultery and, heartbroken, informs the duke of the affair. The doctor leaves for Cuba, the duke, for Seville.

The next day Pepe Vera demands that the Sea Gull attend his bullfight. A feverish Marisalada goes to the arena, where Pepe Vera is killed by a bull. The Sea Gull finds herself not only ill but also alone. Six months later, a conversation in the countess's salon reveals that pneumonia has destroyed Marisalada's operatic voice and Stein has died of yellow fever in Cuba.

The novel ends in the village of Villamar, to which Marisalada has returned. The former opera star, now unkempt and raspy-voiced, has married the local barber, whom she once scorned and with whom she now has two wailing children. The final images are of a decaying fort and the crumbling monastery.

Italian opera and indigenous Spanish music. When the Sea Gull arrives in Seville in 1844, she attends one of the evening gatherings held by the Countess of Algar. Although the assembled nobles have been informed that she has an astonishing voice, they look skeptically at the newcomer, who is neither gracious nor elegant. When asked to sing, to the accompaniment of a piano, Marisalada performs the Italian aria *Casta Diva* from the opera *Norma* by Vincenzo Bellini. She then moves on to a popular Andalusian melody, while playing the guitar. Although the trills from Bellini's *Norma* are met with admiration and applause, it is the Spanish melody that garners the more enthusiastic reception. The members of the audience begin to clap and chant with delight when Marisalada breaks into the Spanish song, then nostalgically reminisce about other indigenous songs of their country. The juxtaposition of an Italian aria and an Andalusian folk tune points to the struggle between foreign and indigenous artistic and literary forms that had been going on in Spain for more than a century.

Italian opera was tremendously popular in Spain in the 1830s and '40s, when *The Sea Gull* takes place, and had in fact long been popular there. Opera companies from Italy began arriving in Spain at the beginning of the eighteenth century. The Spanish royal court at that time, which included Philip V's powerful Italian wife (Elizabeth Farnese, Duchess of Parma) and an Italian prime minister, supported these companies, which proliferated so dramatically that they threatened to squash Spain's indigenous lyric theater.

OPERATIC WORKS IN *THE SEA GULL*

In *The Sea Gull*, there are allusions to the fact that the central female character sings arias from Bellini's *Norma* as well as from Rossini's *Otello* and *Semiramide*. These operatic references may be regarded as warnings about the dire fate of women who rebel—or are even suspected of rebelling—against societal norms. In Bellini's opera, the Druid High Priestess Norma breaks her vow of chastity and bears children with a mortal enemy of her people. In Rossini's *Semiramide*, the queen of Babylon, Semiramis, has her husband murdered and unknowingly falls in love with her own son. In *Otello*, the innocent Desdemona is killed by her husband when he suspects her of adultery. These operatic allusions are not the only musical motifs that refer to the demise of women who resist cultural norms. Marisalada sings an Andalucian folk tune that recounts the murder of an adulterous wife by her husband:

> And thrice he stabbed her through
> The lady was dead by one o'clock
> And her lover was dead by two
> Tura lura lura, tura lura loo.   (*The Sea Gull*, p. 100)

Like most of the women in the musical references above, Marisalada rejects the conventions of society. Unlike the heroines above, however, Caballero's protagonist does not perish but suffers a mundane fate. She is, in other words, denied the status of a tragic heroine.

In an effort to compete with this foreign musical form, Spanish musicians turned to their own popular culture for inspiration. The result was the development in the mid-eighteenth century of the *tonadilla escénica* (scenic *tonadilla*), a short operatic form whose melodies were influenced by rural folk songs and urban street music. The *tonadillas escénicas*—performed by a band of singers accompanied by an orchestra—featured the witty treatment of popular topics, along with character types associated with the lower strata of society, such as barbers or seamstresses. The comic element was essential; trends were often satirized, including the passion for Italian opera in Spain. Later, the foreign tendency to exoticize Spain would be another subject for parody.

CABALLERO'S FATHER REHABILITATES THE REPUTATION OF SPANISH LITERATURE

German Romantics believed that a literary work should not adhere to classical precepts; instead it should represent the essence of a particular people. This was a revolutionary idea for the Spanish when Johann Nikolaus Böhl von Faber (1770-1836), Fernán Caballero's father, came to Spain with his German Romantic theories. In an 1814 article, Böhl defended the works of Golden Age playwright Calderón de la Barca (see *Life Is a Dream*, also in *WLAIT 5:Spanish and Portuguese Literatures and Their Times*), which had been criticized for violating the classical unities, which called for a play to have one main plot that takes place in one location within twenty-four hours. For Böhl, Calderón's dramas, with their themes of knightly courage, religion, and love, were valuable precisely because they did not reflect classical restraint but rather captured the spirit of the Spanish people. In contrast, works modeled after classical Greek or Latin texts could not convey a country's essence and should not be emulated.

Böhl's article triggered a famous literary polemic in which the German scholar exhorted a return to Spanish traditional literary forms. Opposing Böhl was a Spanish scholar, José Joaquín Mora (1783-1864), who, citing "the eternal rules of good taste," advocated adherence to classical rules, as exemplified in the French writings of the Enlightenment (Mora in Flitter, p. 12). The debate became politicized: to look for inspiration to French neoclassical writings, such as those of Voltaire, Böhl implied, indicated a lack of patriotism. Eventually Mora came to agree with the tenets of German Romanticism. In fact, it was Mora who years later translated, edited, and serialized *The Sea Gull*.

The *tonadillas escénicas* proved enormously popular in the mid-to-late eighteenth century. There was competition between indigenous and Italian operatic forms at the time, with each waxing and waning in popularity. By the first decade of the nineteenth century, interest in the *tonadillas* had languished, while Italian opera still flourished. Italian members of the Spanish court continued to support Italian singers, composers, and music, especially operas. A music school—now the Madrid Conservatory—was established (by the fourth wife of Fernando VII, María Christina of Naples), and its students sang solely in Italian, not in Spanish.

With the disappearance of the *tonadillas escénicas*, Spain's indigenous lyric theater had become virtually nonexistent by the 1830s. Spanish musicians still attempted to counter the Italian presence in their country's theaters, achieving a victory of sorts in the late 1840s, when some young Spanish composers revived the *zarzuela*, a traditional Spanish entertainment from the seventeenth century. The modern *zarzuela* was a form of musical theater that included stock characters and spoken dialogue, as well as dances, melodies, and musical instruments regarded as authentically Spanish. Unlike the *tonadilla escénica*, the modern *zarzuela* did not die out but influenced Spanish music for years to come.

Sources. As noted, Fernán Caballero's father, Johann Nikolaus Böhl von Faber, criticized the adoption of French Enlightenment ideals in Spain, propounding instead that artists embrace authentic Spanish traditions. His nationalistic attitude has been regarded as a primary influence on his daughter's work. In the novel, when Marisalada leaves aside the popular melodies of Spain for the arias in the foreign operas, she literally loses her voice. Caballero's father may have in some ways also been a prototype for *The Sea Gull*'s German doctor. The novel's doctor travels to Spain and delights in its picturesque scenery as Böhl did himself.

The Sea Gull draws on oral and textual sources too. Its oral sources include folklore, popular song lyrics, and Andalusian proverbs ("A good fire is half of life; bread and wine the other half," *The Sea Gull*, p. 79). The novel's aristocrats tell anecdotes and use French and English expressions drawn from Caballero's direct observations. Among the novel's literary sources are courtesy books written by eighteenth-century Spanish women. Courtesy books contained tales that warned of punishment for a woman who flaunted society's norms by rejecting the role of committed wife and mother; for her offenses in the novel—adultery and lack of devotion to her elderly father—Marisalada suffers the loss of her gifted voice.

Elements of melodrama, associated at the time with the serial novel, enter into *The Sea Gull* as well. Melodramatic language glamorizes Marisalada's love for Pepe the bullfighter: "María loved that young and handsome man whom she saw facing death so serenely. She savored a love that subjugated her, that made her tremble, that wrung tears from her" (Caballero in Kirkpatrick, p. 332). Other literary influences are the Romantic myth of the genius who wins admiration from a dubious society and fictional tales of heroes who abandon the countryside for the big city in search of fame. This was the first time a Spanish author connected these two literary templates to a female protagonist.

It was not socially acceptable for a woman to be a professional writer in nineteenth-century Europe, and women commonly showed their discomfort at entering a domain reserved for men by employing male pseudonyms. Perhaps this uneasiness explains why women writers usually focused on domestic issues. The author of *The Sea Gull* had a different goal—she aimed instead to portray a nation in transition. Still, her stance is conservative. Caballero herself crossed the boundary that kept upper- and middle-class women from public careers, but her plot upholds a conservative viewpoint: the heroine's pursuit of fame ends in the humiliating loss of her talent.

Literary context. Notoriously difficult to classify, *The Sea Gull* is regarded as a precursor to the famous Spanish Realist novels of the 1870s and '80s, yet it incorporates elements of Romanticism and *costumbrismo*, two currents that already existed in Spain. In the eighteenth and nineteenth centuries, *cuadros de costumbres* (sketches of customs) proved popular. In *The Sea Gull*, several interpolations of folktales and stories that interrupt the main narrative resemble *cuadros de costumbres*. For instance, in the middle of the narrative about Marisalada's recovery from her childhood illness, the story breaks away to recount a didactic fable about a rooster. Fernán Caballero's novel was actually the first in Spain to use the notion of *costumbrismo* (the portrayal of customs characteristic of a certain region), though this had already been done by the French author Honoré de Balzac, whose detailed depictions of contemporary society influenced *The Sea Gull*. Yet, described more as a conglomeration of different genres than a coherent narrative of "life and movement," Caballero's work is not regarded as a true realist novel (Kirkpatrick, p. 334). Because of its didacticism, *The Sea Gull* is viewed rather as a forerunner to an early phase of the realist novel in Spain, the *novela de tesis* (thesis novel), which contained a strong, undisguised message. Finally *The Sea Gull* shares traits with Romantic works, for it defends

traditional life in the villages, in contrast to the foreign-influenced culture of the cities.

Composition and reception. Caballero's facility with French—the result of her education abroad—may explain why she composed *The Sea Gull* in that language. It is also possible that the novel was originally composed for French readers, since in the Prologue to the Spanish edition Caballero states that she wants the European public to have an accurate description of Spain. Various parts of the novel seem directed at a foreign readership; for example, on one occasion, the narrator explains that although the melodies of the Spanish ballads may be monotonous, their charm lies in the way in which the singer modulates his/her voice.

The author's original manuscript was translated into Spanish by an editor. Since the original French version has been lost, it is impossible for scholars to ascertain how much of it was modified in the process of translation. Ironically, a work that appears to be promoting traditional Spanish practices and deriding the imitation of French ones has itself been mediated by this foreign language.

Shortly after being serialized in Madrid's newspaper, *El Heraldo,* in the spring of 1849, *The Sea Gull* was hailed as groundbreaking for its accuracy in depicting Spanish life. A popular as well as a critical success, the serialization prompted curiosity over the author's true identity. Caballero, concerned that the reception of her work would be adversely affected if her gender were known, tried to keep her identity a secret. Despite her fears, her editor's revelation later that year that Fernán Caballero was a woman did not dampen enthusiasm for the work. Within 20 years, five editions of *The Sea Gull* had been published in book form.

One eminent critic of the day, Eugenio de Ochoa, singled out *The Sea Gull* as the first modern Spanish novel to compete with highly regarded realist novels, such as those by Britain's Henry Fielding. While he observed that there was a dearth of action in the novel and lamented its heroine's destiny, Ochoa praised the lifelike characters, and predicted that *The Sea Gull* would provide a literary foundation for the future. In his words, the novel was "the first light of a beautiful day, the first flower of the glorious poetic crown" that would adorn future Spanish novelists, a prediction that would be borne out by the novel's effect on later Spanish literary works (Ochoa, p. 340; trans. M. Tanenbaum).

—Michelle Tanenbaum

For More Information

Bravo-Villasante, Carmen, ed. "Introducción biográfica y crítica" and "Nota previa." In *Fernán Caballero's La Gaviota*. Madrid: Castalia, 1979.

Caballero, Fernán. *The Sea Gull*. Trans. Joan MacLean. Woodbury, N. Y.: Barron, 1965.

Chase, Gilbert. *The Music of Spain*, 2d ed. New York: Dover, 1959.

Cortada, James W. "The United States." In *Spain in the Nineteenth-Century World: Essays on Spanish Diplomacy, 1789-1898*. Ed. James W. Cortada. Westport, Conn.: Greenwood Press, 1994.

Flitter, Derek. *Spanish Romantic Literary Theory and Criticism*. Cambridge: Cambridge University Press, 1992.

Hoffmann, Léon-François. *Romantique Espagne: l'Image de l'Espagne en France entre 1800 et 1850*. Paris: Presses Universitaires de France, 1961.

Johnson, Roberta. "La Gaviota *and Romantic Irony*." In *Cultural Interactions in the Romantic Age*. Ed. Gregory Maertz. Albany: State University of New York Press, 1998.

Kirkpatrick, Susan. "On the Threshold of the Realist Novel: Gender and Genre in *La Gaviota*." *PMLA* 98, no. 3 (1983): 323-40.

Monleón, José B. "Estrategias para entrar y salir del romanticismo (Carmen y La Gaviota)." *Revista Hispánica Moderna* 53, no. 1 (2000): 5-21.

Ochoa, Eugenio de. "La Gaviota: *Juicio crítico*." In *La Gaviota*. Ed. Carmen Bravo-Villasante. Madrid: Castalia, 1979.

Shubert, Adrian. *A Social History of Modern Spain*. London: Unwin Hyman, 1990.

———. *Death and Money in the Afternoon: A History of the Spanish Bullfight*. New York: Oxford University Press, 1999.

Smith, Angel. *Historical Dictionary of Spain*. Lanham, Md.: Scarecrow, 1996.

South of Nowhere

by

António Lobo Antunes

António Lobo Antunes was born in Lisbon on September 1, 1942. A physician with a speciality in psychiatry, he served as a medic in Angola from 1971 to 1973, during the war of liberation. *South of Nowhere* (1979) is his second novel, after *Elephant Memory*, published earlier that same year. Both works address the wars of liberation in Angola, fought between the Portuguese army and the Angolan liberation movement. Of the 13 books he has written since, his latest are often considered more complex and less autobiographical, but he himself disagrees with this idea: "[My novels] are now much more consciously autobiographical. . . . The higher (apparent) complexity relates to the attempt of expressing more deeply what I feel and who I am through my characters" (Antunes, "Confissão," p. 16; trans. A. Ladeira). One of the first novels to denounce the colonialist and nationalist excesses and contradictions of pre-revolutionary Portugal, *South of Nowhere* challenged the official, self-promotional image of a country whose presence in Africa had supposedly been humane, racially tolerant, and welcomed by the colonized.

Events in History at the Time the Novel Takes Place

The New State—inflexible African policy. During the time *South of Nowhere* takes place—from 1971 until 1973—Portugal was experiencing a severe political crisis. The Portuguese dictatorial government, also known as the "New State," was fighting a controversial war in three African

THE LITERARY WORK

A novel set in Lisbon and in Angola from 1971 to 1973; published in Portuguese (as *Os Cus de Judas*) in 1979, in English in 1983.

SYNOPSIS

A Portuguese man reminisces about his two-year campaign as a medic in Angola during the war of liberation. A woman he meets at a bar in Lisbon is the unlikely listener of his two-day confession.

territories (Angola, Mozambique, and Guinea-Bissau) in a desperate attempt to prevent them from achieving the independence that would end centuries-old Portuguese colonial rule. António de Oliveira Salazar, the Portuguese dictator since 1930, had been replaced in 1968 by a more moderate successor who ruled in the same vein: Marcello Caetano. Like his predecessor, Caetano pursued an insistent policy of continued domination in the African territories. By 1974 his regime was being highly criticized for this policy by the rest of the Western world and, in particular, by the North Atlantic Treaty Organization (NATO). The first attempts at repression of the burgeoning 1960s liberation movements in the Portuguese-African colonies had by now turned into a full-blown war, involving at some point the Soviet Union, the United States, Cuba, and China as well as other countries.

António Lobo Antunes

Portugal had distinguished itself as the first expansionist nation, the one that introduced new worlds to the world. In the fifteenth century, the Portuguese scored a series of exploratory milestones. They established an outpost in Ceuta, Africa, in 1415, explored uncharted waters along the Coast of Africa, reaching and rounding the Cape of Good Hope in 1488, became the first to reach India by maritime route in 1498, and officially discovered Brazil in 1500, meanwhile establishing trading outposts and small colonies in Africa, South America, India, and the Far East. In the early 1970s, Portugal was the last imperial nation, an anachronism in the West. Portugal did not follow the lead of other imperial powers, such as Great Britain and Holland, who had decolonized their domains earlier, in the 1960s. Instead, Portugal reinforced its presence in Africa. The reasons behind this strategy are to this day controversial. Some authors claim that Portugal could not have decolonized without self-destructing. Its tenacious hold on its colonies reflected, according to these authors, the unlikeliness of its survival without them due to its own economic frailty, lack of resources, and diminutive size. Unlike other powers, it could not expect to recolonize or neocolonize (i.e., maintain some kind of political and economic presence) in the liberated

nations. The political, economic and—in some respects—mythical basis of the regime rested on empire, and on centuries-old colonial relationships with these African territories. When reprimanded for not following the example of other ex-imperial powers in Europe, Portugal's official justification was a startling one:

> The Portuguese contended that these distant territories were not colonies but "Overseas Portugal." . . . Hence, when Britain, France, and Belgium began liquidating their colonial empires, Portugal felt under no obligation to do the same, because . . . these places . . . had become so completely a part of the home country that Portugal was not a colonial power.
> (Nowell, p. 163)

The situation appeared insolvable. Despite growing political isolation from the rest of the world, Portugal continued in increasingly large numbers to draft soldiers for service in Africa, meanwhile boasting about its "self-sufficiency" as a nation. Echoing Britain's claim to "splendid isolation," imperial Portugal would, as late as the first half of the 1970s, declare its "pride and isolation," or, more accurately, its pride *in* its isolation ("*orgulhosamente sós,*" as Salazar was known to say).

The "New State"—domestic policy and the man who shaped it. At home in Portugal, the dictatorial regime of the early 1970s showed the inflexibility of an authoritarian state. A political police, the PIDE (International and State Defence Police) acted on every suspicion of subversive activities, particularly by members of the Communist Party or those affiliated with workers' organizations. The period witnessed general censorship of the press and of all publications. No new political parties could be formed. Secret societies, including the highly influential Freemasonry Society, had been banned in 1935. Trade unions were controlled by the state and lacked national representation. There was, to be sure, government opposition, but it rested almost exclusively with clandestine groups of workers operating under the direction of the Communist Party.

The New State implemented only social, not political, reforms: the partial rehabilitation of a network of roads, the long-awaited construction of a bridge over the Tagus River, public offices and services. Law courts, hospitals, barracks, post offices, schools, libraries, museums, and the like, which had been operating in abandoned church buildings, were re-established in their own new quarters. New construction occurred too. The regime built airports, modernized harbors, and constructed new dams and power stations. Promoted by continuing low wages in an era of stability, industry developed and production rose steadily. Portugal ceased to be an essentially rural country, and the urban middle class blossomed, particularly in the two main Portuguese cities, Lisbon and Oporto. Thus, changes did occur, but within carefully prescribed limits.

> Salazar administered economically, he planned little. He improved what existed but innovated only slightly; he was attached to the Portuguese society in which he had lived and desired no fundamental alterations. He had no enthusiasm for industrialization and saw it as a breeder of discontent and potential trouble among the masses. He resented the economic subjugation of Portugal to foreigners and took some steps to end it. . . . Most of his efforts for increasing the comforts and amenities of life were concentrated in Lisbon, which became an island of luxury in a sea of national poverty. . . . Three principles dominated his thinking and action: belief in the Catholic religion, distrust of popular government, and abhorrence of communism.
>
> (Nowell, pp. 154-55)

The regime self-destructs. The regime followed a course of intransigent nationalism, pursuing a longstanding diplomatic and military campaign to retain its overseas territories. Social disturbances in the colonies began to take on international dimensions after the Second World War. The United Nations adopted a general stance of defending all peoples' rights to self-determination. Soviet and Afro-Asian blocs were particularly "unimpressed" with Portugal's arguments as to why colonial rule needed to be maintained in the African territories. In response, Portugal accused these critics of having secret, exploitative African plans of their own: "post-war anti-colonial invective was merely a smoke-screen behind which powerful nations intended to take effective economic advantage of countries given political independence but unable to sustain it" (Saraiva, p. 114).

> Anyone who listens to those eloquent defenders of the peoples' liberation will think that the overseas provinces are backlands where sound and prosperous, political and social native organizations existed before colonial times, which ourselves, horrendous colonialists, went ahead and destroyed and oppressed. Do they ignore that those provinces have been part of Portugal for five hundred years? When we found them, they were desolate territories, here and there peopled by extremely primitive tribes,

without the faintest notion of nationality. There the Portuguese established themselves and introduced the natives to commerce, built cities and villages, planted farms, started industries, opened roads, they made the territories liveable by fighting disease. . . . We are not conducting a "colonial war," as the enemies of Portugal insinuate at every step of the way. We are defending order, social harmony and the productive work developed in territories where the great mass of the population shows in its everyday life a determination for remaining Portuguese.

> (Caetano, pp. 37-38, 30; trans. A. Ladeira)

The world had very limited knowledge of the situation in Portuguese Africa under Salazar and Caetano. Portugal kept the territories isolated from global public opinion, keeping a tight rein on "upstarts." The Portuguese colonial government repressed its African subjects with forced labor, demanding they raise export crops and denying them all civil rights. Education in Portuguese Africa was also a highly selective process, and very rarely a fair one. Africans did not have the same rights as a Portuguese citizen born in the home country, unless they entered into a highly demanding and unrealistic process of assimilation into Portuguese society according to its educational standards. (Only with the colonial reforms of 1961 was the "native status" repealed. From then on, Portuguese citizenship was granted to all Africans, regardless of their level of education.) Like other European powers, Portugal had pursued a policy of educating and creating African elites, and the policy backfired, giving rise to early leaders of the rebel movements. Portugal sponsored the schooling of the most promising Africans, educating them in Portuguese institutions, earmarking them to one day serve as representatives of colonial rule. But in practice, the select population shared forbidden anti-colonial ideas, many of the African students later becoming the theoretical and military leaders of the liberation movements. Established in Lisbon in 1951, the Centre for African Studies would in retrospect become known as the "cradle of African leadership." Agostinho Neto and Mário de Andrade of Angola and Marcelino dos Santos of Mozambique are some of the leaders nurtured in this cradle.

Both Portuguese and foreign critics of the regime's African policy were persecuted by the colonial police and sometimes arrested. Yet, with the overthrow of the fascist regime in 1974, all the African territories would win independence—Guinea-Bissau in 1974, followed by

Mozambique, Cape Verde, São Tomé, and Príncipe, and lastly Angola in 1975. Though it appeared sudden to the outside world, this process of independence and self-determination was far from spontaneous. Nationalist movements of liberation had been operating in these countries for more than ten years. In Angola there was the MPLA (Popular Movement for the Liberation of Angola), for example, and in Mozambique, FRELIMO (Front for the Liberation of Mozambique).

The beginning of the armed resistance, or of the wars of liberation, is marked by the repression of an illegal strike in August 1959 in Bissau, the capital of Portuguese Guinea. Portugal responded militarily with an action that cost more than 50 dockworkers their lives and inflicted many more injuries. A few weeks later, at a clandestine meeting in Bissau, the PAIGC (African Party for the Independence of Guinea and Cape Verde) agreed to start an armed offensive against the colonial government. The MPLA followed this decision in Angola in 1961. FRELIMO did the same in Mozambique in 1962. Between 1961 and 1974, Guinea-Bissau, Angola, and Mozambique fought their own wars and at different paces.

Aside from independence for the various colonies, the ultimate consequence of the African Wars would be the fall of the New State in Portugal. The escalating expense of the wars slowed down the rate of investment in the public sector at home and, therefore, in overall development. Meanwhile, the Portuguese citizenry began to balk at having to fight. Intellectual circles and university students protested against military service, and war-weariness set in among the army, who saw no end to a struggle in which guerrilla warfare broke out anew whenever vigilance lapsed. Defeat seemed inevitable, but opinion was divided over what action to take.

After 1968, hope stirred in military circles that Caetano might bring an end to the colonial wars. Under this post-Salazar dictator, the country had seen some economic growth and some signs that political reform was on its way: road networks were constructed; foreign investment was allowed; restrictive industrial policies came to an end; social benefits were extended to rural communities. Yet the formation of new political parties remained illegal. (In the legislative elections of 1973 only members from the National Union—the single legal party—took their seats.) And, more crucial for *South of Nowhere,* African policy did not fundamentally change. Outside

Portugal, the United Nations continued to reiterate opposition to Portugal's colonial policy, while world powers lent moral and political support to the guerrillas. The official count of the Portuguese dead provided by the Armed Forces (Estado-Maior genral das Forças Armadas) was 8,831, including many hundreds of mobilized black African soldiers. Of these casualties 3,455 took place in Angola, 3,136 in Mozambique, and 2,240 in Guinea Bissau (Teixeira, p. 86). Discontent in the Portuguese military finally culminated in the Armed Forces Movement (MFA). Led by a group of army captains, the ensuing bloodless revolution of April 25, 1974, met with no resistance, easily toppling a regime that had oppressed the country for almost half a century. Looking back, some would condemn the half century as a bleak, forgettable era, with unjustified authoritarian restrictions imposed on a society that enjoyed no democratic freedom. Others would speak of the dictatorship as a necessary phase in the evolution of Portuguese society, a period in which a middle class found it possible to blossom. Today's democratic institutions owe their existence to this middle class.

Liberation movements in Portuguese Africa. Angola began resorting to guerrilla warfare in February 1961. Shortly before, in Luanda, the capital, police stations and jails were attacked by rebel groups, followed in March by bloody rioting, then by calculated terrorism involving the massacre of settlers near the border with the republic of Congo. These events seemed to have been entirely unexpected by international observers. The subsequent repression by Portuguese troops temporarily stabilized the situation. This 1961 Portuguese military action marked the beginning of a 13-year anti-guerrilla campaign. In 1963 a revolt broke out in Guinea-Bissau, and in 1964 guerrilla warfare erupted in Mozambique. Addressing these situations as if they were transitory bursts of subversion back home, Portugal sent more and more troops to Africa. The movements of liberation launched a combination of anti-colonial actions: illegal strikes, unauthorized demonstrations, demands for political change. In response, the colonial regime repressed each rebellious act with increasing, ultimately paralyzing force. Salazar himself believed that Portugal had to keep all or it would lose all (in fact its losses had already begun—Goa was annexed by India in 1962). He thought too that either way he would enjoy the support of Western Europe and North America, which for some time he did.

Portugal's relations with the West throughout the wars was always ambivalent and, at times, tense. Western powers did not, though, place any great constraints on Lisbon's colonial policies. Portugal had the geo-strategically important Azores with which to negotiate, thanks to the coveted Lajes air base used by the United States Air Force from World War II to the present day. Also, throughout the 1950s the pressures of the Cold War—the U.S.-Soviet competition for world leadership—tended to mute criticism of Lisbon's African policy. Then, in 1961, the Angola uprising, and especially the violent response to it by the Portuguese, exposed the myth of a benevolent colonial rule.

Early liberation-movement actions. The liberation movements began slowly, indoctrinating the population in the villages, attempting to win their support. To get villagers to condemn colonial rule, the movement appealed to the people's specific demands: to end arbitrary behavior by Portuguese officials, traders, and tax-collectors; to obtain good prices for their produce and reduce the cost of goods; to end forced labor and the obligatory growing of crops for Portuguese export companies. Gradually, in Angola and the other Portuguese territories, the populations were persuaded that their active participation was needed if such demands were to be met.

Portugal began to send an increasing number of troops to Africa in 1963. The total amount was staggering when one considers Portugal's population: "If calculated on the basis of metropolitan populations, [the colonial armies] were more than seven times bigger than the biggest American army sent to Vietnam; and Portugal was having to spend about 45 percent of its national budget on these wars they were fighting in Africa" (Davidson, p. 18).

All of the major western powers and some of the minor ones in NATO supported the Portuguese cause at first. On the other side, the liberation movements received aid from Sweden, from unofficial support groups in the western world, and from the Soviet Union, Cuba, and other communist countries. More support went to Portugal except at the end, when Soviet ground-to-air missiles helped shift the war in favor of the rebel groups, and the United Nations finally registered its disapproval of Portugal's resistance to decolonization. The Portuguese suffered in part from their own overconfident, condescending attitude toward the Africans, as reflected in an infamous, oft-quoted speech by Caetano at the University of Lisbon in 1954:

> The Africans are incapable of developing on their own the countries they have inhabited for thousands of years. . . . The Africans have never invented any useful technology, nor conquered anything for the benefit of mankind. . . . The Africans must be treated as productive elements who are organised, or have to be organised, in an economy governed by whites.
>
> (Caetano in Davidson, p. 18)

The Portuguese suffered too from war tactics that proved ineffective in the long run. One such practice was the forced relocation of villages, the

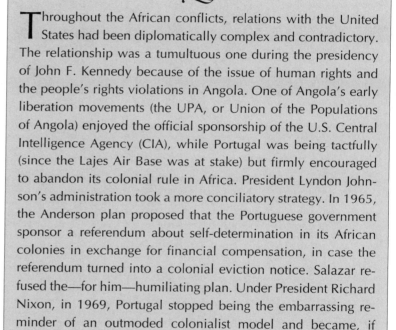

U.S.-PORTUGAL RELATIONS

Throughout the African conflicts, relations with the United States had been diplomatically complex and contradictory. The relationship was a tumultuous one during the presidency of John F. Kennedy because of the issue of human rights and the people's rights violations in Angola. One of Angola's early liberation movements (the UPA, or Union of the Populations of Angola) enjoyed the official sponsorship of the U.S. Central Intelligence Agency (CIA), while Portugal was being tactfully (since the Lajes Air Base was at stake) but firmly encouraged to abandon its colonial rule in Africa. President Lyndon Johnson's administration took a more conciliatory strategy. In 1965, the Anderson plan proposed that the Portuguese government sponsor a referendum about self-determination in its African colonies in exchange for financial compensation, in case the referendum turned into a colonial eviction notice. Salazar refused the—for him—humiliating plan. Under President Richard Nixon, in 1969, Portugal stopped being the embarrassing reminder of an outmoded colonialist model and became, if briefly, an unlikely ally in the war against communism.

aldeamentos, into areas where they would be protected from subversive influence. Another tactic against the liberation movement was the use of African mercenaries, sent in helicopters to raid the "liberated zones," those areas that the rebels had freed of Portuguese influence. Once a zone became "liberated," the rebels would introduce policy welcomed by its people, expelling all colonial officials and traders, eliminating colonial taxes and charges, abolishing forced labor, and establishing schools and hospitals.

Meanwhile, a rising number of Portuguese soldiers began to challenge the colonialist ideology of the New State. Towards the end of the

Portuguese Soldiers in Angola at the end of colonial rule.

war, they instigated important anti-colonial, pro-African, and pro-self-determination movements. It was a party of these soldiers that conducted the military coup d'état igniting the democratic revolution of April 25, 1974, in Portugal. A few months later, on July 29, 1974, responsible military officers issued the following statement:

> The colonised peoples and the people of Portugal are allies. The struggle for national liberation has contributed powerfully to the overthrow of fascism, and, in large degree, has laid at the base of the Armed Forces Movement, whose officers have learned in Africa the horrors of a fruitless war, and have therefore come to understand the roots of the evils which afflict the society of Portugal.
>
> (Davidson, p. 16)

It is unclear whether it is reasonable to speak in terms of a single *national* struggle in Angola. Strife between three nationalist movements often reached an intensity that suggested civil war, even before the collapse of the Lisbon regime. Both the MPLA and the UPA claimed to have initiated the liberation war. During 1959 and 1960 the MPLA was subjected to a campaign of repression by the colonial authorities. Many of its leaders had been arrested and the organization, though much weakened, opted for a dramatic gesture. At dawn, on February 4, 1961, about

200 MPLA members and their supporters attacked the São Paulo de Luanda prison and other government targets. It was the first significant incident of urban guerrilla warfare in the overall struggle. According to UPA, however, the war was ignited by the outbreak of widespread violence in the coffee-growing areas of Northern Angola in March of 1961.

The Novel in Focus

Plot summary. A novel consisting of a frame story and an inner narrative, *South of Nowhere* is divided into chapters, one for each letter of the alphabet. The frame story features the protagonist at a bar, drinking, possibly drunk, in conversation with an unnamed woman, whose responses the reader does not have access to, and with whom he shares a seemingly fragmented series of personal experiences and observations about his time spent as a military doctor during the war in Angola. The setting of the frame is post-revolutionary Lisbon in 1979, from which the reader is intermittently transported back to 1971-73 wartime Angola. The doctor narrates his account to the woman in one sitting, interjecting episodes from his childhood in Portugal as the son of a bourgeois family during the New State dictatorship.

As the doctor progresses through his reminisces, he will at one point address his African washerwoman and lover, Sofia. Another time he talks to his wife in Portugal. None of the addressees talk back. Their function is strictly rhetorical, as is that of the woman who is supposedly listening in the Lisbon bar to the narrator's autobiographical tale.

The novel opens with an account of the narrator's childhood in Portugal, a time back to which he occasionally transports the reader.

> When we used to go to the zoo on Sunday mornings with my father, the animals showed themselves for what they were: the giraffe, in his lofty solitude, had the dimensions of a sad Gulliver; the ostriches resembled spinster gym teachers; the penguins waddled like office boys with bunions. . . . The frantic bark of poodles occasionally filtered up around tombstones in the dog cemetery.
>
> (Antunes, *South of Nowhere*, p. 5)

Later in the first chapter, the first-person narrator's family gathers at a Lisbon harbor to say their goodbyes as the military ship sets off to the colonies. After briefly describing the trip, he reaches his first destination.

The doctor leaves Luanda in a truck filled with troops. As the truck heads to the city of Nova Lisboa, he describes the gigantic scale of everything, "the sky is so vast and ever-changing that you can contemplate it until you fall backward like a great bird in ecstasy" (*South of Nowhere,* p. 23). He suffers a vague sense of guilt connected to his being a Portuguese "man from a narrow country, from a stifling city shimmering in the reflection of its tile façades" (*South of Nowhere,* p. 22). In Nova Lisboa, the Portuguese settlers exhibit bad taste, profound backwardness, and loyalty to petty, outdated colonial customs.

Recurrent references are made to United States culture, mostly in connection with American films, which were an important part of the narrator's upbringing in Lisbon.

A scene in which he is eating with his fellow soldiers while being stared at by a group of locals is described through references to early-twentieth-century American mobsters:

> While eating beefsteak I felt as if I were a protagonist in the St. Valentine's Day Massacre, inclined to gangland prohibition shootouts; I lifted my fork to my mouth with the cool boredom of Al Capone, composing in the mirror a smile of manifest cruelty.
>
> (*South of Nowhere,* p. 24)

From Nova Lisboa, the troops travel to Luso, a territory called "The End of the World," stopping at an outpost near the border with Zambia. The narrator experiences here one of his frequent moments of distress, in which he questions not only the justifications of war but who the real enemy is:

> With every wound from an ambush or a mine, the same distressing question occurred to me, product of the [fascist] Portuguese youth movement, Catholic journals and the monarchist tabloids, nephew of catechists and an intimate of the holy family that visited us at home in a bell jar, now feeling as if he had been jammed into a powder keg: who is killing us? The guerrillas or Lisbon—Lisbon, the Americans, the Russians, the Chinese.
>
> (*South of Nowhere,* p. 29)

In June 1971, the narrator is told of the birth of his first daughter, after which he makes one of his rare references to the story's time frame. The democratic revolution has taken place in Portugal, giving rise to new young Portuguese bureaucrats and bourgeoisie, who in 1979 become the target of the narrator's by now familiar sarcasm.

Let me pay the bill. No, seriously, let me pay the bill so you can take me for the ideal Portuguese '79 technocrat with the cafe-society intelligence, that is, mundane, superficial and inoffensive, garrulous, strange and slight.

(*South of Nowhere,* p. 59)

In 1973 the medic finally makes his way back to Portugal. He attributes a nightmarish quality to Luanda, seen here for the last time, that smacks of his ghostly portrayal of Lisbon. Both cities are presented as unreal places:

> "The plane that flies us to Lisbon transports a cargo of slowly materializing ghosts, officers and soldiers yellow with malaria, fastened to their seats, vacantly looking out the window at blank space. What is real are the sergeants who examine our documents with the laxity of disinterested officials. . . . We spent twenty-seven months . . . of anguish and death together."
>
> (South of Nowhere, p. 153).

ANOTHER KIND OF REVOLUTION

Around the middle of the twentieth century, a weekend trip to the cinema was one of the most common pastimes of the middle class in Portugal. From the 1920s on, American cinema revolutionized the culture. Cowboy and Indian films were extremely popular, especially those featuring actors such as John Wayne. The protagonist recalls another favorite:

> Even today, you know, I walk out of movie houses lighting my cigarette the way Humphrey Bogart did, so much so that I disappoint myself when I look in the mirror; instead of walking into Lauren Bacall's arms I head for my neighborhood and the illusion fades. I put my key in the lock (is it Humphrey Bogart or me?), I hesitate, enter, look at the engraving in the hall (now it's definitely me looking at it) and I sink into the sofa, sighing like a punctured tire, the spell broken.
>
> (*South of Nowhere,* p. 24)

The novel comes full circle, as the medic faces his aunts and they voice their disappointment in him. Subsequently he and the unnamed woman to whom he has told his story take their final leave of each other. From the bar they had retired to his apartment for what turned out to be an unsuccessful attempt at love-making, in which he could not perform, stymied by memories of the war and an associated sense of failure.

"Bourgeois guilt" and the middle-class family. Embedded in *South of Nowhere* is a pervasive pessimism related to the narrator's outlook on love, the tragedy of the colonial wars, and the trauma of the New State in Portugal. He asks the silent woman, "What would happen to us if we were really happy? . . . Have you noticed how frightened we get if someone, spontaneously, with no ulterior motive, loves us, how we cannot stand sincere, unconditional affection?" (*South of Nowhere,* p. 112). How much of this pessimism is bound up with questions of identity is uncertain, but reflections on the identity of the Portuguese, on their idiosyncrasies and shortcomings, continually recur in the novel. For example, along with the bourgeois class he comes from, says the narrator, he shares a "chilling fear of the ridiculous," a characteristically Portuguese trait (*South of Nowhere,* p. 22). Both the protagonist and the author seem to harbor a particular obsession with what they call "bourgeois guilt."

This was a common "affliction" among young intellectuals who had not been revolutionaries during the last days of the dictatorship. When the regime fell, they felt they had been accomplices of it. Many bourgeois youth developed a leftist ideological orientation, adopting the politics and aspirations of the working class as if they were their own. In the cases of Lobo Antunes and his alter-ego protagonist, their guilt embraced the actions of their families, who had resigned themselves to and benefited from the New State:

> Two things, my good friend, I continue to share with the class of people I come from, disappointing [the Latin American revolutionary] Che Guevara, whose poster I have hung over my bed to protect me from bourgeois nightmares: the facile emotion that makes me sniffle at soap operas on the television at the corner café, and the chilling fear of the ridiculous.
> (*South of Nowhere,* p. 22)

The author and his protagonist seem to harbor a guilty conscience connected to their own actions as well. The suffering they experience in the African Wars appears to function as a type of expiation, a delivery of conscience, the only heroic moment available to them, even though they now realize they have been on the wrong side of the conflict:

> Inside myself, I solved the guilty feeling of my bourgeois birth which led me to take sides politically, for example, to have been a candidate by APU, a coalition of left-wing parties, among them, the Portuguese Communist Party. It had to do with the guilt of the bourgeois kid

who felt he had been a coward during the dictatorship. . . . There was a lot of cowardice on my part. I only shed the physical fear in Africa, in the War.
> (Antunes, "Exuberant Confession," p. 17;
> trans. A. Ladeira)

"Fortunately the army will make a man of him," his aunts had hoped before he went off to Africa on his military assignment (*South of Nowhere,* p. 9). At the end, a feeling of inadequacy and deep failure, connected to the absurdity of the war and the deficiencies of the New State, permeates the narrative. Not even the army had made a man out of the protagonist.

> My aunts turned on the lamp to observe me better. . . . A bamboo cane traced a disdainful arabesque before it was stuck on my chest, while a weak, raspy voice said You're thinner than when we last saw you. I always hoped the army would make a man out of you, but I guess there's nothing to be done.
> (*South of Nowhere,* p. 154)

The family's disillusionment and rejection of the ex-soldier at the close of the novel mirrors a similar attitude on the part of Portuguese society in the postwar years. Its "heroes" were not welcomed home, but greeted with insults. Many saw the loss of the colonies as defeat, or more exactly, since in Africa lay the last imperial project, as imperial Portugal's final defeat.

Sources and literary context. In *South of Nowhere,* Lobo Antunes consolidates a new genre in Portugal—the "colonial war novel." He adopts a revolutionary style, invoking slang and scatological images, and using sarcasm and images of violence to depict the death of the Portuguese empire. There is a frenetic, fragmentary quality to his style, a type of stream of consciousness that has been called the "traveling travel narrative" (Madureira, p. 21). Other Portuguese chronicles of the African Wars include *O Capitão Nemo e EU* (1973; Captain Nemo and I) by Álvaro Guerra; *Lugar de Massacre* (1975; The Place of the Massacre) by José Martins Garcia, and *Jornada de África* (1989; African Journey).

Portugal, in the post-revolutionary era, experienced a national crisis of identity that is mirrored in the crisis of this fragmented narrative, a confusing, if rewarding, stream of unpredictable digressions of a drunkard (Peres, p. 189). The novel is a challenge to any patriotic cant, a type of anti-epic. As such, *South of Nowhere* has joined the ranks of such Portuguese famous anti-epics as Fernão Mendes Pinto's seventeenth-century work

Peregrination or Bernardo Gomes de Brito's nine-teenth-century work *The Tragic Story of the Sea*—which are, surprisingly, as famous, as cherished, and as institutionalized in Portugal as its epics.

Events in History at the Time the Novel Was Written

The democratic revolution and its consequences. From the early 1970s setting of *South of Nowhere* to its late 1970s release, Portugal endured a political meandering that recalls the fragmentation and disorientation of the novel. Happily, Portugal's meandering would resolve itself, but not before the novel was published. On April 25, 1974, a group of young military officers from the MFA (Armed Forces Movement) overthrew the New State dictatorship, transferring power to a military provisional government, the Council of National Salvation (Junta de Salvação Nacional). Presiding over this council was General António de Spínola, who was subsequently elected president of the new Portuguese republic.

The backing of the people, without which the coup would not have succeeded, was mostly due to a deep hatred for the New State, not to conscious support for the rebels' ideological positions, which were widely ignored or misunderstood. The Communist Party, still the strongest rebel faction at the time, believed that the national uprising was a prelude to a future socialist revolution. But the real situation was murky.

The first post-revolution contradictions concerned the role played by General Spínola. When the Armed Forces Movement captured the New State dictator Marcello Caetano at Largo do Carmo in Lisbon, he refused to surrender to a junior officer and suggested Spínola instead. Caetano had just chosen his own successor, which made Spínola a problematic figure from the beginning. He would become the symbol of compromise with the old regime, something to which his African policy testified. Spínola supported the colonies' eventual right to independence, but on a delayed schedule, to safeguard Portuguese economics, and to assure that, according to the paternalistic ideology of the day, the "unprepared" Africans were ready for independence.

Presiding over the Council of National Salvation, Spínola objected to what he interpreted as excessively radical clauses in Portugal's new economic policy. He also objected to immediate independence for the colonies. These differences between Spínola and the provisional government he supposedly led ended in his being expelled from its rule. On March 11, 1975, Spínola attempted and failed a counter-coup that would restore some policies of the New State, including a much slower decolonization process. The authors of the April revolution had divided views about the so-called "overseas territories." General Spínola thought their self-determination should be a gradual process to allow for the establishment of a new order in the ex-colonies while preserving of some of Portugal's economic interests there. The communists wanted independence to be granted immediately. The situation in Angola was further complicated by the fact that three rival movements contended for supremacy (MPLA, UNITA [Union for the Total Independence of Angola], and FNLA [National Front for the Liberation of Angola]). Each had different ideologies, international supporters, and national projects. On February 15, 1975, the Portuguese government signed the "Agreements of Alvor" with representatives of all three factions, providing for a period of transition and setting November 11, 1975, as Independence Day. On November 11, the MPLA seized power and rapidly defeated its opponents with military actions. The other groups never accepted MPLA's claims of legitimacy and, to this day, have been fighting a very bloody civil war.

Back in Portugal, although the 1976 Constitution adopted as its objective a progression toward socialism and a classless society, "The allies were reassured of the continuing moderation of the advance towards socialism by the explicit reaffirmation of Portugal's membership of NATO" (Kayman, p. 130). In the end, Portugal would not become a communist country. The elections of April 1976 revealed a trend towards the center. The communists and those parties on the radical left gained less than 20 percent of the votes, the center (Socialist Party and Social Democrats) garnered 6 percent, and representatives designed a Third Republican Constitution to balance presidentialism with parliamentarianism. Elections over the next decade ushered in governments of coalition or compromise through 1979, the year *South of Nowhere* was published. In 1987 the Social Democrats would obtain a large majority that enabled them to both govern in a climate of stability and revitalize the economy. Meanwhile, in January 1986, Portugal would become an official member of the European Economic Community. Since then, Portugal's centuries-old overseas enterprise has been replaced by a very differently focused European enterprise. Portugal's old expansionist imperial projects were by this time abandoned, and the country was restored nearly to its original physical extent. It would retain control of Macau until 1999, when Portugal finally turned the territory over to China.

Reception. *South of Nowhere* met with instant success in Portugal when it was published there in 1979, though critics gave it mixed reviews. Lobo Antunes's first triumph had been *Elephant Memory*, which addressed a similar topic—the colonial war in Angola—and had been published the same year. Thanks to a timely interview conducted by Rodrigues da Silva in the Portuguese newspaper *Diário Popular*, this first novel experienced almost instant fame in the small sphere of Portuguese letters and remarkable sales success. *South of Nowhere* was published to similar acclaim.

Vírgilio Ferreira, pre-eminent novelist of the era, dismissed Lobo Antunes's style as non-literary verbal rambling: "It is worth nothing at all, he is no more than a verbal juggler, no one knows where these inventions come from" (Ferreira in Venâncio; trans. A. Ladeira, p. 18). Lobo Antunes would have to write a few more bestsellers before winning the admiration of the majority of critics and becoming a consecrated writer in the Portuguese contemporary canon. *South of Nowhere* is now known as one of the most representative of Antunes's early, colonial-war-centered novels. Its depiction of the Portuguese war in Angola is seen as both "caricatural and nightmarish, a study in advanced imperialist decrepitude" (Madureira, p. 23). According to many critics, Lobo Antunes and José Saramago (the 1998 Nobel Prize winner; see **Baltasar and Blimunda,** also in *WLAIT 5: Spanish and Portuguese Literatures and Their Times*) constitute "in post-revolutionary Portugal, the two greatest and most universal male revelations of today's narrative writing." (Mourão, p. 672; trans. A. Ladeira).

—António Ladeira

For More Information

Antunes, António Lobo. "Confissão Exuberante/Exuberant Confession." Interview by Robrigues da Silva. *Jornal de Letras, Artes e Ideias* (April 1994): 16-19.

————. *South of Nowhere*. Trans. Elizabeth Lowe. New York: Random House, 1983.

Caetano, Marcello. *Razões da Presença de Portugal no Ultramar: excertos de discursos proferidos pelo presidente do Conselho de Ministros Prof. Doutor Marcello Caetano.* Lisboa, 1973.

Davidson, Basil. "The Movements of National Liberation." *Tarikh* 6, no. 4 (1983): 5-19.

Kayman, Martin. *Revolution and Counter-Revolution in Portugal.* London: Merlin, 1987.

Macqueen, Norrie. *The Decolonisation of Portuguese Africa.* London: Longman, 1997.

Madureira, Luís. "The Discreet Seductiveness of the Crumbling Empire—Sex, Violence and Colonialism in the Fiction of António Lobo Antunes." *Luso-Brazilian Review* 32, no. 1 (1995): 17-29.

Mourão, Luís. "Narrativa contemporánea posterior a la Revolución de los Claveles." In *La Historia de la literatura portuguesa.* Ed. José Luis Gavilanes y António Apolinário. Madrid: Cátedra, 2000.

Nowell, Charles E. *Portugal.* Englewood Cliffs, New Jersey: Spectrum/Prentice Hall, 1973.

Peres, Phillis. "Love and Imagination Among the Ruins of Empire: Anonio Lobo Atunes's *Os Cus de Judas* and *O Fado Alexandrino*." In *After the Revolution.* Ed. Helena Kaufman and Anna Klobucka. Lewisburg: Bucknell University Press, 1997.

Saraiva, José Hermano. *Portugal: A Companion History.* Manchester, U.K.: Carcanet, 1997.

Teixeira, Rui de Azevedo. *A Guerra Colonial e o Romance Português.* Lisboa: Editorial Notícias, 1998.

Venâncio, Fernando. "O Jovem Príncipe." *Jornal de Letras, Artes e Ideas,* 10 September 1997, 18.

Wheeler, Douglas. "Portugal: Prisoners of Glory." *Wilson Quarterly / New Year's 1985* (winter 1985): 48-66.

The Spaniards:
An Introduction to
Their History

by

Américo Castro

Américo Castro (1885-1972) was born in Brazil to Antonio Castro and Carmen Quesada, Spanish merchants who returned to Spain with the family when their infant boy was four. Castro grew up in Granada, earned his doctorate at the University of Madrid, and went on to forge a revolutionary new vision of Spain in respect to its history and culture. The publication of his *El pensamiento de Cervantes* (1925; The Thought of Cervantes) established Castro as a globally influential Cervantes scholar. When the Spanish Civil War broke out in 1936, a void was created by the disappearance of Spain's two foremost journals—the *Revista de Occidente* (Journal of the Occident) founded in 1923 by José Ortega y Gasset and the *Revista de Filología Española* (Journal of Spanish Philology), edited by Ramón Menéndez Pidal. (Castro was a frequent contributor to this last *revista*). Many of the era's intellectuals felt troubled by such developments, and by a sense of disintegration and regression in Europe because of the wars that convulsed the continent, including Spain. Exile became a common, often a necessary, option. Castro himself went into exile in 1936, teaching at various institutions in the United States, including the University of Wisconsin, the University of Texas, and Princeton University. In exile, he wrote his most revolutionary works, *España en su historia: moros, judíos, cristianos* (1948; Spain in its History: Moors, Jews, Christians) and its numerous sequels, most prominent among them *The Spaniards: An Introduction to Their History*, a book with a complex pedigree.

THE LITERARY WORK

A historical treatise set in Spain in the Middle Ages and early modern period; first published in Spain in 1962 (as the revised version of *La realidad histórica de España*); published in English in 1971.

SYNOPSIS

The singular, enigmatic quality of Spanish history can only be understood by looking at the interaction of the three cultures that formed it: Christians, Muslims, and Jews.

Leading up to its publication was *La realidad histórica de España,* or *The Structure of Spanish History,* released in 1954. This work was revised and republished in Spanish in 1962 under the same title but with a new prologue ("Prólogo para españoles"). As one scholar points out, "What most clearly characterizes the 1962 text is its intention of formulating an overall historical vision of Spain and not simply its literature, language or art" (Araya Goubet, p. 49). In 1965 a new introduction was added to create the version that would be revised into *The Spaniards: An Introduction to Their History.* So much more historical is this second English edition than its literature-oriented predecessor, *The Structure of Spanish History,* that it can be thought of as a new work, one that extended Castro's revolutionary approach to Spanish history and that has prompted people to rethink established ideas.

Events in History at the Time of the Treatise

From prehistory to the Reconquest. The historical events treated in this entry begin with the peopling of the Iberian Peninsula and move forward to those events as seen from the points-of-view of historians around the middle of the twentieth century, when Américo Castro advanced his view. Before Castro, the general consensus was "that Spanish culture has fixed characteristics which have remained constant from the time of the [ancient] Iberians to the present"; this perspective, argues Castro, erroneously attributes particularly Spanish traits to all groups that have occupied the peninsula (Glick, p. 290). He maintains that the Spanish are not those who occupied the peninsula from time immemorial, but rather that their culture developed in the centuries following the Muslim invasions of 711.

The Iberian Peninsula has indeed been inhabited by an assortment of peoples since its prehistoric days. Prior to the Muslim invasion in 711, these more or less indigenous peoples (Celtiberians, Galaeci, Turdetanians, Tartessians) played unwilling host to Phoenicians and Carthaginians, among others. Not until the Romans in the 100s B.C.E., however, would any group establish a single political control over the peninsula that the Romans referred to as *Hispania* or *Hispaniae* (plural). Later, in the fifth century C.E., the peninsula came to be dominated by Germanic tribes, the most successful being the Visigoths, who were Arians, or non-Catholic Christians. One of their kings, Recared, converted to Catholicism in 587, paving the way for his own people to follow suit, which, in turn, allowed the larger Catholic Hispano-Roman population of the area, "to rally around the Visigoth monarchy" (Collins in Carr, p. 53). At this point, Catholicism became a common factor that prompted separate groups on the peninsula to identify with each other. Religion had begun to serve as a unifying force among the disparate groups.

The next momentous event in the process was the invasion of Spain by the Muslims, who crossed the Straits of Gibraltar from North Africa in 711. So overwhelming was their assault that in the space of a few short years the North African invaders achieved effective control over all but the most mountainous regions, extending their rule to the west south of the Duero River and to the east almost as far north as what are today Pamplona and Barcelona. The conquerors imposed Arabic culture, making Islam the dominant religion in all the territories they subjugated.

Some small isolated pockets of Christian resistance survived in the north of the peninsula because of the foreboding mountainous terrain, finding an all-encompassing reason for being in the preservation of their faith. Defining themselves collectively as "Christians" (*cristianos*), these holdouts struggled to sustain their faith and to retake the lands that had been seized from them and their kind. Slowly this kernel of Christian resistance, born in the isolated mountainous areas, gathered strength, giving rise over time to new kingdoms that became linked to one another by their opposition to Muslim hegemony. "There is war between Christians and Moors," observed Prince Juan Manuel in the early fourteenth century, "and there will be, until the Christians have regained the lands that the Moors took from them by force" (Juan Manuel in Castro, *The Spaniards*, p. 50).

In a movement known as the "Reconquest" (Reconquista), which spanned several centuries, the Christian kingdoms repossessed areas until they controlled most of the peninsula under the "Catholic Monarchs" Ferdinand and Isabella in 1492. Medieval legend dates the Reconquest from a skirmish in 722, while recent historians say it began in the late eleventh century under Alfonso VI (1065-1109), when the ideology of Crusade was first invoked. From either date, as they reconquered territory, the Christians incorporated into their realm two minority cultures with distinct religious practices and overall outlook: the Muslims and the Jews. Of course, such a population mixture was nothing new in the land. Christians had long been a minority in various reaches of Muslim Spain, becoming known there as Mozarabs (Christians dwelling in Muslim territory). These Mozarabs adapted to the new Muslims rulers and Arabic customs, meanwhile maintaining their own Christian faith and practices. Similarly, Muslims and Jews in the reconquered lands would retain their separate identities, assuming specific minority roles in Christian society—either by law or by established practice.

There was no "secular" government without religious affiliation at the time. In such a world, the distinctions between Christian, Muslim, and Arab cannot properly be viewed in terms of modern ideas such as "discrimination" or "racial segregation." Rather these distinctions enabled society to establish a system of relationships between its majority and minority communities that allowed them to preserve their separate cultural and religious identities. In his works, Castro speaks of three eras in relation to medieval Spain:

The surrender of the Moorish kingdom of Granada to the Christians.

1) an age of the three groups living more or less in harmony (early eighth to the late fourteenth century); 2) disintegration of that harmony (late fourteenth to seventeenth century); 3) total absorption into Christian society (1609 to the present). Historians have since narrowed the first age, speaking of a more or less peaceful coexistence among the three groups in Christian Spain from the late eleventh century (the Jewish migrations to Christian Spain) into the thirteenth century.

In this relatively "cooperative" age, the groups maintained their separate identities by subscribing to a system Castro defines as *convivencia,* or living togetherness. The system—sometimes peaceful, sometimes violent, and not uniform throughout the Christian kingdoms—nevertheless endured without extinguishing the separate cultural identities of the three groups. Religion was but the first of a host of their distinct traits: "By proclaiming oneself a Christian, a Muslim, or a Jew, one espoused specific religious doctrines and also accepted a whole system of cultural values that affected one's daily life, one's habits, traditions, laws, and even language" (O'Callaghan, p. 22).

The three communities in the Christian kingdoms. Medieval society in Christian Spain showed considerable complexity. No one culture was strictly tied to a single set of roles in the larger fabric of society but there were basic tendencies,

as Castro indicates in *The Spaniards.* More exactly, the Christians, Jews, and Muslims tended to assume separate occupational roles. In Castro's words, "a society was gradually being constructed in which . . . certain types of occupations were linked . . . to religious faith" (Castro, *Spaniards,* pp. 81-82). Although there were Christians who in fact engaged in trade, this group held in highest esteem two other pursuits: 1) attaining honor by waging war, and 2) taking holy orders. These were the two main avenues of upward mobility in medieval Christian society. In secular life, agriculture was the next most honorable occupation after the practice of arms, the belief being that farming "strengthens the body and the spirit and prepares [one] for travail and for war" (Sepúlveda in *Spaniards,* p. 81). The statement points to an overriding preoccupation with war in Christian society. Again in Castro's words, "For the Hispano-Christian, peace had never been productive" (*Spaniards,* p. 83). Castile (*Castilla* in Spanish), the kingdom that would provide the central warfaring impetus for the Reconquest, as well as for Spanish imperial expansion beyond the seas, is a case in point. Its very name, notes Castro, harks back to the Latin plural for "castles" or "fortresses" (*castella*), suggesting that the Christians who inhabited the area viewed themselves in relation to a warlike enterprise. Other vital functions (trade, science, and learning), though seen as necessary for the good of society, were considered secondary.

All three societies had proscriptions against intermarriage, a self-preservation tactic in such a mixed society. In Muslim-dominated territories, Islamic men sometimes took Christian wives; in Christian territories, intermarriage did not take place unless one party converted to Christianity.

JEWS AND MUSLIMS IN CASTILIAN LAW

Completed early in the fourteenth century, *Las Siete Partidas* became the law code in Castile. The code prescribed how Jews and Moors were to pass their lives among the Christians.

- Jews . . . practicing their own religious rites . . . [should be] very careful to avoid preaching to, or converting any Christian. . . . Whoever violates this law shall be put to death and lose all his property.

- All Jews male and female living in our dominions shall bear some distinguishing mark upon their heads . . . and . . . shall pay for each time [they are] found without it ten *maravedis* of gold; and if [they have] not the means to do this [they] shall publicly receive ten lashes.

- For the reason that a synagogue is a place where the name of God is praised, we forbid any Christian to deface it, or remove anything from it, or take anything out of it by force.

- Moors shall . . . observe their own [religious] law [but] . . . not have mosques in Christian towns. . . . So long as they live among Christians . . . their property shall not be stolen from them . . . and we order that whoever violates this law shall pay a sum equal to double the value of what he took.

- If a Moor has sexual intercourse with a Christian virgin, we order that he shall be stoned. . . . If a Moor has sexual intercourse with a Christian married woman, he shall be stoned to death.

- Men . . . who . . . renounce the faith of Our Lord Jesus Christ, and become Moors . . . shall lose all their possessions. . . . If any person who has committed such an offense shall be found in any part of our dominions he shall be put to death.

(Constable, pp. 268-75)

The Christian areas formulated laws that forbade Jews from owning Christian slaves, from making love to a Christian, or from cohabiting with or marrying a Christian. Christian parliaments likewise imposed restrictive laws on the Mudéjares,

the Muslims who chose to live in the Christian areas. According to the law, they had to wear their hair short, without a forelock, and their beards long. Mudéjares could not wear bright apparel, employ a Christian, or live in a Christian house. Although they generally enjoyed freedom of worship, certain practices were circumscribed—for example, the *muezzin* calling of the faithful to prayer.

Moors and Jews in Christian Spain. The Muslims of Spain, predicts the epic Christian hero El Cid, shall one day be servants to the Christians (see *Poem of the Cid,* also in *WLAIT 5: Spanish and Portuguese Literatures and Their Times*). His prediction would come to fruition. There were many Muslim slaves in Christian Spain, with little say about where they would reside. The Mudéjares, though, those who elected to remain in Christian-controlled areas of their own free will, commonly chose to live in rural areas. When they settled in the cities, the group often resided in separate Muslim quarters (*Morerías*) with their own courts of law.

Mudéjares won high repute for skill in craftsmanship and in a type of art and architecture that still bears their name (*arte Mudéjar*). Distinguished by intricate carvings and a remarkable sense of proportion, Mudéjar art continues to be regarded as genuinely Spanish. Mudéjares also participated, along with Jews and foreigners, in the School of Translators of Toledo and distinguished themselves for work in astronomy and astrology. Castro associates the Mudéjares with particular service occupations as well. Tailor (*alfayate*), barber (*alfajeme*), muleteer (*arriero*), mason (*albañil*), and inspector of weights and measures (*albéitar*) are all medieval words of Arabic origin that point to Muslim occupations (*Spaniards*, p. 80). While the Mudéjares achieved a veritable monopoly on certain professions in various areas, there was often a high degree of economic cooperation between them and Christians, including joint Christian-Muslim trade unions, such as that of the blacksmiths of Segovia. Rarely, however, were Muslims employed by Christian rulers, perhaps because the Muslims were seen as potential political enemies.

Hispano-Jews became associated with certain occupations too. While Jews had been present on the peninsula at least since their dispersal after the destruction of Jerusalem in 70 C.E., many great personalities appeared in Spain under Muslim rule, including the poet Yehuda Halevi (c. 1080-1140), and the philosopher Moses Maimonides (1135-1204).

First under the Muslims, then in Christian-dominated Spain, Jews often carried out the roles of physicians, scientists, tax-collectors, public officials, diplomats, and administrators of the wealth of the state or nobility, achieving considerable prestige through these privileged positions. The privileged status, along with age-old prejudices, incited animosity against the Jews. Intermittent persecution, a pogrom in Granada in 1066—caused many to flee from Muslim to Christian-controlled zones, bringing with them not only Jewish culture but also the Muslim customs they had assimilated, including the Arabic language, and in the case of the most learned Jews, the languages of Latin and Greek.

The Arabic language used by the Hispano-Jews belonged to a culture that had absorbed through conquest many of the treasures of the Hellenic world. Through the agency of these Hispano-Jews, this culture left its mark on Cordova, which, under the Muslims, became one of the world's most famous centers of learning. In Christian-controlled Castile, a land dedicated to the waging of war, learning was meager, so the educated, multilingual Jews found their way into influential positions working for Christian lords. Extending the work of the translators in Toledo, the Jews of Castile translated Arabic treatises on philosophy, mathematics, and physical science, which were then disseminated to the larger European world. Castilian Jews engaged in a wide variety of other occupations too, from farmer, to doctor, tailor, tax collector, shoemaker, and soldier. The notion of Jews working only in finance, "enjoying high positions in the royal court, or leading uniform lives throughout the peninsula, is misleading and incorrect" (Freund and Ruiz, p. 172).

The Jews mostly lived in urban-centered communities in Christian Spain, often in their own quarters (*juderías*), governed by their own law courts, though legal autonomy varied greatly across kingdoms and eras. In disputes between Jews and members of other communities, Jews often fell under the direct jurisdiction of the king or his representative.

While laws of the land promoted peaceful co-existence, it certainly did not always ensue. Jews were massacred in Christian Spain from time to time, as they had been in Muslim Spain. An especially fierce rash of pogroms raged through the peninsula in 1391, bringing the long cherished tradition of *convivencia*, or living togetherness, to a definitive close. While the tradition had managed to endure through the twelfth and early thirteenth centuries, it began afterwards to deteriorate until it reached a new low in 1391.

Historians generally concur that the pogroms of this year mark an irrevocable turning point. As long as *convivencia* lasted, the situation of minority religious communities in Christian realms was highly structured but also highly interactive. "Despite repeated ecclesiastical condemnation, Christians, Muslims, and Jews drank together, went to war together, lived in the same neighborhoods (sometimes in the same house), established business partnerships, engaged in all forms of commercial exchange, even watched

THE HEBREW CASTILIAN

Referred to as the "Castilian," Yehuda Halevi identified himself as a product of Christian Spain. Halevi, a pre-eminent Jewish poet, was born in Toledo shortly after the Reconquest of that city. He spoke both Arabic and a mixed Arabic and Castilian dialect. Halevi practiced medicine for the aristocracy of Christian Spain—unhappily, it seems. He took comfort in religious philosophy as well as poetry, not sharing the hopes of Jewish leaders about the new Christian rule, his outlook sobered by a rash of pogroms (anti-Jewish massacres) in Castile and Leon around 1109. Instead of placing hope in Christian Spain, Halevi fixed his eyes on Palestine: "A light thing would it seem to me to leave all the good things of Spain—/ Seeing how precious in mine eyes to behold the dust of the desolate sanctuary" (Halevi, p. 2). In 1140 he set out on a pilgrimage to the Holy Land by way of Egypt, only to mysteriously disappear. His legacy survives in poems of love, friendship, and religious passion. Evident in his religious verse is a personal longing for union with God; more than five centuries later, this same longing would surface in the poems of another literary giant of Castile, Saint John of the Cross (see **"Dark Night and Other Poems,"** also in *WLAIT 5: Spanish and Portuguese Literatures and Their Times*):

> O Lord, where shall I find Thee?
> All-hidden and exalted is Thy place;
> And where shall I not find Thee?
> Full of Thy glory is the infinite space.
>
> (Halevi, p. 168)

each other's religious ceremonies" (Nirenberg, p. 157). Relations would only worsen after 1391 until they disintegrated altogether in 1492. In the interim, Jews who converted to Christianity became highly suspect. "In the eyes of lower-class Christians, and of their zealous counterparts in the upper echelons, the *conversos* remained Jews despite their conversion" (Freund and Ruiz, p. 179). This perception helps explain the tension that would continue to exist between Castile's Old and New Christians (the Old Christians being those who claimed no Semitic or *converso* ancestry).

Post-1492 society. In 1492 the Christians conquered the last Muslim kingdom, Granada, cementing Iberia's political unification. That same year, all Spanish Jews who were not willing to accept baptism into the Christian faith were ordered to leave Spain. Having conquered the last Muslim holdout, Spain became a united nation with two religions: Christianity and Islam. Ten years later, in 1502, the king and queen issued an edict calling for all Muslims to convert to Christianity or leave the kingdom. Most felt compelled to convert so that they could stay in their ancestral homeland, but they did not take the new faith to heart and remained suspect in the eyes of their Christian neighbors thereafter. Still a highly rural population, the Moriscos (Christianized Moors) continued to speak Arabic and refused to assimilate into the larger Christian population in other ways as well. The two groups lived together uneasily for another hundred years, until 1609, when, after a series of uprisings and wars, the Christians expelled the Moriscos. This final expulsion converted Spanish society on the peninsula—in contrast to its overseas possessions—into a monocultural entity. But the vestiges of multicultural Spain could not be so easily stamped out. Although in politics and religion, Christians had triumphed, the ensuing society showed an unmistakable fusion of the values of the three "castes" (a term that in Spanish connotes purity of lineage and that Castro uses to differentiate among the three groups).

A reflection of this fusion of values was the widespread concern over "purity of blood" (*limpieza de sangre*). Whether by force or of their own accord, many Jews had converted to Christianity over the centuries. The converts (commonly referred to as "New Christians") were regarded with skepticism and suspected of insincere conversion, of secretly practicing Judaism, and of trying to lure Christians into renouncing their faith. Moriscos too were regarded suspiciously. The ill will engendered by all this suspicion lingered after the Jewish and Muslim expulsions. In particular, the Old Christians showed a fierce respect for pure lineage (*lo castizo*) of people, that is, for their Old Christian ancestry. In fact, the rift between Old and New

Christians increased after 1492, going on to haunt peninsular life, intensifying internal division and conflict in a society that only on the surface appeared to be united.

The Treatise in Focus

Contents summary. *The Spaniards: An Introduction to Their History* is divided into 14 chapters, plus an addendum and an appendix. Though it is a historical investigation, the treatise is arranged not according to a chronological criterion but rather by thematic headings. As noted in the preface, his title *The Spaniards* indicates Castro's "wish to accentuate and emphasize the personal, rather than the structural, nature of [Spanish] history" (*Spaniards,* p. v).

In Chapters 1 and 2, respectively, Castro sets out the terms of the problem: what is the method to be used in studying history and toward what aim should it be employed? The aim is to study a human phenomenon without reducing it to either a justification of current political goals or a series of easily quantifiable data, since neither can adequately take into account acts of human will or volition. The object of examination is a particular nation, Spain, with all its peculiarities and uniqueness. Castro begins with the following premise—the understanding of who Spaniards are has been clouded by historians and philosophers who for centuries have projected the concept of "Spanishness" far back into history on individuals and peoples who had no awareness of being such: the Celtiberians, the Visigoths, and so forth.

In Chapter 3, "The Intermingling of the Three Castes," Castro advances what will become the crux of his new view of Spanish history, perhaps best summarized in the words of Thomas Glick: "The culture we know as Spanish did not exist before, and came into being as a result of, the interaction of Muslims, Christians, and Jews (the 'three castes' as he calls them) in the eighth through the thirteenth centuries" (Glick, p. 7). The chapter makes the case for Castro's central argument regarding the understanding of the individuality of Spain: "Those Peninsular peoples successively conquered by Phoenicians, Carthaginians, Greeks, Romans, Visigoths, Byzantines, and Muslims did not possess the collective or social structure and physiognomy of those who slowly reconquered Peninsular territory [from the Muslims] over a period of eight centuries" (*Spaniards,* p. 38). In other words, the Reconquest of Spain was achieved by the Spaniards—

a people forged from interaction among the three castes.

The next chapter ("Theoretical Assumptions") sets out to delve into the inner life of the people known as the Spaniards. Such an inner life, for Castro, is expressed by the deeds and events that make up their reality. In his eyes, it is the peculiar way that such deeds and events have taken place that constitutes the "vital disposition and way of life" or "dwelling place" that is unique to a given group (*Spaniards*, p. 99). Castro considers "dwelling place" more descriptive than "psychology" or "character," in that it refers to a person's awareness of belonging to a collective life, one that can change and evolve, that is not fixed forever.

Chapter 5, "A History of Inner Confidence and Insecurity," attempts to show how the spirit of struggle and militancy that characterized the people that came to be called "Spanish" provided the basis for an enormous sense of historical "mission," yet also contributed to a sense of historical insecurity. This insecurity, says Castro, can be traced back to a "lack of proportion and congruity between the intensity of [the Spaniard's] impulses and the stability or worth of the results to be achieved" (*Spaniards*, p. 146). It is an insecurity that helps explain the Spanish passion for grand exploits and fame (the Reconquest, the conquest of the Americas, the desire to be seen as *someone*) and the sense of disenchantment that pervades the works of such great writers as Cervantes, Tirso de Molina, Quevedo, and St. Teresa of Avila (see **Don Quixote,** the **Trickster of Seville, The Swindler,** and **Interior Castle,** also in *WLAIT 5: Spanish and Portuguese Literatures and Their Times*).

In Chapter 6, "The Non-Spanish Structure of Roman and Visigothic Hispania," Castro attacks the notion that Spanish life already existed in those peoples who conquered the peninsula before the Moorish invasion of 711. In particular, he takes a close look at the figure of Seneca, the Roman philosopher born in Hispania, whose stoicism has been highlighted as one of his "Spanish" traits. For Castro, the stoicism of Seneca had nothing to do with later forms of Spanish life, nor did it ever really interest Spaniards. In his words, "If the Spaniards had been followers of Seneca, their history would have been different from what it has been and is, because their interest would have been concentrated on the rational analysis of earthly life" (*Spaniards*, p. 178). He then dwells on the Visigothic kingdom, which, though it held political hegemony over

Hispania until 711, had no genealogical or cultural connection with the peoples who undertook the Reconquest, says Castro; nor, to his mind, did the Visigoths provide any lasting traits that could be perceived as Spanish.

Chapters 7 and 8 turn their attention to Islam and its presence in Spain. Castro asserts in Chapter 7 ("Al-Andalus"), "The Christian peoples who finally came to be called Spaniards were the result of the combination of an attitude of submission and wonder in the face of a culturally superior enemy, and the effort to overcome this very position of inferiority" (*Spaniards*, p. 215). The treatise proceeds to examine what Castro holds to be distinctly Islamic elements that have shaped Spanish society, in particular the type of mysticism exemplified in the poetry of St. John of the Cross. The following chapter ("Islamic Tradition and Spanish Life") is an examination of ways of living and speaking in present-day Spanish life that are a result of the centuries-long presence of the Moors in the peninsula.

In Chapter 9 ("In Search of a Better Social Order"), Castro links the nineteenth-century movements called "anarchism" in Spain and their ties to earlier anarchical tendencies in Spanish society. According to Castro, the conflictive state of being that emerged out of the mingling of the three castes and the subsequent amputation of two of them caused Spaniards to turn inward for sources of renewal and hope, rather than outward (to revolutionary movements or alternative forms of government, as in other European countries). Spain's late-nineteenth-century anarchist movements stemmed from a messianic longing that tried to destroy the social order without offering a constructive alternative. There was a similar failure centuries earlier, when the Christian Spaniards expelled the Jews and Muslims. "The Spanish Christian caste fell into the regrettable error of scorning and rejecting the customary occupations of the Moors and Jews instead of taking them over" (*Spaniards*, p. 326).

Chapter 10, "Beginnings of Christian and European Reaction," details the rise of the shrine of Santiago de Compostela, where traditional belief holds that the body of the Apostle St. James (St. James the Great) is buried. Mentioning the strength this belief gave to those who struggled against Islam, the chapter says that the shrine helped rally a type of warlike national self-consciousness. This militant self-consciousness, argues Castro, differed greatly from any other medieval European manifestation of Christianity, since the Spanish were the only European Christian people of the era to feel themselves spiritually isolated and forced to battle for their own existence. In Chapter 11, "Santiago, an International Attraction," Castro details Santiago's function as a contact point with other Christian European nations, one that promoted especially the introduction of French monasticism. Also detailed is Santiago's link to the independence of Portugal.

"The Islamic Perspective of Three Christian Institutions," Chapter 12, is an examination of what Castro deems to be Spanish traditions that arose as a result of the Christian caste's contact with Islam: namely, military orders, Holy War, and religious tolerance. For Castro, the military orders, those knight-monks dedicated to combating the infidel, were not wholly in keeping with the Christian tradition, but rather had more in common with the institution of the hermitages in Islamic lands, in which "holy men who alternated between asceticism and the defense of the borders, lived in retirement" (*Spaniards,* p. 473). Castro also brings his scholarship to bear on a demonstration that the "war against Muslims in Spain and in Palestine, however different its purposes and results may have been, was inspired by the [jihad], or the Muslim doctrine of holy war" (*Spaniards,* p. 488). So too, says Castro, did the relative religious tolerance that held sway in Christian Spain until the end of the fourteenth century spring from contact with ideas in the Muslim's holy text, the Koran, which regarded both Christians and Jews as fellow "peoples of the Book."

Chapter 13, "The Historical Ages Conditioned by the Peculiar Problem of the Spanish Population," examines several issues at once: the reasons why erudition was not cultivated among the Christians of Castile during the Middle Ages; how the Mudéjares related to the other two castes and the role of the Jews in the caste system. Castro finishes the chapter with a section that polemicizes with the American scholar, Otis H. Green and his *Spain in the Western Tradition.* In this last section, Castro takes Green to task for inserting Spain into the Western European cultural tradition and for not taking into account the Semitic (Jewish and Muslim) contributions that shaped the uniqueness of Spain's culture.

In the final chapter (Problems and Periods in Spanish History), Castro addresses the disappearance of the caste system and its effect on Spain's technical and philosophical progress. He finishes by proposing a chronological division for studying Spanish history as follows:

a) Disappearance of the Roman-Visigothic duality and beginning of the reconquest of the eighth and ninth centuries

b) The living togetherness (*convivencia*) in the Christian kingdoms from the tenth to the end of the fifteenth century of people of three castes: Christian, Jewish, and Moorish

c) Religious exclusivism [absence of Islam and Judaism]: imperial, artistic, and literary grandeur from 1500 to 1700 (a conflict between the individual person and collective opinion—Cervantes, Gracián, cultural paralysis)

d) Crisis in the eighteenth century with the rise of a (French) foreign dynasty in Spain, intellectual hermeticism, and attempts at Europeanization; tension between the imported culture and traditional modes of living: Feijoo, Jovellanos, Godoy, Goya

e) From 1800 to the fall of the monarchy in 1931

The Spaniards: An Introduction to Their History ends with an addendum and an appendix. The addendum includes excerpts from two documents: one is a letter from the field marshal of Spanish forces during the War of Mexican Independence. Exhorting the local citizens to remain loyal to the Spanish crown, the marshal explains that "the *Apostle Santiago* [is] always on the side of the Spaniards," thus demonstrating, as Castro explains, that "In the early nineteenth century it was still felt that war in defense of the sovereignty of the king of Spain was holy and of divine origin" (*Spaniards,* p. 586). The second document is from the case of Luis de Carvajal, burned by the Mexican Inquisition in 1596, allegedly for trying to convert a friend to Judaism.

In the appendix, entitled "Observations on Bullfights and Autos da Fe," Castro briefly examines two Spanish spectacles, the latter extinct, the former very much alive today. The point of examining these two institutions, for Castro, is that both "in seventeenth-century Spain came to be spectacles endowed with sacred significance, although in different forms (*Spaniards,* p. 598). The autos da fe, or public executions for deviance from the teachings of the Roman Catholic Church, served to rid Spanish society—symbolically and sometimes literally—of those elements that were deemed foreign to the body of believers.

Castro finishes this volume by reiterating the guiding force behind his conception of history: "Ultimately, to perceive and grasp the dramatic sense of history is as necessary and at least as important as the study of the rising and falling graphs of economy or public and private property" (*Spaniards,* p. 600).

A 1741 intaglio print depicting executions during the Spanish Inquisition.

Caste consciousness. In order to bring into focus the inner life of today's Spaniards, Castro makes use of ancient documents that illustrate how the peoples of the Iberian Peninsula differentiated themselves from one another. Such documents reveal that at the start of the Reconquest, those who opposed the Moors called themselves "Christians," using religion as the distinguishing factor: "The faith in Christ 'conferred nationality' as much as did the faith in Mohammed," whose followers at the time controlled most of the peninsula (*Spaniards,* p. 50). This historical reality helps explain the importance of "caste" to Castro, which, as noted, is the term he uses to differentiate among the three groups. All three groups would live elbow to elbow on the Iberian Peninsula until 1492, each defining itself in opposition to the other two, and despite interaction with the other two, priding itself on the "purity" of its lineage to the extent that it was free from being "tainted" by too much contact with the others. This system of castes, according to Castro, was unique to the Iberian Peninsula, given that other European countries did not undergo the same type of history as Spain—Christian reconquest of lands that had been seized by the Muslims.

For Castro, the concept of caste was not simply an outgrowth of the Christian wars against the Muslims, however; it had deeper, more complex roots and, moreover, "did not proceed from motives peculiar to [the Christian Spaniards]" (*Spaniards,* p. 52). Such a concern for separation, notes Castro, appears often in the literature of the Sephardim, the Spanish Jews. In al-Andalus, as the Muslim-controlled swath of Iberia was called, Jews and Christians were thought inferior for not having accepted Islam and both were excluded from political power (Glick, p. 168). Castro identifies this caste consciousness as the determining factor in Spanish identity, "From the struggle and rivalries among these three groups, from their interconnections and their hatreds, arose the authentic life of the Spaniards" (*Spaniards,* p. 63).

> The history of the Spaniards must begin by determining the identity and procedures of those who initiated new forms of collective life after the Visigothic failure, a life that was tightly bound to the Semitic peoples—Moors and Jews—who for centuries maintained the civilization of the inhabitants of al-Andalus at a high level. Those Semitic peoples deeply affected the vital structure of forms of conduct of the Christians.   (*Spaniards,* p. 64)

Without a firm focus on the "Semitic forms of life" (customs received from Jewish and Islamic peoples) that influenced Spanish Christians, says Castro, one cannot understand their later evolution or their literary achievements. The melding of castes, argues Castro, led to literary greatness. Out of sincere belief or compulsion, many Jews converted to Christianity and much of the finest Spanish literature of the fourteenth to sixteenth century is indebted to the contributions of Jews or Christians of Jewish ancestry.

In Castro's estimation, while the three castes lived side-by-side, each held to a belief in its own worth and a feeling of security in its role in society. The memory of their common life would surface in post-1492 literature. Castro mentions the example of Pármeno's mother in the Spanish drama *La Celestina* (also in *WLAIT 5: Spanish and Portuguese Literatures and Their Times*), who "never failed to attend the burial of Christians, or Moors, or Jews," as well as the literary allusions of the Sephardic Jews, who referred to the social system of the three castes in ballads sung in exile (*Spaniards*, pp. 91-92). The system remained alive in memory. Meanwhile, asserts Castro, the absence of the two castes had a severe consequence. The development of Spanish society was interrupted by the expulsions, cut short by the loss of the Muslims and the Jews, who had contributed so much to the forging of Spanish culture.

Sources and literary context. As far back as the eighteenth century, Spanish authors had begun to question the nature of Spanish history and the Spanish nation. With the influence of French Enlightenment ideas that accompanied the traumatic coming of the French Bourbon family to the Spanish throne, writers such as Benito Jerónimo Feijóo and Gaspar Melchor de Jovellanos began examining the question of what was particularly Spanish (see **Essay on Woman,** also in *WLAIT 5: Spanish and Portuguese Literatures and Their Times*). Such an examination proceeded into the nineteenth century, with the group known as the "Generation of 1898" carrying on the tradition of self-questioning. Writers such as Miguel de Unamuno looked into Spanish history to find features that could explain its rise to imperial grandeur in early modern times and its subsequent fall into "decadence," which reached unprecedented depths in their own times.

Spanish historiography of the late nineteenth and early twentieth centuries saw the emergence of two guiding figures: Marcelino Menéndez Pelayo (1856-1912) and Ramón Menéndez Pidal (1869-1968). Menéndez Pelayo set out to pro-vide a synthesis of the available data that had been maintained regarding the history of Spain. He absorbed many of the prevailing European notions about historical method and searched for a principle to apply to Spain, settling on "Catholic unity" as the central characteristic of the Spanish people throughout history, a conclusion he reached partially in response to the nationalist movements sweeping Europe at that time, movements that tended to focus on ethnicity and particularities instead of factors that transcended race and nationality. While later historians would often view his conclusions as less than scientific, his place in the pantheon of Spanish historians and his contribution to study of Spanish history has never been questioned.

The other towering figure of Spanish historiography is Ramón Menéndez Pidal. His monumental work *Orígenes del español* (The Origins of Spanish) remains to this day the most complete work on the history of the Spanish language. His historico-linguistic approach to the study of the roots of Spanish culture, his innumerable works of scholarship and his dedication to creating the *Revista de filología española* (The Journal of Spanish Philology) formed the school of historians that gave rise to Américo Castro as one of its most illustrious pupils. Menéndez Pidal's scientific rigor was marked by distaste for examining religious questions (in contrast to the approach of Menéndez Pelayo and Américo Castro); in later years he would sometimes disagree with the conclusions reached by his disciple Américo. For Menéndez Pidal, the study of the roots of the Spanish language, along with the earliest forms of its literary tradition (including folk ballads and epic poems) would form the nucleus for understanding the true nature of the Spanish people.

Falling in line with the investigations of these scholars, Castro upset traditional historiography by suddenly dating the origin of the Spaniard from the Muslim invasion. His position was startling in contrast to the long-accepted view that Spanish history started much earlier, with the beginning of peninsular life: "In one way or another, almost all the historians who studied Spain . . . from . . . Father Mariana's *Historia de Espanna* (1601) . . . asserted the existence of a geological "Spaniard" born together with Peninsular geography" (Araya Goubet, pp. 64-65). Castro changed all that, introducing an innovative perspective, one that stirred vigorous controversy.

Reception. Hotly debated before the publication of Castro's theories, the question of Spain's defining characteristics took on new energy with the publication of Castro's theories. *España en su historia: moros, judíos, cristianos*, as well as his later works, proved extremely popular in Spain and abroad, garnering an enormous amount of attention, both positive and negative. In 1957 the Mexican publishing house Porrúa released the book *Juicios y Comentarios* (Judgements and Commentaries), containing reviews of Castro's foundational 1948 book by some of the foremost scholars of the day, culled from journals such as *The Muslim World*, *The Yale Review,* and the Milan daily *Corriere della Sera.*

Back in Spain, in 1953 Ramón Menéndez Pidal published the first volume of the series directed by him, *Historia de España* (History of Spain). In 1956 Claudio Sánchez Albornoz published *España, un enigma histórico* (Spain, a Historical Enigma). The following year, in 1957, the series *Historia social y económica de España y América* (Social and Economic History of Spain and America), directed by J. Vicens Vives, arrived at the bookstores. Each of these studies, either intentionally or unintentionally, entered into polemics with Castro's vision of Spanish history.

In 1966, the medievalist and Cervantes scholar Eugenio Asensio entered into what was perhaps the most biting dispute with Castro's ides. Other authors published ideas that conflicted with Castro's, but Asensio adopted a stance that was anti-Castro (the title of his book *La España imaginada de Américo Castro* [1976; Américo Castro's Imagined Spain] is sufficiently explanatory). For Asensio, "Castro belongs to a line of philosophizing historians that miss that mark by joining historical data with philosophical concepts" (Asensio, p. 10; trans. D. Bacich). Asensio disagreed with Castro's situating Spanish identity in the cultural mix that occurred after 711, and others have too, but none of the criticism has negated the riveting effect his ideas have had on historians and literary scholars: "The impact of his work is . . . equivalent to an intellectual revolution within the scope of Spanish history. . . . One must either yield to his doctrine or have very good reasons for not doing so. But it is impossible to remain impartial; one always has to take a stand in this regard" (Araya Goubet, pp. 64-65).
　　—Damian Bacich and Enrique Rodríguez-Cepeda

For More Information

Araya Goubet, Guillermo. "The Evolution of Castro's Theories." In *Américo Castro and the Meaning of Spanish Civilization.* Ed. José Rubia Barcia and Selma Margaretten. Berkeley: University of California Press, 1976.

Asensio, Eugenio. *La España imaginada de Américo Castro.* Barcelona: Ediciones El Albir, 1976.

Carr, Raymond, ed. *Spain: A History.* Oxford: Oxford University Press, 2000.

Castro, Américo. *The Structure of Spanish History.* Trans. Edmund L. King. Princeton: Princeton University, 1954.

————. *The Spaniards: An Introduction to Their History.* Trans. Willard F. King and Selma Margaretten. Berkeley: University of California Press, 1971.

Constable, Olivia Remie, ed. *Medieval Iberia: Readings From Christian, Muslim, and Jewish Sources.* Philadelphia: University of Pennsylvania Press, 1997.

Freund, Scarlett, and Teofilo F. Ruiz. "Jews, *Conversos,* and the Inquisition in Spain, 1391-1492." In *Jewish-Christian Encounters over the Centuries.* Eds. Marvin Perry and Frederick M. Schweitzer. New York: Peter Lang, 1994.

Glick, Thomas F. *Islamic and Christian Spain in the Early Middle Ages.* Princeton: Princeton University, 1979.

Halevi, Jehudah. *Selected Poems of Jehudah Halevi.* Ed. Heinrich Brody. Philadelphia: The Jewish Publication Society of America, 1952.

Kamen, Henry. *Spain 1469-1714: A Society in Conflict.* London. Longman, 1991.

Nirenberg, David. *Communities of Violence: Persecution of Minorities in the Middle Ages.* Princeton: Princeton University, 1996.

O'Callaghan, Joseph. *A History of Medieval Spain.* Ithaca: Cornell, 1975.

Surtz, Ronald E. et al., eds. *Américo Castro: The Impact of His Thought. Essays to Mark the Centenary of His Birth.* Madison: The Hispanic Seminary of Medieval Studies, 1988.

Stormy Isles—An Azorean Tale

by
Vitorino Nemésio

Vitorino Nemésio was born in the Azores in 1901 in the town of Praia da Vitória, Terceira Island. While still in high school he spent a few years on a different island, Faial, an experience that would influence his future writing. He later attended the universities of Coimbra and Lisbon on the Portuguese mainland, and spent the better part of his teaching career at the University of Lisbon. The experience of immigrating to the mainland impacted him deeply, exerting a strong influence on his reflection about the Azorean islands, which soon became a constant subject in his conversations, lectures, and writings. Nearly every summer he would make the trip by boat back to the Azores so that he might vacation on his home island of Terceira. He wrote about the islands in short stories (in "Paço do Milhafre" [1924], for example) and in poems (such as "Voyelle Promise," first written in French in 1938). They became the subject of important articles by him too that reflect upon the concept of "azoreanness," which means the Azorean worldview, or the Azorean way of life. Nemésio repeated often that for Azoreans, geography is just as important as history. His statement underlines the fact that the formation of the Azorean mentality was due in large part to the geographical location and the physical characteristics of the islands. Nemésio asserted that these were the factors, more than any others, that conditioned the development of a particular dimension of insularity, of isolation and of a kind of social strangulation in the middle of the Atlantic, which, although suffocating,

THE LITERARY WORK

A novel set in the Azores, Portugal (mainly in the city of Horta on the island of Faial), between 1917-19; published in Portuguese (as *Mau Tempo no Canal*) in 1944, in English in 1998.

SYNOPSIS

On a small mid-Atlantic island, Margarida Clark Dulmo, member of a noble yet financially declining family, struggles with the secular fatalism of her culture as she anxiously attempts to overcome it.

was at the same time profoundly rich from a cultural standpoint. It is in this sociocultural and geographical context that Margarida Clark Dulmo's story unfolds.

Events in History at the Time the Novel Takes Place

Imperial harbor. Vitorino Nemésio intended to write a novel that would not be bound to Margarida's story; he purported to study a sort of underlying collective unconscious in Azorean culture as a distinct social reality forged over five centuries within the larger Portuguese cultural space, but significantly far from the mainland. It is therefore necessary to know something of the Azorean history to which he, both implicitly and explicitly, refers throughout the novel. The translator of Nemésio's novel, Francisco Cota Fagundes, confirms this when he writes in the introduction of that work that "the history of the Azores as a whole constitutes the subject matter of *Stormy Isles*" (Cota Fagundes in Nemésio, *Stormy Isles*, p. xix).

Portugal's discovery of the sea route to India took nearly 80 years. It was a cautious yet intrepid process of exploration, first of the Atlantic Ocean, then of the lands that surround it, then of its many islands. Soon after the discovery of the first islands, Madeira and Porto Santo, which together form an archipelago, there appeared to the west another archipelago—the nine Azorean islands, also discovered little by little over a few decades due to the great distances between them. The first of these nine islands appears to have been discovered between 1427 and 1432.

Very early, the Portuguese realized the importance of these islands. As they returned from their South Atlantic excursions, they discovered that the ocean currents and the trade winds would push their ships to the northwest, practically forcing them to call on the Azores. Since Terceira has a natural, safe harbor that is both large and deep, it immediately became the principal port where the Portuguese caravels would anchor. After a long voyage by way of the so-called *rota do largo* (the wide route), which took them far from the African coast, the sailors would inevitably require water, food, and, above all, fresh fruit, since they could only store salted foods in their holds—salting being the only available meat-preserving process that could withstand the torrid heat of the tropics. The sailors would refresh themselves and their supplies, then lift anchor and head from Terceira to Lisbon, which took another three weeks.

Early inhabitants. Such difficulties were anticipated by Henry the Navigator, leader of these maritime expeditions, when he commanded that the Azores be settled shortly after they were discovered. Since they were uninhabited islands and covered with thick vegetation, Henry sent animals (cattle, pigs, chickens, rabbits) so that they might become acclimatized and reproduce in a manner that would provide sustenance for the population that would be sent over a few years later. Almost all settlers came from the Portuguese mainland. It is difficult to ascertain what motivated them to move. It could not have been easy to convince people to leave *terra firma* (firm land, what the mainland was often called) and relocate to small, far-off lands seemingly lost

somewhere in the middle of the ocean with little to offer besides frequent storms and, as the settlers would soon find out, volcanoes and earthquakes. (Because of their volcanic origins, the islands are at the center of periodic seismic activity. Volcanoes commonly erupt underwater and prolonged earthquakes wreak havoc on the islands, so the potential for tragedy coexists with spectacular natural beauty.) On the plus side, the settlement was set up according to a truly impressive plan that was altogether rational, orderly, and intended to help achieve Henry's far-reaching goals.

Among the first settlers on the archipelago were Flemish refugees, who had fled from the fighting that at the time had begun in Flanders (now part Belgium, part The Netherlands). The group established themselves on the westernmost of the Azorean islands, namely on the island of Faial, where there is still today a village called Vale dos Flamengos (Valley of the Flemish). It is difficult to know exactly how many settled there, but some historians estimate the number to have been about 2,000. The name of the main settlement on Faial, the city of Horta, is derived from its Flemish founder, Jos van Huertere. Many other names also derived from Flemish families are still part of Azorean onomastics and toponymy today, such as Dutra, Silveira, Brum, and Terra.

International nexus. In the sixteenth century, Angra, positioned on the southern coast of Terceira along the famous route to India, became the greatest Atlantic port, a sort of way station. However, by the end of that century, Portugal lost its independence to Spain for 60 years (according to dynastical norms, Philip II of Spain, married to a daughter of the king of Portugal, had the rights to the Portuguese throne if the Portuguese monarch were to die without a direct heir). During the reign of Philip II (1580-98) and his successors, Angra continued to play an important role in linking Spanish America and Spain. Philip II ordered that a fortress be built in Angra, and the Azores became a center for control of the Atlantic. The islands proved especially instrumental in defense against the growing number of corsairs, or pirate ships, from northern Europe.

Aside from their function as a fortress of sorts, during the fifteenth and sixteenth centuries, the islands experienced a period of intense commercial and agricultural activity (their volcanic soil was highly fertile and proved well suited for growing fruits and grains). However, when this period ended, the Azorean population was left more or less abandoned in the middle of the Atlantic for a time. Greenland lay to the north, North America to the west, Europe to the east, and Antarctica (then known only as the Glacial Antarctic Ocean) to the south.

Discovered in 1500 by Portuguese explorer Pedro Álvares Cabral, Brazil failed to capture Portugal's interest until many years later. But by the end of the seventeenth century, it had become the center of attention. The mining of gold in Minas Gerais and the production of sugarcane required a great deal of manual labor and attracted many adventurers. Portugal intensified its maritime traffic with Brazil, and the Azores returned to their natural function as a way station. Many Azoreans took advantage of the opportunity and immigrated to that immense colony of the Portuguese Empire.

From the end of the 1700s through the beginning of the 1800s, the whaling industry was developed in North America. Boats from New England ventured out to the South Atlantic Ocean and from there to the Pacific Ocean. Now the whalers found it necessary to use the Azores as a support base. Loaded with supplies, mail, and sometimes with the wives of the captains and crews, whaling ships would travel from Boston to Horta. The ships often needed additional manual labor and frequently recruited sailors among the local population. In his classic novel *Moby-Dick*, Herman Melville mentions these islanders:

> No small number of these whaling seamen belong to the Azores, where the outward bound Nantucket whalers frequently touch to augment their crews from the hardy peasants of those rocky shores. . . . How it is, there is no telling, but Islanders seem to make the best whalemen.
> (Melville, *Moby-Dick*, p. 108)

The islands gained such importance that it even became necessary to establish an American consulate in Horta.

The port of Horta soon became a mandatory port-of-call for ships of all types from America headed to Europe, whether manned by lone sailors or by large crews whose vessels were in need of repair. The city of Horta thus became a cosmopolitan center where many foreigners settled, especially Americans, English, and French. Later, at the turn of the twentieth century, the city played yet another international role. It became necessary to run the first telegraph wire from the United States to Europe through the Azores. Horta was the city chosen for that purpose. Western Union's presence animated the little city on several fronts: economically, culturally, and socially. In the meantime its port

continued to see daily increases in the number of ships that anchored there, significantly invigorating the local economy and facilitating the forming of a local bourgeoisie.

Early-twentieth-century Azorean society. At the end of World War I, the Azores were a conservative society with a population firmly divided into socially stratified classes. The elite, a small number of aristocrats and bourgeoisie, formed a closed social circle. The upper class owned land and tried to keep it in the family, mostly through intermarriage. Family interests prevailed over and above everything else. Even though the glorious past of tremendous wealth had somehow faded a bit, the family name ("the honor of the family") and traditional lifestyle were still fervently maintained. According to tradition, no person of pedigree should have to work. Idleness was in fact a virtue. Parties centered around piano playing, and balls filled many an evening.

The middle class showed more heterogeneity, since it consisted of small landowners, merchants, public officers, and state employees. Very few of them had the chance to rise in the social scale, since it was already congested at the top. In *Stormy Isles,* the Garcia family tries to climb the social ladder. The novel shows the reactions they elicit from the defenders of the status quo, the wealthier Clark Dulmos.

All social classes were profoundly patriarchal. Upper- and middle-class women were supposed to stay home, keeping themselves entertained during the day and often entertaining guests in the evening. Having a professional career was taboo for a woman; that would mean that their husband was not wealthy enough to support her. The novel's protagonist Margarida expresses this quite plainly. Under pressure to marry André Barreto in order to help her family recover financially, she explodes,

> In a land where everything is inheritances and business, what can a girl be worth? It's the dresses, the ball, the birthday, a festival that one attends. . . . If they don't have anything to talk about, why not be a topic of conversation for them? . . . Much more than this is owed by a child to "her progenitors" (isn't that what they call them?). Even more so if one is a "mere female. . . . The mere females are supposed to remain quietly at home, sitting on the floor by the window." I have already received first Communion; I have had my Confirmation . . . we are approaching orange blossom season [wedding season].
> (Nemésio, *Stormy Isles*, p. 157)

Port of Horta

The Novel in Focus

Plot summary. Margarida (Clark-Dulmo) is a well-to-do member of Horta society, born into a family that was the result of the union of descendents of the first settlers and nineteenth-century English merchants. At 20 years of age, she is pretty, vivacious, sharp, a model of feminine aspirations, and cream of the crop of her generation and circle of friends. She shows an awareness of her social status but also a willingness to forego some of the entitlements of her class and a rejection of certain conventions of her social milieu. Not sharing her family's idolatry of family ancestors and its aversion to manual labor, Margarida makes regular contact with workers, something natural and easy for her. She also participates in sports that are normally reserved for men, like tennis, horseback riding, and sailing. Above all, she seems willing to defy family tradition by ignoring the discriminating preferences of her family in matchmaking. She is determined to be the one to choose her own future husband despite the fact that her family, though of noble lineage, is in serious economic decline and in need of the financial revitalization that their daughter might bring them through marriage.

Against her family's wishes, Margarida begins a romantic relationship with João Garcia, a young middle-class man, a parvenu, or social climber, whom in the end she finds to be tepid. Although he studied law at Coimbra he is very attached to the social norms of his time, and possesses little initiative. He did not even display youthful zeal during his college years in Lisbon, far from his family and the social trappings of the island. Bereft of even one redeeming spark and incapable of adventurous overtures, João Garcia does not inspire any enthusiasm in Margarida. She finds nothing attractive about him; even the fact of being in favorable economic circumstances because he is the son of the rising bourgeoisie is lost on Margarida, for she has a romantic and "higher" vision of life. She is a young dreamer with a great desire for freedom and adventure, someone who cannot even define her own aspirations but who knows they go beyond the mere materialistic as well as the sociocultural conventionalisms espoused by her society and especially her family. The more she gets to know him, the more João Garcia impresses her as a man of very weak character, deprived of spontaneity, a man led by rational thinking rather than his heart.

In the little social tapestry in which these characters are woven, there are really no truly dramatic occurrences. The narrator introduces Margarida's personality by way of various small incidents and the intricacies of her daily life, as well as her aversion to family norms and aspira-

A DEEP RELIGIOSITY

As a people, isolated in the middle of the Atlantic Ocean, the Azoreans were subject to the furies of the elements and often powerless to receive aid from outsiders. As a result, solidarity and common sharing of possessions, as well as tribulations, became mainstays, if not essential components, of Azorean society. Also the Azoreans habitually turned to God for relief, developing through the centuries a religiousness that created deep roots in the society's collective unconscious. The Festival of the Holy Ghost is the most widely celebrated on the islands. Though it probably originated on the Portuguese mainland, the festival developed during tragic moments of life on the archipelago, when the people, anxious to placate divine wrath, promised to hold yearly celebrations for the Holy Ghost. *Stormy Isles* devotes a chapter to the Holy Ghost Feast, capturing the continuing importance of the holiday not only to Azorean folk tradition but also to present-day life: "The Holy Ghost celebrations fill springtime with a fantastic excitement" (*Stormy Isles,* p. 194). The celebration was a lower-class event; the upper classes never involved themselves in it. By taking interest in the feast, the novel's Margarida signifies her desire to break with upper-class norms and mingle with the general population.

tions. Little by little, the novel spins its tale, painting a picture of the suffocating atmosphere in which Margarida lives and in which a gossipy social system thrives. Jumping from one small incident to the next (with the exception of natural disasters, nothing really spectacular ever happens on the small island), the narrator slowly reveals the complexity of the novel's characters. Perhaps this is why Francisco Cota Fagundes, the translator of this novel, affirms in his introduction that Vitorino Nemésio "is eminently a storyteller" and that the "title *Stormy Isles: An Azorean Tale* fails on one count: the novel is not a tale; it is a series of tales within a much larger tale, a seemingly endless Chinese-box-of-tales that go on being spun within a fictive world that might be described as a spawning ground for tellers of tales" (Cota Fagundes in *Stormy Isles,* p. xxv). Drawn from the novel are two examples of a seemingly endless set of possibilities:

"Margarida opened the book to a yellowed page with effaced print. It was a single issue of the *Azorean Archives*. It contained a series of documents, relative to the sixteenth century, on earthquakes and volcanic eruptions: an excerpt from Gaspar Frutuoso on the Vila Franca quake, the passage from Garcia de Resende's *Miscellany* on the same catastrophe, and finally, the 'Ballad Written on the Occasion of the Suffering and Damages Brought About by the 1522 Earthquake in Vila Franca do Campo'" (*Stormy Isles,*

pp. 334-35). The novel proceeds to feature a Margarida interested in reading that folk poem.

The other example comes from the chapter "An Embroidered Tablecloth," which brings up a little-known Azorean connection in the life of Portuguese writer Almeida Garrett (see **Travels in My Homeland,** also in *WLAIT 5: Spanish and Portuguese Literatures and Their Times*). The niece of a priest brings sweet ring-bread and vintage Pico wine to two characters in the novel:

> "'Sweet-scented Pico,' in the words of our great poet Almeida Garrett. Did you know that his father was from Fayal? [the Azorean island]" André showed a tepid interest in that historical note. "Well, he was. . . . And the poet, who was raised in Terceira, where he wrote some of his early poetry, actually preached a sermon at Santa Cruz Cathedral in Graciosa."
>
> (*Stormy Isles,* p. 280)

Margarida's life unfolds within a closed circle that she attempts to break, albeit blindly, for she does not even know for certain what she is aiming for, only that her convictions differ from the "prospects" offered to her.

A second possible match for Margarida is one Roberto Clark, her half-uncle, since he was an illegitimate child, who lives in London. For Margarida's father, Clark is a pleasing prospect due to what he would bring the family financially. Margarida feels torn about the matter: on the one hand, she detests her father's pragmatism; on the other, the idea of going off to London, in other words, the prospect of finally leaving the island for good, tantalizes her, especially as she grows increasingly aware of her uncle's appealing, sometimes even romantic personality, which elicits dreams from her and provides her with savory moments of freedom. The possibility of marrying him disappears, however, when Roberto dies.

Now in search of a different path, as the result of a wild yet unconscious impulse, Margarida embarks on an adventure that is somewhat daring for a woman of her time (and obviously symbolic in the author's mind). She sets sail on a whaling ship that by chance brings her to the island of São Jorge. Different from Faial and Pico, where property was more evenly distributed and society exhibited a certain regard for equity, São Jorge was an almost feudal island on which the Baron of Urzelina owned the greater part of the land and wrought a kind of medieval submissiveness out of the island's people.

THE AZORES

The Azorean Archipelago is made up of nine islands which together total 868 square miles spread out over nearly a third of a meridian, and positioned nearly 800 miles off the coast of Portugal and 2,000 miles from the United States. *Stormy Isles* takes place on four islands of the central group, especially on Faial. There are episodes which take place on Pico, the island across from Faial, and on São Jorge, which is behind Pico. At the end of the novel there is one episode that occurs on the island of Terceira.

As the result of her adventure, Margarida finds herself once again caught in the web of insular society, a web from which it seems she cannot really ever escape. She develops an amorous relationship with a young man, André Barreto, the baron's son, who displays a well-to-do, refined social behavior but lacks even a spark of adventurous spirit. At the end of the novel, the two get married. Their union is obviously not a joyous event for Margarida. After the death of her real love, her half-uncle Roberto, she succumbs to family pressures, apparently losing her drive to break free of the social web into which she was born. In the end, Margarida allows herself to be entangled by events, her mind wandering elsewhere, as if she does not live in this world anymore.

A woman's life in "lost islands." The difficulty in summarizing the plot of this novel lies in the peculiar style of a narrator who prefers to construct a kind of "Azorean quilt" in which insular history and geography not only make up the background behind which Margarida's individual history is played out, but at the same time form important strands in a complex web that molds and conditions the subconscious of the protagonist and other characters in *Stormy Isles*. The weight of the past and of these islands' geographical conditions (as the novel insistently reminds us) are factors of fundamental importance for understanding the Azorean people, their horizons of possibilities and expectations, and their attitudes and the steps they take towards their future. Margarida is an island volcanic "geyser" with an intense and molten interior. However, at the peak of her eruption, she is not able to transcend the geographical and societal limits that surround her, no matter how high and far she attempts to do so.

Modern minds find it difficult to accept that an author like Nemésio, who had so much respect for women and defended their right for equality, would let his heroine be entangled in the web of a society that destroys such dreams. But her fate in the novel becomes subordinate to his higher purpose, that of capturing the worldview of 1920s Azorean society, where it was theoretically possible but scarcely plausible to go much further than Margarida does.

Mainland Portugal had suffered a big shake-up in 1910, when the Republicans managed to overthrow the monarchy. Significant changes began occurring in the country, but mostly in Lisbon, although some mid-size cities experienced upheavals. In the Azores, the geographical distance from these events and the isolation from the world at large allowed the old patriarchal society, under heavy influence of the Church, to prolong the status quo, particularly on a small island like Faial. This old order kept tenacious hold of the people, despite the presence of foreigners. As far as their morals were concerned, they remained just that—foreigners—people not to be imitated by the locals.

Sources and literary context. Well-informed critics on Nemésio's biography believe that the author fictionalized in *Stormy Isles* a relationship between himself and the woman who appears to have been the love of his life. It all happened on his home island of Terceira. Taking advantage of his experience as a student in the city of Horta and of his knowledge of the cosmopolitan nature

THE TENTH ISLAND

~

Margarida is the direct descendent of a figure of almost mythic proportions: captain Fernão Dulmo who, according to tradition, discovered an island to the north of Terceira: the alleged tenth Azorean island. This island, which was never really discovered, plays an important symbolic role in *Stormy Isles*, representing something sought but never found. In popular Azorean myth, stories of the sudden appearance and disappearance of islands are very common. Fifteenth-century sailors sought Antillia, or the island of the Seven Cities, an island that appeared on old maps. Although this island was never found, in the search for it, others were discovered. Furthermore, underwater volcanic eruptions caused small islands to appear in the middle of the sea, though they did not last long. One of these islands, Sabrina, sank shortly after an English sailor planted the British flag on its soil.

The most recent of these volcanic islands appeared as the result of the Capelinhos volcano, just off the coast of Faial in 1957-58. This tenth island, then called "Espirito Santo" (Holy Ghost), ended up attaching itself to the land while part of it was submerged. Today all that is left of it is a peninsula attached to the island of Faial. The novel thus takes advantage of one more element of Azorean history, symbolically transforming it. Margarida never is able to find the freedom she so dearly desires, the island of happiness that occupies her dreams and that she so ardently seeks in her youth.

of that city as well, he thought it better to change his story from Angra to Horta, adapting it to an environment that was socioeconomically and culturally similar to his home. Horta provided him with a continual sensation of archipelago, given the proximity of the nearby islands of Pico, whose inhabitants Nemésio so admired for both their vigorous, adventurous whalers and their profound sense of dignity.

Various critics have pointed out the similarity in attributes between Margarida of *Stormy Isles* and her creator, a highly cultured and liberal man engaged in a quest for the freedom of the spirit. Vitorino Nemésio was an artist who, though he possessed a deep understanding of the literary tendencies and esthetics prevalent during his time, always felt like a fish out of the literary waters. Highly informed about not only literature (which was his area of specialty) but also about sciences, philosophy, ethnography, and history, he talked about everything when teaching his university classes. He showed an aversion to particular literary schools of thought, participating in literary circles as an outsider of sorts. His works resembled those of the Presença movement, which favored novels with a psychological bent. However, with the passage of time, Presença began to lose its readership due to the

hegemony then exercised by another movement known in Portugal as Neo-realism, for all intents and purposes, a somewhat modified version of socialist realism.

Curiously, 30 years after the publication of *Stormy Isles*, Vitorino Nemésio had an affair with an aristocrat who, interestingly enough, was named Margarida and whose life was considered scandalous for the conservative environment of São Miguel island. Vitorino Nemésio collaborated with Margarida Victória in the writing of her autobiography. Ironically they were breaking through societal barriers at the time. Portugal had just ended a long dictatorship of nearly 50 years and the Azores were entering a new, more open phase of Portuguese history.

Events in History at the Time the Novel Was Written

Azorean society between World Wars. As noted, Azorean society saw little change after the advent of the Republic. Mainland Portugal experienced 18 years of turmoil, but very little of this turmoil reached the islands, beyond a few, isolated incidents. In 1928 a conservative movement charted the course that Portugal would follow for the next few decades. Allied with the Catholic

Church, it regained control of the country, imposed order, suppressed dissidents, and reinforced the power of the old socioeconomic groups. Even though divorce had been made legal after the Republican revolution and was revoked only in 1940, the Church had never allowed it. Since practically every marriage had taken place within the Church, the temporary liberalization was of little consequence. Also of little consequence was the right of some women to vote (gained in 1931, specifically by those women with university degrees or secondary schooling). Given the fact that Portugal had become a one-party dictatorship, elections were essentially meaningless in any case.

During World War II Portugal's dictator António Salazar opted for neutrality, and the country did not enter the conflict. However, at the end of the war, shortly before *Stormy Isles*'s publication, Portugal ceded to the Allies a stretch of land in Lajes, on the isle of Terceira, a couple of miles from Nemésio's home, for the construction of a military base, which remains today an important strategic location for the North Atlantic Treaty Organization (NATO).

The Azoreans had no say in the matter of building this base, nor in any other matter regarding their destiny. All attempts on the part of the islanders to gain some political control over themselves—there was a movement towards regional autonomy initiated at the end of the nineteenth century—were completely suppressed. Portugal maintained the Azores through the years as a quiet, tamed backyard of the mainland, a sort of Museum of Time and Tradition, until the revolutionary overthrow of Salazar's dictatorship in 1974. Only after this pivotal event would significant social and political change transpire in the Azores.

Reception. When Nemésio published *Stormy Isles,* the Portuguese literary scene was already completely controlled by authors who were either sympathizers of leftist ideologies or directly or indirectly linked to the Communist Party (which in the Portuguese dictatorship of the day was, of course, clandestine). For some time the forefront of the Neo-realist movement had featured authors such as Alves Redol and Soeiro Pereira Gomes. A little before the publication of *Stormy Isles,* these authors were joined by Manuel da Fonseca, Fernando Namora, and Carlos de Oliveira. Therefore, when Vitorino Nemésio's novel appeared, it was received by the Portuguese literary intelligentsia as something completely marginal vis-à-vis the dominant political preoc-

cupations, especially since its story occurred on a remote Azorean island of which most of the mainland Portuguese hardly knew anything at the time. Further encouraging critics to dismiss the novel was the fact that it was focused on the problems of an aristocratic woman who, despite her ruptures with many inherited conventions, did not condemn the class to which she belonged. Rather, she revealed a bourgeois concern with individual freedom with no thought given to the social conditions of the poor in her society. It is obvious that such a work would not be acclaimed by the dominant critics of the day.

João Gaspar Simões, a highly respected critic at the time, was almost the only one to voice praise for this novel. But Simões was one of the contributors of Presença, which was slowly losing ground in the battle between the two above-mentioned Portuguese intellectual camps. Later, David Mourão-Ferreira, also a highly respected independent voice, became the novel's great defender. Mourão-Ferreira slowly gained the support of a group of Nemésio's admirers, which grew after the fall of the dictatorship and the Neo-realists' loss of their ideological hegemony.

Extra-literary factors were paramount in Portuguese society's receptiveness to the novel. A small but growing intellectual class had distanced itself from the Salazar regime by identifying with the strategies of the leftist forces. In such a context, personalities like Nemésio, a "political spectator," as he is called by the critic Heraldo da Silva, could hardly avoid being marginalized by the dominating intelligentsia (Silva, p. 206). Moreover, the "women's question," not part of the left's agenda, within a small insular society to which Portugal had not attributed much importance since the fifteenth-century discoveries, had small chance of attracting much attention, perhaps almost no chance without an advocate such as Nemésio, who spoke incessantly of the islands and of their culture, seeking to draw them to national attention by way of his novel and other writings.

—Onésimo T. Almeida

For More Information

Almeida, Onésimo T. "A Profile of the Azorean." In *Issues in Bilingual Education.* Cambridge, Massachusetts: National Assessment and Dissemination Center, 1980.

Bettencourt, Urbano. "*Mau tempo no Canal*—mulheres cercadas." In *O Gosto das Palavras II.* Ponta Delgada: Jornal de Cultura (1995): 91-101.

Costa Vasco Pereira da. "Lendo o trágico em *Mau*

Tempo no Canal." In *Conhecimento dos Açores Através da Literatura.* Angra do Heroísmo: Instituto Açoriano de Cultura (1988): 115-137.

Fagundes, Francisco Cota. "Introduction." Vitorino Nemésio, *Stormy Isles: An Azorean Tale.* Edited, translated, and annotated by F. C. Fagundes. Providence, R.I.: Gávea Brown, 1998.

Garcia, José Martins. *Vitorino Nemésio: a Obra e o Homem.* Lisboa: Arcádia, 1978.

Lucas, Ancónio C., ed. *Críticas sobre Vitorino Nemésio.* Lisboa: Bertrand, 1974.

Melville, Herman. *Moby-Dick.* Ed. Alfred Kazin. Boston: Houghton Mifflin, 1956.

Moniz, António. *Para uma Leitura de Mau Tempo no Canal de Vitorino Nemésio.* Lisboa: Editorial Presença, 1996.

Moniz, Miguel. *Azores.* Oxford: Clio Press, 1999.

Mourão-Ferreira, David. "Novos elementos sobre a génese de *Mau Tempo no Canal.*" *Colóquio-Letras,* 102 (March-April 1988): 6-17.

Pires et al, ed., António Machado. *Vitorino Nemésio—Vinte Anos Depois.* Lisboa: Cosmos, 1998.

Rogers, Francis Millet. *Atlantic Islanders of the Azores and Madeiras.* North Quincy, Massachusetts: The Christopher Publishing House, 1979.

Silva, Heraldo Gregório da. *Açorianidade na Prosa de Vitorino Nemésio. Realidade, Poesia e Mito.* Lisboa: Imprensa Nacional / Casa da Moeda, 1985.

The Student of Salamanca

by
José de Espronceda

José de Espronceda y Delgado (1808-42) came into the world while his father, a Spanish cavalry officer, was riding to repel the French invasion of Spain during the Napoleonic Wars that shook Europe in the early nineteenth century. Espronceda's mother, accompanying her husband's regiment in a carriage, suffered such a jolting on the hurried journey that the boy was born prematurely—in a shepherd's hut, legend has it, but more likely (scholars suggest) in the mansion of a hospitable aristocrat nearby. The rest of Espronceda's life matched the turbulence of his birth. At age 15 he joined several friends in plotting against the Spanish government. The rebellious act marked the beginning of a continuing defiance; Espronceda would engage in political agitation right up to his premature death from tuberculosis at age 34. His intrigues resulted in years of exile, and critics have traced his Romantic literary style to influences encountered in London and Paris in the 1820s and 1830s. Returning to Spain in the mid-1830s, Espronceda was celebrated as the leading Spanish poet of his generation. His poetry was collected and published in 1840 as *Poesías* (Poems). The long poem *El diablo mundo* (The Devilish World), unfinished when he died, was to have included the shorter *Canto a Teresa* (Song for Teresa), written in 1839, which recounts Espronceda's despair after the death of Teresa Mancha, his estranged lover. Scholars believe that Teresa Mancha also inspired the young virgin Elvira in *The Student of Salamanca*, a supernatural tale of horror and

---

THE LITERARY WORK

A narrative poem set in the Spanish city of Salamanca around the beginning of the seventeenth century; published in Spanish in 1840 (as *El Estudiante de Salamanca*), in English in 1953.

SYNOPSIS

Don Félix de Montemar, a rake and a womanizing student, is led to his death by a phantom after he seduces and abandons a young virgin and kills her brother in a duel.

---

shattered illusions considered to be the fullest expression of Espronceda's Romantic sensibility. The Romantic period's defiant spirit is perfectly exemplified in the uncompromising individuality of the poem's main character, Don Félix de Montemar.

Events in History at the Time the Poem Takes Place

Sex, violence, and honor in Golden Age Spain. The text of *The Student of Salamanca* does not establish the precise time of the poem, but the behavior and accouterments of its characters suggest that it takes place in the late sixteenth or early seventeenth century, during the period known as Spain's Golden Age. Don Diego, a Spanish noble who is killed in a duel

José de Espronceda

by the main character, Don Félix, is said to have fought in Flanders, and Spanish military troops campaigned there intermittently throughout the period. Spain's military might in this era was matched only by its cultural splendor. As Spain's armies imposed Spanish rule on much of Europe, the *conquistadors* took that rule beyond Europe, carving out a worldwide Spanish empire. Meanwhile, painters such as Diego Velazquez (1599-1660) and writers like Miguel de Cervantes (1547-1616) rendered brilliant artistic portrayals of the glories achieved by Spain and the foibles of its society.

Especially characteristic of Spanish society in this period was the idea of honor, *la honra,* which historians have described as the national obsession of Golden Age Spain. While a man's honor could be offended in a variety of ways—a slur on his ancestry or courage, for example—a woman's honor resided primarily in her chastity (if she was unmarried) or her fidelity (if she was married). The works of the period's major dramatists, Lope de Vega (1562-1635) and Pedro Calderón de la Barca (1600-81), reflect this social preoccupation, for they generally turn on the theme of revenge for a male character's offended honor, and most commonly on an offense to his honor arising from the sexual behavior of a female family member. (See Lope's *Fuente Ovejuna,* also in *WLAIT: 5 Spanish and Portuguese Literatures and Their Times.*) As these dramas suggest, a woman's honor was significant only as a essential component of the more important honor of her male family members, be they husband, father, or brothers.

Carefully secluded in the home, women were regarded as precious possessions to be jealously preserved against the sexual predations of outsiders. A woman's seduction was a stain on the honor of all her male relatives, one that remained in place until they took revenge—which could be achieved only when one of them killed the seducer. On stage as in real life, such revenge usually took the form of a duel between two swordsmen. Of the many Golden Age plays that turn on this dramatic combination of sex, violence, and honor, none has had greater resonance through history than Tirso de Molina's *El burlador de Sevilla* (1630; *The Trickster of Seville,* also in *WLAIT: 5 Spanish and Portuguese Literatures and Their Times*), which gave the world a timeless character in its classic version of the womanizing rake, Don Juan. *The Student of Salamanca* would be one of many retellings of this popular tale, and the character of Don Juan himself would provide the model for the poem's hero-villain, the handsome but cold-hearted libertine Don Félix.

Student life. Another element of Golden Age culture, one less central than honor but equally familiar to later generations through vivid depictions in literature, was the colorful and often debauched life of the male university student. (Women generally had no access to higher education.) Education played an increasingly important role in Spanish public life in the Golden Age, until Spanish centers of learning began declining around the middle of the seventeenth century. Founded in the Middle Ages in the northern city of Salamanca, the university there was the largest, oldest, and most prestigious of Spain's educational institutions. Though universities arose in the other major cities during the Golden Age, none threatened Salamanca's top position. The university at Alcalá, located near the capital, Madrid, and known for its aristocratic student body, was Salamanca's closest rival in academic quality, but, catering to no more than 2,000 students, Alcalá was only about a quarter the size. As one modern historian of the Golden Age notes, "the phrase 'student of Salamanca' doubtless meant in real life as well as in the literature of the time,

THE LEGEND OF DON JUAN

The legend of Don Juan originated in medieval folktales but was given permanent definition in Tirso de Molina's play *The Trickster of Seville* (1630), in which the handsome rake Don Juan Tenorio seduces and abandons four different women, including an aristocratic young virgin. The girl's father challenges Don Juan to a duel to avenge the family's honor, and Don Juan kills him; later the father's ghost escorts Don Juan to eternal damnation in hell. The tale has inspired the imaginations of countless European artists over the centuries, in addition to Espronceda. It has been retold in many versions, including Wolfgang Mozart's opera *Don Giovanni* (1787; Austrian), Lord Byron's poem *Don Juan* (1819-24; British), Alexander Dumas the elder's play *Don Juan de Marana* (1836; French), and George Bernard Shaw's play *Man and Superman* (1903; British). Spain itself would invoke the character in literary successors to Molina's play and Espronceda's poem, among them **Don Juan Tenorio** (1844; also in *WLAIT 5: Spanish and Portuguese Literatures and Their Times*) by José Zorrilla.

the very embodiment of the student's way of life" (Defourneaux, p. 165).

In addition to academic learning, that way of life included a regular round of festivals and ceremonies, of which graduation was the largest, with a lavish banquet served at the students' expense. The examination of a doctoral candidate was in some cases preceded by a formal procession of faculty and students in their best finery, and followed by feasting and bullfights (again at the candidate's expense; doctoral candidates would often pool their resources and share the cost). In *The Student of Salamanca*, however, Don Félix is never shown participating in classes, festivals, official ceremonies, or indeed any academic activities. Instead, despite the poem's title, Espronceda describes Don Félix exclusively in a non-academic context, skulking through the streets at night, playing cards, and engaging in sexual escapades. It is true that cards, dice, and sexual liaisons were all common features of student life as depicted in Golden Age literature (though explicitly banned by university statute). Unlike most Golden Age literary depictions, however, Don Félix gambles with men who do not seem to be fellow students. It is also true that, like Don Félix in the poem's opening lines, many students settled their differences with swords, but then so did other males in the honor-obsessed and often violent culture of the Golden Age. In any case, such details matter little in the poem, for regardless of how typical or atypical of a student he is, Don Félix functions here as a symbol of humanity's desire to know.

The Poem in Focus

Plot summary. As published in its final version in 1840 (see below), *The Student of Salamanca* runs to just over 1,700 lines and is divided into four parts of unequal length. Part 4 consists of more than 1,000 lines; it is longer than the other three parts combined. Preceding each part is an epigraph, a brief literary quotation that touches on the dominant theme or action. The poem's narrative structure varies, so that some sections seem addressed to the reader and others to specific characters, while Part 3 (the gambling scene) unfolds in dramatic form, complete with scene divisions and stage directions in the text. The versification varies even more widely, reflecting the disdain for rules and high regard for freedom, including freedom of expression, that typified Espronceda and his peers. Espronceda employs at least 11 distinct meters (ranging from two syllables per line to 12), changing between these meters almost 60 times.

Part 1 opens with an extended and darkly atmospheric description of Salamanca after midnight, when (the narrator tells us in the first few lines) corpses appear to be alive and spectral footsteps can be heard on the streets. Witches meet in a ruined belfry, and a "gothic castle" looms, "its lofty ramparts bristling" over "the tomblike ancient city" (Espronceda, *The Student of Salamanca*, pp. 43-45). Suddenly "a clash of swords" is heard followed by "a shriek of death," as if someone were dying, and as the echo fades a man emerges from the shadow, "his hat brim down, /

Thus to evade / Recognition" (*The Student of Salamanca*, p. 45). Sword in hand, the man moves softly along the gloomy, boxed-in street, called Coffin Street after its appearance. A wispy phantom appears, which this "second Don Juan Tenorio" faces fearlessly with his still bloody sword (*The Student of Salamanca*, p. 47). The swordsman is Don Félix de Montemar: a lover who leaves the women who love him, a gambler who revels in drunken orgies, famous throughout Salamanca for his boldness and fine looks, arrogant, proud, charming, impious. With a change from short, choppy verses to long flowing lines, the poet then introduces "luckless Elvira," more beautiful and pure than the blue of the sky, once loved by Don Félix but now abandoned and unhappy, her "virgin soul. . . . betrayed by love" (*The Student of Salamanca*, pp. 49-51).

Part 2 consists of another nighttime scene, but now supernatural gloom has given way to starry skies and rustling trees with softly moonlit blossoms. Appearing in a white dress and flowing braids, Elvira walks alone in the moonlight, pining for her lost love. As the dawn begins to break, she addresses the moon: what use is its beauty if it cannot heal her heartbreak? By dusk, the poet tells us, Elvira will be dead, her lost reason briefly restored by the knowledge of her approaching death. As she feels the "icy hand" of death, she addresses Don Félix in farewell, calling on him to "Mourn for me, yes; but may thy heart beat free, / Let no remorse knaw [sic] at its liberty" (*The Student of Salamanca*, pp. 63-65).

Part 3 opens with six gamblers seated at a table playing cards in silence, which is broken only by the jangle of gold coins and the gamblers' occasional curses. Don Félix enters, his left hand resting jauntily on the pommel of his sword, and declares that he's tired of love affairs and ready to win some money. He removes a chain he is wearing and demands 2,000 ducats for it, a large amount of cash that he insultingly bullies the others into putting up. When he loses this stake, he wagers a jeweled frame with a portrait of a beautiful woman that the other gamblers admire enviously. Losing the frame, he then wagers the portrait itself. Winning the subsequent bets, he coolly ignores Don Diego, who has entered and approached the table with hatred in his eyes.

Don Diego identifies himself as Elvira's brother and says that his sister is dead, implying that Don Félix is responsible for her death. He challenges Don Félix to a duel, and Don Félix accepts but tells Don Diego to wait while he, Don Félix, counts his winnings. Elvira was beautiful, he says as he counts, and she fell in love with him, but he is not to blame for her death. More important, he has won 1,300 ducats. As they leave to fight their duel, the other gamblers suspect that Don Diego is doomed.

Part 4 returns to the scene at the beginning of Part 1, as Don Félix walks haltingly at night along darkened Coffin Street, having—we now discover—just vanquished Don Diego, who presumably gave the "shriek of death" heard in the opening lines. In the murky gloom Don Félix hears a sound like a sigh and stops, but no one answers his inquiring call. As he starts again, however, the "fateful shape" of the phantom, shrouded in white, emerges from the shadows, leaving a trail of mist behind it (*The Student of Salamanca*, p. 97). The only light comes from a lamp illuminating a statue of Christ, which flares up as Don Félix boldly challenges either God or the Devil, whichever of the two is trying to scare him. In the flaring light he sees a woman in white kneeling before the statue, but when he comes closer, the statue, the lamp, and the woman seem to recede. Tears stream from the eyes in the sculpted face of Jesus, and the scene reels—for a moment Don Félix suspects that he must be drunk—when the lamp suddenly goes out in the wind and the kneeling figure rises and moves away, its white raiment billowing in the mist.

He challenges the apparition, demanding to know if she is beautiful or ugly, since his reputation demands that he follow her if she is beautiful. The phantom glides silently away after answering with only a ghostly groan, which leads the narrator to reflect on the sorrows of shattered love. Lured by the phantom's refusal to answer, Don Félix again challenges her, and this time she answers in a voice that evokes "an immaculate maid's first acquiescence" but that delivers words of warning, which he ignores (*The Student of Salamanca*, p. 105). She can no longer know earthly love, she says. Calling him by name, she warns that he pursues her at his peril, risking the anger of heaven and eternal damnation in hell. He dismisses the warnings, telling her to be done with her sermons. Her coldness only interests him further. Life is for living, he says, and let tomorrow look after itself:

> Is it my concern if tomorrow I perish
> In bad hour, or good one, as the saying is?
> Why! 'Tis the joy in harvesting now that I
>   cherish,
> When dead, then the Devil can have me at
>   will.
>
>   (*The Student of Salamanca*, pp. 107-09)

Bridge in Salamanca, the city in which the story takes place.

A long nightmarish pursuit follows, as the phantom leads the willing but increasingly disoriented Don Félix down street after street, through square after square, over walls and past strange, fantastic towers that leave their foundations and move around him. He encounters cursing witches and sees cavorting spectral skeletons; then without warning this surreal cityscape vanishes and he finds himself in the middle of a stark and desolate plain, lightless, airless, skyless. As lightning flashes, he catches sight of the ghostly woman's eerily lit face. Just as suddenly he is back on the streets of Salamanca again, where a muted, torch-lit procession approaches. It is a funeral procession, bearing the corpses of two men—one is Don Diego's, and the other, Don Félix is amazed to see, is his own dead body. Just for a moment he feels fear, but then he recovers his nerve, laughing aloud on understanding that he and Diego have, it seems, killed each other in the duel. (Presumably, the clash of swords heard in the opening lines spelled both of their deaths, and the reader has been following Félix's disembodied spirit through the course of the poem's action.)

As glowing eyes watch from the darkness, Don Félix follows the phantom lady into an infernal mansion, and along its long deserted galleries, lit only by a few candles. Now enjoying his adventure, for hours he trails behind her, down the mansion's corridors, as spectral apparitions swirl around him, glaring with hostile eyes. Like "a second Lucifer" Don Félix has grown proudly determined to go out in a blaze of defiance, determined to uncover the phantom's face.

At last they come to a narrow spiral staircase of black marble, and without hesitation he follows her down. Disoriented, he seems to tumble down the steps, whirling in a shrieking tempest of sensation until he comes to rest. He gets to his feet and sees the lady alone by a stone tomb that resembles a bed. He approaches her and asks her politely to remove her veil so that he can see her face, and says he would like to know whether he is in the hands of God or the devil. Several lengthy stanzas then evoke a slowly rising crescendo of sights and sounds as Don Félix prepares to pull the veil away. Just as he reaches for it he hears the surrounding apparitions proclaim, "'Tis her husband!" and "At last the consort of the bride is here" (*The Student of Salamanca*, p. 137). Beneath the veil he finds not the face of a beautiful lady but "a grim repulsive skull" (*The Student of Salamanca*, p. 139).

Don Diego appears and reveals that the ghostly woman is Elvira, and that Don Félix must now accept her as his wife. He agrees to do so, and the stinking skeleton embraces him as he drips with sweat. Skeletal apparitions surround them and begin a fantastic dance, whirling like dead leaves in a gale. Elvira's skeleton continues to embrace him ever more tightly, and he begins to lose strength as his senses fade to unconsciousness like a flickering, dying flame.

Meanwhile the city awakes to its normal hubbub, except for a quickly spreading rumor that the Devil, dressed as a pretty woman, had come to Salamanca that night for Don Félix de Montemar. That was the rumor, and to the reader who doesn't believe it, the narrator protests that he has only told the tale as it was told to him.

THE DANCE OF DEATH

The skeletons' dance in Part 4 of *The Student of Salamanca* exemplifies the medieval artistic and literary motif called the *danse macabre* or Dance of Death, in which ghostly skeletons are depicted dancing around the newly dead and escorting them to the underworld. Originating in thirteenth- or fourteenth-century poetry, the concept was popularized during the Black Death of the mid-fourteenth century, an outbreak of bubonic plague in which much of Europe's population perished. The Dance of Death was one of many medieval motifs rediscovered and adapted by Romantic writers and artists in nineteenth-century Spain.

The individual in rebellion against the world. In calling Don Félix "a second Lucifer," the narrator compares him to the rebel archangel of Christian lore, the brightest angel in heaven who arrogantly challenged God and was cast down in defeat to hell, where he became Satan. "A rebel soul who beats fear with disdain," the speaker continues, "Beaten down, yes, but never marred" (*The Student of Salamanca*, p. 125). His self-consciously exultant rebelliousness distinguishes Don Félix from the Don Juan of medieval and Renaissance legend, who was merely an impious libertine, for the rebel who rebels for the sake of rebellion alone is a quintessentially Romantic figure.

Rebellion for its own sake is not as simple as may appear at first glance. Tirso de Molina's seventeenth-century Don Juan is given specific and explicit warnings about his behavior based on Catholic religious doctrine, and he is punished for his refusal to repent for that behavior. While Don Félix certainly seems to share this attitude of sinful and deliberate self-indulgence, in fact he goes far beyond it to question the very foundations of ideas such as sin in the first place. Repeatedly Don Félix claims to find little difference between God and the devil. Even after his unveiling of Elvira's skeleton, for example, he still demands to know whether it is God or the devil who has orchestrated his ordeal: "Happy I'd be," he asserts, "to see if not both, then either" (*The Student of Salamanca*, p. 139). Don Félix insists not upon doing evil, but upon following his own will, and his rebellion is not against God but ultimately against a world that continually acts to restrict his autonomy.

Significantly, Don Félix's will is expressed mainly through his curiosity, his desire to learn the truth about the phantom lady, which represents his general desire to know. Like Faust, another medieval hero who captured the imaginations of Romantic poets, Don Félix risks damnation to pursue knowledge that turns out to be illusory and unobtainable. According to the Romantics, one seeks but cannot find the truth, the answer to life's key questions. In their adaptations of such legends as Faust and Don Juan, Romantic poets like Espronceda reflect not only their age's exaltation of the individual and the individual will, but also their age's abandonment of earlier certainties about religious faith, absolute morality, and the existence of rational explanations for all life's questions. "In the Romantic mind," writes one critic of *The Student of Salamanca*, "any foundation for firm belief or rational conduct is impossible" (Cardwell, p. 45). The absence of such foundations gives Don Félix no reason to prefer the world's standards of conduct to his own.

Sources and literary context. Many critics have suggested that in Don Félix, Espronceda presents an idealized version of himself, and that Don Félix's relationship with Elvira similarly offers Espronceda's own interpretation of his tempestuous and ultimately unhappy love affair with Teresa Mancha. A girl of 17 when the affair began in 1827, Teresa Mancha married an older man in accordance with her father's wishes, but continued the affair, ultimately leaving her husband and having a child with Espronceda. By 1839 he had abandoned her and the child, and shortly after falling into the life of a prostitute, she became ill and died. Espronceda expresses his guilt and misery over this situation in the poem *Song for Teresa* (1839).

Critics have established that Espronceda drew on a number of literary sources for *The Student of Salamanca* in addition to Tirso de Molina's

REBELLION AND ROMANTIC HEROES

Born in the years following the French Revolution of 1789, Romanticism was closely linked to the idea of rebellion against established authority. The movement can be traced back to Sturm und Drang ("storm and stress"), a literary movement of mid-to-late 1700s Germany that rejected rationalism and celebrated instead emotion, intuition, and nature. An early hero of the Romantics was the French revolutionary general Napoleon Bonaparte, who, for many Romantics, symbolized the dynamic potential of the spirited individual. When Napoleon seized dictatorial power and embarked on wars of conquest, however, he himself came to stand for the oppressive power of authority. Romantics found another hero in English poet Lord Byron, who inspired them with his support for the underdog Greek nationalists in their struggle for independence from the Turks. The colorful Byron became the stereotype of the Romantic poet, and people often called Espronceda "the Spanish Byron." Both wrote poems based on the legend of Don Juan, both engaged in political intrigues, and both carried on numerous love affairs—each even had a famous and adulterous relationship with a woman named Teresa.

original seventeenth-century Don Juan story, *The Seducer of Seville*. The poem's major plot elements can all be traced to these sources, the most important of which probably include:

• A story in Spanish author Antonio de Torquemada's *Garden of Curious Flowers* (1570) about a student of Salamanca University named Lisardo, who commits a murder, sees a phantom procession that turns out to be his own funeral, and follows a mysterious female figure to a confrontation with his dead victim.

• Juan de Cárdenas's *Miguel de Mañara* (1680), recounting a libertine's encounter with his own funeral after a duel, and featuring a road named Coffin Street and supernatural apparitions.

• Agostin Moreto's play *Franco de Sena* (1654), a tale of rape and murder that features a gambling episode, a ghostly sigh, and an illuminated statue of Christ. Espronceda quotes from this work at the beginning of *The Student of Salamanca*'s gambling scene.

• Various traditional tales of Spain featuring an alluring female phantom who leads a male hero on a ghostly journey, only to be revealed as a decaying corpse or a skeleton.

• Two contemporary French versions of Cárdenas's 1680 story (see above): Prosper Mérimée's *The Souls of Purgatory* (1834) and Alexandre Dumas's *Don Juan de Marana* (1836), the latter incorporating elements of the Don Juan legend as well.

All of these literary sources end with the main character's repentance, however, and even de Molina's Don Juan intended to repent, but was cast into hell before he could do so. Don Félix, in contrast, unrepentantly preserves his triumphal individualism to the end.

Espronceda worked entirely within the influential European literary and artistic movement known as Romanticism, which is commonly judged to have lasted from roughly the French Revolution (1789) to around the middle of the nineteenth century. Goethe's *Faust* (1790) was the movement's first major literary landmark on the continent; in England the first major Romantic work is considered to have been William Wordsworth's and Samuel Taylor Coleridge's collaboration, *Lyrical Ballads* (1798). While Romanticism was a highly complex phenomenon, Romantic works tend to exalt the potential of the individual, to evoke mysterious or exotic settings in foreign lands (or glorious past eras in an appeal to nationalistic sentiments), and often to involve supernatural forces. Romanticism came late to Spain; in fact, Espronceda and others are sometimes said to have imported it with their return in the 1830s from exile in London and Paris. Some 1,000 Spanish liberal families are thought to have lived in England in the decade 1823-33, after fleeing political persecution in Spain. During the same decade, countless liberals along with some 8,000 *afrancesados* (literally "Frenchified ones") lived in Paris. Together, these two refugee classes comprised nearly all of Spain's intellectual class, which returned only with the death of King Ferdinand in 1833.

In 1834, shortly after his return, Espronceda founded a literary review called *El Siglo* (*The Century*), in which he and his circle of writer friends published poetry, literary criticism, and political commentary. Outside of Espronceda's own poetry, however, Romanticism in Spain during the 1830s is usually considered best represented by dramatists. Examples include Ángel de Saavedra, whose play *Don Alonso or The Force of Destiny* (1835) entailed, like *The Student of Salamanca*, a conscious reworking of themes from Golden Age literature.

Events in History at the Time the Poem Was Written

Revolution and reaction. The Spanish Golden Age ended with Spain's decline in the middle of the seventeenth century. By the end of that century, France had replaced Spain as Europe's leading cultural and political power. This shift in leadership was reflected in the early eighteenth century by Spain's receiving representatives of the French royal family, the Bourbons, as monarchs on the Spanish throne. The French Bourbons were themselves overthrown in the French Revolution of 1789, a pivotal event that often marks the beginning of the modern period in European history. Joining in the reaction of the horrified monarchical governments of Europe, Spain opposed the revolutionaries, but in the so-called French Revolutionary Wars of 1792-1800 the coalition of these horrified governments was defeated. Spain, vanquished early in these wars, was a French satellite by 1796. Despite the defeat, however, in Spain, as in the rest of Europe, a rebellious spirit arose in the political realm, and it would be paralleled by a similar impulse in literature.

A series of tumultuous and militarily aggressive revolutionary republican governments ruled in France until Napoleon Bonaparte, France's most successful and charismatic general, seized power and established a military dictatorship called the Consulate in 1799. In 1804 Napoleon had himself crowned as Emperor Napoleon I, after which he launched a series of further wars that brought much of Europe under his and France's rule within the next decade. Opposing France and its satellites in these Napoleonic Wars was Britain, joined intermittently by Austria. However, by 1809 Austria had surrendered and Napoleon ruled virtually all of continental Europe.

In Spain, meanwhile, popular resentment against French rule had led to an independence movement that would ultimately play a central part in Napoleon's downfall. Forcing the Spanish King Ferdinand VII to abdicate, Napoleon invaded Spain in 1808 and named his own brother Joseph Bonaparte as the country's new ruler on May 5 of that year. Already on May 2, however, the people of the Spanish capital of Madrid had revolted against the invading French. Though harshly and rapidly suppressed in Madrid, the insurrection soon spread to the rest of Spain, with Spanish guerrilla fighters receiving aid from British troops that operated from Portugal under the Duke of Wellington. Fighting continued into 1812, when Napoleon invaded Russia, where he was forced to divert needed manpower from the front in Spain and was disastrously defeated. In 1813 Wellington defeated the French army in Spain at the battle of Vitoria, and the following year Ferdinand returned to claim the Spanish throne. The year after that, in 1815, Wellington defeated Napoleon, decisively and finally, at the battle of Waterloo in Belgium.

Romanticism and liberalism. The turbulent aftermath of the Napoleonic era gave rise to a political philosophy called liberalism that would become a fixture on the European scene for the next century. In Spain liberal ideals were embodied in the Constitution of Cadiz, proclaimed in that Spanish city by the Cortes, or parliament, in 1812, while Ferdinand was still a prisoner in France. The constitution's liberal framers aimed to democratize and modernize the Spanish government, inspired by the egalitarian French revolutionary constitution of 1791. They also wished to minimize the role of the Catholic Church, long a powerful influence in Spanish politics and society. Among other measures, the new constitution abolished the Spanish Inquisition, strictly limited the powers of the monarchy, and established a single-chamber parliament without the parliamentary privileges that the clergy and aristocracy had previously enjoyed.

With the support of a conservative backlash and of the powerful Catholic and military establishments, Ferdinand overturned the Constitution of Cadiz on his return in 1814, ejecting the liberals from power and persecuting the liberal leaders. Ferdinand spent the rest of the decade in an abortive attempt to resurrect Spanish colonial power in the Americas. With the failure of that attempt clear by 1820, and supported by the now-disillusioned army, the liberals regained power and forced the king to accept the Constitution of Cadiz. Again the liberals failed to maintain their position, however, as popular resentment at their curtailment of the Church allowed Ferdinand to repudiate the constitution once more. During the so-called "ominous decade" (1823-33), the king resumed his persecution of liberal leaders and critics of the government. It was during this decade that Espronceda, one of those critics, was exiled in London and Paris, where he was under constant surveillance by Spanish intelligence for his part in conspiracies to overthrow Ferdinand.

Other European artists and writers had already forged a natural alliance between the political ideals of liberalism and the aesthetic ideals of the Romantic movement, an alliance that Espronceda was exposed to while in exile. With Ferdinand's death in 1833, Spanish liberals found a cause in the succession of his young daughter Isabella, proposing that her mother Queen María Cristina act as regent. Conservatives themselves had grown disillusioned with Ferdinand's rule, and already during the king's last years supported his brother Don Carlos as rightful heir to the throne. This struggle would be played out during the rest of the 1830s, but Spanish liberalism as a political force was already spent. On returning to Spain in 1834, Espronceda led the way in attempting to reproduce the alliance between liberal political ideals and the Romantic literary sensibility that he had found in London and Paris. His writings of the period betray a growing disillusionment with Spanish liberalism's inability to gain popular support among the staunchly Catholic Spanish populous.

Critics have suggested that Espronceda's political commentary finds much to rail against but little to put forward in the way of realistic solutions. In his later poetry, too, critics have found a profound disenchantment with the possibility of political progress, a world-weary cynicism that itself harmonized with the Romantic spirit. Richard Cardwell, for example, writes that in the character of Don Félix, who rebels against everything and believes in nothing, "Espronceda translates his disillusioned political revolutionism into the literary response of metaphysical revolt" (Cardwell, p. 60).

Reception. Parts of the poem that became *The Student of Salamanca* appeared in several literary journals between 1836 and 1839 before the final version was published with Espronceda's other works in the collection *Poesías* (*Poems*) in 1840. On its publication the poem was praised in a review by Espronceda's friend, the Spanish Romantic critic Enrique Gil y Carrasco, who singled out its remarkable poetic versatility, linguistic virtuosity, and forceful imagery. In an influential essay in 1854, however, the literary critic Juan Valera suggested that both the poem and Espronceda's style in general were in places artificial and insincere. These two contradictory lines of criticism have been echoed by later reviewers and scholars, with Espronceda's defenders praising the poem's colorful language and poetic variety, and his detractors claiming that the poem is in places shallow, overblown, and bombastic. This ongoing scholarly debate has been complicated by related academic disputes over the nature and impact of Romanticism in Spain. It has also been colored by the idea that the character of Don Félix is an idealized portrait of Espronceda himself, and that Espronceda therefore endorsed what critics have seen as Don Félix's antisocial qualities.

—Colin Wells

For More Information

Cardwell, Richard A., ed. *Espronceda: El Estudiante de Salamanca and Other Poems*. London: Tamesis, 1980.

Carr, Raymond. *Spain: 1808-1939*. Oxford: Oxford University Press, 1966.

Defourneaux, Marcelin. *Daily Life in Spain in the Golden Age*. Trans. Newton Branch. Stanford: Stanford University Press, 1979.

Domínquez Ortiz, Antonio. *The Golden Age of Spain 1516-1659*. Trans. James Casey. New York: Basic Books, 1971.

Espronceda, Jose de. *The Student of Salamanca*. Trans. C. K. Davies. Warminster, England: Aris & Phillips, 1991.

Flitter, Derek. *Spanish Romantic Literary Theory and Criticism*. Cambridge: Cambridge University Press, 1992.

Piñeyro, Enrique. *The Romantics of Spain*. Trans. E. Allison Peers. Liverpool: Institute of Hispanic Studies, 1934.

Rees, Margaret A., ed. *Espronceda: El Estudiante de Salamanca*. London: Grant & Cutler, 1979.

The Swindler

by
Francisco de Quevedo y Villegas

Francisco Gómez de Quevedo y Villegas (1580-1645) was born to aristocratic parents in the Castilian capital of Madrid, where his father was a secretary to the Spanish royal family. Like other young men of his class, Quevedo was educated in classical Greek and Latin literature and in Catholic theology, studying at the universities in Valladolid and Alcalá. He afterward pursued a contentious political career, meanwhile establishing a reputation as one of the most versatile and stylistically gifted writers of his time. His works vary widely in tone, ranging from biting and humorous social satire to lyric love poems, to sophisticated treatises on classical philosophy and theology, but share such features as complex wordplay and ornate, sustained imagery. Quevedo was particularly acknowledged for his mastery of the *conceptismo* or conceit, an extended metaphor employing elaborate puns and double meanings. He also became known in his time as a proponent of Stoic philosophy. Today Quevedo is remembered both for his doctrinal works and his satirical poems and prose. An example is the *Sueños* or *Visions* (1627), five brief satirical prose pieces that attack ignorance and stupidity in a broad range of targets, including bad poets, thieving innkeepers, corrupt constables, and rapacious bankers. Similar satirical elements emerge in *The Swindler*, a work that introduced new dimensions into the then-fashionable genre of the picaresque novel, which focuses on a *pícaro*, or rogue, as its central character.

THE LITERARY WORK

A novel set in the Spanish kingdom of Castile in the early seventeenth century; published in Spanish in 1626 (as *La vida del Buscón llamado don Pablos*), in English in 1657.

SYNOPSIS

From the vantage point of his mature years, Pablos of Segovia tells the story of his life and adventures as a young *pícaro*, or rogue.

Events in History at the Time of the Novel

The twilight of Spain's Golden Age. In the sixteenth century the Spanish enjoyed a period of cultural and imperial vitality known as the Golden Age, during which they dominated Europe and much of the world. In addition to Spain's vast colonies in the Americas and the Pacific, the union of the Spanish royal family with the powerful Habsburg dynasty of central Europe meant that Spanish monarchs also ruled in the Netherlands, Germany, Austria, southern Italy, and Sicily, or benefitted from close family ties to rulers in those lands. Using the famous system of routes known as the "Spanish Road," Spain could send troops deep into central or northern Europe without leaving Habsburg territory. Spanish ships also took the lead in defeating the Turks at the battle of Lepanto (1571) in the Mediterranean Sea, marking the beginning of

Francisco de Quevedo

Turkey's decline as a threat to Christian Europe. Spanish imperial might forms much of the backdrop of *The Swindler*, in which famous sixteenth-century campaigns and battles (such as Lepanto) receive frequent mention.

Spain reached the height of its Golden Age strength under its adept and tireless King Philip II (ruled 1555-98). Philip II's successors, his son Philip III (ruled 1598-1621) and his grandson Philip IV (ruled 1621-65), lacked both the political skill and the energy of their capable and popular predecessor. Whereas Philip II exercised close control in governing his dominions, often working late into the night to ensure that the smallest details received his personal attention, his son and grandson were less inclined to take part directly in making decisions and forming policies. Instead, they preferred recreation and lavish entertainments, delegating responsibility for government to a series of aristocratic court favorites, called *privados* or *validos*. Under Philip III the most influential *privado* was Francisco de Sandoval, the Duke of Lerma, and under Philip IV it was Gaspar de Guzmán, the Count-Duke of Olivares.

Quevedo finished his education and returned to Madrid in 1606 at age 26, hoping to participate in court life. While he had influential friends, including the ambitious Duke of Osuna, Philip III's Viceroy of Sicily (which was under Spanish rule), the often abrasive Quevedo soon made many enemies at court as well; in fact, in 1611 he was forced to flee briefly to Italy after killing another man in a duel. Scholars believe that *The Swindler*, though not published until 1626, had already been written by then and had been circulated among Quevedo's friends at court, most likely around 1608.

By the time Philip III died in 1621, the Duke of Osuna had fallen from grace and Quevedo's political career was at a low ebb. To ingratiate himself with the new regime, Quevedo wrote poems celebrating the 16-year-old Philip IV's accession to the throne. Though Quevedo himself had earlier distributed bribes on Osuna's behalf, his poems on this occasion reflected the feelings of many who were impatient with the bribery and corruption that had dominated court life under Philip III, and to whom the succession seemed like a chance for a fresh start. Philip IV's court favorite, Olivares, announced his intention to clean up the government and transform the court into a center of arts and literature, and Quevedo dedicated a political tract to him: *La Política de Dios* (The Politics of God), published in 1626, the same year as *The Swindler*. Quevedo and Olivares would be linked throughout their careers in the years after *The Swindler*'s publication, with Quevedo repeatedly falling in and out of favor before the deaths of both men in 1645.

Historians rate Olivares as far more capable than his predecessor, the genial but inept and bribable Lerma, yet despite Olivares's undeniable statesmanship, he was ultimately unable to reverse Spain's decline. To be fair, many of the problems had originated in policies pursued by Philip II. For example, Philip II's insistence on making even the smallest decisions personally, while highly effective, also led him to discount the advice of others, deterring the development of anything resembling a cabinet of ministers with officially delegated spheres of authority. His methods left the government ill-prepared to function under a monarch of lesser ability. Nor was Philip II ever able to enforce Spanish rule over the rebellious Dutch, despite massive expenditures of lives as well as weapons in attempting to do so. The Dutch Revolt of Philip II's reign began in 1566 and dragged on for decades, with the Dutch finding willing allies in the English and the French, both of whom were eager to curtail Spanish power. Spilling over into the reign of Philip III, it ended only when Spain recognized the independence of a new Dutch state, the United Provinces of the Netherlands,

NOBLES, CLERICS, AND PEASANTS: THE THREE ESTATES

Spanish society in the Golden Age was divided (in theory at least) into three levels. At the top were the nobles or aristocracy, and the clerics or Church officials. These two classes owned virtually all the land. At the bottom were the peasants who worked the land and paid rent to their landlords; the peasants were the only class that paid taxes. Traditionally, these social classes are known as the "three estates." Within each estate there were further gradations into upper and lower levels. Quevedo belonged to the *hidalgo* class, part of the lesser nobility, ranking above peasants on the social scale but below nobles such as counts and dukes. By Quevedo's time the poor but proud hidalgo, jealously guarding his honor and social rank, had become a stereotypical character in the picaresque novel. In *The Swindler*, fulfilling the demands of the genre, Pablos meets a hidalgo who takes ludicrous pains to conceal the fact that he is dressed in rags.

in 1609. Spain kept its hold only on the part of the so-called Low Countries that later became Belgium. In the novel, Pablos, the narrator, frequently refers to Spanish campaigns in the Low Countries and elsewhere in Europe, and at one point he meets a soldier who took part in these campaigns. The toothless, scarred old veteran boasts, for example, that he was "in the front at the sacking of Antwerp," an important Belgian port captured by the Spanish in 1576 (Quevedo, *The Swindler*, p. 137).

While Olivares inherited serious problems from preceding governments, historians indict him for failing to realize that Spain's resources, in the end, were unequal to Philip II's earlier, grandiose ambitions. Striving to maintain the bellicose stance of a former era, Olivares pursued policies that, for example, led to the spread of hostilities in the Thirty Years' War (1618-48). The war began with a revolt against Habsburg rule in Bohemia, but Olivares's aggressiveness soon rekindled conflict in the Low Countries, and Spain and the Habsburgs were ultimately embroiled in disastrous fighting throughout Europe. The Thirty Years' War resulted in the eclipse of Spanish and Habsburg military preeminence; by the end of the seventeenth century France would replace Spain as Europe's major power. Thus, the years that fell between *The Swindler*'s probable composition and its publication—roughly 1608 to 1626—were among the last years of clear Spanish dominance in Europe.

Religion in Spanish society. The Thirty Years' War marked a time in which religion played a decisive role in the outbreak of a major European war. As a strongly Catholic nation, the

Spanish had resisted the Protestant Reformation that began to sweep much of northern Europe in the first half of the sixteenth century. Dutch Protestantism was a leading factor in the Dutch uprising against Catholic Spain, and the rebellious Bohemian princes whose revolt touched off the Thirty Years' War were also Protestants resentful of Catholic Habsburg rule. Conversely, the parts of the Low Countries over which the Habsburgs kept control were precisely those parts that had remained largely Catholic. In the future, however, strategic national interests would overshadow shared religious bonds in determining Europe's alliances and enmities.

Spain's particular brand of aggressive Catholic militantism sprang from its unique history as the only Western European country to have fallen under Islamic rule. Muslim Arabs and North Africans (or Moors) had conquered Spain in the eighth century, and in the wake of the Muslim conquest came Jewish immigrants who added to the preexisting Jewish population. The resulting culture—called Moorish—blended Muslim, Jewish, and Christian elements under generally tolerant Muslim rulers. Not everyone adapted to the blend. In fact, Christian identity in Spain became closely linked to the idea of reconquering the peninsula from the Muslims, a centuries-long process that was completed when King Ferdinand and Queen Isabella captured the last Muslim city, Granada, in 1492.

Driven by the ideal of a unified Catholic society, in that same year Ferdinand and Isabella—known as the "Catholic Monarchs"—offered Spain's remaining Jews a choice between converting to Christianity or being expelled from

ARBITRISTAS

By the time Quevedo wrote *The Swindler*, Spain's decline had become clear enough for some writers to begin proposing solutions to the nation's various problems. Called *arbitristas* or "projectors," these intellectuals and their sometimes unrealistic *arbitrios*, or schemes, would become popular targets for satire by Quevedo and others. In *The Swindler*, Pablos meets an *arbitrista* who has a plan to help the king's armies capture the Dutch stronghold of Ostend by using sponges to suck up the sea water that protected the city's fortress. The novel's use of the word *arbitrista* to describe this new phenomenon is perhaps the earliest recorded appearance of the word in Spanish literature.

Spain. In the face of long persecution from Spanish Christians, many Spanish Jews had already converted. Some 700,000 Jews who refused to convert after the Catholic Monarchs' decree were expelled, and a decade later, in 1502, Ferdinand and Isabella offered Spanish Muslims the same choice between conversion or expulsion. Muslims who converted to Catholicism were called Moriscos; Jews who converted were called Conversos. Both minority groups suffered hostility from the Catholic establishment, which (often correctly) suspected them of continuing to observe their former religious practices in secret. While some Conversos retained varying degrees of their original Jewish culture, many others assimilated into Spanish society, often into the aristocracy. By contrast, the Moriscos remained a largely segregated underclass in Catholic Spain. Moriscos in Granada revolted in 1569-71, after Philip II ordered them to abandon their customs, and in 1609 the government of Philip III and the Duke of Lerma expelled the Moriscos from Spain altogether.

The Spanish Inquisition. To force the Moriscos and Conversos to conform to Catholic practice, the Catholic Monarchs established the Spanish Inquisition, an arm of the Church that, though under royal control, had broad powers to seek out and punish any deviation from accepted Catholic worship. The Inquisition rapidly became Spain's most feared institution, for its methods ranged from confiscation of property to torture and execution by fire. Originally intended to monitor the Conversos and Moriscos, the Inquisition expanded during the sixteenth century to target suspected witches and heretics as well, and even to monitor converted Indian peoples in the Spanish colonies of Latin America.

In Spain, tens of thousands died in the Inquisition's *autos-da-fé* (literally, "acts of faith"), spectacular public burnings of condemned offenders that were usually attended by large and enthusiastic crowds. The Inquisition appears frequently in *The Swindler*, illustrating its constant presence in the background—and sometimes the foreground—of Spanish daily life. At one point, for example, Pablos (with a characteristic lack of emotion) hears from his uncle that his mother has been arrested by the Inquisition and accused of witchcraft. She is to be burned at an *auto-da-fe*, together "with four hundred other people" (*The Swindler*, p. 121). In another episode Pablos arranges with friends to pretend they are Inquisitors and arrest him, so that he won't have to pay his bill at an inn.

Poverty and honor. Despite the Latin American gold and silver that flowed into its royal treasury, Spain remained essentially a poor nation throughout the Golden Age. Much of its American treasure was transferred directly to German or Italian bankers in order to finance the Spanish Crown's expensive foreign wars. By the time of the novel, these bankers were widely resented as a cause of Spain's growing economic problems. In *The Swindler*, for example, Pablos meets "a Genoese—you know, one of those bankers who've ruined Spain" (*The Swindler*, p. 140). Historians point to a deeper cause for the failing economy, however, one that had roots in the Spanish tendency to despise industry and business as base and dishonorable. "Conscience in businessmen is a bit like virginity in whores," Pablos says after meeting the Genoese banker: "they sell it when they haven't got it anymore. Hardly anyone in business has a conscience" (*The Swindler*, p. 140). That part of the American trea-

Refugees of the Thirty Years' War

sure that did not go to the Crown found its way into the hands of nobles, who made up the viceroys and other colonial officials upon which the Crown relied but who invested very little of their gains in domestic business. As a result, Spain had little industry, so it needed to import most manufactured products, which further drained cash from the Spanish economy.

In the end, the influx of treasure merely exacerbated the poverty of Spanish peasants by driving up prices, which rose steadily throughout the sixteenth century. The peasants, upon whose backs rested both food production and taxation, grew ever worse off, and rural populations throughout Spain began falling. Between 1596 and 1614, the overall population in Castile, Spain's leading kingdom and the setting of the novel, fell by an estimated 600,000-700,000 people, a decline of some 10 percent (Lynch, p. 6). Several factors contributed to this depopulation, including outbreaks of plague starting in 1596 and the expulsion of perhaps 90,000 agriculturally productive Castilian Moriscos in 1609.

In addition, many peasants escaped mounting tax debts in their villages by fleeing to the cities. There they often subsisted, like Pablos in the novel, by begging or engaging in petty theft or robbery. Others, as Pablos does at the end of the novel, might seek their fortunes in the Americas, where they could conceal past indiscretions and fabricate a new identity with perhaps a higher social rank. By the time he goes to America, Pablos has already tried and failed to pass himself off as a hidalgo in Spain. His attempts to ascend in social rank reflect what historians have seen as a pervasive obsession in Spanish society with

nobility and honor, and an equally widespread desire to avoid the harsh economic burdens of peasant life. His personal experience is based largely on his low-class Converso heritage. Pablos wants to work his way up the social ladder, which does not seem possible in Spain itself, or so the novel seems to say.

The Novel in Focus

Plot summary. The text is prefaced by a brief letter "To the Reader," which some modern critics have argued was not written by Quevedo. In it readers are told that the tale about to unfold will teach them "all the tricks of the low life" that people like to read about—and they are warned against themselves trying to trick the bookseller by reading the book without paying for it (*The Swindler*, p. 83).

In keeping with the demands of the picaresque genre, the novel itself opens with a brief account of the narrator's lowly origins and early life. His name, he tells us, is Pablos of Segovia. His father is a barber in that city in central Spain, and his mother is a beautiful woman suspected by the townspeople of having "some Jewish or Moorish blood in her" (*The Swindler*, p. 85). His parents are always in trouble with local authorities, the father for robbing his customers and the mother for practicing witchcraft. His parents argue about which of their careers he should follow, thievery or witchcraft, but Pablos says that even as a boy he thought of himself as a *caballero* or gentleman, a member of the leisured upper classes, so he did not apply himself to either (*The Swindler*, p. 86).

LIMPIEZA DE SANGRE

Unfavorable references to Moriscos or Conversos appear frequently in *The Swindler*, and often in a way that modern readers might find offensive. The references to Conversos typically incorporate anti-Semitic stereotypes (for example, Jews have long noses) and stress historical differences between Judaism and Christianity (like Muslims, for example, Jews do not eat pork, an aversion often maintained in Converso families). "There's no shortage of those people [Moriscos]," Pablos declares, "or the ones who have long noses and only need them to smell out bacon. Of course, I'm not hinting at any impure blood among the aristocracy, oh no!" (*The Swindler*, p. 106). The latter part of this quotation reflects the pervasive Spanish social ideal known as *limpieza de sangre*, literally "purity of blood." According to this principle, it was desirable to come from a family with ancient Christian roots and no Moorish or Jewish ancestors. In Quevedo's day, real or, if necessary, false genealogies could be bought, and Spain's noble families often went to great trouble to proclaim their Christian "purity" in this way. Actually, however, many noble families descended from Jews who had converted to Christianity decades or even centuries earlier. Fewer noble families had ancestors who married Moriscos. Incidents in *The Swindler* betray the Converso origins of the narrator, Pablos, among them his family's contact with the Inquisition, the body authorized to suppress deviation from the Roman Catholic Church.

In school Pablos is befriended by the son of Don Alonso Coronel de Zúñiga, a Segovia aristocrat. The boy's name is Diego; Pablos refers to him with the honorific *don* (from the Latin *dominus*, lord), denoting his higher social rank: Don Diego. When Don Diego begins to attend a boarding school in Segovia, Pablos decides to leave home and go with him as his servant and companion. The school is run by the stingy, penny-pinching Dr. Goat (*licenciado Cabra*), who feeds the boys so little that they are constantly famished. When a boy at the school actually dies of starvation, Don Alonso removes them from Dr. Goat's academy and sends them both to Alcalá, where Don Diego will finish his education at the university and Pablos will continue to act as his servant.

At the university Pablos is at first mercilessly hazed both by the students and by other servants. On the first night, for example, a group of students surrounds him and spits all over him, so that he is completely coated. Later, while he sleeps, the other servants defecate in his bed so that when he rolls over he covers himself in human excrement. However, Pablos decides to join the mischief and soon fits in with the others, specializing in stealing food from the housekeeper of the boarding house where they live in Alcalá.

Pablos's stint at the university comes to an end when he receives a letter from his uncle Alonso, Segovia's hangman, who informs Pablos that his father has been hanged (by the uncle) for theft and his mother has been arrested and condemned to death by the Inquisition for witchcraft. Pablos must return to Segovia and claim his inheritance. On his journey to Segovia, Pablos meets up with a series of characters who represent various social types:

- The *arbitrista*, a crackpot engineer full of projects (*arbitrios*) for solving Spain's problems.

- An inept fencing master, who combines incredible clumsiness with fancy mathematical theories about sword-fighting. (Quevedo's depiction caricatures his enemy Luis Pacheco de Narváez, who wrote a book on sword-fighting and with whom Quevedo engaged in a long-running literary battle.)

- A priest who recites terrible poetry.

- A scarred old veteran who brags about taking part in campaigns in the Low Countries and elsewhere, though Pablos suspects him of lying.

- A gluttonous monk who loves to gamble and cheats at cards.

- A Genoese banker who talks only about money.

On the way into Segovia, Pablos sees his father's quartered remains at the city gate (the bodies of executed criminals were often displayed in this way as a warning to others). He finds his uncle leading a procession of five condemned criminals, flogging them as they go, preceded by the town crier, part of whose job is to walk ahead and call out the crimes of the condemned. During a debauched night of drinking with the uncle's rascally cronies, Pablos suffers his uncle's grim humor; the uncle serves meat pies for dinner and hints that pieces of Pablos's father are ground up in the pies. Next the uncle offers to train Pablos as a hangman, but, disgusted, Pablos declines. As soon as he collects the money his parents have left him, he hires a donkey and leaves for Madrid, which he had passed through on his way from Alcalá to Segovia.

Along the way, Pablos takes up with a poverty-stricken hidalgo, Don Toribio, a gentleman of the lesser nobility whose trousers are so tattered that his buttocks show through unless he covers them with his cloak. Don Toribio, who lives in Madrid, instructs Pablos in how to get by there by passing oneself off as well-heeled when in reality one is penniless. On arriving in the capital, Pablos joins Don Toribio's group of friends, essentially a band of high-born con artists and petty thieves that is headed by an aged woman called Old Lebrusca. One day the police catch her selling stolen goods, and after she confesses where to find her gang of "gentleman thieves" (*caballeros de rapiña*), Pablos and the others are arrested and thrown in jail (*The Swindler*, p. 170). He spends a few nights in jail, then escapes by bribing and smooth-talking the jailer, leaving his friends behind.

Taking a room at an inn, Pablos pretends to be wealthy in order to impress and seduce the attractive daughter of the innkeepers. His plot backfires when he is exposed and beaten in front of the girl by a lawyer who lives next door. Humiliated, Pablos arranges for two accomplices to come to the inn masquerading as agents of the Inquisition and arrest him, so that he can leave without paying his bill. He then decides that he needs to find a wealthy wife. He chooses a beautiful young girl, Doña Ana, for his attentions, and prepares an expensive picnic in order to impress her and her older relatives.

Again, however, his plot backfires, for he unexpectedly bumps into his old friend and master Don Diego, who turns out to be related to Doña Ana. At first, Pablos tries to carry off the fiction that he is "Don Felipe Tristán," who just happens to bear a remarkable resemblance to Don Diego's former servant (*The Swindler*, p. 187). But Don Diego eventually recognizes Pablos and sets a trap to punish him for his deception. He hires two ruffians to beat a man whom he says will be wearing a cloak he shows them. He then tricks Pablos into swapping cloaks and taking the one he has pointed out to the ruffians. This time Pablos is beaten twice, for some enemies of Don Diego's (lying in wait to beat *him* up in an unexplained dispute involving a prostitute) get to Pablos first. Mistaking him for Don Diego, they beat him once, and a few minutes later the two ruffians give him another beating, pounding him with clubs, cutting his face, and covering him with bruises.

After recovering from the beatings, Pablos, now nearly broke, becomes a beggar, employing several child beggars to supplement his takings. Soon he is kidnapping children and waiting till their distraught parents offer a reward, then returning the children and claiming the reward. He decides to leave Madrid for Toledo, and joins a traveling theatrical company that is also going there. By the time they reach Toledo, Pablos is acting in plays, and soon he is writing his own plays for production by the company. The company breaks up, however, and Pablos, who has made some money as a playwright, begins romancing a beautiful nun who saw him act the part of St. John the Apostle in a religious play. He absconds with a valuable needlework she has made, and flees to the port city of Seville, the point of embarkation for Spanish ships sailing to the Americas.

In Seville Pablos joins a group of thugs on a drunken spree in which they hunt policemen. When he kills two officers, he and his companions take refuge in the city's cathedral, which according to custom provides them with temporary immunity from the law as long as they are inside. Fed by the city's prostitutes, Pablos escapes with one of them, La Grajales, and embarks for the Americas, hoping things will go better in a new land. "But they went worse," he concludes his story, "as they always will for anybody who thinks he only has to move his dwelling without changing his life or ways" (*The Swindler*, p. 214).

Class and conservatism. The *arbitrista* in *The Swindler* aspires to rise in social rank, saying that he won't tell the king about his plan to capture the Belgian port of Ostend "unless the king gives me an estate first" (*The Swindler*, p. 124). He says he deserves to be given an estate (*encomienda*) because he has a highly honorable pedigree (*una ejecutoria muy honrada*), by which he means he has no Moriscos or Conversos among his ancestors. By contrast, Pablos, who also wishes to rise socially, does seem to have "some Jewish or Moorish blood," at least on his mother's side (*The Swindler*, p. 85). In practice, however, Pablos's mixed ancestry wouldn't have excluded him from joining the aristocracy. It was common knowledge in Golden Age Spain that many noble families had Converso origins, though the families hid them. Scholars have recently uncovered such origins for a prominent Segovia family named Coronel, for example, which is the name of Don Diego's family in the novel. The Converso origins of the Coronels seem to have been well known at the time, and these scholars argue that Quevedo meant to suggest to his contemporary readers Converso origins for Don Diego's family.

"Pure" ancestry was therefore not the sole arbiter of social class. An autobiography from the year 1600 draws a clear distinction between *limpieza de sangre*, purity of blood, and *hidalguia*, nobility of birth:

> There are two kinds of nobility: the greater is the *hidalguia*, the lesser the *limpieza*. Even though the former carries more honour, it is a great disgrace to be denied the latter; in Spain there is more esteem for a pure-bred commoner than for a *hidalgo* who lacks this purity.
> (Defourneaux, p. 40)

Thus, while not a sufficient criterion for nobility on its own, *limpieza* could enhance nobility immeasurably, and a peasant with *limpieza* could, despite being a peasant, lord it over a noble of known mixed ancestry.

By Quevedo's time, however, the traditional value system that promoted such ideals had started to become subject to various social pressures. Some of these pressures are represented by phenomena such as the *arbitristas* whom Quevedo mocks in *The Swindler*. While many of the *arbitristas'* ideas were in fact impracticable, others amounted to common sense reforms that might have done some good if followed. For example, one suggestion was to reform the antiquated Castilian tax system so that the entire burden did not fall on the peasants but would be shared with the upper classes. Historians in fact see the *arbitrista* movement as a precursor of the modern science of political economy.

While critics disagree on many aspects of *The Swindler*'s meaning, they generally agree that Quevedo's ideology was essentially conserva-

tive. Representing this consensus, for example, William Clamurro writes that "Quevedo, throughout most of his writings and especially in the *Buscón* [i.e., *The Swindler*] can be seen as a spokesman for the ideology of the reigning status quo" (Clamurro, p. 87). Within this status quo, aristocrats such as Quevedo held a privileged position, but one increasingly under threat as, for example, economic problems drove peasants to the cities, threatening the rural tax base on which society depended. Thus, in his edition of the novel, B. W. Ife suggests that in the character of Pablos, Quevedo has created "a representative example of the kind of villainous social upstart which Quevedo saw as the most dangerous threat to the established fabric of Spanish society" (Ife in Quevedo, *La Vida del Buscón llamado Don Pablos,* p. 15). In a similar vein, James Iffland focuses on Pablos's Converso ancestry, arguing that Quevedo shared the anti-Semitism common in Spain, "including resentment at the way many Conversos were still able to attain social and economic prominence at a time when aristocrats of limited means (such as Quevedo) were slowly losing influence and prestige" (Iffland in Quevedo, *El Buscón*, p. xix). These insights may help explain such disparate elements in *The Swindler* as Quevedo's contemptuous depiction of the *arbitristas*, Pablos's farcical and brutally punished attempts to break into the nobility, and especially the constantly reiterated preoccupation with *limpieza de sangre*.

Sources and literary context. *The Swindler* is the last written of the three canonical works frequently cited as defining the genre of the Spanish picaresque novel. The genre was inaugurated by the highly popular and anonymously written ***Lazarillo de Tormes*** (1554; also in *WLAIT 5: Spanish and Portuguese Literatures and Their Times*), which served as a model for a spate of lesser works that followed. Not until 1599 did a worthy successor appear in the form of Mateo Alemán's *Guzmán de Alfarache*, narrated by the adventurous son of a ruined moneylender. Though lively critical discussion about the genre persists, critics have discerned three major elements that distinguish the picaresque novel:

- The central character's lowly origins and, from society's point of view at the time, shameful Converso background

- First-person narration by the central character

- An episodic, autobiographical structure, telling the narrator's life story in order of events

The Swindler follows Lazarillo de Tormes more closely than it does Guzmán, and the two former works share several additional features that distinguish them from the latter. For example, they are brief and concise where it is lengthy and digressive, and their central characters defy conventional morality, with the tale itself imparting no clear moral lesson, where Guzmán's sententious narrator frequently moralizes directly to the reader.

The Swindler was written during a time of immense cultural vitality in Spain, for Golden Age culture continued to flourish long past the onset of Spain's political and economic decline. Miguel de Cervantes (1547-1616), whose masterpiece **Don Quixote** (1605 and 1615; also in WLAIT 5: Spanish and Portuguese Literatures and Their Times) is regarded as establishing the form of the modern novel, dominated the field of letters. His own contributions to the picaresque genre, Rinconete and Cortadillo and Colloquy of the Dogs were both published in 1613, after The Swindler was written but before it was published. In drama, Lope de Vega wrote his play **Fuente Ovejuna** (also in WLAIT 5: Spanish and Portuguese Literatures and Their Times) around the same time. More generally, the prolific Lope de Vega (1562-1635), who wrote some 800 plays altogether, founded the popular comedia tradition, which combines high drama with lively farce, music, and dance.

Quevedo was highly conscious of The Swindler's rich literary context, and the contemporary literary scene features twice in the novel, first when Pablos meets the priest who recites awful poetry and again when he works briefly as a playwright. In the first instance Pablos reads aloud "A Proclamation Against All Idiot, Useless, and Rubbishy Poets," a mock legal decree banning poets and playwrights who use clichés and hackneyed plot devices in their works. For example, the decree singles out love poets who, imitating Italian Renaissance romantic verse, "continually worship eyebrows, teeth, ribbons and slippers" (The Swindler, p. 133). The poets mocked in Quevedo's decree would have been among the growing ranks of professional writers who earned their living in the expanded literary marketplace of the Golden Age.

Publication and reception. From references to specific historical events in the text (for example, the siege of Ostend, which ended in 1604), literary historians have concluded that The Swindler was probably written in the first decade of the seventeenth century, with an early draft completed by perhaps 1603-04 and a revised draft perhaps a decade later. Other scholars, however, have cautioned that such internal references need not necessarily correspond to the time of composition.

More revealing than an exact date of composition is the fact that Quevedo, having written the novel, did not want to publish it. Instead, he distributed handwritten copies to his friends at court and to other literary figures, and may (as B. W. Ife stresses) have read all or part of it aloud at gatherings of his social circle. In keeping with The Swindler's mock decree banning bad poets, the aristocratic writer would have looked down on the growing ranks of professional authors, opposing as dishonorable the idea of deriving income from his literary efforts. Finally, by not publishing the novel, Quevedo ensured his own safety from the powerful censors of the Spanish Inquisition, whose legal reach extended only to published works. For all these reasons, Quevedo resisted The Swindler's initial publication in 1626 by the printer Roberto Duport in Zaragoza, and refused to acknowledge authorship thereafter. His refusal mattered little, though, for readers recognized his biting, witty style.

In his introduction to the first edition, Roberto Duport indicates The Swindler's appeal to contemporary readers. Comparing the novel to Don Quixote in its wit and grace, Duport invokes two classical Latin authors, assuring the reader that the novel lies closer to the careless wickedness of the poet Martial than to the serious moralizing of the playwright Seneca. Despite Quevedo's disavowal of authorship the novel was highly popular, as evidenced by the many subsequent editions that appeared not only in Spain but also in France, the Low Countries, and England, both in the original Spanish and in translation.

—Colin Wells

For More Information

Chandler, Frank Wadleigh. Romances of Roguery. New York: Lenox Hill, 1974.

Clamurro, William. Language and Ideology in the Prose of Quevedo. Newark, Delaware: Juan de la Cuesta, 1991.

Defourneaux, Marcel. Daily Life in Spain in the Golden Age. Trans. Newton Branch. Stanford: Stanford University Press, 1979.

Domínguez Ortiz, Antonio. The Golden Age of Spain 1516-1659. Trans. James Casey. New York: Basic Books, 1971.

Dunn, Peter. Spanish Picareque Fiction: A New Literary History. Ithaca: Cornell University Press, 1993.

Time of Silence

by

Luis Martín-Santos

L uis Martín-Santos, son of a military officer, was born in Larache, Morocco, in 1924, and raised in San Sebastian, in the Spanish Basque country, where he resided most of his life. He was both a practicing psychiatrist and a writer of two books, as well as articles on psychiatry, a book of essays and short stories, and two novels, *Time of Silence* and the incomplete *Time of Destruction* (*Tiempo de destrucción*, 1975). Also politically active, Martín-Santos was jailed several times for his participation in the banned Spanish Socialist Party. Circumstances prevented him from enjoying the acclaim of *Time of Silence* for very long; in 1964, two years after its release, he died in an automobile accident. A searing indictment of Francoist society, *Time of Silence* also marks a turning point in the development of contemporary Spanish prose. The novel dramatically blends the social realism of the late 1950s with the experimental style of stream-of-consciousness writing that was destined to dominate the Spanish novel of the 1960s. While the experimental element reflected the author's frustrations with social realist conventions, the plot of his novel illustrates his growing impatience with social conditions in Franco's Spain.

Events in History at the Time the Novel Takes Place

Post-Civil War society. After his victory in the Spanish Civil War (1936-39), Nationalist leader General Francisco Franco became absolute dictator of Spain. His government tolerated only a

> ## THE LITERARY WORK
>
> A novel set in Madrid in the fall of 1949; published in Spanish (as *Tiempo de Silencio*) in 1962, in English in 1964.
>
> ## SYNOPSIS
>
> A medical researcher strives for a cure for cancer in hopes of a Nobel Prize for Spain. While searching for mice for his experiments, he crosses rigid class barriers, breaks social taboos, finds himself implicated in crime and incest, and discovers that the whole society is afflicted with moral and intellectual cancer.

single party, the Falange, or Spanish fascist party, which remained under Franco's control. Though officially neutral during World War II, the Franco government supported the war efforts of the fascist dictators Adolf Hitler in Germany and Benito Mussolini in Italy, both of whom had helped arm Franco during the Spanish Civil War.

As victors in World War II in 1945, the United States, Britain, and France ostracized Spain. The only surviving fascist dictatorship in the postwar period, Franco's Spain found itself excluded from the U.S. Marshall Plan, which supplied aid to rebuild war-torn Western Europe in the late 1940s. In the same vein, the newly formed United Nations refused admittance to Spain. Meanwhile, the Spanish economy and infrastructure lay in shambles in the post-Civil War period. Economist París Eguilaz points out that "the national

Luis Martín-Santos

tainers or tar barrels, . . . bricks stolen one by one from building sites . . . scraps of wicker from what had formerly been hats . . . all this amalgamated by human flesh, sweat, and tears" (Martín-Santos, *Time of Silence*, p. 40). A blight on Spain's urban centers, the shantytowns lacked running water, electricity, basic sewerage, and any semblance of law. When their existence was even known to the authorities, they posed a threat to the authoritarian regime, which viewed their residents as difficult to control. As in the case of the Vallecas shantytown in the novel, these accumulations of hovels sat right beside the city dump, their residents foraging in the refuse of the city for sustenance. The novel portrays the shantytown as a cancer of a sick society, much like the cancerous mice that the character Muecas breeds for Pedro's medical research.

"Years of Hunger"—urban survival. With the arrival of unskilled laborers in such throngs, unemployment increased dramatically, despite the execution, imprisonment, or economic ostracism of those who had fought against Franco in the Civil War. As shown in the novel, many of the poor sold what they could to survive: from individual cigarettes, to lighter flints near the subway stations and in the large plazas of the city. A permanent underclass of criminals, pimps, and prostitutes flourished.

By the late 1940s, under the rule of fascism, established Spanish society displayed a rigid social hierarchy, comparable to that of medieval times, making it virtually impossible to cross class boundaries. Landowning nobles still held sway at the top, joined now by high military and civilian officials of the regime and by the industrial leaders, many of whom had used their money and influence to buy government support.

> The idea of conflict-of-interest between government and business did not exist. Anyone who did not line their pockets when given the chance was considered deranged. Juan March was probably the ultimate product of the system; his smuggled cigarettes almost broke the government monopoly, and it was said he had 40,000 Spaniards on his payroll from customs officials to ministers. When he died in 1962 . . . he was reputedly the world's seventh richest man.
>
> (Williams, p. 236)

Fascist Spain prohibited labor unions independent of government control. Instead, the Falange organized the industrial working class into "vertical syndicates," which included management and a representative tied to the govern-

income, at constant prices [in 1940], had fallen back to that of 1914, but since the population had increased the per capita income fell to nineteenth century levels" (Eguilaz in Carr, p. 156). Not until 1952 would the standard of living return to its level at outbreak of the Spanish Civil War in 1936.

Plagued by food shortages, unrelieved even by imports from its few remaining allies, Spain suffered years of famine. Among the many references to this era of hunger in *Time of Silence*, most noteworthy are the allusions to it in the inner monologue of old Dora, owner of the boardinghouse in which Pedro resides. In real-life, prodded by hunger, country folk migrated to the cities at an ever-increasing rate, far exceeding the capacity of urban communities to absorb them. Franco's Ministry of Housing financed construction of low-income dwellings, but their production "fell far short of the need" (Payne, p. 392). Most of the migrants were landless, illiterate laborers or subsistence farmers, like Muecas in the novel, who hails from the outskirts of Toledo in La Mancha, an impoverished region south of Madrid.

Many of the poor newcomers were forced to build shanties on the outskirts of the major cities. The makeshift dwellings were "nightmarish constructions of orange boxes, flattened condensed-milk tins, metal sheets made from gasoline con-ment. The Law of the Bases of Syndical Organization (1940) declared that "the social discipline of the producers should be established upon the principles of unity and cooperation" (Babiano Mora, p. 51). Strikes were considered acts of sedition, but "workers gained a plethora of benefits like Social Security, numerous paid holidays and bonuses, and job security so sacred that only the most heinous offense warranted dismissal" (Williams, p. 235). This created apathy toward social justice among those fortunate enough to find jobs in the first place. In Madrid in 1949, there were 34,632 unemployed (Soto Carmona, p. 88). "The idea was to replace class struggle with cooperation in a kind of state-run paternalistic world" (Williams, p. 232).

A struggling middle class, comprised of government functionaries, shopkeepers and their clerks, schoolteachers, mechanics, and tradesmen—formed perhaps the only group with some social mobility. Members of the working class could ascend to middle-class status, either by holding down several different low-paying jobs or by marriage; and children of the middle class, either through personal effort or higher education, could ascend to the professional class of businessmen, doctors, and lawyers. The professions, however, were mostly dominated by the upper classes, and a family's clean ideological background (no significant activity on the losing, Republican side of the Civil War), or more importantly an *enchufe* (connection), was often necessary to attain the academic degrees or business permits required to attain professional status. Some individuals managed to breach the rigid boundaries and cross into other social classes. But it was generally dangerous to ignore the rigid class system. Whether aspiring upward or attempting to mix with those below, the individual always ran the risk of losing hard-fought gains.

Malcontents—from war "widows" to intellectuals. The case of prostitution was particularly grave in Franco Spain. The cause lay partly in the circumstances of the times, and partly in Spanish tradition, which kept economic power in the hands of men and codified that paternalism into law. Also, the Catholic Church exercised a strong influence on prostitution: taboos on premarital sex often led to the expulsion of a young girl from the family if she became pregnant. Abortion was illegal and therefore difficult to obtain. All these conditions converged to produce an army of young, single mothers who resorted to prostitution as their only means of support

(Hooper, p. 165). Other prostitutes came from the ranks of women whose marriages had failed and who likewise had little choice. There were restrictions on how they could earn an income. The regime made it illegal for a married woman to seek any employment outside the home without her husband's permission; nor could she control the family's money, even the portion she brought into the marriage. Following Church dogma, the state made divorce illegal, leaving the unhappily married woman with few other options than to simply abandon her husband. As for the children, the so-called *patria potestad,* or paternal authority, guaranteed that the husband maintained custody. One curious solution to the question of honor, an eternal obsession in Spanish culture, was the phenomenon of the young "widow" (exemplified by the mother Dora in *Time of Silence*). In the relative anonymity of the city, especially in the years just after the Civil War, young widows abounded. It became easy to invent the martyred soldier husband, a Nationalist, of course, lost in the "Great Crusade," and thus to hide the shame of a child born out of wedlock.

Abortion and divorce were not the only areas in which the Catholic Church exercised influence. Under Franco's regime, the Church hierarchy regained power and prerogatives it had enjoyed before the Second Republic had come to power in 1931. The regime banned civil marriages, "bishops sat in parliament and on the Council of the Realm, and laws had to conform to Catholic dogma" (Williams, p. 231). In addition, the Church assumed control of the educational system and, though the Falange took responsibility for censorship and propaganda, by the mid-1940s the Church monitored these facets of daily life too.

The Civil War and postwar repression had an indelible effect on social and intellectual conditions. A majority of Spain's greatest thinkers were executed, jailed, or forced into exile. Just two months after the Nationalist uprising, the poet-playwright Federico García Lorca was shot by Falangists in the fields outside Granada. The poet Antonio Machado died of pneumonia in a French village after his arduous escape across the Pyrenees. The poet Miguel Hernández languished in various prisons before eventually dying in one. Those who survived and remained in the country experienced what has been called an "inner exile." They found themselves silenced by the Nationalist Catholic coalition that supported Franco, or censored beyond recognition. A "majority of

SPAIN'S ONLY NOBEL

The picture opposite me of the man with the beard, the man who saw everything and who freed the Iberian people from their native inferiority in the field of science, gazes down silently, a witness of the lack of mice.

(Time of Silence, p. 3)

Time of Silence begins with Pedro, the protagonist, meditating on his frustrated cancer research, beneath the benevolent gaze of a photograph of Santiago Ramón y Cajal. Spain's only Nobel laureate in science before 1949, when the novel takes place, Ramón y Cajal shared the prize in 1906 with Camillo Golgi for their research on the nervous system. Born in Aragon in 1852, Ramón y Cajal became not only one of Europe's most respected physicians, but also a leading expert on micrography and histology, the microscopic study of human tissue. In the novel, Pedro despairs that under the conditions of Franco's dictatorship no Spanish scientist would ever again achieve as much. However, Spaniards did win several Nobels for literature before the novel was published: Fréderic Mistral and José Echegary y Eizaguirre shared the 1904 prize, Jacinto Benavente won the award in 1922, and Juan Ramón Jiménez in 1956. Spanish writers have since won two more: Vicente Aleixandre in 1977 and Camilo José Cela in 1989. There was another scientific winner too, but a generation after the novel. In 1949, Pedro could not have known that only ten years later Severo Ochoa would win the prize for his study of the synthetic processes of DNA.

university professors had been enthusiastic Republicans [anti-Francoists] . . . so purging those that remained was a priority" (Grugel and Rees, p. 138). The ranks of teachers were filled by members of Catholic Action, and a growing branch of conservative Catholicism, founded in 1929, the Opus Dei (Work of God), began to assert itself in science and technology. The Opus dominated the Consejo Superior de Investigaciones Científicas (CSIC or Council for Scientific Investigation), the organization that funds Pedro's cancer research in *Time of Silence*. Founded in 1939, just after the war ended, CSIC "defined its goal as 'the necessary reestablishment of the basic Christian unity of the sciences, destroyed in the eighteenth century'" (Payne, p. 366). The declaration places blame on the rationalist philosophy of the Enlightenment, which rejected religious dogma when it proved inconsistent with empirical scientific evidence.

Clearly, any aspiration toward the sort of probing, groundbreaking research achieved by Santiago Ramón y Cajal, Spain's only Nobel laureate in science, would encounter obstacles in this anti-intellectual atmosphere.

In the arts and literature, the salons of the rich continued, as is illustrated in *Time of Silence*, but they were purged of avant-garde voices that had

flourished in the pre-Civil War Republic. Poetry was dominated by champions of the regime such as José María Pemán and Agostín de Foxá, who returned to bucolic verse that celebrated simple country life and emulated the Renaissance poet Garcilaso de la Vega. It was only in the literary cafés, such as Café Gijón, where Pedro meets his wealthy friend Matías, that some semblance of genuine literary ambition surfaced. Books from around the world, often smuggled in from France, were cautiously discussed in these cafés, as were antiestablishment ideas. But the mixture of alcohol, self-glorification, and dilettantism within the framework of the regime often undermined pretensions to progressiveness, a phenomenon brought into visible relief in *Time of Silence*.

Meanwhile, the vast majority of the population spent its free time in what historian Raymond Carr refers to as the culture of evasion: bullfights, the music hall, soccer, radio serials, kiosk literature, and the tightly controlled movies. As Carr points out, these phenomena, along with the more benign coercion in politics and the occupational sphere that replaced the terror of the early years, worked "to keep the ordinary citizen a passive member of the new consumer society" (Carr, p. 164).

It is the collection of these conditions—social rigidity, religious control, imposed passivity, abhorrent living standards for the underclass, scientific backwardness, intellectual paralysis, sexual, marital, and economic precariousness for all but the wealthiest—that gives rise to the searing indictment of Spanish society in *Time of Silence*.

The Novel in Focus

Plot summary. Although the basic narrative structure of *Time of Silence* follows Pedro, the protagonist, through Madrid, his movement is frequently interrupted by meditative passages, philosophical digressions, mock-epic descriptions, and the inner monologues of three characters: Pedro himself, the boardinghouse owner and grandmother Dora, and a young tough from the slums named Cartucho ("Cartridge").

The action spans six days in the fall of 1949 in Madrid. Pedro, a young, middle-class doctor, exhausts his supply of the special, cancerous mice imported from the United States for his experiments on the cause of cancer. He is exploring whether genes or environment causes the disease. His laboratory assistant, Amador, reveals that his cousin Muecas, hustling king of the shantytown, has stolen a mating pair of mice to resell their offspring. In the shantytown of Vallecas to which Amador leads Pedro, Muecas, his wife, and two daughters live in misery and breed those mice.

Pedro himself is hardly better off in his shabby boardinghouse in a working-class neighborhood in mid-Madrid. The novel flashes back to describe his dismal living conditions, along with the subtle seduction plotted by the owner Dora and her daughter to unite Pedro and Dorita, the granddaughter, in order to improve the family's economic and social status. Pedro divides his leisure between the boardinghouse and the Café Gijón. At the café, he meets his wealthy friend Matías, as well as a young woman and a German painter. They set out for the painter's studio, continue drinking until drunk, then Pedro and Matías head for Doña Luisa's brothel. The two spend a great deal of time socializing with the prostitutes but never sleep with any. Upon his return to the boardinghouse, still quite drunk, Pedro finds Dorita naked in her bed. In a dreamlike state, he sleeps with her, telling her over and over that he loves her. He later recognizes that he has sealed his connection to her and her family and, envisioning his sordid future, he washes himself compulsively, seeking some kind of purification.

At dawn, a frantic Muecas seeks Pedro's services. He takes Pedro to his shack where his older daughter Florita is bleeding to death from a botched abortion. Muecas himself is the abortionist and the father of the fetus. Pedro cannot reverse the damage and Florita dies. Cartucho, her boyfriend, having already killed one rival for Florita's affections, threatens Amador into revealing who was responsible for her death. Amador lies and blames Pedro. Cartucho swears revenge.

Later that day, Pedro visits the home of Matías in the wealthy district. In Matías's room they contemplate a print of Goya's *Witches' Sabbath,* a work also known as *The Great Billygoat.* In Pedro's mind, the animal comes to symbolize the male-dominated, patriarchal Spanish society, whose narrow-mindedness, based on sexual dominance, spills over into intellectual life. In Goya's painting, the goat is surrounded by admiring female worshippers:

> The great goat, the great male, the great buck, the scapegoat, the well-made Hispanic billygoat. The stinking expiatory goat? No! The great buck in the splendor of his glory, in the supreme power of his dominion, the center of female adoration, his horn no longer ominous but a sign of glorious phallic domination.
> (*Time of Silence,* p. 127)

Laced with irony, the speech on the painting constitutes a thinly veiled critique of the philosopher José Ortega y Gasset. In real life, women flocked to Ortega's public lectures on philosophy. In the novel, Pedro and Matías arrive at one of these lectures, delivered at the Barceló Theater on the theme of point-of-view in philosophy and life. The audience contains upper-class women and well-meaning young intellectuals. Sarcastically described as a "well-arranged cosmos," the theater is divided into three sections, a metaphor for social divisions in Spain (*Time of Silence,* p. 131). The basement is a dance hall for the workers, the main floor serves as a lecture-hall for the wealthier classes, and the stage, like a throne, has "only a virtual or allegorical existence until the precise moment of the Master's appearance on his doctoral pinnacle," a mocking reference perhaps to Ortega's elitist philosophy (*Time of Silence,* p. 132).

After the lecture, at a reception for the philosopher in Matías's home, the superficiality of the upper class, especially of the women, concerns Pedro. He recognizes his own ambivalence: "Did he despise that way of living because it was really despicable or because he was incapable of getting

One of two paintings by Francisco de Goya called *The Witches Sabbath*. Also one of Goya's 14 Black Paintings, this *Witches' Sabbath* (1820-23) hangs in the Prado Museum.

close enough to take part in it. . . ?" (*Time of Silence,* p. 141). Yet he takes little solace when he escapes the party to attend the funeral of Florita. There follows a mordant satire in technological terms of burial practices at the municipal cemetery of Madrid, with the suggestion that death is the only industry Spain carries off successfully.

Pedro's troubles with the law begin with an exhumation of Florita's body, ordered because Pedro had failed to sign a death certificate. Pursued by the authorities, Pedro takes refuge at Doña Luisa's brothel. His friend Matías blunders, turning to Amador for help, unaware of his treachery. Amador betrays Pedro once again, this time by divulging his hiding place to the police, who arrest the fugitive.

In an inner monologue in jail, Pedro recriminates himself by criticizing his every act, including his passive compliance, which he regards as cowardice. In time, however, he comes to see his condition as a liberation from all cares, especially from his ambition for the Nobel Prize, which had led to his being in this current fix. Pedro's liberation from prison ironically emanates from the dregs of society. His upper-class friend Matías fails in trying to secure Pedro's release through influence in the higher echelons of society in the city. His middle-class fiancée Dorita and her grandmother harbor the idea of freeing Pedro only to enslave him themselves. Dorita's grandmother sees his current circumstances as one more step in his fall into their clutches: "The old woman knew that a little humiliation makes a man more amenable" (*Time of Silence,* p. 182). Only the lowly earth-mother Ricarda, wife of Muecas, comes successfully to Pedro's rescue. Ricarda witnesses the autopsy of her daughter Florita and considers the situation. Reflecting on her own life of suffering with the incestuous Muecas, she informs the authorities of Pedro's innocence.

Once released from jail, Pedro finds himself dismissed from his post at the research institute, fired by the director of research for unsavory deeds. His only recourse lies in practicing medicine in some obscure village of the provinces. Overcome with apathy about his fate, he takes his fiancée to a musical revue, part of the Spanish "culture of evasion," and later to a fair. Here the vengeful Cartucho murders Dorita in cold blood. The novel ends with Pedro's inner monologue of resignation to his fate as he arrives at the train station, bound for medical practice in the provinces. With Dorita dead and his research position lost, he explains why he has allowed society "to castrate" him (*Time of Silence,* p. 244). Comparing his silent acquiescence to the agonized screams of the eunuchs castrated on the beaches of Anatolia by the Turks, he points out that his is an "age of anesthesia" (*Time of Silence,* p. 244). In the end, gazing on the Escorial Palace as his train heads out into the countryside of Castile, he compares himself to the martyr St. Lawrence, patron saint of El Escorial: "St. Lawrence was a man, he didn't cry out, he lay there silently while the pagans roasted him over the fire, and history tells us that all he said was: 'Turn me over, for I'm done on this side,' and the executioner turned him over merely as a matter of symmetry" (*Time of Silence,* p. 247).

Madrid: metaphor. As if it were a specimen under a microscope, Luis Martín Santos dissects the city of Madrid, examining its every nook and cranny, in order to diagnose the cancerous society it reflects. The novel follows Pedro's movements through the city, much as the British writer James Joyce described Leopold Bloom's movements through Dublin in *Ulysses*. Both literary works, of course, are ultimately based on Homer's ancient Greek classic the *Odyssey*.

THE PHILOSOPHER RETURNS

José Ortega y Gasset, a major twentieth-century Spanish philosopher, was born in Madrid in 1883. He became a writer and publisher, founding such important journals as *España*, *Revista de Occidente* and the newspaper *El Sol*. A brilliant essayist, he was perhaps best known for his books of essays *The Revolt of the Masses*, *Invertebrate Spain*, and *The Dehumanization of Art*, which included the ideas on perspective and relativism parodied in *Time of Silence*. A liberal Republican, upon the outbreak of the Civil War in 1936, Ortega went into voluntary exile. In 1948 he returned to Madrid and founded the Institute for the Humanities. The lecture depicted in the novel is one in a series he delivered at the Teatro Barceló in Madrid in 1949. But times had changed. Ortega's notions of society as a meritocracy, a project of a moral and mental elite, as set out in essays like *The Dehumanization of Art* and *The Revolt of the Masses*, had undergone perversion in Franco Spain as justification for fascism. Younger leftward-leaning intellectuals like Luis Martín-Santos, though highly influenced by Ortega, found his apparent elitism repugnant, and regarded his reappearance on the intellectual scene as evidence of what seemed to them to be his tacit complicity with Franco.

As Pedro moves around the city, the author finds frequent opportunities to characterize Spanish society in general as reflected by the city's elements. He makes his intent clear at the start. As Pedro and Amador set out for Muecas's shack, the novel spends an entire page on one paragraph that is, especially in the original Spanish, one of the most scathing indictments ever written of a city. It begins with "The city is so stunted" and ends with "in this city with no cathedral" (*Time of Silence*, p. 11-12). In between are mentioned so many of Spain's historical pretensions, inadequacies, and failed longings for greatness as to leave the reader gasping for breath. And of course, in this most Catholic of societies, where all great cities have their one main cathedral, nothing could prove Madrid's shortcomings more than its unfinished Almudena Cathedral.

Included in the city are smoky taverns, street prostitutes, dwarves selling lighter flints, swindler taxi drivers, smooth talkers exploiting tourists, bars refrying squid in old olive oil, pharmacies producing cut-rate cure-alls, and the decrepit shantytown lurking on the outskirts. If the foregoing images represent the illness of Spanish society, the shantytown is the festering, open sore.

Doña Luisa's brothel, the Café Gijón, Matías's home, the Teatro Barceló, the music hall, the prison, and especially Pedro's boardinghouse, are likewise described in long-winded, epic fashion, complete with Homeric epithets. Through the grandmother's inner monologues and the third-person narration, the boardinghouse is treated almost as a complete microcosm of the decadence of the city and, in turn, of mid-twentieth-century Spanish society.

Emasculation and political impotence. Within this microcosm, the author equates sexual seduction and emasculation with the social and political impotence of society, one of the central metaphors of the novel. Manhood is identified with the city itself: "A man is the image of a city, and . . . a city is a man's entrails turned inside out, . . . a man finds in a city, not only his justification, his reason for being, but also the stumbling blocks as well as the invincible obstacles that destroy his manhood" (*Time of Silence*, p. 13).

In the Madrid of *Time of Silence* these "invincible obstacles" are most frequently represented by the women who come into Pedro's life. Foreshadowing his victimization, Pedro's life with the "three [female] generations" of the boardinghouse (Dorita, her mother, and her grandmother) illustrates his sense of impotence:

During this silence the hidden intentions of the three women became more clearly perceptible to Pedro, as though the three Fates were whispering the meaning of the web of his life . . . and he was troubled by a slight anguish as he felt himself yielding to temptation.
(*Time of Silence*, p. 39)

The calculating nature of women, and men's incapacity to escape them, are illustrated in the monologue of Dorita's grandmother and in her actions as well as those of her daughter, Dora. Dorita's own seductive powers may not be so innocent, suspects Pedro, a suspicion that the novel underlines by equating her powers with those of a Venus Flytrap: "He must not fall into this half-open flower like a fly and remain caught by the feet" (*Time of Silence*, p. 95).

Mythic figures, carnivorous plants, and insects are all employed to describe the women in the novel, which also associates them with witchcraft through the discourse on Goya's painting *The Great Billygoat* also called The Witches' Sabbath (1797-98). While it originally may have been an Enlightenment-inspired attempt to undermine superstition, in *Time of Silence* the painting serves as a scathing example of misogyny in a novel that casts women as one of the roots of man's incapacity to transcend his circumstances. The novel's Philosopher, based on Ortega y Gasset, author of the famous statement "I am myself and my circumstances," is set up as the Great Goat; the women who adore him as the witches, the source of his power: "The women press toward him to hear that truth. And it is precisely these women who are completely indifferent to the truth" (*Time of Silence*, p. 128).

Even the one female worthy of praise, the source of Pedro's redemption from the charges against him, is hardly spared the author's contempt. Ricarda, Florita's mother, is referred to as an "earthlike creature," little more than a large stone, "almost circular," with a "strikingly smooth and expressionless face" (*Time of Silence*, pp. 205, 49, 51). Her epiphany, which leads to Pedro's release, is like a simple force of nature, "not from love of the truth, nor from love of decency . . . but because she thought she was doing her duty in speaking like that" (*Time of Silence*, p. 206).

As Ronald Rapin points out, sexual dysfunction operates in the novel as a metaphor for repression by the dictatorial regime. This elaborate and at times contradictory metaphor was affected by the ideological restrictions imposed by Franco's censors. Since the institution of the 1938 Press Law (established by the Nationalists' provisional government even before it had taken complete control of Spain), it was "the obligation for all printed, visual or broadcast materials to be submitted for censorship before publication" (Labanyi, p. 208). Censors were given a set of rules to apply: Did the work attack Catholic dogma, morality, the Church or its ministers?

Did it attack the regime, its institutions, or those who cooperate with it? And finally, do objectionable passages compromise the work as a whole? (Rapin, p. 240). Most censorable of all was any mention of censorship itself.

According to Rapin, the harsh description of the brothel in *Time of Silence* is in reality an indictment of the dictatorial regime, and of the government's support of the brothels as an escape valve for otherwise dangerous urges (Rapin, pp. 238-39). As such, it was excised from the original 1962 Spanish edition and did not appear in Spain until the 1971 edition. Curiously a passage referring to the Papal See was excised in this later edition (*Time of Silence*, p. 85). It had slipped past the censors in the original, but Rapin speculates that when the editors were about to re-issue the novel, they cut it themselves. If sexual themes were handled more leniently by then, political and religious themes were treated more strictly (Rapin, p. 238). Fines could be quite high, which made publishers cautious; more importantly, their works would be vigilantly combed for offenses in the future if they slipped, which made them, as well as their writers, careful. All this effort proved effective. One of the few avenues of cultural satisfaction under Franco, literature was also a significant instrument of social change.

Sources and literary context. *Time of Silence* has been continually cited as a turning point in the modern Spanish novel. It has the curious distinction, as Suárez Granda points out, of combining "an *unoriginal* theme and an *original* style" (Suárez Granda, p. 5). The author clearly takes his cues from the *Odyssey* of Homer and from James Joyce's *Ulysses*, as well as the Bible and classical mythology, alluded to in numerous references, usually employed ironically. In much of the novel, the lowliest situations are described in the most grandiloquent terms: "just as Moses had stood on a much higher mountain" (*Time of Silence*, p. 39).

There is also a clear similarity between Pedro's relationship with Amador and Don Quixote's with his squire, Sancho Panza in Miguel de Cervantes's **Don Quixote** (also in *WLAIT 5: Spanish and Portuguese Literatures and Their Times*). Their walk through the streets of Madrid, as they head toward the shantytown, mirrors Don Quixote and Sancho's travels, sharply contrasting Pedro's high-minded analysis of the decadent society surrounding them with Amador's *sanchoesque* cravings for a meal, a drink, the embrace of one of the young women they pass. Cervantes is in fact mentioned directly various times. Ricardo Doménech has also noted the influences of Jean-Paul Sartre in the existential philosophy of the protagonist; the absurd, nightmare quality inspired by Franz Kafka, and the provocative sense of memory reminiscent of Marcel Proust (Doménech, pp. 290-91).

More generally, the novel is striking in its amalgamation of different literary genres: "testimonial, serial literature . . . philosophical discourse, parody, clinical report, regenerationist reflection, naked dialogue, interior monologue, erudition" (Suárez, p. 7). *Time of Silence* is also noted for its use of dialectical realism, the synthesis between objectivist tendencies of 1950s Neorealism (which sought to deal realistically with post-World War II social problems) and experimental aesthetic techniques and psychological analysis (Winecoff Díaz, p. 234). In fact, readers of Spanish novels in the 1960s were able to accustom themselves to the linguistic and ideological experiments of Juan and Luis Goytisolo, Juan Benet, and Juan Marsé precisely because of the impact of *Time of Silence* (Suárez, pp. 6-7; see Juan Goytisolo's **Marks of Identity**, also in *WLAIT 5: Spanish and Portuguese Literatures and Their Times*).

Events in History at the Time the Novel Was Written

Franco relaxes his grip. By 1962, the year in which *Time of Silence* was published, many changes had come about since its setting in 1949. In 1952 *Bienvenido Mr. Marshall* (Welcome, Mr. Marshall), a parody of Spanish pretensions to Marshall Plan funding, found its way uncensored to the screen. With the intensification of the Cold War (the competition between the United States and the Soviet Union for world leadership), and Spain's strategic location at the entrance to the Mediterranean, the United States signed an agreement with Franco in 1953. The agreement allowed American bases in Spain, in exchange for liberalized trade relations and substantial financial assistance—millions in foreign aid flowed into Spain from the U.S. government (Williams, p. 237). Franco's regime was further legitimized when Franco signed a concordat with the Vatican in 1954. In 1955 Spain was finally admitted into the United Nations.

Most importantly, Spain reorganized its economy with the Development Plan of 1959. Much of this effort was stimulated by the founding, and instant success, of the European Common Market in 1958. Hoping for eventual admittance, the regime saw it had to liberalize its economy, which, not incidentally, was in a shambles. The regime began to allow local collective bargaining of workers, though still within the framework of its verticalist Syndical Organization. Also, the Opus Dei, with its hundreds of so-called *technocrats*, had by this time worked its way into key positions both in industry and in the administration. There were indications that government change was in the offing too. Since the days of the novel's setting, Juan Carlos, the grandson of the last king, Alfonso XIII, had been living in Spain and was educated under Franco's wing, a clear indication that the dictator would keep his promise to someday restore the monarchy. Yet 1962 Spain was still a dictatorship, authoritarian in nature, characterized by censorship, a rubber-stamp parliament, a restrictive social structure, and a second-rate economy.

Reviews. *Time of Silence* was hailed at its publication for its break with the social realism then in vogue. Writing in *Ínsula* magazine, Ricardo Doménech saluted its originality, its variance from the "monotony of character, situation and action" of its contemporaries. Despite its "apparent multiplicity of styles," the whole novel seemed to him to be "astonishingly unified" (Doménech, pp. 290-91). In the *New York Times Book Review*, Thomas Curley praised the novel in translation: "the bravura and lyricism of the prose . . . the casual deftness of the symbols and most of all the brilliant concluding monologue. . . . The fact that the novel was published in Spain only after much cutting is evidence that their censors have neither common nor aesthetic sense" (Curley, p. 57). A year later a review in the London *Times* summed up *Time of Silence* as "an extraordinarily good study of a nation in the midst of decay" (*Times of London*, p. 83).

—Eric M. Thau

For More Information

Babiano Mora, José. *Emigrantes, cronómetros y huelgas*. Madrid: Siglo XXI de España Editores, 1995.

Carr, Raymond. *Modern Spain: 1875-1980*. Oxford, New York: Oxford University Press, 1980.

Curley, Thomas. "Man Lost in Madrid." *The New York Times Book Review,* 29 November 1964, 57.

Doménech, Ricardo. "Luis Martín Santos." *Modern Spanish and Portuguese Literatures*. Ed. and trans. Marshall J. Schneider and Irwin Stern. New York: Continuum, 1988.

Grugel, Jean, and Tim Rees. *Franco's Spain*. London: Arnold, 1997.

Hooper, John. *The New Spaniards*. London: Penguin, 1986.

Labanyi, Jo. "Censorship or the Fear of Mass Culture." In *Spanish Cultural Studies, An Introduction*.

Travels in
My Homeland

by
Almeida Garrett

Portuguese writer Almeida Garrett (1799-1854) was born in Oporto but spent most of his adolescence in the Azores, where he was deeply influenced by his well-read Franciscan uncle, the bishop Father Alexandre da Sagrada Família. On returning to mainland Portugal, Garrett studied law from 1816-21 at the university in Coimbra, where he was at the heart of the sociopolitical debates on the drafting of the first Portuguese constitution. Extremely active in favor of the liberal revolution, he is known to have charismatically proclaimed discourses on the streets of Coimbra and to have rallied together groups of students and political activists around the liberal ideals that he preached. Twice forced into exile for political reasons (in 1823 and 1828), Almeida Garrett came into direct contact with the works of seasoned Romantic writers such as Lord Byron and Walter Scott. His epic poem *Camões* (1825), a tribute to the persecuted sixteenth-century Portuguese epic poet who was also forced into exile, is nowadays considered the first Romantic poem of the Portuguese language. (See *The Lusiads* by Camões, also in *WLAIT 5: Spanish and Portuguese Literatures and Their Times*.)

Always seeking to punctuate his writing with personal convictions, Garrett worked in journalism, serving as editor and main writer for several political periodicals. In 1822 he established and entirely wrote one of the first feminist periodicals to ever be published in Portugal, *O Toucador* (The Hairdresser). Hoping to draw attention to the lack of modernization in Portugal, he also

THE LITERARY WORK

A novel set in Santarém, a provincial town northeast of Lisbon, Portugal, in the first part of the nineteenth century; first published in Portuguese (as *Viagens na minha terra*) in 1846, in English in 1987.

SYNOPSIS

A traveler journeys to Santarém, where he is told a romantic story intertwined with a mysterious family tragedy set against the Portuguese civil war.

published an extensive essay on political history, *Portugal na balança da Europa* (1830; Portugal in Relation to the Rest of Europe). Garrett contributed as well to Portuguese theater, which stood in desperate need of drastic restructuring at the time, lacking actors, plays, stages, and funding. Along with the many initiatives he undertook in this area, Garrett founded the Conservatory of Dramatic Arts (O Conservatório Dramático) and acted in and wrote plays himself, winning most renown for his *Frei Luís de Sousa* (1844; *Brother Luís de Sousa*, 1907). His interest in preserving national culture as expressed in oral tradition led to his compilation of poems, legends, and folktales in the collection *Romanceiro* (1843), the first of its kind in Portuguese literature. Garrett's novels are embedded in nationalistic ideas too, for example, his two-part historical novel *O Arco de Santana* (The Sant'Ana

Almeida Garrett

Arch, 1845, 1850). By far the most famous of his writings, *Travels in My Homeland* combines the popular nineteenth-century tastes for travel literature with eclectic digressions on arts, culture, history and politics, a romantic tale of unhappy love, and an acute assessment of Portugal in the civil war era.

Events in History at the Time of the Novel

The constitutional struggle. *Travels in My Homeland* is set during the constitutional fight and the Portuguese civil war that devastated the country in the first part of the nineteenth century. The liberals fought the monarchists, with the two groups following the leads of King John VI's sons Dom Pedro and Dom Miguel, respectively. At the outset, the liberals favored a constitution; the monarchists, kingly rule—that is, Portuguese kingly rule, after years of foreign governance.

The years prior to the 1832-34 civil war are significant in order to fully understand the political backdrop of *Travels*. In 1807 the invasion of the Napoleonic troops led the Portuguese royal family to flee to Brazil, where they arrived the following year (1808), setting up court in Rio de Janeiro. Portugal, aided by its ally England, successfully ousted the French in 1812, whereupon in the absence of King John VI, the country was governed by the English marshal William Carr Beresford. The Portuguese, feeling abandoned by the monarchy and resenting the British rule, promoted the growth of the liberal movement, to which Almeida Garrett's generation enthusiastically adhered. On August 24, 1820, the military revolted in Oporto, claimed full sovereignty in the north of Portugal, and formed a provisional junta. The instigators of this revolt, known as the Oporto Liberal Revolution, looked forward to adopting a constitution, holding elections, and welcoming back King John VI to act as the first Portuguese constitutional monarch.

In 1821 John VI returned to Portugal and, taken prisoner by the liberals, was forced to accept the new constitution. Meanwhile his son Dom Pedro declared the independence of Brazil and became Brazil's first emperor. The Portuguese constitution of 1822 took effect for only about a year before the absolutists waged a counter-revolution known as the "Vilafrancada" in May of 1823, proclaiming the restoration of absolute monarchy. Dom John VI was again forced to act according to the dictates of the rebels, this time to abolish the constitution, and many liberals, including Garrett, were driven abroad in search of refuge. The conflict would persist despite their absence. The counter-revolution had begun a seesaw epoch of action and reaction: "This necessary and inevitable upheaval the world is going through will take a long time and will be resisted by a good deal of reaction before it is complete" (Garrett, *Travels in My Homeland*, p. 23).

Upon the death of John VI, the liberals rallied together around the second Portuguese constitution, the "Constitutional Charter," sent from Brazil by the Emperor Dom Pedro. It was less democratic and extreme than the first constitution and so promoted a spirit of compromise between the absolutists and liberals. Approved in 1827, the Charter enabled exiled liberals to return to Portugal. Dom Pedro placed his seven-year-old daughter on the throne, having her marry her uncle Miguel, who was to be acting regent of the kingdom. The atmosphere of conciliation quickly disintegrated, however. The following year the absolutists proclaimed Dom Miguel the legitimate heir, forcing the liberals out of the country again and marking the beginning of Dom Miguel's repressive six-year rule.

Thousands left the country, thousands were arrested and kept in jail in the worst possible conditions, dozens were executed and murdered. Repression hit every aspect of Portuguese life. . . . Yet the majority of the population applauded such measures, because they regarded the liberals as pure atheists, enemies of the country and guilty of the worst crimes.

(Marques, p. 60)

The Portuguese civil war. In the late 1820s, under the reign of Dom Miguel, many liberals fled to England and France. However, they did not give up hope and in exile organized an expedition to the island of Terceira (in the Azores) early in 1829. This explains the itinerary of the protagonist Carlos in *Travels in My Homeland,* who joins the liberals: "That night he was in Lisbon, a few days later in England and some months afterwards on the island of Terceira" (*Travels*, p. 100). At this point in the conflict, Emperor Pedro left Brazil in the hands of his son to undertake the direct leadership of the liberal cause in Europe, organizing troops in England and France. Following the French revolution of 1830, Dom Pedro's strategy to liberate Portugal was well received by the French government; hundreds of French volunteers and mercenaries accompanied the sovereign to Terceira in March of 1832. Three months later Pedro formed an expedition of 7,500 men that landed on mainland Portugal near Oporto, taking the absolutist forces by surprise. In the novel, Friar Dinis condemns Carlos for his involvement in this attack.

Despite an outbreak of cholera, the liberals held strong in Oporto for about a year as the absolutists besieged the town. The liberal cause spread throughout the country, demoralizing the absolutists who were badly beaten in July of 1833. Dom Pedro assumed control of the government, and the absolutists evacuated the capital, suffering defeat after defeat as they retreated. Following the bloody battle of Asseiceira in May of 1834, Dom Miguel and his army finally conceded ultimate defeat. A general amnesty was granted on May 26 in the village of Évora-Monte, northeast of Évora.

Portuguese liberalism and disillusionment. Echoing the doctrines and privileges that had triumphed in America and France several years earlier, the ideals of Portuguese liberalism promised much needed progress: freedom of religion, press, speech, trade and industry; the restriction of royal prerogatives; the right of individual property; equality of rights and laws for all; the abolition of feudal rights; the end of property

confiscations, torture, and other physical penalties; the union of Church and state, which weakened the heretofore dominant power of the Church; and the establishment of a hereditary constitutional monarchy.

Though initially these promises and the constitutions united liberals around shared ideals, the only partial implementation of hoped-for structural changes together with egoistic and diverging interests caused dissension and internal division among the constitutionalists after their 1834 victory. The situation was aggravated by

the often unreasonable expectations of the military who, having played leading roles in the war, wanted rewards for their services and considered themselves the natural leaders of the country. These deep-rooted internal divisions within the liberal ranks came to a head in September of 1836 when a rising in favor of the more radical constitution of 1822 was organized by extreme liberals, thereafter referred to as "Septembrists." Their opponents, the more conservative liberals, or "Chartists," were in favor of Pedro's 1826 constitution, the Charter, that granted more extensive powers to the king. The victory of the Septembrist movement was short-lived, lasting only until 1842, when more internal divisions led to the dissolution of the Septembrist Party.

The secretary of Justice and the Chartist politician António Bernarda da Costa Cabral stepped in to take over the country by a bloodless coup d'état and, prompting a political about-face, created a radical right-wing reform government. Costa Cabral ruthlessly imposed order and economic development in an unashamed despotic authoritarian rule. Those for whom the revolution and the principles for which it stood were still valued ideals deeply despised the "cabralist" political dictatorship and the liberal factions who let themselves be manipulated by financial benefits and lamentable political games.

Travels in My Homeland has a frame story containing the novel proper. In this frame story, the traveler journeys to Santarém approximately ten years after the signing of the amnesty of Évora-Monte. Comments made during the narration reflect the disillusionment with the state of affairs in Portugal in contrast to the protagonist Carlos's enthusiasm for the liberal cause, expressed in the novel within the novel. In Garrett's own life this contrast is equally apparent. Once an adamant liberal, following the liberal victory of 1834 Garrett came to realize that ungodliness, greed, ambition, and immorality had replaced freedom and equality, mere ideals of a thwarted liberal cause.

The history and monuments of Santarém.

Travels in my Homeland is set in the town of Santarém and its surrounding valley, situated along the Tagus River, approximately 50 miles northeast of Lisbon. Santarém is the capital of the Ribatejo (banks of the Tagus) province, a fertile region that is one of the gentlest and greenest in Portugal. Once a flourishing medieval center of 15 convents, this provincial town is known for its abundance of monuments and ruins, each disclosing part of the town's history. Over the centuries the richness of Santarém's history and legends has maintained a captivated audience, inspiring visitors, writers and artists from all walks of life.

Travels in My Homeland combines an appreciation of historical and cultural markers in Santarém with its significance as a metaphor for the glorious past of Portugal. The narrator's visit becomes a pilgrimage to historical places as well as a motive for exploring the Portugal of today and yesterday.

During the medieval era, in the course of the wars between Moors and Christians, Santarém became a capital fortress city, with the Christians effecting Reconquest and renewed control in 1147. Some of the buildings retain a distinctively Mozarabic style, that is, the adaptation by Christian artists of many Islamic features creating a unique colorful style; the style recalls the years of the Muslim occupation in Portugal (from 711 to 1249), which left an indelible mark on the architecture of the town. A strategic stronghold, Santarém became fundamental in expelling the Moors from Portuguese territory; from Santarém Afonso Henriques, the first king of Portugal, and his warriors progressively gained ground, conquering Lisbon and moving southward. In *Travels* references to Afonso Henriques as the founder of Portugal in connection with Santarém emphasize the historical origins of the town, symbolizing a new beginning, nostalgically evoking the memory of a united country heralded around the still vital ideals of freedom and independence.

Travels in My Homeland mentions a host of people of historic importance, including the following:

Friar Gil (1190-1265) An infamous friar who allegedly made a pact with the devil and lived a licentious life set on accumulating wealth and fame, until, smitten with remorse, he repented and entered the Dominican order in Paris.

King Fernando (1345-83) and Queen Leonor Teles (?-1386) Widow of King Fernando I, Leonor Teles arrived at Santarém and from here sought revenge for usurpation of the throne and for the assassination of the widow's lover, appealing to her daughter Beatriz and son-in-law, John I, king of Castile, to come to aid her against Portugal. For over a year Leonor and her partisans held strong in the Castle of Santarém and Alcáçova until their defeat in the Battle of Aljubarrota in 1385.

Nun' Álvares Pereira (1360-1431) A heroic soldier and constable of the Portuguese kingdom. His warfare strategy was fundamental in helping John of Avís secure the throne from the threat of John of Castile, the son-in-law of Leonor Teles and the deceased King Fernando I.

Pedro Álvares Cabral (1467-1520) A key navigator during the Age of the Discoveries mostly remembered as the founder of Brazil. He landed there April 22, 1500, then returned to Portugal. Several years before his death, he moved to Santarém, where he was buried.

Friar Luís de Sousa (1555-1632). A monk formerly named Manuel de Sousa Coutinho, who served as a knight against the Moors and, after being imprisoned, returned to Portugal to marry the widow of King John of Portugal, who had been presumed dead but later was discovered alive in the Holy Land. On mutual accord, Sousa Coutinho and his wife decided to take religious vows, after which he became a convent chronicler known for his eloquent prose and adamant patriotism.

Luís de Camões (1524?-80) Author of the great Portuguese epic poem *The Lusiads* and corpus of lyric poetry. The poet was allegedly sent into exile from Santarém. He is frequently mentioned in *Travels in my Homeland* as the father of all Portuguese literature and the essence of the Portuguese era of glory and prosperity.

The Novel in Focus

Plot summary. Divided into 49 short chapters, each prefaced by a brief synopsis, the narrative of *Travels* progresses on several different levels. First there is the narrator's journey from Lisbon to Santarém, interspersed with digressive comments on what he sees and thinks. The story of Joaninha and Carlos told to the narrator by his traveling companion in the valley of Santarém brings in a second level. Finally, there is the letter that Carlos writes to Joaninha and that the narrator comes across at the conclusion of the narrative.

In 1843 the narrator travels by boat up the Tagus River from Lisbon to Azambuja and then on to Cartaxo by mule. Along the way, he discusses a wide variety of topics, seemingly unrelated, imparting a distinct casualness throughout the rambling discourse. The issues he raises range from the question of whether civilization progresses through spiritualism or materialism, to the perfect recipe for composing original literature, to the work of the Portuguese writer Camões, to philosophical considerations. Leaving Cartaxo, the traveler passes the site of one of the civil war battles and condemns the senselessness of war. These digressions set the scene for the story he is about to hear.

At this point of the narrative, the traveler discovers the paradisiacal valley of Santarém and becomes intrigued by an old cottage whose half-open window sparks his interest. As he conjectures about the inhabitants of the cottage he becomes lost in his meditations, transported by the chirping of the nightingales. With his travel companion he dismounts, and the companion proceeds to relay a tale about the maiden of the nightingales.

The story begins in the summer of 1832 with an old blind woman spinning her reel of yarn on the porch of the cottage. She lives with her 16-year-old granddaughter Joaninha, who is "the embodiment of sweetness, the ideal of spirituality," raised amidst the natural setting of Santarém and for whom "nature had done it all, or nearly all, and education nothing, or close to nothing" (*Travels*, p. 74).

The only regular visitor to the cottage is Friar Dinis, who stops by the home of the old lady Francisca every Friday. It becomes apparent during one of the conversations between Friar Dinis and Francisca that there is an absent member of the family. It is Francisca's grandson, Carlos, whom Friar Dinis accuses of being "with those miscreants who have come from the [Azorean] islands [and] who disembarked in Oporto" (*Travels*, p. 86). Friar Dinis heartlessly claims that because of Carlos's political affiliation with the liberals, the "boy is damned and between him and [them] is the abyss of hell" (*Travels*, p. 88). It is evident that Friar Dinis represents the voice of the Old Regime. He defends the principles of the monarchy and regards the doctrines of the constitutionalists as mere senseless abstractions.

In a flashback the narrator reverts to Friar Dinis's secular life before he entered the monastery and explains his transformation from Dinis de Ataíde to Friar Dinis da Cruz, and the settlement he gave to provide for Dona Francisca and her family because of some past injury. Presently her family consists of her orphaned granddaughter Joaninha, the only child of her son, and her orphaned grandson, Carlos, the issue of her daughter. Carlos was born after his father's death and his birth cost his mother her life. Anxiously concerned with Carlos's upbringing, Friar Dinis grew utterly dismayed at the boy's transformation in the summer of 1830 from a God-fearing, truthful, cheerful youth into a politically engaged liberal, set on emigrating to England after publicly declaring his allegiance to the liberal cause. On the Friday following Carlos's departure Friar Dinis came to speak with Dona Francisca; for the next three days she remained locked up in her room and from then on lost her sight. Since then the friar briefly visits the old cottage each Friday, bringing news of the civil war. Though Carlos departed thinking he knew the family secret concerning the deaths of his father and uncle, he really only knows part of the mystery and Dona Francisca vows that one day she will reveal all the truth to her grandson, against the will of Friar Dinis.

Following this flashback, the story continues as the valley of Santarém becomes a strategic point in the civil war—"before long all the power and interest of the war centred on that once peaceful and delightful, now desolate and turbulent, valley" (*Travels*, p. 110). Despite the proximity of the war, Dona Francisca refuses to leave the only house she has ever known. Also, deep in her soul, she entertains the hope that her grandson will soon find his way back to the family cottage. "Joaninha's frank, innocent dignity and the old woman's sober appearance and serene, kindly melancholy made them so respected by the soldiers that . . . they were as safe and undisturbed, in the small part of the house they had reserved for themselves, as was possible in such circumstances" (*Travels*, p. 111). War and its consequences become a familiar sight, and Joaninha, always accompanied by chirping nightingales as she wanders through the valley, is known to both camps by the suggestive and poetic name "maiden of the nightingales." She wins their respect for her altruism as she cares for the sick and the wounded, wandering freely among both camps.

One afternoon as the constitutional army is receiving reinforcements, Joaninha falls asleep on the hillside near the cottage and to her surprise is awoken by her cousin, Carlos, now an officer in the constitutional army. When the army leaves, Joaninha promises, on Carlos's request, to say nothing of his presence in the valley to their rapidly failing grandmother. Carlos reflects on the transformation of his cousin, two years ago still a child, but now "a sweet, beautiful young woman. . . . He did not expect . . . the impression he received: it was a surprise, a shock, a confused upset of all his ideas and feeling" (*Travels*, p. 125). His heart is spoken for by another, a beautiful young Englishwoman named Georgina who preferred him, a lowly foreign fugitive, to other, higher-born suitors. Through the protagonist's meandering thoughts the reader learns partial truths about the past and Carlos's feelings towards his grandmother and Friar Dinis. As much as he loves his grandmother, Carlos has promised himself never to return to the family cottage that he believes to be "contaminated, dishonoured, blood-stained, and defiled with shame and disgrace" (*Travels*, p. 129). In order to justify not seeing his grandmother, he uses the excuse of the war and his military affiliation with the liberals (at this point the monarchists occupy Santarém and going to the cottage is fraught with danger). The next day he returns to meet Joaninha. They discuss the past, Friar Dinis's role in their grandmother's blindness, and Friar Dinis's accusations against Carlos. Relieved, Carlos realizes that his cousin completely ignores the family's deepest secrets. Joaninha declares that she loves him, only him, and that she will never love any man but him.

At this point, the narrator leaves the story of Joaninha and Carlos and reverts back to his trip to Santarém, interspersed with diverse digressions. He draws attention to the charm and strength of narrating a story in the actual place where it took place. That is why he remains in Santarém listening to his traveling companion and writing down the "fascinating story of the maiden of the nightingales" (*Travels*, p. 148).

When the narrator resumes the tale of Joaninha and Carlos, preparations for battle are underway. Carlos envisions death as the only way out of such tragic circumstances, preferring to die rather than face the bizarre love triangle in which he is now involved and the truth of his family's misfortune. In the battle Carlos is wounded. He awakens in a cell in the convent of St. Francis in Santarém, where he is being tended by Georgina and Friar Dinis. As Carlos recuperates, Georgina explains the events of the past few weeks and how she came to be nursing him in Portugal. Georgina reveals that though she loves him dearly, she now realizes that he loves his cousin Joaninha. Friar Dinis begs Carlos for his forgiveness and mercy, beseeching him to lift the curse placed upon him, preferring to die by Carlos's hand than continue to live under his curse. The reader then learns that Friar Dinis had an affair with Carlos's mother. He was the one who murdered her husband, blinded Carlos's grandmother, and covered the whole family with ignominy. After a moment of tenderness between Carlos, Friar Dinis, and Georgina, Carlos recalls his mother and throws himself at the monk, intending to kill him. Dona Francisca and Joaninha arrive at the crucial moment, revealing a truth about Friar Dinis that stops Carlos in the heat of his fury: Friar Dinis is Carlos's father. Georgina bids Joaninha farewell and leaves Carlos in his cousin's loving hands, whereupon the whole truth concerning the deaths of Carlos's mother's husband and his uncle (Joaninha's father) is revealed: Dinis killed them both in self-defense, not knowing who the two men were who intended to murder him on that dark night. "The two of them joined together to murder me and ambushed me on the heath. I did not recognize them—it was night and pitch black. I defended myself not knowing against whom and had the misfortune to save my life at the cost of theirs" (*Travels*, p. 185). Friar Dinis confesses, and expresses his remorse and pain at prompting and witnessing the death of Carlos's mother and the sorrow heaped on the grandmother. Carlos then takes his leave, rejoining the constitutional army to be stationed in the proximity of Évora.

Once again the narrator pauses before continuing with the story. He wanders through Santarém, recounting legends and historical facts related to the sights and monuments he sees. The following day, weary of the town, he heads back to the valley, attracted again by the window that had previously caught his attention. Here both levels of the narrative merge as the traveler encounters Dona Francisca winding her skein of yarn in the company of Friar Dinis. Friar Dinis hands the traveler a letter that Carlos wrote to Joaninha from Évora. In this letter Carlos reveals his past, his adventures in England with the three young ladies of a rich, highly sophisticated family—Julia, Laura, and Georgina—and the false persona he adopted to be accepted by them: "my true spirit and character were not what they were taken for. I lied: men are always lying. . . . So I lied and I was liked because I lied" (*Travels*, p. 225). Though fond of all three sisters, at first Carlos loved Laura. She, however, was engaged to be wed. After her departure, he fell more in love with Georgina than he had been with Laura, a romance that lasted for three months until he departed to the Azores. Then, on returning to Santarém, he fell in love with Joaninha: "I realized, the moment I saw you among those trees, in the starlight, I realized that it was you I had always loved, that I was born to love you, if my soul was capable and worthy of being united with the angelic soul that dwells in you" (*Travels*, p. 242). But he explains that he could not pursue this love, for any woman whom he loves "will inevitably be unhappy" (*Travels*, p. 242).

The novel concludes as the narrator hands the letter back to Friar Dinis and identifies himself as one of Carlos's comrades. Carlos is now a fat, rich baron, Joaninha died in a state of madness, and Georgina confined herself to a convent in England where she became a Catholic abbess. As Friar Dinis returns to his breviary and the old woman continues her winding, the narrator departs and rides to Cartaxo and then travels on to Lisbon. He concludes that "I have seen some parts of the world and recorded something of what I saw. Of all my travels, however, those which have interested me most were still my travels in my homeland" (*Travels*, p. 246).

Of barons and monks. The clergy, often considered a dangerous and powerful symbol of past injustices, is embodied in *Travels in my Homeland* by Friar Dinis. "The monk was the first to err, by not understanding us, our century, our inspirations and aspirations; that way he put himself in a false position, cut himself off from social life and made his demise a necessity. . . . He was afraid of freedom, which was friendly to him, but meant to reform him, and he joined forces with despotism. . . ." (*Travels*, p. 81). The monk, destitute of the political and social power once conferred upon him, becomes a figure of yesterday, and the baron, a symbol of the rising bourgeois society, takes his place. "An awful substitute!" says the monk (*Travels*, p. 245).

Carlos embodies the baron, the successor. He belongs to the generation that applauded the liberal revolution, refuses to take ecclesiastical vows, and ultimately joins the ranks of the minor nobility. As portrayed in *Travels in My Homeland*, the barons represented the material corruption that distorted the liberal ideals and characterized this new social class. Lisbon, under the government of Costa Cabral, became the domain of the hated barons. "The monk did not understand us, and so he died, and we did not understand the monk, so we made the barons, and we shall die from them. They are the disease of the century: it is they, the barons, who are the cholera morbus of present-day society, not the Jesuits" (*Travels*, pp. 80-81). The narrator laments the lack of spiritualism that he witnesses in Portugal, as well as the lack of respect for the values of the past as materialism comes to dominate the newly founded society. "In Portugal there is no religion of any sort. Even its false shadow, hypocrisy, has disappeared. Another ten years of barons and their materialist regime and the last sigh of the spirit will inevitably flee from Portugal's dying body" (*Travels*, p. 217). The baron, "usuriously revolutionary and revolutionarily usurious," is presented as opposed to the march of progress which the narrator associates with liberal ideals (*Travels*, p. 80).

On a par with the general sentiment widespread throughout other parts of Europe, anticlerical feeling had slowly emerged in Portugal during the late eighteenth century and the beginning of the nineteenth century. As the liberal movement gained momentum and came into power, several reforms directly affected the power of the ecclesiastical orders. Among the measures implemented by the constitutionalists were the abolition of tithes, along with several other taxes, that deprived clerics of important sources of revenue. The Church also became subject to land reform. In a series of decrees enacted during the early 1830s, victorious liberals confiscated the extensive properties and estates of the Church. The desired land-reform resulted in the rise of a new class of wealthy landowners, the barons. Their landownership would confer on this group a dominant position in political life for the rest of the century.

Sources and literary context. Of all his writings, *Travels in My Homeland* seems by far the work most closely inspired by Almeida Garrett's personal life. The first chapter of *Travels* appeared in 1843, just weeks after Garrett set out to visit his old university friend, Passos Manuel, in Santarém. The narrator of *Travels in My Homeland* states: "For a long time I had had this vague idea, more of a notion than a plan, of touring the rich plains of our Ribatejo and paying my respects to the most historical and monumental of our towns on its lofty height. I am prevailed upon by the insistence of a friend" (*Travels*, p. 22). Passos Manuel's letter of invitation is dated July 6 of that year, thus it is most likely that the literary rendition of the trip to Santarém was inspired by the author's visit with him.

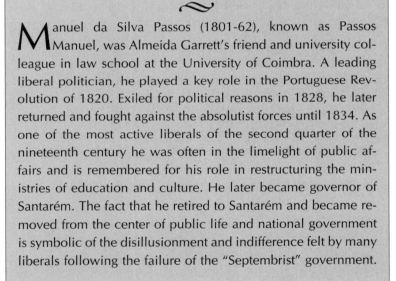

PASSOS MANUEL

Manuel da Silva Passos (1801-62), known as Passos Manuel, was Almeida Garrett's friend and university colleague in law school at the University of Coimbra. A leading liberal politician, he played a key role in the Portuguese Revolution of 1820. Exiled for political reasons in 1828, he later returned and fought against the absolutist forces until 1834. As one of the most active liberals of the second quarter of the nineteenth century he was often in the limelight of public affairs and is remembered for his role in restructuring the ministries of education and culture. He later became governor of Santarém. The fact that he retired to Santarém and became removed from the center of public life and national government is symbolic of the disillusionment and indifference felt by many liberals following the failure of the "Septembrist" government.

Garrett's political affiliations vibrate strongly throughout the work, with his views closely paralleling those of the protagonist Carlos. Both received a traditional education before going on to study law at the University of Coimbra, and it is during these Coimbra years that author and protagonist alike became enthusiastically involved with the liberal cause. Dom Miguel's victory and the triumph of absolutism forced Garrett into exile first in 1823 and then in 1828, which happens also to the fictional Carlos. Similarly, in March of 1832 Garrett joined Dom Pedro's constitutional army that had taken refuge in the Azores, as Carlos does: "The tyrannical law of honour obliged . . . me to leave for the Azores. I went. . . . I still do not know how I left, how I arrived, how I lived those first weeks of my stay on that rock in the middle of the sea called Terceira Island, where the unhappy remains of the constitutional army had taken refuge" (*Travels*, p. 241). Both author and protagonist belonged to the small constitutional army of 7,500 men who landed in northern Portugal in July 1832 and occupied Portugal's second largest city, Oporto.

There are similarities in the romantic lives of author and character too. As a young man, the fictional Carlos flutters from passion to passion. Garrett's marriage to the young and beautiful Luisa Midosi in 1822, when she was merely 15, did not prevent his becoming a philanderer, and the marriage finally ended 14 years later. Garrett would engage in several different love affairs at once, the most famous of which was his adulterous relationship with the Viscountess da Luz, caricaturized in the newspapers of the period. "He always loved many woman who easily surrendered to his charming gallantries. He loved each and every one of them and had a notable preference for younger women. . . . While in close association with a respectable English family he courted three charming sisters at the same time and was seriously involved with one of them" (Santos, p. 11). Indeed, when Garrett was in exile in England in 1823 he stayed in the home of Thomas Haddley in Warwick and his relationship with the Haddley daughters was more than just friendship, a reality echoed by Carlos's relationships with the three English sisters in the novel.

As noted, Garrett was strongly influenced by his uncle Friar Alexandre da Sagrada Família while living in the Azores as a teenager. Friar Dinis may well have been inspired by this association; the novel's description of Friar Dinis points very clearly to Garrett's Franciscan uncle: "Such was Friar Dinis, a man of austere principles, of rigid beliefs and of a stubborn, inflexible logic" (*Travels*, p. 90). Friar Alexandre da Sagrada Família is described by his nephew in a letter written to a friend in April of 1853 as the man "who educated me and taught me the humanities. An austere and even violent character. A true Bishop and religious man" (Garrett in Monteiro, p. 1). Garrett also referred to his uncle as his educator, and a second father. In the novel Friar Dinis fulfills the role of a "second father" in relation to

Carlos's education and upbringing, until it is revealed that he is in fact Carlos's real father. Furthermore, on a political level, Friar Dinis's opposition to the liberal ideology echoes that of Friar Alexandre: both saw the constitutionalists as visionaries ultimately driven by material gain.

Generally considered the first contemporary Portuguese novel, *Travels in My Homeland* distinguished itself in the context of Portuguese Romanticism for its innovative structure and modern use of colloquial language. The narrator converses freely with the reader, moving loosely from theme to theme as the short chapters progress, and it is this level of colloquiality that dominates the discourse. As Carlos Felipe Moisés states, "all of the great modern Portuguese prose, from Camilo to Eça, from Júlio Dinis to Saramago, stems from the mold generously distributed by Garrett in the apparently unpretentious pages of these *Travels in my Homeland*" (Moisés in Garrett, *Viagens,* p. 16; trans. K. Bishop Sanchez).

Publication and reception. The circumstances of the original publication of *Travels* seem to reveal a certain hesitance on behalf of the Portuguese readers to accept this ideologically eclectic novel. The first chapters of the novel initially appeared in a weekly magazine, the *Revista Universal Lisbonense,* in 1843. However, either due to the lack of response from the readers or possibly to reservations on behalf of the magazine's director, the poet António Feliciano Castilho, publication of the novel was suspended. In June of 1845, with the magazine under new ownership, it undertook a second publication of the novel, this time printing a revised version of the first chapters, followed by the remaining chapters periodically through the end of 1846, at which time *Travels in My Homeland* also appeared in book form. As the prologue of the original edition of the book states (a prologue that does not appear in the English translation), "the editors of this work, seeing the extraordinary popularity that it received when published in fragments in the *Revista,* thought it fit to render a service to the letters and glory of this country, printing it now in book form" (Garrett, *Viagens,* p. 19; trans. K. Bishop Sanchez). This prologue, thought to have been written by Garrett himself, suggests that the second publication in the *Revista Universal Lisbonense* met with some success.

Multifaceted and complex, *Travels* is the first novel of its kind in the Portuguese language and this may explain the readers' initial reluctant response: "Because of the complex narrative structure, the audacity of many of the ideological affirmations, the eclecticism of the discursive genres and the diversity of the themes evoked, and even the casual interpolations to the reader and lady reader. . . . *Travels in My Homeland* was indeed an eccentric work, that did not correspond to readership expectancies of the time period" (Reis, p. 20). Yet, despite its complexity, *Travels in My Homeland* remains an essential work in the Portuguese literary canon, because of its richness as a testament to Portuguese culture and literary legacy. With this novel, Garrett becomes the "creator of modern literary Portuguese prose, rejecting typical archaisms and linguistic conventionalities. This revolution, initiated by Garrett and continued by Eça [see **The Maias,** also in *WLAIT 5: Spanish and Portuguese Literatures and Their Times*], opened the way to the current form of writing in Portuguese" (Silvestre in Cruz, p. 39).

—Kathryn Bishop Sanchez

For More Information

Bell, Aubrey F. G. *Studies in Portuguese Literature.* New York: Gordon Press, 1975.

Cruz, Valdemar. "Almeida Garrett, liberal e romântico." *Expresso* 6 (February 1999): 32-40.

Gallagher, Tom. *Portugal. A Twentieth-Century Interpretation.* Manchester: Manchester University Press, 1983.

Garrett, Almeida. *Travels in My Homeland.* Trans. John M. Parker. London: Peter Owen Publishers, 1987.

———. *Viagens na minha terra.* Pref. Carlos Felipe Moisés. São Paulo: Nova Alexandria, 1992.

Ledford-Miller, Linda. "Voyage to the Land of the Novel: Narrative Voices in *Viagens na Minha Terra.*" *Luso-Brazilian Review* 21, no. 2 (1984): 1-8.

Livermore, H. V. *A New History of Portugal.* Cambridge: Cambridge University Press, 1967.

Marques, A. H. de Oliveira. *History of Portugal.* 2d ed. Vol. 2. New York: Columbia University Press, 1976.

Monteiro, Ofélia Milheiro Paiva. *D. Frei Alexandre da Sagrada Família.* Coimbra: Editoria, 1974.

Nowell, Charles E. *A History of Portugal.* New York: D. Van Nostrand, 1952.

Reis, Carlos. *Introdução à leitura das Viagens na minha terra.* 3d ed. Coimbra: Livraria Almedina, 1993.

Santos, António Almeida. "Almeida Garrett Um Quase Retrato." *Camões Revista de Letras e Culturas Lusófonas* 4 (Janeiro/Março 1999): 6-19.

The Trickster of Seville and the Stone Guest

by
Tirso de Molina

abriel Téllez, better known by his pseudonym Tirso de Molina, was born in Madrid around 1583. His parentage is unknown, although some scholars have claimed that Tirso was actually the bastard son of the Duke of Osuna. Information on Tirso's early years is likewise sketchy. After studying at the University of Alcalá, he entered the monastic order of Our Lady of Mercy (Mercederian order) at Guadalajara in 1601. In 1610, while living in Madrid, the young monk first began to write for the theater, adopting his pseudonym in 1616. Between 1616 and 1618, Tirso taught theology and tended to Mercederian affairs in Santo Domingo in the West Indies. Around 1620, Tirso moved back to Madrid and began the major phase of his literary activity, writing an estimated 300 to 400 plays, 80 of which are extant today, although questions of authorship have not been settled with regard to all. In 1625, Tirso was censured by the Castilian Junta de reformación (Committee for Reform) for what was considered his unseemly choice of language and subject matter in his plays. Forced to leave Madrid, he essentially gave up writing to concentrate on his religious career. His literary works, however, were collected and published in installments from 1627 to 1639. *El burlador of Sevilla y convidado de piedra* (*The Trickster of Seville and the Stone Guest*) is among Tirso's best-known plays, notable for its deft handling of strong religious themes and for its introduction of the character of Don Juan into world literature.

THE LITERARY WORK

A tragic play set in Naples, Tarragona, Seville, and Dos Hermanas during the fourteenth century; published in Spanish (as *El burlador de Sevilla y convidado de piedra*) c. 1630, In English in 1923.

SYNOPSIS

A young Spaniard deceives, seduces, and abandons several young women but is ultimately punished by supernatural forces for his misdeeds.

Events in History at the Time the Play Takes Place

Don Juan—history and legend. Although the story of a rakish trickster who tries to outwit death itself already existed in various songs and ballads, Tirso de Molina was apparently the first to give the character a name and identity as Don Juan Tenorio. Since then, many scholars have speculated as to whether Tirso's Don Juan truly existed, under this name or that of another of the playwright's contemporaries. Certainly, libertines were not unknown in either the fourteenth century—during which *The Trickster of Seville* takes place—or the seventeenth century, when Tirso composed his play. While admired by contemporary readers for their virility and audacity, libertines were not necessarily held up as heroic figures to emulate. Indeed, during the

SPANISH AND PORTUGUESE LITERATURES AND THEIR TIMES

527

Tirso de Molina

Although later versions of the Don Juan legend focus on the character as a famous lover, Tirso's play concentrates on Don Juan the trickster instead. Far from being a great lover, Tirso's Don Juan cares more about duping women and outwitting his rivals than about engaging in sensual pleasures. He prides himself on his own cleverness and his ability to deceive his intended victims by one elaborate ploy after another, declaring, "Not for nothing am I / Labelled the greatest trickster of Seville. / My very favorite pastime, my delight's / To trick a woman, steal away her honour, / Deprive her of her cherished reputation" (Molina, *Trickster of Seville*, 2.269-73).

The reign of Alfonso XI. In *The Trickster of Seville*, Tirso de Molina employs the device of putting royalty onstage, which was popularized by Spanish playwright Lope de Vega. The king in question is Alfonso XI of Castile and León, who reigned from 1312-50. After the death of his father, Ferdinand IV, Alfonso XI acceded to the throne as a one-year-old infant. The young king's grandmother, María de Molina, who had retired from court life, emerged from retirement to protect and defend his rights from untrustworthy kinsmen and rival claimants to the throne. After her death in 1321, however, rivalries between factions of nobles nearly tore the realm apart.

Achieving his majority in 1325, Alfonso XI worked diligently to restore order to his troubled kingdom. He gave new powers to the municipalities and to the Cortes (parliament) in exchange for their support against the nobles. He also chose officials who had no competing aristocratic affiliations, thus strengthening the power of the Crown. During his reign, Alfonso XI earned the nickname of Alfonso el Justiciero ("Alfonso the Just"). His foreign policy was mostly successful too. Despite losing Gibraltar in 1333 to the Moors of Granada and their Moroccan allies, the Marinids, Alfonso XI mounted several effective campaigns against the Moors in the 1340s. Forming a Christian coalition with the kingdoms of Portugal, Navarre, and Aragon, Alfonso XI helped defeat Moorish invaders from North Africa at the Battle of Río Salado in 1340. In 1344, Castilian and Portuguese forces recaptured the seaport of Algeciras, which had been in Moorish hands since 1340.

Tirso de Molina's play mentions neither King Alfonso's triumphs in battle nor the efficacy of his domestic policies. Indeed, the play departs significantly from dramatic tradition, which at

thirteenth century, the ideal hero bore a closer resemblance to the legendary Cid, who was portrayed in various poems and romances as not only a perfect warrior but as a faithful, devoted husband and father.

Several theories have been advanced as to Don Juan's historical identity. One possible model might have been Mateo Vázquez de Leca, who was a native of Seville, the nephew of King Philip II's secretary, and, apparently, a scandalous rake in his youth. Arguably the most credible candidate is Don Pedro Téllez Girón (1579-1624), Marquis of Peñafiel and, later, the Duke of Osuna. As an adolescent, Don Pedro resisted his father's attempts to control him; he married young, but then philandered frequently, indulging in sexual trickery. He also lied and broke his word repeatedly, obtained money under false pretenses, and killed a man in a brawl. Don Pedro made Seville—close to his own residence in Osuna—his particular territory, conducting many of his misdeeds in the crime-ridden city. The extent to which Tirso was familiar with Don Pedro's exploits remains unclear. It has been suggested by at least one source, however, that Tirso may have been Don Pedro's illegitimate half-brother and that *The Trickster of Seville* might have been intended as a judgment on an unacknowledged kinsman's scandalous behavior.

the time presented historical stage monarchs as idealized figures. *The Trickster of Seville*, in contrast, presents Alfonso XI as well-intentioned but somewhat ineffectual, always a step behind Don Juan. Although the king sincerely attempts to appease the rake's outraged victims by arranging socially advantageous marriages for them, Alfonso is continually forced to abandon or revise his plans in response to further havoc wreaked by the young rake. The play's harmonious ending owes less to King Alfonso's efficiency than to the fortunate happenstance of Don Juan's sudden death and descent into hell. It may be worth noting the irony of King Alfonso's role in Tirso's play as a proponent of honorable marriage and domestic virtues: the historical Alfonso XI enjoyed a longstanding adulterous affair with Leonor de Guzmán, a beautiful widow of Seville, by whom he had several illegitimate children.

The Play in Focus

Plot summary. At the court of Naples, Don Juan Tenorio, a rakish young Spaniard, seduces Duchess Isabela by pretending to be her betrothed, the Duke Octavio. On discovering the ruse, the horrified Isabela raises an alarm and the King of Naples has Don Juan arrested. Don Pedro Tenorio, the Spanish ambassador at court and Don Juan's uncle, rebukes his nephew for his misdeeds, reminding Don Juan that he was sent to Italy in the first place because of his lewd behavior in Spain. For the sake of the Tenorio good name, however, Don Pedro lets his nephew escape, advising him to take refuge in Sicily or Milan. Don Pedro then deflects scandal from his family. First he implicates Duke Octavio in Isabela's seduction to the king; then he convinces Octavio that Isabela was unfaithful to him. The grief-stricken duke vows to sail for Spain and leave his former beloved to her disgrace.

Shipwrecked off the coast of Tarragona, Don Juan and his servant Catalinón are aided by Tisbea, a beautiful but disdainful fisher-girl. Having long prided herself on her indifference to her many suitors, Tisbea finds herself falling in love with Don Juan, who seduces her with promises of marriage, then abandons her, setting fire to her cottage and escaping on a horse that she gave him. Meanwhile, back in Seville, King Alfonso XI greets Don Gonzalo de Ulloa, Grand Commander of the Order of Calatrava, who has returned from a royal embassy to Portugal to settle an exchange of territories between the two nations.

The king listens to Don Gonzalo's extravagant praise of the city of Lisbon, then raises the subject of arranging a marriage between Don Gonzalo's daughter, Doña Ana, with a gentleman of Seville: Don Juan Tenorio. Don Gonzalo is amenable to the suggestion and agrees to inform his daughter.

The king's plans for the marriage fall through, however, when he learns from Don Diego Tenorio, Don Juan's father, of the young man's amorous misadventure in Naples. Furious, King Alfonso exiles Don Juan from Seville to Lebrija,

THE AUTHORSHIP QUESTION

Like many prolific playwrights of the Spanish Golden Age, Tirso initially gave preservation and publication of his plays little thought. Later in his life, after he had stopped writing for the theater, Tirso undertook the task of collecting his scattered manuscripts for publication. Five volumes, or *partes*, of Tirso's works were printed between 1627 and 1639. *The Trickster of Seville*, however, was not included in any of those volumes, which has led to the question of whether Tirso was indeed the author. But another collection of plays by several authors—printed c. 1630—included a copy of *The Trickster of Seville* with a title page that assigned authorship to Tirso. An alternate version of the play, *Tan largo me lo fiáis* (What Long Credit You Give Me) was first published under the name of the Spanish dramatist Calderón de la Barca. Most scholars now agree that *Tan largo* was in fact an earlier version of the play written by Tirso himself. *The Trickster of Seville* is the version better known to modern readers and audiences.

arranges to bring the disgraced Isabela to Spain as Don Juan's prospective bride, and makes Don Gonzalo major-domo of the palace to compensate for the dissolution of Doña Ana's betrothal to Don Juan. When Duke Octavio arrives in Seville, King Alfonso welcomes the jilted duke and suggests him as a possible husband for Doña Ana; the duke agrees and rejoices in his good fortune. Back in Seville, unaware of his impending banishment, Don Juan ingratiates himself to Duke Octavio, who never suspects that the young Spaniard was the man who cuckolded him with Isabela. Don Juan also renews his acquaintance with the Marquis of Mota. The two young men trade sallies about the prostitutes of Seville; then Mota imprudently reveals to Don Juan that he is actually in love with Doña Ana, who is his cousin and newly arrived in Seville. Moreover, Doña Ana returns Mota's love and the two of them have been engaging in a clandestine courtship, writing each other love letters and planning assignations. By chance, Don Juan intercepts one of Doña Ana's notes in which she invites Mota to a tryst with her at eleven o'clock that night. Don Juan immediately schemes to trick and seduce Doña Ana himself, dismissing his servant Catalinón's warnings that he will ultimately pay the penalty for his trickery.

On encountering Mota again, Don Juan tells him about Doña Ana's note but deliberately gives him the wrong hour for the assignation. That night, Don Juan borrows Mota's cloak and visits Doña Ana at the appointed hour, but the girl instantly discovers the deception and screams for help. Don Gonzalo comes to his daughter's aid and is fatally stabbed by a fleeing Don Juan. An hour later, the bewildered Mota appears on the scene and is arrested for Don Juan's crimes. Doña Ana takes sanctuary in the queen's royal chapel, while King Alfonso decrees that Don Gonzalo be buried with the pomp and ceremony befitting his personal merit and noble rank.

En route to Lebrija, Don Juan and Catalinón arrive at the village of Dos Hermanas, where a wedding between two young people is in progress. Invited to attend the festivities, Don Juan sets his sights on the pretty bride, Aminta, deciding to make her his latest conquest. Before the marriage can be consummated, Don Juan plays upon the insecurities of Batricio, the bridegroom, who is persuaded to abandon Aminta. Don Juan then presents himself to Aminta as her new "husband," promising her wealth, status, and eternal devotion. Initially suspicious of him, Aminta eventually capitulates. Meanwhile, Isabela, lamenting her impending marriage to Don Juan, passes through Tarragona on her way to Seville and meets a similarly embittered Tisbea. The fisher-girl relates her tale of woe to Isabela, who is appalled by this further evidence of Don Juan's perfidy and invites Tisbea to accompany her.

While journeying back to Seville himself, Don Juan learns from his servant Catalinón that the wronged suitors Octavio and Mota now know of his treachery and that King Alfonso wishes him to marry Isabela. On their way to lodgings, master and servant come across the church in which Don Gonzalo's tomb is located. Entering the church, Don Juan taunts Don Gonzalo's statue, pulling its stone beard and facetiously inviting it

to dine with him that evening. To the horror of Don Juan and his servants, the statue turns up at the appointed hour and issues a return invitation to Don Juan for the following night. Not wishing to be thought a coward, Don Juan agrees to sup with the stone guest the next night at ten. They clasp hands in parting; then the statue withdraws and disappears. Alone, Don Juan remembers the stone guest's icy handshake and experiences a sudden fear of death and damnation. He quickly silences those fears, however, and resolves to keep the appointment.

On learning of Isabela's arrival in Seville, King Alfonso and Don Diego discuss what is to be done about Don Juan. They agree that Don Juan will be made to wed Isabela and receive the title of Count of Lebrija. The king also intends for Doña Ana to marry the marquis of Mota, for whom the girl has obtained Alfonso's forgiveness for his alleged involvement in Don Gonzalo's death. The meeting between Don Diego and the king is now interrupted by Octavio, who asks the king for permission to challenge Don Juan and make him pay for his treachery in Naples. King Alfonso prevents a brewing quarrel between Don Diego and Octavio, and forbids the duke to harm Don Juan. Octavio grudgingly complies; alone, the duke encounters Aminta and her father Gaseno and learns from them of Don Juan's latest deceit in Dos Hermanas. Seeing an opportunity for revenge on Don Juan, Octavio promises to array Aminta in fine clothes and bring her to court to meet her errant bridegroom.

Meanwhile, Don Juan and Catalinón keep their appointed tryst at Don Gonzalo's tomb. Waited upon by the dead, master and servant sit down to a feast of snakes, scorpions, vinegar, and gall. A fearful Catalinón is further unnerved by the dead's songs of judgment and damnation; Don Juan, too, is frightened but attempts to conceal it. When the feast ends, Don Gonzalo's statue enjoins Don Juan to take his hand; obeying, Don Juan finds the statue's grasp burning hot and struggles in vain to free himself. Don Gonzalo informs the young man that he is now eternally damned for his crimes and, ignoring Don Juan's pleas for a last-minute confession, drags him down to hell. Catalinón hauls himself to safety as the tomb sinks into the earth after the statue and Don Juan.

In Seville, the various men and women whom Don Juan has betrayed converge before the king and demand Don Juan's punishment. Confronted with all the evidence of the young man's wickedness, the king finally pronounces a death sentence upon Don Juan that even Don Diego does not contest. Just then, Catalinón enters with the news of Don Juan's fate at the hand of the stone guest. The king declares that Don Juan has received his just punishment by God and arranges a series of marriages to compensate for Don Juan's villainy. Mota and Ana are reunited, as are Batricio and Aminta, while Octavio asks for and is granted the hand of the now-available Isabela. King Alfonso then issues a final command that Don Gonzalo's tomb be moved to Madrid as the play concludes.

Women—conquests or conquerors? While it is tempting to brand Tirso's Don Juan as misogynistic, it is probably more accurate to describe him as oblivious to women as anything other than the instruments of his own pleasure. Significantly, that pleasure seems to lie less in the indulgence of his sexual appetites than in the demonstration of his own cleverness and ingenuity. It is the reputation of being "the greatest trickster"—not the "greatest lover"—of Seville that Don Juan values most.

Don Juan is not immune to women's beauty; indeed, their physical charms provide the impetus for his sexual pursuit of them. Attracted to the fisher-girl, Tisbea, who has saved him from drowning, Don Juan declares to his servant, "Oh, I can hardly wait to have Tisbea! / What a fine body of a girl!" (*Trickster of Seville*, 2.896-97). Similarly, Don Juan later sings the praises of Aminta, the country bride he plans to seduce away from her new husband: "What lovely eyes she has! Her hands like snow! / Already her beauty burns within my soul!" (*Trickster of Seville*, 2.743-44). Nonetheless, it is the game of deceit and seduction that Don Juan truly finds irresistible. He barely catches a glimpse of Doña Ana through the bars of her window when her love letter to Mota falls into his hands, yet his determination to have her is as strong as with his other conquests: "This trick delights me even as I think / Of how I'll see it through! I'll have this girl / With all the ingenuity with which / The Duchess Isabela succumbed in Naples!" (*Trickster of Seville*, 2.301-04). To Don Juan, women are essentially interchangeable; it never occurs to him to consider that the sexual trickery that succeeded with Duchess Isabela might fail with Doña Ana, as indeed proves to be the case.

In contrast with his protagonist's blithely arrogant categorization of all women as potential conquests, Tirso takes pains to depict each of

Don Juan's female victims as an individual in her own right. Granted, none of them are presented as blameless for the situations in which they find themselves. Both Isabela and Doña Ana are involved in secret romances with the men they love—Duke Octavio and the Marquis of Mota, respectively—which provides Don Juan with the opportunity to attempt their seduction. Meanwhile, the credulous Aminta, at first determined to remain faithful to her absent husband, finds herself swayed by Don Juan's

---

THE KNIGHTLY ORDERS

During the Middle Ages, the monastic knightly orders of Calatrava (1158), Alcántara (1166), and Santiago (1170) were created to defend Spain's Christian states against the Muslims. Intended to embody the religious and secular ideals of chivalry, these orders were headed by a Grand Master and his high-ranking subordinates. The *comendador mayor,* a position held by the play's Don Gonzalo, was second only to the Grand Master. As religious knights, members of the orders enjoyed clerical and aristocratic privileges. They were entrusted with administering the lands (known as *encomiendas*) they had reconquered from the Moors, and were allowed to retain income from those lands. Over the years, the three orders acquired great wealth and power, attracting many nobles as members. Towards the end of the fifteenth century, the orders lost much of their power—Queen Isabella came to regard them as a possible threat to royal authority. Nevertheless, to hold high rank within the orders continued to be very prestigious, even in Tirso's lifetime.

---

protestations of love and even more by his extravagant promises of wealth. Tisbea, on the other hand, falls, like her seducer, through pride and overconfidence. As Don Juan prides himself on his reputation as the trickster of Seville, so Tisbea initially rejoices in being immune to the attentions of her many love-struck suitors: "I alone am free from love's harsh tyranny, / And only I can boast I'm really happy! / For I can speak with pride of liberty, / And of my rejection of passion's bonds" (*Trickster of Seville*, 1.379-82). Don Juan's betrayal leaves the suddenly love-struck fisher-girl, literally, in ashes—with her cottage on fire and Tisbea herself burning with humiliation: "My soul's on fire too. It burns. Have pity! / I am the one who always mocked all men / And took delight in all their suffering. / The truth is those who think they fool all others / Are in the end the ones who fool themselves" (*Trickster of Seville*, 1.1012-16).

Intriguingly, despite their victimization by Don Juan, the women in Tirso's play attempt to fight back or at least seek redress for their wrongs. Forced into a betrothal with Don Juan,

---

VARIATIONS ON THE "STONE GUEST" SUBPLOT

Literary scholar Gwynne Edwards provides his own translation of an old ballad that Spanish intellectual Ramón Menéndez Pidal first heard in 1905 in the province of Segovia:

There was a young man, the story says,
Who went to church to say his prayers.
Once there he knelt, his prayer began,
Close to the figure of a stone man.
The youngster pulled the statue's beard,
And said to him, as though he heard:
"You're a respectable old sod!
Who would have thought that this young bod
Would one day have the nerve to dare
To tug the thin and scrawny hair
Of your chin? Why don't you tonight
Turn up at my place for a bite
To eat? I know you won't agree.
Your belly's not exactly pretty.
On the contrary, it's long and thin,
I doubt that you'll eat anything."
At that the young man took his leave;
How could he, after all, conceive
What the consequences might be
Of that outrageous affrontery?
And so it was around nightfall
The dead man came to pay his call.

(Edwards in Molina, pp. xxii-xxiii)

Isabela encounters Tisbea by chance and the two women travel to Seville together in hopes of exposing his villainy to the king. Sequestered in a convent after Don Juan kills her father, Doña Ana successfully intercedes for Mota, who has been imprisoned for his former friend's crimes, and wins his freedom and his hand in marriage. Even Aminta, finding herself deserted by Don Juan,

takes the initiative to follow him to Seville and demand her rights as his legal wife. Although supernatural forces decide Don Juan's ultimate fate and King Alfonso assumes responsibility for all the marriages at the end of the play, the women's attempts to determine their own futures still represents a brave step towards autonomy and independence.

The plight shared by the women of Tirso's play and their efforts to counteract their disgrace have their basis in history. In medieval and early modern Spain, it was necessary that a woman's sexual dishonor be avenged, because her shame reflected upon not only her reputation but also that of her husband, her male relatives, and even her entire community. It mattered little whether or not the woman had been a willing participant in her own disgrace:

> Whether women engaged in transgressive behaviour or were victims of male predatory practices—rape, seduction, kidnapping, or mere slander—they were expected to pay the price demanded by strict codes of honour. Banishment or revenge, often the killing of the seducer and the seduced, followed swiftly upon dishonour. The family's honour could not be restored until these actions had been carried out.
>
> (Ruiz, p. 239)

Sources and literary context. As previously discussed, Tirso may well have found the inspiration for his Don Juan among his contemporaries or perhaps in accounts of past libertines of Seville. The "stone guest" subplot of Tirso's play, however, seems to have been derived from medieval ballads and folktales that circulated throughout Europe, and possibly from an Italian religious drama, *Leonzio, overra la terrible benmdetta di un morto* (c. 1615). Other elements of the play, such as the details regarding the port cities of Lisbon and Seville, may have originated from Tirso's own travel experiences.

Overall, Tirso's dramatic works seem to fall into three categories: 1) historical plays, 2) cloak-and-dagger comedies (*comedias de capa y espada*) involving love intrigues among the nobility, and 3) religious dramas. Although *The Trickster of Seville* contains some elements common to cloak-and-dagger comedies (love, intrigue, mistaken identity), it is usually considered a religious drama, as Don Juan is ultimately called to account not just for his rakish behavior but for his willful defiance of God in pursuit of his desires. Tirso's plays frequently evoke comparisons with those of Lope de Vega (1562-1635), his dramatic precursor and the play-

The Council of Trent

wright most responsible for the form and shape of Spanish *comedia* during the seventeenth century. While Lope's plays are often considered more inventive than and technically superior to those of his younger compatriot, Tirso's plays nonetheless garner praise for their psychological insight into characters—especially female characters—and their thoughtful exploration of such profound religious themes as sin, penance, redemption, and free will.

Events in History at the Time the Play Was Written

The Counter-Reformation in Spain. During the sixteenth and early seventeenth centuries, many Christian nations in Europe, including Spain, became involved in the religious movement known as the Counter-Reformation. Also known as the Catholic Reformation, the Counter-Reformation denoted the response of the Roman Catholic Church to the Protestant Reformation, which had gained momentum since 1517, when the German theologian Martin Luther had first nailed to the church door his Ninety-Five Theses calling for sweeping reforms. Overall, the Counter-Reformation may be said to have had two major objectives: internal religious reform within the Church itself and the restoration of Catholicism in Protestant northern Europe.

Pope Paul III (reigned 1534-1549), considered to be the first pope of the Counter-Reformation, convened the Council of Trent in 1545 to settle the most pressing issues resulting from the ongoing religious controversy in Europe. Although the Council encountered many difficulties and met only intermittently during sessions held from 1545 to 1563, it nonetheless proved to be an effective force for stabilizing and revitalizing Roman Catholicism. For example, the council clarified the Catholic doctrine on the nature of the sacraments, a point that had been challenged by Protestants. The council also implemented disciplinary measures targeting luxurious living among the clergy, the nepotistic appointment of relatives to Church office, and the absence of bishops from their dioceses. Special attention was given to the education of future priests: diocesan seminaries were founded to train and foster an educated clergy. Moreover, variations in the liturgy were abolished, the Roman Missal and Breviary (decreed in 1568 and 1570 to establish uniformity in prayers) was implemented, and the authority of bishops over parish clergy was strengthened. The measures effected significant changes in clerical practice.

As a predominantly Catholic country, Spain became an early and primary supporter of the Counter-Reformation. In 1540, a Spanish nobleman, Ignatius Loyola, founded an important new religious order: the Society of Jesus or the Jesuits. The duties of the Jesuits were to defend and advance the Catholic faith through education and discipline. Like many of their Protestant opponents, the Jesuits encouraged literary endeavors. Soon after their inception, they appeared an active force in Northern Europe, setting up schools, preaching, and spreading their influence through court circles. A strong central organization, selectivity in admitting new members, and sincere religious fervor all contributed to the Jesuits' becoming a particularly effective force for promoting the new Catholicism in Spain.

The Counter-Reformation in Spain was also aided by the notorious Spanish Inquisition, which tried to expel Protestants from the country altogether. Historian Henry Kamen observes that together with bishops and religious orders, the Inquisition gradually brought Spaniards into the fold of the new Catholicism over the course of the late sixteenth and early seventeenth centuries.

> In all fundamentals nothing had changed; there were nevertheless profound differences between the new Catholicism and the old. Trent imposed upon Spanish religion a revolutionary sense of the sacred that endured into the twentieth century. Where the church had been used for communal meetings and festivities, it was now totally separated from all secular use; all religious rites, and all baptisms, were to be performed in the church and in no other place.
>
> (Kamen, pp. 182-83)

The Counter-Reformation affected not only political and religious but artistic and intellectual life in Spain as well. Despite Spain's reputation as a staunchly Catholic country, troubling ideas introduced by the Protestant Reformation could not be easily dismissed there or in any other European nation exposed to them. It has been argued that while the Counter-Reformation scored some notable successes, it could hardly expect to succeed in its general attempt to abort the movement of European thought away from a God-centered medieval world order towards an evolving man-centered world order. In such an environment, devout Catholics might find themselves torn between their individual consciences—which tempted them to explore a new religious sensibility—and their traditional loyalties to habitual religious practices. According to one literary historian, the conflict influenced creative expression:

> A resultant state of paradoxical doubt, or paralyzed confusion, is a recurrent motif of Spanish

literature in the Counter Reformation, and it gave great stimulus to a theater which frequently probed deeply in its formulation of problematic situations, but usually reached timid, "safe" and reconciliatory conclusions. . . . The Spanish *comedia* could consequently serve a double function in its society: a) homeopathically to purge a doubt-filled collective conscience of its feelings of confusion, and b) to leave the spectator restored in himself at play's end by concluding on a note of reaffirmation. Thus the *comedia* operated as a very effective safety-valve for all sectors of society and its success was correspondingly great.
>
> (Sullivan, p. 14)

In *The Trickster of Seville*, Tirso—writing during the later years of the Counter-Reformation—does indeed appear to reaffirm and uphold the view of a theocentric or God-centered world-order. While Tirso's Don Juan is not a religious skeptic or a heretic, he nonetheless reveals an arrogant misunderstanding of the true nature of sin and repentance. Although his family and his plain-spoken manservant continually warn the young man that his misdeeds could result in his eternal damnation, Don Juan refuses to mend his way, remarking carelessly, "Plenty of time for me to pay that debt!" (*Trickster of Seville*, 1.904). He "trusts nonchalantly that an eleventh-hour recantation in old age will suffice, leaving him free to indulge his libertine lusts in youth" (Sullivan, p. 39). Believing that a last-minute confession to a priest will cleanse his soul and allow him to die in a state of grace, Don Juan is horrified to find himself on the brink of eternal damnation with no priest in sight. Struggling in the deadly grasp of Don Gonzalo's stone statue, Don Juan beseeches his foe, "Give me confession! Grant me absolution!" only to be sternly informed by the statue, "No time, my friend! No time! Your time runs out" (*Trickster of Seville*, 3.967-68). The chorus of the dead whose songs accompany the final encounter between Don Juan and Don Gonzalo utter what might be considered the moral of *The Trickster of Seville*: "As long as man lives out his total span, / Let him avoid this boast, as best he can: / 'Plenty of time to pay the final debt.' / No sooner said, the payment must be met" (*Trickster of Seville*, 3.939-42).

Impact. The number of subsequent versions of the Don Juan legend reveals the lasting impact of Tirso's play, although all authors undertaking the story have added their own twists to the tale. *Dom Juan ou le Festin de Pierre*—by the French dramatist Jean-Baptiste Poquelin Molière—appeared only 35 years after Tirso's play and portrayed Don Juan as "a thinking, sophisticated, self-justifying seducer rather than as a man of action," an interpretation that proved more intellectual but less passionate than Tirso's (Edwards in Molina, p. xxxvi). By contrast, the composer Wolfgang Amadeus Mozart attempted to merge Molière's witty, cynical rake with Tirso's passionate, reckless one in his opera *Don Giovanni*, first performed in 1787. This and other eighteenth-century versions tended to focus more on Don Juan's pursuit of sensual pleasures than on the religious ramifications of that pursuit. During the nineteenth century, the Don Juan story was altered by writers influenced by the Romantic movement. In his short story "Don Juan," German author August Heinrich Hoffman depicts the character as irresistible to women yet frustrated in his vain quest for the ideal woman and taking his frustration out on man and God. The British poet George Gordon, Lord Byron, took an entirely different and more irreverent approach in his mock-epic *Don Juan*, in which his hero, unlike the aggressive lover of legend, drifts passively from affair to affair; in Spain itself, José Zorrilla composed his drama **Don Juan Tenorio** (also in *WLAIT 5: Spanish and Portuguese Literatures and Their Times*). Zorilla's drama resurrects the ruthless, reckless seducer of Tirso's play but makes Don Juan a religious skeptic as well and has him ultimately saved from damnation by the love of a pure woman.

Although many of these later versions of the Don Juan story have become famous in their own right, *The Trickster of Seville*—while seldom performed today—remains vitally important as a prototype. As Gwynne Edwards writes, "It was left to Tirso to create the character of Don Juan. . . . The measure of his success may be gauged by the extent to which Tirso's protagonist, the first-ever Don Juan, inspired so many later writers and musicians to produce their variations on the original" (Edwards in Molina, p. xxiv).

—Pamela S. Loy

For More Information

Gerstinger, Heinz. *Lope de Vega and Spanish Drama*. Trans. Samuel R. Rosenbaum. New York: Frederick Ungar, 1974.

Hughes, Ann Nickerson. *Religious Imagery in the Theatre of Tirso de Molina*. Macon: Mercer University Press, 1984.

Kamen, Henry. *Spain 1469-1714*. London: Longman, 1983.

Molina, Tirso de. *The Trickster of Seville and the Stone Guest*. Ed. Gwynne Edwards. Warminster: Aris & Phillips, 1986.

Ruiz, Teofilo. *Spanish Society 1400-1600*. Harlow, England: Longman, 2001.

Sola-Solé, Josep M., and George E. Gingras. *Tirso's Don Juan: The Metamorphosis of a Theme*. Washington, D.C.: Catholic University of America Press, 1988.

Sullivan, Henry W. *Tirso de Molina and the Drama of the Counter Reformation*. Amsterdam: Rodopi, 1976.

Index

O

P

Q